WINDOWS XP
COMMAND LINE

CAROLYN Z. GILLAY
Saddleback College

BETTE A. PEAT

Franklin, Beedle & Associates, Inc.
8536 SW St. Helens Drive, Suite D
Wilsonville, Oregon 97070
503-682-7668
www.fbeedle.com

President and Publisher	Jim Leisy (jimleisy@fbeedle.com)
Production	Stephanie Welch
	Tom Sumner
Cover	Ian Shadburne
Marketing	Christine Collier
Order Processing	Krista Brown

Printed in the U.S.A.

Library of Congress cataloging-in-publication data is available from the publisher.

Dedication

To Jim and Linda Winter—the best in-laws ever—
whose wonderful love, loyalty, and support have been
my sustenance through the years.

—C.Z.G.

For Jean—my sister in all the ways that count.

—B.A.P.

CONTENTS

CHAPTER 2   COMMAND SYNTAX   39

CHAPTER 3   DISKS AND FORMATTING   95

CHAPTER 7   USING ATTRIB, SUBST, XCOPY,   309
DOSKEY, AND THE TEXT EDITOR

CHAPTER 8   ORGANIZING AND MANAGING YOUR HARD DISK   373

CHAPTER 9   PIPES, FILTERS, AND REDIRECTION   439

CHAPTER 10   INTRODUCTION TO BATCH FILES   483

CHAPTER 11   ADVANCED BATCH FILES   547

CHAPTER 12   CONNECTIVITY   633

CHAPTER 13   FILE AND DISK MAINTENANCE   719

APPENDIX A   INSTALLING THE WUGXP DIRECTORY AND SHAREWARE REGISTRATION   783

APPENDIX B   HARDWARE OVERVIEW   790

This book introduces the hardware, software, and operating system concepts of today's computer systems. The reader is presented with a system-level experience through problem-solving exercises at the command line. The book can be used in many settings: as the core book for a course that focuses exclusively on DOS, for the DOS portion of a network or programming class, as a supplement to a Windows XP Professional course, for a class that follows an introduction to Windows XP Professional, or for self-directed study.

Why Learn DOS when It's a Windows World?

Many people with little or no computer experience believe DOS is "dead." However, the rise of network computing and the vast number of businesses running legacy DOS applications make knowledge of DOS and the Windows XP command line essential. Command syntax, parameters, parsing commands, and troubleshooting are all handled better from the command line interface rather than the graphical user interface.

The command line interface exists in Windows 95, Windows 98, Windows Me, Windows NT 4.0, Windows NT 4.5, Windows 2000, Windows XP, and Novell. Batch files are useful in all these operating systems. Batch file skills are critical in the networking world, as well as on the stand-alone computer system.

Begins with the Basics and Leads to the Advanced

This book spans basic to sophisticated uses of the command line interface. Each chapter has been written with both novice and advanced users in mind, so it challenges advanced students without sacrificing the needs of beginning students. Furthermore, while this book does present the various character-based commands, it also stresses the concepts, theory, and understanding of operating systems in general.

The book demonstrates the command line interface and explains when and why one would use it instead of the graphical user interface (GUI) of Windows XP Professional. It provides numerous examples to allow students to master operating systems. This book teaches these concepts using the Command Prompt window, referred to as the MS-DOS Prompt window in earlier versions of Windows. Though this book deals primarily with those commands and functions that are available at the command prompt, it also deals with commands and functions necessary to understand, maintain, and troubleshoot a system that are available only in the GUI.

Pipes, filters, and redirection used with batch files are covered in a thorough, step-by-step methodology. Advanced batch files are covered in detail, building on programming logic in a comprehensible way. Students cover all batch file commands and are introduced to DEBUG.

Setting up computer systems, optimizing performance, and troubleshooting require students to have good command line skills. To this end, the student learns how to create an Automated System Recovery (ASR) disk, boot into Safe Mode, and use Last Known Good Configuration.

This book also covers two major forms of connectivity: networking and the Internet. We have found that there is a gap in too many students' knowledge of networks. Students often take a Windows and/or DOS class and then, if on a networking career path, jump into a large-systems networking class. This can be an intimidating jump. There are many other students who work in small offices that do not have network administrators; others may work in environments where they only need to access a network or share files, folders, and devices on their own systems at home. These students are not going to follow the networking program. To address the needs of all these students, this book introduces some basic networking concepts and then leads the students into setting up a peer-to-peer network (where possible) and shows them how to share files, folders, and devices. Students also learn general networking techniques, such as mapping drives, which will serve them in good stead if they are on the networking career path. Furthermore, for students using the NTFS file system, permissions and rights are introduced.

Another connectivity topic is the Internet. In our book, students learn various ways to connect to the Internet and then do some simple activities using Internet Explorer. A brief introduction to TCP/IP concepts is included because, when using the Internet, so many students are lost at the first mention of such terms as "protocol" and "IP address." This overview gives them an understanding of some of these important terms so that they have a better comprehension of online activities. Students learn how to use simple Internet-related commands that can be run at the command line, such as FTP. In addition, certain troubleshooting commands such as ping and telnet are covered.

The last chapter covers a much too neglected topic—maintaining and troubleshooting a computer system. This chapter includes backing up a computer system and recovering a damaged system using such tools as System Restore and Safe Mode.

In addition, there are extensive appendices. These appendices cover the installation of the WUGXP directory; a basic look at hardware terminology; the Recovery console; a look at CMOS; the purpose, function, and structure of the Registry; FDISK; the keyboard scan codes; and an alphabetical list of all the commands used at the command line. These topics were placed in appendices as instructors may not have the capability in a lab network environment to allow the students to use such tools as the Recovery Console. The Recovery Console is a command line repair tool that needs to be installed or used with the original Windows CD. Thus, the instructor may only be able to demonstrate the use of this important tool The same is true for the Registry. Most labs environments do not allow the student to work with the Registry. Hence, a comprehensive overview is presented with one simple activity

This book takes up where other Windows books leave off. Although no prior knowledge or experience with computers, software, operating systems, or Windows 95/98/Me/2000/XP is necessary, it helps if the students have completed a basic Windows 95/98/Me/2000/XP class.

ACTIVITIES Disk with Shareware Programs and Data Files

The esoteric nature of operating systems is one of the biggest obstacles in teaching the command line interface to students. Many students find the material interesting and stimulating. However, there is always a group that asks, "What good is DOS? It doesn't do anything." Using discussion and example, this book demonstrates the importance of the command line interface.

In order to see how the command line works in the real world, the student uses Excel to load and look at files. Students have the opportunity to load an application program and prewritten data files, as well as create simple data files. In doing so, students better understand the differences between data files and program files and are able to use operating system commands to manipulate both types of files. Although most students and lab environments include the Microsoft Office Suite, if the student does not have Excel, the student can see how a data file works in conjunction with an application program by seeing the extensive screen captures that are provided in the book. In addition, the book includes several educationally sound shareware games that reinforce certain DOS concepts in an enjoyable manner.

These shareware files are on the ACTIVITIES disk along with data files students use for the exercises in the book. The ACTIVITIES disk's files are easily installed on a computer system's hard disk or network server. The exercises do not direct students to save files to the hard disk or network server. Early on, students create a DATA disk, and all files are written to the DATA disk. This approach provides real-life experience in working with the hard disk or server without risking damage to either. There are numerous warnings and cautions alerting students when a possible network conflict could arise. The students save all their homework files to a different disk so that the book activities and homework assignments are kept separate.

An Integrated Presentation of Concepts and Skills

Each section of the book is presented in a careful, student-oriented, step-by-step approach. Interspersed between the steps in the exercises are the reasons for and results of each action. At the end of each chapter, there are homework assignments that allow students to apply their knowledge and prove mastery of the subject area through critical-thinking skills. Each command is presented in a syntactically correct manner so that when the students have finished the course, they will be able to not only use software documentation, but also be comfortable in a network/Internet environment that requires the use of syntax and commands. This also assists the students in their ability to learn how to solve problems using the documentation at hand. This skill also transfers to the use of application packages and other operating system environments. No matter what changes are made to future versions of the operating system, students will be able to use the new commands.

Uses a Self-Mastery Approach

Each chapter includes a chapter overview, a list of key terms, a chapter summary, discussion questions, true-and-false questions, completion questions, multiple-choice questions, and problems where students are asked to write the commands. Each chapter also includes three sets of application assignments that focus on the skills learned in the chapter. The first two require the use of the computer. The first problem set requires students to complete activities on the computer and write the resulting answers on a Scantron form; the second problem set requires students to use the computer and print out the answers.

For the second problem set, the student results are sent to a batch file provided with the ACTIVITIES disk. The batch file is an easy-to-follow program. The students supply their solutions to the problems, and the batch file formats the answers in a consistent manner and includes the students' names and other instructor-directed identifying information. The printouts typically print on two pages or less.

The last set of assignments are brief essay questions that encourage students to integrate what they have accomplished in the chapter with their improved understanding of the command line interface of the Windows XP Professional operating system. All three types of assignments reinforce critical-thinking skills. The instructor can use all of the assignments or any part of them as homework assignments. The homework assignments are intended to be turned in as homework. Where hands-on assignments are not possible, students still have an opportunity to answer brief essay questions that encourage them to explain their understanding of the topic at hand.

Supplementary Material

This book comes with an instructor's manual that includes teaching suggestions for each chapter as well as the answers for every question and application exercise. A complete PowerPoint presentation for each chapter is included as well. There are additional chapter tests. A midterm and a final are included.

Reference Tools

This book is useful as a reference for MS-DOS commands. The first appendix provides instructions to install the subdirectory containing the shareware programs and data files to the hard disk. This feature is particularly useful for students who work at home or in an office. The rest of the appendices include an introduction to hardware, the Recovery Console, a look at CMOS, an overview of the Registry, a look at FDISK, keyboard scan codes, and a complete command reference. There is also a glossary.

Acknowledgments

A project of this scope is difficult to complete successfully without the contributions of many individuals. Thank you to all who contributed. A special thanks to:

- Kathryn Maurdeff for providing questions, answers, and PowerPoint presentations.
- All the authors of the shareware included with this book.
- My students at Saddleback College, who make writing worthwhile.
- My colleagues in the Computer Information Management Department at Saddleback College.
- The California Business Education Association and the National Business Education Association for providing forums for professional growth as well as inviting me to make presentations sharing my teaching experiences.
- A big thanks to everyone at Franklin, Beedle & Associates—Tom Sumner, Stephanie Welch, Ian Shadburne, Christine Collier, Krista Brown, Bran Bond, Dean Lake, and Stephen Mosberg.
    - An extra big thanks to Jim Leisy—publisher extraordinaire.
- And, as always, to my husband, Frank Panezich. Without a doubt, I'd choose you again.

Anyone who wants to offer suggestions or improvements or just share ideas can reach me at **czg@bookbiz.com**.

—C.Z.G.

My sincere thanks to those who helped along the way. Special thanks to:

- My family—Parkers, Peats, and Farneths—for their support and most of all for their love. They make "Grandma" believe she can do anything!
- Jean and Mac for, once again, adjusting their schedule to accommodate mine.
- The wonderful crew at Franklin, Beedle & Associates for their phenomenal patience and encouragement.
- First, last, and foremost, to Carolyn—for listening to me vent, for finding answers to my crazy questions, for sharing tears and laughter, and changing my life.

Anyone who wishes to offer suggestions, share ideas, or ask a question can contact me at **wugbook@pacbell.net**.

—B.A.P.

CHAPTER 1

GETTING STARTED WITH
THE OPERATING SYSTEM

Learning Objectives

After completing this chapter, you will be able to:

1. Define *operating system*.
2. Define *enhancements*.
3. Explain the function and purpose of OS version numbers.
4. List some of the types of system configurations.
5. Explain the need and procedure for booting the system.
6. Explain the function of disk files.
7. Explain the function of and rules for file specifications.
8. List and explain the importance of the two types of computer files.
9. Describe the function and purpose of commands.
10. Compare and contrast internal and external commands.
11. Explain the function and purpose of the DIR, VER, and CLS commands.
12. Explain the purpose of and the procedure for using the DATE and TIME commands.
13. Explain the legal and ethical ramifications of copying disks that were not purchased.
14. Explain the purpose and function of the DISKCOPY command.
15. Explain the necessary steps to end a work session.

Student Outcomes

1. Identify your system configuration.
2. Boot the system.
3. Use the DIR command to display the files on the screen.
4. Use the VER command to determine which version of Windows is being used.
5. Use the CLS command to clear the screen.
6. Use the DATE and TIME commands to set or change the date and time on the computer.
7. Make a copy of a disk.
8. End a computer work session.

Chapter Overview

Most people who use computers are really interested in application software. They want programs that are easy to use and that help them solve specific problems. However, before you can use application software, you must know at least the basics of using the operating system. No computer can work without an operating system in RAM. The Windows operating system takes care of mandatory functions for computer operations such as handling the input and output of the computer, managing computer resources, and running application software. It enables the user to communicate with the computer.

In this chapter you will learn about loading the operating system into the computer, use some basic commands, make a copy of the ACTIVITIES disk to use in future activities, learn your system configuration, and identify the version of Windows you are using.

1.1   What Is an Operating System?

An *operating system* is a software program. If you have a microcomputer, commonly referred to as a PC, that conforms to the standards developed by IBM and uses a microprocessor in the Intel family, you are probably using a version of the Windows operating system. In fact, these computers are sometimes called *Wintel* machines because they use the Intel processor and run the Windows operating system.

You need to load the Windows operating system (the OS) into memory (RAM) before you can use other software programs. The OS is in charge of the hardware components of the computer—the monitor, the keyboard, the printer, etc. You, the user, communicate what you want the computer to do through the OS. These commands are issued by pointing and clicking when in the GUI (Graphical User Interface) or by keying in commands such as TYPE or CLS at the command line prompt.

1.2   Versions of the Operating System (OS)

Microsoft periodically releases new versions of the OS to take advantage of new technology. These new upgrades contain enhancements. The term *enhancements* simply means that more functions and/or commands are available. In addition, new versions of software and operating systems fix problems, called *bugs*, that appeared in earlier versions. To keep track of these versions, each new version is assigned a number. The first version of Windows 95 was Windows 95 4.00.950, released in 1995. The last Windows 95 version was 95 4.00.1111, known as Windows 95B or OSR2. Also available is a major update of Windows 95 called Windows 98, SE version 4.10.1998. The next version of Windows was Windows Millennium Edition, referred to as Windows Me. These versions of Windows are and were primarily used on personal desktop computers.

Windows NT Workstation was a desktop operating system designed primarily for software developers and "power users," such as engineers who worked on large, powerful applications such as CAD (Computer-Aided Design). Microsoft's network operating system, Windows NT Server, was primarily used in large corporate environments where it provided network administrators with the ability to manage many networked computers with various security needs.

Windows 2000 Professional was the replacement for Windows NT Workstation 4. It was used as a desktop operating system in a networked environment or as a stand-alone operating system.

The current version of the Windows operating system is Windows XP. It comes in two distinct versions—Windows XP Home Edition and Windows XP Professional. The two versions are very similar with the primary difference being that in Windows XP Home Edition, certain features are disabled. There are also some cosmetic changes that make it easier for the home user. The major differences in the Windows XP Home Edition are:

- Backup—Must be installed separately.
- Multiprocessor support—Not supported.
- Domain-based network support—Not supported.

- User Administration—Less control over user accounts. Windows XP Home Edition does provide the ability to set up user accounts for multiple users on the same computer as well as providing levels of security. However, Windows XP Professional has a much more robust set of user account administration.
- File Encryption—Not supported on NTFS formatted disks.
- Remote Desktop—Not supported. This feature allows a user to see the desktop of another computer.
- Offline Files and Folders—Not supported. This feature allows you to copy files from a server to a notebook computer or to work offline from a server.
- Upgrades—Cannot upgrade to Windows XP Home Edition from Windows NT or 2000. You can upgrade from Windows 98 or Windows Me to either version of Windows XP.

There are also other versions of XP designed either for very fast processing of large amounts of data or for server-based computing. These include Windows XP 64-bit Edition which runs on the (now) new version of Intel's 64-bit Itanium processor. The 64 Bit Edition supports not only 32-bit applications but provides a much more efficient environment for the processing of very large amounts of data, such as those used on high-end engineering, scientific, and graphics workstations. In this light are the releases of the Windows .NET Server and Advanced Server. These are designed to run on servers rather than on workstations. Servers are those computers that provide services to other computers on network. There will be releases of 32-bit server versions as well but they will be labeled Windows .NET Servers.

This text will focus on Windows XP Professional, though much of the information is applicable to most versions of the Windows operating system. It is assumed in this textbook that Windows XP Professional is installed on your computer. If you are working on your own computer and have not installed or upgraded to Windows XP Professional, refer to the documentation that came with the Windows software so you can initiate the installation or upgrade. If you are in a laboratory environment, a version of Windows will be available for you.

1.3 Overview of Files and Disks

You need a way to store information permanently. In the computer world, the primary way to save data and programs permanently is to store them on a disk. After you have booted your computer, the OS reads the programs or data it needs from the disk into its memory. However, in order for Windows to find this information, it has to have a way of organizing it, which it does by keeping programs and data in files on the disk. Just as you organize your written work in files, Windows organizes computer information in disk files.

A *disk file* is much like a file folder stored in a file cabinet. The file cabinet is the floppy disk or the hard disk. A file consists of related information stored on the disk in a "folder" or directory with a unique name. Information with which a computer works is contained and stored in files on the disk. (See Figure 1.1.)

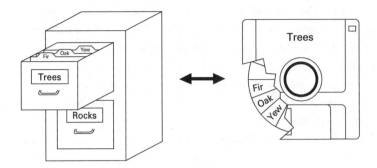

Figure 1.1—Disks and Files

1.4 File Names, File Types, and Folders

Because computers must follow very specific rules, there is a specific format for file names. Technically, a file name is called the *file specification*. The first rule is that the file specification must be unique. Second, the file specification is broken into two parts, a *file name* and a *file extension*. The file name typically describes or identifies the file, and the file extension typically identifies the kind of data in the file. Since the term "file specification" is rather awkward, most people simply refer to the file name, meaning both the file name and its extension. In versions of the OS before Windows, referred to simply as DOS, the file name size was limited by what was called the 8.3 (eight-dot-three) rule, which was a limit of eight characters for the file name and three characters for the file extension). In Windows, the 8.3 rule is gone. Now file names can have a maximum of 255 characters, referred to as LFNs (long file names). The three-letter file extension, known as the file type, remains in Windows. However, some software does not recognize long file names (LFNs), and some network operating systems have difficulty dealing with them. Because storing long file names takes additional space, consider using the 8.3 rule when saving to floppy disks with limited capacity.

There are two major types of computer files: *data files* and *program files*. Data files contain information that is usually generated by an application program. Most often, only an application program can use a data file directly. Program files are application programs that allow a user to perform specific tasks, for example, a payroll program that lets you create and maintain a payroll system for a company.

You do not purchase a computer to run the Windows operating system. You purchase a computer so that you may use application packages to help with tasks such as gaining access to the Internet, writing letters, managing your checkbook, doing your taxes, or creating a budget. If you needed to employ someone to do these tasks for you, you might go to a temporary employment agency and hire a secretary to write your letters or an accountant to manage your checkbook and taxes.

In the computer world, you purchase application packages, so that you can do the work. These application packages fall into generic categories such as word-processing or spreadsheet programs. In the same way you would choose a specific temporary employee such as Mr. Woo for your letter writing, in the computer world, you choose application packages by their names. They have brand names such as Word, Quicken, or Excel. These application packages are "employees" you choose to do the work.

In order for these application programs to do work, they must be copied from where they are installed (usually the hard drive, or the network drive) into RAM, the workspace of the computer. They are "temporary" employees because you call on them only when you need to do a specific task that they can accomplish. Windows is like an office manager who goes to the disk to get the correct file and place it in RAM. This process is known as loading the program from disk into memory. Windows then lets the program do its job. This process is known as executing the program. Program files are step-by-step instructions that direct the computer to do something.

Even though Word can create letters for anyone, you are interested only in the letters *you* create—the information that *you* want. Once you create your data, you also want to keep it. Remember, all the work occurs in RAM, and RAM is volatile (temporary). In order to keep information permanently, you direct Word to write (save) the information to a disk as a data file. Word actually does not save the data; instead, it turns to the operating system, which does the actual work of writing the file to disk. When you need to retrieve the information to alter it, Word again turns to the OS to retrieve the file. Windows then reads the disk to retrieve the appropriate data file and gives it to Word.

A unique name must be assigned to each file so that it can be identified by the OS. Program files have predetermined names such as WINWORD.EXE for Word, QW.EXE for Quicken, or EXCEL.EXE for Excel. WINWORD is the file name and .EXE is the file extension. Clicking on the application icon tells Windows to retrieve the program from the disk and place it in memory so you may work. When you install the application program you wish to use, it creates the icon, which actually is a reference to the name and location of the program file so that Windows can find and load it. Data files, on the other hand, are named by you, the user. You may call the files anything you want. For instance, a file name for a letter to your sister might be SISTER.LET or a name for your budget file might be BUDGET02.JAN. Typically, in the Windows environment, application programs assign a file extension such as .DOC or .XLS to identify the data file as a document file belonging to a specific application program. So, the filename SISTER.LET would be saved as SISTER.LET.DOC and BUDGET02.JAN would be filed as BUDGET02.JAN.XLS. The Word and Excel programs would assign their own file extensions—.DOC and .XLS, respectively.

A file name is mandatory, but a file extension is not. A file name typically identifies the file, such as WP for word processing or SISTER for your letter. The file name tells you about the file, and the file type (extension) identifies the kind of data in a file. For instance, .EXE is reserved for programs so that Windows knows the file is a worker; in a program like WINWORD.EXE, the extension .EXE stands for executable code.

Data files are generated by specific application programs, and the information or data in them can be altered or viewed only within the application package. You would not give your tax information to an administrative assistant to make changes. You would give that data to the accountant, who knows how to make the changes.

Data files do not stand alone. They can be used only in conjunction with an application program. Again, the job of the operating system is to fetch and carry both program files and data files in and out of memory and to and from the disk (reading and writing). In addition, since the OS is the "office manager," you may also use it to do office-related tasks such as copying or deleting a file. The OS does not know what is in the file folder, nor can it make changes to the information in the file folder. It can manipulate the file folder by such tasks as copying the information in it or throwing it away.

To assist you in organizing your information further, the OS can divide or structure your disks into what are called folders or directories. Technically they are subdirectories, but the terms *directory, subdirectory,* and *folder* are used interchangeably. Folders allow you to group related program or data files so they will be easy to locate later. For instance, all the files related to a spreadsheet program such as Excel could be stored in a folder named EXCEL. You might then group any data files you created with EXCEL, such as BUDGET02.XLS and APRIL01.XLS, in another folder called BUDGETS.

A primary directory (root) is automatically created when you prepare a disk to store information. It is named and called the root directory, but its symbol is \ (the backslash). You can create additional folders (subdirectories) for storing related files. Directories, including the root, will be discussed in full detail in later chapters.

1.5   Identifying Your System Configuration

All computers come with disk drives: the floppy disk drive, the hard or fixed disk drive, usually a CD-ROM drive or a DVD drive, and sometimes a large capacity removable drive, such as a Zip drive. Today there are many ways that computer systems can be configured:

- One hard disk drive, one CD-ROM drive, and one floppy disk drive.
- One hard disk drive, one CD-ROM drive, one floppy disk drive, and one Zip drive.
- Two hard disk drives, one CD-ROM drive, and one floppy disk drive.
- One hard disk drive, one CD-ROM drive, one read-write CD-ROM drive, and one floppy disk drive.

The possibilities are numerous. Computers are configured to suit the needs of the individual user.

1.6   Computer Configuration Guide

This textbook is based on a specific computer configuration model—one that is most common to PC users. However, there are some differences depending on whether you upgraded from a previous version of Windows or whether you have a new, or fresh, install of Windows XP Professional. These are:

Location and Prompts	All Versions	Upgrade from Previous Versions of Windows	New Version of Windows XP
Hard disk	C:\		
Floppy disk drive	A:\		
Location of Windows utility files		C:\WINNT\SYSTEM32	C:\WINDOWS\ SYSTEM32
Other Windows files		C:\WINNT	C:\WINDOWS
Displayed prompt for Drive C	C:\>		
Activities folder on Drive C	C:\WUGXP		
Displayed prompt for floppy disk	A:\>		

Note: When you open a Command Line session, your initial displayed screen prompt will probably be something like C:\Documents and Settings\ YourName. This will vary, depending on how your system was set up by your lab administrator. Again, if your administrator upgraded from a previous version of Windows, your initial displayed screens might be C:\WINNT\Profiles\YourName.

If your computer configuration conforms to the above, you can follow the textbook without making any adjustments. However, computer configuration setups vary, particularly on network systems. Thus, your system configuration may be different, and you might have to substitute what is on your system for the setups used in this textbook. Complete the following table so that the substitutions will be readily identifiable for your computer:

Description	Book Reference	Your System
Hard drive	C:	
Floppy drive	A:	
Location of OS utility files	C:\WINDOWS\SYSTEM32	
Displayed prompt for Drive C	C:\>	
Activities folder on Drive C	C:\WUGXP	
Prompt for floppy disk	A:\>	

1.7   Booting the System

You need to know how to get the operating system files from the bootable disk into memory (RAM) so that you can use the computer. With the Windows operating system, this happens automatically when you turn the system on. This process is known as *booting the system*. These files reside on the hard disk. The following activity allows you to have your first hands-on experience with the computer. You are going to load Windows or "boot the system."

Note: Since laboratory procedures will vary, check with your instructor before proceeding with these activities. A special process may be needed to boot the system if you are on a network.

1.8   Activity: Booting the System

1   Check to see if the monitor has a separate on/off switch. If it does, turn on the monitor.

2   Be sure there is no disk in Drive A. If your Drive A has a door that shuts or latches, be sure it is open. (Remember that your instructions may be different if you are booting to a network. You will need to get your user name and password from your instructor if you are in a lab environment.) Power on the computer by locating the **Power** button and pressing it. The **Power** button location can vary, depending on the design of the computer.

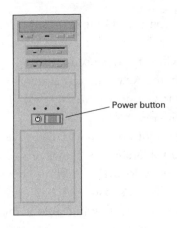
Power button

Figure 1.2—Powering on the Computer

WHAT'S
HAPPENING?   In Windows XP Professional, the startup sequence when booting from the primary hard disk is as follows:

- The BIOS initiates the Power-on self-test (POST)
- The BIOS finds the boot device (usually the C drive)
- The BIOS loads the first physical sector of the booting device into memory
- The executable code in the Master Boot Record finds, and loads Ntldr (the file that loads the operating system files from the boot volume)
- Ntldr loads Ntdetct.com for hardware detection
- Hardware configuration selection if the user is using more than one hardware profile (boot.ini)
- Ntldr loads the Windows Kernel Ntoskrnl.exe into memory, which also loads the support files it needs
- Hardware scanning files, which ask which Plug and Play devices are installed as well as their capabilities
- Media support files for the hard drive and other media storage devices
- Any special video drivers are loaded

- It then loads drivers for all the services your system supports. A service, in this case, refers to a program, routine, or process that performs a specific system function to support other programs, particularly at a low level (hardware).
- Operating system logon process

The POST determines the amount of memory and checks that the hardware devices are present and working. Then the computer system BIOS (Basic Input Output System) begins the process of starting the operating system. The normal search order is for the system to first look in Drive A and then, if no disk is present in Drive A, to look to Drive C. It may also look to your CD drive. The BIOS looks for the active partition of the hard drive and reads the MBR (Master Boot Record) into memory. The MBR then looks for the system partition information. The Windows XP partition boot sector reads the file system to find the bootstrap loader. It then loads the bootstrap loader into memory and starts the bootstrap loader (ntldr—NT loader). The hidden system file NTLDR uses another file, BOOT.INI, which identifies the location of the default operating system to load or gives you a choice of which operating system you wish to use if you have multiple operating systems installed. The NTLDR loads and executes another hidden system file called NTDETECT.COM. This file checks your hardware so that Windows XP Professional can configure the computer correctly. Then the core components of the operating system are loaded into memory, such as the kernel (NTOSKRNEL.EXE) and the Hardware Abstraction Layer (HAL.DLL). Lastly, the Windows subsystem automatically starts WINLOGON.EXE, which presents the dialog box for you to enter your user name and password. Depending on how your system is configured, you may first have to press **Ctrl** + **Alt** + **Delete** in order to log on to the system.

3   Press **Ctrl** + **Alt** + **Delete** if necessary.

4   Enter your user name and password.

5   Click **OK**.

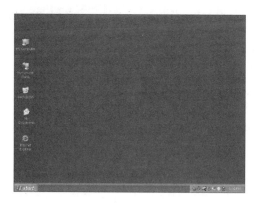 

WHAT'S HAPPENING?   You have successfully booted the system. Your opening screen may appear as one of the above, or it may look quite different. Windows XP has endless combinations of possible desktop appearances.

1.9 Shutting Down the System

It is very important that you shut down Windows XP Professional computers correctly every time. When you go through the shut-down process, Windows writes certain information to the disk. If you just turn off the computer, Windows will not have an opportunity to take care of the process it needs to go through to shut down. Simply turning off the computer could "crash" the system and it might be unable to boot the next time it is turned on.

1.10 Activity: The Windows Shut-Down Procedure

1 Click the **Start** button on the lower-left corner of the screen. ("Click" means to place the point of the arrow over the word **Start** and press the left button on the mouse once.)

2 Click **Turn Off Computer**.

WHAT'S
HAPPENING?   Your dialog box may vary, depending on the version of Windows you are using or if you are on a network. If **Shut down** does not appear in the drop-down window, click and hold on the down arrow and slide down to **Shut down**. On many computers today, the power will shut off automatically. On a computer that automatically shuts down, the screen will simply go blank, and you may not have to physically turn the computer off. You will probably, however, have to turn off the monitor.

3 Turn off the **Power** switch if necessary. Turn off the monitor.

WHAT'S
HAPPENING?   You have successfully shut down Windows.

1.11 Why DOS?

Since Windows is a GUI (graphical user interface), when you boot the system, you open the desktop with icons, menus, and pictures. You will run your programs and open your data files by clicking or double-clicking icons or menu choices. You accomplish tasks such as copying a file by opening the Windows Explorer window, selecting a file with your mouse, and dragging it to a different location, a procedure known as drag-and-drop. These are the reasons why a GUI is so popular. It is "user friendly."

In character-based operating systems, with DOS being the most common, all you would see on the screen after you booted would be a prompt such as C:\>—no picture, no icons, no drag-and-drop. In order to accomplish any task, you need to know what command to use. For instance, to copy a file in a character-based operating system, you would need to key in **COPY *THIS.FIL THAT.FIL***. This means you would need to know the command and how to use it. Hardly as easy as a drag-and-drop operation!

Why then, you may ask yourself, would you ever need to learn the "hard, archaic way" of using your computer when you can easily use the new, improved way? In fact, if you talk to many people, they would say to you, "DOS is dead; long live Windows." They would also say, "You don't need to know DOS anymore because it is all Windows." Those people are only somewhat right. They are correct in saying that DOS as a stand-alone operating system is dead. A new computer comes with Windows as its operating system, not DOS. But they are wrong in assuming that you do not need to know DOS.

What they do not understand, and you will after completing this text, is that what they refer to as DOS is really the Command Line interface. In fact, the GUI is simply a pretty face on top of what is really going on under the hood. Windows is like the gauges on the dashboard of an automobile. When the red light goes on, there is trouble under the hood. The red light only alerts you to a problem. Sometimes, you may fix the problem simply by responding to the evidence given. For instance, if you see the red oil light come on, that information only requires you to put oil in your engine. Other times, you must dig deeper to solve the problem. You must go to the engine and run diagnostic tests to identify the problem. Then you can fix the problem.

The same is true in Windows. Windows will alert you to a problem like the red light on the dashboard. Sometimes you can fix it at the GUI level, and other times you must open the hood and go to the command line interface to run diagnostic software to identify the problem. Once you have identified the problem, you can fix it either by running the problem-solving software you are given with Windows or by making small fixes at the system level.

Microsoft, even though it expects you to use the GUI for your day-to-day computer operations, still knows the importance of a character-based interface—the command line. That is why, with Windows 95, Windows 98, Windows Me, Windows NT, Windows 2000 Server, Windows 2000 Professional, and Windows XP, one of the choices is the availability of the command line interface. In Windows Me, it is a menu choice called the MS-DOS Prompt. In Windows 2000 and Windows XP Professional, it is simply called the Command Prompt. You open what used to be called a DOS window and is now called a Command Prompt window, but where you really are is right back to a character-based interface.

Why, then, did Microsoft leave this option available to the user? There are many reasons. For instance, you will find that there are many tasks that still cannot be accomplished from the GUI. In addition, Windows provides utility programs that can only be run at the command line to help you solve problems with Windows itself. Furthermore, there are other tasks that, although they can be done from the GUI, are accomplished easier and faster from the command line, and most users will use the command line in those instances. You will also find that even in the Windows environment, there is an assumption that the user "knows" DOS. For instance, you will find that error messages you receive are couched in DOS terms, such as "The system can not find the path specified." Likewise, you will still find that there are programs, especially if you are involved in developing Web pages for use on the Internet, that can only be run from the *DOS system level* (another way of saying *command line interface* or *command line prompt*).

Additionally, if you are a user of the Internet, which often runs on Unix- or Linux-based computers, you often will be once again at the command line. Although Unix and Linux (both of which are command line interface operating systems—Linux is based on Unix-like commands) do not use commands identical to DOS commands, they are in fact similar enough that, if you know one, you can figure out the other.

If you work with networks or plan a career in network administration, knowledge of the command line is a necessity. Network operating systems rely on the command line interface. Even the Windows family of operating systems, Microsoft's GUI networking operating system, absolutely relies on command line interfaces. Windows XP Professional provides you with an expanded list of commands that are available to you from the command line. In addition, Windows Operating systems allow you to write batch files, which are usually written, tested, and run at the command line interface, to automate many routine tasks. In fact, Windows XP Professional has even more powerful batch file commands available to you than Windows Me and Windows 98. Furthermore, if a career in a computer-related field is in your future, you must know the command line interface. Almost all networking classes have as a prerequisite a working knowledge of DOS. Remember that "DOS" is a shorthand way of saying "command line interface." If you are working towards A+ Certification, knowing "DOS" is a must. It is much easier to say "go to DOS" than to say "go to the command prompt" or "the command line interface."

You will also find that the knowledge that you gain in this text by learning the command line interface will help you understand what is going on in the Windows environment. Perhaps an analogy might be your automobile. Most of us are not auto mechanics and do not know how to do engine repair. Nonetheless, if you have an understanding of what is going on under the hood, you may be able to do minor repairs and preventative maintenance so you can avoid more costly major repairs. At the very least, you will be able to explain problems to professional auto technicians in intelligent terms that will allow them to identify problems so that they may spend their expensive time fixing, not identifying, problems. In this text, you are going to use the command line prompt, and you will learn what's under the hood of Windows. This will give you, as with an automobile, the ability to do minor repairs and preventative maintenance as well as to explain complex problems to a software technician.

1.12   Accessing the Command Line Prompt

In order to use the command line interface, you first need to access it. You must open the Command Line window from a menu, or you may create a shortcut to it.

One thing you must remember is not to turn off the computer when you are in a Command Line window. You must exit the window and then follow the Windows shut-down procedure.

Note: What you see on your screen may differ from the examples shown in this book. While almost all of the examples shown are done on a computer with a standard installation of Windows XP Professional, some may be from another version of Windows. You can ignore these minor differences. If there is a significant difference, it will be noted and explained.

1.13   Activity: The Command Line Prompt

1   Boot the system.

2   Click **Start**. Click **Programs**. Click **Accessories**. Click **Command Prompt**.

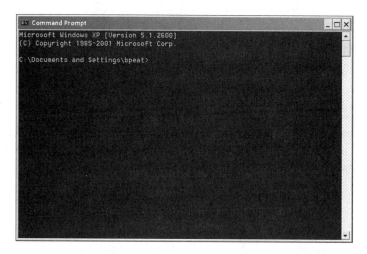

Note: If you do not see the title bar, press [Alt] + [Enter]

WHAT'S HAPPENING?   You have opened the Command Prompt window. This is the character-based interface. You may close this window and return to the desktop.

3   Click the ⊠ on the title bar in the right corner.

WHAT'S HAPPENING?   You have returned to the desktop. You can also create a shortcut to the command line. A shortcut is an icon on the desktop that points to an application or command.

Note: If you are in a lab environment, check with your administrator or lab technician to see if there are any special instructions for creating shortcuts.

4   Right-click the desktop.

5   Point to **New**.

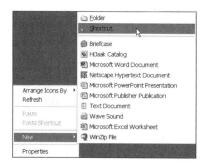

6   Click **Shortcut**.

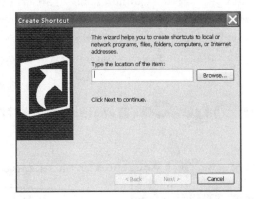

WHAT'S ▇▇▇▇
▇▇▇ **HAPPENING?**   You opened the dialog box for the Create Shortcut wizard. A wizard is a tool that leads you through the steps you need to take to accomplish your goal. In order to create a shortcut, you need to know the name and location of the program of interest.

7   In the text box, key in the following: **C:\WINDOWS\SYSTEM32\CMD.EXE** (Remember, if you have upgraded from Windows 2000, all references to the WINDOWS directory will be WINNT on your system.)

8   Click **Next**.

WHAT'S ▇▇▇▇
▇▇▇ **HAPPENING?**   You may use any name you wish for your shortcut. However, in this example, Windows automatically gives the shortcut the name of **CMD.EXE**. In this way, Windows is telling you that **CMD.EXE** is the Command Prompt.

9   Key in the following: **Command Prompt**

10   Click **Finish**.

WHAT'S ▇▇▇▇
▇▇▇ **HAPPENING?**   You have created a shortcut and placed it on the desktop. By double-clicking it, you can go to the command line, referred to as the "Command Prompt."

11   Double-click the **Command Prompt** shortcut.

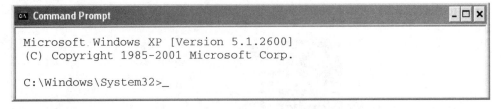

WHAT'S ▇▇▇▇
▇▇▇ **HAPPENING?**   The Command Prompt window opens with the default prompt (in this example, that is **C:\WINDOWS\SYSTEM32**). You would prefer it to open with the prompt **C:**. You may alter this.

12 Click the ☒ on the title bar in the right corner to close the Command Line window.

13 Right-click the **Command Prompt** shortcut. Click **Properties**.

WHAT'S ▓▓▓▓▓▓
▓▓▓ HAPPENING?   In Windows XP Professional, when you open the shortcut, you may be taken to either **C:\WINDOWS\SYSTEM32** or to **C:**, depending on how your lab technician set up your environment. This is determined by the entry in the Start in: text box. In this example, the Command Prompt window will open in **C:\WINDOWS\SYSTEM32**.

14 Select the text in the **Start in:** text box.

15 Key in the following: **C:**

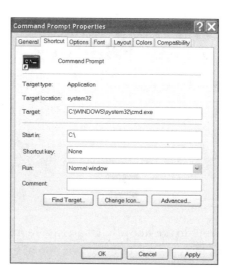

WHAT'S ▓▓▓▓▓▓
▓▓▓ HAPPENING?   You have altered the properties of the Command Prompt window so that it will always start at **C:**.

16 Click **OK**.

17 Double-click the **Command Prompt** icon.

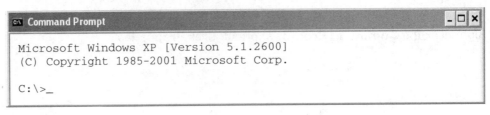

WHAT'S
HAPPENING?   Now your shortcut will open with **C:\>** as the default.

18 Click the ⊠ on the title bar in the right corner.

1.14 Controlling the Appearance of the Command Line Window

In the Windows environment, everything initially appears in a window with a title bar and a toolbar, but this look can be changed. You can leave the Command Prompt in a window. When it is in a window, you can use the Minimize button (⎯), the Maximize button (□), or the Restore button (🗗), all on the right side of the title bar. The Minimize button will make the window a button on the taskbar. The Maximize button will fill the entire screen with the window, and the Restore button will return the window to its previous size. While in window view, you may alter the size of the text in the window. You may also dispense with the window altogether and view the command line in full-screen mode by clicking on the icon on the far left side of the title bar, selecting Properties, selecting Options, and selecting Full Screen under Display Options. To toggle (switch) between a window and full-screen mode, you may press the **Alt** and **Enter** keys.

1.15 Activity: Altering the Command Line Window

1 Double-click the **Command Prompt** shortcut on the desktop.

2 Place and hold your mouse pointer over the Minimize button in the upper-right corner of the Command Prompt window.

WHAT'S
HAPPENING?   When you do not know what an icon represents, placing the mouse pointer over the object causes a brief description of the object to appear. This description is called a *ToolTip*.

3 Click the Minimize button on the title bar.

WHAT'S
HAPPENING?   The Command Prompt window has become a button on the
taskbar. It is still open but not active.

4   Click the **Command Prompt** button on the taskbar.

5   Click the Maximize button on the title bar.

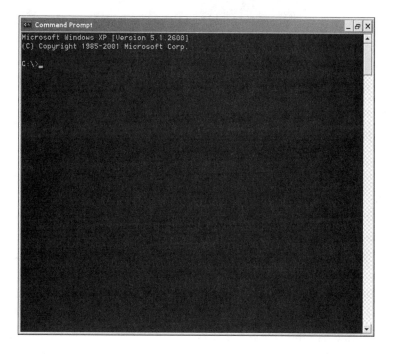

WHAT'S
HAPPENING?   Now the Command Prompt window is at its maximum size.
Depending on the resolution of your monitor and the text size setting, the display
may fill the entire screen.

6   Click the Restore button.

7   Click on the icon in the upper-left corner of the Command Prompt screen, .
You will open a menu.

Command Pr
Restore
Move
Size
Minimize
Maximize
Close
Edit   ▸
Defaults
Properties

8   Select **Properties** from the menu. Click on **Font**.

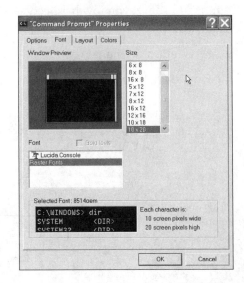

HAPPENING?   While you are in this window, you may choose a font size. The fonts that have Tt in front of them are called TrueType fonts. The other choice is raster or bit-mapped fonts. Typically, a bit-mapped font will be clearer and sharper in a Command Prompt window, and a TrueType font is better for use in application programs such as Word or Excel. Your choices of font sizes will depend on your monitor and available resolutions.

9   Click **Cancel** to close the Properties box.

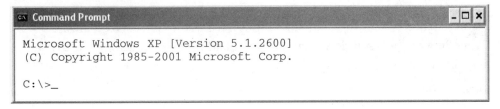

HAPPENING?   You have returned the display to a window. The actual displays you will see on the screen are white text on a black background, but in this text, dark text on a lighter background will be used for easier reading. Remember *never* turn off the computer when at the Command Prompt. You must first close the Command Prompt window and return to the Windows desktop or type EXIT at the prompt to return to the desktop. Then you must shut down the computer using the Windows shut-down procedure, learned previously.

10   Key in the following: C:\>**EXIT** Enter

HAPPENING?   You have closed the Command Prompt window and returned to the desktop.

1.16   The Default Drive and Default Directory

The command prompt is where you key in your commands. You normally do not use a pointing device when in command prompt mode. Command prompt mode is character-based, which means that you must explicitly tell the operating system what you want it to do by keying in the instruction (command). Where you key in your command is indicated by a blinking *cursor* following the prompt. The prompt usually looks like C:\>_ or sometimes [C:\]_. (The _ represents the blinking cursor.) The letter and colon behind the greater-than sign or in brackets is the default drive. The \ has two functions. It indicates the root directory when proceeded by a colon (:) and acts as a separator between directories, in a prompt such as C:\WINDOWS\SYSTEM32>. The *default* drive and directory is your current location. This will change depending on where you are. The default drive and directory that is displayed when you go to the command line prompt depends on the setup of your particular computer, how many hard drives you have, and what software is currently running. The most common prompt will be C:\>, C:\WINDOWS>, or C:\WINDOWS\SYSTEM32>, but many other variations are possible. The operating system names drives using a letter followed by a colon, such as A:, C:, or J:. All drives, no matter the type—CD-ROM drives, floppy drives, removable drives such as Zip drives or Jaz drives, and hard drives—follow this naming rule. The default drive is the one where the operating system is currently pointing. It can be changed easily.

1.17   Activity: Changing the Default Drive

Note 1:   You should be at the Windows desktop.

Note 2:   Though your Command Line window may open to a different default
            drive and directory, in this text, the prompt used will be C:\>.

1   Click **Start,** point to **Programs,** point to **Accessories,** and click **Command
Prompt** or double-click the **Command Prompt** shortcut on the desktop.

2   Get the disk labeled **Activities** that came with the textbook.

3   To insert a 3½-inch disk properly into the disk drive, place your thumb on the
label with the metal shutter facing away from you and toward the floppy disk
drive (see Figure 1.3). On some computers, the floppy disk drive is installed
vertically. To determine which way to insert the disk it is helpful to know that the
side of the disk with the circular metal disk is the bottom of the disk. The bottom
of the disk always faces the button on the drive. Slip the disk into the slot and
gently push the disk into the drive until you hear it click and/or feel it snap into
place. When the disk is properly in place, the small rectangular button on the
floppy drive will pop out.

Figure 1.3—Inserting a Disk

Note 1:   Remember, when you see the notation [Enter], it means to press the [Enter] key located towards the right side of the keyboard and labeled "Enter" and/or "Return."

Note 2:   The prompt will be in the following font: C: What you key in will be in the following font: **C:** Key in only what follows the prompt, not the prompt itself.

Note 3:   You will need to refer to your Configuration Table in Section 1.6 from time to time to ensure that your operating procedures for this, and all other activities, are correct for the computer you are using.

4   Key in the following: C:\>**A:** [Enter]

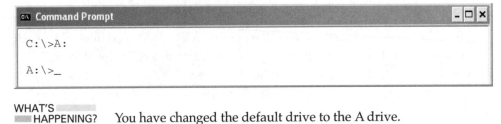

```
C:\>A:

A:\>_
```

WHAT'S
HAPPENING?   You have changed the default drive to the A drive.

1.18 Understanding Commands

Windows operating system *commands* are programs. Like application programs, they perform specific tasks. OS commands are of two types: internal or external. When you boot the system, internal commands are automatically loaded and stored into memory (RAM). These internal commands are built into the command processor, CMD.EXE. This file, and hence, these internal commands, are always placed in memory and remain in RAM the entire time your computer is on.

To use an internal command, you key in the command name at the command line or click the command's icon. For an internal command, Windows checks memory, finds the program, loads it into RAM, and executes it. Internal commands are also called resident commands because they reside in memory or inside the computer. Internal commands are limited in number because they take up valuable space in memory.

External commands are stored as files on a disk. When you wish to use an external command, you call upon the operating system to load the program into RAM by keying in the program's name or clicking its icon. Since it is an external command, the OS cannot find the program internally, so it must go to the disk, locate the file, load it into RAM, and then execute it. If the OS cannot find the file, the program cannot be run. These commands are called external or transient commands because they reside in a file on a disk and must be read into RAM each time you key them in.

Windows loads and executes programs such as Word or Quicken. Clicking or double-clicking a program icon or choosing a program from a menu loads an external command. You do not have to key in a command name, but the process is the same. For instance, the icon for Word stores the location and name of the program file such as C:\PROGRAM FILES\MICROSOFT OFFICE\WINWORD.EXE. The operating system looks first for the program in memory. When it cannot find it in memory, it goes to the specified location, including the disk drive as well as the directory. In the example given, Windows looks to Drive C in a folder called MICROSOFT OFFICE, which is in a folder called PROGRAM FILES, for a file called WINWORD.EXE. When it finds it, it loads it, and you have Word available to you. You are letting the GUI do the work. You could do the work yourself at the command prompt by simply keying in WINWORD.EXE. The end result would be the same. The OS would find and load Word for you. If the icon were set up incorrectly, Windows would not load (execute) the program you wanted, no matter how often you chose the icon or the menu choice. The icon or menu choice is only a pointer to the program file.

If the icon had stored incorrect information, such as an incorrect program location, Windows would give you the error message that it could not load Word because it could not find it. If you did not understand this process, you would not be able to use Word because all you would see would be the error message. If you did understand the operating system process, you would either correct the pointer or run Word from the command prompt.

Although all program files are external, including application programs, the term *external command* is reserved for the group of programs that perform operating system functions. These programs are files that come with Windows and are copied to a subdirectory called C:\WINDOWS\SYSTEM32 on the hard disk when Windows is installed. This group of files is generically referred to as the command line utility files or system utility files.

In the Command Prompt window, unlike the Windows GUI environment, you have no icons. In order to use commands, you must know their file names. The DIR command, an internal command that stands for directory, is provided so that you may look for files on a disk from the command line. In Windows, Explorer is the equivalent of the DIR command. When you key in DIR and press the Enter key, you are asking the operating system to run the directory program. The purpose or task of the DIR command is to display the names of all the files in a directory on the disk onto the screen. You see what could be described as a table of contents of the disk. The DIR command is the first internal command you will use.

1.19 Activity: Using the DIR Command

Note: Be sure the disk labeled ACTIVITIES is in Drive A and you are at the A:\> prompt.

1   Key in the following: A:\>**DIR** Enter

```
Command Prompt                                                    _ □ ✕

    11/24/2001    11:24  AM                   194  PLANETS.TXT
    10/30/2001    03:18  PM                   758  RIGHT.UP
    07/31/2000    04:32  PM                   260  STATE.CAP
    10/31/2001    07:08  PM                   478  VEN.NEW
    05/14/2002    08:07  AM                    64  WILD2.YYY
    10/30/2001    01:46  PM                   148  ASTRO.TMP
    08/01/2002    09:28  AM      <DIR>             DATA
    10/31/2001    07:08  PM                   478  VEN.TMP
    10/31/2001    05:37  PM                   383  EARTH.THR
    12/11/2002    09:10  AM                   294  EXP02JAN.dta
    10/31/2001    04:50  PM                   138  FILE3.SWT
    05/30/2000    04:32  PM                   182  OLDAUTO.MAK
```

```
10/31/2001   12:00 PM                  115  RIGHT.RED
12/06/2001   12:13 AM                  138  AWARD.MOV
10/12/2002   09:31 AM    <DIR>              SPORTS
05/14/2001   11:28 AM                4,843  GO.BAT
05/27/2001   10:08 PM                   76  LONGFILENAME
11/16/2002   09:36 AM    <DIR>              LEVEL-1
10/31/2001   01:08 PM                  406  MER.99
12/06/2001   12:25 AM                  465  person.fil
07/31/1999   12:53 PM                   46  STEVEN.FIL
10/31/2001   07:08 PM                  478  VENUS.TXT
12/31/2001   04:32 PM                   93  WILDONE
10/31/2001   06:40 PM                  188  ZODIAC.FIL
               91 File(s)         47,396 bytes
                7 Dir(s)         287,744 bytes free

A:\>_
```

WHAT'S HAPPENING?   This graphic represents the last part of the screen you will see (91 files and 7 directories will be listed). You may see more or fewer files displayed, depending on how your Command Prompt window is set up. Nonetheless, you will see text moving vertically on the screen. This movement is known as *scrolling*, the result of executing the DIR command. The operating system is displaying, or listing, all the files on the root of the disk in Drive A and stops scrolling when the list ends. The last subdirectory on the list is **LEVEL-1**. You can tell it is a subdirectory by the **<DIR>** entry to the left of the name. The last file listed is called **ZODIAC.FIL**. The file name is **ZODIAC**. The file extension is **FIL**.

The order of the file information differs significantly from some versions of Windows. You will use the file **ZODIAC.FIL** as your example. First, you will see the date that the file was created, **10/31/2001**; and the time, **06:40 PM**. The date and time indicate either when this file was created or when it was last modified. Next is the number **188**, the size of the file in bytes. Then you will see the file name.

Now look at the bottom two lines of the screen. One line states: **91 File(s)   47,396** bytes. This line indicates how many files are in the current directory and how much room they occupy. The next line, **7 Dir(s)   287,744 bytes free**, indicates first how many directories are below the current directory and second how much room is left on the disk for more files. All the files listed on the disk are practice files so that you may practice using the operating system commands without harming any of your own files.

1.20   Software Versions

Software companies regularly release new versions of software to take advantage of new technology. These upgrades also contain enhancements. The term *enhancements* simply means more features. In addition, new versions of software fix problems in older versions. This process is known as fixing bugs. To keep track of the versions, companies assign them version numbers. For instance, there is WordPerfect 8 and WordPerfect 9 and Word 2000 and Word 2002.

As previously explained, version numbers are also assigned to operating systems. For MS-DOS, 1.0 was the first version, released in 1981, and DOS 6.22 was the last stand-alone, character-based operating system. Windows 95 replaced DOS 6.22. Windows Millennium Edition replaced Windows 98 and Windows 95, and

Windows 2000 Professional replaced Windows NT. Windows XP Home Edition is an UpGrade of Windows Millennium and Windows XP Professional is an upgrade to Windows 2000 Professional. Beginning with Windows 95, DOS has been integrated into the Windows operating system.

1.21 Activity: Using the VER Command

1 Key in the following: A:\>**VER** Enter

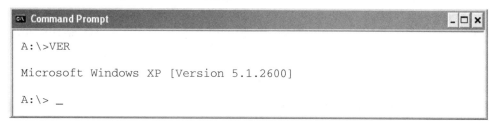

WHAT'S
HAPPENING?   In this example, the computer is running the operating system Windows XP [Version 5.1.2600]. The version number you see depends on the version of Windows you have on your computer.

1.22 The CLS Command

Your screen is filled with the display of the directory from the DIR command that you keyed in. You may want to have a "fresh" screen, with nothing displayed except the C:\> prompt and the cursor in its "home" position (the upper left-hand corner of the screen). The internal command CLS clears the screen. Whatever is displayed on the screen will go away, as if you erased a chalkboard. The command erases the screen display, not your files.

1.23 Activity: Using the CLS Command

1 Key in the following: A:\>**CLS** Enter

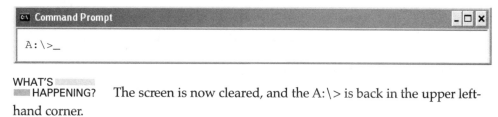

WHAT'S
HAPPENING?   The screen is now cleared, and the A:\> is back in the upper left-hand corner.

1.24 The DATE and TIME Commands

The computer, via a battery, keeps track of the current date and time. Date and time are known as the *system date* and the *system time*. The system date and time are the date and time the computer uses when it opens and closes files (last date/time accessed) or when another program asks for the date and time. Today's computers have a built-in clock. It is simply a built-in, 24-hour, battery-operated clock that sets the date and time automatically when you boot the system. You can change or check the system date and system time whenever you wish by using the internal DATE and TIME commands at the command line, or from within the Windows desktop by clicking the time displayed at the far right of the taskbar.

1.25   Activity: Using DATE/TIME Commands at the Command Line

WARNING: If you are logged on to a DOMAIN be SURE and return the date and time to the current date and time before you shut down. If you do not do this, you may not be able to log on to that station.

1   Key in the following: A:\>**DATE** Enter

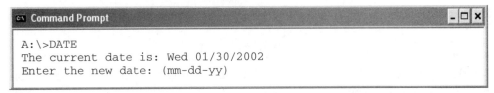

```
Command Prompt                                            _ □ x
A:\>DATE
The current date is: Wed 01/30/2002
Enter the new date: (mm-dd-yy)
```

WHAT'S HAPPENING?   The date displayed on your screen is the current date, not the above example. If you did not wish to change the date, you would just press <Enter>, retaining the date displayed and returning you to A:\>. However, if you do want to change the date, respond to the prompt. You must key in the date in the proper format, such as **11-15-02**. You may not key in character data such as **November 15, 2002**. Furthermore, you are allowed to use some other separators that are not stated. You may key in **11/15/02** using the forward slash, or you may use periods such as **11.15.02**. No other characters can be used.

2   Key in the following: **12-31-02** Enter

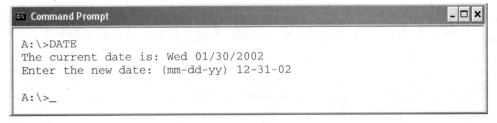

```
Command Prompt                                            _ □ x
A:\>DATE
The current date is: Wed 01/30/2002
Enter the new date: (mm-dd-yy) 12-31-02

A:\>_
```

WHAT'S HAPPENING?   You did change the date, and we will examine this change in a moment. You can also change the time in the same fashion with the TIME command.

3   Key in the following: A:\>**TIME** Enter

```
Command Prompt                                            _ □ x
A:\>TIME
The current time is: 10:45:47.15
Enter the new time:
```

WHAT'S HAPPENING?   The time displayed on your screen is the current time, not the above example. If you did not wish to change the time, you would just press Enter, retaining the time displayed and returning you to A:\>. However, if you do want to change the time, you respond to the prompt. You may use only the colon (:) to separate the numbers. Although in this case you are going to key in the seconds, most people usually key in only the hour and minutes. If you wish the time to be in the P.M., you add a "p" after the time. You may also use a 24-hour clock.

4   Key in the following: **23:59:59** [Enter]

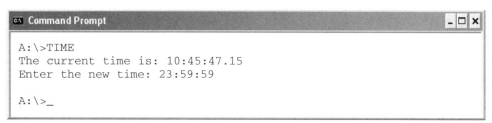

```
A:\>TIME
The current time is: 10:45:47.15
Enter the new time: 23:59:59

A:\>_
```

WHAT'S
HAPPENING?   You have just reset the computer clock with the DATE and TIME commands. These are internal commands. How do you know the system date and time have been changed? You can check by keying in the commands using a parameter that displays only the date and time.

5   Key in the following: A:\>**DATE /T** [Enter]

6   Key in the following: A:\>**TIME /T** [Enter]

```
A:\>DATE /T
Wed 01/01/2003

A:\>TIME /T
12:02 AM

A:\> _
```

WHAT'S
HAPPENING?   Your time display numbers may be slightly different. What have you done? You have changed the system date and time. You entered the date of December 31, 2002 (12-31-02), prior to changing the time. The date now displayed is Wed, January 1, 2003. How did that happen? Why is the displayed date different from the keyed-in date? After you entered the date of 12/31/02, you entered the time of 11:59 p.m. (23:59:59). Seconds went by; the time passed midnight, and, when you are passed midnight, you are into a new day. Hence, the day "rolled over" from December 31, 2002 to January 1, 2003. In other words, the system keeps the date and time current based on the information you give. The /T parameter used with the DATE and TIME commands displayed the system date and time.

The day of the week is displayed in the date. You can experiment with the DATE and TIME commands. For instance, you can find the day of your birthday in any future or past year by using the DATE command and entering your birthday.

7   Key in the following: A:\>**DATE** [Enter]

8   At the prompt on the screen key in your birthday for 2002:
A:\> **12-11-02** [Enter]
(In this example, I used my birthday.)

9   Key in the following: A:\>**DATE** **/T** Enter

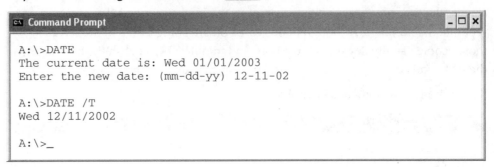

```
CN  Command Prompt                                                    - □ ×

A:\>DATE
The current date is: Wed 01/01/2003
Enter the new date: (mm-dd-yy) 12-11-02

A:\>DATE /T
Wed 12/11/2002

A:\>_
```

WHAT'S
HAPPENING?   The screen display shows you the day of your birthday in 2002. In this case, my birthday falls on a Wednesday. If you wish to see or change the system date or time, you can also use the clock on the taskbar.

10   Click the Close button in the Command Prompt window.

1.26   Activity: Changing the Date and Time Using the Taskbar

1   Right-click the time display on the right of the taskbar. Click **Adjust Date/Time**.

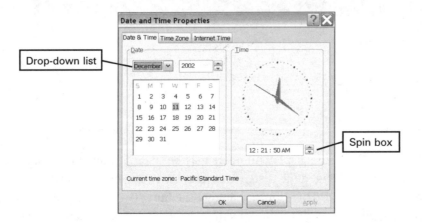

WHAT'S
HAPPENING?   You have opened the Date/Time Properties dialog box. You can change the date by clicking on any one of the numbers in the calendar. You can change the time either by clicking in the spin box under the clock, deleting any part of the time, and keying in the correct time, or by using the up and down arrows in the spin box. A spin box is a control that allows you to move ("spin") through a set of fixed values such as dates or times. In a spin box, you may also key in a valid value in the box. You can change the month or year by using the drop-down list box. You may either key in the new value or use the up or down arrows. A drop-down list box is a control that has the current value in it. When you click the up or down arrow, you open the drop-down list box to display a pre-determined list of choices, from which you can make a seletion.

2   Change the date, month, and time to the current values. *(Do not skip this step.)*

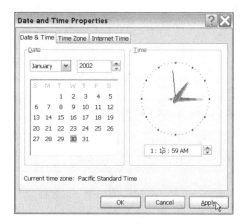

WHAT'S HAPPENING?   You have returned the system time and date to the current values. A feature of the clock on the taskbar is to show you the current date without opening the dialog box.

3   Click **OK**.

4   Place the mouse pointer over the time on the taskbar. Do not click, just point the arrow.

WHAT'S HAPPENING?   The day and date are briefly displayed. The display remains only for a few seconds and then disappears.

1.27 Media Objects: Their Properties and Values

What is an object? What is a property? To Windows, *everything* is an object. This is true for all versions of Windows. A file, the keyboard, a disk drive—all are objects. Each object has properties, and the properties may have values.

To explain the object-property-value relationship, you can use a person. A person is an object. All objects of that same type (human) have the same properties. Some properties of this person object are *name, height,* and *eye color*. The values of person objects, however, differ. One person's name property value is John Jones; another person's name property value is Olivia Wu. A newborn person has the property of name, but no value has been assigned to that property.

To discover information about an object in Windows, you examine that object's property sheet. Most objects' property sheets can be displayed by right-clicking on the object icon and choosing Properties from the shortcut menu. For example, when you copy a disk, it is very important that you know what type of media you are using. Furthermore, it is important to know what type of floppy disk drive or hard drive you have on your system. You need to know the "native" format of the disk drive, whether or not you have a high-density disk drive, and which drive is

Drive A. In Windows, this information is ascertained by examining a drive's property sheet.

1.28 Activity: Examining Disk Properties and Values

1   Click the Start menu. Click **My Computer**. (If you have the My Computer icon on your desktop, you may double-click the icon.)

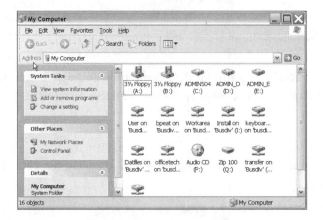

WHAT'S HAPPENING?   You have opened the My Computer window. In this example, the system is logged onto a Domain, and there are many network drives shown, as well as the local drives. In My Computer, you see all the drives available on your system. You can identify the type of drive by its icon:

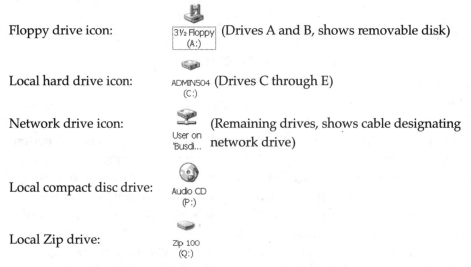

Floppy drive icon: (Drives A and B, shows removable disk)

Local hard drive icon: (Drives C through E)

Network drive icon: (Remaining drives, shows cable designating network drive)

Local compact disc drive:

Local Zip drive:

This view is the default view for Windows XP Professional. You may also see the following display as shown in Figure 1.4, where the Folder options have been changed to a classic Windows display.

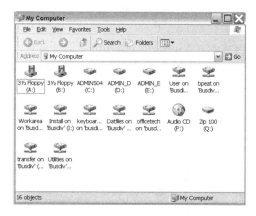

Figure 1.4—My Computer in a Classic Windows Display

In this text, different views on different computer systems will be shown. The appearance of your desktop and windows will depend on your particular lab or home computing environment.

2   Right-click the A drive icon.

WHAT'S
HAPPENING?   A drop-down menu has opened. The last item on the menu is Properties. Depending on the configuration of your system, your drop down menu may have more or less options available to you.

3   Click **Properties**.

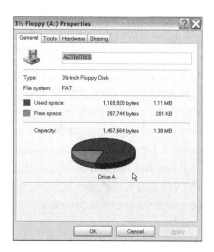

WHAT'S ▓▓▓▓▓
▓▓▓ HAPPENING?   The property sheet for the A drive displays the properties of the ACTIVITIES disk. You can see many things about the disk: the label or electronic name, the amount of used space, and the amount of free space displayed in numbers and in a graphic pie chart. You can also see the disk type and its total capacity. This is a 3½-inch diskette with a total capacity of 1,457,664 bytes.

4   Click **Cancel**.

5   Close My Computer.

1.29   Ethical Considerations in Copying Disks

It is *unethical* and *illegal* to make a copy of a program or a disk that you did not purchase and do not own. Making a copy of a program or receiving a copy of a program is stealing someone else's work. If you did not personally purchase the program, even if you are using it at work, it is still illegal to copy it and use it. However, most software manufacturers allow you and encourage you to make backup copies of program disks for your own personal use in case something happens to the original. Remember, however, you need to have purchased the program or have permission to copy the disk in order for the copy to be both legal and ethical. If your program came on a CD-ROM, as is most usual today, it is possible to copy it if you have a recording CD-ROM (CDRW) drive, but once again, this is legal *only if you purchased the CD*.

In the following activity, you are going to copy the ACTIVITIES disk that comes with this book so that you have a working copy of it. You will work from a copy of the ACTIVITIES disk so that, if anything happens, you can use the original ACTIVITIES disk to make another copy. Whenever possible, always work from a copy, never an original. This copy of the ACTIVITIES disk will be used in all future exercises. It is legal to make a copy for your personal use only. If you are in a computer lab, check with your instructor for the procedures in your specific lab.

1.30   Making a Copy of the ACTIVITIES Disk: DISKCOPY

When making an exact copy of a disk, you must have like media. This means the disk you are copying *from* and the disk you are copying *to* must be *exactly* the same type and capacity. You are now going to make a working copy of the ACTIVITIES disk. You will use an external program called DISKCOPY. It is stored as a file called DISKCOPY.COM in the WINDOWS\SYSTEM32 (or WINNT\SYSTEM32) subdirectory. It does exactly what it says; it copies all the information from one floppy disk to another. Before it copies a disk, it formats it. You can never use the DISKCOPY command to copy from a hard disk to a floppy disk or from a floppy disk to a hard disk. You could copy the disk from the desktop. Notice the menu in the previous Activity 1.28, step 2. One of the options is **Copy Disk. . .** In the following activity however, you will use the command line method. Please follow the instructions precisely. The ACTIVITIES disk is a high-density, 3½-inch floppy disk. Your blank disk must be the same media type in order to do the next activity.

1.31 Activity: Using DISKCOPY

Note: If you are in a lab environment, check with your instructor to see if there are any special procedures.

1 Get a new paper label. On the label write "ACTIVITIES Disk—Working Copy" and your name. Make sure you are using either a new disk or one that you no longer want the information on, and that is the same type and capacity as the ACTIVITIES disk. Affix the label to the disk. See Figure 1.5 for the correct location of the label.

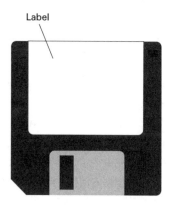

Figure 1.5—Floppy Disk Label Placement

2 Place the ACTIVITIES disk that came with the textbook in Drive A.

3 Click **Start**. Point to **Programs**. Point to **Accessories**. Click **Command Prompt**.

4 Key in the following: `C:\ >`**CD \WINDOWS\SYSTEM32** Enter

Note: Refer to your configuration table, if necessary, to locate the correct directory.

5 Key in the following: `C:\WINDOWS\SYSTEM32>`**DISKCOPY A: A:** Enter

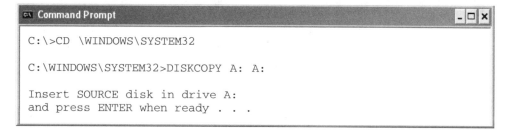

WHAT'S
HAPPENING?   By keying in **DISKCOPY**, you asked the command processor to find a program called DISKCOPY. It first looked in memory in the internal table of commands. When it could not find a match, it went to the disk in Drive **C** and the subdirectory **WINDOWS\SYSTEM32**, found the program, loaded it into memory, and started executing it. This program has some prompts, which are instructions to follow. The program asks you to put the SOURCE disk that you wish to copy in Drive A. In this case, the ACTIVITIES disk, which you want to copy, is already in Drive A. You are telling the operating system to make a copy from the disk in

Drive A to the disk in Drive A. To make the copy or begin executing the command DISKCOPY, press the [Enter] key.

6   Press [Enter]

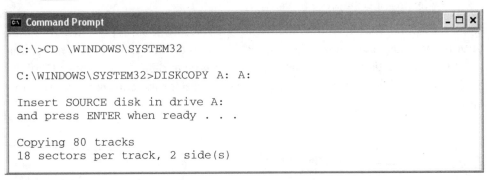

```
C:\>CD \WINDOWS\SYSTEM32

C:\WINDOWS\SYSTEM32>DISKCOPY A: A:

Insert SOURCE disk in drive A:
and press ENTER when ready . . .

Copying 80 tracks
18 sectors per track, 2 side(s)
```

WHAT'S HAPPENING?   Track and sector numbers will vary depending on the type of disk used. The DISKCOPY command tells the operating system to copy everything on the disk in Drive A (the SOURCE) to RAM. While this program is doing the copying, the cursor flashes onscreen. When the command is completed or the copying is finished, you will need to take another step. You see the following prompt:

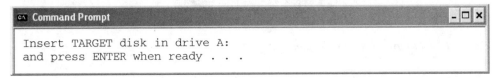

```
Insert TARGET disk in drive A:
and press ENTER when ready . . .
```

WHAT'S HAPPENING?   This prompt tells you to remove the SOURCE disk from Drive A and insert the blank or TARGET disk in Drive A so the operating system has a place to copy the information.

7   Remove the master ACTIVITIES disk from Drive A. Insert the blank disk labeled "ACTIVITIES Disk—Working Copy" into Drive A. Close or latch the drive door. Press [Enter]

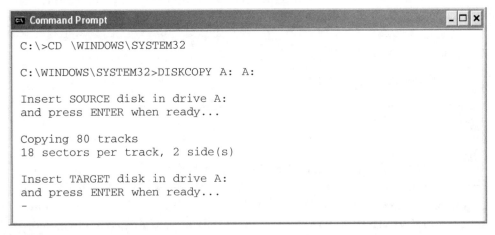

```
C:\>CD \WINDOWS\SYSTEM32

C:\WINDOWS\SYSTEM32>DISKCOPY A: A:

Insert SOURCE disk in drive A:
and press ENTER when ready...

Copying 80 tracks
18 sectors per track, 2 side(s)

Insert TARGET disk in drive A:
and press ENTER when ready...
-
```

WHAT'S HAPPENING?   Again, you see the flashing cursor. After DISKCOPY formats the TARGET disk, whatever was copied into RAM is copied or written to the blank disk in Drive A. When the process is complete, you will see the following message:

**WHAT'S
HAPPENING?**   The system wants to know if you wish to copy another disk.

8   Press N Enter

**WHAT'S
HAPPENING?**   The prompt tells you that the program has finished executing. The volume serial number changes with each DISKCOPY command and will not be the same as the example.

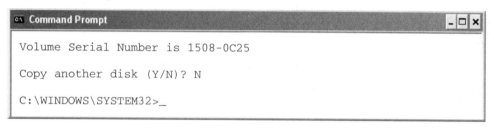

**WHAT'S
HAPPENING?**   You are returned to the C:\WINDOWS\SYSTEM32> prompt. The operating system is now ready for a new command.

9   Close the Command Prompt window.

1.32 How to End the Work Session

You can stop working with the computer at any time. Since your programs are stored on disks, you will not lose them. Remember, if you stop in the middle of an Activity, you will have to remember what the prompt was when you stopped, and return to it when you begin again. For example, if the default prompt was A:\> when you stop, it would be helpful to write that down. Then, when you begin again, you will be able to return to the place you were when you stopped. You must always exit Windows properly and completely; otherwise you could do serious, sometimes irreparable, damage to the system.

1.33 Activity: Ending the Work Session

Note: Check with your lab instructor to see what special procedures you might need to follow in your lab environment.

1   Close any remaining open windows, including the Command Prompt window.

2   Click Start.

3   Click Shut Down. Be sure Shut down is the choice on the drop-down menu.

4   Click **OK**.

WHATS
HAPPENING?   You have initiated the shut-down procedure.

5   New computers may be set to power down automatically, but if this does not
     happen, wait until you see the screen telling you it is safe to turn off the com-
     puter.

6   Turn off the system unit and (if necessary).

Chapter Summary

1. An operating system is a software program that is required in order to run
   application software and to oversee the hardware components of the computer
   system.
2. Windows is the major operating system in use today on Wintel microcomputers.
3. All microcomputers come with disk drives. There three basic types of disk
   drives are the floppy disk drive, the hard disk drive, and the CD-ROM drive.
4. Computer systems are configured in various ways, such as: One hard disk
   drive, one CD-ROM drive, and one floppy disk drive; one hard disk drive, one
   CD-ROM drive, one floppy disk drive, and one Zip drive; two hard disk drives,
   one CD-ROM drive, and one floppy disk drive, one hard disk drive, one CD-
   ROM drive, one read-write CD-ROM drive, and one floppy disk drive.
5. Booting the system, also known as a cold start, means more than powering on
   the system. It loads the operating system into memory and executes the self-
   diagnostic test routine.
6. Internal commands are programs loaded in CMD.EXE with the operating
   system. They remain in memory until the power is turned off.
7. External commands are stored on a disk and must be loaded into memory each
   time they are used. They are transient and do not remain in memory after being
   executed.
8. Programs and data are stored on disks as files. The formal name for this is file
   specification, which includes the file name and the file extension.
9. A command is a program. A program is the set of instructions telling the computer what to do.
10. Programs (commands) must be loaded into memory in order to be executed.
11. To load a program into memory, the user can key in the command name at the
    system prompt or click on the command's icon.
12. The DIR command is an internal command that displays the directory (table of
    contents) of a disk.

13. Internal commands include VER, CLS, DATE, and TIME.
    - VER displays the current version of the OS that is in memory
    - CLS clears the screen.
    - DATE and TIME allow you to look at and/or change the system date and system time, a process that can also be done from the desktop taskbar. Using the /T parameter with the DATE or TIME command will display the system date or time.
14. DISKCOPY is an external command that makes an identical copy of any disk, track for track, sector for sector. It was used to make a working copy of the ACTIVITIES disk but can be used to make exact copies with any two floppy disks that are the same media type. It formats a disk prior to copying to it.
15. To end a work session with the computer, Windows must be shut down in the proper sequence and shouldn't be turned off until a message on the screen tells you it is safe to do so.

Key Terms

booting the system	file extension	operating system
bug	file name	program file
command	file specification	system date
cursor	function key	system time
data file	LFN	ToolTip
disk file		

Discussion Questions

1. What is an operating system?
2. What are enhancements?
3. Define system configuration.
4. List two common ways that computer systems are configured.
5. Why is it necessary to boot the system?
6. How would you boot the system?
7. What is an object?
8. What is a property?
9. What is a value?
10. Identify and explain the function and purpose of the two parts of a file specification.
11. What is the difference between a command and a program?
12. Compare and contrast internal and external commands.
13. What is the purpose of the DIR command?
14. What is the function of the VER command?
15. What is the function of the CLS command?
16. How can you set the date and time?
17. How do you set the time when using the TIME command?
18. What is the purpose of making a backup copy of a program?
19. Why should you work with a copy of a program rather than with the original?
20. Why is it important to know what type of media you are using when copying disks?

21. What is the purpose of the DISKCOPY command?
22. What are the necessary steps to ending a work session?

True/False Questions

For each question, circle the letter T if the statement is true and the letter F if the statement is false.

T   F   1. To identify what version of the operating system you are using, you could, at the command line, use the VER command.

T   F   2. A correct way to key in a date would be **2/4/01.**

T   F   3. When you see the computer notation $\boxed{\text{Ctrl}}$ + C, it means you should key in the word Control and then the letter C.

T   F   4. LFN is an acronym for Last File Noted.

T   F   5. DISKCOPY.COM is a program that is stored on the disk as a file.

Completion Questions

Write the correct answer in each blank space.

6. One way to communicate with the computer is by _____ commands on the keyboard.

7. Programs, data, and text are stored on disks as _____.

8. The operating system is in charge of the _____ components of the computer.

9. If you wanted to see the table of contents of a disk in the Command Prompt window, you would key in _____.

10. When you wish to end your computer session, you would first click on the _____ button.

Multiple Choice Questions

For each question, write the letter for the correct answer in the blank space.

____   11. To display the contents of a disk, key in the following command:
a. TOC
b. DIR
c. DIS
d. Directory

____   12. To change the date to May 7, 2001, after you key in DATE, you could key in:
a. 5/7/01
b. 5-7-01
c. 5.7.01
d. any of the above

____   13. To clear the screen, key in:
a. CLS
b. CLR
c. CLEAR
d. Clear the screen

_____ 14. Which of the following is a type of disk drive?
   a. hard disk drive
   b. soft disk drive
   c. both a and b
   d. neither a nor b

_____ 15. To make a duplicate of a floppy disk, you use the command:
   a. DISKCOPY
   b. COPY
   c. DISKCMP
   d. D-COPY

Homework Assignments

Problem Set I—At the Computer

Problem A

A-a   Boot the system, if it is not booted.

A-b   Go to the Command Prompt window.

A-c   Make sure the prompt is C:\>.

A-d   Change the date to 5/8/01.

A-e   Re-enter the same command.

_____ 1. The day of the week that appears on the screen is:
   a. Tue
   b. Wed
   c. Thu
   d. Fri

A-f   Change the date to the current date.

_____ 2. The command you used was:
   a. DISKCOPY
   b. TIME
   c. DATE
   d. none of the above

A-g   Key in **Time** Enter

A-h   At the time prompt, key in **27:00** Enter

_____ 3. What error message is displayed on the screen?
   a. Not a valid time.
   b. The system cannot accept the time entered.
   c. Please key in the correct time.
   d. Do not use a colon.

A-i   Press Enter

Problem B

B-a   Place the working copy of the ACTIVITIES disk in Drive A.

B-b   Key in C:\>**A:** Enter

B-c   Key in A:\>**DIR** Enter

_____ 4. What date is listed for **WILD2.YYY**?
  a. 8/12/1999
  b. 5/14/2002
  c. 8/12/1998
  d. 8/12/2000

B-d   If the Command Prompt is not in a window, place it in one now.

B-e   Click on the icon at the left of the title bar. Select **Properties**.

_____ 5. What Property sheet is on the top?
  a. Options
  b. Font
  c. Layout
  d. Colors

B-f   Click **Cancel**.

B-g   Close the Command Prompt window.

_____ 6. You may close the Command Prompt window by clicking the
  a. ☒ button on the title bar.
  b. ☐ button on the title bar.
  c. ▨ on the title bar and click Close.
  d. either a or c

B-h   Exit Windows properly.

_____ 7. The fastest way to exit Windows correctly is to
  a. turn off the computer.
  b. click Start, then click Shut Down.

B-i   Be sure to remove your ACTIVITIES Disk—Working Copy from Drive A.

Problem Set II—Brief Essay

1. When DOS was a stand-alone operating system, file specifications were limited to the 8.3 file-naming rules. Windows 95 introduced the use of LFNs. Compare and contrast these two sets of rules. List any reasons for still retaining the use of 8.3 file names.

2. You can change the system time and date either from the command line or from Windows. List the advantages and disadvantages of each method. Which do you prefer? Explain your answer.

COMMAND SYNTAX: USING THE DIR COMMAND WITH PARAMETERS AND WILDCARDS

Learning Objectives

After completing this chapter you will be able to:

1. Define command syntax.
2. Explain what parameters are and how they are used.
3. Explain the purpose and use of the DIR command.
4. Define prompts and explain how they are used.
5. Explain the purpose of the CD command.
6. Explain the purpose and function of a device.
7. Explain the purpose and function of device names.
8. Explain the purpose and function of defaults.
9. Explain the function and purpose of subdirectories (paths).
10. Explain the use and purpose of wildcards.
11. Define global specifications and identify their symbols.
12. Explain the purpose and function of redirection.

Student Outcomes

1. Read a syntax diagram and be able to name and explain what each part signifies.
2. Use both fixed and variable parameters with the DIR command.
3. Give the names of the disk drives on your computer.
4. Change the default drive and the directory.
5. Use subdirectories (paths) with the DIR command.

6. Use global specifications with the DIR command.
7. Use wildcards with the DIR command.
8. Redirect the output of the DIR command to either a file or a printer.
9. Use online Help.

Chapter Overview

To communicate with the computer at the command line prompt, you need to learn the computer's language. You must follow the syntax of the language and use punctuation marks the computer understands. As in mastering any new language, new vocabulary words must be learned, word order (syntax) must be determined, and the method of separating statements into syntactic units must be understood. The computer has a very limited use of language, so it is very important to be precise when you are speaking to it.

In this chapter, you will learn some basic computer commands, the syntax or order of these commands, and where the commands begin and end. You will learn how to make your commands specific, how to use wildcards to affect a command, and how to determine which disk you want to write to or read from. You will also learn how to use the online Help feature.

2.1   Command Syntax

All languages have rules or conventions for speaking and writing. The *syntax*, or word order, and punctuation of a language is important. For example, in English the noun (person, place, or thing) is usually followed by the verb (the action). In Latin the verb most often ends a sentence, because Latin had no punctuation marks and the subject could be anywhere in the sentence, even within the verb. When you learn a language, you learn its syntax.

Anything you key into the computer must be in a language and syntax that the computer understands. The words you key in are actually *commands* ordering the computer to perform a specific task. These commands must also be in the correct order; that is, they must have the proper syntax. The computer cannot guess what you mean. People can understand "Going I store," but if you key in an incorrect word or put correct words in the wrong order, a computer will not understand.

In computer language, a command can be compared to a verb, the action you wish to take. In Chapter 1, you used the command DIR. In other words, when you keyed in DIR, you were asking the system to take an action: run the program called DIR that lets you see the directory (table of contents) of a disk.

Using the graphical user interface in the Windows OS does not change things—there are still syntax and rules. An icon that points to a program is based on the rules of syntax. Certainly, it is easier from a user's perspective to click an icon to accomplish a task rather than having to know the command and the appropriate syntax. However, it is important to understand what is actually taking place so when things do not work, you the user know how to go under the hood, so to speak, and fix the problem so that you can "click" on your desktop successfully.

2.2   What Are Parameters?

A *parameter* is information you can use to modify or qualify a command. Some commands *require* parameters, while other commands let you add them when needed. Some parameters are variable. A *variable parameter* is one to which you the user supply the value. This process is similar to a math formula. For instance, $x + y = z$ is a simple formula. You can plug in whatever values you wish for x and y. If $x = 1$ and $y = 2$, you know the value of z, which is 3. These values can change or are *variable* so that x can equal 5 and y can equal 3, which makes z equal to 8. These variables can have any other numerical value you wish. You can also have $z = 10$, $x = 5$, and mathematically establish the value of y. No matter what numbers x, y, or z are, you will be able to establish the value of each.

Other parameters are *fixed*. For instance, if the formula reads $x + 5 = z$, then x is the variable parameter and 5 is the fixed parameter. You can change the value of x but not the value of 5.

When you are working with some command line commands, you are allowed to add one or more parameters to make the action of a command more specific. This process is the same in English. If I give my granddaughter my Visa card and tell her, "Go buy," I have given her an open-ended statement—she can buy anything (making her one happy camper!). However, if I add a qualifier, "Go buy *shoes*," I have

limited what she can do. The word "shoes" is the parameter. This pattern exempli-
fies precisely what parameters do to a command.

2.3   Reading a Syntax Diagram

A command line interface is a language that has a vocabulary, grammar, and syntax.
To use the language of the command line, you must learn the vocabulary (commands) and understand the grammar (punctuation) and syntax (order). The syntax
information is provided through online Help. The *command syntax* diagrams tell
you how to enter a command with its optional or *mandatory parameters*. However,
you need to be able to interpret these *syntax diagrams*.

Here is the formal command syntax diagram for the DIR command you used
earlier:

```
DIR [drive:][path][filename] [/A[[:]attributes]] [/B] [/C] [/D] [/L]
    [/N] [/O[[:]sortorder]] [/P] [/Q] [/S] [/T[[:]timefield]] [/W]
    [/X] [/4]
```

The first entry is the command name, DIR. You must use this name only. You
cannot substitute another word such as DIRECTORY or INDEX. The parameters
that follow the command are in brackets [ ]. Brackets indicate that these parameters
are optional—not required for the command. The DIR command has *optional
parameters* only. There are no required, or mandatory, parameters for the DIR
command.

2.4   Using Fixed Parameters
with the DIR Command

The DIR command is one of the oldest commands available to the command line. It
has changed significantly since the "old days" of the 1980's but it has not changed at
all from Windows 2000. DIR is a command with optional parameters. Most often, a
fixed parameter is referred to as a *switch* and typically begins with / (the slash).

In the **DIR** command syntax diagram, **/W** and **/P** are in brackets. You never key in
the brackets, only / (the forward slash or slash) and the **W** or **P**. You must be careful;
there is only one slash—the forward slash /. The \ is a *backslash* and is always
referred to as the backslash. When a mark is referred to as a slash, it always means
the forward slash.

When you key in **DIR** and the files scroll by, they move so quickly that you
cannot read them. There is an efficient way to solve this problem by using the **/P**
parameter. The **/P** parameter will display one screen of information at a time. It will
also give you a prompt that you must respond to before it will display another
screenful of information.

Note 1:   There are times you may find it necessary to quit before you have com-
            pleted the entire chapter. Each activity begins with a note indicating which
            diskette is in the drive and the current directory and drive. Thus, if you
            complete an activity, you may pick up where you left off. When you stop
            working, be sure to return to the Windows desktop and initiate the Win-
            dows shut-down procedure.

Note 2:   Be sure you know what your computer laboratory procedures are.

Note 3:   If your system varies from the textbook, refer to the Configuration Table in Chapter 1, section 1.6.

2.5   Activity: Using Fixed Parameters with the DIR Command

Note: Whenever the textbook refers to the ACTIVITIES disk, you will use the working copy that you made in Chapter 1 and labeled "ACTIVITIES Disk—Working Copy."

1   If it is not on, turn on the computer.

2   Open a **Command Prompt** window.

3   Key in the following: C:\>**CD ** Enter

4   Key in the following: C:\>**CLS** Enter

```
Command Prompt                                         - □ ×

C:\>_
```

WHAT'S HAPPENING?   You have successfully booted the system. To ensure that you were at the root of Drive C, you keyed in **CD **. You are at the root directory of Drive C. You have also cleared the screen.

5   Insert the "ACTIVITIES Disk—Working Copy" in Drive A. (Remember, this means your working copy.)

6   Key in the following: C:\>**A:** Enter

```
Command Prompt                                         - □ ×

C:\>A:
A:\>_
```

WHAT'S HAPPENING?   The default drive is now Drive A. The default directory is the root of A.

7   Key in the following: A:\>**DIR** **/P** Enter

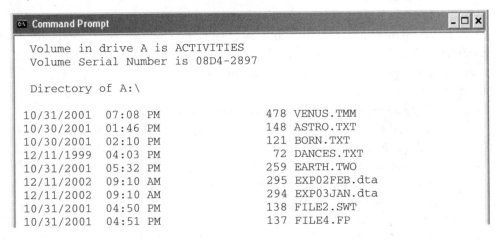

```
Command Prompt                                         - □ ×

 Volume in drive A is ACTIVITIES
 Volume Serial Number is 08D4-2897

 Directory of A:\

10/31/2001  07:08 PM              478 VENUS.TMM
10/30/2001  01:46 PM              148 ASTRO.TXT
10/30/2001  02:10 PM              121 BORN.TXT
12/11/1999  04:03 PM               72 DANCES.TXT
10/31/2001  05:32 PM              259 EARTH.TWO
12/11/2002  09:10 AM              295 EXP02FEB.dta
12/11/2002  09:10 AM              294 EXP03JAN.dta
10/31/2001  04:50 PM              138 FILE2.SWT
10/31/2001  04:51 PM              137 FILE4.FP
```

```
05/02/1994   12:57 AM                     26 GETYN.COM
05/30/2000   04:32 PM                     53 HELLO.TXT
05/07/2002   07:41 AM                    190 JUPITER.TMP
05/27/2001   10:09 PM                    122 LONGFILENAME.EXTENSION
08/12/2000   04:12 PM                     73 MARK.FIL
10/31/2001   01:08 PM                    406 MERCURY.TMP
05/14/2001   10:16 AM                  2,273 NAME.BAT
10/31/2001   01:49 PM                    219 ORION.NEB
10/31/2001   02:16 PM                 11,264 QUASARS.DOC
11/16/2000   12:00 PM                     59 Sandy and Patty.txt
10/31/2001   02:43 PM                    529 TITAN.TXT
10/30/2001   01:46 PM                    148 AST.99
05/14/2002   08:07 AM                     64 WILD3.ZZZ
12/31/2001   04:32 PM                    182 WILDTWO.DOS
12/06/2001   09:14 AM       <DIR>           GAMES
11/16/2000   12:00 PM                     53 Sandy and Nicki.txt
10/31/2001   06:51 PM                    125 BLUE.JAZ
08/12/2000   04:12 PM                    314 CASES.FIL
10/31/2001   05:28 PM                    165 EARTH.ONE
12/11/2002   09:10 AM                    295 EXP01FEB.dta
Press any key to continue . . .
```

Note: The number of files displayed will vary, depending on the size of your command line window.

WHAT'S HAPPENING?   You keyed in the command **DIR** followed by a slash / and the parameter **P**. The slash, which must be included with a fixed parameter, is commonly referred as a switch. However, the slash (/) is really a *delimiter*. A delimiter is a signal that one thing is ending and another is beginning. The number of files on your screen may differ from the figure above, depending on the size of your open Command Prompt window. Command line commands use different punctuation marks, such as delimiters, but the punctuation marks that they use are very specific. Remember, / is used only with fixed parameters.

In this example, the slash is the signal to the DIR command that additional instructions follow. The parameter P is the additional instruction. There can be no space between the slash and the P. The slash and the P stop the directory from scrolling. Thus, /P told the DIR command to fill the screen and then pause until the user takes some action. The message at the bottom of the screen tells you to press any key to continue.

8   Press ⌶Enter⌶

```
▣ Command Prompt                                                    - □ ×

12/11/2002   09:10 AM                    292 EXP02MAR.dta
10/31/2001   04:51 PM                    137 FILE2.FP
10/31/2001   04:51 PM                    137 FILE3.FP
07/31/1999   12:53 PM                     44 FRANK.FIL
10/31/2001   11:57 AM                  1,334 GRAMMY.REC
05/07/2002   07:41 AM                    190 JUP.TMP
10/31/2001   12:02 PM                    166 LEFT.RED
05/27/2001   10:08 PM                     81 LONGFILENAME.TXT
10/31/2001   01:08 PM                    406 MER.NEW
10/30/2001   03:05 PM                    193 MIDDLE.UP
07/31/1999   12:53 PM                  2,672 NEWPRSON.FIL
10/31/2001   01:38 PM                  4,064 NEW-SUVS.XLS
07/31/2000   04:32 PM                  2,307 PERSONAL.FIL
10/30/2001   01:46 PM                    148 AST.NEW
07/31/2000   04:32 PM                  1,228 STATES.USA
10/31/2001   07:08 PM                    478 VEN.99
```

```
05/14/2002   08:07 AM                     64  WILD1.XXX
12/31/2001   04:32 PM                    181  WILDTHR.DOS
08/12/2000   04:12 PM                      3  Y.FIL
12/06/2001   09:18 AM     <DIR>               TEST
12/06/2001   09:18 AM     <DIR>               MUSIC
10/30/2001   02:47 PM                     86  BONJOUR.TMP
07/31/1999   12:53 PM                     47  CAROLYN.FIL
10/30/2001   03:03 PM                    286  DRESS.UP
12/11/2002   09:10 AM                    294  EXP01JAN.dta
12/11/2002   09:10 AM                    295  EXP03FEB.dta
10/31/2001   02:49 PM                    138  FILE2.CZG
10/31/2001   02:49 PM                    138  FILE3.CZG
10/31/2001   11:33 AM                    152  GALAXY.TMP
10/31/2001   06:52 PM                    105  GREEN.JAZ
10/30/2001   03:42 PM                    190  JUP.NEW
10/30/2001   03:42 PM        .           190  JUPITER.TXT
12/06/2001   12:15 AM                     97  LONGFILENAMED.TXT
10/31/2001   01:08 PM                    406  MER.TMP
Press any key to continue . . .
```

WHAT'S HAPPENING?   When you pressed **Enter**, the display continued scrolling. Because there are still more files, the DIR command asks you to press any key again to continue the display. As you can see, the display stops each time the screen fills.

9 Press **Enter**

10 Continue pressing **Enter** until you reach the end of the display.

```
C:\ Command Prompt                                    _ □ ✕

10/30/2001   03:18 PM                    758  RIGHT.UP
07/31/2000   04:32 PM                    260  STATE.CAP
10/31/2001   07:08 PM                    478  VEN.NEW
05/14/2002   08:07 AM                     64  WILD2.YYY
10/30/2001   01:46 PM                    148  ASTRO.TMP
08/01/2002   09:28 AM     <DIR>               DATA
10/31/2001   07:08 PM                    478  VEN.TMP
10/31/2001   05:37 PM                    383  EARTH.THR
12/11/2002   09:10 AM                    294  EXP02JAN.dta
10/31/2001   04:50 PM                    138  FILE3.SWT
05/30/2000   04:32 PM                    182  OLDAUTO.MAK
10/31/2001   12:00 PM                    115  RIGHT.RED
12/06/2001   12:13 AM                    138  AWARD.MOV
10/12/2002   09:31 AM     <DIR>               SPORTS
05/14/2001   11:28 AM                  4,843  GO.BAT
05/27/2001   10:08 PM                     76  LONGFILENAME
11/16/2002   09:36 AM     <DIR>               LEVEL-1
10/31/2001   01:08 PM                    406  MER.99
12/06/2001   12:25 AM                    465  person.fil
07/31/1999   12:53 PM                     46  STEVEN.FIL
10/31/2001   07:08 PM                    478  VENUS.TXT
12/31/2001   04:32 PM                     93  WILDONE
Press any key to continue . . .
10/31/2001   06:40 PM                    188  ZODIAC.FIL
              91 File(s)          47,396 bytes
               7 Dir(s)          287,744 bytes free

A:\>_
```

WHAT'S HAPPENING?   You kept pressing **Enter** until there were no more files to display. The system prompt (A:\>) appears to signal that there are no more files on this disk and that the OS is waiting for you to key in the next command. There is another way to display the files on the screen. You may use the /W parameter to display the directory in a wide format.

11 Key in the following: A:\>**DIR /W** Enter

```
Command Prompt                                                    - □ ×

EXP03JAN.dta             FILE2.SWT              FILE4.FP
GETYN.COM                HELLO.TXT              JUPITER.TMP
LONGFILENAME.EXTENSION   MARK.FIL               MERCURY.TMP
NAME.BAT                 ORION.NEB              QUASARS.DOC
Sandy and Patty.txt      TITAN.TXT              AST.99
WILD3.ZZZ                WILDTWO.DOS            [GAMES]
Sandy and Nicki.txt      BLUE.JAZ               CASES.FIL
EARTH.ONE                EXP01FEB.dta           EXP02MAR.dta
FILE2.FP                 FILE3.FP               FRANK.FIL
GRAMMY.REC               JUP.TMP                LEFT.RED
LONGFILENAME.TXT         MER.NEW                MIDDLE.UP
NEWPRSON.FIL             NEW-SUVS.XLS           PERSONAL.FIL
AST.NEW                  STATES.USA             VEN.99
WILD1.XXX                WILDTHR.DOS            Y.FIL
[TEST]                   [MUSIC]                BONJOUR.TMP
CAROLYN.FIL              DRESS.UP               EXP01JAN.dta
EXP03FEB.dta             FILE2.CZG              FILE3.CZG
GALAXY.TMP               GREEN.JAZ              JUP.NEW
JUPITER.TXT              LONGFILENAMED.TXT      MER.TMP
MIDDLE.RED               AST.TMP                [MEDIA]
WILDONE.DOS              BORN.TYP               EXP01MAR.dta
EXP03MAR.dta             GALAXY.TXT             JUP.99
LONGFILENAMING.TXT       MERCURY.TXT            PLANETS.TXT
RIGHT.UP                 STATE.CAP              VEN.NEW
WILD2.YYY                ASTRO.TMP              [DATA]
VEN.TMP                  EARTH.THR              EXP02JAN.dta
FILE3.SWT                OLDAUTO.MAK            RIGHT.RED
AWARD.MOV                [SPORTS]               GO.BAT
LONGFILENAME             [LEVEL-1]              MER.99
person.fil               STEVEN.FIL             VENUS.TXT
WILDONE                  ZODIAC.FIL
              91 File(s)          47,396 bytes
               7 Dir(s)          287,744 bytes free

A:\>_
```

WHAT'S HAPPENING? The directory display is now across the screen, three columns wide. In addition, the information about the files is not as comprehensive. All you see is the file specification—the file name and its extension. You do not see the file size, date, or time, but you still see the total number of files and the number of bytes free. You can also identify the directories by the brackets around them such as **[MEDIA]**. Thus, /W allows you to see the files side by side. You can use more than one parameter at a time. Since there are so many files on this disk, the entire directory does not fit on one screen.

12 Key in the following: A:\>**DIR /P /W** Enter

```
Command Prompt                                                    - □ ×

A:\>DIR /P /W
 Volume in drive A is ACTIVITIES
 Volume Serial Number is 08D4-2897

 Directory of A:\
```

```
VENUS.TMM              ASTRO.TXT              BORN.TXT
DANCES.TXT             EARTH.TWO              EXP02FEB.dta
EXP03JAN.dta           FILE2.SWT              FILE4.FP
GETYN.COM              HELLO.TXT              JUPITER.TMP
LONGFILENAME.EXTENSION MARK.FIL               MERCURY.TMP
NAME.BAT               ORION.NEB              QUASARS.DOC
Sandy and Patty.txt    TITAN.TXT              AST.99
WILD3.ZZZ              WILDTWO.DOS            [GAMES]
Sandy and Nicki.txt    BLUE.JAZ               CASES.FIL
EARTH.ONE             EXP01FEB.dta           EXP02MAR.dta
FILE2.FP              FILE3.FP               FRANK.FIL
GRAMMY.REC            JUP.TMP                LEFT.RED
LONGFILENAME.TXT      MER.NEW                MIDDLE.UP
NEWPRSON.FIL          NEW-SUVS.XLS           PERSONAL.FIL
AST.NEW              STATES.USA             VEN.99
WILD1.XXX            WILDTHR.DOS            Y.FIL
[TEST]              [MUSIC]                BONJOUR.TMP
CAROLYN.FIL          DRESS.UP               EXP01JAN.dta
EXP03FEB.dta         FILE2.CZG              FILE3.CZG
GALAXY.TMP           GREEN.JAZ              JUP.NEW
JUPITER.TXT          LONGFILENAMED.TXT      MER.TMP
MIDDLE.RED           AST.TMP                [MEDIA]
WILDONE.DOS          BORN.TYP               EXP01MAR.dta
EXP03MAR.dta         GALAXY.TXT             JUP.99
LONGFILENAMING.TXT   MERCURY.TXT            PLANETS.TXT
RIGHT.UP            STATE.CAP              VEN.NEW
WILD2.YYY           ASTRO.TMP              [DATA]
VEN.TMP             EARTH.THR              EXP02JAN.dta
FILE3.SWT           OLDAUTO.MAK            RIGHT.RED
Press any key to continue . . .
```

WHAT'S HAPPENING?   By using these parameters together, you could see the files in a wide display, one screenful at a time.

13 Press Enter

```
┌─────────────────────────────────────────────────────────────┐
│ C:\ Command Prompt                              _ □ ✕         │
├─────────────────────────────────────────────────────────────┤
│ MIDDLE.RED            AST.TMP               [MEDIA]           │
│ WILDONE.DOS           BORN.TYP              EXP01MAR.dta      │
│ EXP03MAR.dta          GALAXY.TXT            JUP.99            │
│ LONGFILENAMING.TXT    MERCURY.TXT           PLANETS.TXT       │
│ RIGHT.UP             STATE.CAP             VEN.NEW            │
│ WILD2.YYY            ASTRO.TMP             [DATA]             │
│ VEN.TMP             EARTH.THR             EXP02JAN.dta       │
│ FILE3.SWT           OLDAUTO.MAK           RIGHT.RED          │
│ Press any key to continue . . .                              │
│ AWARD.MOV           [SPORTS]              GO.BAT             │
│ LONGFILENAME        [LEVEL-1]             MER.99             │
│ person.fil          STEVEN.FIL            VENUS.TXT          │
│ WILDONE             ZODIAC.FIL                               │
│          91 File(s)         47,396 bytes                     │
│           7 Dir(s)      287,744 bytes free                   │
│                                                              │
│ A:\>_                                                        │
└─────────────────────────────────────────────────────────────┘
```

WHAT'S HAPPENING?   You have returned to the system prompt.

2.6   Using File Names as Variable Parameters

In the previous activities, you used the DIR command with two different optional fixed parameters, /P and /W. These optional fixed parameters have specific meanings. There is another parameter you can use with the DIR command: the name of the file.

File names are formally called file specifications. A file specification is broken into two parts, the file name and the file extension. When people refer to a *file* or file name, they really mean the file specification: the file name and file extension together. It is much like a person's name. When someone refers to Ramon, he usually means someone specific such as Ramon Rodreiquez. In the computer world, when you refer to a file name, you must give both its first name (file name) and its last name (file extension). When you create files in an application program, you are allowed to name the file. On this disk the files already exist and are already named. You cannot call them anything else. However, when you have the opportunity for naming files, you must follow the rules. Windows has rules called *naming conventions* for naming files. They are the same in Windows XP as they were in Windows 2000. These are:

1. All files in a directory (subdirectory) must have unique names.
2. File names are mandatory. All files must have file names less than but no more than 256 characters long. However, it is recommended that you do not use very long file names, as most programs cannot interpret them.
3. File extensions are usually three characters long.
4. The following are *illegal characters*, and may *not* be used in a file name:
   \   /   :   *   ?   "   <   >   ¦

5. All other characters, including periods and spaces, are legal in Windows file names.

Typically, a file name reflects the subject of the file, for example, EMPLOYEE or TAXES. The file extension is usually given by the application creating the file. For example, Microsoft Word uses .DOC for its extension, Lotus 1-2-3 uses .WK1, and Microsoft Excel uses .XLS.

Keep in mind that many older, 16-bit application packages created before Windows 95 cannot deal with long file names (LFN's), spaces in file names, or periods in file names. These packages adhere to the older DOS rules, which limit the name to eight characters and the optional extension to three characters, and cannot include spaces. You will also find that files on the Internet tend to adhere to the older DOS rule—also called the 8.3 (eight-dot-three) rule.

When you key in the DIR command, you get the entire table of contents of the disk, known as the directory. Usually, you do not care about all the files. Most often, you are interested only in whether or not one specific file is located or stored on the disk. If you use one of the parameters /P or /W, you still have to look through all the files. You can locate a specific file quickly by using the file name. Simply give the DIR command specific information about what file you seek. Look at the syntax diagram:

```
DIR [drive:][path][filename] [/P] [/W]
```

The file name, indicated above in brackets, is a variable optional parameter. To use the optional parameter, you must plug in the value or the name of the file for [filename]. In some syntax diagrams, you will see [filename[.ext]]. The .ext is in separate brackets within the file name brackets because it is part of the file name syntax. A file may not have an extension, but if it does have an extension, you must include it. When you include it, there must be no spaces between the file name and the file extension.

The delimiter that is used between a file name and a file extension is a period, or what is called the *dot*. A dot, as a delimiter, is used between a file name and a file extension. To verbalize a file name keyed in as MYFILE.TXT, you would say "MY FILE dot TEXT."

2.7 Activity: Using a File Name as a Variable Parameter

Note: You should be at the command line at the A:\> prompt.

1   Key in the following: A:\>**DIR VENUS.TXT** [Enter]

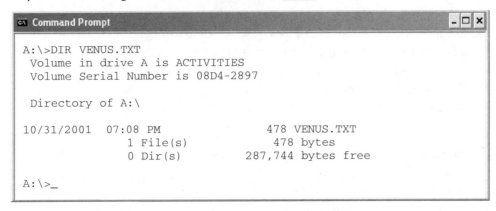

```
Command Prompt                                          _ □ ✕

A:\>DIR VENUS.TXT
 Volume in drive A is ACTIVITIES
 Volume Serial Number is 08D4-2897

 Directory of A:\

10/31/2001  07:08 PM                 478 VENUS.TXT
               1 File(s)             478 bytes
               0 Dir(s)         287,744 bytes free

A:\>_
```

WHAT'S
HAPPENING?   The DIR command returned exactly what you asked for—a single file that met your criteria. This command did find the file **VENUS.TXT** on the disk in Drive A. **VENUS.TXT** is the variable parameter. You substituted **VENUS.TXT** for [filename]. You are told the Volume name is ACTIVITIES. The generic name for drives is *Volume*. The date and time **VENUS.TXT** was last updated appears first (**10/31/2001 07:08 PM**), then the size of the file is listed in bytes (**478**) followed last by the file name (**VENUS.TXT**). The line beneath (**1 File(s) 478 bytes**) told you that you only have one file that matched that criteria. The last line states that there are no directories (**0 Dir (s)**) and how much space is free on the disk for more data (**287,744 bytes free**). What if the system could not find the file you asked for?

2   Key in the following: A:\>**DIR NOFILE.TXT** [Enter]

```
Command Prompt                                          _ □ ✕

A:\>DIR NOFILE.TXT
 Volume in drive A is ACTIVITIES
 Volume Serial Number is 08D4-2897
```

```
 Directory of A:\

File Not Found
A:\>_
```

HAPPENING?   **File Not Found** is a system message. Sometimes it is referred to as an error message. DIR is telling you that it looked through the entire list of files in the root directory of the disk in Drive A and could not find a "match" for the file called **NOFILE.TXT**. You may also enter more than one file specification with the DIR command.

3   Key in the following:

   A:\>**DIR STEVEN.FIL C:\WINDOWS\SYSTEM32\DISKCOPY.COM** [Enter]

```
☒ Command Prompt                                          _ □ x

A:\>DIR STEVEN.FIL C:\WINDOWS\SYSTEM32\DISKCOPY.COM
 Volume in drive A is ACTIVITIES
 Volume Serial Number is 08D4-2897

 Directory of A:\

07/31/1999  12:53 PM                 46 STEVEN.FIL
               1 File(s)             46 bytes
               0 Dir(s)         287,774 bytes free

 Volume in drive C is ADMIN504
 Volume Serial Number is 0E38-11FF

 Directory of C:\WINNT\SYSTEM32

08/23/2001  12:00 PM              7,168 diskcopy.com
               1 File(s)          7,168 bytes
               0 Dir(s)   8,539,275,264 bytes free

A:\>_
```

HAPPENING?   The Command Prompt allows you to enter more than one parameter at a time when using the DIR command. This feature was introduced in Windows 2000 Professional. You asked the Operating System to display two files from two different locations. Both were displayed with their individual file names and file information listed under their respective locations (**Directory of A:** and **Directory of C:\WINDOWS\SYSTEM32**).

4   Key in the following: A:\>**DIR LONGFILENAME** [Enter]

```
☒ Command Prompt                                          _ □ x

A:\>DIR LONGFILENAME
 Volume in drive A is ACTIVITIES
 Volume Serial Number is 08D4-2897

 Directory of A:\

05/27/2001  10:08 PM                 76 LONGFILENAME
               1 File(s)             76 bytes
               0 Dir(s)         287,744 bytes free
A:\>_
```

WHAT'S ▓▓▓▓
▓▓▓ HAPPENING?   As you can see, you may use the DIR command with long file
names.

5   Key in the following: A:\>**DIR LONGFILENAME.EXTENSION** [Enter]

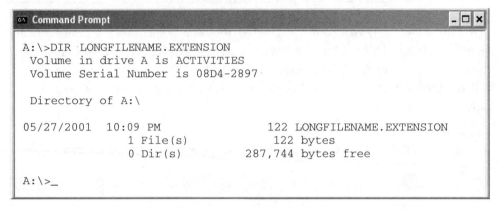

```
A:\>DIR LONGFILENAME.EXTENSION
 Volume in drive A is ACTIVITIES
 Volume Serial Number is 08D4-2897

 Directory of A:\

05/27/2001  10:09 PM                 122 LONGFILENAME.EXTENSION
               1 File(s)            122 bytes
               0 Dir(s)         287,744 bytes free

A:\>_
```

WHAT'S ▓▓▓▓
▓▓▓ HAPPENING?   You may also have a file extension that is longer than three
characters, as is shown here.

6   Key in the following: A:\>**DIR Sandy and Patty.txt** [Enter]

```
A:\>DIR Sandy and Patty.txt
 Volume in drive A is ACTIVITIES
 Volume Serial Number is 08D4-2897

 Directory of A:\

 Directory of A:\

 Directory of A:\

File Not Found

A:\>_
```

WHAT'S ▓▓▓▓
▓▓▓ HAPPENING?   It appears that the file you requested could not be found. Note
that Directory of A:\ appears three times. This is a long file name with spaces in it.
The DIR command read or parsed (interpreted the parameters) as three separate
files—first "Sandy," then "and," and last "Patty.txt." It could find no files by those
names. If you want a long file name with spaces in it treated as one unit, you must
enclose the file name in quotation marks.

7   Key in the following: A:\>**DIR "Sandy and Patty.txt"** [Enter]

```
A:\>DIR "Sandy and Patty.txt"
 Volume in drive A is ACTIVITIES
 Volume Serial Number is 08D4-2897

 Directory of A:\

11/16/2000  12:00 PM                  59 Sandy and Patty.txt
               1 File(s)             59 bytes
               0 Dir(s)         287,744 bytes free
```

```
A:\>_
```

**WHAT'S ▓▓▓▓▓▓
▓▓▓HAPPENING?**   The parameter you used was very specific. By enclosing the
filename in quotes, called "quoting," the operating system did not treat the spaces
as delimiters, but as part of one file name. Every file that has a long file name also
has a name that adheres to the 8.3 naming convention. This name is called an *alias*.
Windows assigns this alias automatically. If you want to see the 8.3 names, you must
use the /X parameter.

8   Key in the following: A:\>**DIR /X /P** Enter

```
⌐x⌐ Command Prompt                                                    - □ ×

 Volume in drive A is ACTIVITIES
 Volume Serial Number is 08D4-2897

 Directory of A:\

10/31/2001  07:08 PM                478                     VENUS.TMM
10/30/2001  01:46 PM                148                     ASTRO.TXT
10/30/2001  02:10 PM                121                     BORN.TXT
12/11/1999  04:03 PM                 72                     DANCES.TXT
10/31/2001  05:32 PM                259                     EARTH.TWO
12/11/2002  09:10 AM                295                     EXP02FEB.dta
12/11/2002  09:10 AM                294                     EXP03JAN.dta
10/31/2001  04:50 PM                138                     FILE2.SWT
10/31/2001  04:51 PM                137                     FILE4.FP
05/02/1994  12:57 AM                 26                     GETYN.COM
05/30/2000  04:32 PM                 53                     HELLO.TXT
05/07/2002  07:41 AM                190                     JUPITER.TMP
05/27/2001  10:09 PM                122 LONGFI~1.EXT LONGFILENAME.EXTENSION
08/12/2000  04:12 PM                 73                     MARK.FIL
10/31/2001  01:08 PM                406                     MERCURY.TMP
05/14/2001  10:16 AM              2,273                     NAME.BAT
10/31/2001  01:49 PM                219                     ORION.NEB
10/31/2001  02:16 PM             11,264                     QUASARS.DOC
11/16/2000  12:00 PM                 59 SANDYA~1.TXT Sandy and Patty.txt
10/31/2001  02:43 PM                529                     TITAN.TXT
10/30/2001  01:46 PM                148                     AST.99
05/14/2002  08:07 AM                 64                     WILD3.ZZZ
12/31/2001  04:32 PM                182                     WILDTWO.DOS
12/06/2001  09:14 AM     <DIR>                              GAMES
11/16/2000  12:00 PM                 53 SANDYA~2.TXT Sandy and Nicki.txt
10/31/2001  06:51 PM                125                     BLUE.JAZ
08/12/2000  04:12 PM                314                     CASES.FIL
10/31/2001  05:28 PM                165                     EARTH.ONE
12/11/2002  09:10 AM                295                     EXP01FEB.dta
Press any key to continue . . .
A:\>_
```

**WHAT'S ▓▓▓▓▓▓
▓▓▓HAPPENING?**   The 8.3 file name is always derived from the long file name by
removing any spaces from the file name, taking the first six characters of the file
name, and adding a tilde (~) and a number. When there is more than one file with
the same first six characters in its name, Windows handles it. If you look at the
display for the two files that begin with "Sandy" (**Sandy and Nicki.txt** and **Sandy
and Patty.txt**), the first file placed on the disk is given the number 1 following the
tilde, and the second file, the number 2.

9 Continue pressing the [Enter] key, paying attention to the files that begin with **LONGFILE** and end with **.TXT,** until you reach the end of the display.

```
 Command Prompt                                                          _ □ ✕

12/11/2002   09:10 AM                  292                    EXP01MAR.dta
12/11/2002   09:10 AM                  292                    EXP03MAR.dta
10/31/2001   11:37 AM                  253                    GALAXY.TXT
10/30/2001   03:42 PM                  190                    JUP.99
12/06/2001   12:16 AM                   99 LONGFI~3.TXT LONGFILENAMING.TX
10/31/2001   01:08 PM                  406                    MERCURY.TXT
11/24/2001   11:24 AM                  194                    PLANETS.TXT
10/30/2001   03:18 PM                  758                    RIGHT.UP
07/31/2000   04:32 PM                  260                    STATE.CAP
10/31/2001   07:08 PM                  478                    VEN.NEW
05/14/2002   08:07 AM                   64                    WILD2.YYY
10/30/2001   01:46 PM                  148                    ASTRO.TMP
08/01/2002   09:28 AM     <DIR>                               DATA
10/31/2001   07:08 PM                  478                    VEN.TMP
10/31/2001   05:37 PM                  383                    EARTH.THR
12/11/2002   09:10 AM                  294                    EXP02JAN.dta
10/31/2001   04:50 PM                  138                    FILE3.SWT
05/30/2000   04:32 PM                  182                    OLDAUTO.MAK
10/31/2001   12:00 PM                  115                    RIGHT.RED
12/06/2001   12:13 AM                  138                    AWARD.MOV
10/12/2002   09:31 AM     <DIR>                               SPORTS
05/14/2001   11:28 AM                4,843                    GO.BAT
05/27/2001   10:08 PM                   76 LONGFI~1     LONGFILENAME
11/16/2002   09:36 AM     <DIR>                               LEVEL-1
10/31/2001   01:08 PM                  406                    MER.99
12/06/2001   12:25 AM                  465                    person.fil
07/31/1999   12:53 PM                   46                    STEVEN.FIL
10/31/2001   07:08 PM                  478                    VENUS.TXT
12/31/2001   04:32 PM                   93                    WILDONE
Press any key to continue . . .
10/31/2001   06:40 PM                  188                    ZODIAC.FIL
              91 File(s)           47,396 bytes
               7 Dir(s)          287,744 bytes free

A:\>_
```

**WHAT'S ▨▨▨▨
▨▨HAPPENING?**   There are three files that begin with **LONGFILE** and end with the **TXT** (**LONGFILENAME.TXT**, **LONGFILENAMING.TXT**, and **LONGFILENAMED.TXT**). The first file, **LONGFLENAME.TXT**, is assigned the 8.3 name of **LONGFI~1.TXT**. The second file, **LONGFILENAMING.TXT**, is assigned the next number—**LONGFI~2.TXT**. And the last file, **LONGFILENAMED.TXT**, is assigned the next number—**LONGFI~3.TXT**.

If you cannot see the long file names, these names become very confusing, as it is difficult to distinguish one file from another. You want to be able to identify the contents of a file quickly by looking at the file names. Older versions of DOS and older application software will not allow you to use or view long file names. In the real world, the more you have to key in, the more likely you will make a typographical error. Thus, even though you can use spaces and long names, it may be a better idea to keep the file names short and concise. This is especially important when using floppy disks. Long file names take up needed room on floppies.

2.8   Command Line Editing

You may reuse the last command you keyed in on a line without re-keying it. When you key in a command, it is stored in a memory buffer until it is replaced by the next keyed in command. The last command line you keyed in can be recalled to the screen so you may edit it. To recall the command line one letter at a time, press the **F1** key once for each keystroke you wish to repeat. To recall the entire command line, press the **F3** key. In addition, Windows lets you use the up and down arrow keys to recall commands used in a command prompt session. Furthermore, you may also recall command lines by number, edit them, keep a command history, find commands by number, and so on. The following table illustrates the keys you may use to edit a command history. This feature functions in the same way it did in Windows 2000.

Key	Editing Function
F7	Displays a list of commands.
Alt + **F7**	Clears the list of commands.
↑	Allows you to scroll up through the commands.
↓	Allows you to scroll down through the commands.
F8	Searches the list for the command that starts with the text you provided before pressing the function key.
F9	Selects the command from the list by number.
PgUp	Displays the oldest command in the list.
PgDn	Displays the newest command in the list.
Esc	Erases the displayed command from the screen.
Home	Moves the cursor to the beginning of the displayed command.
End	Moves the cursor to the end of the displayed command.
←	Moves the cursor back one character.
→	Moves the cursor forward one character.
Ctrl + **←**	Moves the cursor back one word.
Ctrl + **→**	Moves the cursor forward one word.
Backspace	Moves the cursor back one character and deletes the character preceding the cursor.
Delete	Deletes the character at the cursor.
Ctrl + **End**	Deletes all characters from the cursor to the end of the line.
Ctrl + **Home**	Deletes all characters from the cursor to the beginning of the line.
Insert	Toggles between insert and overstrike mode.

Table 2.1—Editing Keys Command Summary

2.9   Activity: Using Command Line Editing

Note: The ACTIVITIES Disk—Working Copy is in Drive A. You are at the Command Prompt screen. A:\> is the default drive and directory.

1   Key in the following, including the error: A:\>**DIIR /p** [Enter]

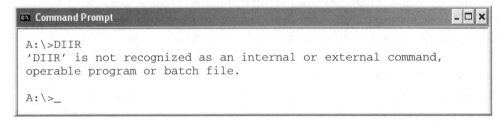

```
A:\>DIIR
'DIIR' is not recognized as an internal or external command,
operable program or batch file.

A:\>_
```

WHAT'S HAPPENING?   Your command was keyed in incorrectly and was not understood by the system. You received the error message "'DIIR' is not recognized as an internal or external command, operable program or batch file." This error message informs you that the OS did not understand what it is you asked for. It is important to read the messages so that you understand what is happening.

2   Press the [F1] key twice.

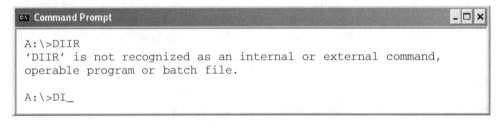

```
A:\>DIIR
'DIIR' is not recognized as an internal or external command,
operable program or batch file.

A:\>DI_
```

WHAT'S HAPPENING?   The characters that you keyed in previously are being recalled from the buffer. If you were to press the [F1] key once more, the incorrectly entered second "I" would appear, the character error you want to eliminate.

3   Press the [Esc] key to cancel the command.

4   Press [Alt] + [F7] to clear the memory of the command line editor.

5   Key in the following: A:\>**CLS** [Enter]

6   Key in the following: A:\>**DIR FRANK.FIL** [Enter]

7   Key in the following: A:\>**DIR VEN.99** [Enter]

8   Key in the following: A:\>**VOL** [Enter]

9   Key in the following: A:\>**DIR JUP.99** [Enter]

10 Key in the following: A:\>**DIR ORION.NEB** [Enter]

11 Key in the following: A:\>**DIR DRESS.UP RIGHT.UP** [Enter]

```
A:\>DIR ORION.NEB
 Volume in drive A is ACTIVITIES
 Volume Serial Number is 08D4-2897
```

```
     Directory of A:\

10/31/2001  01:49 PM                  219 ORION.NEB
               1 File(s)              219 bytes
               0 Dir(s)          287,744 bytes free

A:\>DIR DRESS.UP RIGHT.UP
 Volume in drive A is ACTIVITIES
 Volume Serial Number is 08D4-2897

 Directory of A:\

10/30/2001  03:03 PM                  286 DRESS.UP

 Directory of A:\

10/30/2001  03:18 PM                  758 RIGHT.UP
               2 File(s)            1,044 bytes
               0 Dir(s)          287,744 bytes free

A:\>_
```

WHAT'S
HAPPENING?   (This graphic represents the tail end of what you see scroll by on your screen.) You have executed several commands and can now use the editing keys to recall and edit commands.

12 Press the ⬆ key twice.

```
A:\>DIR ORION.NEB
```

WHAT'S
HAPPENING?   You have recalled, in descending order, the commands you previously entered.

13 Press the ⬇ key once.

```
A:\>DIR DRESS.UP RIGHT.UP
```

WHAT'S
HAPPENING?   You recalled, in ascending order, the last command you keyed in.

14 Press **Ctrl** + ⬅ once.

```
A:\>DIR DRESS.UP RIGHT.UP
```

WHAT'S
HAPPENING?   Your cursor is now on the **R** in **RIGHT.UP**. Using the **Ctrl** and ⬅ keys moved you back one word.

15 Press the **Insert** key.

```
A:\>DIR DRESS.UP RIGHT.UP
```

WHAT'S ▓▓▓
▓▓▓HAPPENING?   When you pressed the **Insert** key, you toggled into what is called
overstrike mode. Overstrike will replace each character as you key in data. The
cursor also changed to a thicker block underline.

16 At the cursor, key in **FILE3.FP**.

```
A:\>DIR DRESS.UP FILE3.FP
```

WHAT'S ▓▓▓
▓▓▓HAPPENING?   Notice how you did not have to delete the **RIGHT.UP** characters.
As you keyed in data, it replaced what was there.

17 Press **Enter**. Press **↑** twice.

```
A:\>DIR DRESS.UP RIGHT.UP
```

WHAT'S ▓▓▓
▓▓▓HAPPENING?   You recalled the prior command you keyed in.

18 Press **Ctrl** + **←** once. Key in **FILE3.FP**.

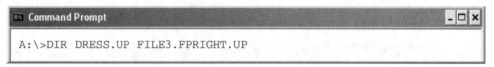

```
A:\>DIR DRESS.UP FILE3.FPRIGHT.UP
```

WHAT'S ▓▓▓
▓▓▓HAPPENING?   When you are in insert mode, you are "inserting" data at the
cursor.

19 Press **F7**

WHAT'S ▓▓▓
▓▓▓HAPPENING?   Pressing the **F7** key lists all the commands that you have keyed
in. You may edit any line you wish by selecting the line number, but you must press
the **F9** key first.

20 Press **F9**. Press the number that appears before **DIR VEN.99** (in this
example, it is **2**). Press **Enter**

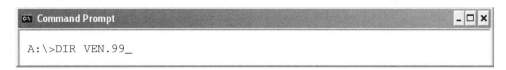

```
A:\>DIR VEN.99_
```

**WHAT'S
HAPPENING?**   By pressing **F9**, you saw the **Enter command number:** prompt. You then keyed in the line number (**2**) of the command you wished to edit. You can edit this line or simply execute it again. If you wish to delete a line quickly, there is a shortcut—the **Esc** key. You can also search for a previously entered command by pressing the first letter or letters of the command you are interested in.

21 Press **Esc**. Press **D**. Press **F8**

```
A:\>DIR FRANK.FIL
```

**WHAT'S
HAPPENING?**   You selected a command by keying in the first letter and then pressing **F8**. If you continued to press **F8**, you would cycle through all the commands that begin with D.

22 Press **Esc**. Press **Alt** + **F7**. Press **↑** once.

```
A:\>_
```

**WHAT'S
HAPPENING?**   By pressing **Alt** + **F7**, you cleared the commands that were in the buffer. There are no commands to scroll through or to edit. When you are working at the Command Prompt, remember these editing commands. They can save you many keystrokes.

23 Close the Command Prompt window.

**WHAT'S
HAPPENING?**   You have returned to the desktop.

2.10 Drives as Device Names

A disk drive is an example of a device. A device is a place to send information (write) or a place from which to receive information (read). Disk drives have assigned *device names*. These are letters of the alphabet followed by a colon. Using these names, Windows knows which disk drive to read from or write to. When you are at the command prompt, the prompt displayed on the screen tells you where the system is currently *pointing* and from which device data will be read from or written to. If you are using a stand-alone computer, your drive names will typically be A: and C: and then drive letters from D on, depending on what devices you have attached to your system. However, if you are on a network, disk drive letters can vary. They can include such drive letters as J: or P: or W: and represent storage areas that are somewhere on the network, not on your local system. Again, the displayed prompt will tell you on what drive (device) the operating system is going to take an action. Disk drives are not the only places where the system sends or receives information. Other common devices are the keyboard, the printer, and the monitor.

2.11   Defaults

In addition to understanding names of devices, it is also important to understand the concept of *defaults*. Computers must have very specific instructions for everything they do. However, there are *implied* instructions that the system falls back on or *defaults* to in the absence of other instructions. Default, by computer definition, is the value used unless another value is specified. If you do not specify what you want, the system will make the assumption for you. For example, when A:\> is displayed on the screen, it is called the A prompt, but it is also the *default drive*. When you want any activity to occur but do not specify where you want it to happen, the system assumes the activity will occur on the default drive, the A:\> that is displayed on the screen.

When you key in DIR after A:\>, how does the operating system know that you are asking for a table of contents of the disk in Drive A? When a specific direction is given, the operating system must have a specific place to look. A:\>, the default drive, is displayed on the screen. Since you did *not* specify which disk you wanted DIR to check, it defaulted to the default drive—the drive displayed in the prompt on the screen. It deduced that you want the table of contents or directory listing for the default drive, the disk in Drive A.

The prompt displayed on the screen is also known as the *designated drive* or the *logged drive*. All commands, if given no other instructions to the contrary, assume that all reads and writes to the disk drive must take place on the default drive, the drive indicated by the prompt on the screen. When you are not in the Command Prompt window, the same rules apply. There is indeed a default drive, and in Windows Explorer it is indicated on the title bar, if you have set the Folder option to "Display the full path in the title bar."

2.12   Activity: Working with Defaults

Note: The ACTIVITIES Disk—Working Copy should be in Drive A. You should be at the Windows desktop.

1   Click **Start**. Point at **Programs**. Point at **Accessories**. Click **Command Prompt**.

2   Key in the following: C:\>**A:** Enter

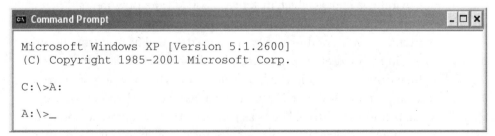

```
Command Prompt                                                    _ □ x

Microsoft Windows XP [Version 5.1.2600]
(C) Copyright 1985-2001 Microsoft Corp.

C:\>A:

A:\>_
```

WHAT'S ▓▓▓▓▓
▓▓▓▓HAPPENING?   You have opened the Command Prompt window and changed the
default drive to A. Opening this window is often referred to as "shelling out to
DOS" or "shelling out to the command line."

3   Key in the following: A:\>**DIR** ⌷Enter⌷

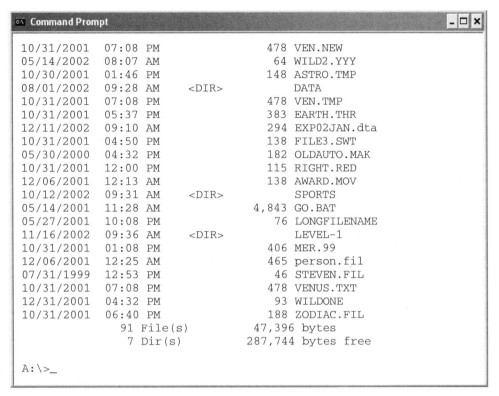

WHAT'S ▓▓▓▓▓▓
▓▓▓▓HAPPENING?   Displayed on the screen is the result of the DIR command you
executed. (The graphic represents the tail end of that listing.) Since you did not
specify which disk drive DIR should look into, it assumed or defaulted to the disk in
Drive A. Review the syntax diagram: The syntax diagram has [*drive*:], which is
another optional variable parameter. You can substitute the letter of the drive you
wish DIR to look into.

4   Key in the following: A:\>**DIR A:** ⌷Enter⌷

```
 C:\  Command Prompt                                          _ □ ✕

   10/31/2001   07:08  PM                      478  VEN.NEW
   05/14/2002   08:07  AM                       64  WILD2.YYY
   10/30/2001   01:46  PM                      148  ASTRO.TMP
   08/01/2002   09:28  AM       <DIR>               DATA
   10/31/2001   07:08  PM                      478  VEN.TMP
   10/31/2001   05:37  PM                      383  EARTH.THR
   12/11/2002   09:10  AM                      294  EXP02JAN.dta
   10/31/2001   04:50  PM                      138  FILE3.SWT
   05/30/2000   04:32  PM                      182  OLDAUTO.MAK
   10/31/2001   12:00  PM                      115  RIGHT.RED
   12/06/2001   12:13  AM                      138  AWARD.MOV
   10/12/2002   09:31  AM       <DIR>               SPORTS
   05/14/2001   11:28  AM                    4,843  GO.BAT
   05/27/2001   10:08  PM                       76  LONGFILENAME
   11/16/2002   09:36  AM       <DIR>               LEVEL-1
   10/31/2001   01:08  PM                      406  MER.99
   12/06/2001   12:25  AM                      465  person.fil
   07/31/1999   12:53  PM                       46  STEVEN.FIL
```

```
10/31/2001   07:08 PM                    478 VENUS.TXT
12/31/2001   04:32 PM                     93 WILDONE
10/31/2001   06:40 PM                    188 ZODIAC.FIL
             91 File(s)              47,396 bytes
              7 Dir(s)              287,744 bytes free


A:\>_
```

WHAT'S ▨▨▨▨
▨▨▨▨ HAPPENING?   You substituted **A:** for the variable optional parameter, [*drive*:]. The
display, however, is exactly the same as DIR without specifying the drive because
A:\> is the default drive. It is unnecessary to key in **A:**, but not wrong to do so. (The
graphic represents the tail end of your listing.) If you want to see what files are on
Drive C or Drive R, you must tell DIR to look on the drive you are interested in.

Note: Remember that if you are on a network, your hard drive letter may not be
          C:. Refer to your Configuration Table in Chapter 1 for the correct drive
          letter for your system.

5   Key in the following: A:\>**C:** Enter

6   Key in the following: C:\>**CD** \ Enter

```
A:\>C:

C:\>CD \

C:\>_
```

WHAT'S ▨▨▨▨
▨▨▨▨ HAPPENING?   You have changed the default drive to the hard disk, Drive C. You
then changed the directory to the root of C. In this example, you were already at the
root of C. Keying in **CD** \ confirmed that location.

7   Key in the following: C:\>**DIR A:** Enter

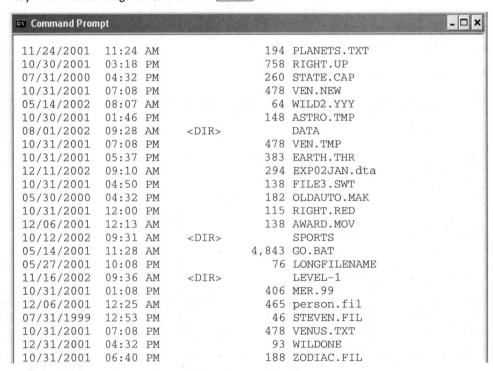

```
11/24/2001   11:24 AM                    194 PLANETS.TXT
10/30/2001   03:18 PM                    758 RIGHT.UP
07/31/2000   04:32 PM                    260 STATE.CAP
10/31/2001   07:08 PM                    478 VEN.NEW
05/14/2002   08:07 AM                     64 WILD2.YYY
10/30/2001   01:46 PM                    148 ASTRO.TMP
08/01/2002   09:28 AM     <DIR>              DATA
10/31/2001   07:08 PM                    478 VEN.TMP
10/31/2001   05:37 PM                    383 EARTH.THR
12/11/2002   09:10 AM                    294 EXP02JAN.dta
10/31/2001   04:50 PM                    138 FILE3.SWT
05/30/2000   04:32 PM                    182 OLDAUTO.MAK
10/31/2001   12:00 PM                    115 RIGHT.RED
12/06/2001   12:13 AM                    138 AWARD.MOV
10/12/2002   09:31 AM     <DIR>              SPORTS
05/14/2001   11:28 AM                  4,843 GO.BAT
05/27/2001   10:08 PM                     76 LONGFILENAME
11/16/2002   09:36 AM     <DIR>              LEVEL-1
10/31/2001   01:08 PM                    406 MER.99
12/06/2001   12:25 AM                    465 person.fil
07/31/1999   12:53 PM                     46 STEVEN.FIL
10/31/2001   07:08 PM                    478 VENUS.TXT
12/31/2001   04:32 PM                     93 WILDONE
10/31/2001   06:40 PM                    188 ZODIAC.FIL
```

```
        91 File(s)          47,396 bytes
         7 Dir(s)         287,744 bytes free

C:\>_
```

WHAT'S HAPPENING?   (The graphic represents the tail end of your listing.) The display of files, which scrolled by quickly, is still of the files on Drive A, but this time you *had* to specify the drive because the default drive was no longer A. Keying in **DIR** and a drive letter, **A:**, told the command line, "I want a display of the directory (DIR), but this time I don't want you to display the files on the default drive. I want you to look only on the disk that is in Drive A." As long as you tell the command DIR where you want it to look, you can work *with* and *from* any drive you wish. If you are not specific, the command will execute on the default drive shown by the prompt on the screen (A:\>, B:\>, C:\>, etc.).

8   Key in the following: C:\>**DIR HELLO.TXT** [Enter]

9   Key in the following: C:\>**DIR A:HELLO.TXT** [Enter]

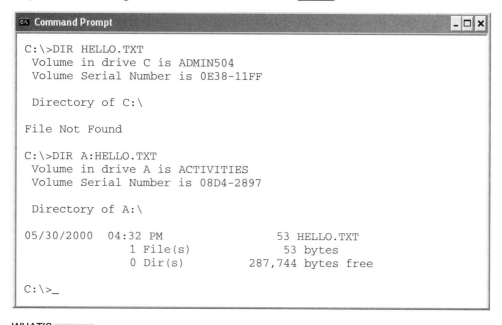

```
C:\>DIR HELLO.TXT
 Volume in drive C is ADMIN504
 Volume Serial Number is 0E38-11FF

 Directory of C:\

File Not Found

C:\>DIR A:HELLO.TXT
 Volume in drive A is ACTIVITIES
 Volume Serial Number is 08D4-2897

 Directory of A:\

05/30/2000  04:32 PM                    53 HELLO.TXT
             1 File(s)             53 bytes
             0 Dir(s)        287,744 bytes free

C:\>_
```

WHAT'S HAPPENING?   You first asked DIR to look on the default drive for a file called **HELLO.TXT**. The default drive is Drive C. The prompt displayed on the screen, C:\>, is the default drive. Since you did not specify which drive to check for the file called **HELLO.TXT**, DIR assumed the default drive. DIR could not find the **HELLO.TXT** file on the default drive, so it responded with **File Not Found**. The operating system is not smart enough to say, "Oh, this file is not on the default drive. Let me go check the ACTIVITIES disk in a different disk drive." The operating system followed your instructions exactly.

Your next step was more specific. You made a clearer request: "Look for a file called HELLO.TXT." However, you first told DIR what disk drive to look into—A:. The drive designator (**A:**) preceded the file name (**HELLO.TXT**) because you always tell DIR which "file cabinet" to look in (the disk drive **A:**) before you tell it which "folder" you want (**HELLO.TXT**). By looking at the syntax diagram, you see that you can combine optional variable parameters. You gave DIR [*drive:*][*path*][*filename*] some specific values—**DIR A:HELLO.TXT**. The **A:** was substituted for the [*drive*:], and **HELLO.TXT** was substituted for [*filename*]. So far, you have used the optional variable parameters [*drive*:] and [*filename*] and the optional fixed parameters [/P] and [/W]. You have not used [*path*].

2.13 A Brief Introduction to Subdirectories: The Path

Subdirectories are used primarily, but not exclusively, with hard disks and other large storage media such as read/writable-CDs or Zip disks. Hard disks have a large storage capacity (current common values are from 8 to 20 GB or more), and are therefore more difficult to manage than floppy disks. This is also true of RW-CDs and Zip disks. In general, users like to have similar files grouped together. Subdirectories allow a disk to be divided into smaller, more manageable portions. Windows refers to *subdirectories* as *folders*, and they are graphically represented with folder icons. In the command line shell, folders are referred to as directories and subdirectories.

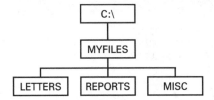

The full path name of a file called REP.DOC that is in the REPORTS directory is C:\MYFILES\REPORTS\REP.DOC. The first \ (backslash) always represents the root directory. The following backslashes without spaces are delimiters—separators between elements in the path, elements being subdirectories and the ending file.

Subdirectories can be used on floppy disks. If you think of a disk as a file cabinet, a subdirectory can be thought of as a drawer in the file cabinet. These file cabinet drawers (subdirectories) also hold disk files. Just as disk drives have a name, such as A:, B:, or C:, subdirectories must also have names so the system will know where to look. Since subdirectories are part of a disk, their names should not be a single letter of the alphabet. Single letters of the alphabet should be reserved for disk drives.

Every disk comes with one directory that is named by the operating system. This directory is called the **root directory** and is indicated by the backslash (\). The prompt displays the default directory as well as the default drive, as in A:\> or C:\>. Technically, there is only one *directory* on any disk—the root directory, referred to only as \. All others are *subdirectories*. However, the terms *directories* and *subdirectories*, *folders* and *subfolders* are used interchangeably. This textbook will also use the terms *directory* and *subdirectory* interchangeably. All subdirectories on a disk have names such as UTILITY or SAMPLE, or any other name you choose or a program chooses. The rules for naming subdirectories are the same as for naming files, although subdirectory names do not usually have extensions.

When working with files on a disk, you need to perform certain tasks that can be summarized as finding a file, storing a file, and retrieving a file. Because there are subdirectories on a disk, simply supplying the DIR command with the drive that the file might be on is insufficient information. You must also tell DIR the path to the file. The **path** is the route followed by the operating system to locate, save, and retrieve a file. Thus, in a syntax diagram, the path refers to the course leading from the root directory of a drive to a specific file. Simply stated, when you see *path* in a syntax diagram, you substitute the directory name or names. In essence, you are being very specific by telling the DIR command not to go just to the file cabinet (the disk) but to go to a drawer (subdirectory) in the file cabinet.

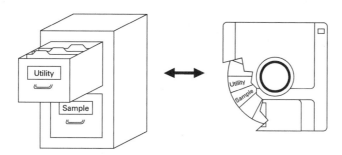

Figure 2.1—File Cabinets and Subdirectories

2.14   Activity: Using Path with the DIR Command

Note: You are at the command line screen. The ACTIVITIES Disk—Working Copy is in Drive A. C:\> is displayed as the default drive and the default directory.

1   Key in the following: C:\>**DIR A:** (Enter)

```
Command Prompt                                                    _ □ ✕

 08/01/2002    09:28 AM    <DIR>            DATA
 10/31/2001    07:08 PM            478 VEN.TMP
 10/31/2001    05:37 PM            383 EARTH.THR
 12/11/2002    09:10 AM            294 EXP02JAN.dta
 10/31/2001    04:50 PM            138 FILE3.SWT
 05/30/2000    04:32 PM            182 OLDAUTO.MAK
 10/31/2001    12:00 PM            115 RIGHT.RED
 12/06/2001    12:13 AM            138 AWARD.MOV
 10/12/2002    09:31 AM    <DIR>            SPORTS
 05/14/2001    11:28 AM          4,843 GO.BAT
 05/27/2001    10:08 PM             76 LONGFILENAME
 11/16/2002    09:36 AM    <DIR>            LEVEL-1
 10/31/2001    01:08 PM            406 MER.99
 12/06/2001    12:25 AM            465 person.fil
 07/31/1999    12:53 PM             46 STEVEN.FIL
 10/31/2001    07:08 PM            478 VENUS.TXT
 12/31/2001    04:32 PM             93 WILDONE
 10/31/2001    06:40 PM            188 ZODIAC.FIL
               91 File(s)       47,396 bytes
                7 Dir(s)       287,744 bytes free

 C:\>_
```

WHAT'S ▨▨▨▨▨
▨▨▨ **HAPPENING?**   (The graphic represents the tail end of your listing.) On the screen display there are entries with **<DIR>** following their name, indicating subdirectories. How do you know what files are inside a subdirectory? Look at the beginning of the syntax diagram: DIR [*drive:*][*path*][*filename*]. You will substitute the specific drive letter for [*drive:*] and substitute the specific subdirectory name for

[*path*]. You include \ to indicate that you want to begin at the top of the directory and look down. You want to see what is in the **DATA** subdirectory.

2   Key in the following: C:\>**DIR A:\DATA** Enter

```
┌─────────────────────────────────────────────────────────────────────┐
│ ▭ Command Prompt                                         - □ × │
├─────────────────────────────────────────────────────────────────────┤
│                                                                       │
│  C:\>DIR A:\DATA                                                      │
│   Volume in drive A is ACTIVITIES                                     │
│   Volume Serial Number is 08D4-2897                                   │
│                                                                       │
│   Directory of A:\DATA                                                │
│                                                                       │
│  08/01/2002   09:28 AM     <DIR>              .                       │
│  08/01/2002   09:28 AM     <DIR>              ..                      │
│  10/30/2001   02:47 PM                 86 BONJOUR.TXT                 │
│  08/01/2002   09:43 AM                 75 GOOD.TXT                    │
│  10/30/2001   03:26 PM                111 HIGHEST.TXT                 │
│  08/01/2002   09:43 AM                256 MOTHER.LET                  │
│  10/30/2001   03:33 PM                201 TEA.TAX                     │
│  10/30/2001   03:29 PM                274 THANK.YOU                   │
│  08/01/2002   09:43 AM                129 THIN.EST                    │
│                  7 File(s)          1,132 bytes                       │
│                  2 Dir(s)         287,744 bytes free                  │
│                                                                       │
│  C:\>_                                                                │
│                                                                       │
└─────────────────────────────────────────────────────────────────────┘
```

WHAT'S HAPPENING?   You keyed in the command you wanted to execute, the drive letter you were interested in, the backslash to indicate that you wanted to start at the root directory, and finally the name of the subdirectory. Remember, the first backslash always indicates the root directory. The screen display shows you only what files are in the subdirectory (file drawer) called **DATA**. The third line of the display (**Directory of A:\DATA**) tells you the subdirectory you are looking in. What if you wanted to look for a specific file in a subdirectory? Once again, look at the syntax diagram: DIR [*drive*][*path*][*filename*]. You will substitute the drive letter, the path name, and the file name you wish to locate. You need to use a delimiter to separate the file name from the directory name. The delimiter reserved for path names is the backslash. It separates the path name from the file name so that DIR knows which is which.

Note: It is ***very important*** to remember that the first backslash always represents the root directory, and any subsequent backslashes are delimiters separating file names from directory names. The command in Step 2 above tells the operating system (in English) to do a DIRectory of the files found by starting at the root of Drive A, and going down one level into the subdirectory DATA.

3   Key in the following: C:\>**DIR A:\DATA\THIN.EST** Enter

```
┌─────────────────────────────────────────────────────────────────────┐
│ ▭ Command Prompt                                         - □ × │
├─────────────────────────────────────────────────────────────────────┤
│                                                                       │
│  C:\>DIR A:\DATA\THIN.EST                                            │
│   Volume in drive A is ACTIVITIES                                     │
│   Volume Serial Number is 08D4-2897                                   │
│                                                                       │
│   Directory of A:\DATA                                                │
│                                                                       │
│  08/01/2002   09:43 AM                129 THIN.EST                    │
```

```
                   1 File(s)            129 bytes
                   0 Dir(s)         287,744 bytes free

C:\>_
```

**WHAT'S
HAPPENING?**   You keyed in the command you wanted to execute, the drive letter
you were interested in, the first backslash indicating the root directory, the name of
the subdirectory, then a backslash used as a delimiter, and finally the name of the
file. The screen display shows you only the file called **THIN.EST** located on the
ACTIVITIES disk in the subdirectory **DATA**.

2.15   Changing Defaults

Since you generally work on a specific drive, instead of keying in the drive letter
every time, you can change the default drive so that the operating system *automatically* uses the drive displayed on the screen as the default drive.

   Refer to your Configuration Table in Chapter 1.6, or consult your instructor to see
where the Windows system utility files are located. If they are in a subdirectory
other than C:\Windows\system32, you will have to know the name of that location,
and you will have to substitute that path for C:\Windows\System32. For example,
if your system command files are located on a network in
F:\APPS\WINDOWS\SYSTEM32, you would substitute that drive and path each
time you see C:\Windows\system32 in this text. (Also, remember it does not matter
if you key in C:\WINDOWS or c:\windows. The command line is not case sensitive.)

   During the writing of this text book, different computers with Windows XP
installed in different ways are used, and the appearance of the prompt will vary.
Your own prompt may show in a different case, depending on whether you have
upgraded to Windows XP from Windows 2000, upgraded from Millennium or
Windows 98, are using a version installed by the computer manufacturer (called an
OEM [*O*riginal *E*quipment *M*anufaturer] version) or have installed from a full
version onto an empty computer. In addition, if you are in a lab environment, the
display may vary depending on how the network was set up. If you have not filled
out the information on your Configuration Table in Chapter 1, you may wish to do
so at this time.

2.16   Activity: Changing the Default Drive

Note: You are in the Command Prompt window. The "ACTIVITIES Disk—
           Working Copy" is in Drive A. C:\> is displayed as the default drive and
           the default directory.

1   Key in the following: C:\>**A:** [Enter]

```
┌────────────────────────────────────────────────────────────────────┐
│ ▣ Command Prompt                                         _ □ ✕       │
├────────────────────────────────────────────────────────────────────┤
│  C:\>A:                                                              │
│                                                                      │
│  A:\>_                                                               │
│                                                                      │
└────────────────────────────────────────────────────────────────────┘
```

WHAT'S ▨▨▨▨
▨▨HAPPENING?   By simply keying in a letter followed by a colon, you are telling the system that you want to change your work area to that designated drive. Thus, when you keyed in **A:**, you changed the work area from the hard disk, Drive C, to the floppy disk in Drive A. You have now made A: the default drive. The assumption the DIR command will make is that all files will come from the disk in Drive A. It will not look at the hard disk, Drive C.

2   Key in the following: A:\>**DIR DISKCOPY.COM** Enter

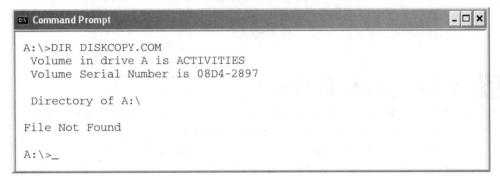

```
A:\>DIR DISKCOPY.COM
 Volume in drive A is ACTIVITIES
 Volume Serial Number is 08D4-2897

 Directory of A:\

File Not Found

A:\>_
```

WHAT'S ▨▨▨▨
▨▨HAPPENING?   Because the default drive is the drive with the ACTIVITIES disk, DIR looked for this file only on the ACTIVITIES disk in Drive A. You *must* be aware of where you are (what the default drive and subdirectory are) and where your files are located.

3   Key in the following: A:\>**DIR C:\DISKCOPY.COM** Enter

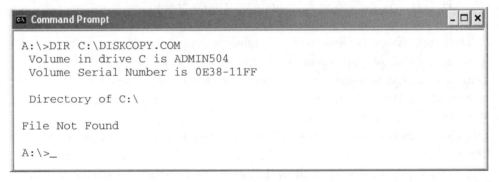

```
A:\>DIR C:\DISKCOPY.COM
 Volume in drive C is ADMIN504
 Volume Serial Number is 0E38-11FF

 Directory of C:\

File Not Found

A:\>_
```

WHAT'S ▨▨▨▨
▨▨HAPPENING?   Although you did tell DIR to look on Drive C, you were not specific enough. DIR looked only in the root directory of C and could not find the file of interest.

4   Key in the following:
        A:\>**DIR C:\WINDOWS\SYSTEM32\DISKCOPY.COM** Enter
Note: Substitute your drive and/or subdirectory that contains your system utility files if it is different from this example.

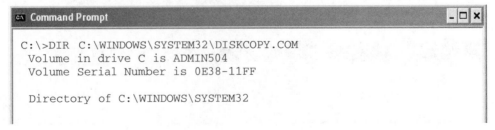

```
C:\>DIR C:\WINDOWS\SYSTEM32\DISKCOPY.COM
 Volume in drive C is ADMIN504
 Volume Serial Number is 0E38-11FF

 Directory of C:\WINDOWS\SYSTEM32
```

```
08/23/2001   12:00 PM                 7,168 diskcopy.com
                  1 File(s)           7,168 bytes
                  0 Dir(s)    8,572,444,672 bytes free

C:\>_
```

WHAT'S HAPPENING?   The dates and times for the diskcopy.com file may vary depending on which version of Windows you are using. In this case, because you specified the drive and subdirectory as well as the file name, DIR knew where to look and located the file. You asked DIR not only to look on Drive C, but more specifically to look on Drive C in the subdirectory called **WINDOWS\SYSTEM32** for the file called **DISKCOPY.COM**.

2.17   Changing Directories

In addition to changing drives, you can also change directories. When you work on a hard disk, it is usually divided into subdirectories. Once you establish your default drive, you can also establish your default directory. Then, instead of keying in the path name every time, you can change the default directory so that the operating system will use the directory displayed on the screen as the default directory. To change directories, you key in the command CD (which stands for "change directory") followed by the directory (path) name. The partial command syntax is: CD [/D] [drive:][path].

If you key in **CD** with no parameters, it tells you the directory that is currently the default directory. If you wish to change the default, you follow CD with a path name such as **CD \WINDOWS\SYSTEM32**. If you wish to change drives at the same time you change directories, you use the /D parameter. Thus, if your default prompt were A:\> and you keyed in **CD /D C:\WINDOWS\SYSTEM32**, you would change drives as well as directories.

2.18   Activity: Changing Directories

Note: You are at the command line screen. The ACTIVITIES Disk—Working Copy is in Drive A. A:\> is displayed as the default drive and the default directory.

1   Key in the following: A:\>**C:** ⏎Enter⏎

2   Key in the following: C:\>**CD** ⏎Enter⏎

```
A:\>C:

C:\>CD
C:\

C:\>_
```

WHAT'S HAPPENING?   When you keyed in **CD**, C:\ displayed, telling you that your current default drive is C and the current default directory is the root or \. In the last activity, when you wanted to locate the file called **DISKCOPY.COM**, you had to precede it with the path name **\WINDOWS\SYSTEM32**. If you change to that directory, the only place that DIR will look for that file is in the current default directory.

3　Key in the following: `C:\>`**CD \WINDOWS\SYSTEM32** `Enter`

```
C:\>CD \WINDOWS\SYSTEM32

C:\WINDOWS\SYSTEM32>_
```

WHAT'S HAPPENING?　You told Windows to change from the current directory to a directory called **SYSTEM32** under a directory called **WINDOWS** under the root (****) of the default drive (**C:**). You changed directories so that **WINDOWS\SYSTEM32** is now the default directory. Notice how the prompt displays both the default drive and directory. Whenever you execute any command, the command will look only in the current directory for the file of interest.

4　Key in the following: `C:\WINDOWS\SYSTEM32>`**DIR DISKCOPY.COM** `Enter`

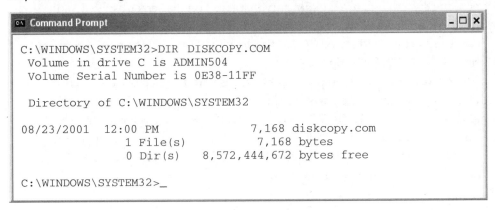

```
C:\WINDOWS\SYSTEM32>DIR DISKCOPY.COM
 Volume in drive C is ADMIN504
 Volume Serial Number is 0E38-11FF

 Directory of C:\WINDOWS\SYSTEM32

08/23/2001  12:00 PM             7,168 diskcopy.com
             1 File(s)          7,168 bytes
             0 Dir(s)   8,572,444,672 bytes free

C:\WINDOWS\SYSTEM32>_
```

WHAT'S HAPPENING?　The command DIR looked only in the **\WINDOWS\SYSTEM32** directory and located the file called **DISKCOPY.COM**. Look at the line that states **Directory of C:\WINDOWS\SYSTEM32**. DIR always tells you where it has looked. This procedure works with any directory.

5　Key in the following: `C:\WINDOWS\SYSTEM32>`**CD ** `Enter`

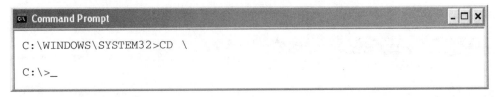

```
C:\WINDOWS\SYSTEM32>CD \

C:\>_
```

WHAT'S HAPPENING?　Whenever you key in **CD **, it always takes you to the root directory of the drive you are on.

6　Key in the following: `C:\>`**CD /D A:\DATA** `Enter`

7　Key in the following: `A:\DATA>`**DIR** `Enter`

```
██ Command Prompt                                                    _ □ x

C:\>CD /D A:\DATA


A:\DATA>DIR
 Volume in drive A is ACTIVITIES
 Volume Serial Number is 08D4-2897

 Directory of A:\DATA

08/01/2002   09:28 AM    <DIR>            .
08/01/2002   09:28 AM    <DIR>            ..
10/30/2001   02:47 PM              86 BONJOUR.TXT
08/01/2002   09:43 AM              75 GOOD.TXT
10/30/2001   03:26 PM             111 HIGHEST.TXT
08/01/2002   09:43 AM             256 MOTHER.LET
10/30/2001   03:33 PM             201 TEA.TAX
10/30/2001   03:29 PM             274 THANK.YOU
08/01/2002   09:43 AM             129 THIN.EST
                 7 File(s)        1,132 bytes
                 2 Dir(s)       287,744 bytes free

A:\DATA>_
```

WHAT'S ▦▦▦
▦▦ **HAPPENING?**   You used two commands. With the first command, you changed
the default drive to A and the default directory to **DATA** on Drive A. You could do
this because you used the /D parameter. Then you changed from the root of the A
drive to the **DATA** directory. With the second command, you executed the DIR
command. All files in the **DATA** directory are displayed. You could have looked for
a particular file, but, since there are only a few files in the **DATA** directory, you
could find any file you are looking for easily.

8   Key in the following: A:\DATA>**CD** \ [Enter]

WHAT'S ▦▦▦
▦▦ **HAPPENING?**   You have now returned to the root directory of Drive A.

2.19   Global File Specifications: Wildcards, the ?, and the *

Using the DIR command and a file specification, you can find one specific file that
matches what you keyed. Every time you wish to locate a file, you can key the entire
file specification. Often, however, you wish to work with a group of files that have
similar names or a group of files whose names you do not know. There is a "shorthand" system that allows you to operate on a group of files rather than a single file.
This system is formally called *global file specifications*; informally, it is called using
wildcards. Sometimes it is referred to as using ambiguous file references. Conceptually, they are similar to playing cards, where the joker can stand for another card of

your choice. In Windows, the question mark (?) and the asterisk (*) are the wildcards. These symbols stand for unknowns. The * represents or substitutes for a group or *string* of characters; the ? represents or substitutes for a *single* character. Many commands allow you to use global file specifications. You will use the DIR command to demonstrate the use of wildcards. You will find that the techniques you learn here will also apply when you use Search in the GUI (the Windows desktop).

2.20   Activity: DIR and Wildcards

Note: The ACTIVITIES Disk—Working Copy is in Drive A. A:\> is displayed as the default drive and the default directory.

1   Key in the following: A:\>**C:** [Enter]

2   Key in the following: C:\>**CD \WINDOWS\SYSTEM32** [Enter]

Note: Remember that if the system utility files are in a subdirectory with a different name, you will have to substitute your subdirectory name.

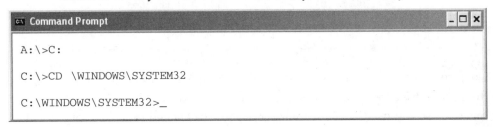

```
A:\>C:

C:\>CD \WINDOWS\SYSTEM32

C:\WINDOWS\SYSTEM32>_
```

WHAT'S HAPPENING?   You have changed the default directory to where the system utility files are located. If you wanted to locate a file and all you remembered about the file name was that it began with the letter G and that it was located on the default drive and subdirectory, you would not be able to find that file. You have insufficient information.

3   Key in the following: C:\WINDOWS\SYSTEM32>**DIR   G** [Enter]

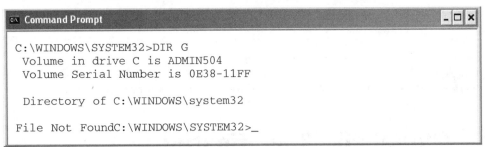

```
C:\WINDOWS\SYSTEM32>DIR G
 Volume in drive C is ADMIN504
 Volume Serial Number is 0E38-11FF

 Directory of C:\WINDOWS\system32

File Not FoundC:\WINDOWS\SYSTEM32>_
```

WHAT'S HAPPENING?   First, note how the prompt reflects the subdirectory **\WINDOWS\SYSTEM32**. When you keyed in **DIR G**, you were correct, but only somewhat. You first entered the work you wanted done, the command DIR. You did not need to enter the drive letter. DIR assumed both the default drive and default subdirectory. However, DIR specifically looked for a file called G. There was no file called G; that was simply the first letter of the file name. You could find files that begin with G by using the wildcard symbol * to represent all other characters—both the file name (*) and the file extension (.*).

4   Key in the following: `C:\WINDOWS\SYSTEM32>`**DIR G*.*** [Enter]

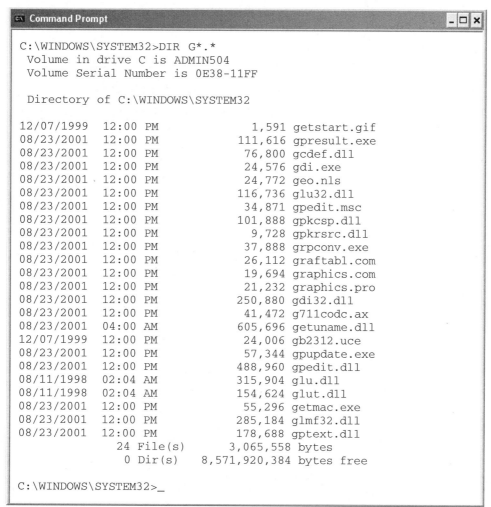

```
Command Prompt                                              _ □ ×

C:\WINDOWS\SYSTEM32>DIR G*.*
 Volume in drive C is ADMIN504
 Volume Serial Number is 0E38-11FF

 Directory of C:\WINDOWS\SYSTEM32

12/07/1999  12:00 PM              1,591 getstart.gif
08/23/2001  12:00 PM            111,616 gpresult.exe
08/23/2001  12:00 PM             76,800 gcdef.dll
08/23/2001  12:00 PM             24,576 gdi.exe
08/23/2001  12:00 PM             24,772 geo.nls
08/23/2001  12:00 PM            116,736 glu32.dll
08/23/2001  12:00 PM             34,871 gpedit.msc
08/23/2001  12:00 PM            101,888 gpkcsp.dll
08/23/2001  12:00 PM              9,728 gpkrsrc.dll
08/23/2001  12:00 PM             37,888 grpconv.exe
08/23/2001  12:00 PM             26,112 graftabl.com
08/23/2001  12:00 PM             19,694 graphics.com
08/23/2001  12:00 PM             21,232 graphics.pro
08/23/2001  12:00 PM            250,880 gdi32.dll
08/23/2001  12:00 PM             41,472 g711codc.ax
08/23/2001  04:00 AM            605,696 getuname.dll
12/07/1999  12:00 PM             24,006 gb2312.uce
08/23/2001  12:00 PM             57,344 gpupdate.exe
08/23/2001  12:00 PM            488,960 gpedit.dll
08/11/1998  02:04 AM            315,904 glu.dll
08/11/1998  02:04 AM            154,624 glut.dll
08/23/2001  12:00 PM             55,296 getmac.exe
08/23/2001  12:00 PM            285,184 glmf32.dll
08/23/2001  12:00 PM            178,688 gptext.dll
              24 File(s)      3,065,558 bytes
               0 Dir(s)   8,571,920,384 bytes free

C:\WINDOWS\SYSTEM32>_
```

**WHAT'S
HAPPENING?**   The files listed in the subdirectory vary, depending on the release or version of the OS, so do not worry if your screen display is different. You asked DIR to find files beginning with the letter G on the default drive and default subdirectory. You did not know anything else about the file names or even how many files you might have that begin with the letter G. You represented any and all characters following the letter G with the asterisk, separated the file name from the file extension with a period, and represented all the characters in the file extension with the second asterisk. Thus, **G*.*** (read as "G star dot star") means all the files that start with the letter G having any or no characters following the letter G, and can have any or no file extension. Now DIR could look for a match.

In this example, the first file DIR found that had the G you specified was **getstart.gif**. DIR returned this file because the asterisk (*) following the G matched the remainder of the file name, **etstart**. Remember, * represents any group of characters. The second *, representing the file extension, matched **gif** because, again, the * represents any group of characters. The second file DIR found that began with G was **gpresult.exe**. DIR displayed this file because the * following the G matched the remainder of the file name, **presult**. The second * representing the file extension matched **exe** because, again, the * represents any group of characters. The third file matches **G*.*** for the same reasons. You could have more or fewer files listed in very different order depending on how your system is set up.

There are other ways of requesting information using the *. If all you know about a group of files on the disk in the default drive is that the group has the common file extension **.SYS**, you could display these files on the screen using wildcards.

5   Key in the following: C:\WINDOWS\SYSTEM32>**DIR *.SYS** [Enter]

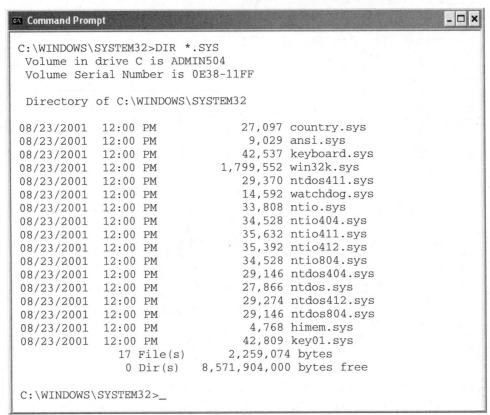

```
C:\WINDOWS\SYSTEM32>DIR *.SYS
 Volume in drive C is ADMIN504
 Volume Serial Number is 0E38-11FF

 Directory of C:\WINDOWS\SYSTEM32

08/23/2001  12:00 PM               27,097 country.sys
08/23/2001  12:00 PM                9,029 ansi.sys
08/23/2001  12:00 PM               42,537 keyboard.sys
08/23/2001  12:00 PM            1,799,552 win32k.sys
08/23/2001  12:00 PM               29,370 ntdos411.sys
08/23/2001  12:00 PM               14,592 watchdog.sys
08/23/2001  12:00 PM               33,808 ntio.sys
08/23/2001  12:00 PM               34,528 ntio404.sys
08/23/2001  12:00 PM               35,632 ntio411.sys
08/23/2001  12:00 PM               35,392 ntio412.sys
08/23/2001  12:00 PM               34,528 ntio804.sys
08/23/2001  12:00 PM               29,146 ntdos404.sys
08/23/2001  12:00 PM               27,866 ntdos.sys
08/23/2001  12:00 PM               29,274 ntdos412.sys
08/23/2001  12:00 PM               29,146 ntdos804.sys
08/23/2001  12:00 PM                4,768 himem.sys
08/23/2001  12:00 PM               42,809 key01.sys
              17 File(s)      2,259,074 bytes
               0 Dir(s)   8,571,904,000 bytes free

C:\WINDOWS\SYSTEM32>_
```

WHAT'S HAPPENING?   The * represented any file name, but all the files must have **.SYS** as a file extension. Again, the number of files displayed may vary. In addition, if your hard disk is using the NTFS file system, your display will be in alphabetical order by file name. The next activities will demonstrate the differences between the two wildcards, * and ?.

6   Key in the following: C:\WINDOWS\SYSTEM32>**DIR A:*.TXT** [Enter]

```
C:\WINDOWS\SYSTEM32>DIR A:*.TXT
 Volume in drive A is ACTIVITIES
 Volume Serial Number is 08D4-2897

 Directory of A:\

10/30/2001  01:46 PM              148 ASTRO.TXT
10/30/2001  02:10 PM              121 BORN.TXT
12/11/1999  04:03 PM               72 DANCES.TXT
05/30/2000  04:32 PM               53 HELLO.TXT
11/16/2000  12:00 PM               59 Sandy and Patty.txt
10/31/2001  02:43 PM              529 TITAN.TXT
11/16/2000  12:00 PM               53 Sandy and Nicki.txt
```

```
05/27/2001  10:08 PM                81 LONGFILENAME.TXT
10/30/2001  03:42 PM               190 JUPITER.TXT
12/06/2001  12:15 AM                97 LONGFILENAMED.TXT
10/31/2001  11:37 AM               253 GALAXY.TXT
12/06/2001  12:16 AM                99 LONGFILENAMING.TXT
10/31/2001  01:08 PM               406 MERCURY.TXT
11/24/2001  11:24 AM               194 PLANETS.TXT
10/31/2001  07:08 PM               478 VENUS.TXT
              15 File(s)         2,833 bytes
               0 Dir(s)        287,744 bytes free

C:\WINDOWS\SYSTEM32>_
```

WHAT'S HAPPENING?   You asked DIR what files had an extension of **.TXT** and were located on the ACTIVITIES disk. You did not know anything about the file names, only the file extension. DIR searched the table of contents in Drive A since you placed an **A:** prior to ***.TXT**. It looked only in the root directory of the disk since you preceded ***.TXT** with ****. The command found 15 files that matched ***.TXT**. Now, how does the question mark differ from the asterisk?

7   Key in the following: C:\WINDOWS\SYSTEM32>**DIR A:\?????.TXT** [Enter]

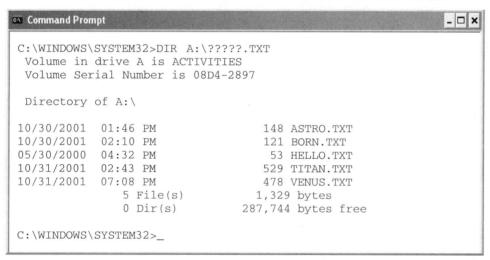

```
C:\WINDOWS\SYSTEM32>DIR A:\?????.TXT
 Volume in drive A is ACTIVITIES
 Volume Serial Number is 08D4-2897

 Directory of A:\

10/30/2001  01:46 PM               148 ASTRO.TXT
10/30/2001  02:10 PM               121 BORN.TXT
05/30/2000  04:32 PM                53 HELLO.TXT
10/31/2001  02:43 PM               529 TITAN.TXT
10/31/2001  07:08 PM               478 VENUS.TXT
               5 File(s)         1,329 bytes
               0 Dir(s)        287,744 bytes free

C:\WINDOWS\SYSTEM32>_
```

WHAT'S HAPPENING?   This time you asked your question differently. You still asked for files that had the file extension of **.TXT** in the root directory of the ACTIVITIES disk. However, instead of using the asterisk representing "any number of characters," you used the question mark (?) five times. You asked for a file name with five characters and DIR displayed files with five *or fewer* characters in their file name. You then separated the file name from the file extension with a period saying that the file not only needed to have that size name, but also the extension **.TXT**. This time five files matched your request. Note how the above screen display differs from the screen display in Step 6. This time you do not see the files **PLANETS.TXT, GALAXY.TXT, JUPITER.TXT, DANCES.TXT, Sandy and Nicki.txt, Sandy and Patty.txt, LONGFILENAME.TXT, LONGFILENAMING.TXT, MERCURY.TXT,** or **LONGFILENAMED.TXT** on the screen. Those file names were longer than five characters.

8   Key in the following: C:\WINDOWS\SYSTEM32>**DIR A:\EXP*.*** [Enter]

```
[ca] Command Prompt                                          [-][□][×]

C:\WINDOWS\SYSTEM32>DIR A:\EXP*.*
 Volume in drive A is ACTIVITIES
 Volume Serial Number is 08D4-2897

 Directory of A:\

12/11/2002  09:10 AM                 295 EXP02FEB.dta
12/11/2002  09:10 AM                 294 EXP03JAN.dta
12/11/2002  09:10 AM                 295 EXP01FEB.dta
12/11/2002  09:10 AM                 292 EXP02MAR.dta
12/11/2002  09:10 AM                 294 EXP01JAN.dta
12/11/2002  09:10 AM                 295 EXP03FEB.dta
12/11/2002  09:10 AM                 292 EXP01MAR.dta
12/11/2002  09:10 AM                 292 EXP03MAR.dta
12/11/2002  09:10 AM                 294 EXP02JAN.dta
                 9 File(s)         2,643 bytes
                 0 Dir(s)        287,744 bytes free

C:\WINDOWS\SYSTEM32>_
```

WHAT'S
HAPPENING?   This time you asked to see all the files located on the ACTIVITIES
disk (Drive A) in the root directory (\) that start with the letters EXP (**EXP*.***). The
. following the **EXP** represents the rest of the file name and the file extension.
These file names were created with a pattern in mind. All the files having to do with
the Budget start with EXP, which stands for "expenses," followed by the last two
digits of the year (99, 00, or 01), followed by the month (JANuary, FEBruary, or
MARch). The file extension is .dta to indicate these are data files, not program files.
However, often you are not interested in all the files. You want only some of them.
For example, you might want to know what expense files you have on the ACTIVI-
TIES disk for the year 2001.

9   Key in the following: C:\WINDOWS\SYSTEM32>**DIR A:\EXP01*.*** [Enter]

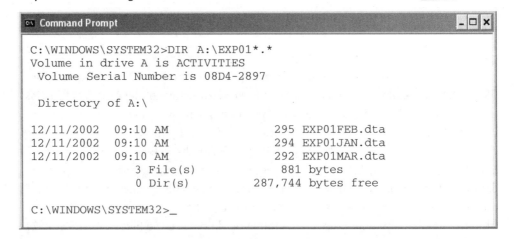

```
[ca] Command Prompt                                          [-][□][×]

C:\WINDOWS\SYSTEM32>DIR A:\EXP01*.*
Volume in drive A is ACTIVITIES
 Volume Serial Number is 08D4-2897

 Directory of A:\

12/11/2002  09:10 AM                 295 EXP01FEB.dta
12/11/2002  09:10 AM                 294 EXP01JAN.dta
12/11/2002  09:10 AM                 292 EXP01MAR.dta
                 3 File(s)           881 bytes
                 0 Dir(s)        287,744 bytes free

C:\WINDOWS\SYSTEM32>_
```

WHAT'S
HAPPENING?   Here you asked for all the files (**DIR**) on the ACTIVITIES disk in
Drive A in the root directory that were expense files for 2001 (**EXP01**). The rest of the
file names were represented by ***.***. On your screen display you got only the 2001
files. However, suppose your interest is in all the January files. You no longer care
which year, only which month.

10   Key in the following: C:\WINDOWS\SYSTEM32>**DIR A:\EXP??JAN.*** [Enter]

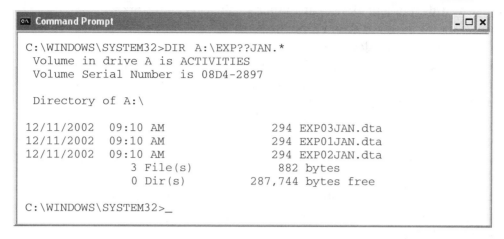

```
C:\WINDOWS\SYSTEM32>DIR  A:\EXP??JAN.*
 Volume in drive A is ACTIVITIES
 Volume Serial Number is 08D4-2897

 Directory of A:\

12/11/2002   09:10 AM                 294 EXP03JAN.dta
12/11/2002   09:10 AM                 294 EXP01JAN.dta
12/11/2002   09:10 AM                 294 EXP02JAN.dta
               3 File(s)             882 bytes
               0 Dir(s)        287,744 bytes free

C:\WINDOWS\SYSTEM32>_
```

WHAT'S HAPPENING?   The two question marks represented the two characters within the file name. The characters could have been any characters, but they would be limited to two characters. You could have also keyed in **DIR A:\exp*jan.*** because remember, Windows is not case sensitive, and will recognize characters entered after a wildcard. Previous versions of the operating system would have ignored all characters after the asterisk, allowing any and all characters to fill the remaining spaces. In those versions, the command **DIR *JAN.*** would have resulted in the same display as **DIR *.***. Both Windows XP and Windows 2000 Professional, however, recognize characters following the asterisk wildcard, and the resulting display shows you the files you were looking for.

11   Key in the following: C:\WINDOWS\SYSTEM32>**CD ** [Enter]

```
C:\WINDOWS\SYSTEM32>CD \

C:\>_
```

WHAT'S HAPPENING?   You have returned to the root directory of C.

2.21   Redirection

The system knows what you want to do when you key in commands. In the Command Prompt window, input is expected from the keyboard, which is considered the *standard input* device. In addition, the results of a command's execution are written to the screen. The screen, or monitor, is considered the *standard output* device.

You can change where input is coming from, and where output is going to through a feature called *redirection*. Redirection allows you to tell the operating system to, instead of writing the output to the standard output device (the screen), write the information somewhere else. Typically, this is to a file or printer. For redirection to work with a printer, the printer must be a local printer—a printer that is attached directly to the computer you are working with—and not a network printer. Redirection *does not work with all commands,* only with those commands that write their output to standard output. Redirection does work with the DIR command because DIR gets its input from the standard input device, the keyboard, and writes to the standard output device, the screen. The syntax for redirection is COMMAND > DESTINATION. The command is what you key in, such as DIR *.TXT. You then use the greater-than symbol (>) to redirect the results of that command to where you specify, instead of to the screen. The command would be keyed in as DIR *.TXT > MY.FIL to send the results, or output of the DIR command, to a file named MY.FIL. The command would be keyed in as DIR *.TXT > LPT1 if you wanted the output to go to the printer attached to the first printer port. You must use the actual device name for the printer, PRN for the default printer, or LPT1, LPT2, or LPT3 for a printer attached to a specific port on your computer. If you are using a network printer, you cannot redirect unless you know the name of the network printer.

2.22   Activity: Redirecting Output to a File

Note: The system is booted. You have shelled out to the command prompt screen. The ACTIVITIES Disk—Working Copy is in Drive A. C:\> is displayed as the default drive and the default directory.

1   Key in the following: C:\>**A:** Enter

2   Key in the following: A:\>**DIR *.NEW** Enter

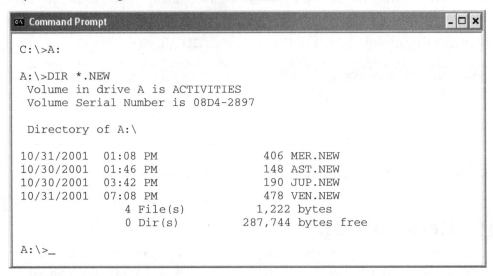

```
C:\>A:

A:\>DIR *.NEW
 Volume in drive A is ACTIVITIES
 Volume Serial Number is 08D4-2897

 Directory of A:\

10/31/2001  01:08 PM                406 MER.NEW
10/30/2001  01:46 PM                148 AST.NEW
10/30/2001  03:42 PM                190 JUP.NEW
10/31/2001  07:08 PM                478 VEN.NEW
               4 File(s)          1,222 bytes
               0 Dir(s)       287,744 bytes free

A:\>_
```

WHAT'S HAPPENING?   You changed the default drive to the A drive. You then asked for all the files on the ACTIVITIES disk that have the file extension of **.NEW.** You saw the output displayed on the screen. You have four files that meet the criteria. You keyed in a command and the results were sent to the screen.

You are now going to create a file on your ACTIVITIES Disk—Working Copy using redirection. Remember that when the instructions in this text say "ACTIVI-TIES disk," they mean the copy of the ACTIVITIES disk you made in Chapter 1. It is this disk that is in the A drive.

3   Key in the following: A:\>**DIR *.NEW > MY.HW** Enter

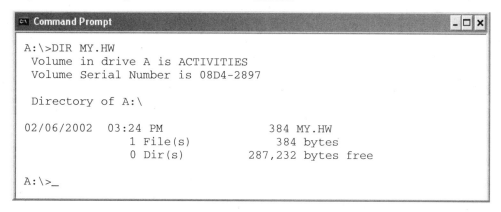

```
c:\ Command Prompt                                          - □ x

A:\>DIR *.NEW > MY.HW

A:\>_
```

WHAT'S ▓▓▓▓▓
▓▓▓ HAPPENING?   This time you instructed the system to send the output of the DIR
command to a file called **MY.HW**, instead of sending the output to the screen.
Redirection is an "instead of" procedure. You either have the results of the DIR
command displayed on the screen, or you send it to a file.

Note: If you see a dialog box that says "The disk cannot be written to because it is
write protected. Please remove the write protection from the volume
ACTIVITIES in drive A:," your disk is write protected. Remove the disk
and move the sliding tab to cover the small hole in the corner to unprotect
it. Reinsert the disk and click **Try Again** in the dialog box to complete the
task.

4   Key in the following: A:\>**DIR MY.HW** Enter

```
c:\ Command Prompt                                          - □ x

A:\>DIR MY.HW
 Volume in drive A is ACTIVITIES
 Volume Serial Number is 08D4-2897

 Directory of A:\

02/06/2002   03:24 PM                  384 MY.HW
               1 File(s)               384 bytes
               0 Dir(s)          287,232 bytes free

A:\>_
```

WHAT'S ▓▓▓▓▓
▓▓▓ HAPPENING?   You now have a file that contains the output from the DIR command stored on your disk.

2.23 Redirecting Output to the Printer

You have seen that you can redirect output to a file. You can also redirect output to a
local printer. Since the DIR command normally writes to the screen, you can redirect
the output of the DIR command to the printer to get a printout of what normally
would be written to the screen. However, you cannot use just any name with a
device, as you can with a file name. Windows has very specific names for its devices. You already know that a letter of the alphabet followed by a colon (:) is always
a disk drive. Printers have names also. The printer device names are PRN, LPT1,
LPT2, and sometimes LPT3. PRN is the default printer, usually LPT1. These are the
names for local printers. Network printers also have specific names. The network
administrator assigns the network printer name. Unless you know your network
printer name, you may not be able to redirect output to the printer.

**CAUTION: Before doing the next activity, check with your lab instructor to see if
you have a local printer. If you have access to only a network printer, you may not**

be able to do the next activity unless you have received other instructions. If you do have a local printer, and you use LPT1, be sure to use the number one, not the lowercase L.

2.24 Activity: Redirecting the Output to the Printer

Note 1:   DO NOT do this activity until you have checked with your lab instructor for any special instructions. In fact, you may be unable to do the activity. If you cannot do it, read the activity.

Note 2:   The ACTIVITIES Disk—Working Copy is in Drive A. A:\> is displayed as the default drive and the default directory. Be sure the printer is turned on and online before beginning this activity.

1   Key in the following: A:\>**DIR *.TXT** Enter

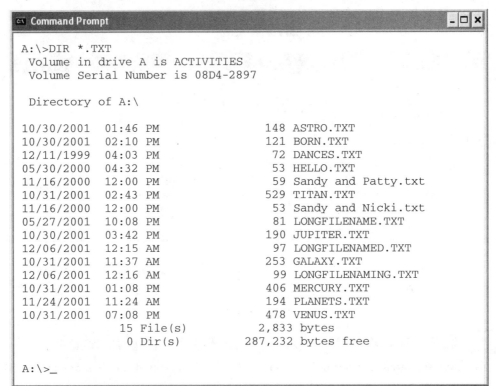

```
Command Prompt                                           _ □ ×

A:\>DIR *.TXT
 Volume in drive A is ACTIVITIES
 Volume Serial Number is 08D4-2897

 Directory of A:\

10/30/2001  01:46 PM               148 ASTRO.TXT
10/30/2001  02:10 PM               121 BORN.TXT
12/11/1999  04:03 PM                72 DANCES.TXT
05/30/2000  04:32 PM                53 HELLO.TXT
11/16/2000  12:00 PM                59 Sandy and Patty.txt
10/31/2001  02:43 PM               529 TITAN.TXT
11/16/2000  12:00 PM                53 Sandy and Nicki.txt
05/27/2001  10:08 PM                81 LONGFILENAME.TXT
10/30/2001  03:42 PM               190 JUPITER.TXT
12/06/2001  12:15 AM                97 LONGFILENAMED.TXT
10/31/2001  11:37 AM               253 GALAXY.TXT
12/06/2001  12:16 AM                99 LONGFILENAMING.TXT
10/31/2001  01:08 PM               406 MERCURY.TXT
11/24/2001  11:24 AM               194 PLANETS.TXT
10/31/2001  07:08 PM               478 VENUS.TXT
              15 File(s)         2,833 bytes
               0 Dir(s)     287,232 bytes free

A:\>_
```

WHAT'S ▨▨▨▨
▨▨▨HAPPENING?   You asked to see a listing of all the files on the ACTIVITIES disk that had the file extension of **.TXT**.

2   Key in the following: A:\>**DIR *.TXT > PRN** Enter

WHAT'S ▨▨▨▨
▨▨▨HAPPENING?   You instructed the operating system to send the output to an alternate output device, specifically the printer, instead of displaying it on the screen. The printer should be printing, and nothing should be on the screen. Remember, redirection is an "instead of" procedure. You either display the results of the DIR command on the screen, or send the results to the printer. See Figure 2.2.

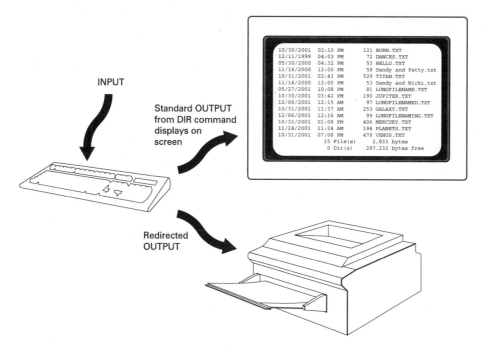

```
10/30/2001  02:10 PM        121  BORN.TXT
12/11/1999  04:03 PM         72  DANCES.TXT
05/30/2000  04:32 PM         53  HELLO.TXT
11/16/2000  12:00 PM         59  Sandy and Patty.txt
10/31/2001  02:43 PM        529  TITAN.TXT
11/16/2000  12:00 PM         53  Sandy and Nicki.txt
05/27/2001  10:08 PM         81  LONGFILENAME.TXT
10/30/2001  03:42 PM        190  JUPITER.TXT
12/06/2001  12:15 AM         97  LONGFILENAMED.TXT
10/31/2001  11:37 AM        253  GALAXY.TXT
12/06/2001  12:16 AM         99  LONGFILENAMING.TXT
10/31/2001  01:08 PM        406  MERCURY.TXT
11/24/2001  11:24 AM        194  PLANETS.TXT
10/31/2001  07:08 PM        478  VENUS.TXT
               15 File(s)       2,833 bytes
                0 Dir(s)    287,232 bytes free
```

INPUT

Standard OUTPUT
from DIR command
displays on
screen

Redirected
OUTPUT

Figure 2.2—Redirected Output

Your page may not have ejected from your local printer. If you have a dot-matrix printer, it printed the lines in the file and then it stopped. The printer did not advance to the beginning of a new page.

You have to go to the printer and roll the platen until the perforated line appears so that you can tear off the page. If you have an inkjet printer or a laser printer, the situation is even stranger. No paper appears at all. In order to feed the paper manually with an inkjet printer, you have to press the **Reset** button. With a laser printer, you have to go to the printer, turn the **Online** button off, press the form feed (**FF**) button, and then turn the **Online** button back on. In all these cases, you are doing what is called a *hardware solution* to a problem. You are manipulating the hardware to get the desired results.

2.25   Getting Help

As you begin to use commands, their names, purposes, and proper syntax become familiar. Initially, however, these commands are new to users. Prior to DOS 5.0, the only way to become familiar with a command or to check the proper syntax was to locate the command in the manual. The reference manual that comes with any software package is called *documentation*. The completeness of the documentation can vary from software package to software package. The documentation that comes with an operating system consists of at least the installation instructions and occasionally a command reference manual, which is a list of commands with a brief description and syntax for each. For the Windows operating systems, documenta-tion is in the form of text files on the CD. In DOS 6.0 and above, the documentation has been provided less and less in written form, and more and more online. There is a very good database of information that can be accessed via the Help choice on the Start menu from the desktop, but this help is for procedures and methods used in the Windows GUI. You may also get help on command line commands in the GUI help. But to get help with a command and its syntax within the DOS environment, key in the name of the command followed by a space, a forward slash (/), and a question mark (?). You may also use HELP followed by the command name, such as HELP DIR. For reference, the commands and syntax are listed in Appendix B.

2.26 Activity: Getting Help with a Command

Note: The ACTIVITIES Disk—Working Copy is in Drive A. A:\> is displayed as the default drive and the default directory.

1   Key in the following: A:\>**DIR** /? [Enter]

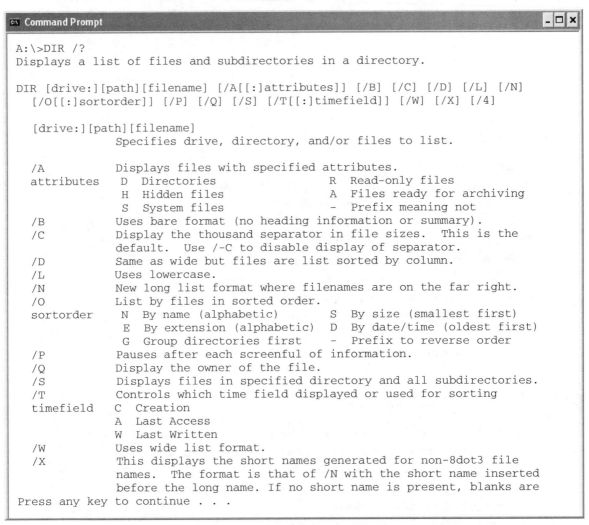

```
Command Prompt                                                    _ □ ✕

A:\>DIR /?
Displays a list of files and subdirectories in a directory.

DIR [drive:][path][filename] [/A[[:]attributes]] [/B] [/C] [/D] [/L] [/N]
  [/O[[:]sortorder]] [/P] [/Q] [/S] [/T[[:]timefield]] [/W] [/X] [/4]

  [drive:][path][filename]
              Specifies drive, directory, and/or files to list.

  /A          Displays files with specified attributes.
  attributes  D  Directories              R  Read-only files
              H  Hidden files             A  Files ready for archiving
              S  System files             -  Prefix meaning not
  /B          Uses bare format (no heading information or summary).
  /C          Display the thousand separator in file sizes.  This is the
              default.  Use /-C to disable display of separator.
  /D          Same as wide but files are list sorted by column.
  /L          Uses lowercase.
  /N          New long list format where filenames are on the far right.
  /O          List by files in sorted order.
  sortorder   N  By name (alphabetic)      S  By size (smallest first)
              E  By extension (alphabetic) D  By date/time (oldest first)
              G  Group directories first   -  Prefix to reverse order
  /P          Pauses after each screenful of information.
  /Q          Display the owner of the file.
  /S          Displays files in specified directory and all subdirectories.
  /T          Controls which time field displayed or used for sorting
  timefield   C  Creation
              A  Last Access
              W  Last Written
  /W          Uses wide list format.
  /X          This displays the short names generated for non-8dot3 file
              names.  The format is that of /N with the short name inserted
              before the long name. If no short name is present, blanks are
Press any key to continue . . .
```

WHAT'S HAPPENING?   This will display the complete syntax explanation for the DIR command. Previously, you looked at only a partial syntax diagram for the DIR command. Notice the first line of the complete diagram:
DIR [drive:][path][filename] [/A[[:]attributes]] [/B] [/C] [/D] [/L] [/N].
The entire line is in brackets, **[ ]**, meaning that all of the parameters or switches are optional. The DIR command can stand alone—it requires no parameters. You may include the drive, path, and file name, and you may specify the order (**/O**) in which you wish the files displayed. Look at the diagram at the line that begins with **/O List**

ed order. Below that are the orders available. **N** is by name, **S** by size,
D by date, and so on.

r key see the remaining few lines of the DIR syntax.

owing: A:\>**DIR /ON** Enter

```
mpt                                                        _ □ ×

       01:38 PM               4,064 NEW-SUVS.XLS
       04:32 PM                 182 OLDAUTO.MAK
       01:49 PM                 219 ORION.NEB
       12:25 AM                 465 person.fil
       04:32 PM               2,307 PERSONAL.FIL
       11:24 AM                 194 PLANETS.TXT
       02:16 PM              11,264 QUASARS.DOC
       12:00 PM                 115 RIGHT.RED
       03:18 PM                 758 RIGHT.UP
       12:00 PM                  53 Sandy and Nicki.txt
       12:00 PM                  59 Sandy and Patty.txt
10/12/2002  09:31 AM    <DIR>        SPORTS
07/31/2000  04:32 PM             260 STATE.CAP
07/31/2000  04:32 PM           1,228 STATES.USA
07/31/1999  12:53 PM              46 STEVEN.FIL
12/06/2001  09:18 AM    <DIR>        TEST
10/31/2001  02:43 PM             529 TITAN.TXT
10/31/2001  07:08 PM             478 VEN.99
10/31/2001  07:08 PM             478 VEN.NEW
10/31/2001  07:08 PM             478 VEN.TMP
10/31/2001  07:08 PM             478 VENUS.TMM
10/31/2001  07:08 PM             478 VENUS.TXT
05/14/2002  08:07 AM              64 WILD1.XXX
05/14/2002  08:07 AM              64 WILD2.YYY
05/14/2002  08:07 AM              64 WILD3.ZZZ
12/31/2001  04:32 PM              93 WILDONE
12/31/2001  04:32 PM             181 WILDONE.DOS
12/31/2001  04:32 PM             181 WILDTHR.DOS
12/31/2001  04:32 PM             182 WILDTWO.DOS
08/12/2000  04:12 PM               3 Y.FIL
10/31/2001  06:40 PM             188 ZODIAC.FIL
            92 File(s)       47,780 bytes
             7 Dir(s)       287,232 bytes free

A:\>_
```

WHAT'S
HAPPENING?   (As with previous examples, this graphic represents the tail end of
your listing.) Notice that the files are displayed in alphabetical order. You can
reverse the order.

4   Key in the following: A:\>**DIR /O-N** Enter

```
📟 Command Prompt                                           _ □ ×

10/31/2001  04:51 PM             137 FILE2.FP
10/31/2001  02:49 PM             138 FILE2.CZG
12/11/2002  09:10 AM             292 EXP03MAR.dta
12/11/2002  09:10 AM             294 EXP03JAN.dta
12/11/2002  09:10 AM             295 EXP03FEB.dta
12/11/2002  09:10 AM             292 EXP02MAR.dta
12/11/2002  09:10 AM             294 EXP02JAN.dta
12/11/2002  09:10 AM             295 EXP02FEB.dta
12/11/2002  09:10 AM             292 EXP01MAR.dta
12/11/2002  09:10 AM             294 EXP01JAN.dta
12/11/2002  09:10 AM             295 EXP01FEB.dta
```

```
10/31/2001    05:32 PM                    259 EARTH.TWO
10/31/2001    05:37 PM                    383 EARTH.THR
10/31/2001    05:28 PM                    165 EARTH.ONE
10/30/2001    03:03 PM                    286 DRESS.UP
08/01/2002    09:28 AM      <DIR>             DATA
12/11/1999    04:03 PM                     72 DANCES.TXT
08/12/2000    04:12 PM                    314 CASES.FIL
07/31/1999    12:53 PM                     47 CAROLYN.FIL
10/30/2001    02:10 PM                    121 BORN.TYP
10/30/2001    02:10 PM                    121 BORN.TXT
10/30/2001    02:47 PM                     86 BONJOUR.TMP
10/31/2001    06:51 PM                    125 BLUE.JAZ
12/06/2001    12:13 AM                    138 AWARD.MOV
10/30/2001    01:46 PM                    148 ASTRO.TXT
10/30/2001    01:46 PM                    148 ASTRO.TMP
10/30/2001    01:46 PM                    148 AST.TMP
10/30/2001    01:46 PM                    148 AST.NEW
10/30/2001    01:46 PM                    148 AST.99
                 92 File(s)          47,780 bytes
                  7 Dir(s)          287,232 bytes free

A:\>_
```

WHAT'S
HAPPENING?   The file names scrolled by quickly, but they were in reverse alphabetical order, from Z to A. Thus, by using the parameters **/O-N** (**O** for order, the **-** for reverse, and **N** for file name), you accomplished your task.

5   Key in the following: A:\>**DIR** **/S** Enter

```
Command Prompt                                            _ □ ✕

12/25/1999    11:36 AM                    227 FOOT-COL.TMS
12/25/1999    11:36 AM                    207 FOOT-PRO.TMS
                  5 File(s)           1,089 bytes

 Directory of A:\LEVEL-1

11/16/2002    09:36 AM      <DIR>             .
11/16/2002    09:36 AM      <DIR>             ..
09/09/2000    04:39 PM                     80 HELLO.TXT
11/16/2002    09:36 AM      <DIR>             LEVEL-2
                  1 File(s)              80 bytes

 Directory of A:\LEVEL-1\LEVEL-2

11/16/2002    09:36 AM      <DIR>             .
11/16/2002    09:36 AM      <DIR>             ..
09/09/2001    04:39 PM                     76 HELLO.TXT
11/16/2002    09:36 AM      <DIR>             LEVEL-3
                  1 File(s)              76 bytes

 Directory of A:\LEVEL-1\LEVEL-2\LEVEL-3

11/16/2002    09:36 AM      <DIR>             .
11/16/2002    09:36 AM      <DIR>             ..
08/08/2000    04:39 PM                     80 HELLO.TXT
                  1 File(s)              80 bytes

     Total Files Listed:
                189 File(s)       1,107,655 bytes
                 45 Dir(s)          287,232 bytes free

A:\>_
```

WHAT'S HAPPENING?   This time the file names scrolled by for a much longer time. This is because the /S in the command said you wanted to see a DIRectory of not only the files on the root of A (A:\) but also in all of the Sub directories (/S) The /S parameter displays all the files from the default or specified directory and all its subdirectories.

Using the different parameters available with the DIR command, you can display files sorted by their *attributes* (covered in a later chapter), display only the names of the files with no additional information (/B), or display the information in lower case (/L). However, if you use more than one parameter, each parameter must be preceded by the forward slash.

6   Key in the following: A:\>**DIR /blp** [Enter]

```
A:\>DIR /BLP
Parameter format not correct - "BLP".

A:\>_
```

WHAT'S HAPPENING?   As you can see, although B, L, and P are all valid parameters, they must be separated.

7   Key in the following: A:\>**DIR /B /L /P** [Enter]

8   Press [Enter] until you reach the end of the display.

```
born.typ
Press any key to continue . . .
exp01mar.dta
exp03mar.dta
galaxy.txt
jup.99
longfilenaming.txt
mercury.txt
planets.txt
right.up
state.cap
ven.new
wild2.yyy
astro.tmp
data
ven.tmp
earth.thr
exp02jan.dta
file3.swt
oldauto.mak
right.red
award.mov
sports
go.bat
longfilename
level-1
mer.99
```

```
person.fil
steven.fil
venus.txt
wildone
zodiac.fil
my.hw

A:\>_
```

WHAT'S HAPPENING?   Now that you have separated the parameters, you have the directory listing you wanted—a bare listing in lower case letters that pauses so you can see one screenful of information at a time.

9   Key in the following: `A:\>`**EXIT** `Enter`

10 Initiate and complete the Windows shut-down procedure.

Chapter Summary

1. Command syntax means the correct command and the proper order for keying in commands.
2. A parameter is some piece of information that you want to include in a command. It allows a command to be specific.
3. A delimiter indicates where parts of a command begin or end. It is similar to punctuation marks in English.
4. Some commands require parameters. They are called mandatory or required parameters. Other commands allow parameters; these are called optional parameters.
5. A variable parameter or switch is one that requires the user to supply a value. A fixed parameter or switch has its value determined by the OS.
6. A syntax diagram is a representation of a command and its syntax.
7. The DIR command is an internal command that displays the directory (table of contents) of a disk.
8. DIR has many parameters, all of which are optional.
9. A file specification has two parts, the file name and the file extension. A file name is mandatory; however, a file extension is optional. If you use a file extension, separate it from the file name by a period, called a dot.
10. A valid file name contains legal characters, most often alphanumeric characters. It cannot contain illegal characters.
11. You may use keys such as the <up arrow> or <Down arrow> to perform command line editing.
12. Every device attached to the computer has a reserved, specific, and unique name so that the operating system knows what it is communicating with.
13. Disk drives are designated by a letter followed by a colon, as in A:.
14. A local printer is connected directly to your computer and has the device name of PRN, LPT1, LPT2, or LPT3.
15. Defaults are implied instructions the operating system falls back to when no specific instructions are given.
16. The root directory's name is represented by the \ (backslash).
17. With some commands, such as DIR, parameters are preceded by a / (slash).

18. Subdirectories allow a disk to be divided into areas that can hold files.
19. Subdirectories are named by the user or by an application program.
20. The system prompt displayed on the screen is the default drive and directory.
21. You can change the default drive and default subdirectory.
22. To change the default drive, you key in the drive letter followed by a colon, as in A: or C:.
23. To change the default subdirectory, you key in CD followed by the subdirectory name, such as CD \DATA or CD \WINDOWS\SYSTEM32.
24. To change directories and drives at the same time, you use the /D parameter, such as CD /D A:\DATA.
25. The subdirectory that contains the system utility files is usually \WINDOWS\SYSTEM32 or \WINNT\SYSTEM32.
26. You can look for files on drives and subdirectories other than the default if you tell the OS where to look by prefacing the file names with a drive designator and/or path name.
27. If the file is in a subdirectory, the file specification must be prefaced by the drive designator and followed by the subdirectory name. If the default drive\directory is different than the location of the needed file, a user must include the subdirectory name in the command, as in C:\WINDOWS\SYSTEM32\FILENAME.EXT.
28. Global file specifications (* or ?) allow a user to substitute a wildcard for unknown characters.
29. The ? represents one single character in a file name; the * matches a string of characters.
30. A command's output that normally is displayed on the screen may be redirected to a file. You key in the command, add the redirection symbol (>), and then key in the file name.
31. A command's output that is normally displayed on the screen may be redirected to a local printer. You key in the command, add the redirection symbol (>), and then key in the device name (PRN or LPT*n*).
32. To get help on a command, key in the name of the command followed by a forward slash and a question mark, such as DIR /?.
32. The DIR command allows you to sort the directory listing by use of the parameter /O followed by the sort order letter you are interested in. For instance, to sort by name, you would key in DIR /ON.

Key Terms

alias	device name	insert mode
attributes	documentation	logged drive
backslash	eight-dot-three	mandatory parameter
command line editing	extension	OEM
convention	FF button	online button
default	fixed parameter	optional parameter
default drive	folders	overstrike mode
delimiter	global file specifications	parameter
designated drive	GUI	path
device	illegal characters	redirection

reset button	subdirectory	syntax diagram
root directory	subfolders	variable parameter
standard input	switch	volume
standard output	syntax	wildcards

Discussion Questions

1. Define *command syntax*.
2. Why is syntax important when using a command?
3. Define *parameters*.
4. What is the difference between a variable and a fixed parameter?
5. How would you use a syntax diagram? Why is the diagram important?
6. Name two parameters that can be used with the DIR command. Explain why you would use the parameters.
7. Define *delimiters*. Give an example of a delimiter.
8. Define *file specifications*.
9. How do you separate a file name and a file extension?
10. What is used to separate a file specification from a path name?
11. What is the function and purpose of a device?
12. Explain the function and purpose of the default drive.
13. How can you tell which drive is the default drive?
14. Define *default subdirectory*.
15. How can you tell which directory is the default subdirectory?
16. What steps must be done to change the default drive? Why would you change drives?
17. What does A:\> mean?
18. If you keyed in 10 commands and wanted to reuse a command previously keyed in, what could you do?
19. What steps must be done to change a directory? Why would you change a directory?
20. What is the significance of the first backslash in a command?
21. Define *global file specifications*.
22. How are wildcards used?
23. If you see C:\WINDOWS\SYSTEM32> on the screen, what does it mean?
24. What is the purpose and function of redirection?
25. What would you do if you forgot the parameter for a wide DIR display?

True/False Questions

For each question, circle the letter T if the statement is true and the letter F if the statement is false.

T   F   1. Command syntax is the proper order or sequence for keying in commands.

T   F   2. When working at the Command Prompt, you are allowed to add one parameter to every command.

T   F   3. The standard input device is the monitor or screen.

T   F   4. The * is a wildcard that represents a group of characters.

T   F   5. If you see brackets in a syntax diagram, you do not use the parameters.

Completion Questions

Write the correct answer in each blank space.

6. A variable parameter is one in which the _____ provides the value.

7. A mark that separates characters (much like a punctuation mark in English) is known as a(n) _____.

8. All files in a directory must have a(n) _____ name.

9. The first \ symbol represents the _____.

10. If you keyed in _____, you would see all the files displayed across the screen, rather than down the screen.

Multiple Choice Questions

For each question, write the letter for the correct answer in the blank space.

_____ 11. Which of the following is a global file specification?

    a. "

    b. /

    c. *

    d. .

_____ 12. In a Command line window, the prompt displayed on the screen will display

    a. the only drive the computer can ever use.

    b. the default drive.

    c. always the floppy disk drive.

    d. always the hard disk drive.

_____ 13. To display the directories for Drive A and Drive C at the same time, key in:

    a. DIR A: C:

    b. DIR A:/C

    c. DIR A: /DIR C:

    d. none of the above

_____ 14. The default drive can be changed by

    a. pressing **Enter** twice.

    b. using the DIR command.

    c. entering the new drive letter followed by a colon.

    d. The default drive cannot be changed.

_____ 15. If the system prompt is A:\> and you wanted to display all the files that are in the subdirectory called **CHAIRS** on Drive C, you would key in:

    a. CHAIRS

    b. DIR C:\CHAIRS

    c. DIR CHAIRS

    d. DIR A:\CHAIRS

Writing Commands

Write the correct steps or commands to perform the required action *as if you were at the computer*. The scenarios do not necessarily represent actual files on the disk. The prompt will indicate the default drive and directory.

16. A directory of all files that have the extension of **.TXT** on the root of Drive A.

    `C:\>`

17. A directory listing of the file called **MYFILE.TXT** located in the subdirectory **NEWS** on Drive C.

    `A:\>`

18. Clear the screen.

    `C:\WINDOWS\SYSTEM32>`

19. Display all the file names on the default drive and directory so only the file names and extensions are listed. (*Hint:* See the syntax diagram.)

    `A:\>`

20. Display all the files on the default drive that begin with the letter E, are five or fewer characters in length, and have no extension.

    `A:\>`

Homework Assignments

Problem Set I—At the Computer

Open a Command Prompt window. Insert the ACTIVITIES Disk—Working Copy in Drive A.

1. On the ACTIVITIES disk in the root directory, find the file called **PERSONAL.FIL**. What is its size in bytes?
   a. 3
   b. 315
   c. 2307
   d. 3055

2. On the ACTIVITIES disk in the root directory, find all the files that have the file extension **.NEW**. How many files are there?
   a. one
   b. two
   c. three
   d. four

3. On the ACTIVITIES disk in the subdirectory called **GAMES**, find the file called **LS.PAS**. What is the file date?
   a. 6-23-89
   b. 8-13-98
   c. 3-1-97
   d. none of the above

4. Do a paused, wide display of the root directory of the ACTIVITIES disk. The fourth file down in the second column is:
   a. FILE2.FP

    b. MAR.NEW

    c. HELLO.TXT

    d. DRESS.UP

5. Display the syntax diagram and help for the DIR command. What command could you have used?

    a. DIR /HELP

    b. HELP DIR

    c. DIR /?

    d. either b or c

6. From the root of the ACTIVITIES disk, change the default directory to **SPORTS**. What command did you use?

    a. CD :

    b. CD ..

    c. CD SPORTS or CD \SPORTS

    d. DIR \SPORTS

7. On the ACTIVITIES disk, change back to the root from the **SPORTS** directory. What command did you use?

    a. CD ROOT

    b. CD \

    c. CD \ROOT

    d. none of the above

8. On the hard disk in the **WINDOWS\SYSTEM32** subdirectory, locate the file called **MEM**. What is the file extension?

    a. .BAT

    b. .COM

    c. .EXE

    d. .SYS

9. On the ACTIVITIES disk in the root directory, find all the files that have a file name that is at most four characters long and have the file extension **.TXT**. Which of the following files is displayed?

    a. BORN.TXT

    b. YOUR.TXT

    c. TEST.TXT

    d. NAME.TXT

10. On the ACTIVITIES disk in the root directory, how many files have a file name that is two characters or fewer in length and have any file extension?

    a. two

    b. three

    c. six

    d. none of the above

11. On the ACTIVITIES disk in the subdirectory **DATA**, find all the files that have names beginning with the letter T and have any extension. What files are displayed?

    a. THIN.EST and TEA.TAX

    b. TEA.TAX and THANK.YOU

    c. THIN.EST and TEA.TAX and THANK.YOU
    d. none of the above

____ 12. On the hard disk in the **WINDOWS\SYSTEM32** subdirectory, what file
        extension does *not* appear?
    a. .CZG
    b. .SYS
    c. .COM
    d. .EXE

____ 13. When using the sort order parameter (/O), what additional parameter lets
        you sort files by file extension?
    a. X
    b. N
    c. D
    d. E

____ 14. On the ACTIVITIES disk in the root directory, display all the files by file
        name in alphabetical order and pause the display. Which file appears first?
    a. AWARD.MOV
    b. BLUE.JAZ
    c. AST.99
    d. VENUS.TMM

____ 15. Key in the command to display the syntax and help for the DATE command.
        What is the last line in the first paragraph that appears on the screen?
    a. Displays or sets the date.
    b. current date, without prompting for a new date.
    c. Press ENTER to keep the same date.
    d. DATE [date]

Problem Set II—At the Computer

Note 1: Before proceeding with these assignments, check with your lab technician
        or instructor to see if there are any special procedures for your lab environ-
        ment.

Note 2: The ACTIVITIES Disk—Working Copy disk is in Drive A. The A:\>
        prompt is displayed as the default drive and directory. All work will occur
        from the root of the ACTIVITIES disk. *You may not change drives or
        directories*.

Note 3: The first homework activity may seem confusing and unclear. It is just a
        way to create a file containing your name and class information, which you
        will use for turning in your homework.

1 Key in the following: **NAME** Enter

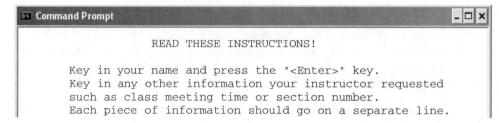

```
Command Prompt                                              _ □ ×

                    READ THESE INSTRUCTIONS!

     Key in your name and press the "<Enter>" key.
     Key in any other information your instructor requested
     such as class meeting time or section number.
     Each piece of information should go on a separate line.
```

```
Press the "<Enter>" key each time you are done with a line.
When you are completely through keying in information,
press the F6 key and the "<Enter>" key.

Once you press "<Enter>", you cannot return to a previous
line to make corrections. Later you will be given an
opportunity to correct errors.

You will see a blank screen. Begin keying in data at the
blinking cursor.

_
```

2   Here is an example to key in, but your instructor will have other specific information that applies to your class. Key in the following:

Bette Peat Enter   (*Your* name goes here)
CIS 55 Enter   (*Your* class goes here)
M-W-F 8-9 Enter   (*Your* day and time go here)
Chapter 2 Enter   (*Your* assignment goes here)

3   Press F6 Enter

WHAT'S ▨▨▨
▨▨ HAPPENING?   You will see the following on the screen:

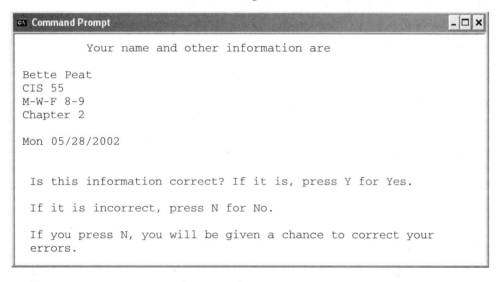

```
🔲 Command Prompt                                          _ □ ✕

         Your name and other information are

Bette Peat
CIS 55
M-W-F 8-9
Chapter 2

Mon 05/28/2002


 Is this information correct? If it is, press Y for Yes.

 If it is incorrect, press N for No.

 If you press N, you will be given a chance to correct your
 errors.
```

This program gives you a chance to check your data entry—what you have keyed in. The current date is inserted automatically. If it is correct, you press **Y**. If it is incorrect, you press **N**. In this case, the printout was correct.

4   Press **Y**.

```
🔲 Command Prompt                                          _ □ ✕

A:\>_
```

WHAT'S ▨▨▨
▨▨ HAPPENING?   You have completed the program and returned to the command line prompt. You now have a file called **NAME.FIL** in the root directory of the working copy of the ACTIVITIES disk that contains the above data. (*Hint:* Remember redirection; see 2.21 and 2.22 to refresh your memory.) Now you are ready to

complete Problem Set II. Remember to pay attention to the default directory. All the homework files need to be created in the root directory of the ACTIVITIES disk. If you do not create them there, you will not be able to find or print them.

To Create 1.HW

1 The root directory of the ACTIVITIES disk is the default.

2 Locate all the files in the root directory that have a **.99** file extension.

3 Place the output in a file called **1.HW**.

To Create 2.HW

1 The root directory of the ACTIVITIES disk is the default.

2 Locate all the files in the **GAMES** directory that begin with the letter A and have any file extension.

3 Place the output in a file called **2.HW**.

To Create 3.HW

1 The root directory of the ACTIVITIES disk is the default.

2 Find the files in the root directory that have file names up to five characters in length and have the file extension of **.TMP**.

3 Place the output in a file called **3.HW**.

To Create 4.HW

1 The root directory of the ACTIVITIES disk is the default.

2 Display all the files in the **MUSIC** directory across the screen.

3 Place the output in a file called **4.HW**.

To Create 5.HW

1 The root directory of the ACTIVITIES disk is the default.

2 Display all the files with the file extension of **.TXT** in sorted order by file name.

3 Place the output in a file called **5.HW**.

CAUTION: Do not proceed with this step unless it is okayed by your lab instructor.

To Print Your Homework

1 Be sure the printer is on and ready to accept print jobs from your computer.

2 Key in the following (be very careful to make no typing errors):
GO NAME.FIL 1.HW 2.HW 3.HW 4.HW 5.HW Enter

WHAT'S ▓▓▓▓▓▓
▓▓HAPPENING?   If one of the files you requested, 1.HW, 2.HW, etc., does not exist in the default directory, you will see the following two-line message on the screen:

```
File Not Found
The system cannot find the file specified.
```

Followed by this message:

```
Is there a message that says "File Not Found. The system cannot
find the file specified."

If so, press Y to find out what could be wrong.

Otherwise, press N to continue.
```

The operating system is telling you that the file cannot be found. If you see the first two-line message at any time, press **Y** to see what could be wrong, and repeat the print procedure after you have corrected the problem. You will go through this sequence for each .HW file. If you have made no errors, you will not see the "File Not Found" message at all. For Chapter 2, you have five .HW files, so you will see the second message that begins "Is there a message . . ." five times.

3   Keep pressing **N**, and follow the messages on the screen until the Notepad program opens with a screen similar to the following:

WHAT'S ▒▒▒▒
▒▒▒HAPPENING?   All the requested files have been found and placed in a Notepad document. Your homework is now ready to print.

4   On the Notepad menu bar, click **File**. Click **Print**.

WHAT'S HAPPENING? The print dialog box opens. If you have more than one printer, all your printer choices will be displayed. The default printer is the highlighted printer.

5 Click the **Print** button.

6 In the Notepad window, click **File**. Click **Exit**.

WHAT'S HAPPENING? The following will appear on the Command Prompt screen:

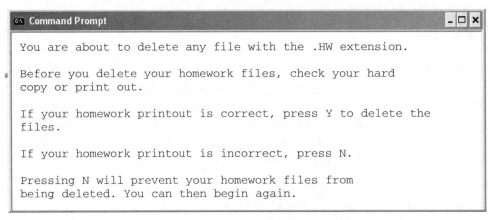

```
You are about to delete any file with the .HW extension.

Before you delete your homework files, check your hard
copy or print out.

If your homework printout is correct, press Y to delete the
files.

If your homework printout is incorrect, press N.

Pressing N will prevent your homework files from
being deleted. You can then begin again.
```

At this point, look at your printout. If it is correct, you can press **Y** to delete the homework files for this chapter. If your printout is incorrect, you can press **N**. That will preserve your homework and you will need to redo only the problem that was incorrect, not all the homework assignments.

7 Press **Y** Enter

8 Close the Command Prompt session.

9 Execute the shut-down procedure.

Problem Set III—Brief Essay

1. *Although the Windows operating system is a graphical user environment, it is still important to learn how to use the command line interface.*
   Agree or disagree with the above statement and explain your answer.

2. You have keyed in the following commands:
   C:\WINDOWS\SYSTEM32>**CD **
   C:\>**A:**
   A:\>**DIR HOUSE*.TXT**
   Describe the output and purpose of each command you keyed in. Could you have accomplished this task by using any other commands? If so, write the command(s).

CHAPTER 3

DISKS AND
FORMATTING

Learning Objectives

After completing this chapter you will be able to:

1. Explain the need for formatting a disk.
2. Describe the structure of a disk.
3. Name and explain the purpose of each section of a disk.
4. Define *formatting*.
5. Explain the difference between internal and external commands.
6. List and explain the steps in formatting a floppy disk.
7. Explain the purpose and function of the /Q parameter and other parameters used with the FORMAT command

Student Outcomes

1. Format a floppy disk.
2. Use the LABEL command to change the volume label on a disk.
3. View the current volume label using the VOL command.
4. Use the /Q parameter to format a disk.

Chapter Overview

Disks are the mainstays of the computer workstation. They are used for storing data and programs and for distributing data from one computer to another. In order to be used, disks must be formatted, a process by which an operating system sets up the guidelines for reading from and writing to a disk. In Windows, you can still format a disk by using the FORMAT command from the command line.

In this chapter you will learn how a disk is structured, how the operating system uses disks, and how to format and electronically label a disk. In addition, you will learn how to change the electronic label. Throughout, remember that formatting a disk is a dangerous operation because it removes all existing data from the disk.

3.1   Why Format a Disk?

So far, the disks you have used with this text have been already prepared for your environment. Although most floppy disks come preformatted, you may still purchase unformatted disks. And if you purchase a new hard disk, it too must be formatted. When you want to prepare a disk for use, you will use a system utility command called FORMAT.COM. But prior to using the format command, which can also be accessed from the GUI, you should have some understanding of what this process is all about.

3.2   Partitioning and Formatting Disks

Before Windows XP Professional can use a disk, the disk must be prepared for use. A hard disk requires a special process. It must first be partitioned, or divided, into one or more logical divisions and then formatted with a file system. A *primary partition* is a section of a hard disk. When a disk is partitioned, it allocates a fixed amount of space for each primary partition. This information is stored in what is called a *partition table* that is located in the first physical sector of a hard disk. The partition table tells where each partition begins and ends. The physical locations of the partitions are given as the beginning and ending head, sector, and cylinder number. In addition, the partition table identifies the type of file system used for each partition and identifies whether the partition is bootable. Note that each partition on a drive is called a Volume, and has its own volume label.

One partition is marked as the *active partition*, and you may boot from only the active partition. Hard disks are limited to a maximum of four primary partitions per physical disk. Only one primary partition can be designated as an extended partition. An *extended partition* can contain logical drives (volumes). Thus, if you had two physical drives, each could be partitioned as one primary partition and would be assigned the drive letters C and D. Drive C would be partitioned, formatted, and bootable. Drive D would be partitioned and formatted but not bootable. If you had one hard drive, as many users do, the hard drive might be partitioned as only one primary partition, Drive C, that, of course, would be bootable. In another instance, the single hard drive could be partitioned with one primary partition and an extended partition. In that case, you would then have Drive C (the bootable drive) and logical drive D. Each drive would have to be formatted.

Only one operating system can be active at a time. If you had a dual-booting system, (a system with two operating systems) using, for example, Windows XP Professional and Linux, you could create a *partition* for each operating system. You would then choose and boot the computer from the active partition where the operating system you wished to use was located. Each operating system formats disks in its own, unique way. Depending on the operating system you use and the file system you select, the operating system you are using might be able to recognize the other drive, but not read the files on it.

If you are interested in running multiple operating systems on a single computer, there are precautions you need to be aware of. For example, there are some operating systems that are not compatible. You cannot have both Windows 95 and Windows 98 in a multiple-boot configuration. Windows 98 was intended to be an upgrade to Windows 95, and both systems will attempt to use the same boot file. Also, the order in which the Operating Systems are installed is important. The combinations are numerous and varied. The necessary, specific information to install multiple-operating systems is beyond the scope of this text.

Each operating system has a unique way of recording information on a disk. The organizational scheme is known as a *file system*. One factor that makes one computer compatible with another is not the brand name such as Apple, IBM, or Compaq, but rather the operating system, part of which is the file system that each operating system brand uses. Disk formatting is based almost entirely on which operating system the computer uses. Operating systems prepare disks so that information can be read from and written to them. The disk manufacturers cannot prepare a disk in advance without knowing what kind of operating system will be used. The process of preparing a disk so that it will be compatible with an operating system is known as *formatting* or *initializing the disk*.

Since this textbook is for Windows XP Professional users, the only kind of formatting that you are interested in is Windows-based. Although there are many file systems in use for readable/writable disks, such as Unix and HPFS (OS2), Windows XP Professional supports four file systems for readable/writable disks, the NTFS file system and three FAT file systems (FAT12, FAT16, and FAT32). FAT12 is used only on floppy disks. Essentially, you have two file system types to choose from—FAT and NTFS. FAT is an acronym for *file allocation table*, and *NTFS* is an acronym for *New Technology File System*. Windows XP also supports two types of file systems on CD-ROM and DVD (Compact Disc File systems [CDFS] and Universal Disk Format [UDF]). The CDFS and UDF file systems are beyond the scope of this text.

All disks, including hard disks, must be formatted. In general, when you purchase a computer, the hard drive or drives have already been partitioned and formatted. When you purchase floppy disks for a Wintel computer (a computer that has an Intel or clone-Intel processor and is running the Windows operating system), the floppy disks are almost always preformatted, although non-formatted disks are also available. Even if you purchase preformatted disks, it is inevitable that you will want to reuse them. Disks that have been used and possess information that is no longer needed can be erased or re-prepared with the FORMAT command. Hard disks are typically formatted once, when they are new, and are rarely reformatted because formatting eliminates what is on the disk. Although you may format both hard and floppy disks, this textbook deals only with formatting floppy disks using the FORMAT command in Windows XP Professional.

Windows XP provides two types of disk storage configurations, basic disk and dynamic disk. *Basic disk* is a physical disk that contains primary partitions and/or extended partitions with logical drives and a partition table. Windows XP, by default, initializes all disks as basic. New to the operating system with the Windows 2000 version are dynamic disks. *Dynamic disks* are physical disks that have been upgraded by and are managed by the Disk Management utility program. Dynamic disks do not use partitions or logical drives, and only computers running Windows 2000 and above can use dynamic disks. Dynamic disks are beyond the scope of this text. Discussion will be limited to basic disks.

3.2.1   The Structure of a Disk

Formatting a disk consists of two parts: *low-level formatting*, or *physical formatting*, and *high-level formatting*, or *logical formatting*. Low-level (physical) formatting creates and sequentially numbers tracks and sectors for identification purposes. Tracks are concentric circles on a disk. Each track is divided into smaller units called sectors. A sector, which is the smallest unit on a disk, is usually 512 bytes, the industry standard. The number of tracks and sectors varies depending on the type of disk. When data needs to be written to or read from a disk, the identification number of the track and sector tells the read/write head where to position itself. This process accounts for every space on the disk. It is similar to assigning every house a unique address so that it can be instantly identifiable. However, even after a disk is physically prepared to hold data, it is not ready for use.

The second part of formatting is high-level (logical) formatting. In logical formatting, the operating system creates a file system on a disk so it can keep track of the location of files. Formatting a hard disk involves only logical formatting. Low-level formatting of a hard disk is usually done as part of the manufacturing process. Low-level formatting can also be done by the computer system vendor, or you may purchase special software programs to low-level format your hard disk, although this is a rare occurrence. Most commonly, when you purchase a computer system, the high-level and low-level formatting of the hard disk are done. However, when you format a floppy disk, both the physical and logical formatting processes occur.

Logical formatting determines how the operating system uses a disk by building a structure to manage files on the disk so they can be easily saved and retrieved. The FORMAT command performs both high- and low-level formatting on a floppy disk. On a hard disk, only high-level formatting is performed.

Windows XP Professional needs to monitor the status of all of a disk's data sectors so it can answer critical questions. Does a sector already have information in it? Is it damaged? In either case, it cannot be used. Is it an empty sector, available for data storage? Since there can be many sectors on a disk, particularly on a hard disk, it would be too time-consuming for Windows XP Professional to manage them one sector at a time. Instead, it combines one or more sectors into logical units called *clusters*, also called *allocation units* since these units allocate disk space. When Windows XP Professional writes a file to a disk, it copies the file's contents to unused clusters in the data sectors. The smallest unit that Windows XP Professional works with when reading or writing to a disk is a cluster. To be able to read from and write files to a disk, Windows tracks locations in the file system you have chosen, either the FAT file system or the NTFS file system.

Floppy disks only use FAT. Thus, since the smallest unit Windows can deal with is a cluster, a file that is only 100 bytes long saved to a 3½-inch, 1.44-MB disk will actually occupy 512 bytes on the floppy disk. If you were using the FAT file system and the file were saved to a 2-MB hard disk, it would actually occupy 32,768 bytes. The portion of a cluster that is not being used by the data in the file is still allocated to the file; that space can be claimed by no other file. It is wasted space on your disk and is called *cluster overhang*. Furthermore, as you can imagine, a data file is rarely ever *exactly* one cluster in size, nor would its size necessarily be an even number. How the data is managed depends on whether you are using FAT or NTFS.

3.2.2   The Master Boot Record and the Boot Sector

The first part of any hard disk is the *master boot record (MBR)*. The master boot record is the mechanism required to find a hard disk and launch any necessary code to load drivers located on the boot record. The MBR of a hard disk resides at the first physical sector of the disk. The *boot sector* is the first sector on every logical drive. It contains a table of that drive's characteristics and contains a short program, called the bootstrap loader, that begins loading Windows, copying the necessary system files from the disk into memory. If you are using FAT, and the disk the system is trying to boot from is not a system disk, you see the message:

```
Non-System disk or disk error
Replace the disk and press any key when ready
```

If you are using NTFS, and the disk the system is trying to boot from is not a system disk, you may see one of the following messages:

- Invalid partition table
- Error loading operating system
- Missing operating system

If you have a floppy disk in Drive A that is not a system disk, you may see the message

```
NTLDR is missing
Press any key to restart
```

Some computers have a setting called Boot Device Priority that will boot the system from any disk that has the operating system on it and will ignore a non-booting disk in the floppy disk drive. Even if a disk is not a system disk (one capable of booting the system), it still has a boot sector. (There is no MBR on a floppy disk. The first sector on a floppy disk is the boot sector.) On any disk, the boot sector contains information about the physical characteristics of the disk: the number of tracks, the number of bytes per sector, the number of sectors per track, the version of the operating system used to format the disk, the root directory, the volume serial number, etc. The boot sector allows Windows to identify the type of disk.

3.2.3   FAT16, VFAT, and FAT32

When you format a disk using FAT, the formatting program creates three critical elements: the boot record, the file allocation table (two copies), and the root directory. These elements occupy the first portion of the disk and take only about one to two percent of the disk space. The remainder of the disk is used for file storage. See Figure 3.1.

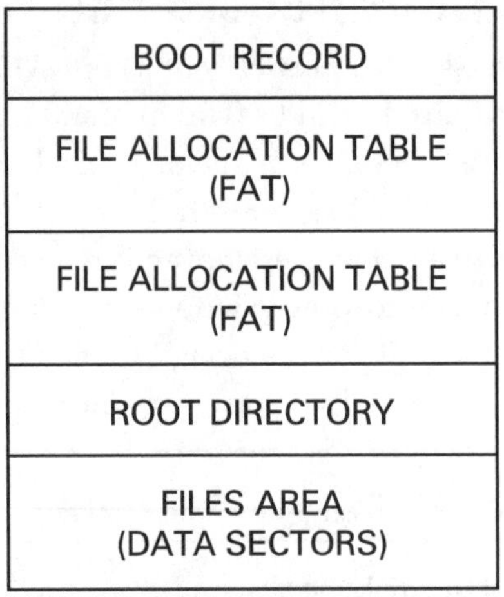

```
┌─────────────────────────────────┐
│           BOOT RECORD           │
├─────────────────────────────────┤
│     FILE ALLOCATION TABLE       │
│             (FAT)               │
├─────────────────────────────────┤
│     FILE ALLOCATION TABLE       │
│             (FAT)               │
├─────────────────────────────────┤
│         ROOT DIRECTORY          │
├─────────────────────────────────┤
│          FILES AREA             │
│        (DATA SECTORS)           │
└─────────────────────────────────┘
```

Figure 3.1—The Logical Structure of a Disk

The order of the sections is always the same. The boot record, two copies of the FAT, and the root directory table are always located in the first sectors. These elements control how the files are stored on a disk and how Windows saves and retrieves files. The data sectors are where the data or files are actually stored.

A map of a disk's data clusters, the FAT, is made up of entries that correspond to every cluster on the disk. The number of clusters varies from one type of disk to another. Cluster size on a hard disk is not determined by the disk's overall capacity, but by the partition size. Table 3.1 indicates the relationship between cluster size and disk size.

Disk Size	Number of Sectors in a Cluster	Cluster Size in Bytes	Cluster Size in KB
3½-inch 1.44 MB	1 sector	512 bytes	½KB
3½-inch 2.88 MB	2 sectors	1,024 bytes	1KB
33 MB–64 MB	2 sectors	1,024 bytes	1KB
65 MB–128 MB	4 sectors	2,048 bytes	2KB
129 MB–256 MB	8 sectors	4,096 bytes	4KB
257 MB–512 MB	16 sectors	8,192 bytes	8KB
513 MB–1,024 MB	32 sectors	16,384 bytes	16KB
1,025 MB–2,048 MB	64 sectors	32,768 bytes	32KB

Table 3.1—Cluster Size and Disk Size

To manage the data, each entry in the FAT is a number that indicates the status of a cluster. A 0 (zero) in the FAT means the cluster is empty and available for use. Other specific numbers indicate that a cluster is reserved (not available for use) or bad (also not available for use). Any other number indicates that a cluster is in use.

To follow the trail of a data file longer than one cluster, the number in the FAT is a pointer to the next cluster that holds data for that file. That entry becomes a pointer to the next cluster that holds data in the same file. A special entry in the FAT indicates where the file ends and that no more data is in the file. Thus, the numbers in the FAT are used to link, or chain, clusters that belong to the same file. The FAT works in conjunction with the root directory table. Since the FAT is used to control the entire disk, two copies of the FAT are kept on the disk in case one is damaged. The FAT occupies as many sectors as it needs to map the disk. The FAT is always located on the first sectors of the disk.

Windows 95 introduced a special version of FAT called *VFAT*, or *virtual file allocation table*, which allowed Windows 95 to maintain backward compatibility and to accommodate long file names. VFAT is a variation of the original 16-bit FAT. It is a virtual 32-bit FAT, meaning that it is not really a 32-bit FAT. A reserved area of the VFAT keeps directory block information for long file names. In Windows 2000 and Windows XP, the 32-bit VFAT is the primary file system. The VFAT is still referred to as the FAT and you rarely hear the term "VFAT." The FAT file system can maintain a maximum of 65,536 clusters, which means that the largest hard drive that can be supported is 2.1 GB. When you purchase a new computer today, it is common to have a hard drive of 20, 40, 60, or more GB. On older computer systems can get around this limitation by partitioning a hard drive into 2-GB sizes and creating the logical drive letters C, D, E, and F (for an 8-GB drive, for instance).

To overcome this limitation, FAT32 was introduced in Windows 95 OSR2, which is also referred to as Windows 95 B. It was enhanced in Windows 98. FAT32 is an enhancement of the FAT file system and is based on 32-bit file allocation table entries, rather than the 16-bit file entries the FAT file system used in DOS and the first version of Windows 95. FAT16 is usually referred to simply as FAT on disks greater than 5 MB. As a result, FAT32 will support larger hard drives (up to 2 terabytes). A terabyte is a trillion bytes, or 1,000 billion bytes. An 8-GB drive would simply be Drive C under FAT32. FAT32 also uses smaller clusters than the FAT file system. However, FAT32 is for drives over 512 MB and does not apply to floppy disks. See Table 3.2 for a comparison.

Drive Size	FAT Cluster Size	FAT32 Cluster Size
257 MB–512 MB	8KB	4 KB
513 MB–1,024 MB	16KB	4KB
1,025 MB–2 GB	32KB	4KB
2GB–4GB	64KB	4KB
4 GB–8 GB	Not supported	4KB
8 GB–16 GB	Not supported	8KB
16 GB–32 GB	Not supported	16KB
Greater than 32 GB	Not supported	Not supported

Table 3.2—Comparison of FAT and FAT32

FAT32 provides some further enhancements. It allows a moveable root directory, the ability to use the backup copy of the file allocation table (FAT maintains two copies of the table but can use only one of them), and an internal backup copy of some critical FAT data structures. Unlike FAT, FAT32 does impose a restriction on the number of entries in the root directory table, but the number is over 64,000 and thus, does not restrict users as the 512 file limit did. It also allows the root directory table to be located anywhere on the hard disk.

There are advantages and disadvantages to both FAT and FAT32. With FAT32, you have smaller clusters. Therefore, there are more clusters on a partition, and you can store more data on your hard disk. However, the more clusters there are, the bigger the FAT must be. It takes Windows longer to search the table in order to find the information that it needs so it can access a file. On the other hand, with larger clusters, the table is much smaller and Windows needs less time to search to locate the information it needs to access a file. Unfortunately, you also increase the amount of wasted disk space from cluster overhang.

If you have many small files, using FAT32 is probably best. If you have mostly large files such as graphics or video files, then FAT is fine. You could have one drive FAT and another FAT32, depending on your needs. Remember, FAT32 can be used only on drives larger than 512 MB. In addition, DOS, Windows 3.1, Windows NT, and the original version of Windows 95 will *not* recognize FAT32 and cannot boot or use files on any drive that has FAT32. However, Windows 2000 and Windows XP can recognize FAT 32. If, for example, your C drive used FAT32 and you wanted to use another operating system such as DOS 6.22 to boot from the A drive, you would not be able to "see" the C drive at all. Remember as well, floppy disks are always FAT and can be read by all of the above operating systems.

3.2.4   The Root Directory

The root directory is a table that records information about each file on a disk. When you use Windows Explorer or My Computer, the information displayed on the screen comes from this root directory table.

In order to make Windows XP Professional compatible with older Windows and DOS programs, some changes had to be made in the root directory table. The DOS directory structure only recognized 8.3 file names. Windows 95, Windows 98, Windows 2000, and Windows XP needed to allow long file names while still permitting the use of DOS or Windows 3.1 or 3.11 programs with the 8.3 file name limitation. The DOS root directory stores information in a table about every file on a disk, including the file name, the file extension, the size of the file in bytes, the date and time the file was last modified, and the file's attributes. The Windows 2000 and Windows XP, root directory tables still include this information, but they also use previously unused areas in the table, particularly the file attribute, to handle long file names. In addition to the file attributes you have learned about, Windows uses a special combination of attributes to signal that an entry is the first of a series of directory entries. This feature allows a series of directory entries to be chained together so that long file names can be used.

To maintain compatibility with DOS or Windows 3.1 or 3.11 programs, Windows XP gives every file both a long file name and a short file name. The short file name, an alias, is based on the long file name and is stored in the first directory entry using the DOS 8.3 name. Neither a user nor an application can control the name created by the alias process.

Another critical entry in the root directory table is the starting cluster number. This number indicates which cluster holds the first portion of the file, or the first

FAT address. In this way, the root directory tells the operating system *what* is on the disk, and the FAT tells the operating system *where* data is on the disk.

3.2.5   The FAT and the Root Directory

Imagine a book on computers with a table of contents. Like the root directory, the table of contents tells you what is in the book. One chapter could be listed as "The Hard Disk" starting on page number 30. The page number is a pointer to the place you must go to find the information about the hard disk. The page number is similar to the FAT.

You must turn to page 30 to begin reading about the hard disk. However, the information about the hard disk is not located only on page 30. You must read page 31, then page 32, and so on, until you have all the information about the hard disk. The pages are linked, or have a trail. If a book were like a disk, the table of contents (the root directory) would be followed by a chart (the FAT) instructing you to begin on page 30, then go to page 31, then to page 32, and so on. The number in the FAT is a pointer to the next cluster that holds data in the file, enabling the system to follow the trail of a file longer than one cluster. A special entry in the FAT, called an *EOF (end-of-file) marker*, indicates when there is no more data in the file. Other data indicates when the cluster is available or has bad sectors in it. See Figure 3.2.

ROOT DIRECTORY

File Name	File Extension	Date	Time	File Size	Starting Cluster
MYFILE	TXT	1/23/98	11:13 PM	41,364	1
YOUR	XLS	11/7/99	1:00 AM	98,509	3
THIS	DOC	5/7/00	2:13 AM	38,949	7

FAT

Cluster	Pointer	Data in Cluster
1	2	MYFILE.TXT
2	EOF	MYFILE.TXT
3	4	YOUR.XLS
4	5	YOUR.XLS
5	6	YOUR.XLS
6	EOF	YOUR.XLS
7	8	THIS.DOC
8	EOF	THIS.DOC
9	0	Unused
10	BAD	Contains bad sectors

Figure 3.2—The Root Directory and the FAT

The FAT works in conjunction with the root directory table. The FAT can occupy as many sectors as it needs to map out the disk.

3.2.6   The Data Portion or the Files Area

The rest of the disk, which is the largest part, is used for storing files or data. As far as Windows XP is concerned, all files, programs, and data are chains of bytes laid out in sequence. Space is allocated to files on an as-needed basis, one cluster at a time. When a file is written to a disk, Windows begins writing to the first available cluster. It writes in adjacent, or *contiguous*, clusters if possible, but, if any adjacent sectors are already in use (allocated by the FAT), Windows skips to the next available (unallocated) space. Thus, a file can be *noncontiguous*, physically scattered around a disk.

3.2.7   Understanding the FAT and the Root Directory Table

To illustrate how the root directory table and the FAT work, imagine you want to create a file called MYFILE.TXT, which will occupy three clusters on a disk. Let us say that clusters 3, 4, and 6 are free. The operating system first creates an entry in the root directory table and fills in the file information (file name, file extension, date, time, etc.). Then data is written to the first free cluster, number 3, as the starting cluster number in the root directory table. Windows knows it will need three clusters and must link or chain them. It does this by placing a 4 (a pointer) in the number 3 cluster pointing to the next available cluster. When it gets to cluster 4, it places a 6 (another pointer) pointing to the next available cluster. The FAT continues to cluster 6. When it gets to cluster 6, it places an end-of-file marker, a note indicating that the file ends there.

To make an analogy, imagine a self-storage facility comprised of storage bins that hold things (the data). The front office that manages the self-storage facility does not care what is in the bins. The front office only has to know how many bins there are, where they are located, and if they are in use. The front office has a map of all its numbered storage bins (the FAT). The bins are numbered so that the front office knows where the bins are located. The front office also needs a list (the root directory) of all the people who have rented bins. Thus, I walk in and say that I want the boxes stored for Gillay. The front office first looks up Gillay in the list to be sure they have stored my boxes. In this case, they find the name Gillay, so they know that the user Gillay has rented at least one bin. Besides having the name in their directory, their list points to another list that says to go to the map (the FAT), starting with bin 3. The front office goes to the map (the FAT) and sees that storage bin 3 is linked to storage bin 4, which is linked to storage bin 6. Storage bin 6 has no links. Now the front office knows that Gillay has bins 3, 4, and 6 full of boxes. The front office can send someone (rotate the disk) to bins 3, 4, and 6 to retrieve the boxes. To look at this process graphically, see Figure 3.3.

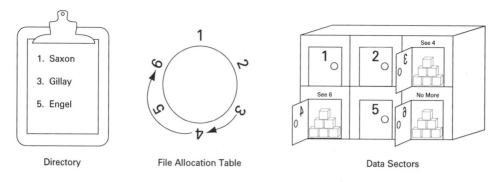

Directory   File Allocation Table   Data Sectors

Figure 3.3—Storing Files

This analogy gives you some of the basic information you need in order to understand the FAT structure of a disk.

3.2.8   NTFS

The file system that you use with Windows XP determines which of the operating system's advanced features that you can use. If you are concerned with disk security, performance, and efficiency, or are using very large hard drives, you may want to choose to use the NTFS (New Technology File System). NTFS, first introduced in Windows NT, is the preferred file system to FAT, VFAT, and FAT32. What NTFS offers, besides the performance needed for the much larger disk drives seen today, is a secure file system. With NTFS, you can manage the security of files and folders for your machine. NTFS also offers other major advantages. These include:

- The ability to assign permissions to each file and folder on the disk.
- More efficient storage of data on large hard disks.
- Faster access to files and folders.
- Better data recovery because a log file is kept of disk activities. Thus, if there is a disk failure, Windows can restore the disk based on the log file.
- Ability to compress files, allowing more data to be stored on a disk.
- Ability to assign disk quotas, which allow you to set limits on how much disk space a user may have.
- Encryption of files for better security.

3.2.9   Clusters and NTFS

NTFS uses the cluster scheme that you have seen in FAT for allocating data, but for a given drive, it has less overhead. Every business has expenses that do not directly make a profit, such as rent or utilities, and the business must pay these costs so it can stay in business. These expenses are known as overhead. A computer system's overhead is its cost of doing business because it must use processing time and memory to run the operating system. Computer overhead does not directly relate to the task at hand, but is mandatory so that the computer system can operate. In business, reducing overhead means that you can make a larger profit. With computers, reducing operating overhead means that you can allocate more computer resources to the work you wish to do. Table 3.3 shows the cluster sizes for NTFS volumes.

Partition Size	Cluster Size in Bytes	Sectors in a Cluster
7 MB–512 MB	512	1
513 MB–1,024 MB	1,024 (1 KB)	2
1,025 MB–2 GB	2,048 (2 KB)	4
2 GB–2 TB*	4,096 (4 KB)	8

*A terabyte is 1,099,511,627,776 bytes or 1,024 gigabytes and is abbreviated as TB.

Table 3.3—NTFS Cluster Size

The structure of an NTFS volume looks similar to FAT, but there are differences, as you can see in Figure 3.4.

Partition boot information	Master File Table (MFT)	System files and folders

Figure 3.4—Structure of an NTFS Volume

3.2.10 Master File Table (MFT)

The MFT is the first file on an NTFS volume. Instead of using the FAT, NTFS uses a special file called the *Master File Table (MFT)* that tracks all the files and directories in a volume. The MFT is really a database file of all the files on the system. A database is a way of finding information quickly. For instance, libraries, long before computers, used databases. The card catalog was a database. The card catalog did not have books in it, but it instead had a card that pointed to the physical location of the book on a shelf. Databases are used heavily in the computer world. When using NTFS, the MFT is dynamic and will change size when necessary. The first 16 records, called the metadata files, contain information about the volume itself and are considered the overhead for maintaining the file system. The MFT has an entry for the MFT itself (just another file) and other metadata files such as the log file, marked bad clusters, and the root directory.

After the volume information, each record in the MFT corresponds to one file or one folder in the file system. The record for the file or folder contains the attributes of the file or folder, including such attributes as the file name, the status of the read-only bit, the file creation and last accessed date, and so on. One major attribute that MFT adds to the file system is the security descriptor. The security descriptor provides information on who has what access to what files or folders and what they can or cannot do to the file or folder, i.e., who can read the file, write to the file, and so on. NTFS is considered a secure file system, and you can assign a permission for every file and folder on your system.

In addition, and very different from FAT, the data in the file is considered just an attribute in the file and, if the amount of data is small enough, the entire file will fit in the MFT. This feature not only allows very fast access to files but also eliminates file fragmentation. However, there is a limit to how much data will fit into the MFT (about 750 bytes) and most files are too large to have all their data fit into the MFT.

In that case, NTFS also allocates files in cluster units. If any attribute (usually the data) does not fit into the MFT record, NTFS stores it a new, separate set of clusters, called a *run* or an *extent*. Any attribute stored in the MFT is considered a resident attribute and any attribute forced out to an extent is called a nonresident attribute. When the extent needs to become larger (usually because data is added to a file), NTFS again tries to allocate contiguous clusters to the same extent. If that is not possible, then NTFS will allocate an extent somewhere else on the disk. This process continues as the file becomes larger.

Folders (directories) are treated much as files are in NTFS. If the folder is small enough, the index to the files in the folder is kept in its entirety in the MFT. This too is an attribute called the Index Root attribute. If the folder entries are larger than what will fit into the MFT, then NTFS creates a new extent with a nonresident attribute called an index buffer. The index buffer contains a data structure called a b-tree. A b-tree stores indexes to information in a sorted order. This makes locating information on the volume much quicker because the entry is more easily found.

3.2.11   Deciding on a File System

You may choose your file system when you install Windows XP Professional. You may also convert a FAT file system to FAT32 or NTFS at any time with special utility programs that come with Windows XP Professional. However, these are one way conversions. You cannot convert from NTFS or FAT32 to FAT. When you format a floppy disk, it will always be the FAT file system. With a hard disk, you make the decision. Remember, every disk has a file system assigned to it. If you look at the properties of a disk, you will see which file system has been assigned to it.

3.3   Clarifying Procedures

1. **System utility files subdirectory.** You will be at the command prompt screen. You may have to change your directory so that you are in the subdirectory that has the system utility files. Remember to refer to your Configuration Table in Chapter 1 to ensure that all substitutions have been made before you begin this activity.
2. **A blank or new disk.** Whenever a new or blank disk is referred to, you may use a brand new disk or an old disk containing information you no longer wish to keep. Any information will be written over in the format process.
3. If you are in a lab environment, you need to check with your instructor to see if there are any particular procedures that need to be followed in your lab. For instance, in some networked environments, you cannot format a floppy disk in Drive A.

3.4   Activity: Formatting a Floppy Disk

WARNING: Never format an application disk or a disk that has data you wish to keep. Also, if you have a hard disk, you must be exceedingly careful. Never, never key in C:\>FORMAT C:. If you do, you may completely erase, forever, all the information on the hard disk.

1 Shell out to the command prompt screen. (This means to open a Command Prompt window.) Make certain that you have no disk in your A drive.

Note: Your starting prompt may differ from the examples in this text. Your initial prompt upon shelling out to the Command Prompt screen may be C:\WINDOWS\SYSTEM32> or perhaps a network drive, such as G:\>.

2 Key in the following: C:\>**CD \WINDOWS\SYSTEM32** [Enter]

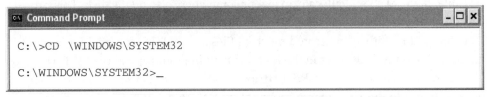

WHAT'S
HAPPENING?   You have changed the default directory to the
\WINDOWS\SYSTEM32 subdirectory. The prompt should now display
C:\WINDOWS\SYSTEM32>.

To format a disk, you use the FORMAT command. FORMAT is another example of a system utility program, also called an external command, stored as a file in the **WINDOWS\SYSTEM32** subdirectory. The default drive and subdirectory, in this situation, become very important. Whenever you use an external command, you are telling the operating system to look for a file that matches what you keyed in. Remember that the prompt on the screen represents the default drive and subdirectory. When the operating system looks for an external command, it will look on the default drive only (in this case, Drive C) and in the default subdirectory (in this case, **\WINDOWS\SYSTEM32**) for the command or file name that you keyed in. You can instruct the operating system to look or do something on a different disk drive or different subdirectory, but you must specify that disk drive and/or subdirectory. In this case, you are looking for the command FORMAT. You can see whether or not this command, stored as a file called **FORMAT.COM**, is located on the disk in the default drive and in the default subdirectory.

3 Key in the following: C:\WINDOWS\SYSTEM32>**DIR FORMAT.COM** [Enter]

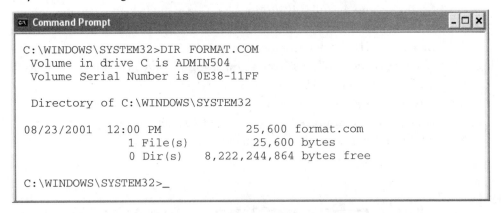

WHAT'S
HAPPENING?   The screen display tells you that the FORMAT command, stored as the file named **FORMAT.COM**, is located on the default drive, Drive C. In addition, since your system utility files are in a subdirectory, you will not only be on Drive C but also in a subdirectory called **\WINDOWS\SYSTEM32**. To use (or execute or run) the FORMAT program, you key in the name of the command.

4 Key in the following (be sure to include the drive letter A):

C:\WINDOWS\SYSTEM32>**FORMAT A:** [Enter]

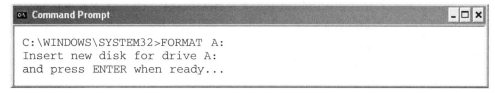

```
C:\WINDOWS\SYSTEM32>FORMAT A:
Insert new disk for drive A:
and press ENTER when ready...
```

WHAT'S
HAPPENING?   In step 3 you used the DIR command to locate the file. You called
the program by keying in the name of the file. When you do that, you are asking the
operating system to find the file called **FORMAT.COM** and load it into memory.
FORMAT is the command that tells the system what work you want it to do. The **A:**
tells the system that the disk you want to format is in Drive A. If you did not specify
a lettered drive, A:, B:, or C:, you would receive a message that you were missing a
parameter—the drive letter. In earlier versions of DOS, the FORMAT command
would not ask for a drive letter and would format the default drive. Since the
default drive is C and C is the hard disk, FORMAT would have unintentionally
erased everything on the hard disk. You never want this to happen. *Never!*

   In addition, you get a message or prompt that tells you what to do. Before you
get involved in the following activity, it is exceedingly important that you know
what kind of disk drive you have so that you can choose the correct disk with the
correct format. It is assumed that you have a 3½-inch high-density disk drive and
floppy disk. If you have any other type of floppy disk or drive, ask your instructor
for further instructions. If you are not sure, refer to your Configuration Table in
Chapter 1.6. If you do not use the correct floppy disk, you will have problems.

5 Get a blank disk out and prepare a sticky paper label for it. Do *not* use either the
ACTIVITIES disk or the ACTIVITIES Disk—Working Copy. Write your name and
the words "DATA disk" on the label. Place the label on the disk. Insert the disk
into Drive A. Be sure that this disk either is blank or contains data you no longer
want. Everything on the disk will be eliminated after you press [Enter].

6 Press [Enter]

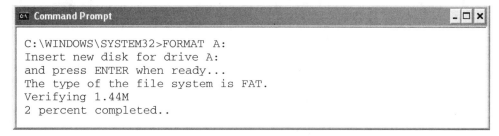

```
C:\WINDOWS\SYSTEM32>FORMAT A:
Insert new disk for drive A:
and press ENTER when ready...
The type of the file system is FAT.
Verifying 1.44M
2 percent completed..
```

WHAT'S
HAPPENING?   The light on the floppy disk drive is glowing, indicating that
activity is taking place on the disk. The FORMAT command displays what media
type it is formatting. The message will vary depending on whether the disk has or
has not been formatted before. You are informed that your file system is FAT. All
floppy disks are formatted as FAT. The **Verifying 1.44M** that appears in the above
screen display will vary depending on the type of floppy disk you are formatting.

The message *"nn percent completed"* tells you that the formatting is taking place and, at that moment, *nn* percent of the formatting process is completed (the *nn* represents a number that changes as the disk is formatted) until it reaches 100 percent. Do not do anything until you see the following message displayed on the screen:

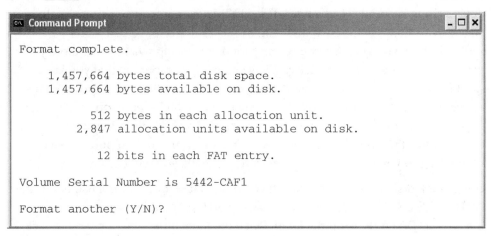

```
C:\WINDOWS\SYSTEM32>FORMAT A:
Insert new disk for drive A:
and press ENTER when ready...
The type of the file system is FAT.
Verifying 1.44M
Initializing the File Allocation Table (FAT)...
Volume label (11 characters, ENTER for none)?
```

You are being asked for a volume label, an electronic name. However, you are not going to place a volume label on the disk at this time.

7   Press **Enter**

```
Format complete.

    1,457,664 bytes total disk space.
    1,457,664 bytes available on disk.

        512 bytes in each allocation unit.
    2,847 allocation units available on disk.

        12 bits in each FAT entry.

Volume Serial Number is 5442-CAF1

Format another (Y/N)?
```

WHAT'S HAPPENING?   You are being asked if you wish to format another disk.

8   Press N. Press **Enter**

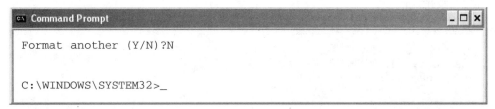

```
Format another (Y/N)?N

C:\WINDOWS\SYSTEM32>_
```

WHAT'S HAPPENING?   You have completed formatting your disk. The FORMAT command was executed, formatting the disk in Drive A. The bytes available will vary depending on what your disk capacity is. You also see a report that FAT12 is being used. You also receive a status report that tells you how many spots were bad on the disk, if any. In addition, the report tells you about the allocation units on the disk. In this case, the allocation unit—the cluster—is 512 bytes, so you know that one sector on a 3½-inch high-density disk is a cluster. If you multiplied the size of the allocation unit by the number of allocations units available, you would come up with the number of available bytes (512 * 2,847 = 1,457,664 bytes). The OS can now read from and write to this disk because it has set up the tracks and sectors, the boot record, the FAT, the root directory, and the data section as needed. Notice the line **Volume Serial Number is 5442-CAF1**. This is a hexadecimal number, randomly generated by the formatting process. Each volume serial number is unique. It is used for disk identification by application programs. For example, if you open a WordPerfect document file from a floppy disk and, while it is in memory, replace that disk with another, WordPerfect will be aware of the disk change by virtue of this number. Programmers can use *volume serial numbers* to identify the disks they use to distribute their programs.

9   Key in the following: C:\WINDOWS\SYSTEM32>**CD** \ [Enter]

```
C:\WINDOWS\SYSTEM32>CD \

C:\>_
```

WHAT'S
HAPPENING?   You have returned to the root directory. The root directory of any disk is always the \.

3.5   Formatting a Disk with a Volume Label

You can use parameters other than the disk drive letter with the FORMAT command. The FORMAT command has many parameters, some of which are used more than others. The syntax for the FORMAT command is:

```
Formats a disk for use with Windows XP.

FORMAT volume [/FS:file-system] [/V:label] [/Q] [/A:size] [/C] [/X]
FORMAT volume [/V:label] [/Q] [/F:size]
FORMAT volume [/V:label] [/Q] [/T:tracks /N:sectors]
FORMAT volume [/V:label] [/Q]
FORMAT volume [/Q]

  volume        Specifies the drive letter (followed by a colon),
                mount point, or volume name.
  /FS:filesystem Specifies the type of the file system (FAT, FAT32, or NTFS).
  /V:label      Specifies the volume label.
  /Q            Performs a quick format.
  /C            NTFS only: Files created on the new volume will be compressed
                by default.
  /X            Forces the volume to dismount first if necessary.  All opened
                handles to the volume would no longer be valid.
  /A:size       Overrides the default allocation unit size. Default settings
                are strongly recommended for general use.
                NTFS supports 512, 1024, 2048, 4096, 8192, 16K, 32K, 64K.
                FAT supports 512, 1024, 2048, 4096, 8192, 16K, 32K, 64K,
                (128K, 256K for sector size > 512 bytes).
                FAT32 supports 512, 1024, 2048, 4096, 8192, 16K, 32K, 64K,
                (128K, 256K for sector size > 512 bytes).

                Note that the FAT and FAT32 files systems impose the
                following restrictions on the number of clusters on a volume:
                FAT: Number of clusters <= 65526
                FAT32: 65526 < Number of clusters < 4177918

                Format will immediately stop processing if it decides that
                the above requirements cannot be met using the specified
                cluster size.
```

```
              NTFS compression is not supported for allocation unit sizes
              above 4096.

/F:size       Specifies the size of the floppy disk to format (1.44)
/T:tracks     Specifies the number of tracks per disk side.
/N:sectors    Specifies the number of sectors per track.
```

Although this syntax diagram may look intimidating, it really is not. The parameters that are important to remember are as follows are the /V for Volume name, and /Q for Quick.

```
FORMAT volume [/V:label] [/Q]
```

Beginning with MS-DOS version 3.3, the volume: or drive letter is mandatory. It must be included. This mandatory drive letter prohibits you from accidentally formatting the disk in the default drive. In addition, many of the options such as /C (compressed), /X (dismount), and /A (cluster size) are really only relevant when managing a network.

The /V allows you to place a volume label on a disk, but as you have already seen, the FORMAT command asks you for a volume label even if you don't include the /V. The /Q performs a quick format, but a quick format can be used only on a disk that has been previously formatted. It is "quick" because it simply deletes the entries from the FAT and the root directory and essentially leaves the files area untouched.

The /F:*size* parameter is an easy way to format floppy disks that do not match the capacity of a floppy disk drive. For instance, if you have a high-density disk drive but wish to format a 720KB disk, you would inform the FORMAT command using /F:720. However, /F:*size* does not solve all your mismatching problems. If you have a 720KB disk drive, you cannot format a high-density, 1.44-MB floppy disk in that drive. The 720KB disk drive is older technology and does not recognize the new high-density media type. Do not format a floppy disk at a size higher than it was designed for. In general, however, the older capacity disks are disappearing and you will rarely, if ever, have the need to use these numbers.

In the next activity, you are going to use the /V parameter to place a volume label on the disk you are formatting. A *volume label* is an electronic name. It is very much like labeling a file drawer so you know what it contains. The switch is /V, which tells the FORMAT command that it is to format a disk and place an electronic volume label on it. Whenever you format a disk in recent versions of the OS, you are automatically asked for a volume label, even if you do not include /V, so why use the parameter at all? When you don't use it, the formatting process stops and asks you for the volume label. When you use the /V (a fixed parameter), you can provide the label itself (a variable parameter) at the time you enter the command, rendering it unnecessary for the FORMAT command to ask you to enter it after the formatting process. In the partial command diagram, **FORMAT A: /V[:*label*]** notice that the bracketed item [:label] includes both the colon and the label with no spaces between.

3.6   Activity: Using the /V Option

Note: Your default directory is the root of C and C:\> is displayed. The disk just
formatted is in Drive A.

1   Key in the following: C:\>**CD \WINDOWS\SYSTEM32** Enter

```
C:\>CD \WINDOWS\SYSTEM32

C:\WINDOWS\SYSTEM32>_
```

WHAT'S
HAPPENING?   You made **\WINDOWS\SYSTEM32** the default subdirectory.

2   Key in the following:
C:\WINDOWS\SYSTEM32>**FORMAT A: /V:SAMPLEDATA** Enter

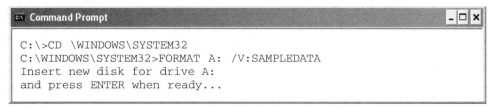

```
C:\>CD \WINDOWS\SYSTEM32
C:\WINDOWS\SYSTEM32>FORMAT A: /V:SAMPLEDATA
Insert new disk for drive A:
and press ENTER when ready...
```

WHAT'S
HAPPENING?   The FORMAT command was loaded from the disk into memory.
The data contained in any files on the disk is not actually deleted, but instead the
FAT and the root directory table are "zeroed out." Also, the disk area is scanned for
bad surfaces that might have appeared since the last time you formatted the disk.

3   Press Enter

```
C:\WINDOWS\SYSTEM32>FORMAT A: /V:SAMPLEDATA
Insert new disk for drive A:
and press ENTER when ready...
The type of the file system is FAT.
Verifying 1.44M
10 percent completed.
```

WHAT'S
HAPPENING?   You have begun the process of formatting the DATA disk.

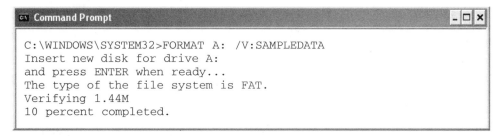

```
Initializing the File Allocation Table (FAT) . .
Format complete.

   1,457,664 bytes total disk space
   1,457,664 bytes available on disk

        512 bytes in each allocation unit.
      2,847 allocation units available on disk.

        12 bits in each FAT entry.
```

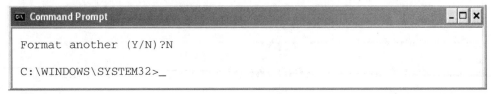

Volume Serial Number is A067-7C79

Format another (Y/N)?

WHAT'S HAPPENING?   You were not asked to enter the volume label, as the label was provided within the command.

4   Key in the following: **N** Enter

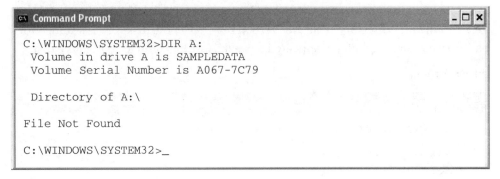

C:\ Command Prompt   _ □ ✕

Format another (Y/N)?N

C:\WINDOWS\SYSTEM32>_

WHAT'S HAPPENING?   Since you do not want to format another disk, you pressed **N** for "no." You named your disk SAMPLEDATA because on this disk you are going to store samples. Whenever you use a volume label, make it as meaningful as possible so that you do not have to look at all the files on the disk to know what is on the disk. Examples of meaningful names (volume labels) could include ENGLISH to indicate the disk is for your English homework or INCOMETAX for a disk that contains your income tax data. There are two ways to see your volume label.

5   Key in the following: C:\WINDOWS\SYSTEM32>**DIR A:** Enter

C:\ Command Prompt   _ □ ✕

C:\WINDOWS\SYSTEM32>DIR A:
 Volume in drive A is SAMPLEDATA
 Volume Serial Number is A067-7C79

 Directory of A:\

File Not Found

C:\WINDOWS\SYSTEM32>_

WHAT'S HAPPENING?   You can see displayed the label you entered, SAMPLEDATA. The internal command VOL lets you look at the volume label on any disk or check to see if there is a label. By using this command, you can quickly see what is on a disk without having to execute the directory command. The syntax is:

VOL [drive:]

6   Key in the following: C:\WINDOWS\SYSTEM32>**VOL** Enter

C:\ Command Prompt   _ □ ✕

C:\WINDOWS\SYSTEM32>VOL
 Volume in drive C is ADMIN504
 Volume Serial Number is 0E38-11FF
C:\>WINDOWS\SYSTEM32>_

WHAT'S
HAPPENING?   The volume label on your hard disk will be different depending on whether a volume label was entered when the hard disk was formatted. In this example, a volume label was placed on the hard disk, so you see the message **Volume in drive C is ADMIN504**. When you used the VOL command, the operating system looked only on Drive C, the default drive. To look at the volume label on Drive A, you must specifically request Drive A by giving VOL another parameter, the variable parameter [*drive*:], which represents the drive letter.

7   Key in the following: C:\WINDOWS\SYSTEM32>**VOL A:** Enter

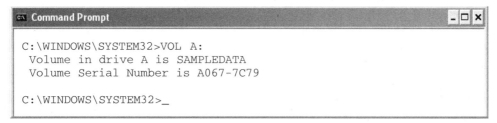

```
C:\WINDOWS\SYSTEM32>VOL A:
 Volume in drive A is SAMPLEDATA
 Volume Serial Number is A067-7C79

C:\WINDOWS\SYSTEM32>_
```

WHAT'S
HAPPENING?   Since you placed a volume label on the DATA disk, you can see it with the VOL command. If a volume label is meaningful, it clearly identifies what files are on the disk.

3.7   The LABEL Command

It would be very inconvenient if every time you wanted to change the volume label on a disk you had to reformat the disk. Not only is this fatal to your data, but it takes time to format disks. In MS-DOS version 3.3, the LABEL command was introduced. It is an external command that lets you change the volume label without reformatting the disk. Remember, VOL, an internal command, lets you *see* the volume label, but LABEL lets you *change* the volume label. Bracketed items are always optional. The partial syntax is:

```
LABEL [drive:][label]
```

3.8   Activity: Using the LABEL Command

Note: Your default directory is the **\WINDOWS\SYSTEM32** subdirectory on Drive C, and you have C:\WINDOWS\SYSTEM32> displayed. The disk you just formatted is in Drive A.

1   Key in the following: C:\WINDOWS\SYSTEM32>**LABEL A:** Enter

Note: Be certain to include the A: parameter, or the OS will assume you want to change the electronic name of the C drive. This action can cause problems on networked computers.

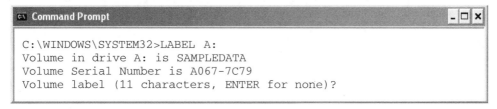

```
C:\WINDOWS\SYSTEM32>LABEL A:
Volume in drive A: is SAMPLEDATA
Volume Serial Number is A067-7C79
Volume label (11 characters, ENTER for none)?
```

WHAT'S ▨▨▨▨▨
▨▨▨HAPPENING?   This message looks exactly like the one you saw when you used
the FORMAT command without the /V parameter. At this point, you can key in a
new volume label.

2   Press `Enter`

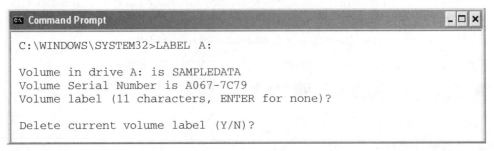

```
C:\WINDOWS\SYSTEM32>LABEL A:

Volume in drive A: is SAMPLEDATA
Volume Serial Number is A067-7C79
Volume label (11 characters, ENTER for none)?

Delete current volume label (Y/N)?
```

WHAT'S ▨▨▨▨▨
▨▨▨HAPPENING?   The LABEL command knows that you already have a volume
label, so it is asking you if you want to remove it.

3   Key in the following: **Y** `Enter`

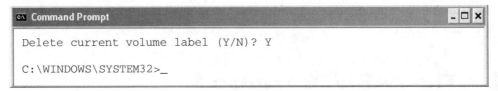

```
Delete current volume label (Y/N)? Y

C:\WINDOWS\SYSTEM32>_
```

WHAT'S ▨▨▨▨▨
▨▨▨HAPPENING?   You deleted the current volume label.

4   Key in the following: C:\WINDOWS\SYSTEM32>**VOL A:** `Enter`

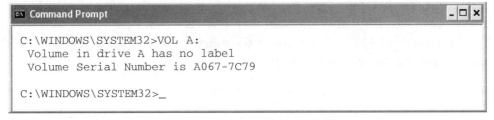

```
C:\WINDOWS\SYSTEM32>VOL A:
 Volume in drive A has no label
 Volume Serial Number is A067-7C79

C:\WINDOWS\SYSTEM32>_
```

WHAT'S ▨▨▨▨▨
▨▨▨HAPPENING?   You no longer have a volume label on the disk. In the next step
you are going to place a volume label on the DATA disk, but you are going to take a
shortcut. You are going to use the volume label SAMPLE DATA. Since you already
know what you want to key in, you do not have to wait for the LABEL command to
ask you what label you want. The LABEL command allows the use of spaces,
whereas the /V parameter with FORMAT does not allow spaces.

5   Key in the following:
C:\WINDOWS\SYSTEM32>**LABEL A:SAMPLE DATA** `Enter`

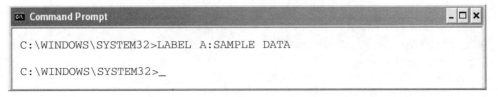

```
C:\WINDOWS\SYSTEM32>LABEL A:SAMPLE DATA

C:\WINDOWS\SYSTEM32>_
```

WHATʼS
HAPPENING? You are returned to the system level prompt. Did your volume label change on the DATA disk?

6 Key in the following: C:\WINDOWS\SYSTEM32>**VOL A:** Enter

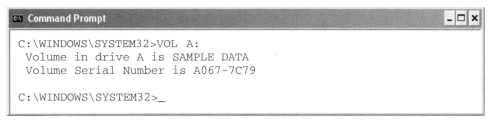

```
ca Command Prompt                                            _ □ ×

C:\WINDOWS\SYSTEM32>VOL A:
 Volume in drive A is SAMPLE DATA
 Volume Serial Number is A067-7C79

C:\WINDOWS\SYSTEM32>_
```

WHATʼS
HAPPENING? Using the VOL command, you can see the new volume label.

3.9 Formatting a Disk Using the /Q Parameter

Often you will want to clear a disk totally to ensure that there is really nothing on the disk and you know the tracks and sectors are already there from a previous formatting. There is no need to take the time to reformat the disk. You can use the /Q parameter. The /Q parameter stands for "quick" format. The /Q works *only* on a disk that has been previously formatted. It works like the usual FORMAT command, but skips the low-level formatting. It clears the FAT and root directory as it prepares a disk for new files. However, in order to clear the disk rapidly, /Q will not check for *bad sectors* on a disk. Using /Q is a very fast way to erase a disk.

3.10 Activity: Using the /Q Parameter

Note: Your default directory is the **WINDOWS****SYSTEM32** subdirectory on Drive C, and C:\WINDOWS\SYSTEM32> is displayed. The SAMPLE DATA disk is in Drive A.

1 Key in the following: C:\WINDOWS\SYSTEM32>**FORMAT A: /Q** Enter

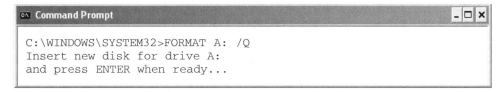

```
ca Command Prompt                                            _ □ ×

C:\WINDOWS\SYSTEM32>FORMAT A: /Q
Insert new disk for drive A:
and press ENTER when ready...
```

WHATʼS
HAPPENING? FORMAT is asking you for a disk to format. Since you already have a disk in the drive, you may proceed.

2 Be sure the DATA disk is in Drive A. Then press Enter

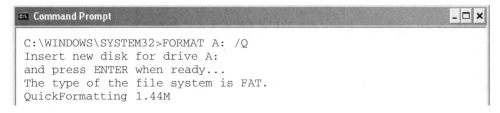

```
ca Command Prompt                                            _ □ ×

C:\WINDOWS\SYSTEM32>FORMAT A: /Q
Insert new disk for drive A:
and press ENTER when ready...
The type of the file system is FAT.
QuickFormatting 1.44M
```

```
Initializing the File Allocation Table (FAT) . . .
Volume label (11 characters, ENTER for none)?
```

WHAT'S HAPPENING?   Notice how fast the formatting occurred. FORMAT is asking you for a volume label. You will use this disk throughout the remainder of this text for the DATA disk.

3   Key in the following: C:\WINDOWS\SYSTEM32>**DATA** [Enter]

4   Key in **N** [Enter]

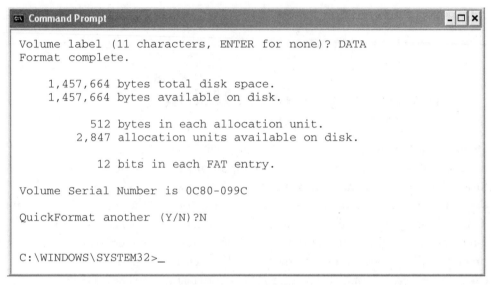

```
Command Prompt                                              _ □ ×

Volume label (11 characters, ENTER for none)? DATA
Format complete.

    1,457,664 bytes total disk space.
    1,457,664 bytes available on disk.

        512 bytes in each allocation unit.
    2,847 allocation units available on disk.

        12 bits in each FAT entry.

Volume Serial Number is 0C80-099C

QuickFormat another (Y/N)?N


C:\WINDOWS\SYSTEM32>_
```

WHAT'S HAPPENING?   The FORMAT command wanted to know if you had any more disks to quick format. You responded **N** for "no." You returned to the system prompt. What happened to the volume label?

5   Key in the following: C:\WINDOWS\SYSTEM32>**VOL A:** [Enter]

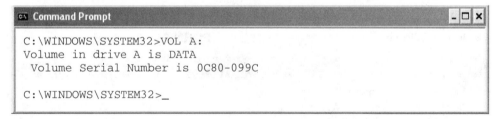

```
Command Prompt                                              _ □ ×

C:\WINDOWS\SYSTEM32>VOL A:
Volume in drive A is DATA
 Volume Serial Number is 0C80-099C

C:\WINDOWS\SYSTEM32>_
```

WHAT'S HAPPENING?   As you did not press enter, but entered the new volume label DATA, your disk has been electronically "renamed" to DATA. You have finished creating the disk you will use each time the instructions tell you to be sure your DATA disk is in the drive.

6   Key in the following: C:\WINDOWS\SYSTEM32>**CD ** [Enter]

```
Command Prompt                                              _ □ ×

C:\WINDOWS\SYSTEM32>CD \

C:\>_
```

WHATS **■■■■■**
■■■HAPPENING?   You returned to the root directory of the hard disk.

7   Key in the following: C:\>**EXIT** Enter

WHATS **■■■■■**
■■■HAPPENING?   You have closed the Command Prompt window and have returned to the desktop. Remember, the appearance of the desktop will differ from
computer to computer.

8   Click **Start**. Click **Turn Off Computer**. Click **Turn Off**.

WHATS **■■■■■**
■■■HAPPENING?   You have completed the Windows shut-down procedure.

Chapter Summary

1. Floppy disks that are purchased are sometimes not ready to use. They must first
    be prepared for use.
2. Each type of computer has its own specific way of recording information on a
    disk. This text is only concerned with Windows-based computers.
3. Disks are the means to store data and programs permanently.
4. All disks must be formatted by a utility program stored as a file called
    FORMAT.COM so that data and programs can be read from and written to
    them.
5. Disks that have information on them can be formatted again.
6. If a disk has files on it, formatting the disk will remove all of those files.
7. Since the FORMAT command removes all data, formatting a hard disk can be
    dangerous.
8. Formatting a disk means that the physical layout of the disk is defined to
    determine how the information is stored on the disk so that the OS can locate
    what is stored.
9. Each operating system has a unique way of recording information on a disk.
    This is known as a file system.
10. The OS uses sections of a disk, whether it is a hard disk or a floppy disk. A disk
    is divided into concentric circles called tracks. Each track is divided into sectors.
    The number of tracks, sectors, and sides of a disk determine the capacity of the
    disk.
11. The two major types of files systems that Windows XP Professional supports is
    FAT and NTFS.
12. All floppy disks are formatted as FAT disks.
13. The smallest unit that the operating system will read from or write to is a
    cluster. A cluster is made up of one or more adjacent sectors, depending on the
    type of disk.
14. Each disk that is formatted with FAT has a root directory and two copies of a file
    allocation table (FAT).
15. All disks that are formatted with FAT have a boot record, a FAT, a directory, and
    data sectors.
16. All FAT-formatted disks use the file allocation table. The FAT (file allocation
    table) is a map of every track and sector on the disk. The FAT tells the OS where
    files are on the disk. The FAT links a file together by pointing to the next cluster
    that holds the file's data.

17. On a FAT-formatted disk, the root directory has information about files including the file name and the file's starting cluster entry in the FAT.
18. The data sectors are where files are actually stored.
19. Files are chains of bytes laid out in sequence.
20. NTFS is the preferred file system for Windows XP Professional.
21. Major advantages of using NTFS include that it is a secure file system that provides more efficient storage of data on hard disks and faster access to files and folders.
22. Insead of using FAT, NTFS uses a special file called the Master File Table (MFT) that tracks all the files and directories in a volume. It is a database of all the files on the system.
23. Files are written to a disk in the first available cluster and, if possible, in adjacent or contiguous clusters. If the adjacent clusters are already in use, the OS skips to the next available noncontiguous cluster.
24. A disk is formatted with the FORMAT command, an external utility program.
25. The basic syntax of the FORMAT command is:

```
FORMAT volume: [/V:label] [/Q] [/F:size]
```

26. The internal VOL command allows you to view the internal electronic label.
27. The external LABEL command allows you to change the internal electronic label.
28. The /Q parameter performs a quick format that does not check for bad sectors on a disk. In addition, it can be used only on a disk that has been previously formatted.
29. Always use the correct media type when formatting disks.

Key Terms

active partition	file allocation table	New Technology File
allocation unit	(FAT)	System (NTFS)
bad sectors	file system	partition
basic disk	formatting	partition table
boot sector	high-level formatting	physical formatting
cluster	initializing the disk	primary partition
cluster overhang	logical formatting	run
contiguous	low-level formatting	virtual file alloction
dynamic disk	master boot record	table (VFAT)
end-of-file (EOF) marker	(MBR)	volume label
extended partition	master file table (MFT)	volume serial number
extent	noncontiguous	

Discussion Questions

1. What purpose do disks serve?
2. Why must you format a disk?
3. Compare and contrast physical (low-level) formatting with logical (high-level) formatting of a disk.
4. Define *tracks*, *sectors*, and *clusters*.

5. What is the purpose and function of the boot record?
6. Define *FAT*. How is it used on a disk?
7. Compare and contrast FAT, FAT32, and NTFS.
8. What is the purpose and function of the root directory in a FAT file system?
9. How is space allocated to files in FAT? In NTFS?
10. FORMAT can be a dangerous command. Explain.
11. What does the prompt on the screen represent?
12. Compare and contrast internal and external commands.
13. What steps can you take when you see error messages ?
14. What is a volume label?
15. When formatting a disk, the drive letter is a mandatory parameter. Why?
16. Give the basic syntax for the FORMAT command and explain each item.
17. Explain the purpose and function of a quick format.
18. When using the FORMAT command, what are the purpose and function of the parameter /V?
19. What is the purpose and function of the VOL command?
20. What is the purpose and function of the LABEL command?
21. When using the FORMAT command, when would you use the /Q parameter?

True/False Questions

For each question, circle the letter T if the statement is true or the letter F if the statement is false.

T   F   1. Each track is divided into smaller units called sectors.
T   F   2. You may format any disk with the FORMAT command.
T   F   3. DIR FORMAT.COM will execute the command FORMAT and format a disk.
T   F   4. The DOS directory structure only recognized 8.3 file names.
T   F   5. All floppy disks are formatted as FAT.

Completion Questions

Write the correct answer in each blank space.

6. The smallest unit of disk space the operating system will work with is called a(n) _____.
7. The information in files is stored in the _____ sectors of a disk.
8. In a FAT-formatted disk, where a file is located is kept track of by the _____, while the _____ keeps track of the files and attributes.
9. NTFS keeps track of all its files and directories in the _____.
10. In order to be usable, a disk must first be _____.

Multiple Choice Questions

For each question, write the letter for the correct answer in the blank space.

____ 11. When you format a disk, you

   a. erase everything on that disk.

   b. prepare it so the operating system can read from and write to it.

   c. both a and b

   d. neither a nor b

____ 12. On a hard disk, you may only boot from the _____ partition.

   a. active

   b. extended

   c. expanded

   d. primary

____ 13. To name a disk when you are formatting it, you can use

   a. the /V parameter.

   b. the VOL command.

   c. /L for label.

   d. /N for name.

____ 14. NTFS and FAT are examples of

   a. operating systems.

   b. partition tables.

   c. file systems.

   d. none of the above

____ 15. To change the volume label of the disk currently in Drive A without eliminating any information on it, key in:

   a. LABEL A:

   b. VOL A:

   c. VOLUME A:

   d. none of the above

Writing Commands

Write the correct steps or commands to perform the required action as if you were at the computer. The prompt will indicate the default drive and directory.

16. View the name of the disk in the default drive.

   `A:\>`

17. Format and place the volume label MYDISK on the disk in Drive A, in one step.

   `C:\WINDOWS\SYSTEM32>`

18. Display the volume label on Drive A.

   `C:\>`

19. Locate the FORMAT command on the hard drive.

   `A:\>`

20. Change the label on the disk in Drive A from DATA to ACTION.

   `C:\WINDOWS\SYSTEM32>`

Homework Assignments

Problem Set I—At the Computer

Note 1: Your DATA disk is in Drive A. C:\> is displayed as the default drive and the default directory.

Note 2: Remember, be very careful when using the FORMAT command. *Never* issue the command without a drive parameter specified, A: or B:, and do not use the C drive as a parameter.

Problem A

A-a   Format the DATA disk the fastest way.

A-b   Key in the following at the volume label prompt: **MYDATA DISK**

____   1. In addition to the drive letter, what parameter did you use with the FORMAT command?
  a. /U
  b. /Q
  c. /S
  d. none of the above

A-c   Display the volume label of the DATA disk.

____   2. In addition to the drive letter, what command did you use?
  a. VOL
  b. NAME
  c. FORMAT
  d. all of the above

____   3. What volume label is displayed?
  a. MY DATA DISK
  b. MYDISK
  c. MYDATADISK
  d. none of the above

Problem B

B-a   Change the name of the disk in the A drive without using the FORMAT command.

B-b   Use the name **CLASSDISK**.

____   4. Which command did you use?
  a. NAME
  b. LABEL
  c. VOL
  d. none of the above

B-c   Check to see that the name has actually changed.

_____ 5. What volume label is displayed?
    a. DATA
    b. CLASSDISK
    c. MYDATADISKVERY_OWN
    d. none of the above

B-d   Change the volume label to **DATA**.

_____ 6. In addition to the drive letter, what command did you use?
    a. VOL
    b. FORMAT
    c. LABEL
    d. none of the above

Problem Set II—Brief Essay

1. You have taught a friend how to format a disk, and she is happy to find that the process is simple. However, she does not understand why she must format a disk and what is happening when it is formatted. Briefly answer her questions. Include an explanation of the purpose of the boot record, the directory table, the FAT, and the data sectors.
2. You have just keyed in **FORMAT A:/V:CLEAN**. What is it that you did, and why did you do it?

CHAPTER 4

PROGRAM FILES, DATA FILES, AND SUBDIRECTORIES

Learning Objectives

After completing this chapter you will be able to:

1. List and explain the major reasons for learning about the operating system.
2. Explain the difference between program files and data files.
3. Explain the difference between freeware and shareware programs.
4. Define "real mode" and "protected mode" operations.
5. Explain the hierarchical filing system of a tree-structured directory.
6. Define the CD, MD, and RD commands.
7. Explain the purpose and function of a root directory and tell how and when it is created.
8. Explain what subdirectories are and tell how they are named, created, and used.
9. Explain the purpose and use of subdirectory markers.
10. Identify the commands that can be used with subdirectories.
11. Explain the purpose of the PROMPT command.
12. Explain the purpose and function of the MOVE command.
13. List the steps to remove a directory.
14. Explain the purpose of the path.

6. Use subdirectory markers with commands.
7. Use the PROMPT command to change the display of the prompt.
8. Rename a directory using the MOVE command.
9. Use the RD command to eliminate a directory.
10. Explain how to remove an entire tree structure.
11. Understand the purpose of the path command.

Student Outcomes

1. Understand the difference between data files and program files.
2. Create subdirectories using the MD command.
3. Understand Hierarchical Filing Systems
4. Display the default directory using the CD command.
5. Change directories using the CD command.

Chapter Overview

You do not purchase a computer to use the operating system. You purchase a computer to help you be more efficient in doing work you want to do. Work on a computer is comprised of two aspects—the programs that do the work and the information you create. When you work with a computer, you accumulate many programs and data files. If you are going to be an efficient user, you must have a way to manage these files. Part of the power of the Windows operating system is its ability to manage files. From the desktop, you can use Windows Explorer and My Computer to view the location of your files and to manage them. In this text, you will learn how to manage your files from the command prompt. There are things that you cannot do easily (and some things you cannot do at all) from the Windows GUI.

In this chapter you will learn to use a program file and a data file. You will also learn the subdirectory commands to help you manage your files.

4.1   Why Use the Command Prompt Window?

So far, you have used commands to prepare a disk for use (FORMAT), to copy a disk (DISKCOPY), to see what files are on a disk (DIR), and to clear the screen (CLS). Each of these commands is useful, but no one buys a computer to use the operating system. You purchase a computer to assist you in work, and the way you work on a computer is by using application programs. The major categories of application programs include word processors to make writing easier, spreadsheets to manage budgets and do financial projections, databases to manage and manipulate collections of data, and graphics to create artistic drawings and designs. The application programs that use graphics include CAD (computer-aided design), desktop publishing, photo-editing programs, and scanning or camera programs. Each program has its own instructions that must be learned. If this is true, why are you learning about the operating system? There are two important reasons.

First and foremost, you cannot run an application program without Windows. It is the manager of the system, supervising the hardware and software components and allowing you to load and execute specific application packages. All application programs run under the supervision of the operating system.

The second reason for learning about the operating system is that application programs are stored as files on disks and usually generate data files. Windows has a variety of commands that allow you to manage and manipulate program and data files. Be aware that the operating system manages the files—their location, movement, etc.—but not the information you put *into* files.

4.2   Program Files, Data Files, and the Operating System

On the hard disk is a subdirectory called WUGXP. This subdirectory was created by installing the files and directories from the ACTIVITIES disk to the hard disk. It was placed on the hard disk or network server by the lab technician or the instructor. If you are using your own computer, you will have to create the directory and place the files there yourself—see Appendix A for instructions on how to do this. The subdirectory WUGXP contains other subdirectories, among which is GAMES. This subdirectory has a subdirectory called BOG2 in which there is an application program called BOG that will help you understand how operating systems work in the "real world." BOG is a simple game program. The object of Bog 2 is to find as many words as possible in the grid, formed from adjacent cubes.

The Windows operating system, because it is downward compatible, allows for the use of older software, referred to as *legacy software*. You are going to use the Command Prompt window to execute this program by loading the program file.

An application or program file is an executable file that is loaded from disk into memory. The operating system then turns control over to the application program. With software written for DOS or earlier versions of Windows, when the application program needed to interface with the hardware, such as when it wanted to write a character to the screen, print, or respond to mouse movement, there were two choices. The application program could "talk" directly to the device or it could talk to DOS and let DOS do the actual labor of writing to the screen or sending a job to the printer. This is called *real mode* operation. With software written for the Windows operating system, this is not the case. Windows software runs in protected mode. In *protected mode*, no communication exists between the application software and the actual hardware itself. *Device drivers* (the software that comes with peripheral devices, such as a mouse or a modem) are also called mini-drivers. Instead of having the manufacturer's device drivers talk to the hardware or to the core of the operating system itself, these drivers talk to virtual device drivers, which are part of the Windows operating system. These virtual device drivers are outside of the core operations of the operating system, which remains "protected" from the actions of the devices and device drivers.

As an example, assume you bought a fancy ACME video card with all the new bells and whistles. It has the magic words "Plug and Play" on the package. When you install it, you may have to insert the disk that came with it in order to install a mini-driver that talks to the Windows virtual video card driver and tells it how to blow the whistles and ring the bells. The core of the Windows operating system, however, is *not* touched by the software driver written by ACME. The Windows virtual video driver will make sure nothing gets through to the core of the operating system that could cause problems. Thus the term "protected mode."

An application program cannot load itself into memory. The operating system is the means by which the application program gets loaded into memory. Remember that work takes place only in memory. The operating system also assists in loading the data file into memory so that the application program can use the data. Ensuring the cooperative effort between the OS and the application program and its data files is the work of the operating system. You, the user, do not directly interface with the operating system at the application level.

There is another component: the command line commands that Windows provides. Commands are also programs. These commands allow you, the user, to interface directly with the operating system to manage your program and data files.

4.3   Shareware

Some of you may have already purchased commercial application packages such as WordPerfect, Word, or PageMaker. There are hundreds of different programs to choose from that will meet almost any computer user's needs, from managing a checkbook (Quicken) to playing a game (Flight Simulator).

The subdirectory WUGXP contains data files, freeware programs, and shareware programs. Freeware and shareware programs are available from a wide variety of sources. One of the most common sources today is the Internet. Friends and acquaintances may pass programs to you; members of computer clubs share their programs; or you can receive them from a source such as this textbook.

Freeware is software that is in the public domain. The authors (programmers) of these programs have donated the programs to anyone who wants to use them with the understanding that people will use them but not alter them. The programmers do not expect to be paid in any way—although sometimes they will ask for a small donation for expenses.

Shareware is a trial version of a program. The program is not distributed through commercial channels, thus saving the programmer the costs of marketing and distribution. After you purchase commercial software, if you do not like it or it does not meet your needs, you usually cannot return it. On the other hand, shareware is something you can try out. If you like it, you then register it with the programmer for a nominal fee. If you do not like it, you simply delete the file or files from your disk. Trying these programs costs you nothing. If you decide to retain and use the program, the programmer *does* expect to be paid. The programmer or programmers who write shareware are professional programmers, students, and people who just enjoy programming.

Sometimes, to encourage people to register, the program will be a limited version without all the features of the shareware program. Sometimes called "crippleware," it may lose features after a certain date or have annoying screens that pop up to remind you to register it. When you do register it, you receive the full version or the latest version of the program, the documentation (a manual of commands and instructions), and notices of updates and technical support. The update notices will provide you with the latest version of corrections to the program. Technical support means you can call the programmer(s) for help if something is not working correctly.

This textbook includes both freeware and shareware. Appendix A lists all the shareware programs with the fees and addresses necessary to register them. If, after you complete the textbook, you wish to continue using the shareware programs, please pay the appropriate fees and register the programs. Otherwise, delete the files. Shareware provides some really great programs and by registering them, you are encouraging the programmer to write shareware. Who knows, you may be assisting the next Bill Gates or Steve Jobs.

4.4   Activity: Using DIR to Locate the BOG Program

Note 1:   Check with your lab technician or network administrator to be sure that the subdirectory **WUGXP** has been installed for you, either on the C:\ drive or on a network drive. Be sure to fill in your Configuration Table in Chapter 1 with your specific location of this subdirectory. This text is written with the assumption that the **WUGXP** subdirectory is directly off the root of the C drive. If you are working on your own computer, you will have to install the subdirectory **WUGXP**. Complete instructions on how to do this are in Appendix A.

Note 2:   It is assumed that your computer is booted and Windows is loaded. You have shelled out to the Command Prompt. You have changed the directory to the root directory of C. C:\> is displayed on the screen as the default drive and directory.

Note 3:   When keying in commands, you may use the command line editing keys to correct typographical errors, as shown in Chapter 2.

1   Key in the following: C:\>**DIR WUG*.*** [Enter]

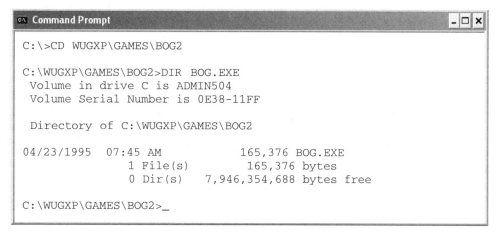

```
C:\>DIR WUG*.*
 Volume in drive C is ADMIN504
 Volume Serial Number is 0E38-11FF

 Directory of C:\

02/04/2002  09:20 AM    <DIR>          WUGXP
                0 File(s)            0 bytes
                1 Dir(s)   7,946,362,880 bytes free

C:\>_
```

WHAT'S
HAPPENING?   You are verifying that you have a subdirectory called **WUGXP**. In
this example, only one entry matches the criterion you requested. You asked DIR to
find any file or any directory on the hard disk that begins with **WUG** and has any
other characters in the file name and any file extension. Your display may vary
depending on how many other files you have that begin with **WUG**. If the entry
named **WUGXP** is not displayed, refer to Appendix A and take the necessary steps
before continuing.

2   Key in the following: C:\>**CD \WUGXP\GAMES\BOG2** Enter

3   Key in the following: C:\WUGXP\GAMES\BOG2\>**DIR BOG.EXE** Enter

```
C:\>CD WUGXP\GAMES\BOG2

C:\WUGXP\GAMES\BOG2>DIR BOG.EXE
 Volume in drive C is ADMIN504
 Volume Serial Number is 0E38-11FF

 Directory of C:\WUGXP\GAMES\BOG2

04/23/1995  07:45 AM           165,376 BOG.EXE
                1 File(s)        165,376 bytes
                0 Dir(s)   7,946,354,688 bytes free

C:\WUGXP\GAMES\BOG2>_
```

WHAT'S
HAPPENING?   You changed the default directory to **WUGXP\GAMES\BOG2**
subdirectory where the BOG program is located. You used the DIR command to see
if the file called **BOG.EXE** is on the hard disk C: off of the *root directory* (\) in the
subdirectory called **WUGXP\GAMES\BOG2**. DIR is the command,
WUGXP\GAMES\BOG2 is the *path,* and **BOG.EXE** is the file name of the program. The DIR command just allows you to see if the file is on the disk; it does not
let you use the program. The name of the file is **BOG**. The name of the extension is
.EXE. The **.EXE** file extension has a special meaning: executable code. This informs
the OS the file is a program. The file extension **.EXE** always indicates an executable
program.

4   Key in the following: C:\WUGXP\GAMES\BOG2>**DIR BOG.DAT** Enter

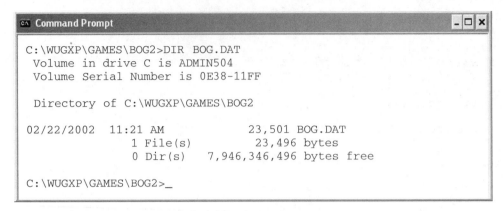

```
C:\WUGXP\GAMES\BOG2>DIR BOG.DAT
 Volume in drive C is ADMIN504
 Volume Serial Number is 0E38-11FF

 Directory of C:\WUGXP\GAMES\BOG2

02/22/2002  11:21 AM              23,501 BOG.DAT
              1 File(s)          23,496 bytes
              0 Dir(s)    7,946,346,496 bytes free

C:\WUGXP\GAMES\BOG2>_
```

WHAT'S HAPPENING?   You used the DIR command to see if the file called **BOG.DAT** is in this subdirectory. DIR is the command, **BOG** is the file name, and **DAT** is the file extension. DIR does not let you use the data; it just lets you see if it is there.

4.5   Using Application Programs and Data Files

In the above activity, you used the command DIR to see if there were two files on the disk, BOG.EXE and BOG.DAT. All DIR did was let you know that these files exist. To make use of these files, you have to load them into memory. Remember that the application program is BOG.EXE, which has the instructions to tell the computer what to do. The BOG.DAT data file cannot be used by itself. You must load the application program first, then the program will be able to get to and use the data.

4.6   Activity: Using Application Programs and Data Files

Note: C:\WUGXP\GAMES\BOG2> is displayed on your screen.

1   Key in the following: C:\WUGXP\GAMES\BOG2>**BOG.DAT** [Enter]

WHAT'S HAPPENING?   You opened up a dialog box that warned you against trying to open the file. The file called **BOG.DAT** is a data file. It is not a program, so it cannot execute. It does not have a program file extension **.EXE**, **.COM**, or **.BAT**. It is a data file. Data files cannot execute.

2   Click **Cancel**. Key in the following: C:\WUGXP\GAMES\BOG2>**BOG** [Enter]

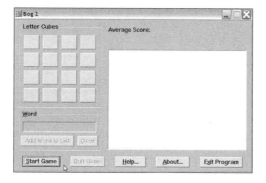

WHAT'S HAPPENING? When you keyed in **BOG**, the operating system looked for a file with the name of **BOG** and an extension of **.COM**, **.EXE**, or **.BAT** or other executable file extensions because those are the extensions that mean "execute." Because **BOG** is a file with an **.EXE** file extension, it was found. The operating system took an image copy of the program from the disk and loaded it into memory. Control was turned over to the BOG program. BOG is a shareware game program with its own commands and instructions. It is a word programs where the user tries to make up lots of words from a random group of letters. The program's data file (BOG.DAT) is a long list of words from which the letters are gathered, and against which your words are compared. If you like this program, remember to register it with the author.

3 Click **Exit Program**.

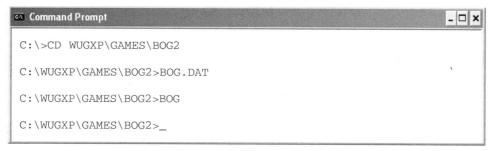

```
C:\>CD WUGXP\GAMES\BOG2

C:\WUGXP\GAMES\BOG2>BOG.DAT

C:\WUGXP\GAMES\BOG2>BOG

C:\WUGXP\GAMES\BOG2>_
```

WHAT'S HAPPENING? You have returned to the Command prompt window. Most programs today are written to run under the Windows GUI system. Most computer systems today have Microsoft Office installed, which includes the program Word. The following assumes you have Word on your computer.

4 Key in the following: C:\WUGXP\GAMES\BOG2>**CD ** [Enter]

5 Key in the following: C:\>**DIR WINWORD.EXE /S** [Enter]

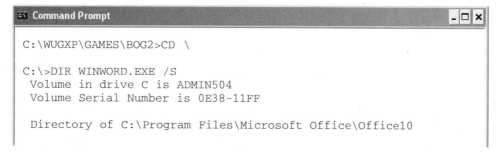

```
C:\WUGXP\GAMES\BOG2>CD \

C:\>DIR WINWORD.EXE /S
 Volume in drive C is ADMIN504
 Volume Serial Number is 0E38-11FF

 Directory of C:\Program Files\Microsoft Office\Office10
```

```
06/01/2001  10:07 AM          10,578,248 WINWORD.EXE
                   1 File(s)     10,578,248 bytes

      Total Files Listed:
                   1 File(s)     10,578,248 bytes
                   0 Dir(s)   7,906,836,480 bytes free
C:\>_
```

WHAT'S
HAPPENING?   You have used the DIR command with an optional parameter, /S, to discover if the Word program is installed on your system. The directory found in this example is the standard directory for Microsoft Word, but your system may be different.

WARNING: If you found something other than the directory found in this exercise, take careful note of what you found and use that directory instead of the one listed here. If the directory you found was not on your local system (not on the C:\ drive), be sure and check with your lab administrator to be sure you may complete this exercise.

WARNING: If WINWORD was not found on your system, go directly to step 11.

6   Key in the following:
C:\>**CD PROGRAM FILES\MICROSOFT OFFICE\OFFICE10** [Enter]

WHAT'S
HAPPENING?   You have changed directories to the directory where the Word program (Winword.exe) is located.

7   Key in the following:
C:\Program Files\Microsoft Office\Office10>**WINWORD** [Enter]

WHAT'S HAPPENING?   You have opened the Word Program. Word is *not* a shareware program, and you must purchase it to be able to use it on your system. (Your display may be very different from the one shown, depending on your version of Word installed in your lab.)

8   Click the ⊠ in the upper-right corner of the window to close the Word Program.

9   Key in the following:

`C:\Program Files\Microsoft Office\Office10>`**CD \ ⏎Enter**

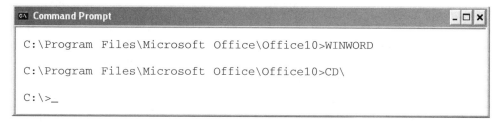

```
 Command Prompt                                              _ □ x

C:\Program Files\Microsoft Office\Office10>WINWORD

C:\Program Files\Microsoft Office\Office10>CD\

C:\>_
```

WHAT'S HAPPENING?   You have returned to the root drive.

10   Key in the following: `C:\>`**CD WUGXP ⏎Enter**

11   Key in the following: `C:\WUGXP>`**QUASARS.DOC ⏎Enter**

WARNING: If Winword was not found on your system, this will bring up the WordPad program—the applet that comes with Windows XP Professional—instead of Microsoft Word, as shown in the image below. The exercise will still work for you.

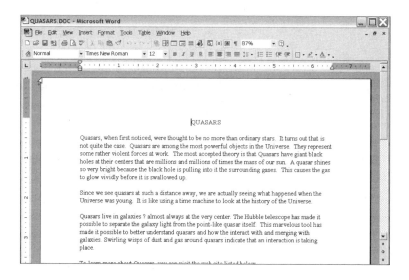

WHAT'S HAPPENING?   The Windows operating system knew which program you wanted to enter because the .DOC file extension is *associated* with the Word program, if Microsoft Word is installed, or the WordPad program if it is not. This association process happens during program installation. The operating system found the associated program and used it to open the requested file QUASARS.DOC.

12   Click the ⊠ in the right corner to close the Word (or WordPad) program.

4.7 Managing Program and Data Files at the Command Prompt

In the last few activities, you moved around the hard disk and loaded both program files and data files. Although you did not spend much time working with each program, the experience should give you some idea of how many different types of programs there are. With each new program, you generate new data files. Windows does a very good job managing your program files so that you can launch them from the Start/Programs menu. You need to manage the data files you create in these programs so that you can quickly locate what you need and get to work.

As an example of what you are faced with, imagine that you own 10 books. By reading each spine, you can quickly peruse the authors and titles and locate the book you wish to read. Suppose your library grows, and you now have 100 books. You do not want to read every author and title looking for just one book, so you classify the information. A common classification scheme is to arrange the books alphabetically by the author's last name. Now you have shortened your search time. If you are looking for a book by Peat, you go to the letter P. You may have more than one book by an author that begins with P, but, by going to the letter P, you have narrowed your search. Now imagine you have 10,000 books—arranging alphabetically by author is still not enough. You may have 200 books by authors whose last names begin with P. So you further classify your books. You first divide them into categories like computer or fiction. Then, within the category, you arrange alphabetically by last name. So, if you wanted a computer book by Peat, you would first go to the computer section, then to the letter P. If you wanted a novel by Peters, you would first go to the fiction section and then the letter P. As you can see, you are classifying and categorizing information so that you can find it quickly.

This process is exactly what you want to do with files. Remember, you have many data files. You want to be able to locate them quickly by grouping them logically. The way you do this in the OS is by the means of subdirectories.

Some programs, upon installation, create a directory for your files. For example, Microsoft Office places all the files you create with Word, Excel, and PowerPoint, to a directory called My Documents. On this system, My Documents is a subdirectory under C:\Documents and Settings\bpeat. However, if you save all of your documents to this single folder, it will soon become very crowded and your documents will be very, very hard to find. Most programs will allow you to specify a default folder to use for saving your files, and will also allow you to save to a folder other than the default during the saving process.

4.8 Hierarchical Filing Systems or Tree-structured Directories

As shown in Chapter 3, every disk must be formatted. Formatting a disk automatically creates a directory known as the root directory. Every disk must have a root directory so that files can be located on the disk. The root directory table is the area of the disk that contains information about what is stored there. It is like an index to the disk. However, there is a limit to the number of files or entries that can be placed in the root directory table if your disk is formatted as FAT16. See Table 4.1. Under FAT16, the root directory is a fixed size and location on the disk. This is no longer true with FAT32. Under FAT32 the root directory is now free to grow as necessary and can be located anywhere on a disk. There is no longer a limit on the number of directory entries in the root directory because the root directory is now an ordinary cluster chain and can grow as large as needed, limited only by the physical size of your disk.

Disk Size	Number of Root Directory Entries
3½-inch DS/DD disks	112
Hard disk	512

Table 4.1—FAT16 Root Directory File Limits

Although the limits of the root directory table on a floppy disk may be adequate, the limits on a FAT16 root directory of a hard disk were not. If you had a 1-GB hard disk, 512 entries were not enough space to store all the files the drive can accumulate. Normally, people work more efficiently when they group files and programs together logically. Subdirectories give you the capability of "fooling" the system so that you can create as many file entries as you need. The only limitation is the capacity of the disk. Even though FAT32 no longer limits the size of the root directory, subdirectories are still an important part of organizing a disk. This is also true if you are using the NTFS file system. It too no longer limits how many files or directories are located in the root directory.

This capability is called the hierarchical or tree-structured filing system. In this system, the root directory has entries not only for files but also for other directories called subdirectories, which can contain any number of entries. Windows refers to the subdirectories as folders.

The root directory is represented by a backslash. (Do not confuse the backslash \ with the forward slash /.) All directories other than the root directory are technically called subdirectories, yet the terms *directory* and *subdirectory* are used interchangeably. Windows uses the terms *folders* and *subfolders*. All of these terms—*folders, subfolders, directories,* and *subdirectories*—are used interchangeably. Subdirectories are not limited to a specific number of files. Subdirectories may have subdirectories of their own. Subdirectories divide the disk into different areas.

The directory structure of a disk is like an inverted family tree with the root directory at the top and the subdirectories branching off from the root. The root directory is the point of entry in the hierarchical directory structure. In Figure 4.1, the example on the left is a family tree showing a parent who has two children; the one on the right is a root directory with two subdirectories. The two subdirectories contain all files and programs having to do with sales and accounting. Again, what you are doing is classifying and further classifying information.

Figure 4.1—A Directory Is Like a Family Tree

A child can have only one biological mother, but a child can become a parent and have children. Those children can also become parents and have children. Likewise, ACCOUNTING can be a *child directory* of the root directory, but also a parent directory to subdirectories beneath it (see Figure 4.2).

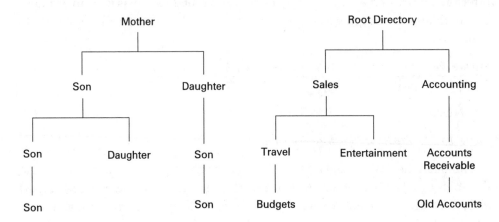

Figure 4.2—Hierarchical Structure of a Directory

The children are dependent on the parent above. Each subdirectory is listed in its *parent directory*, but not in any directory above the parent. Note the absolute *hierarchical structure*. You cannot skip a subdirectory any more than you can have a grandparent and grandchild with no parent in between. You move around in the directories via the path that tells the operating system where to go for a particular file.

Think of a disk as a building. When a structure is built, it has a finite size, which is also true of a disk. For example, you can have a 1.44-MB floppy disk or a 20-GB hard disk. The size is fixed. You cannot make it larger or smaller, but you can divide it into rooms. However, you first have to get inside. To open the door, you need a drive letter (volume). Once inside, you are in a room that is equivalent to the fixed size of a disk. This undivided room is the root directory. Every disk has a root directory that may or may not be subdivided. The name of the root directory is always \ (backslash). Thus, the structure could look like Figure 4.3.

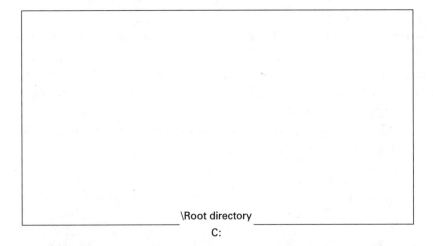

Figure 4.3—A Disk as a Building

Since it is difficult to find things when they are scattered about a large room, you want to put up walls (subdirectories) so that like things can be grouped together. When the walls go up, the root directory becomes the main lobby—backslash (\). In the rooms (subdirectories) you plan to have games, names and addresses in phone books, and the operating system commands. You post a sign (label) indicating what you plan to put inside each room (see Figure 4.4).

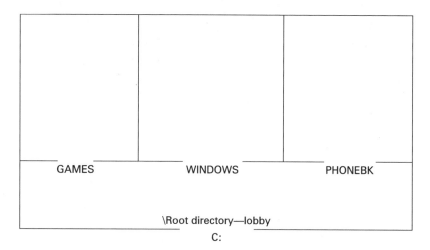

Figure 4.4—Subdirectories as Rooms

Each room is off the main lobby, the \. You cannot go from the GAMES room to the PHONEBK room without first going through the main lobby (\). Furthermore, the lobby (\) sees only the entryways to the rooms. It does not know what is in the rooms, only that there are rooms (subdirectories). In addition, each room can be further divided (see Figure 4.5).

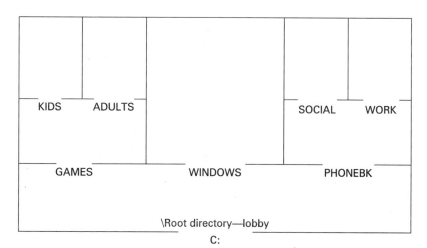

Figure 4.5—More Subdirectories

Each new room (subdirectory) is off another room (subdirectory). The GAMES room, for example, now has two new rooms—KIDS and ADULTS. The GAMES room (subdirectory) now becomes a lobby. You can get to the KIDS and ADULTS rooms (subdirectories) only through the GAMES lobby. Furthermore, in order to get to the GAMES room, you must pass through the main lobby \ (root directory).

The GAMES lobby knows that there are two new rooms but does not know what is inside each. The main lobby (\) knows the GAMES room but does not know what is inside GAMES. The KIDS and ADULTS rooms know only the GAMES lobby.

The same relationship exists for all other new rooms (subdirectories). A subdirectory knows only its parent lobby and any children it may create. There are no shortcuts. If you are in the KIDS room and wish to go the SOCIAL room, you must return to the GAMES lobby, then you must pass through the main lobby (root directory) to the PHONEBK lobby. Only then can you enter the SOCIAL room.

You do not have to subdivide rooms. GAMES is subdivided, while Windows is not. Remember, you are not changing the size of the structure; you are merely organizing it. Presently, these rooms have nothing in them, but they are ready to receive something. That something is files. The files are like the furniture (see Figure 4.6).

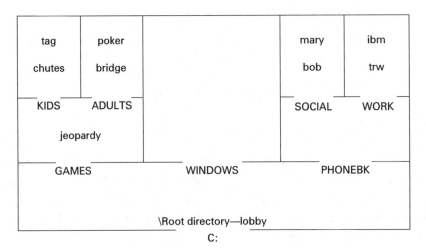

Figure 4.6—Files in Subdirectories

You now have not only created the rooms (subdirectories), but you have also filled them with furniture (files). Thus, using subdirectories is a way to manage the numerous files and programs you collect and create. Again, this is a classification scheme, and you expect there to be some logic to it. Just as you would not expect to find a stove in a room called bedroom, you would not expect to find a file called WINWORD.EXE in a subdirectory called GAMES. This does not mean there cannot be a mistake—that someone could, indeed place the stove in the bedroom—but that would make the stove *very* hard to find.

There is another component to using subdirectories. When you use subdirectories, you can change your work area, much like using a room. If you are going to cook, you will go to the kitchen because you expect the tools that you need to be in that location. You expect not only the stove to be there but also all the tools you need—the sink, the spices, and the pots and pans. If you want to go to sleep, you will go to the bedroom because that is where you expect to find the bed. Subdirectories have names that you or a program choose. The only exception is the root directory, which is created when you format the disk and is always known as \ (backslash). The root directory *always* has the same name on every disk (\).

Because computers are so rigid, they must follow certain rules when naming anything. Subdirectories follow the same naming conventions as files. Usually, subdirectory names do not have extensions. Although the Windows operating system treats subdirectories as files, the subdirectories themselves cannot, for the most part, be manipulated with the standard file manipulation commands. Subdirectories have their own special commands. Table 4.2 lists the directory management commands.

Command	Function
CHDIR or CD	Changes a directory.
MKDIR or MD	Makes or creates a directory.
RMDIR or RD	Removes or erases a directory and its subdirectories.
PATH	Defines the search paths.
PROMPT	Changes the look of the prompt to identify what subdirectory is the default.
MOVE	Allows you to rename a directory.

Table 4.2—Directory Management Commands

4.9 Creating Subdirectories

When you create a subdirectory, you are setting up an area where files can be stored. There is nothing in the subdirectory initially. The internal MD command creates a subdirectory. When you format a disk, you are preparing it to hold files. When you set up a subdirectory, you are preparing it to hold a logical group of files. The syntax of the command is:

MKDIR [drive:]path

or

MD [drive:]path

MD and MKDIR perform exactly the same function. You will use MD, because it requires fewer keystrokes. In the following activity, you will create two subdirectories under the root directory on the DATA disk. These subdirectories will be for two classes: one in political science and the other in physical education.

4.10 Activity: How to Create Subdirectories

Note: Make sure you are at the Command Prompt. C:\> is displayed as the default drive and directory.

1 Place the DATA disk created in Chapter 3 into Drive A.

2 Key in the following: C:\>**FORMAT A: /Q /V:DATA** Enter

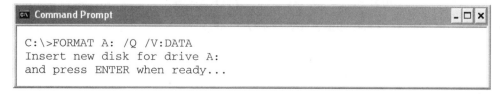

```
C:\>FORMAT A: /Q /V:DATA
Insert new disk for drive A:
and press ENTER when ready...
```

WHAT'S ░░░░
░░░░HAPPENING?   You are going to format the DATA disk again. In addition to using the /Q parameter to format the disk quickly, you also used a shortcut to place a volume label on the disk, so you do not have to wait for the volume label prompt. If you want to include a volume label on a disk, you can do it at the time of issuing the FORMAT command. However, when you use /V (followed by a colon), you cannot have spaces in the volume label name.

3   Press [Enter]

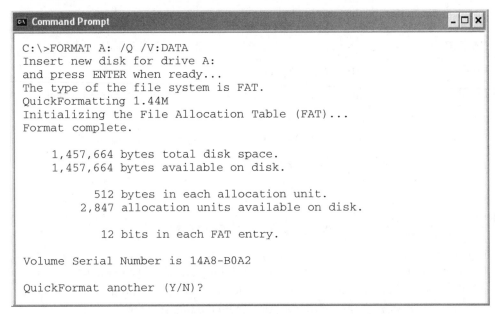

```
C:\>FORMAT A: /Q /V:DATA
Insert new disk for drive A:
and press ENTER when ready...
The type of the file system is FAT.
QuickFormatting 1.44M
Initializing the File Allocation Table (FAT)...
Format complete.

    1,457,664 bytes total disk space.
    1,457,664 bytes available on disk.

          512 bytes in each allocation unit.
        2,847 allocation units available on disk.

           12 bits in each FAT entry.

Volume Serial Number is 14A8-B0A2

QuickFormat another (Y/N)?
```

WHAT'S ░░░░
░░░░HAPPENING?   You formatted the disk and placed a volume label on it.

4   Press **N** [Enter]

5   Key in the following: C:\>**A:** [Enter]

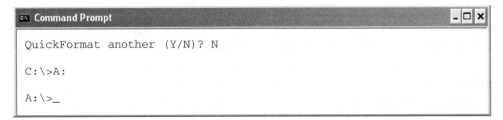

```
QuickFormat another (Y/N)? N

C:\>A:

A:\>_
```

WHAT'S ░░░░
░░░░HAPPENING?   You told the operating system you did not wish to format any more disks. You have changed the default drive. However, you are in more than a default *drive*, you are in a default *directory*—the root of A. This is the only directory on this disk and was created when you formatted it. You can tell that you are in the root directory because when you look at the prompt, it displays not just A: but also \, indicating the root.

6   Key in the following: A:\>**MD ASTRONOMY** [Enter]

7   Key in the following: A:\>**MD PHYSED** [Enter]

```
A:\>MD ASTRONOMY

A:\>MD PHYSED

A:\>_
```

WHAT'S HAPPENING?   You created two subdirectories called **ASTRONOMY** and **PHYSED** under the root directory on the DATA disk. **ASTRONOMY** will hold all the files that involve classes in astrological science, and **PHYSED** will hold files that involve classes in physical education. Although you have created the subdirectories to hold the files, they are now "empty" file cabinets. When you used the MD command, all you saw on the screen was the system prompt. How do you know that you created subdirectories? You can see the subdirectories you just created by using the DIR command.

8   Key in the following: A:\>**DIR** Enter

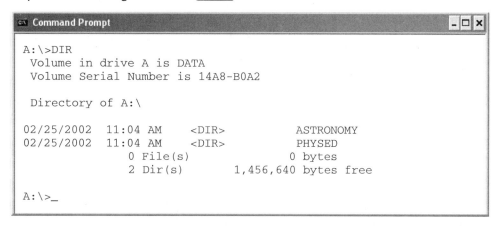

```
A:\>DIR
 Volume in drive A is DATA
 Volume Serial Number is 14A8-B0A2

 Directory of A:\

02/25/2002  11:04 AM    <DIR>          ASTRONOMY
02/25/2002  11:04 AM    <DIR>          PHYSED
              0 File(s)              0 bytes
              2 Dir(s)       1,456,640 bytes free

A:\>_
```

WHAT'S HAPPENING?   The DIR command displayed the contents of the disk. In this case, there are only the two subdirectory files you just created. It is the <DIR> after each file name that indicates a subdirectory. **ASTRONOMY** and **PHYSED** are subdirectories. It is also important to note that the \ following the **Directory of A:** on the screen indicates the root directory of the disk.

One of the parameters for the DIR command is /A for attributes. The only attribute you are interested in is D for directories. If you look at the syntax diagram, it indicates the /A followed by a list of the attributes you can request. The D is for directories:

```
/A          Displays files with specified attributes.
  attributes   D  Directories          R  Read-only files
               H  Hidden files         A  Files ready for archiving
               S  System files         -  Prefix meaning not
```

9   Key in the following: A:\>**DIR /AD** Enter

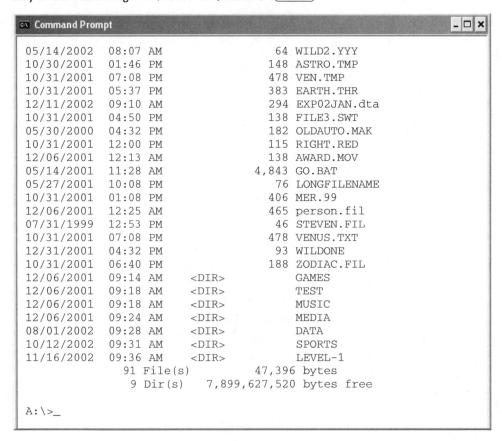

```
Command Prompt                                                    _ □ ×

A:\>DIR /AD
 Volume in drive A is DATA
 Volume Serial Number is 14A8-B0A2

 Directory of A:\

02/25/2002  11:04 AM    <DIR>          ASTRONOMY
02/25/2002  11:04 AM    <DIR>          PHYSED
               0 File(s)              0 bytes
               2 Dir(s)        1,456,640 bytes free

A:\>_
```

WHAT'S HAPPENING?   You see displayed only the directories on the DATA disk because that is all that the disk contains. What if you want to look at a disk that already has directories and files on it?

10 Key in the following: A:\>**DIR C:\WUGXP** [Enter]

```
Command Prompt                                                    _ □ ×

 05/14/2002   08:07 AM                  64 WILD2.YYY
 10/30/2001   01:46 PM                 148 ASTRO.TMP
 10/31/2001   07:08 PM                 478 VEN.TMP
 10/31/2001   05:37 PM                 383 EARTH.THR
 12/11/2002   09:10 AM                 294 EXP02JAN.dta
 10/31/2001   04:50 PM                 138 FILE3.SWT
 05/30/2000   04:32 PM                 182 OLDAUTO.MAK
 10/31/2001   12:00 PM                 115 RIGHT.RED
 12/06/2001   12:13 AM                 138 AWARD.MOV
 05/14/2001   11:28 AM               4,843 GO.BAT
 05/27/2001   10:08 PM                  76 LONGFILENAME
 10/31/2001   01:08 PM                 406 MER.99
 12/06/2001   12:25 AM                 465 person.fil
 07/31/1999   12:53 PM                  46 STEVEN.FIL
 10/31/2001   07:08 PM                 478 VENUS.TXT
 12/31/2001   04:32 PM                  93 WILDONE
 10/31/2001   06:40 PM                 188 ZODIAC.FIL
 12/06/2001   09:14 AM    <DIR>          GAMES
 12/06/2001   09:18 AM    <DIR>          TEST
 12/06/2001   09:18 AM    <DIR>          MUSIC
 12/06/2001   09:24 AM    <DIR>          MEDIA
 08/01/2002   09:28 AM    <DIR>          DATA
 10/12/2002   09:31 AM    <DIR>          SPORTS
 11/16/2002   09:36 AM    <DIR>          LEVEL-1
              91 File(s)          47,396 bytes
               9 Dir(s)    7,899,627,520 bytes free

A:\>_
```

WHAT'S HAPPENING?   (This graphic represents the tail end of your listing.) As you can see, using DIR with no parameters shows you all files, not just directories. Notice the subdirectories are at the bottom of the listing. This is the way Windows XP, by default, shows you directory listings. Windows XP Professional showed the directory listings as they were stored in the directory entry table, which, to the viewer, was in no particular order. However, if you are using NTFS, the files and directories are listed alphabetically by default. Remember, the displayed results from DIR will be very different if you have a FAT16 or NTFS file system. Most displays in this text are on a FAT32 system.

11 Key in the following: A:\>**DIR C:\WUGXP /AD** Enter

```
┌─────────────────────────────────────────────────────────────────┐
│ ▆ Command Prompt                                      _ □ x       │
├─────────────────────────────────────────────────────────────────┤
│                                                                   │
│ A:\>DIR C:\WUGXP /AD                                              │
│  Volume in drive C is ADMIN504                                    │
│  Volume Serial Number is 0E38-11FF                                │
│                                                                   │
│  Directory of C:\WUGXP                                            │
│                                                                   │
│ 02/04/2002  09:20 AM    <DIR>          .                          │
│ 02/04/2002  09:20 AM    <DIR>          ..                         │
│ 12/06/2001  09:14 AM    <DIR>          GAMES                      │
│ 12/06/2001  09:18 AM    <DIR>          TEST                       │
│ 12/06/2001  09:18 AM    <DIR>          MUSIC                      │
│ 12/06/2001  09:24 AM    <DIR>          MEDIA                      │
│ 08/01/2002  09:28 AM    <DIR>          DATA                       │
│ 10/12/2002  09:31 AM    <DIR>          SPORTS                     │
│ 11/16/2002  09:36 AM    <DIR>          LEVEL-1                    │
│               0 File(s)            0 bytes                         │
│               9 Dir(s)    7,898,628,096 bytes free                │
│                                                                   │
│ A:\>_                                                             │
│                                                                   │
└─────────────────────────────────────────────────────────────────┘
```

WHAT'S ▓▓▓▓▓▓
▓▓▓▓ **HAPPENING?**   The above command listed only the directories on the hard disk in the subdirectory called **WUGXP**. Do not be concerned if the order is different on your computer. What if you wish to see the names of the files inside the directory? Since **ASTRONOMY** is a subdirectory on the A drive, not just a file, you can display the contents of the directory with the DIR command. Remember, the terms *directory* and *subdirectory* are interchangeable. Actually there is only one directory—the root directory. Although others may be called directories, they are really subdirectories. Again, the syntax of the DIR command is DIR [*drive:*][*path*]. You use the subdirectory name for *path*.

12 Key in the following: A:\>**DIR ASTRONOMY** Enter

```
┌─────────────────────────────────────────────────────────────────┐
│ ▆ Command Prompt                                      _ □ x       │
├─────────────────────────────────────────────────────────────────┤
│                                                                   │
│ A:\>DIR ASTRONOMY                                                 │
│  Volume in drive A is DATA                                        │
│  Volume Serial Number is 14A8-B0A2                                │
│                                                                   │
│  Directory of A:\ASTRONOMY                                        │
│                                                                   │
│ 02/25/2002  11:04 AM    <DIR>          .                          │
│ 02/25/2002  11:04 AM    <DIR>          ..                         │
│               0 File(s)            0 bytes                         │
│               2 Dir(s)      1,456,640 bytes free                  │
│                                                                   │
│ A:\>_                                                             │
│                                                                   │
└─────────────────────────────────────────────────────────────────┘
```

WHAT'S ▓▓▓▓▓▓
▓▓▓▓ **HAPPENING?**   The directory line, **Directory of A:\ASTRONOMY**, tells you the path. You are looking from the root directory into the subdirectory called **ASTRONOMY**. Even though you just created the subdirectory **ASTRONOMY**, it

seems to have two subdirectories in it already, . (one period, also called the *dot*) and . . (two periods, also called the *double dot*). Every subdirectory, except the root directory, has two named subdirectories, always. The subdirectory named . is another name or abbreviation for the current directory, **ASTRONOMY**. The subdirectory name . . is an abbreviation for the parent directory of the current directory, in this case the root directory \. The . (dot) and . . (double dot) are called *subdirectory markers* or *dot notation*. This always holds true—the single dot is the name of the subdirectory you are currently in, the default directory, and the double dot is the name of the directory immediately above the current directory, the parent directory.

13 Key in the following: A:\>**DIR PHYSED** [Enter]

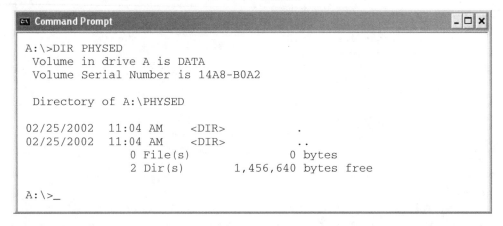

```
A:\>DIR PHYSED
 Volume in drive A is DATA
 Volume Serial Number is 14A8-B0A2

 Directory of A:\PHYSED

02/25/2002  11:04 AM    <DIR>          .
02/25/2002  11:04 AM    <DIR>          ..
               0 File(s)              0 bytes
               2 Dir(s)       1,456,640 bytes free

A:\>_
```

WHAT'S
HAPPENING?   The line that reads **Directory of A:\PHYSED** tells you the path. You are looking from the root directory into the subdirectory called **PHYSED**, the same way you looked when you asked for a directory on another drive. If, for instance, you asked for a directory of the disk in Drive B, that line would read **Directory of B:**. If you had asked for a directory of Drive C, that line would have read **Directory of C:**. It tells you not only what drive but also what subdirectory is displayed on the screen.

4.11 The Current Directory

Just as the operating system keeps track of the default drive, it also keeps track of the *current directory*, or default directory of each drive. When you boot the system, the default drive is the drive you load the operating system from, usually C, and the default directory is the root directory of the current drive. You can change the directory just as you can change the drive. Doing so makes a specific subdirectory the default. In previous chapters you used the CD command to change the default directory to the \WINDOWS\SYSTEM32 subdirectory on the hard disk. It was important to have that as the default subdirectory so that you could use the external commands.

The change directory command (CHDIR or CD) has two purposes. If you key in CD with no parameters, the name of the current default directory is displayed. If you include a parameter after the CD command, the default directory will be changed to the directory you request. The CD command does not use spaces as delimiters, so it is possible to change to a directory that contains a space in its name, such as My Documents, without using quotes. This process is similar to changing drives by keying in the desired drive letter followed by a colon, e.g., A:, B:, and C:.

However, do not be fooled. If your default drive and directory is the root of A so that the displayed prompt is A:\> and you key in CD C:\WUGXP, you *will not* change drives. What you will do is change the default directory on Drive C to \WUGXP. Your current default drive and directory will still be the root of A and your displayed prompt will still be A:\>. However, if you change to the C drive by keying in C:, you will go to the current default directory on the C drive, which is now C:\WUGXP. But if you use the /D parameter with the CD command, you will change drives and directories with one command. The command would be CD /D C:\WUGXP. The commands CHDIR and CD are exactly the same. You will use CD because it requires fewer keystrokes. The syntax for the CD command is as follows:

```
CD [/D] [drive:][path]
```

4.12 **Activity: Using the CD Command**

Note: The DATA disk is in Drive A. The default drive is Drive A, and A:\> is
           displayed on the screen.

1   Key in the following: A:\>**CD** Enter

WHAT'S HAPPENING?   This display tells you that you are in the root directory of the DATA disk and that any command you enter will apply to this root directory, which is also the default directory. You can change this default using the CD command. You are going to change the default subdirectory from the root to the subdirectory called **ASTRONOMY**.

2   Key in the following: A:\>**CD ASTRONOMY** Enter

3   Key in the following: A:\ASTRONOMY>**CD** Enter

WHAT'S HAPPENING?   In step 2, CD followed by the name of the subdirectory changed the default from the root directory to the subdirectory **ASTRONOMY**. Since you changed the default directory, the prompt then said A:\ASTRONOMY>. However,

you can always confirm that you changed the default directory by keying in **CD**.
CD with no parameters always displays the default drive and default subdirectory.
When you keyed in **CD**, it displayed **A:\ASTRONOMY**, which tells you that you
are in the subdirectory **\ASTRONOMY** on the DATA disk in Drive A and that any
command you enter with no parameters will apply to this default subdirectory. You
can think of the command this way: CD with no parameters shows you the current
drive and directory; CD followed by a subdirectory name changes the subdirectory.
CD alone *cannot* be used to change drives.

4   Key in the following: A:\ASTRONOMY>**DIR** Enter

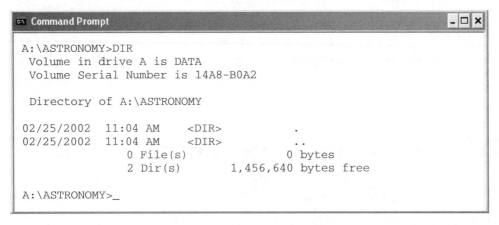

```
Command Prompt                                                    _ □ ×

A:\ASTRONOMY>DIR
 Volume in drive A is DATA
 Volume Serial Number is 14A8-B0A2

 Directory of A:\ASTRONOMY

02/25/2002  11:04 AM    <DIR>            .
02/25/2002  11:04 AM    <DIR>            ..
              0 File(s)            0 bytes
              2 Dir(s)     1,456,640 bytes free

A:\ASTRONOMY>_
```

**WHAT'S
HAPPENING?**   You are displaying the contents of the current default directory,
\ASTRONOMY. When you use a command, in this case DIR, it always assumes the
default drive and default subdirectory, unless you specify another drive and/or
subdirectory.

5   Key in the following: A:\ASTRONOMY>**CD** \ Enter

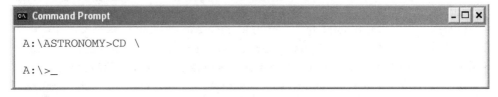

```
Command Prompt                                                    _ □ ×

A:\ASTRONOMY>CD \

A:\>_
```

**WHAT'S
HAPPENING?**   By keying in **CD **, you moved to the root directory of the DATA
disk. The first backslash always means the root directory.

4.13   Relative and Absolute Paths

You are going to add subdirectories to the *tree structure* so that the levels will look
like those in Figure 4.7. To create these additional subdirectories, you use the MD, or
make directory, command. The command syntax allows these parameters: MD
[*drive:*]*path.*

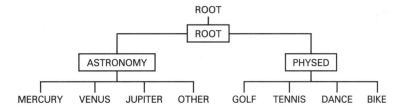

Figure 4.7—Directory with Subdirectories

The *drive:* is the letter of the drive that contains the disk on which the subdirectory is to be created (such as A:, B:, or C:). If you omit the drive designator, the subdirectory will be created on the default or current drive. The path is the path name of the directory in which the subdirectory is to be created. If you omit the path name, the subdirectory is created in the default or current subdirectory.

It is important to understand the concept of **absolute path** and **relative path**. The absolute path is the complete and total hierarchical structure. You start at the top and work your way down through every subdirectory without skipping a directory. The absolute path is *always* absolutely correct.

As an analogy, if you were living in Los Angeles, California, you could get a bus ticket to Santa Barbara. It would not be necessary to use the absolute path to ask for a ticket—the United States, California, Los Angeles, and then Santa Barbara—you could use the relative path of just Santa Barbara. If you were in London, England, and were flying to Los Angeles and needed to buy your connecting bus ticket from the airport to Santa Barbara before you left England, you would indeed need to give the English ticket broker complete information about the ticket that you wanted. You would need to give the absolute path of where you wanted to leave from and where you wanted to go to—you would ask for a ticket to the United States, state of California, city of Los Angeles, and then a bus ticket from the airport to the city of Santa Barbara.

Just as the ticket salesperson in Los Angeles knows where Santa Barbara is, the current directory also knows information about its immediate surroundings. However, a directory knows *only* about the files and subdirectories within itself and the files and directory immediately above it. There can be many directories beneath it (many child directories) but only one directory above it (the parent directory). Each directory knows only its immediate child directories and its parent directory—no more. If you want to move to a different parent subdirectory, you must return to the root. The root is the common "ancestor" of all the directories on the disk.

Thus, if you wanted to go from the subdirectory GOLF in the above figure to the subdirectory VENUS, you would need to go via ROOT. Once you get to the root, you can choose where you want to go. There are many places to go. It is like a subway—you must pass through all the stations along the path to get to your destination.

4.14   Activity: Creating More Subdirectories

Note: The DATA disk is in Drive A. A:\> is displayed as the default drive and the default directory.

1   Key in the following: A:\>**CD** [Enter]

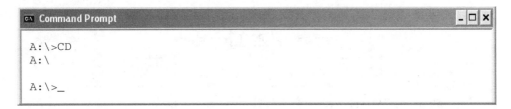

WHAT'S HAPPENING?   You confirmed that the default directory is the root of the DATA disk. To create three subdirectories under **ASTRONOMY**, you will use the MD command along with the subdirectory names. The subdirectories will be called **MERCURY, VENUS, JUPITER,** and **OTHER**. You will begin with an absolute path and then use a relative path.

2   Key in the following: A:\>**MD A:\ASTRONOMY\MERCURY** Enter

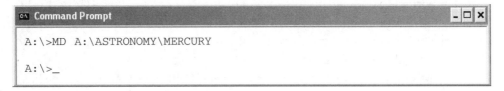

WHAT'S HAPPENING?   You have given absolute instructions as to where to create the directory. You issued the command MD (make a directory) followed by the location (go to Drive A, under the root directory (\), under the directory called **AS-TRONOMY**). The next backslash is a delimiter to separate **ASTRONOMY** from the next entry. Then you can add your new subdirectory called **MERCURY**. You could not create **MERCURY** until you created **ASTRONOMY** because it is a hierarchy. Looking at the screen, however, nothing seems to have happened.

3   Key in the following: A:\>**DIR ASTRONOMY** Enter

```
Command Prompt                                              _ □ ×

A:\>DIR ASTRONOMY
 Volume in drive A is DATA
 Volume Serial Number is 14A8-B0A2

 Directory of A:\ASTRONOMY

02/25/2002  11:04 AM    <DIR>          .
02/25/2002  11:04 AM    <DIR>          ..
02/25/2002  12:20 PM    <DIR>          MERCURY
              0 File(s)          0 bytes
              3 Dir(s)     1,456,128 bytes free

A:\>_
```

WHAT'S HAPPENING?   You indeed have a subdirectory called **MERCURY** under the root, under **ASTRONOMY**. You are now going to create the subdirectory called **VENUS**. Here you can use a relative path. The default prompt shows you that you are already in Drive A. If you are already in Drive A, it is the default directory. Therefore, you do not need to include the drive letter because the operating system assumes the default drive, unless you tell it otherwise. The default directory is the root. The \ is shown in the prompt, which tells you that you are in the root directory and that it is your default. Since you are already in the root, you do not need to include it. The first backslash is implied.

4 Key in the following: A:\>**MD ASTRONOMY\VENUS** [Enter]

5 Key in the following: A:\>**DIR ASTRONOMY** [Enter]

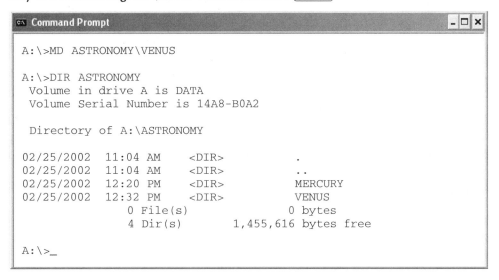

```
A:\>MD ASTRONOMY\VENUS

A:\>DIR ASTRONOMY
 Volume in drive A is DATA
 Volume Serial Number is 14A8-B0A2

 Directory of A:\ASTRONOMY

02/25/2002  11:04 AM    <DIR>          .
02/25/2002  11:04 AM    <DIR>          ..
02/25/2002  12:20 PM    <DIR>          MERCURY
02/25/2002  12:32 PM    <DIR>          VENUS
               0 File(s)              0 bytes
               4 Dir(s)      1,455,616 bytes free

A:\>_
```

WHAT'S HAPPENING?   You created the subdirectory **VENUS** under **ASTRONOMY** and then you used the DIR command to see that **VENUS** was, indeed, created. As you can see, in step 2, you used the absolute path to create the directory. In step 4, you used the default values and created a subdirectory using the relative path.

6 Key in the following: A:\>**CD ASTRONOMY** [Enter]

```
A:\>CD ASTRONOMY

A:\ASTRONOMY>_
```

WHAT'S HAPPENING?   You have changed the default directory to **ASTRONOMY**, which is under the root directory. Using the relative path, you are going to create two more subdirectories, **JUPITER** and **OTHER** , under **ASTRONOMY**. Remember, you are in **ASTRONOMY** under the root on the DATA disk, so all you need to use is a relative path name—relative to where you are.

7 Key in the following: A:\ASTRONOMY>**MD JUPITER** [Enter]

8 Key in the following: A:\ASTRONOMY>**MD OTHER** [Enter]

9 Key in the following: A:\ASTRONOMY>**DIR** [Enter]

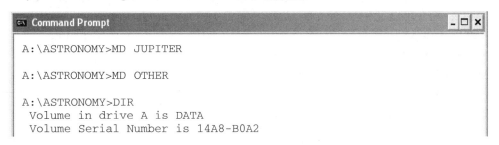

```
A:\ASTRONOMY>MD JUPITER

A:\ASTRONOMY>MD OTHER

A:\ASTRONOMY>DIR
 Volume in drive A is DATA
 Volume Serial Number is 14A8-B0A2
```

```
 Directory of A:\ASTRONOMY

02/25/2002  11:04 AM    <DIR>          .
02/25/2002  11:04 AM    <DIR>          ..
02/25/2002  12:20 PM    <DIR>          MERCURY
02/25/2002  12:32 PM    <DIR>          VENUS
02/25/2002  12:34 PM    <DIR>          JUPITER
02/25/2002  12:34 PM    <DIR>          OTHER
               0 File(s)              0 bytes
               6 Dir(s)       1,454,592 bytes free

A:\ASTRONOMY>_
```

WHAT'S ▓▓▓▓▓▓
▓▓▓HAPPENING?   You needed only to key in the subdirectory names, **JUPITER** and **OTHER**. The path was assumed from the position relative to where you were. In other words, as the current directory displayed, **A:\ASTRONOMY** was where the new directories were added. Because you gave no other path in your command, the default drive and directory were assumed.

10   Key in the following: A:\ASTRONOMY>**MD \PLANETS** ⌜Enter⌝

11   Key in the following: A:\ASTRONOMY>**DIR** ⌜Enter⌝

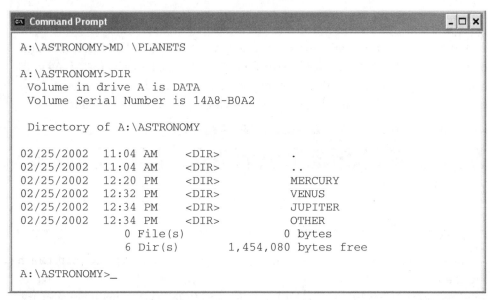

```
Command Prompt                                      _ □ x

A:\ASTRONOMY>MD  \PLANETS

A:\ASTRONOMY>DIR
 Volume in drive A is DATA
 Volume Serial Number is 14A8-B0A2

 Directory of A:\ASTRONOMY

02/25/2002  11:04 AM    <DIR>          .
02/25/2002  11:04 AM    <DIR>          ..
02/25/2002  12:20 PM    <DIR>          MERCURY
02/25/2002  12:32 PM    <DIR>          VENUS
02/25/2002  12:34 PM    <DIR>          JUPITER
02/25/2002  12:34 PM    <DIR>          OTHER
               0 File(s)              0 bytes
               6 Dir(s)       1,454,080 bytes free

A:\ASTRONOMY>_
```

WHAT'S ▓▓▓▓▓▓
▓▓▓HAPPENING?   You created the subdirectory **PLANETS**, but where is it? Here is a common mistake users make. When you keyed in **\PLANETS**, you were keying in an absolute path. Remember, the first backslash always means the root. You created the directory called **PLANETS** under the root (\), not under **ASTRONOMY**. The term *first backslash* can be misleading. In the path statement **ASTRONOMY\MERCURY**, some users would think that the first backslash is the one separating **ASTRONOMY** from **MERCURY**. This is not true. You are separating **ASTRONOMY** from **MERCURY**; hence, this backslash is a delimiter. The first backslash is the one that begins any path statement such as **\ASTRONOMY\MERCURY**. The backslash preceding **ASTRONOMY** is the first backslash.

12   Key in the following: A:\ASTRONOMY>**DIR ** ⌜Enter⌝

```
Command Prompt                                          _ □ ×

A:\ASTRONOMY>DIR \
 Volume in drive A is DATA
 Volume Serial Number is 14A8-B0A2

 Directory of A:\

02/25/2002  11:04 AM    <DIR>          ASTRONOMY
02/25/2002  11:04 AM    <DIR>          PHYSED
02/25/2002  12:37 PM    <DIR>          PLANETS
              0 File(s)              0 bytes
              3 Dir(s)       1,454,080 bytes free

A:\ASTRONOMY>_
```

**WHAT'S
HAPPENING?**   By keying in **DIR **, you asked to look at the root directory. As you
can see, looking at the screen display of the DATA disk, **PLANETS** is under the root
directory. Windows simply followed your instructions. Remember, there are no files
in the newly created subdirectories. You have made "rooms" for "furniture." As of
now, they are empty. You can create subdirectories wherever you wish as long as the
proper path is included. You *must* pay attention to where you are and whether you
are keying in an absolute path or a relative path. If you key in an absolute path of
the directory you want to create, you will always be correct. If you key in a relative
path, you must remember that you will create the subdirectory *relative* to where you
are.

13 Key in the following: A:\ASTRONOMY>**MD \PHYSED\TENNIS** Enter

```
Command Prompt                                          _ □ ×

A:\ASTRONOMY>MD \PHYSED\TENNIS

A:\ASTRONOMY>_
```

**WHAT'S
HAPPENING?**   Since the default, or current, directory is **ASTRONOMY**, you first
had to tell the operating system to return to the root (\) and then go to the
subdirectory called **PHYSED**. Remember, the relative path only looks down or
under **ASTRONOMY**. Thus, the path is **PHYSED**. You told the system that under
PHYSED the name for the new subdirectory was **TENNIS**. The second backslash
(**PHYSED\TENNIS**) is a separator or delimiter, separating the first subdirectory
name from the second subdirectory name. The first backslash indicates the root. Any
other backslash in the line is a delimiter. This is *always* true. The MD command does
not change the current or default directory. You can verify that you created the
subdirectory **TENNIS** under the subdirectory **PHYSED** by using the DIR command with the path name.

14 Key in the following: A:\ASTRONOMY>**DIR \PHYSED** Enter

```
Command Prompt                                          _ □ ×

A:\ASTRONOMY>DIR \PHYSED
 Volume in drive A is DATA
 Volume Serial Number is 14A8-B0A2
```

```
 Directory of A:\PHYSED

02/25/2002  11:04 AM     <DIR>            .
02/25/2002  11:04 AM     <DIR>            ..
02/25/2002  12:42 PM     <DIR>            TENNIS
              0 File(s)               0 bytes
              3 Dir(s)        1,453,568 bytes free

A:\ASTRONOMY>_
```

WHAT'S ▦▦▦▦▦
▦▦ HAPPENING?   The subdirectory **PHYSED** is displayed with the **TENNIS**
subdirectory listed. It was very important to key in the backslash in **PHYSED** in
order to tell DIR to go up to the root and then down to the subdirectory **PHYSED**. If
you had not included the backslash (\) and had keyed in **DIR PHYSED** only, you
would have seen the message "File Not Found" because DIR would have looked
below **ASTRONOMY** only. **PHYSED** is under the root directory, not under the
subdirectory **ASTRONOMY**.

4.15 Knowing the Default Directory

Since Windows, and any operating system, always uses default values unless you
specify otherwise, knowing the current default is very important. Recognizing the
default drive and directory is easy because the screen displays the prompt or disk
drive letter, A:\ or C:\. You know the default directory or subdirectory the same
way. The screen displays the full path, but that was not always the case. In versions
of DOS prior to DOS 6, the default prompt did not display the path—only the drive.
If you were currently in C:\WINDOWS\SYSTEM32>, all you would have seen was
C>—no path indicators at all. You change the way the prompt appears with the
PROMPT command. In operating systems prior to Windows XP Professional, the
PROMPT command, issued without any parameters, returned only the current
drive and the greater-than sign (>). It eliminated the path display from the prompt.
Now, the prompt command issued without parameters has no effect.

4.16 The PROMPT Command

The system or command prompt is a letter of the alphabet designating the default or
disk drive, followed by the greater-than sign, such as A> or C>. As previously
noted, this was the prompt displayed automatically in versions of DOS prior to DOS
6.0. Since the introduction of DOS 6.0, if no prompt is specified, the prompt includes
the path as well as the greater-than sign, such as A:\> or C:\>. However, the
prompt can be changed to reflect what you want to be displayed during a command
line session. All you are changing with the PROMPT command is the way the
prompt *looks*, not the function of the prompt. PROMPT is an internal command—it
is contained in CMD.EXE. The syntax for the PROMPT command is as follows:

```
PROMPT [text]
    text    Specifies a new command prompt.
```

The PROMPT command also has some special characters, called *metastrings*,
that mean specific things. When you include one of these metastrings, it establishes

a specific value. Metastrings always have the syntax $x where x represents any of the values in the following table:

Character	Description
$A	& (Ampersand)
$B	¦ (Pipe)
$C	((Left parenthesis)
$D	Current date
$E	Escape code (ASCII code 27)
$F	) (Right parenthesis)
$G	> (Greater-than sign)
$H	Backspace (Erases previous character)
$L	< (Less-than sign)
$N	Current drive
$P	Current drive and path
$Q	= (Equal sign)
$S	(Space)
$T	Current time
$V	Windows XP version number
$_	Carriage return and linefeed
$$	$ (Dollar sign)

The following activity allows you to change the prompt and use text data as well as metastrings. PROMPT, when keyed in without any parameters, returns the default prompt value (A:\>, B:\>, or C:\>) and will include the current path.

4.17   Activity: Changing the Prompt

Note: The DATA disk is in Drive A. The default drive is Drive A. The default subdirectory is ASTRONOMY. The prompt A:\ASTRONOMY> is displayed.

1   Key in the following: A:\ASTRONOMY>**PROMPT HELLO$G** [Enter]

WHATS ▓▓▓▓
▓▓▓HAPPENING?   You changed the way the prompt looks. You no longer see A:\ASTRONOMY> but, instead, the text you supplied, HELLO. The greater-than sign, >, appeared because you keyed in **$G**. When the operating system sees **$G**, it returns the metastring value for G, which is **>**. The function of the prompt has not

changed, only its appearance. The new prompt works just as if A>, B>, or C> were displayed. Any command keyed in works the same way.

2   Key in the following: HELLO>**VOL** Enter

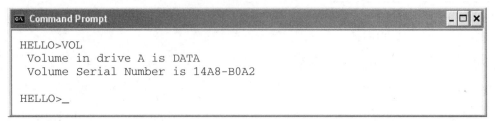

```
HELLO>VOL
 Volume in drive A is DATA
 Volume Serial Number is 14A8-B0A2

HELLO>_
```

WHAT'S ▓▓▓▓▓
▓▓▓HAPPENING?   As you can see, the VOL command works the same way. What if you change drives?

3   Key in the following: HELLO>**C:** Enter

```
HELLO>C:

HELLO>_
```

WHAT'S ▓▓▓▓▓
▓▓▓HAPPENING?   You changed the default drive to C, but, by looking at the screen, there is no way to tell what the default drive is.

4   Key in the following: HELLO>**VOL** Enter

```
HELLO>VOL
 Volume in drive C is ADMIN504
 Volume Serial Number is 0E38-11FF

HELLO>_
```

WHAT'S ▓▓▓▓▓
▓▓▓HAPPENING?   You can now see that you changed the designated drive. This exercise shows you that having the default drive letter displayed on the screen is very important. You can return the prompt to the default value by keying in the command with no parameters.

5   Key in the following: HELLO>**PROMPT** Enter

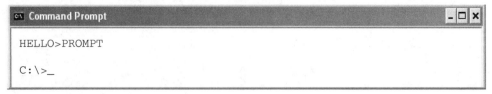

```
HELLO>PROMPT

C:\>_
```

WHAT'S ▓▓▓▓▓
▓▓▓HAPPENING?   Now you know what drive you are in. You can see the default drive, which is Drive C, displayed in the prompt.

6   Key in the following: C:\>**A:** Enter

```
Command Prompt                                    _ □ ×

C:\>A:

A:\ASTRONOMY>_
```

WHAT'S HAPPENING?   With the prompt back to the default value, you know what drive you are in, and you know what subdirectory you are in.

4.18   Subdirectory Markers

The single **.** (one period) in a subdirectory is the specific name of the current directory, which is a way to refer to the current subdirectory. The **. .** (two periods) is the specific name of the parent directory of the current subdirectory. The parent directory is the one immediately above the current subdirectory. You can use **. .** as a shorthand version of the parent directory name to move up the subdirectory tree structure. You can move up the hierarchy because a child always has only one parent. However, you cannot use a shorthand symbol to move down the hierarchy because a parent directory can have many child directories, and the operating system will have no way of knowing which child directory you are referring to.

4.19   Activity: Using Subdirectory Markers

Note: The DATA disk is in Drive A. The default drive is Drive A. The default subdirectory is **ASTRONOMY**. The prompt A:\ASTRONOMY> is displayed.

1   Key in the following: A:\ASTRONOMY>**CD . .** ⏎Enter⏎

Note: With the CD or MD commands, the space after the command (CD) and before the backslash (\) or the directory marker (. or . .) is optional.

```
Command Prompt                                    _ □ ×

A:\ASTRONOMY>CD  . .

A:\>_
```

WHAT'S HAPPENING?   You used **. .** to move up to the root directory. The root directory is the parent of the subdirectory **\ASTRONOMY**.

2   Key in the following: A:\>**MD PHYSED\GOLF** ⏎Enter⏎

```
Command Prompt                                    _ □ ×

A:\>MD  PHYSED\GOLF

A:\>_
```

WHAT'S HAPPENING?   You created a subdirectory called **GOLF** under the subdirectory called **PHYSED**. Since you were at the root directory of the DATA disk, you needed to include the relative path name, **PHYSED\GOLF**. Had you keyed in **MD \GOLF**, the **GOLF** subdirectory would have been created in the root directory because the root directory is the default directory. However, you do not need to include the path name of **PHYSED** if you change directories and make **PHYSED** the default directory.

3   Key in the following: A:\>**CD PHYSED** [Enter]

```
A:\>CD PHYSED

A:\PHYSED>_
```

WHAT'S ▨▨▨▨
▨▨▨ **HAPPENING?**   **PHYSED** is now the default directory. Any activity that occurs will automatically default to this directory, unless otherwise specified. You may use a relative path name.

4   Key in the following: A:\PHYSED>**MD DANCE** [Enter]

5   Key in the following: A:\PHYSED>**DIR** [Enter]

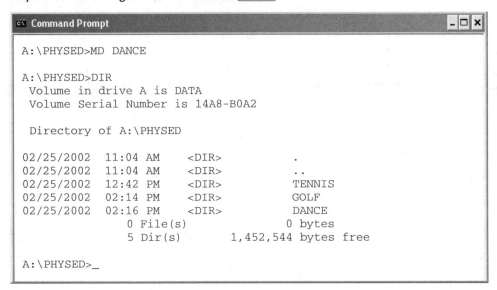

```
A:\PHYSED>MD DANCE

A:\PHYSED>DIR
 Volume in drive A is DATA
 Volume Serial Number is 14A8-B0A2

 Directory of A:\PHYSED

02/25/2002  11:04 AM    <DIR>          .
02/25/2002  11:04 AM    <DIR>          ..
02/25/2002  12:42 PM    <DIR>          TENNIS
02/25/2002  02:14 PM    <DIR>          GOLF
02/25/2002  02:16 PM    <DIR>          DANCE
               0 File(s)              0 bytes
               5 Dir(s)       1,452,544 bytes free

A:\PHYSED>_
```

WHAT'S ▨▨▨▨
▨▨▨ **HAPPENING?**   You used the relative path name. You did not have to key in the drive letter or the first backslash (the root), only the name of the directory **DANCE** that now is under the subdirectory called **PHYSED**.

6   Key in the following: A:\PHYSED>**CD DANCE** [Enter]

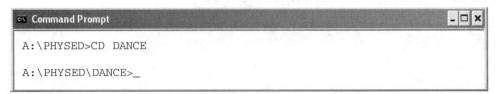

```
A:\PHYSED>CD DANCE

A:\PHYSED\DANCE>_
```

WHAT'S ▨▨▨▨
▨▨▨ **HAPPENING?**   You used the relative path to move to the subdirectory **DANCE** under **PHYSED**, which is under the root. You are going to create one more directory

under **PHYSED** called **CYCLING**, but you are going to use the subdirectory markers.

7 Key in the following: A:\PHYSED\DANCE>**MD ..\CYCLING** [Enter]

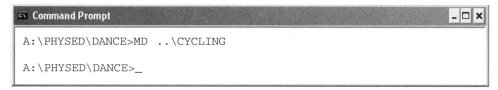

```
A:\PHYSED\DANCE>MD  ..\CYCLING

A:\PHYSED\DANCE>_
```

WHAT'S
HAPPENING?   You used the markers to move up to the parent directory of
DANCE, which is PHYSED, and you created the directory CYCLING in that directory.

8 Key in the following: A:\PHYSED\DANCE>**DIR** [Enter]

```
A:\PHYSED\DANCE>DIR
 Volume in drive A is DATA
 Volume Serial Number is 14A8-B0A2

 Directory of A:\PHYSED\DANCE

02/25/2002  02:16 PM    <DIR>          .
02/25/2002  02:16 PM    <DIR>          ..
              0 File(s)              0 bytes
              2 Dir(s)       1,452,032 bytes free

A:\PHYSED\DANCE>_
```

WHAT'S
HAPPENING?   When you keyed in the DIR command, you were looking at the
default directory **DANCE**. **CYCLING** does not appear there because you did not
put it there.

9 Key in the following: A:\PHYSED\DANCE>**DIR ..** [Enter]

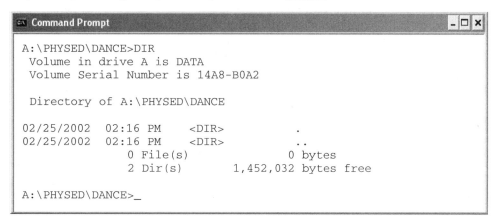

```
A:\PHYSED\DANCE>DIR ..
 Volume in drive A is DATA
 Volume Serial Number is 14A8-B0A2

 Directory of A:\PHYSED

02/25/2002  11:04 AM    <DIR>          .
02/25/2002  11:04 AM    <DIR>          ..
02/25/2002  12:42 PM    <DIR>          TENNIS
02/25/2002  02:14 PM    <DIR>          GOLF
02/25/2002  02:16 PM    <DIR>          DANCE
02/25/2002  02:18 PM    <DIR>          CYCLING
              0 File(s)              0 bytes
              6 Dir(s)       1,452,032 bytes free

A:\PHYSED\DANCE>_
```

WHAT'S ▒▒▒▒▒
▒▒▒HAPPENING?   When you keyed the DIR command followed by **. .** you looked at the parent directory of **DANCE**, which was **PHYSED**. **CYCLING**, indeed, appears there.

10 Key in the following: A:\PHYSED\DANCE>**CD .. Enter**

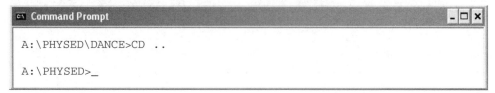

WHAT'S ▒▒▒▒▒
▒▒▒HAPPENING?   You used the subdirectory marker to move to the parent of **DANCE**, which is **PHYSED**.

11 Key in the following: A:\PHYSED>**CD\ Enter**

WHAT'S ▒▒▒▒▒
▒▒▒HAPPENING?   You moved to the root directory of the DATA disk. (You did not use a space between CD and \, as you did in the prior example; the space is optional.) Using the command **CD** or **CD ** will always take you to the root directory of the default disk. The following figures demonstrate what the DATA disk now looks like.

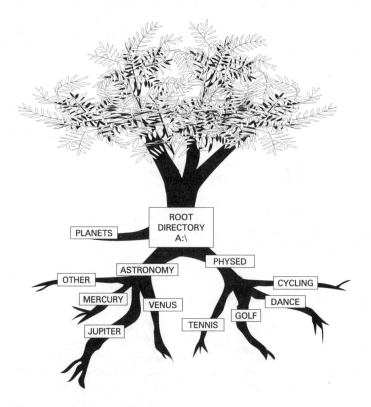

Figure 4.8—Structure of the DATA Disk

Another way to illustrate the subdirectory structure pictorially is as follows:

```
                              ROOT DIRECTORY (A:\)

                              ASTRONOMY    <DIR>
                              PHYSED       <DIR>
                              PLANETS      <DIR>


    SUBDIRECTORY (A:\ASTRONOMY)          SUBDIRECTORY (A:\PHYSED)              PLANETS

    subdirectories   MERCURY  <DIR>      subdirectories   TENNIS   <DIR>
                     JUPITER  <DIR>                       GOLF     <DIR>
                     VENUS    <DIR>                       DANCE    <DIR>
                     OTHER    <DIR>                       CYCLING  <DIR>


              A:\POLYSCI\MERCURY                    A:\PHYSED\TENNIS


              A:\POLYSCI\JUPITER                    A:\PHYSED\GOLF


              A:\POLYSCI\VENUS                      A:\PHYSED\DANCE


              A:\POLYSCI\OTHER                      A:\PHYSED\CYCLING
```

Figure 4.9—Subdirectories: Another View

4.20 Changing the Names of Directories

Prior to MS-DOS version 6.0, the only way the operating system had to rename a directory was to eliminate the old directory and create a new one. Beginning with MS-DOS version 6.0, you could use the MOVE command. In the Windows operating system, you can rename a file or a directory from Windows Explorer. To rename a directory from the Command Prompt, you can still use the MOVE command, though MOVE is not often used for this purpose. The syntax of the MOVE command to rename a directory is:

```
To rename a directory:
MOVE [/Y ¦ /-Y] [drive:][path]dirname1 dirname2
```

4.21 Activity: Using MOVE to Rename a Directory

Note: The DATA disk is in Drive A. A:\> is displayed as the default drive and the default directory.

1   Key in the following: A:\>**MOVE PHYSED GYM** [Enter]

2   Key in the following: A:\>**DIR** [Enter]

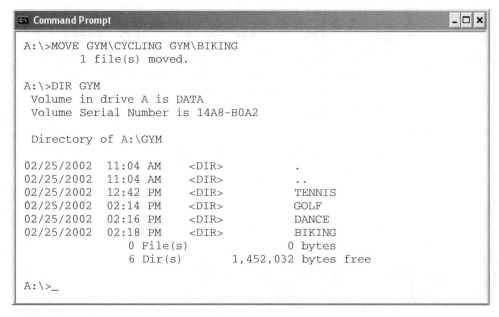

```
Command Prompt                                                      _ □ ✕

A:\>MOVE PHYSED GYM
        1 file(s) moved.

A:\>DIR
 Volume in drive A is DATA
 Volume Serial Number is 14A8-B0A2

 Directory of A:\

02/25/2002  11:04 AM    <DIR>          ASTRONOMY
02/25/2002  11:04 AM    <DIR>          GYM
02/25/2002  12:37 PM    <DIR>          PLANETS
              0 File(s)              0 bytes
              3 Dir(s)       1,452,032 bytes free

A:\>_
```

WHAT'S HAPPENING?   You used the MOVE command to change the name of the
PHYSED directory to **GYM**. You got a confirmation message on the screen that the
renaming process was successful. You then used DIR to confirm that the directory
name was changed. Indeed, **PHYSED** is no longer there, but **GYM** is.

3   Key in the following: A:\>**MOVE GYM\CYCLING GYM\BIKING** Enter

4   Key in the following: A:\>**DIR GYM** Enter

```
Command Prompt                                                      _ □ ✕

A:\>MOVE GYM\CYCLING GYM\BIKING
        1 file(s) moved.

A:\>DIR GYM
 Volume in drive A is DATA
 Volume Serial Number is 14A8-B0A2

 Directory of A:\GYM

02/25/2002  11:04 AM    <DIR>          .
02/25/2002  11:04 AM    <DIR>          ..
02/25/2002  12:42 PM    <DIR>          TENNIS
02/25/2002  02:14 PM    <DIR>          GOLF
02/25/2002  02:16 PM    <DIR>          DANCE
02/25/2002  02:18 PM    <DIR>          BIKING
              0 File(s)              0 bytes
              6 Dir(s)       1,452,032 bytes free

A:\>_
```

WHAT'S HAPPENING?   You used the MOVE command to change the name of the **CY-
CLING** directory under **GYM** to **BIKING**. Although the message says **1 file(s)
moved**, you actually renamed the directory. As long as you give the correct path
name, either absolute or relative, you can be anywhere and rename a directory. You
got a confirmation message on the screen that the renaming process was successful.
You then used DIR to confirm the name change. Indeed, **CYCLING** is no longer
there, but **BIKING** is.

4.22 Removing Directories

In the same way a disk can be cluttered with files, so can it be cluttered with subdirectories. Removing subdirectories requires a special command, the remove directory command (RD or RMDIR). As with CD and CHDIR, RD and RMDIR are exactly the same. RD is used because it requires fewer keystrokes. You cannot use the RD command to delete a directory that contains hidden or system files. Using it alone, without parameters, limits its use to empty subdirectories. In addition, you can never remove the default directory—the current directory. In order to remove a subdirectory, you must be in another directory. Furthermore, since you created the directories from the top down, you must remove them from the bottom up. This means using RD one directory at a time unless you use the /S parameter. The /S parameter allows you to traverse the directory tree from the top down. You cannot use wildcards with RD. The command syntax is:

```
RMDIR [/S] [/Q] [drive:]path
RD [/S] [/Q] [drive:]path
```

    /S   Removes all directories and files in the specified
              directory in addition to the directory itself. Used to
              remove a directory tree.

    /Q   Quiet mode, do not ask if ok to remove a directory tree
              with /S

   If you do not include the drive designator, the default drive will be used. The remove directory command will not remove the directory you are currently in (the default directory), nor can it ever remove the root directory.

4.23 Activity: Using the RD Command

Note: The DATA disk is in Drive A. A:\> is displayed as the default drive and the default directory.

1   Key in the following: A:\>**RD PLANETS** [Enter]

2   Key in the following: A:\>**DIR** [Enter]

```
A:\>RD PLANETS

A:\>DIR
 Volume in drive A is DATA
 Volume Serial Number is 14A8-B0A2

 Directory of A:\

02/25/2002  11:04 AM    <DIR>          ASTRONOMY
02/25/2002  11:04 AM    <DIR>          GYM
              0 File(s)              0 bytes
              2 Dir(s)       1,452,544 bytes free

A:\>_
```

WHAT'S ▓▓▓
▓▓▓ HAPPENING?   You, indeed, removed the directory called **PLANETS** from the root directory of the DATA disk.

3   Key in the following: A:\>**CD ASTRONOMY\OTHER** [Enter]

4   Key in the following: A:\ASTRONOMY\OTHER>**RD OTHER** [Enter]

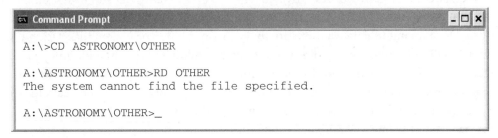

```
Command Prompt                                              _ □ ×

A:\>CD ASTRONOMY\OTHER

A:\ASTRONOMY\OTHER>RD OTHER
The system cannot find the file specified.

A:\ASTRONOMY\OTHER>_
```

WHAT'S ▓▓▓
▓▓▓ HAPPENING?   RD did not remove the directory **\ASTRONOMY\OTHER**. You got an error message. In this case, the path is valid. **OTHER** is a directory. A directory is simply a special type of file. But the OS is looking for a directory (file) named **OTHER** *in the current directory.* The current directory is \ASTRONOMY\OTHER. There is no OTHER directory in OTHER. You cannot remove a directory you are in. RD will never remove the default directory. Remember, the root directory can also never be removed.

5   Key in the following: A:\ASTRONOMY\OTHER>**CD ..** [Enter]

6   Key in the following: A:\ASTRONOMY>**DIR** [Enter]

7   Key in the following: A:\ASTRONOMY>**RD OTHER** [Enter]

8   Key in the following: A:\ASTRONOMY>**DIR** [Enter]

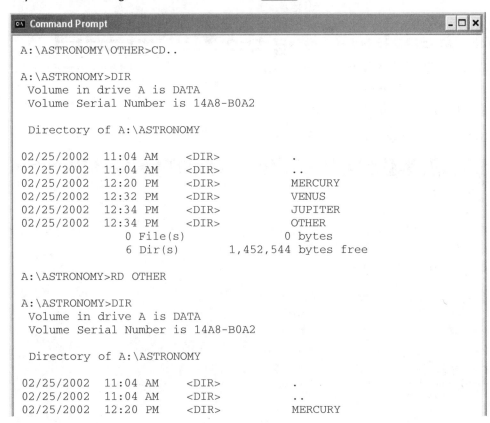

```
Command Prompt                                              _ □ ×

A:\ASTRONOMY\OTHER>CD..

A:\ASTRONOMY>DIR
 Volume in drive A is DATA
 Volume Serial Number is 14A8-B0A2

 Directory of A:\ASTRONOMY

02/25/2002  11:04 AM    <DIR>          .
02/25/2002  11:04 AM    <DIR>          ..
02/25/2002  12:20 PM    <DIR>          MERCURY
02/25/2002  12:32 PM    <DIR>          VENUS
02/25/2002  12:34 PM    <DIR>          JUPITER
02/25/2002  12:34 PM    <DIR>          OTHER
               0 File(s)              0 bytes
               6 Dir(s)      1,452,544 bytes free

A:\ASTRONOMY>RD OTHER

A:\ASTRONOMY>DIR
 Volume in drive A is DATA
 Volume Serial Number is 14A8-B0A2

 Directory of A:\ASTRONOMY

02/25/2002  11:04 AM    <DIR>          .
02/25/2002  11:04 AM    <DIR>          ..
02/25/2002  12:20 PM    <DIR>          MERCURY
```

```
02/25/2002  12:32 PM   <DIR>              VENUS
02/25/2002  12:34 PM   <DIR>              JUPITER
             0 File(s)                 0 bytes
             5 Dir(s)        1,453,056 bytes free

A:\ASTRONOMY>_
```

**WHAT'S
HAPPENING?**   You moved to the parent of **OTHER**, which is **ASTRONOMY**. You used the DIR command to see that **OTHER** was there. You then used the RD command to remove **OTHER** and the DIR command again. The subdirectory entry **OTHER** was not displayed. You did, indeed, remove it. Remember, you create directories in a hierarchical fashion, top down, and you must remove directories bottom-up using RD without parameters. If **OTHER** had a subdirectory beneath it, such as **OTHER\ASTEROIDS**, you would have needed to remove the **ASTEROIDS** subdirectory before you could remove the **OTHER** subdirectory.

9   Key in the following: A:\ASTRONOMY>**CD** \ Enter

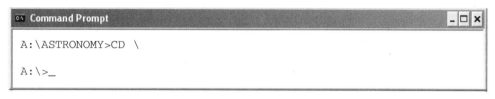

```
A:\ASTRONOMY>CD \

A:\>_
```

**WHAT'S
HAPPENING?**   You have moved to the root directory of the DATA disk.

4.24 Deleting a Directory and Its Subdirectories

The RD command is useful for deleting an empty directory, but what if you want to delete a directory and its contents with a single command? This can be done by using the parameter /S with the RD command. The syntax is as follows:

```
RMDIR [drive:]path [/S] [/Q]
```

or

```
RD [drive:]path [/S] [/Q]
```

The variable /S will remove the specified directory and all subdirectories, including any files. It is used to remove a tree. The variable /Q means to run RD in quiet mode. Adding this variable will make your system delete directories without confirmation.

4.25 Activity: Using RD with the /S Parameter

Note: The DATA disk is in Drive A. The Command Prompt window is open, and A:\> is displayed as the default drive and the default directory.

1   Key in the following: A:\>**DIR GYM /S** Enter

```
Command Prompt                                                      _ □ ×

A:\>DIR GYM /S
 Volume in drive A is DATA
 Volume Serial Number is 14A8-B0A2

 Directory of A:\GYM

02/25/2002  11:04 AM    <DIR>          .
02/25/2002  11:04 AM    <DIR>          ..
02/25/2002  12:42 PM    <DIR>          TENNIS
02/25/2002  02:14 PM    <DIR>          GOLF
02/25/2002  02:16 PM    <DIR>          DANCE
02/25/2002  02:18 PM    <DIR>          BIKING
               0 File(s)              0 bytes

 Directory of A:\GYM\TENNIS

02/25/2002  12:42 PM    <DIR>          .
02/25/2002  12:42 PM    <DIR>          ..
               0 File(s)              0 bytes

 Directory of A:\GYM\GOLF

02/25/2002  02:14 PM    <DIR>          .
02/25/2002  02:14 PM    <DIR>          ..
               0 File(s)              0 bytes

 Directory of A:\GYM\DANCE

02/25/2002  02:16 PM    <DIR>          .
Press any key to continue . . .
02/25/2002  02:16 PM    <DIR>          ..
               0 File(s)              0 bytes

 Directory of A:\GYM\BIKING

02/25/2002  02:18 PM    <DIR>          .
02/25/2002  02:18 PM    <DIR>          ..
               0 File(s)              0 bytes

    Total Files Listed:
               0 File(s)              0 bytes
              14 Dir(s)      1,453,056 bytes free

A:\>_
```

WHAT'S HAPPENING?   In your display, the beginning information will have scrolled off the screen. You can see that there are no files in **GYM** or any of its subdirectories. Therefore, there is nothing in **GYM** that you wish to keep.

2   Key in the following: A:\>**RD GYM /S** [Enter]

```
Command Prompt                                                      _ □ ×

A:\>RD GYM /S
GYM, Are you sure (Y/N)? _
```

WHAT'S HAPPENING?   You get a chance to back out of the RD /S command by pressing **N** for "No." In this case, you do want to proceed.

3   Press **Y** Enter

```
GYM, Are you sure (Y/N)? Y
A:\>_
```

WHAT'S HAPPENING?   The RD /S command deleted **GYM**. You can use the DIR command to confirm that **GYM** is gone.

4   Key in the following: A:\>**DIR** Enter

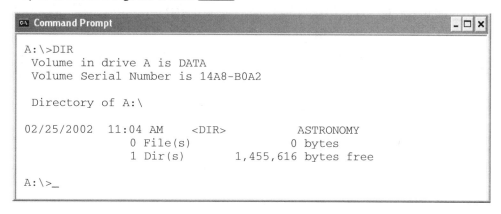

```
A:\>DIR
 Volume in drive A is DATA
 Volume Serial Number is 14A8-B0A2

 Directory of A:\

02/25/2002  11:04 AM    <DIR>          ASTRONOMY
              0 File(s)              0 bytes
              1 Dir(s)       1,455,616 bytes free

A:\>_
```

WHAT'S HAPPENING?   You removed **GYM** and all its subdirectories with one command. RD /S is very useful, very fast, very powerful, and *very dangerous*.

4.26 Using Multiple Parameters with MD and RD

You can make or remove more than one directory on the same command line. Both RD and MD allow you to create or remove more than one directory with one command line. In addition, the MD command allows you to create a parent and a child directory with one command. If the parent directory does not exist, the OS will create the child directories and any necessary intermediate directories.

4.27 Activity: Using Multiple Parameters with MD and RD

1   Key in the following: A:\>**MD FIRST SECOND** Enter

2   Key in the following: A:\>**DIR** Enter

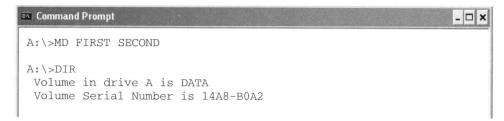

```
A:\>MD FIRST SECOND

A:\>DIR
 Volume in drive A is DATA
 Volume Serial Number is 14A8-B0A2
```

```
Directory of A:\

02/25/2002   11:04 AM    <DIR>            ASTRONOMY
02/25/2002   03:05 PM    <DIR>            FIRST
02/25/2002   03:05 PM    <DIR>            SECOND
                 0 File(s)           0 bytes
                 3 Dir(s)     1,454,592 bytes free

A:\>_
```

WHAT'S
HAPPENING?   Both subdirectories were created.

3   Key in the following: A:\>**RD FIRST SECOND** [Enter]

4   Key in the following: A:\>**DIR** [Enter]

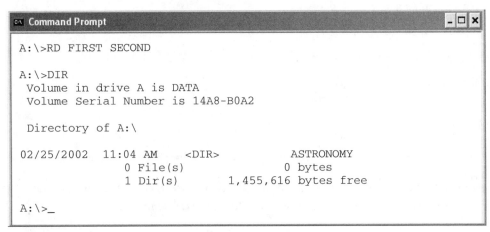

```
CA Command Prompt                                            _ □ ×

A:\>RD FIRST SECOND

A:\>DIR
 Volume in drive A is DATA
 Volume Serial Number is 14A8-B0A2

 Directory of A:\

02/25/2002   11:04 AM    <DIR>            ASTRONOMY
                 0 File(s)           0 bytes
                 1 Dir(s)     1,455,616 bytes free

A:\>_
```

WHAT'S
HAPPENING?   Both subdirectories were removed.

5   Key in the following: A:\>**MD THIS\THAT\WHAT** [Enter]

6   Key in the following: A:\>**DIR THIS /S** [Enter]

```
CA Command Prompt                                            _ □ ×

A:\>DIR THIS /S
 Volume in drive A is DATA
 Volume Serial Number is 14A8-B0A2

 Directory of A:\THIS

02/25/2002   03:07 PM    <DIR>            .
02/25/2002   03:07 PM    <DIR>            ..
02/25/2002   03:07 PM    <DIR>            THAT
                 0 File(s)           0 bytes

 Directory of A:\THIS\THAT

02/25/2002   03:07 PM    <DIR>            .
02/25/2002   03:07 PM    <DIR>            ..
02/25/2002   03:07 PM    <DIR>            WHAT
                 0 File(s)           0 bytes

 Directory of A:\THIS\THAT\WHAT

02/25/2002   03:07 PM    <DIR>            .
02/25/2002   03:07 PM    <DIR>            ..
                 0 File(s)           0 bytes
```

```
      Total Files Listed:
               0 File(s)                    0 bytes
               8 Dir(s)        1,454,080 bytes free

A:\>_
```

WHAT'S ▒▒▒▒▒
▒▒▒**HAPPENING?**   When you created the child directory **WHAT**, it had no existing parent directories (**THIS\THAT**). Since **THIS** and **THAT** had to exist before WHAT could be created, the OS created them for you.

7   Key in the following: A:\>**RD THIS /S /Q** ⌷Enter⌷

8   Key in A:\>**DIR** ⌷Enter⌷

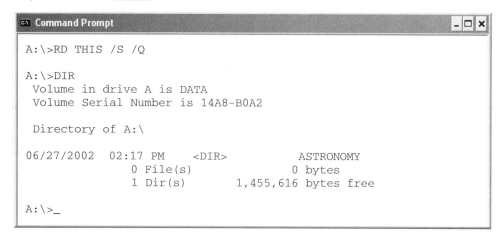

```
⌨ Command Prompt                                                    ▬◻✕

A:\>RD THIS /S /Q

A:\>DIR
 Volume in drive A is DATA
 Volume Serial Number is 14A8-B0A2

 Directory of A:\

06/27/2002  02:17 PM    <DIR>              ASTRONOMY
               0 File(s)                    0 bytes
               1 Dir(s)        1,455,616 bytes free

A:\>_
```

WHAT'S ▒▒▒▒▒
▒▒▒**HAPPENING?**   You used the /S parameter to remove the entire directory structure for the **THIS** directory. In addition, you used the /Q parameter so that you would not be prompted for confirmation of the deletion of the directories. Note, you could also have stated the command **RD /S /Q THIS** as in the case of the RD command, the order does not matter.

4.28 Understanding the PATH Command

You have, so far, changed the current or default subdirectory using the CD command, which works well for locating various data files. In addition, in this chapter you executed the application program, BOG. You changed to the subdirectory where program file was located. You needed to do this in order to execute or run the program.

The process of executing a program is simple and always the same. You key in the file name of the program, and the operating system looks for the file first in memory. If you keyed in DIR, for example, that program is in memory, and, since it is an internal program, the OS would look no further. If you keyed in BOG, it would not find it in memory, and the operating system would look for the file only in the current default drive and directory. First, it would look for BOG.COM. If no file by that name existed, it would look for BOG.EXE. If it found no file by that name, its last search would be for BOG.BAT. If it found no file by any of those names, it would return an error message. That would be the operating system's way of telling you it could not find a file by one of those names in the current drive or directory.

If the OS found a file with the correct name, as it did with BOG.EXE, it would take a copy of the file, place it in memory, and turn control over to that application program. A program is executed at the command prompt in this way. In the Windows GUI, you double-click the icon or choose an item off a menu to execute a program. However, the GUI is just a pretty face that does *exactly* what you did from the command prompt. When you work from the Windows interface, the Windows operating system first looks in memory and then on the disk for the program. The only difference is that when a program is installed through the GUI interface, the program tells the Windows operating system where it is being installed and what the path to the program is. Windows then keeps track of the location of the file. If there were an error in installation or a program file was somehow moved, Windows would not be able to execute the program because the path would be incorrect. Windows has a hard time fixing its mistakes; that is why managing Windows at the system level is so important.

The operating system's search for the correct file is limited to the following file extensions in the order listed:

Extension	Meaning
.COM	Command file
.EXE	Executable file
.BAT	Batch file
.CMD	Command script file
.VBS	VBScript file (Visual Basic)
.VBE	VBScript Encoded Script file (Visual Basic)
.JS	JScript file (JavaScript)
.JSE	JScript Encoded Script file (JavaScript)
.WSF	Windows Script file
.WSH	Windows Script Host Settings file

If the command interpreter does not find any of these in your default drive and directory, it then searches your search path as set in the PATH statement, in the file extension order listed above. If your file name does not meet any of these criteria, then you see the error message, "Filename is not recognized as an internal or external command, operable program or batch file."

These are the only file extensions that indicate programs and are sometimes called *executables*. You have previously executed programs. You have also used external commands such as FORMAT, DISKCOPY, and MOVE, which, being external commands, are also programs stored as files with either a .COM or .EXE file extension. These are examples of the system's utility files. They are just programs you want to execute (executables). When you use these programs, you do not have to key in C: and then CD\WINDOWS\SYSTEM32 in order to execute them.

Why, then, when the root of the directory was the default drive and default directory, did those commands work? The files were not on the DATA disk. Based on this information, since those files were not in the default drive and subdirectory, you should have seen an error message. Why didn't this happen? Because of the PATH command.

The PATH command sets a *search path* to other drives and directories. This command tells the system what other drives and directories you want it to look in for a program file not in the current drive or directory. The PATH command looks only for program files that can be executed. All this means is that, when you key in a command and you have set the path, the operating system will search for the program first in memory, second in the current directory, and then in the subdirectories you have specified with the PATH command. When it finds the program, it will load and execute it. You can set the path for command files to another subdirectory or disk drive. In the Windows operating system, the default PATH includes the subdirectory where the system utility files are located—C:\WINDOWS\SYSTEM32. The command syntax for the path command is as follows:

```
PATH [[drive:]path[;...][;%PATH%]]
PATH ;

Type PATH ; to clear all search-path settings and direct cmd.exe to
search only in the current directory.
Type PATH without parameters to display the current path.
Including %PATH% in the new path setting causes the old path to be
appended to the new setting.
```

PATH is the command. PATH with no parameters displays the current path. Choosing a *drive*: indicates which drive designator you want the path to follow. If you omit the drive designator, the default drive will be used. You can have more than one subdirectory in the search path by using the semicolon (;) between each path element (with no spaces between the semicolon and the paths). The semicolon (;) used as the only parameter, without the drive or path, cancels any paths you have set. The current path is represented by %PATH%.

4.29   Activity: Using the PATH Command

WARNING: Do not do this activity if you are on a network unless instructed to do so or until you have cleared it with your lab technician.

Note: The DATA disk is in Drive A. A:\> is displayed as the default drive and the default directory.

1   Key in the following: A:\>**PATH > HOLDPATH.BAT** Enter

WHAT'S
HAPPENING?   You have captured the current path and placed it in a batch file called **HOLDPATH.BAT**. Doing activities with the PATH command will destroy the path that is set up in your lab environment. By placing the current path in a batch file, you will be able to return to the proper path when the activities are done. Batch files will be discussed later in this text.

2   Key in the following: A:\>**DIR** Enter

```
Command Prompt                                                  _ □ ×

A:\>DIR
 Volume in drive A is DATA
 Volume Serial Number is 14A8-B0A2

 Directory of A:\

02/25/2002  11:04 AM    <DIR>          ASTRONOMY
03/04/2002  08:15 AM                56 HOLDPATH.BAT
              1 File(s)              56 bytes
              1 Dir(s)       1,455,104 bytes free

A:\>_
```

**WHAT'S
HAPPENING?**   You now have the file **HOLDPATH.BAT** on the root of the DATA
disk. With this file, you will later be able to return the path to where it was set by
your lab administrator.

3   Key in the following: A:\>**PATH** Enter

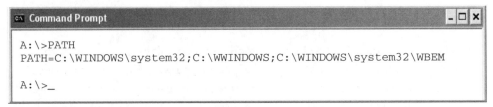

```
Command Prompt                                                  _ □ ×

A:\>PATH
PATH=C:\WINDOWS\system32;C:\WWINDOWS;C:\WINDOWS\system32\WBEM

A:\>_
```

**WHAT'S
HAPPENING?**   You have displayed the current search path. Your display may be
different depending on what programs you have on your disk and their locations.

4   (Note that a semicolon follows the command PATH in this step.) Key in the
following: A:\>**PATH;** Enter

5   Key in the following: A:\>**PATH** Enter

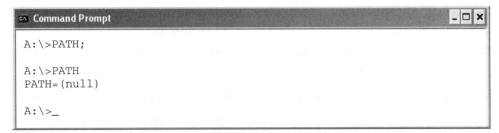

```
Command Prompt                                                  _ □ ×

A:\>PATH;

A:\>PATH
PATH=(null)

A:\>_
```

**WHAT'S
HAPPENING?**   By using the semicolon (;) following the command word PATH,
you eliminated all possible existing search paths. The second PATH command, with
no parameters, showed that there is now no path set.

6   Key in the following: A:\>**PATH C:\WUGXP\GAMES\MATCH32** Enter

Note: Remember, if the system utility programs are in a subdirectory on the hard
          disk other than **C:\WINDOWS\SYSTEM32**, you must key in the appro-
          priate path name. Refer to your Configuration Table in Chapter 1,
          section 1.6.

7   Key in the following: A:\>**PATH** Enter

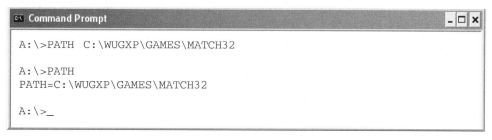

WHAT'S HAPPENING?   When you first keyed in the **PATH C:\WUGXP\GAMES\MATCH32** command, it appeared that nothing happened, but something did. The second PATH command shows that you have set a path the operating system will search. If it does not find a command (file) in the default drive and subdirectory, in this case A:\, it will go to the path set, the subdirectory called **\WUGXP\GAMES\MATCH32** under the root directory of Drive C.

8 Key in the following: A:\>**BOG** [Enter]

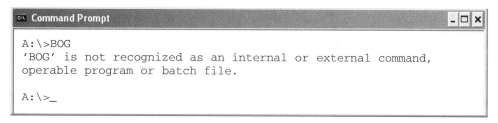

WHAT'S HAPPENING?   Bog is a game program, but it is not located in the root of the A drive nor in the **\WUGXP\GAMES\MATCH32** subdirectory. So, even though the search path is set, it is not set to the directory that holds the **BOG.EXE** file. In the beginning of this chapter, you found that this program was located in the **C:\WUGXP\GAMES\BOG2** directory and was called **BOG.EXE**. You had to change drives and directories in order to execute the program. If you do not want to change the default drive and subdirectory to use this program, you can use the PATH command instead.

9 Key in the following: A:\>**MATCH32** [Enter]

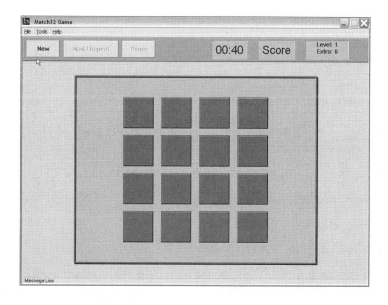

WHAT'S
HAPPENING?   You set the search path to the **C:\WUGXP\GAMES\MATCH32** subdirectory on the hard disk, and so the Match32 game was found and executed.

10 Click **File**. Click **Exit**.

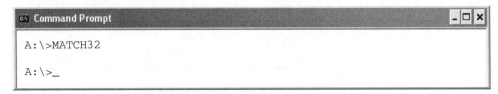

```
A:\>MATCH32

A:\>_
```

WHAT'S
HAPPENING?   You exited the MATCH32 program. By setting the path to **C:\WUGXP\GAMES\MATCH32,** you canceled the path that included the **C:\WINDOWS\SYSTEM32** subdirectory, where the utility files reside. You do not have to replace an existing PATH to change it. You can add to, or append to the path.

11 Key in the following: A:\>**HOLDPATH** Enter

12 Key in the following: A:\>**PATH** Enter

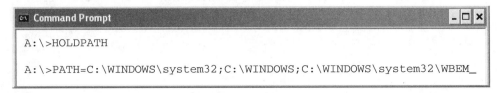

```
A:\>HOLDPATH

A:\>PATH=C:\WINDOWS\system32;C:\WINDOWS;C:\WINDOWS\system32\WBEM_
```

WHAT'S
HAPPENING?   By executing the HOLDPATH batch file, you returned the path to the default.

13 Key in the following:
A:\>**PATH=%PATH%;C:\WUGXP\GAMES\MATCH32** Enter

Note: Elements of the path are separated by a semi-colon (;) %PATH% is the way you refer to the existing path.

14 Key in the following: A:\>**PATH** Enter

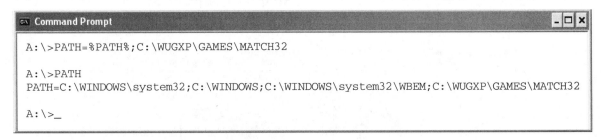

```
A:\>PATH=%PATH%;C:\WUGXP\GAMES\MATCH32

A:\>PATH
PATH=C:\WINDOWS\system32;C:\WINDOWS;C:\WINDOWS\system32\WBEM;C:\WUGXP\GAMES\MATCH32

A:\>_
```

WHAT'S
HAPPENING?   You have added the directory where the game MATCH32 is stored to the existing path.

15 Click the ☒ in the upper-right corner of the Command window to close it.

16 Open another Command line window.

17 Key in the following: C:\>**A:** Enter

18 Key in the following: A:\>**PATH** Enter

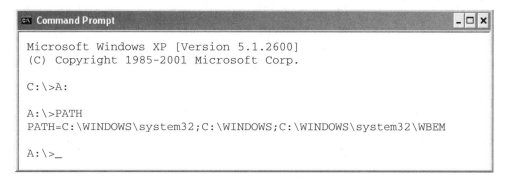

WHAT'S HAPPENING? You are back to the default path. Paths set in a command line window are in effect only through that session. When you close the window, the session ends, and the path returns to the default.

19 Key in the following: A:\>**DEL HOLDPATH.BAT** Enter

20 Key in the following: A:\>**C:** Enter

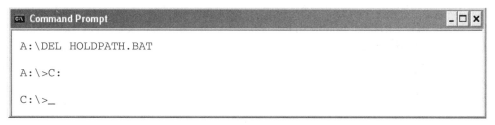

WHAT'S HAPPENING? You have deleted the **HOLDPATH.BAT** file and changed the default directory to the hard drive C.

21 Execute the Windows shut-down procedure.

Chapter Summary

1. Software designed for use with Windows operates in protected mode.
2. When running software created for older versions of DOS or Windows 3.x, Windows operates in real mode.
3. Subdirectories are created to help organize files on a disk as well as to defeat the number-of-files limitation of the root directory imposed by FAT16.
4. Whenever a disk is formatted, one directory is always created. It is called the root directory.
5. MD is an internal command that allows the user to create a subdirectory.
6. Subdirectory-naming conventions follow Windows file-naming conventions. Programs written for previous versions of DOS and Windows follow the "eight-dot-three" file-naming convention.
7. A <DIR> next to a file name indicates that it is a subdirectory.
8. CD is an internal command that, when keyed in by itself, will show the user the current or default directory.
9. CD followed by a directory name will change the current directory to the named directory.
10. CD used with the /D parameter will allow you to change drives at the same time you change directories.

11. When managing subdirectories and file names, you must use the backslash (\) as a delimiter to separate subdirectory and/or file names.

12. You may use either an absolute path name or a relative path name. The absolute path name is the entire subdirectory name or names. The relative path requires only the path name relative to your current directory.

13. The way the prompt looks can be changed using the PROMPT command. The PROMPT command followed by a text string will show that text.

14. The PROMPT command has metastrings. When included following the PROMPT command, the metastrings will return a value. For instance, the metastrings PG will set the prompt to display the default drive and subdirectory. To return the prompt to the default value, key in PROMPT with no parameters.

15. Subdirectory markers, also called dot notation, are shortcuts to using subdirectories. The single dot (.) represents the current directory itself. The double dot (..) represents the name of the parent directory.

16. You can move up the tree with subdirectory markers, but not down the tree.

17. The MOVE command allows you to rename subdirectories.

18. RD is an internal command that allows users to eliminate subdirectories.

19. Subdirectories must be empty of files before you can use the RD command without parameters.

20. The root directory can never be eliminated.

21. RD used with the /S parameter allows you to remove an entire directory, including all its files and subdirectories, with one command.

22. PATH is an internal command that allows you to tell the operating system on what disk and in what subdirectory to search for command files.

23. PATH keyed in by itself will display the current path.

24. PATH keyed in with a semicolon following it will cancel the path.

Key Terms

absolute path	executable	real mode
child directory	hierarchical structure	relative path
current directory	legacy software	root directory
device driver	metastring	search path
dot (.)	parent directory	subdirectory marker
dot notation	path	tree structure
double dot (..)	protected mode	

Discussion Questions

1. List three of the major categories of application software and briefly explain their functions.

2. What is the purpose and function of a program file (application program)?

3. Explain the purpose and function of the operating system when working with program files and data files.

4. Briefly explain the difference between real-mode and protected-mode operation.

5. Explain documentation, update notices, and technical support.

6. Name at least three file extensions that indicate an executable program.

7. What is the purpose and function of the root directory? What symbol is used to represent the root directory?
8. What is a subdirectory?
9. Why would you want to create a subdirectory?
10. What is a parent directory?
11. Explain the purpose and function of three directory management commands.
12. Give the syntax for creating a subdirectory.
13. Give the syntax for the CD command.
14. What is the difference between an absolute path and a relative path?
15. If you wanted to create a subdirectory called **JAIL** under the subdirectory called **COURT** on Drive A:, would you get the same result by keying in either **MD A:\COURT\JAIL** or **MD A:\JAIL**? Why or why not?
16. What are subdirectory markers? How can they be used?
17. What are metastrings?
18. How can you return the prompt to the default value? Would you want to? Why or why not?
19. Explain the purpose and function of the MOVE command. Explain each part of the syntax.
20. Why will the RD command without parameters not remove a directory if there is a file in it?
21. What steps must be followed to remove a directory with RD?
22. What is the purpose and function of the PATH command?
23. How can you cancel the current path?
24. How can you set a multiple search path?
25. What is the difference between the path to a file and using the PATH command?

True/False Questions

For each question, circle the letter T if the statement is true and the letter F if the statement is false.

T   F   1. A subdirectory can hold a maximum of 112 files.
T   F   2. The RD /S command deletes a specified directory structure and all the files and subdirectories beneath it.
T   F   3. The MOVE command allows you to delete subdirectories.
T   F   4. If the default directory is the root directory, you do not need to include the path name for creating a new subdirectory under a subdirectory called **MEDIA**.
T   F   5. The double dot is a shorthand name for the parent directory.

Completion Questions

Write the correct answer in each blank space.

6. Two files can have the same name on the same disk so long as they are in _____ subdirectories.
7. When using MOVE to rename a directory, you need to use two parameters: the old directory name and the _____ directory name.
8. If the current default subdirectory is MEDIA, the directory above MEDIA is known as the _____ directory.

9. When looking at a directory display, you can identify a subdirectory because the name appears with _____ by it.

10. To place the current path in a batch file called HOLDPATH.BAT, you would key in _____ .

Multiple Choice Questions

For each question, write the letter for the correct answer in the blank space.

____   11. Formatting a floppy disk automatically creates
       a. subdirectories.
       b. a root directory.
       c. command files.
       d. none of the above

____   12. A subdirectory is created by using the
       a. MD command.
       b. CD command.
       c. MAKEDIR command.
       d. both a and c

____   13. When you create subdirectories under existing subdirectories,
       a. omitting the drive designator or path name means that the operating system will perform the task using the default values.
       b. omitting the new subdirectory name means that the operating system will name the new subdirectory after its parent directory.
       c. you must return to the root directory.
       d. no more than 32 subdirectories may be contained in any one subdirectory.

____   14. One of the major purposes in creating subdirectories is to be able to
       a. use the DIR command.
       b. use relative and absolute paths.
       c. group files together logically.
       d. none of the above

____   15. When you create subdirectories, you are allowed
       a. eight characters in the subdirectory name.
       b. to use the same naming conventions as for files.
       c. to save as many files as the disk space will allow.
       d. both b and c

Writing Commands

Write the correct steps or commands to perform the required action as if you were at the computer. The prompt will indicate the default drive and directory. *Use the relative path whenever possible.*

16. Locate the file called **BETTE.TXT** in the **ARCHIE** directory that is under **COMICS**.

```
A:\COMICS>
```

17. Display the name of the current directory.

```
A:\TEXT>
```

18. Change the prompt to = followed by the greater-than sign.
    ```
    A:\>
    ```

19. Locate the file called **FISH.FIL** in the parent directory of the default directory using subdirectory markers.
    ```
    C:\ZOO\AQUARIUM>
    ```

20. Set up a search path that will look in the root directory of Drive C, and then the \BOOK directory also located on Drive C.
    ```
    A:\TEXT>
    ```

Homework Assignments

Note 1:   Remember, if you are logged on to a network, do not use the PATH command without instructions and/or assistance from your lab administrator.

Note 2:   You will format a new disk, the HOMEWORK disk.

CAUTION: You will not use the DATA disk. The DATA disk will be used only for the chapter activities. You will format a new disk, called the HOMEWORK disk, and this disk will be used for the Homework Assignments.

Note 3:   The homework problems will use Drive A as the drive where the HOMEWORK disk is located.

Note 4:   The homework problems will use the **WINDOWS\SYSTEM32** subdirectory as the directory where the operating system utility files are located. If you have a different drive or directory, substitute that drive or directory.

Note 5:   Windows is running, and you have shelled out to the Command Prompt window. The visible prompt is C:\>.

Problem Set I—At the Computer

Problem A

A-a   **Do not use the DATA disk for these homework problems.**

A-b   Write your name and the word "HOMEWORK" on a label for a blank disk or a disk you no longer want; then insert the disk in Drive A. Be *sure* either the disk is blank or you no longer need the data that it contains. Everything on it will be eliminated after you press the [Enter] key.

A-c   Key in the following: C:\>**FORMAT A: /V:HOMEWORK** [Enter]

A-d   Press [Enter]

A-e   When the message appears asking if you wish to format another disk, press **N** [Enter]

A-f   Key in the following: C:\>**A:** [Enter]

A-g   With the root directory of the HOMEWORK disk as the default, use the *relative* path to create a directory called **NEW** on the HOMEWORK disk.

____   1. What command did you use to create the directory?
      a. MD NEW
      b. MD C:\NEW
      c. CD NEW
      d. CD C:\NEW

A-h   Using the *relative* path, make **NEW** the default directory.

____   2. What command did you use to make **NEW** the default directory?
      a. MD NEW
      b. MD C:\NEW
      c. CD NEW
      d. CD C:\NEW

A-i   Do a directory listing of the default directory.

____   3. Look at the directory display. How many bytes do the two directories occupy?
      a. 2,048
      b. 1,024
      c. 512
      d. none of the above

A-j   Remove the **NEW** directory.

____   4. What command did you execute *first*?
      a. RD NEW
      b. CD NEW
      c. RD \
      d. CD \

Problem B

B-a   Change the prompt so it reads only **HELLO THERE**.

____   5. What command did you use?
      a. PROMPT PG
      b. PROMPT HELLO THERE
      c. PROMPT $HELLO $THERE
      d. none of the above

B-b   Key in the following: **PROMPT VG** [Enter]

____   6. What word is included in the prompt?
      a. Version
      b. Date
      c. Time
      d. Volume

B-c   Key in the following: **PROMPT** [Enter]

Problem C

C-a   Get help on the PROMPT command.

_____   7. What symbol will display the = sign in the prompt?
   a. $D
   b. $E
   c. $Q
   d. $T

C-b   Key in the following: **PROMPT D_PG** [Enter]

_____   8. What appears in the prompt?
   a. the current OS version
   b. the current date
   c. the current time
   d. the current volume label

C-c   Key in the following: **PROMPT** [Enter]

C-d   Key in the following: **CD ASTRONOMY** [Enter]

_____   9. What message appears?
   a. Incorrect DOS version.
   b. Invalid subdirectory.
   c. The system cannot find the path specified.
   d. Invalid command.

Problem D

D-a   With the root directory of the HOMEWORK disk as the default, create a directory called **HISTORY** off the root.

D-b   With the root directory of the HOMEWORK disk as the default, create two subdirectories under **HISTORY**. One will be called **US**, and the other will be called **EUROPE**.

D-c   With the root directory of the HOMEWORK disk as the default, create a directory called **OLD** off the root.

D-d   Make **OLD** the default directory.

D-e   With **OLD** as the default directory, create a subdirectory called **LETTERS** under the **\HISTORY\US** subdirectory.

_____   10. What command did you use?
   a. MD LETTERS
   b. MD HISTORY\LETTERS
   c. MD HISTORY\US\LETTERS
   d. MD \HISTORY\US\LETTERS

D-f   With **OLD** as the default directory, remove the subdirectory called **LETTERS** that you just created.

____ 11. The command you used was:
   a. CD LETTERS
   b. CD HISTORY\LETTERS
   c. RD HISTORY\US\LETTERS
   d. RD \HISTORY\US\LETTERS

D-g   Use the subdirectory markers to move to the parent directory of **OLD**.

____ 12. The command you used was:
   a. CD ..
   b. CD \
   c. MD..
   d. MD \

____ 13. The parent of **OLD** is:
   a. HISTORY
   b. LETTERS
   c. the root of the HOMEWORK disk—the \
   d. the root of the hard disk—the \

D-h   Remove the directory **OLD**.

____ 14. Which of the following command(s) could you have used?
   a. RD OLD
   b. RD \OLD
   c. both a and b
   d. neither a nor b

Problem E

E-a   Create a directory called **PHONE** under the root directory of the HOMEWORK disk.

E-b   With the root directory as the default directory, create two subdirectories under the **PHONE** directory called **BUSINESS** and **PERSONAL**.

____ 15. The command you used to create **PERSONAL** was:
   a. MD PERSONAL
   b. MD \PERSONAL
   c. MD PHONE\PERSONAL or MD \PHONE\PERSONAL
   d. MD PERSONAL\PHONE or MD \PERSONAL\PHONE

E-c   Do a directory listing of the **PHONE** directory.

____ 16. How many files and directories are listed?
   a. 0 File(s)
      2 Dir(s)
   b. 0 File(s)
      4 Dir(s)
   c. 4 File(s)
      4 Dir(s)
   d. 2 File(s)
      2 Dir(s)

E-d   Using the relative path, change the default directory to **PHONE**.

____   17. The command you used was:
- a. CD PHONE
- b. MD PHONE
- c. RD PHONE

E-e   With **PHONE** as the current default directory, use the relative path to change the default directory to **BUSINESS**.

____   18. The command you used was:
- a. CD \PHONE
- b. CD \BUSINESS
- c. CD BUSINESS
- d. RD BUSINESS

E-f   Use the subdirectory markers to move to the parent directory of **BUSINESS**.

____   19. The command you used was:
- a. CD ..
- b. CD \
- c. MD ..
- d. MD \

____   20. The parent of **BUSINESS** is:
- a. PERSONAL
- b. PHONE
- c. the root directory of the HOMEWORK disk—the \
- d. none of the above

E-g   Move to the root directory of the HOMEWORK disk.

____   21. The command you used was:
- a. CD ROOT
- b. CD \..
- c. CD ..\
- d. CD \

Problem F

F-a   With the root directory as the default directory, create a directory called **BOOKS** under the root of the HOMEWORK disk.

____   22. Which of the following command(s) could you have used?
- a. MD BOOKS
- b. MD \BOOKS
- c. either a or b
- d. neither a nor b

F-b   With the root directory as the default directory, create two subdirectories under the **BOOKS** directory called **MYSTERY** and **LITERATURE**.

____   23. Which of the following command(s) could you have used to create the
        MYSTERY subdirectory?
        a. MD BOOKS\MYSTERY
        b. MD \BOOKS\LITERATURE\MYSTERY
        c. either a or b
        d. neither a nor b

F-c   With the root directory as the default directory and using the method learned
        in this chapter, rename the **LITERATURE** directory to **AM_LIT**.

____   24. Which of the following command(s) could you have used to rename
        LITERATURE?
        a. MOVE \BOOKS \BOOKS\AM_LIT
        b. MOVE LITERATURE MYSTERY
        c. MOVE BOOKS\LITERATURE BOOKS\AM_LIT
        d. either a or c

F-d   Use the RD command to remove the **BOOKS** directory in one step.

____   25. What parameter did you use?
        a. /N
        b. /O
        c. /S
        d. none

____   26. If you wanted to know what the current path was on your system, what
        command would you use?
        a. DIR
        b. PATH
        c. PATH /?
        d. PATH ?/

Problem Set II—At the Computer

Problem A

A-a   With the root directory of the HOMEWORK disk as the default, create a
        directory called **CLASS**.

        1. Write the command(s) you used to create the directory.

A-b   Make **CLASS** the default directory.

        2. Write the command(s) you used to change the default directory to **CLASS**.

A-c   Change the default directory to the root of the HOMEWORK disk.

A-d   With the root of the HOMEWORK disk as the default directory, using the
        relative path, rename **CLASS** to **ORDERS**.

        3. Write any message(s) that appeared on the screen.

4. Write the command(s) you used to rename the directory.

A-e   Remove the directory called **ORDERS**.

5. Write the command(s) you used to remove the directory.

Problem B

B-a   Key in the following: A:\>**PROMPT TP$G** [Enter]

6. Look at the screen display and write the displayed prompt.

B-b   Key in the following: **PROMPT** [Enter]

7. Look at the screen display and write the displayed prompt.

Problem Set III—Brief Essay

1. A friend is watching you work at the command line. You key in the following:
   C:\WINDOWS>**CD **
   C:\>**A:**
   A:\>**CD HOUSE\UTILS**
   A:\HOUSE\UTILS>**DIR**
   A:\HOUSE\UTILS>**DIR \HOMEWORK\PROBLEM**
   Your friend asks you how you know when and where to place the backslashes.
   Explain to her how to determine the positioning of the backslashes and the
   differences between the placements. Include a brief description of relative and
   absolute paths.
2. Windows, and thus the command prompt, uses a hierarchical filing system.
   Briefly describe this system and justify why it is used.

CHAPTER 5

INTERNAL COMMANDS:
COPY AND TYPE

Learning Objectives

After completing this chapter you will be able to:

1. Explain the purpose and function of internal commands.
2. Explain the purpose and function of the COPY command.
3. List the file-naming rules.
4. Explain the purpose and function of the TYPE command.
5. Explain when and how to use wildcards with the COPY command.
6. Explain the purpose and use of subdirectory markers.
7. Identify the commands that can be used with subdirectories.
8. Explain when and how files are overwritten.
9. Explain the function, purpose, and dangers of concatenating files.
10. Explain setting up Command Line printing in a network lab environment.
11. Compare and contrast printing files using the TYPE and COPY commands.

5. Use wildcards with the COPY command to copy files on the same disk to a different subdirectory.
6. Use the COPY and DIR commands with subdirectories.
7. Use subdirectory markers with commands.
8. Overwrite a file using the COPY command.
9. Combine the contents of two or more files using the COPY command.
10. Explain setting up Command Line printing in some networked lab environments.
11. Print files.

Student Outcomes

1. Copy a file on the same disk using the COPY command.
2. Use wildcards with the COPY command to copy files on the same disk.
3. Display a text file using the TYPE command.
4. Use the COPY command to make additional files on the same disk but in different subdirectories.

Chapter Overview

In this chapter you will review the Windows operating system rules used to create unique names for files and learn some essential internal commands that will help you manage and manipulate your files. You will learn about the COPY command, which allows you to make additional copies of files and to back up files by copying them to another disk or directory. You will learn the consequences of overwriting files and of combining the contents of files. You will copy dummy files that are in the WUGXP directory to your DATA disk so that you can have experience in naming, managing, manipulating, viewing, and printing files.

5.1   Why Learn Command Line Commands?

In the last chapter, you learned how to manipulate subdirectories. You learned MD, CD, and RD, which are directory management commands that handle subdirectories. However, directories are places to hold files. With the directory management commands, you have built the bookshelves, but you have not as yet put any books on them. If shelves are directories, books are files. In a library, you are interested in locating, reading, and using books, not admiring the shelves. In the same way, on your computer, you are interested in locating, reading, and using files, not admiring the directories you created.

You will have many files and directories on a disk. The directories will be used to organize both your program and data files. Directories are the largest units of information management, but you need to manage information in smaller quantities—at the file level. You will generate many data files with your programs. You will need a way to perform "housekeeping tasks" such as copying files from one directory or one disk to another and eliminating files you no longer need. These tasks are different from creating or changing the data within the files. You must use the application program that created a data file to change the data in that file.

For instance, if you are the accountant who created Ms. Woo's tax return, you know how to manage the information correctly in her tax return. You also have other clients for whom you perform the same service. You, the accountant, are analogous to an application program such as TurboTax. The data for Ms. Woo's tax return is in a data file created by TurboTax. The other clients such as Mr. Rodriguez and Mr. Markiw need separate data files, also generated in TurboTax. Those data files have to be named according to the rules of the operating system in which TurboTax works. If your version of TurboTax was created for the Windows OS, you will be able to use up to 255 characters in a file name, including blank spaces. If your version was created for DOS 6.22 or older operating systems, you will be limited to eight-character names with three-character extensions.

In addition to the accounting work, there are other tasks that must be performed. For instance, Ms. Woo might get married and want her data file under her married name. This does not require a change to the accounting data itself. You, as the accountant, do not need to perform these low-level tasks. You hire a clerk to perform them. In the computer world, you use the operating system to perform these tasks.

In Windows, you can use Windows Explorer and My Computer to manage your files. You can drag files from one place to another, cut and paste them, rename them, and delete them with the click of a mouse button. Using the command line will help you understand file manipulation as well as disk and subdirectory structure. You will also learn that there are some tasks that you can accomplish more easily and quickly at the command line than in the GUI. For instance, in the GUI, in order to copy a file and give it a new name, you must take two steps—first copy the file, second rename it. At the command line, you can accomplish this task with one step. The COPY command allows you to change the name of the destination file as it is copied.

In addition, several major internal commands will help manage your files on disks and in directories. These file-management commands include DIR, COPY, REN, DEL, and TYPE. These commands are internal, meaning that once you have booted the system and opened a Command line session, they are always available to use. They are contained within the file CMD.EXE, which is in the WINDOWS\SYSTEM32 subdirectory; they are not separate files. These commands deal only with files as objects; you are not working with the *contents* of files, just manipulating the files. The commands allow you to see what files you have on a disk or in a directory (DIR), copy files from here to there (COPY), change their names (REN), throw files away (DEL), and take a quick peek at what is inside a file (TYPE). The following activities in this chapter will show you how to use the COPY and TYPE commands.

5.2   The COPY Command

COPY, one of the most frequently used internal commands, is used to copy files from one place to another. COPY does exactly what it says—it takes an original *source file*, makes an identical copy of that file, and places the copy where you want it: its destination. In a sense, it is similar to a photocopy machine. You place your original on the copy plate, press the appropriate button, and receive a copy of your document. Nothing has happened to your original document. If it has a smudge on it, so does your copy. The same is true with the COPY command—it makes an exact copy of the file, and the original file remains intact. Copying a file *does not* alter the original file in any way.

Why might you want to copy files? You might want to copy a file from one disk to another. For example, you might create an inventory of all your household goods for your homeowner's insurance policy. It would be stored as a file on your disk. If your home burned down, so would your disk with your inventory file. It makes sense to copy this file to another disk and store it somewhere else, perhaps in a safe-deposit box.

You might want to make a second copy of an existing file on the same disk. Why would you want to do this? If you are going to be making changes to a data file with the program that created it, you might like a copy of the original just in case you do not like the changes you make. You cannot have two files with the same name in the *same* directory, but you can have them in *different* directories.

You might want to copy a file to a device. One of the most common devices is the printer. You can use the COPY command to copy a file to the printer to get a hard copy, but the file must be an ASCII file, a special kind of text file that contains no codes such as bold or italic—just keyed in characters.

You have used the BOG program and the MATCH32 program. You might wish to make another copy of those program files in case something happens to the original, presuming you are the legal owner. Those programs also had data files with information in them. You might like to have another copy, a backup copy of the various data files, so that if anything goes wrong, you still have a copy to work with.

COPY has a very specific syntax. Its basic syntax is always:

```
COPY [parameters][drive:][path]filename [drive:][path]filename
[parameters]
```

or conceptually:

```
COPY source destination
```

COPY is the command or the work you want the system to do. The *source* is what you want copied, your original. The *destination* is where you want it copied to. The command, the source, and the destination are separated by spaces. In the formal syntax, the variables are as follows: *[drive:]* stands for the drive letter where the file is located; *[path]* is the subdirectory where the file is located; and *filename* is the name of the file you wish to copy. The file name is made up of two parts: the file name and the file extension. If a file has an extension, it is separated from the file name by the period or dot at the command line. If you are using a version of the operating system prior to Windows 95, when you key in a file name, you must have no spaces between the file name and the file extension. In Windows, if you wish to use a long file name that includes spaces, you must enclose the entire name in quotes. All three portions of the command—COPY, source, and destination—are mandatory. Drive and path do not need to be specified if you are using the default drive and subdirectory.

You use file-management commands to manage files. When you are learning how to use these commands, you do not want to worry about harming "real" programs or "real" data files. The WUGXP subdirectory, therefore, contains practice data files and program files. In the following activities, you will write data to your DATA disk only. You will never write to the hard disk. In this way you can enjoy the next activities and not worry about making mistakes. Mistakes are part of the learning process.

5.3   Review of File-naming Rules

To name any file, whether it is an application or a data file, you must follow the operating system file-naming rules. A file name is technically called a file specification. The file specification is comprised of two parts: the file name itself and the file extension. The file-naming rules are:

1. The names of files in a directory must be unique.
2. No file name can be longer than 256 characters, including the file extension.
3. File extensions are optional.
4. A file name must be separated from its extension with a period, called a dot.
5. All alphanumeric characters can be used in file names and file extensions except the following nine illegal or forbidden characters:

   "   /   \   :   ¦   <   >   *   ?

You cannot alter the rules. Usually, you will not get an opportunity to name program files. You purchase these programs, and the file names are those that were assigned by a programmer. Remember, a program file commonly has the file extension of .COM, .EXE, or .BAT. However, you will be naming your data files all the time. You name a data file from within the application program, usually when you save it to a disk.

You should apply some common sense when you are naming files. For instance, naming a file ABCDEF.GHI does not tell you much about the contents of the file, but a file named TAXES99.XLS does give you a clear idea of what is in the data file. File names should reflect file contents. However, you must know how your application program works. Most application programs let you assign the file name, but not the file extension. The programs themselves usually assign the extension to data files.

5.4   Activity: Making Copies of Files

Note 1:   The DATA disk is in Drive A. Be sure it is the DATA disk and not the HOMEWORK disk.

Note 2:   You have opened a Command Prompt window, and changed (if necessary) the default directory to the root of the hard drive so that C:\ > is displayed as the default drive and the default directory. Remember to check your Configuration Table in Chapter 1.6 if your system configuration varies from the textbook.

Note 3:   It is assumed that the **WUGXP** directory with its files has been installed on the hard disk. If it has not, refer to Appendix A for instructions on how to install it at home or see your lab administrator.

Note 4:   When keying in commands, you may use the editing keys to correct typographical errors and to recall previously used commands. Refer to Chapter 2 for details.

1   Key in the following: C:\>**CD WUGXP** [Enter]

2   Key in the following: C:\WUGXP>**DIR *.TMP** [Enter]

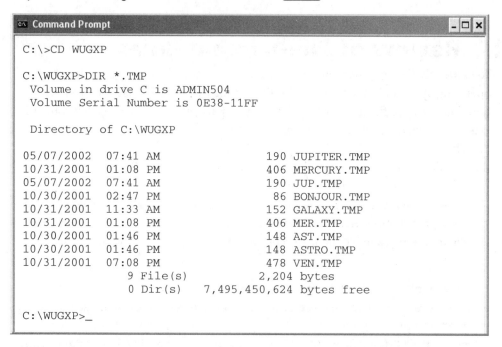

```
C:\>CD WUGXP

C:\WUGXP>DIR *.TMP
 Volume in drive C is ADMIN504
 Volume Serial Number is 0E38-11FF

 Directory of C:\WUGXP

05/07/2002  07:41 AM              190 JUPITER.TMP
10/31/2001  01:08 PM              406 MERCURY.TMP
05/07/2002  07:41 AM              190 JUP.TMP
10/30/2001  02:47 PM               86 BONJOUR.TMP
10/31/2001  11:33 AM              152 GALAXY.TMP
10/31/2001  01:08 PM              406 MER.TMP
10/30/2001  01:46 PM              148 AST.TMP
10/30/2001  01:46 PM              148 ASTRO.TMP
10/31/2001  07:08 PM              478 VEN.TMP
               9 File(s)          2,204 bytes
               0 Dir(s)   7,495,450,624 bytes free

C:\WUGXP>_
```

WHAT'S HAPPENING?   You changed the default directory to **WUGXP**. You then used the DIR command to see what files had a **.TMP** file extension in this directory. If your file system is NTFS, your files will be displayed in alphabetic order. You want to make a copy of the file called **JUP.TMP** and place it on the DATA disk. You are going to use the absolute path for both the source file and the *destination file*.

3   Key in the following:
C:\WUGXP>**COPY C:\WUGXP\JUP.TMP A:\JUP.TMP** [Enter]

```
ca  Command Prompt                                                  _ □ x
C:\WUGXP>COPY C:\WUGXP\JUP.TMP A:\JUP.TMP
        1 file(s) copied.

C:\WUGXP> _
```

WHAT'S
HAPPENING?   You see a message on the screen telling you that the file was copied. If you look at your command, following the syntax diagram, **COPY** is the command and **JUP.TMP** is the source file or what you want to copy. It is located in the subdirectory called **WUGXP**, which is under the root directory of the hard disk. **C:** was substituted for *[drive:]*. The subdirectory name **\WUGXP** was substituted for *[path]* (remembering that \ indicates the root directory). The next \ is a delimiter separating the subdirectory name from the file name. The second backslash (\) is only a separator. **JUP.TMP** was substituted for *filename*. A . (dot), not a space, separates the file name from the file extension.

The destination file also followed the syntax diagram. **A:** was substituted for *[drive:]*; \ was substituted for *[path]*; **JUP.TMP** was substituted for *filename*. Each file followed the file-naming rules; each is a unique name with no illegal characters. Each file extension has no illegal characters. You used a period to separate the file name from the file extension. The period is not part of the file specification. It is a delimiter telling the operating system that you are done with the file name; get ready for the file extension. Thus, **JUP** is the source file name and **.TMP** is the source file extension. **JUP** is the destination file name, and **.TMP** is the destination file extension.

4 Key in the following: C:\WUGXP>**DIR A:** [Enter]

```
ca  Command Prompt                                                  _ □ x
C:\WUGXP>DIR A:
 Volume in drive A is DATA
 Volume Serial Number is 30B8-DA1D

 Directory of A:\

02/25/2002  11:04 AM    <DIR>             ASTRONOMY
05/07/2002  07:41 AM              190 JUP.TMP
             1 File(s)            190 bytes
             1 Dir(s)       1,455,104 bytes free

C:\WUGXP>_
```

WHAT'S
HAPPENING?   You used the DIR command to confirm that you copied **JUP.TMP** to the DATA disk. You have one file and one subdirectory in the root directory of the DATA disk. In step 3, you used the absolute path name. You can save yourself a lot of time by using relative path names.

5 Key in the following: C:\WUGXP>**COPY MER.TMP A:** [Enter]

6 Key in the following: C:\WUGXP>**COPY AST.TMP A:** [Enter]

7 Key in the following: C:\WUGXP>**COPY VEN.TMP A:** [Enter]

8   Key in the following: C:\WUGXP>**DIR A:** Enter

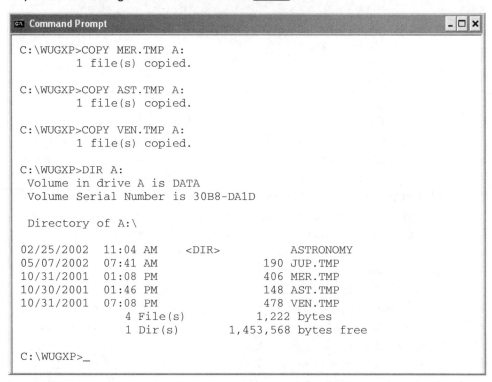

```
C:\WUGXP>COPY MER.TMP A:
        1 file(s) copied.

C:\WUGXP>COPY AST.TMP A:
        1 file(s) copied.

C:\WUGXP>COPY VEN.TMP A:
        1 file(s) copied.

C:\WUGXP>DIR A:
 Volume in drive A is DATA
 Volume Serial Number is 30B8-DA1D

 Directory of A:\

02/25/2002  11:04 AM    <DIR>          ASTRONOMY
05/07/2002  07:41 AM              190 JUP.TMP
10/31/2001  01:08 PM              406 MER.TMP
10/30/2001  01:46 PM              148 AST.TMP
10/31/2001  07:08 PM              478 VEN.TMP
              4 File(s)         1,222 bytes
              1 Dir(s)      1,453,568 bytes free

C:\WUGXP>_
```

WHAT'S HAPPENING?   You executed several COPY commands and used DIR to confirm
that you copied the files. You copied the file called **MER.TMP** to the root directory
of the DATA disk, but you did not need to key in all the information. Since the
default drive and directory are already **C:\WUGXP**, the command will always look
in the default drive and directory and no place else, unless you tell it otherwise.
Since the destination you wanted the file copied to was the DATA disk, which in this
case is Drive A, you had to key in the drive letter followed by a colon. The colon lets
the operating system know the destination is a drive. If you just keyed in **A**, the
COPY command would think that you wanted to name the file A. You did not give
the destination file a name, because if you do not supply a file name, the COPY
command will use the source file name as the destination file name. In this case the
source file name was **MER.TMP**, and that is what the copy of the file on the DATA
disk is called. You then proceeded to perform the same task with **AST.TMP** and
VEN.TMP. Next, you will give the destination file a different name and override the
defaults. Remember, in Windows Explorer or My Computer, you can copy files, but
you cannot give them a new name when you copy them. Hence, you must copy the
files, then rename each one. At the command line, you can copy and give the files a
new name in one command. This is one of the reasons users like the command line.

9   Key in the following: C:\WUGXP>**COPY AST.TMP A:\ASTROLGY.FIL** Enter

10   Key in the following: C:\WUGXP>**DIR A:** Enter

```
Command Prompt                                            _ □ x

C:\WUGXP>COPY AST.TMP A:\ASTROLGY.FIL
        1 file(s) copied.

C:\WUGXP>DIR A:
 Volume in drive A is DATA
 Volume Serial Number is 30B8-DA1D

 Directory of A:\

02/25/2002  11:04 AM    <DIR>              ASTRONOMY
05/07/2002  07:41 AM              190 JUP.TMP
10/31/2001  01:08 PM              406 MER.TMP
10/30/2001  01:46 PM              148 AST.TMP
10/31/2001  07:08 PM              478 VEN.TMP
10/30/2001  01:46 PM              148 ASTROLGY.FIL
              5 File(s)          1,370 bytes
              1 Dir(s)      1,453,248 bytes free

C:\WUGXP>_
```

WHAT'S ▓▓▓▓▓
▓▓▓**HAPPENING?**   You executed the COPY command and used DIR to confirm that
you copied the file. Following the syntax diagram, **COPY** is the command.
AST.TMP is the source file or what you want to copy. **ASTROLGY.FIL** is the new
destination file name. The destination file name followed the file-naming rules; it is
a unique name with no illegal characters. You used a period to separate the file
name from the file extension. The period is a delimiter, not part of the file specification. You did not need to use the drive letter or path name (subdirectory name) in
the source file, but you did need to specify the drive letter in the destination. The
default drive and subdirectory are always assumed unless you specify otherwise. In
this case, you overrode the defaults by telling the COPY command to call the
destination file on the DATA disk **ASTROLGY.FIL**.

5.5   Using Long File Names

You may consider using long files names (LFNs) with files on floppy disks, but only
when really necessary. On a 1.44-MB floppy disk, the directory entry table has room
for only 224 file names. Floppy disks use the old FAT filing system. In reality, you
can rarely save more than 212 actual files or subdirectory names on the root of a
floppy disk. Floppy disks were "designed" to hold files that complied with the old
eight-dot-three naming convention based on the FAT. Even if the files are very small
(without much data in them) and there is still ample room in the data sectors on the
diskette for information, once the directory entry table is filled, you can no longer
place more files on the disk, even though there is room. Once the root directory table
is full, as far as the operating system is concerned, the disk is full regardless of how
much actual space remains on the disk.

     For example, assume you saved two files to the root of a floppy disk. One file is
named FIRST.FIL, and the second is named TWENTY.FIL. If you saved the same
files to another floppy disk, but with the names FIRST.FIL and TWENTYFIRST.FIL,
the amount of space taken up by the actual data files would be the same. However,

there would be a difference in the root directory table entries. Compare the two directory entry tables in Figure 5.1.

```
Disk 1 Directory Table        Disk 2 Directory Table
FIRST.FIL                     FIRST.FIL
TWENTY.FIL                    TWENTYF
                             IRST.FIL
```

Figure 5.1—Two Directory Entry Tables

Notice that on the second disk, the long file name took two entries in the directory entry table. Disk 2 will "fill" faster than Disk 1, even though the amount of data is identical! A file with 20 characters in its name can take the space of three eight-dot-three named files. Although it is possible to have files with up to 255 characters in their names, you can see how quickly the root directory entry table of a floppy disk could be filled, thus limiting your ability to save files to a disk.

When referring to files that contain spaces in their long file name at the command line, you need to enclose the entire file specification in quotes. To see both the short and long name in a directory listing, you need to use the /X parameter with DIR. See Figure 5.2.

```
05/27/2001  10:08 PM           81 LONGFI~1.TXT LONGFILENAME.TXT
12/06/2001  12:15 AM           97 LONGFI~2.TXT LONGFILENAMED.TXT
12/06/2001  12:16 AM           99 LONGFI~3.TXT LONGFILENAMING.TXT
```

Figure 5.2—Directory Listing Showing Short and Long File Names

Notice the second file listed. The file LONGFILENAME.TXT has an alias of LONGFI~1.TXT. The digit is assigned by the operating system. The LONGFILENAMED.TXT file is assigned the digit 2 following the tilde. The digit is assigned by the operating system. The third file, LONGFILENAMING.TXT, in the same directory, gets another digit, 3.

When dealing with long file names, it is helpful to have meaningful, unique characters within the first six characters of the name to avoid this confusion when using short file names.

5.6 Activity: Copying Files with Long File Names

Note: The DATA disk is in Drive A. C:\WUGXP is displayed.

1 Key in the following:

C:\WUGXP>**COPY "SANDY AND NICKI.TXT" A:** Enter

```
C:\WUGXP>COPY "SANDY AND NICKI.TXT" A:
        1 file(s) copied.

C:\WUGXP>_
```

WHAT'S
HAPPENING?   You have successfully copied the file to the DATA disk.

2   Key in the following: C:\WUGXP>**DIR A: /X** Enter

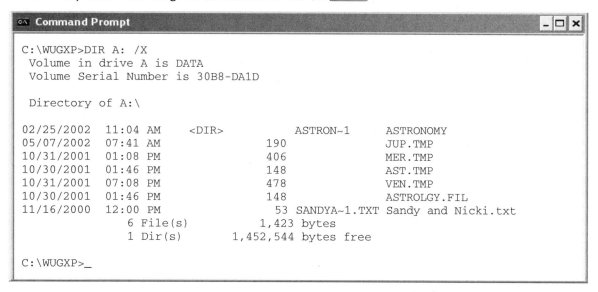

```
C:\WUGXP>DIR A: /X
 Volume in drive A is DATA
 Volume Serial Number is 30B8-DA1D

 Directory of A:\

02/25/2002  11:04 AM    <DIR>             ASTRON~1      ASTRONOMY
05/07/2002  07:41 AM              190                   JUP.TMP
10/31/2001  01:08 PM              406                   MER.TMP
10/30/2001  01:46 PM              148                   AST.TMP
10/31/2001  07:08 PM              478                   VEN.TMP
10/30/2001  01:46 PM              148                   ASTROLGY.FIL
11/16/2000  12:00 PM               53  SANDYA~1.TXT Sandy and Nicki.txt
               6 File(s)        1,423 bytes
               1 Dir(s)     1,452,544 bytes free

C:\WUGXP>_
```

WHAT'S
HAPPENING?   Notice the display on the right contains the entire directory and
file names, **ASTRONOMY** and **Sandy and Nicki.txt**, whereas the display in the
center does not. The operating system has assigned the directory **ASTRONOMY** an
alias in the eight-dot-three file name format of **ASTRON~1**, and the file **Sandy and
Nicki.txt** the alias **SANDYA~1**.

5.7   Using Wildcards with the COPY Command

In Chapter 2, you used global file specifications, or wildcards (* and ?), with the DIR
command so that you could display a group of files. You can also use wildcards to
copy files. In the previous activity you copied one file at a time. You then proceeded
to key in a command line for each file you copied. Since each of the files you wished
to copy had the same file extension, instead of keying in each source file and destination file, you could have used the wildcards to key in the command line and
reduced three commands to one. You can also use wildcards when changing the
destination name.

5.8   Activity: Using Wildcards with the COPY Command

Note: The DATA disk is in Drive A. C:\WUGXP> is displayed.

1   Key in the following: C:\WUGXP>**COPY *.TMP A:*.NEW** Enter

```
Command Prompt                                                    _ □ ×

C:\WUGXP>COPY *.TMP A:*.NEW
JUPITER.TMP
MERCURY.TMP
JUP.TMP
BONJOUR.TMP
GALAXY.TMP
MER.TMP
AST.TMP
ASTRO.TMP
VEN.TMP
        9 file(s) copied.

C:\WUGXP>_
```

WHAT'S ▒▒▒▒
▒▒▒ HAPPENING?   As each file is copied, it is displayed on the screen. Your command line instructed the operating system to copy any file in the **WUGXP** subdirectory that has the file extension **.TMP**, regardless of its file name, to a new set of files that will have the same file name but a different extension, **.NEW**. The * represented any file name. The operating system knew that you were referring to file extensions because you preceded the file extension with the delimiter, the period. These files will be copied to the DATA disk.

You could have keyed in the absolute path name,

COPY *C:\WUGXP**.TMP A:*.NEW

but once again, it is unnecessary to specify the source drive (default drive) and source subdirectory (default directory). Since you did not tell it otherwise, the COPY command assumed the default drive and subdirectory for the source. You needed to key in the destination drive and the destination file extension since you were not using the default values.

2   Key in the following: C:\WUGXP>**DIR A:*.NEW** [Enter]

```
Command Prompt                                                    _ □ ×

C:\WUGXP>DIR A:*.NEW
 Volume in drive A is DATA
 Volume Serial Number is 30B8-DA1D

 Directory of A:\

05/07/2002  07:41 AM              190 JUPITER.NEW
10/31/2001  01:08 PM              406 MERCURY.NEW
05/07/2002  07:41 AM              190 JUP.NEW
10/30/2001  02:47 PM               86 BONJOUR.NEW
10/31/2001  11:33 AM              152 GALAXY.NEW
10/31/2001  01:08 PM              406 MER.NEW
10/30/2001  01:46 PM              148 AST.NEW
10/30/2001  01:46 PM              148 ASTRO.NEW
10/31/2001  07:08 PM              478 VEN.NEW
              9 File(s)        2,204 bytes
              0 Dir(s)     1,447,936 bytes free

C:\WUGXP_
```

WHAT'S
HAPPENING?   You keyed in the command **DIR A:*.NEW**. You used the wildcards to display the **.NEW** files, instead of displaying the entire directory. You also used the wildcard * to make copies of the **.TMP** files. The file names are identical, but the extensions are different. You successfully copied nine files with the extension **.TMP** to nine new files with the extension **.NEW** from the hard disk to the DATA disk. However, the directory display merely shows that the files are there. How can you tell if the contents of the files are the same? You will also see a difference in the order of the display. If you are using NTFS as your file system, copy will copy the files in alphabetic order to the disk you are copying to. The files are the same. It is simply the order that is different. You can use the TYPE command.

5.9   The TYPE Command

The DIR command allowed you to determine that, indeed, there are files with the .TMP and .NEW extensions on the DATA disk. Using the DIR command is like opening your file drawer (the disk) and looking at the labels on the files. DIR does not show you what is in the files. An internal command called TYPE opens a file and displays the contents of the file on the screen. However, although the TYPE command will display the contents of any file on the screen, a file must be an ASCII file for the data to be meaningful. The TYPE command displays the file on the screen without stopping (scrolling). If the file is longer than one full screen, you can stop the scrolling using the MORE filter (which will be explained fully in a later chapter.) The syntax for the TYPE command is:

```
TYPE [drive:][path]filename
```

To stop the scrolling when using TYPE with a long file, add:

```
TYPE [drive:][path] filename | more
```

TYPE is the command (the work) you want the system to perform. The brackets, [and], indicate that what is between the brackets is optional. You do not key in the brackets, only what is inside them. *[drive:]* represents the drive letter. You must substitute the drive letter where the file is located (A:, B:, or C:). Another name for the drive letter is the "designated disk drive." This letter tells the command on which disk drive to look for the information. *[path]* is the name of the subdirectory where the file is located. You do not key in "path." You substitute the name of the path or subdirectory name, as in \WINDOWS \SYSTEM32 or \PHONE. The file name is mandatory. If the file has an extension, it must be included as part of the file name. You do not key in "filename" but substitute the actual name of the file. *Filename* is the parameter that the TYPE command expects. In addition, the file must be a text file to be readable. The TYPE command will not display the contents of a document file created with a word-processing program such as WordPerfect or Word.

It is interesting to note that although the TYPE command works in the same manner in Windows XP Professional as it did in Windows 2000 Professional, it behaves quite differently than it did in versions of the operating system previous Windows 2000 Professional. In previous versions, you could not use multiple files with TYPE, nor could you use wildcards. Both of these options came available with Windows 2000 Professional.

5.10 Activity: Displaying Files Using the TYPE Command

Note: The DATA disk is in Drive A. C:\WUGXP> is displayed.

1   Key in the following: C:\WUGXP>**TYPE** Enter

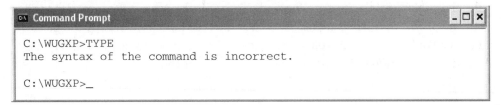

```
C:\WUGXP>TYPE
The syntax of the command is incorrect.

C:\WUGXP>_
```

WHAT'S
HAPPENING?   The message displayed on the screen tells you that TYPE does not know what to do. The operating system is asking you, "TYPE or display what?" Since you did not give a file name, as the syntax mandates, the TYPE command cannot show the contents of a file.

2   Key in the following: C:\WUGXP>**TYPE GAMES\MLINK\MLOTRA.EXE** Enter

```
C:\WUGXP>TYPE GAMES\MLINK\MLOTRA.EXE
MZ  ] -?¦ ???«-¶ @  °)  ?    ¤   ?   +    9   G   U   ¦   ¦   ??  .?  A?  T?  ¦?
î?  ƒ?  +?
  µ?  ÷?  ??  §?  $?  3?  B?  Q?  _?  m?  ¦?  ï?  Ü?  ¬?  +?  ¦?  ¦?  =?  ??
+?  9?  I?
z?  ê?  P?  ¦?  -?  +?  Ù¦  ²¦  >¦  #¦  0¦  {¦  ç?  ¡?  +?  ð¦  -¦  ^¦  ê?  É?
¦?  -?  +?
  -¦  Ã¦  ·¦    +  ¦  ¦     -  2  8  a  ü  ù  á  +  +  ·        *        ~
-
&
  I
  \
  +
  ±
  ??  ,?  ??  I?  S?  ]?  g?  q?  {?  Ç?  +?  ??  Ö?  ¦?  +?  =?  ?
C:\WUGXP>_
```

WHAT'S
HAPPENING?   Your display may be slightly different, depending on your system. What you see on screen is, indeed, the contents of a file named **MLOTRA.EXE** in the **GAMES\MLINK** subdirectory. This program or executable code is in machine language and not meaningful to you in this format. However, the TYPE command will display the contents of any file, even if it looks like nonsense characters to you. Using the TYPE command on an executable file has no value, as the results are not meaningful.

Programs or executable code files are recognized by their file extensions, such as **.COM**, **.EXE**, or **.SYS**, as well as those extensions listed in Chapter 4. **COM** stands for command file. **EXE** stands for executable code. **SYS** stands for system file. There are also other support files that programs need such as those files that have the .DLL (dynamic link library) extension. These types of files are not text files and not readable using the TYPE command. However, the TYPE command will do whatever you ask, even if it means displaying nonsense. Remember, a file must be a text file to be readable.

Another name for a text file is an ASCII (pronounced "ask-ee") file. *ASCII* is an acronym for American Standard Code for Information Interchange. ASCII is a code that translates the bits of information into readable letters. All you need to remember is that an ASCII file is a readable text file. Another name for an ASCII file is an *unformatted text file*. ASCII files are in a common language that almost all programs can recognize.

The data files that programs use or generate are usually not readable either. Each program has a special way of reading and writing the information in a data file so that the program knows what to do with the data. Usually, no other program can read the data file except the program that generated it. It would be like wanting to write a letter in Japanese if you didn't speak, read, or write Japanese. You would hire a translator (the program). He would write the letter (the data file). You still could not read the letter. You would give it to the translator to know what is in the letter. Furthermore, if you had another translator—say a French translator (another program)—you could not give your Japanese letter (data file) to the French translator. She would not be able to read it either.

3   Key in the following:

C:\WUGXP>**TYPE GAMES\MATCH32\TUNE1.MID** [Enter]

```
C:\WUGXP>TYPE GAMES\MATCH32\TUNE1.MID
MThd  ¦ O ¦OáMTrk   ,  ¦¦  A O¦Seq-1 T¦'      X¦¦  Q¦b¡  / MTrk  ¦[  Od#7
Harpsichord -
[P+??¦dÄyÉ(B?¦@ üpÉ47?¦@¦ümÉ;@üpÉ<>¶Ç;@ü\ÉA>üZÇ<@¶É;-
üoÉ<@)Ç;@üJÉ9@(Ç(@¶Ç4@:ÇA@pÉ(@üp¦@  É
47?Ç9@zÇ<@X¦@¦  É;?ürÉ<>üpÉA>¶Ç;@üYÉ;7§Ç<@ü\É<?>Ç;@ü2É9<(Ç(@PÇA@¶Ç4@f¦@
É(@üHÇ9@?Ç<@?¦@¦  É
Ç<@üaÉ<9#Ç;@üHÉ98<Ç(@(Ç4@ü¤É(@?¦@  üké4??¦@¦?Ç9@?Ç@@(Ç<@ü?É;CüpÉ<<üpÇ;@?¦@
?É@@üi¦@¦?É;9¤Ç<
@ü^É<:&Ç;@üJÉ98(Ç@@  Ç(@¶Ç4@ü4É(>?¦@  üié45?¦@¦#Ç9@*Ç<@ü É;DüpÉ<9?¦@ ümÇ;@
É?4?¦@¦ükÇ<@?É;7ü
Ç;@ü'¦@¦  É;>?Ç<@üUÉ<8(Ç;@üHÉ9=:Ç(@?Ç4@ü2Ç<@?Ç?@ É(B?¦@ üYÇ9@¶¦@¦
É4@üpÉ8@üpÉ;=üp¦@  É@>?Ç8
@üJÇ;@?¦@¦  É9=ütÉ;58Ç9@ü8É8>(Ç;@8Ç(@?Ç4@xÉ(@?¦@
ün¦@¦?É4@NÇ8@(Ç@@zÉ9@üpÉ;8(Ç9@üF¦@  É@@ür¦
@¦  É9>?Ç;@ü^É;C?Ç9@(Ç(@fÇ4@LÉ8C*Ç;@_Ç8@RÇ@@?¦@    É-Düp¦@¦
É98üpÉ@LünÉA:ürÉGD?Ç@@ü7ÇA@(É@Büp
ÉA>?Ç@@ü]É>>=Ç-@¶Ç9@ü#É-??¦@
ük¦@¦?É9.4Ç>@ü<É@I?ÇA@?ÇG@üpÉA@ünÉG@¶Ç@@ü[É@@)ÇA@üJÉA:%Ç@@ü#Ç
9@(Ç-@ É>@üpÉ,9?¦@ ükÇ>@?¦@¦?É8DMÇG@PÇA@OÉ@@üqÉA>üpÇ@@ ÉG@?¦@ üm¦@¦
É@@?ÇA@ü\ÉAB(Ç@@üJÉ>C¶
Ç,@¶Ç8@üH¦@    É,@üp¦@¦ É8-<Ç>@ü2É@B>ÇA@PÇG@aÉABüsÇ@@ ÉGDüpÇA@
É@>üqÉA@'Ç@@dÇ8@:Ç,@(É>DüpÉ+C
?¦@ dÇA@ü?ÇG@ É7@?¦@¦KÇ>@ü"É>DüpÉ@?ünÉE@?¦@
?Ç>@ü[¦@¦?É>@?Ç@@ü^É@@(Ç>@üHÉ<@<Ç+@¶Ç7@ü ¦@  É
+?ünÉ7>?¦@¦&Ç<@ü?ÇE@<É>G%Ç@@üKÉ@>üpÇ>@  ÉEBüpÉ>B?Ç@@ü\É@>(Ç>@ü?Ç7@(Ç+@?É<>üp¦@
É)Büp¦@¦ É5
B¤Ç<@üFÇ@@?É;G#ÇE@üLÉ@BünÇ>@?ÉECükÇ@@?É<8ümÉ>G&Ç<@ü  Ç5@¶Ç)@¶Ç>@?É;B¤ÇE@ü'É(>?¦@
ülÉ48?¦@¦5
Ç;@ü6É;@ünÉ>@(Ç;@üHÉD:üJÇ>@(É;9üpÉ>D¶ÇD@(Ç;@ü  Ç>@¶É;B<Ç4@¶Ç(@NÇ;@P¦@    / MTrk
á  O0#104
Star Theme ¦[P¤-
g?¦xÜ§æL<ç7æTüL@ç6æS>?üT@ÄjæJ<(üS@ç?æS?¤üJ@ç,üS@?æQ=ÄeüQ@?æH9ç>üH@  æQ7¢BüQ
üM@ç.üL@?æH:û¦üH@?æG9ÄxüG@?æJ@ÄiüJ@?æM@ç,üM@?æLBÄ¦æJ@(üL@ç?æH<%üJ@âsüH@&æQ7Æaæp-
"üQ@îjüP@
 /
C:\WUGXP>_
```

WHAT'S
HAPPENING?   You are looking at a music file for the **MATCH32.EXE** program. This is a file is formatted so that it can be read and used by the MATCH32 game. This program has its data in a somewhat recognizable form, in that you can at least read some of it. There is a Seq1, which you may assume means Sequence 1, and the word Harpsichord suggests that this file sounds like a Harpsichord, but that is about the extent of the information you can derive from the file.

Format, in this case, does not mean format as in format a disk but format in the sense of how the data is arranged. Only the program **MATCH32.EXE** knows how to use this data.

TYPE can sometimes be useful with files like these because it may give you an idea of what the file actually holds. Nearly all the files in the **WUGXP** directory are ASCII files, which means that you can read them using the TYPE command.

4   Key in the following: C:\WUGXP>**TYPE JUP.TMP** (Enter)

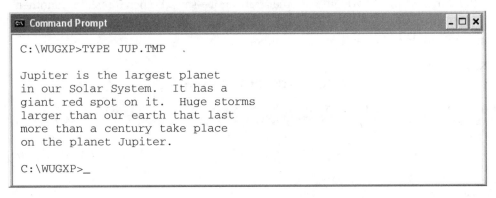

WHAT'S
HAPPENING?   In this case, the above is a text file (ASCII file), so you can read it. Using the TYPE command, you "opened" your file, **JUP.TMP**, and saw the contents displayed on the screen. Whenever a file is readable on the screen, as this one is, you know it is an ASCII file. You did not need to include the drive or path since **JUP.TMP** was on the hard disk in the **WUGXP** subdirectory and the TYPE command used the default values. You copied this file to the DATA disk in Activity 5.4. Is the content of the file the same on the DATA disk as it is in the **WUGXP** subdirectory? If it is, you will know that the COPY command makes no changes to any information in a file when it copies it.

5   Key in the following: C:\WUGXP>**TYPE A:JUP.TMP** (Enter)

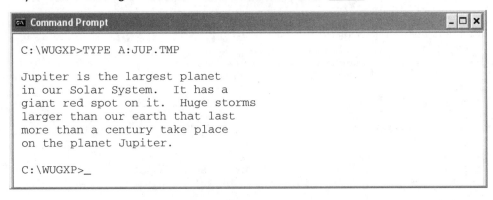

**WHAT'S
HAPPENING?**   The contents of the two files are the same. Copying the file from one disk to another had no impact on the contents. This is also true no matter what type of file you copy. But you would still need to include the drive designator **A:** in front of the file name **JUP.TMP** because that told the operating system which disk drive to select. Had you not included the drive designator, the operating system would have looked for the file **JUP.TMP** on the default hard disk and in the default subdirectory **\WUGXP**. After the TYPE command has executed, you are returned to the system prompt, ready for the next command.

6   Key in the following: C:\WUGXP>**CD** \ Enter

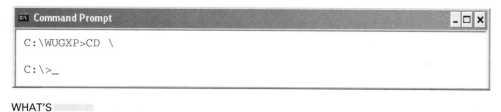

```
Command Prompt                                           _ □ ×

C:\WUGXP>CD \

C:\>_
```

**WHAT'S
HAPPENING?**   You have returned to the root directory of the hard disk.

5.11 Dummy Files

You are going to use some dummy files. "Dummy" refers to the fact that these files have no particular meaning and are of no importance. You can use these files to practice file-management commands without worrying about harming your "real" program and data files. The concept of dummy files and/or dummy data is common in data processing. Often data-processing professionals wish to test different portions of systems or programs. For instance, if you were writing a program about employee benefits, rather than looking at every employee, you would create dummy files and data in order to have a smaller representative sample that is manageable and easily tested. Not only are the files smaller, they are samples. If the data gets harmed in any way, it has no impact on the "real" data.

The following activities allow you to do the same. Following the instructions, you will use the COPY command to make copies of different files either on the DATA disk or from the WUGXP subdirectory to the DATA disk. You will then display the contents of the file on the screen with the TYPE command.

5.12 Activity: Using the COPY and TYPE Commands

Note 1:   C:\> is displayed and the DATA disk is in Drive A.

Note 2:   Remember that if your DATA disk is in a drive other than A, you will have to substitute the proper drive letter. Check your Configuration Table in Chapter 1.6 for the appropriate substitutions.

1   Key in the following: C:\>**A:** Enter

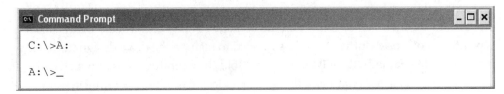

WHAT'S HAPPENING?   You changed the default drive so that all activities will automatically occur or default to the DATA disk.

2   Key in the following: `A:\>`**COPY JUP.TMP JUP.OLD** Enter

```
A:\>COPY JUP.TMP JUP.OLD
        1 file(s) copied.

A:\>_
```

WHAT'S HAPPENING?   You keyed in the command and its required parameters to accomplish the work you wanted done. You did not need to specify the drive letter or the path name preceding either the source file or the destination file name. Because you did not, the COPY command automatically read **JUP.TMP** from and wrote **JUP.OLD** to the default drive and directory, which is the root directory of the DATA disk.

3   Key in the following: `A:\>`**TYPE JUP.TMP JUP.OLD** Enter

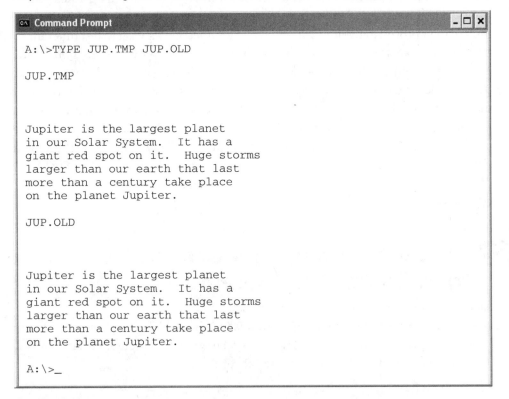

```
A:\>TYPE JUP.TMP JUP.OLD

JUP.TMP



Jupiter is the largest planet
in our Solar System.  It has a
giant red spot on it.  Huge storms
larger than our earth that last
more than a century take place
on the planet Jupiter.

JUP.OLD



Jupiter is the largest planet
in our Solar System.  It has a
giant red spot on it.  Huge storms
larger than our earth that last
more than a century take place
on the planet Jupiter.

A:\>_
```

WHAT'S HAPPENING?   You can see that you made a copy of the **JUP.TMP** file to a new file called **JUP.OLD**, but the contents of the files are identical. Also, rather than keying in the TYPE command twice, TYPE allows you use more than one parameter.

4 Key in the following: A:\>**COPY AST.TMP AST.TMP** [Enter]

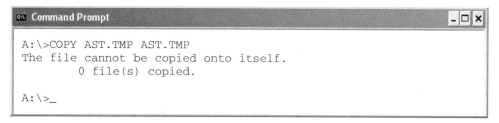

```
A:\>COPY AST.TMP AST.TMP
The file cannot be copied onto itself.
        0 file(s) copied.

A:\>_
```

WHAT'S HAPPENING?   You must give new files on the same disk and in the same subdirectory unique names. Just as you should not label two file folders the same in a file drawer, you would not label two disk files with the same names.

5 Key in the following: A:\>**COPY AST.TMP ASTROLGY.TXT** [Enter]

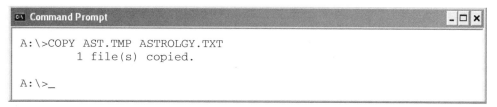

```
A:\>COPY AST.TMP ASTROLGY.TXT
        1 file(s) copied.

A:\>_
```

WHAT'S HAPPENING?   Here you are making a copy of the contents of the file on the DATA disk called **AST.TMP**, copying the contents to the DATA disk, and calling this new file **ASTROLGY.TXT**. You could have used the absolute path and file name by keying in **COPY A:\AST.TMP A:\ASTROLGY.TXT**. Either is correct, but it is not necessary to specify the disk drive since the default drive is assumed. Nor is it necessary to specify the path or directory because the root directory (\) is the default directory.

6 Key in the following: A:\>**TYPE ASTROLGY.TXT AST.TMP** [Enter]

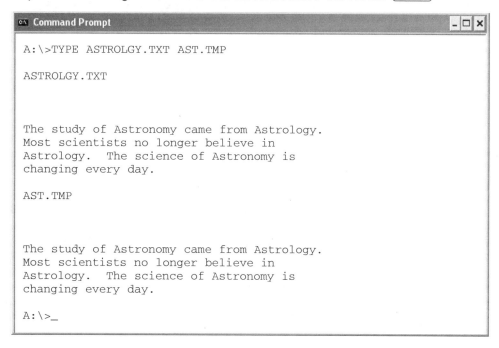

```
A:\>TYPE ASTROLGY.TXT AST.TMP

ASTROLGY.TXT


The study of Astronomy came from Astrology.
Most scientists no longer believe in
Astrology.  The science of Astronomy is
changing every day.

AST.TMP


The study of Astronomy came from Astrology.
Most scientists no longer believe in
Astrology.  The science of Astronomy is
changing every day.

A:\>_
```

WHATS
HAPPENING?   The contents of each file are identical even though the file names are different. The COPY command does nothing to the original; the contents of the original file remain the same. As far as the system is concerned, what makes a file different is its unique file name. To the operating system, **AST.TMP** and **ASTROLGY.TXT** are unique, separate files.

7   Key in the following: A:\>**COPY JUP.TMP JUPITER.TXT** Enter

8   Key in the following: A:\>**COPY MER.TMP MERCURY.TXT** Enter

9   Key in the following: A:\>**COPY VEN.TMP VENUS.TXT** Enter

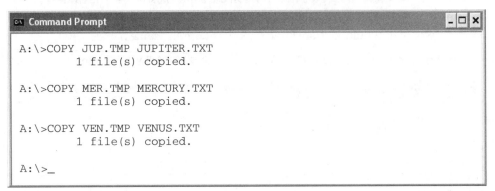

```
A:\>COPY JUP.TMP JUPITER.TXT
        1 file(s) copied.

A:\>COPY MER.TMP MERCURY.TXT
        1 file(s) copied.

A:\>COPY VEN.TMP VENUS.TXT
        1 file(s) copied.

A:\>_
```

10   Key in the following: A:\>**DIR *.TMP *.TXT** Enter

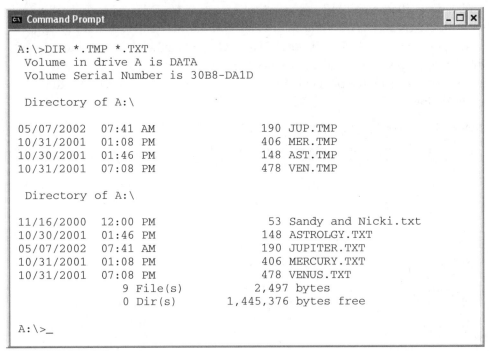

```
A:\>DIR *.TMP *.TXT
 Volume in drive A is DATA
 Volume Serial Number is 30B8-DA1D

 Directory of A:\

05/07/2002  07:41 AM              190 JUP.TMP
10/31/2001  01:08 PM              406 MER.TMP
10/30/2001  01:46 PM              148 AST.TMP
10/31/2001  07:08 PM              478 VEN.TMP

 Directory of A:\

11/16/2000  12:00 PM               53 Sandy and Nicki.txt
10/30/2001  01:46 PM              148 ASTROLGY.TXT
05/07/2002  07:41 AM              190 JUPITER.TXT
10/31/2001  01:08 PM              406 MERCURY.TXT
10/31/2001  07:08 PM              478 VENUS.TXT
             9 File(s)        2,497 bytes
             0 Dir(s)     1,445,376 bytes free

A:\>_
```

WHATS
HAPPENING?   You had four files with the extension **.TMP**. You still have those files, but, in addition, you now have four more files you just "created" with the copy command that have the extension **.TXT**.

5.13 Making Additional Files on the Same Disk

You often want to have extra copies of files on the same disk but in a different subdirectory. You may want to keep your backup files in the same file cabinet (disk) but in a different drawer (subdirectory). In this way you can group similar files together. When you make a copy of a file on the same disk, in a different subdirectory, it may have the same file name. Every file on a disk must have a unique name. However, a copy of a file in a different subdirectory, even though the file name is the same, has a different path name and is therefore unique.

You sometimes want to have extra copies of the same files on the same disk. Often, you may wish to make copies of files created when you use other software application packages. You choose to make copies because you want to leave your original files intact. For instance, if you created an extensive client list with a database-management package and needed to update it, rather than working on the original file, you could re-key in the entire client list. If you made a mistake, you would still have your original list.

However, an easier method would be to copy the client list, stored as a file, to a new file with a new name and make changes to the new file. When you make a copy of a file on the same disk in the same subdirectory, you must give it a different name. Every file name in a directory must be unique.

5.14 Activity: Using the COPY Command

Note: The DATA disk is in Drive A. A:\> is displayed.

1 Key in the following: A:\>**MD \CLASS** [Enter]

```
A:\>MD \CLASS

A:\>_
```

WHAT'S HAPPENING? You created a subdirectory called **CLASS** on the DATA disk. Remember, MD, which means "make directory," is the command to create a place for additional files. The first backslash (\) is the name of the root directory. **CLASS** is the name of the subdirectory. The only reserved name for a directory is \. You may use any name for the subdirectory you create, provided that you follow the file-naming rules.

2 Key in the following: A:\>**DIR** [Enter]

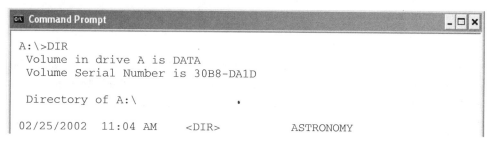

```
A:\>DIR
 Volume in drive A is DATA
 Volume Serial Number is 30B8-DA1D

 Directory of A:\

02/25/2002  11:04 AM    <DIR>            ASTRONOMY
```

```
05/07/2002   07:41 AM                  190 JUP.TMP
10/31/2001   01:08 PM                  406 MER.TMP
10/30/2001   01:46 PM                  148 AST.TMP
10/31/2001   07:08 PM                  478 VEN.TMP
10/30/2001   01:46 PM                  148 ASTROLGY.FIL
11/16/2000   12:00 PM                   53 Sandy and Nicki.txt
05/07/2002   07:41 AM                  190 JUPITER.NEW
10/31/2001   01:08 PM                  406 MERCURY.NEW
05/07/2002   07:41 AM                  190 JUP.NEW
10/30/2001   02:47 PM                   86 BONJOUR.NEW
10/31/2001   11:33 AM                  152 GALAXY.NEW
10/31/2001   01:08 PM                  406 MER.NEW
10/30/2001   01:46 PM                  148 AST.NEW
10/30/2001   01:46 PM                  148 ASTRO.NEW
10/31/2001   07:08 PM                  478 VEN.NEW
05/07/2002   07:41 AM                  190 JUP.OLD
10/30/2001   01:46 PM                  148 ASTROLGY.TXT
05/07/2002   07:41 AM                  190 JUPITER.TXT
10/31/2001   01:08 PM                  406 MERCURY.TXT
10/31/2001   07:08 PM                  478 VENUS.TXT
03/15/2002   01:38 PM   <DIR>              CLASS
              20 File(s)          5,039 bytes
               2 Dir(s)       1,444,854 bytes free

A:\>
```

WHAT'S HAPPENING?   The directory display shows the subdirectory called **CLASS**. You know it is a subdirectory because it has **<DIR>** by the file name. To see what is inside that subdirectory, or "file cabinet," you must use DIR with the path name. A review of the syntax is:

```
DIR [drive:][path][filename]
```

You do not need to include the drive letter since the default drive is where the DATA disk is. Nor do you need to include \ for the root directory, since the root directory of the DATA disk is the default. You do need to include the path name. The path name is the subdirectory name, **CLASS**.

3   Key in the following: A:\>**DIR CLASS** Enter

```
A:\>DIR CLASS
 Volume in drive A is DATA
 Volume Serial Number is 30B8-DA1D

 Directory of A:\CLASS

03/15/2002   01:38 PM   <DIR>          .
03/15/2002   01:38 PM   <DIR>          ..
              0 File(s)              0 bytes
              2 Dir(s)       1,444,500 bytes free

A:\>_
```

WHAT'S HAPPENING?   This directory listing is not for the root directory. The display tells you what you are looking at. The third line of the display reads **Directory of A:\CLASS**, telling you that you are looking at the subdirectory called **CLASS** on the DATA disk. There is nothing yet in this subdirectory. The . and the .. are created when you create a subdirectory. The . tells the operating system that this is a subdirectory. The .. is a shorthand name for the directory above **CLASS**, in this case the root directory (\). How do you copy a file into this subdirectory? You can always use the absolute path. You do this by following the syntax of the COPY command:

```
COPY [drive:][path]filename [drive:][path]filename
```

4   Key in the following: A:\>**COPY A:\JUP.TMP A:\CLASS\JUP.PAR** Enter

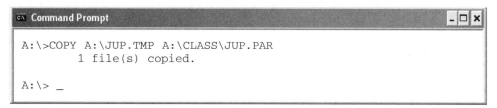

```
A:\>COPY A:\JUP.TMP A:\CLASS\JUP.PAR
        1 file(s) copied.

A:\> _
```

WHAT'S
HAPPENING?   You copied the source file, **JUP.TMP**, from the root directory on the DATA disk, to the destination, the subdirectory **CLASS**; you also gave the destination file a new name, **JUP.PAR**. By looking at the syntax diagram, you can follow how you substituted the values you wanted:

```
COPY [drive:] [path] [filename] [drive:]  [path]   [file name]
COPY    A:      \     JUP.TMP      A:     \CLASS\    JUP.PAR
```

In the destination syntax, what is the second backslash? The first backslash is the name of the root directory. The second backslash is used as a delimiter between the subdirectory name and the file name. This delimiter tells the operating system that the subdirectory name is over and the file name is about to begin. Backslashes are used as delimiters separating subdirectory and file names.

Keying in the absolute path is not as easy as using the relative path. With the relative path, you don't have to key in the default drive and directory. The system will make these assumptions for you. You must include the command COPY. Since the DATA disk is the default drive, you do not need to include the drive letter, and, since the root directory is the default directory, you do not need to include the first \. However, you do need to include the source file name.

The same is true with the destination file. You do not need to include the drive letter or root directory, but you must include the path name and the new file name. The shorthand way of copying is done in Step 5.

5   Key in the following: A:\>**COPY MER.TMP CLASS\MER.PAR** Enter

```
A:\>COPY MER.TMP CLASS\MER.PAR
        1 file(s) copied.

A:\>_
```

WHAT'S
HAPPENING?   In this case, you kept your typing to a minimum by using the relative path, observing your default drive and directory and keying in only what was necessary to execute the command.

6   Key in the following: A:\>**DIR CLASS** Enter

```
A:\>DIR CLASS
 Volume in drive A is DATA
 Volume Serial Number is 30B8-DA1D

 Directory of A:\CLASS

03/15/2002  01:38 PM    <DIR>          .
03/15/2002  01:38 PM    <DIR>          ..
05/07/2002  07:41 AM              190 JUP.PAR
10/31/2001  01:08 PM              406 MER.PAR
               2 File(s)          596 bytes
               2 Dir(s)     1,443,840 bytes free

A:\>_
```

**WHAT'S
HAPPENING?**   You copied the files **JUP.TMP** and **MER.TMP** from the root
directory to the subdirectory **CLASS** on the DATA disk. You gave the copies new
names, **JUP.PAR** and **MER.PAR**. Are the files the same? You can use the TYPE
command to compare the contents visually, TYPE supports wildcards, but since the
files are in different directories, you must look at each file individually. Again, since
you want to look at the contents of two files in different subdirectories, you must
follow the TYPE syntax:

```
TYPE [drive:][path]filename[.ext]
```

7   Key in the following: A:\>**TYPE JUP.TMP CLASS\JUP.PAR** [Enter]

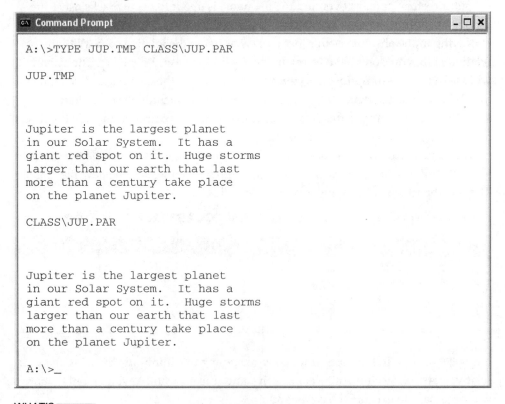

```
A:\>TYPE JUP.TMP CLASS\JUP.PAR

JUP.TMP



Jupiter is the largest planet
in our Solar System.  It has a
giant red spot on it.  Huge storms
larger than our earth that last
more than a century take place
on the planet Jupiter.

CLASS\JUP.PAR



Jupiter is the largest planet
in our Solar System.  It has a
giant red spot on it.  Huge storms
larger than our earth that last
more than a century take place
on the planet Jupiter.

A:\>_
```

**WHAT'S
HAPPENING?**   The contents of the files are the same, even though they are in
different directories. The same is true for the **MER** files.

8   Key in the following: A:\>**TYPE MER.TMP** Enter

9   Key in the following: A:\>**TYPE CLASS\MER.PAR** Enter

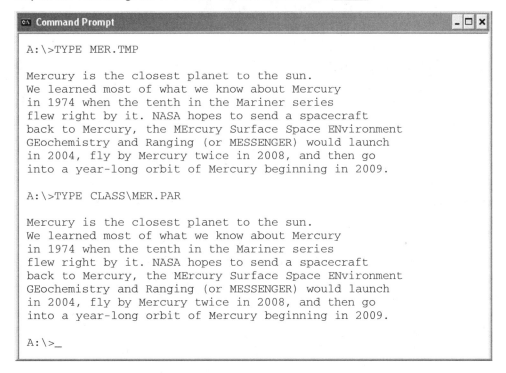

```
Command Prompt                                                    - □ x

A:\>TYPE MER.TMP

Mercury is the closest planet to the sun.
We learned most of what we know about Mercury
in 1974 when the tenth in the Mariner series
flew right by it. NASA hopes to send a spacecraft
back to Mercury, the MErcury Surface Space ENvironment
GEochemistry and Ranging (or MESSENGER) would launch
in 2004, fly by Mercury twice in 2008, and then go
into a year-long orbit of Mercury beginning in 2009.

A:\>TYPE CLASS\MER.PAR

Mercury is the closest planet to the sun.
We learned most of what we know about Mercury
in 1974 when the tenth in the Mariner series
flew right by it. NASA hopes to send a spacecraft
back to Mercury, the MErcury Surface Space ENvironment
GEochemistry and Ranging (or MESSENGER) would launch
in 2004, fly by Mercury twice in 2008, and then go
into a year-long orbit of Mercury beginning in 2009.

A:\>_
```

WHAT'S
HAPPENING?   The file contents are the same.

5.15   Using Wildcards with the COPY Command

You can also use wildcards to copy files on the same drive to a different
subdirectory. Again, the important point to remember when using the command line
is that you can never violate syntax. It is always COPY *source destination*. Computers
and commands always do what you tell them to. Users sometimes think that the
"computer lost their files." More often than not, files are misplaced because the user
gave an instruction that he or she thought meant one thing but, in reality, meant
something else. For instance, when the default drive and directory was A:\>, you
keyed in COPY THIS.FIL YOUR.FIL. You wanted YOUR.FIL to be copied to the root
of Drive C. Since you did not key that in (C:\YOUR.FIL), the default drive and
directory were used, and YOUR.FIL was copied to the default drive and directory
(A:\) instead of where you wanted it to go.

5.16   Activity: Using Wildcards with the COPY Command

Note: The DATA disk is in Drive A. A:\> is displayed.

1   Key in the following: A:\>**COPY *.TMP CLASS*.ABC** Enter

```
A:\>COPY *.TMP CLASS\*.ABC
JUP.TMP
MER.TMP
AST.TMP
VEN.TMP
        4 file(s) copied.

A:\>_
```

WHAT'S HAPPENING?   As each file is copied, it is displayed on the screen. Your command line says COPY any file on the DATA disk in the root directory (the default directory) that has the file extension **.TMP**, regardless of its file name, to a new set of files that will have the same file name but a different extension, **.ABC**. These files were copied to the subdirectory called **CLASS** on the DATA disk.

You could have keyed in **COPY A:*.TMP A:\CLASS*.ABC**. Once again, for the source files (***.TMP**), it is unnecessary to specify the designated drive and directory. Since you did not tell it otherwise, the default drive and default directory were assumed. However, for the destination you had to include the subdirectory name, **CLASS**; otherwise, the files would have been copied to the default drive and directory instead of to the subdirectory **CLASS**.

This is another area where using the command line is much quicker and easier than using the GUI. In order to accomplish what you did with one command, you would have had to take many more steps in Windows Explorer. You would have had to select the files individually, drag them to their new location, and then rename each file individually. You can see why users like the command line for certain tasks.

2   Key in the following: A:\>**DIR *.TMP** Enter

3   Key in the following: A:\>**DIR CLASS*.ABC** Enter

```
A:\>DIR *.TMP
 Volume in drive A is DATA
 Volume Serial Number is 30B8-DA1D

 Directory of A:\

05/07/2002  07:41 AM               190 JUP.TMP
10/31/2001  01:08 PM               406 MER.TMP
10/30/2001  01:46 PM               148 AST.TMP
10/31/2001  07:08 PM               478 VEN.TMP
               4 File(s)         1,222 bytes
               0 Dir(s)      1,441,792 bytes free

A:\>DIR CLASS\*.ABC
 Volume in drive A is DATA
 Volume Serial Number is 30B8-DA1D

 Directory of A:\CLASS

05/07/2002  07:41 AM               190 JUP.ABC
10/31/2001  01:08 PM               406 MER.ABC
10/30/2001  01:46 PM               148 AST.ABC
10/31/2001  07:08 PM               478 VEN.ABC
```

```
        4 File(s)          1,222 bytes
        0 Dir(s)       1,441,792 bytes free

A:\> _
```

WHAT'S HAPPENING? You keyed in two commands, **DIR *.TMP** and **DIR CLASS *.ABC**, although you could have used one command. You used wildcards to display the **.ABC** files in the subdirectory **CLASS** and the **.TMP** files in the root directory. You also used the wildcard * to make copies of the **.TMP** files. The file names are identical, but the extensions are different. The files were copied to the subdirectory **CLASS**. However, the directory display merely shows that the files are there. To see that the contents of the original files and copied files are the same, use the TYPE command. Remember, you must specify the subdirectory where the **.ABC** files are located.

4 Key in the following: A:\>**TYPE MER.TMP** [Enter]

5 Key in the following: A:\>**TYPE CLASS\MER.ABC** [Enter]

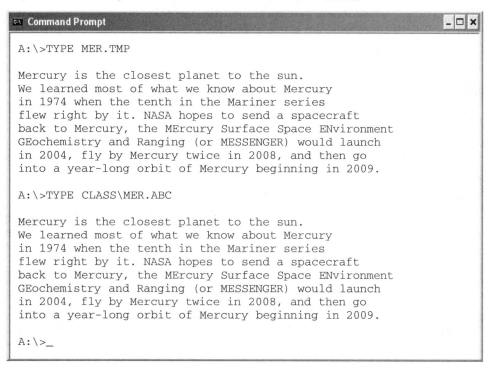

```
A:\>TYPE MER.TMP

Mercury is the closest planet to the sun.
We learned most of what we know about Mercury
in 1974 when the tenth in the Mariner series
flew right by it. NASA hopes to send a spacecraft
back to Mercury, the MErcury Surface Space ENvironment
GEochemistry and Ranging (or MESSENGER) would launch
in 2004, fly by Mercury twice in 2008, and then go
into a year-long orbit of Mercury beginning in 2009.

A:\>TYPE CLASS\MER.ABC

Mercury is the closest planet to the sun.
We learned most of what we know about Mercury
in 1974 when the tenth in the Mariner series
flew right by it. NASA hopes to send a spacecraft
back to Mercury, the MErcury Surface Space ENvironment
GEochemistry and Ranging (or MESSENGER) would launch
in 2004, fly by Mercury twice in 2008, and then go
into a year-long orbit of Mercury beginning in 2009.

A:\>_
```

WHAT'S HAPPENING? The file contents are identical, even though the file names are different and the files are in different directories.

5.17 Using COPY and DIR with Subdirectories

You are going to see how commands work with subdirectories by using the COPY command to place files in the subdirectories and by using the DIR command to see that the files were copied.

5.18 Activity: Using COPY with Subdirectories

Note: The DATA disk is in Drive A. A:\> is displayed.

1 Key in the following: A:\>**CD ASTRONOMY\MERCURY** [Enter]

2 Key in the following: A:\ASTRONOMY\MERCURY>**DIR** [Enter]

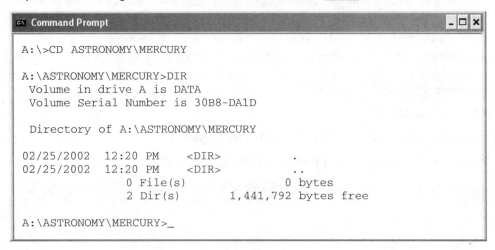

```
A:\>CD ASTRONOMY\MERCURY

A:\ASTRONOMY\MERCURY>DIR
 Volume in drive A is DATA
 Volume Serial Number is 30B8-DA1D

 Directory of A:\ASTRONOMY\MERCURY

02/25/2002  12:20 PM    <DIR>          .
02/25/2002  12:20 PM    <DIR>          ..
              0 File(s)              0 bytes
              2 Dir(s)       1,441,792 bytes free

A:\ASTRONOMY\MERCURY>_
```

WHAT'S HAPPENING?   You changed the default directory to the **MERCURY** directory, which is under the **ASTRONOMY** directory under the root of the DATA disk. The prompt should display **A:\ASTRONOMY\MERCURY>** as the default drive and subdirectory. The prompt is quite lengthy because it shows you the default drive as well as the default subdirectory. *Remember:* All activities will occur in the subdirectory **\ASTRONOMY\MERCURY**, unless you specify another path. When you keyed in DIR, it showed you the contents of only the current default directory. The directory is empty of files but has the two subdirectory markers, dot and double dot.

3 Key in the following:
A:\ASTRONOMY\MERCURY>**COPY \CLASS\JUP.PAR FINAL.RPT** [Enter]

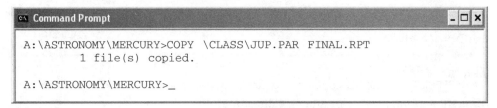

```
A:\ASTRONOMY\MERCURY>COPY \CLASS\JUP.PAR FINAL.RPT
        1 file(s) copied.

A:\ASTRONOMY\MERCURY>_
```

WHAT'S HAPPENING?   The file called **JUP.PAR** in the subdirectory **\CLASS** was successfully copied to the subdirectory **\ASTRONOMY\MERCURY**, but is now called **FINAL.RPT**. Spacing is very important when keying in commands.

```
Command  Space   Source (no spaces)   Space   Destination (no spaces)
COPY             \CLASS\JUP.PAR                FINAL.RPT
```

The syntax of the COPY command remained the same—COPY *source destination*. First, you issued the COPY command, but it was not enough to list just the file name

JUP.PAR as the source. You had to include the path so that the operating system would know in which subdirectory the file was located; hence, the source was **\CLASS\JUP.PAR**. Users often get confused when using \. Here is a simple rule: The first \ in any command line always means the root directory. Any other \ in the command is simply a delimiter.

Thus, in the example, the first \ tells the operating system to go to the root and then go down to **CLASS**. The second \ is the delimiter between the subdirectory name and the file name, **JUP.PAR**. The destination is a file called **FINAL.RPT**. You did not have to key in the path for the destination because the default (**\ASTRONOMY\MERCURY**) was assumed. Remember, you can always key in the command using the absolute path. In this instance, the command would have read as follows:

COPY A:\CLASS\JUP.PAR A:\ASTRONOMY\MERCURY\FINAL.RPT

Next, you are going to make a copy of the file in the current directory, so you do not need to include the absolute path name; here, you can use the relative path name.

4 Key in the following:

A:\ASTRONOMY\MERCURY>**COPY FINAL.RPT NOTE2.TMP** Enter

5 Key in the following:

A:\ASTRONOMY\MERCURY>**COPY FINAL.RPT NOTE3.TMP** Enter

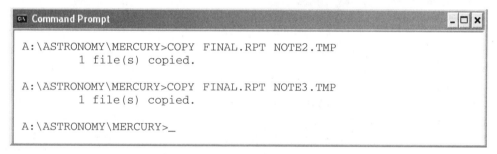

WHAT'S HAPPENING? You copied two files. You did not have to include the absolute path name because the default path was assumed. You used the relative path name. The operating system always assumes the default drive and directory, unless you tell it otherwise. Technically, the commands looked like this:

COPY A:\ASTRONOMY\MERCURY\FINAL.RPT A:\ASTRONOMY\MERCURY\NOTE2.TMP
COPY A:\ASTRONOMY\MERCURY\FINAL.RPT A:\ASTRONOMY\MERCURY\NOTE3.TMP

You can see that using the relative path eliminates a lot of keystrokes.

6 Key in the following: A:\ASTRONOMY\MERCURY>**DIR** Enter

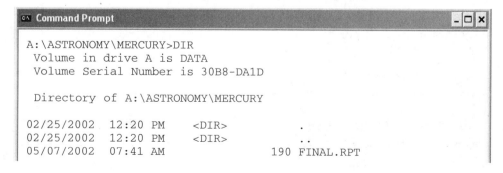

```
05/07/2002  07:41 AM                   190 NOTE2.TMP
05/07/2002  07:41 AM                   190 NOTE3.TMP
               3 File(s)               570 bytes
               2 Dir(s)          1,440,256 bytes free

A:\ASTRONOMY\MERCURY>_
```

WHAT'S
HAPPENING?   You see only the files that are in the default subdirectory. You can create subdirectories from the current directory. Do not forget about the command line editing keys. As you use them, you become familiar with how they work and you save yourself unneeded keystrokes.

7   Key in the following: A:\ASTRONOMY\MERCURY>**MD \WORK** Enter

8   Key in the following: A:\ASTRONOMY\MERCURY>**MD \WORK\CLIENTS** Enter

9   Key in the following: A:\ASTRONOMY\MERCURY>**MD \WORK\ADS** Enter

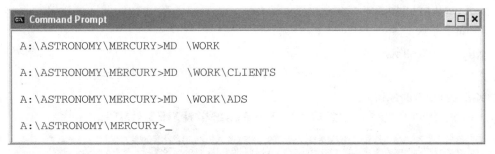

```
A:\ASTRONOMY\MERCURY>MD  \WORK

A:\ASTRONOMY\MERCURY>MD  \WORK\CLIENTS

A:\ASTRONOMY\MERCURY>MD  \WORK\ADS

A:\ASTRONOMY\MERCURY>_
```

WHAT'S
HAPPENING?   You had to include the first backslash so that the **WORK** directory would be under the root instead of under ASTRONOMY\MERCURY. **WORK** had to be created before you could create its subdirectories, **CLIENTS** and **ADS**. However, you could have created **WORK** and **CLIENTS** with one command by keying in **MD\WORK\CLIENTS**. You could have also created the directories with two commands, keying in MD \WORK\CLIENTS and MD \WORK\ADS. Work is considered the parent directory and clients and ads are the children to work. If you use the MD command to create a child directory and there is no parent directory, Windows will create the parent directory at the same time it creates the child directory. Now that you have created the directories of interest, you can use wildcards to copy files to them.

10   Key in the following:
A:\ASTRONOMY\MERCURY>**COPY *.* \WORK\CLIENTS** Enter

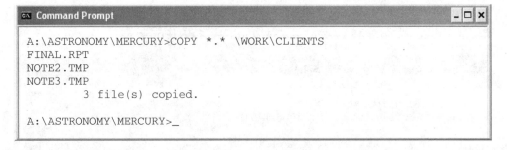

```
A:\ASTRONOMY\MERCURY>COPY *.* \WORK\CLIENTS
FINAL.RPT
NOTE2.TMP
NOTE3.TMP
        3 file(s) copied.

A:\ASTRONOMY\MERCURY>_
```

WHAT'S
HAPPENING?   As the files were copied to the **\WORK\CLIENTS** subdirectory, they were listed on the screen. Again, the syntax is the same: the command (COPY),

the source (*.* meaning all the files in the default subdirectory **\ASTRONOMY \MERCURY**), the destination (**\WORK\CLIENTS**). You had to include the absolute path name in the destination. The first \ in the destination is very important because it tells the OS to go to the top of the tree structure and *then* go down to the **\WORK\CLIENTS** subdirectory. If you had not included that first backslash, the operating system would have looked under the subdirectory **\ASTRONOMY\MERCURY**. Since you wanted to have the files with the same name in the destination subdirectory, **\WORK\CLIENTS**, you did not have to specify new file names. The operating system used or *defaulted* to the current file names.

11 Key in the following: A:\ASTRONOMY\MERCURY>**DIR \WORK\CLIENTS** [Enter]

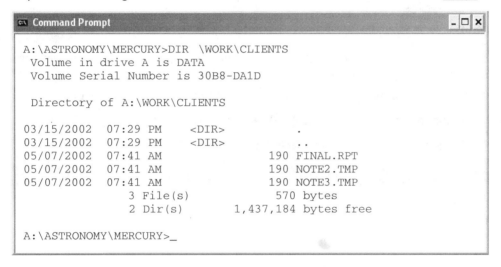

```
A:\ASTRONOMY\MERCURY>DIR  \WORK\CLIENTS
 Volume in drive A is DATA
 Volume Serial Number is 30B8-DA1D

 Directory of A:\WORK\CLIENTS

03/15/2002  07:29 PM    <DIR>          .
03/15/2002  07:29 PM    <DIR>          ..
05/07/2002  07:41 AM               190 FINAL.RPT
05/07/2002  07:41 AM               190 NOTE2.TMP
05/07/2002  07:41 AM               190 NOTE3.TMP
              3 File(s)            570 bytes
              2 Dir(s)       1,437,184 bytes free

A:\ASTRONOMY\MERCURY>_
```

WHAT'S HAPPENING?   You can copy files from anywhere to anywhere, provided you give the source and destination locations. If you use the relative path, be sure you are aware of the current default drive and directory.

12 Key in the following: A:\ASTRONOMY\MERCURY>
COPY \WORK\CLIENTS\NOTE?.TMP \WORK\ADS\EXAM?.QZ [Enter]

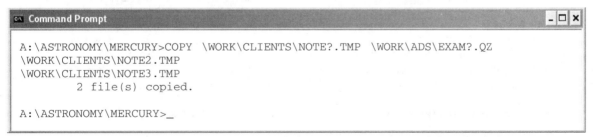

```
A:\ASTRONOMY\MERCURY>COPY  \WORK\CLIENTS\NOTE?.TMP  \WORK\ADS\EXAM?.QZ
\WORK\CLIENTS\NOTE2.TMP
\WORK\CLIENTS\NOTE3.TMP
        2 file(s) copied.

A:\ASTRONOMY\MERCURY>_
```

WHAT'S HAPPENING?   The operating system displayed the entire path name as it copied all the **.TMP** files from the subdirectory **\WORK\CLIENTS** to the subdirectory **\WORK\ADS**. So that you could retain the number in the source file name in the destination file names, you used the **?** wildcard as a place holder. Thus, **NOTE2.TMP** copied as **EXAM2.QZ**, and **NOTE3.TMP** copied as **EXAM3.QZ**. To see if the files were copied correctly, you will use the DIR command.

13 Key in the following: A:\ASTRONOMY\MERCURY>**DIR \WORK\ADS** [Enter]

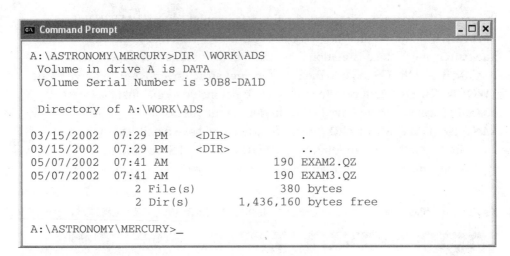

WHAT'S HAPPENING?   You successfully copied the files because you used the proper path name. You have been using the COPY and DIR commands to exemplify how to use the path. Any command will work if you use the proper syntax and the proper path.

14 Key in the following: A:\ASTRONOMY\MERCURY>**C:** Enter

15 Key in the following: C:\>**CD \WUGXP** Enter

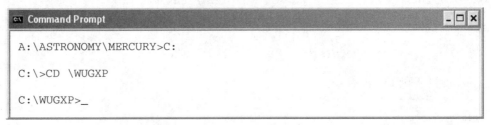

Note: The prompt you saw as you began step 15 (**C:\ >**) may be different on your system if you have been interrupted while following the steps in this chapter. It does not matter; the command **CD \WUGXP** specifies to change directories to the root (\) of the current drive, and *then* to the subdirectory **WUGXP**. Regardless of what directory you went to when you keyed in step 14, you will end up in **C:\WUGXP** after step 15.

WHAT'S HAPPENING?   You changed the default drive to C. In this example, you were in the root directory of C. You then changed the default directory to **WUGXP**. Note that it took two steps. You must first change drives, then change directories.

16 Key in the following: C:\WUGXP>**COPY DRESS.UP A:** Enter

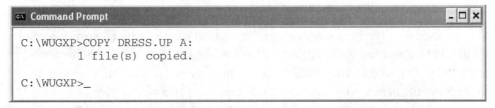

WHAT'S HAPPENING?   You executed a simple COPY command. You asked the OS to copy the file called **DRESS.UP** from the **\WUGXP** directory to the DATA disk in the A drive, but where on the DATA disk did the file get copied? Since the last place you

were on the DATA disk was the **MERCURY** subdirectory (under **ASTRONOMY**, under the root), that is where the file was copied. You did not specify a destination directory and consequently, the current default directory was used. If you wanted the file copied to the root directory of the DATA disk, you would have had to key in **COPY DRESS.UP A:**.

17 Key in the following: C:\WUGXP>**DIR A:DRESS.UP** Enter

18 Key in the following: C:\WUGXP>**DIR A:\DRESS.UP** Enter

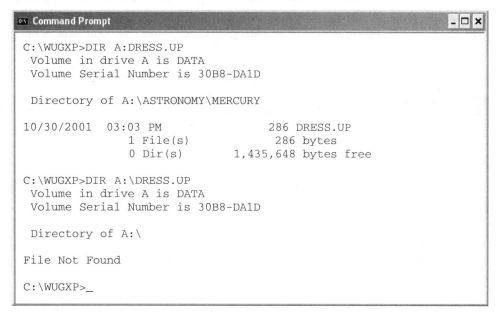

```
C:\WUGXP>DIR A:DRESS.UP
 Volume in drive A is DATA
 Volume Serial Number is 30B8-DA1D

 Directory of A:\ASTRONOMY\MERCURY

10/30/2001  03:03 PM                 286 DRESS.UP
               1 File(s)             286 bytes
               0 Dir(s)        1,435,648 bytes free

C:\WUGXP>DIR A:\DRESS.UP
 Volume in drive A is DATA
 Volume Serial Number is 30B8-DA1D

 Directory of A:\

File Not Found

C:\WUGXP>_
```

WHAT'S HAPPENING?   The last place you were on the DATA disk was in the subdirectory **\ASTRONOMY\MERCURY**. The operating system "remembered" where you last were and copied the file to the **MERCURY** subdirectory (currently, the default directory), not to the root directory. When you asked DIR to locate the file **DRESS.UP** and preceded **DRESS.UP** only with **A:**, the operating system looked in the default directory of **A:**, which was **\ASTRONOMY\MERCURY**. In order to look at the root directory, you had to request **A:\DRESS.UP**. When you did, the file was not found because that was not where it was copied.

19 Key in the following: C:\WUGXP>**A:** Enter

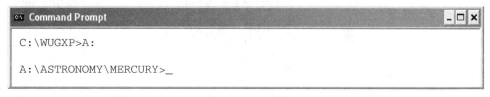

```
C:\WUGXP>A:

A:\ASTRONOMY\MERCURY>_
```

WHAT'S HAPPENING?   Your default drive is now the A drive, where the DATA disk is located. Look at the default directory. Note that you are not in the root directory of the DATA disk but were returned to the **MERCURY** subdirectory (under **ASTRONOMY**, under the root directory). As you can see, if you change drives during various activities, Windows will remember the last default subdirectory of the drive you were on. On the hard disk, the default directory is still **\WUGXP**.

20 Key in the following: A:\ASTRONOMY\MERCURY>**CD C:** [Enter]

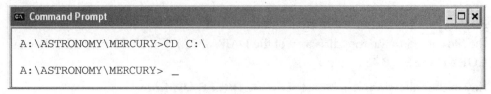

```
A:\ASTRONOMY\MERCURY>CD  C:\

A:\ASTRONOMY\MERCURY>  _
```

WHAT'S
HAPPENING?   You issued the command to change the directory to the root on the hard disk, in this case Drive C, but your prompt shows that you are still in the **MERCURY** subdirectory on the DATA disk. Did you accomplish anything with the command?

21 Key in the following: A:\ASTRONOMY\MERCURY>**DIR C:ZZZ*.*** [Enter]

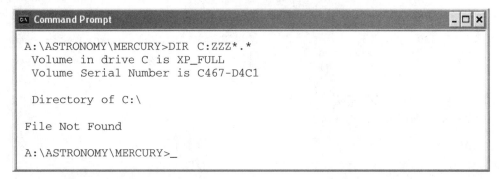

```
A:\ASTRONOMY\MERCURY>DIR  C:ZZZ*.*
 Volume in drive C is XP_FULL
 Volume Serial Number is C467-D4C1

 Directory of C:\

File Not Found

A:\ASTRONOMY\MERCURY>_
```

WHAT'S
HAPPENING?   You used a made-up file name to see the current default directory on the C drive. Notice the directory line **Directory of C:**. You did, indeed, change directories on C drive. When you issued the command **CD C:**, you changed the default directory from **\WUGXP** to the root of C on the hard disk without leaving the DATA disk in the A drive.

5.19 Using Subdirectory Markers with the COPY Command

Because the command line can get unmanageably long, using the subdirectory markers dot and double dot is a convenient shorthand way of writing commands. The **. .** (double dot) represents the parent of the current directory. The only directory that does not have a parent is the root directory because it is the ultimate parent of all the directories on a disk. You are going to use COPY as an example, but any system command that uses directory names works with subdirectory markers. Subdirectory markers are sometimes also called "dot notation."

5.20 Activity: Using Shortcuts: The Subdirectory Markers

Note: The DATA disk is in Drive A. A:\ASTRONOMY\MERCURY> is displayed.

1 Key in the following:
A:\ASTRONOMY\MERCURY>**COPY FINAL.RPT . .\FIRST.TST** [Enter]

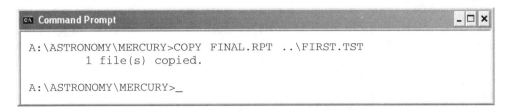

WHAT'S HAPPENING?   You copied the file called **FINAL.RPT** located in the current directory, **MERCURY**, to the parent of **MERCURY**, which is **ASTRONOMY**. You gave it a new name, **FIRST.TST**. Instead of having to key in **\ASTRONOMY\FIRST.TST**, you used the shorthand name for **\ASTRONOMY**, which is . .. This means the parent of **MERCURY**. You included \ between . . and **FIRST.TST** as a delimiter.

2   Key in the following:

A:\ASTRONOMY\MERCURY>**COPY . .\FIRST.TST . .\VENUS\LAST.TST** [Enter]

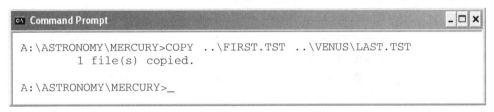

WHAT'S HAPPENING?   You copied the file called **FIRST.TST** from the **ASTRONOMY** subdirectory to the **VENUS** subdirectory, which is a child directory of **AS-TRONOMY**. The long way to key in the command is to use the absolute path. If you issued the command using the absolute path, it would look like the following:

COPY A:\ASTRONOMY\FIRST.TST A:\ASTRONOMY\VENUS\LAST.TST

In the source file, the first . . represented the parent of MERCURY. You did not have to key in **\ASTRONOMY**. However, you did need to key in the delimiter \ preceding the file name. You also did not need to key in **\ASTRONOMY** in the destination file. Instead you used the subdirectory marker . . (double dot). You did need to key in \ preceding **VENUS** and \ preceding **LAST.TST** because they were needed as delimiters to separate subdirectory names and file names. You can use subdirectory markers to save keystrokes. You can now verify that the files are in the **VENUS** subdirectory.

3   Key in the following: A:\ASTRONOMY\MERCURY>**DIR . .\VENUS** [Enter]

```
 Command Prompt                                             _ □ ×

A:\ASTRONOMY\MERCURY>DIR  ..\VENUS
 Volume in drive A is DATA
 Volume Serial Number is 30B8-DA1D

 Directory of A:\ASTRONOMY\VENUS

02/25/2002  12:32 PM    <DIR>            .
02/25/2002  12:32 PM    <DIR>            ..
05/07/2002  07:41 AM                190 LAST.TST
              1 File(s)              190 bytes
              2 Dir(s)       1,434,624 bytes free

A:\ASTRONOMY\MERCURY>_
```

WHAT'S ▨▨▨▨
▨▨▨ HAPPENING?   You used the DIR command with the subdirectory markers to verify that you successfully copied the file using subdirectory markers. The double dot (..) represents the immediate parent directory.

4 Key in the following: A:\ASTRONOMY\MERCURY>**CD** \ [Enter]

WHAT'S ▨▨▨▨
▨▨▨ HAPPENING?   You returned to the root of the DATA disk.

5.21 Overwriting Files with the COPY Command

When you made copies of files, you gave the files on the same disk and in the same subdirectory unique names. One of the reasons for doing this is that, when you tried to use the same file name on the same disk and directory, you got an error message:

```
File cannot be copied onto itself,
    0 file(s) copied.
```

The operating system would not permit you to make that error. However, the rule of unique file names is true only if the files are on the same disk and in the same subdirectory. If you are using more than one disk or more than one subdirectory, the system *will* let you use the same file name. There have been no problems so far because, when you copied the source file from one disk to the destination file on another disk, it was a new file on the destination disk.

Overwrite means just what it says; it writes over or replaces what used to be in a file. If the contents of the source file are different from the contents of the destination file, when you overwrite the destination file this will change. Both files will now have not only the same file *name* but also the same file *contents*. The previous contents of the destination file will be gone. Overwriting also happens on the same disk when the destination file name already exists. The same rules apply to subdirectories. See Figure 5.4 for a graphic representation of this.

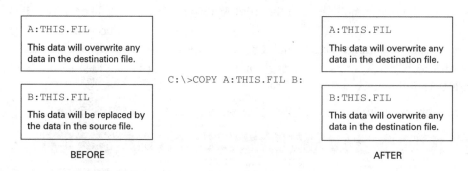

BEFORE   AFTER

Figure 5.4—Overwriting Files

The overwrite process seems dangerous because you will lose the data in the destination file when you replace it with the source file. Why are you not protected from this error? Because, when working with computers, this is typically *not* an error. Usually, you *do* want to overwrite files. That is, you want to replace the old contents of a file with the new, revised contents.

Data changes all the time. For example, if you have a customer list stored as a file named CUSTOMER.LST on a disk, the information in the file (the data) changes as you add, delete, and update information about customers. When you have completed your work for the day, you want to back up your file or copy it to another disk because you are working with it on a daily basis. Thus, you have a file called CUSTOMER.LST on your source disk and a file called CUSTOMER.LST on your destination disk. Since CUSTOMER.LST is clearly a descriptive file name, you really do not want to create a new file name every time you copy the file to the destination disk because creating new file names and then tracking current files can be time-consuming and confusing. In addition, if you are working with a file on a daily basis, you could end up with hundreds of files. In reality, you do not care about last week's or yesterday's customer information or the old file; you care about the current version and its backup file. When copying a file for backup purposes, you do want the source file to overwrite the destination file. Windows warns you that this is an overwrite—that you are about to overwrite the data in the older file. The same is true at the command line. In earlier versions of the operating system, prior to DOS 6.2, you were not made aware of the existence of a file on the destination disk that has the same name—DOS simply overwrote the destination file contents with the source file contents without a warning.

5.22   Activity: Overwriting Files Using the COPY Command

Note: The DATA disk is in Drive A. A:\> is displayed.

1   Key in the following: A:\>**TYPE GALAXY.NEW** Enter

2   Key in the following: A:\>**TYPE JUP.OLD** Enter

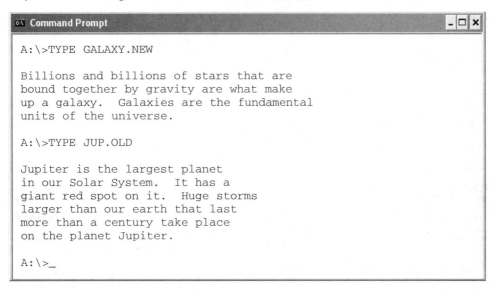

```
A:\>TYPE GALAXY.NEW

Billions and billions of stars that are
bound together by gravity are what make
up a galaxy.  Galaxies are the fundamental
units of the universe.

A:\>TYPE JUP.OLD

Jupiter is the largest planet
in our Solar System.  It has a
giant red spot on it.  Huge storms
larger than our earth that last
more than a century take place
on the planet Jupiter.

A:\>_
```

WHAT'S ▓▓▓▓▓
▓▓▓▓HAPPENING?   You have displayed the contents of two files and can see that each file contains different data.

3   Key in the following: A:\>**COPY GALAXY.NEW JUP.OLD** Enter

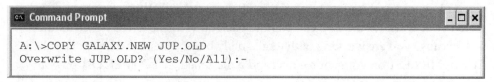

```
A:\>COPY GALAXY.NEW JUP.OLD
Overwrite JUP.OLD? (Yes/No/All):-
```

WHAT'S ▇▇▇▇
▇▇▇HAPPENING?   You get a message telling you that you already have a file by the name of **JUP.OLD**.

4   Key in the following: **Y** [Enter]

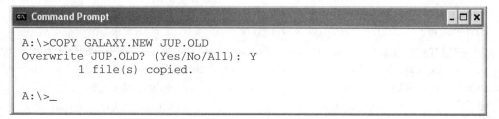

```
A:\>COPY GALAXY.NEW JUP.OLD
Overwrite JUP.OLD? (Yes/No/All): Y
        1 file(s) copied.

A:\>_
```

WHAT'S ▇▇▇▇
▇▇▇HAPPENING?   The file **GALAXY.NEW** was successfully copied to the file called **JUP.OLD**, but what about the contents of the file? Did anything change?

5   Key in the following: A:\>**TYPE GALAXY.NEW** [Enter]

6   Key in the following: A:\>**TYPE JUP.OLD** [Enter]

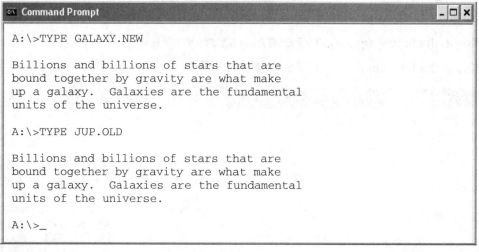

```
A:\>TYPE GALAXY.NEW

Billions and billions of stars that are
bound together by gravity are what make
up a galaxy.  Galaxies are the fundamental
units of the universe.

A:\>TYPE JUP.OLD

Billions and billions of stars that are
bound together by gravity are what make
up a galaxy.  Galaxies are the fundamental
units of the universe.

A:\>_
```

WHAT'S ▇▇▇▇
▇▇▇HAPPENING?   The file contents are now identical. What used to be inside the file called **JUP.OLD** located on the DATA disk was overwritten or replaced (i.e., is gone forever) by the contents of the file called **GALAXY.NEW**. You need to be aware of how this procedure works so that you do not accidentally overwrite a file.

    The operating system does not allow you to overwrite or copy a file when the source file and the destination file are on the same disk and in the same subdirectory and have exactly the same file name.

7   Key in the following: A:\>**COPY JUP.OLD JUP.OLD** [Enter]

```
C:\ Command Prompt                                          - □ ×

A:\>COPY JUP.OLD JUP.OLD
The file cannot be copied onto itself.
        0 file(s) copied.

A:\>_
```

WHAT'S HAPPENING?   You tried to copy (overwrite) a file onto itself and got an error message. This process works the same when you are dealing with subdirectories.

In Activity 5.14, you copied **JUP.TMP** and **MER.TMP** to the **CLASS** directory with the same file names but different extensions, so that in the **CLASS** directory the files were now called **JUP.PAR** and **MER.PAR**. You are going to use wildcards to copy the rest of the **.TMP** files to the **CLASS** directory. In the process, you will overwrite the existing files.

8   Key in the following: A:\>**COPY *.TMP CLASS*.PAR** [Enter]

```
C:\ Command Prompt                                          - □ ×

A:\>COPY *.TMP CLASS\*.PAR
JUP.TMP
Overwrite CLASS\JUP.PAR? (Yes/No/All):
```

WHAT'S HAPPENING?   The OS does not know the contents of the file; it only knows you already have a file by that name. Rather than prompting you each time, one of the choices is A for "all." Thus, if you intend to overwrite all the **.TMP** files, you can choose A.

9   Key in the following: **A** [Enter]

```
C:\ Command Prompt                                          - □ ×

A:\>COPY *.TMP CLASS\*.PAR
JUP.TMP
Overwrite CLASS\JUP.PAR? (Yes/No/All):A
MER.TMP
AST.TMP
VEN.TMP
        4 file(s) copied.

A:\>_
```

WHAT'S HAPPENING?   The OS has overwritten the **JUP.PAR** and **MER.PAR** files in the **CLASS** directory with the **JUP.TMP** and **MER.TMP** files in the root directory. You can prove this occurred by using the TYPE command.

10   Key in the following: A:\>**TYPE JUP.TMP CLASS\JUP.PAR** [Enter]

```
C:\ Command Prompt                                          - □ ×

A:\>TYPE JUP.TMP CLASS\JUP.PAR

JUP.TMP
```

```
Jupiter is the largest planet
in our Solar System.  It has a
giant red spot on it.  Huge storms
larger than our earth that last
more than a century take place
on the planet Jupiter.

CLASS\JUP.PAR


Jupiter is the largest planet
in our Solar System.  It has a
giant red spot on it.  Huge storms
larger than our earth that last
more than a century take place
on the planet Jupiter.

A:\>_
```

WHAT'S HAPPENING?   As you can see, the contents of the two files are identical. You did overwrite the destination file with the contents of the source file. You can verify that all the files have been copied by using the DIR command.

11 Key in the following: A:\>**DIR CLASS*.PAR** Enter

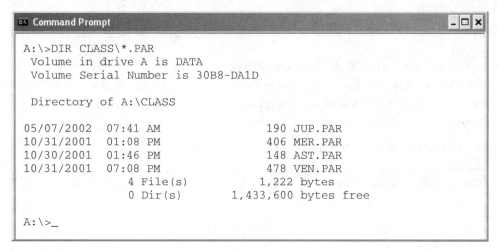

```
A:\>DIR CLASS\*.PAR
 Volume in drive A is DATA
 Volume Serial Number is 30B8-DA1D

 Directory of A:\CLASS

05/07/2002  07:41 AM             190 JUP.PAR
10/31/2001  01:08 PM             406 MER.PAR
10/30/2001  01:46 PM             148 AST.PAR
10/31/2001  07:08 PM             478 VEN.PAR
              4 File(s)         1,222 bytes
              0 Dir(s)      1,433,600 bytes free

A:\>_
```

WHAT'S HAPPENING?   Now all the **.TMP** files are in the **CLASS** directory. They have the same file names but different file extensions.

5.23 Combining Text Files with the COPY Command

Sometimes, but rarely, it is useful to combine the contents of two or more text (ASCII) files. This process is known as file *concatenation*. To concatenate means to "put together." You might wish to concatenate when you have several short text files that would be easier to work with if they were combined into one file. When you combine files, nothing happens to the original files; they remain intact. You just create a new file from the original files.

However, most often users concatenate files accidentally and are unaware of it until they attempt to retrieve the file. *Concatenation should never be done with either program files or the data files generated by programs*. Programs are binary code and combining any of these files makes the binary code useless and the program incapable of being executed. The same is true for the data files that programs generate. When you create a data file with a program, that program "formats" the data in such a way that the program knows how to interpret that data. That data file format is different for each program. A data file can be read only by the program that created it. If another program can read a foreign data file, it is because the program converts the foreign data into its own native format. The classic example of that is converting data files created in WordPerfect so that these files can be used in Word and the reverse.

Why learn concatenation if you should not use it? You need to learn concatenation because accidental concatenation of files can occur. The clue is to read the messages displayed on the screen. In the following activity you will see the results of concatenation. The COPY command never changes. The syntax never changes. It is always COPY *source destination*. Look at the syntax diagram:

```
COPY [/D] [/V] [/N] [/Y ¦ /-Y] [/Z] [/A ¦ /B ] source [/A ¦ /B]
[+ source [/A ¦ /B] [+ ...]] [destination [/A ¦ /B]]
```

/A indicates an ASCII file, whereas /B indicates a binary file. In addition, whenever you see the notation in a syntax diagram of two or more items separated by the pipe symbol (¦) as in [/A ¦ /B], it is an either/or choice. Either you may use /A or you may use /B, but you may not use both.

5.24 Activity: Combining Files Using the COPY Command

Note: The DATA disk is in Drive A. A:\> is displayed.

1   Key in the following: A:\>**DIR C:\WUGXP\MUSIC /P** Enter

```
Command Prompt                                          _ □ ×

Directory of C:\WUGXP\MUSIC

12/09/2001  11:04 AM    <DIR>          .
12/09/2001  11:04 AM    <DIR>          ..
12/05/2001  09:53 AM            282 Ballad1960.txt
12/05/2001  09:54 AM            451 Ballad1960Hits.txt
12/05/2001  08:41 AM            247 CalifSurf.txt
12/05/2001  08:41 AM            368 CalifSurfHits.txt
12/11/2001  09:41 AM            852 Doo-wopWest.txt
12/11/2001  09:41 AM            451 Doo-wopWestHits.txt
12/11/2001  09:41 AM            271 Doo-wop2.txt
12/11/2001  09:41 AM            760 Doo-wop2hits.txt
12/11/2001  09:41 AM            357 Doo-wopEast.txt
12/11/2001  09:41 AM            444 Doo-wopEastHits.txt
12/04/2001  09:33 AM            222 Idols1950.txt
12/04/2001  09:34 AM            725 Idols1950hits.txt
12/04/2001  09:28 AM            258 Idols1960.txt
12/04/2001  09:28 AM            876 Idols1960hits.txt
12/05/2001  08:44 AM            227 JazzEvans.txt
12/05/2001  08:45 AM            311 JazzEvansHits.txt
01/24/2002  09:42 AM            427 RB1958.txt
Press any key to continue . . .
```

WHAT'S
HAPPENING?   You displayed the files in the MUSIC directory. The third and
fourth file on the list have "Calif" in their names.

2   Hold down the **Ctrl** key and press **C** to cancel the command.

3   Key in the following: A:\>**TYPE C:\WUGXP\MUSIC\CALIFSURF.TXT** Enter

4   Key in the following:
    A:\>**TYPE C:\WUGXP\MUSIC\CALIFSURFHITS.TXT** Enter

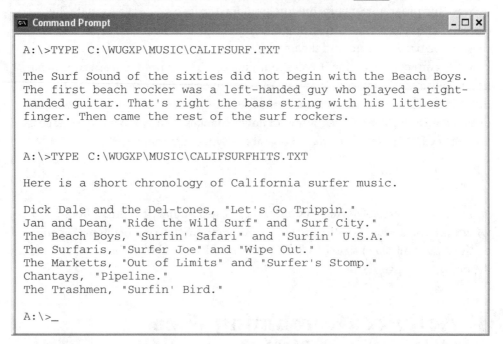

WHAT'S
HAPPENING?   You displayed the contents of one of the files. The first file has
information about surfing music, and the second file has a list of surfer music hits.
You want all of this information to be in one file, called CalSurf.MUS. The new file
will reside on the DATA disk.

Note: In the following step, there are spaces between COPY and the source file
           specification, before and after the + sign, and before the destination file
           name. Though it appears here that the command is on two different lines,
           the entire command must go on one line.

5   Key in the following (press the **Enter** key only when you see **Enter**):
    A:\>**COPY C:\WUGXP\MUSIC\CALIFSURF.TXT +**
    C:\WUGXP\MUSIC\CALIFSURFHITS.TXT CalifSurf.MUS Enter

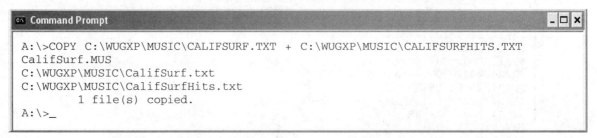

Note: As shown in the screen above, the command will probably have wrapped
           to the next line on your screen. Just be sure you do not press the **Enter** key
           until you see **Enter**, even if your command line wraps to the next line.

WHAT'S
HAPPENING?   The message is **1 file(s) copied**. It seems as if you have too many parameters because the syntax is COPY *source destination*. However, you are still following the correct syntax for the COPY command. You are creating one destination file out of two source files. What you did here was say COPY (the command) the contents of the file called **C:\WUGXP\MUSIC\CALIFSURF.TXT** *and* the contents of the file called **C:\WUGXP\MUSIC\CALIFSURFHITS.TXT** (the source) to a new file called **CalifSurf.MUS** that will reside on the root of the DATA disk (the destination). The plus sign (+) told the operating system that the source had more to it than just one file. It also told the OS that you were joining files. The destination file is the last file name on the command line that does not have a plus sign in front. Look at step 3 and note that **CalifSurf.MUS** has just a space in front of it, not a plus sign, making **CalifSurf.MUS** the destination. Also note, the use of the combination of upper and lower case letters in the destination file name is for the benefit of the user—the reader. The operating system does not care if you use upper or lower case letters, but it will remember and display the file in the case you choose.

6   Key in the following: A:\>**DIR CALIFSURF.MUS** [Enter]

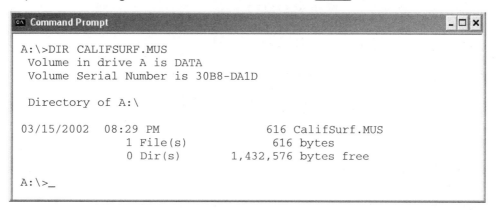

```
A:\>DIR CALIFSURF.MUS
 Volume in drive A is DATA
 Volume Serial Number is 30B8-DA1D

 Directory of A:\

03/15/2002  08:29 PM                616 CalifSurf.MUS
              1 File(s)             616 bytes
              0 Dir(s)        1,432,576 bytes free

A:\>_
```

WHAT'S
HAPPENING?   The file CALIFSURF.MUS was *requested* with the DIR command using uppercase letters, and displayed in mixed case. When it was created with the COPY command, the name was specified with mixed case.

7   Key in the following: A:\>**TYPE CALIFSURF.MUS** [Enter]

```
A:\>TYPE CALIFSURF.MUS

The Surf Sound of the sixties did not begin with the Beach Boys.
The first beach rocker was a left-handed guy who played a right-
handed guitar. That's right the bass string with his littlest
finger. Then came the rest of the surf rockers.


Here is a short chronology of California surfer music.

Dick Dale and the Del-tones, "Let's Go Trippin."
Jan and Dean, "Ride the Wild Surf" and "Surf City."
The Beach Boys, "Surfin' Safari" and "Surfin' U.S.A."
The Surfaris, "Surfer Joe" and "Wipe Out."
The Marketts, "Out of Limits" and "Surfer's Stomp."
Chantays, "Pipeline."
```

```
The Trashmen, "Surfin' Bird."

A:\>_
```

As you can see, the information that was contained in both the files is now contained in this one file. But, did the contents of the original two files change?

8   Key in the following: A:\>**TYPE   C:\WUGXP\MUSIC\CALIFSURF.TXT** Enter

9   Key in the following:
A:\>**TYPE   C:\WUGXP\MUSIC\CALIFSURFHITS.TXT** Enter

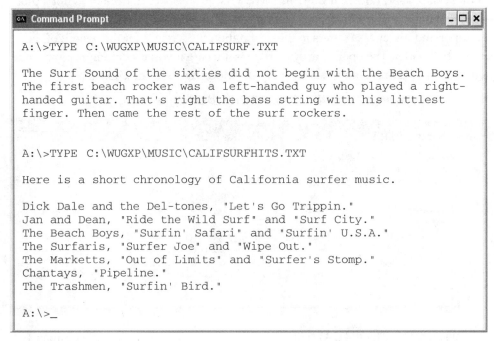

```
A:\>TYPE  C:\WUGXP\MUSIC\CALIFSURF.TXT

The Surf Sound of the sixties did not begin with the Beach Boys.
The first beach rocker was a left-handed guy who played a right-
handed guitar. That's right the bass string with his littlest
finger. Then came the rest of the surf rockers.


A:\>TYPE  C:\WUGXP\MUSIC\CALIFSURFHITS.TXT

Here is a short chronology of California surfer music.

Dick Dale and the Del-tones, "Let's Go Trippin."
Jan and Dean, "Ride the Wild Surf" and "Surf City."
The Beach Boys, "Surfin' Safari" and "Surfin' U.S.A."
The Surfaris, "Surfer Joe" and "Wipe Out."
The Marketts, "Out of Limits" and "Surfer's Stomp."
Chantays, "Pipeline."
The Trashmen, "Surfin' Bird."

A:\>_
```

As you can see, the source files remain unchanged. You merely created a third file from the contents of two files. Although you *can* join files with the plus sign, remember that this is useful for text files *only*. If you try to join two data files created by an application program using the COPY command, the application program will no longer be able to read the combined data file. You may also use wildcards to concatenate text files.

10   Key in the following: A:\>**DIR C:\WUGXP*.99** Enter

```
A:\>DIR  C:\WUGXP\*.99
 Volume in drive C is XP_FULL
 Volume Serial Number is C467-D4C1

 Directory of C:\WUGXP

10/30/2001  01:46 PM                148 AST.99
10/31/2001  07:08 PM                478 VEN.99
10/30/2001  03:42 PM                190 JUP.99
10/31/2001  01:08 PM                406 MER.99
```

```
        4 File(s)              1,222 bytes
        0 Dir(s)   21,416,771,584 bytes free

A:\>_
```

WHAT'S
HAPPENING?   Using the wildcards, you have shows that there are four files in the C:\WUGXP directory with the .99 extension. You want all of the information in one file. You could key in:

COPY AST.99 + VEN.99 + JUP.99 + MER.99 NINE.TXT

but there is a much easier way.

11 Key in the following: A:\>**COPY C:\WUGXP*.99 NINE.TXT** Enter

12 Key in the following: A:\>**TYPE NINE.TXT** Enter

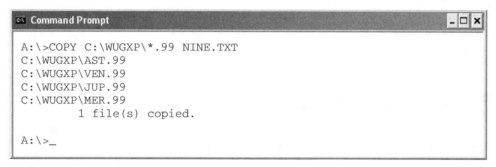

```
A:\>COPY C:\WUGXP\*.99 NINE.TXT
C:\WUGXP\AST.99
C:\WUGXP\VEN.99
C:\WUGXP\JUP.99
C:\WUGXP\MER.99
        1 file(s) copied.

A:\>_
```

WHAT'S
HAPPENING?   As you can see, you get the message "1 file(s) copied" which tells you that the contents of the four files has been placed into 1 file.

13 Key in the following: A:\>**TYPE NINE.TXT** Enter

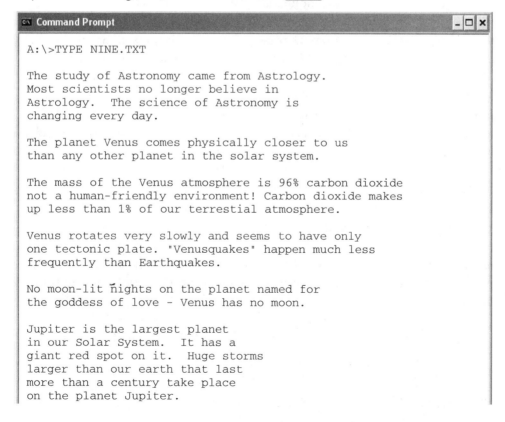

```
A:\>TYPE NINE.TXT

The study of Astronomy came from Astrology.
Most scientists no longer believe in
Astrology.  The science of Astronomy is
changing every day.

The planet Venus comes physically closer to us
than any other planet in the solar system.

The mass of the Venus atmosphere is 96% carbon dioxide
not a human-friendly environment! Carbon dioxide makes
up less than 1% of our terrestial atmosphere.

Venus rotates very slowly and seems to have only
one tectonic plate. "Venusquakes" happen much less
frequently than Earthquakes.

No moon-lit nights on the planet named for
the goddess of love - Venus has no moon.

Jupiter is the largest planet
in our Solar System.  It has a
giant red spot on it.  Huge storms
larger than our earth that last
more than a century take place
on the planet Jupiter.
```

```
Mercury is the closest planet to the sun.
We learned most of what we know about Mercury
in 1974 when the tenth in the Mariner series
flew right by it. NASA hopes to send a spacecraft
back to Mercury, the MErcury Surface Space ENvironment
GEochemistry and Ranging (or MESSENGER) would launch
in 2004, fly by Mercury twice in 2008,  and then go
into a year-long orbit of Mercury beginning in 2009.

A:\>_
```

**WHAT'S
HAPPENING?**   As you can see, the file now contains information about Astronomy, Venus, Jupiter, and Mercury. You have successfully concatenated the four files with a simple, short command line using a wildcard character (*). Again, the contents may differ if you are using the NTFS file system. The files will be copied alphabetically rather than as they were found on Drive C. If you are using FAT32, the files will be copied in the order they are found on the disk.

5.25 Printing Files

So far, you have not printed the contents of any files. You may have redirected the output of the DIR command to the printer, but this printed only file *names*, not file *contents*. You could redirect the output of the TYPE command to the printer by keying in TYPE MY.FIL > PRN, if you were not on a network that prevented it. You may also copy a file to a printer by keying in COPY MY.FIL PRN. Note here that with the COPY command, there is no redirection, but merely copying a file to a device. Again, if you are in a computer lab and printing to a network printer, this may not work. However, using either redirection or the COPY command, you need to manually eject the paper from the printer. The PRINT command makes it easier to print the contents of text files. The PRINT command will print the contents of files, not their names, and it will automatically eject the page. However, these techniques work only for ASCII files. Again, data files generated by application programs can be printed only from within the application program because the application program must send special signals to the printer so that the data prints correctly.

There are times you wish to print an ASCII file. You often will want a hard copy of configuration information on your computer. There are also other reasons for printing text files; for instance, if you have a printer problem from within an application program, the first thing you want to do is verify that it is a software problem, not a hardware problem. To test this, you return to the command line interface level and print an ASCII file. If the ASCII file prints, you now know you have a software problem within the application program and not a connection problem with your printer.

There are three ways to print a text file from the command line:

■ Use the PRINT command. The syntax of the PRINT command is as follows:

```
PRINT [/D:device] [[drive:][path]filename[...]]
/D:device    Specifies a print device.
```

■ Use redirection as you did in Chapter 2 with the DIR command.

■ Copy the contents of a file to a printer. The destination is a device, not a file. The device is the printer. Since the printer is a device, it has a reserved name: *PRN*. Sometimes this name causes problems when you are printing on a network, so you will use *LPT1* for Line Printer 1. When you use LPT1, be sure to key in the letter L, the letter P, the letter T, and the number 1. You cannot use the letter l ("ell") as the number 1. These are the names for local printers. Network printers also have specific names. The network administrator assigns the network printer name. Unless you know your network printer name, you may not be able to copy a file to the printer.

5.26   Printing in a Lab Environment

Without a local printer, printing can be complicated. In a lab environment, it takes special preparation. If you have access to only a network printer, you will have to determine if accommodation has been made for command line printing. It is probable that you will have special needs in your own lab environment for printing from the Command line. The following activity will set up printing in many lab situations. Once again, *BE SURE TO CHECK WITH YOUR LAB INSTRUCTOR BEFORE DOING THE FOLLOWING ACTIVITY!*

5.27   Activity: Setting Up Printing in a Lab Environment

1 Determine the name of the network server\printer (in this example, BUSDIV\HP504-1).

WHAT'S HAPPENING?   Now you will create two short cuts on the desktop: one to enable command line printing, and one to disable it when you are finished.

2 Return to the desktop by closing the command line window.

3 Right click the desktop, click **New**, and click **Shortcut**.

WHAT'S HAPPENING?   You have opened the Create Shortcut dialog box.

4   Fill in the location box with the information shown below, substituting the name of your server for BUSDIV and your printer for HP504-1 (all of the line may not be visible): **NET.EXE USE LPT1: \\BUSDIV\HP504-1 /YES**

5   Click **Next**.

6   Key in the following in the Shortcut name box: **Print From Command Line**

7   Click **Finish**.

WHAT'S [blank] HAPPENING?   You have created a shortcut to enable printing on the desktop.

8   Repeat step 3.

9   Repeat step 4, changing the location box information to **NET.EXE USE LPT1 /D**.

10   Repeat step 5.

11   Repeat step 6, changing the Shortcut name box information to **Stop Printing From Command Line**.

12   Click **Finish**.

WHAT'S [blank] HAPPENING?   You have created a second shortcut on the desktop to disable command line printing. In this example lab environment, before printing from the command line, double click on the Print From.... icon. When the command line printing is finished, double click on the Stop Print from... icon. In many circumstances, normal application printing will not resume until you have disabled command line printing.

REMEMBER: The previous activity is an example of the type of preparation that needs to be done to enable you to print from the command line in a networked lab environment.

13   Open a Command Line window and make A:\> the default prompt.

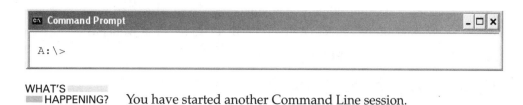

You have started another Command Line session.

5.28 Activity: Printing Files

CAUTION: Do not do this activity if you are on a network unless instructed to do so.

Note 1:   The DATA disk is in Drive A. **A:\>** is displayed.

Note 2:   Check with your lab instructor for any special instructions. (If necessary, enable command line printing.)

Note 3:   Remember, many times in a lab environment, you can use **LPT1,** the hardware name of the printer port. When **LPT1** does not work, you may try **PRN.** Other times, you need to use the printer object's *URL (Uniform Resource Locator)*, such as **\\SERVER\HP.** Once again, check with your lab instructor for what is needed in your lab.

1   Key in the following: A:\>**TYPE MER.TMP** [Enter]

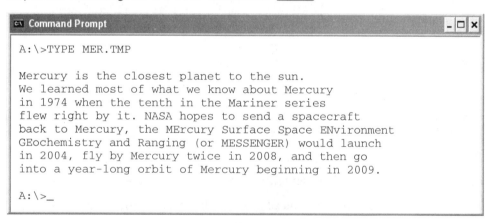

**WHAT'S
HAPPENING?**   You see the contents of the file. To print it, you may use the PRINT command.

2   Key in the following: A:\>**PRINT MER.TMP** [Enter]

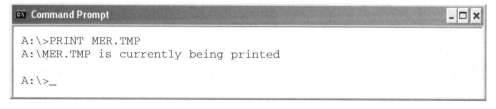

**WHAT'S
HAPPENING?**   The PRINT command tells you the status of your print job. A print job is something that you sent to the printer to be printed. If you check your printer, you should have a hard copy of the contents of the file **MER.TMP**. Note that you see

only the contents of the file, not any of the file information such as its name or size. Another advantage of the PRINT command is that you may use wildcards.

3 Key in the following: A:\>**PRINT *.TMP** Enter

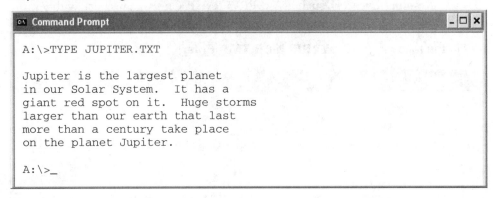

```
Command Prompt                                                    _ □ ✕

A:\>PRINT *.TMP
A:\JUP.TMP is currently being printed
A:\MER.TMP is currently being printed
A:\AST.TMP is currently being printed
A:\VEN.TMP is currently being printed

A:\>_
```

WHAT'S
HAPPENING?   Again, you see a status report. Each file's contents will have printed on a separate piece of paper and each page was automatically ejected. You may also key in multiple files names as in **PRINT VEN.TMP JUP.99**, and so on. You may also use redirection.

4 Key in the following: A:\>**TYPE JUPITER.TXT** Enter

```
Command Prompt                                                    _ □ ✕

A:\>TYPE JUPITER.TXT

Jupiter is the largest planet
in our Solar System.  It has a
giant red spot on it.  Huge storms
larger than our earth that last
more than a century take place
on the planet Jupiter.

A:\>_
```

WHAT'S
HAPPENING?   The contents of the TYPE command are written to the standard output device, the screen. You can redirect the output to another device—the printer.

5 Turn the printer on. Make sure the printer is online, or command line printing is enabled.

6 Key in the following: A:\>**TYPE JUPITER.TXT > LPT1** Enter

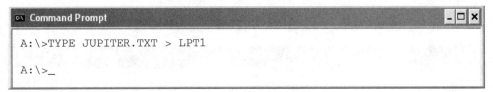

```
Command Prompt                                                    _ □ ✕
A:\>TYPE JUPITER.TXT > LPT1

A:\>_
```

WHAT'S
HAPPENING?   Nothing was written to the screen because you redirected the output to the printer. Now you want to eject the page. Depending on how your printer is set up, it may automatically eject the page without your having to take the next step. Check your printer to see if your page printed and ejected; otherwise, manually eject the page. See Activity 2.24 for the steps to take to manually eject a page. It would seem that, if this works as it did, you could also use redirection with the COPY command, but you cannot. The only output that is actually a *product* of

the copy command itself is **1 file(s) copied**. If you redirected that output, you would have only the printed message **1 file(s) copied**, not the contents of the file. Instead of using redirection, you copy the file to a device, the printer.

7 Key in the following: A:\>**COPY JUPITER.TXT LPT1** Enter

```
A:\>COPY JUPITER.TXT LPT1
        1 file(s) copied.

A:\>_
```

WHAT'S HAPPENING?   Even though you are using a device, the syntax for the COPY command remains the same. COPY is the command, the work you want done. **JUPITER.TXT** is the source, the file you want copied. You do not need to enter a drive designator in front of the file name because the operating system will assume the default. **LPT1** is the device name for the printer. The printer is the destination, where you want the contents of the file to go. As soon as you press Enter, you may hear and see the printer begin to print. If your page does not eject, manually eject it. You then see your hard copy:

```
Jupiter is the largest planet
in our Solar System.  It has a
giant red spot on it.  Huge storms
larger than our earth that last
more than a century take place
on the planet Jupiter.
```

8 If you enabled Print From Command Line, disable it now by double-clicking the Stop Print from Command Line icon.

9 Close the Command Line window.

Chapter Summary

1. One of the major reasons people buy computers is for using application programs that assist people in different tasks.
2. Application software usually generates data. Both application software and data are stored as disk files.
3. Usually, only a program can use the data files it creates. A data file without the application program cannot be used.
4. Another component of the operating system is the commands that allow the user to manage and manipulate program and data files.
5. The internal commands DIR, COPY, and TYPE allow you to manage the files on a disk.
6. The file extensions .COM (command file) and .EXE (executable code) tell the operating system that the file is a program.
7. COPY allows you to copy files selectively.
8. The syntax of the copy command is:

```
COPY [drive:][path] filename [drive:][path] filename
```

A simple way to remember the COPY syntax is

```
COPY source destination
```

Source is what you want to copy. Destination is where you want it copied.

9. The COPY command never changes the source file.

10. When naming files, it is best to stick to alphanumeric characters. Certain characters are illegal, such as the colon (:) and the asterisk (*).

11. When copying a file to a subdirectory, you must include the path name. The path name and the file name are separated by the backslash, which is used as a delimiter. The one exception is that the root directory's name is \ (backslash).

12. Wildcards may be used with the COPY command.

13. Files must have unique names when on the same drive and in the same subdirectory, but files that are copied to different subdirectories may have identical names because the path makes those file names unique.

14. TYPE allows you to display the contents of a file on the screen. The syntax is:

```
TYPE [drive:][path]filename
```

15. Wildcards may be used with the TYPE command.

16. You may use subdirectory markers with the DIR, COPY, and TYPE commands.

17. If you use *.* with a command, it chooses all the files. Thus, DIR *.* would display all the files. COPY C:\WHAT*.* A:\ would copy all the files in the WHAT directory to the disk in Drive A.

18. When you move between drives, the operating system remembers the last directory you were in.

19. Overwriting files with the COPY command is the process in which the contents of the source file copy over the contents of the destination file.

20. Concatenation means combining the contents of files using the COPY command with either + or a wildcard. There is only one destination file. You should not concatenate program files or data files generated from program files.

21. You may print the contents of an ASCII file by using the PRINT command with the name of the file or files. You may use multiple file names or use wildcards. Usually the PRINT command automatically ejects the pages.

22. Printing in a networked lab environment requires special accommodations.

23. You may also print the contents of an ASCII file by keying in TYPE filename > LPT1 or TYPE filename > PRN. If you are on a network, you may need to know the name of your device. You will probably have to manually eject the page.

24. You may also print the contents of an ASCII file by keying in COPY filename LPT1 or TYPE filename PRN. If you are on a network, you may need to know the name of your device. You will probably have to manually eject the page.

Key Terms

ASCII	overwrite	unformatted text file
concatenation	PRN	Uniform Resource
destination file	source file	Locator (URL)
LPT1		

Discussion Questions

1. Explain the function and purpose of internal commands.
2. Give two reasons for making a copy of a file on the same disk.
3. Give the syntax for the COPY command and explain each part of the syntax.
4. Is a file extension mandatory when naming a file?
5. What is the maximum number of characters that may be used when naming a file?
6. List three characters that cannot be used when naming files.
7. List three examples of legal file names.
8. When would you use a wildcard with the COPY command?
9. What is the purpose and function of the TYPE command? Explain each part of the syntax diagram.
10. How can you recognize an executable file?
11. What are ASCII files?
12. What is the purpose and function of dummy files?
13. Every file on a disk must have a unique name. Yet, when you make a copy of a file on the same disk in a different subdirectory, it may have the same file name. Explain.
14. Under what circumstances could a user think that the computer has "lost" its files?
15. Can you use wildcards with the TYPE command? Why or why not?
16. What does the first \ in any command line mean?
17. What does it mean to "overwrite" a file? What are some of the dangers of overwriting files?
18. Why would you make a copy of a file on the same disk? On another disk?
19. What would happen if you tried to copy a file from one disk to another and the destination disk already had a file with the same name?
20. How would you combine the contents of two files? Why would you?
21. What happens to the original files when you combine two or more files?
22. What are some of the dangers of concatenating program files or data files?
23. What message on the screen informs you that you have concatenated several files?
24. Name two ways that you may print the contents of an ASCII file.
25. Identify two advantages to using the PRINT command to print the contents of ASCII files.

True/False Questions

For each question, circle the letter T if the statement is true and the letter F if the statement is false.

T   F   1. The contents of two files on the same disk can be identical even though the file names are different.

T   F   2. It is a good idea to concatenate text files and program files.

T   F   3. The COPY command is an internal command.

T   F   4. The contents of files are not affected by displaying them with the TYPE command.

T   F   5. To save time when copying multiple files to a different disk, you can use wildcards.

Completion Questions

Write the correct answer in each blank space.

6. There are two mandatory parameters for the COPY command. They are the _____ and the _____.

7. When you replace the contents of a file with the contents of a different file, this process is known as _____.

8. You can differentiate between a program file and a data file by the file _____.

9. If you wish to display the contents of a text file on the screen, you would use the _____ command.

10. The delimiter that is used to separate a file name from a file extension is _____.

Multiple Choice Questions

For each question, write the letter for the correct answer in the blank space.

____   11. The COPY command can be used to
   a. copy a file from one disk to another.
   b. make a second copy of an existing file on the same disk with a new name.
   c. copy a file from one directory to another directory.
   d. all of the above

____   12. Files may be copied to another disk in order to
   a. make backup copies.
   b. copy a program to another disk.
   c. share data files with others.
   d. all of the above

____   13. To display the contents of an ASCII file on the screen, you use the
   a. DIR command.
   b. TYPE command.
   c. VIEW command.
   d. SEE command.

____   14. COPY *.TXT THE.FIL will result in
   a. joining together all files with the .TXT extension to a file called THE.FIL.
   b. joining THE.FIL to all files with the .TXT extension.
   c. creating a new set of files with the same file name having .FIL as an extension.
   d. none of the above

____   15. COPY MY.TXT \DATA\OLD.TXT will
   a. copy the file MY.TXT to a new file called DATA.
   b. copy the file MY.TXT to a new file called OLD.TXT in the subdirectory DATA.
   c. copy the file OLD.TXT to a file called MY.TXT in the subdirectory DATA.
   d. copy the file called DATA to a file called MY.TXT in the subdirectory called OLD.TXT.

Writing Commands

Write the correct steps or commands to perform the required action *as if* you were at the computer. The prompt will indicate the default drive and directory.

16. Copy the file called OLD.FIL from the root of Drive C to the root of Drive A, keeping the same file name.

    A:\>

17. Copy all files in the default directory with the .TXT file extension to files with the same names but with the .DOC file extension.

    A:\>

18. On the default drive, copy the file JOE from the root directory to the INFO directory, and call the new file NAMES.

    A:\>

19. Copy the contents of two files, one named DOG *and* one named CAT from the default directory to a file called ANIMALS in the \MYFILES directory.

    A:\>

20. Copy all files from the default directory with the extension .TXT to the subdirectory TXTFILES.

    A:\>

Homework Assignments

Note 1: Place the HOMEWORK disk in Drive A. Be sure to work on the HOME-WORK disk, not the DATA disk.

Note 2: The homework problems will assume Drive C is the hard disk and the HOMEWORK disk is in Drive A. If you are using another drive, such as floppy Drive B or hard Drive D, be sure to substitute that drive letter when reading the questions and answers.

Note 3: All subdirectories will be created under the root directory unless otherwise specified.

Problem Set I

Problem A

Note: If the DATA disk is in Drive A, remove it and place it in a safe place. *Do not* use the DATA disk for these homework problems.

A-a Insert the HOMEWORK disk into Drive A.

A-b Copy the file called **GRAMMY.REC** from the **WUGXP** subdirectory to the root directory of the HOMEWORK disk keeping the same file name.

A-c Copy the file called **GRAMMY.REC** from the **WUGXP** subdirectory to the root directory of the HOMEWORK disk but call the new file **GRAMMY.TAP**.

A-d   Execute the DIR command to display only the **GRAMMY** files on the HOME-
WORK disk.

_____   1. What date is listed for the files?
  - a. 10/31/2002
  - b. 10/31/2001
  - c. 10/01/2001
  - d. 10/01/2002

_____   2. What are the sizes of the GRAMMY files in bytes?
  - a. GRAMMY.REC = 1,334 and GRAMMY.TAP = 1,434
  - b. GRAMMY.REC = 1,335and GRAMMY.TAP = 1,534
  - c. both files are 1,334 bytes
  - d. GRAMMY.REC = 1,434and GRAMMY.TAP = 1,434

A-e   While in the root of the HOMEWORK disk, copy the file **GRAMMY.REC** to
GRAM:.REC.

_____   3. What message appears on the screen?
  - a. File(s) copied
  - b. Invalid file name
  - c. The filename, directory name, or volume label syntax is incorrect.
  - d. no message was displayed

Problem B

B-a   Copy any files with the file extension **.99** from the **WUGXP** subdirectory to
the root directory of the HOMEWORK disk keeping the same file names.

_____   4. How many files were copied?
  - a. two
  - b. four
  - c. six
  - d. eight

B-b   Execute the DIR command to display only the files with the extension of **.99**
on the HOMEWORK disk.

_____   5. What date is displayed for the files?
  - a. 10/30/2001 and 10/31/2001
  - b. 10/30/2000 and 10/31/2000
  - c. 10/30/1999 and 10/31/1999
  - d. 10/30/1998 and 10/31/1998

B-c   Create a subdirectory on the HOMEWORK disk called **FILES**.

B-d   Copy all the files with the extension of **.99** from the root directory of the
HOMEWORK disk into this subdirectory but give them the new extension of
.FIL.

B-e   Do a directory display of the **FILES** directory.

____ 6. There is a line in the resulting display that states
   a. 2 File(s)   1,222 bytes
   b. 4 File(s)   1,222 bytes
   c. 6 File(s)   1,222 bytes
   d. 8 File(s)   1,222 bytes

B-f   Create a subdirectory on the HOMEWORK disk called **BOOKS**.

B-g   Copy all the files in the **WUGXP\MEDIA\BOOKS** directory to the **BOOKS** directory keeping the same file name(s).

____ 7. How many files were copied?
   a. seven
   b. five
   c. three
   d. one

Problem C

C-a   Display the contents of the **GRAMMY.REC** file located in the root directory of the HOMEWORK disk.

____ 8. Who received the Pop Dance Recording award?
   a. Sting
   b. Rob Thomas
   c. Santana
   d. Cher

C-b   Display the contents of the **GOLD_OLD.MOV** file located in the **C:\WUGXP\MEDIA\MOVIES** directory.

____ 9. What movie title is displayed?
   a. Citizen Kane
   b. Desk Set
   c. Key Largo
   d. Shane

C-c   Display the contents of the **MYSTERY.BKS** file located in the **BOOKS** directory of the HOMEWORK disk.

____ 10. What author's name is NOT displayed?
   a. Josephine Tey
   b. Sue Grafton
   c. Peter Robinson
   d. Janet Dawson

Problem D

D-a   Create a subdirectory called **ROOM** on the HOMEWORK disk under the **FILES** directory created in Problem B.

D-b   On the HOMEWORK disk change the default directory to **ROOM**.

D-c   Using subdirectory markers, copy the file called **VEN.FIL** from the **FILES** directory to the **ROOM** directory keeping the same name but giving it the new extension of **.RMS**.

___   11. Which command did you use?
        a. COPY \..\VEN.FIL \VEN.RMS
        b. COPY ..\VEN.FIL VEN.RMS
        c. COPY ..\VEN.FIL \VEN.RMS
        d. COPY ..\VEN.FIL ..\VEN.RMS

Problem E

E-a   Change to the root directory of the HOMEWORK disk.
    Note: The root directory of the HOMEWORK disk is the default drive and directory.

E-b   Copy any file with a **.TMP** extension from the **WUGXP** directory to the root of the HOMEWORK disk, keeping the same file names but giving them the extension of **.TRP**.

E-c   Copy the file called **VEN.99** from the root directory of the HOMEWORK disk to the subdirectory called **HISTORY** giving the file the new name of **VEN.ICE**.

E-d   Copy any files with a **.99** file extension from the root directory of the HOME-WORK disk to the **HISTORY** subdirectory, but give the files the new extension of **.ICE**.

___   12. Which command did you use?
        a. COPY *.99 HISTORY
        b. COPY *.99 HISTORY*.ICE
        c. COPY *.99 *.ICE
        d. COPY .ICE \HISTORY\.99

___   13. What message was displayed?
        a. 1 file(s) copied
        b. Overwrite HISTORY\VEN.ICE? (Yes/No/All):
        c. Overwrite VEN.ICE (Yes/No/All)?
        d. no message was displayed

E-e   Take any steps necessary to copy the files.
    Note: The root directory of the HOMEWORK disk is the default drive and directory.

E-f   Overwrite the file **A:\BONJOUR.TRP** with the contents of the file called **RIGHT.UP**, which is located in the **WUGXP** directory.

___   14. Which command did you use?
        a. COPY C:\BONJOUR.TRP RIGHT.UP
        b. COPY C:\WUGXP\RIGHT.UP BONJOUR.TRP
        c. COPY C:\WUGXP\BONJOUR.TRP C:\WUGXP\RIGHT.UP
        d. COPY C:\WUGXP\RIGHT.UP RIGHT.UP

E-g Display the contents of the file called **BONJOUR.TRP** on the HOMEWORK disk.

_____ 15. What is the first line in the file?
- a. HELLO, GUTEN TAG
- b. BUONGIORNO,BONJOUR
- c. Forces associated with the rotation of Earth cause the planet
- d. Precession of Earth's Axis

Problem F

Note: The root directory of the HOMEWORK disk is the default drive and directory.

F-a Copy all the files that begin with **EX** and have **FEB** within the name and have the extension **.dta** from the **WUGXP** directory to the root directory of the HOMEWORK disk.

_____ 16. Which command did you use?
- a. COPY C:\WUGXP\EX*FEB*.DTA
- b. COPY C:\WUGXP\EXFEB*.DTA
- c. COPY C:\WUGXP\EX*F.DTA
- d. COPY C:\WUGXP\?EX*FEB.DTA

_____ 17. How many files were copies?
- a. one.
- b. two.
- c. three.
- d. four.

F-b Concatenate the files called **EXP01FEB.DTA** and **EXP02FEB.DTA** and **EXP03FEB.DTA** (in that order) to the root directory of the HOMEWORK disk, calling the new file **FEBEXP.DTA**

_____ 18. Which command did you use?
- a. COPY EXP*FEB*.DTA FEBEXP.DTA
- b. COPY EXP01FEB.DTA + EXP02FEB.DTA + EXP03FEB.DTA
   FEBEXP.DTA
- c. COPY *FEB*.DTA FEBEXP.DTA
- d. COPY EX*.* EX*.*

F-c Display the contents of the file **FEBEXP.DTA** on the HOMEWORK disk.

_____ 19. What is the last line in the file?
- a. TOTAL   2340.00
- b. TOTAL   2245.00
- c. TOTAL   2270.00
- d. MONTHLY EXPENSES FOR FEBRUARY, 2003

Note: The root directory of the HOMEWORK disk is the default drive and directory.

F-d Concatenate all the files from the WUGXP directory that have the filename **EARTH** with any extension to the subdirectory **FILES** on the HOMEWORK disk. The new file should be named **EARTH.ALL**. Use a wildcard.

____ 20. Which command did you use?
  a. COPY C:\EARTH* A:FILES\EARTH*
  b. COPY C:\WUGXP\EARTH.* A:\FILES\EARTH.ALL
  c. COPY EARTH.ALL FILES\EARTH.ALL
  d. COPY C:\WUGXP\EARTH.ALL A:\FILES

Note: The root directory of the HOMEWORK disk is the default drive and directory.

F-e   Display the contents of the file **EARTH.ALL** created in **F-d** above.

____ 21. The EARTH.ALL contains the contents of
  a. the first Earth file.
  b. the second Earth file.
  c. the third Earth file.
  d. the first, second, and third Earth files.

Problem G

Note 1:   Check with your lab instructor prior to proceeding with this problem.

Note 2:   Remember, use the method of printing (LPT1, PRN, or the URL of your printer) that works in your particular lab environment.

Note 3:   You may not be able to do this activity in your lab environment. Check with your instructor to see if you should proceed.

Note 4:   The root directory of the HOMEWORK disk is the default drive and directory.

Print the files whose names begin with called **AST** located on the root of the HOMEWORK disk using the TYPE command and redirection (>) (*Note:* If you used **PRN** or a URL instead of **LPT1**, substitute what you use for **LPT1** in the answers.)

____ 22. Which command did you use? (*Note:* If you are in a lab environment that uses a URL, assume that LPT1 is your URL.)
  a. TYPE > AST*.* LPT1
  b. TYPE > LPT1 AST*.*
  c. TYPE AST*.* > LPT1
  d. All of the above commands work.

Problem H

Note: The root directory of the HOMEWORK disk is the default drive and directory.

H-a   Copy all the files from the **WUGXP** directory that have the file extension of **.BAT** to the root of the HOMEWORK disk.

____ 23. How many files were copied?
  a. two
  b. four
  c. six
  d. eight

H-b   Copy the file called **MARK.FIL** and the file called **GETYN.COM** from the **WUGXP** directory to the root of the HOMEWORK disk.

____ 24. Is there a way use one command to copy both of these files simultaneously from the command line?

  a. yes

  b. no

____ 25. What is the size, in bytes, of GETYN.COM?

  a. 326

  b. 226

  c. 126

  d. 26

____ 26. What kind of file is GETYN.COM?

  a. data

  b. text

  c. program

  d. none of the above

Problem Set II—At the Computer

Note 1:   Before proceeding with these assignments, check with your lab instructor to see if there are any special procedures you should follow.

Note 2:   The HOMEWORK disk is in Drive A. A:\> is displayed as the default drive and the default directory. All work will occur on the HOMEWORK disk.

Note 3:   Make sure that **NAME.BAT**, **MARK.FIL**, **GETYN.COM**, and **GO.BAT** are all present in the root directory of the HOMEWORK disk before proceeding with these problems.

Note 4:   All files with the **.HW** extension *must* be created in the root directory of the HOMEWORK disk.

1   Key in the following: A:\>**NAME** Enter

2   Here is an example to key in, but your instructor will have other information that applies to your class. Key in the following:

Bette A. Peat Enter   (*Your* name goes here.)

CIS 55 Enter   (*Your* class goes here.)

T-Th 8-9:30 Enter   (*Your* day and time go here.)

Chapter 5 Homework Enter

3   Press F6 Enter

4   If the information is correct, press **Y** and you are back to A:\>.

WHAT'S ▒▒▒▒
▒▒ HAPPENING?   You have returned to the system level. You now have a file called **NAME.FIL** with your name and other pertinent information. *Hint*: Remember redirection.

To Create 1.HW

1   Create a subdirectory called **MOVIES** under the root directory of the HOME-WORK disk.

2   Copy all the files in the **WUGXP\MEDIA\MOVIES** directory to the **MOVIES** directory on the HOMEWORK disk and keep the same file names.

3   Locate all the files in the **MOVIES** directory on the HOMEWORK disk.

4   Place the names of the files in a file called **1.HW**.

To Create 2.HW

1   On the HOMEWORK disk, make a copy of all the files in the **MOVIES** directory in the **MOVIES** directory, keeping the same file names but having a new extension of **.FLM**.

2   Locate only the files in the **MOVIES** directory that have the extension of **.FLM** on the HOMEWORK disk.

3   Place the names of the files with only an extension of **.FLM** in a file called **2.HW**.

To Create 3.HW

Redirect the contents (not the file name) of the file called **BESTPIC.FLM** in the **MOVIES** directory on the HOMEWORK disk to a file called **3.HW**.

To Create 4.HW

1   Overwrite the file called **BESTPIC.FLM** in the **MOVIES** directory on the HOME-WORK disk with the contents of the file called **VEN.99** located in the root directory of the HOMEWORK disk.

2   Redirect the contents (not the file name) of the file called **BESTPIC.FLM** in the **MOVIES** directory on the HOMEWORK disk to a file called **4.HW**.

To Create 5.HW

1   Concatenate all the files that have the extension **.RED** from the **WUGXP** directory to the **MOVIES** directory on the HOMEWORK disk.

2   Call the new file **MYRED.FIL**.

3   Redirect the contents (not the file name) of the file called **MYRED.FIL** to a file called **5.HW**.

To Print Your Homework

1   Be sure the printer is on and ready to accept print jobs from your computer.

2   Key in the following (be very careful to make no typing errors):
   GO NAME.FIL 1.HW 2.HW 3.HW 4.HW 5.HW Enter

> WHATS ▨▨▨▨
> ▨▨HAPPENING?   If the files you requested, 1.HW, 2.HW, etc., do not exist in the default directory, you will see the following message on the screen:

```
File Not Found
The system cannot find the file specified.

Is there a message that says "File Not Found. The system cannot
find the file specified."

If so, press Y to find out what could be wrong.

Otherwise, press N to continue.
```

The operating system is telling you that the file cannot be found. If you see this screen, press **Y** to see what could be wrong, and repeat the print procedure after you have corrected the problem.

If the default directory contains the specified files, the following message will appear on the screen:

```
Is there a message that say "File Not Found. The system cannot
find the file specified."

If so, press Y to find out what could be wrong.

Otherwise, press N to continue.
```

You will need to press **N** once for each file you are printing.

3 Follow the messages on the screen until the Notepad program opens with a screen similar to the following:

WHAT'S HAPPENING?   All the requested files have been found and placed in a Notepad document. Your homework is now ready to print.

4 On the Notepad menu bar, click **File**. Click **Print**.

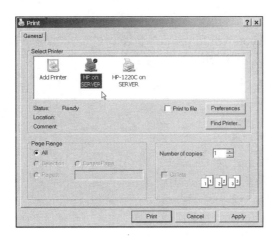

WHAT'S HAPPENING?   The print dialog box opens. If you have more than one printer, all your printer choices will be displayed. The default printer is the highlighted printer.

5   Click the **Print** button.

6   In the Notepad window, click **File**. Click **Exit**.

WHAT'S ▨▨▨
▨▨ HAPPENING?   The following will appear on the Command Prompt screen:

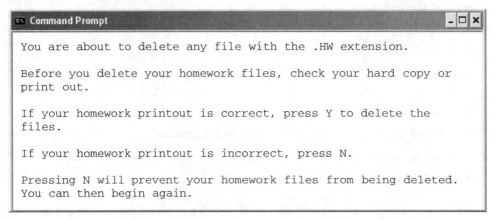

At this point, look at your printout. If it is correct, you can press **Y** to delete the homework files for this chapter. If your printout is incorrect, you can press **N**. That will preserve your homework and you will need to redo only the problem that was incorrect, not all the homework assignments.

7   Press **Y** [Enter]

WHAT'S ▨▨▨
▨▨ HAPPENING?   You have returned to the default prompt.

8   Close the Command Prompt session.

9   Execute the shut-down procedure.

Problem Set III—Brief Essay

1. Copying and printing files can be done from My Computer or Windows Explorer. Why or why not might you use the command line to accomplish these tasks?
2. Briefly explain the purpose and function of subdirectory markers. Give three examples of how you would use subdirectory markers. Include commands that can be used with subdirectory markers.

CHAPTER 6

USING
DEL, REN, MOVE, AND RD /S

Learning Objectives

After completing this chapter you will be able to:

1. Explain why it is necessary to eliminate files from a disk.
2. Explain when and how to use wildcards with the DEL command.
3. Explain the use of the /P parameter with the DEL command.
4. Explain the purpose and function of the RENAME/REN command.
5. Explain the purpose and function of the MOVE command.
6. Explain the purpose and function of the RD /S command.
7. Explain the importance of backing up data.

9. Back up a data disk using the DISKCOPY command.
10. Back up files using the COPY command.

Student Outcomes

1. Use the DEL command to eliminate files on disks and in directories.
2. Use wildcards appropriately with the DEL command.
3. Use parameters with the DEL command.
4. Use the RENAME/REN command to change the names of file and subdirectories.
5. Use the RENAME/REN command with wildcards to change the names of files and subdirectories.
6. Use the MOVE command to move files and subdirectories.
7. Use the RD command without parameters to delete empty directories.
8. Use the RD command with parameters to delete directories with files and other directories.

Chapter Overview

The more work you do with computers, the more files you create, and the harder it is to manage them. It becomes increasingly difficult to keep track of what disks have which files and which files are needed. In addition, as new data is keyed into existing files, the names given to the files may no longer be appropriate. It is also important to be able to make a copy of an entire disk or specific files on a disk so that data is not lost due to a power failure, a power surge, or a bad disk.

In this chapter, you will continue to work with commands that help you manage and manipulate your files. This chapter will focus on the DEL command, which allows you to delete files you no longer need or want; the RENAME command, which is used to rename files; and the MOVE command, which allows you to move files and subdirectories from one location to another. In addition, you will look at the RD /S command, which allows you to quickly eliminate a subdirectory and all its files. You will also learn why and how to back up specific files or an entire disk so that you do not lose important data.

6.1   Eliminating Files with the DEL Command

In the various activities completed previously, you copied many files. The DATA disk began as a disk absent of files. As you have been working, the number of files on the disk has increased dramatically. This is typical when working with computers. There is a kind of Murphy's Law that says you create as many files as you have disk space. However, you do not want to keep files forever. The more files and/or disks you have, the harder it is to keep track of what disks have which files and which files are the ones you need. If you have floppy disks, you end up with many floppies, and if you have a hard disk, you end up with many subdirectories and many files. Often, you are not quite sure what files are where. By keeping only the files you need on your disk, you will decrease the number of files you have to manage.

Logic tells you that, if you can copy and create files, you should be able to eliminate files by deleting or erasing them. You can do these tasks with the DEL command, which is identical to another command, ERASE (for the purposes of this book, the DEL command will be discussed with the understanding that ERASE works the same way). This command is internal, always resident in memory. You do need to be careful with this command. Once you press **Enter** after the DEL command, the file is gone forever. The operating system does not ask you if this is really the file you want to get rid of; it simply obeys your instructions.

When a file is deleted at the command line, it cannot be recovered except by certain special utility programs. Even then, recovery is not necessarily complete or even possible. Technically, when you delete a file, the file is not actually physically removed from the disk. Instead, the first character of the file name is replaced with a special byte—the symbol **s**—that marks the file as deleted in the directory entry table. Then a 0 is placed in each cluster entry in the FAT (file allocation table). The value of 0 in each cluster means to the operating system that the space is now available for reuse by other files, even though, in fact, the data is still on the disk. When you create the next file, the operating system sees that there is space available in the directory entry table and the FAT and assigns the new file to that space. The old file is overwritten by the new file. If you are using the NTFS file system, the process is similar; instead of the FAT, the file's MFT entry, directory entry, and data clusters are marked as available. The file's data remains, though, until the clusters get recycled to store some other file.

Special utility programs, such as Norton Utilities, can occasionally help you recover deleted files, particularly if you realize immediately that you inadvertently erased a file. In versions of the operating system from MS-DOS version 5.0 through MS-DOS version 6.22, the UNDELETE command was available. UNDELETE was an operating system utility supplied to recover deleted files. However, once a file was overwritten by new data, nothing could recover the previous data. It was gone forever. When you use the DEL command in the Windows operating system, you cannot recover deleted files. UNDELETE is not supported by Windows XP Professional, nor was is supported by Windows 2000 Professional. In Windows 9x versions, you could boot to the command line, and occasionally recover deleted files, but that is no longer the case. Thus, you should consider that, for all practical purposes, when you use DEL, you have indeed permanently removed the file or files.

When you delete a file from a hard drive using My Computer or Windows Explorer (using the Windows GUI), the file goes to the Recycle Bin and is then recoverable. You can open the Recycle Bin, select the file you deleted, and restore it. However, if you never empty your Recycle Bin, eventually it becomes full and Windows begins deleting the oldest files in the Recycle Bin. Files are not recoverable if you delete them from a removable disk, such as a Zip drive or a floppy disk. Files deleted from the command prompt bypass the Recycle Bin and cannot be recovered by the operating system.

The syntax of the DEL command (identical to ERASE) is:

```
DEL [/P] [/F] [/S] [/Q] [/A[[:]attributes]] names
ERASE [/P] [/F] [/S] [/Q] [/A[[:]attributes]] names
```

The /P parameter prompts you before each file is deleted. /F forces the deletion of read-only files. /S deletes specified files from the current directory and all subdirectories. /Q puts the command in quiet mode; you are not prompted to confirm the deletion. /A deletes files based on specified attributes. The attributes are abbreviated as follows: R, read-only; A, archive; s, system; h, hidden; -, a prefix meaning "not."

6.2   Activity: Using the DEL Command

Note 1:   When keying in commands, you may use the editing keys to correct typographical errors.

Note 2:   Be sure the DATA disk, not the HOMEWORK disk, is in Drive A.

Note 3:   C:\> is displayed as the default drive and directory.

1   Key in the following: C:\>**A:** [Enter]

2   Key in the following: A:\>**COPY C:\WUGXP*.DOS *.AAA** [Enter]

```
Command Prompt                                        _ □ ✕

C:\>A:

C:\WUGXP>A:

A:\>COPY C:\WUGXP\*.DOS *.AAA
C:\WUGXP\WILDTWO.DOS
C:\WUGXP\WILDTHR.DOS
C:\WUGXP\WILDONE.DOS
         3 file(s) copied.

A:\>_
```

WHAT'S HAPPENING?   You changed the default drive to A. You then copied the files with a **.DOS** extension from the **\WUGXP** directory, keeping the same file names but giving them a different extension (**.AAA**), to the root of the DATA disk.

3   Key in the following: A:\>**DIR *.AAA** Enter

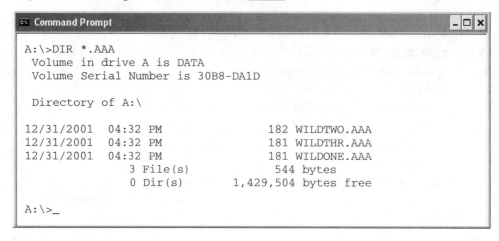

```
A:\>DIR *.AAA
 Volume in drive A is DATA
 Volume Serial Number is 30B8-DA1D

 Directory of A:\

12/31/2001  04:32 PM                182 WILDTWO.AAA
12/31/2001  04:32 PM                181 WILDTHR.AAA
12/31/2001  04:32 PM                181 WILDONE.AAA
               3 File(s)            544 bytes
               0 Dir(s)      1,429,504 bytes free

A:\>_
```

WHAT'S ▓▓▓▓▓▓▓
▓▓▓▓HAPPENING?   You used the DIR command to confirm that the **.AAA** files are on the DATA disk. The work you wish to do is delete files. The DEL command is an internal command and was installed in memory (RAM) when you booted the system. It will remain in memory until you turn off the power. It is a good practice to use DIR before DEL with the same parameters. In this way, you can be extra sure which files you will be deleting.

4   Key in the following: A:\>**DIR WILDONE.AAA** Enter

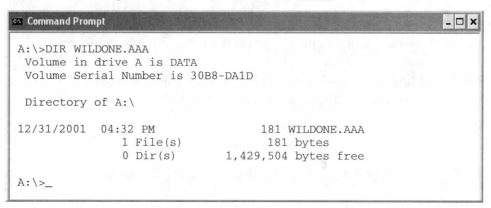

```
A:\>DIR WILDONE.AAA
 Volume in drive A is DATA
 Volume Serial Number is 30B8-DA1D

 Directory of A:\

12/31/2001  04:32 PM                181 WILDONE.AAA
               1 File(s)            181 bytes
               0 Dir(s)      1,429,504 bytes free

A:\>_
```

WHAT'S ▓▓▓▓▓▓▓
▓▓▓▓HAPPENING?   The DIR command verified that the file called **WILDONE.AAA** is located on the DATA disk.

5   Key in the following: A:\>**DEL WILDONE.AAA** Enter

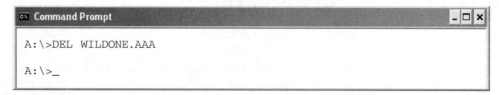

```
A:\>DEL WILDONE.AAA

A:\>_
```

WHAT'S ▓▓▓▓▓▓▓
▓▓▓▓HAPPENING?   You asked the DEL command to eliminate the file called **WILDONE.AAA**, located on the DATA disk. You did not need to include the drive letter or \ because the operating system assumed the default drive and directory and looked only for the file called **WILDONE.AAA** on the DATA disk in the root.

However, it appears that nothing happened. All you got on the screen was the system prompt.

6   Key in the following: A:\>**DIR WILDONE.AAA** [Enter]

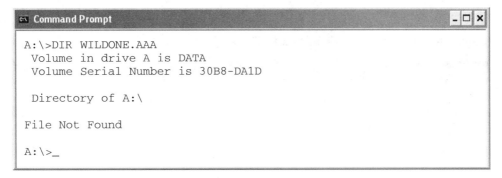

```
A:\>DIR WILDONE.AAA
 Volume in drive A is DATA
 Volume Serial Number is 30B8-DA1D

 Directory of A:\

File Not Found

A:\>_
```

WHAT'S HAPPENING?   The DIR command confirmed that the file is gone. You now know that the DEL command was executed and that it removed the file called **WILDONE.AAA**. It is no longer on the DATA disk. What if the file you wanted to delete was not on the disk?

7   Key in the following: A:\>**DEL NOFILE.XXX** [Enter]

```
A:\>DEL NOFILE.XXX
Could Not Find A:\NOFILE.XXX

A:\>_
```

WHAT'S HAPPENING?   In order for the DEL command to execute, it must be able to find the file to delete. Here, the file was not found.

8   Key in the following: A:\>**DEL** [Enter]

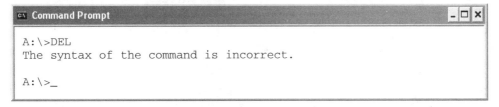

```
A:\>DEL
The syntax of the command is incorrect.

A:\>_
```

WHAT'S HAPPENING?   Not only must the operating system find the file but it also must know what file to look for. Remember, the syntax is DEL *names*.

6.3   Deleting Multiple Files

You can delete more than one file at a time with the DEL command. List the files you want to delete after the DEL command, separated by spaces. Remember, it is always a good idea to use the DIR command first.

6.4   Activity: Using DEL with Multiple Parameters

1   Key in the following: A:\>**COPY C:\WUGXP*.DOS *.BBB** [Enter]

2   Key in the following: A:\>**DIR *.BBB** [Enter]

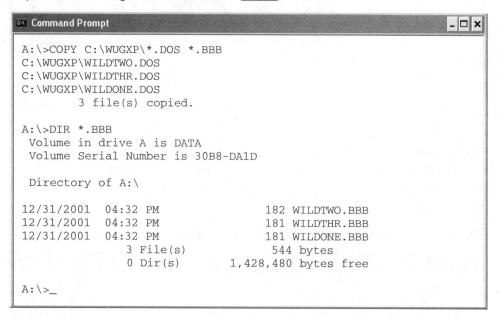

```
A:\>COPY C:\WUGXP\*.DOS *.BBB
C:\WUGXP\WILDTWO.DOS
C:\WUGXP\WILDTHR.DOS
C:\WUGXP\WILDONE.DOS
        3 file(s) copied.

A:\>DIR *.BBB
 Volume in drive A is DATA
 Volume Serial Number is 30B8-DA1D

 Directory of A:\

12/31/2001  04:32 PM                182 WILDTWO.BBB
12/31/2001  04:32 PM                181 WILDTHR.BBB
12/31/2001  04:32 PM                181 WILDONE.BBB
               3 File(s)            544 bytes
               0 Dir(s)       1,428,480 bytes free

A:\>_
```

WHAT'S HAPPENING?   You copied the same files from the previous exercise and used the DIR command to verify their presence on the DATA disk.

3   Key in the following:

A:\>**DIR WILDONE.BBB WILDTWO.BBB WILDTHR.BBB** [Enter]

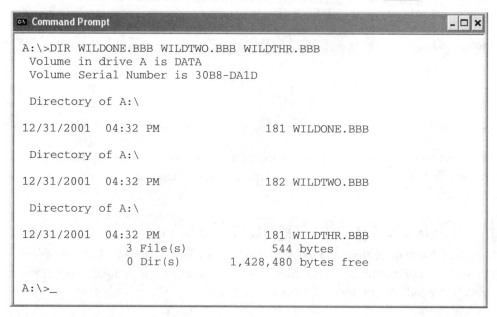

```
A:\>DIR WILDONE.BBB WILDTWO.BBB WILDTHR.BBB
 Volume in drive A is DATA
 Volume Serial Number is 30B8-DA1D

 Directory of A:\

12/31/2001  04:32 PM                181 WILDONE.BBB

 Directory of A:\

12/31/2001  04:32 PM                182 WILDTWO.BBB

 Directory of A:\

12/31/2001  04:32 PM                181 WILDTHR.BBB
               3 File(s)            544 bytes
               0 Dir(s)       1,428,480 bytes free

A:\>_
```

WHAT'S HAPPENING?   You have identified the three files you want to delete.

4   Key in the following:

A:\>**DEL WILDONE.BBB WILDTWO.BBB WILDTHR.BBB** [Enter]

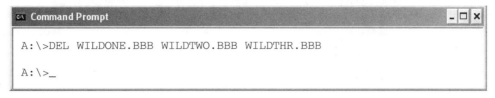

```
A:\>DEL WILDONE.BBB WILDTWO.BBB WILDTHR.BBB

A:\>_
```

WHAT'S HAPPENING?   No message appears on the screen. Were the files in fact deleted?

5   Key in the following: A:\>**DIR *.BBB** [Enter]

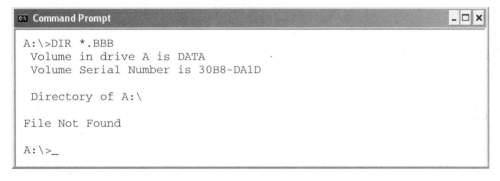

```
A:\>DIR *.BBB
 Volume in drive A is DATA
 Volume Serial Number is 30B8-DA1D

 Directory of A:\

File Not Found

A:\>_
```

WHAT'S HAPPENING?   The DIR command has confirmed that the files were deleted.

6.5   Deleting Files on Other Drives and Directories

Using the DEL command to eliminate files works exactly the same on other drives and subdirectories as it did in the previous activities. The syntax of the command remains DEL *names*. The only difference is that you must specify which disk drive and which directory you want to look on. Once again, the operating system follows your instructions exactly as keyed in; it does not check with you to see if you are deleting the correct file. One of the most common mistakes computer users make is placing the drive designator or subdirectory in the wrong place, which can completely change the meaning and results of an instruction. Again, the syntax of the command is:

DEL *names*

DEL is the command; *names* represents the designated drives, subdirectories, and names of the files you wish to delete. Notice that DEL and names are not in brackets, so they are required parts of the command.

6.6   Activity: Using the DEL Command with Individual Files

Note: The DATA disk is in Drive A. A:\> is displayed.

1   Key in the following: A:\>**MD TRIP** [Enter]

2   Key in the following: A:\>**COPY C:\WUGXP*.99 TRIP** [Enter]

3   Key in the following: A:\>**COPY C:\WUGXP*.JAZ TRIP** [Enter]

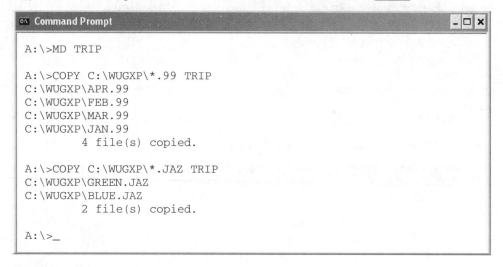

```
A:\>MD TRIP

A:\>COPY C:\WUGXP\*.99 TRIP
C:\WUGXP\APR.99
C:\WUGXP\FEB.99
C:\WUGXP\MAR.99
C:\WUGXP\JAN.99
        4 file(s) copied.

A:\>COPY C:\WUGXP\*.JAZ TRIP
C:\WUGXP\GREEN.JAZ
C:\WUGXP\BLUE.JAZ
        2 file(s) copied.

A:\>_
```

WHAT'S
HAPPENING?   You created another subdirectory on the DATA disk called **TRIP**.
You then copied files from the **\WUGXP** subdirectory on the hard disk to the
subdirectory called **TRIP** on the DATA disk. You used the COPY command. You had
to specify where the source files were located, **C:\WUGXP**. However, for the
destination of these files, since the default drive is A and the default directory is the
root, the OS assumed the default, and you did not have to specify either the destination drive or the root directory in the destination. If you had not included the name
of the subdirectory **TRIP**, where you wanted the files copied, the operating system
would have assumed the default and copied the files to the root directory of the
DATA disk. The longhand or absolute path version of the command is
A:\>**COPY C:\WUGXP*.99 A:\TRIP*.99**.

4   Key in the following: A:\>**DIR TRIP\JUP.99** [Enter]

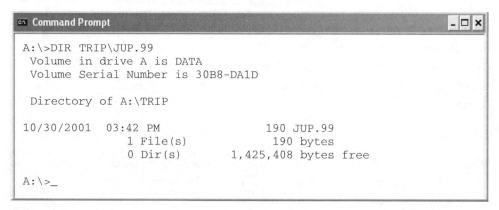

```
A:\>DIR TRIP\JUP.99
 Volume in drive A is DATA
 Volume Serial Number is 30B8-DA1D

 Directory of A:\TRIP

10/30/2001  03:42 PM              190 JUP.99
               1 File(s)          190 bytes
               0 Dir(s)     1,425,408 bytes free

A:\>_
```

WHAT'S
HAPPENING?   The file is there. You successfully copied it.

5   Key in the following: A:\>**DEL TRIP\JUP.99** [Enter]

```
A:\>DEL TRIP\JUP.99

A:\>_
```

**WHAT'S
HAPPENING?**   You had to provide the proper syntax to tell the DEL command where the **JUP.99** file was located. It was located in the subdirectory **TRIP** under the root directory on the DATA disk. Since the default drive is A, you did not need to include the drive letter. Since the default subdirectory is the root (\), the \ is assumed and does not need to be keyed in. However, the \ between the subdirectory **TRIP** and the file name **JUP.99** does need to be keyed in. In this case \ is used as a delimiter between the subdirectory name and the file name. Has the file been deleted?

6   Key in the following: A:\>**DIR TRIP\JUP.99** [Enter]

```
A:\>DIR TRIP\JUP.99
 Volume in drive A is DATA
 Volume Serial Number is 30B8-DA1D

 Directory of A:\TRIP

File Not Found

A:\>_
```

**WHAT'S
HAPPENING?**   The file called **JUP.99** is gone from the subdirectory called **TRIP** on the DATA disk. Look at the display. The third line returned by the command, **Directory of A:\TRIP**, tells you that DIR looked only in the subdirectory called **TRIP**.

7   Key in the following: A:\>**CD /D C:\WUGXP** [Enter]

8   Key in the following: C:\WUGXP>**COPY HELLO.TXT A:** [Enter]

```
A:\>CD /D C:\WUGXP

C:\WUGXP>COPY HELLO.TXT A:\
        1 file(s) copied.

C:\WUGXP>_
```

**WHAT'S
HAPPENING?**   You changed the default drive and the default subdirectory from the root of the hard disk to the subdirectory called **\WUGXP** on Drive C. You then copied the file called **HELLO.TXT** from the **\WUGXP** directory to the root directory of the DATA disk. The purpose of this activity is to have two identically named files on different drives.

9   Key in the following: C:\WUGXP>**DIR HELLO.TXT** [Enter]

10 Key in the following: C:\WUGXP>**DIR A:\HELLO.TXT** Enter

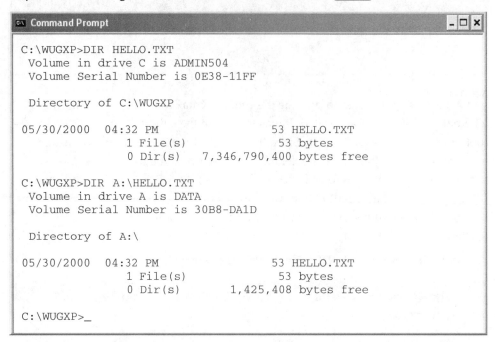

```
C:\WUGXP>DIR HELLO.TXT
 Volume in drive C is ADMIN504
 Volume Serial Number is 0E38-11FF

 Directory of C:\WUGXP

05/30/2000  04:32 PM                 53 HELLO.TXT
               1 File(s)             53 bytes
               0 Dir(s)    7,346,790,400 bytes free

C:\WUGXP>DIR A:\HELLO.TXT
 Volume in drive A is DATA
 Volume Serial Number is 30B8-DA1D

 Directory of A:\

05/30/2000  04:32 PM                 53 HELLO.TXT
               1 File(s)             53 bytes
               0 Dir(s)        1,425,408 bytes free

C:\WUGXP>_
```

WHAT'S HAPPENING?   You have two files called **HELLO.TXT**. One file is on the hard disk in the subdirectory **\WUGXP**. The other file is on the DATA disk. You want to delete the file on the DATA disk, *not* on the hard disk.

11 Key in the following: C:\WUGXP>**DEL A:\HELLO.TXT** Enter

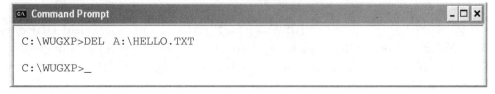

```
C:\WUGXP>DEL A:\HELLO.TXT

C:\WUGXP>_
```

WHAT'S HAPPENING?   You asked DEL to erase the file on the DATA disk called **HELLO.TXT**. The file should be gone from the DATA disk, but the file called **HELLO.TXT** on the hard disk (Drive C, subdirectory **\WUGXP**) should still be there.

12 Key in the following: C:\WUGXP>**DIR HELLO.TXT** Enter

13 Key in the following: C:\WUGXP>**DIR A:\HELLO.TXT** Enter

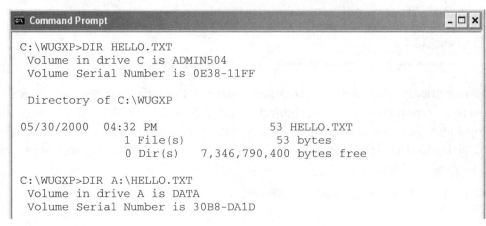

```
C:\WUGXP>DIR HELLO.TXT
 Volume in drive C is ADMIN504
 Volume Serial Number is 0E38-11FF

 Directory of C:\WUGXP

05/30/2000  04:32 PM                 53 HELLO.TXT
               1 File(s)             53 bytes
               0 Dir(s)    7,346,790,400 bytes free

C:\WUGXP>DIR A:\HELLO.TXT
 Volume in drive A is DATA
 Volume Serial Number is 30B8-DA1D
```

```
 Directory of A:\

File Not Found

C:\WUGXP>_
```

WHAT'S ▒▒▒▒▒
▒▒▒▒ **HAPPENING?**   The file called **HELLO.TXT** is still in the subdirectory **\WUGXP** on the hard disk, but the file called **HELLO.TXT** on the DATA disk is gone.

14 Key in the following: C:\WUGXP>**DIR A:\TRIP\BLUE.JAZ** [Enter]

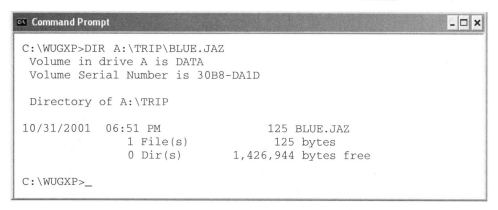

```
 Command Prompt                                            – □ ×

C:\WUGXP>DIR A:\TRIP\BLUE.JAZ
 Volume in drive A is DATA
 Volume Serial Number is 30B8-DA1D

 Directory of A:\TRIP

10/31/2001  06:51 PM                125 BLUE.JAZ
               1 File(s)            125 bytes
               0 Dir(s)       1,426,944 bytes free

C:\WUGXP>_
```

WHAT'S ▒▒▒▒▒
▒▒▒▒ **HAPPENING?**   There is a file called **BLUE.JAZ** in the subdirectory **TRIP** on the DATA disk. To delete this file, you once again follow the same command you used with the DIR command DEL command, substituting DEL for DIR. In this way, you can be sure you of exactly what you will delete.

15 Key in the following: C:\WUGXP>**DEL A:\TRIP\BLUE.JAZ** [Enter]

```
 Command Prompt                                            – □ ×

C:\WUGXP>DEL A:\TRIP\BLUE.JAZ

C:\WUGXP>_
```

WHAT'S ▒▒▒▒▒
▒▒▒▒ **HAPPENING?**   The syntax for the DEL command is DEL *names*. You used the drive letter of the DATA disk, then **TRIP** and **BLUE.JAZ** for the name. The second backslash was mandatory because you needed a delimiter between the file name and the subdirectory name. This backslash is similar to the period that you used to separate the file name from the file extension. Is the file gone?

16 Key in the following: C:\WUGXP>**DIR A:\TRIP\BLUE.JAZ** [Enter]

```
 Command Prompt                                            – □ ×

C:\WUGXP>DIR A:\TRIP\BLUE.JAZ
 Volume in drive A is DATA
 Volume Serial Number is 30B8-DA1D

 Directory of A:\TRIP

File Not Found

C:\WUGXP>_
```

WHAT'S
HAPPENING?   The file **BLUE.JAZ** from the directory **TRIP** on the DATA disk is indeed gone.

17 Key in the following: C:\WUGXP>**CD** \ Enter

18 Key in the following: C:\>**A:** Enter

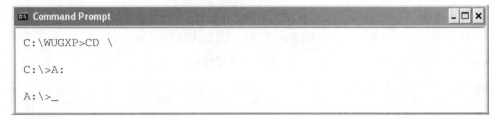

```
C:\WUGXP>CD \

C:\>A:

A:\>_
```

WHAT'S
HAPPENING?   You returned to the root directory of the hard disk. You then made the root directory of the DATA disk the default drive and directory.

6.7   Using Wildcards with the DEL Command

You have been erasing or deleting files either one at a time, or by listing each file's complete name. Often you want to erase many files. It is tedious to erase many files one at a time. You can use the wildcards with the DEL command to delete several files at one time. Wildcards allow you to erase a group of files with a one-line command. Although you can certainly delete files in My Computer, you must select each file to be deleted, which takes time. It is simply quicker and easier deleting files from the command line. However, at the command line, be *exceedingly* careful when using wildcards with the DEL command. Once again, the strength of wildcards is also their weakness. A global file specification means global. You can eliminate a group of files very quickly. If you are not careful, you could erase files you want to keep. In fact, you probably will some day say, "Oh no, those files are gone." However, this does not mean you should never use wildcards. They are far too useful. Just be very, *very* careful.

6.8   Activity: Using the DEL Command

Note 1:   The DATA disk is in Drive A. A:\> is displayed.
Note 2:   If the .TMP files are not on the root of the DATA disk, they may be copied from the \WUGXP subdirectory.

1 Key in the following: A:\>**DIR *.TMP** Enter

```
A:\>DIR *.TMP
 Volume in drive A is DATA
 Volume Serial Number is 30B8-DA1D

 Directory of A:\

05/07/2002  07:41 AM              190 JUP.TMP
10/31/2001  01:08 PM              406 MER.TMP
10/30/2001  01:46 PM              148 AST.TMP
10/31/2001  07:08 PM              478 VEN.TMP
```

```
                  4 File(s)              1,222 bytes
                  0 Dir(s)           1,427,456 bytes free

  A:\>_
```

WHAT'S ▒▒▒▒▒▒▒
▒▒▒▒ **HAPPENING?**   You should see four files with **.TMP** as the file extension displayed on the screen. Remember, prior to doing a global erase, it is always wise to key in DIR with the same global file specification you are going to use with the DEL command. In this way, you can see ahead of time *exactly* which files will be deleted.

2   Key in the following: A:\>**DEL *.TMP** [Enter]

```
A:\>DEL *.TMP

A:\>_
```

WHAT'S ▒▒▒▒▒▒▒
▒▒▒▒ **HAPPENING?**   You asked DEL to erase or delete every file with the **.TMP** file extension on the DATA disk in the root directory. The wildcard * represented any file name. Only the system prompt appears on the screen. The DEL command executed, erasing those ***.TMP** files quickly and permanently. To verify this, use the DIR command.

3   Key in the following: A:\>**DIR *.TMP** [Enter]

```
 Command Prompt                                             _ □ ×

A:\>DIR *.TMP
 Volume in drive A is DATA
 Volume Serial Number is 30B8-DA1D

 Directory of A:\

File Not Found

A:\>_
```

WHAT'S ▒▒▒▒▒▒▒
▒▒▒▒ **HAPPENING?**   Those ***.TMP** files are, indeed, gone from the root directory on the DATA disk. They are not recoverable by the operating system. It must be emphasized that before you use a wildcard to delete a group of files you should use the DIR command to see the files you are going to delete. For instance, if you had a file called **TEST.TMP** that you had forgotten about and that you did not want to delete, the directory display would include it as follows:

```
 Directory of A:\

 05/07/2002   07:41 AM              190 JUP.TMP
 10/31/2001   01:08 PM              406 MER.TMP
 10/30/2001   01:46 PM              148 AST.TMP
 10/31/2001   07:08 PM              478 VEN.TMP
 05/01/1998   05:00p               500 TEST.TMP
                  5 File(s)        1,722 bytes
```

You would have been made aware of the presence of the **TEST.TMP** file using the DIR command, and would thus have avoided losing a needed file. Using the

DIR command with wildcards will let you display on the screen all the files that have been selected by ***.TMP**, which includes the **TEST.TMP** file that you do not want to erase. If you had keyed in **DEL *.TMP**, all those **.TMP** files would have been deleted. Remember, the computer does not come back and tell you, "Oh, by the way, **TEST.TMP** was included with the ***.TMP** files; did you want to erase that file?" The DEL command simply eliminates all the **.TMP** files because that is what you told it to do. You can also use wildcards when files are in a subdirectory.

4   Key in the following: A:\>**DIR TRIP*.99** [Enter]

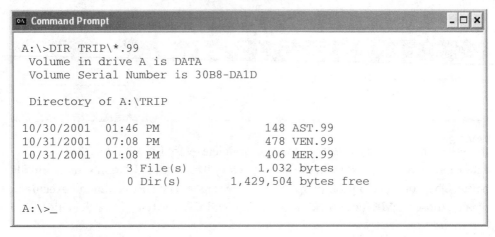

```
A:\>DIR TRIP\*.99
 Volume in drive A is DATA
 Volume Serial Number is 30B8-DA1D

 Directory of A:\TRIP

10/30/2001  01:46 PM              148 AST.99
10/31/2001  07:08 PM              478 VEN.99
10/31/2001  01:08 PM              406 MER.99
             3 File(s)          1,032 bytes
             0 Dir(s)     1,429,504 bytes free

A:\>_
```

WHAT'S HAPPENING?   There are three files with the extension **.99** on the DATA disk in the subdirectory **TRIP**. The DEL command works the same way.

5   Key in the following: A:\>**DEL TRIP*.99** [Enter]

```
A:\>DEL TRIP\*.99

A:\>_
```

WHAT'S HAPPENING?   You asked DEL to erase or delete every file on the DATA disk in the subdirectory **TRIP** that has any file name and has the file extension **.99**. The wildcard ***** represented any file name. Only the system prompt appears on the screen. The DEL command executed, erasing those ***.99** files quickly and permanently. To verify this, you can use the DIR command.

6   Key in the following: A:\>**DIR TRIP*.99** [Enter]

```
A:\>DIR TRIP\*.99
 Volume in drive A is DATA
 Volume Serial Number is 30B8-DA1D

 Directory of A:\TRIP

File Not Found

A:\>_
```

WHAT'S
▓▓▓HAPPENING?   The ***.99** files are indeed gone from the **TRIP** directory.

6.9 The /P and /S Parameters with the DEL Command

Prior to DOS 4.0, the DEL command provided no way for you to confirm deletions. The file was simply erased. In DOS 4.0 an enhancement was introduced—the /P parameter. This parameter allows you to tell the DEL command to prompt you with the file name prior to deleting the file. The syntax is:

```
DEL [/P] [/S] names
```

/P is one of the optional fixed parameters that work with the DEL command. Its purpose is to display each file name to verify that you really want to delete it. You can think of the P as standing for "prompt you for an answer." This parameter is particularly useful when you are using wildcards. It minimizes the risk of accidental file deletions. The /S parameter is also exceedingly useful, as it will traverse the directory tree so you do not have to delete files individually throughout your disk structure. Several new parameters were also added in Windows 2000 Professional, and remain available in Windows XP. These include the ability to force the deletion of read-only files (/F), to delete files based on certain attributes (/A), and to not ask for confirmation of a deletion (/Q).

6.10 Activity: Using /P and /S with the DEL Command

Note: The DATA disk is in Drive A. A:\> is displayed.

1   Key in the following: A:\>**COPY C:\WUGXP*.99** [Enter]

2   Key in the following: A:\>**MD TRIP\CHINA** [Enter]

```
C:\ Command Prompt                                    _ □ ✕

A:\>COPY C:\WUGXP\*.99
C:\WUGXP\AST.99
C:\WUGXP\VEN.99
C:\WUGXP\JUP.99
C:\WUGXP\MER.99
        4 file(s) copied.

A:\>MD TRIP\CHINA

A:\>_
```

WHAT'S
▓▓▓HAPPENING?   You have copied the files with the **.99** extension from the **WUGXP** directory to the root of the DATA disk and kept the file names the same.

3   Key in the following: A:\>**COPY *.99 TRIP** [Enter]

4   Key in the following: A:\>**COPY *.99 TRIP\CHINA** [Enter]

5   Key in the following: A:\>**DIR TRIP TRIP\CHINA** [Enter]

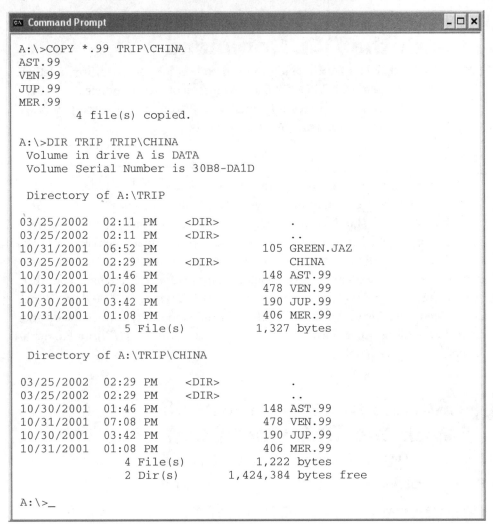

```
A:\>COPY *.99 TRIP\CHINA
AST.99
VEN.99
JUP.99
MER.99
        4 file(s) copied.

A:\>DIR TRIP TRIP\CHINA
 Volume in drive A is DATA
 Volume Serial Number is 30B8-DA1D

 Directory of A:\TRIP

03/25/2002  02:11 PM    <DIR>          .
03/25/2002  02:11 PM    <DIR>          ..
10/31/2001  06:52 PM                105 GREEN.JAZ
03/25/2002  02:29 PM    <DIR>          CHINA
10/30/2001  01:46 PM                148 AST.99
10/31/2001  07:08 PM                478 VEN.99
10/30/2001  03:42 PM                190 JUP.99
10/31/2001  01:08 PM                406 MER.99
               5 File(s)        1,327 bytes

 Directory of A:\TRIP\CHINA

03/25/2002  02:29 PM    <DIR>          .
03/25/2002  02:29 PM    <DIR>          ..
10/30/2001  01:46 PM                148 AST.99
10/31/2001  07:08 PM                478 VEN.99
10/30/2001  03:42 PM                190 JUP.99
10/31/2001  01:08 PM                406 MER.99
               4 File(s)        1,222 bytes
               2 Dir(s)     1,424,384 bytes free

A:\>_
```

WHAT'S HAPPENING?   You copied the files with the extension of **.99** to the **TRIP** and the **TRIP\CHINA** subdirectories on the DATA disk and confirmed that they are there. The file called **GREEN.JAZ** is also in that subdirectory. Next, you are going to choose *some* of the **.99** files to delete.

6   Key in the following: A:\>**DEL TRIP*.99 /P** [Enter]

```
A:\>DEL TRIP\*.99 /P
A:\TRIP\AST.99, Delete (Y/N)?
```

WHAT'S HAPPENING?   The **/P** parameter, when included in the command line, prompts you by asking if you want to delete the file called **AST.99** in the subdirectory **TRIP** on the DATA disk. When you have a **Y/N** choice, press either **Y** for "Yes" or **N** for "No." Pressing [Enter] takes no action.

7   Key in the following: **N** [Enter]

```
Command Prompt                                                    - □ ×

A:\>DEL TRIP\*.99 /P
TRIP\AST.99,    Delete (Y/N)?N
TRIP\VEN.99,    Delete (Y/N)?
```

**WHAT'S
HAPPENING?**   DEL found the next file and asked if you wanted to delete the file
called **VEN.99**. If you are using NTFS, the next file that will be found will be JUP.99
because of the order the files were copied to the floppy disk.

8   If **VEN.99** is displayed, key in **Y**. If **JUP.99** is displayed, key in **N**.

```
Command Prompt                                                    - □ ×

A:\>DEL TRIP\*.99 /P

TRIP\AST.99,    Delete (Y/N)?N
TRIP\VEN.99,    Delete (Y/N)?Y
TRIP\JUP.99,    Delete (Y/N)?
```

**WHAT'S
HAPPENING?**   DEL found the next file and asked if you wanted to delete the file
called **JUP.99** or if you are using NTFS, the file will be **MER.99**.

9   If the displayed file is **JUP.99**, key in **N**. If the file displayed is **MER.99**, key in **Y**.

```
Command Prompt                                                    - □ ×

A:\>DEL TRIP\*.99 /P
A:\>DEL TRIP\*.99 /P
A:\TRIP\AST.99, Delete (Y/N)? N
A:\TRIP\VEN.99, Delete (Y/N)? Y
A:\TRIP\JUP.99, Delete (Y/N)? N
A:\TRIP\MER.99, Delete (Y/N)
```

**WHAT'S
HAPPENING?**   DEL found the next file and asked you if you wanted to delete the
file called **MER.99**. If you are using NTFS, the displayed file will be **VEN.99**.

10 If the displayed file is **MER.99**, key in **Y**. If the displayed file is **VEN.99**, key in **Y**.

```
Command Prompt                                                    - □ ×

A:\>DEL TRIP\*.99 /P
A:\TRIP\AST.99, Delete (Y/N)? N
A:\TRIP\VEN.99, Delete (Y/N)? Y
A:\TRIP\JUP.99, Delete (Y/N)? N
A:\TRIP\MER.99, Delete (Y/N)? Y

A:\>_
```

**WHAT'S
HAPPENING?**   You were returned to the system prompt because there were no
more files with the extension **.99** on the DATA disk in the subdirectory **TRIP**. You
were able to delete files selectively. You deleted the files **VEN.99** and **MER.99** but
kept the files **AST.99** and **JUP.99**. You can verify this by using the DIR command.

11 Key in the following: A:\>**DIR TRIP** Enter

```
Command Prompt                                              _ □ ×

A:\>DIR TRIP
 Volume in drive A is DATA
 Volume Serial Number is 30B8-DA1D

 Directory of A:\TRIP

03/25/2002  02:11 PM    <DIR>          .
03/25/2002  02:11 PM    <DIR>          ..
10/31/2001  06:52 PM              105 GREEN.JAZ
03/25/2002  02:29 PM    <DIR>          CHINA
10/30/2001  01:46 PM              148 AST.99
10/30/2001  03:42 PM              190 JUP.99
             3 File(s)             443 bytes
             3 Dir(s)        1,425,408 bytes free

A:\>_
```

WHAT'S HAPPENING?   You retained the files **AST.99** and **JUP.99** but deleted **VEN.99** and **MER.99**. The file **GREEN.JAZ** was not deleted because it did not have the file extension **.99**. You can use the /S parameter to traverse the directory tree. You can also use more than one parameter at a time.

12 Key in the following: A:\>**DEL TRIP*.99 /P /S** Enter

13 Key in **N** Enter, then **N** Enter again.

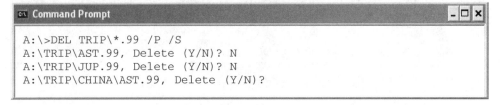

```
Command Prompt                                              _ □ ×

A:\>DEL TRIP\*.99 /P /S
A:\TRIP\AST.99, Delete (Y/N)? N
A:\TRIP\JUP.99, Delete (Y/N)? N
A:\TRIP\CHINA\AST.99, Delete (Y/N)?
```

WHAT'S HAPPENING?   You answered "No, do not delete the files **AST.99** and **JUP.99** in the **TRIP** directory," but since you included the /S parameter, the DEL command continued down the tree looking for all files that ended in **.99**.

14 Press **Y** and Enter until there are no more prompts.

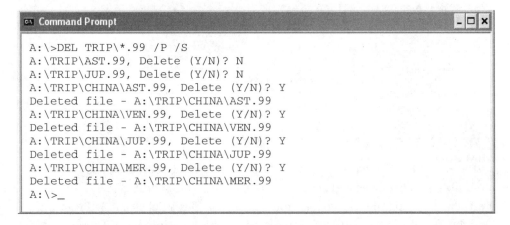

```
Command Prompt                                              _ □ ×

A:\>DEL TRIP\*.99 /P /S
A:\TRIP\AST.99, Delete (Y/N)? N
A:\TRIP\JUP.99, Delete (Y/N)? N
A:\TRIP\CHINA\AST.99, Delete (Y/N)? Y
Deleted file - A:\TRIP\CHINA\AST.99
A:\TRIP\CHINA\VEN.99, Delete (Y/N)? Y
Deleted file - A:\TRIP\CHINA\VEN.99
A:\TRIP\CHINA\JUP.99, Delete (Y/N)? Y
Deleted file - A:\TRIP\CHINA\JUP.99
A:\TRIP\CHINA\MER.99, Delete (Y/N)? Y
Deleted file - A:\TRIP\CHINA\MER.99
A:\>_
```

WHAT'S HAPPENING?   Each time you pressed **Y**, you deleted the ***.99** files in the **TRIP\CHINA** directory. You also see a more complete message that tells you which files have been deleted. Again, your order of files will be different, if your hard disk is using NTFS.

15 Key in the following: A:\>**RD TRIP\CHINA** Enter

```
A:\>RD TRIP\CHINA

A:\>_
```

WHAT'S HAPPENING?   You have removed the **CHINA** directory. If there had been any files left in the **CHINA** directory, you would not have been able to use the **RD** command to remove it.

6.11 Changing File Names

Often when working with files, you want to change a file name. For example, you may wish to change the name of a file to indicate an older version. You might also think of a more descriptive file name. As the contents of a file change, the old name may no longer reflect the contents. When you make a typographical error, you want to be able to correct it. One way to change the name of a file is to copy it to a different name. The COPY command can, in this way, help to change the name of a file. You could, for example, copy the file A:\JUP.99 to A:\TRIP\JUP.00. You did not change the name of an existing file—you created a new file with the same contents under a different name.

The operating system supplies a way to change existing file names using the internal command RENAME. RENAME does exactly what it says; it changes the name of a file. The contents of the file do not change, only the name of the file. The syntax for this command is:

```
RENAME [drive:][path][directoryname1 ¦ filename1]
[directoryname2 ¦ filename2]
```

or

```
REN [drive:][path][directoryname1 ¦ filename1]
[directoryname2 ¦ filename2]
```

RENAME does not let you specify a new drive or path for *filename2* or *directoryname2*. Remember, you are not making a copy of a file. It is like pasting a new label on an existing file folder. That file folder does not get moved in the process. You are dealing with only one file when using REN. In the syntax diagram, *filename1* and *filename2* refer to the same file—*filename1* will be changed to *filename2*. You are changing the file name only, not creating another copy of it with a new name.

The RENAME command has two forms, RENAME or REN, with exactly the same syntax. Most computer users choose REN, simply because it has fewer keystrokes. The syntax is the command REN, the first parameter (the old file name), and the second parameter (the new file name).

Renaming files at the command line is especially useful. In My Computer or Windows Explorer, renaming files is always a two-step process. First, you must select the file; then, you must rename it. At the command line, you can accomplish this task in one step.

6.12 Activity: Using the REN Command to Rename Files

Note: The DATA disk is in Drive A. A:\> is displayed.

1   Key in the following: A:\>**COPY C:\WUGXP\MEDIA\TV** Enter

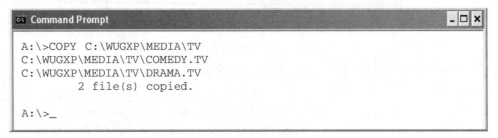

```
A:\>COPY C:\WUGXP\MEDIA\TV
C:\WUGXP\MEDIA\TV\COMEDY.TV
C:\WUGXP\MEDIA\TV\DRAMA.TV
        2 file(s) copied.

A:\>_
```

WHAT'S HAPPENING?   You copied two files from the subdirectory **\WUGXP\MEDIA\TV** from the hard disk to the root directory of the DATA disk. Notice that after **TV** did not have to specify a file name. When you key in a command ending in the name of a directory rather than a file specification, ***.*** is assumed. The destination is also assumed. It is the default drive and directory—in this case the root directory of the DATA disk.

2   Key in the following: A:\>**TYPE COMEDY.TV** Enter

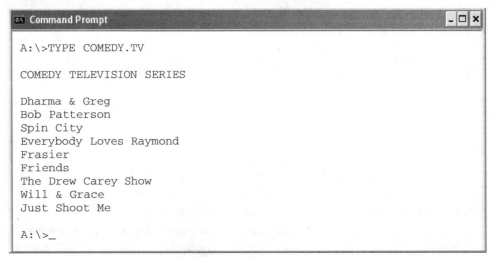

```
A:\>TYPE COMEDY.TV

COMEDY TELEVISION SERIES

Dharma & Greg
Bob Patterson
Spin City
Everybody Loves Raymond
Frasier
Friends
The Drew Carey Show
Will & Grace
Just Shoot Me

A:\>_
```

WHAT'S HAPPENING?   You are displaying the contents of the file called **COMEDY.TV** located in the root directory on the DATA disk. You opened the file folder called **COMEDY.TV** and looked inside.

3   Key in the following: A:\>**REN COMEDY.TV FUNNY.TV** Enter

```
A:\>REN COMEDY.TV FUNNY.TV

A:\>_
```

WHAT'S HAPPENING?   Using the command REN changed the name of the file called **COMEDY.TV** to **FUNNY.TV**. Since the default was the DATA disk and the default directory was the root, the operating system looked only on the root directory of the DATA disk for the file called **COMEDY.TV**. Once you pressed [Enter], you got back only the system prompt. Did anything happen?

4   Key in the following: A:\>**DIR COMEDY.TV** [Enter]

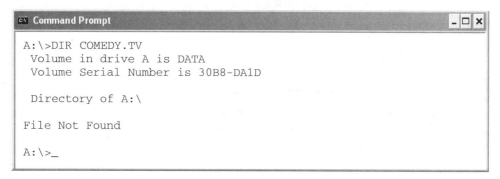

```
A:\>DIR COMEDY.TV
 Volume in drive A is DATA
 Volume Serial Number is 30B8-DA1D

 Directory of A:\

File Not Found

A:\>_
```

WHAT'S HAPPENING?   Once you have renamed a file, it no longer exists under its old file name.

5   Key in the following: A:\>**DIR FUNNY.TV** [Enter]

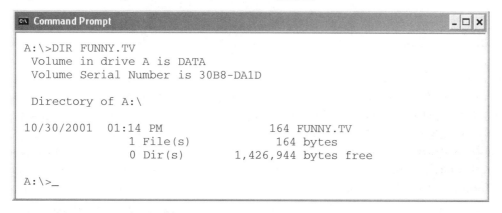

```
A:\>DIR FUNNY.TV
 Volume in drive A is DATA
 Volume Serial Number is 30B8-DA1D

 Directory of A:\

10/30/2001  01:14 PM                164 FUNNY.TV
               1 File(s)            164 bytes
               0 Dir(s)       1,426,944 bytes free

A:\>_
```

WHAT'S HAPPENING?   The above display demonstrates that the file called **FUNNY.TV** is on the DATA disk in the root directory. You know that the file named **COMEDY.TV** is no longer on the DATA disk. Are the contents of the file **FUNNY.TV** the same as the contents of the file that was named **COMEDY.TV**?

6   Key in the following: A:\>**TYPE FUNNY.TV** [Enter]

```
A:\>TYPE FUNNY.TV

COMEDY TELEVISION SERIES
```

```
Dharma & Greg
Bob Patterson
Spin City
Everybody Loves Raymond
Frasier
Friends
The Drew Carey Show
Will & Grace
Just Shoot Me

A:\>_
```

WHAT'S HAPPENING?   As you can see, you changed the file name from **COMEDY.TV** to **FUNNY.TV**, but the contents of the file did not change. REN works the same way with a file in a subdirectory. You just have to follow the syntax (only the partial syntax, that which refers to renaming files, is shown here):

```
REN [drive:][path][filename1] [filename2]
```

7   Key in the following: A:\>**DIR TRIP\GREEN.JAZ** Enter

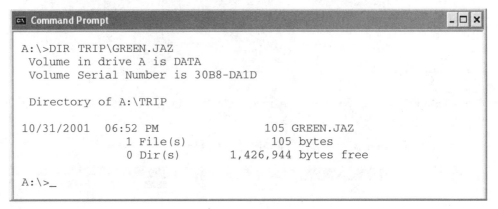

```
Command Prompt                                              _ □ ×

A:\>DIR TRIP\GREEN.JAZ
 Volume in drive A is DATA
 Volume Serial Number is 30B8-DA1D

 Directory of A:\TRIP

10/31/2001  06:52 PM                 105 GREEN.JAZ
               1 File(s)             105 bytes
               0 Dir(s)        1,426,944 bytes free

A:\>_
```

WHAT'S HAPPENING?   The file called **GREEN.JAZ** is in the subdirectory called **TRIP** on the DATA disk. Using REN is different from using COPY. The COPY syntax requires that you place the path name in front of the source file and the destination file. You are dealing with two files; thus, each file could be in a separate location. This situation is not true with REN. You are dealing with only one file and are changing only one file name. You are not moving the file; thus, the path name is placed in front of the source file only.

8   Key in the following: A:\>**REN TRIP\GREEN.JAZ TRIP\RED.JAZ** Enter

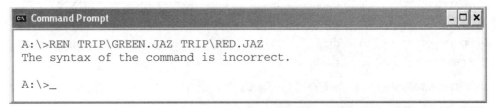

```
Command Prompt                                              _ □ ×

A:\>REN TRIP\GREEN.JAZ TRIP\RED.JAZ
The syntax of the command is incorrect.

A:\>_
```

WHAT'S HAPPENING?   The message is descriptive. The error message refers to second part of the command, **TRIP\RED.JAZ**. That portion of the command syntax is incorrect. It is incorrect because you placed a subdirectory before the new file name.

The REN command already knew where the file to be renamed, GREEN.JAZ, was located. It did not the location repeated.

9   Key in the following: `A:\>`**REN TRIP\GREEN.JAZ RED.JAZ** [Enter]

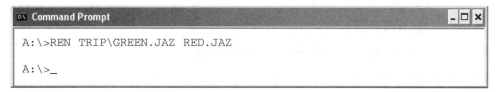

```
A:\>REN TRIP\GREEN.JAZ RED.JAZ

A:\>_
```

WHAT'S ▓▓▓▓▓
▓▓▓**HAPPENING?**   You received no error message, indicating that this command was executed. All the REN command needed to correctly execute the command was the location in the first part of the command, TRIP\GREEN.JAZ, and the new name, RED.JAZ. You will confirm that the file name was changed from **GREEN.JAZ** to **RED.JAZ** using the DIR command.

10   Key in the following: `A:\>`**DIR TRIP*.JAZ** [Enter]

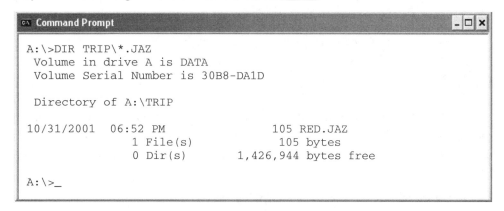

```
A:\>DIR TRIP\*.JAZ
 Volume in drive A is DATA
 Volume Serial Number is 30B8-DA1D

 Directory of A:\TRIP

10/31/2001  06:52 PM               105 RED.JAZ
              1 File(s)            105 bytes
              0 Dir(s)       1,426,944 bytes free

A:\>_
```

WHAT'S ▓▓▓▓▓
▓▓▓**HAPPENING?**   You can see that the file in the **TRIP** subdirectory with the extension **.JAZ** is now called **RED.JAZ** instead of **GREEN.JAZ**.

6.13 Changing the Names of Subdirectories

In previous versions of MS-DOS, the REN command worked only with files. With the release of Windows 95, it became possible to use the REN command to rename subdirectories. Previously, you used the MOVE command to rename subdirectories. Remember the syntax.

```
REN [drive:][path][directoryname1 | filename1]
[directoryname2 | filename2]
```

When renaming subdirectories, the partial syntax is:

```
REN [drive:][path][directoryname1] [directoryname2]
```

6.14 Activity: Using the REN Command to Rename Subdirectories

Note: The DATA disk is in Drive A. A:\> is displayed as the default drive and the default directory.

1   Key in the following: A:\>**MD PAGEONE** Enter

2   Key in the following: A:\>**DIR P*.*** Enter

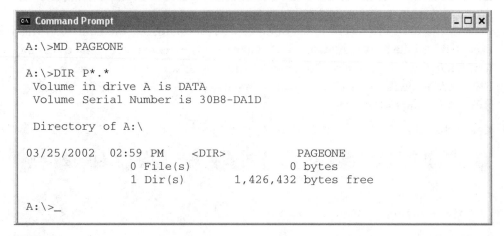

```
A:\>MD PAGEONE

A:\>DIR P*.*
 Volume in drive A is DATA
 Volume Serial Number is 30B8-DA1D

 Directory of A:\

03/25/2002  02:59 PM    <DIR>            PAGEONE
              0 File(s)             0 bytes
              1 Dir(s)      1,426,432 bytes free

A:\>_
```

WHAT'S HAPPENING?   You have created a new directory called **PAGEONE** on the root of the DATA disk in the A drive. You have verified its existence by using the DIR command. There is only one entry on the root of the DATA disk that begins with the letter **P**.

3   Key in the following: A:\>**REN PAGEONE PAGETWO** Enter

```
A:\>REN PAGEONE PAGETWO

A:\>_
```

WHAT'S HAPPENING?   You received no error messages, so the command executed. Was the subdirectory **PAGEONE** actually renamed to **PAGETWO**?

4   Key in the following: A:\>**DIR P*.*** Enter

```
A:\>DIR P*.*
 Volume in drive A is DATA
 Volume Serial Number is 30B8-DA1D

 Directory of A:\

03/25/2002  02:59 PM    <DIR>            PAGETWO
              0 File(s)             0 bytes
              1 Dir(s)      1,426,432 bytes free

A:\>_
```

WHAT'S
HAPPENING?   You have verified that the REN command successfully renamed the directory **PAGEONE** to **PAGETWO**. **PAGEONE** no longer exists under its original name. It is now **PAGETWO**. You can also rename subdirectories that are within other subdirectories.

5   Key in the following: A:\>**MD PAGETWO\DIRONE** [Enter]

6   Key in the following: A:\>**DIR PAGETWO** [Enter]

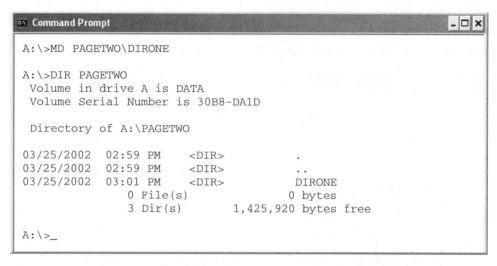

```
A:\>MD PAGETWO\DIRONE

A:\>DIR PAGETWO
 Volume in drive A is DATA
 Volume Serial Number is 30B8-DA1D

 Directory of A:\PAGETWO

03/25/2002  02:59 PM    <DIR>          .
03/25/2002  02:59 PM    <DIR>          ..
03/25/2002  03:01 PM    <DIR>          DIRONE
              0 File(s)              0 bytes
              3 Dir(s)       1,425,920 bytes free

A:\>_
```

WHAT'S
HAPPENING?   You have created a subdirectory called **DIRONE** in the existing subdirectory **PAGETWO**. You have also used the DIR command to display the contents of the **PAGETWO** directory to verify the new subdirectory just created called **DIRONE**. You will now rename the new directory.

7   Key in the following: A:\>**REN PAGETWO\DIRONE DIRTWO** [Enter]

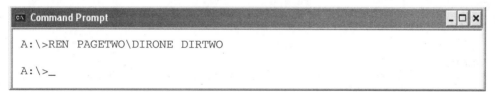

```
A:\>REN PAGETWO\DIRONE DIRTWO

A:\>_
```

WHAT'S
HAPPENING?   You have renamed the subdirectory **DIRONE** to **DIRTWO**. Again, you see no error messages, so the command executed. You can verify the change with the DIR command.

8   Key in the following: A:\>**DIR PAGETWO** [Enter]

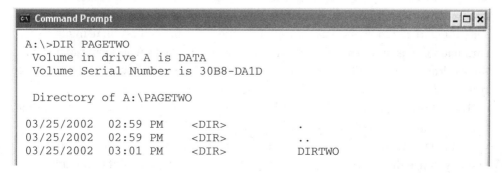

```
A:\>DIR PAGETWO
 Volume in drive A is DATA
 Volume Serial Number is 30B8-DA1D

 Directory of A:\PAGETWO

03/25/2002  02:59 PM    <DIR>          .
03/25/2002  02:59 PM    <DIR>          ..
03/25/2002  03:01 PM    <DIR>          DIRTWO
```

```
              0 File(s)              0 bytes
              3 Dir(s)      1,425,920 bytes free

A:\>_
```

**WHAT'S
HAPPENING?**   You have used the DIR command to confirm that you have,
indeed, renamed the subdirectory **DIRONE** to the new name of **DIRTWO**. This
subdirectory structure will no longer be used. You will use the RD /S command,
covered later in this chapter, to remove the entire structure.

9   Key in the following: A:\>**RD PAGETWO /S** [Enter]

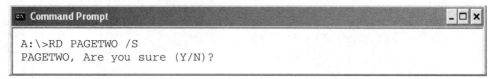

```
A:\>RD PAGETWO /S
PAGETWO, Are you sure (Y/N)?
```

**WHAT'S
HAPPENING?**   The RD /S command is asking you if you are sure you want to
delete the **PAGETWO** subdirectory and all of its contents.

10   Key in the following: **Y** [Enter]

11   Key in the following: A:\>**DIR P*.*** [Enter]

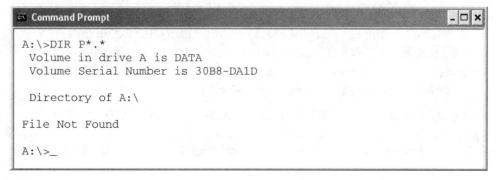

```
A:\>DIR P*.*
 Volume in drive A is DATA
 Volume Serial Number is 30B8-DA1D

 Directory of A:\

File Not Found

A:\>_
```

**WHAT'S
HAPPENING?**   As you can see with the DIR command, you have successfully
removed the **NAMETWO** directory structure.

6.15 Using REN with Wildcards

When you wish to change the name of a single file or directory, you can use My
Computer from the GUI. It is easy to do—just right-click the file or folder and
choose Rename. If, however, you have numerous files to rename and they have
something in common, such as they all have the .ABC file extension, using the
command line is more efficient. You can use the REN or RENAME command with
the wildcards ? and *, allowing you to change many file names with a one-line
command.

    The wildcards or global file specifications are so "global" that, prior to renaming
files, it is wise to do a directory display with the wildcards you want to use so that
you can see what files are going to be renamed, just as you use a directory display
before you use the DEL command with wildcards. You do not want to rename a
subdirectory accidentally along with a group of files. This can happen all too easily.

Once a file is renamed, you can never find the file under its old name. This rule has caused havoc for users because it seems as if the file is lost. The file is still on the disk, and you can find it, but only under its new name.

6.16   Activity: Using REN with Wildcards

Note 1:   The DATA disk is in Drive A. A:\> is displayed.

Note 2:   This activity assumes you have files on the DATA disk with the file extension .**NEW**. If you do not, you may copy them from \ **WUGXP** to the DATA disk.

1   Key in the following: A:\>**DIR ???.NEW** [Enter]

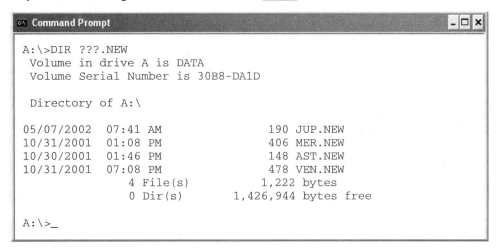

```
A:\>DIR ???.NEW
 Volume in drive A is DATA
 Volume Serial Number is 30B8-DA1D

 Directory of A:\

05/07/2002  07:41 AM               190 JUP.NEW
10/31/2001  01:08 PM               406 MER.NEW
10/30/2001  01:46 PM               148 AST.NEW
10/31/2001  07:08 PM               478 VEN.NEW
               4 File(s)         1,222 bytes
               0 Dir(s)      1,426,944 bytes free

A:\>_
```

WHAT'S HAPPENING?   You have four files with file names of three characters and with the extension .**NEW**. You used **???** instead of *****. When you used **???.NEW**, the **???** selected only files that had a file name of three characters or less. Had you used ***** instead of **???**, you would have selected all file names that had an extension of .**NEW**. That would have included such files as **BONJOUR .NEW**. Your objective is to rename these four files, keeping their file names but changing the file extension from .**NEW** to .**BUD**. You could rename these files one at a time, **REN JUP.NEW JUP.BUD**, then **REN MER.NEW MER.BUD**, then **REN AST.NEW AST.BUD**, and **REN VEN.NEW VEN.BUD**. However, this repetition becomes very tiresome. Using wildcards allows you to rename these four files at one time.

2   Key in the following: A:\>**REN ???.NEW *.BUD** [Enter]

```
A:\>REN ???.NEW *.BUD

A:\>_
```

WHAT'S HAPPENING?   All that is displayed is the system prompt. Was the work done? Are the files renamed? To verify that you did rename these files, use the DIR command.

3   Key in the following: A:\>**DIR ???.NEW *.BUD** Enter

```
🖳 Command Prompt                                              _ □ ✕

A:\>DIR ???.NEW *.BUD
 Volume in drive A is DATA
 Volume Serial Number is 30B8-DA1D

 Directory of A:\


 Directory of A:\

05/07/2002  07:41 AM                 190 JUP.BUD
10/31/2001  01:08 PM                 406 MER.BUD
10/30/2001  01:46 PM                 148 AST.BUD
10/31/2001  07:08 PM                 478 VEN.BUD
                4 File(s)          1,222 bytes
                0 Dir(s)       1,426,944 bytes free

A:\>_
```

**WHAT'S
HAPPENING?**   Files with file names of three characters and the extension **.NEW**
no longer exist on the DATA disk. With the REN command and the use of the
wildcards, you renamed four files with one command. When you use multiple
parameters on the command line, you do not see the message **File Not Found**. You
simply see the **A:** prompt with no file name following it. You can also use wildcards
with subdirectories.

4   Key in the following: A:\>**COPY *.BUD TRIP** Enter

```
🖳 Command Prompt                                              _ □ ✕

A:\>COPY *.BUD TRIP
JUP.BUD
MER.BUD
AST.BUD
VEN.BUD
        4 file(s) copied.

A:\>_
```

**WHAT'S
HAPPENING?**   You copied files with the **.BUD** extension from the root directory
of the DATA disk to a subdirectory called **TRIP** on the DATA disk.

5   Key in the following: A:\>**REN TRIP*.BUD *.PEN** Enter

6   Key in the following: A:\>**DIR TRIP*.BUD** Enter

7   Key in the following: A:\>**DIR TRIP*.PEN** Enter

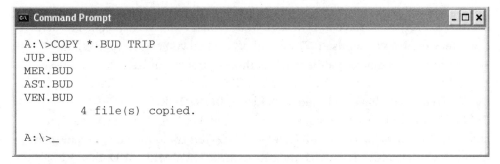

```
🖳 Command Prompt                                              _ □ ✕

A:\>REN TRIP\*.BUD *.PEN

A:\>DIR TRIP\*.BUD
 Volume in drive A is DATA
 Volume Serial Number is 30B8-DA1D

 Directory of A:\TRIP
```

```
File Not Found

A:\>DIR TRIP\*.PEN
 Volume in drive A is DATA
 Volume Serial Number is 30B8-DA1D

 Directory of A:\TRIP

10/31/2001  07:08 PM                 478 VEN.PEN
05/07/2002  07:41 AM                 190 JUP.PEN
10/31/2001  01:08 PM                 406 MER.PEN
10/30/2001  01:46 PM                 148 AST.PEN
               4 File(s)           1,222 bytes
               0 Dir(s)        1,424,896 bytes free

A:\>_
```

WHAT'S
HAPPENING?   You successfully renamed all the files with the **.BUD** extension in
the subdirectory **TRIP** on the DATA disk to a new set of files with the same file
name but with the file extension of **.PEN**.

6.17   Using RENAME on Different Drives and Directories

Since REN is an internal command, you can use it at any time, for any file, in any
drive, and in any directory. If you wish to rename a file on a different drive, you
must specify on which drive the old file is located. If you want the file renamed in a
different directory, you must specify in which directory the file is located. In the
syntax of REN OLDFILE.EXT NEWFILE.EXT, the operating system looks for
OLDFILE.EXT on the designated drive and directory. It renames the file and leaves
the file where it found it unless you preface OLDFILE.EXT with a drive letter. When
you key in the command REN B:OLDFILE.EXT NEWFILE.EXT, only the disk in
Drive B will be searched for the file called OLDFILE.EXT. If a directory is involved,
you must also include its name, so the command would read

REN C:\JUNK\OLDFILE.EXT NEWFILE.EXT

There is a substantial difference between the COPY command and the REN
command. With the COPY command, you can copy a file from one disk to another
disk or one directory to another directory, ending up with two identical files in
different locations. You *cannot* do this with the REN command because it changes
the names of files in only one directory or disk at a time. Remember, with REN you
are changing the name of an existing file in a specific location. REN finds a file by its
name, which is the first parameter in the REN command, on the designated disk or
directory. The second parameter must be the new name *only*, not including a repeat
of the location. REN cannot move a file from one location to another, nor can it copy
a file. It simply renames a file, leaving it where it found it.

6.18 Activity: Using RENAME on Different Drives

Note: The DATA disk is in Drive A. A:\> is displayed.

1   Key in the following: A:\>**CD /D C:\WUGXP** Enter

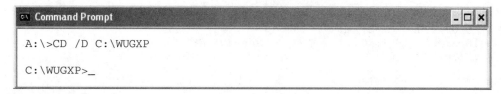

```
A:\>CD /D C:\WUGXP

C:\WUGXP>_
```

WHAT'S
HAPPENING?   You have changed the default drive to **C:** and have made
\WUGXP the default directory.

2   Key in the following: C:\WUGXP>**DIR ASTRO.TXT** Enter

3   Key in the following: C:\WUGXP>**COPY ASTRO.TXT A:** Enter

4   Key in the following: C:\WUGXP>**DIR A:\ASTRO.TXT** Enter

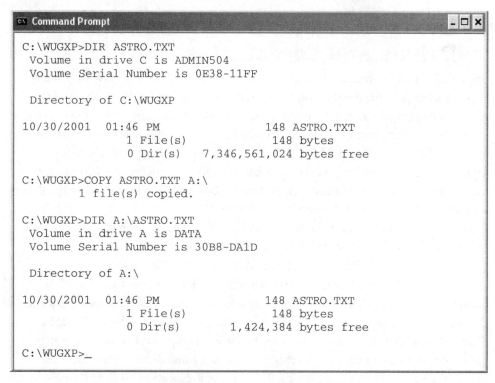

```
C:\WUGXP>DIR ASTRO.TXT
 Volume in drive C is ADMIN504
 Volume Serial Number is 0E38-11FF

 Directory of C:\WUGXP

10/30/2001  01:46 PM                148 ASTRO.TXT
               1 File(s)            148 bytes
               0 Dir(s)    7,346,561,024 bytes free

C:\WUGXP>COPY ASTRO.TXT A:\
        1 file(s) copied.

C:\WUGXP>DIR A:\ASTRO.TXT
 Volume in drive A is DATA
 Volume Serial Number is 30B8-DA1D

 Directory of A:\

10/30/2001  01:46 PM                148 ASTRO.TXT
               1 File(s)            148 bytes
               0 Dir(s)      1,424,384 bytes free

C:\WUGXP>_
```

WHAT'S
HAPPENING?   The directory display tells you that the file called **ASTRO.TXT**
does now exist on both the root of the DATA disk in the A drive and in the
\WUGXP subdirectory on the C drive.

5   Key in the following: C:\WUGXP>**TYPE A:\ASTRO.TXT** Enter

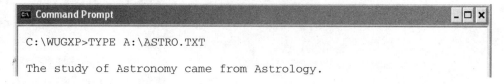

```
C:\WUGXP>TYPE A:\ASTRO.TXT

The study of Astronomy came from Astrology.
```

```
Most scientists no longer believe in
Astrology.  The science of Astronomy is
changing every day.

C:\WUGXP>_
```

WHAT'S HAPPENING?   You used the TYPE command to see the contents of the file called **ASTRO.TXT** located on the DATA disk.

6   Key in the following: `C:\WUGXP>`**REN A:\ASTRO.TXT A:\AST.TST** Enter

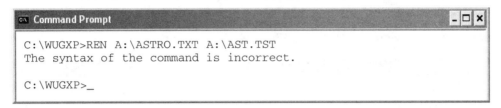

```
C:\WUGXP>REN A:\ASTRO.TXT A:\AST.TST
The syntax of the command is incorrect.

C:\WUGXP>_
```

WHAT'S HAPPENING?   Remember, the syntax of this command is:

```
REN [drive:][path]oldfile.ext newfile.ext
```

Since the operating system knows you cannot change a file name on any other disk except where the original file is located, it will not allow you to put a drive designator before the new file name.

7   Key in the following: `C:\WUGXP>`**REN A:\ASTRO.TXT AST.TST** Enter

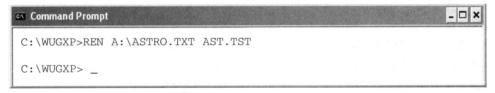

```
C:\WUGXP>REN A:\ASTRO.TXT AST.TST

C:\WUGXP> _
```

WHAT'S HAPPENING?   You see no messages because the syntax of the command you issued is correct. The file called **ASTRO.TXT** is in the root directory of the DATA disk. You requested that REN change the name of this file from **ASTRO.TXT** to a new file name **AST.TST**.

8   Key in the following: `C:\WUGXP>`**DIR ASTRO.TXT** Enter

9   Key in the following: `C:\WUGXP>`**DIR A:\ASTRO.TXT** Enter

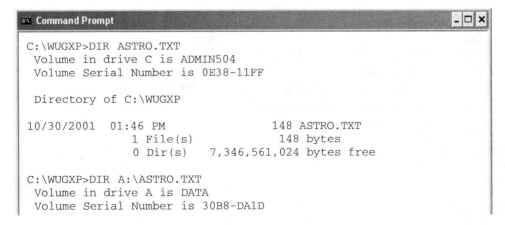

```
C:\WUGXP>DIR ASTRO.TXT
 Volume in drive C is ADMIN504
 Volume Serial Number is 0E38-11FF

 Directory of C:\WUGXP

10/30/2001  01:46 PM                 148 ASTRO.TXT
               1 File(s)             148 bytes
               0 Dir(s)    7,346,561,024 bytes free

C:\WUGXP>DIR A:\ASTRO.TXT
 Volume in drive A is DATA
 Volume Serial Number is 30B8-DA1D
```

```
Directory of A:\

File Not Found

C:\WUGXP>_
```

WHAT'S
HAPPENING?   You did not rename the file **ASTRO.TXT** on the hard disk in the
\WUGXP directory, only the one on the DATA disk. You got the message **File Not
Found** for the DATA disk because the file no longer exists under the file name
A:\ASTRO.TXT.

10   Key in the following: C:\WUGXP>**DIR A:\AST.TST** Enter

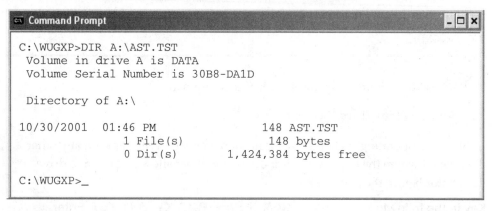

```
C:\WUGXP>DIR A:\AST.TST
 Volume in drive A is DATA
 Volume Serial Number is 30B8-DA1D

 Directory of A:\

10/30/2001  01:46 PM                 148 AST.TST
               1 File(s)            148 bytes
               0 Dir(s)       1,424,384 bytes free

C:\WUGXP>_
```

WHAT'S
HAPPENING?   You successfully renamed the file in the root directory of the DATA
disk from **ASTRO.TXT** to **AST.TST**. Does the file **AST.TST** have the same contents
as **ASTRO.TXT**? It should because renaming changes only the file name, not the
contents. To verify this, you can use the TYPE command.

11   Key in the following: C:\WUGXP>**TYPE A:\AST.TST** Enter

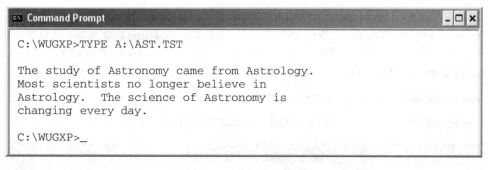

```
C:\WUGXP>TYPE A:\AST.TST

The study of Astronomy came from Astrology.
Most scientists no longer believe in
Astrology.  The science of Astronomy is
changing every day.

C:\WUGXP>_
```

WHAT'S
HAPPENING?   If you check the screen display following Step 4, you will see that
the file contents are identical. REN works the same way with subdirectories on other
drives. In Activity 6.16, you copied the files with the **.BUD** extension to the
subdirectory **TRIP** on the DATA disk; you then renamed them with the same file
name but with the **.PEN** file extension.

12   Key in the following: C:\WUGXP>**DIR A:\TRIP*.PEN** Enter

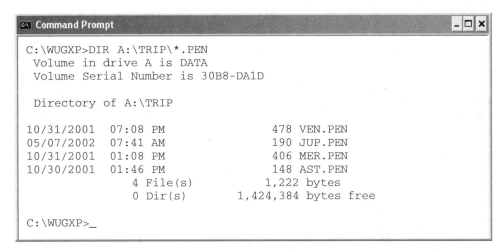

```
C:\WUGXP>DIR A:\TRIP\*.PEN
 Volume in drive A is DATA
 Volume Serial Number is 30B8-DA1D

 Directory of A:\TRIP

10/31/2001  07:08 PM               478 VEN.PEN
05/07/2002  07:41 AM               190 JUP.PEN
10/31/2001  01:08 PM               406 MER.PEN
10/30/2001  01:46 PM               148 AST.PEN
               4 File(s)         1,222 bytes
               0 Dir(s)      1,424,384 bytes free

C:\WUGXP>_
```

WHAT'S HAPPENING?   The files are there in the subdirectory **TRIP** on the DATA disk.

13 Key in the following: `C:\WUGXP>`**REN A:\TRIP*.PEN *.INK** [Enter]

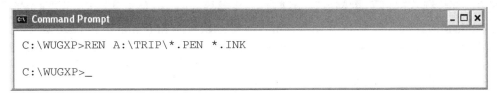

```
C:\WUGXP>REN A:\TRIP\*.PEN *.INK

C:\WUGXP>_
```

WHAT'S HAPPENING?   Once again, all that appears is the system prompt. Notice how you placed the drive and path in front of *only* the file names that you wanted to change (the old file names). These files can be renamed only on the DATA disk in the subdirectory **TRIP**. The REN command does not move files; it only changes file names.

14 Key in the following: `C:\WUGXP>`**DIR A:\TRIP*.PEN** [Enter]

15 Key in the following: `C:\WUGXP>`**DIR A:\TRIP*.INK** [Enter]

```
C:\WUGXP>DIR A:\TRIP\*.PEN
 Volume in drive A is DATA
 Volume Serial Number is 30B8-DA1D

 Directory of A:\TRIP

File Not Found

C:\WUGXP>DIR A:\TRIP\*.INK
 Volume in drive A is DATA
 Volume Serial Number is 30B8-DA1D

 Directory of A:\TRIP

10/31/2001  07:08 PM               478 VEN.INK
05/07/2002  07:41 AM               190 JUP.INK
10/31/2001  01:08 PM               406 MER.INK
10/30/2001  01:46 PM               148 AST.INK
               4 File(s)         1,222 bytes
               0 Dir(s)      1,424,384 bytes free

C:\WUGXP>_
```

WHAT'S ▓▓▓▓▓
▓▓▓▓ **HAPPENING?**   You successfully renamed all the **.PEN** files in the subdirectory
TRIP on the DATA disk. These files no longer exist with the **.PEN** file extension.

16 Key in the following: C:\WUGXP>**CD** \ Enter

17 Key in the following: C:\>**A:** Enter

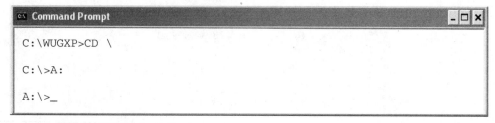

WHAT'S ▓▓▓▓▓
▓▓▓▓ **HAPPENING?**   You returned to the root directory of the hard disk and also
changed the default drive to the DATA disk location.

6.19   Moving Files and Renaming Directories

You learned in Chapter 4 that you could use the MOVE command to rename a
directory. In this chapter, you learned to use the RENAME command for renaming
both files and subdirectories. The REN command renames files and subdirectories;
it does not move them from one location to another.

The MOVE command was introduced in DOS 6.0. MOVE allows you to move
files and subdirectories from one location to another. If you move a file or
subdirectory individually, you can change the name as you move it. If you move a
group of files and/or subdirectories, you cannot change their names. The MOVE
command includes a prompt that will warn you that you are about to overwrite a
file. However, if you desire, you can turn off the warning. The full syntax diagram
for the MOVE command is:

```
Moves files and renames files and directories.

To move one or more files:
MOVE [/Y | /-Y] [drive:][path]filename1[,...] destination

To rename a directory:
MOVE [/Y | /-Y] [drive:][path]dirname1 dirname2

  [drive:][path]filename1 Specifies the location and name of the
                          file or files you want to move.
  destination             Specifies the new location of the file.
                          Destination can consist of a drive letter
                          and colon, a directory name, or a
                          combination. If you are moving only one
                          file, you can also include a filename if
                          you want to rename the file when you move
                          it.
  [drive:][path]dirname1  Specifies the directory you want to
                          rename.
  dirname2                Specifies the new name of the directory.

  /Y                      Suppresses prompting to confirm you want
                          to overwrite an existing destination file.
  /-Y                     Causes prompting to confirm you want to
                          overwrite an existing destination file.
```

```
The switch /Y may be present in the COPYCMD environment variable.
This may be overridden with /-Y on the command line.  Default is
to prompt on overwrites unless MOVE command is being executed from
within a batch script.
```

The MOVE command will not only move files and directories from one directory to another, but will also allow you to move them from one drive to another. This feature is especially useful in maintaining your hard disk.

6.20 Activity: Moving Files and Renaming Directories

Note: The DATA disk is in Drive A. A:\> is displayed.

1   Key in the following: A:\>**MD FILES** [Enter]

2   Key in the following: A:\>**COPY *.99 FILES*.FIL** [Enter]

3   Key in the following: A:\>**MD FILES\ROOM** [Enter]

4   Key in the following: A:\>**COPY GALAXY.NEW FILES** [Enter]

```
Command Prompt                                              _ □ x

A:\>MD FILES

A:\>COPY *.99 FILES\*.FIL
AST.99
VEN.99
JUP.99
MER.99
        4 file(s) copied.

A:\>MD FILES\ROOM

A:\>COPY GALAXY.NEW FILES
        1 file(s) copied.

A:\>_
```

WHAT'S HAPPENING?   You have created the **FILES** directory with a directory beneath it called **ROOM**. You copied some files from the root directory of the DATA disk into the **FILES** directory.

5   Key in the following: A:\>**DIR FILES** [Enter]

```
Command Prompt                                              _ □ x

A:\>DIR FILES
 Volume in drive A is DATA
 Volume Serial Number is 30B8-DA1D

 Directory of A:\FILES

03/25/2002  03:42 PM    <DIR>          .
03/25/2002  03:42 PM    <DIR>          ..
10/30/2001  01:46 PM               148 AST.FIL
10/31/2001  07:08 PM               478 VEN.FIL
10/30/2001  03:42 PM               190 JUP.FIL
10/31/2001  01:08 PM               406 MER.FIL
```

```
03/25/2002   03:42 PM    <DIR>          ROOM
10/31/2001   11:33 AM              152 GALAXY.NEW
              5 File(s)          1,374 bytes
              3 Dir(s)       1,420,800 bytes free

A:\>_
```

WHAT'S HAPPENING?   You have a subdirectory called **ROOM** under the **FILES** directory on the DATA disk. You decide that you no longer care for the name **ROOM** and wish to call the directory **MYROOM**.

6   Key in the following: A:\>**MOVE FILES\ROOM FILES\MYROOM** [Enter]

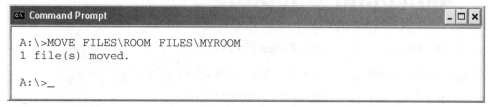

```
A:\>MOVE FILES\ROOM FILES\MYROOM
1 file(s) moved.

A:\>_
```

WHAT'S HAPPENING?   You have renamed a subdirectory from **FILES\ROOM** to **FILES\MYROOM**. Notice the difference between the MOVE and REN syntax. When using REN, you do not give the path with the new name. When using MOVE to rename a directory, you do give the full path with the new name.

7   Key in the following: A:\>**REN FILES\MYROOM PLACE** [Enter]

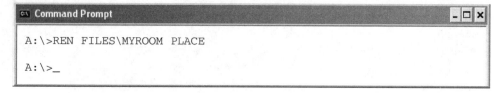

```
A:\>REN FILES\MYROOM PLACE

A:\>_
```

WHAT'S HAPPENING?   You can verify that the subdirectory **MYROOM** was, indeed, renamed to **PLACE**.

8   Key in the following: A:\>**DIR FILES** [Enter]

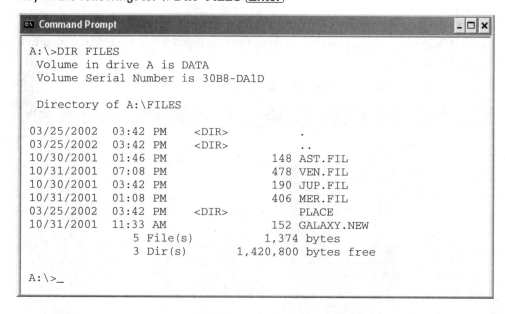

```
A:\>DIR FILES
 Volume in drive A is DATA
 Volume Serial Number is 30B8-DA1D

 Directory of A:\FILES

03/25/2002   03:42 PM    <DIR>          .
03/25/2002   03:42 PM    <DIR>          ..
10/30/2001   01:46 PM              148 AST.FIL
10/31/2001   07:08 PM              478 VEN.FIL
10/30/2001   03:42 PM              190 JUP.FIL
10/31/2001   01:08 PM              406 MER.FIL
03/25/2002   03:42 PM    <DIR>          PLACE
10/31/2001   11:33 AM              152 GALAXY.NEW
              5 File(s)          1,374 bytes
              3 Dir(s)       1,420,800 bytes free

A:\>_
```

WHAT'S
WHAT'S
HAPPENING?   The directory name has again changed. Now you want to move a file. You use MOVE to move files from one location to another. If you try to move a file in the same drive and the same directory, it has the effect of eliminating the first file and replacing the contents of the second file with the contents of the first file. In the next steps you will see the results of such a task.

9 Key in the following: A:\>**TYPE FILES\AST.FIL** ⎡Enter⎤

10 Key in the following: A:\>**TYPE FILES\JUP.FIL** ⎡Enter⎤

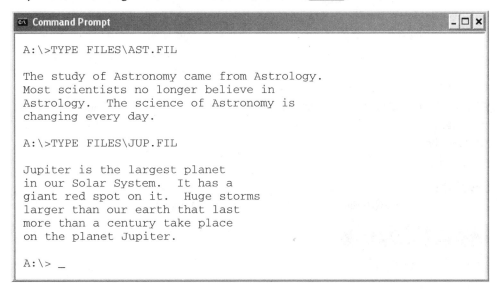

```
A:\>TYPE FILES\AST.FIL

The study of Astronomy came from Astrology.
Most scientists no longer believe in
Astrology.  The science of Astronomy is
changing every day.

A:\>TYPE FILES\JUP.FIL

Jupiter is the largest planet
in our Solar System.  It has a
giant red spot on it.  Huge storms
larger than our earth that last
more than a century take place
on the planet Jupiter.

A:\> _
```

WHAT'S
HAPPENING?   You can see that the contents are different as well as the file names.

11 Key in the following: A:\>**MOVE FILES\AST.FIL FILES\JUP.FIL** ⎡Enter⎤

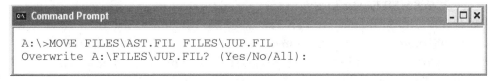

```
A:\>MOVE FILES\AST.FIL FILES\JUP.FIL
Overwrite A:\FILES\JUP.FIL? (Yes/No/All):
```

WHAT'S
HAPPENING?   This warning by the MOVE command tells you that you are about to overwrite a file.

12 Press **Y** ⎡Enter⎤

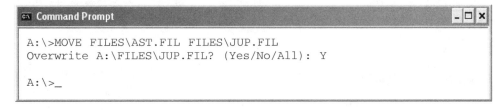

```
A:\>MOVE FILES\AST.FIL FILES\JUP.FIL
Overwrite A:\FILES\JUP.FIL? (Yes/No/All): Y

A:\>_
```

WHAT'S
HAPPENING?   Because you entered **Y** for "yes," the file was overwritten.

13 Key in the following: A:\>**TYPE FILES\AST.FIL** ⎡Enter⎤

14 Key in the following: A:\>**TYPE FILES\JUP.FIL** ⎡Enter⎤

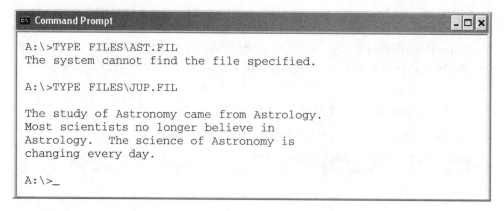

```
A:\>TYPE FILES\AST.FIL
The system cannot find the file specified.

A:\>TYPE FILES\JUP.FIL

The study of Astronomy came from Astrology.
Most scientists no longer believe in
Astrology.  The science of Astronomy is
changing every day.

A:\>_
```

WHAT'S HAPPENING?   The file **AST.FIL** no longer exists. It "moved" to a new file, **JUP.FIL**. Thus, **JUP.FIL** now holds the contents of the old **AST.FIL**. The old contents of **JUP.FIL** are gone. If this sounds confusing, it is. The lesson here is do not use MOVE when you mean REN. The following steps will show you how MOVE is useful when it is used wisely.

15 Key in the following:

A:\>**MOVE FILES\VEN.FIL FILES\PLACE\VEN.NEW** Enter

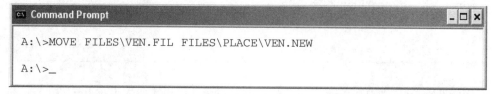

```
A:\>MOVE FILES\VEN.FIL FILES\PLACE\VEN.NEW

A:\>_
```

WHAT'S HAPPENING?   You have, in essence, accomplished three separate functions with one command. First, you copied the file called **VEN.FIL** located in the **FILES** directory to the **FILES\PLACE** directory. Second, you gave it a new name, **VEN.NEW**. Third, you deleted **VEN.FIL** from the **FILES** directory. All this occurred using one command, MOVE, not three—COPY, REN, and DEL. If you used Windows Explorer, you would have to take two steps: first move the file, and then rename it. The command line provided a one-step solution.

16 Key in the following: A:\>**DIR FILES** Enter

17 Key in the following: A:\>**DIR FILES\PLACE** Enter

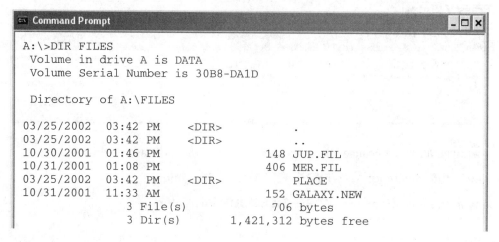

```
A:\>DIR FILES
 Volume in drive A is DATA
 Volume Serial Number is 30B8-DA1D

 Directory of A:\FILES

03/25/2002  03:42 PM    <DIR>          .
03/25/2002  03:42 PM    <DIR>          ..
10/30/2001  01:46 PM               148 JUP.FIL
10/31/2001  01:08 PM               406 MER.FIL
03/25/2002  03:42 PM    <DIR>          PLACE
10/31/2001  11:33 AM               152 GALAXY.NEW
               3 File(s)            706 bytes
               3 Dir(s)       1,421,312 bytes free
```

```
A:\>DIR FILES\PLACE
 Volume in drive A is DATA
 Volume Serial Number is 30B8-DA1D

 Directory of A:\FILES\PLACE

03/25/2002  03:42 PM    <DIR>          .
03/25/2002  03:42 PM    <DIR>          ..
10/31/2001  07:08 PM              478 VEN.NEW
              1 File(s)            478 bytes
              2 Dir(s)       1,421,312 bytes free

A:\>_
```

WHAT'S HAPPENING?   The file called **VEN.FIL** is no longer in the **FILES** directory. It is, however, in the **FILES\PLACE** directory with the name of **VEN.NEW**. MOVE also works well with wildcards. However, when you use wildcards with the MOVE command, you cannot change file names.

18 Key in the following: A:\>**MOVE FILES*.FIL FILES\PLACE*.TXT** [Enter]

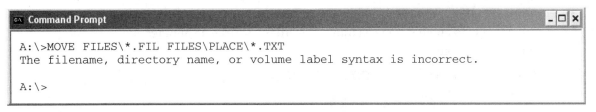

```
Command Prompt                                          _ □ ×

A:\>MOVE FILES\*.FIL FILES\PLACE\*.TXT
The filename, directory name, or volume label syntax is incorrect.

A:\>
```

WHAT'S HAPPENING?   MOVE cannot combine the contents of files (concatenate files) and therefore cannot place these files into one file called ***.TXT**.

19 Key in the following: A:\>**MOVE FILES*.FIL FILES\PLACE** [Enter]

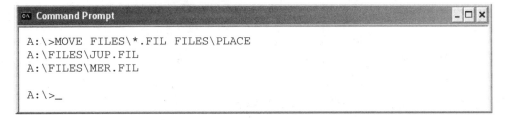

```
Command Prompt                                          _ □ ×

A:\>MOVE FILES\*.FIL FILES\PLACE
A:\FILES\JUP.FIL
A:\FILES\MER.FIL

A:\>_
```

WHAT'S HAPPENING?   Now that you have issued the command correctly, the files with the **.FIL** extension are no longer in the **FILES** directory but in the **PLACE** directory.

20 Key in the following: A:\>**DIR FILES** [Enter]

21 Key in the following: A:\>**DIR FILES\PLACE** [Enter]

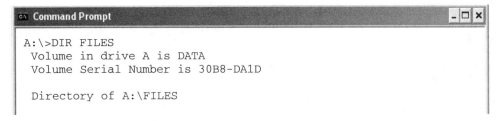

```
Command Prompt                                          _ □ ×

A:\>DIR FILES
 Volume in drive A is DATA
 Volume Serial Number is 30B8-DA1D

 Directory of A:\FILES
```

```
03/25/2002  03:42 PM      <DIR>               .
03/25/2002  03:42 PM      <DIR>               ..
03/25/2002  03:42 PM      <DIR>               PLACE
10/31/2001  11:33 AM                  152 GALAXY.NEW
              1 File(s)               152 bytes
              3 Dir(s)         1,421,312 bytes free

A:\>DIR FILES\PLACE
 Volume in drive A is DATA
 Volume Serial Number is 30B8-DA1D

 Directory of A:\FILES\PLACE

03/25/2002  03:42 PM      <DIR>               .
03/25/2002  03:42 PM      <DIR>               ..
10/31/2001  07:08 PM                  478 VEN.NEW
10/30/2001  01:46 PM                  148 JUP.FIL
10/31/2001  01:08 PM                  406 MER.FIL
              3 File(s)             1,032 bytes
              2 Dir(s)          1,421,312 bytes freeee

A:\>_
```

WHAT'S HAPPENING?   The files with the **.FIL** extension were successfully moved from one location to another. You can move files from one drive to another and from one directory to another.

22 Key in the following: A:\>**MOVE FILES\PLACE*.FIL CLASS** Enter

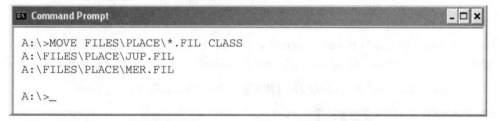

```
A:\>MOVE FILES\PLACE\*.FIL CLASS
A:\FILES\PLACE\JUP.FIL
A:\FILES\PLACE\MER.FIL

A:\>_
```

WHAT'S HAPPENING?   The files with the **.FIL** extension are no longer located in the **FILES\PLACE** directory but were moved to the **CLASS** directory, keeping the same file names.

23 Key in the following: A:\>**DIR FILES\PLACE*.FIL** Enter

24 Key in the following: A:\>**DIR CLASS*.FIL** Enter

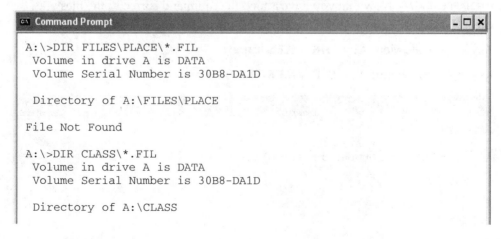

```
A:\>DIR FILES\PLACE\*.FIL
 Volume in drive A is DATA
 Volume Serial Number is 30B8-DA1D

 Directory of A:\FILES\PLACE

File Not Found

A:\>DIR CLASS\*.FIL
 Volume in drive A is DATA
 Volume Serial Number is 30B8-DA1D

 Directory of A:\CLASS
```

```
10/30/2001  01:46 PM                  148 JUP.FIL
10/31/2001  01:08 PM                  406 MER.FIL
              2 File(s)               554 bytes
              0 Dir(s)          1,421,312 bytes free

A:\>_
```

WHAT'S HAPPENING?   The files were successfully moved. You can see that the MOVE command is very useful and very powerful. You can move entire subdirectory structures, along with the files in them, with one command.

25 Key in the following: A:\>**MD START\SUBDIR** [Enter]

26 Key in the following: A:\>**COPY *.FIL START\SUBDIR** [Enter]

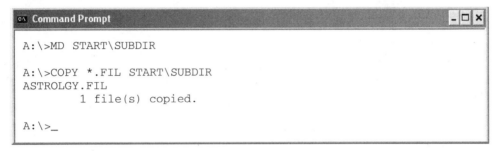

```
Command Prompt                                    _ □ x

A:\>MD START\SUBDIR

A:\>COPY *.FIL START\SUBDIR
ASTROLGY.FIL
        1 file(s) copied.

A:\>_
```

WHAT'S HAPPENING?   You have created a new directory, **START**, that contains a child directory, **SUBDIR,** in which there is one file, **ASTROLOGY.FIL**. To see everything in the **START** directory structure, you will use the DIR command with two of its parameters: /S to view all the contents in the subdirectories and /B to see only the file and subdirectory names with none of the other information.

27 Key in the following: A:\>**DIR START /S /B** [Enter]

```
Command Prompt                                    _ □ x

A:\>DIR START /S /B
A:\START\SUBDIR
A:\START\SUBDIR\ASTROLGY.FIL

A:\>_
```

WHAT'S HAPPENING?   You can see that with this bare (/B) display, you do not see "Volume in drive A is DATA," "Volume Serial Number is 30B8-DA1D," or "Directory of A:\START." Nor do you see the amounts of drive space used or free. The bare display shows you directory names and file names only. You can see that the **START** directory contains only one subdirectory, **SUBDIR,** and no files. The subdirectory **SUBDIR** contains one file, **ASTROLOGY.FIL.** But you made a mistake. You actually wanted to place this entire directory structure beginning with **START** under the subdirectory **FILES**. You can move the entire structure with the MOVE command.

28 Key in the following: A:\>**MOVE START FILES** [Enter]

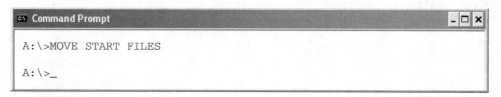

```
A:\>MOVE START FILES

A:\>_
```

WHAT'S ▒▒▒▒▒▒
▒▒▒▒HAPPENING?   The command has properly executed. What actually happened? You can use the DIR command to verify that the **START** directory is no longer under the root, but that it and all of its contents are now under the **FILES** directory.

29 Key in the following: A:\>**DIR START** [Enter]

30 Key in the following: A:\>**DIR FILES** [Enter]

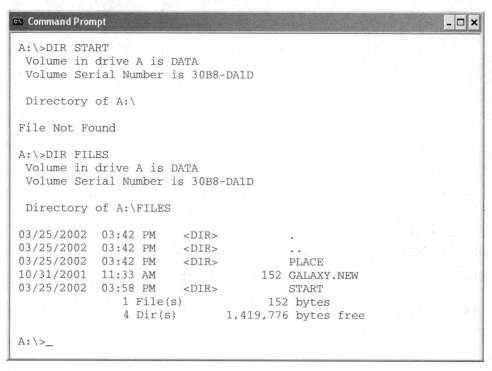

```
A:\>DIR START
 Volume in drive A is DATA
 Volume Serial Number is 30B8-DA1D

 Directory of A:\

File Not Found

A:\>DIR FILES
 Volume in drive A is DATA
 Volume Serial Number is 30B8-DA1D

 Directory of A:\FILES

03/25/2002  03:42 PM    <DIR>          .
03/25/2002  03:42 PM    <DIR>          ..
03/25/2002  03:42 PM    <DIR>          PLACE
10/31/2001  11:33 AM              152 GALAXY.NEW
03/25/2002  03:58 PM    <DIR>          START
               1 File(s)            152 bytes
               4 Dir(s)      1,419,776 bytes free

A:\>_
```

WHAT'S ▒▒▒▒▒▒
▒▒▒▒HAPPENING?   As you can see, the **START** subdirectory is no longer on the root of the DATA disk. It is now in the **FILES** directory. But has the entire subdirectory structure been moved? You can verify this further with the DIR /S /B command.

31 Key in the following: A:\>**DIR FILES\START /S /B** [Enter]

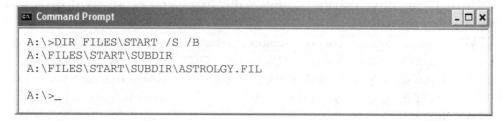

```
A:\>DIR FILES\START /S /B
A:\FILES\START\SUBDIR
A:\FILES\START\SUBDIR\ASTROLGY.FIL

A:\>_
```

WHAT'S ▒▒▒▒▒▒
▒▒▒▒HAPPENING?   You can see that the entire **START** directory structure was moved successfully to the **FILES** directory.

6.21 RD /S Revisited

In Chapter 4, you learned how to remove a directory. You could use the RD command with no parameters. This was the bottom-up approach. Since you create directories from the top down, you had to delete directories from the bottom up. If the subdirectory you wished to remove had more subdirectories beneath it, you had to remove those subdirectories first. RD with the parameter /S allows you to delete directories from the top down with one command. In addition, when you use RD on its own, you must first remove any subdirectories and any files that are in each subdirectory. Thus, removing directories with RD by itself is a two-step process—first delete files (DEL), then eliminate the directory (RD). Removing directories from the GUI is also a two-step process—delete and empty the Recycle Bin. RD /S has the advantage that in one fell swoop, you eliminate files and directories—no second step is required. It is a very powerful, but also an *extremely* dangerous, command.

6.22 Activity: Using RD and RD /S

Note: The DATA disk is in Drive A. A:\> is displayed.

1 Key in the following: A:\>**RD FILES\PLACE** Enter

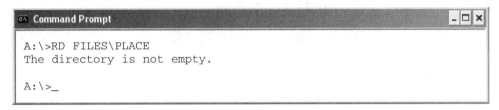

```
A:\>RD FILES\PLACE
The directory is not empty.

A:\>_
```

**WHAT'S
HAPPENING?** The portion of the message that applies here is that the **FILES\PLACE** directory is not empty of files. Thus, you have to take a step preceding the RD command.

2 Key in the following: A:\>**DEL FILES\PLACE** Enter

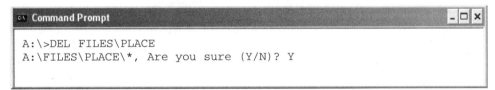

```
A:\>DEL FILES\PLACE
A:\FILES\PLACE\*, Are you sure (Y/N)? Y
```

**WHAT'S
HAPPENING?** You had to use the DEL command to eliminate the files. The command **DEL FILES\PLACE** implied or defaulted to all the files in the **PLACE** directory. You could have keyed in **DEL FILES\PLACE*.***, but *.* wasn't necessary since, if you do not use a value with DEL, the default is all files.

3 Press **Y** Enter

4 Key in the following: A:\>**RD FILES\PLACE** Enter

5 Key in the following: A:\>**DIR FILES** Enter

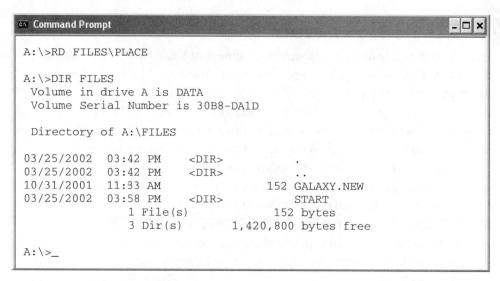

```
A:\>RD FILES\PLACE

A:\>DIR FILES
 Volume in drive A is DATA
 Volume Serial Number is 30B8-DA1D

 Directory of A:\FILES

03/25/2002  03:42 PM    <DIR>          .
03/25/2002  03:42 PM    <DIR>          ..
10/31/2001  11:33 AM                152 GALAXY.NEW
03/25/2002  03:58 PM    <DIR>          START
               1 File(s)            152 bytes
               3 Dir(s)       1,420,800 bytes free

A:\>_
```

WHAT'S ▦▦▦
▦▦▦HAPPENING?   Once you eliminated the files from the **PLACE** directory using
DEL, you could remove the directory using the RD command without the /S
parameter. Using RD /S is much faster because it is a one-step process. In addition,
if you had any hidden or system files, they would be deleted as well.

6   Key in the following: A:\>**RD FILES /S** [Enter]

```
A:\>RD FILES /S
FILES, Are you sure (Y/N)?
```

WHAT'S ▦▦▦
▦▦▦HAPPENING?   As you can see, RD /S is offering to delete files and directories.

7   Press **Y** [Enter]

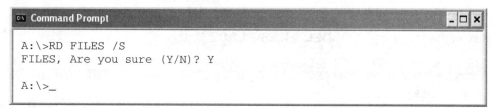

```
A:\>RD FILES /S
FILES, Are you sure (Y/N)? Y

A:\>_
```

WHAT'S ▦▦▦
▦▦▦HAPPENING?   You saw no message stating that the files or subdirectory were
deleted. Were they?

8   Key in the following: A:\>**DIR FILES** [Enter]

```
A:\>DIR FILES
 Volume in drive A is DATA
 Volume Serial Number is 30B8-DA1D

 Directory of A:\

File Not Found

A:\>_
```

WHAT'S
HAPPENING?   The directory **FILES** was removed. RD /S is fast, but keep in mind that "fast" can be "dangerous."

6.23 Backing Up Your DATA Disk

You should get into the habit of backing up your data files so that if something happens to the original data, you have a copy of the original material. In data-processing circles, this habit is called "Disaster and Recovery Planning." It means exactly what it says. If there is a disaster—fire, flood, power surge, theft, head crash, coffee spilled on a disk—what is your plan to recover your programs and data?

Most application programs today come on a CD-ROM disc, but there are still programs that come on diskette. Backing up application program disks can be tricky, especially on *copy-protected* disks (which means you cannot back them up with regular operating system commands). You should never back up your program or software Application disks until you understand how the application programs work. Application software that comes on diskettes provides documentation that instructs you how to back up the specific application program disk you own.

Backing up a hard disk is a special circumstance, using special operating commands and procedures. You cannot and should not back up the hard disk using the techniques that will be described here because the contents of a hard disk will not fit on one floppy disk or on a zip disk.

However, you can and should back up all the data on any data disk with the following techniques. There are three ways to back up data files. One way is to back up the entire data disk—this backs up all the files and all the subdirectories. To do this, you use the DISKCOPY command, which makes an identical copy of a disk, track for track and sector for sector. You can use DISKCOPY on floppy disks.

You can also use the COPY command, which backs up files from floppy disk to floppy disk or other storage media or specific files in specific directories on the hard disk. The third method, using the XCOPY command, will be discussed later. Never use the MOVE command for backup purposes. The MOVE command, although useful in placing files onto a floppy disk from a hard disk, removes the files from their original location. Thus, you end up with only one copy of your data files, which defeats the purpose of backing up.

Typically, data files are backed up at the end of every work session so that you can keep your data files current. It is very important to acquire a regular backup routine so that it becomes an automatic process.

Usually with application software you are not so worried about backing up the programs. If something happens to the hard disk, you can recover and reinstall the programs from the original, purchased CDs or disks. However, the data that you create is unrecoverable unless you have backed it up. A common technique to back up data from a hard disk is to purchase a device called a "tape backup." This device allows the user the ease of backing up the hard disk without having to sit in front of the computer and keep inserting blank floppy disks. In addition, if you have a writable CD, you can also copy files to a CD. However, the important message is that whatever technique you use, *back up your data files!*

In this text, you have been placing all your data files on a floppy disk. Backing up this disk is the easiest kind of backup to perform. It is also extremely useful. With a backup copy of the DATA disk, if you should have a problem, you would not have to go back to Chapter 2 and redo all the activities and homework. In the next activity, you will back up your DATA disk.

6.24 Activity: Backing Up with the DISKCOPY Command

Note 1:   The DATA disk is in Drive A. C:\> is displayed.

Note 2:   DISKCOPY requires that media types be the same.

1   If you are not at the C prompt, change to the C drive now. Get either a blank disk, a disk that has not been used, or a disk that has data on it that you no longer want. Label it "BACKUP DATA disk."

2   Key in the following: C:\>**DISKCOPY A: A:** [Enter]

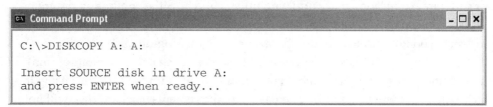

```
Command Prompt                                              _ □ ✕

C:\>DISKCOPY A: A:

Insert SOURCE disk in drive A:
and press ENTER when ready...
```

WHAT'S HAPPENING?   You are asked to put the SOURCE disk that you wish to copy in Drive A. In this case, the DATA disk, which you want to copy, is already in Drive A. You keyed in two disk drives, **A** and **A**, to ensure that you do not accidentally copy the hard disk. You are telling DISKCOPY to make a copy from the disk in Drive A to the disk in Drive A.

3   Press [Enter]

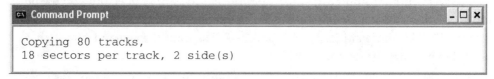

```
Command Prompt                                              _ □ ✕

Copying 80 tracks,
18 sectors per track, 2 side(s)
```

WHAT'S HAPPENING?   The number of tracks and sectors will vary depending on the disk media type. The DISKCOPY command tells the operating system to copy everything on the disk in Drive A (the SOURCE) to RAM. While this program is doing the copying, the cursor flashes on the screen. When the command is completed or the program has finished executing (copying), you need to take another step. You receive the following prompt:

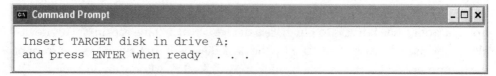

```
Command Prompt                                              _ □ ✕

Insert TARGET disk in drive A:
and press ENTER when ready  . . .
```

This prompt tells you to remove the SOURCE disk from Drive A and insert the blank or TARGET disk in Drive A so that the operating system has a place to copy the information.

4   Remove your original DATA disk from Drive A. Insert the blank disk labeled "BACKUP DATA disk" into Drive A. This is your target disk. Close or latch the drive door. Press **Enter**

```
Volume Serial Number is 843B-9D87
Copy another disk (Y/N)?
```

WHAT'S
HAPPENING?   You saw a only a flashing cursor while whatever was in RAM was being copied or written to the blank disk in Drive A. Now you see a question: Do you want to execute DISKCOPY again to copy another disk? In this case, you do not wish to make another copy, so you key in **N**. The Volume Serial Number changes each time you use the DISKCOPY command.

5   Press **N**

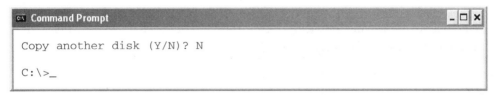

```
Copy another disk (Y/N)? N

C:\>_
```

WHAT'S
HAPPENING?   Because of the DISKCOPY command, you now have two copies of the DATA disk, the original and the backup. At the end of each work session, you should follow these steps to back up your DATA disk. You do not need a new backup disk each time. Keep using the same backup disk over and over. You are merely keeping current; you do not need an archival or historical record of each day's work. You should also make a backup copy of your HOMEWORK disk. However, if you wish to be prudent, it is wise to have more than one backup copy of your disks. As you can imagine, the only time you need your copy of the data is when something has gone wrong. This is not the time you want to find out that your only copy of the data is bad. It is also a good idea to check your backed up data periodically to ensure that it is good data and that you can recover it if you need to. Remember, DISKCOPY makes an exact duplicate of the source diskette. Anything that was previously on the target diskette is destroyed in this process.

Some organizations, such as banks and the IRS, may need to recreate records, so they will have not only a *Disaster and Recovery Plan* but also *archival data* or an *archival backup*. This is sometimes called a "transaction history." Organizations like this need far more than a simple backup copy. For instance, if you go into the bank today and say you are missing the $100.00 deposit you made last week, the bank cannot tell you that they do not know what happened last week. The bank needs to be able to recreate all the transactions that occurred on the day in question. Just having a backup copy of your account for today or even yesterday is not sufficient. Most PC users, however, do not need archival data. Simply backing up their data is sufficient.

6   Remove the disk labeled "BACKUP DATA disk" and keep it in a safe place until you need it again to make another backup.

WHAT'S ▓▓▓▓
▓▓▓HAPPENING?   You now have a backup copy of your DATA disk. You may wish to repeat the steps with another disk to back up your HOMEWORK disk too, as well as for any floppy disks you have important data stored on, such as your papers for your English class. In this class, every time you complete a chapter, it is a good idea to update your backups so that they are kept current. In this way, if something happens to one of the original disks, you have lost only one chapter's work.

6.25 Backing Up Files with the COPY Command

Note: The following material is informational and meant *to be read only*. It is not an activity.

Using the DISKCOPY command backs up an entire floppy disk. More often than not, however, you need to back up only specific files, or you want to back up files from the hard disk to a floppy disk or a removable drive such as a Zip drive. Remember that you can also use the COPY command to back up specific files. The basic syntax does not change. It is as follows:

```
COPY [drive:][path]SOURCE.FIL [drive:][path]DESTINATION.FIL
```

You can also back up files from one floppy disk to another with the COPY command. Be sure that the destination disk is already formatted because COPY does not format a new disk as DISKCOPY does. Furthermore, COPY can be used only if you have two removable drives such as a floppy disk and a Zip drive. Since you are using two disk drives, COPY does not require identical disk media types. For example, you can copy from a 3½-inch, 1.44 MB disk to a Zip disk. You would place the source disk in Drive A and the destination disk in Drive F or whatever your removable drive letter is, and key in

A:\>**COPY *.* F:**

A:\> is the default drive. COPY is the command. *.* means every file with every file extension—the first * represents any file name, the second * represents any file extension. COPY goes to the source disk to find each file in the root directory. As it copies the source file, it lists the file name on the screen. F:\ represents the root directory of the destination disk. Since you give no file names following F:\, COPY assumes that you want the same file names on the destination disk. If there is a file with the same name on the destination disk, COPY overwrites it.

If you want to back up files from a hard disk, you can also use the COPY command to copy the files in the individual subdirectories. However, you must be sure that there are not too many files in a subdirectory to fit on a floppy disk. Look at the following display:

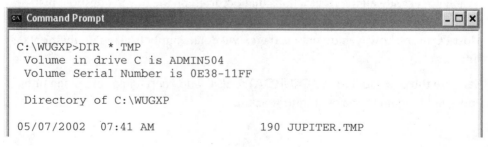

```
C:\WUGXP>DIR *.TMP
 Volume in drive C is ADMIN504
 Volume Serial Number is 0E38-11FF

 Directory of C:\WUGXP

05/07/2002  07:41 AM                 190 JUPITER.TMP
```

```
10/31/2001    01:08 PM                    406 MERCURY.TMP
05/07/2002    07:41 AM                    190 JUP.TMP
10/30/2001    02:47 PM                     86 BONJOUR.TMP
10/31/2001    11:33 AM                    152 GALAXY.TMP
10/31/2001    01:08 PM                    406 MER.TMP
10/30/2001    01:46 PM                    148 AST.TMP
10/30/2001    01:46 PM                    148 ASTRO.TMP
10/31/2001    07:08 PM                    478 VEN.TMP
               9 File(s)            2,204 bytes
               0 Dir(s)    7,209,746,432 bytes free

C:\WUGXP>_
```

After **9 File(s)**, the number is **2,024 bytes**. This number tells you that these nine files require only 2,204 bytes and will easily fit on a floppy disk. On the other hand, you may get a display like the one that follows:

```
[C:\] Command Prompt                                          _ □ ✕

  Volume in drive H is BETTES H
  Volume Serial Number is 2F4B-16FD

  Directory of H:\ENCARTA

04/23/2000    04:03p                     72 APRIL.TMP
07/03/2000    01:53p      <DIR>             WORKING
10/22/1997    4:31p       <DIR>             .
10/22/1997    4:31p       <DIR>             ..
08/12/1996    8:47p               2,681,344 ENCRES97.DLL
08/12/1996    2:34p                 134,144 DECO_32.DLL
08/12/1996    2:40p                   1,434 E97SPAM.INI
08/12/1996    8:47p                 355,328 ENCTITLE.DLL
08/12/1996    2:43p                  13,204 YBBST97A.DAT
08/12/1996    2:34p                 526,336 EEUIL10.DLL
08/12/1996    2:36p                 212,992 SUBSCRIB.EXE
08/12/1996    8:45p                  17,258 DISCS.HLP
08/12/1996    8:46p                 863,913 ENC97.HLP
08/12/1996    8:45p                   6,429 ENC97.CNT
08/12/1996    2:36p                  60,053 WEBTIPS.HLP
08/12/1996    2:34p                  84,343 README.HLP
11/16/1997    3:42p                  20,848 INST97A.LOG
08/12/1996    8:46p               1,520,354 ENC97F.STR
08/12/1996    8:46p               3,429,346 ENCART97.DAT
08/12/1996    8:53p                  78,188 UNINSTAL.EXE
08/12/1996    8:45p               1,715,200 ENC97.EXE
10/05/1996   11:49a                       4 ENCART97.ANN
10/22/1997    4:31p       <DIR>             UPDATES
              18 File(s)    11,720,718 bytes
               3 Dir(s)    921,403,392 bytes free

H:\ENCARTA>_
```

The number is now **18 File(s)** that occupy **11,720,718 bytes**, which will not fit on a single floppy disk. However, the files would fit on a 100-MB Zip cartridge. Only if the files will fit on a floppy disk can you use the COPY command. Thus, if you wanted to back up the subdirectory \WUGXP, the command would be keyed in as

C:\>COPY C:\WUGXP*.* A:

This command, however, would not copy files in any subdirectories under the \WUGXP subdirectory, only the files in the \WUGXP directory. You would have to key in another command such as

C:\>**COPY \WUGXP\DATA*.* A:**

You cannot and must not copy all the files from a hard disk to a floppy disk with the COPY command. There are too many files on the hard disk, and they will not fit on a single floppy disk. There are backup utilities to back up large volumes, but they need a destination other than a floppy disk.

A question that arises is how often should you back up data? If you have backed up files to floppies or a tape and have not changed your original files, you do not need to back them up again. The files you are interested in backing up are those that have changed or those that are new. A rule of thumb to follow is to think of how long it would take you to recreate your data. If you think in those terms, you will make regular backups.

Chapter Summary

1. DEL eliminates files.
2. Deleting files helps you manage your disks and directories.
3. The syntax for the DEL command is:
   ```
   DEL names
   ```
4. Wildcards can be used with DEL.
5. DEL does not eliminate the data on the disk, only the entry in the directory table.
6. Once a file has been deleted, it cannot be recovered except with special utility programs.
7. Before you use wildcards with DEL, it is wise to use the DIR command to see what is going to be erased.
8. The /P parameter prompts you to confirm whether or not you wish to delete a file, and the /S parameter allows you to delete files in the directory hierarchy.
9. You can change the names of files or directories with the RENAME or REN command.
10. The syntax for renaming is:
    ```
    RENAME [drive:][path][directoryname1 | filename1]
    [directoryname2 | filename2]
    REN [drive:][path][directoryname1 | filename1]
    [directoryname2 | filename2]
    ```
11. Renaming can be done only on one drive or directory. RENAME does not move files.
12. Renaming changes only file names, not contents of files.
13. With the REN command, you use the path only with the original file name and do not repeat it with the new file name.
14. Wildcards can be used with the REN command.
15. Before you use wildcards with the REN command, it is wise to use the DIR command to see what files are going to be affected by renaming.
16. Once a file is renamed, it cannot be found under its old name.
17. The MOVE command can be used either to change the name of a subdirectory or to move files from one location to another. When you use MOVE, two steps are taken: the files are copied to the new location and deleted from the old location.

18. You may remove directories with either RD or RD /S. With RD alone, you must remove files first and then any directories. RD /S does it all in one command.

19. It is wise to make backup copies of data files so that if something happens, you have another source of data.

20. You can back up a floppy disk with the DISKCOPY command, or you can back up files on your disk using the COPY command. The wildcard *.* allows you to back up all the files in a directory.

Key Terms

archival backup   copy-protected   Disaster and Recovery Plan
archival data

Discussion Questions

1. Explain why you may want to eliminate files from a disk.

2. When you delete a file, the file is not actually removed from the disk. What really happens?

3. Give the syntax of the DEL command and explain each part of the syntax.

4. Explain the following statement, with regards to the DEL command. *The strength of wildcards is also a weakness.*

5. When deleting files, why should you key in DIR with global file specifications first?

6. Explain the purpose and function of the /P parameter with the DEL command. The /S?

7. Why would you want to change the name of a file?

8. Explain the purpose and function of the RENAME or REN command.

9. Give the syntax of the REN command and explain each part of the syntax.

10. What is the difference between the REN and RENAME commands?

11. What is the difference between the RENAME and COPY commands?

12. If you are using the REN command and get the message, "A duplicate file name exists, or the file name cannot be found," what could it mean?

13. What is the function and purpose of the MOVE command?

14. Give the syntax of the MOVE command and explain each part of the syntax.

15. Compare and contrast MOVE and COPY.

16. What is the difference between the MOVE and the REN commands?

17. Compare and contrast the RD /S command with the RD command without the /S parameter.

18. What process could you use to back up specific files?

19. What process could you use to back up a subdirectory?

20. Why would you not copy all the files from the hard disk to a floppy disk with the DISKCOPY command?

21. Why would you not copy all the files from a hard disk to a floppy disk with the COPY command?

True/False Questions

For each question, circle the letter T if the statement is true and the letter F if the statement is false.

T   F   1. REN and RENAME perform identical functions.

T   F   2. It is not possible to find a file that has been renamed if you do not know its new name.

T   F   3. When using wildcards with the MOVE command, you cannot change the destination file name.

T   F   4. You cannot use REN on subdirectories.

T   F   5. If you use the command DEL TRIP and TRIP is a subdirectory name, the default parameter is all files (*.*).

Completion Questions

Write the correct answer in each blank space.

6. One way to verify that a file has been deleted is to use the _____ command.

7. The REN command does not move files. Its only function is to _____ a file name.

8. The command for making an exact duplicate of a floppy disk is

   _____.

9. After you complete a work session, an important procedure to follow to ensure not losing your data is to _____ your original disk.

10. The parameter that allows you to confirm whether or not you wish to delete a file is _____.

Multiple Choice Questions

For each question, write the letter for the correct answer in the blank space.

____   11. DEL is a command that
   a. removes a subdirectory.
   b. can delete only one file at a time.
   c. can be used with wildcards.
   d. none of the above

____   12. Prior to using wildcards with the DEL command,
   a. it is a good idea to confirm visually the files to be erased using DIR.
   b. it is wise to remember that wildcards have opposite meanings when used with DIR and COPY.
   c. remember that only data files can be removed with the DEL command.
   d. remember that only program files can be removed with the DEL command.

____   13. When A:\> is the default and DEL CLASS.DBF is keyed in,
   a. the file CLASS.DBF will be deleted from the default drive.
   b. the file CLASS.DBF will be deleted from Drive C.
   c. nothing will happen.
   d. none of the above

____   14. Using the command RD *directory_name* /S only
  a. deletes the files from the specified directory.
  b. deletes the files from the specified directory and files from its child directories.
  c. deletes the specified directory and all subdirectories and files contained therein.
  d. deletes the subdirectories contained in the specified directory.

____   15. The MOVE command
  a. can be used to rename a directory.
  b. can be used to make multiple copies of files.
  c. can move an entire directory structure to a new location.
  d. both a and c

Writing Commands

Write the correct steps or commands to perform the required action as if you were at the computer. The prompt will indicate the default drive and directory.

16. Remove the file called **CATS** in the directory called **ANIMALS** located under the root directory of Drive A.

    A:\TEST>

17. Delete all the files with the **.OLD** file extension in the subdirectory **WHAT** located under the current directory on the default drive.

    C:\JUNK>

18. Change the extension of the **COLOR** file from **.DOT** to **.DOC**. The file is located in the **PAINT** directory under the root directory on Drive A.

    C:\>

19. Change the file extension from **.FIL** to **.TXT** for all the files in the **FURN** subdirectory located under the root directory on Drive C.

    A:\>

20. Eliminate the file called **MYFILE.TXT**, located in the subdirectory **JUNK** on Drive C.

    C:\JUNK>

Homework Assignments

Note 1: Place the HOMEWORK disk in Drive A. Be sure to work on the HOME-WORK disk, not the DATA disk.

Note 2: The homework problems will assume Drive C is the hard disk and the HOMEWORK disk is in Drive A. If you are using another drive, such as floppy Drive B or hard Drive D, be sure and substitute that drive letter when reading the questions and creating the answers.

Note 3: All subdirectories that are created will be under the root directory unless otherwise specified.

Problem Set I

Problem A

Note: If the DATA disk is in Drive A, remove it and place it in a safe place.

CAUTION: Do not use the DATA disk for these HOMEWORK problems. Use the HOMEWORK disk.

A-a   Insert the HOMEWORK disk into Drive A.

A-b   Copy all the files from the **WUGXP\MEDIA\TV** subdirectory to the root directory of the HOMEWORK disk.

A-c   On the HOMEWORK disk, rename the file called **DRAMA.TV** to **SERIOUS.TV**.

_____   1. Which command did you use to rename the file?
      a. REN DRAMA.TV SERIOUS.TV
      b. REN SERIOUS.TV DRAMA.TV
      c. COPY DRAMA.TV SERIOUS.TV
      d. COPY SERIOUS.TV DRAMA.TV

A-d   Execute the DIR command looking only for the file called **DRAMA.TV**.

_____   2. What message is displayed?
      a. Invalid File Parameter
      b. File Not Found
      c. Required parameter missing
      d. no message is displayed

A-e   Rename the file called **SERIOUS.TV** to **DRAMA.TV**.

_____   3. Which command did you use?
      a. REN DRAMA.TV SERIOUS.TV
      b. REN SERIOUS.TV DRAMA.TV
      c. COPY DRAMA.TV SERIOUS.TV
      d. COPY SERIOUS.TV DRAMA.TV

A-f   Key in the following: **TYPE SERIOUS.TV** [Enter]

_____   4. What message is displayed?
      a. The system cannot find the file specified
      b. File Not Found
      c. Required parameter missing
      d. no message is displayed

A-g   Key in the following: **TYPE DRAMA.TV** [Enter]

_____   5. What television series is displayed?
      a. The Rosie O'Donnell Show
      b. Seinfeld
      c. The Practice
      d. Dallas

Problem B

Note: The exercises in Problem B assume the root directory of the HOME-WORK disk is the default drive and directory.

B-a Copy all files from the **WUGXP** subdirectory that have the file extension of **.DOS** to the root directory of the HOMEWORK disk, keeping the file names the same.

6. How many files were copied?
   - a. one
   - b. two
   - c. three
   - d. four

B-b Rename all the files that have a file extension of **.DOS** to the same file name but with **.WG** as the file extension (remember wildcards).

7. Which command did you use?
   - a. COPY *.DOS *.WG
   - b. REN *.DOS *.WG
   - c. COPY ?.DOS ?.WG
   - d. REN ?.DOS ?.WG

B-c Make copies of all the **.WG** files on the root of the HOMEWORK disk keeping the same file name but with a new extension of **.RRR**.

8. Which command did you use?
   - a. DIR *.RRR
   - b. REN *.WG *.RRR
   - c. DIR *.WG
   - d. COPY *.WG *.RRR

B-d Make copies of all the **.WG** files on the HOMEWORK disk keeping the same file names but with a new extension of **.MMM**.

9. What date is listed for the WILDTWO.MMM file?
   - a. 02/13/2000
   - b. 12/31/2001
   - c. 12/31/2000
   - d. 02/13/1999

B-e Using the relative path, move all the files with the **.RRR** file extension to the **PHONE** subdirectory.

10. What command did you use?
    - a. COPY *.RRR PHONE
    - b. REN *.RRR PHONE
    - c. MOVE *.RRR PHONE
    - d. MOVE PHONE *.RRR

B-f Execute the DIR command looking only for files in the root directory of the HOMEWORK disk that have the **.RRR** file extension.

___   11. How many files were located?
        a. one
        b. two
        c. three
        d. zero

B-g   Execute the DIR command looking only for files in the **PHONE** subdirectory that have the **.RRR** file extension.

___   12. How many files were located?
        a. one
        b. two
        c. three
        d. zero

B-h   Rename all the files that have the extension of **.WG** to the same file name but with **.DOS** as the file extension. Use a wildcard.

___   13. Which command did you use?
        a. COPY *.DOS *.WG
        b. REN *.DOS *.WG
        c. COPY *.WG *.DOS
        d. REN *.WG *.DOS

B-i   Key in the following:
MOVE WILDONE.MMM PHONE\OLD\WILD.MMM [Enter]

___   14. What message is displayed?
        a. A:\WILDONE.MMM => a:\phone\old\wild.mmm [ok]
        b. The system cannot find the path specified.
        c. A:\WILDONE.MMM => a:\phone\old\wild.mmm [No such directory]
        d. no message is displayed

B-j   Delete all the files on the HOMEWORK disk with the **.MMM** extension. Use a wildcard.

___   15. Which command did you use?
        a. DEL *.MMM /S or DEL /S *.MMM
        b. DEL PHONE*.MMM or DEL /S PHONE*.MMM
        c. RD PHONE*.MMM or RD /S PHONE*.MMM
        d. MOVE *.MMM or MOVE /S *.MMM

___   16. What is displayed when you have finished executing the command?
        a. 3 file(s) deleted
        b. File not found
        c. Deleted file - A:\WILDTWO.MMM
           Deleted file - A:\WILDTHR.MMM
           Deleted file - A:\WILDONE.MMM
        d. none of the above

B-k   Ascertain how many files there are on the HOMEWORK disk with the extension **.RRR**. (*Hint:* Remember DIR /S.)

____ 17. Which command did you use?
   a. DIR /S *.RRR or DIR *.RRR /S
   b. DIR PHONE*.RRR
   c. FIND PHONE*.RRR
   d. none of the above

B-l Delete all the files with the **.RRR** extension on the HOMEWORK disk. Use a wildcard.

____ 18. Which commands could you have used?
   a. DEL /S *.RRR or DIR *.RRR /S
   b. DEL PHONE*.RRR
   c. MOVE PHONE*.RRR
   d. either a or b

Problem C

Note: The exercises in Problem C assume the root directory of the HOME-WORK disk is the default drive and directory.

C-a Copy the file from the **WUGXP** directory called **PLANETS.TXT** to the root of the HOMEWORK disk.

C-b Create a subdirectory called **SERIES** under the root of the HOMEWORK disk.

C-c Copy all the files on the root of the HOMEWORK disk with the extension **.99** to the **SERIES** directory.

C-d Using the relative path, move the file called **PLANETS.TXT** from the root directory of the HOMEWORK disk to the **SERIES** directory.

____ 19. Which command did you use with PLANETS.TXT?
   a. COPY PLANETS.TXT SERIES
   b. DEL SERIES\PLANETS.TXT
   c. REN PLANETS.TXT SERIES
   d. MOVE PLANETS.TXT SERIES

____ 20. The file PLANETS.TXT is now in
   a. only the SERIES directory on the HOMEWORK disk.
   b. only the root of the HOMEWORK disk.
   c. the WUGXP directory on the hard drive and the SERIES directory on the HOMEWORK disk.
   d. none of the above

C-e From the root of the HOMEWORK disk using the relative path, delete the file **PLANETS.TXT** on the HOMEWORK disk.

____ 21. Which command did you use?
   a. DEL PLANETS.TXT
   b. DEL SERIES\PLANETS.TXT
   c. MOVE PLANETS.TXT
   d. REN PLANETS.TXT

C-f Eliminate the **SERIES** directory from the HOMEWORK disk *without* using the /S parameter with the RD command.

_____ 22. Which command did you use *first?*
   a. RD SERIES
   b. DEL SERIES or DEL \SERIES*.*
   c. DELETE SERIES or DELETE \SERIES*.*
   d. MOVE SERIES or MOVE \SERIES*.*

_____ 23. Which command did you use *second?*
   a. RD SERIES
   b. DEL SERIES or DEL \SERIES*.*
   c. DELETE SERIES or DELETE \SERIES*.*
   d. MOVE SERIES or MOVE \SERIES*.*

Problem D

Note: The exercises in Problem D assume the root directory of the HOME-WORK disk is the default drive and directory.

D-a   You wish to use a wildcard, but you want to select only some files to eliminate in the **FILES** subdirectory that have the file extension **.FIL**.

_____ 24. What parameter would you use with the DEL command?
   a. /K
   b. /P
   c. /S
   d. /T

D-b   Use the correct parameter from the above question with the DEL command to selectively eliminate the files with **JUP** or **MER** as a file name and **.FIL** as a file extension from the **FILES** subdirectory.

_____ 25. Beside the file names, which message was displayed?
   a. Delete [ok]?
   b. Delete (Y/N)?
   c. Invalid parameter
   d. no message was displayed

D-c   Rename all the files in the **FILES** subdirectory that have a file extension of **.FIL** to the same file name but with **.AAA** as the file extension.

_____ 26. Which command did you use?
   a. REN FILES*.FIL *.AAA
   b. REN FILES*.FIL FILES*.AAA
   c. REN FILES*.AAA FILES*.FIL
   d. REN FILES*.AAA *.FIL

Problem E

Note: The root directory of the HOMEWORK disk is the default drive and directory.

E-a   Copy all the files from the **\WUGXP** directory that have the file extension of **.TMP** to the root directory of the HOMEWORK disk.

_____ 27. How many files were copied?
   a. 3
   b. 6
   c. 9
   d. 12

E-b Rename all the files on the root of the HOMEWORK disk with the **.TMP** file extension to have the same names with the file extension of **.AST**. Use a wildcard.

_____ 28. Which command did you use?
   a. REN *.AST *.TMP
   b. COPY *.AST *.TMP
   c. REN *.TMP *.AST
   d. COPY *.TMP *.AST

E-c Eliminate all the **.AST** files _except_ **BONJOUR.AST**.

_____ 29. Which command did you use?
   a. DEL *.AST
   b. DEL *.AST /P
   c. DEL *.AST /Y
   d. DEL *.AST /S

Problem Set II—At the Computer

Note 1: Before proceeding with these assignments, check with your lab instructor to see if there are any special procedures you should follow.

Note 2: The HOMEWORK disk is in Drive A. The A:\> prompt is displayed as the default drive and the default directory. _All work will occur on the HOMEWORK disk._

Note 3: Make sure that **NAME.BAT**, **MARK.FIL**, **GETYN.COM**, and **GO.BAT** are all present in the root directory of the HOMEWORK disk before proceeding with these problems.

Note 4: All files with the **.HW** extension _must_ be created in the root directory of the HOMEWORK disk.

1 Key in the following: A:\>**NAME** [Enter]

2 Here is an example to key in, but your instructor will have other information that applies to your class. Key in the following:
Bette A. Peat [Enter]   (_Your_ name goes here.)
CIS 55 [Enter]   (_Your_ class goes here.)
T-Th 8-9:30 [Enter]   (_Your_ day and time go here.)
Chapter 6 Homework [Enter]

3 Press [F6] [Enter]

4 If the information is correct, press **Y** and you are back to A:\>.

WHAT'S ▓▓▓▓▓
▓▓ HAPPENING?   You have returned to the system level. You now have a file called **NAME.FIL** with your name and other pertinent information. _Hint:_ Remember redirection.

To Create 1.HW

1   The root directory of the HOMEWORK disk is the default drive and directory.

2   Key in the following: **DIR EXP*.* > 1.HW** [Enter]

3   Eliminate all the files that begin with **EXP** and have any file extension.

4   Note the double >> and note that there is no space with between the two >>. Key in the following: **DIR EXP*.* >> 1.HW** [Enter]

To Create 2.HW

1   The root directory of the HOMEWORK disk is the default drive and directory.

2   Move all the files with a **.TV** extension to the **PHONE** directory.

3   Locate only the files in the **PHONE** directory on the HOMEWORK disk that have the extension of **.TV** and place the names of the files in a file called **2.HW**.

To Create 3.HW

1   The root directory of the HOMEWORK disk is the default drive and directory.

2   Locate all the files in the root directory of the HOMEWORK disk that have an extension of **.TV**, if any, placing the output of the command in a file called **3.HW**.

To Create 4.HW

1   The root directory of the HOMEWORK disk is the default drive and directory.

2   Rename all the files in the **FILES** subdirectory that have the extension **.AAA** to the same name but with the extension of **.PLA**.

3   Locate all the files in the **FILES** directory that have an extension of **.PLA**.

4   Place the output of the command in a file called **4.HW**.

To Create 5.HW

1   The root directory of the HOMEWORK disk is the default drive and directory.

2   Eliminate all the files in the root directory of the HOMEWORK disk that have the **.MAK** extension, if any.

3   Locate any files in the root directory of the HOMEWORK disk with the **.MAK** extension, if any, and place the output of the command in a file called **5.HW**.

To Print Your Homework

1   Be sure the printer is on and ready to accept print jobs from your computer.

2   Key in the following (be very careful to make no typing errors): **GO NAME.FIL 1.HW 2.HW 3.HW 4.HW 5.HW** [Enter]

WHAT'S ▓▓▓▓
▓▓▓▓HAPPENING?   If the files you requested, **1.HW**, **2.HW**, etc., do not exist in the default directory, you will see the following message on the screen:

```
File Not Found
The system cannot find the file specified.

  Is there a message that says "File Not Found. The system cannot
  find the file specified."

  If so, press Y to find out what could be wrong.

  Otherwise, press N to continue.
```

The operating system is telling you that the file cannot be found. If you see this screen, press **Y** to see what could be wrong, and repeat the print procedure after you have corrected the problem.

If the default directory contains the specified files, the following message will appear on the screen:

```
  Is there a message that says "File Not Found. The system cannot
  find the file specified."

  If so, press Y to find out what could be wrong.

  Otherwise, press N to continue.
```

You will need to press **N** once for each file you are printing.

3   Follow the messages on the screen until the Notepad program opens with a screen similar to the following:

WHAT'S
HAPPENING?   All the requested files have been found and placed in a Notepad document. Your homework is now ready to print.

4   On the Notepad menu bar, click **File**. Click **Print**.

5   Click the **Print** button.

6   In the Notepad window, click **File**. Click **Exit**.

WHATS HAPPENING?   The following will appear on the Command Prompt screen:

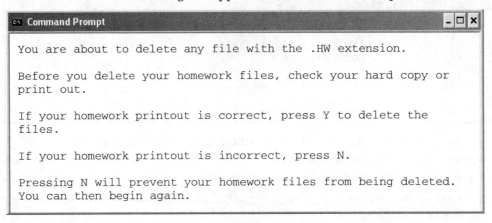

At this point, look at your printout. If it is correct, you can press **Y** to delete the homework files for this chapter. If your printout is incorrect, you can press **N**. That will preserve your homework and you will need to redo only the problem that was incorrect and not all the homework assignments.

7   Press **Y** Enter

WHATS HAPPENING?   You have returned to the default prompt.

8   Close the Command Prompt session.

Problem Set III—Brief Essay

1. What are the advantages of using the commands REN, DEL, COPY, and MOVE from the command line instead of using Windows Explorer? What are the disadvantages?

2. *Deleting files and directories can have serious consequences and should never be done.* Agree or disagree with this statement and explain the rationale for your answer.

CHAPTER 7

USING ATTRIB, SUBST, XCOPY, DOSKEY, AND THE TEXT EDITOR

Learning Objectives

After finishing this chapter, you will be able to:

1. Explain the purpose and function of the ATTRIB command.
2. Explain the purpose and function of the SUBST command.
3. Explain the purpose and function of the XCOPY command.
4. Explain the purpose and function of DOSKEY.
5. Use the text editor to create and edit text files.

Student Outcomes

1. Use the ATTRIB command to protect files.
2. Use the SUBST command to simplify long path names.
3. Use XCOPY to copy files and subdirectories.
4. Use the XCOPY parameters to copy hidden files and retain file attributes.
5. Use DOSKEY to be more efficient at the command line.
6. Create text files using the text editor.

Chapter Overview

By using different utility commands and programs, you can manipulate files and subdirectories to help make tasks at the command line much easier. You can make the DEL *.* command safer by using the ATTRIB command to hide files that you don't want to delete. You will learn what file attributes are and how to manipulate them with the ATTRIB command. You can copy files and subdirectories at the same time with the XCOPY command. You can even copy hidden files and empty subdirectories. By understanding how DOSKEY functions, you can further use command line editing keys. By using the text editor, you can quickly create simple text files. In this chapter, you will take a look at these commands and programs.

7.1 File Attributes and the ATTRIB Command

The root directory keeps track of information about every file on a disk. This information includes the file name, file extension, file size, date and time the file was last modified, and a pointer to the file's starting cluster in the file allocation table. In addition, each file in the directory has attributes. Each attribute is a "bit" of information that is either on or off. A bit is 1/8 of a byte, and can store only a 1 or a 0, representing True or False, Yes or No, or On or Off. These attributes describe the status of a file. The attributes are represented by a single letter. These attributes include whether or not a file is a system file (S), a hidden file (H), a read-only file (R), or an archived file (A). Attributes are sometimes referred to as flags. If you are using the NTFS file system, there are also other attributes. These include an attribute indicating a compressed or encrypted file and whether the file contents should be indexed for fast file searching. However, at the command line, the only attributes you can change with the ATTRIB command are the S, H, R, and A.

The *system attribute* is a special signal to the operating system that the file is a system file. Files with this attribute are usually operating system files, but some application programs may set a bit to indicate that a particular program is a system file. The *hidden attribute* means that, when you key in DIR, the file name is not displayed. Hidden files cannot be deleted using the DEL command without parameters, copied with the COPY command, or renamed. For example, hidden files such as the operating system files NTLDR and NTDETECT.COM are on a disk, but when you execute DIR, they are not displayed. The same is true in Windows Explorer or My Computer. Unless you change the folder options, hidden files are not displayed.

When a file is marked as read-only, it means exactly that. A user can only read the file, not modify or delete it. Sometimes application programs will set the *read-only attribute* bit to "on" for important files so that a user cannot easily or accidentally delete them.

Finally, the *archive attribute* is used to indicate the backup history (archive status) of a file. When you create or modify a file, an archive bit is turned on or set. When a file has its archive bit turned on, that signifies that it has not been backed up. Certain commands and programs, such as those that back up, can modify the archive bit and reset it (turn it off or on).

The ATTRIB command allows you to manipulate *file attributes*. You can view, set, and reset all the file attributes for one file or many files. ATTRIB is an external command. The syntax for the ATTRIB command is the same as it was in Windows 2000:

```
ATTRIB [+R | -R] [+A | -A] [+S | -S] [+H | -H]
[[drive:][path]filename] [/S [/D]]
```

When you see a parameter in brackets, as you know, it is an optional parameter. When you see a parameter displayed as [+R | -R], the bar (called a pipe) signifies that there is a choice. The parameter can be one thing or the other, not both—the choices are mutually exclusive. Thus, you can set a file with +R or -R, but not both at the same time. When you see two sets of brackets such as [/S [/D]], it means that the /S can be used alone but the /D must be used with the /S and cannot be used alone. The parameters are as follows:

+ Sets an attribute.

- Clears an attribute.

R Read-only file attribute.

A Archive file attribute.

S System file attribute.

H Hidden file attribute.

/S Processes matching files in the current folder and all subfolders.

/D Processes folders as well.

The attributes that you will find most useful to set or unset are read-only (R) and hidden (H). By making a file read-only, no one, including you, will be able to delete or overwrite the file accidentally. If a data file is marked read-only, even when you are in an application program, you cannot alter the data.

When you use the H attribute to make a file hidden, it will not be displayed when using the DIR command. If you cannot see a file displayed in the directory listing, you also cannot copy, delete, or rename it. This feature, as you will see, will allow you great flexibility in manipulating and managing files.

The A attribute is called the archive bit. The A attribute is a signal that the file has not been backed up. However, merely using the COPY command does not turn off the A attribute. You must use certain programs, such as XCOPY, which can read and manipulate the archive bit. Unlike COPY, XCOPY will determine whether or not a file has changed since the last time it was backed up, based on whether or not the archive bit is set. Then, XCOPY can make a decision on whether or not the file needs to be backed up. Rarely, if ever, will you use the ATTRIB command to change the attribute of a file marked as a system file (S).

You will find that, although you can change file attributes from Windows Explorer, it is much easier to do these kinds of tasks from the command prompt.

7.2 Activity: Using ATTRIB to Make Files Read-only

Note 1: Be sure you have opened the Command Prompt window.

Note 2: Be sure the DATA disk is in Drive A and A:\> is displayed.

Note 3: If specified files are not on your DATA disk, you can copy them from the **WUGXP** subdirectory.

1 Key in the following: A:\>**ATTRIB** *.99 Enter

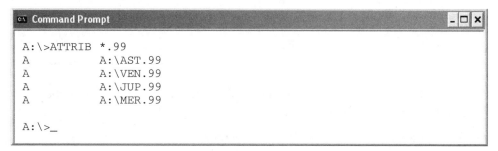

```
A:\>ATTRIB  *.99
A           A:\AST.99
A           A:\VEN.99
A           A:\JUP.99
A           A:\MER.99

A:\>_
```

WHAT'S ▓▓▓▓
▓▓▓**HAPPENING?**   You asked the ATTRIB command to show you all the files with the
.99 extension in the root directory of the DATA disk. The only file attribute that is
visible or "on" for these files is A, the archive bit. The display tells you that the
archive bit is set for each file that has a .99 file extension.

2   Key in the following: A:\>**ATTRIB C:*.*** [Enter]

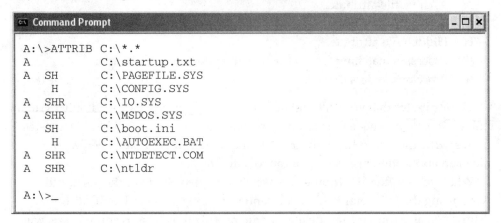

```
A:\>ATTRIB  C:\*.*
A               C:\startup.txt
A   SH          C:\PAGEFILE.SYS
    H           C:\CONFIG.SYS
A   SHR         C:\IO.SYS
A   SHR         C:\MSDOS.SYS
    SH          C:\boot.ini
    H           C:\AUTOEXEC.BAT
A   SHR         C:\NTDETECT.COM
A   SHR         C:\ntldr

A:\>_
```

WHAT'S ▓▓▓▓
▓▓▓**HAPPENING?**   You are looking at the files in the root directory of C. Your display
will be different depending on what files are in your root directory. Also, if you are
using a network drive instead of a local hard disk, you may not be able to access the
root directory of the network drive. You can see that in this display, **io.sys**,
MSDOS.SYS, **ntldr**, and **NTDETECT.COM** are marked with an S for the system
attribute, an H for the hidden attribute, and an R for the read-only attribute. Since
you cannot boot the computer from the hard disk without these files, they are triple-
protected. Other critical files are marked with one or more of the S, H, and R attributes.

3   Key in the following: A:\>**COPY C:\WUGXP*.FIL** [Enter]
     Note: Overwrite any files if you are prompted to do so.

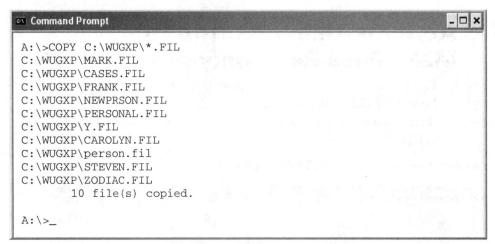

```
A:\>COPY  C:\WUGXP\*.FIL
C:\WUGXP\MARK.FIL
C:\WUGXP\CASES.FIL
C:\WUGXP\FRANK.FIL
C:\WUGXP\NEWPRSON.FIL
C:\WUGXP\PERSONAL.FIL
C:\WUGXP\Y.FIL
C:\WUGXP\CAROLYN.FIL
C:\WUGXP\person.fil
C:\WUGXP\STEVEN.FIL
C:\WUGXP\ZODIAC.FIL
        10 file(s) copied.

A:\>_
```

WHAT'S ▓▓▓▓
▓▓▓**HAPPENING?**   You have copied all the files with the **.FIL** extension from the
\WUGXP subdirectory to the DATA disk.

4   Key in the following: A:\>**ATTRIB *.FIL** [Enter]

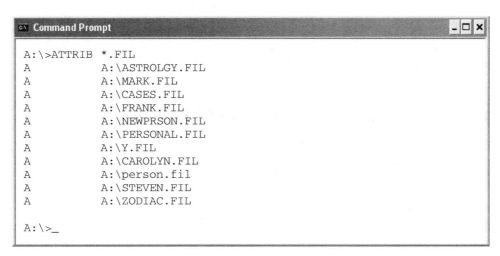

```
A:\>ATTRIB *.FIL
A           A:\ASTROLGY.FIL
A           A:\MARK.FIL
A           A:\CASES.FIL
A           A:\FRANK.FIL
A           A:\NEWPRSON.FIL
A           A:\PERSONAL.FIL
A           A:\Y.FIL
A           A:\CAROLYN.FIL
A           A:\person.fil
A           A:\STEVEN.FIL
A           A:\ZODIAC.FIL

A:\>_
```

WHAT'S HAPPENING?   The only attribute that is set (turned on) for these files is the archive bit (A).

5   Key in the following: A:\>**ATTRIB +R STEVEN.FIL** Enter

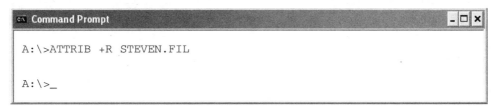

```
A:\>ATTRIB +R STEVEN.FIL

A:\>_
```

WHAT'S HAPPENING?   You asked the ATTRIB command to make **STEVEN.FIL** a read-only file.

6   Key in the following: A:\>**ATTRIB STEVEN.FIL** Enter

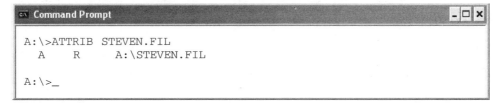

```
A:\>ATTRIB STEVEN.FIL
  A    R     A:\STEVEN.FIL

A:\>_
```

WHAT'S HAPPENING?   Now you have flagged or marked **STEVEN.FIL** as a read-only file.

7   Key in the following: A:\>**DEL STEVEN.FIL** Enter

```
A:\>DEL STEVEN.FIL
A:\STEVEN.FIL
Access is denied.

A:\>_
```

WHAT'S HAPPENING?   You cannot delete this file because it is marked read-only. You can also protect against other kinds of file destruction. Once a file is marked read-only, even when you are in an application program, the operating system will stop you from overwriting the file.

Note: Steps 8 through 24 can be completed only if you have Microsoft Excel installed on your computer. If Excel is not available, read through the exercise and study the screen images.

8   Key in the following: A:\>**COPY C:\WUGXP*.XLS** [Enter]

9   Key in the following: A:\>**DIR *.XLS** [Enter]

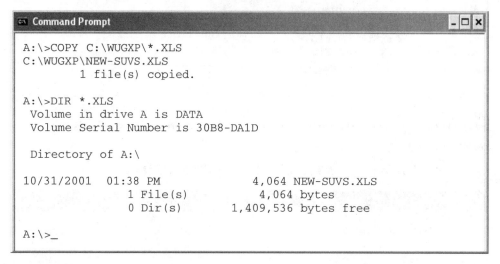

```
A:\>COPY C:\WUGXP\*.XLS
C:\WUGXP\NEW-SUVS.XLS
        1 file(s) copied.

A:\>DIR *.XLS
 Volume in drive A is DATA
 Volume Serial Number is 30B8-DA1D

 Directory of A:\

10/31/2001  01:38 PM              4,064 NEW-SUVS.XLS
             1 File(s)            4,064 bytes
             0 Dir(s)         1,409,536 bytes free

A:\>_
```

WHAT'S ▓▓▓▓▓▓▓
▓▓▓▓ HAPPENING?   You have the file NEW-SUVS.XLS on the DATA disk.

10   Key in the following: A:\>**ATTRIB +R *.XLS** [Enter]

11   Key in the following: A:\>**ATTRIB *.XLS** [Enter]

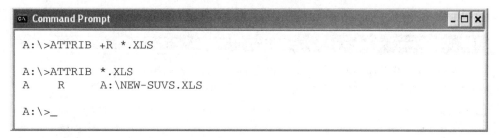

```
A:\>ATTRIB +R *.XLS

A:\>ATTRIB *.XLS
A    R     A:\NEW-SUVS.XLS

A:\>_
```

WHAT'S ▓▓▓▓▓▓▓
▓▓▓▓ HAPPENING?   You have made NEW-SUVS.XLS a read-only file.

12   Minimize the command line window:

13   Click **Start**. Click **My Computer**. Double-click the A drive icon. Click **Tools** on the menu bar. Click **Folder Options**.

14 Click the **View** Tab. Scroll down and remove the check from **Hide extensions for known file types**. Click **OK**.

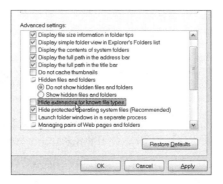

WHAT'S HAPPENING?   You have made it possible to see the .XLS file extension on the New-SUVs file.

15 Scroll down until you can see the **NEW-SUV.XLS** file. Double-click on the **NEW-SUV.XLS** file to open both Excel and the file.

WHAT'S HAPPENING?   You have opened the file in Excel. Notice the title bar says [Read-Only].

16 Click in cell A-30 (the box right below **Toyota**).

17 Key in the following: **Latest Thing** [Enter]

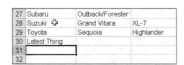

WHAT'S HAPPENING?   You have added data to the file.

18 Click **File** on the menu bar. Click **Save**.

WHATS
HAPPENING?   You are told that the file is read-only.

19   Click **OK**.

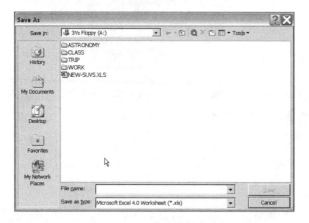

WHATS
HAPPENING?   Excel brought up the Save As dialog box. Notice that there is no
name in the File name box. In order to save the file, you would have to give it a
different name, as NEW-SUV.XLS is read only and can not be overwritten.
In less sophisticated software, when you try and save over a read-only file you may
get an error that is not at all descriptive, or worse, the program may simply "crash."
Excel provides you with an easy solution.

20   Click **Cancel** to close the dialog box.

21   Click **File**. Click **Exit**.

WHATS
HAPPENING?   Excel prompts you to save your changes. You do not want to save.

22   Click **No** to return to the desktop.

23   Close the My Computer window.

24   Click the minimized Command Line button on the taskbar.

25   Key in the following: A:\>**CLS** Enter

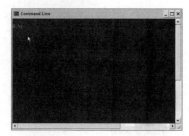

WHAT'S HAPPENING?   You have returned to the command line window and cleared the screen.

26   Key in the following: A:\>**COPY STEVEN.FIL BETTE.FIL** Enter

27   Key in the following: A:\>**ATTRIB +R BETTE.FIL** Enter

28   Key in the following: A:\>**DEL BETTE.FIL** Enter

29   Key in the following: A:\>**DEL /F BETTE.FIL** Enter

30   Key in the following: A:\>**DIR BETTE.FIL** Enter

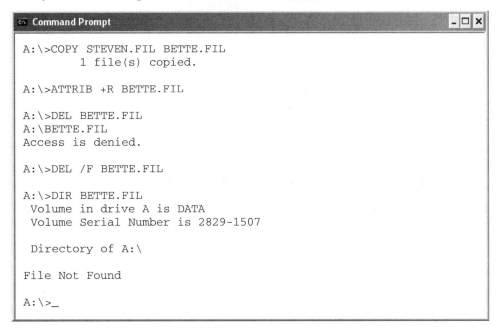

```
A:\>COPY STEVEN.FIL BETTE.FIL
        1 file(s) copied.

A:\>ATTRIB +R BETTE.FIL

A:\>DEL BETTE.FIL
A:\BETTE.FIL
Access is denied.

A:\>DEL /F BETTE.FIL

A:\>DIR BETTE.FIL
 Volume in drive A is DATA
 Volume Serial Number is 2829-1507

 Directory of A:\

File Not Found

A:\>_
```

WHAT'S HAPPENING?   You created a new file called **BETTE.FIL**. You made it read-only and then attempted to delete it. Since it was read-only, you could not delete it with the DEL command ("Access is denied"). However, when you added the /F parameter to the DEL command to force deletion of a read-only file, you could successfully delete **BETTE.FIL**.

7.3   Using the Hidden and Archive Attributes with ATTRIB

The purpose of the H attribute is to hide a file so that when you use the DIR command, you will not see it displayed. Why would you want to hide a file? The most likely person you are going to hide the file from is yourself, and this seems to make no sense. The real advantage to using the hidden attribute is that it allows you to manipulate files. For instance, when you use the COPY or the MOVE command with wildcards, you may not want to move or copy specific files. When you hide files, neither COPY nor MOVE can see them so they are protected from manipulation. These are tasks you cannot perform in Windows Explorer. Although you can hide files and folders by right-clicking the file name, then clicking Properties, and then choosing the Hide attribute, it is much more difficult to perform file operations on groups of files simultaneously in Windows Explorer.

The A attribute uses certain commands to flag a file as changed since the last time you backed it up. These commands can read the attribute bit (A) and can identify if it has been set. If it is set (on), the commands that can read the archive bit know whether the file has changed since the last time it was copied. With the ATTRIB command, you can set and unset this flag to help identify what files you changed since the last time you backed them up. The following activity will demonstrate how you can use the H and A attributes.

7.4   Activity: Using the H and the A Attributes

Note: The DATA disk is in Drive A. A:\> is displayed.

1   Key in the following: A:\>**COPY C:\WUGXP\FI*.*** [Enter]

```
Command Prompt                                                    _ □ x

A:\>COPY  C:\WUGXP\FI*.*
C:\WUGXP\FILE2.SWT
C:\WUGXP\FILE4.FP
C:\WUGXP\FILE2.FP
C:\WUGXP\FILE3.FP
C:\WUGXP\FILE2.CZG
C:\WUGXP\FILE3.CZG
C:\WUGXP\FILE3.SWT
        7 file(s) copied.

A:\>_
```

2   Key in the following: A:\>**DIR F*.*** [Enter]

```
Command Prompt                                                    _ □ x

A:\>DIR F*.*
 Volume in drive A is DATA
 Volume Serial Number is 30B8-DA1D

 Directory of A:\

10/30/2001  01:14 PM              164 FUNNY.TV
07/31/1999  12:53 PM               44 FRANK.FIL
10/31/2001  04:50 PM              138 FILE2.SWT
10/31/2001  04:51 PM              137 FILE4.FP
10/31/2001  04:51 PM              137 FILE2.FP
10/31/2001  04:51 PM              137 FILE3.FP
10/31/2001  02:49 PM              138 FILE2.CZG
10/31/2001  02:49 PM              138 FILE3.CZG
10/31/2001  04:50 PM              138 FILE3.SWT
               9 File(s)          1,171 bytes
               0 Dir(s)       1,405,952 bytes free

A:\>_
```

WHAT'S
HAPPENING?   You copied all the files that begin with **FI** from the **WUGXP** subdirectory to the root directory of the DATA disk. Now you want to move all the files that begin with F to the **TRIP** subdirectory, but you do not want to move the files you just copied. The problem is that, if you use **MOVE F*.* TRIP**, all the files that begin with F will be moved, not just the ones you desire. You cannot say, "Move all the files that begin with F except the files that begin with FI." Here, the ability to hide files is useful.

3 Key in the following: A:\>**ATTRIB FI*.* +H** [Enter]

4 Key in the following: A:\>**DIR F*.*** [Enter]

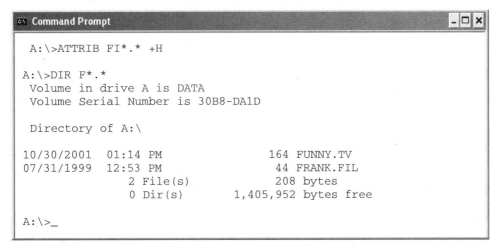

```
A:\>ATTRIB FI*.* +H

A:\>DIR F*.*
 Volume in drive A is DATA
 Volume Serial Number is 30B8-DA1D

 Directory of A:\

10/30/2001  01:14 PM                164 FUNNY.TV
07/31/1999  12:53 PM                 44 FRANK.FIL
              2 File(s)             208 bytes
              0 Dir(s)        1,405,952 bytes free

A:\>_
```

WHAT'S
HAPPENING?   The files that begin with FI are hidden and will not be displayed by the DIR command. Note that you could have keyed the command in with the parameter +H before the file specification as well as after. (**ATTRIB +H FI*.***) With the ATTRIB command, the order does not matter. Now when you use the MOVE command, none of the hidden files, the **FI*.*** files, will be moved.

5   Key in the following: A:\>**MOVE F*.* TRIP** [Enter]

```
A:\>MOVE F*.* TRIP
A:\FUNNY.TV
A:\FRANK.FIL

A:\>_
```

WHAT'S
HAPPENING?   You see that you accomplished your mission. The files you hid were not moved. What if you forget which files you hid? The **/A** parameter, which can be used with the DIR command, allows you to specify the kind of file you want to look for. The attribute choices are:

D	Directories	**H**	Hidden files
R	Read-only files	**A**	Files ready to archive

6 Key in the following: A:\>**DIR /AH** [Enter]

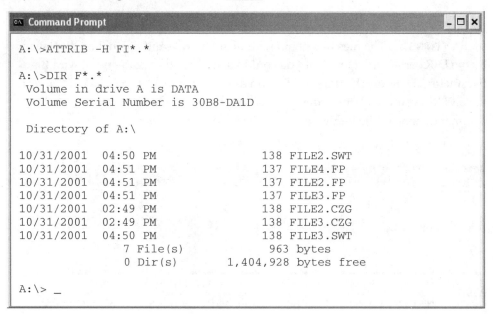

```
Command Prompt                                                    _ □ ✕

A:\>DIR /AH
 Volume in drive A is DATA
 Volume Serial Number is 30B8-DA1D

 Directory of A:\

10/31/2001  04:50 PM                138 FILE2.SWT
10/31/2001  04:51 PM                137 FILE4.FP
10/31/2001  04:51 PM                137 FILE2.FP
10/31/2001  04:51 PM                137 FILE3.FP
10/31/2001  02:49 PM                138 FILE2.CZG
10/31/2001  02:49 PM                138 FILE3.CZG
10/31/2001  04:50 PM                138 FILE3.SWT
              7 File(s)             963 bytes
              0 Dir(s)        1,405,952 bytes free

A:\>_
```

WHAT'S
HAPPENING?   The attribute you wanted to use was the hidden attribute (H). As you can see, the DIR /AH command displays only the hidden files. Now you can "unhide" the files.

7   Key in the following: A:\>**ATTRIB -H FI*.*** [Enter]

8   Key in the following: A:\>**DIR F*.*** [Enter]

```
Command Prompt                                                    _ □ ✕

A:\>ATTRIB -H FI*.*

A:\>DIR F*.*
 Volume in drive A is DATA
 Volume Serial Number is 30B8-DA1D

 Directory of A:\

10/31/2001  04:50 PM                138 FILE2.SWT
10/31/2001  04:51 PM                137 FILE4.FP
10/31/2001  04:51 PM                137 FILE2.FP
10/31/2001  04:51 PM                137 FILE3.FP
10/31/2001  02:49 PM                138 FILE2.CZG
10/31/2001  02:49 PM                138 FILE3.CZG
10/31/2001  04:50 PM                138 FILE3.SWT
              7 File(s)             963 bytes
              0 Dir(s)        1,404,928 bytes free

A:\> _
```

WHAT'S
HAPPENING?   The **FI*.*** files are no longer hidden. Notice that this time, you placed the parameter before the file specification.

You can manipulate other file attributes to assist you in managing your files. You can indicate what files have changed since the last time you copied them by changing the A, or archive, bit. When you create a file, the operating system automatically turns on the A attribute or "flags" it as new and not backed up. When you use certain commands, such as XCOPY, that command will turn off the A flag to indicate that the file has been backed up. Whenever you make a change to a file, the A attribute bit is turned on again or "re-flagged" to indicate that there has been a change since the last time you backed it up. You will learn later how this works when using the XCOPY command. You can also manipulate the archive bit directly with the ATTRIB command to let you know if you changed a file.

9 Key in the following: A:\>**TYPE STEVEN.FIL** Enter

10 Key in the following: A:\>**ATTRIB STEVEN.FIL** Enter

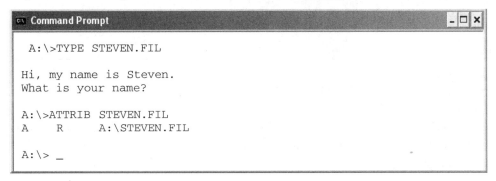

```
A:\>TYPE STEVEN.FIL

Hi, my name is Steven.
What is your name?

A:\>ATTRIB STEVEN.FIL
A    R      A:\STEVEN.FIL

A:\> _
```

WHAT'S HAPPENING?   This file is protected with the R attribute. You can see the contents of it using the TYPE command. Setting the R attribute does not prevent the file from being viewed, neither with the TYPE command, nor with a program such as Excel. You set the R attribute—the operating system automatically set the A attribute.

11 Key in the following: A:\>**ATTRIB -A -R STEVEN.FIL** Enter

12 Key in the following: A:\>**ATTRIB STEVEN.FIL** Enter

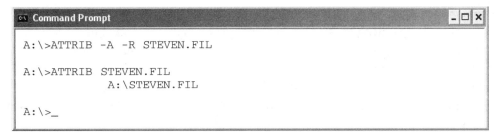

```
A:\>ATTRIB -A -R STEVEN.FIL

A:\>ATTRIB STEVEN.FIL
          A:\STEVEN.FIL

A:\>_
```

WHAT'S HAPPENING?   You have turned off all the attributes of this file.

13 Key in the following: A:\>**COPY TRIP\FRANK.FIL STEVEN.FIL** Enter

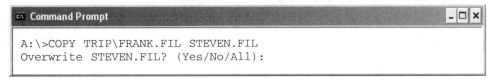

```
A:\>COPY TRIP\FRANK.FIL STEVEN.FIL
Overwrite STEVEN.FIL? (Yes/No/All):
```

WHAT'S HAPPENING?   Since the file is no longer read-only, you are asked if you want to overwrite the contents of **STEVEN.FIL** with **FRANK.FIL**.

14 Press **Y** Enter

15 Key in the following: A:\>**TYPE STEVEN.FIL** Enter

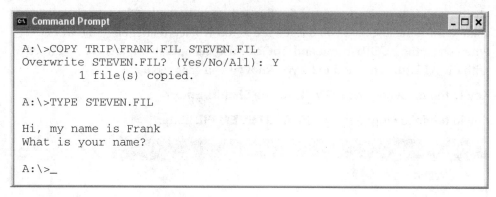

```
A:\>COPY TRIP\FRANK.FIL STEVEN.FIL
Overwrite STEVEN.FIL? (Yes/No/All): Y
        1 file(s) copied.

A:\>TYPE STEVEN.FIL

Hi, my name is Frank
What is your name?

A:\>_
```

WHAT'S ▨▨▨
▨▨▨ **HAPPENING?**   The file contents have clearly changed. This file is an ASCII or text file and can be read on the screen with the TYPE command. If this were a data file generated by a program, you could not use the TYPE command to see if the contents had changed. By looking at the attributes of a data file, you could see that the file had changed.

16 Key in the following: A:\>**ATTRIB STEVEN.FIL** [Enter]

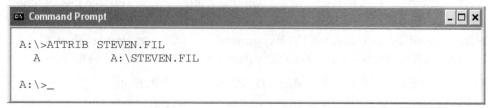

```
A:\>ATTRIB STEVEN.FIL
  A         A:\STEVEN.FIL

A:\>_
```

WHAT'S ▨▨▨
▨▨▨ **HAPPENING?**   The A attribute or archive bit is once again turned on so that you know the file has changed. Another way of saying it is that **STEVEN.FIL** is flagged by the archive bit. If you had protected **STEVEN.FIL** with the read-only attribute, you would be protected from accidentally overwriting the file. Other operations do not work the same way. If you rename a file, it keeps the same file attributes, but if you copy the file, it does not carry the read-only attribute to the copy. Since this is a "new" file, the archive bit will be set automatically.

17 Key in the following: A:\>**ATTRIB +R -A STEVEN.FIL** [Enter]

18 Key in the following: A:\>**ATTRIB STEVEN.FIL** [Enter]

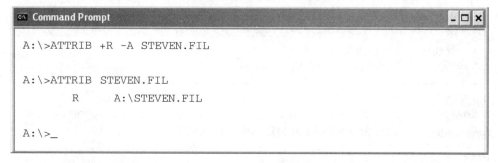

```
A:\>ATTRIB +R -A STEVEN.FIL

A:\>ATTRIB STEVEN.FIL
      R     A:\STEVEN.FIL

A:\>_
```

WHAT'S ▨▨▨
▨▨▨ **HAPPENING?**   **STEVEN.FIL** is now read-only and has had the A flag turned off.

19 Key in the following: A:\>**REN STEVEN.FIL BRIAN.FIL** [Enter]

20 Key in the following: A:\>**ATTRIB BRIAN.FIL** [Enter]

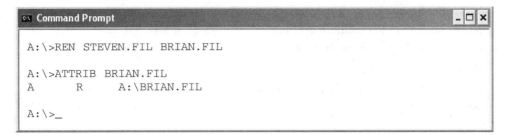

```
A:\>REN STEVEN.FIL BRIAN.FIL

A:\>ATTRIB BRIAN.FIL
A      R      A:\BRIAN.FIL

A:\>_
```

WHAT'S HAPPENING?   You can rename a file marked Read-only. The read-only attributes protects the *contents* of a file—not the filename. Even though you renamed **STEVEN.FIL** to **BRIAN.FIL**, **BRIAN.FIL** retained the read-only attribute that **STEVEN.FIL** had, plus the A attribute was added. It is the same file; you just renamed it. However, things change when you copy a file because you are creating a new, different file.

21 Key in the following: A:\>**COPY BRIAN.FIL STEVEN.FIL** Enter

22 Key in the following: A:\>**ATTRIB STEVEN.FIL** Enter

23 Key in the following: A:\>**ATTRIB BRIAN.FIL** Enter

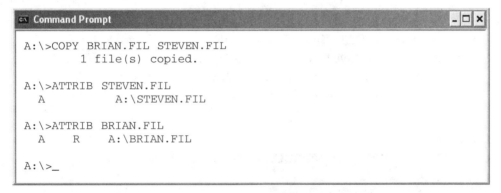

```
A:\>COPY BRIAN.FIL STEVEN.FIL
        1 file(s) copied.

A:\>ATTRIB STEVEN.FIL
  A           A:\STEVEN.FIL

A:\>ATTRIB BRIAN.FIL
  A    R     A:\BRIAN.FIL

A:\>_
```

WHAT'S HAPPENING?   When you copied **BRIAN.FIL**, which had a read-only file attribute, to a new file called **STEVEN.FIL**, the operating system removed the read-only attribute of the new file. **STEVEN.FIL** is not a read-only file. Thus, setting the read-only attribute is really most valuable for protecting you against accidental erasure of a file, not for any particular security reason. Remember that you set file attributes with the plus sign (+). You can unset file attributes with the minus sign (-). You can eliminate or add several file attributes with a one-line command, but there must be a space between each parameter, so follow the spacing of the command syntax carefully.

7.5   The SUBST Command

SUBST is an external command that allows you to substitute a drive letter for a path name. This command can be used to avoid having to key in a long path name. It can also be used to install programs that do not recognize a subdirectory but do recognize a disk drive. You can also use SUBST if you need information from a drive that a program does not recognize.

CAUTION: Be cautious when you use SUBST when logged on to a network. You may not be able to use SUBST on the network. As networks use letter drive specifications, be SURE to check with your lab administrator to see if you can use this command successfully, and if so, what drive letter you are free to use.

On a stand-alone system, when you use SUBST and while a substitution is in effect, you should not use the commands LABEL, CHKDSK, FORMAT, DISKCOPY, DISKCOM, RECOVER, or FDISK. These commands expect a drive letter to represent an actual disk drive. The syntax for the SUBST command is:

```
SUBST [drive1: [drive2:]path]
```

or to undo a substitution:

```
SUBST    drive1: /D
```

and to see what you have substituted:

```
SUBST
```

7.6   Activity: Using SUBST

Note 1:   You have the DATA disk in Drive A with A:\> displayed.

Note 2:   If you have a Drive E on your own computer system you should pick a drive letter that is not being used, such as H: or K:. Remember that if you are in a lab environment you must check with your instructor to see if you can do this activity.

1   Key in the following:
A:\>**TYPE ASTRONOMY\MERCURY\DRESS.UP** Enter

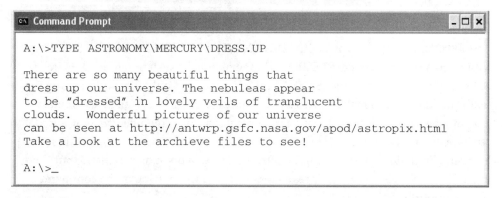

```
A:\>TYPE ASTRONOMY\MERCURY\DRESS.UP

There are so many beautiful things that
dress up our universe. The nebuleas appear
to be "dressed" in lovely veils of translucent
clouds.  Wonderful pictures of our universe
can be seen at http://antwrp.gsfc.nasa.gov/apod/astropix.html
Take a look at the archieve files to see!

A:\>_
```

WHAT'S HAPPENING?   You displayed the contents of the file called **DRESS.UP** in the subdirectory called **MERCURY** under the subdirectory called **ASTRONOMY** in the root directory. Even though you left the first backslash off, since the default directory is the root, you still have a lot of keying in to do. If you use the SUBST command, you need to key in only the logical or virtual drive letter. In this example, E: is selected.

You are creating a *virtual* drive, one that exists temporarily. A virtual drive is also known as a logical drive. You are letting a drive letter represent an actual physical drive and path. Thus, you must be sure to use a drive letter that is not being used by an actual physical disk drive. If you have a floppy disk Drive A; a floppy disk Drive B; a hard disk that is logically divided into Drives C, D, and E; a removable drive such as a Zip drive that is Drive G; and a CD-ROM that is Drive H; your first available letter would be I. If, on the other hand, you had all the above drives except an actual physical Drive B, you could use B. Conceptually, this is how networks operate—a network takes a path name and substitutes a drive letter for the path. It appears to the user as a "real" drive and behaves like a real drive for COPY, MOVE, and other file and directory commands. However, since it is not a "real" drive, you cannot perform disk actions on it such as SCANDISK, format, or DISKCOPY. (*Note:* If you have a Drive E on your own computer system, you should pick a drive letter that is not being used, such as H: or K:. Remember, if you are in a lab environment, you *must* check with your instructor to see if you can do this activity.) Often, Drive B is not assigned to a drive letter and you may use B: instead of E:.

2   Key in the following: A:\>**SUBST E: A:\ASTRONOMY\MERCURY** [Enter]

3   Key in the following: A:\>**TYPE E:DRESS.UP** [Enter]

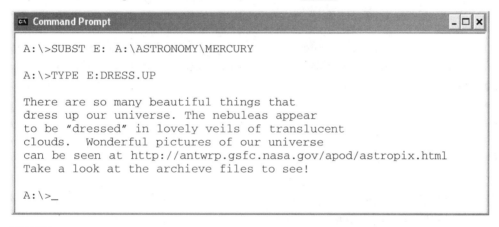

```
A:\>SUBST E:  A:\ASTRONOMY\MERCURY

A:\>TYPE E:DRESS.UP

There are so many beautiful things that
dress up our universe. The nebuleas appear
to be "dressed" in lovely veils of translucent
clouds.  Wonderful pictures of our universe
can be seen at http://antwrp.gsfc.nasa.gov/apod/astropix.html
Take a look at the archieve files to see!

A:\>_
```

WHAT'S HAPPENING?   You first set up the substitution. You said substitute the letter E for the path name **A:\ASTRONOMY\MERCURY**. Now, every time you want to refer to the subdirectory called **A:\ASTRONOMY\MERCURY**, you can just use the letter E, which refers to logical Drive E. You can use this logical drive just like a physical drive. You can use the DIR command, the COPY command, the DEL command, and just about any other command you wish.

4   Key in the following: A:\>**SUBST** [Enter]

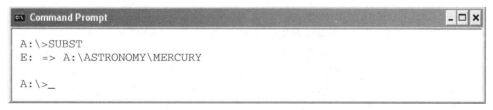

```
A:\>SUBST
E:  => A:\ASTRONOMY\MERCURY

A:\>_
```

WHAT'S HAPPENING?   SUBST, when used alone, tells you what substitution you have used.

5   Key in the following: A:\>**SUBST E: /D** [Enter]

6   Key in the following: A:\>**SUBST** [Enter]

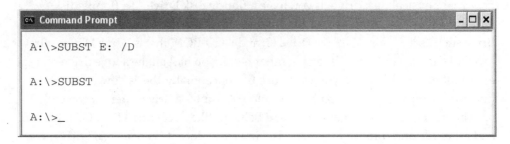

WHAT'S ▓▓▓▓▓▓
▓▓▓▓ HAPPENING?   The /D parameter disabled or "undid" the SUBST command so
that logical Drive E no longer refers to the subdirectory **A:\ASTRONOMY
\MERCURY**. The SUBST that was keyed in with no parameters showed that no
substitution was in effect. Most software today is quite sophisticated. For instance, if
you have an older program that comes on a 5¼-inch disk and insists on running
from Drive A but Drive A is a 3½-inch disk drive, you can solve the problem with
SUBST. The biggest offenders are game programs and older installation programs.
The solution would be as follows:

SUBST A: B:

This command would reroute every disk request intended for Drive A to Drive B.
The only tricky thing about this command is that you must include \ after **B:**.
SUBST does not recognize a drive letter alone as a destination, so you must include
the path.

7.7   The XCOPY Command

Although COPY is a useful internal command, it has some drawbacks, as you have
seen. COPY copies one file at a time, even with wildcards. If you issue the command
COPY *.FIL and there are four files ending in .FIL, the operating system finds the
first file and reads it, then rights it to the destination. Then it finds the second file,
reads it, and writes that one to the destination, and so on. This is the slowest way to
copy files. In addition, you cannot copy a subdirectory structure with the COPY
command. If you have disks with different formats such as a 3½ inch disk and Zip
disk, you cannot use DISKCOPY because the media types must be the same. You
can, however, use XCOPY. Unlike COPY, XCOPY is an external command that
allows you to copy files that exist in different subdirectories as well as the contents
of a subdirectory, including both files and subdirectories beneath a parent
subdirectory. It allows you to specify a drive as a source and assumes you want to
copy all files on the drive in the default directory. With XCOPY you can copy files
created on or after a certain date, or files with the archive bit set. XCOPY provides
overwrite protection so that, if there is a file with the same name, XCOPY will
request permission before overwriting the destination file with the source file.
Furthermore, XCOPY operates faster than the COPY command. In the previous
example copying the four files ending in .FIL, the XCOPY command finds all the
files meeting the criteria, reads them all into memory, and then writes them out to
the destination disk. This method saves time. The XCOPY command will not, by
default, copy system or hidden files.

XCOPY is a very powerful and useful command. With it you can copy files and subdirectories that have any attributes. You can also specify that the files and subdirectories copied *retain* their attributes. As you remember, when you use COPY to make a copy of a file, the copy does not have the same attributes as the source file. The attributes are lost when the file is copied. There are further advantages to using the command line over using Windows Explorer. When dragging and dropping to copy files and directory structures, it is easy to "miss" your destination. If you want to be specific, it is easier to key in commands than to drag and drop. In addition, you can perform file operations on a group of files rather than one file at a time.

There are many parameters available when using the XCOPY command. The full syntax is:

```
Copies files and directory trees.

XCOPY source [destination] [/A ¦ /M] [/D[:date]] [/P] [/S [/E]]
                           [/V] [/W] [/C] [/I] [/Q] [/F] [/L]
                           [/G] [/H] [/R] [/T] [/U] [/K] [/N]
                           [/O] [/X] [/Y] [/-Y] [/Z]
                           [/EXCLUDE:file1[+file2][+file3]...]

  source       Specifies the file(s) to copy.
  destination  Specifies the location and/or name of new files.
  /A           Copies only files with the archive attribute set,
               doesn't change the attribute.
  /M           Copies only files with the archive attribute set,
               turns off the archive attribute.
  /D:m-d-y     Copies files changed on or after the specified date.
               If no date is given, copies only those files whose
               source time is newer than the destination time.
  /EXCLUDE:file1[+file2][+file3]...
               Specifies a list of files containing strings.  Each
               string should be in a separate line in the files.
               When any of the strings match any part of the
               absolute path of the file to be copied, that file
               will be excluded from being copied.  For example,
               specifying a string like \obj\ or .obj will exclude
               all files underneath the directory obj or all files
               with the .obj extension respectively.
  /P           Prompts you before creating each destination file.
  /S           Copies directories and subdirectories except empty
               ones.
  /E           Copies directories and subdirectories, including
               empty ones.
               Same as /S /E. May be used to modify /T.
  /V           Verifies each new file.
  /W           Prompts you to press a key before copying.
  /C           Continues copying even if errors occur.
  /I           If destination does not exist and copying more than
               one file, assumes that destination must be a
               directory.
  /Q           Does not display file names while copying.
  /F           Displays full source and destination file names while
               copying.
  /L           Displays files that would be copied.
  /G           Allows the copying of encrypted files to destination
               that does not support encryption.
  /H           Copies hidden and system files also.
  /R           Overwrites read-only files.
  /T           Creates directory structure, but does not copy files.
               Does not include empty directories or subdirectories.
               /T /E includes empty directories and subdirectories.
```

```
/U              Copies only files that already exist in destination.
/K              Copies attributes. Normal Xcopy will reset read-only
                attributes.
/N              Copies using the generated short names.
/O              Copies file ownership and ACL information.
/X              Copies file audit settings (implies /O).
/Y              Suppresses prompting to confirm you want to overwrite
                an existing destination file.
/-Y             Causes prompting to confirm you want to overwrite an
                existing destination file.
/Z              Copies networked files in restartable mode.
```

The switch /Y may be preset in the COPYCMD environment variable. This may be overridden with /-Y on the command line.

These many parameters give XCOPY a great deal of versatility.

7.8   Activity: Using the XCOPY Command

Note: You have the DATA disk in Drive A with A:\> displayed.

1   Key in the following: A:\>**DIR C:\WUGXP\MEDIA** [Enter]

2   Key in the following: A:\>**DIR C:\WUGXP\MEDIA\BOOKS** [Enter]

```
🖳 Command Prompt                                               _ □ ✕

A:\>DIR C:\WUGXP\MEDIA
 Volume in drive C is ADMIN504
 Volume Serial Number is 0E38-11FF

 Directory of C:\WUGXP\MEDIA

02/04/2002  09:21 AM    <DIR>          .
02/04/2002  09:21 AM    <DIR>          ..
12/06/2001  09:24 AM    <DIR>          TV
12/06/2001  09:24 AM    <DIR>          MOVIES
12/06/2001  09:25 AM    <DIR>          BOOKS
              0 File(s)              0 bytes
              5 Dir(s)    7,033,864,192 bytes free

A:\>DIR C:\WUGXP\MEDIA\BOOKS
 Volume in drive C is ADMIN504
 Volume Serial Number is 0E38-11FF

 Directory of C:\WUGXP\MEDIA\BOOKS

02/04/2002  09:21 AM    <DIR>          .
02/04/2002  09:21 AM    <DIR>          ..
12/06/2001  12:12 AM             1,260 PULITZER.BKS
12/06/2001  12:04 AM               370 MYSTERY.BKS
12/06/2001  12:09 AM               437 AME-LIT.BKS
              3 File(s)          2,067 bytes
              2 Dir(s)    7,033,864,192 bytes free

A:\>_
```

WHAT'S ▒▒▒▒▒
▒▒▒HAPPENING?   As you can see, the **MEDIA** subdirectory has three subdirectories: **TV**, **MOVIES**, and **BOOKS**. Each subdirectory has files in it as well. If you were going to use the COPY command to recreate this structure on your DATA disk, you would have to create the directories with the MD command and then copy the files

in the **TV, MOVIES,** and **BOOKS** subdirectories. XCOPY can do all this work for you. You are still copying files, but you can consider XCOPY as a smart COPY command. When working with computers, you want the computer to do all the work, when possible.

3   Key in the following: A:\>**XCOPY   C:\WUGXP\MEDIA   MEDIA   /S** Enter

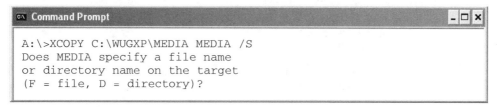

```
Command Prompt                                    _ □ ×

A:\>XCOPY C:\WUGXP\MEDIA MEDIA /S
Does MEDIA specify a file name
or directory name on the target
(F = file, D = directory)?
```

WHAT'S
HAPPENING?   You asked XCOPY to copy all the files from the **WUGXP\MEDIA** subdirectory located on the hard disk to the **\MEDIA** subdirectory under the root directory of the DATA disk. In this case, XCOPY is a smart command. It asks you if you want to place all these files in one file or to create a subdirectory structure. In this case, you want to create the subdirectory structure. The /S parameter means to copy all the subdirectories and their files to the **MEDIA** subdirectory on the DATA disk. XCOPY is a command that does not care where you place /S. The command could have been written as **XCOPY /S C:\WUGXP\MEDIA MEDIA**, and it would also have been correct.

4   Key in the following: **D**

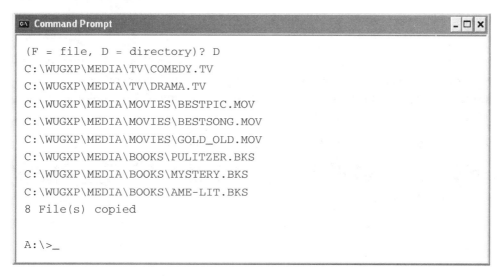

```
Command Prompt                                    _ □ ×

(F = file, D = directory)? D
C:\WUGXP\MEDIA\TV\COMEDY.TV
C:\WUGXP\MEDIA\TV\DRAMA.TV
C:\WUGXP\MEDIA\MOVIES\BESTPIC.MOV
C:\WUGXP\MEDIA\MOVIES\BESTSONG.MOV
C:\WUGXP\MEDIA\MOVIES\GOLD_OLD.MOV
C:\WUGXP\MEDIA\BOOKS\PULITZER.BKS
C:\WUGXP\MEDIA\BOOKS\MYSTERY.BKS
C:\WUGXP\MEDIA\BOOKS\AME-LIT.BKS
8 File(s) copied

A:\>_
```

WHAT'S
HAPPENING?   Since you included the /S parameter, XCOPY copied all the files from the subdirectory **\WUGXP\MEDIA**, including the subdirectories called **BOOKS, TV,** and **MOVIES** and their contents.

5   Key in the following: A:\>**DIR   MEDIA** Enter

6   Key in the following: A:\>**DIR   MEDIA\BOOKS** Enter

```
Command Prompt                                                    _ □ ×

A:\>DIR MEDIA
 Volume in drive A is DATA
 Volume Serial Number is 30B8-DA1D

 Directory of A:\MEDIA

04/10/2002  02:36 PM    <DIR>          .
04/10/2002  02:36 PM    <DIR>          ..
12/06/2001  09:24 AM    <DIR>          TV
12/06/2001  09:24 AM    <DIR>          MOVIES
12/06/2001  09:25 AM    <DIR>          BOOKS
               0 File(s)              0 bytes
               5 Dir(s)       1,396,736 bytes free

A:\>DIR MEDIA\BOOKS
 Volume in drive A is DATA
 Volume Serial Number is 30B8-DA1D

 Directory of A:\MEDIA\BOOKS

04/10/2002  02:36 PM    <DIR>          .
04/10/2002  02:36 PM    <DIR>          ..
12/06/2001  12:12 AM         1,260 PULITZER.BKS
12/06/2001  12:04 AM           370 MYSTERY.BKS
12/06/2001  12:09 AM           437 AME-LIT.BKS
               3 File(s)         2,067 bytes
               2 Dir(s)       1,397,760 bytes free

A:\>_
```

WHAT'S HAPPENING?   All the files and subdirectories were copied, and the subdirectory structure was retained. As you can see, XCOPY is a smart command with many useful parameters. One of the more useful ones is copying files modified or created after a certain date.

7 Key in the following: A:\>**DIR C:\WUGXP*.TXT** [Enter]

```
Command Prompt                                                    _ □ ×

A:\>DIR C:\WUGXP\*.TXT
 Volume in drive C is ADMIN504
 Volume Serial Number is 0E38-11FF

 Directory of C:\WUGXP

10/30/2001  01:46 PM          148 ASTRO.TXT
10/30/2001  02:10 PM          121 BORN.TXT
12/11/1999  04:03 PM           72 DANCES.TXT
05/30/2000  04:32 PM           53 HELLO.TXT
11/16/2000  12:00 PM           59 Sandy and Patty.txt
10/31/2001  02:43 PM          529 TITAN.TXT
11/16/2000  12:00 PM           53 Sandy and Nicki.txt
05/27/2001  10:08 PM           81 LONGFILENAME.TXT
10/30/2001  03:42 PM          190 JUPITER.TXT
12/06/2001  12:15 AM           97 LONGFILENAMED.TXT
10/31/2001  11:37 AM          253 GALAXY.TXT
12/06/2001  12:16 AM           99 LONGFILENAMING.TXT
10/31/2001  01:08 PM          406 MERCURY.TXT
11/24/2001  11:24 AM          194 PLANETS.TXT
10/31/2001  07:08 PM          478 VENUS.TXT
```

```
          15 File(s)          2,833 bytes
           0 Dir(s)   7,033,864,192 bytes free

A:\>_
```

WHAT'S HAPPENING?   You want to copy all the .**TXT** files that were created on or after 06-01-00 to the root directory of the DATA disk. You do not want to copy the files **DANCES.TXT** and **HELLO.TXT**. The XCOPY command allows you to make choices by date. In the following step, overwrite files if necessary.

8   Key in the following: A:\>**XCOPY C:\WUGXP*.TXT /D:06-01-00** [Enter]

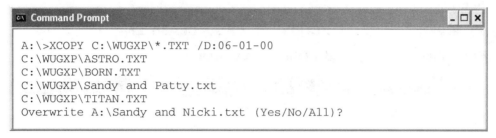

```
A:\>XCOPY C:\WUGXP\*.TXT /D:06-01-00
C:\WUGXP\ASTRO.TXT
C:\WUGXP\BORN.TXT
C:\WUGXP\Sandy and Patty.txt
C:\WUGXP\TITAN.TXT
Overwrite A:\Sandy and Nicki.txt (Yes/No/All)?
```

WHAT'S HAPPENING?   Remember the default for XCOPY is to confirm overwrites. The command is telling you that **Sandy and Nicki.txt** already exists. Again, your choice may be different if you are using the NTFS file system. In that case, the first file that queries you as to overwriting is JUPITER.TXT. In this case, you want to overwrite all the files.

9   Press **A**.

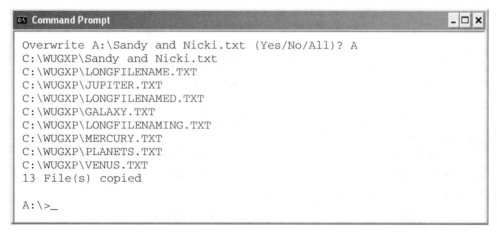

```
Overwrite A:\Sandy and Nicki.txt (Yes/No/All)? A
C:\WUGXP\Sandy and Nicki.txt
C:\WUGXP\LONGFILENAME.TXT
C:\WUGXP\JUPITER.TXT
C:\WUGXP\LONGFILENAMED.TXT
C:\WUGXP\GALAXY.TXT
C:\WUGXP\LONGFILENAMING.TXT
C:\WUGXP\MERCURY.TXT
C:\WUGXP\PLANETS.TXT
C:\WUGXP\VENUS.TXT
13 File(s) copied

A:\>_
```

WHAT'S HAPPENING?   You copied only the 13 files of interest and not all 15 files that were in the **WUGXP** subdirectory. Furthermore, you can use the XCOPY command to copy only files that have changed since the last time you copied them with XCOPY. Remember, XCOPY can manipulate the A attribute (archive bit).

10 Key in the following: A:\>**ATTRIB *.BUD** [Enter]

Note: Do not be concerned if your files display in a different order than shown here.

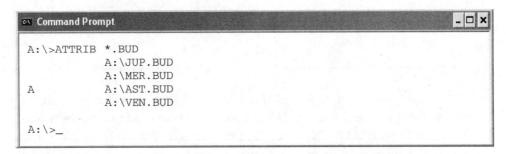

```
A:\>ATTRIB *.BUD
            A:\JUP.BUD
            A:\MER.BUD
A           A:\AST.BUD
            A:\VEN.BUD

A:\>_
```

WHAT'S HAPPENING?   The files with the extension of **.BUD** have the archive attribute turned on.

11 Key in the following: A:\>**XCOPY /M *.BUD CLASS** [Enter]

12 Key in the following: A:\>**ATTRIB *.BUD** [Enter]

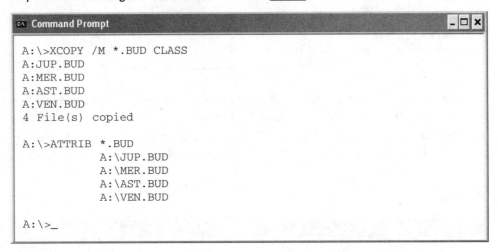

```
A:\>XCOPY /M *.BUD CLASS
A:JUP.BUD
A:MER.BUD
A:AST.BUD
A:VEN.BUD
4 File(s) copied

A:\>ATTRIB *.BUD
            A:\JUP.BUD
            A:\MER.BUD
            A:\AST.BUD
            A:\VEN.BUD

A:\>_
```

WHAT'S HAPPENING?   When you used the /M parameter, it read the attribute bit for the ***.BUD** files and, as it copied each file to the **CLASS** directory, it turned off the archive bit on the source file.

To see how XCOPY can use the archive bit, you are going to make a change to the **AST.BUD** file by using COPY to copy over the contents of **AST.BUD** with the contents of **FILE2.FP**. You will then use the ATTRIB command to see that the A bit is back on because the file contents changed. When you next use XCOPY with the /M parameter, it will copy only the file that changed.

13 Key in the following: A:\>**COPY FILE2.FP AST.BUD** [Enter]

14 Press **Y** [Enter]

15 Key in the following: A:\>**ATTRIB *.BUD** [Enter]

```
A:\>COPY FILE2.FP AST.BUD
Overwrite AST.BUD? (Yes/No/All): Y
        1 file(s) copied.

A:\>ATTRIB *.BUD
            A:\JUP.BUD
            A:\MER.BUD
            A:\AST.BUD
```

```
            A:\VEN.BUD

A:\>_
```

Since **AST.BUD** already existed, COPY asked if you really wanted to overwrite it. You keyed in **Y** for "Yes." The **AST.BUD** file has changed since the last time you used XCOPY. When you used the ATTRIB command, you saw that the A bit for **AST.BUD** was turned back on.

16 Key in the following: A:\>**XCOPY *.BUD CLASS /M** [Enter]

17 Press **Y**

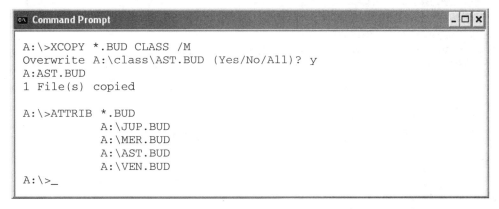

```
A:\>XCOPY *.BUD CLASS /M
Overwrite A:\class\AST.BUD (Yes/No/All)? y
A:AST.BUD
1 File(s) copied

A:\>ATTRIB *.BUD
            A:\JUP.BUD
            A:\MER.BUD
            A:\AST.BUD
            A:\VEN.BUD
A:\>_
```

Once again, XCOPY informed you that you were about to overwrite an existing file in the **CLASS** subdirectory. You told XCOPY you wanted to do that. Notice that only one file was copied, **AST.BUD**, to the **CLASS** subdirectory. XCOPY read the attribute bit, saw that only **AST.BUD** had changed, and copied only one file, not all of the **.BUD** files. The XCOPY command then turned off the A attribute so that, if you make any further changes to any of the **.BUD** files, XCOPY will know to copy only the files that changed. XCOPY can also copy files that are hidden.

18 Key in the following: A:\>**ATTRIB *.BUD** [Enter]

19 Key in the following: A:\>**COPY C:\WUGXP*.TXT** [Enter]

20 Key in the following: **A** [Enter]

```
A:\>COPY C:\WUGXP\*.TXT
C:\WUGXP\ASTRO.TXT
Overwrite A:\ASTRO.TXT? (Yes/No/All): A
C:\WUGXP\BORN.TXT
C:\WUGXP\DANCES.TXT
C:\WUGXP\HELLO.TXT
C:\WUGXP\Sandy and Patty.txt
C:\WUGXP\TITAN.TXT
C:\WUGXP\Sandy and Nicki.txt
C:\WUGXP\LONGFILENAME.TXT
C:\WUGXP\JUPITER.TXT
C:\WUGXP\LONGFILENAMED.TXT
C:\WUGXP\GALAXY.TXT
C:\WUGXP\LONGFILENAMING.TXT
C:\WUGXP\MERCURY.TXT
```

```
C:\WUGXP\PLANETS.TXT
C:\WUGXP\VENUS.TXT
        15 file(s) copied.

A:\>_
```

**WHAT'S
HAPPENING?**   You have copied all the files with the extension **.TXT** from the
WUGXP directory to the root of the DATA disk.

21 Key in the following: A:\>**DIR *.TXT** Enter

22 Key in the following: A:\>**ATTRIB +H SAN*.TXT** Enter

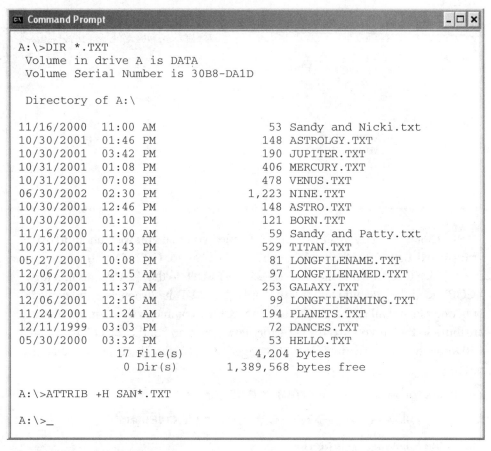

```
A:\>DIR *.TXT
 Volume in drive A is DATA
 Volume Serial Number is 30B8-DA1D

 Directory of A:\

11/16/2000  11:00 AM               53 Sandy and Nicki.txt
10/30/2001  01:46 PM              148 ASTROLGY.TXT
10/30/2001  03:42 PM              190 JUPITER.TXT
10/31/2001  01:08 PM              406 MERCURY.TXT
10/31/2001  07:08 PM              478 VENUS.TXT
06/30/2002  02:30 PM            1,223 NINE.TXT
10/30/2001  12:46 PM              148 ASTRO.TXT
10/30/2001  01:10 PM              121 BORN.TXT
11/16/2000  11:00 AM               59 Sandy and Patty.txt
10/31/2001  01:43 PM              529 TITAN.TXT
05/27/2001  10:08 PM               81 LONGFILENAME.TXT
12/06/2001  12:15 AM               97 LONGFILENAMED.TXT
10/31/2001  11:37 AM              253 GALAXY.TXT
12/06/2001  12:16 AM               99 LONGFILENAMING.TXT
11/24/2001  11:24 AM              194 PLANETS.TXT
12/11/1999  03:03 PM               72 DANCES.TXT
05/30/2000  03:32 PM               53 HELLO.TXT
              17 File(s)        4,204 bytes
               0 Dir(s)     1,389,568 bytes free

A:\>ATTRIB +H SAN*.TXT

A:\>_
```

**WHAT'S
HAPPENING?**   You have used the DIR command to display all 18 files ending in
.TXT. You have set the H attribute on for the two **.TXT** files that begin with SAN.
Those files will no longer be listed by the DIR command.

23 Key in the following: A:\>**DIR *.TXT** Enter

```
A:\>DIR *.TXT
 Volume in drive A is DATA
 Volume Serial Number is 2829-1507

 Directory of A:\

10/30/2001  01:46 PM              148 ASTROLGY.TXT
10/30/2001  03:42 PM              190 JUPITER.TXT
10/31/2001  01:08 PM              406 MERCURY.TXT
10/31/2001  07:08 PM              478 VENUS.TXT
```

```
06/30/2002  02:30 PM                1,223 NINE.TXT
10/30/2001  12:46 PM                  148 ASTRO.TXT
10/30/2001  01:10 PM                  121 BORN.TXT
10/31/2001  01:43 PM                  529 TITAN.TXT
05/27/2001  10:08 PM                   81 LONGFILENAME.TXT
12/06/2001  12:15 AM                   97 LONGFILENAMED.TXT
10/31/2001  11:37 AM                  253 GALAXY.TXT
12/06/2001  12:16 AM                   99 LONGFILENAMING.TXT
11/24/2001  11:24 AM                  194 PLANETS.TXT
12/11/1999  03:03 PM                   72 DANCES.TXT
05/30/2000  03:32 PM                   53 HELLO.TXT
             15 File(s)         4,092 bytes
              0 Dir(s)      1,389,568 bytes free


A:\>_
```

WHAT'S HAPPENING?   You have displayed all the files ending with **.TXT**, but only 16 files are displayed. The DIR command does not display hidden files.

24 Key in the following: A:\>**MD HIDDEN** Enter

25 Key in the following: A:\>**COPY *.TXT HIDDEN** Enter

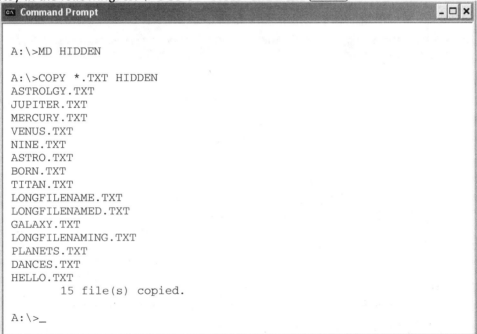

```
A:\>MD HIDDEN

A:\>COPY *.TXT HIDDEN
ASTROLGY.TXT
JUPITER.TXT
MERCURY.TXT
VENUS.TXT
NINE.TXT
ASTRO.TXT
BORN.TXT
TITAN.TXT
LONGFILENAME.TXT
LONGFILENAMED.TXT
GALAXY.TXT
LONGFILENAMING.TXT
PLANETS.TXT
DANCES.TXT
HELLO.TXT
       15 file(s) copied.

A:\>_
```

WHAT'S HAPPENING?   Only 16 files were copied. The two hidden files were not copied.

26 Key in the following: A:\>**XCOPY *.TXT HIDDEN /H** Enter

27 Key in the following: **A**

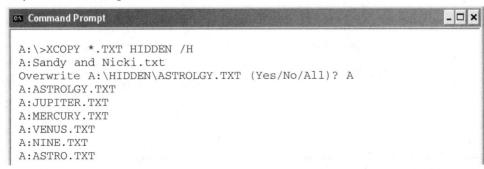

```
A:\>XCOPY *.TXT HIDDEN /H
A:Sandy and Nicki.txt
Overwrite A:\HIDDEN\ASTROLGY.TXT (Yes/No/All)? A
A:ASTROLGY.TXT
A:JUPITER.TXT
A:MERCURY.TXT
A:VENUS.TXT
A:NINE.TXT
A:ASTRO.TXT
```

```
A:BORN.TXT
A:Sandy and Patty.txt
A:TITAN.TXT
A:LONGFILENAME.TXT
A:LONGFILENAMED.TXT
A:GALAXY.TXT
A:LONGFILENAMING.TXT
A:PLANETS.TXT
A:DANCES.TXT
A:HELLO.TXT
17 File(s) copied

A:\>_
```

WHAT'S
HAPPENING?   All the files ending with **.TXT** were copied, including the two files
with the H attribute set.

28 Key in the following: A:\>**CD HIDDEN** [Enter]

29 Key in the following: A:\HIDDEN>**DEL *.*** [Enter]

30 Key in the following: **Y** [Enter]

31 Key in the following: A:\HIDDEN>**DIR** [Enter]

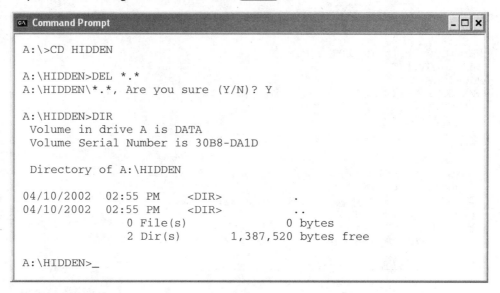

```
A:\>CD HIDDEN

A:\HIDDEN>DEL *.*
A:\HIDDEN\*.*, Are you sure (Y/N)? Y

A:\HIDDEN>DIR
 Volume in drive A is DATA
 Volume Serial Number is 30B8-DA1D

 Directory of A:\HIDDEN

04/10/2002  02:55 PM    <DIR>          .
04/10/2002  02:55 PM    <DIR>          ..
              0 File(s)              0 bytes
              2 Dir(s)       1,387,520 bytes free

A:\HIDDEN>_
```

WHAT'S
HAPPENING?   It would appear that all the files have been deleted.

32 Key in the following: A:\HIDDEN>**DIR /AH** [Enter]

```
A:\HIDDEN>DIR /AH
 Volume in drive A is DATA
 Volume Serial Number is 30B8-DA1D

 Directory of A:\HIDDEN

11/16/2000  12:00 PM                53 Sandy and Nicki.txt
11/16/2000  12:00 PM                59 Sandy and Patty.txt
              2 File(s)            112 bytes
              0 Dir(s)       1,387,520 bytes free

A:\HIDDEN>_
```

WHAT'S ▓▓▓▓▓▓
▓▓▓ HAPPENING?   You have used the DIR command, asking it to display all files with the hidden attribute (/AH). You can see that there are still two files in the **HIDDEN** subdirectory. You did not delete them.

7.9   Multiple XCOPY Parameters

One of the advantages of using XCOPY is the ability to perform file operations on hidden, system, and even read-only files. You can use XCOPY to manipulate files that have one or more attributes set. As you become a more sophisticated computer user, you will find that you need to troubleshoot different kinds of computer problems to protect your Windows environment. Here you will find commands like XCOPY invaluable because you can accomplish tasks at the command line that you cannot accomplish in the graphical user interface.

In the last activity, in the A:\HIDDEN directory, there were two files that had the hidden attribute set. Now you want to copy these files to a new directory without removing the H attribute.

7.10   Activity: Using Multiple XCOPY Parameters

Note: The DATA disk is in Drive A and A:\HIDDEN> is displayed.

1   Key in the following: A:\HIDDEN>**MD HOLD** [Enter]

2   Key in the following: A:\HIDDEN>**XCOPY *.TXT HOLD /H** [Enter]

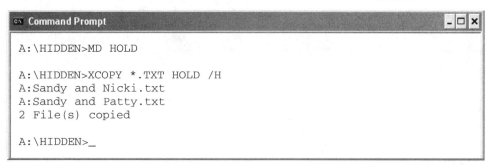

```
A:\HIDDEN>MD HOLD

A:\HIDDEN>XCOPY *.TXT HOLD /H
A:Sandy and Nicki.txt
A:Sandy and Patty.txt
2 File(s) copied

A:\HIDDEN>_
```

WHAT'S ▓▓▓▓▓▓
▓▓▓ HAPPENING?   You can see from the display that the two hidden files were copied to the new **HOLD** directory. Did the copies of the files retain the hidden attribute?

3   Key in the following: A:\HIDDEN>**DIR HOLD** [Enter]

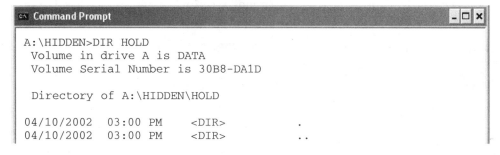

```
A:\HIDDEN>DIR HOLD
 Volume in drive A is DATA
 Volume Serial Number is 30B8-DA1D

 Directory of A:\HIDDEN\HOLD

04/10/2002  03:00 PM    <DIR>          .
04/10/2002  03:00 PM    <DIR>          ..
```

```
                          0 File(s)                  0 bytes
                          2 Dir(s)          1,385,984 bytes free

A:\HIDDEN>_
```

WHAT'S
HAPPENING?   You know you copied files into the HOLD directory, yet there are
no files shown.

4   Key in the following: A:\HIDDEN>**DIR HOLD /AH** [Enter]

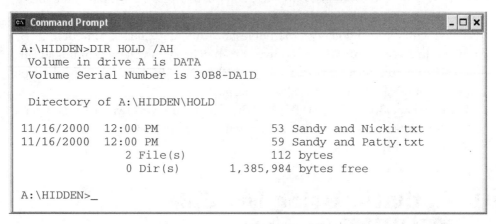

```
A:\HIDDEN>DIR HOLD /AH
 Volume in drive A is DATA
 Volume Serial Number is 30B8-DA1D

 Directory of A:\HIDDEN\HOLD

11/16/2000   12:00 PM                    53 Sandy and Nicki.txt
11/16/2000   12:00 PM                    59 Sandy and Patty.txt
                  2 File(s)             112 bytes
                  0 Dir(s)        1,385,984 bytes free

A:\HIDDEN>_
```

WHAT'S
HAPPENING?   The hidden attribute on the two files copied was retained. You can
manipulate files with other attributes. You can also find out which files *would* be
copied by using the /L parameter. The /L parameter tells you what files would be
copied by the issued command. It does not copy them.

5   Key in the following: A:\HIDDEN>**XCOPY \FILE*.* /L** [Enter]

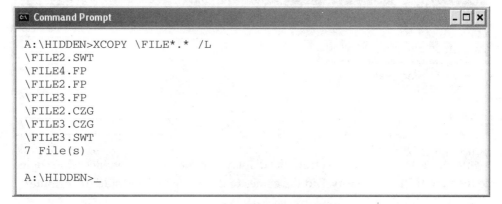

```
A:\HIDDEN>XCOPY \FILE*.* /L
\FILE2.SWT
\FILE4.FP
\FILE2.FP
\FILE3.FP
\FILE2.CZG
\FILE3.CZG
\FILE3.SWT
7 File(s)

A:\HIDDEN>_
```

WHAT'S
HAPPENING?   Notice there was no sound. No actual copying took place. Using
/L with the XCOPY command allows you to "preview" the files that will be copied.

6   Key in the following: A:\HIDDEN>**COPY \FILE*.*** [Enter]

```
A:\HIDDEN>COPY \FILE*.*
\FILE2.SWT
\FILE4.FP
\FILE2.FP
\FILE3.FP
\FILE2.CZG
```

```
\FILE3.CZG
\FILE3.SWT
        7 file(s) copied.

A:\HIDDEN>_
```

WHAT'S
HAPPENING?   Indeed, the files that were listed in the preview were copied. You have copied all the files that begin with FILE from the root directory to the **HIDDEN** subdirectory.

7 Key in the following: A:\HIDDEN>**ATTRIB *.FP +R** [Enter]

8 Key in the following: A:\HIDDEN>**ATTRIB +S *.CZG** [Enter]

9 Key in the following: A:\HIDDEN>**ATTRIB *.SWT +S +H +R** [Enter]

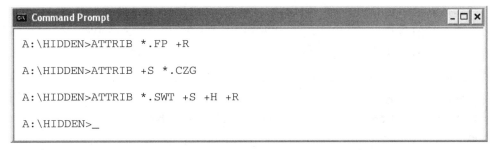

```
A:\HIDDEN>ATTRIB *.FP +R

A:\HIDDEN>ATTRIB +S *.CZG

A:\HIDDEN>ATTRIB *.SWT +S +H +R

A:\HIDDEN>_
```

WHAT'S
HAPPENING?   You have applied different attributes to the files you copied from the root directory. Notice that in Step 8, the file specification is listed last, while in steps 7 and 9, it is listed first. Remember that, although this is not the case with most commands, with ATTRIB, the order of the parameters does not matter.

10 Key in the following: A:\HIDDEN>**DIR** [Enter]

```
 A:\HIDDEN>DIR
 Volume in drive A is DATA
 Volume Serial Number is 30B8-DA1D

 Directory of A:\HIDDEN

04/10/2002  02:55 PM    <DIR>          .
04/10/2002  02:55 PM    <DIR>          ..
10/31/2001  04:51 PM              137 FILE4.FP
10/31/2001  04:51 PM              137 FILE2.FP
10/31/2001  04:51 PM              137 FILE3.FP
04/10/2002  03:00 PM    <DIR>          HOLD
              3 File(s)            411 bytes
              3 Dir(s)       1,381,376 bytes free

 A:\HIDDEN>_
```

WHAT'S
HAPPENING?   Only the files ending with **.FP** are displayed. You can verify that all the files are there, as well as look at all the file attributes.

11 Key in the following: A:\HIDDEN>**ATTRIB** [Enter]

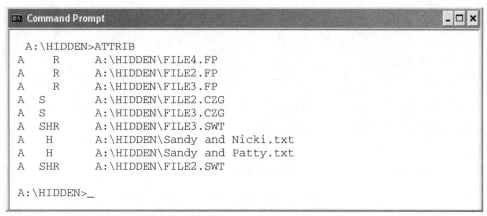

```
A:\HIDDEN>ATTRIB
A    R       A:\HIDDEN\FILE4.FP
A    R       A:\HIDDEN\FILE2.FP
A    R       A:\HIDDEN\FILE3.FP
A  S         A:\HIDDEN\FILE2.CZG
A  S         A:\HIDDEN\FILE3.CZG
A  SHR       A:\HIDDEN\FILE3.SWT
A    H       A:\HIDDEN\Sandy and Nicki.txt
A    H       A:\HIDDEN\Sandy and Patty.txt
A  SHR       A:\HIDDEN\FILE2.SWT

A:\HIDDEN>_
```

Note: Do not be concerned it the order of your directory listings differ from those shown in the text. You have copied and deleted many files from your DATA disk, and the order copied from the hard drive will differ, depending on the file system (FAT32, NTFS) used on your computer.

WHAT'S
HAPPENING?   You can see that all but five of the files have the hidden attribute set. You have discovered that files with only the S attribute set (the system attribute) are also hidden. Can you manipulate all of these files with different attributes at the same time?

12   Key in the following: A:\HIDDEN>**CD** \ Enter

13   Key in the following: A:\>**MD HIDDEN2** Enter

```
A:\HIDDEN>CD \

A:\>MD HIDDEN2

A:\>_
```

WHAT'S
HAPPENING?   You have returned to the root of the DATA disk and created a new subdirectory named **HIDDEN2**.

You are going to copy the **HIDDEN** subdirectory with all its files and subdirectories to the new subdirectory **HIDDEN2**. To do this, you will use multiple parameters with the XCOPY command. The parameters you will use are as follows:

/S   Copies directories and subdirectories except empty ones.

/H   Copies hidden and system files.

/R   Overwrites read-only files.

/I   If the destination does not exist and you are copying more than one file, assumes that the destination must be a directory. If you do not include this parameter, you will be asked if you are copying to a directory or a file.

/E   Copies directories and subdirectories, including empty ones.

/K   Copies attributes. XCOPY will automatically reset read-only attributes.

These six parameters used together will copy everything, retaining all attributes. It may help you to remember them as SHRIEK. If the destination does exist, and you do not need the **/I** parameter, remember "SHREK." In this case, you know you have already created the directory, **HIDDEN2** so you do not need the /I. If you had not created it, you would be queried whether the destination name was a file or a directory. Including the /I means that XCOPY will assume the destination is a directory.

14 Key in the following:

A:\>**XCOPY HIDDEN HIDDEN2 /S /H /R /E /K** [Enter]

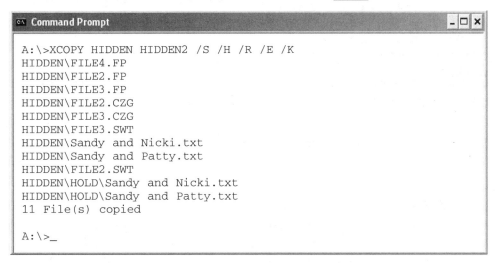

```
A:\>XCOPY HIDDEN HIDDEN2 /S /H /R /E /K
HIDDEN\FILE4.FP
HIDDEN\FILE2.FP
HIDDEN\FILE3.FP
HIDDEN\FILE2.CZG
HIDDEN\FILE3.CZG
HIDDEN\FILE3.SWT
HIDDEN\Sandy and Nicki.txt
HIDDEN\Sandy and Patty.txt
HIDDEN\FILE2.SWT
HIDDEN\HOLD\Sandy and Nicki.txt
HIDDEN\HOLD\Sandy and Patty.txt
11 File(s) copied

A:\>_
```

WHAT'S HAPPENING?   You copied all the files and subdirectories with one command. Did the copies of the files retain their attributes?

15 Key in the following: A:\>**CD HIDDEN2** [Enter]

16 Key in the following: A:\HIDDEN2>**ATTRIB /S** [Enter]

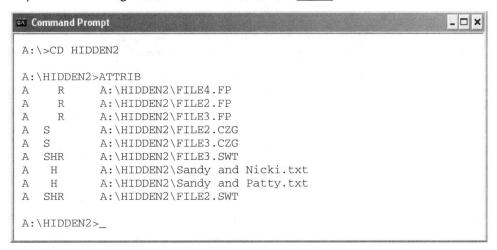

```
A:\>CD HIDDEN2

A:\HIDDEN2>ATTRIB
A    R      A:\HIDDEN2\FILE4.FP
A    R      A:\HIDDEN2\FILE2.FP
A    R      A:\HIDDEN2\FILE3.FP
A  S        A:\HIDDEN2\FILE2.CZG
A  S        A:\HIDDEN2\FILE3.CZG
A  SHR      A:\HIDDEN2\FILE3.SWT
A    H      A:\HIDDEN2\Sandy and Nicki.txt
A    H      A:\HIDDEN2\Sandy and Patty.txt
A  SHR      A:\HIDDEN2\FILE2.SWT

A:\HIDDEN2>_
```

WHAT'S HAPPENING?   You have verified that all the files you copied from the **HIDDEN** subdirectory to the **HIDDEN2** subdirectory have retained their attributes.

17 Key in the following: A:\HIDDEN2>**CD ** [Enter]

18 Key in the following: A:\>**RD HIDDEN /S** [Enter]

19 Key in the following: **Y** [Enter]

20 Key in the following: A:\>**RD HIDDEN2 /S** [Enter]

21 Key in the following: **Y** [Enter]

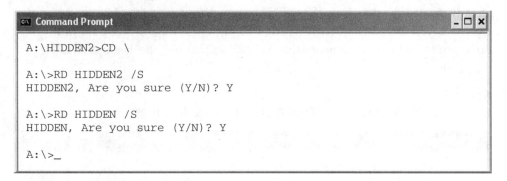

```
A:\HIDDEN2>CD \

A:\>RD HIDDEN2 /S
HIDDEN2, Are you sure (Y/N)? Y

A:\>RD HIDDEN /S
HIDDEN, Are you sure (Y/N)? Y

A:\>_
```

WHAT'S ▦▦▦▦
▦▦HAPPENING?   You returned to the root of the DATA disk and deleted the **HID-DEN** and **HIDDEN2** subdirectories along with all the files and subdirectories they contained.

22 Close the Command Prompt window.

7.11 DOSKEY

DOSKEY enhances command line editing. You may already have used it to correct keystroke errors. DOSKEY is an external, memory-resident command that in Windows XP Professional is loaded automatically (as it was in Windows 2000) when you open a Command Prompt window. It keeps track of the last 50 commands that you enter when you are in the Command Prompt window and stores them in area of memory called the command history. You can, as you have been doing, recall those command from the command history and edit them. (See Table 2.1 in Chapter 2.) When you exceed 50 commands, the oldest commands are eliminated and replaced by the new commands. When you exit the Command Prompt window, all entries made during that work session are gone.

DOSKEY, though an external command, acts like an internal command, which means that you need not reload it from disk each time you wish to use it. Memory-resident commands are also referred to as *TSR* commands (*Terminate Stay Resident*). The normal process with any external command (program) is to execute it by keying in the command name. The operating system goes to the disk and looks for a program with that name, loads it into memory, and executes that program. When loaded, that program occupies and uses RAM. When you exit the program, the operating system reclaims the memory.

When you load a TSR, the process works initially as it does with any external command. You execute it by keying in the command name. The operating system goes to the specified or default drive and path and looks for the program with that name. The program is loaded into memory and executed. However, a TSR holds on to the memory it occupies, even while it is not actually being used or accessed. It does not release the memory for the duration of the Command Prompt work session. You may still load other programs, but the other programs will not use the memory that the TSR has claimed.

DOSKEY is loaded into memory when a Command Prompt window is opened. It remains there until you close the Command Prompt window. DOSKEY lets you recall command lines, edit them, keep a command history, and write macros. A

macro is a command that you can define to automate a set of commands you often
use. You may also increase the size the command history or see what is in the
history file. The full syntax is as follows:

```
Edits command lines, recalls Windows XP commands, and creates
macros.

DOSKEY [/REINSTALL] [/LISTSIZE=size] [/MACROS[:ALL ¦ :exename]]
  [/HISTORY] [/INSERT ¦ /OVERSTRIKE] [/EXENAME=exename]
  [/MACROFILE=filename] [macroname=[text]]

  /REINSTALL          Installs a new copy of Doskey.
  /LISTSIZE=size      Sets size of command history buffer.
  /MACROS             Displays all Doskey macros.
  /MACROS:ALL         Displays all Doskey macros for all executables
                      which have Doskey macros.
  /MACROS:exename     Displays all Doskey macros for the given
                      executable.
  /HISTORY            Displays all commands stored in memory.
  /INSERT             Specifies that new text you type is inserted
                      in old text.
  /OVERSTRIKE         Specifies that new text overwrites old text.
  /EXENAME=exename    Specifies the executable.
  /MACROFILE=filename Specifies a file of macros to install.
  macroname           Specifies a name for a macro you create.
  text                Specifies commands you want to record.

UP and DOWN ARROWS recall commands; ESC clears command line; F7
displays command history; ALT+F7 clears command history; F8 searches
command history; F9 selects a command by number; ALT+F10 clears
macro definitions.

The following are some special codes in Doskey macro definitions:
$T      Command separator.  Allows multiple commands in a macro.
$1-$9   Batch parameters.  Equivalent to %1-%9 in batch programs.
$*      Symbol replaced by everything following macro name on command
        line.
```

7.12   Activity: Using DOSKEY

1   Close current Command Prompt window.

2   Open a new Command Prompt window.

3   Key in the following:

C:\>**A:**

A:\>**DIR *.TXT** [Enter]

A:\>**DIR C:\WUGXP*.99** [Enter]

A:\>**VOL** [Enter]

```
Command Prompt                                       _ □ ×

10/31/2001   01:08 PM              406 MERCURY.TXT
10/31/2001   07:08 PM              478 VENUS.TXT
06/30/2002   02:30 PM            1,223 NINE.TXT
10/30/2001   12:46 PM              148 ASTRO.TXT
10/30/2001   01:10 PM              121 BORN.TXT
10/31/2001   01:43 PM              529 TITAN.TXT
05/27/2001   10:08 PM               81 LONGFILENAME.TXT
12/06/2001   12:15 AM               97 LONGFILENAMED.TXT
```

```
10/31/2001   11:37 AM                 253 GALAXY.TXT
12/06/2001   12:16 AM                  99 LONGFILENAMING.TXT
11/24/2001   11:24 AM                 194 PLANETS.TXT
12/11/1999   03:03 PM                  72 DANCES.TXT
05/30/2000   03:32 PM                  53 HELLO.TXT
                15 File(s)          4,092 bytes
                 0 Dir(s)       1,389,568 bytes free

A:\>DIR C:\WUGXP\*.99
 Volume in drive C is XP_FULL
 Volume Serial Number is C467-D4C1

 Directory of C:\WUGXP

10/30/2001   12:46 PM                 148 AST.99
10/31/2001   07:08 PM                 478 VEN.99
10/30/2001   03:42 PM                 190 JUP.99
10/31/2001   01:08 PM                 406 MER.99
                 4 File(s)          1,222 bytes
                 0 Dir(s)   20,680,916,992 bytes free

A:\>VOL
 Volume in drive A is DATA
 Volume Serial Number is 2829-1507

A:\>_
```

WHAT'S HAPPENING?   (This graphic represents the tail end of what you see scroll by on your screen.) You have executed several commands and can now use the DOSKEY editing keys to recall and edit commands. If you want to see what is in the command history buffer, you can use the /HISTORY parameter.

4   Key in the following: A:\>**DOSKEY /HISTORY** [Enter]

```
🖳 Command Prompt                                                    _ □ ×

A:\>DOSKEY /HISTORY
A:
DIR *.TXT
DIR C:\WUGXP\*.99
VOL
DOSKEY /HISTORY

A:\>_
```

WHAT'S HAPPENING?   You used the /HISTORY parameter to recall what commands you keyed in. Although this seems no different than using the F7 key, there is one major advantage. Since this command writes the output to the screen, you could redirect the output to a file. If you do a certain series of repetitive tasks with a complicated set of commands, you can save those commands in a file. Later, when you learn about batch files, you could execute those series of commands with one command.

5   Key in the following: A:\>**DOSKEY /HISTORY > TEST.BAT** [Enter]

6   Key in the following: A:\>**TYPE TEST.BAT** [Enter]

```
cx  Command Prompt                                           - □ x

A:\>DOSKEY /HISTORY > TEST.BAT

A:\>TYPE TEST.BAT
A:
DIR *.TXT
DIR C:\WUGXP\*.99
VOL
DOSKEY /HISTORY > TEST.BAT

A:\>_
```

WHAT'S HAPPENING? You have saved the series of keystrokes you made in a batch file. Batch files (Chapter 10–11) are executable files. You may also create a macro that will run a series of often-used commands. You, in essence, can create an alias for a command. You may also, in your macro, have more than one command on a line. (You may actually have more than one command on a line in a Command Prompt window if you separate the commands with the ampersand (&). If you wish to do this in a macro, you must use $T.

7 Key in the following: A:\>**CD CLASS & DIR *.BUD & CD ** Enter

```
cx  Command Prompt                                           - □ x

A:\>CD CLASS & DIR *.BUD & CD \
 Volume in drive A is DATA
 Volume Serial Number is 30B8-DA1D

 Directory of A:\CLASS

05/07/2002  07:41 AM                 190 JUP.BUD
10/31/2001  01:08 PM                 406 MER.BUD
10/31/2001  04:51 PM                 137 AST.BUD
10/31/2001  07:08 PM                 478 VEN.BUD
               4 File(s)           1,211 bytes
               0 Dir(s)        1,389,056 bytes free

A:\>_
```

WHAT'S HAPPENING? You issued more than one command on the command line using the & as a separator between the commands. Nonetheless, you needed to key all of the commands. If you used this command all the time, you could create a macro that would execute it for you.

8 Key in the following:
A:\>**DOSKEY bb=CD CLASS$TDIR *.BUD$TCD ** Enter

9 Key in the following: A:\>**bb** Enter

```
cx  Command Prompt                                           - □ x

A:\>DOSKEY bb=CD CLASS$TDIR *.BUD$TCD\

A:\>bb

A:\CLASS> Volume in drive A is DATA
 Volume Serial Number is 30B8-DA1D
```

```
 Directory of A:\CLASS

05/07/2002  07:41 AM                190 JUP.BUD
10/31/2001  01:08 PM                406 MER.BUD
10/31/2001  04:51 PM                137 AST.BUD
10/31/2001  07:08 PM                478 VEN.BUD
              4 File(s)          1,211 bytes
              0 Dir(s)       1,389,056 bytes free

A:\CLASS>
A:\>_
```

WHAT'S HAPPENING?   Since you saved those series of commands in a macro called **bb**, every time you wanted to execute those series of commands, you would only need to key in **bb**. However, once you close this particular Command Prompt window, macros created in this window no longer exist. If you want to be able to reuse them, you can redirect the macros into a batch file.

10 Key in the following: A:\>**DOSKEY /MACROS > b.bat** [Enter]

11 Key in the following: A:\>**TYPE b.bat** [Enter]

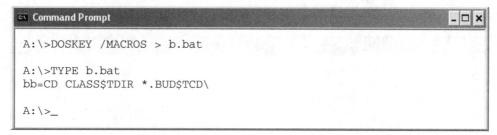

```
 Command Prompt                                        _ □ ✕

A:\>DOSKEY /MACROS > b.bat

A:\>TYPE b.bat
bb=CD CLASS$TDIR *.BUD$TCD\

A:\>_
```

WHAT'S HAPPENING?   When you close the Command Prompt window, your macros are not saved. However, you have saved this macro in a batch file which you will edit in the next activity so you may reuse it.

7.13 The Command Prompt Text Editor

There is no doubt that, for your writing needs, you will use a word-processing program such as Word or WordPerfect. Word-processing programs are extremely sophisticated and allow you full flexibility in creating and editing documents, including inserting graphics or using different fonts such as Century Schoolbook or Times New Roman. In order to retain all of your selections in your word-processing documents, there are special codes that only the word-processing program can read. These codes are entered as the document is formatted. Most word-processing programs will, however, allow you to save your document files as ASCII text, also referred to as text, MS-DOS text, or as unformatted text, by stripping the formatting and saving only the keyed in text. This may puzzle you since, if you are creating a letter or a report, you want the formatting included when you print it. However, you will find that sometimes you need to "talk" to your computer. The only way you can talk to it or give the operating system instructions is by using a text file. Computers do not understand margins, italics, bold, or any other formatting instructions. Those instructions are meant for the word processing program—not the operating system. Now you know why every operating system includes a *text editor*.

The Windows operating system includes the applet called Notepad, which allows you to create text documents. If you are having troubles with Windows, you may need to edit certain text documents that the Windows operating system requires to operate. In addition, you will want to write batch files. These can be written only with a text editor. The command-line interface contains a text editor called Edit. It is a full-screen text editor for use in the Command Prompt window. It is not a word processor—it has no ability to format the data in documents.

Edit cannot manipulate the environment with margin-size or page-length adjustments. The Edit screen has a menu bar at the top and a status bar at the bottom. The status bar shows you the column and line where the cursor is currently positioned. Each menu contains further choices.

From the File menu, you can begin a New document, Open an existing document, Save a document, save a document under a new name (Save As), Print a document, and Exit the editor.

From the Edit menu, you can Cut selected text, Copy selected text, Paste previously cut or copied text, or Clear (delete) selected text.

From the Search menu, you can Find a specified string of text, Repeat the Last Find, and search for a specified string of text and Replace it with another specified string of text.

From the View menu, you can Split, Size, or Close the Edit window.

From the Options menu, you can change the Printer Port or the tab Stops and choose the Colors for the Edit window.

From the Help menu, you can click Commands to get a list of all available Edit commands and About to view the version information for Edit.

Aside from using the menus, there are many keystrokes you can use to edit a text file in the Edit window. Table 7.1 lists most of the cursor movement keys and shortcuts.

Cursor Action	Shortcut	Alternate Shortcut
Character left	←	Ctrl + S
Character right	→	Ctrl + D
Word left	Ctrl + ←	Ctrl + A
Word right	Ctrl + →	Ctrl + F
Line up	↑	Ctrl + Enter
Line down	↓	
Beginning of current line	Home	Ctrl + Q, S
End of current line	End	Ctrl + Q, D
Top of file	Ctrl + Home	
End of file	Ctrl + End	

Table 7.1—Desired Cursor Movement Key(s) to Use Keyboard Shortcuts

7.14 Activity: Using the Command Prompt Text Editor

Note 1:   The DATA disk is in the A drive. A:\> is displayed.

Note 2:   VERY IMPORTANT—In this section you will be editing, creating, and overwriting files with the text editor. The file size, bytes, and bytes free numbers shown in the directory listings will vary and will most likely not match the examples shown in the text.

Note 3:   In order to make the mouse work in a window, you need to make some alterations to the properties of the window.

1   Close any open Command Prompt windows.

2   Open a Command Prompt window. Right-click the title bar. Click **Properties**.

3   Click the **Options** tab.

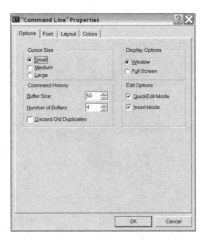

WHAT'S HAPPENING?   If the QuickEdit Mode, under Edit Options has a check mark in it, the mouse will not work in Edit. The mouse will work in full-screen mode. But by clearing the QuickEdit Mode check box, you will always be able to use the mouse no matter if you are in a window or in full-screen mode.

4   Clear the QuickEdit Mode check box by clicking it, if necessary. Click **OK**.

WHAT'S HAPPENING?   You see another dialog box. You must choose the option of **Modify shortcut that started this window**. This will then allow the mouse to always work.

5   Click **Modify shortcut that started in this window**. Click **OK**.

6   Key in the following: C:\>**A:** Enter

7   Key in the following: **EDIT** Enter

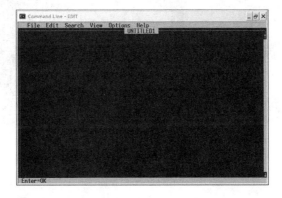

WHAT'S ▓▓▓▓
▓▓▓ HAPPENING?   This is the opening screen to the editor. If this is the first time the program has been executed, you will see a welcome message in the middle of the screen, with instructions on how to remove the welcome message.

6 Close the welcome message if necessary, so your screen is blank. Then key in the following:

This is a test. Enter
This is more test data.

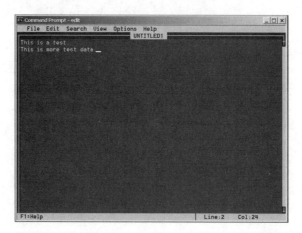

WHAT'S ▓▓▓▓
▓▓▓ HAPPENING?   You have keyed in some data. If you did not press **Enter** and kept keying in data, you would move to character column 25. If you look at the bottom of the screen, you see that the status line tells you what line and what character position you are in. As you can see, you are on the second line, and the cursor is in the 24th position.

You have two modes of operation: *insert mode* and *overstrike mode*. Insert mode is the default. You can tell you are in insert mode because the cursor is a small blinking line. Insert mode means that, as you key in data on an existing line, any data following the cursor will not be replaced, just pushed along.

7 Press Ctrl + Home

8 Key in the following: **THIS IS MORE DATA.**

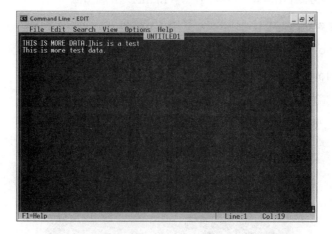

WHAT'S
WHAT'S HAPPENING?   The new data is there in front of the old data. Overstrike mode permits you to replace the characters that are there. You can toggle between overstrike mode and insert mode by pressing the [Insert] key.

9   Press the [Insert] key.

10   Key in **My second**.

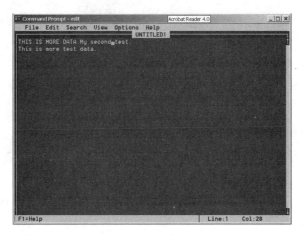

WHAT'S HAPPENING?   Notice the shape of the cursor. It is a vertical rectangle. This cursor shape indicates that you are in overstrike mode. You have replaced old text data with new.

11   Press the [Insert] key to return to insert mode.

WHAT'S HAPPENING?   Full-screen editing can be done either with the cursor keys or with the mouse. You can position the mouse and click to reposition the point of insertion. You can select text by clicking the mouse at the beginning of the text you wish to select, holding down the left mouse button, and dragging it to the end of the text you wish to select.

12   Click under the first **t** in the phrase **test data**.

13   Hold down the left mouse button and drag to the end of the sentence, not including the period.

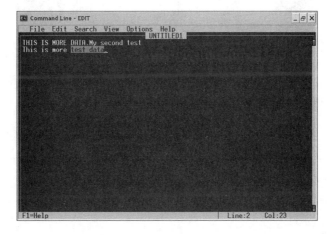

WHAT'S
HAPPENING?   You have selected the phrase **test data**.

16 Key in the following: **meaningless data**

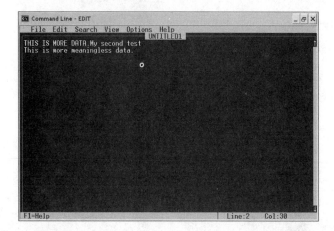

WHAT'S
HAPPENING?   You have used the mouse to edit data. You can also use the Command Prompt editor to edit existing files. *Note:* You can always use keystrokes if you do not want to use the mouse. Pressing the [**Alt**] key and the first letter of a menu will drop down the menu. Once you open the menu, you select the highlighted letter of the task you want to perform.

17 On the menu bar at the top of the editor, click **File**. Click **Open**.

18 Key in the following: **A:\PERSONAL.FIL**

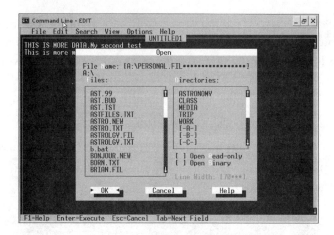

WHAT'S
HAPPENING?   You have chosen to open the **PERSONAL.FIL** file from the DATA disk in the A drive.

19 Click **OK**.

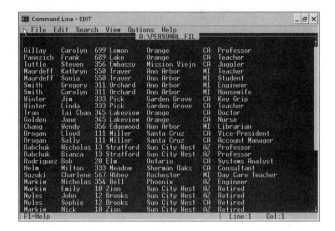

WHAT'S HAPPENING?   You have opened the **PERSONAL.FIL** file in the editor. You can search for text strings in the editor. You are going to look for Ervin Jones.

20 On the menu bar, click **Search**.

21 Click **Find**.

22 In the **Find What** area, key in **Jones**.

23 Click **OK**.

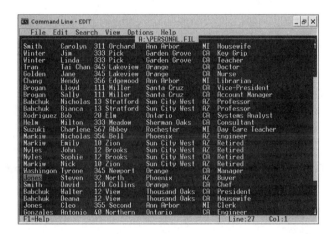

WHAT'S HAPPENING?   You found a Jones, but not the right one. You can repeat the search with a function key.

24 Press the **F3** key three times.

WHAT'S HAPPENING?   You have cycled from Jones to Jones until you reached the one you were looking for. You can also add text to the file.

25 Press the ⬇ key four times.

26 Key in the following (use the spacebar to align the data):

Peat	**Brian**	**125 Second**	**Vacaville**	**CA**	**Athlete**
Farneth	**Nichole**	**237 Arbor**	**Vacaville**	**CA**	**Dancer**

27 On the menu bar, click **File**.

28 Click **Exit**.

WHAT'S HAPPENING?   A dialog box appears asking you if you want to save the file **UNTITLED1**. This file has the first data you keyed in. You do not want this file.

29 Click **No**.

WHAT'S HAPPENING?   You are now asked if you want to save **A:\PERSONAL.FIL**. You do want to save the changes you made.

30 Click **Yes**.

HAPPENING? You have exited the editor and returned to the Command Prompt window.

31 Open the Command Prompt editor.

32 Click **File**. Click **Open**.

33 Key in **A:\STEVEN.FIL** [Enter]

34 Click **View**. Click **Split Window**.

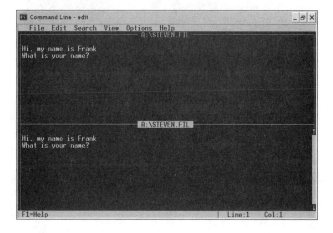

HAPPENING? You can see the file data displayed in two windows.

35 Change the word **Frank** in the top screen to **Steven**.

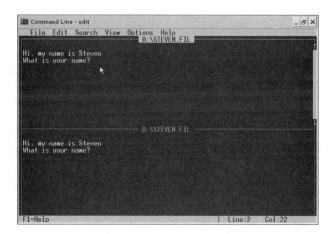

HAPPENING? You can see that the word was changed in both sections. When you split the screen, you can look at the same file data in both windows.

36 Click **File**. Click **Save**.

37 Click **File**. Click **Close**.

38 Place your cursor in the top window. Click **File**. Click **Open**.

39 Key in **A:\TEST.BAT**. Click **OK**.

40 Place your cursor in the bottom window. Click **File**. Click **Open**.

41 Key in **A:\B.BAT**. Click **OK**.

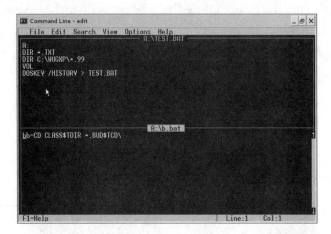

WHAT'S ████████ ████ HAPPENING?   You have opened two separate files and can view them simultaneously on the split screen.

42 In the top window, delete the first line (**A:**) and the last two lines (**DOSKEY /HISTORY** and **DOSKEY /HISTORY > TEST.BAT**).

43 In the bottom window, alter the line to read as follows: **DOSKEY bb=CD CLASS $TDIR *.BUD$TCD **

44 Save both files. Close both files. Exit the editor.

WHAT'S ████████ ████ HAPPENING?   You now have two batch files. Batch files, which will be covered in much more detail in Chapters 10 and 11, are programs that you can write. You execute a batch file by keying in its name. You have one batch file (**TEST.BAT**) that runs a series of commands. The other batch file (**B.BAT**) will set up a macro.

45 Close the Command Prompt window. Open a Command Prompt window. Make A:\ the default drive.

46 Key in the following: A:\>**bb** **Enter**

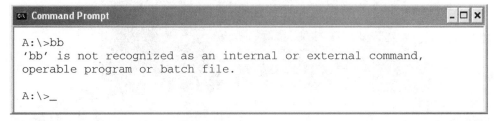

WHAT'S ████████ ████ HAPPENING?   Because you closed the Command Prompt window, your macros are no longer in effect.

47 Key in the following: A:\>**B** **Enter**

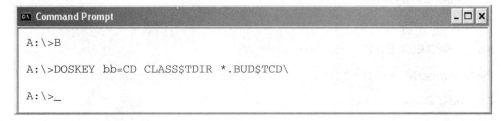

WHAT'S
HAPPENING?   Since you executed your batch file, you enabled your macro. Now if you keyed in **bb**, you would see the screen that follows Step 9 in Activity 7.12.

48   Close the Command Prompt window.

7.15 Using Text Data Files

When there are so many application programs available that create their own particular data files, why use a text editor to create data? The program you wish to use may not be available to you at the time and place you want to create the data. Many programs will allow you to import text files directly, and will in interpret them into the format needed. Thus, where ever you are, and regardless of the software available to you, if you have a computer, you have the ability to record the data you need in a text file. As you have seen, text files take very little space on a disk, so you can save your file to floppy, and take it with you to a workstation that has the software you need.

In the next activity, you will use the Excel spreadsheet program and import text data into a usable spreadsheet. Microsoft Excel 2002, from the Microsoft Office XP suite, is used here. Other versions of Excel and other spreadsheet programs work in a very similar fashion, though the dialog boxes and menus shown here will appear different and may be used in a different order.

7.16 Activity: Importing a Text File

Note 1:   You are at the desktop, with no open command line windows.
Note 2:   This exercise assumes the class files are installed at C:\WUGXP. If this is not the case, substitute the appropriate directory for your environment.

1   Open the Microsoft Excel Program.

2   On the menu bar, click **Data**.

3   Point to **Import External Data** (or **Get External Data**).

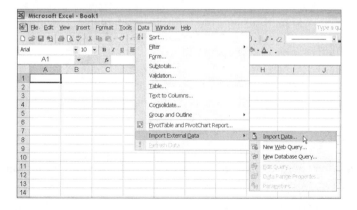

WHAT'S
HAPPENING?   You have opened Excel, and began the process of importing the data.

4   On the menu, click **Import data** (or **Import Text File**).

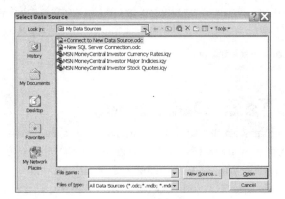

WHAT'S HAPPENING?   The Select Data Source (or Import Text File) dialog box is opened.

5   Click the arrow by the **Look in:** drop down box and navigate to **C:\WUGXP**.

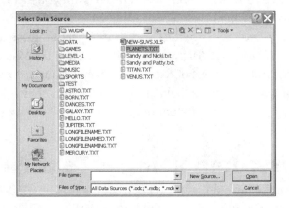

WHAT'S HAPPENING?   You have chosen your Data Source folder.

6   Double click **PLANETS.TXT**.

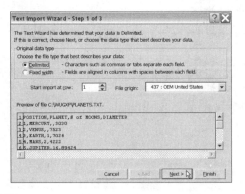

WHAT'S HAPPENING?   You have started to import the text data into Excel. The Text Import Wizard dialog box is open. This screen is the first of three screens which will enable you to you will tell Excel about your text data file. Notice you have a preview window in the bottom portion of the dialog box. You can see the text file in the same way Excel "sees" it. You want to begin importing at row 1, and this file is a "Delimited" file. Each element of the data is separated, or delimited by commas.

7   Click **Next**.

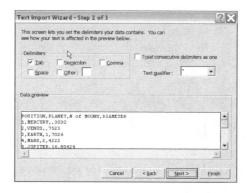

WHAT'S HAPPENING?   This is the second screen of the Text Import Wizard. The default delimiter is a Tab character, but your text file is using commas for delimiters.

8   Click the **Tab** check box to clear it.

9   Click the **Comma** check box to select it.

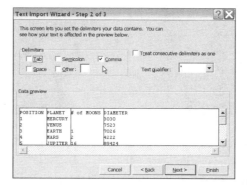

WHAT'S HAPPENING?   You have told Excel that you are using commas for data delimiters. Notice how the preview screen changes. You are shown how Excel is interpreting your text data file.

10   Click **Next**.

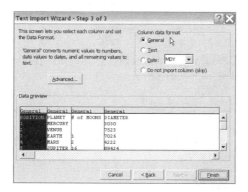

WHAT'S HAPPENING?   You have opened the last Text Import Wizard screen. Here you can further refine your data. The first column is the Data preview window is selected. If this column contained only text, no numbers, you could define it as a Text column. If it were a column of dates, you could give Excel that information on this screen. You will leave all the columns under General format.

11   Click **Finish**.

WHAT'S
HAPPENING?   Now Excel is asking you where you want to place your data in the
worksheet. A is the first column, 1 is the first row. Your data will be placed beginning at the upper left corner of the worksheet.

12   Click **OK**.

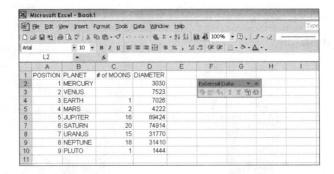

WHAT'S
HAPPENING?   You have successfully imported your data. The commas are gone,
and each element of data is in its own cell.

    You also could have imported this delimited text data file into other types of
application software, such as a data base program like Access or Paradox, or a word
processing program such as WordPerfect or Word.

13 Click **File**. Click **Exit**.

WHAT'S
HAPPENING?   Excel is asking if you want to save the newly created worksheet
file.

14 Click **No**.

WHAT'S
HAPPENING?   You have closed the Excel program, and returned to the desktop.

Chapter Summary

1. File attributes are tracked by the operating system.
2. There are four file attributes: A (archive), H (hidden), S (system), and R (read-
    only).
3. The ATTRIB command allows you to manipulate file attributes.

4. The SUBST command allows you to substitute an unused drive letter for a long, unwieldy path name.

5. The XCOPY command allows you to copy files and subdirectories.

6. There are many parameters available to the XCOPY command. Among them are parameters that enable you to:
   a. copy by date (/D)
   b. copy hidden files (/H)
   c. copy subdirectories (/S)
   d. overwrite read-only files (/R)
   e. copy empty directories (/E)
   f. keep file attributes (/K)

7. DOSKEY is an external, memory-resident program that loads automatically in Windows XP Professional. It allows you to do command line editing.

8. A memory-resident program is commonly referred to as a TSR program. Once loaded into memory, it remains in memory for the duration of the session.

9. The arrow and function keys in DOSKEY allow you to do command-line editing by recalling and listing the previously keyed in commands.

10. You can create macros in a command line window.

11. On the desktop, you use Notepad to edit text files. In the Command Prompt window, you use the Edit editor.

12. Edit can be used to edit or create ASCII text files.

13. In Edit, you can use menus, the mouse, and keystrokes to edit text.

14. Text files can be imported into application programs.

Key Terms

archive attribute	overstrike mode	Terminate Stay Resident
file attribute	read-only attribute	(TSR)
hidden attribute	system attribute	text editor
insert mode		

Discussion Questions

1. What is the purpose and function of the ATTRIB command?
2. Give two parameters for the ATTRIB command and describe the function and purpose of each.
3. What are file attributes?
4. What effect does a file marked "hidden" have for a user? How can you "unhide" the file?
5. What does a file marked "read-only" mean to a user?
6. What is the function of the archive bit?
7. What is the purpose of the SUBST command?
8. Under what circumstances would the SUBST command be useful?
9. What is the purpose of the XCOPY command?
10. What advantages does the XCOPY command have over the COPY command?
11. List four XCOPY parameters, and explain their function and their syntax.
12. Explain the purpose and function of the DOSKEY command.
13. What is a memory-resident program, and how does it work?

14. Explain what a macro is and how you would create one.
15. Discuss how to execute commands from the history list.
15. How could you use the Editor program to create useful data information?
16. Compare and contrast a word-processing program, Notepad, and Edit.

True/False Questions

For each question, circle the letter T if the statement is true and the letter F if the statement is false.

T   F   1. The ATTRIB command allows you to add and remove file attributes.

T   F   2. You should not use the DIR command when the drive letter has been assigned with the SUBST command.

T   F   3. You cannot copy empty subdirectories with the XCOPY command.

T   F   4. You should use caution when using SUBST while logged on to a network.

T   F   5. The Edit editor can be used in place of Notepad.

Completion Questions

Write the correct answer in each blank space.

6. If you key in the command ATTRIB +H THIS.ONE, you have marked the file THIS.ONE as _____.

7. The XCOPY parameter(s) that allow(s) you to copy hidden, system, and read-only files is/are _____.

8. To see what commands you have keyed in, key in _____.

9. If you have to key in a long path name repeatedly, you can use the _____ command to assign a drive letter to the path.

10. To go to the beginning of a file in Edit, press _____.

Multiple Choice Questions

For each question, write the letter for the correct answer in the blank space.

____   11. Once installed, a TSR acts like an
    a. external command.
    b. internal command.
    c. both a and b
    d. neither a nor b

____   12. The /D parameter of the SUBST command
    a. displays the true name of the logical drive.
    b. will have no effect on the SUBST command.
    c. will confirm that the substitution has occurred.
    d. will disable the SUBST command.

____   13. XCOPY will copy _____ than COPY.
    a. faster, with more options
    b. slower, with more options
    c. with fewer options
    d. none of the above

_____ 14. If you wanted to protect the file **MY.FIL** from being accidentally erased, you would key in the following:
   a. ATTRIB -R MY.FIL
   b. ATTRIB +R MY.FIL
   c. ATTRIB +S MY.FIL
   d. ATTRIB -S MY.FIL

_____ 15. To XCOPY a file marked read-only and to be sure that the destination file retained the read-only attribute, you would use the parameters
   a. /S /R
   b. /R /K
   c. /R /E
   d. /T /E

Writing Commands

Write the correct step(s) or command(s) necessary to perform the action listed *as if* you were at the keyboard.

16. Copy all the files and subdirectories, regardless of their attributes, from the TEMP directory on the root of the default directory to the OLDTEMP directory on the root directory of the disk in the A drive.

   `C:\>`

17. Create a macro called X that will allow you to change your drive to C: and your directory to the WUGXP.

   `A:\>`

18. Allow the letter J to stand for C:\WUGXP\SPORTS.

   `C:\>`

19. Prevent the DIR command from seeing all the files ending with .99 in the root directory of the disk in the A drive.

   `C:\TEST>`

20. In the Edit text editor, view and edit two text files simultaneously.

Homework Assignments

Note 1: Be sure to work on the HOMEWORK disk, not the DATA disk.

Note 2: The homework problems will assume Drive C is the hard disk and the HOMEWORK disk is in Drive A. If you are using another drive, such as a floppy drive B or a hard drive D, be sure to substitute that drive letter when reading the questions and answers.

Note 3: All subdirectories that are created will be under the root directory unless otherwise specified.

Problem Set I

Note: The prompt is A:\>.

Problem A

A-a   If necessary, remove the DATA disk and insert the HOMEWORK disk in Drive A.

A-b   Copy any files with the **.TV** extension from the **PHONE** directory to the root directory of the HOMEWORK disk.

A-c   Copy the file in the root directory called **DRAMA.TV** to a new file called **GRAVE.TV**, also in the root directory.

A-d   Using the relative path, display the attributes of the **GRAVE.TV** file.

_____   1. Which command did you use?
      a. DIR GRAVE.TV
      b. ATTRIB GRAVE.TV
      c. ATTRIB +R GRAVE.TV or ATTRIB GRAVE.TV +R
      d. ATTRIB -R GRAVE.TV or ATTRIB GRAVE.TV -R

_____   2. What file attribute is *not* displayed?
      a. S
      b. H
      c. A
      d. both a and b

A-e   Make the **GRAVE.TV** file read-only.

_____   3. Which command did you use?
      a. DIR GRAVE.TV
      b. ATTRIB GRAVE.TV
      c. ATTRIB -R GRAVE.TV or ATTRIB GRAVE.TV -R
      d. ATTRIB +R GRAVE.TV or ATTRIB GRAVE.TV +R

A-f   Key in the following: **DEL GRAVE.TV**

_____   4. What message is displayed?
      a. Access is denied.
      b. This is a read-only file.
      c. This file is read-only, delete anyway?
      d. no message is displayed

A-g   Display the attributes of the **GRAVE.TV** file.

_____   5. Which attributes are set on the **GRAVE.TV** file?
      a. A and S
      b. A and R
      c. A and H
      d. A, H, and R

A-h   Copy **GRAVE.TV** to **GRAVEST.TV**.

A-i   Delete **GRAVE.TV** with the DEL command.

_____   6. What parameter did you have to use with DEL?
      a. /X
      b. /P

      c. /F

      d. /Q

A-j   Make **GRAVEST.TV** a hidden, read-only file.

____   7. Which command did you use?

      a. ATTRIB +A +R GRAVEST.TV

      b. ATTRIB +H +A GRAVEST.TV

      c. ATTRIB +H +R GRAVEST.TV

      d. ATTRIB +S +H +R GRAVEST.TV

A-k   Use the DIR command (with no parameters) to display **GRAVEST.TV**.

____   8. Which of the following lines do you see on the screen?

      a. GRAVEST.TV is a hidden file.

      b. File Not Found.

      c. Not found - GRAVEST.TV.

      d. none of the above

Problem B

B-a   Make a subdirectory on the root of the HOMEWORK disk called **FIRST**.

B-b   From the root of the HOMEWORK disk, make a subdirectory under **FIRST** called **SECOND**.

B-c   From the root of the HOMEWORK disk, make a subdirectory under **SECOND** called **THIRD**.

____   9. Which command did you use to make the THIRD subdirectory?

      a. MD THIRD

      b. MD FIRST\THIRD

      c. MD FIRST\SECOND\THIRD

      d. MD SECOND\THIRD

B-d   Copy all the files ending in **.99** from the **WUGXP** directory on the C drive to **FIRST**.

B-e   Copy the files in the **FIRST** subdirectory to the **SECOND** subdirectory keeping the same names but with the new file extension of **.BRI**.

B-f   Copy the files in the **SECOND** subdirectory to the **THIRD** subdirectory keeping the same names but with the new file extension of **.NIC**.

B-g   From the root of the HOMEWORK disk, display all the files and subdirectories in and under the **FIRST** subdirectory, but not the entire disk.

____   10. Which command did you use?

      a. DIR /S

      b. DIR FIRST SECOND THIRD

      c. DIR FIRST /S

      d. DIR FIRST/SECOND/THIRD

B-h   Make all the files in the **FIRST** directory read-only.

B-i   Make all the files in the **THIRD** directory hidden.

_____ 11. Which command did you use to mark the files in the **THIRD** subdirectory as hidden?

      a. ATTRIB *.* +H THIRD

      b. ATTRIB THIRD +H

      c. ATTRIB FIRST\SECOND\THIRD*.* +H

      d. either a or b

B-j   With the root directory of the HOMEWORK disk as the default, make a directory called **FIRST-2**.

B-k   With the root directory of the HOMEWORK disk as the default, duplicate the **FIRST** subdirectory, including all files and subdirectories beneath it, to the subdirectory **FIRST-2**. (Be sure to duplicate all files and retain their attributes in **FIRST-2**.)

_____ 12. Which command and parameters did you use?

      a. XCOPY FIRST FIRST-2 /S /E

      b. XCOPY FIRST FIRST-2 /S /H /R /E /K

      c. XCOPY FIRST FIRST-2 /R /H /K

      d. XCOPY FIRST FIRST-2 /S /E

_____ 13. How many files were copied?

      a. 4

      b. 8

      c. 12

      d. 16

Problem C

    Note: Check with your lab administrator before proceeding with the next step.

C-a   With the root directory of the HOMEWORK disk as the default, assign the letter **E** (if available) to represent the path to the **THIRD** subdirectory on the HOMEWORK disk under **FIRST**.

    Note: If Drive E is not available, choose another drive letter and substitute it in the answers.

_____ 14. Which command did you use?

      a. SUBST E A:\FIRST\SECOND\THIRD

      b. SUBST E: A:\FIRST\SECOND\THIRD

      c. SUBST E THIRD

      d. SUBST E: THIRD

C-b   Key in the following: **SUBST** [Enter]

_____ 15. What line is displayed on the screen?

      a. E:\: => A:\FIRST\SECOND\THIRD

      b. E = FIRST\SECOND\THIRD

      c. E: = THIRD

      d. none of the above

C-c   With the root directory of the HOMEWORK disk as the default, display the directory of the E drive.

____ 16. How many files are displayed?

    a. zero

    b. two

    c. four

    d. eight

C-d With the root directory of the HOMEWORK disk as the default and without using the ATTRIB command to determine which attributes are set, issue a command that will remove the attributes from the files in the **THIRD** directory.

____ 17. Which command did you use?

    a. ATTRIB E:*.* -A -H

    b. ATTRIB -ALL E:

    c. ATTRIB -*.* E:

    d. none of the above

C-e Remove the virtual Drive E.

____ 18. Which command did you use?

    a. SUBST /D

    b. SUBST E: /D

    c. SUBST E /D

    d. SUBST /D [Enter]

Problem D

D-a Create a macro called FIRST that will display the directory of the FIRST directory and then will display the directory of the FIRST\SECOND\THIRD directory.

____ 19. Which command did you use?

    a. DOSKEY /MACRO=FIRST=DIR FIRST & DIR FIRST\SECOND\THIRD

    b. DOSKEY DIR FIRST & DIR FIRST\SECOND\THIRD

    c. DOSKEY FIRST=DIR FIRST $TDIR FIRST\SECOND\THIRD

    d. DOSKEY /MACRO FIRST=DIR FIRST $TDIR FIRST\SECOND\THIRD

D-b Redirect the macro you created into a batch file called **FIRST.BAT**.

____ 20. Which command did you use?

    a. DOSKEY /MACROS > FIRST.BAT

    b. DOSKEY /HISTORY > FIRST.BAT

    c. DOSKEY > FIRST.BAT

    d. DOSKEY *.* > FIRST.BAT

D-c Edit the **FIRST.BAT** file so that it can be executed whenever you open a command prompt window. Delete any unnecessary lines.

____ 21. What did you add to the batch file macro line?

    a. DOSKEY /MACROS

    b. DOSKEY

    c. DOSKEY /MACROS > FIRST.BAT

    d. none of the above

Problem E

> *Note:*   The HOMEWORK disk is in the A drive and A:\> is the default drive. If
> necessary, press **Alt** + **Enter** to operate in full-screen mode or clear the
> QuickEdit option button.

E-a   Copy **FRANK.FIL** from the **WUGXP** directory to the root of the A drive.

E-b   Copy **CAROLYN.FIL** from the **WUGXP** directory to the root of the A drive.

E-c   Using Edit, edit **FRANK.FIL** to say "Hi, my name is Bob." instead of "Hi, my
name is Frank."

E-d   Save the file as **BOB.FIL**.

_____   22. To save the file as **BOB.FIL**,
        a. you clicked File and then Save As, keyed in BOB.FIL, and clicked OK.
        b. you clicked File and then Save, keyed in BOB.FIL, and clicked OK.
        c. you clicked Edit and then Save As, keyed in BOB.FIL, and clicked OK.
        d. you clicked Edit and then Save, keyed in BOB.FIL, and clicked OK.

E-e   Close the file.

E-f   Open **CAROLYN.FIL** with the text editor.

E-g   Edit the file to read:

```
Hi, my name is Bette.
I like learning about operating systems.
I hope you like it too.
```

E-h   Save the file as **BETTE.FIL**.

E-i   Close the editor.

_____   23. The current contents of **CAROLYN.FIL** are:
        a. Hi, my name is Carolyn.
            What is your name?
        b. Hi, my name is Bette.
            What is your name?
        c. Hi, my name is Bette.
            I like learning about operating systems.
            I hope you like it too.
        d. none of the above

E-j   Copy any files with the name **BORN** and any extension from the **\WUGXP**
directory to the root of the A drive.

E-k   Open the text editor and split the window into two sections.

_____   24. After the editor was open, which procedure did you follow?
        a. Click File, click Two Windows.
        b. Click Edit, click Split Screen.
        c. Click View, click Split Window.
        d. Click Options, click Split View.

E-l   With the cursor in the top window, open the file **AST.99** from the root of the
A drive.

E-m   Move the cursor to the bottom window and open the file **BORN.TYP** from the root of the A drive.

_____   25. What is the last line in the bottom window?
   a. changing every day.
   b. BLASTS AWAY ITS WOMB OF DUST, AND SHINES!
   c. A STAR IS BORN WHEN IT'S CORE REACHES
   d. Most scientists no longer believe in

E-n   Close Edit.

Problem Set II

Note 1:   Before proceeding with these assignments, check with your lab instructor to see if there are any special procedures you should follow.

Note 2:   The HOMEWORK disk is in Drive A. The A:\> prompt is displayed as the default drive and the default directory. *All work will occur on the HOME-WORK disk.*

Note 3:   Make sure that **NAME.BAT**, **MARK.FIL**, **GETYN.COM**, and **GO.BAT** are all present in the root directory of the HOMEWORK disk before proceeding with these problems.

Note 4:   All files with the **.HW** extension *must* be created in the root directory of the HOMEWORK disk.

1   Key in the following: A:\>**NAME** [Enter]

2   Here is an example to key in, but your instructor will have other information that applies to your class. Key in the following:
Bette A. Peat [Enter]   (*Your* name goes here.)
CIS 55 [Enter]   (*Your* class goes here.)
T-Th 8-9:30 [Enter]   (*Your* day and time go here.)
Chapter 7 Homework [Enter]

3   Press [F6] [Enter]

4   If the information is correct, press **Y** and you are back to A:\>.

WHAT'S ▒▒▒▒▒
▒▒▒HAPPENING?   You have returned to the system level. You now have a file called **NAME.FIL** with your name and other pertinent information. (*Hint*: Remember redirection.)

To Create 1.HW

Display the names of all files in only the root of the HOMEWORK disk that are hidden and redirect the output of the command to a file called **1.HW**.

To Create 2.HW

1   Remove the hidden attribute from all the files in only the root directory of the HOMEWORK disk.

2   Remove the **FIRST-2** subdirectory from the root of the HOMEWORK disk.

3   Change the default directory to **A:\FIRST>**.

4   Remove all the attributes from all files and subdirectories *under* the **FIRST** subdirectory but not *in* the **FIRST** subdirectory.

5   Key in the following: `A:\FIRST>`**ATTRIB /S > \2.HW** Enter

To Create 3.HW

1   Change the default directory to **A:\>**.

2   Perform the step necessary to be able to refer to the directory **A:\FIRST\SECOND\THIRD** as **E:** or a drive letter you can use.

3   Key in the following: `A:\>`**DIR E: > 3.HW** Enter

4   Remove the virtual Drive E.

To Create 4.HW

1   Concatenate the files **BETTE.FIL** and **BOB.FIL** to a new file named **PEAT.FIL**.

2   Open the file **PEAT.FIL** with the text editor and make sure there is a single blank line between **I hope you like it too.** and **Hi, my name is Bob.**

3   Add a new blank line to the bottom of the file, then add another line that reads: **Are we having fun yet?**

4   Save the file and exit the text editor.

5   Display the contents of **PEAT.FIL** and redirect it to a file called **4.HW**.

To Create 5.HW

1   From the root of the A drive, set the read-only and hidden attributes for all the files in the **FILES** subdirectory but not in any of the subdirectories of **FILES**.

2   Make an exact duplicate of the **FILES** subdirectory and any subdirectories to another subdirectory off of the root called **MORFILES**. (*Hint:* You need to copy all files, regardless of their attributes, and the new files should retain their attributes.)

3   Create a new file with the text editor on the root of the HOMEWORK disk called **5.HW**. In the file, key in the command you used to copy **FILES** to **MORFILES** in the previous step.

4   Remove any hidden or read-only attributes on any file on the entire HOMEWORK disk.

To Print Your Homework

1   Be sure the printer is on and ready to accept print jobs from your computer.

2   Key in the following (be very careful to make no typing errors): **GO NAME.FIL 1.HW 2.HW 3.HW 4.HW 5.HW** Enter

WHAT'S ▓▓▓▓▓
▓▓▓▓ HAPPENING?   If the files you requested, 1.HW, 2.HW, etc., do not exist in the default directory, you will see the following message on the screen:

```
File Not Found
The system cannot find the file specified.

  Is there a message that says "File Not Found. The system cannot
  find the file specified."

  If so, press Y to find out what could be wrong.

  Otherwise, press N to continue.
```

The operating system is telling you that the file cannot be found. If you see this screen, press **Y** to see what could be wrong, and repeat the print procedure after you have corrected the problem.

If the default directory contains the specified files, the following message will appear on the screen:

```
Is there a message that says "File Not Found. The system cannot
find the file specified."

If so, press Y to find out what could be wrong.

Otherwise, press N to continue.
```

You will need to press **N** once for each file you are printing.

3 Follow the messages on the screen until the Notepad program opens with a screen similar to the following:

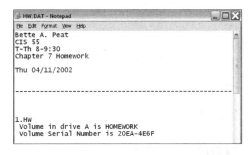

WHAT'S ▒▒▒▒▒
▒▒▒▒**HAPPENING?**   All the requested files have been found and placed in a Notepad document. Your homework is now ready to print.

4 On the Notepad menu bar, click **File**. Click **Print**.

WHAT'S
▓▓HAPPENING?   The print dialog box opens. If you have more than one printer, all your printer choices will be displayed. The default printer is the highlighted printer.

5   Click the **Print** button.

6   In the Notepad window, click **File**. Click **Exit**.

WHAT'S
▓▓HAPPENING?   The following will appear on the Command Prompt screen:

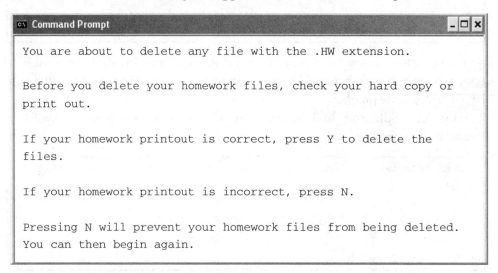

```
You are about to delete any file with the .HW extension.

Before you delete your homework files, check your hard copy or
print out.

If your homework printout is correct, press Y to delete the
files.

If your homework printout is incorrect, press N.

Pressing N will prevent your homework files from being deleted.
You can then begin again.
```

At this point, look at your printout. If it is correct, you can press **Y** to delete the homework files for this chapter. If your printout is incorrect, you can press **N**. That will preserve your homework and you will need to redo only the problem that was incorrect, not all the homework assignments.

7   Press **Y** [Enter]

WHAT'S
▓▓HAPPENING?   You have returned to the default prompt.

8   Close the Command Prompt session.

9   Execute the shut-down procedure.

Problem Set III—Brief Essay

1. The attributes most often set by the user are H and R. Describe two scenarios where you might find it advantageous to set the hidden and/or read-only attributes to a file or group of files.
2. The XCOPY command's many parameters make it a versatile command. Choose two of the parameters and describe, in detail, how, why, and when you would use them.

CHAPTER 8

ORGANIZING AND
MANAGING
YOUR HARD DISK

Learning Objectives

After completing this chapter, you will be able to:

1. Explain the purpose of organizing a hard disk.
2. Explain the purpose and function of the TREE command.
3. List criteria for organizing a hard disk efficiently and logically.
4. Explain the role XCOPY can play in organizing a hard disk.
5. Explain the difference between contiguous and noncontiguous files.
6. Explain the purpose and function of the CHKDSK command.
7. Explain lost clusters and cross-linked files.
8. Explain the ways you can repair a disk.
9. Explain the purpose and function of using the Disk Defragmenter program.

Student Outcomes

1. Reorganize the DATA disk.
2. Use the TREE command to view the organization of a disk.
3. Use the XCOPY command with its parameters to copy files.
4. Use the CHKDSK command to elicit statistical information about disks and memory.
5. Interpret the statistical information obtained by using the CHKDSK command.
6. Use CHKDSK to see if files are contiguous.
7. Repair a disk, if possible.
8. Use the Disk Defragmenter utility program.

Chapter Overview

The more efficiently and logically a hard disk is organized, the easier it becomes for you to know where to store a new file or how to access an existing one. Subdirectories (folders that group files together under one heading) help you organize a hard disk so that you can easily locate a specific file.

An inefficient but typical hard disk organizational scheme is to divide the disk into major application programs (e.g., word-processing program, spreadsheet program, etc.) and place the data files for those applications in the same subdirectory. This organizational scheme can create problems when you try to locate a specific data file. To locate a specific data file, you have to remember under which program the data file was listed. It makes sense to never place program files and data files in the same subdirectory. Program files rarely change, and data files are always changing. The majority of computer users are working with application programs to help them do their work projects more easily and efficiently. It makes better sense to organize the disk the way most people work—by project, not by software application.

This chapter demonstrates ways to use the hard disk efficiently. You will learn how to organize a hard disk to serve your specific needs, use directories to keep track of the files on your disk, and determine the best command to use to locate a specific file. You will learn what a logical disk is and what commands can be used with a logical disk. In addition, you will learn some useful commands to manage the hard disk itself and keep it healthy.

8.1   Why Organize a Hard Disk?

You will accumulate many programs, and with each program you usually generate many data files. What you have is an information explosion. Organization of information is a constant process in the world; whether in a library or an office, items need to be organized so that information can be found. People have been managing paper files and folders with many office-related tools such as file cabinets, folders, and other organizational labels. However, managing files and folders on a computer system is a much neglected topic of discussion. No one would think of taking paper files and folders and throwing them into a room, yet that is exactly what happens with a computer system. People "throw" their files and folders on the computer system with no thought of organization or the ability to retrieve the information they need. You need to manage these programs and data files so that you can not only locate what you need but also be able to identify what is located. Grouping files logically is the best way to organize. With Windows XP Professional, you create subdirectories for storing related files. In addition, you want to name your files and directories in some meaningful way so that you can identify what is in each.

When Windows XP Professional is installed, certain folders are created. These include at the very least My Documents, with at least two subfolders of My Music and My Pictures. In addition, the subdirectories named Documents and Settings, Program Files and Windows (or WINNT) are created. Each of these folders holds other directories and files. Windows is used for the operating system files; Program Files is used for different programs you may install, as well as programs included with Windows such as Outlook Express. Documents and Settings is used to hold your preferences for your system. My Documents is the default folder for data files with specifically named directories for types of documents, i.e, My Pictures. As you can see, if you have nothing on your computer but Windows XP Professional, there is an organizational scheme using directories to hold significant files needed for the operating system and the utility programs that come with Windows. There are also critical files and folders placed in the root directory that Windows needs to boot the system. These files and folders are normally hidden from view.

Obviously, you did not purchase a computer to have only an operating system to use. You purchase programs that you will use in your work. People often purchase or receive with their computer purchases some kind of integrated program that provides tools for the most common types of work. Integrated programs, sometimes called suites, usually include a program for word processing, a spreadsheet program, a database program, some kind of presentation software, and other related tools.

The two most popular choices are Microsoft Office (which includes Word, Excel, Access, PowerPoint, and other office-related programs) or WordPerfect Office (which includes WordPerfect, QuattroPro, Paradox, Corel Presentations, and other office-related programs). Sometimes, people choose individual programs rather than a suite, particularly if they do not need all the programs in the suite. For instance, you might choose to use Word as your word-processing program but Lotus 1-2-3 as your spreadsheet program. Other critical programs that users should absolutely purchase or download include virus-checking programs such as Norton

AntiVirus or McAfee VirusScan and a file compression utility such as WinZip. After these programs, you will purchase programs that meet your needs—graphics, games, Web-related software, financial management software, etc. The list is endless as to the kinds of tools (software) you will want to have on your computer.

When you purchase these additional programs for your computer system, you must install them on your hard disk in order to use them. In general, most people use the installation program that comes with their new program. In general, most programs today come on a CD. The CD will have an installation program, usually with a file with a name like SETUP or INSTALL. You may double-click that file name to start the installation process. Often, when you insert the CD into the CD-ROM drive, the program will automatically ask you if you want to install it.

An installation program creates a directory or directories for the application program you are installing and then copies the files from the CD-ROM (or floppy disks, in rare cases) to the named directories. Many of these application programs have such huge files that, when they are placed on the disk by the manufacturer, the files are compressed. In the process of copying the files to the named subdirectory, the setup or install programs must first decompress those program files. As part of the installation, these programs may or may not create a directory for data. If not, your data files may, by default, end up being saved to the directory that holds the application program files or to the My Documents folder. In addition, the installation program will usually make entries in the Windows Registry that accomplish such tasks as adding the program name to your menus, registering file extensions, and so forth. However, if you do not tell the installation program where you want the files and folders located, the program will decide what the folders are called and where the files and folders are to be located. Many programs, including Microsoft programs, will install their program folders under the Program Files folder. Other programs will install the program folders and files to the root directory.

If, when you use the DIR command, the many files and subdirectory names in the root directory scroll by endlessly, it becomes very difficult to know what files are on the hard disk and where they are located. Furthermore, in many cases, you will look at a directory name and have no idea if it contains a program you use. If you look inside the directory, you also will have no idea if the files in it are your data files or program files. You do not know what you can safely delete or what you should back up. This problem does not change in the Windows GUI. Even in a graphical environment, a disorganized disk is not a pretty sight. To further complicate the organization of your hard drive, the installation of programs is only the beginning. You will be creating data files and the location of those data files will be critical to you and your work. If you do not have some organizational scheme, you will spend your time looking for data files instead of working with them.

The use of long file names on floppy disks, which are sometimes used for backing up files from the hard disk can be a problem. Remember, floppy disks always use FAT. Thus, if you are using a 1.44-MB floppy disk, the root directory table is limited to 224 entries. Disks were originally designed to hold files that complied to the old 8.3 naming convention. Even if the files are very small (not much data in them) and there is still ample room in the data sectors for new information, once the directory table is filled you can no longer place more files on the disk. Once the root directory table is full, as far as the operating system is concerned, the disk is full, regardless of how much actual space remains on the disk.

On the hard disk, you do not have this problem unless you are using FAT16 as your file system. In that case, the root directory table on your hard disk has a limit of 512 entries. If every file was located in the root directory, you would ultimately get a message that the disk was full. The root directory table would be what was actually full, not the disk, but you would still not be able to place anything else on the disk. However, today, most hard disks use either FAT32 or NTFS. If you are using FAT32 as your file system, your root directory table on the hard disk has a capacity of 65,535 entries. Although this number may seem sufficient, it is still not a good idea to place all your directories and data and program files in the root directory. Just think of scrolling through 65,535 entries to find a file of interest. Although the NTFS file system does not have these limitations, organization of a disk is still a concern for ease in locating files and directories.

Most programs written for the Windows environment install themselves to the C:\Program Files folder. As you can imagine, this directory fills rapidly. Other setup programs handle it differently. For example, when you install a program like WordPerfect using the setup program, a subdirectory is created called C:\Corel, and all products written by Corel are installed in that same directory. Most setup programs allow you to change the directory you wish to install in. If you have a second drive or partition with extra space on it, you may want to install your software to a subdirectory of your own choosing. Perhaps you have three drawing and graphics programs, PCDraw, PCPaint, and Paint Shop Pro. You might want to create a subdirectory called DRAW, and then install the programs in C:\DRAW\PCDraw, C:\DRAW\PCPaint, and C:\DRAW\PSP, respectively. In this way, all your drawing programs would be in one location.

There can be, however, one disadvantage to choosing your own installation location. If you have technical problems with an installed program and need to call that company's tech support, the person you speak to will undoubtedly expect the software to be installed to the setup program's default directory. If you have installed it somewhere else, the support person may have difficulty helping you.

You typically have more than one program on your computer system. The programs may have come with the computer when you purchased it, or you may have purchased additional programs. For instance, a typical user might have a word-processing program (Word), a spreadsheet program (Lotus 1-2-3), a database program (FoxPro), the operating system (Windows XP Professional), and a checkbook management program (Quicken). If you were that user, your hard disk might look like Figure 8.1.

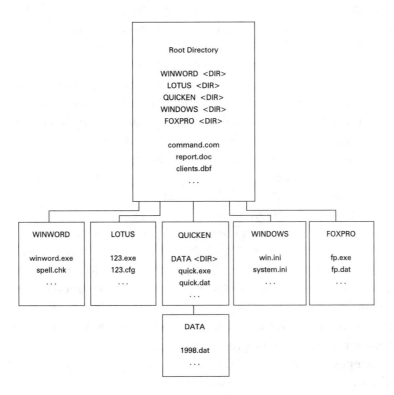

Figure 8.1—A Typical Hard Disk Configuration

In Figure 8.1, an ellipsis (...) represents the rest of the files. You or the program would create each subdirectory and place the program files that belong to the application program in the proper subdirectory. Notice the Quicken program has automatically created a subdirectory for data files.

The point is you want to use the programs to do work. As an example, let us say you are a salesperson and you have two products to sell: widgets and bangles. You use Word to write letters to clients and to make proposals. You use Lotus 1-2-3 to do budget projections for clients. You use Quicken to manage your expenses. You use the operating system to manage your files and disks. You use FoxPro to manage your clients' names and addresses (a database). You know enough that you know you do not want the data files (such as REPORT.DOC or CLIENTS.DBF) in the root directory. You could use the MOVE command to move the REPORT.DOC file to the WINWORD subdirectory and to move CLIENTS.DBF to the FOXPRO subdirectory.

First an foremost, you do not want to save your data files to the program folders. Placing data files in the program folders is not a good organizational technique for several reasons. Program files do not change, while data files change as often as you add or delete information. You also add and delete files. You will want to back up your data files from the hard disk to a floppy disk, a tape, a CD, or a Zip drive to ensure you do not lose your data. If you have placed your data files in the program folders, you will have to sort through many program and support files to back up your data and identify which is a program file and which is a data file. Furthermore, part of the rationale for folders is to categorize information; data files are information.

Part of a good organizational scheme is creating meaningful names for your data files so you can identify at a later date what they contain without having to open each file. Naming data files requires more thought than most beginning users realize. Having a *naming convention*, a scheme for naming your files, helps you determine what is in files. It also requires knowledge of how your application programs work. For instance, if the programs you are using are Word and PowerPoint you first need to know that Word automatically assigns the file extension of .doc to each file you create in Word, and PowerPoint assigns the file extension of .ppt to each file you create in PowerPoint. With that knowledge, you now can name your files. Thus, if you were writing a book on Windows XP Professional, your naming convention could be to preface every file name with a code to indicate that it had to do with that book. Thus, your file names could be **wxpch01.doc** (Windows XP Professional Chapter 1 document) and **wxpch02.doc** for the chapter documents and **wxpch01.ppt** (Windows XP Professional Chapter 1 PowerPoint presentation) and **wxpch02.ppt** for your presentations and **wxppub1.doc** (Windows XP Professional publisher document 1) and **wxppub2.doc** for your correspondence with your publisher. With this convention, it would be easy to locate all your files that dealt with the book or only the files that dealt with your correspondence to your publisher.

Because Windows XP Professional allows up to 255 characters for a file name, it might seem easy to create meaningful names. In fact, you might ask why not call the document **Windows XP Professional Chapter 1.doc** rather than **wxpch01.doc**? Certainly reading the file's name will tell you what is in it and what program created it (Word because of the .doc file extension). However, the availability of long file names can actually be problematic, and not only because of the limitations of the root directory table. Certainly, if you are using older programs, you must still use the 8.3 file-naming rule. Windows XP Professional creates an MS-DOS alias for a long file name which is a truncated version of the long file name. Thus, **Windows XP Professional Chapter 1.doc** will have an MS-DOS name of **window~01.doc** and **Windows XP Professional Chapter 2.doc** would have an MS-DOS name of **window~02.doc**. Although, when using long file names, it is helpful to know the 8.3 file name, it is not too critical today as most people will have programs written for the Windows world that do support long file names.

But there are also other reasons for using an 8.3 name. Some utility programs will not work with long file names. *Utility programs* include such types of programs as virus-scanning programs and disk-repair utilities. Many of these types of programs cannot work with long file names. A strong recommendation is also to not use spaces in file names, although Windows XP Professional allows you to so. There are two primary reasons for this. Again, you will find that sometimes utility programs, the Internet, and even Windows XP Professional itself do not like spaces in file names, even though spaces are allowed characters. A program could "choke" (not work) if it finds a file name with spaces. But more importantly, as a user, it is difficult to remember whether or not you placed spaces in a file name and where you placed the spaces. **My new file.doc** and **mynew file.doc** and **mynewfile.doc** are all considered unique file names by Windows XP Professional. If you never use spaces, you never have to remember where and what spaces you used. For this reason, another recommendation is always to use lowercase letters.

Long file names can pose a problem in Windows XP Professional. Although a file name can be up to 255 characters in length, the full file name also includes the path name. Remember that the folder name is part of the file name so that a file called bud.wk1 full name is C:\LOTUS\WIDGETS\bud.wk1. Another consideration is that file names that are too long make browsing a list of files in the Command Prompt window or even Windows Explorer very difficult. Even if you only use Windows XP Professional programs that allow long file names, there is still a problem. You are the user who is going to key in the file name. The more characters you have to key in, the more likely it is that you are going to make a typographical error. It is also difficult to remember your naming strategy when you use very long file names.

Again, the importance of creating meaningful file names cannot be overemphasized. Your naming convention should be easy to use so that when you create a new file, you know what name you are going to give it so that it fits into your scheme. You should be able to identify a file's contents by its name. You do not want to have to open each file to see what its contents are. For example, you are using your database program and you want to keep track of your clients for the bangles product line. You name the data file CLIENTS.DBF. However, you have two products to sell, bangles and widgets. Each product has different clients, so each product requires a separate client file. You now have two files you want to call CLIENTS.DBF. You do not want to overwrite one file with another, so you must uniquely identify each file. An efficient way to do this is to create a subdirectory called BANGLES and a subdirectory called WIDGETS and place each CLIENTS.DBF file in the appropriate subdirectory. It is the subdirectory name that clarifies which product client file you work with. An example of an inefficient but typical hard disk organizational scheme with subdirectories for data might look like Figure 8.2.

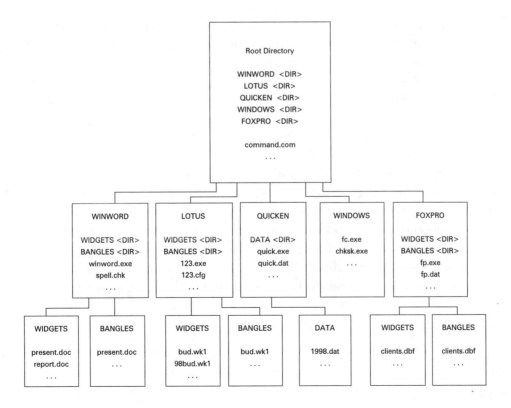

Figure 8.23—Organizing a Disk by Software Application Package

Although the organizational scheme in Figure 8.2 is better than placing the data files in the root directory or in the program subdirectories, it is still very inefficient. There are too many repeated subdirectory names. In addition, every time you want a data file, you will have to remember not only what application you are working on, but also where the appropriate data file is located. Furthermore, at this point you must key in long path names. For example, when you want to retrieve REPORT.DOC in Word, you need to key in **C:\WINWORD\WIDGETS\ REPORT.DOC.** In addition, when you need to find a file two or three levels down the hierarchical tree, the operating system must look at every subdirectory on the way down. The heads on the disk drive are constantly going back and forth reading the entries and looking for the files.

As you become a more sophisticated user, you will find that you can use data files in conjunction with different application programs. For instance, you can use FoxPro to generate a mailing list from your CLIENTS.DBF file so that you can use it with Word to send out a form letter. When you begin doing this, you end up with data in two places: the word-processing subdirectory and the database subdirectory. More importantly, when you find a new program you want to purchase, such as a presentation package like Harvard Graphics, you need to add a new subdirectory for that program, and you need to add further subdirectories for your products, bangles and widgets. Or you could decide that you want a different word processor, such as WordPerfect. How do you handle those data files in the WIDGETS and BANGLES subdirectories? You do not want to delete them because WordPerfect will be able to read them. An even worse nightmare is if you pick up a new product line such as beads. Now you have to create a BEADS subdirectory under each application program. You have created a logistical nightmare for finding out where files are located and deciding what data files should be kept.

The real problem with this all-too-typical organizational scheme is the logic behind it. Remember, programs are tools. Before computers, you still used tools—a pencil, a calculator, a typewriter. But did you file your output from these tools by the tool name? When you wrote a letter using a typewriter, did you file it in a folder labeled TYPEWRITER? When you calculated some numbers with your calculator, did you place your totals in a file folder called CALCULATOR? Of course not. It sounds silly to even suggest that. But in the above organizational scheme, that is *exactly* what you are doing!

Programs are simply tools. People do not work by software package; they work by projects. Software is a tool to help you do work easily and efficiently. Hence, it makes much better sense to organize a hard disk by the way you work rather than by the application package—the tool. In addition, with an efficient organizational scheme, it is easier to add and delete projects and software. The following section will recommend some guidelines to assist you in organizing your hard disk. However, you must always remember that any organizational scheme you devise is to assist you in saving, retrieving, and backing up your data files easily. A good organizational scheme for one user will not necessarily work for another.

8.2   Methods of Organizing a Hard Disk

Certain criteria can give a hard disk an efficient and logical organization. These include the following suggestions:

- *The root directory should be a map to the rest of the disk.* The only files that should be in the root directory are the files placed there by the operating system. All other files in the root directory should be subdirectory listings. Look at the root directory as the index or table of contents to your entire hard disk. Ideally, when you execute the DIR command, you should not see more than a screenful of information. With today's very large hard disks, it is difficult to keep to this ideal. In reality, you may have 30 or more subdirectories off the root, which cannot fit on one screen. Nonetheless, the principle remains valid. Keep the root directory clear of unnecessary files.

- *Plan the organization of your hard disk.* Think about the work you do and how it would be easiest for you to find your work files. This is especially true prior to installing new software.

- Develop a naming convention for files and directories. It should be easy to follow so that when you create new files or directories, you can logically name them to fit your convention and when you look at a file name, you will know approximately what data is in it.

- Create as many directories and subdirectories as you need before copying files into them.

- There is no risk in creating or deleting folders for data files. Nor is there any risk in moving, copying, or deleting data files. However, if your application software has already been installed on your computer for you, you *cannot* and *must not* rename or move program files or any program support files. If you do either, the programs will not work!

- *Create subdirectories that are shallow and wide instead of compact and deep.* The reason is that it is easier for the operating system to find files that are not buried several levels down. Also, it is much easier for you to keep track of the subdirectories when the organizational scheme is simple. Remember the old programmer's principle: "KISS—Keep It Simple, Stupid." Short path names are easier to key in than long path names.

- *Do not place data files in the same subdirectory as program files.* Although you are constantly changing, creating, and deleting data files, you rarely, if ever, create or delete program files.

- *Many small subdirectories with few files are better than a large subdirectory with many files.* Remember, you are categorizing data. If you begin to get too many files in a subdirectory, think about breaking the subdirectory into two or more subdirectories. It is easier to manage and update a subdirectory with a limited number of files because there is less likelihood of having to determine on a file-by-file basis which file belongs where. In addition, if you have too few files in many subdirectories, think about combining them into one subdirectory.

- *Keep subdirectory names short but descriptive.* Try to stay away from generic and meaningless subdirectory names such as DATA. The shorter the subdirectory name, the less there is to key in. For instance, using the subdirectory name WIDGETS for your widgets data files is easy. If you simply use W, that is too short and cryptic for you to remember easily what the W subdirectory holds. On the other hand, the name WIDGETS.FIL is a little long to key in. You rarely, if ever, use extensions with subdirectory names. Again, remember you will be keying in these path names.

- *Create a separate subdirectory for batch files.* Batch files are files that you will learn to write to help automate processes you do often. Place the subdirectory for batch files under the root directory. A popular name for this subdirectory is BATCH.

- *Create a subdirectory called UTILS (utilities) in which you will create further separate subdirectories for each utility program you own or purchase.* As you work with computers, you start collecting utility software. Utility software programs provide commonly needed services. An example of this is Norton Utilities. Utility software would also include any shareware utilities that you might acquire from a download site on the World Wide Web. In many instances, utility software and shareware packages have similar file names, making it imperative that each has its own separate and readily identifiable subdirectory. You can place these subdirectories under the UTILS directory. You could place the UTILS directory under the Program Files directory.

- *Learn how to install programs to your hard drive.* Typically programs will have a setup or install command. For instance, if you were going to install a file-compression program called WinZip, you would key in SETUP, and the setup program would tell you that it is going to install the program to C:\WINZIP. You can change that to C:\UTILS\WINZIP or D:\WINZIP. In other words, you can create your own organizational scheme and do not have to let the installation programs put the programs anywhere they wish.

- *Learn how to use the application package, and also learn how the application package works.* For instance, find out if the application package assigns a file extension. Lotus 1-2-3 assigns an extension of .WK1 for its files, whereas WordPerfect assigns a file extension of .WPD. If an application does not assign file extensions to data files, you can be extremely flexible and create file extensions that will apply to the work that you do with that application program's data files. For instance, you could assign the file extension .LET to letter files that deal with all your correspondence or .MYS to data files that deal with a mystery book you are writing. However, nearly all programs written for Windows will assign file extensions. With the addition of long file names introduced in Windows 95, you can name a file CHAPTER8.MYS in Word, and the .DOC extension will be added, leaving the full file name as CHAPTER8.MYS.DOC. But be aware of your application programs file extension assignments. For instance, graphic programs such as Paint Shop Pro will use common file extensions such as .TIF. If you first install a program such as Paint Shop Pro, which uses the .TIF file extension, then install a program such as SnagIt that also uses that file extension, now all .TIF files will be assigned to SnagIt instead of Paint Shop Pro. Many software programs allow you to choose a custom installation where you can choose what file extension will be used for that program.

- *Find out how the application package works with subdirectories.* For instance, does it recognize subdirectories for data files? Very few programs today do not recognize subdirectories. However, most programs will have a default subdirectory where that program saves its data files. You should know what that subdirectory is and if you can change the default directory.

■ *Analyze the way you work.* If you always use an application program's default data directory when you save and retrieve files, then organizing your hard disk around projects will not work for you. In that case, perhaps you do want to create data directories. Figure 8.3 is another way to organize your hard disk.

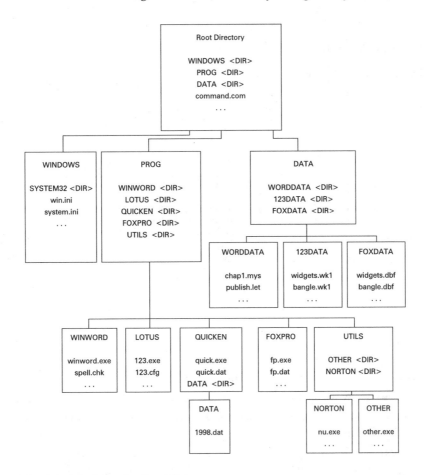

Figure 8.3—Another Organizational Scheme

■ *Analyze your environment.* If, for instance, you are in an educational environment, organization by application package makes sense. You are teaching only that one application package, and all data created by students will be saved to floppy disks. Hence, your focus is the package, and organizing around the application package in this instance is logical.

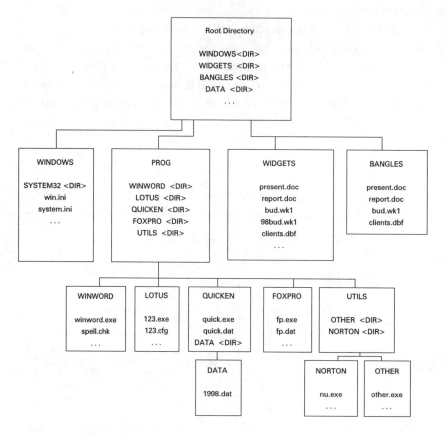

Figure 8.4—Organization by Project

An organizational scheme for a project-oriented environment based on our salesperson scenario could look something like Figure 8.4. In Figure 8.4, you know where all your software application programs are located. In addition, it is much easier to add a new software package or to update an existing one because all the program files are located in one place. For instance, when you want to add a presentation software application program, such as Harvard Graphics, you can create a subdirectory called C:\PROG\HG and install all the files in that location. If you have a suite of software, such as Corel Perfect Office or Microsoft Office, its installation makes subdirectories that act like PROG in the example. Microsoft creates MICROSOFT OFFICE under Program Files, and Corel creates COREL. Under these directories are subdirectories holding the individual programs. Also, since this scheme is organized by project, it is easy to add a new project or delete an old one. If, for example, you are now selling beads, you can create a subdirectory called C:\BEADS. If you no longer are selling widgets, you can use RD /S to eliminate the WIDGETS subdirectory. It is also easy to know which data files belong to what project. You also can tell which data files belong to which program by virtue of the file extension. In this example, if you look at the subdirectory called WIDGETS, you know that the data files PRESENT.DOC and REPORT.DOC were created with Word. You know that the data files BUD.WK1 and 98BUD.WK1 were created with Lotus 1-2-3, whereas CLIENTS.DBF was created with FoxPro. The same would be true for the BANGLES subdirectory. This example also shows that you leave the DATA subdirectory as is for Quicken because that is where Quicken prefers the data files.

This, of course, is not the only way to organize a hard disk. You can organize your hard disk any way you wish, but there should be organization. Although it may take some time in the beginning, ultimately organization will make more effective use of the hard disk. Primarily you want to organize your data files into meaningful directories. You do not want to save all your data files to a subdirectory called My Documents. You want to be able to go directly to the subdirectory that holds the files you wish to work on. Except when you create a new file, you will find that if you properly organize your data files, you will rarely use the Start/All Programs menu. Instead, you will go directly to the directory that holds the files you wish to work on. For instance, if you were working with the bangles product line, you could open the directory BANGLES, which would have all of your files that deal with bangles, regardless of the application program that created them. The two major considerations for any organizational scheme are first, how do *you* work, and second, how do the *application programs* work?

8.3 Organizing a Disk

Most users do not begin with an organized hard disk. What may seem organized to one user is chaos to another. In this instance, the user needs to reorganize the hard disk, a process that can be done without reformatting the hard disk. To master this process, you are going to take the DATA disk and reorganize it. This exercise will give you some idea of how the process works without having to worry about inadvertently deleting files from the hard disk. (You may like to back up your Data disk before the reorganization process.)

8.4 Viewing the Disk Structure with the TREE Command

You have looked at disk structures in the figures shown in this chapter. These have been pictorial representations of how a disk was organized. The TREE command allows you to see a graphic representation of the disk structure on the screen in the command prompt window. The syntax of the TREE command is:

```
TREE [drive:][path] [/F] [/A]

    /F   Display the names of the files in each folder.
    /A   Use ASCII instead of extended characters.
```

8.5 Activity: Using the TREE Command

1   Open a Command Line window.

2   Make the **C:\WUGXP** directory the default.

3   Key in the following: C:\WUGXP>**TREE** Enter

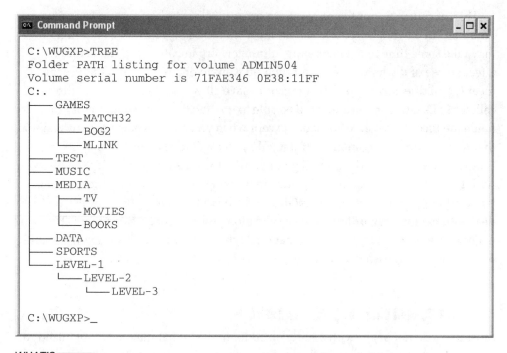

```
C:\WUGXP>TREE
Folder PATH listing for volume ADMIN504
Volume serial number is 71FAE346 0E38:11FF
C:.
├──── GAMES
│       ├───── MATCH32
│       ├───── BOG2
│       └───── MLINK
├──── TEST
├──── MUSIC
├──── MEDIA
│       ├──── TV
│       ├───── MOVIES
│       └──── BOOKS
├──── DATA
├──── SPORTS
└──── LEVEL-1
         └────LEVEL-2
                 └──── LEVEL-3

C:\WUGXP>_
```

WHAT'S **HAPPENING?**   You can see a graphical representation of the folder structure under the **C:\WUGXP** directory. Your order may be different. The subdirectories **GAMES, TEST, MUSIC, MEDIA, DATA, SPORTS,** and **LEVEL-1** are directly under **WUGXP.** The subdirectories **MATCH32, BOG2,** and **MLINK** are under **GAMES; TV, MOVIES,** and **BOOKS** are under **MEDIA;** and **LEVEL-2** and **LEVEL-3** are under **LEVEL-1**. With this graphic, it is easy to see how the **WUGXP** directory is organized.

4   Key in the following: C:\WUGXP>**TREE /A** Enter

```
C:\WUGXP>TREE /A
Folder PATH listing for volume ADMIN504
Volume serial number is 71FAE346 0E38:11FF
C:.
+---GAMES
¦     +---MATCH32
¦     +---BOG2
¦     \---MLINK
+---TEST
+---MUSIC
+---MEDIA
¦     +---TV
¦     +---MOVIES
¦     \---BOOKS
+---DATA
+---SPORTS
\---LEVEL-1
      \---LEVEL-2
            \---LEVEL-3

C:\WUGXP>_
```

WHAT'S HAPPENING?   You used the TREE command with the / A parameter. Instead of the solid graphic lines, you got only those lines that you could create with the keyboard using only ASCII characters, not the extended character set, which is able to draw solid, unbroken lines on the screen. The information displayed, however, is exactly the same.

5   Key in the following: C:\WUGXP>**TREE** **/F** Enter

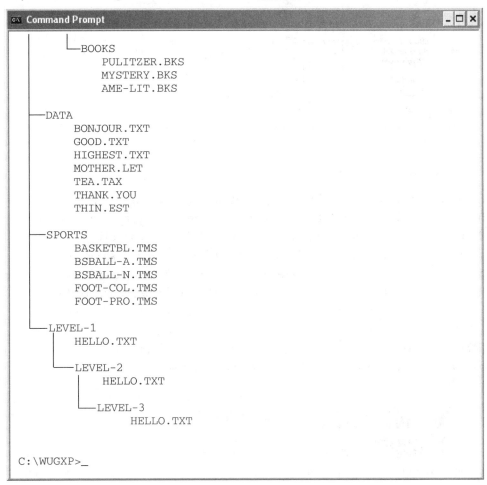

WHAT'S HAPPENING?   The screen display above is the end of your display as it scrolled. All the file names were listed within their respective directories. You can use redirection to place this information in a file, use the MORE filter.

6   Key in the following: C:\WUGXP>**CD** \ Enter

8.6   Organizing the DATA Disk

The DATA disk has minimal organization. The . . . in the figure below represents file names. (*Note:* If you did not do all the chapter activities, your disk could look different. It is not important that your disk is exactly as the one pictured. If you have additional files or are missing some files, you can delete, copy, or create files as needed. The contents of the text files do not matter.) Its structure is as follows:

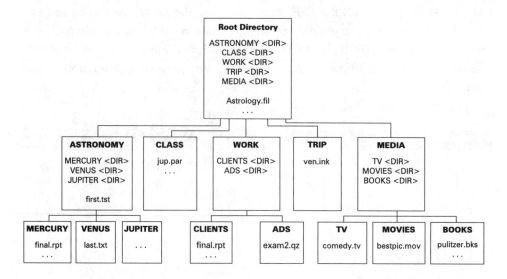

Figure 8.5—Current DATA Disk Structure

In addition to organizing this disk, you are also going to copy some programs from the \WUGXP directory to the disk so that there will be programs as well as data files on it. At this moment, you really cannot tell what is on this disk. There are so many files in the root directory that when you key in DIR, you see many, many files scrolling by on the screen. Therefore, you are going to reorganize the disk so that it will be easier to manage. You are going to create the necessary subdirectories and copy the appropriate files to the correct subdirectories. You will create a GAMES subdirectory, which will be a map to the game programs on the DATA disk. (*Warning:* If you have installed programs on your hard disk, you do not move or copy them elsewhere. You may do so here as these are special examples.)

8.7   Activity: Setting Up the GAMES Subdirectory

Note: The DATA disk is in Drive A. You have shelled out to the Command Line.
C:\> is displayed as the default drive and the default directory.

1   Key in the following: `C:\>`**A:** (Enter)

2   Key in the following: `A:\>`**MD GAMES** (Enter)

3   Key in the following: `A:\>`**MD GAMES\ARGH** (Enter)

4   Key in the following: `A:\>`**MD GAMES\MLINK** (Enter)

5   Key in the following: `A:\>`**MD GAMES\OTHER** (Enter)

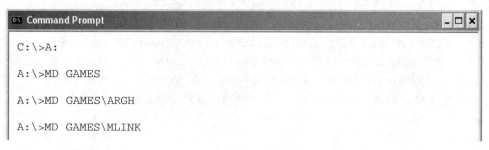

```
A:\>MD GAMES\OTHER

A:\>_
```

WHAT'S HAPPENING?   You created a generic program subdirectory and identified the specific subdirectories that reflect the programs you will have on the DATA disk. Now you need to copy the proper files to the proper subdirectory.

6   Key in the following:
A:\>**COPY C:\WUGXP\GAMES\MLINK*.* GAMES\MLINK** Enter

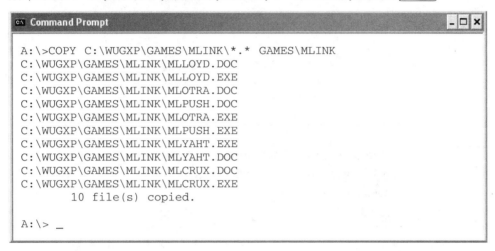

```
A:\>COPY C:\WUGXP\GAMES\MLINK\*.* GAMES\MLINK
C:\WUGXP\GAMES\MLINK\MLLOYD.DOC
C:\WUGXP\GAMES\MLINK\MLLOYD.EXE
C:\WUGXP\GAMES\MLINK\MLOTRA.DOC
C:\WUGXP\GAMES\MLINK\MLPUSH.DOC
C:\WUGXP\GAMES\MLINK\MLOTRA.EXE
C:\WUGXP\GAMES\MLINK\MLPUSH.EXE
C:\WUGXP\GAMES\MLINK\MLYAHT.EXE
C:\WUGXP\GAMES\MLINK\MLYAHT.DOC
C:\WUGXP\GAMES\MLINK\MLCRUX.DOC
C:\WUGXP\GAMES\MLINK\MLCRUX.EXE
      10 file(s) copied.

A:\> _
```

WHAT'S HAPPENING?   You copied all the files necessary for the MLINK game into the proper directory on the DATA disk.

7   Key in the following: A:\>**DIR C:\WUGXP\GAMES\MLINK** Enter

8   Key in the following: A:\>**DIR A:\GAMES\MLINK** Enter

```
A:\>DIR C:\WUGXP\GAMES\MLINK
 Volume in drive C is ADMIN504
 Volume Serial Number is 0E38-11FF

 Directory of C:\WUGXP\GAMES\MLINK

02/04/2002  09:21 AM    <DIR>          .
02/04/2002  09:21 AM    <DIR>          ..
03/13/1990  10:34 PM            13,093 MLLOYD.DOC
03/13/1990  10:31 PM            46,128 MLLOYD.EXE
10/28/1989  12:10 PM            12,988 MLOTRA.DOC
07/07/1990  01:28 PM            12,534 MLPUSH.DOC
10/28/1989  12:09 PM            47,136 MLOTRA.EXE
07/06/1990  06:03 PM            45,632 MLPUSH.EXE
09/22/1989  11:59 AM            37,088 MLYAHT.EXE
09/22/1989  12:19 PM            10,962 MLYAHT.DOC
01/10/1992  07:11 PM            19,191 MLCRUX.DOC
01/10/1992  07:04 PM            26,368 MLCRUX.EXE
              10 File(s)        271,120 bytes
               2 Dir(s)   6,878,904,320 bytes free
```

```
A:\>DIR GAMES\MLINK
 Volume in drive A is DATA
 Volume Serial Number is 30B8-DA1D

 Directory of A:\GAMES\MLINK

04/17/2002  01:07 PM    <DIR>          .
04/17/2002  01:07 PM    <DIR>          ..
03/13/1990  10:34 PM         13,093 MLLOYD.DOC
03/13/1990  10:31 PM         46,128 MLLOYD.EXE
10/28/1989  12:10 PM         12,988 MLOTRA.DOC
07/07/1990  01:28 PM         12,534 MLPUSH.DOC
10/28/1989  12:09 PM         47,136 MLOTRA.EXE
07/06/1990  06:03 PM         45,632 MLPUSH.EXE
09/22/1989  11:59 AM         37,088 MLYAHT.EXE
09/22/1989  12:19 PM         10,962 MLYAHT.DOC
01/10/1992  07:11 PM         19,191 MLCRUX.DOC
01/10/1992  07:04 PM         26,368 MLCRUX.EXE
              10 File(s)        271,120 bytes
               2 Dir(s)      1,112,064 bytes free

A:\>_
```

WHAT'S HAPPENING?   You used the COPY command in step 6 to request all the MLINK files on the C drive be copied to the GAMES\MLINK directory on the DATA disk, and they were indeed copied.

9 Key in the following: `A:\>`**CD GAMES\OTHER** [Enter]

10 Key in the following: `A:\GAMES\OTHER>`**CD C:\WUGXP\GAMES** [Enter]

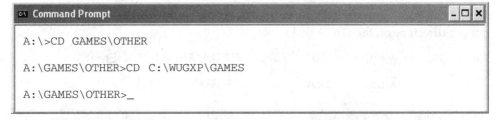

```
Command Prompt                                          _ □ ✕

A:\>CD  GAMES\OTHER

A:\GAMES\OTHER>CD  C:\WUGXP\GAMES

A:\GAMES\OTHER>_
```

WHAT'S HAPPENING?   You changed to the newly created OTHER directory under GAMES on the root of the DATA disk. Then, you switched the default directory on the C drive to WUGXP\GAMES. Did the default directory on C change?

11 Key in the following: `A:\GAMES\OTHER>`**C:** [Enter]

```
Command Prompt                                          _ □ ✕

A:\GAMES\OTHER>C:

C:\WUGXP\GAMES>_
```

WHAT'S HAPPENING?   As you can see, the default directory on the C drive has changed to WUGXP\GAMES.

12 Key in the following: `C:\WUGXP\GAMES>`**A:** [Enter]

13 Key in the following: `A:\GAMES\OTHER>`**COPY C:LS*.*** [Enter]
Note: ***Do not*** key in the \ after **C:**

```
Command Prompt                                                    _ □ ✕

C:\WUGXP\GAMES>A:

A:\GAMES\OTHER>COPY C:LS*.*
C:LS.DOC
C:LS.EXE
C:LS.PAS
        3 file(s) copied.

A:\GAMES\OTHER>_
```

**WHAT'S
HAPPENING?**   Notice the copy display. There is no \ after the C:. The copy is
taking place from the default directory on C, which you changed to
WUGXP\GAMES. By manipulating your default directory, you can shorten the path
name that you have to key in.

14 Key in the following: A:\GAMES\OTHER>**DIR C:** `Enter`

```
Command Prompt                                                    _ □ ✕

A:\GAMES\OTHER>DIR C:
 Volume in drive C is ADMIN504
 Volume Serial Number is 0E38-11FF

 Directory of C:\WUGXP\GAMES

02/04/2002  09:20 AM    <DIR>          .
02/04/2002  09:20 AM    <DIR>          ..
06/23/1989  11:34 PM             2,611 LS.DOC
06/23/1989  11:40 PM            12,576 LS.EXE
08/19/1990  04:00 AM             8,729 ARGH.DOC
08/19/1990  04:00 AM            69,728 ARGH.EXE
08/14/1989  10:31 PM            43,776 MLSHUT.EXE
08/14/1989  10:48 PM            15,049 MLSHUT.DOC
05/09/1989  03:51 PM            34,645 MAZE.EXE
06/23/1989  11:41 PM             8,404 LS.PAS
12/06/2001  09:14 AM    <DIR>          MATCH32
12/06/2001  09:15 AM    <DIR>          BOG2
12/06/2001  09:15 AM    <DIR>          MLINK
              8 File(s)        195,518 bytes
              5 Dir(s)   6,802,833,408 bytes free

A:\GAMES\OTHER>_
```

**WHAT'S
HAPPENING?**   There are two other files to place in the OTHER directory, and
both begin with ML. But, there is also a directory that begins with ML that you do
not want to copy.

15 Key in the following: A:\GAMES\OTHER>**COPY C:ML*.*** `Enter`

```
Command Prompt                                                    _ □ ✕

A:\GAMES\OTHER>COPY C:ML*.*
C:MLSHUT.EXE
C:MLSHUT.DOC
        2 file(s) copied.

A:\GAMES\OTHER>_
```

WHAT'S
HAPPENING?   As you can see, the COPY command ignored the subdirectory.

16 Key in the following: A:\GAMES\OTHER>**CD** [Enter]

17 Key in the following: A:\>**TREE GAMES /F** [Enter]

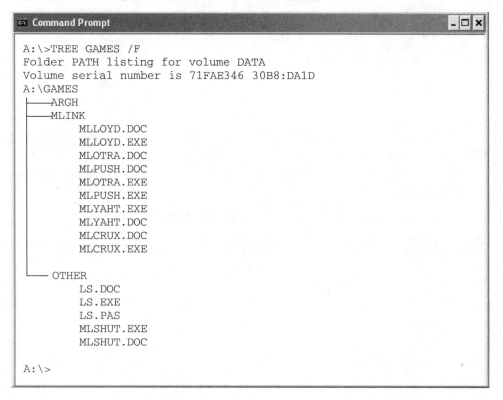

```
A:\>TREE GAMES /F
Folder PATH listing for volume DATA
Volume serial number is 71FAE346 30B8:DA1D
A:\GAMES
├────ARGH
├────MLINK
│        MLLOYD.DOC
│        MLLOYD.EXE
│        MLOTRA.DOC
│        MLPUSH.DOC
│        MLOTRA.EXE
│        MLPUSH.EXE
│        MLYAHT.EXE
│        MLYAHT.DOC
│        MLCRUX.DOC
│        MLCRUX.EXE
│
└────OTHER
         LS.DOC
         LS.EXE
         LS.PAS
         MLSHUT.EXE
         MLSHUT.DOC

A:\>
```

WHAT'S
HAPPENING?   You displayed the directory structure and files starting at the
GAMES directory and including all directories and files beneath. All that is remaining to copy is the ARGH game.

18 Key in the following: A:\>**COPY C:ARG*.* GAMES\ARGH** [Enter]

```
A:\>COPY C:ARG*.* GAMES\ARGH
C:ARGH.DOC
C:ARGH.EXE
        2 file(s) copied.

A:\>
```

19 Key in the following: A:\>**CD C:** [Enter]

20 Key in the following: A:\>**TREE GAMES /F** [Enter]

```
A:\>TREE GAMES /F
Folder PATH listing for volume DATA
Volume serial number is 71FAE346 30B8:DA1D
A:\GAMES
├────ARGH
│        ARGH.DOC
│        ARGH.EXE
```

```
  ┌──MLINK
  │        MLLOYD.DOC
  │        MLLOYD.EXE
  │        MLOTRA.DOC
  │        MLPUSH.DOC
  │        MLOTRA.EXE
  │        MLPUSH.EXE
  │        MLYAHT.EXE
  │        MLYAHT.DOC
  │        MLCRUX.DOC
  │        MLCRUX.EXE
  │
  └──OTHER
           LS.DOC
           LS.EXE
           LS.PAS
           MLSHUT.EXE
           MLSHUT.DOC

A:\> CD C:\

A:\>_
```

WHAT'S ▓▓▓▓▓▓▓▓
▓▓▓▓HAPPENING?   You have completed copying your game files and they are arranged in a logical manner. You then returned the default directory on the hard drive to the root.

21 Key in the following: A:\>**DIR C:\WUGXP*.TXT** [Enter]

```
◼▧ Command Prompt                                                   ─ ☐ ✕

A:\>DIR C:\WUGXP\*.TXT
 Volume in drive C is ADMIN504
 Volume Serial Number is 0E38-11FF


 Directory of C:\WUGXP

10/30/2001  01:46 PM                 148 ASTRO.TXT
10/30/2001  02:10 PM                 121 BORN.TXT
12/11/1999  04:03 PM                  72 DANCES.TXT
05/30/2000  04:32 PM                  53 HELLO.TXT
11/16/2000  12:00 PM                  59 Sandy and Patty.txt
10/31/2001  02:43 PM                 529 TITAN.TXT
11/16/2000  12:00 PM                  53 Sandy and Nicki.txt
05/27/2001  10:08 PM                  81 LONGFILENAME.TXT
10/30/2001  03:42 PM                 190 JUPITER.TXT
12/06/2001  12:15 AM                  97 LONGFILENAMED.TXT
10/31/2001  11:37 AM                 253 GALAXY.TXT
12/06/2001  12:16 AM                  99 LONGFILENAMING.TXT
10/31/2001  01:08 PM                 406 MERCURY.TXT
11/24/2001  11:24 AM                 194 PLANETS.TXT
10/31/2001  07:08 PM                 478 VENUS.TXT
              15 File(s)        2,833 bytes
               0 Dir(s)   6,878,904,320 bytes free

A:\>_
```

WHAT'S ▓▓▓▓▓▓▓▓
▓▓▓▓HAPPENING?   You displayed all the **.TXT** files in the **WUGXP** directory. You want to copy all the **.TXT** files that were created on or after 05-30-00 to the root

directory of the DATA disk. You do not want to copy the files **HELLO.TXT** or **DANCES.TXT**. XCOPY allows you to make choices by date.

22 Key in the following: A:\>**ATTRIB -S -H -R *.*** [Enter]

23 Key in the following: A:\>**DEL *.TXT** [Enter]

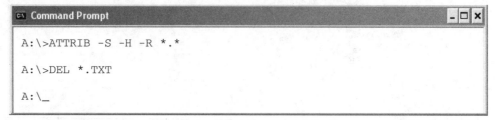

```
cmd Command Prompt                                                 _ □ ×

A:\>ATTRIB -S -H -R *.*

A:\>DEL *.TXT

A:\_
```

WHAT'S
HAPPENING?   You removed any system, hidden, and read-only attributes that were set for the files on the root of the A drive. You did not have to key in A:*.* as the root of A is the default directory. You then deleted all files ending in .TXT from the DATA disk. This time, to be cautious, you did key in the drive specification. When using DEL with a wild card, it is usually best to be absolutely sure what you are deleting, and from where you are deleting it.

24 Key in the following: A:\>**XCOPY C:\WUGXP*.TXT /D:05-31-00** [Enter]

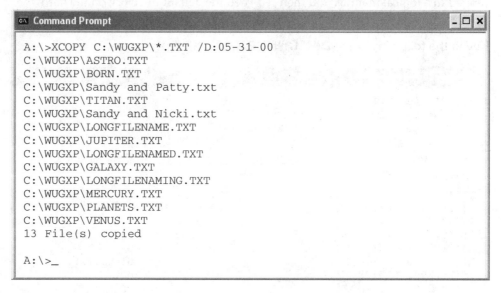

```
cmd Command Prompt                                                 _ □ ×

A:\>XCOPY C:\WUGXP\*.TXT /D:05-31-00
C:\WUGXP\ASTRO.TXT
C:\WUGXP\BORN.TXT
C:\WUGXP\Sandy and Patty.txt
C:\WUGXP\TITAN.TXT
C:\WUGXP\Sandy and Nicki.txt
C:\WUGXP\LONGFILENAME.TXT
C:\WUGXP\JUPITER.TXT
C:\WUGXP\LONGFILENAMED.TXT
C:\WUGXP\GALAXY.TXT
C:\WUGXP\LONGFILENAMING.TXT
C:\WUGXP\MERCURY.TXT
C:\WUGXP\PLANETS.TXT
C:\WUGXP\VENUS.TXT
13 File(s) copied

A:\>_
```

WHAT'S
HAPPENING?   You copied only the 13 files of interest, not all 15 that were in the **\WUGXP** subdirectory.

8.8   The MOVE Command Revisited

When reorganizing your hard disk, you sometimes do need to copy files and/or subdirectory structures from one place to another and replace existing files. In terms of reorganizing your hard disk, you do not necessarily want to actually *copy* files and directories. Most often, what you really want to do is either move files from one location to another or simply rename the subdirectory.

You have used the MOVE command in previous chapters to move files from one directory to another. Clearly, using the MOVE command is an easy way to manipulate your files. However, there is an important precaution to take before moving files and directories wholesale. Moving *data* files and *data* directories is usually a safe procedure that rarely impacts your programs. However, moving *program* files and renaming *program* directories is not "safe." Windows registers program files, their names, and their locations in the Registry. If they are moved or renamed at the Command Line or in the GUI, the Registry will not be able to find them. Program files are not generally *copied* to a location—they are *installed* in a location with a setup program. Files pertaining to the program are placed in many different locations. Moving or renaming these Windows program files and directories will almost certainly cause the program to fail.

When dealing with small programs that are completely contained within one directory and were created to run under DOS rather than Windows, problems can still occur. Moving the entire directory or renaming it *may* be safe—the program may still run. If you do decide to manipulate program files and directories, be sure and take note of which directory the program files are in before you start. Does this mean that you should not organize your hard disk? It does not, but you must do it with extreme caution. You can and will be primarily concerned with organizing your data files. These files can be easily and safely rearranged to meet your needs.

In the next activity you will move files and rename subdirectories so you can see how easy it is with data files.

8.9 Activity: Using MOVE to Organize Your Disk

Note: You have the DATA disk in Drive A with A:\> displayed.

1 Key in the following: A:\>**DIR *VEN*.*** [Enter]

```
Command Prompt                                                    _ □ ✕

A:\>DIR *VEN*.*
 Volume in drive A is DATA
 Volume Serial Number is 30B8-DA1D

 Directory of A:\

10/31/2001  07:08 PM                 478 VEN.BUD
10/31/2001  07:08 PM                 478 VEN.99
04/11/2002  12:17 PM                  45 STEVEN.FIL
10/31/2001  07:08 PM                 478 VENUS.TXT
               4 File(s)           1,479 bytes
               0 Dir(s)          951,808 bytes free

A:\>_
```

WHAT'S HAPPENING? By using the wildcard character you were able to see all files that contained VEN in filename. You want the files that are about VENUS, however you do not want STEVEN.FIL.

2 Key in the following: A:\>**ATTRIB +H STEVEN.FIL** [Enter]

3   Key in the following: A:\>**MOVE *VEN*.* ASTRONOMY\VENUS** [Enter]

4   Key in the following: A:\>**DIR *VEN*.*** [Enter]

5   Key in the following: A:\>**ATTRIB –H STEVEN.FIL** [Enter]

6   Key in the following: A:\>**DIR *VEN*.*** [Enter]

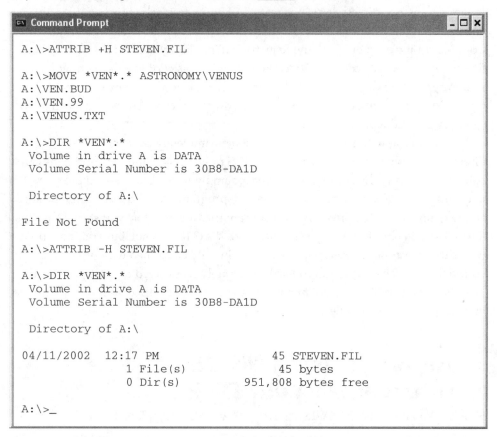

```
A:\>ATTRIB +H STEVEN.FIL

A:\>MOVE *VEN*.* ASTRONOMY\VENUS
A:\VEN.BUD
A:\VEN.99
A:\VENUS.TXT

A:\>DIR *VEN*.*
 Volume in drive A is DATA
 Volume Serial Number is 30B8-DA1D

 Directory of A:\

File Not Found

A:\>ATTRIB -H STEVEN.FIL

A:\>DIR *VEN*.*
 Volume in drive A is DATA
 Volume Serial Number is 30B8-DA1D

 Directory of A:\

04/11/2002  12:17 PM                 45 STEVEN.FIL
               1 File(s)             45 bytes
               0 Dir(s)         951,808 bytes free

A:\>_
```

WHAT'S
HAPPENING?   You used the ATTRIB command to hide the file you did not want
to move. You then moved the files pertaining to VENUS to the VENUS subdirectory
under the ASTRONOMY subdirectory. When the files were moved, you removed
the hidden flag from STEVEN.FIL. You want to move the files pertaining to JUPI-
TER and MERCURY to their own directories also.

7   Key in the following: A:\>**DIR *MER*.*** [Enter]

8   Key in the following: A:\>**DIR *JUP*.*** [Enter]

```
A:\>DIR *MER*.*
 Volume in drive A is DATA
 Volume Serial Number is 30B8-DA1D

 Directory of A:\

10/31/2001  01:08 PM                406 MERCURY.NEW
10/31/2001  01:08 PM                406 MER.BUD
10/31/2001  01:08 PM                406 MER.99
10/31/2001  01:08 PM                406 MERCURY.TXT
               4 File(s)          1,624 bytes
               0 Dir(s)         951,808 bytes free
```

```
A:\>DIR *JUP*.*
 Volume in drive A is DATA
 Volume Serial Number is 30B8-DA1D


 Directory of A:\

05/07/2002  07:41 AM                 190 JUPITER.NEW
05/07/2002  07:41 AM                 190 JUP.BUD
10/31/2001  11:33 AM                 152 JUP.OLD
10/30/2001  03:42 PM                 190 JUP.99
10/30/2001  03:42 PM                 190 JUPITER.TXT
               5 File(s)             912 bytes
               0 Dir(s)          951,808 bytes free


A:\>_
```

**WHAT'S ▓▓▓▓▓▓
▓▓▓HAPPENING?**   You see there are no files listed that you do not want to include in
your move, so it is not necessary to use the ATTRIB command to hide files.

9   Key in the following:
A:\>**MOVE *MER*.* ASTRONOMY\MERCURY** Enter

10   Key in the following: A:\>**MOVE *JUP*.* ASTRONOMY\JUPITER** Enter

11   Key in the following: A:\>**TREE ASTRONOMY /F** Enter

```
Command Prompt                                                          _ □ ✕

A:\>MOVE *MER*.* ASTRONOMY\MERCURY
A:\MERCURY.NEW
A:\MER.BUD
A:\MER.99
A:\MERCURY.TXT

A:\>MOVE *JUP*.* ASTRONOMY\JUPITER
A:\JUPITER.NEW
A:\JUP.BUD
A:\JUP.OLD
A:\JUP.99
A:\JUPITER.TXT

A:\>TREE ASTRONOMY /F
Folder PATH listing for volume DATA
Volume serial number is 71FAE346 30B8:DA1D
A:\ASTRONOMY
    FIRST.TST

────MERCURY
        FINAL.RPT
        NOTE2.TMP
        NOTE3.TMP
        DRESS.UP
        MERCURY.NEW
        MER.BUD
        MER.99
        MERCURY.TXT

────VENUS
        LAST.TST
        VEN.BUD
        VEN.99
        VENUS.TXT
```

```
└── JUPITER
         JUPITER.NEW
         JUP.BUD
         JUP.OLD
         JUP.99
         JUPITER.TXT


A:\>_
```

**WHAT'S
HAPPENING?**   You completed the moves successfully, as shown by the TREE
command. You decide that ASTRONOMY is not an accurate name for this directory.

12 Key in the following: A:\>**REN ASTRONOMY 3PLANETS** [Enter]

13 Key in the following: A:\>**DIR ASTRONOMY** [Enter]

14 Key in the following: A:\>**DIR 3PLANETS** [Enter]

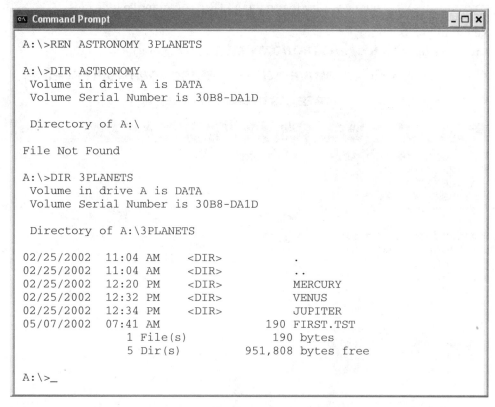

```
A:\>REN ASTRONOMY 3PLANETS

A:\>DIR ASTRONOMY
 Volume in drive A is DATA
 Volume Serial Number is 30B8-DA1D

 Directory of A:\

File Not Found

A:\>DIR 3PLANETS
 Volume in drive A is DATA
 Volume Serial Number is 30B8-DA1D

 Directory of A:\3PLANETS

02/25/2002  11:04 AM    <DIR>          .
02/25/2002  11:04 AM    <DIR>          ..
02/25/2002  12:20 PM    <DIR>          MERCURY
02/25/2002  12:32 PM    <DIR>          VENUS
02/25/2002  12:34 PM    <DIR>          JUPITER
05/07/2002  07:41 AM           190 FIRST.TST
              1 File(s)        190 bytes
              5 Dir(s)     951,808 bytes free

A:\>_
```

**WHAT'S
HAPPENING?**   You successfully renamed the **ASTRONOMY** directory to
3PLANETS. As previously stated, in versions of DOS previous to Windows 95, the
REN command would not rename subdirectories; you had to use the MOVE command. Using the MOVE command for this purpose was confusing given that, if you
keyed it in one way, you moved files, but, if you keyed it another way, you renamed
subdirectories. There are still files on the root which have to do with Astronomy.

15 Key in the following: A:\>**DIR /W** [Enter]

```
A:\>DIR /W
 Volume in drive A is DATA
```

```
Volume Serial Number is 2829-1507

Directory of A:\

ASTROLGY.FIL          BONJOUR.NEW           GALAXY.NEW
AST.BUD               ASTRO.NEW             [CLASS]
[WORK]                CalifSurf.MUS         WILDTWO.AAA
WILDTHR.AAA           [TRIP]                AST.99
DRAMA.TV              AST.TST               MARK.FIL
CASES.FIL             NEWPRSON.FIL          Y.FIL
CAROLYN.FIL           person.fil            BRIAN.FIL
ZODIAC.FIL            NEW-SUVS.XLS          FILE2.SWT
FILE4.FP             FILE2.FP               FILE3.FP
FILE2.CZG            FILE3.CZG              FILE3.SWT
[MEDIA]              PERSONAL.FIL           STEVEN.FIL
TEST.BAT            b.bat                  [GAMES]
ASTRO.TXT           BORN.TXT               Sandy and Patty.txt
TITAN.TXT           Sandy and Nicki.txt    LONGFILENAME.TXT
LONGFILENAMED.TXT   GALAXY.TXT             LONGFILENAMING.TXT
PLANETS.TXT          [3PLANETS]
                41 File(s)            15,115 bytes
                 6 Dir(s)          951,808 bytes free

A:\>_
```

WHAT'S HAPPENING?   There are some files that are related Astronomy and Astrology, but they do not have enough in common to group them when copying. It would take a lot of keying in to copy them one by one. This is a time that using the GUI is most efficient. You will first create a directory to hold the remaining Astro... files, and then move on to the desktop.

16 Key in the following: A:\>**MD ASTRO** Enter

17 Close the command line window.

18 Open My Computer and double-click Drive A. Click **View**. Click **Icons**. Click **View**. Click **Status Bar** to set it.

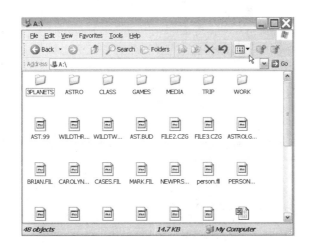

WHAT'S HAPPENING?   You are looking at the root of the A drive in the GUI.

19 Click the View button (the cursor is pointing to it in the above figure) and select **List**.

20 Size the window so you can see all of the files.

WHAT'S HAPPENING?   You are now looking at all the file names. If you can not see all the file extensions, go to the Tools menu, select Folder Options, then View, and uncheck Hide extensions for known file types.

21 Hold down the [Ctrl] key and, without releasing it, click each of the following 11 files:

AST.99	**AST.BUD**	**ASTROLOGY.FIL**	**ZODIAC.FIL**
ASTRO.NEW	**GALAXY.NEW**	**ASTRO.TXT**	**GALAXY.TXT**
PLANETS.TXT	**TITAN.TXT**	**AST.TST**	

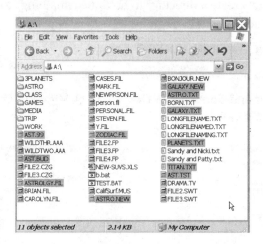

WHAT'S HAPPENING?   You have singled out the files you want to copy to the new ASTRO directory.

22 Release the [Ctrl] key. Move the mouse pointer over any one of the selected files and click the RIGHT mouse button.

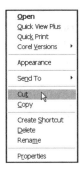

**WHAT'S
HAPPENING?**   The shortcut menu appears.

23 Click **Cut**.

24 Double-click the **ASTRO** directory.

25 Right-click in the blank area of the folder.

**WHAT'S
HAPPENING?**   You opened another shortcut menu.

26 Click **Paste**.

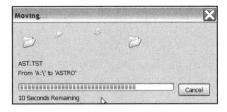

**WHAT'S
HAPPENING?**   The Moving dialog box shows you the files are being moved from
the root of A, 'A:\' , to the ASTRO directory.

27 Click in the blank area of the window to deselect the files.

28 Click the **View** button. Select **List**.

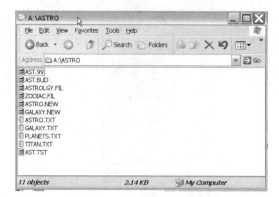

WHAT'S HAPPENING?   You have indeed moved all the files into the ASTRO directory.

29 Close all open windows

30 Open a Command Line window and make A:\ the default directory.

31 Key in the following: `A:\>`**TREE** **/F** Enter

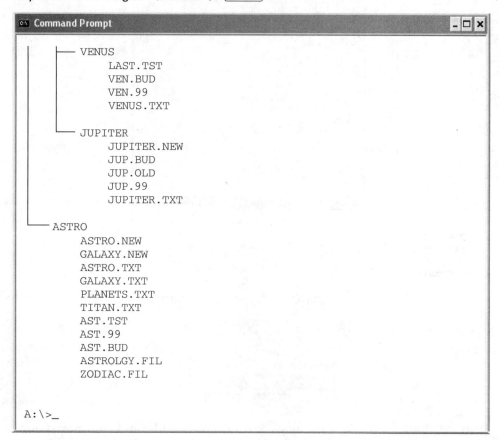

WHAT'S HAPPENING?   Most of the display will scroll off the screen, but the end of the display shows you that you have successfully organized your Astronomy files.

8.10   Checking a Disk: FAT and NTFS

CHKDSK is an operating system utility that dates back to very early versions of MS-DOS. CHKDSK is an external command stored in the C:\WINDOWS\ SYSTEM32 subdirectory. CHKDSK can be used on disks with any file system supported by Windows XP Professional: FAT12 (floppy disks), FAT16, FAT32, and NTFS. CHKDSK examines disk space and use for the NTFS and FAT file systems. A status report is provided with information specific to the file system on the drive you checked. CHKDSK also locates errors on a disk and can correct those errors when you use the proper parameters.

The information provided by the reports is information you need to know about your disks. You need to know how much room is left on the disk so that you can add a new file. You want to know if there are any bad spots on a disk, which can mean the loss of a file. Bad spots can come from a variety of sources, such as a mishandled disk or a manufacturing defect. You may want to know if the files are being stored efficiently on a disk or if you have problems with the logical structure of the disk.

If your disk is using the FAT file system, the CHKDSK command analyzes both FATs (file allocation tables) on the disk, the directory table for the root directory, the directory structure, and the integrity of the files, including the validity of any long file names. Part of the process of checking the FAT includes tracing out the chain of data for each file. This ensures that the directory entries match the location and lengths of files with the file allocation table on the specified drive. It ensures that all the directories are readable. After checking the disk, CHKDSK reports how many files are on a disk and how much space is taken. CHKDSK establishes the space left on the disk for additional files.

As you learned in Chapter 3, NTFS uses an MFT (Master File Table) to track every file on the disk rather than a FAT. The CHKDSK utility when used with an NTFS file system works in three stages. Stage 1: CHKDSK looks at each file record segment in the MFT for consistency. It also identifies which file segments and clusters are currently being used. At the end of Stage 1, the CHKDSK command then compares the information it collected against the information that NTFS keeps on the disk. CHKDSK is looking for any discrepancies or problems. Stage 2: It verifies what NTFS calls "indexes" (directories), again checking for internal consistency. It ensures that every directory and file belongs to at least one directory and that the reference to that file in the MFT is valid. It also verifies file times and dates as well as file size. This is the most time-consuming portion of CHKDSK. Stage 3: CHKDSK checks and verifies the security for each directory and file. The security information includes the file's owner, permissions granted to users and groups, and any auditing that is to occur for that file or directory.

You should regularly run the CHKDSK command for each disk to ensure that your file structures have integrity. No files should be open when you run CHKDSK on a disk. This means you need to close all programs, including programs such as screen savers. If CHKDSK cannot lock the drive—prevent access—it will tell you that it will run CHKDSK the next time you start your system.

The syntax for CHKDSK is:

Checks a disk and displays a status report.

CHKDSK [volume[[path]filename]]] [/F] [/V] [/R] [/X] [/I] [/C]
[/L[:size]]

volume	Specifies the drive letter (followed by a colon), mount point, or volume name.
filename	FAT/FAT32 only: Specifies the files to check for fragmentation.
/F	Fixes errors on the disk.
/V	On FAT/FAT32: Displays the full path and name of every file on the disk. On NTFS: Displays cleanup messages if any.
/R	Locates bad sectors and recovers readable information (implies /F).
/L:size	NTFS only: Changes the log file size to the specified number of kilobytes. If size is not specified, displays current size.
/X	Forces the volume to dismount first if necessary. All opened handles to the volume would then be invalid (implies /F).
/I	NTFS only: Performs a less vigorous check of index entries.
/C	NTFS only: Skips checking of cycles within the folder structure.

The /I or /C switch reduces the amount of time required to run
Chkdsk by skipping certain checks of the volume.

Note that there are parameters that are valid only with FAT file systems and
other parameters that are valid only with NTFS drives. In addition, on a hard disk,
you need to have administrator privileges to run CHKDSK.

8.11 Activity: Using CHKDSK on Hard and Floppy Drives

Note: The DATA disk is in Drive A. A:\> is displayed.

1   Key in the following: A:\>**C:** `Enter`

2   Key in the following: C:\>**CD WINDOWS\SYSTEM32** `Enter`

3   Key in the following: C:\WINDOWS\SYSTEM32>**DIR CHKDSK.*** `Enter`

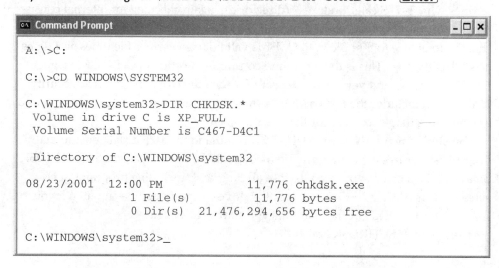

```
A:\>C:

C:\>CD WINDOWS\SYSTEM32

C:\WINDOWS\system32>DIR CHKDSK.*
 Volume in drive C is XP_FULL
 Volume Serial Number is C467-D4C1

 Directory of C:\WINDOWS\system32

08/23/2001  12:00 PM             11,776 chkdsk.exe
              1 File(s)         11,776 bytes
              0 Dir(s)  21,476,294,656 bytes free

C:\WINDOWS\system32>_
```

WHATS
WHAT'S
HAPPENING?   The DIR command told you that the program **CHKDSK.EXE** is
indeed stored as a file in the **\WINDOWS\SYSTEM32** subdirectory.

4   Key in the following: C:\WINDOWS\SYSTEM32>**CHKDSK** Enter

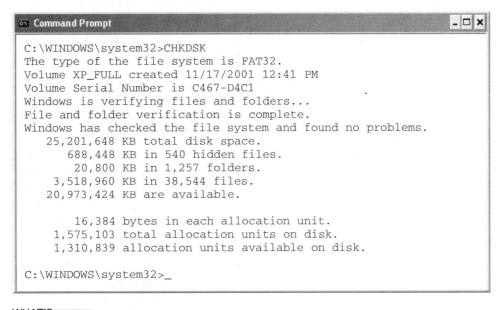

```
Command Prompt                                                  _ □ ×

C:\WINDOWS\system32>CHKDSK
The type of the file system is FAT32.
Volume XP_FULL created 11/17/2001 12:41 PM
Volume Serial Number is C467-D4C1
Windows is verifying files and folders...
File and folder verification is complete.
Windows has checked the file system and found no problems.
   25,201,648 KB total disk space.
      688,448 KB in 540 hidden files.
       20,800 KB in 1,257 folders.
    3,518,960 KB in 38,544 files.
   20,973,424 KB are available.

       16,384 bytes in each allocation unit.
    1,575,103 total allocation units on disk.
    1,310,839 allocation units available on disk.

C:\WINDOWS\system32>_
```

WHAT'S
HAPPENING?   The operating system tells you it has checked this file system
(FAT32) for errors and found none. Valuable information has been provided. You
know the total disk capacity (25,201,648 KB), the remaining space (20,973,424 KB),
the total number of allocation units (1,575,103), the number of allocation units
available for use (1,310,839), and the number of bytes in each allocation unit
(16,384). Do not worry if you do not see the same numbers displayed on your
screen. These numbers are related to how the disk was formatted, the size of the
hard disk, and how much internal memory is installed in a specific computer. What
is important is what the status report is telling you. Let us look at this example, line
by line:

25,204,648 KB total disk space	This number is the entire capacity of a specific disk.
688,488 KB in 540 hidden files	What are hidden files? The Registry files are hidden files. Many Help files are hidden files, as well as system and information files from both the operating system and software applications. The number of hidden files will vary from disk to disk.
20,800 KB in 1,257 folders	Nearly all hard disks have subdirectories. This number is for subdirectory entries only.
3,518,960 KB in 38,544 files	These are the files that are stored on the disk. They are not necessarily files that you created. User files include all program or application files you have on a disk.

20,973,424 KB are available

This line establishes how much room remains on the disk in Drive C for new data or program files in bytes. A KB is 1,024 bytes. A byte is one character. It can be the letter "b," the letter "c," the number "3," or the punctuation mark "?," for example. To give you a rough idea of what a byte means, a page of a printed novel contains about 3,000 bytes. Thus, a disk with a total capacity of 360,000 bytes could hold or store a maximum of about 120 pages of a novel. A 20-MB hard disk (1 megabyte means 1,000,000 bytes) would hold approximately 20,000,000 bytes or 6,667 pages of text; if the average novel has about 400 pages, you could store about 16½ novels. A 2-GB hard drive could hold about 1,800 books! This approximation is not entirely accurate because it does not take into account that often information is stored in such a way as to be compressed. However, it does give you an idea of the disk capacity in "human terms." As you work with computers, you become accustomed to thinking in bytes.

16,384 bytes in each allocation unit

As discussed earlier, the smallest unit that the OS actually reads is a cluster. A cluster is made up of sectors. A cluster is also referred to as an allocation unit. The number of sectors that make up a cluster (allocation unit) vary depending on the type of disk.

1,575,103 total allocation units on disk

This indicates the total number of clusters available.

1,310,839 allocation units available on disk

This line tells you how much room is available on the disk by cluster.

Sometimes you will see a line reporting how many bad sectors a disk may have. Having bad sectors is not uncommon on hard disks. If you had bad sectors, the line might read "65,536 bytes in bad sectors." The number would, of course, vary depending on the disk that is checked. On a 20-GB hard disk, for instance, 65,536 bytes in bad sectors is not that significant. However, if you had a smaller hard disk, the number would be significant and you might want to determine if your hard disk needs to be replaced. The next step cannot be done unless you have a disk that is formatted with NTFS. If you do not, simply read the steps.

5   Key in the following: C:\WINDOWS\SYSTEM32>**CD ** Enter

6   Key in the following: C:\>**CHKDSK E:** Enter

```
┌──────────────────────────────────────────────────────────────┐
│ ▣ Command Prompt                                      _ □ ✕    │
├──────────────────────────────────────────────────────────────┤
│ C:\>CHKDSK E:                                                  │
│ The type of the file system is NTFS.                           │
│ Volume label is NTFS.                                          │
│                                                                │
│ WARNING!  F parameter not specified.                           │
│ Running CHKDSK in read-only mode.                              │
│                                                                │
│ CHKDSK is verifying files (stage 1 of 3)...                    │
│ File verification completed.                                   │
│ CHKDSK is verifying indexes (stage 2 of 3)...                  │
│ Index verification completed.                                  │
│ CHKDSK is verifying security descriptors (stage 3 of 3)...     │
│ Security descriptor verification completed.                    │
│                                                                │
│    4795370 KB total disk space.                                │
│     105440 KB in 813 files.                                    │
│        256 KB in 64 indexes.                                   │
│          0 KB in bad sectors.                                  │
│      27826 KB in use by the system.                            │
│      26032 KB occupied by the log file.                        │
│    4661848 KB available on disk.                               │
│                                                                │
│       4096 bytes in each allocation unit.                      │
│    1198842 total allocation units on disk.                     │
│    1165462 allocation units available on disk.                 │
│                                                                │
│ C:\>_                                                          │
│                                                                │
└──────────────────────────────────────────────────────────────┘
```

WHAT'S HAPPENING?   In order to repair a disk, you need to include a parameter, and CHKDSK informs you of that fact. Then each stage is executed. Then, again, you see the statistical report.

4795370 KB total disk space	This number is the entire capacity of a specific disk.
105440 KB in 813 files	These are the files that are stored on the disk. They are not necessarily files that you created. User files include all program or application files you have on a disk.
256 KB in 64 indexes	This refers to indexes, which are like subdirectories.
0 KB in bad sectors	The report tells you that you have no bad sectors.
27826 KB in use by the system	This is information being used by the system.
26032 KB occupied by the log file	The log file is a transaction log of disk activities. Windows XP Professional uses this file so it can recover files if you have disk problems. It can even repair itself if necessary.
4661848 KB available on disk	This line establishes how much room remains on the disk.

4096 bytes in each allocation unit   As discussed earlier, the smallest unit that the OS actually reads is a cluster. A cluster is made up of sectors. A cluster is also referred to as an "allocation unit."

1198842 total allocation units on disk available.   This indicates the total number of clusters

1165462 allocation units available on disk   This line tells you how much room is available on the disk by cluster.

7   Key in the following: C:\>**A:** Enter

```
C:\>A:

A:\>_
```

WHAT'S HAPPENING?   You have changed the default drive to the A drive. The DATA disk is in the A drive.

8   Key in the following: A:\>**CHKDSK** Enter

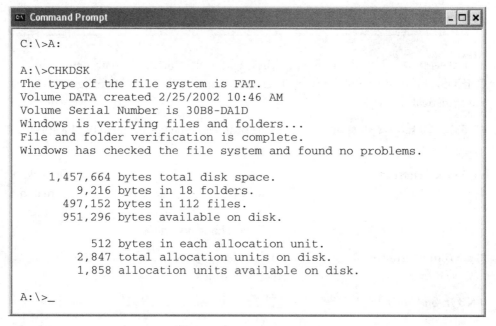

```
C:\>A:

A:\>CHKDSK
The type of the file system is FAT.
Volume DATA created 2/25/2002 10:46 AM
Volume Serial Number is 30B8-DA1D
Windows is verifying files and folders...
File and folder verification is complete.
Windows has checked the file system and found no problems.

    1,457,664 bytes total disk space.
        9,216 bytes in 18 folders.
      497,152 bytes in 112 files.
      951,296 bytes available on disk.

          512 bytes in each allocation unit.
        2,847 total allocation units on disk.
        1,858 allocation units available on disk.

A:\>_
```

WHAT'S HAPPENING?   This display looks similar to the screen displayed when you used CHKDSK on the FAT hard drive. The numbers are, of course, very different. You have 1,457,664 bytes total disk space because this is a 1.44-MB disk. The files and bytes available will vary based on what is on the DATA disk. If you placed another disk in Drive A, you would get different information about files and free bytes remaining on that particular disk.

8.12 The Verbose Parameter with the CHKDSK Command

The CHKDSK command has a very useful parameter, /V. Using /V on a FAT drive is known as running in verbose mode. This parameter, in conjunction with the CHKDSK command, not only gives the usual status report, but also lists every file on the disk including hidden files. On an NTFS drive, it displays clean-up messages, if any.

An important thing to remember about parameters is that they are associated with specific commands and perform specific tasks for those commands. The same parameter does not do the same thing with other commands. For instance, if you use the parameter /V with the FORMAT command, it means put a volume label on the disk. However, when you use /V with the CHKDSK command, it displays all the files on the disk if it is FAT and displays clean-up messages if it is NTFS.

8.13 Activity: Using the /V Parameter and Using DIR Parameters

Note 1: The DATA disk is in Drive A. A:\> is displayed.

Note 2: When you press **Enter** in step 1, the screen display will scroll by too fast to see. Even hitting the **Pause** key immediately will not stop the screen.

Note 3: Your files may appear in a different order.

Note 4: To facilitate mouse usage, click on the Command Line icon, go to Properties, and disable QuickEdit mode.

1 Key in the following: A:\>**CHKDSK /V** **Enter**

```
\CLASS\MER.PAR
\CLASS\JUP.ABC
\CLASS\MER.ABC
\CLASS\AST.ABC
99 percent completed.
\CLASS\VEN.ABC
\CLASS\AST.PAR
\CLASS\VEN.PAR
\CLASS\JUP.FIL
\CLASS\MER.FIL
\CLASS\JUP.BUD
\CLASS\MER.BUD
\CLASS\AST.BUD
\CLASS\VEN.BUD
100 percent completed.
File and folder verification is complete.
Windows has checked the file system and found no problems.

   1,457,664 bytes total disk space.
       9,216 bytes in 18 folders.
     497,152 bytes in 112 files.
     951,296 bytes available on disk.

         512 bytes in each allocation unit.
       2,847 total allocation units on disk.
       1,858 allocation units available on disk.


A:\>_
```

WHAT'S
HAPPENING?   The output from the command you entered scrolled by so quickly that you were unable to see that all the files on the disk were listed. You can see only the last few files and the statistical and memory information at the end of the display. In order to view the information returned by this command, you are going to use an operating system feature that will be covered in the next chapter—redirection. You have, however, used this feature in previous chapters to direct the Homework Assignments to the printer. You will redirect the output of the CHKDSK /V command to a file instead of the screen, and then use the command line editor to see it.

2   Key in the following: A:\>**CHKDSK /V > CHKDSK.TXT** Enter

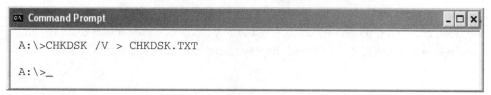

```
A:\>CHKDSK /V > CHKDSK.TXT

A:\>_
```

WHAT'S
HAPPENING?   Nothing is displayed on the screen. You have redirected the display to the file **CHKDSK.TXT** on the default drive.

3   Key in the following: A:\>**EDIT CHKDSK.TXT** Enter

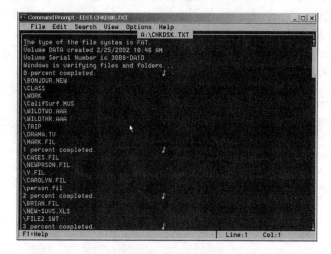

WHAT'S
HAPPENING?   You can see the output of the CHKDSK /V command that you have redirected to the **CHKDSK.TXT** file.

4   Move the scroll bar at the right edge of the screen approximately halfway down the screen, as shown in the following screen.

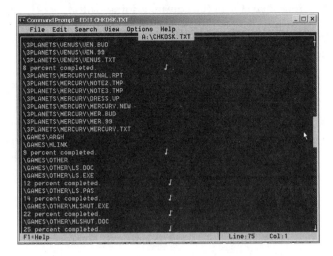

HAPPENING? The subdirectory names are displayed, along with all the files each subdirectory contains. You can use this command on any FAT drive to see the files and directories. You could, for instance, key in **CHKDSK C: /V**. However, since the display on a hard disk is typically large, it is not as useful as you would like. The DIR command has the /S parameter, which allows you to look at all your subdirectories on any disk. Furthermore, the DIR command has the /P parameter to pause the display, and CHKDSK does not.

5 Scroll down to the bottom of the file.

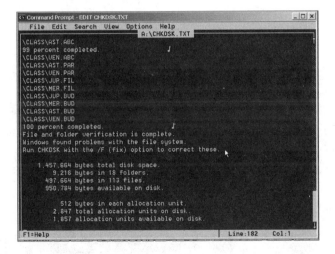

WHAT'S **HAPPENING?** Notice that Windows found errors on this disk. Your display may or may not report errors.

6 On the Edit menu bar, click **File**. Click **Exit**.

WHATS
■■■HAPPENING?   You have closed the command line editor.

7   Key in the following: A:\>**DIR /S** Enter

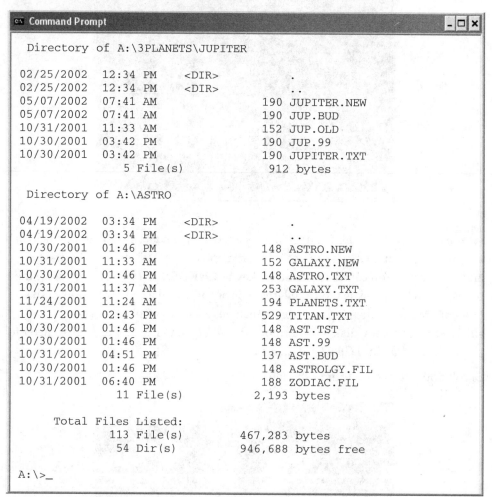

```
Command Prompt                                                    _ □ ×

  Directory of A:\3PLANETS\JUPITER

02/25/2002   12:34 PM    <DIR>           .
02/25/2002   12:34 PM    <DIR>           ..
05/07/2002   07:41 AM              190 JUPITER.NEW
05/07/2002   07:41 AM              190 JUP.BUD
10/31/2001   11:33 AM              152 JUP.OLD
10/30/2001   03:42 PM              190 JUP.99
10/30/2001   03:42 PM              190 JUPITER.TXT
              5 File(s)            912 bytes

  Directory of A:\ASTRO

04/19/2002   03:34 PM    <DIR>           .
04/19/2002   03:34 PM    <DIR>           ..
10/30/2001   01:46 PM              148 ASTRO.NEW
10/31/2001   11:33 AM              152 GALAXY.NEW
10/30/2001   01:46 PM              148 ASTRO.TXT
10/31/2001   11:37 AM              253 GALAXY.TXT
11/24/2001   11:24 AM              194 PLANETS.TXT
10/31/2001   02:43 PM              529 TITAN.TXT
10/30/2001   01:46 PM              148 AST.TST
10/30/2001   01:46 PM              148 AST.99
10/31/2001   04:51 PM              137 AST.BUD
10/30/2001   01:46 PM              148 ASTROLGY.FIL
10/31/2001   06:40 PM              188 ZODIAC.FIL
             11 File(s)          2,193 bytes


    Total Files Listed:
             113 File(s)        467,283 bytes
              54 Dir(s)         946,688 bytes free

A:\>_
```

WHATS ■■■■
■■■HAPPENING?   (This graphic represents the end portion of the scrolling display.)
This parameter allows you to view the files in all your directories. If you added the
/P parameter, you would pause the display. You can also view specific files in all
subdirectories.

8   Key in the following: A:\>**DIR *.NEW /S** Enter

```
Command Prompt                                                    _ □ ×

A:\>DIR *.NEW /S
 Volume in drive A is DATA
 Volume Serial Number is 30B8-DA1D

 Directory of A:\

10/30/2001   02:47 PM               86 BONJOUR.NEW
              1 File(s)             86 bytes

 Directory of A:\3PLANETS\MERCURY

10/31/2001   01:08 PM              406 MERCURY.NEW
              1 File(s)            406 bytes
```

```
    Directory of A:\3PLANETS\JUPITER

05/07/2002  07:41 AM                190 JUPITER.NEW
               1 File(s)            190 bytes

    Directory of A:\ASTRO

10/30/2001  01:46 PM                148 ASTRO.NEW
10/31/2001  11:33 AM                152 GALAXY.NEW
               2 File(s)            300 bytes

      Total Files Listed:
               5 File(s)            982 bytes
               0 Dir(s)         946,688 bytes free

A:\>_
```

WHAT'S
HAPPENING?   This command allows you to be even more specific and locate a file anywhere on the disk by searching all the subdirectories. Thus, DIR /S supplants CHKDSK /V in its ability to show every file on the disk in every subdirectory.

The CHKDSK /V command can also show any hidden files, but the parameters in the DIR command are better for that purpose. Using the /A parameter (attribute) with the attribute you wish, you can determine what you will see. You can use D (directories), R (read-only files), H (hidden files), S (system files), and A (files ready to archive). If you use the - sign before an attribute, you can select all the files except those that have that attribute.

9   Key in the following: A:\>**DIR /AD** Enter

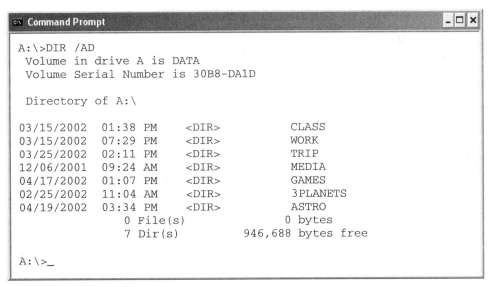

```
 ◼ Command Prompt                                                    _ □ ✕

A:\>DIR /AD
 Volume in drive A is DATA
 Volume Serial Number is 30B8-DA1D

 Directory of A:\

03/15/2002  01:38 PM    <DIR>          CLASS
03/15/2002  07:29 PM    <DIR>          WORK
03/25/2002  02:11 PM    <DIR>          TRIP
12/06/2001  09:24 AM    <DIR>          MEDIA
04/17/2002  01:07 PM    <DIR>          GAMES
02/25/2002  11:04 AM    <DIR>          3PLANETS
04/19/2002  03:34 PM    <DIR>          ASTRO
               0 File(s)            0 bytes
               7 Dir(s)        946,688 bytes free

A:\>_
```

WHAT'S
HAPPENING?   You selected the /A parameter and used the D attribute for directories to control the output of the DIR command. Remember, the order in which your directories and files are displayed may vary.

8.14 Using CHKDSK to Repair Disk Problems

On a FAT disk, the file allocation table (FAT) and the directory work in conjunction. Every file has an entry in the directory table. The file entry in the directory table points to the starting cluster in the FAT. If the file is longer than one cluster, which it usually is, the file allocation table has a pointer that leads it to the next cluster, then the next cluster, and so on. These pointers *chain* all the data together in a file. If the chain is broken (i.e., there is a lost pointer), the disk ends up with lost clusters, which means that these clusters are marked as used in the FAT and not available for new data. Look at Figure 8.6; clusters 3, 4, and 6 are a chain, but the FAT does not know to which file this chain belongs. There is no entry in the root directory. Hence, these are *lost clusters*.

Root Directory Table

File Name	File Extension	Date	Time	Other Info	Starting Cluster Number
MY	FIL	5-7-99	11:23a		1
HIS	DOC	5-7-99	11:50a		5
					3

File Allocation Table

Cluster Number	Status
1	in use
2	in use
3	4
4	6
5	in use
6	end

Clusters 3, 4, and 6 have data, are linked together,
but have no file entry in the directory table.

Figure 8.6—Lost Clusters

Since these lost clusters belong to no specific file, they cannot be retrieved. The data becomes useless, yet the operating system cannot write other data to these lost clusters. Thus, you lose space on the disk. This phenomenon occurs for a variety of reasons, the most common being a user who does not exit a program properly. If you simply turn off the computer, you are interrupting the shut-down process of the application program. Often, when you interrupt this process, the data will not be properly written to the disk. Other times power failures or power surges are the cause. Not exiting an application properly can be damaging to the operating system and can leave lost clusters on the hard disk.

On an NTFS disk, CHKDSK, in Stage 2, looks for orphaned files. An orphaned file is one that has an entry in the MFT but is not listed in any directory. It is similar to a lost cluster in the FAT file system.

If one of these events happens, you may not be able to boot back into Windows. You would then boot with your Windows boot disks and use your ASR (Automated System Recovery Disk) to try to repair the damage or use System Restore. When Windows XP Professional is running, you cannot run CHKDSK with the /F parameter and attempt to repair disk errors. When you execute the CHKDSK /F command, you will get a message at the beginning of the CHKDSK display similar to this:

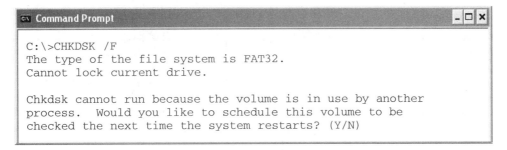

```
C:\>CHKDSK /F
The type of the file system is FAT32.
Cannot lock current drive.

Chkdsk cannot run because the volume is in use by another
process.  Would you like to schedule this volume to be
checked the next time the system restarts? (Y/N)
```

The message "Cannot lock the current drive" means the current drive is the default drive. However, even switching to another drive before running the command will not work.

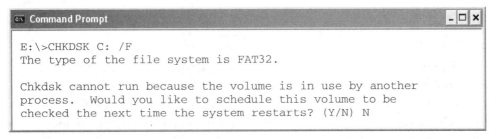

```
E:\>CHKDSK C: /F
The type of the file system is FAT32.

Chkdsk cannot run because the volume is in use by another
process.  Would you like to schedule this volume to be
checked the next time the system restarts? (Y/N) N
```

"Cannot lock the current drive" does not appear, but the rest of the message is the same. The message means that you can schedule CHKDSK with the /F parameter to run when your computer starts up the next time. The utility will run *before* most of the system loads, eliminating the problem of other processes running. You can, however, use the /F and /R parameters with CHKDSK on a floppy disk. If you have multiple hard drives, you can run CHKDSK on a hard drive that is not the default drive, and that is not currently in use. If you did use it on an active partition, it may report erroneous error messages since it cannot lock the drive. The /F is used to repair logical errors, and the /R is used to locate bad sectors and recover readable information. Using /R implies /F.

Be careful when running this utility program. First, you should always regularly back up your data files in case the "fix" behaves improperly. You could lose data. Actually, you should be backing up your hard disk on a regular basis. Even after backing up, it may be advisable to "schedule" CHKDSK /F to run when the system next boots. It is faster this way, as the system is not loaded. Secondly, if you use /F on a large disk or on a disk with a very large number of files (in the millions), CHKDSK can take a very, very long time (even days) to complete. During this time, you will not have access to the drive you are repairing since CHKDSK does not give up control of the disk until it is finished executing. If the drive (system volume) is being checked during the startup process, your computer will not be available to you until the CHKDSK process is complete.

Another type of error that occurs infrequently is cross-linked files. Cross-linked files usually occur on FAT disks. *Cross-linked files* are two files that claim the same cluster in the FAT.

Root Directory Table

File Name	File Extension	Date	Time	Other Info	Starting Cluster Number
MY	FIL	4-15-94	11:23		1
HIS	FIL	4-15-94	11:23		3

File Allocation Table

Cluster Number	Status
1	MY.FIL
2	MY.FIL
3	HIS.FIL
4	MY.FIL HIS.FIL
5	HIS FIL
6	MY.FIL

Figure 8.7—Cross-linked Files

In Figure 8.7, MY.FIL thinks it owns clusters 1, 2, 4, and 6. HIS.FIL thinks it owns clusters 3, 4, and 5. Thus, both MY.FIL and HIS.FIL think that cluster 4 is part of their chain. If you edit MY.FIL, the file will contain its own data as well as some part of HIS.FIL. Even worse, if you delete MY.FIL, you will be deleting part of the HIS.FIL data. Usually, to recover data from cross-linked files, you copy each file to a new location so they are no longer cross-linked. One of the files is usually bad, but at least you have one file that is good.

8.15 Activity: Using CHKDSK to Repair Disk Problems

Note: The DATA disk is in Drive A. A:\> is displayed.

1   Key in the following: A:>**CHKDSK** **/R** [Enter]

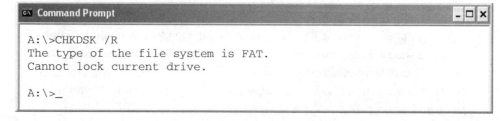

```
A:\>CHKDSK /R
The type of the file system is FAT.
Cannot lock current drive.

A:\>_
```

WHAT'S HAPPENING?   The A drive is the default drive, so you received the message "Cannot lock current drive." Windows XP Professional needs total access to the disk.

2   Key in the following: A:\>**CD** **/D** **C:** [Enter]

3   Key in the following: C:\>**CHKDSK** **A:** **/R** [Enter]

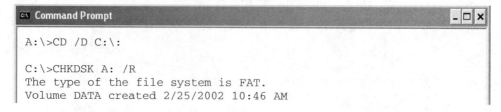

```
A:\>CD /D C:\:

C:\>CHKDSK A: /R
The type of the file system is FAT.
Volume DATA created 2/25/2002 10:46 AM
```

```
Volume Serial Number is 30B8-DA1D
Windows is verifying files and folders...
File and folder verification is complete.
Windows is verifying free space...
Free space verification is complete.
Windows has checked the file system and found no problems.

   1,457,664 bytes total disk space.
       9,216 bytes in 18 folders.
     501,760 bytes in 113 files.
     946,688 bytes available on disk.

         512 bytes in each allocation unit.
       2,847 total allocation units on disk.
       1,849 allocation units available on disk.

C:\>_
```

WHAT'S
HAPPENING?   You needed to change drives so that CHKDSK could lock Drive A.
The status reports that there is "no problem" with this drive. Again, if you do not
have an NTFS drive (or one with errors), you cannot do the next steps. However,
read the steps.

4   Key in the following: C:\>**CHKDSK E:** Enter

```
━━ Command Prompt                                              _ □ x

C:\>CHKDSK E:
The type of the file system is NTFS.
Volume label is NTFS.

WARNING!  F parameter not specified.
Running CHKDSK in read-only mode.

CHKDSK is verifying files (stage 1 of 3)...
File verification completed.
CHKDSK is verifying indexes (stage 2 of 3)...
Index verification completed.
CHKDSK is verifying security descriptors (stage 3 of 3)...
Security descriptor verification completed.

   4795370 KB total disk space.
    105428 KB in 813 files.
       256 KB in 64 indexes.
         0 KB in bad sectors.
     27826 KB in use by the system.
     26032 KB occupied by the log file.
   4661860 KB available on disk.

      4096 bytes in each allocation unit.
   1198842 total allocation units on disk.
   1165465 allocation units available on disk.

C:\>_
```

WHAT'S
HAPPENING?   If Windows had found errors on this disk, it would have recommended running CHKDSK with the /F parameter. Windows would then make the
necessary corrections to the file system. If you had errors on a FAT disk, Windows
XP Professional, would ask if you wanted to convert the lost files to fragments. You
would see the following error message:

```
Convert lost chains to files (Y/N?)
```

If you answered yes, then Windows would place those file fragments in files labeled **FILE0000.CHK**, **FILE0001.CHK**, **FILE0002.CHK**, and so on, depending on how many chains were found. If you opened the file with a program like Notepad, you would likely see that the file was a garbage file, as shown in Figure 8.8.

Figure 8.8—A Lost Cluster Opened in Notepad

Normally those files are useless and can be safely deleted, as well as any **FOUND** directories.

8.16 Checking Disks with System Tools

Windows XP Professional provides another way to check a disk. You may use the GUI and use System Tools. The three system tools that are provided in the GUI are Error-checking (CHKDSK), Backup, and Defragmentation.

8.17 Activity: Checking Disks with System Tools

Note: The DATA disk is in the A drive.

1   Key in the following: C:\>**EXIT** Enter

WHATS HAPPENING?   You have terminated the command line session and returned to the Windows XP Professional "GUI" screen. Your screen display may be different depending on how Windows XP was installed.

2   Open **My Computer** (either from the Start menu, or the Desktop Icon, depending on your system configuration.)

3   Right-click on the A drive icon.

WHATS HAPPENING?   You have opened the shortcut menu for the A drive.

4   Click **Properties**. Click the **Tools** tab.

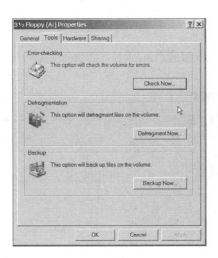

WHAT'S
HAPPENING?   You have displayed the Tools dialog box, showing you three options. You can check the disk for errors, back it up, or defragment it. Defragmenting will eliminate noncontiguous files from a hard disk. In Windows 2000 and Windows XP, floppy disks can not be defragmented. Error-checking will perform in a similar manner to CHKDSK.

5   Click the **Check Now** button.

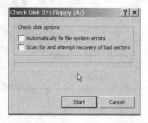

WHAT'S
HAPPENING?   You are give two options—to fix the errors if any are found and to try and fix any bad sectors discovered during the check. This second option is very time-consuming. In general, if there are bad sectors on a floppy disk, it is best to copy the files to another disk and throw the disk with bad sectors away. Floppy disks are very inexpensive, and data is very valuable.

6   Click **Automatically fix file system errors**.

7   Click **Start**.

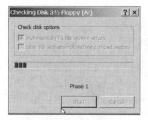

WHAT'S
HAPPENING?   The disk checking begins. Phase 1 is checking for errors. Scanning for and attempting the recovery of bad sectors is Phase 2, which was not requested. The completion dialog box appears when the check is complete.

No errors were found, and the check is complete. These options are available on the property sheet for the hard drive as well, but if you attempt to check the hard drive, you will receive the following message:

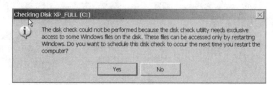

Just as at the command line, the checks cannot be performed while other processes are active. To check the hard drive, you would have to click **Yes** and shut down and restart your computer.

8   Close all open windows.

8.18 Contiguous and Noncontiguous Files

"Contiguous" means being in contact with or touching. What does this have to do with files? As far as the operating system is concerned, data is a string of bytes that it keeps track of by grouping the data into a file. In order to manage storing and retrieving files, a disk is divided into numbered blocks called "sectors." Sectors are then grouped into clusters. A cluster is the smallest unit that the operating system deals with, and it is always a set of contiguous sectors. Clusters on a 1.44-MB floppy disk consist of one 512-byte sector. The number of sectors that make up a cluster on a hard disk varies depending on the size of the hard disk and the FAT being used. On a 2-GB hard disk, a sector consists of 32,768 bytes. Most often, a data file will take up more space on a disk than one cluster. Thus, the operating system has to keep track of the location of all the parts of the file that are on the disk. It does so by means of the directory and the FAT. If you are using NTFS, then it tracks the files by means of the MFT.

The original release of Windows 95 used the standard FAT—a 16-bit version. A 32-bit FAT was introduced with release B of Windows 95. From that version through Millennium, you have the choice of using the standard FAT or the 32-bit version, referred to as FAT32. Beginning with Windows 2000, NTFS (New Technology File System) is supported, which was previously supported only by Windows NT. This file system allows local security. With NTFS, access to areas of the partition can be blocked to some users, and allowed for others. This is useful in an environment where more than one user has sensitive files stored on the same computer. It also can block access to the operating system files. The decision on which file system to use is made when the disk volume is originally partitioned. All floppy drives are FAT12.

The FAT keeps a record of the cluster numbers each file occupies. As the operating system begins to write files on a new disk, it makes an entry in the disk's directory for that file and updates the FAT with the cluster numbers used to store that file. Data is written to the disk based on the next empty cluster. Files being written to a disk are written in adjacent clusters. The operating system wants all the pieces of file information to be next to each other and tries to write to adjacent clusters whenever possible. It is easier to retrieve or store information when it is together. When this occurs, the file is considered contiguous. For example, if you began writing a letter to your United States senator, it would be stored on your disk in the manner shown in Figure 8.9.

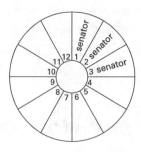

Figure 8.9—One File in Clusters

The clusters with nothing in them are simply empty spaces on the disk. If you now decide to write a letter to your mother, this new file is written to the next group of adjacent clusters, which would begin with cluster 4 as shown in Figure 8.10.

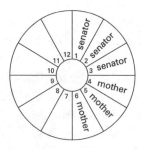

Figure 8.10—Contiguous Files in Clusters

These two files, SENATOR and MOTHER, are contiguous. Each part of each file follows on the disk. Now you decide to add a comment to your senator letter, making the SENATOR file bigger. When the operating system goes to write the file to the disk, the FAT looks for the next empty clusters, which are clusters 7 and 8. The FAT would appear as shown in Figure 8.11.

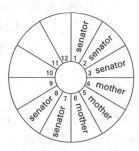

Figure 8.11—Noncontiguous Files in Clusters

The parts of the file named SENATOR are separated, making this file noncontiguous, or fragmented. The process becomes more complicated as you add and delete files. For example, if you delete the file SENATOR, the FAT marks clusters 1, 2, 3, 7, and 8 as available even though the data actually remains on the disk. You then decide to develop a PHONE file, as shown in Figure 8.12.

Figure 8.12—Adding a File

Next, you decide to write a letter to your friend Joe, to write a letter to your friend Mary, to add to the PHONE file, and to add to the letter to your mother. The disk would look like Figure 8.13.

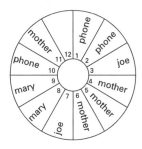

Figure 8.13—Adding More Files

The parts of these files are broken up and are no longer stored in adjacent clusters. They are now known as noncontiguous or *fragmented files*. If the disk is comprised of noncontiguous files, it can be called a fragmented disk. It will take longer to read noncontiguous files because the read/write heads must move around the disk to find all the parts of a file. You can see if files are contiguous or noncontiguous by using a parameter with the CHKDSK command, but only on FAT volumes.

8.19 Activity: Using CHKDSK to See If Files Are Contiguous

Note: The DATA disk is in Drive A. You are shelled out to the Command Line.
A:\> is displayed.

1   Key in the following: A:\>**CHKDSK BORN.TXT** [Enter]

```
🖳 Command Prompt                                           _ □ ✗

A:\>CHKDSK BORN.TXT
The type of the file system is FAT.
Volume DATA created 2/25/2002 10:46 AM
Volume Serial Number is 30B8-DA1D
Windows is verifying files and folders...
File and folder verification is complete.
Windows has checked the file system and found no problems.

    1,457,664 bytes total disk space.
        9,216 bytes in 18 folders.
      501,760 bytes in 113 files.
```

```
            946,688 bytes available on disk.

                512 bytes in each allocation unit.
              2,847 total allocation units on disk.
              1,849 allocation units available on disk.
All specified files are contiguous.

A:\>_
```

WHAT'S HAPPENING?   The screen display supplies all the statistical information about the DATA disk and computer memory. In addition, the last line states, "All specified file(s) are contiguous." By adding the parameter of the file name **BORN.TXT** after the CHKDSK command, you asked not only to check the disk but also to look at the file **BORN.TXT** to see if all the parts of this file are next to one another on the DATA disk. Are they contiguous? The message indicates that they are.

2   Key in the following: A:\>**CHKDSK   *.TXT** Enter

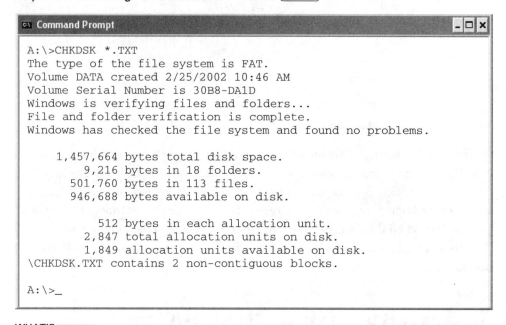

```
A:\>CHKDSK *.TXT
The type of the file system is FAT.
Volume DATA created 2/25/2002 10:46 AM
Volume Serial Number is 30B8-DA1D
Windows is verifying files and folders...
File and folder verification is complete.
Windows has checked the file system and found no problems.

      1,457,664 bytes total disk space.
          9,216 bytes in 18 folders.
        501,760 bytes in 113 files.
        946,688 bytes available on disk.

            512 bytes in each allocation unit.
          2,847 total allocation units on disk.
          1,849 allocation units available on disk.
\CHKDSK.TXT contains 2 non-contiguous blocks.

A:\>_
```

WHAT'S HAPPENING?   CHKDSK not only gave you the usual statistical information but also checked to see if all the files in the root directory that have **.TXT** as an extension are contiguous. By using wildcards, you can check a group of files with a common denominator. In this case, the common denominator is the file extension **.TXT**. The message on the screen verifies that one file, **CHKDSK.TXT** from all the files with the extension **.TXT**, has two noncontiguous blocks.

3   Key in the following: A:\>**CHKDSK   *.*** Enter

```
A:\>CHKDSK *.*
The type of the file system is FAT.
Volume DATA created 2/25/2002 10:46 AM
Volume Serial Number is 30B8-DA1D
Windows is verifying files and folders...
File and folder verification is complete.
Windows has checked the file system and found no problems.
```

```
     1,457,664 bytes total disk space.
         9,216 bytes in 18 folders.
       501,760 bytes in 113 files.
       946,688 bytes available on disk.

           512 bytes in each allocation unit.
         2,847 total allocation units on disk.
         1,849 allocation units available on disk.
\CHKDSK.TXT contains 2 non-contiguous blocks.

A:\> _
```

WHAT'S
HAPPENING? The screen display shows only the same noncontiguous file. If you had no fragmented files, you would have received the message, "All specified files are contiguous." The CHKDSK command, followed by star dot star (***.***), checked every file in the root directory on the DATA disk to see if all the files were contiguous. The ***.*** represents all files in the root directory.

4 Key in the following: A:\>**CHKDSK CLASS*.*** Enter

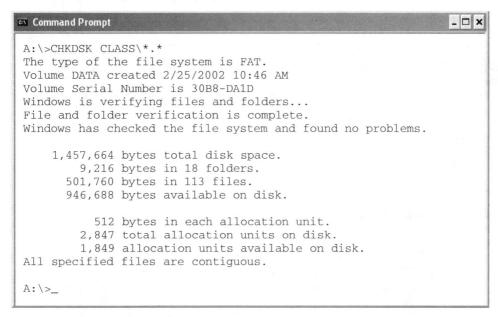

```
A:\>CHKDSK CLASS\*.*
The type of the file system is FAT.
Volume DATA created 2/25/2002 10:46 AM
Volume Serial Number is 30B8-DA1D
Windows is verifying files and folders...
File and folder verification is complete.
Windows has checked the file system and found no problems.

     1,457,664 bytes total disk space.
         9,216 bytes in 18 folders.
       501,760 bytes in 113 files.
       946,688 bytes available on disk.

           512 bytes in each allocation unit.
         2,847 total allocation units on disk.
         1,849 allocation units available on disk.
All specified files are contiguous.

A:\>_
```

WHAT'S
HAPPENING? You are checking to see if all the files in the subdirectory **CLASS** are contiguous. In this case, they are.

What difference does it make if files are contiguous or not? Only to the extent that noncontiguous files or a fragmented disk can slow performance. In other words, if a file is contiguous, all of its parts can be found quickly, minimizing the amount of time the heads need to read and write to the disk. If files are noncontiguous, the operating system has to look for all the parts of the file, causing the read/write heads to fly about the disk. The longer the disk is used, the more fragmented it becomes, slowing its performance. However, performance on a floppy disk is usually not that important because most of the time you are working on the hard disk.

You do notice a big decline in performance on a hard disk system. The solution most hard disk users opt for is to use the disk defragmenter program. This program is listed as Disk Defragmenter on the Start menu, under Programs, under Accessories, under System Tools. This program, referred to generically as a *disk optimization* program, rearranges the storage on the hard disk so that each file is stored in sequentially numbered clusters. Before using disk optimization, the disk must be free of errors.

8.20   Defragmenting Your Hard Disk

To make your programs run faster and better, you need to perform disk maintenance. One way to maintain your disk is to run the Defragmenter program from the Tools menu on the disks drive property sheet. The other is to run it from the Start Menu, choose All Programs, choose Accessories, choose System Tools, and choose Disk Defragmenter. Either way, it will rearrange files and unused space on your hard disk. Although the Windows operating system allows you to run Disk Defragmenter without closing all your programs, it is better, faster, and safer to close any open programs you have running, including any screen savers or virus-protection programs. As stated previously, it is no longer possible to defragment your floppy disk.

8.21   Activity: Using Disk Defragmenter

Note: Be sure to check with your lab administrator before completing the following hard disk defragmenting exercise.

1   Click **Start**.

2   Point to **All Programs**.

3   Point to **Accessories**.

4   Point to **System Tools**.

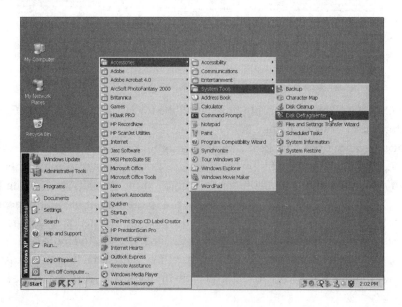

WHAT'S
HAPPENING?   You opened the System Tools menu. You will choose Disk
Defragmenter.

5   Click **Disk Defragmenter**.

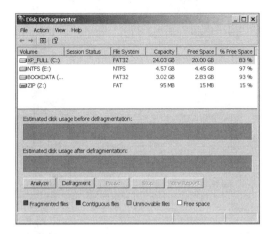

WHAT'S
HAPPENING?   Although this computer has an A drive, it is not listed in the Disk
Defragmenter options box. Attempting to defragment the A drive from its property
sheet menu would give the following results:

6   Highlight your hard drive C and click **Analyze**.

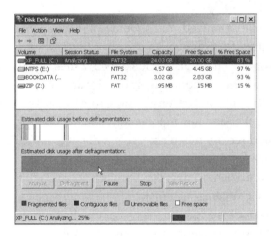

WHAT'S
HAPPENING?   You will first see a graphical display of your disk, and then a
dialog box where you can choose to defragment or to view the analysis report.

7   Click **View Report**.

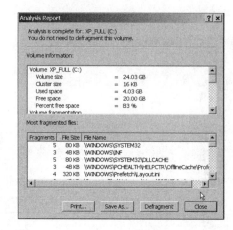

WHAT'S
HAPPENING?   You can see the information on your hard drive. You can scroll up and down in the Volume information window and the Most fragmented files window, or you can click the Save As button and save the report for printing or examination at a later time. You will also get a recommendation to defragment or not to defragment. It is good practice to defragment your hard drive regularly, as it improves the performance of your system.

7   Click **Close**.

8   Close all open windows.

Chapter Summary

1. All disks should be organized. You should not place all your programs and data in the root directory.
2. The root directory of a hard disk holds only 512 files if you are using FAT16.
3. Many users inefficiently organize their disk by application programs. This often leads to a repetition of subdirectory names, forcing users to remember where they placed their files and key in long path names. The operating system must search every subdirectory when accessing a file. It is difficult to add and delete application programs and data files in this scheme.
4. One way to organize a hard disk is by project.
5. Some guidelines to organizing a disk:
   a. The root directory is a map to the rest of the disk.
   b. Plan the organization before installing software.
   c. Develop and use a naming convention for files and directories.
   d. Create as many directories and subdirectores as you need before copying files into them.
   e. Remember that it is safe to work with data files but dangerous to move or rename program files.
   f. Subdirectories should be shallow and wide.
   g. Do not place data files in program subdirectories.
   h. It is better to have small subdirectories with only a few files.
   i. Keep subdirectory names short and descriptive.
   j. Create a separate subdirectory for batch files and utility programs.
   k. Learn how the install programs work before you install software.

     l. Learn how each application program works.

     m. Analyze the way you work.

6. If a disk is unorganized, you can organize it by planning it, creating the new organizational scheme and any necessary subdirectories, copying files to the new subdirectories, and deleting those files from the old subdirectories.

7. The XCOPY command allows you to copy files and the subdirectories beneath them. Among the options available with XCOPY, you may choose:

     a. to copy subdirectories and the files in them (/S).

     b. to keep the read-only attribute (/R).

     c. to copy hidden files (/H).

     d. to create an empty subdirectory (/E).

     e. to keep file attributes (/K)

8. The command line editor is a full-screen editor that allows you to modify text files. It is a menu-driven program.

9. MOVE is used to move files. Although it can rename directories, it is better to use the REN command to rename objects and the MOVE command to move these objects. You must be cautious when you use MOVE to ensure you are performing the task that you wish.

10. Utility programs include the ones that come with the operating system, such as the external command MOVE.

11. CHKDSK will search your drives for errors and give you a statistical report on the integrity of your drives.

12. You can use CHKDSK to check and repair FAT, FAT32, and NTFS drives but it must not be the default drive.

13. You must not use CHKDSK /F while on a network drive or on any substituted drives or the default drive.

14. Disk Defragmenter is a program used to optimize performance of a disk by rewriting files so the clusters are contiguous. When files are contiguous, computer performance is enhanced.

15. You can not defragment a floppy disk in Windows XP Professional.

Key Terms

chain	fragmented file	naming convention
cross-linked files	lost cluster	utility program
disk optimization		

Discussion Questions

1. Why would you want to organize a hard disk?

2. What are the advantages and disadvantages of organizing a hard disk by application program rather than by project?

3. Why would you not want to place data files in a program subdirectory?

4. List five criteria that can be used for organizing a hard disk and explain the rationale for each.

5. What are two major considerations for any disk organizational scheme?

6. What are some of the drawbacks of using the COPY command for organizing your disk?

7. Why is moving program files and renaming program directories not as safe as moving data files and renaming data file directories?
8. What steps would you take to move a directory?
9. Why would you want to own utility programs that do not come with the operating system?
10. What is the function and purpose of the CHKDSK command?
11. CHKDSK informs you of two types of errors. Explain.
12. What is a lost cluster? A cross-linked file? What impact does either of these have on available disk space?
13. Give the syntax for CHKDSK and explain two parameters when used with FAT volumes. With NTFS volumes.
14. What is verbose mode? Explain the use of the /V parameter with the CHKDSK command with a FAT file system and an NTFS file system.
15. Compare and contrast contiguous files with noncontiguous (fragmented) files.
16. Why would you use the parameter of the file name with the CHKDSK command?
17. What is the purpose and function of the /F parameter when it is used with the CHKDSK command, and under what circumstances would you use it?
18. Explain the function and purpose of disk-optimization programs.

True/False Questions

For each question, circle the letter T if the statement is true, and the letter F if the statement is false.

T   F   1. The number of files that can be stored in the root of a hard drive is unlimited if the file system is FAT16.
T   F   2. It is a good idea to have your data files and program files in the same subdirectory so you can keep track of your files easily.
T   F   3. To repair FAT drives, you can use CHKDSK.
T   F   4. The operating system writes files to disk based on the next empty cluster.
T   F   5. To optimize a disk, you should use CHKDSK.

Completion Questions

Write the correct answer in each blank space.
6. To change the name of a subdirectory, you can use the _____ command or the _____ command.
7. Two commands that can help you organize your disk are _____ and _____.
8. When you use the MOVE *.* command, subdirectories contained in the default directory _____ (are or are not) moved.
9. When you use the CHKDSK command, the parameter that will list every file on the disk, including hidden files, is the _____ parameter if the disk is using the FAT16 or FAT32 file system.
10. To solve the problem of having noncontiguous files on a hard disk, use _____.

Multiple Choice Questions

For each question, write the letter for the correct answer in the blank space.

____   11. A good rule of thumb when organizing a hard disk is

    a. to create compact and deep subdirectories rather than shallow and wide ones.

    b. to place data files in the same subdirectories with their associated program files.

    c. to use the root directory as a map to the rest of the disk.

    d. to have no files, only subdirectories, in the root directory.

____   12. When organizing a hard disk, XCOPY is _____ to use than COPY.

    a. faster

    b. slower

    c. neither faster nor slower

    d. less reliable

____   13. CHKDSK will not

    a. tell how many files are on a floppy disk.

    b. tell whether or not a floppy disk has hidden files.

    c. remove damaged files from a floppy disk.

    d. tell how much room is left on a floppy disk.

____   14. A noncontiguous file is one that

    a. occupies more than one cluster.

    b. occupies nonconsecutive clusters.

    c. has a directory entry table that is missing certain numbers.

    d. contains a document that hasn't been finished.

____   15. To help your disk perform quickly and reliably, you should

    a. rename the directories that hold program files after they have been installed, so that they are all in the same directory.

    b. use deep subdirectories.

    c. run Disk Defragmenter.

    d. use long file names.

Writing Commands

Write the correct steps or commands to perform the required action as if you were at the computer. The prompt will indicate the default drive and directory. If there is no prompt indicated, assume you are at the desktop and not in the Command Line window.

16. You need statistical information about the disk in Drive A.

```
C:\WINDOWS>
```

17. You want to see if the file called GALAXY.NEW in the 3PLANETS directory on the disk in Drive A is contiguous.

```
C:\WINDOWS>
```

18. You want to fix lost clusters and cross-linked files on the disk in Drive A.

```
C:\WINDOWS>
```

19. You want to display all the files on the disk in Drive A. (Do not use the DIR command.)

    C:\>

20. You want to locate bad sectors and recover any readable information on Drive E.

    C:\>

Homework Assignments

Note 1: Place the HOMEWORK disk in Drive A. Be sure to work on the HOMEWORK disk, not the DATA disk.

Note 2: The homework problems will assume that Drive C is the hard disk and the HOMEWORK disk is in Drive A. If you are using another drive, such as floppy Drive B or hard Drive D, be sure and substitute that drive letter when reading the questions and answers.

Note 3: All subdirectories that are created will be under the root directory unless otherwise specified.

Problem Set 1

Problem A

A-a On the HOMEWORK disk, under the subdirectory called **HISTORY**, create a subdirectory called **ROMAN**.

A-b With the root directory of the HOMEWORK disk as the default, use the XCOPY command with the relative path to copy all the files in the root directory that begin with W to the subdirectory called **ROMAN** that you just created.

____ 1. Which command did you use?
    a. XCOPY W*.* HISTORY
    b. XCOPY W*.* HISTORY\ROMAN
    c. XCOPY W*.* ROMAN\HISTORY
    d. XCOPY W*.* ROMAN

____ 2. What message(s) was/were displayed on the screen?
    a. Reading source file(s).
    b. Copying source file(s).
    c. 3 File(s) copied
    d. none of the above

____ 3. Are there any files that begin with W in the root directory of the HOME-WORK disk?
    a. yes
    b. no

A-c With the root directory of the HOMEWORK disk as the default, move all the files that begin with W to the subdirectory called **ROMAN** you created above.

_____ 4. Which command did you use?

    a. MOVE W*.* HISTORY\ROMAN

    b. MOVE W*.* ROMAN\HISTORY

    c. MOVE W*.* ROMAN

    d. none of the above

A-d   Take the necessary steps to complete the move.

_____ 5. Are there any files that begin with W in the root directory of the HOME-WORK disk?

    a. yes

    b. no

Problem B

B-a   With the root directory of the HOMEWORK disk as the default, under the subdirectory called **PHONE** create a subdirectory called **FILES**.

B-b   With the root directory of the HOMEWORK disk as the default, move all the files in the root directory that begin with F to the subdirectory called **PHONE\FILES** that you just created.

_____ 6. What items beginning with F remain in the root directory?

    a. the FILES and FIRST subdirectories

    b. nothing is remaining that begins with F

    c. the FEB.99 and FEB.TRP files

    d. FILES, FIRST, FEB.99, and FEB.TRP

B-c   With the root directory of the HOMEWORK disk as the default, move all the files in the root directory that have the file extension of **.FIL** to the **PHONE\FILES** subdirectory.

_____ 7. How many files were moved?

    a. one

    b. four

    c. six

    d. eight

Problem C

Note: The root directory of the HOMEWORK disk is the default.

C-a   Copy from the **WUGXP** directory the **LEVEL-1**, **LEVEL-2**, and **LEVEL-3** subdirectories and all the files in those directories to the root directory of the HOMEWORK disk. There are no empty directories. Maintain the hierarchical structure.

_____ 8. Which of the following commands did you use?

    a. XCOPY C:\WUGXP\LEVEL-1*.* LEVEL-1

    b. XCOPY C:\WUGXP\LEVEL-1*.* /O

    c. XCOPY C:\WUGXP\LEVEL-1 LEVEL-1 /S

    d. XCOPY C:\WUGXP\LEVEL-1*.* LEVEL-1 /D

___   9. What is the *first* message displayed?

    a. Reading source file(s) . . . .

    b. Does LEVEL-1 specify a file name or directory name on the target (F = file, D = directory)?

    c. LEVEL-1 directory being created.

    d. no message was displayed

C-b   Complete the command. Then, with the root directory of the HOMEWORK disk as the default, use Edit to create a new file called **PLANET.RED**. The contents of the file will be as follows:

```
This is a new red file.
Mars is called the red planet.
I wonder who painted it?
```

C-c   Make a directory called **TRAVEL** on the root of the HOMEWORK disk.

C-d   Copy all the files from the **WUGXP** directory ending with the extension **.RED** to the **TRAVEL** subdirectory on the HOMEWORK disk.

C-e   With the root directory of the HOMEWORK disk as the default, move the **PLANET.RED** file to the **TRAVEL** subdirectory on the HOMEWORK disk.

C-f   With the root directory of the HOMEWORK disk as the default, use Edit to alter and save the **PLANET.RED** file with the following text added to the current content:

```
Maybe the red comes from rust.
Maybe the red comes from Rubies!
If it comes from Rubies, I want to go there!
```

C-g   With the root directory of the HOMEWORK disk as the default, use Edit to create a new file in the **TRAVEL** directory called **ANSWERS.RED**. The contents should read:

```
How disappointing! The red of Mars is caused by rust,
called iron oxide.  Rubies would have been more fun!
```

___   10. How many files are on the root of the HOMEWORK disk with the file extension of .RED?

    a. one

    b. three

    c. five

    d. zero

___   11. How many files are in the TRAVEL subdirectory with the file extension of .RED?

    a. one

    b. three

    c. five

    d. zero

C-h   With the root of the HOMEWORK disk as the default, rename the file called **ANSWERS.RED** to **WHY-MARS.RED** in the **TRAVEL** subdirectory.

C-i   With the root of the HOMEWORK disk as the default, copy all the files from the **TRAVEL** directory to the **BOOKS** subdirectory.

____   12. What is the total number of files with the extension .RED on the HOME-WORK disk?

        a. 2

        b. 4

        c. 8

        d. 10

____   13. What command did you use to answer question 12?

        a. CHKDSK A:

        b. DIR *.RED

        c. DIR *.RED /S

        d. DIR *.RED TRAVEL BOOKS

Problem Set II

Note 1:   Before proceeding with these assignments, check with your lab instructor to see if there are any special procedures you should follow.

Note 2:   The HOMEWORK disk is in Drive A. A:\> is displayed as the default drive and the default directory. *All work will occur on the HOMEWORK disk.*

Note 3:   **NAME.BAT**, **MARK.FIL**, **GETYN.COM**, **GO.BAT**, and **NAME.FIL** need to be present in the root directory of the HOMEWORK disk before proceeding with these problems. In steps 1 and 2, you will move the files MARK.FIL and NAME.FIL that were moved from the PHONE\FILES directory back to the root directory. If these files are not there, you can copy them from the WUGXP directory.

Note 4:   All files with the **.HW** extension *must* be created in the root directory of the HOMEWORK disk.

1   Key in the following: A:\>**MOVE PHONE\FILES\MARK.FIL** [Enter]

2   Key in the following: A:\>**MOVE PHONE\FILES\NAME.FIL** [Enter]

3   Use the editor to edit **NAME.FIL**.

4   Change **Chapter 7** to **Chapter 8**.

5   Change the date to the current date.

WHAT'S HAPPENING?   You have updated **NAME.FIL**.

To Create 1.HW

Locate *all* of the files ending with **.RED** on the HOMEWORK disk and place the results of the command in a file called **1.HW**.

To Create 2.HW

1   Copy only the files with the **.TXT** extension that were created on or after 5-31-00 in the **WUGXP** subdirectory to the root of the HOMEWORK disk (overwrite if necessary).

2   Locate only the files in the root of the HOMEWORK disk that have the extension **.TXT**. Place the names of the files in a file called **2.HW**.

To Create 3.HW

1   Copy all the files that have the extension **.RED** from the **BOOKS** subdirectory to the root of the HOMEWORK disk.

2   Edit the file **PLANET.RED** in the **TRAVEL** directory. Remove the last three lines, add two blank lines (press [Enter] twice) and save the file.

3   Display the contents (not the file name) of the **PLANET.RED** file you just edited to a file called **3.HW**.

4   From the root of the A drive, Key in the following:
    TYPE A:\PLANET.RED >> 3.HW [Enter]

To Create 4.HW

Locate *all* the files that have the extension **.TXT** on the HOMEWORK disk and place the results of the command in a file called **4.HW**.

To Create 5.HW

In the root directory, see if the files that have the **.TRP** file extension are contiguous and place results of the command in a file called **5.HW**.

To Print Your Homework

1   Be sure the printer is on and ready to accept print jobs from your computer.

2   Key in the following (be very careful to make no typing errors):
    GO NAME.FIL 1.HW 2.HW 3.HW 4.HW 5.HW [Enter]

WHAT'S
HAPPENING?   If the files you requested, 1.HW, 2.HW, etc., do not exist in the default directory, you will see the following message on the screen:

```
File Not Found
The system cannot find the file specified.

  Is there a message that says "File Not Found. The system cannot
  find the file specified."

  If so, press Y to find out what could be wrong.

  Otherwise, press N to continue.
```

The operating system is telling you that the file cannot be found. If you see this screen, press **Y** to see what could be wrong, and repeat the print procedure after you have corrected the problem.

If the default directory contains the specified files, the following message will appear on the screen:

```
  Is there a message that say "File Not Found. The system cannot
  find the file specified."

  If so, press Y to find out what could be wrong.

  Otherwise, press N to continue.
```

You will need to press **N** once for each file you are printing.

3 Follow the messages on the screen until the Notepad program opens with a screen similar to the following:

WHAT'S HAPPENING?   All the requested files have been found and placed in a Notepad document. Your homework is now ready to print.

4 On the Notepad menu bar, click **File**. Click **Print**.

5 Click the **Print** button.

6 In the Notepad window, click **File**. Click **Exit**.

WHAT'S HAPPENING?   The following will appear on the Command Prompt screen:

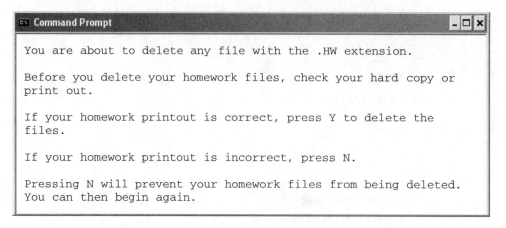

```
You are about to delete any file with the .HW extension.

Before you delete your homework files, check your hard copy or
print out.

If your homework printout is correct, press Y to delete the
files.

If your homework printout is incorrect, press N.

Pressing N will prevent your homework files from being deleted.
You can then begin again.
```

At this point, look at your printout. If it is correct, you can press **Y** to delete the homework files for this chapter. If your printout is incorrect, you can press **N**. That will preserve your homework and you will need to redo only the problem that was incorrect, not all the homework assignments.

7   Press **Y** ⌷**Enter**⌷

**WHAT'S ▩▩▩▩
▩▩HAPPENING?**   You have returned to the default prompt.

8   Close the Command Line session.

9   Execute the shut-down procedure.

Problem Set III—Brief Essay

1. Plan and organize the HOMEWORK disk *on paper only*. Write a brief explanation to justify your organizational scheme.
2. One way to organize a hard disk is by project. Another way to organize it is by program. Which way do you prefer? What advantages/disadvantages do you see to each method? Explain your answer.

PIPES, FILTERS, AND
REDIRECTION

Learning Objectives

After completing this chapter, you will be able to:

1. List the standard input and output devices.
2. Explain redirection.
3. Explain what filters are and when they are used.
4. Formulate and explain the syntax of the three filter commands SORT, FIND, and MORE.
5. Explain when and how to use the SORT, FIND, and MORE commands.
6. Explain what shell extensions are and how you may use them.
7. Explain what pipes are and how they are used.

Student Outcomes

1. Use > and >> to redirect standard output.
2. Use < to redirect standard input.
3. Use filter commands to manipulate information.
4. Enable shell extensions and use extended features.
5. Combine commands using pipes, filters, and redirection.

Chapter Overview

The operating system usually expects to read information from the keyboard. The keyboard is the standard input device. The standard output device, where the results of commands and the output of programs is displayed, is the screen. However, there are times when it is desirable to *redirect* input and output. Changing the standard input or standard output from one device to another is a process known as redirection. There are three external commands, called filters, which allow the user to manipulate data input and output. Pipes, used with filters, allow the user to link commands. Pipes, filters, and redirection give the user choices in determining where information is read from (input) and written to (output). You have been using redirection each time you placed the result of a command into your homework files (1.HW, 2.HW, etc.).

In this chapter you will learn how to use redirection. You will learn to use pipes to connect programs and filters to manipulate data.

9.1 Redirection of Standard I/O (Input/Output)

You have already used input and output. When you keyed in something on the keyboard, the operating system recognized it as input. After the input was processed, it was written to an output device—usually the screen. In other words, if you key in TYPE MYFILE.TXT, the input is what you key in. The output is the content of the file that is displayed on the screen. See Figure 9.1.

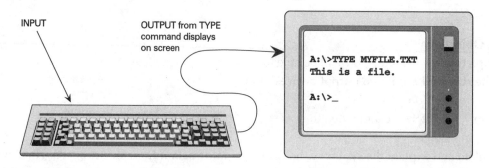

Figure 9.1—Input and Output Devices

In the data processing world, this **input/output** process is commonly referred to as **I/O**.

The operating system gets information from or sends information to three places: standard input, standard output, and standard error. **Standard input** is the keyboard. **Standard output** is the display screen. **Standard error** is the place from which the operating system writes error messages to the screen, e.g., "File Not Found."

Not all commands deal with standard input and standard output. For instance, the result or output of many of the commands you have used has been some action that occurred, such as copying a file with the COPY command. There is no standard input or output except the messages written to the screen. See Figure 9.2.

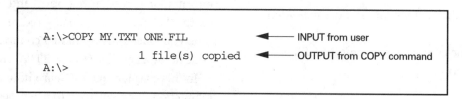

Figure 9.2—Results of COPY Command

On the other hand, the output of commands like DIR has been a screen display of all the files on a disk. The information was received from the standard input device, the keyboard, and the results of the DIR command were sent to the standard output device, the screen. I/O *redirection* means that you tell the operating system you want information read from or written to a device *other than* the standard ones. With the DIR command, you can write the output to a file. This process is called redirecting the output of a command. See Figure 9.3.

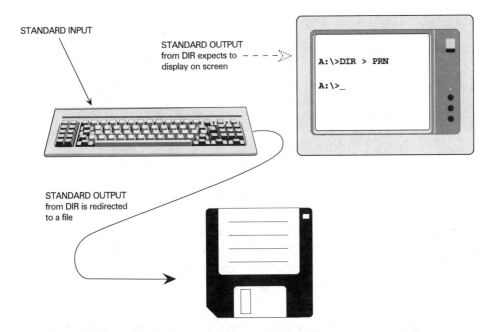

Figure 9.3—Redirecting Standard Output

Redirection works only when the command expects to send its results to the standard output device or receive the information from the standard input device.

The following symbols are used for redirection:

>   The greater-than symbol redirects the output of a command to someplace other than the screen, the standard output.

<   The less-than symbol tells the operating system to get its input from somewhere other than the keyboard.

>>   The double greater-than symbol is used to redirect the output of a command to an existing file, but it appends the information to the bottom of the file. It does not overwrite the existing file. It appends the output to the bottom of the existing file.

9.2   Activity: Using > to Redirect Standard Output

Note: The DATA disk is in Drive A with A:\> displayed.

1   Key in the following: A:\>**DIR C:\WUGXP*.TXT** [Enter]

```
Command Prompt                                                    _ □ ×

A:\>DIR C:\WUGXP\*.TXT
 Volume in drive C is ADMIN504
 Volume Serial Number is 0E38-11FF

 Directory of C:\WUGXP

10/30/2001  01:46 PM                148 ASTRO.TXT
10/30/2001  02:10 PM                121 BORN.TXT
12/11/1999  04:03 PM                 72 DANCES.TXT
05/30/2000  04:32 PM                 53 HELLO.TXT
11/16/2000  12:00 PM                 59 Sandy and Patty.txt
```

```
10/31/2001   02:43 PM              529 TITAN.TXT
11/16/2000   12:00 PM               53 Sandy and Nicki.txt
05/27/2001   10:08 PM               81 LONGFILENAME.TXT
10/30/2001   03:42 PM              190 JUPITER.TXT
12/06/2001   12:15 AM               97 LONGFILENAMED.TXT
10/31/2001   11:37 AM              253 GALAXY.TXT
12/06/2001   12:16 AM               99 LONGFILENAMING.TXT
10/31/2001   01:08 PM              406 MERCURY.TXT
11/24/2001   11:24 AM              194 PLANETS.TXT
10/31/2001   07:08 PM              478 VENUS.TXT
              15 File(s)          2,833 bytes
               0 Dir(s)   6,784,942,080 bytes free

A:\>_
```

WHAT'S
HAPPENING?   This command behaved in the "normal" way. You asked for a
display of all the files in the **WUGXP** directory that had a **.TXT** file extension. The
selected files were displayed on the screen. Because the DIR command writes its
results to the screen, the standard output device, redirection can be used with this
command.

2 Key in the following: A:\>**DIR C:\WUGXP*.TXT > TXTFILES.TXT** [Enter]

```
A:\>DIR C:\WUGXP\*.TXT > TXTFILES.TXT

A:\>_
```

WHAT'S
HAPPENING?   The output of the command has been sent to the file
TXTFILES.TXT on the DATA disk. Nothing appears on the screen. When you key in
DIR C:\WUGXP*.TXT, you normally see the directory listing of all the ***.TXT** files
on the screen, as you did in the display following step 1. The > sign tells the operating system that instead of sending the standard output to the screen, you want to
redirect that output elsewhere.

3 Key in the following: A:\>**TYPE TXTFILES.TXT** [Enter]

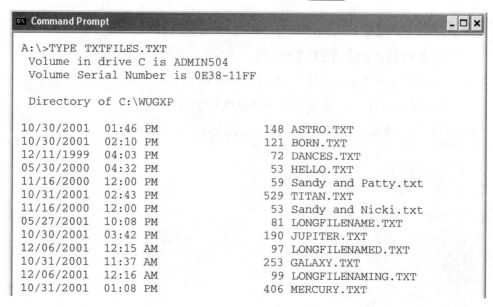

```
A:\>TYPE TXTFILES.TXT
 Volume in drive C is ADMIN504
 Volume Serial Number is 0E38-11FF

 Directory of C:\WUGXP

10/30/2001   01:46 PM              148 ASTRO.TXT
10/30/2001   02:10 PM              121 BORN.TXT
12/11/1999   04:03 PM               72 DANCES.TXT
05/30/2000   04:32 PM               53 HELLO.TXT
11/16/2000   12:00 PM               59 Sandy and Patty.txt
10/31/2001   02:43 PM              529 TITAN.TXT
11/16/2000   12:00 PM               53 Sandy and Nicki.txt
05/27/2001   10:08 PM               81 LONGFILENAME.TXT
10/30/2001   03:42 PM              190 JUPITER.TXT
12/06/2001   12:15 AM               97 LONGFILENAMED.TXT
10/31/2001   11:37 AM              253 GALAXY.TXT
12/06/2001   12:16 AM               99 LONGFILENAMING.TXT
10/31/2001   01:08 PM              406 MERCURY.TXT
```

```
11/24/2001  11:24 AM                 194 PLANETS.TXT
10/31/2001  07:08 PM                 478 VENUS.TXT
              15 File(s)           2,833 bytes
               0 Dir(s)    6,784,942,080 bytes free

A:\>_
```

WHAT'S
HAPPENING?   As you can see, the TXTFILES.TXT file contains the same information that would have appeared on the screen. Redirection is very useful. For example, if you wanted a file copy of the directory of a disk, you could not key in **COPY DIR filename** because DIR is a command, not a file. You cannot copy a command to a file. COPY is for use with files only. Redirection, used properly, gets you that hard copy.

9.3 Activity: Using < to Redirect Standard Input

Note: The DATA disk is in Drive A with A:\> displayed.

1   Key in the following: A:\>**MD TEST** Enter

2   Key in the following: A:\>**COPY C:\WUGXP*.NEW TEST** Enter

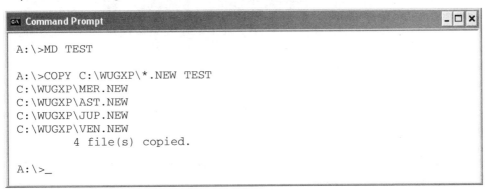

```
A:\>MD TEST

A:\>COPY C:\WUGXP\*.NEW TEST
C:\WUGXP\MER.NEW
C:\WUGXP\AST.NEW
C:\WUGXP\JUP.NEW
C:\WUGXP\VEN.NEW
        4 file(s) copied.

A:\>_
```

WHAT'S
HAPPENING?   You have a created a subdirectory called **TEST** on the DATA disk and copied four files into it.

Standard input is from the keyboard. The DEL command uses standard input.

3   Key in the following: A:\>**DEL TEST*.*** Enter

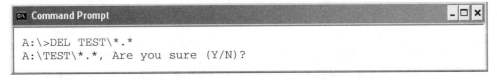

```
A:\>DEL TEST\*.*
A:\TEST\*.*, Are you sure (Y/N)?
```

WHAT'S
HAPPENING?   You asked the DEL command to delete all the files in the **TEST** subdirectory. DEL is asking you if you are really sure that you want to delete these files. DEL is expecting input from the standard input device, the keyboard.

4   Key in the following: **N** Enter

```
CX  Command Prompt                                                        _ □ x

A:\>DEL TEST\*.*
A:\TEST\*.*, Are you sure (Y/N)? N

A:\>_
```

WHAT'S HAPPENING?   You were returned to the system prompt without deleting the files in the **TEST** subdirectory because you answered **N** for "No, don't delete." As you can see, the operating system took no action until it received input from you via the keyboard, **N**. The input was **N**. You can prove that the files are still there by keying in **DIR TEST**.

5   Key in the following: A:\>**DIR TEST** Enter

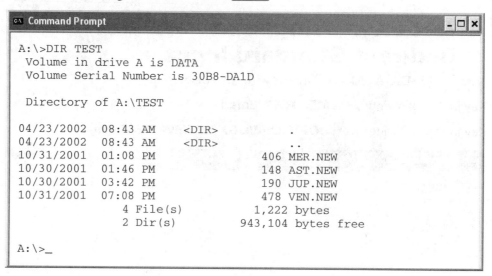

```
CX  Command Prompt                                                        _ □ x

A:\>DIR TEST
 Volume in drive A is DATA
 Volume Serial Number is 30B8-DA1D

 Directory of A:\TEST

04/23/2002  08:43 AM    <DIR>              .
04/23/2002  08:43 AM    <DIR>              ..
10/31/2001  01:08 PM              406 MER.NEW
10/30/2001  01:46 PM              148 AST.NEW
10/30/2001  03:42 PM              190 JUP.NEW
10/31/2001  07:08 PM              478 VEN.NEW
              4 File(s)         1,222 bytes
              2 Dir(s)      943,104 bytes free

A:\>_
```

WHAT'S HAPPENING?   From the display you can see that you did not delete the files in the **TEST** directory.

6   Key in the following: A:\>**TYPE Y.FIL** Enter

```
CX  Command Prompt                                                        _ □ x

A:\>TYPE Y.FIL
y

A:\>_
```

WHAT'S HAPPENING?   The **Y.FIL** file is a simple file that contains the letter y followed by a carriage return (Enter). If you do not have this file on the DATA disk, you can copy it from the **WUGXP** directory to the DATA disk.

7   Key in the following: A:\>**DEL TEST*.* < Y.FIL** Enter

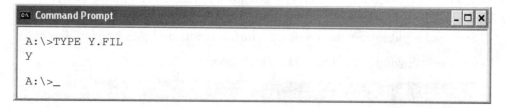

```
CX  Command Prompt                                                        _ □ x

A:\>DEL TEST\*.* < Y.FIL
A:\TEST\*.*, Are you sure (Y/N)? y

A:\>_
```

WHAT'S
HAPPENING?   This time you told the operating system to get input from a file called Y.FIL (< Y.FIL), instead of from the standard input device, the keyboard. When DEL TEST*.* was executed and displayed the message "Are you sure (Y/N)?" it still needed input, a Y or N followed by **Enter**. The operating system found the file you told it to look for, Y.FIL, which had the "y **Enter**" answer. This file provided a response to the question, so the operating system proceeded to delete the files in the subdirectory **TEST**.

You must be very careful with redirection of input. When you tell the operating system to take input from a file, any input from the keyboard will be ignored. In this example, if the **Y.FIL** contents were "X," this would not be a valid answer to the question posed, "Are you sure (Y/N)?" Only **Y** or **N** is an acceptable response. Any other letter would be unacceptable, and the question would be asked again, and then the system would assume the response was **N** and you would be returned to the command prompt. You would see the following on the screen:

```
A:\TEST\*.*, Are you sure (Y/N)?X
A:\TEST\*.*, Are you sure (Y/N)?
```

and the files would not have been deleted.

8   Key in the following: A:\>**DIR TEST** **Enter**

```
Command Prompt                                              _ □ x

A:\>DIR TEST
 Volume in drive A is DATA
 Volume Serial Number is 30B8-DA1D

 Directory of A:\TEST

04/23/2002  08:43 AM    <DIR>          .
04/23/2002  08:43 AM    <DIR>          ..
              0 File(s)              0 bytes
              2 Dir(s)         945,152 bytes free

A:\>_
```

WHAT'S
HAPPENING?   The files were deleted. You did it with one command line, and you did not have to key in the **Y**. The Y came from the contents of the file called **Y.FIL**.

9.4   Activity: Using >> to Add Redirected Output to a File

Note: The DATA disk is in Drive A with A:\> displayed.

1   Key in the following: A:\>**COPY C:\WUGXP*.TXT** **Enter**
(Overwrite files as necessary.)

```
Command Prompt                                              _ □ x

A:\>COPY C:\WUGXP\*.TXT
C:\WUGXP\ASTRO.TXT
C:\WUGXP\BORN.TXT
Overwrite A:\BORN.TXT? (Yes/No/All): A
C:\WUGXP\DANCES.TXT
```

```
C:\WUGXP\HELLO.TXT
C:\WUGXP\Sandy and Patty.txt
C:\WUGXP\TITAN.TXT
C:\WUGXP\Sandy and Nicki.txt
C:\WUGXP\LONGFILENAME.TXT
C:\WUGXP\JUPITER.TXT
C:\WUGXP\LONGFILENAMED.TXT
C:\WUGXP\GALAXY.TXT
C:\WUGXP\LONGFILENAMING.TXT
C:\WUGXP\MERCURY.TXT
C:\WUGXP\PLANETS.TXT
C:\WUGXP\VENUS.TXT
        15 file(s) copied.

A:\>
```

WHAT'S HAPPENING?   You have copied all the .TXT files to the root of the DATA disk.

2   Key in the following: A:\>**TYPE JUPITER.TXT** [Enter]

3   Key in the following: A:\>**TYPE MERCURY.TXT** [Enter]

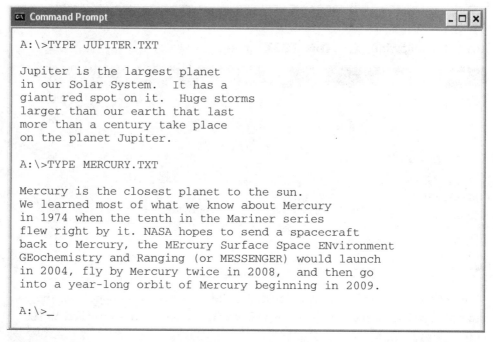

```
Command Prompt                                                    _ □ ✕

A:\>TYPE JUPITER.TXT

Jupiter is the largest planet
in our Solar System.  It has a
giant red spot on it.  Huge storms
larger than our earth that last
more than a century take place
on the planet Jupiter.

A:\>TYPE MERCURY.TXT

Mercury is the closest planet to the sun.
We learned most of what we know about Mercury
in 1974 when the tenth in the Mariner series
flew right by it. NASA hopes to send a spacecraft
back to Mercury, the MErcury Surface Space ENvironment
GEochemistry and Ranging (or MESSENGER) would launch
in 2004, fly by Mercury twice in 2008,  and then go
into a year-long orbit of Mercury beginning in 2009.

A:\>_
```

WHAT'S HAPPENING?   You have two separate files. You want to add **MERCURY.TXT** to the end of **JUPITER.TXT**. If you keyed in **TYPE MERCURY.TXT > JUPITER.TXT**, you would *overwrite* the contents of **JUPITER.TXT** with the contents of **MERCURY.TXT**. To *append* to the end of an existing file, you use the double redirection symbol, >>.

4   Key in the following: A:\>**TYPE MERCURY.TXT >> JUPITER.TXT** [Enter]

5   Key in the following: A:\>**TYPE JUPITER.TXT** [Enter]

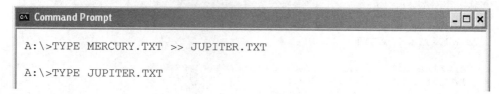

```
Command Prompt                                                    _ □ ✕

A:\>TYPE MERCURY.TXT >> JUPITER.TXT

A:\>TYPE JUPITER.TXT
```

```
Jupiter is the largest planet
in our Solar System.  It has a
giant red spot on it.  Huge storms
larger than our earth that last
more than a century take place
on the planet Jupiter.

Mercury is the closest planet to the sun.
We learned most of what we know about Mercury
in 1974 when the tenth in the Mariner series
flew right by it. NASA hopes to send a spacecraft
back to Mercury, the MErcury Surface Space ENvironment
GEochemistry and Ranging (or MESSENGER) would launch
in 2004, fly by Mercury twice in 2008,  and then go
into a year-long orbit of Mercury beginning in 2009.

A:\>_
```

WHAT'S HAPPENING?   Instead of overwriting the contents of **JUPITER.TXT** with the contents of **MERCURY.TXT**, the contents of **MERCURY.TXT** were added to the end of the **JUPITER.TXT** file.

9.5 Filters

Filter commands manipulate information. *Filters* read information from the keyboard (standard input), change the input in a specified way, and write the results to the screen (standard output). Filter commands function like filters in a water purification system. They remove the unwanted elements from the water (data) and send the purified water (data) on its way. There are three filters, all of which are external commands:

SORT   Arranges lines in ascending or descending order.

FIND   Searches for a particular group of characters, also called a *character string*.

MORE   Temporarily halts the screen display after each screenful.

The operating system creates temporary files while it "filters" data with the **SORT** command, so during this process it is important that there be access to the disk and the filters. You must be sure that the floppy disk is not write-protected or, if you are using a Network drive, that you have write access to that drive. If a disk is write-protected, or if you do not have the write "permission," the operating system will not be able to execute the SORT filter command.

9.6 The SORT Command

The SORT filter command arranges or sorts lines of input (text) and sends them to standard output (the screen), unless you redirect it. The default SORT is in ascending order (A to Z or lowest to highest numbers), starting in the first column. The SORT command has many parameters. The syntax for the command is:

```
SORT [/R] [/+n] [/M kilobytes] [/L locale] [/REC recordbytes]
  [[drive1:][path1]filename1] [/T [drive2:][path2]]
  [/O [drive3:][path3]filename3]
```

The full syntax is listed in the command summary in Appendix H.

9.7   Activity: Using SORT

Note 1:   The DATA disk is in Drive A with A:\> displayed.

Note 2:   Remember when you see [F6], it means to press the [F6] key.

1   Key in the following: A:\>**SORT** [Enter]
                                       MERCURY [Enter]
                                       VENUS [Enter]
                                       EARTH [Enter]
                                       3 [Enter]
                                       MARS [Enter]
                                       JUPITER [Enter]
                                       [F6] [Enter]

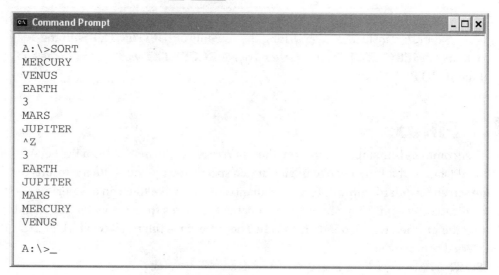

```
Command Prompt                                            _ □ ✕

A:\>SORT
MERCURY
VENUS
EARTH
3
MARS
JUPITER
^Z
3
EARTH
JUPITER
MARS
MERCURY
VENUS

A:\>_
```

WHAT'S HAPPENING?   As you can see, the SORT command took input from the keyboard. When you pressed the [F6] key (identical to pressing [Ctrl] + **Z**), you told the SORT command that you were finished entering data. Then the SORT command "filtered" the data and wrote the keyboard input alphabetically to the standard output device (the screen). See Figure 9.4 for a graphical representation of this filter.

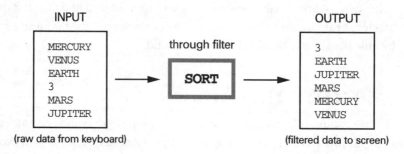

Figure 9.4—Filtering Data

2   Key in the following: A:\>**SORT** [Enter]
                                       333 [Enter]
                                       3 [Enter]

23 Enter
124 Enter
F6 Enter

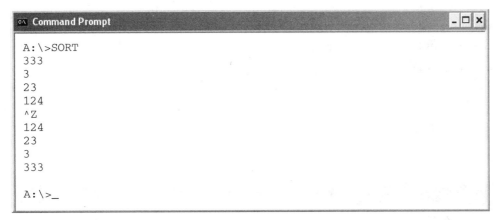

```
A:\>SORT
333
3
23
124
^Z
124
23
3
333

A:\>_
```

WHAT'S HAPPENING? The SORT command does not seem very smart because these numbers are certainly not in numeric order. This data is not actually numeric data. Numbers, in this case, are really character data and not numeric values that are manipulated mathematically. Numbers are often used as character data. For instance, a zip code or a phone number, although they use numbers, really are character data and are not treated mathematically. You would not think of adding your address to your phone number and dividing by your zip code, for example.

Character data is sorted from left to right. Numeric data is sorted by units. Thus, if you look at "Smith" and "Smythe," you read character data from left to right and would place "Smith" before "Smythe." If you had the numbers 124, 222, 22, 23, 31, 9, and 6, the numeric order would be, of course, 6, 9, 22, 23, 31, 124, and 222. You first sort all the single-digit numbers. You then sort the two-digit numbers by looking at the first digit—thus you know that 22 and 23 come before 32. Since 22 and 23 have the same first digit, you then go to the second digit to determine that the 2 in 22 comes before the 3 in 23.

A human knows that 12 comes before 13 because that person has learned how numbers work. The operating system is different. It relies on something called the *ASCII sort sequence*. ASCII is a standard code that assigns values to letters, numbers, and punctuation marks—from the *left*, in the same way we read characters. The ASCII sort sequence is determined by the number assigned to the ASCII character. The sort order is punctuation marks (including spaces), then numbers, then letters (lowercase preceding uppercase). If you had a series of characters such as BB, aa, #, 123, bb, 13, and AA, the ASCII sort order would be:

   #   123   13   aa   AA   bb   BB

Notice that with the new sort sequence the relative position of aa and AA did not change, but the relative position of BB and bb did change.

There is another point about using the SORT command. Not only does it follow the ASCII sort sequence, but it also sorts entire lines from left to right. Thus, the sort sequence of "Carolyn Smith" and "Robert Nesler" is:

Carolyn Smith
Robert Nesler

Because the SORT command looks at the entire line, "Carolyn" comes before "Robert."

In our numeric example, SORT looked at the entire line, and, since the "1" in "124" preceded the "2" in "23," it placed the "124" before the "23." You can force the operating system to sort numbers correctly using the spacebar to add the space character (indicated here by a #).

3   Key in the following: A:\>**SORT** [Enter]
                             333 [Enter]
                             ##3 [Enter]
                             #23 [Enter]
                             124 [Enter]
                             [F6] [Enter]

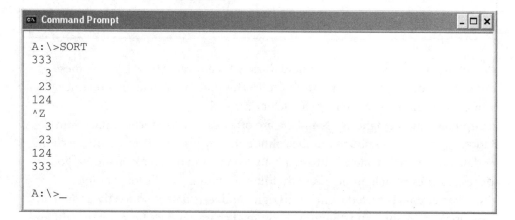

```
A:\>SORT
333
  3
 23
124
^Z
  3
 23
124
333

A:\>_
```

WHAT'S HAPPENING?   By entering spaces, you forced the lines to be the same length, placing the number digits in their proper position. Since spaces precede numbers in the ASCII sort sequence, the SORT command could sort the entire line and place it in proper numeric order. Indeed, you made numeric data character data. Essentially, you left-justify character data and right-justify numeric data.

9.8   Filters and Redirection

The standard output of filters is a screen display. Hence, you can redirect both the output and input of these filter commands. The filter commands are not usually used with actual keyboard input, but with input redirected from a file, a device, or another command.

9.9   Activity: Using the SORT Command with Redirection

Note: The DATA disk is in Drive A with A:\> displayed.

1   Key in the following: A:\>**COPY C:\WUGXP\STATE.CAP** [Enter]

2   Key in the following: A:\>**SORT < STATE.CAP** [Enter]

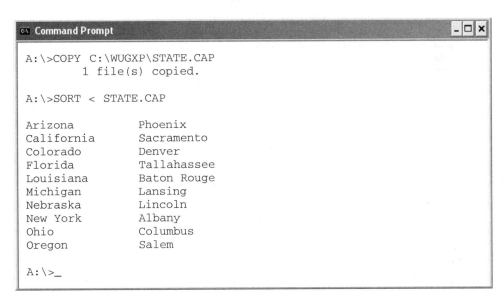

```
A:\>COPY C:\WUGXP\STATE.CAP
        1 file(s) copied.

A:\>SORT < STATE.CAP

Arizona         Phoenix
California       Sacramento
Colorado        Denver
Florida         Tallahassee
Louisiana       Baton Rouge
Michigan        Lansing
Nebraska        Lincoln
New York        Albany
Ohio            Columbus
Oregon          Salem

A:\>_
```

WHAT'S
HAPPENING?   You copied the **STATE.CAP** file from the **WUGXP** directory to the
DATA disk. You then keyed in the **SORT** command. You used the symbol < for
taking data from a source other than the keyboard, the file called **STATE.CAP**, and
fed it into the SORT command. Displayed on your screen (the standard output) is
the **STATE.CAP** file arranged in alphabetical order, with **Arizona** and **Phoenix** at
the top. Another SORT command feature is the /R parameter, which allows you to
sort in reverse or descending order (Z to A). In Windows XP Professional, the SORT
command no longer requires the < prior to the file being sorted.

3   Key in the following: A:\>**SORT STATE.CAP** [Enter]

```
A:\>SORT STATE.CAP

Arizona         Phoenix
California       Sacramento
Colorado        Denver
Florida         Tallahassee
Louisiana       Baton Rouge
Michigan        Lansing
Nebraska        Lincoln
New York        Albany
Ohio            Columbus
Oregon          Salem

A:\>_
```

WHAT'S
HAPPENING?   As you can see, the command worked the same even without the
< symbol. SORT expects either keyboard input or a file.

4   Key in the following: A:\>**SORT /R < STATE.CAP** [Enter]

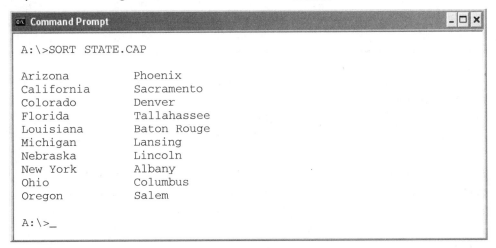

```
A:\>SORT /R < STATE.CAP
Oregon          Salem
Ohio            Columbus
New York        Albany
```

```
Nebraska        Lincoln
Michigan        Lansing
Louisiana       Baton Rouge
Florida         Tallahassee
Colorado        Denver
California      Sacramento
Arizona         Phoenix


A:\>_
```

WHAT'S ▒▒▒▒▒▒
▒▒▒▒HAPPENING?   The file **STATE.CAP** that the SORT command used as input is displayed on the screen in reverse alphabetical order. The standard output, the results of the SORT command, is written to the screen. The SORT parameter that sorts by a column number is /+n. (A column, on the screen, is the place occupied by one character.)

5   Key in the following: A:\>**SORT /+17 STATE.CAP** [Enter]

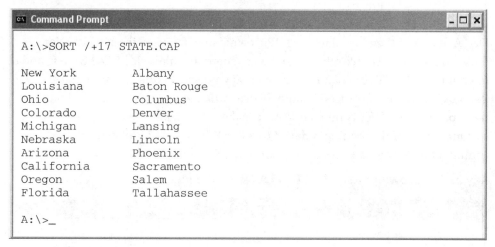

```
A:\>SORT /+17 STATE.CAP

New York        Albany
Louisiana       Baton Rouge
Ohio            Columbus
Colorado        Denver
Michigan        Lansing
Nebraska        Lincoln
Arizona         Phoenix
California      Sacramento
Oregon          Salem
Florida         Tallahassee

A:\>_
```

WHAT'S ▒▒▒▒▒▒
▒▒▒▒HAPPENING?   This time you sorted by the character in the column number you specified, the seventeenth position in the line in this example. The first letter of the city is in the seventeenth column. The file is now ordered by city rather than by state. It is important to note that the SORT command does not understand columns in the usual sense. A person would say that the "city" column is the second column, going from left to right. The SORT command counts each character (letters and spaces) from left to right and counts each character as a column. Thus, "city" is located by counting the number of characters, including the spaces between the characters. The total number was 17.

In these examples, you have been "massaging the data." The actual data in **STATE.CAP** has not changed at all. It remains exactly as it was written. The only thing that has changed is the way it is displayed—the way you are *looking* at the data. This alphabetic arrangement is temporary. If you want to change the data in the file, you need to save the altered data to a new file.

6   Key in the following: A:\>**SORT /+17 STATE.CAP > SORTED.CAP** [Enter]

7   Key in the following: A:\>**TYPE SORTED.CAP** [Enter]

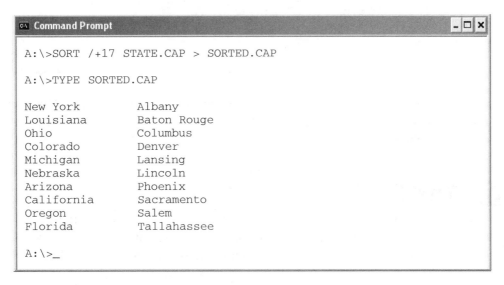

```
A:\>SORT /+17 STATE.CAP > SORTED.CAP

A:\>TYPE SORTED.CAP

New York        Albany
Louisiana       Baton Rouge
Ohio            Columbus
Colorado        Denver
Michigan        Lansing
Nebraska        Lincoln
Arizona         Phoenix
California       Sacramento
Oregon          Salem
Florida         Tallahassee

A:\>_
```

WHAT'S HAPPENING?   You used redirection and saved the sorted output to a new file called **SORTED.CAP**. The standard output of the command **SORT STATE.CAP** would be written to the screen (the standard output device). Since standard output writes to the screen, you can redirect it to a file called **SORTED.CAP** with the command line **SORT STATE.CAP > SORTED.CAP**. In this case, you *do* need the > symbol. Otherwise SORT will not know what to do with the output. The SORT command includes a parameter to store the sorted data in a file that works faster than using redirection. The parameter is /O.

8   Key in the following. A:\>**SORT /+17 STATE.CAP /O BYCITY.CAP** Enter

9   Key in the following. A:\>**TYPE SORTED.CAP** Enter

10 Key in the following: A:\>**TYPE BYCITY.CAP** Enter

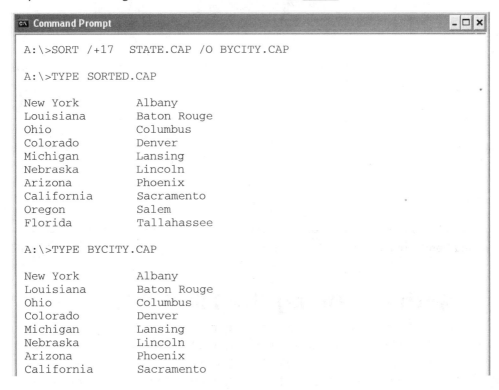

```
A:\>SORT /+17   STATE.CAP /O BYCITY.CAP

A:\>TYPE SORTED.CAP

New York        Albany
Louisiana       Baton Rouge
Ohio            Columbus
Colorado        Denver
Michigan        Lansing
Nebraska        Lincoln
Arizona         Phoenix
California       Sacramento
Oregon          Salem
Florida         Tallahassee

A:\>TYPE BYCITY.CAP

New York        Albany
Louisiana       Baton Rouge
Ohio            Columbus
Colorado        Denver
Michigan        Lansing
Nebraska        Lincoln
Arizona         Phoenix
California       Sacramento
```

```
Oregon          Salem
Florida         Tallahassee

A:\>_
```

HAPPENING?   As you can see, both files are the same. With this small file, the time difference is not discernable, but with a large data file, using /O is considerably faster than using redirection.

9.10 The FIND Filter

The FIND command allows you to search a file for a specific character string by enclosing it in quotation marks. Although intended for use with ASCII text files, this command can be useful with some data files produced by application software. For example, let's say you used a program to create five documents. One of the documents was a paper on law enforcement in which you know you used the word "indictment" but you can't remember the name of the file. You could, of course, open each one of the five documents, or you could use the FIND command to search for the word "indictment." Although much of the document would appear as funny characters if you used the TYPE command, the FIND command might be able to tell you whether or not the word "indictment" is in the file.

On the desktop, there is a Search option in the Start menu, which can search files for textbook as well. In this text you are using the command line, but it is not as reliable in Windows XP Professional as it was in Windows 2000. Using the FIND command at the command line can help you find a file based on content.

The FIND command is *case sensitive* unless you use the parameter /I, which means ignore case. The syntax is:

```
FIND [/V] [/C] [/N] [/I] [/OFF[LINE]] "string"
[drive:][path]filename[ ...]]

    /V        Displays all lines NOT containing the specified string.
    /C        Displays only the count of lines containing the string.
    /N        Displays line numbers with the displayed lines.
    /I        Ignores the case of characters when searching for the
              string.
    /OFF[LINE] Do not skip files with offline attribute set.
    "string"  Specifies the text string to find.
    [drive:][path]filename
              Specifies a file or files to search.

If a path is not specified, FIND searches the text typed at the
prompt or piped from another command.
```

If a file name is not specified, FIND searches the text typed at the prompt or piped from another command.

9.11 Activity: Using the FIND Filter

Note 1:   The DATA disk is in Drive A with the A:\> displayed.

Note 2:   *Only* if PERSONAL.FIL is not on the root of the DATA disk, copy it from WUGXP to the root of the DATA disk. Use the text editor to open A:\PERSONAL.FIL. Go to Chapter 7, Activity 7.14, step 26. Add the data listed there to the bottom of the file. Save the edited file.

Note 3: You *must* use double quotes. Single quotes are invalid.

1 Key in the following: A:\>**FIND "Smith" PERSONAL.FIL** [Enter]

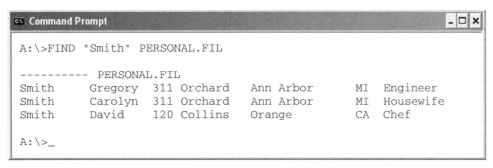

```
A:\>FIND "Smith" PERSONAL.FIL

---------- PERSONAL.FIL
Smith      Gregory  311 Orchard   Ann Arbor    MI   Engineer
Smith      Carolyn  311 Orchard   Ann Arbor    MI   Housewife
Smith      David    120 Collins   Orange       CA   Chef

A:\>_
```

WHAT'S
HAPPENING?   The FIND command found every occurrence of the character string "Smith" in **PERSONAL.FIL** on the DATA disk. A character string must be enclosed in quotation marks. Since FIND is case sensitive, you must key in the word exactly as it appears in the file. The character string SMITH would not be found because FIND would be looking for uppercase letters. If you use the parameter /I, the command would find SMITH, smith, or Smith. The FIND command "filtered" the file **PERSONAL.FIL** to extract the character string that matched the specification. With the use of the /V parameter, you can search a file for anything *except* what is in quotation marks.

2 Key in the following: A:\>**FIND /V "Smith" PERSONAL.FIL** [Enter]

```
Suzuki     Charlene 567 Abbey      Rochester     MI   Day Care Teacher
Markiw     Nicholas 354 Bell       Phoenix       AZ   Engineer
Markiw     Emily    10 Zion        Sun City West AZ   Retired
Nyles      John     12 Brooks      Sun City West AZ   Retired
Nyles      Sophie   12 Brooks      Sun City West CA   Retired
Markiw     Nick     10 Zion        Sun City West AZ   Retired
Washingon  Tyrone   345 Newport    Orange        CA   Manager
Jones      Steven   32 North       Phoenix       AZ   Buyer
Babchuk    Walter   12 View        Thousand Oaks CA   President
Babchuk    Deana    12 View        Thousand Oaks CA   Housewife
Jones      Cleo     355 Second     Ann Arbor     MI   Clerk
Gonzales   Antonio  40 Northern    Ontario       CA   Engineer
JONES      JERRY    244 East       Mission Viejo CA   Systems Analyst
Lo         Ophelia  1213 Wick      Phoenix       AZ   Writer
Jones      Ervin    15 Fourth      Santa Cruz    CA   Banker
Perez      Sergio   134 Seventh    Ann Arbor     MI   Editor
Yuan       Suelin   56 Twin Leaf   Orange        CA   Artist
Markiw     Nicholas 12 Fifth       Glendale      AZ   Engineer
Peat       Brian    123 Second     Vacaville     CA   Athlete
Farneth    Nichole  456 Stage      Davis         CA   Biologist

A:\>_
```

WHAT'S
HAPPENING?   (This graphic represents the last part of what you will see on your screen.) Though the output is so long it scrolled off the screen, you can see that FIND located everyone *except* Smith. Furthermore, you can find the specific line number of each occurrence by using the /N parameter.

3 Key in the following: A:\>**FIND /N "Smith" PERSONAL.FIL** [Enter]

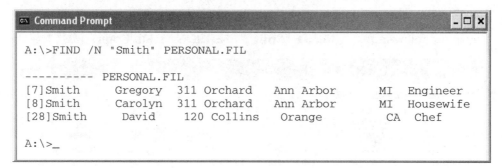

```
A:\>FIND /N "Smith" PERSONAL.FIL

---------- PERSONAL.FIL
[7]Smith      Gregory   311 Orchard    Ann Arbor      MI  Engineer
[8]Smith      Carolyn   311 Orchard    Ann Arbor      MI  Housewife
[28]Smith      David     120 Collins    Orange         CA  Chef

A:\>_
```

WHAT'S HAPPENING?   Displayed on the screen are not only all the people named Smith, but also the line numbers where their names appear in the file. You can also have a numeric count of the number of times a specific character string appears in a file. The FIND command will not display the actual lines, but it will tell you how many occurrences there are of that specific string.

4   Key in the following: A:\>**FIND /C "Smith" PERSONAL.FIL** [Enter]

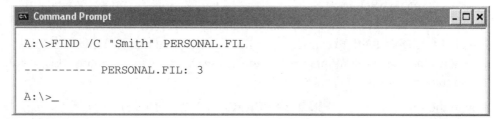

```
A:\>FIND /C "Smith" PERSONAL.FIL

---------- PERSONAL.FIL: 3

A:\>_
```

WHAT'S HAPPENING?   The number 3 follows the file name. The name Smith, (capital "S," small "mith") appears three times in the file **PERSONAL.FIL**. You can also tell the FIND command to ignore case.

5   Key in the following: A:\>**FIND /I "Jones" PERSONAL.FIL** [Enter]

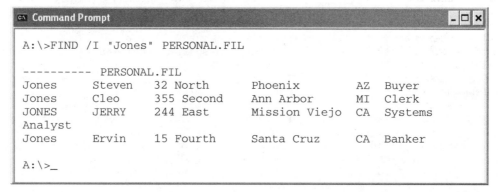

```
A:\>FIND /I "Jones" PERSONAL.FIL

---------- PERSONAL.FIL
Jones      Steven    32 North       Phoenix        AZ  Buyer
Jones      Cleo      355 Second     Ann Arbor      MI  Clerk
JONES      JERRY     244 East       Mission Viejo  CA  Systems
Analyst
Jones      Ervin     15 Fourth      Santa Cruz     CA  Banker

A:\>_
```

WHAT'S HAPPENING?   By using the /I parameter, which told the FIND command to ignore the case, you found both Jones and JONES. The parameters can come at the end of the command.

6   Key in the following: A:\>**FIND "Jones" PERSONAL.FIL /I** [Enter]

```
A:\>FIND "Jones" PERSONAL.FIL /I

---------- PERSONAL.FIL
```

```
Jones      Steven     32 North     Phoenix        AZ  Buyer
Jones      Cleo       355 Second   Ann Arbor      MI  Clerk
JONES      JERRY      244 East     Mission Viejo  CA  Systems
Analyst
Jones      Ervin      15 Fourth    Santa Cruz     CA  Banker

A:\>_
```

**WHAT'S
HAPPENING?**   As you can see, the results of step 5 and step 6 are exactly the
same.

9.12 Pipes

Pipes allow the standard output of one program to be used as standard input to the
next program. When you use pipes, you are not limited to two programs. You may
pipe together many programs. The term "pipe" reflects the flow of information from
one command to the next. Pipes are used with filter commands. You may take any
command that has standard output and pipe it to a filter. The filter will "do"
something to the standard output of the previous command, such as sort it. Since
filters always write to standard output, you may use pipes and filters to further
refine your data. Essentially, you may use filters to transform data to meet your
needs.

The pipe symbol is the vertical broken bar (¦) used between two commands. The
standard output from a command is written to a temporary file. Then the next
command in the pipeline, typically a filter, reads the temporary file as standard
input. See Figure 9.5.

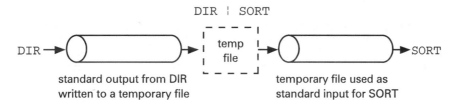

Figure 9.5—Piping Commands

On the original IBM keyboard, the pipe symbol is located between the **Shift** key
and the letter Z. On some computers, the pipe symbol is located along with the
backslash. Some other keyboards have the ¦ symbol next to the **Ctrl** and **Alt** keys
on the right side of the keyboard. The location of the pipe is not standard and could
appear in other locations, particularly on notebook computers. The pipe is the
connection between two commands, like a pipe in a water system. Since filters are
external commands, the operating system must be able to access the commands. If a
disk is write-protected, filter commands will not work because these commands
read and write temporary files to the disk.

After using pipes with filters, you may see some strange files on the directory
listing labeled:

```
%PIPE1.$$$
%PIPE2.$$$
%PIPE3.$$$
```

or

```
11002649
1100274E
```

All files must be named—even temporary files. These are the names the operating system gives for the files that it creates when you use piping. These temporary files "hold" the data until the next command can process it. These temporary files are automatically deleted by the operating system when you have finished your chain of commands. You will not see these names displayed on the screen, and probably will not see them at all. Remember, you must be able to write to the disk to use the pipe. The floppy can not be write-protected, and you must have write permission on a network drive.

9.13 The MORE Filter

The MORE command displays one screenful of data at a time with a prompt that reads **-- More --**. The MORE command pauses after the screen is full. How the display continues depends on what key is touched. When there is no more data in the file, the MORE command finishes by returning you to the system prompt. The purpose of the MORE command is to allow you to be able to read a long text file, one that would not fit onto the screen, one screenful at a time. Many new features have been were added to the MORE command with Windows 2000 Professional and are retained in Windows XP Professional. The syntax is:

```
MORE [/E [/C] [/P] [/S] [/Tn] [+n]] < [drive:][path]filename
command-name ¦ MORE [/E [/C] [/P] [/S] [/Tn] [+n]]
MORE /E [/C] [/P] [/S] [/Tn] [+n] [files]

    [drive:][path]filename  Specifies a file to display one
                            screen at a time.

    command-name            Specifies a command whose output
                            will be displayed.

    /E      Enable extended features
    /C      Clear screen before displaying page
    /P      Expand FormFeed characters
    /S      Squeeze multiple blank lines into a single line
    /Tn     Expand tabs to n spaces (default 8)

            Switches can be present in the MORE environment
            variable.

    +n      Start displaying the first file at line n

    files   List of files to be displayed. Files in the list
            are separated by blanks.

    If extended features are enabled, the following commands
    are accepted at the -- More -- prompt:

    P n     Display next n lines
    S n     Skip next n lines
    F       Display next file
    Q       Quit
    =       Show line number
    ?       Show help line
```

```
<space> Display next page
<ret>   Display next line
```

By default, in Windows XP Professional, extended features are enabled. The following exercises assume extended features are enabled. As the syntax diagram indicates, MORE can be both redirected and used with a pipe.

9.14 Activity: Using the MORE Filter

Note: The DATA disk is in Drive A with the A:\> displayed.

1 You will use the pipe symbol ¦, so be sure you locate it on the keyboard. Key in the following: A:\>**DIR ¦ MORE** Enter

```
Command Prompt                                              - □ ×

A:\>DIR ¦ MORE
 Volume in drive A is DATA
 Volume Serial Number is 30B8-DA1D

 Directory of A:\

10/30/2001  02:47 PM                86 BONJOUR.NEW
03/15/2002  01:38 PM    <DIR>          CLASS
03/15/2002  07:29 PM    <DIR>          WORK
03/15/2002  08:29 PM               616 CalifSurf.MUS
12/31/2001  04:32 PM               182 WILDTWO.AAA
12/31/2001  04:32 PM               181 WILDTHR.AAA
03/25/2002  02:11 PM    <DIR>          TRIP
10/30/2001  01:41 PM               155 DRAMA.TV
08/12/2000  04:12 PM                73 MARK.FIL
08/12/2000  04:12 PM               314 CASES.FIL
07/31/1999  12:53 PM             2,672 NEWPRSON.FIL
08/12/2000  04:12 PM                 3 Y.FIL
07/31/1999  12:53 PM                47 CAROLYN.FIL
12/06/2001  12:25 AM               465 person.fil
07/31/1999  12:53 PM                44 BRIAN.FIL
10/31/2001  01:38 PM             4,064 NEW-SUVS.XLS
10/31/2001  04:50 PM               138 FILE2.SWT
10/31/2001  04:51 PM               137 FILE4.FP
10/31/2001  04:51 PM               137 FILE2.FP
10/31/2001  04:51 PM               137 FILE3.FP
10/31/2001  02:49 PM               138 FILE2.CZG
10/31/2001  02:49 PM               138 FILE3.CZG
10/31/2001  04:50 PM               138 FILE3.SWT
12/06/2001  09:24 AM    <DIR>          MEDIA
04/11/2002  11:40 AM             2,431 PERSONAL.FIL
04/11/2002  12:17 PM                45 STEVEN.FIL
04/11/2002  12:20 PM                36 b.bat
04/11/2002  12:20 PM                30 TEST.BAT
04/17/2002  01:07 PM    <DIR>          GAMES
10/30/2001  02:10 PM               121 BORN.TXT
11/16/2000  12:00 PM                59 Sandy and Patty.txt
11/16/2000  12:00 PM                53 Sandy and Nicki.txt
 -- More  --
```

WHAT'S
HAPPENING?   Your file listing may vary. The Command Line window height shown in these displays has been adjusted to provide a varied range of displays. By using the pipe symbol, you asked that the output of the DIR command be used as input to the MORE command. The **-- More --** on the bottom of the screen tells you

that there are more screens of data. Press the spacebar and the next page of data appears. Pressing the **Enter** key displays the next line in the file.

2   Press the **Enter** key until you are back at the system prompt. You may have to press several times until you are returned to the system prompt, as with extended features, the **Enter** key continues the display one line at a time.

3   Key in the following: A:\>**DIR ¦ MORE** **Enter**

4   Press the **Space Bar**

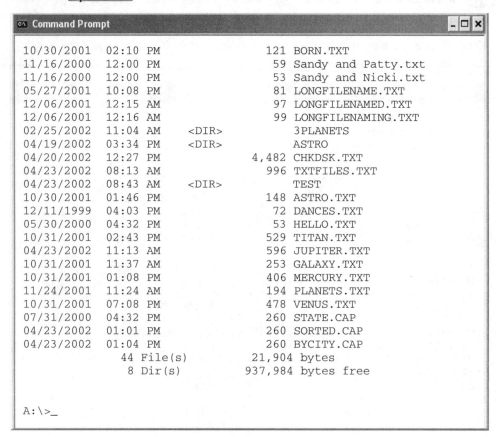

```
Command Prompt                                                      _ □ ×
10/30/2001  02:10 PM                   121 BORN.TXT
11/16/2000  12:00 PM                    59 Sandy and Patty.txt
11/16/2000  12:00 PM                    53 Sandy and Nicki.txt
05/27/2001  10:08 PM                    81 LONGFILENAME.TXT
12/06/2001  12:15 AM                    97 LONGFILENAMED.TXT
12/06/2001  12:16 AM                    99 LONGFILENAMING.TXT
02/25/2002  11:04 AM     <DIR>             3PLANETS
04/19/2002  03:34 PM     <DIR>             ASTRO
04/20/2002  12:27 PM                 4,482 CHKDSK.TXT
04/23/2002  08:13 AM                   996 TXTFILES.TXT
04/23/2002  08:43 AM     <DIR>             TEST
10/30/2001  01:46 PM                   148 ASTRO.TXT
12/11/1999  04:03 PM                    72 DANCES.TXT
05/30/2000  04:32 PM                    53 HELLO.TXT
10/31/2001  02:43 PM                   529 TITAN.TXT
04/23/2002  11:13 AM                   596 JUPITER.TXT
10/31/2001  11:37 AM                   253 GALAXY.TXT
10/31/2001  01:08 PM                   406 MERCURY.TXT
11/24/2001  11:24 AM                   194 PLANETS.TXT
10/31/2001  07:08 PM                   478 VENUS.TXT
07/31/2000  04:32 PM                   260 STATE.CAP
04/23/2002  01:01 PM                   260 SORTED.CAP
04/23/2002  01:04 PM                   260 BYCITY.CAP
             44 File(s)          21,904 bytes
              8 Dir(s)          937,984 bytes free


A:\>_
```

WHATS
HAPPENING?   You displayed the next page of information. (If necessary, press the spacebar again until you are returned to the A:\> prompt.) With extended features, you can also use Q to break the command and return to the system prompt.

5   Key in the following: A:\>**DIR ¦ MORE** **Enter**

6   Press the **Q** key.

```
Command Prompt                                                      _ □ ×
A:\>DIR ¦ MORE
 Volume in drive A is DATA
 Volume Serial Number is 30B8-DA1D

 Directory of A:\

10/30/2001  02:47 PM                    86 BONJOUR.NEW
03/15/2002  01:38 PM     <DIR>             CLASS
03/15/2002  07:29 PM     <DIR>             WORK
03/15/2002  08:29 PM                   616 CalifSurf.MUS
```

```
12/31/2001   04:32 PM                    182 WILDTWO.AAA
12/31/2001   04:32 PM                    181 WILDTHR.AAA
03/25/2002   02:11 PM    <DIR>               TRIP
10/30/2001   01:41 PM                    155 DRAMA.TV
08/12/2000   04:12 PM                     73 MARK.FIL
08/12/2000   04:12 PM                    314 CASES.FIL
07/31/1999   12:53 PM                  2,672 NEWPRSON.FIL
08/12/2000   04:12 PM                      3 Y.FIL
07/31/1999   12:53 PM                     47 CAROLYN.FIL
12/06/2001   12:25 AM                    465 person.fil
07/31/1999   12:53 PM                     44 BRIAN.FIL
10/31/2001   01:38 PM                  4,064 NEW-SUVS.XLS
10/31/2001   04:50 PM                    138 FILE2.SWT
10/31/2001   04:51 PM                    137 FILE4.FP
10/31/2001   04:51 PM                    137 FILE2.FP
10/31/2001   04:51 PM                    137 FILE3.FP
10/31/2001   02:49 PM                    138 FILE2.CZG
10/31/2001   02:49 PM                    138 FILE3.CZG
10/31/2001   04:50 PM                    138 FILE3.SWT
12/06/2001   09:24 AM    <DIR>               MEDIA
04/11/2002   11:40 AM                  2,431 PERSONAL.FIL
04/11/2002   12:17 PM                     45 STEVEN.FIL
04/11/2002   12:20 PM                     36 b.bat
04/11/2002   12:20 PM                     30 TEST.BAT
04/17/2002   01:07 PM    <DIR>               GAMES
10/30/2001   02:10 PM                    121 BORN.TXT
11/16/2000   12:00 PM                     59 Sandy and Patty.txt
11/16/2000   12:00 PM                     53 Sandy and Nicki.txt

A:\>_
```

Note: The size (number of bytes) listed may be different from the display due to the difference in files you created.

WHAT'S
HAPPENING?   The display halted and returned you to the system level. You may ask yourself, why do this when the same effect is achieved by using DIR /P? There are two reasons. The first is that you can connect several commands with pipes and filters. The second is that /P works only with the DIR command.

7   Key in the following: A:\>**DIR ¦ SORT /+39 ¦ MORE** [Enter]

```
Command Prompt                                                    _ □ ✕

A:\>DIR ¦ SORT +39 ¦ MORE


              8 Dir(s)         937,984 bytes free
             44 File(s)         21,904 bytes
Directory of A:\

 Volume Serial Number is 2829-1507
 Volume in drive A is DATA
06/27/2002   02:17 PM    <DIR>               3PLANETS
07/04/2002   11:05 PM    <DIR>               ASTRO
10/30/2001   12:46 PM                    148 ASTRO.TXT
07/04/2002   02:24 PM                     37 b.bat
10/30/2001   02:47 PM                     86 BONJOUR.NEW
10/30/2001   01:10 PM                    121 BORN.TXT
07/31/1999   12:53 PM                     44 BRIAN.FIL
07/05/2002   01:42 PM                    260 BYCITY.CAP
06/27/2002   07:22 PM                    616 CalifSurf.MUS
```

```
07/31/1999    12:53 PM                     47 CAROLYN.FIL
08/12/2000    03:12 PM                    314 CASES.FIL
07/04/2002    11:18 PM                  4,481 CHKDSK.TXT
06/27/2002    07:00 PM      <DIR>           CLASS
12/11/1999    03:03 PM                     72 DANCES.TXT
10/30/2001    01:41 PM                    155 DRAMA.TV
10/31/2001    02:49 PM                    138 FILE2.CZG
10/31/2001    03:51 PM                    137 FILE2.FP
10/31/2001    03:50 PM                    138 FILE2.SWT
10/31/2001    02:49 PM                    138 FILE3.CZG
10/31/2001    04:51 PM                    137 FILE3.FP
10/31/2001    04:50 PM                    138 FILE3.SWT
10/31/2001    03:51 PM                    137 FILE4.FP
10/31/2001    11:37 AM                    253 GALAXY.TXT
07/04/2002    10:43 PM      <DIR>           GAMES
05/30/2000    03:32 PM                     53 HELLO.TXT
07/05/2002    01:26 PM                    596 JUPITER.TXT
— More —
```

WHAT'S HAPPENING?   You now have a sorted directory listing. The filename begins in column 40. You used column 39 to begin the SORT on the space before the file name, thus preventing the lines with bytes and bytes free sizes, which contain numbers in column 40, from being listed at the top of the display.

8 Continue pressing the **Space Bar** until you have returned to the system prompt or press **Q**.

```
━━ Command Prompt                                              _ □ ✕

07/05/2002    01:26 PM                    596 JUPITER.TXT
05/27/2001    10:08 PM                     81 LONGFILENAME.TXT
12/06/2001    12:15 AM                     97 LONGFILENAMED.TXT
12/06/2001    12:16 AM                     99 LONGFILENAMING.TXT
08/12/2000    03:12 PM                     73 MARK.FIL
10/30/2001    03:33 PM      <DIR>           MEDIA
10/31/2001    01:08 PM                    406 MERCURY.TXT
10/31/2001    01:38 PM                  4,064 NEW-SUVS.XLS
07/31/1999    12:53 PM                  2,672 NEWPRSON.FIL
12/06/2001    12:25 AM                    465 person.fil
07/04/2002    02:22 PM                  2,428 PERSONAL.FIL
11/24/2001    11:24 AM                    194 PLANETS.TXT
11/16/2000    11:00 AM                     53 Sandy and Nicki.txt
11/16/2000    11:00 AM                     59 Sandy and Patty.txt
07/05/2002    01:36 PM                    260 SORTED.CAP
07/31/2000    04:32 PM                    260 STATE.CAP
07/04/2002    02:22 PM                     45 STEVEN.FIL
07/05/2002    01:24 PM      <DIR>           TEST
07/04/2002    02:24 PM                     37 TEST.BAT
10/31/2001    01:43 PM                    529 TITAN.TXT
06/30/2002    02:45 PM      <DIR>           TRIP
07/05/2002    01:23 PM                    995 TXTFILES.TXT
10/31/2001    07:08 PM                    478 VENUS.TXT
12/31/2001    04:32 PM                    181 WILDTHR.AAA
12/31/2001    03:32 PM                    182 WILDTWO.AAA
06/27/2002    07:07 PM      <DIR>           WORK
08/12/2000    04:12 PM                      3 Y.FIL
              8 Dir(s)          937,984 bytes free
             44 File(s)          21,907 bytes



A:\>_
```

WHAT'S
HAPPENING?   You returned to the system prompt. Pipes are extremely useful with long ASCII text files. Often a program will come with a **Read.me** or **Readme.txt** file and this command can be used to read the file. A Readme file holds late-breaking information about the program. If you have a text file that is more than one screenful (or page) of data, you cannot use **TYPE /P filename.ext** because /P is not a valid TYPE parameter. You can use the MORE command with a file as input. You can enter the name of the text file to be used with the MORE command, or you can pipe it. In the next step, the command used with the file name will be used first.

9   Key in the following: A:\>**MORE PERSONAL.FIL** Enter

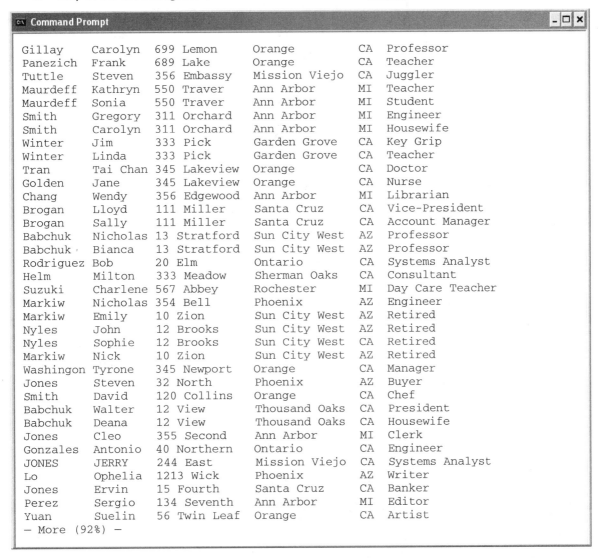

```
Command Prompt                                                        _ □ x

Gillay     Carolyn  699 Lemon      Orange          CA  Professor
Panezich   Frank    689 Lake       Orange          CA  Teacher
Tuttle     Steven   356 Embassy    Mission Viejo   CA  Juggler
Maurdeff   Kathryn  550 Traver     Ann Arbor       MI  Teacher
Maurdeff   Sonia    550 Traver     Ann Arbor       MI  Student
Smith      Gregory  311 Orchard    Ann Arbor       MI  Engineer
Smith      Carolyn  311 Orchard    Ann Arbor       MI  Housewife
Winter     Jim      333 Pick       Garden Grove    CA  Key Grip
Winter     Linda    333 Pick       Garden Grove    CA  Teacher
Tran       Tai Chan 345 Lakeview   Orange          CA  Doctor
Golden     Jane     345 Lakeview   Orange          CA  Nurse
Chang      Wendy    356 Edgewood   Ann Arbor       MI  Librarian
Brogan     Lloyd    111 Miller     Santa Cruz      CA  Vice-President
Brogan     Sally    111 Miller     Santa Cruz      CA  Account Manager
Babchuk    Nicholas 13 Stratford   Sun City West   AZ  Professor
Babchuk    Bianca   13 Stratford   Sun City West   AZ  Professor
Rodriguez  Bob      20 Elm         Ontario         CA  Systems Analyst
Helm       Milton   333 Meadow     Sherman Oaks    CA  Consultant
Suzuki     Charlene 567 Abbey      Rochester       MI  Day Care Teacher
Markiw     Nicholas 354 Bell       Phoenix         AZ  Engineer
Markiw     Emily    10 Zion        Sun City West   AZ  Retired
Nyles      John     12 Brooks      Sun City West   AZ  Retired
Nyles      Sophie   12 Brooks      Sun City West   CA  Retired
Markiw     Nick     10 Zion        Sun City West   AZ  Retired
Washingon  Tyrone   345 Newport    Orange          CA  Manager
Jones      Steven   32 North       Phoenix         AZ  Buyer
Smith      David    120 Collins    Orange          CA  Chef
Babchuk    Walter   12 View        Thousand Oaks   CA  President
Babchuk    Deana    12 View        Thousand Oaks   CA  Housewife
Jones      Cleo     355 Second     Ann Arbor       MI  Clerk
Gonzales   Antonio  40 Northern    Ontario         CA  Engineer
JONES      JERRY    244 East       Mission Viejo   CA  Systems Analyst
Lo         Ophelia  1213 Wick      Phoenix         AZ  Writer
Jones      Ervin    15 Fourth      Santa Cruz      CA  Banker
Perez      Sergio   134 Seventh    Ann Arbor       MI  Editor
Yuan       Suelin   56 Twin Leaf   Orange          CA  Artist
— More (92%) —
```

WHAT'S
HAPPENING?   You asked that the file from the DATA disk called **PERSONAL.FIL** be used as the file to be sent to the MORE command. The MORE command then displayed a screenful of this file. You will see more or less of the file depending on the size of your Command Line window. There is an alternative way to produce the same results. You can pipe the output of the file to the MORE command.

10   Continue to press the SpaceBar until you have returned to the system prompt or press **Q**.

11 Key in the following: A:\>**TYPE PERSONAL.FIL ¦ MORE** Enter

```
Command Prompt                                                    _ □ ×

Gillay      Carolyn   699 Lemon      Orange         CA   Professor
Panezich    Frank     689 Lake       Orange         CA   Teacher
Tuttle      Steven    356 Embassy    Mission Viejo  CA   Juggler
Maurdeff    Kathryn   550 Traver     Ann Arbor      MI   Teacher
Maurdeff    Sonia     550 Traver     Ann Arbor      MI   Student
Smith       Gregory   311 Orchard    Ann Arbor      MI   Engineer
Smith       Carolyn   311 Orchard    Ann Arbor      MI   Housewife
Winter      Jim       333 Pick       Garden Grove   CA   Key Grip
Winter      Linda     333 Pick       Garden Grove   CA   Teacher
Tran        Tai Chan  345 Lakeview   Orange         CA   Doctor
Golden      Jane      345 Lakeview   Orange         CA   Nurse
Chang       Wendy     356 Edgewood   Ann Arbor      MI   Librarian
Brogan      Lloyd     111 Miller     Santa Cruz     CA   Vice-President
Brogan      Sally     111 Miller     Santa Cruz     CA   Account Manager
Babchuk     Nicholas  13 Stratford   Sun City West  AZ   Professor
Babchuk     Bianca    13 Stratford   Sun City West  AZ   Professor
Rodriguez   Bob       20 Elm         Ontario        CA   Systems Analyst
Helm        Milton    333 Meadow     Sherman Oaks   CA   Consultant
Suzuki      Charlene  567 Abbey      Rochester      MI   Day Care Teacher
Markiw      Nicholas  354 Bell       Phoenix        AZ   Engineer
Markiw      Emily     10 Zion        Sun City West  AZ   Retired
Nyles       John      12 Brooks      Sun City West  AZ   Retired
Nyles       Sophie    12 Brooks      Sun City West  CA   Retired
-- More   --
```

WHAT'S HAPPENING? You took the output from the TYPE command, which is normally a screen display, and piped it as input to the MORE command. The MORE command then displayed a screenful of this file. Remember that there must be a command on either side of the pipe. You could not key in **PERSONAL.FIL ¦ MORE** because **PERSONAL.FIL** is a file and not a command.

12 Continue to press the SpaceBar or press Q to return you to the system prompt.

WHAT'S HAPPENING? You returned to the system prompt. PERSONAL.FIL is more than one screenful of information. Lines of information in a data file are called records. Each person listed in the file, and all the information on that same line, is one record. MORE will allow you to start viewing the file at a specified line, or record number. Also, to help avoid confusion, you can clear the screen before the display begins.

13 Key in the following: A:\>**MORE PERSONAL.FIL /C +20** Enter

```
Command Prompt                                                    _ □ ×

Markiw     Nicholas  354 Bell      Phoenix        AZ   Engineer
Markiw     Emily     10 Zion       Sun City West  AZ   Retired
Nyles      John      12 Brooks     Sun City West  AZ   Retired
Nyles      Sophie    12 Brooks     Sun City West  CA   Retired
Markiw     Nick      10 Zion       Sun City West  AZ   Retired
Washingon  Tyrone    345 Newport   Orange         CA   Manager
Jones      Steven    32 North      Phoenix        AZ   Buyer
Smith      David     120 Collins   Orange         CA   Chef
Babchuk    Walter    12 View       Thousand Oaks  CA   President
Babchuk    Deana     12 View       Thousand Oaks  CA   Housewife
Jones      Cleo      355 Second    Ann Arbor      MI   Clerk
Gonzales   Antonio   40 Northern   Ontario        CA   Engineer
```

```
JONES      JERRY      244 East      Mission Viejo  CA  Systems Analyst
Lo         Ophelia    1213 Wick     Phoenix        AZ  Writer
Jones      Ervin      15 Fourth     Santa Cruz     CA  Banker
Perez      Sergio     134 Seventh   Ann Arbor      MI  Editor
Yuan       Suelin     56 Twin Leaf  Orange         CA  Artist
Markiw     Nicholas   12 Fifth      Glendale       AZ  Engineer
Peat       Brian      123 Second    Vacaville      CA  Athlete
Farneth    Nichole    456 Stage     Davis          CA  Biologist

A:\>_
```

WHAT'S HAPPENING?   Markiw's record is the twentieth record in **PERSONAL.FIL** (+20). The display began at that point in the file. Also, the screen was cleared (/C) before the display began. Notice, not even the command you keyed in is visible. You can use the MORE filter with more than one file.

14 Key in the following: A:\>**MORE SORTED.CAP BYCITY.CAP /C** [Enter]

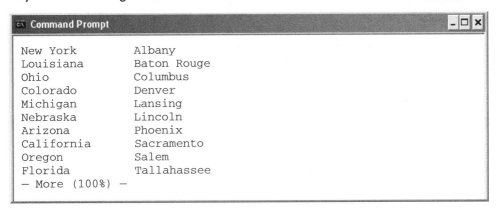

WHAT'S HAPPENING?   The command does not appear on the screen, as the /C parameter cleared the screen before the display began. The entire file, **SORTED.CAP** is on the screen, signified by the 100%.

15 Press the [Space Bar]

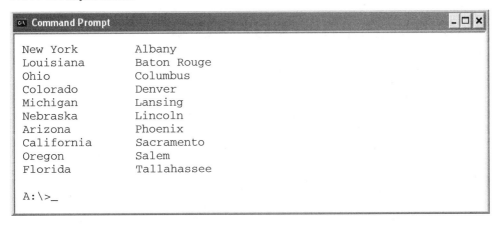

WHAT'S HAPPENING?   Because **SORTED.CAP** and **BYCITY.CAP** contained the same information and the /C parameter cleared the screen before each display, the information does not seem to have changed. There are times when clearing the screen can become confusing.

16 Key in the following: A:\>**MORE SORTED.CAP BYCITY.CAP** [Enter]

17 Press the [Space Bar]

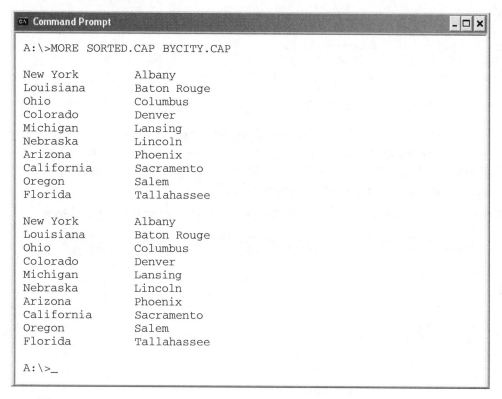

```
     Command Prompt                                                   _ □ ×

    A:\>MORE SORTED.CAP BYCITY.CAP

    New York         Albany
    Louisiana        Baton Rouge
    Ohio             Columbus
    Colorado         Denver
    Michigan         Lansing
    Nebraska         Lincoln
    Arizona          Phoenix
    California       Sacramento
    Oregon           Salem
    Florida          Tallahassee

    New York         Albany
    Louisiana        Baton Rouge
    Ohio             Columbus
    Colorado         Denver
    Michigan         Lansing
    Nebraska         Lincoln
    Arizona          Phoenix
    California       Sacramento
    Oregon           Salem
    Florida          Tallahassee

    A:\>_
```

WHAT'S ▒▒▒▒▒
▒▒▒▒ HAPPENING?   The first file displayed, and then the message **-- More (100%) --**
was displayed. When you pressed the spacebar, the message disappeared, and the
second file was displayed. In this case, not using the /C parameter made it possible
to compare the two files.

18 Close all open windows and return to the desktop environment, the GUI.

9.15 Other Features of MORE

If you look at the bottom of the syntax diagram of the MORE command,

```
If extended features are enabled, the following commands
are accepted at the -- More -- prompt:

 P n Display next n lines
 S n Skip next n lines
 F         Display next file
 Q         Quit
 =         Show line number
 ?         Show help line
 <space>   Display next page
 <ret>     Display next line
```

it states that if extended features are enabled, you have more choices available to
you with the MORE command. *Extensions* in this case means that Windows XP
Professional provides more features to CMD.EXE, which provides a richer, more
powerful shell programming environment. When you open a Command Prompt

window, you are running a shell. A shell is the command interpreter used to pass commands to the operating system. The Command Prompt, by default, enables the shell extensions. If your system did not, by default, enable shell extensions, part of the previous exercise would not have worked correctly. You can enable extended features by keying in CMD /X. If you wanted the shell extensions disabled, you could key in CMD /Y. The commands that use the shell extensions are DEL, COLOR, CD, MD, PROMPT, PUSHD, POPD, SET, SETLOCAL, ENDLOCAL, IF, FOR, CALL, SHIFT, GOTO, STARTS, ASSOC, and FTYPE. If you wanted full details on what you may do with each command, you would key in the command name with /? . In this case, you are going to continue to use some of the extended features of the MORE command.

9.16 Activity: Using the Extended Features of MORE

Note: The DATA disk is in Drive A. You are on the desktop.

1 Click **Start**. Click **Run**.

WHAT'S HAPPENING? You may run a program from the Run dialog box. You may have data already in the Open text box. Run remembers the last command that was keyed in. In this case, the command you want to execute is the shell, **CMD.EXE**.

2 If there is any text in the Open text box, clear it. Then key in **CMD.EXE /X**.

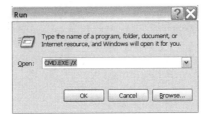

WHAT'S HAPPENING? You are now going to execute the program CMD /X. The /X ensures that you are going to be able to use the extensions to commands.

3 Click **OK**.

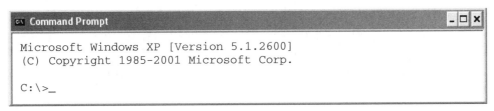

```
Command Prompt                                          _ □ ×

Microsoft Windows XP [Version 5.1.2600]
(C) Copyright 1985-2001 Microsoft Corp.

C:\>_
```

WHAT'S
HAPPENING?   You have opened a Command Prompt window. The prompt in
your new window will vary. If you are not in the root directory of C, key in CD \.

4   Key in the following: C:\>**A:** Enter

5   Key in the following: A:\>**MORE PERSONAL.FIL** Enter

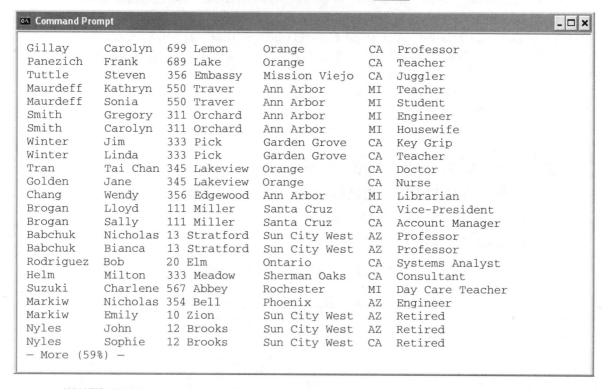

```
🖳 Command Prompt                                                    - □ ×

Gillay      Carolyn    699 Lemon      Orange         CA  Professor
Panezich    Frank      689 Lake       Orange         CA  Teacher
Tuttle      Steven     356 Embassy    Mission Viejo  CA  Juggler
Maurdeff    Kathryn    550 Traver     Ann Arbor      MI  Teacher
Maurdeff    Sonia      550 Traver     Ann Arbor      MI  Student
Smith       Gregory    311 Orchard    Ann Arbor      MI  Engineer
Smith       Carolyn    311 Orchard    Ann Arbor      MI  Housewife
Winter      Jim        333 Pick       Garden Grove   CA  Key Grip
Winter      Linda      333 Pick       Garden Grove   CA  Teacher
Tran        Tai Chan   345 Lakeview   Orange         CA  Doctor
Golden      Jane       345 Lakeview   Orange         CA  Nurse
Chang       Wendy      356 Edgewood   Ann Arbor      MI  Librarian
Brogan      Lloyd      111 Miller     Santa Cruz     CA  Vice-President
Brogan      Sally      111 Miller     Santa Cruz     CA  Account Manager
Babchuk     Nicholas   13 Stratford   Sun City West  AZ  Professor
Babchuk     Bianca     13 Stratford   Sun City West  AZ  Professor
Rodriguez   Bob        20 Elm         Ontario        CA  Systems Analyst
Helm        Milton     333 Meadow     Sherman Oaks   CA  Consultant
Suzuki      Charlene   567 Abbey      Rochester      MI  Day Care Teacher
Markiw      Nicholas   354 Bell       Phoenix        AZ  Engineer
Markiw      Emily      10 Zion        Sun City West  AZ  Retired
Nyles       John       12 Brooks      Sun City West  AZ  Retired
Nyles       Sophie     12 Brooks      Sun City West  CA  Retired
— More (59%) —
```

WHAT'S
HAPPENING?   So far the MORE command is working in the usual way. With
extensions enabled, if you press the **Space Bar**, referred to as <space> in the syntax
diagram, you will display the next page. If you press the **Enter** key, referred to as
<ret> in the syntax diagram, you will display the next line in the file.

6   Press **Enter** twice.

```
🖳 Command Prompt                                                    - □ ×

Panezich    Frank      689 Lake       Orange         CA  Teacher
Tuttle      Steven     356 Embassy    Mission Viejo  CA  Juggler
Maurdeff    Kathryn    550 Traver     Ann Arbor      MI  Teacher
Maurdeff    Sonia      550 Traver     Ann Arbor      MI  Student
Smith       Gregory    311 Orchard    Ann Arbor      MI  Engineer
Smith       Carolyn    311 Orchard    Ann Arbor      MI  Housewife
Winter      Jim        333 Pick       Garden Grove   CA  Key Grip
Winter      Linda      333 Pick       Garden Grove   CA  Teacher
Tran        Tai Chan   345 Lakeview   Orange         CA  Doctor
Golden      Jane       345 Lakeview   Orange         CA  Nurse
Chang       Wendy      356 Edgewood   Ann Arbor      MI  Librarian
Brogan      Lloyd      111 Miller     Santa Cruz     CA  Vice-President
Brogan      Sally      111 Miller     Santa Cruz     CA  Account Manager
Babchuk     Nicholas   13 Stratford   Sun City West  AZ  Professor
Babchuk     Bianca     13 Stratford   Sun City West  AZ  Professor
Rodriguez   Bob        20 Elm         Ontario        CA  Systems Analyst
Helm        Milton     333 Meadow     Sherman Oaks   CA  Consultant
Suzuki      Charlene   567 Abbey      Rochester      MI  Day Care Teacher
Markiw      Nicholas   354 Bell       Phoenix        AZ  Engineer
Markiw      Emily      10 Zion        Sun City West  AZ  Retired
```

```
Nyles      John      12 Brooks      Sun City West   AZ   Retired
Nyles      Sophie    12 Brooks      Sun City West   CA   Retired
Markiw     Nick      10 Zion        Sun City West   AZ   Retired
Washingon  Tyrone    345 Newport    Orange          CA   Manager
— More (64%) —
```

WHAT'S HAPPENING?   By pressing [Enter] twice, you moved two lines down in the file. You may exit the MORE command by keying in **Q**.

7   Press **Q**.

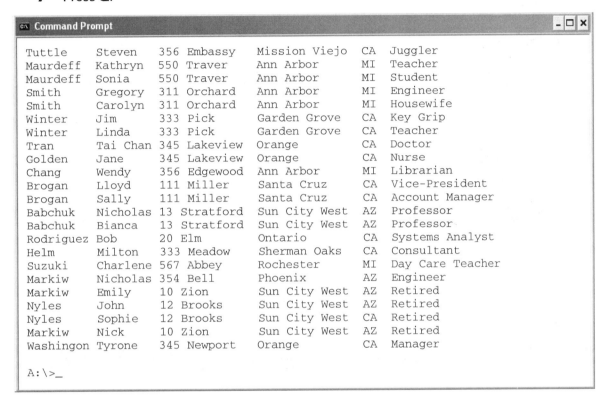

```
Tuttle     Steven     356 Embassy    Mission Viejo   CA   Juggler
Maurdeff   Kathryn    550 Traver     Ann Arbor       MI   Teacher
Maurdeff   Sonia      550 Traver     Ann Arbor       MI   Student
Smith      Gregory    311 Orchard    Ann Arbor       MI   Engineer
Smith      Carolyn    311 Orchard    Ann Arbor       MI   Housewife
Winter     Jim        333 Pick       Garden Grove    CA   Key Grip
Winter     Linda      333 Pick       Garden Grove    CA   Teacher
Tran       Tai Chan   345 Lakeview   Orange          CA   Doctor
Golden     Jane       345 Lakeview   Orange          CA   Nurse
Chang      Wendy      356 Edgewood   Ann Arbor       MI   Librarian
Brogan     Lloyd      111 Miller     Santa Cruz      CA   Vice-President
Brogan     Sally      111 Miller     Santa Cruz      CA   Account Manager
Babchuk    Nicholas   13 Stratford   Sun City West   AZ   Professor
Babchuk    Bianca     13 Stratford   Sun City West   AZ   Professor
Rodriguez  Bob        20 Elm         Ontario         CA   Systems Analyst
Helm       Milton     333 Meadow     Sherman Oaks    CA   Consultant
Suzuki     Charlene   567 Abbey      Rochester       MI   Day Care Teacher
Markiw     Nicholas   354 Bell       Phoenix         AZ   Engineer
Markiw     Emily      10 Zion        Sun City West   AZ   Retired
Nyles      John       12 Brooks      Sun City West   AZ   Retired
Nyles      Sophie     12 Brooks      Sun City West   CA   Retired
Markiw     Nick       10 Zion        Sun City West   AZ   Retired
Washingon  Tyrone     345 Newport    Orange          CA   Manager

A:\>_
```

WHAT'S HAPPENING?   By pressing **Q**, you exited the MORE command and returned to the system prompt.

8   Key in the following: A:>**MORE PERSONAL.FIL** [Enter]

9   Key in the following: **P**

```
Nyles      Sophie     12 Brooks      Sun City West   CA   Retired
-- More (59%) -- Lines:
```

WHAT'S HAPPENING?   By pressing **P** where MORE stopped, you can now request how many lines you want displayed.

10 Key in the following: **5** [Enter]

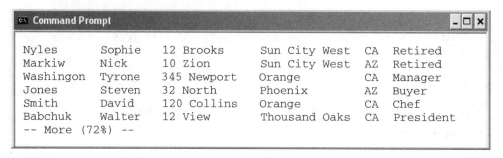

```
c:\  Command Prompt                                                    _ □ ×

Nyles        Sophie     12 Brooks      Sun City West   CA   Retired
Markiw       Nick       10 Zion        Sun City West   AZ   Retired
Washingon    Tyrone     345 Newport    Orange          CA   Manager
Jones        Steven     32 North       Phoenix         AZ   Buyer
Smith        David      120 Collins    Orange          CA   Chef
Babchuk      Walter     12 View        Thousand Oaks   CA   President
-- More (72%) --
```

WHAT'S
HAPPENING?   You have displayed the next five lines.

11 Press the = sign.

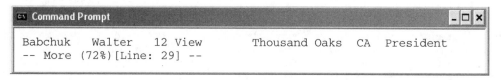

```
c:\  Command Prompt                                                    _ □ ×

Babchuk     Walter     12 View           Thousand Oaks  CA   President
-- More (72%)[Line: 29] --
```

WHAT'S
HAPPENING?   Pressing the = sign displays which line number you are on.

12 Press **S**.

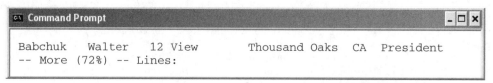

```
c:\  Command Prompt                                                    _ □ ×

Babchuk     Walter     12 View           Thousand Oaks  CA   President
-- More (72%) -- Lines:
```

WHAT'S
HAPPENING?   You are asked how many lines you want to skip in your display.

13 Key in the following: **3** Enter

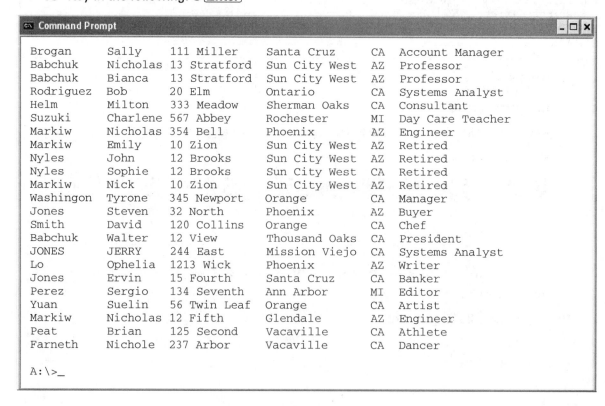

```
c:\  Command Prompt                                                            _ □ ×

Brogan      Sally      111 Miller     Santa Cruz     CA   Account Manager
Babchuk     Nicholas   13 Stratford   Sun City West  AZ   Professor
Babchuk     Bianca     13 Stratford   Sun City West  AZ   Professor
Rodriguez   Bob        20 Elm         Ontario        CA   Systems Analyst
Helm        Milton     333 Meadow     Sherman Oaks   CA   Consultant
Suzuki      Charlene   567 Abbey      Rochester      MI   Day Care Teacher
Markiw      Nicholas   354 Bell       Phoenix        AZ   Engineer
Markiw      Emily      10 Zion        Sun City West  AZ   Retired
Nyles       John       12 Brooks      Sun City West  AZ   Retired
Nyles       Sophie     12 Brooks      Sun City West  CA   Retired
Markiw      Nick       10 Zion        Sun City West  AZ   Retired
Washingon   Tyrone     345 Newport    Orange         CA   Manager
Jones       Steven     32 North       Phoenix        AZ   Buyer
Smith       David      120 Collins    Orange         CA   Chef
Babchuk     Walter     12 View        Thousand Oaks  CA   President
JONES       JERRY      244 East       Mission Viejo  CA   Systems Analyst
Lo          Ophelia    1213 Wick      Phoenix        AZ   Writer
Jones       Ervin      15 Fourth      Santa Cruz     CA   Banker
Perez       Sergio     134 Seventh    Ann Arbor      MI   Editor
Yuan        Suelin     56 Twin Leaf   Orange         CA   Artist
Markiw      Nicholas   12 Fifth       Glendale       AZ   Engineer
Peat        Brian      125 Second     Vacaville      CA   Athlete
Farneth     Nichole    237 Arbor      Vacaville      CA   Dancer


A:\>_
```

WHAT'S
HAPPENING?   You skipped three lines, which in this case took you to the end of the file.

14 Close all open windows.

WHAT'S
HAPPENING?   You have returned to the desktop.

9.17 Combining Commands with Pipes and Filters

You can use the pipe symbol to join commands where the standard output of one command is the standard input of the next command. The pipe symbol allows you to connect two or more programs and create a flow of data. When you use the pipe symbol, there must be a command on both sides of the actual symbol. If you use redirection with the "pipeline," a command does not have to be on either side of the > or >>. Remember, when you are redirecting output from a command, it is an "instead of" process. For instance, instead of writing the output of a command to the screen, you are redirecting the output to a file. When you combine the use of pipes and the >, the redirection becomes the end of the pipeline, the last step in the process.

9.18 Activity: Combining Commands

Note 1:   Open a Command Prompt window.
Note 2:   The DATA disk is in Drive A. A:\> is displayed.

1 Key in the following:
  A:\>**FIND "Teacher" PERSONAL.FIL ¦ FIND "CA"** Enter

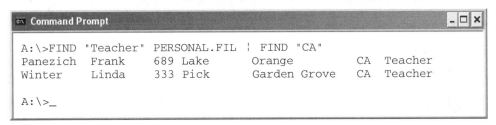

```
A:\>FIND "Teacher" PERSONAL.FIL ¦ FIND "CA"
Panezich   Frank    689 Lake     Orange         CA   Teacher
Winter     Linda    333 Pick     Garden Grove   CA   Teacher

A:\>_
```

WHAT'S
HAPPENING?   You asked the FIND command to locate the lines that contained "Teacher" in the **PERSONAL.FIL**, and to take the output from that command and pipe it back through the FIND command again, locating the lines from that output that contained "CA." The results were that only the teachers who live in California were displayed. Remember, the data in **PERSONAL.FIL** has not changed. You have merely searched that data so you could display only those lines, or records, that met your requirements. If you want to save the data you displayed, you must save it to a file.

2 Key in the following: A:\>
  FIND "Teacher" PERSONAL.FIL ¦ FIND "CA" > TEACHER.FIL Enter

3 Key in the following: A:\>**TYPE TEACHER.FIL** Enter

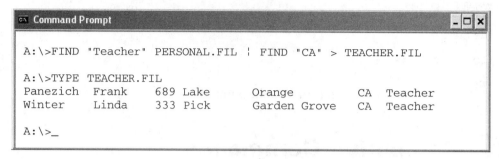

```
A:\>FIND "Teacher" PERSONAL.FIL | FIND "CA" > TEACHER.FIL

A:\>TYPE TEACHER.FIL
Panezich   Frank     689 Lake      Orange        CA  Teacher
Winter     Linda     333 Pick      Garden Grove  CA  Teacher

A:\>_
```

WHAT'S ▒▒▒▒▒
▒▒▒▒HAPPENING?   You used FIND to locate all the teachers in California in the same way you did in step 1. Since the FIND command sends its output to the screen, you were able to redirect it. The results of the command did not appear on the screen because you redirected the output to a file called **TEACHER.FIL**. You then used the TYPE command to display that file on the screen. You can use the same filter more than once in the same command line. You can also use filters in combination in the same command line.

4   Key in the following:
   A:\>**FIND "PrOfeSSor" PERSONAL.FIL | FIND "AZ" | SORT** Enter

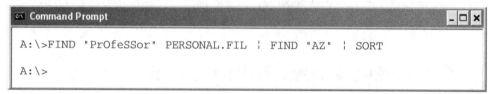

```
A:\>FIND "PrOfeSSor" PERSONAL.FIL | FIND "AZ" | SORT

A:\>
```

WHAT'S ▒▒▒▒▒
▒▒▒▒HAPPENING?   The command found nothing, as it is case sensitive.

5   Press the up arrow key once.

6   Use the left arrow key until the cursor is under the P in PERSONAL.FIL.

7   Key in the following: **/I** Space Bar

8   Press the End key.

9   Press Enter

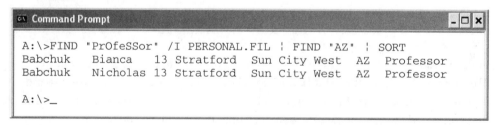

```
A:\>FIND "PrOfeSSor" /I PERSONAL.FIL | FIND "AZ" | SORT
Babchuk    Bianca    13 Stratford  Sun City West  AZ  Professor
Babchuk    Nicholas  13 Stratford  Sun City West  AZ  Professor

A:\>_
```

WHAT'S ▒▒▒▒▒
▒▒▒▒HAPPENING?   This time the FIND command ignored the case and located professor, regardless of how it was keyed in. You then piped (had the standard output of the FIND command sent as standard input to the next FIND command) to select only those who lived in Arizona ("AZ"). You then piped the standard output of FIND to the SORT command because you wanted all the professors who live in Arizona sorted in alphabetical order.

If you wanted a permanent copy of this list, you could have redirected the standard output (normally displayed on the screen) to a file. For instance, if you had keyed in the command as **FIND "PrOfeSSor" /I PERSONAL.FIL ¦ FIND "AZ" ¦ SORT > AZ.FIL**, the output of the command would have been placed in a file called **AZ.FIL**.

Perhaps the easiest way to remember the rules of pipes, filters, and redirection is that, when you use a pipe, there must be a command on either side of the pipe. Remember, you are taking the standard output of a command and using it as standard input to the next command. Remember also that not every command has standard output. For instance, when you key in **DEL filename** at the system level, there is no output that appears or is written to the screen. The file is simply deleted. When you key in **COPY MYFILE YOURFILE**, the only item written to the screen is the message "1 file(s) copied." The standard output from the COPY command is that message. Nothing else is written to the screen.

Conversely, when you use redirection, it is an "instead of" action. Instead of the standard output being written to the screen, you are redirecting (sending) it somewhere else, such as a file or a device. You only get one output place. Since it is an "instead of" action, you cannot say instead of displaying the output of the DIR command on the screen, redirect the output to a file *and* redirect the output to the screen. Your choice is either the screen or a file, not both. The device name for the screen is CON. If you keyed in **DIR > CON > TESTFILE**, the output would not appear on the screen, but would go to the file **TESTFILE**. If you keyed in **DIR > TESTFILE > CON** the output would go to the screen. The output will go to the last place it is directed to go. The primary use of pipes and filters is manipulating the standard output and standard input of commands. You rarely use pipes and filters to sort or find data in text or data files.

10 Key in the following: A:\>**DIR ¦ SORT /+39 ¦ MORE** Enter

```
⌐¬ Command Prompt                                          _ □ ✕

A:\>DIR ¦ SORT /+39 ¦ MORE

 Directory of A:\

 Volume Serial Number is 30B8-DA1D
 Volume in drive A is DATA
02/25/2002  11:04 AM    <DIR>          3PLANETS
04/19/2002  03:34 PM    <DIR>          ASTRO
10/30/2001  01:46 PM             148   ASTRO.TXT
04/11/2002  12:20 PM              36   b.bat
10/30/2001  02:47 PM              86   BONJOUR.NEW
10/30/2001  02:10 PM             121   BORN.TXT
07/31/1999  12:53 PM              44   BRIAN.FIL
04/23/2002  01:04 PM             260   BYCITY.CAP
03/15/2002  08:29 PM             616   CalifSurf.MUS
07/31/1999  12:53 PM              47   CAROLYN.FIL
08/12/2000  04:12 PM             314   CASES.FIL
04/20/2002  12:27 PM           4,482   CHKDSK.TXT
03/15/2002  01:38 PM    <DIR>          CLASS
12/11/1999  04:03 PM              72   DANCES.TXT
10/30/2001  01:41 PM             155   DRAMA.TV
10/31/2001  02:49 PM             138   FILE2.CZG
10/31/2001  04:51 PM             137   FILE2.FP
10/31/2001  04:50 PM             138   FILE2.SWT
10/31/2001  02:49 PM             138   FILE3.CZG
10/31/2001  04:51 PM             137   FILE3.FP
10/31/2001  04:50 PM             138   FILE3.SWT
10/31/2001  04:51 PM             137   FILE4.FP
```

```
10/31/2001  11:37 AM                253 GALAXY.TXT
04/17/2002  01:07 PM    <DIR>           GAMES
 — More  —
```

Note: Your screen display will vary based on the work you did as well as the date and time you created the files.

WHAT'S HAPPENING?   You took the directory display and piped the output to the SORT command. You then sorted by the file name, which begins in the 39th column. You then piped the output to the MORE command so that you could see the output one screenful at a time. You can perform the same task with the parameters of the DIR command. The command line **DIR /ON /P** would provide the same results.

11 Continue pressing the [Space Bar] until you have returned to the system prompt or press **Q** to quit.

12 Key in the following: A:\>**DIR ¦ FIND "<DIR>" ¦ SORT /+39** [Enter]

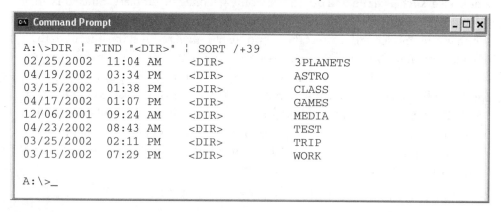

```
Command Prompt                                              _ □ ✕

A:\>DIR ¦ FIND "<DIR>" ¦ SORT /+39
02/25/2002  11:04 AM    <DIR>           3 PLANETS
04/19/2002  03:34 PM    <DIR>           ASTRO
03/15/2002  01:38 PM    <DIR>           CLASS
04/17/2002  01:07 PM    <DIR>           GAMES
12/06/2001  09:24 AM    <DIR>           MEDIA
04/23/2002  08:43 AM    <DIR>           TEST
03/25/2002  02:11 PM    <DIR>           TRIP
03/15/2002  07:29 PM    <DIR>           WORK

A:\>_
```

WHAT'S HAPPENING?   You sent the output of DIR to FIND. You were looking for any file that had **<DIR>** in it. You used uppercase letters since that is how <DIR> is displayed. You had to use quotation marks to enclose <DIR>. Had you not done that, the command line would have read the < and the > as redirection symbols. By enclosing them, you ensured those symbols were read as character data. You then sent that output to the SORT command with the /+39 parameter. Now you have an alphabetical list of the subdirectories on your DATA disk. Again, you can do the same task with the parameters of the DIR command. The command line **DIR /AD /ON** would provide the same results, except you would see information about bytes and volume label.

Chapter Summary

1. The redirection symbols are >, <, and >>.
2. The >> appends output redirected from standard output to the end of a file.
3. Redirection, pipes, and filters have to do with standard input and standard output.
4. Any command that expects its input from the keyboard has standard input.
5. Any command that normally displays its output on the screen has standard output.
6. Standard error means that the operating system writes error messages to the screen.

7. You can redirect standard input and output to and from devices or files.
8. The pipe symbol is ¦.
9. The pipe takes standard output from one command and uses it as standard input for the next command.
10. You can pipe many programs together.
11. Filters take data, change it in some fashion, and send the output to the screen.
12. The three filters are SORT, FIND, and MORE.
13. Two of the SORT command parameters are /R for reverse order and /+n for column number.
14. FIND has four parameters: /V for everything except the specified item, /C for the number of occurrences of the item, /N for the line number where the item appears in the file, and /I for results regardless of case.
15. MORE lets you look at text files one screenful at a time. The parameter /C clears the screen before the display begins.
16. You may enable shell extensions (extended features) in a command prompt window. However they are enabled by default. Extensions give you more options with commands.
17. You must have a command on both ends of the pipe.
18. Redirection is the last action you can take. You write either to the screen or to a file, not to both. You either accept input from the keyboard or from a file.
19. You can string together pipes and filters to create your own commands.
20. Each part of a command must be able to stand alone on the command line.
21. Redirection performs an "instead of" action.

Key Terms

ASCII sort sequence	filter	standard error
case sensitive	input/output (I/O)	standard input
character string	pipe	standard output
extension	redirection	

Discussion Questions

1. Explain redirection.
2. Explain the terms standard input, standard output, and standard error.
3. Does every operating system command use standard input and standard output? If not, why not?
4. What is the difference between > and >> when redirecting output?
5. Explain how the symbol < is used.
6. Keying in **COPY DIR filename** will not give you a file containing the directory display. Why?
7. What are filters?
8. What do the three SORT parameters covered in this chapter—/n, /O, and /R—represent?
9. Explain how the SORT command works. Describe any limitations of the SORT command.
10. Identify one place to which standard output can be written.
11. What is the purpose of the FIND command?

12. What are four parameters that can be used with the FIND command, and what do they represent?

13. Why must a character string be enclosed in quotation marks when using the FIND command?

14. What are pipes?

15. Are there any restrictions on the use of pipes? If so, what are they?

16. How is the MORE command used?

17. What are two useful features that extended features provides for the MORE command?

18. How can combining filters be useful?

True/False Questions

For each question, circle the letter T if the statement is true or the letter F if the statement is false.

T   F   1. All system commands use standard input and standard output.

T   F   2. Standard output can be directed to a file.

T   F   3. There are only two filter commands: FIND and SORT.

T   F   4. You can use the FIND command to find data either with or without a specified string enclosed in double-quotes.

T   F   5. The SORT command allows you to sort data from the keyboard.

Completion Questions

Write the correct answer in each blank space.

6. The standard input device is the _____.

7. The standard output device is the _____.

8. In the syntax SORT [/R] [/+n], the letter n represents a(n) _____.

9. The filter command used to display information one screenful at a time is the _____ command.

10. The redirection symbols are _____, _____, and _____.

Multiple Choice Questions

For each question, write the letter for the correct answer in the blank space.

____   11. The command that redirects the output of the DIR command to the file **DIRTXT.TXT** is
    a. DIR ¦ DIRTXT.TXT
    b. DIR < DIRTXT.TXT
    c. DIR >DIRTXT.TXT
    d. COPY DIR DIRTXT.TXT

____   12. The parameter used with the command SORT to sort a list by the fifth column of data in a file (where the fifth column begins at character number 25) would be:
    a. /+5
    b. /+25
    c. /+5-25
    d. /+R=25

_____ 13. To display **MYFILE.FIL** one screenful at a time, you would use:
   a. MORE MYFILE.FIL
   b. TYPE MYFILE.FIL ¦ MORE
   c. COPY MYFILE.FIL > MORE
   d. either a or b

_____ 14. The command to display the files **FIRST.FIL** and **SECOND.FIL** on the screen, each one screenful at a time, is:
   a. MORE FIRST.FIL SECOND.FIL
   b. MORE > FIRST.FIL > SECOND.FIL
   c. FIRST.FIL >> SECOND.FIL >> MORE
   d. none of the above

_____ 15. When using the SORT command, if you key in 1234, 96, 4, and 789, the order returned would be:

a. 4	96	789	1234
b. 1234	789	96	4
c. 1234	4	789	96
d. 96	789	4	1234

Writing Commands

Note: If you find it necessary to perform some of the steps in order to write your answers, do the work on a new disk, *not* on your DATA or HOMEWORK disk. To be able to perform the steps, you will need to copy the files **\WUGXP\STATES.USA**, **\WUGXP\PERSONAL.FIL**, **\WUGXP\STEVEN.FIL**, and **\WUGXP\CASES.FIL** to the root of the new disk.

Write the step(s) or command(s) to perform the required action as if you were at the computer. The prompt will indicate the default drive and directory.

16. Without changing the default directory, make a directory on the A drive named **WORK**. Without changing the default directory, locate every occurrence of "Teacher" in the file **PERSONAL.FIL** located in the root directory of the disk in the A drive, and send the output to a file called **TEACHER.FIL**, which is in the **WORK** directory of the disk in the A drive.

   `C:\>`

17. Display the contents of **PERSONAL.FIL**, located on the root of the disk in the A drive, one screenful at a time.

   `C:\TEMP>`

18. Display the contents of **PERSONAL.FIL**, located on the root of the disk in the A drive, one screenful at a time beginning with the 25th record (line), on a clear screen.

   `A:\>`

19. Append the contents of **STEVEN.FIL** to the file called **CASES.FIL**. Both files are on the root of the disk in Drive A.

   `C:\>`

20. Find out how many occurrences of "Teacher" appear in the file
    PERSONAL.FIL, which is located on the root of the disk in Drive A.

    C:\>

Homework Assignments

Note 1:   Place the HOMEWORK disk in Drive A. Be sure to work on the
            HOMEWORK disk, not the DATA disk.

Note 2:   The homework problems assume that Drive C is the hard disk and that
            the HOMEWORK disk is in Drive A. If you are using another drive,
            such as floppy Drive B or hard Drive D, be sure to substitute that drive
            letter when reading the questions and answers.

Note 3:   All subdirectories that are created will be under the root directory
            unless otherwise specified.

Note 4:   The homework problems will use **C:\WINDOWS\SYSTEM32** as the
            directory where the system utility files are located.

Note 5:   It is assumed that the path includes **C:\WINDOWS\SYSTEM32**.

Note 6:   Do not save the output from the commands to a file unless specifically
            asked to do so.

Problem Set I

Problem A

A-a   Place the HOMEWORK disk in Drive A.

A-b   Copy all the files from the **WUGXP\SPORTS** directory to the HOMEWORK
          disk, maintaining the same directory structure on the HOMEWORK disk. (*Hint:*
          Remember XCOPY.)

A-c   With the root directory of the A drive as the default directory and using the
          relative path, sort the file called **BASKETBL.TMS** in the **SPORTS**
          subdirectory.

____   1. Which command(s) could you have used?
           a. SORT SPORTS\BASKETBL.TMS
           b. TYPE BASKETBL.TMS ¦ SORT
           c. both a and b
           d. neither a nor b

____   2. What team is listed first?
           a. Atlanta Hawks
           b. Boston Celtics
           c. Charlotte Hornets
           d. Los Angeles Lakers

A-d   Key in the following:

          A:\>**COPY \SPORTS*.TMS \SPORTS\ALL.SPT** Enter

A-e   With the root directory of the HOMEWORK disk as the default and using the relative path, display the contents of the **SPORTS\ALL.SPT** file one screenful at a time.

_____   3. Which command did you use?
     a. TYPE SPORTS\ALL.SPT < MORE
     b. TYPE SPORTS\ALL.SPT /P
     c. MORE SPORTS\ALL.SPT
     d. MORE < TYPE SPORTS\ALL.SPT

A-f   Press **Q** to exit.

A-g   Sort the **ALL.SPT** file in reverse order and display the output one screenful at a time.

_____   4. What team appeared first on the first screen display?
     a. Utah Jazz
     b. Washington Bullets
     c. USC Trojans
     d. Washington Redskins

A-h   Press **Q** to exit.

A-i   In the **ALL.SPT** file, find all the teams that have "Los" in their names. Do not ignore case.

_____   5. What results are displayed?
     a. Los Angeles Lakers
     b. Los Angeles Dodgers
     c. neither a nor b appears
     d. both a and b appear

Problem B

B-a   Be sure you have the **ALL.SPT** file from Problem A above. In the **ALL.SPT** file, find all the teams that have "go" in their names. Do not ignore case.

_____   6. What team appears that _is not_ from Chicago?
     a. Michigan Gophers
     b. San Diego Padres
     c. San Diego Chargers
     d. all teams are from Chicago

B-b   Copy **PERSONAL.FIL** from **C:\WUGXP** to **A:\TRAVEL**. Sort the **TRAVEL\PERSONAL.FIL** file in alphabetical order.

_____   7. What name appears last?
     a. Winter
     b. Wyse
     c. Yuan
     d. Zola

B-c   From **TRAVEL\PERSONAL.FIL**, create a file sorted by city (city starts in column 34) called **CALIF.FIL** that will be saved to the **TRAVEL** subdirectory. This file will contain only people who live in California (CA). Begin your command with the FIND command.

_____   8. What street name is listed *last* in **CALIF.FIL**?
        a. Brooks
        b. Lake
        c. Pick
        d. View

B-d   Copy the **STATES.USA** file from the **WUGXP** directory to the subdirectory called **TRAVEL** on the HOMEWORK disk keeping the same file name.

B-e   In the **STATES.USA** file, find all the states that are located in the South and sort the output in reverse alphabetical order.

_____   9. What state is displayed first?
        a. South Carolina
        b. North Carolina
        c. Louisiana
        d. Florida

Problem Set II

Note 1:   Before proceeding with these assignments, check with your lab instructor to see if there are any special procedures you should follow.

Note 2:   The HOMEWORK disk is in Drive A. A:\> is displayed as the default drive and the default directory. *All work will occur on the HOMEWORK disk.*

Note 3:   Make sure that **NAME.BAT**, **MARK.FIL**, **GETYN.COM**, **GO.BAT**, and **NAME.FIL** are all present in the root directory of the HOMEWORK disk before proceeding with these problems.

Note 4:   All files with the **.HW** extension *must* be created in the root directory of the HOMEWORK disk.

1   Use the text editor (Edit) to edit **NAME.FIL** with current information. Here is an example, but your instructor will have other information that applies to your class.
Bette A. Peat
CIS 55
T-Th 8-9:30
Chapter 9 Homework

2   Save the file and close the editor.

WHAT'S ▓▓▓▓▓
▓▓▓▓HAPPENING?   You have returned to the system level. The file called **NAME.FIL** has been updated with the current pertinent information.

To Create 1.HW

While the root directory of the HOMEWORK disk is the default, locate all the people who live in Orange in the **TRAVEL\PERSONAL.FIL** file and sort them in descending order (*Hint:* Z to A) sending the output to a file called **1.HW**.

To Create 2.HW

1 Sort the files in the **TRAVEL** directory of the HOMEWORK disk. Sort in file name order. Use the SORT command. File name begins in column 40. Save the output to a file called **2.HW**.

2 Sort the files in the **SPORTS** directory of the HOMEWORK disk. Sort in file name order. Use the SORT command. Base your sort on column 40. **Append** the output to the file called **2.HW**.

To Create 3.HW

In the **SPORTS\ALL.SPT** file, find all the teams that have "in" within their names, regardless of case, and direct the output to a file called **3.HW**.

To Create 4.HW

In the **TRAVEL\PERSONAL.FIL** file, find all occurrences, regardless of case, of the name Jones, sort them by occupation (column 53) and direct the output to a file called **4.HW**.

To Create 5.HW

In the **SPORTS\ALL.SPT** file, locate all the lines that *do not* have an "r" in them, regardless of case, and direct the output to a file called **5.HW**.

To Print Your Homework

1 Be sure the printer is on and ready to accept print jobs from your computer.

2 Key in the following (be very careful to make no typing errors):
   GO NAME.FIL 1.HW 2.HW 3.HW 4.HW 5.HW [Enter]

WHAT'S
HAPPENING?   If the files you requested, **1.HW**, **2.HW**, etc. do not exist in the default directory, you will see the following message on the screen:

```
File Not Found
The system cannot find the file specified.

Is there a message that says "File Not Found. The system cannot
find the file specified."

 If so, press Y to find out what could be wrong.

 Otherwise, press N to continue.
```

The operating system is telling you that the file cannot be found. If you see this screen, press **Y** to see what could be wrong, and repeat the print procedure after you have corrected the problem.

If the default directory contains the specified files, the following message will appear on the screen:

```
Is there a message that say "File Not Found. The system cannot
find the file specified."

If so, press Y to find out what could be wrong.

Otherwise, press N to continue.
```

You will need to press **N** once for each file you are printing.

3   Follow the messages on the screen until the Notepad program opens. Your homework is now ready to print.

4   On the Notepad menu bar, click **File**. Click **Print**. The print dialog box opens. If you have more than one printer, your printer choices will be displayed. The default printer is the highlighted printer.

5   Click the **Print** button.

6   In the Notepad window, click **File**. Click **Exit**.

WHAT'S ▒▒▒▒
▒▒▒HAPPENING?   The following will appear on the Command Prompt screen:

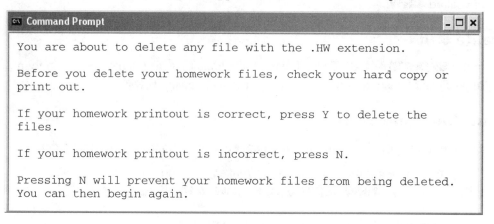

At this point, look at your printout. If it is correct, you can press **Y** to delete the homework files for this chapter. If your printout is incorrect, you can press **N**. That will preserve your homework and you will need to redo only the problem that was incorrect, not all the homework assignments.

7   Press **Y** Enter

WHAT'S ▒▒▒▒
▒▒▒HAPPENING?   You have returned to the default prompt.

8   Close the Command Prompt session.

9   Execute the shut-down procedure.

Problem Set III—Brief Essay

1. List and explain the syntax and at least two parameters for the three filter commands (FIND, SORT, and MORE). Also explain how redirection and piping can work with each of them.

2. Discuss two real-world scenarios where you would use pipes, a filters, and redirection. Include one example of a pipe, a filter, and a use of redirection.

INTRODUCTION TO
BATCH FILES

Learning Objectives

After completing this chapter you will be able to:

1. Compare and contrast batch and interactive processing.
2. Explain how batch files work.
3. Explain the purpose and function of the REM, ECHO, and PAUSE commands.
4. Explain how to stop or interrupt the batch file process.
5. Explain the function and use of replaceable parameters in batch files.
6. Explain the function of pipes, filters, and redirection in batch files.

Student Outcomes

1. Use Edit to write batch files.
2. Use COPY CON to write batch files.
3. Write and execute a simple batch file.
4. Write a batch file to load an application program.
5. Use the REM, PAUSE, and ECHO commands in batch files.
6. Terminate a batch file while it is executing.
7. Write batch files using replaceable parameters.
8. Write a batch file using pipes, filters, and redirection.

Chapter Overview

You have used many command line commands throughout this textbook. Many of these commands are repeated in the same sequence. If more than one command is needed to execute a program, you have to key in each command at the system prompt. This repetitive, time-consuming process increases the possibility of human error.

A batch file is a text file that contains a series of commands stored in the order the user wants them carried out. It executes a series of commands with a minimum number of keystrokes. Batch files allow you to automate a process and, at the same time, create more powerful commands, which increases productivity.

In this chapter, you will learn to create batch files to automate a sequence of commands, to write and use batch files for complex tasks, to use batch file subcommands, to halt the execution of a batch file, and to write batch files using replaceable parameters. You will also learn how batch files can be used from the desktop.

10.1   Concepts of Batch and Interactive Processing

Operating system commands used at the command line are programs that are executed or run when you key in the command name. If you wish to run more than one command, you need to key in each command at the system prompt. You can, however, customize and automate the sequence of commands by writing a command sequence, called a *batch file* or a command file, to be executed with a minimum number of keystrokes. Any command you can enter at the system prompt can be included in a batch file. You can even execute an application program from a batch file. When you string together a sequence of steps in an application program, it is called a "macro," which is conceptually similar to a batch file.

A batch file contains one or more commands. To create this file of commands, you write a text file using Edit, COPY CON, or a text editor such as Notepad. You can also use a word processor providing it has a "Save as text file" option. The file that you write and name will run any command that the operating system can execute. This file *must* have the file extension .BAT if you are using a version of Windows earlier than Windows 2000 Professional. Beginning with Windows 2000 Professional, you may also use the extension .CMD. The file must be an ASCII file. Once you have written this command file, you execute or run it by simply keying in the name of the batch file, just as you key in the name of a command. The operating system reads and executes each line of the batch file, as if you were sitting at the terminal and separately keying in each command line. Once you start running a batch file, your attention or input is not needed until the batch file has finished executing.

Batch files are used for several reasons. They allow you to minimize keystrokes, and they minimize the possibility of errors, as you do not have to key in the commands over and over. Batch files are used to put together a complex sequence of commands and store them under an easily remembered name. They automate any frequent and/or consistent procedures that you always want to do in the same manner, such as backing up critical data to an alternate location. In addition, you can execute application programs by calling them with a batch file.

"Batch" is an old data-processing term. In the early days of computing, work was done by submitting a job (or all the instructions needed to run the job successfully) to a data-processing department, which would run these jobs in *batches*. There was no chance for anyone to interact with the program. The job was run, and the output was delivered. Thus, when you run a batch job, you are running a computer routine without interruption.

Batch jobs are still run today. An example of a batch job would be running a payroll—issuing paychecks. The computer program that calculates and prints paychecks is run without interruption. The output or results are the paychecks. This job can be run at any time. If a company decides that payday will be Friday, the data-processing department can run the payroll Thursday night. If the company decides payday will be Monday, the data-processing department can run the payroll Sunday night. This is *batch processing*.

Batch processing is in contrast to an interactive mode of data processing. Sometimes called online or real time mode, interactive mode means you are interacting directly with the computer. An automated teller machine (ATM) that a bank uses so that you can withdraw or deposit money without human intervention is an example of *interactive processing*. The bank needs instant updating of its records. It cannot wait until next week to run a batch job to find out how much money you have deposited or withdrawn. If you withdraw $100, the bank first wants to be sure that you have $100 in your account, and then it wants the $100 subtracted immediately from your balance. You are dealing with the computer in an interactive, real time mode—the data is processed without delay.

In the PC world, you can work in interactive mode, but this usually requires a connection to another computer, over phone lines, DSL, or a cable modem. The Internet allows you to communicate directly with other computers and perform such functions as reviewing airline flight schedules and booking an airline ticket. Although interactive mode can be exciting, most of the time you are working one-on-one with your computer and are not in interactive mode. Hence, the batch mode is the area of emphasis.

10.2   How Batch Files Work

You will be creating and executing batch files in this chapter. By now you should know that data and programs are stored as files, but how does the operating system know the difference between a data file and a program file? As mentioned in previous chapters, it knows the difference based on the file extension. When you key in something at the prompt, the operating system first checks in RAM to compare what you keyed in to the internal table of commands. If it finds a match, the program is executed. If what you keyed in does not match an internal command, the operating system looks on the default drive and directory for the extension .COM, meaning command file, first. Then the operating system looks for the file extension .EXE, meaning executable file (this extension is used for system utility programs and most application software).

If what you keyed in does not match either .COM or .EXE, the operating system looks on the default drive and directory for the file extension .BAT, meaning batch file. If it finds a match, it loads and executes the batch file, one line at a time. It then looks for .CMD, meaning command file. If it finds a match, it loads and executes the command file, one line at a time. If what you keyed in does not match any of the above criteria, it continues to search in your default directory for files with the following extensions: .VBS, .VBE, JS, JSE, WSF and WSH. Table 10.1 lists the search order for extensions.

Extension	Meaning
.COM	Command file
.EXE	Executable file
.BAT	Batch file
.CMD	Command script file
.VB	VBScript file (Visual Basic)
.VBE	VBScript Encoded Script file (Visual Basic)
.JS	JScript file (JavaScript)

.JSE	JScript Encoded Script file (JavaScript)
.WSF	Windows Script file
.WSH	Windows Script Host Settings file

Table 10.1—Search Order for Extensions

If the command interpreter does not find any of these in your default drive and directory, it then searches your search path as set in the PATH statement, in the file extension order listed above. If your file name does not meet any of these criteria, then you see the error message, "*filename* is not recognized as an internal or external command, operable program or batch file."

What if you had files on a disk that had the same file name but three different file extensions, such as CHKDSK.COM, CHKDSK.EXE, and CHKDSK.BAT? How would the operating system know which program to load and execute? Priority rules are followed. The operating system looks for the program with the .COM file extension first and, if found, would never get to the other files. However, if you were more specific and keyed in both the file name *and* the file extension, such as CHKDSK.BAT, the operating system would then execute the file name you specified.

Remember that, since the batch file is a program, either the .BAT file must be on the default drive and directory or the path must be set to the location of the batch file so you may invoke it. Most importantly, each line in a batch file must contain only one command.

10.3 Using Edit to Write Batch Files

To write batch files, you need a mechanism to create an ASCII text file, since that is what a batch file is. You should remember that ASCII is a code used by the operating system to interpret the letters, numbers, and punctuation marks that you key in. In simple terms, if a file is readable with the TYPE command, it is an ASCII text file. You can use a word-processing program to write a batch file if it has a nondocument or text mode. However, most word-processing programs are quite large and take time to load into memory. Most batch files are not very long, nor do they need the features of a word processor. Using a word processor to write a batch file is like using a sledgehammer to kill a fly.

Having a small, simple text editor is so important that the operating system includes one as part of the system utility programs. This is the Command Line editor, called Edit. Edit is simple to use and universal. You will write some batch files using Edit. Remember, Edit is only a tool to create the file; it does not run or execute it. You execute the file when you key in the file name at the system prompt in the Command Line window. Each line in a batch file must contain only one command. A batch file can have any legal file name but the file extension must always be .BAT or .CMD.

If you are in the Windows interface, the text editor is Notepad. Like Edit, Notepad creates text-only files and may be used to write batch files. However, if you are having problems with Windows, you will not have Notepad available to you because you need a graphical user interface to use Notepad. Edit, on the other hand, can work at the command line. In fact, you will later see that when you create your startup disk, Edit is on the disk, but not Notepad. Thus, in the following activities, you will be using Edit.

10.4   Activity: Writing and Executing a Batch File

Note 1:   The DATA disk is in Drive A. A:\> is displayed.

Note 2:   Although you may use a mouse with the MS-DOS editor, the instructions will show the keystroke steps, not the mouse steps.

Note 3:   In some systems, the mouse will not work in Edit unless you change the properties of Edit to open Edit in full-screen mode or clear the Quick Edit Mode check box in the Command Line property sheet (Options tab).

Note 4:   The amount of space shown as remaining on the disk will vary, depending on the size and placement of the batch files on your disk.

1   Key in the following: A:\>**EDIT EXAMPLE.BAT** [Enter]

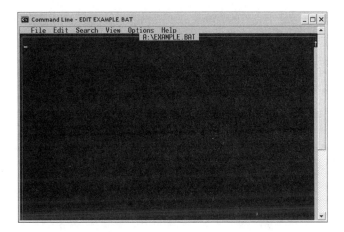

WHATS HAPPENING?   You are now using the Command Line editor. You are going to create a batch file named **EXAMPLE**. The file extension must be **.BAT** or **.CMD**.

2   Key in the following: **DIR *.NEW** [Enter]

3   Key in the following: **DIR C:\WUGXP*.FIL** [Enter]

WHATS HAPPENING?   Look at each line. Each one is a legitimate operating system command that could be keyed in at the prompt. Each command is on a separate line. The first line asks for a listing of all the files on the disk in the default drive that have the file extension **.TXT**. The second line asks for all the files in the WUGXP directory in the C drive that have the file extension **FIL**. At this point, you have written the batch file. Next, you need to exit Edit and save the file to disk.

4   Press **Alt** + **F**.

5   Press **X**.

WHAT'S HAPPENING?   Since you have not saved the file, Edit reminds you with a dialog box that, if you want this file on the disk, you must save it.

6   Press **Y**.

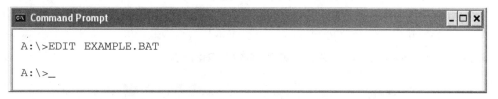

```
A:\>EDIT EXAMPLE.BAT

A:\>_
```

WHAT'S HAPPENING?   You have saved your file, exited Edit, and returned to the system prompt.

7   Key in the following: A:\>**DIR EXAMPLE.BAT** **Enter**

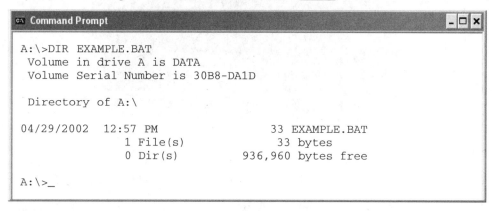

```
A:\>DIR EXAMPLE.BAT
 Volume in drive A is DATA
 Volume Serial Number is 30B8-DA1D

 Directory of A:\

04/29/2002  12:57 PM                 33 EXAMPLE.BAT
               1 File(s)             33 bytes
               0 Dir(s)         936,960 bytes free

A:\>_
```

WHAT'S HAPPENING?   The **DIR EXAMPLE.BAT** command shows that there is a file on the DATA disk called **EXAMPLE.BAT**. It looks like any other text file.

How do you make the operating system treat it like a program so that you can execute it? You simply key in the name of the file at the prompt. You do not need to key in the extension, just the name. The operating system first looks for a file in its internal table called **EXAMPLE**. It does not find it. It then looks for a file called **EXAMPLE.COM** on the default disk, the DATA disk. No file exists called **EXAMPLE.COM**. Next, it looks for a file on the default disk called **EXAMPLE.EXE**. No file exists called **EXAMPLE.EXE**. It then looks for a file called **EXAMPLE.BAT** on the default disk. It does find a file by this name. It loads it into memory and executes each line, one at a time. Thus, to execute the batch file called **EXAMPLE**, key in the name of the file at the prompt. Watch what happens on the screen after you key in the file name.

8   Key in the following: A:\>**EXAMPLE** Enter

```
A:\>EXAMPLE

A:\>DIR *.NEW
 Volume in drive A is DATA
 Volume Serial Number is 30B8-DA1D

 Directory of A:\

10/30/2001  02:47 PM                86 BONJOUR.NEW
              1 File(s)             86 bytes
              0 Dir(s)         936,960 bytes free

A:\>DIR C:\WUGXP\*.FIL
 Volume in drive C is ADMIN504
 Volume Serial Number is 0E38-11FF

 Directory of C:\WUGXP

08/12/2000  04:12 PM                73 MARK.FIL
08/12/2000  04:12 PM               314 CASES.FIL
07/31/1999  12:53 PM                44 FRANK.FIL
07/31/1999  12:53 PM             2,672 NEWPRSON.FIL
07/31/2000  04:32 PM             2,307 PERSONAL.FIL
08/12/2000  04:12 PM                 3 Y.FIL
07/31/1999  12:53 PM                47 CAROLYN.FIL
12/06/2001  12:25 AM               465 person.fil
07/31/1999  12:53 PM                46 STEVEN.FIL
10/31/2001  06:40 PM               188 ZODIAC.FIL
             10 File(s)         6,159 bytes
              0 Dir(s)  6,785,228,800 bytes free
A:\>_
```

WHAT'S HAPPENING?   (*Note:* Part of the display may have scrolled off of your screen.)
The operating system read and executed each line of the batch file you wrote, one
line at a time. The screen displayed each command line and the results of the
command line as it executed. Each line executed as if you had sat in front of the
keyboard and keyed in each command individually. You did key in the commands
when you wrote the batch file, but you had to key them in only once. The first line
was **DIR *.NEW**. When the operating system read that line, it executed it and
showed on the screen the file on the DATA disk with the file extension **.NEW**. It then
read the next line of the batch file and looked in the root directory of Drive C for any
file that had the file extension **.FIL**. It found 10 files with that extension, and displayed their names on the screen. Now that you have written the file
EXAMPLE.BAT, you can execute this batch file's commands over and over again by
keying in **EXAMPLE** at the prompt.

10.5 Writing and Executing a Batch File to Save Keystrokes

The previous example showed you how to write and execute a batch file, but that
file is not especially useful. The next batch file to be written will allow you to key in
only one keystroke instead of seven. As you know, the command DIR /AD will

quickly show you any subdirectories on the DATA disk. The /A switch means attribute, and the attribute you want displayed is D for directories. This command is composed of seven keystrokes, and you must have the proper parameters. With a batch file, you can do the same task by pressing only one key.

The DIR command has other parameters that are very useful. One of these is O for order. There are many kinds of order you can achieve. One kind that is useful is the arrangement of files by size. The command line would be DIR /OS. The O is for order, and the S is to arrange by size from the smallest to the largest file. If you wanted to reverse the order so that the files would be displayed from the largest to smallest, the command would be DIR /O-S. The O is still for order, but the - is for reverse order, placing smallest files at the end of the listing. The S is for file size. This command would take eight keystrokes. You can reduce it to one.

These batch files you are going to write are very small—one line. It seems like a lot of trouble to load Edit just to accomplish this task. If you would rather not load Edit, you can use the COPY command to write a simple ASCII file. The syntax is:

```
COPY CON filename
```

What you are doing here is copying what you key in (CON) to a file name. CON is the operating system's name for the keyboard/console devices of your computer. You are still following the syntax of the COPY command; it is just that now you are copying from a device—the console (CON)—to a file. Remember that in an early chapter, you copied to a device, the printer (COPY filename PRN). Just as PRN, LPT1, and LPT2 are reserved device names, so is CON.

When you are done keying in text, you must tell the COPY command you are finished. You do this by pressing the **F6** key and then the **Enter** key. This writes the data you keyed in to the file name you specified. This is what you have been doing in your Homework assignments when you have entered data in NAME.FIL. The only problem with COPY CON, as it is informally referred to, is that you cannot correct errors once you press **Enter** at the end of a command line. Nor can you use COPY CON to correct errors in an existing file. To do that, you need an editor, such as Edit. But nothing is faster than using COPY CON.

10.6 Activity: Writing and Executing a One-letter Batch File

Note 1: The DATA disk is in Drive A. A:\> is displayed.
Note 2: For these examples, the use of COPY CON will be shown. If you make errors, you can either use COPY CON and key in all the data again or use the MS-DOS editor to correct the errors.
Note 3: In earlier chapters you may have used DOSKEY and the function keys to correct errors. Either of these methods will work with COPY CON.

1 Key in the following: A:\>**COPY CON D.BAT** **Enter**

```
A:\>COPY CON D.BAT
_
```

WHAT'S HAPPENING?   When you keyed in **COPY CON D.BAT**, you were informing the COPY command that you wanted to make the keyboard the source. The cursor is blinking right below the prompt, and the screen is blank.

2   Key in the following: **DIR /AD** Enter

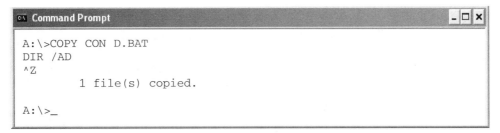

```
A:\>COPY CON D.BAT
DIR /AD
_
```

WHAT'S HAPPENING?   You have one line. You are finished keying in data and you wish this line to be saved to a file called **D.BAT**. First, however, you must tell COPY you are finished.

3   Press F6 Enter

```
A:\>COPY CON D.BAT
DIR /AD
^Z
        1 file(s) copied.

A:\>_
```

WHAT'S HAPPENING?   By pressing F6 and then Enter, you sent a signal to COPY that you were done. The F6 appeared on the screen as ^Z. Pressing Ctrl + Z will produce the same results as F6. You then got the message "1 file(s) copied" and were returned to the system level.

4   Key in the following: A:\>**TYPE D.BAT** Enter

```
A:\>TYPE D.BAT
DIR /AD

A:\>_
```

WHAT'S HAPPENING?   You wrote a one-line batch file named **D.BAT** with COPY CON and saved the file **D.BAT** to the disk. Once you returned to the system prompt, you displayed the contents of **D.BAT** with the TYPE command. The fact that you could display this file with the TYPE command is another indication that it is indeed an ASCII file. All COPY CON did was allow you to create the file, and TYPE merely displayed what is inside the file. To execute the file, you must key in the file name. Now, whenever you want to see the subdirectories on the DATA disk in Drive A, you only have to key in one letter to execute this command.

5   Key in the following: A:\>**D** Enter

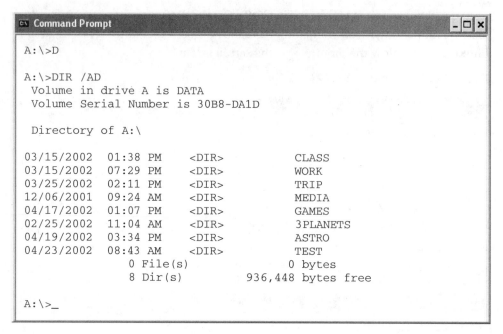

```
A:\>D

A:\>DIR /AD
 Volume in drive A is DATA
 Volume Serial Number is 30B8-DA1D

 Directory of A:\

03/15/2002  01:38 PM    <DIR>         CLASS
03/15/2002  07:29 PM    <DIR>         WORK
03/25/2002  02:11 PM    <DIR>         TRIP
12/06/2001  09:24 AM    <DIR>         MEDIA
04/17/2002  01:07 PM    <DIR>         GAMES
02/25/2002  11:04 AM    <DIR>         3PLANETS
04/19/2002  03:34 PM    <DIR>         ASTRO
04/23/2002  08:43 AM    <DIR>         TEST
               0 File(s)              0 bytes
               8 Dir(s)        936,448 bytes free

A:\>_
```

WHAT'S HAPPENING?   Your display may vary based on what subdirectories are on the DATA disk and in what order they were created. As you can see, you set up a command sequence in a batch file called **D.BAT**. You can run this batch file whenever the need arises, simply by keying in the name of the batch file at the system prompt. You can also display the files by size, with the smallest file at the end of the list.

6   Key in the following: A:\>**COPY CON S.BAT** [Enter]
                        DIR /O-S [Enter]
                        [F6] [Enter]

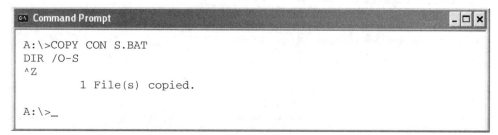

```
A:\>COPY CON S.BAT
DIR /O-S
^Z
        1 File(s) copied.

A:\>_
```

WHAT'S HAPPENING?   You have written another simple one-line batch file and saved it to the default directory.

7   Key in the following: A:\>**TYPE S.BAT** [Enter]

```
A:\>TYPE S.BAT
DIR /O-S

A:\>_
```

WHATʼS▦▦▦▦
▦▦HAPPENING?   After saving the file to disk, you looked at its contents with the
TYPE command. To execute the batch file, you must key in the batch file name (**S**) at
the system prompt.

8   Key in the following: `A:\>`**S** `Enter`

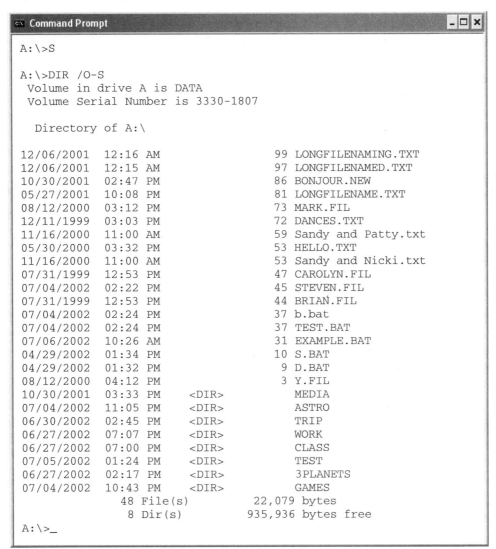

```
 ◉ Command Prompt                                             _ □ ✕

 A:\>S

 A:\>DIR /O-S
  Volume in drive A is DATA
  Volume Serial Number is 3330-1807

  Directory of A:\

 12/06/2001  12:16 AM                     99 LONGFILENAMING.TXT
 12/06/2001  12:15 AM                     97 LONGFILENAMED.TXT
 10/30/2001  02:47 PM                     86 BONJOUR.NEW
 05/27/2001  10:08 PM                     81 LONGFILENAME.TXT
 08/12/2000  03:12 PM                     73 MARK.FIL
 12/11/1999  03:03 PM                     72 DANCES.TXT
 11/16/2000  11:00 AM                     59 Sandy and Patty.txt
 05/30/2000  03:32 PM                     53 HELLO.TXT
 11/16/2000  11:00 AM                     53 Sandy and Nicki.txt
 07/31/1999  12:53 PM                     47 CAROLYN.FIL
 07/04/2002  02:22 PM                     45 STEVEN.FIL
 07/31/1999  12:53 PM                     44 BRIAŃ.FIL
 07/04/2002  02:24 PM                     37 b.bat
 07/04/2002  02:24 PM                     37 TEST.BAT
 07/06/2002  10:26 AM                     31 EXAMPLE.BAT
 04/29/2002  01:34 PM                     10 S.BAT
 04/29/2002  01:32 PM                      9 D.BAT
 08/12/2000  04:12 PM                      3 Y.FIL
 10/30/2001  03:33 PM      <DIR>            MEDIA
 07/04/2002  11:05 PM      <DIR>            ASTRO
 06/30/2002  02:45 PM      <DIR>            TRIP
 06/27/2002  07:07 PM      <DIR>            WORK
 06/27/2002  07:00 PM      <DIR>            CLASS
 07/05/2002  01:24 PM      <DIR>            TEST
 06/27/2002  02:17 PM      <DIR>            3PLANETS
 07/04/2002  10:43 PM      <DIR>            GAMES
                48 File(s)          22,079 bytes
                 8 Dir(s)          935,936 bytes free
 A:\>_
```

WHATʼS▦▦▦▦
▦▦HAPPENING?   (The graphic represents the top and bottom of what you will see
scroll by on your screen.) The files are listed by size, and all the subdirectories are
grouped at the bottom of the display. Because directories have no size, they are
listed last as the smallest files.

10.7   Using Batch Files to Alter Your Command Line Environment

Today, in the Windows environment, you typically open a command line session by
clicking on the icon on the Start Menu. The window can be opened from a short cut
as well. The short cut can then be altered to run in a customized way.

In Chapter 8, disk organization was discussed. It was suggested that, on your own system, you might create a subdirectory called Batch to hold your batch files, and Utils to hold utility files. These two user-created directories will not be part of the normal path in a command line window. If you have batch files that you like to use when in a command line session, it would be helpful if the default path included these two directories.

You will first create two subdirectories on the DATA disk, and then add them to the path for use in your command line sessions. Note: To be truly useful, the directories would be on your own system on the hard drive. Using the DATA disk to do this could, in the real world, present a serious problem, in that the DATA disk that contained the two subdirectories would have to be in the A drive each and every time you used your short cut to begin a command line session.

10.8 Activity: Creating a Batch File to Alter the Command Line Session Environment

Note: The DATA disk is in Drive A. A:\> is displayed.

1   Key in the following: A:\>**MD Batch** **Enter**

2   Key in the following: A:\>**MD Utils** **Enter**

3   Key in the following: A:\>**DIR /AD** **Enter**

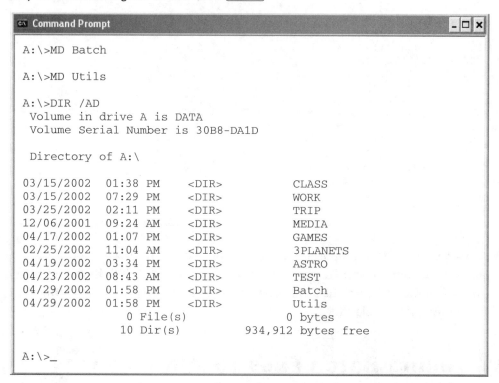

```
A:\>MD Batch

A:\>MD Utils

A:\>DIR /AD
 Volume in drive A is DATA
 Volume Serial Number is 30B8-DA1D

 Directory of A:\

03/15/2002  01:38 PM    <DIR>          CLASS
03/15/2002  07:29 PM    <DIR>          WORK
03/25/2002  02:11 PM    <DIR>          TRIP
12/06/2001  09:24 AM    <DIR>          MEDIA
04/17/2002  01:07 PM    <DIR>          GAMES
02/25/2002  11:04 AM    <DIR>          3PLANETS
04/19/2002  03:34 PM    <DIR>          ASTRO
04/23/2002  08:43 AM    <DIR>          TEST
04/29/2002  01:58 PM    <DIR>          Batch
04/29/2002  01:58 PM    <DIR>          Utils
              0 File(s)              0 bytes
             10 Dir(s)        934,912 bytes free

A:\>_
```

WHAT'S HAPPENING?   You have created two subdirectories on the DATA disk and used the DIR command to verify their existence. Notice that the operating system remembers the case you used when you created the directories.

You would like the directory names to be in upper case. You can use the REN command to change the case.

4   Key in the following: `A:\>`**REN Batch BATCH** `Enter`

5   Key in the following: `A:\>`**REN Utils UTILS** `Enter`

6   Key in the following: `A:\>`**DIR /AD** `Enter`

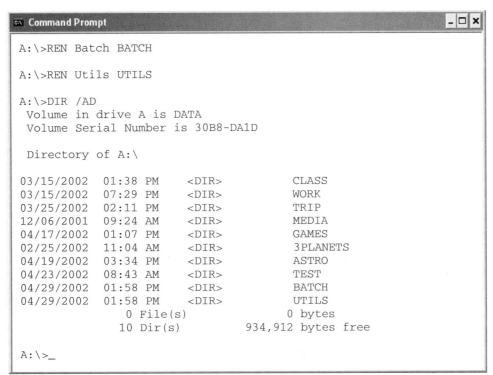

```
A:\>REN Batch BATCH

A:\>REN Utils UTILS

A:\>DIR /AD
 Volume in drive A is DATA
 Volume Serial Number is 30B8-DA1D

 Directory of A:\

03/15/2002  01:38 PM    <DIR>          CLASS
03/15/2002  07:29 PM    <DIR>          WORK
03/25/2002  02:11 PM    <DIR>          TRIP
12/06/2001  09:24 AM    <DIR>          MEDIA
04/17/2002  01:07 PM    <DIR>          GAMES
02/25/2002  11:04 AM    <DIR>          3PLANETS
04/19/2002  03:34 PM    <DIR>          ASTRO
04/23/2002  08:43 AM    <DIR>          TEST
04/29/2002  01:58 PM    <DIR>          BATCH
04/29/2002  01:58 PM    <DIR>          UTILS
               0 File(s)              0 bytes
              10 Dir(s)         934,912 bytes free

A:\>_
```

WHAT'S HAPPENING?   You have used the REN command to change the case of the directory names.

7   Key in the following: `A:\>`**EDIT A:\BATCH\SETPATH.BAT** `Enter`

8   In the Edit screen, Key in the following:
PATH = %PATH%;A:\BATCH;A:\UTILS

9   Press `Alt` + **F.**

10   Press **X.**

11   Press the **Y** key to save the file.

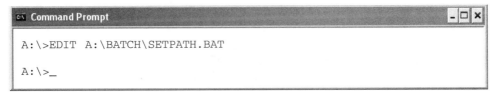

```
A:\>EDIT A:\BATCH\SETPATH.BAT

A:\>_
```

WHAT'S HAPPENING?   You have completed creating the SETPATH.BAT file, and returned to the command line window.

12   Close the Command line window.

Note: If you still have the shortcut to the command line window on your desktop, do not do Steps 13 through 17; go directly to Step 18.

13 Point to **Programs**. Point to **Accessories**.

14 Point to the Command Prompt icon.

WHAT'S ▓▓▓▓
▓▓ HAPPENING?   You have displayed the Icon to start a command line session.

15 Hold down the right mouse button and drag the command icon onto the desktop.

16 Release the right mouse button.

WHAT'S ▓▓▓▓
▓▓ HAPPENING?   You see a shortcut menu appear.

17 Click **Copy Here**.

WHAT'S ▓▓▓▓
▓▓ HAPPENING?   You now have a short cut to open a command line session on the desk top.

18 Right-click the shortcut icon, and click **Properties**.

19 Click the **Shortcut** tab.

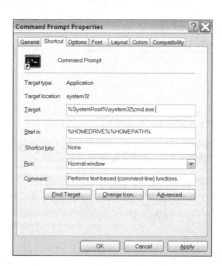

WHAT'S HAPPENING? You have opened the property sheet for the shortcut to the CMD.EXE program. Notice entry in the Target text box. When you click this Icon, the operating system goes to the root of this system (%SystemRoot%), to the system32 subdirectory, and runs the program file cmd.exe. Also, notice the Start In text box. In this example, the computer is part of a Domain network, which assigns a particular home directory to the user. The line %HOMEDRIVE%%HOMEPATH% causes the initial default directory to be the directory assigned by the network administrator to the user. On this particular computer, that will be a directory on the server addressed as G.

In your own home environment, you could change this to say C:\ or C:\DATA or whatever directory you wished to be the default directory when you open a command session.

20 Click in the Target text box. Press the **End** key.

21 Press the spacebar once.

22 Key in the following: **/k A:\BATCH\SETPATH.BAT**

WHAT'S HAPPENING? You have given additional instructions to the Target command line. You have told the operating system to go to the specified drive, run cmd.exe to open a command line session, and then to run the file **SETPATH.BAT** residing in the specified A:\BATCH directory.

23 Click **Apply**.

24 Click **OK**.

25 Double-click the shortcut to the Command line icon on the desktop.

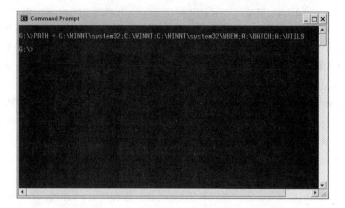

WHAT'S ▒▒▒
▒▒▒ **HAPPENING?**   As you can see, the batch file executed. But, did it work?

26 Key in the following from the default prompt: **A:** Enter

27 Key in the following: A:\>**PATH** Enter

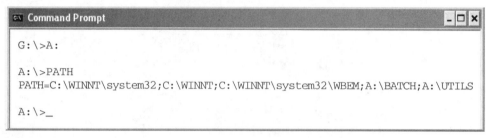

WHAT'S ▒▒▒
▒▒▒ **HAPPENING?**   As you can see by the path returned, the batch file did indeed work. Each time you use this shortcut icon to open a command line session, the path will include the specified directories on the A drive. Once again, this will only be helpful if this particular disk is in the A drive.

28 Close the command line window.

29 Remove the DATA disk from the A drive.

30 Double-click the shortcut icon.

WHAT'S ▒▒▒
▒▒▒ **HAPPENING?**   The message box tells you that it is running the program cmd.exe and that program is reporting there is No Disk in the drive.

31 Insert the DATA disk into the A drive.

32 Click **Try Again**.

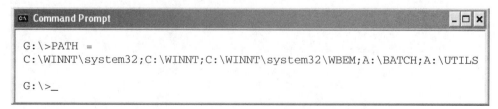

WHAT'S
HAPPENING?   The operating system found the specified disk and directories, and executed the batch file requested.

With the /k parameter, you can include a batch file with any number of commands that you would like to execute each time you open a command line session. Once again, the use of this technique on a floppy has limited value, but on your own system, referencing directories on the hard drive, it can be very valuable.

33 Close all open windows.

34 Drag the shortcut to the Recycle bin to delete it.

10.9   Writing a Batch File to Load an Application Program

Previously, in order to execute the BOG game, you had to take three separate steps. First you had to change to the directory where the program file was located. Second, you had to load the program, BOG.EXE. Third, after you exited the game, you returned to the root directory. A batch file is an ideal place to put all of these commands. In the following activity, you will run the BOG game from its location on the hard drive. Remember, if your WUGXP directory is somewhere other than C:\, substitute that location in your batch file.

10.10   Activity: Writing a Batch File to Execute the BOG Game

Note: You may use any text editor you wish for creating the batch files. You may use COPY CON, but when you have more than one line, using an editor is easier. Remember, you cannot edit lines when you use COPY CON. The operating system's Edit program will be used in this text. Instructions for keyboard use will be shown, but if you prefer using a mouse, do so.

1   Open a command line window.

2   Change directories to the root of the A drive.

3   Key in the following: A:\>**EDIT BOG.BAT** [Enter]

4   Key in the following: **CD /D C:\WUGXP\GAMES\BOG2** [Enter]
             BOG [Enter]
             A: [Enter]

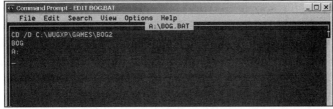

WHAT'S
HAPPENING?   You have just written a batch file to load the BOG application program. You can give the file the name **BOG.BAT**, because it is in the root directory

of the DATA disk and **BOG.EXE** is in a subdirectory on the hard drive. The two file names will not conflict, and you will not have to be specific and key in **BOG.BAT**. Furthermore, the first line tells the operating system to change drives and directories. The full path name is necessary in to change to the desired directory, but even if it had not been, you want the batch file to run no matter where you are when you execute it, so commands the require a particular location should always be referenced by their full file specification.

5   Press [Alt] + **F**.

6   Press **X**.

7   Press **Y**.

8   Key in the following: A:\>**TYPE BOG.BAT** [Enter]

```
A:\>TYPE BOG.BAT
CD /D C:\WUGXP\GAMES\BOG2
BOG
A:


A:\>_
```

WHAT'S
HAPPENING?   You created the batch file **BOG.BAT** in Edit and then returned to the system prompt. Now you can execute this file.

9   Key in the following: A:\>**BOG** [Enter]

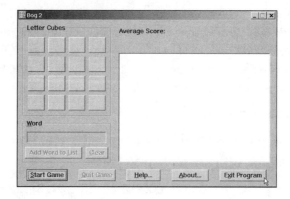

WHAT'S
HAPPENING?   When you keyed in BOG at the root directory, the operating system looked for changed directories, looked for and found the BOG program, and executed it. It read the lines in the order they appeared. It read the first line, which said to change the drive and directory to the **C:\WUGXP\GAMES\BOG2** subdirectory. It then read the second line, which told it to look for a program called **BOG.EXE**, and then it loaded BOG. The BOG game then appeared on the screen.

10   Click the **Exit Program** button.

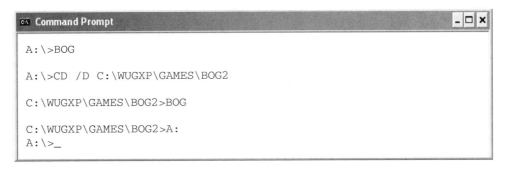

```
A:\>BOG

A:\>CD /D C:\WUGXP\GAMES\BOG2

C:\WUGXP\GAMES\BOG2>BOG

C:\WUGXP\GAMES\BOG2>A:
A:\>_
```

**WHAT'S ▒▒▒▒▒▒▒
▒▒▒HAPPENING?**   You can see on the command line screen how the lines were
executed, one at a time. It does not matter if played the game for one minute, one
hour, or one entire day. Whenever you exit the program, the command line continues with the execution of the batch file where it last was and simply reads and
executes the next line. The operating system finished executing your batch file by
changing the drive back to the A drive.

10.11 Creating Shortcuts for Batch Files on the Desktop

Any batch file can be run from the Windows environment. One way to do it is to
locate the batch file name in Windows Explorer or My Computer, then double-click
the file name. You can also create a shortcut for it and place it on the desktop or in a
folder. Again, once it is a shortcut, the shortcut can be clicked to execute the batch
file. However, there are things that you can do with the shortcut that you cannot do
in the command line interface. You can also change the icon for the shortcut.

10.12 Activity: Creating a Shortcut on the Desktop

Note: The DATA disk is in Drive A. A:\> is displayed.

1   Key in the following: A:\>**EXIT** Enter

2   Right-click in any blank area of the desktop.

3   Point to **New**.

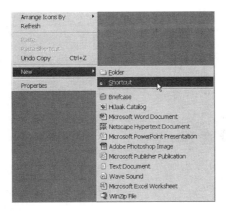

WHAT'S HAPPENING?   You opened the shortcut menu for the desktop, and the pop out menu for New.

4   Click **Shortcut**.

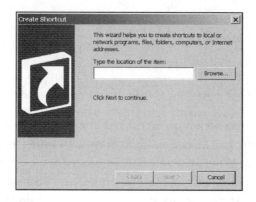

WHAT'S HAPPENING?   You started the Create a shortcut wizard.

5   In the location box, key in **C:\WUGXP\GAMES\BOG2\BOG.EXE**.

WHAT'S HAPPENING?   Notice that, as you type, the operating system anticipates what you mean. Once you key in the B of BOG, the BOG2 directory was shown below. As you continued to key in the full name, the B of BOG.EXE brought up 4 possibilities. You could have, at this point, double clicked on BOG.EXE and populated the location box in this way. However, in this example, you keyed in the entire file specification.

6   Click **Next**.

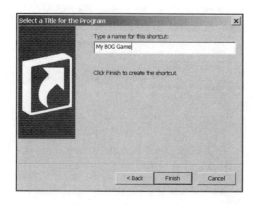

WHAT'S HAPPENING?   You are asked to supply a name for the shortcut. Once again, Windows XP anticipates what you want. This time, however, the assumption is incorrect.

7   In the name box, key in **My BOG Game** as shown in the figure above.

8   Click **Finish**.

WHAT'S HAPPENING?   You now have a shortcut to the batch file you created. Notice the Icon. Many executable files written for the Windows environment contain an icon that represents the program. If this program had not contained an icon, you would see the default windows icon. You can change the icon for short cuts..

9   Right-click the shortcut.

10   Click **Properties**.

WHAT'S HAPPENING?   You have opened the property sheet for the shortcut to the BOG program.

11   Click the **Shortcut** tab, if it is not already selected.

12   Click the **Change Icon** button.

WHAT'S ▓▓▓▓▓▓
▓▓▓▓**HAPPENING?**   As you can see, the program file BOG.EXE has its own icons. You want to change this.

13 Click **Browse**.

14 Click the down arrow of the **Look for icons in this file:** text box.

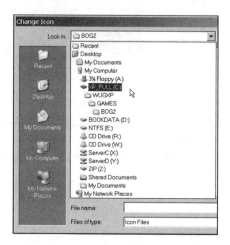

15 Click the C drive icon.

16 Click the **Windows** directory.

17 Click the **system32** directory. Click **shell32.dll**. (If you cannot see these directory names, you may have to go to the Tools menu of My Computer, Folder Options, View, and select Show all files.)

WHAT'S ▓▓▓▓▓▓
▓▓▓▓**HAPPENING?**   Windows provides a set of icons in a file named **SHELL32.DLL**. You are going to choose this file by either double clicking it, or selecting it and clicking the open button.

18 Click **Open**. Scroll until you an icon you like. (In this example, a Star was chosen.) Double-click the icon.

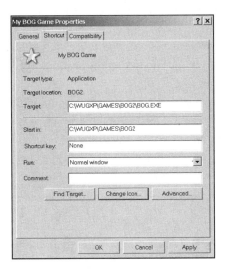

Now your shortcut to BOG is represented by the icon you selected.

19 Click **Apply**. Click **OK**.

Your shortcut appears on the desktop with the new icon.

20 Double-click the icon.

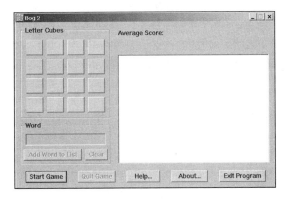

You have used the icon to run the BOG program.

21 Click **Exit Program**.

22 Drag the shortcut to BOG to the **Recycle Bin**.

10.13 Batch Files to Run Windows Programs

The Windows system files will reside in a different directory, depending on how the Windows XP operating system was installed. If the installation was an upgrade to Windows 2000, you will have a WINNT directory. It you upgraded Windows 98 or have a new installation, it will have a Windows directory. The drive may be C:\ or D:\, or another drive. Windows "keeps notes" about itself in the system environment. Remember that the path was stored in the *environmental variable* %Path%. The drive is referred to, in the environment, as "%SystemDrive%" and the directory where the system files are located is referred to as "%SystemRoot%." You can use this information to create a batch file to run the small programs that come with Windows, such as Notepad or Calculator.

Perhaps you prefer to use Notepad when writing batch files, but find it bothersome to have to return to the GUI to start the Notepad program. You can create a batch file that will allow you to run the program without having to return to the desktop. You can also use special features of Notepad to create a log file that will add the current date and time to a file created with Notepad. In order to use this feature, you must create a file with Notepad whose first line is .LOG.

10.14 Activity: Creating a Batch File to Run Notepad

Note: You have shelled out to the Command Line. The DATA disk is in Drive A. A:\> is displayed.

1   Key in the following: A:\>**EDIT N.BAT** Enter
                                        %SYSTEMROOT%\NOTEPAD.EXE Enter
                                        A: Enter

2   Key in the following: Alt + **F**. Press **X**.

3   Key in the following: **Y** Enter

WHAT'S
HAPPENING?   You have written a batch file to start a Windows applet, Notepad. You used an environmental variable, **%SYSTEMROOT%**. Case does not matter. You could key in an absolute path such as **C:\WINDOWS\NOTEPAD.EXE** or **C:\WINNT\NOTEPAD.EXE** if you knew the name of your Windows directory. However, if you use the environmental variable, Windows knows where the Windows files are located and will substitute the correct name. You did not need to use %SYSTEMDRIVE% as that variable knows which drive the %SYTEMROOT% is on.

4   Key in the following: A:\>**N** Enter

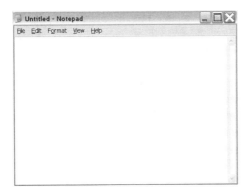

You have opened Notepad without returning to the desktop.

5 Key in the following in the Notepad window: **.LOG** [Enter]

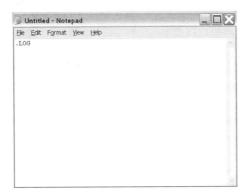

WHAT'S HAPPENING? You are creating a log file using Notepad. Here case *does* matter and you must use uppercase letters preceded by a period.

6 Click **File**. Click **Save As**.

7 In the File name text box, key in the following: **A:\log.txt** [Enter]

8 Click **Save**. Click **File**. Click **Exit**.

WHAT'S HAPPENING? You have closed Notepad and returned to the Command Line window.

9 Key in the following: **Edit log.bat** [Enter]
%systemroot%\notepad log.txt [Enter]
DIR *.AAA [Enter]

10 Press [Alt] + **F**. Press **X**. Press **Y**.

11 Key in the following: A:\>**LOG** [Enter]

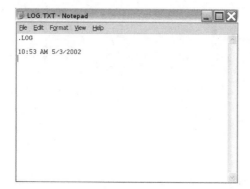

WHAT'S ▒▒▒▒
▒▒▒HAPPENING?   When you supplied a file name with Notepad, it opened the file you specified. As you can see, Notepad has placed the current date and time in the **log.txt** file. However, your second command has not executed. Your batch file requires that you finish using Notepad before it will read the next line and execute it (**DIR *.AAA**).

12 In Notepad, key in the following: **The first entry in my log file.** [Enter]

13 Press [Alt] + **F**. Press **X**. Key in the following: **Y**

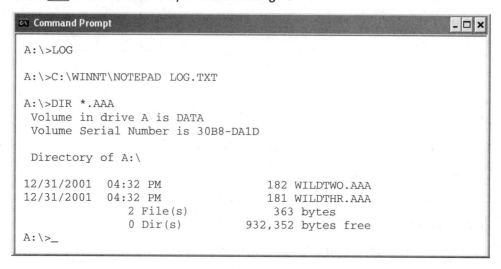

```
A:\>LOG

A:\>C:\WINNT\NOTEPAD LOG.TXT

A:\>DIR *.AAA
 Volume in drive A is DATA
 Volume Serial Number is 30B8-DA1D

 Directory of A:\

12/31/2001  04:32 PM               182 WILDTWO.AAA
12/31/2001  04:32 PM               181 WILDTHR.AAA
                2 File(s)          363 bytes
                0 Dir(s)       932,352 bytes free
A:\>_
```

WHAT'S ▒▒▒▒
▒▒▒HAPPENING?   Now that you exited Notepad, your other command could execute. There is a command called START that allows you to start a program in a new window and at the same time, continue executing your batch file in the previous window. You may also change the title of the Command Line window.

14 Edit and save the LOG.BAT file so it reads as follows and only has these two lines:
START notepad log.txt
START "THE .AAA FILES WINDOW" DIR *.AAA

WHAT'S ▒▒▒▒
▒▒▒HAPPENING?   The START command will start a new command window so that LOG.TXT will open in one window. The second command accomplishes two tasks. It will open another window, and it will give the window the title enclosed in quotation marks.

15 Key in the following: **LOG** [Enter]

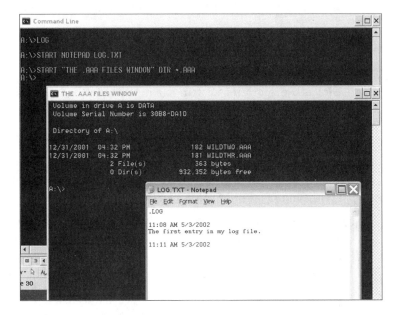

WHAT'S HAPPENING? You have three windows open, your original Command Line, your Notepad window, and "THE .AAA FILES WINDOW." The Notepad window is waiting for you to make an entry.

16 Make the Notepad window active. In the Notepad window, key in the following: **The second entry in my log file.**

17 Click **File**. Click **Save**. Click **File**. Click **Exit**.

WHAT'S HAPPENING? You still have THE AAA FILES WINDOW open. The DIR command executed.

18 Key in the following in each of the command line windows: **Exit** [Enter]

WHAT'S HAPPENING? You have closed the Command Line windows.

10.15 Special Batch File Commands

There are commands specifically designed to be used in batch files. They are the same for Windows XP as they were for Windows 2000. These commands can make batch files extremely versatile. They are listed in Table 10.2 below:

Command	Purpose
CALL	Calls one batch program from another without causing the first batch program to stop. The CALL command now accepts labels as the target of the call.
ECHO	Displays or hides the text in batch programs while the program is running. Also used to determine whether or not commands will be *echoed* to the screen while the program file is running.

ENDLOCAL	Ends localization of environment changes in a batch file, restoring environment variables to their values before the matching SETLOCAL command.
FOR	Runs a specified command for each file in a set of files. This command can also be used at the command line.
GOTO	Directs the operating system to a new line in the program that you specify with a label.
IF	Performs conditional processing in a batch program, based on whether or not a specified condition is true or false.
PAUSE	Suspends processing of a batch file and displays a message prompting the user to press a key to continue.
REM	Used to document your batch files. The operating system ignores any line that begins with REM, allowing you to place lines of information in your batch program or to prevent a line from running.
SETLOCAL	Begins localization of environmental variables in a batch file. Localization lasts until a matching ENDLOCAL command is encountered or the end of the batch file is reached.
SHIFT	Changes the position of the replaceable parameter in a batch program.

Table 10.2—Batch File Commands

You will examine and use some of these commands in the following activities.

10.16 The REM Command

The REM command, which stands for "remarks," is a special command that allows the user to key in explanatory text that will be displayed on the screen. Nothing else happens. REM does not cause the operating system to take any action, but it is very useful. When a line begins with REM, the operating system knows that anything following the REM is not a command and, thus, is not supposed to be executed, just displayed on the screen. REM allows a batch file to be *documented*. In a data-processing environment, "to document" means to give an explanation about the purpose of a program. This process can be very important when there are many batch files on a disk, especially when someone who did not write the batch file would like to use it. The REM statements should tell anyone what the purpose of the batch file is. The remarks can also include the name of the batch file, the time and date it was last updated, and the author of the batch file.

10.17 Activity: Using REM

Note: You have shelled out to a Command Line window. The DATA disk is in Drive A. A:\> is displayed.

1   Key in the following: A:\>**COPY CLASS\JUP.*** (Enter)

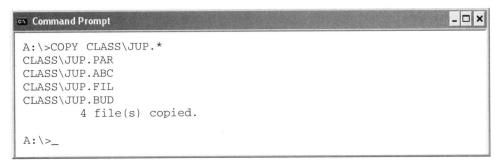

```
 Command Prompt                                    _ □ ×
A:\>COPY CLASS\JUP.*
CLASS\JUP.PAR
CLASS\JUP.ABC
CLASS\JUP.FIL
CLASS\JUP.BUD
        4 file(s) copied.

A:\>_
```

WHAT'S HAPPENING?   You have copied some files that were previously moved to the CLASS directory to the root of the DATA disk.

2   Key in the following: A:\>**EDIT TEST2.BAT** Enter
                         REM This is a test file Enter
                         REM to see how the REM Enter
                         REM command works. Enter
                         TYPE JUP.BUD Enter
                         COPY JUP.BUD JUP.XYZ

WHAT'S HAPPENING?   You are using Edit to write another batch file called **TEST2.BAT**. You have inserted some text with REM preceding each line. You keyed in two command line commands, TYPE and COPY. Now you want to save this file to the disk and return to the system level.

3   Press Alt + **F**. Press **X**. Press **Y**.

4   Key in the following: A:\>**TYPE TEST2.BAT** Enter

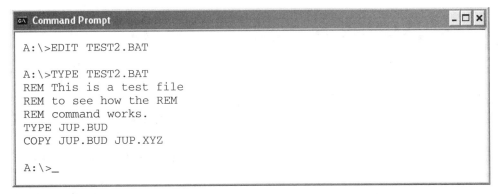

```
 Command Prompt                                    _ □ ×
A:\>EDIT  TEST2.BAT

A:\>TYPE  TEST2.BAT
REM This is a test file
REM to see how the REM
REM command works.
TYPE JUP.BUD
COPY JUP.BUD JUP.XYZ

A:\>_
```

WHAT'S HAPPENING?   This batch file was created as a test case. The remarks just keyed in explain the purpose of this batch file. You created **TEST2.BAT** in Edit and returned to the system prompt. You then displayed **TEST2.BAT** with the TYPE command. To execute the **TEST2.BAT** batch file, you must run it.

5   Key in the following: A:\>**TEST2** Enter

```
 Command Prompt                                    _ □ ×
A:\>TEST2

A:\>REM This is a test file

A:\>REM to see how the REM
```

```
A:\>REM command works.

A:\>TYPE JUP.BUD

Jupiter is the largest planet
in our Solar System.  It has a
giant red spot on it.  Huge storms
larger than our earth that last
more than a century take place
on the planet Jupiter.

A:\>COPY JUP.BUD JUP.XYZ
        1 file(s) copied.

A:\>_
```

WHAT'S
HAPPENING?   When you keyed in **TEST2**, the batch file was executed. The operating system read the first line of the batch file, *REM This is a test file*. It knew that it was supposed to do nothing but display the text following REM on the screen. Then the next line in the batch file was read, *REM to see how the REM*, and the same procedure was followed. The operating system kept reading and displaying the REM lines until it got to the line that had the command TYPE. To the operating system, TYPE is a command, so it executed or ran the TYPE command with the parameter JUP.BUD. Then the next line was read, which was another command, COPY, so it was executed. The file **JUP.BUD** was copied to a new file called **JUP.XYZ**. Then the operating system looked for another line in the batch file but could find no more lines, so it returned to the system level. The purpose of REM is to provide explanatory remarks about the batch file.

10.18 The ECHO Command

Notice in the above activity, when you ran TEST2.BAT you saw the command on the screen, and then the command executed. You saw the words "TYPE JUP.BUD" which was the command, and then saw the typed-out file, the results of the command. Both the command and the output of the command were "echoed" to the screen. ECHO is a command that means display to the screen. The default value for ECHO is on. Unless specifically told otherwise, both commands and their results will show on the screen. In a batch file, you can turn off the display of the command and see only the output of a command—not the command itself. For instance, COPY THIS.FIL THAT.FIL is a command. The output of the command is **1 File(s) copied**. The work of the command is the actual copying of the file. See Table 10.3.

	Echo On Display	Echo Off Display
Command:	COPY THIS.FIL THAT.FIL	
Output:	1 File(s) copied	1 File(s) copied

Table 10.3—ECHO On or Off

If the purpose of the REM command is to document a batch file, what is the purpose of the ECHO command? One purpose of the ECHO command is, by turning it off, you can minimize screen clutter. For instance, although you want to use the REM command to document your batch file, you really only want to see this documentation when you type out the contents of the file, or edit it to make changes. You do not need to see your documentation on the screen every time you run the batch file. ECHO OFF allows you to suppress the display of the commands.

10.19 Activity: Using ECHO

Note: The DATA disk is in Drive A. A:\> is displayed.

1   Key in the following: A:\>**COPY TEST2.BAT TESTING.BAT** Enter

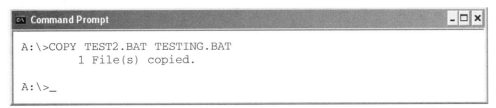

```
A:\>COPY TEST2.BAT TESTING.BAT
        1 File(s) copied.

A:\>_
```

WHAT'S
HAPPENING?   You made a copy of the file **TEST2.BAT**.

2   Key in the following: A:\>**EDIT TESTING.BAT** Enter

3   At the top of the file, key in the following: **ECHO OFF** Enter

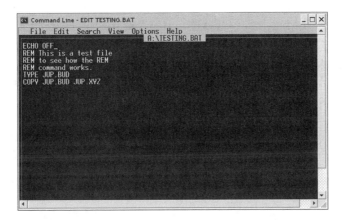

WHAT'S
HAPPENING?   You are using a copy of the batch file from the previous activity. The only difference is that you added one line at the top of the batch file to turn ECHO off. You are going to run the batch file so that only the output of each command is displayed, not the actual commands. First you must exit Edit and save the file to the disk.

4   Press Alt + **F**. Press **X**. Press **Y**.

5   Key in the following: A:\>**TYPE TESTING.BAT** Enter

```
A:\>TYPE TESTING.BAT
ECHO OFF
REM This is a test file
REM to see how the REM
REM command works.
```

```
TYPE JUP.BUD
COPY JUP.BUD JUP.XYZ

A:\>_
```

WHAT'S ▓▓▓▓▓
▓▓▓▓ **HAPPENING?**   You saved the file as **TESTING.BAT** and displayed the contents on the screen. Now you wish to execute the file.

6   Key in the following: A:\>**TESTING** [Enter]

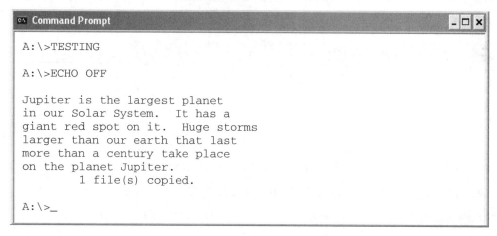

WHAT'S ▓▓▓▓▓
▓▓▓▓ **HAPPENING?**   The batch file **TESTING.BAT** has the same commands as **TEST2.BAT**, but this time you saw only the output of the commands, not the actual commands themselves. You saw the ECHO OFF command on the screen, but you did not see the REM commands displayed on the screen. You saw the results of the TYPE JUP.BUD command, the contents of the file on the screen, but you never saw the TYPE JUP.BUD command on the screen. You also did not see the COPY JUP.BUD JUP.XYZ command, only the results of the command—the message "1 file(s) copied."

You can eliminate the display of the ECHO OFF command.

7   Key in the following: A:\>**EDIT TESTING.BAT** [Enter]
                                @ (do not press [Enter])

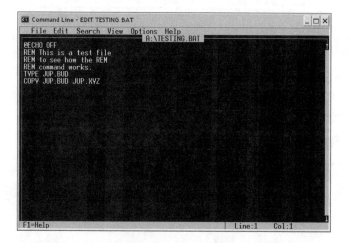

WHAT'S ▓▓▓▓▓
▓▓▓▓ **HAPPENING?**   You have inserted the @ symbol in front of ECHO OFF to prevent the command from echoing to the screen.

8   Press [Alt] + **F**. Press **X**. Press **Y**.

9   Key in the following: A:\>**TESTING** [Enter]

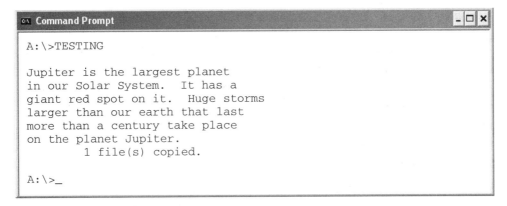

```
A:\>TESTING

Jupiter is the largest planet
in our Solar System.  It has a
giant red spot on it.  Huge storms
larger than our earth that last
more than a century take place
on the planet Jupiter.
        1 file(s) copied.

A:\>_
```

WHAT'S
HAPPENING?   The ECHO OFF display was suppressed. All you see at the end of
the display is 1 file(s) copied. This may be misleading. You want to see the names of
the source and destination files used in the copy process.

10   Key in the following: **EDIT TESTING.BAT** [Enter]

11   Place the cursor under the C in COPY and press the [Enter] key.

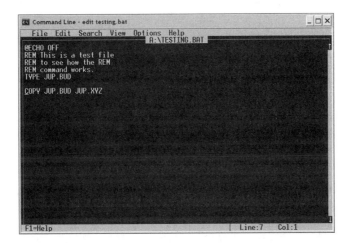

WHAT'S
HAPPENING?   There is now a blank line in the file.

12   Place the cursor in the blank line and Key in the following: **ECHO ON**

13   Press [Alt] + **F**. Press **X**. Press **Y**.

14   Key in the following: **TESTING** [Enter]

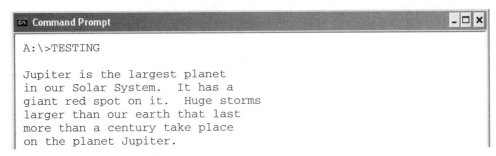

```
A:\>TESTING

Jupiter is the largest planet
in our Solar System.  It has a
giant red spot on it.  Huge storms
larger than our earth that last
more than a century take place
on the planet Jupiter.
```

```
A:\>COPY JUP.BUD JUP.XYZ
        1 file(s) copied.

A:\>_
```

**WHAT'S ▓▓▓▓▓▓
▓▓▓ HAPPENING?**   You have manipulated the screen display to better suit your needs using ECHO OFF and ECHO ON.

You already have a file by the name of **JUP.XYZ**, but, even though you are using the COPY command, it did not tell you that the file already exists (overwrite protection). The purpose of using a batch program would be defeated if there were interaction required by the user, so the warning is not there. The differences between ECHO ON and ECHO OFF are exemplified in Table 10.4.

	TEST2.BAT— ECHO ON Display	TESTING.BAT— ECHO OFF Display
Command:	ECHO ON	ECHO OFF
Command:	REM This is a test file	
Command:	REM to see how the REM	
Command:	REM command works.	
Command:	TYPE JUP.BUD	
Output:	Jupiter is the largest planet in our Solar System. It has a giant red spot on it. Huge storms larger than our earth that last more than a century take place on the planet Jupiter.	Jupiter is the largest planet in our Solar System. It has a giant red spot on it. Huge storms larger than our earth that last more than a century take place on the planet Jupiter.
Command:	COPY JUP.BUD JUP.XYZ	
Output:	1 File(s) copied	1 File(s) copied

(*Note:* Although commands and file names are shown as uppercase letters, the case does not matter.)

Table 10.4—ECHO ON and ECHO OFF: A Comparison of Screen Displays

10.20 The CLS Command

In the previous exercise, running the batch file TESTING caused the output of that file to be placed on the screen directly below the request (TESTING) for the file to execute. In many instances, the screen already contained previously executed commands and outputs. The purpose of this batch file is to 1) display the contents of a file and 2) to copy that file to another file. Having the display appear on a screen that already contains information can be difficult to read. Using the CLS (CLear Screen) command after turning the ECHO off eliminates this problem.

10.21 Activity: Using CLS

1   Key in the following: **EDIT TESTING.BAT** [Enter]

2   Place the cursor under the R in the first REM command and press the [Enter] key.

3   In the blank line created, key in the following: **CLS**

4   Press [Alt] + **F**. Press **X**. Press **Y**.

5   Key in the following: **TESTING** [Enter]

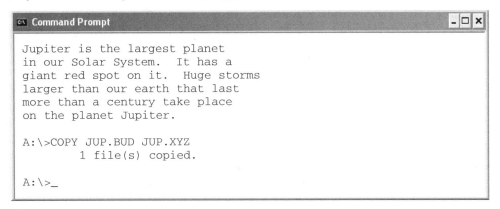

```
Jupiter is the largest planet
in our Solar System.  It has a
giant red spot on it.  Huge storms
larger than our earth that last
more than a century take place
on the planet Jupiter.

A:\>COPY JUP.BUD JUP.XYZ
        1 file(s) copied.

A:\>_
```

WHAT'S HAPPENING?   The first "action" taken by the batch file after the ECHO was turned off was to clear the screen. When and if to turn the ECHO off and on, and when and if to clear the screen depends on the purpose and function of each batch file.

10.22 The PAUSE Command

Another batch file command is PAUSE, which does *exactly* what its name implies: It tells the batch file to stop executing until the user takes some action. Batch file processing is suspended, and no other batch command will be executed until the user presses a key. The PAUSE command will wait forever until the user takes some action.

10.23 Activity: Using PAUSE

Note: The DATA disk is in Drive A. A:\> is displayed.

1   Key in the following: A:\>**EDIT TEST2.BAT** [Enter]

2   Press [Ctrl] + [End]

3   Key in the following: **PAUSE You are going to delete JUP.XYZ** [Enter]
                           DEL JUP.XYZ

4   Press [Alt] + **F**. Press **X**. Press **Y**.

5   Key in the following: A:\>**TYPE TEST2.BAT** [Enter]

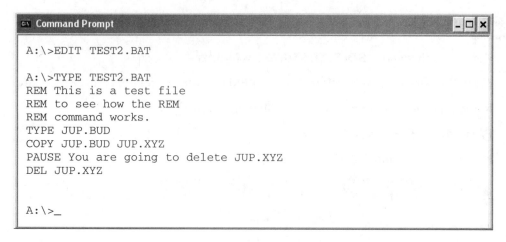

```
A:\>EDIT TEST2.BAT

A:\>TYPE TEST2.BAT
REM This is a test file
REM to see how the REM
REM command works.
TYPE JUP.BUD
COPY JUP.BUD JUP.XYZ
PAUSE You are going to delete JUP.XYZ
DEL JUP.XYZ


A:\>_
```

WHATS
HAPPENING?   You saved the file to disk with the changes you made. You then looked at the contents of the file with the TYPE command. You edited the batch file **TEST2.BAT**. When the file is executed, the first three lines of the file, the **REM** statements, explain the purpose of **TEST2.BAT**. Then the batch file displays the contents of **JUP.BUD** on the screen and copies the file **JUP.BUD** to a new file, **JUP.XYZ**. The PAUSE statement tells you that the file is going to be deleted and gives you a chance to change your mind. After you take action by pressing a key, the file **JUP.XYZ** is erased.

To execute **TEST2.BAT**, you must key in **TEST2** at the prompt.

6   Key in the following: A:\>**TEST2** [Enter]

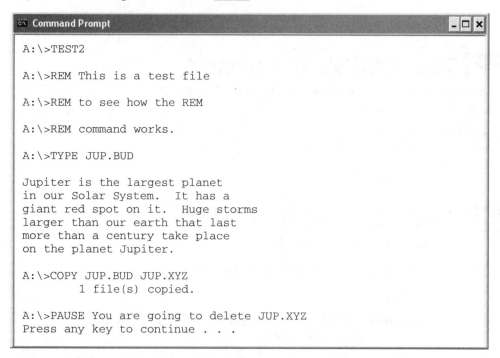

```
A:\>TEST2

A:\>REM This is a test file

A:\>REM to see how the REM

A:\>REM command works.

A:\>TYPE JUP.BUD

Jupiter is the largest planet
in our Solar System.  It has a
giant red spot on it.  Huge storms
larger than our earth that last
more than a century take place
on the planet Jupiter.

A:\>COPY JUP.BUD JUP.XYZ
        1 file(s) copied.

A:\>PAUSE You are going to delete JUP.XYZ
Press any key to continue . . .
```

WHATS
HAPPENING?   The batch file TEST2 has stopped running or "paused." It has halted execution until some action is taken. When you press a key, the operating system will read and execute the next line of the batch file. PAUSE just stops; it is

not an order. If ECHO were off, all you would see is the message, "Press any key to continue ...". You would not see the message, "You are going to delete JUP.XYZ."

7   Press [Enter]

```
A:\>PAUSE You are going to delete JUP.XYZ
Press any key to continue . . .

A:\>DEL JUP.XYZ
A:\>_
```

WHAT'S HAPPENING?   The batch file continued executing all the steps and deleted the file called **JUP.XYZ.**

8   Key in the following: A:\>**DIR JUP.XYZ** [Enter]

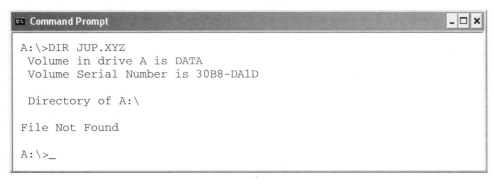

```
A:\>DIR JUP.XYZ
 Volume in drive A is DATA
 Volume Serial Number is 30B8-DA1D

 Directory of A:\

File Not Found

A:\>_
```

WHAT'S HAPPENING?   The file **JUP.XYZ** was deleted.

10.24 Stopping a Batch File from Executing

In the above activity, you pressed a key after the PAUSE command was displayed so that the batch file continued to execute. What if you wanted to stop running the batch file? You can do this by interrupting or exiting from a running batch file. You do this by pressing the [Ctrl] key, and while pressing the [Ctrl] key, pressing the letter C ([Ctrl] + C or [Ctrl] + [Break]). At whatever point [Ctrl] + C is pressed, you leave the batch file and return to the system prompt. The rest of the lines in the batch file do not execute.

10.25 Activity: Quitting a Batch File

Note: The DATA disk is in Drive A. A:\> is displayed.

1   Key in the following: A:\>**TEST2** [Enter]

```
A:\>REM This is a test file

A:\>REM to see how the REM

A:\>REM command works.
```

```
A:\>TYPE JUP.BUD

Jupiter is the largest planet
in our Solar System.  It has a
giant red spot on it.  Huge storms
larger than our earth that last
more than a century take place
on the planet Jupiter.

A:\>COPY JUP.BUD JUP.XYZ
        1 file(s) copied.

A:\>PAUSE You are going to delete JUP.XYZ
Press any key to continue . . .
```

WHAT'S HAPPENING?   You are at the same point as you were in the last activity. The batch file reached the PAUSE command. It has momentarily stopped running. You do not want to erase **JUP.XYZ**. You want the batch file to cease operation. Previous experience with the PAUSE command showed that pressing any key would continue running the program. If any key were pressed here, the next line in the file, **DEL JUP.XYZ**, would execute and the file **JUP.XYZ** would be erased. To stop this from happening, another action must be taken to interrupt the batch file process.

2   Hold down the Ctrl key, and while it is down, press the letter **C**. Then release both keys.

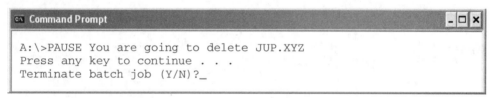

```
A:\>PAUSE You are going to delete JUP.XYZ
Press any key to continue . . .
Terminate batch job (Y/N)?_
```

WHAT'S HAPPENING?   The message is giving you a choice: either stop the batch file from running (**Y** for "yes") or continue with the batch file (**N** for "no"). If you press **Y**, the last line in the batch file, DEL JUP.XYZ, will not execute.

3   Press **Y** Enter

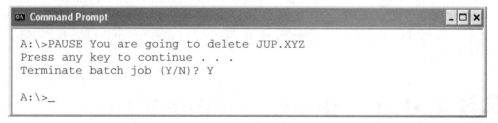

```
A:\>PAUSE You are going to delete JUP.XYZ
Press any key to continue . . .
Terminate batch job (Y/N)? Y

A:\>_
```

WHAT'S HAPPENING?   The system prompt is displayed. If the batch file was interrupted properly, **JUP.XYZ** should not have been deleted because the line, DEL JUP.XYZ should not have executed.

4   Key in the following: A:\>**DIR JUP.XYZ** Enter

```
Command Prompt                                                    - □ ×

A:\>DIR JUP.XYZ
 Volume in drive A is DATA
 Volume Serial Number is 30B8-DA1D

 Directory of A:\

05/07/2002  07:41 AM                 190 JUP.XYZ
               1 File(s)             190 bytes
               0 Dir(s)        928,768 bytes free

A:\>_
```

**WHAT'S
HAPPENING?**   The file **JUP.XYZ** is still on the DATA disk. Pressing [Ctrl] + **C** at the
line *PAUSE You are going to delete JUP.XYZ* broke into the batch file **TEST2.BAT** and
stopped it from running. Because **TEST2.BAT** stopped executing and returned you
to the system prompt, it never got to the command line DEL JUP.XYZ. Therefore, the
file **JUP.XYZ** is still on the DATA disk. Although in this activity you broke into the
batch file at the PAUSE statement, you can press [Ctrl] + **C** any time during the
execution of a batch file. The batch file will stop when it has completed the current
command before executing the next one. The problem is, with the speed of today's
computers, it is difficult to ascertain how many lines of the batch file have been read
by the operating system when you press [Ctrl] + C.

10.26 Replaceable Parameters in Batch Files

In the same way that you use parameters with system commands, you can use
parameters effectively in batch files. For instance, look at the command DIR A: /W.

```
Command       Command Line Parameter
DIR           A: /W
```

In the above example, the space and the / are delimiters. DIR is the command. A:
and W are parameters that tell the operating system that you want a directory of A:
and that you want it displayed in a wide mode. Parameters give the command
additional instructions on what to do. When you use the DIR command as used
above, the /W parameter is fixed; you cannot choose another letter to accomplish a
wide mode display.

   Many commands use *variable* or *replaceable parameters*. An example of a
command that uses a replaceable parameter is TYPE. TYPE requires one parameter,
a file name, but the file name you use will vary; hence, it is a variable parameter.
The TYPE command uses the parameter that you keyed in to choose the file to
display on the screen. You can key in TYPE THIS.FIL or TYPE TEST.TXT or whatever file name you want. You replace the file name for the parameter, hence the term
replaceable parameter.

```
Command                Replaceable Command Line Parameter
 TYPE                        THIS. FIL
```

or

```
Command                 Replaceable Command Line Parameter
   TYPE                         TEST.TXT
```

Batch files can also use replaceable parameters, also called *dummy parameters*, *substitute parameters*, or *positional parameters*. When you write the batch file, you insert *place holders* that will hold information that is keyed in at the time the batch file is executed. When you execute the batch file by keying in the batch file name, you also key in additional information on the command line that will be inserted where the placeholders are in the batch file. The batch file looks to the command line and selects which information you desire by its position (positional parameters) on the command line. What you are doing is parsing a command. To *parse* is to analyze something in an orderly way. In linguistics, to parse is to divide words and phrases into different parts in order to understand relationships and meanings. In computers, to parse is to divide the computer language statement into parts that can be made useful for the computer. In the above example, the TYPE command had the argument TEST.TXT passed to it so that it can display the contents of that variable. When you write the batch file, you supply the place holder or marker to let the batch file know that something, a variable, will be keyed in with the batch file name at execution time. The place holder, marker, or blank parameter used in a batch file is the percent sign (%) followed by a number from **0** through **9**. The % sign is the signal to the operating system that a parameter is coming. The numbers indicate what position the parameter is on the command line. Whatever is first is **%0**, usually the command itself. Thus, the command occupies the position of %0. The next item on the command line is in the first position (%1) and the next item on the command line is in the second position (%2) and so on.

The batch files that you have written so far deal with specific commands and specific file names, but the real power of batch files is their ability to use replaceable parameters. You are going to write a batch file in the usual way with specific file names, and then use the batch file to see how replaceable parameters work.

10.27 Activity: Using Replaceable Parameters

Note: The DATA disk is in Drive A. A:\> is displayed.

1   Key in the following: A:\>**TYPE JUP.XYZ** [Enter]

2   Key in the following: A:\>**DIR JUP.XYZ** [Enter]

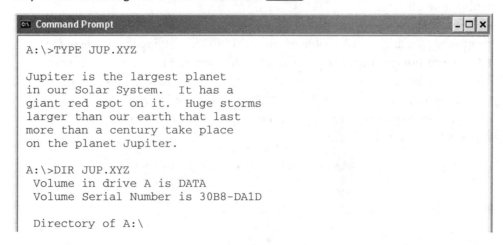

```
05/07/2002   07:41 AM                190 JUP.XYZ
              1 File(s)               190 bytes
              0 Dir(s)           928,768 bytes free

A:\>_
```

**WHAT'S
HAPPENING?**   This file was created in the last activity. It has data in it and
occupies 190 bytes of space on the disk. (Your file size may differ slightly.) If you
remember, when you delete a file, the data is still on the disk. What if you wanted a
way to delete the data completely so that it cannot ever be recovered? You can
overwrite the file with new data. If you key in ECHO at the command line, you get
a status report of whether ECHO is on or off. You can redirect the output of the
ECHO command to your file, making it 13 bytes long and replacing the data in the
file with the output of the ECHO command. You are going to first try this at the
command line.

3   Key in the following: A:\>**ECHO > JUP.XYZ** Enter

4   Key in the following: A:\>**TYPE JUP.XYZ** Enter

5   Key in the following: A:\>**DIR JUP.XYZ** Enter

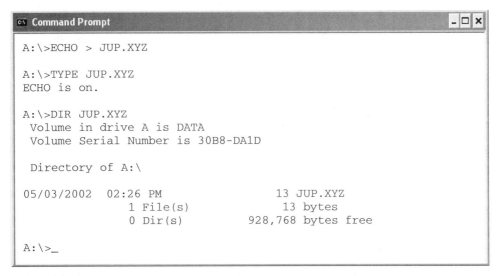

```
A:\>ECHO > JUP.XYZ

A:\>TYPE JUP.XYZ
ECHO is on.

A:\>DIR JUP.XYZ
 Volume in drive A is DATA
 Volume Serial Number is 30B8-DA1D

 Directory of A:\

05/03/2002   02:26 PM                 13 JUP.XYZ
              1 File(s)                13 bytes
              0 Dir(s)           928,768 bytes free

A:\>_
```

**WHAT'S
HAPPENING?**   As you can see, it worked. You have *really* overwritten this file.
Your data is no longer in the file to recover. This command would be useful when
deleting files of a confidential nature. It would prevent most data recovery programs from being able to recover the data from your file. It can also be used in a
batch file.

6   Key in the following: A:\>**EDIT KILLIT.BAT** Enter
                                     ECHO > JUP.XYZ Enter
                                     TYPE JUP.XYZ Enter
                                     DEL JUP.XYZ

7   Press Alt + **F**. Press **X**.

8   Press **Y**.

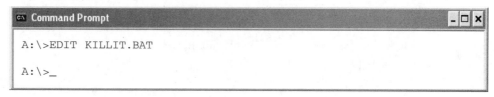

```
Command Prompt                                    _ □ ×

A:\>EDIT KILLIT.BAT

A:\>_
```

WHAT'S HAPPENING?   Edit is the tool you used to write the batch file. You created a simple batch file that sends data to **JUP.XYZ,** displays the file contents, and then deletes the file called **JUP.XYZ.** You then used the Edit menu to exit and save **KILLIT.BAT** to your disk.

9   Key in the following: A:\>**TYPE KILLIT.BAT** Enter

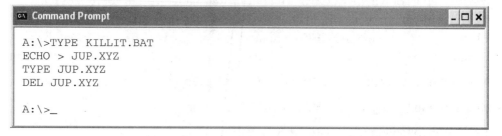

```
Command Prompt                                    _ □ ×

A:\>TYPE KILLIT.BAT
ECHO > JUP.XYZ
TYPE JUP.XYZ
DEL JUP.XYZ

A:\>_
```

WHAT'S HAPPENING?   You displayed the contents of the **KILLIT.BAT** file. To execute this batch file, you must *call* it, which is another way of saying key in the command name—the name of the batch file.

10   Key in the following: A:\>**KILLIT** Enter

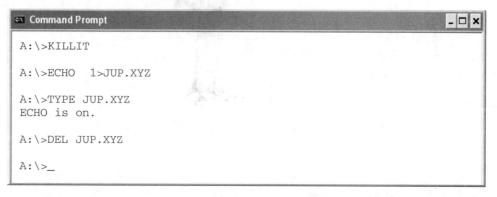

```
Command Prompt                                    _ □ ×

A:\>KILLIT

A:\>ECHO  1>JUP.XYZ

A:\>TYPE JUP.XYZ
ECHO is on.

A:\>DEL JUP.XYZ

A:\>_
```

WHAT'S HAPPENING?   The batch file called **KILLIT** ran successfully. (The 1 before the directional sign (>) indicates the numerical value of Standard Output, indicating that the Standard Ouput of the Echo command is redirected to the object of the directional sign.) However, this batch file is not useful, as it can be used only for the file called **JUP.XYZ.** You have deleted **JUP.XYZ** so now **KILLIT.BAT** is no longer useful.

What if you wanted to do the same sequence of commands for a file called **JUP.TMP** or **PERSONAL.FIL** or any other file on the disk? Until now, you would have to create another batch file using **JUP.TMP** instead of **JUP.XYZ**. You would write another batch file for **PERSONAL.FIL**. You can quickly clutter up your disks with many batch files, all doing the same thing but using different file names and having no value after they have executed. An easier way is to have a batch file that does the same steps—a generic batch file. When you execute it, you supply the specific parameter or file name that interests you. When you write this batch file, you need to supply a place for the name of the file. These places are called "replaceable parameters." They are percent signs followed by numbers.

You are going to edit **KILLIT.BAT** so that it uses replaceable parameters. In addition, you will document it and add some protection for yourself. When you key in the replaceable parameters, be sure to use the percent sign (%), then the number **1**, and not the lowercase of the letter L (**l**). Also note that there is no space between % and the number **1**.

11 Key in the following:

A:\>**EDIT KILLIT.BAT** [Enter]
       REM This batch file will make [Enter]
       REM the data in a file difficult to recover. [Enter]
       DIR %1 [Enter]
       PAUSE You are going to kill the file, %1. Are you sure? [Enter]

12 Replace **ECHO > JUP.XYZ** with **ECHO > %1**.

13 Delete the line **TYPE JUP.XYZ**.

14 Replace **DEL JUP.XYZ** with **DEL %1**.

15 Press [Alt] + **F**. Press **X**.

16 Press **Y**.

17 Key in the following: A:\>**TYPE KILLIT.BAT** [Enter]

```
Command Prompt                                            _ □ x
A:\>TYPE KILLIT.BAT
REM This batch file will make
REM the data in a file difficult to recover.
DIR %1
PAUSE You are going to kill the file, %1. Are you sure?
ECHO > %1
DEL %1

A:\>_
```

WHAT'S ▓▓▓▓
▓▓▓▓ **HAPPENING?**   You used Edit to edit the file **KILLIT.BAT**. You then saved it to the disk. You displayed the contents of the file on the screen. The contents of the batch file **KILLIT.BAT** are different from the previous version of **KILLIT.BAT**. By using the place holder **%1**, instead of a specific file name, you are saying that you do not yet know what file name (**%1**) you want these commands to apply to. When you run the batch file **KILLIT**, you will provide a value or parameter on the command line that the batch file will substitute for **%1**. For instance, if you key in on the command line, **KILLIT MY.FIL**, **KILLIT** is in the zero position on the command line (**%0**) and **MY.FIL** is in the first position on the command line (**%1**). Remember, you used %1 as a place holder in the KILLIT.BAT file. You will fill that place holder at the time of execution.

For you to understand the purpose of replaceable parameters, it is helpful to view them as *positional* parameters. The operating system gets the information or knows what to substitute by the position on the command line. The first piece of data on the command line is always in position 0; the second piece of data on the command line is always in position 1; the third piece of data on the command line is always in position 2, and so on.

18 Key in the following: A:\>**KILLIT JUP.BUD** [Enter]

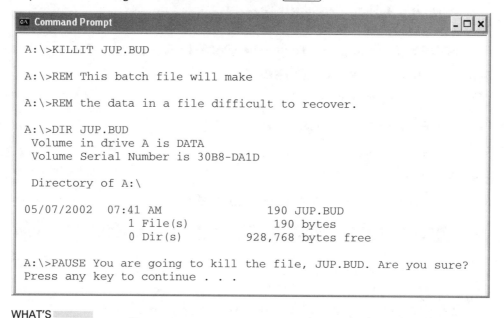

```
A:\>KILLIT JUP.BUD

A:\>REM This batch file will make

A:\>REM the data in a file difficult to recover.

A:\>DIR JUP.BUD
 Volume in drive A is DATA
 Volume Serial Number is 30B8-DA1D

 Directory of A:\

05/07/2002  07:41 AM                190 JUP.BUD
               1 File(s)            190 bytes
               0 Dir(s)         928,768 bytes free

A:\>PAUSE You are going to kill the file, JUP.BUD. Are you sure?
Press any key to continue . . .
```

WHAT'S ▓▓▓▓
▓▓▓▓ **HAPPENING?**   In the command line **KILLIT JUP.BUD**, **KILLIT** is position 0 and **JUP.BUD** is position 1. The batch file **KILLIT** executed each command line. However, when it found **%1** in the batch file, it looked for the first position after **KILLIT** on the command line, which was **JUP.BUD**. It substituted **JUP.BUD** every time it found **%1**. You placed the **DIR %1** in the batch file to confirm that it is on the disk. The PAUSE statement allows you to change your mind. The **%1** in the PAUSE line identifies which file is to be killed.

19 Press [Enter]

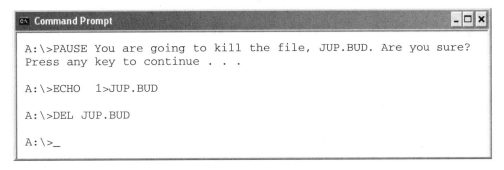

```
A:\>PAUSE You are going to kill the file, JUP.BUD. Are you sure?
Press any key to continue . . .

A:\>ECHO  1>JUP.BUD

A:\>DEL JUP.BUD

A:\>_
```

WHAT'S HAPPENING?   You have deleted the file. Even if you, or anyone else, try to recover it, the data is truly gone. You have written a generic or "plain wrap" batch file that allows you to use the same batch file over and over. All you have to supply is a value or parameter after the batch file name on the command line. Thus, you could key in **KILLIT BUSINESS.APP**, **KILLIT SALES.LET**, **KILLIT FEB.99**, **KILLIT TELE.SET**, or any other file name. The batch file will execute the same commands over and over, using the position 1 (%1) value (the file name) you key in after the batch file name. You can see that because this file is versatile, it is infinitely more useful than it was without positional parameters.

10.28 Multiple Replaceable Parameters in Batch Files

In the above example, you used one replaceable parameter. What happens if you need more than one parameter? For instance, if you want to include the COPY command in a batch file, COPY needs two parameters: *source* and *destination*. Many commands require more than one parameter. You may also use multiple parameters in batch files. You can have up to 10 dummy parameters (%0 through %9). Remember, replaceable parameters are sometimes called positional parameters because the operating system uses the position number in the command line to determine which parameter to use. The parameters are placed in order from left to right. For example, examine the command line:

COPY MYFILE.TXT YOUR.FIL

COPY is in the first position, %0 (computers always count beginning with 0, not 1). MYFILE.TXT is in the second position, %1, and YOUR.FIL is in the third position, %2.

The next activity will allow you to create a simple batch file with multiple replaceable parameters so you will see how the positional process works. Then you will write another batch file, and in it you will create a command that the operating system does not have. Your new command will copy all files *except* the ones you specify.

10.29 Activity: Using Multiple Replaceable Parameters

Note: The DATA disk is in Drive A. A:\> is displayed.

1   Key in the following:

A:\>**EDIT MULTI.BAT** Enter
      REM This is a sample batch file Enter
      REM using more than one replaceable parameter. Enter
      TYPE %3 Enter
      COPY %1 %2 Enter
      TYPE %1

2   Press Alt + **F**. Press **X**.

3   Press **Y**.

4   Key in the following: A:\>**TYPE MULTI.BAT** Enter

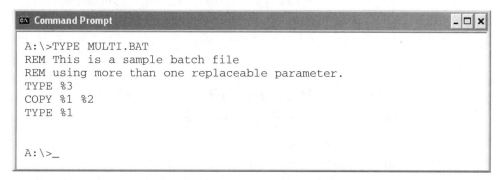

```
A:\>TYPE MULTI.BAT
REM This is a sample batch file
REM using more than one replaceable parameter.
TYPE %3
COPY %1 %2
TYPE %1


A:\>_
```

WHAT'S
HAPPENING?   You keyed in and saved a batch file called **MULTI.BAT** on the root of the DATA disk. You then displayed the contents of **MULTI.BAT** on the screen. To execute it you must not only key in the command name **MULTI** but must also provide the command with the positional parameters that are referred to in the file. First you will copy some files to the root of the DATA disk.

5   Key in the following: A:\>**COPY CLASS\VEN.*** Enter

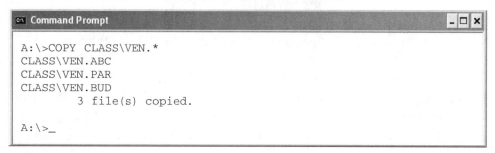

```
A:\>COPY CLASS\VEN.*
CLASS\VEN.ABC
CLASS\VEN.PAR
CLASS\VEN.BUD
        3 file(s) copied.

A:\>_
```

WHAT'S
HAPPENING?   You copied some files from the CLASS directory that had been moved from the root directory during disk organization (Chapter 8). In the next step, you will key in **MULTI VEN.ABC JUP.ABC FILE2.SWT**. The batch file knows what to put in each percent sign because it looks at the position on the command line. It does not matter which order you use the %1 or %2 or %3 in the batch file, only the order you use on the command line. See Table 10.5.

Position 0 on the Command Line	Position 1 on the Command Line	Position 2 on the Command Line	Position 3 on the Command Line
MULTI	**VEN.ABC**	**JUP.ABC**	**FILE2.SWT**
When the batch file needs a value for %0, it uses **MULTI**	When the batch file needs a value for %1, it uses **VEN.ABC**	When the batch file needs a value for %2, it uses **JUP.ABC**	When the batch file needs a value for %3, it uses **FILE2.SWT**
Command	**Parameter**	**Parameter**	**Parameter**

Table 10.5—Positional Parameters

6   Key in the following: A:\>**MULTI VEN.ABC JUP.ABC FILE2.SWT** Enter

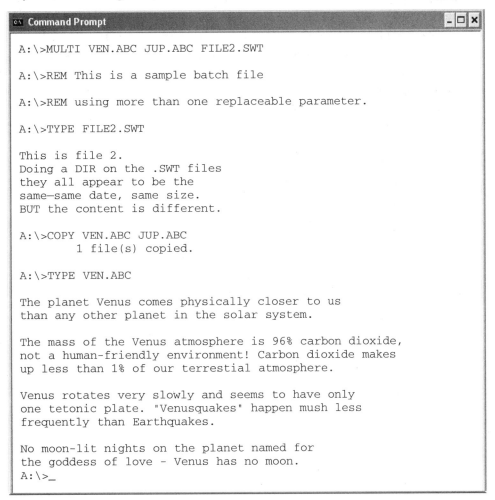

```
A:\>MULTI VEN.ABC JUP.ABC FILE2.SWT

A:\>REM This is a sample batch file

A:\>REM using more than one replaceable parameter.

A:\>TYPE FILE2.SWT

This is file 2.
Doing a DIR on the .SWT files
they all appear to be the
same—same date, same size.
BUT the content is different.

A:\>COPY VEN.ABC JUP.ABC
        1 file(s) copied.

A:\>TYPE VEN.ABC

The planet Venus comes physically closer to us
than any other planet in the solar system.

The mass of the Venus atmosphere is 96% carbon dioxide,
not a human-friendly environment! Carbon dioxide makes
up less than 1% of our terrestial atmosphere.

Venus rotates very slowly and seems to have only
one tetonic plate. "Venusquakes" happen mush less
frequently than Earthquakes.

No moon-lit nights on the planet named for
the goddess of love - Venus has no moon.
A:\>_
```

WHAT'S HAPPENING?   Each time the batch file came to a command line and needed a value for a replaceable parameter (%1, %2, or %3), it looked to the command line as it was keyed in by you, and it counted over (by position or location on the command line) until it found the value to replace for the percent sign. **MULTI.BAT** is actually in the first position, which is counted as %0. The command itself is always first, or %0. Thus, to indicate the position of the replaceable parameters, %1 refers to the first position after the command, not the first item on the command line. %2 refers to the second position after the command, not the second item on the command line, and so on. Hence, when you refer to %1, you are referring to the first position after the command. When it needed a value for %1, it used **VEN.ABC** because that was in the first position on the command line. When it needed a value for %2, it used **JUP.ABC** because that was in the second position on the command line, and, when it needed a value for %3, it used **FILE2.SWT** because that was in the third position on the command line. Instead of calling them replaceable parameters, it is easier to remember them as positional parameters because it is the position on the command line that matters, not where it occurs in the batch file. Although this batch file may show you how the positional parameters work, it is not very useful. It does not accomplish any logical task. You are going to use the same principle to create a command that the operating system does not have.

7   Key in the following:

A:\>**EDIT NOCOPY.BAT** [Enter]

    REM This batch file, NOCOPY.BAT, will hide specified files, [Enter]
    REM then copy all other files from one location to another, [Enter]
    REM then unhide the original files. [Enter]
    ATTRIB +H %1 [Enter]
    COPY %3*.* %2 [Enter]
    ATTRIB -H %1

WHAT'S ▨▨▨▨▨
▨▨▨HAPPENING?   You created a batch file called **NOCOPY.BAT** using multiple positional parameters. You have created a command that the operating system does not have. It copies files selectively, allowing you to copy all files except those you hid. You must save the file to disk.

8   Press [Alt] + **F**. Press **X**.

9   Press **Y**.

10   Key in the following: A:\>**TYPE NOCOPY.BAT** [Enter]

```
A:\>TYPE NOCOPY.BAT
REM This batch file, NOCOPY.BAT, will hide specified files,
REM then copy all other files from one location to another,
REM then unhide the original files.
ATTRIB +H %1
COPY %3\*.* %2
ATTRIB -H %1

A:\>_
```

WHAT'S ▨▨▨▨▨
▨▨▨HAPPENING?   You are displaying the contents of **NOCOPY.BAT**. To execute it, you must not only key in the command name—NOCOPY—but also provide the command with values for all the positional parameters. You want to copy all the files from the **CLASS** directory to the **TRIP** subdirectory except the files that have the **.ABC** file extension. Remember, parameters are separated by a space. On the command line you will key in **NOCOPY CLASS*.ABC TRIP CLASS**. The value *CLASS*.ABC* replaces parameter %1, *TRIP* replaces %2, and CLASS replaces %3. Notice that %1 will be used to represent a subdirectory and files ending with **.ABC**, while %2 and %3 will represent subdirectory names only.

11 Key in the following: A:\>**NOCOPY CLASS*.ABC TRIP CLASS** Enter

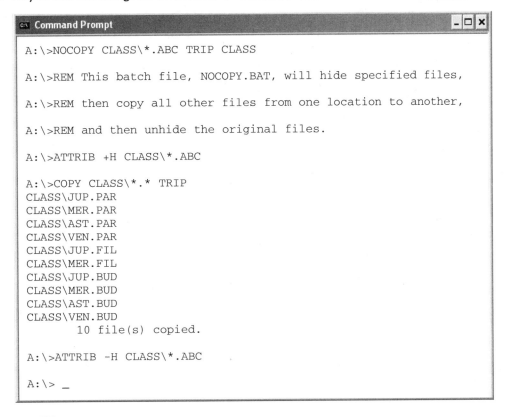

```
A:\>NOCOPY CLASS\*.ABC TRIP CLASS

A:\>REM This batch file, NOCOPY.BAT, will hide specified files,

A:\>REM then copy all other files from one location to another,

A:\>REM and then unhide the original files.

A:\>ATTRIB +H CLASS\*.ABC

A:\>COPY CLASS\*.* TRIP
CLASS\JUP.PAR
CLASS\MER.PAR
CLASS\AST.PAR
CLASS\VEN.PAR
CLASS\JUP.FIL
CLASS\MER.FIL
CLASS\JUP.BUD
CLASS\MER.BUD
CLASS\AST.BUD
CLASS\VEN.BUD
       10 file(s) copied.

A:\>ATTRIB -H CLASS\*.ABC

A:\> _
```

WHAT'S HAPPENING? (*Note:* You may not see the command line you keyed in, as it may scroll off the screen.) You ran the batch file called **NOCOPY**. You substituted or provided the values: CLASS*.ABC (%1), TRIP (%2), and CLASS (%3). To check that the ***.ABC** files are not hidden in the **CLASS** directory and that they have not been copied to the **TRIP** directory, do the following:

12 Key in the following: A:\>**DIR CLASS*.ABC** Enter

13 Key in the following: A:\>**DIR TRIP*.ABC** Enter

```
A:\>DIR CLASS\*.ABC
 Volume in drive A is DATA
 Volume Serial Number is 30B8-DA1D

 Directory of A:\CLASS

05/07/2002  07:41 AM              190 JUP.ABC
10/31/2001  01:08 PM              406 MER.ABC
10/30/2001  01:46 PM              148 AST.ABC
10/31/2001  07:08 PM              478 VEN.ABC
               4 File(s)        1,222 bytes
               0 Dir(s)       921,088 bytes free

A:\>DIR TRIP\*.ABC
 Volume in drive A is DATA
 Volume Serial Number is 30B8-DA1D

 Directory of A:\TRIP
```

```
File Not Found

A:\>_
```

WHAT'S
HAPPENING?   Your goal was achieved. To the operating system, the command
sequence or string of commands looked like this:

    ATTRIB +H CLASS*.ABC
    COPY CLASS*.* TRIP
    ATTRIB -H CLASS*.ABC

When you keyed in **NOCOPY CLASS*.ABC TRIP CLASS**, you asked the
operating system to load the batch file called **NOCOPY.BAT**. The first position after
NOCOPY has the value of **CLASS*.ABC**. The second position has the value of
TRIP, and the third position has the value of **CLASS**. Then the lines were executed
in order:

1. **REM This batch file, NOCOPY.BAT, will hide specified files,**
   This line is documentation for you to know why you wrote this batch file.

2. **REM then copy all other files from one location to another,**
   This line is a continuation of the documentation for you to know why you wrote
   this batch file.

3. **REM then unhide the original files.**
   This line is a continuation of the documentation for you to know why you wrote
   this batch file.

4. **ATTRIB +H CLASS*.ABC**
   This line tells ATTRIB to hide all the files in the **CLASS** directory with the file
   extension of **.ABC**. The operating system knew which file and which directory
   were %1 and could substitute CLASS*.ABC for %1 because CLASS*.ABC
   held the first position (%1) after the command NOCOPY.

5. **COPY CLASS*.* TRIP**
   This line tells the operating system to copy files in a directory. It knew in which
   directory to get the files because CLASS was %3, so it substituted CLASS for
   %3. The operating system knew it could substitute CLASS for %3 because
   CLASS was in the third position after NOCOPY. It knew to copy all the files
   because you included *.*. It knew which directory to copy the files to because it
   substituted TRIP for %2. It could substitute TRIP for %2 because TRIP was in
   the second position after NOCOPY.

6. **ATTRIB -H CLASS*.ABC**
   This line tells the operating system to unhide all the files in the **CLASS** directory with the file extension of **.ABC**. It knew which files and which directory
   were %1 and could substitute CLASS*.ABC for %1 because CLASS*.ABC
   held the first position after the command NOCOPY.

This command, which you just wrote as a batch file with replaceable parameters,
can be very useful. You can use it to copy files selectively from one disk to another
or from one subdirectory to another. You do not need to take separate steps because
all the steps are included in the batch file.

10.30 Creating Useful Batch Files

Batch files are used to automate processes that otherwise take numerous commands in succession. With batch files you can, in essence, create new commands—commands that are not provided with the operating system. Or, as in the following example, re-create an old favorite command that isn't there anymore.

10.31 Activity: Writing Useful Batch Files

Note: The DATA disk is in Drive A with A:\> displayed.

1 Key in the following:
EDIT DELTREE.BAT Enter
REM This file will delete entire directory structures Enter
REM making use of the newer command, RD /S with the Enter
REM old command name, DELTREE Enter
RD /S %1

2 Press Alt + **F**. Press **X**.

3 Press **Y**.

4 Key in the following: A:\>**TYPE DELTREE.BAT** Enter

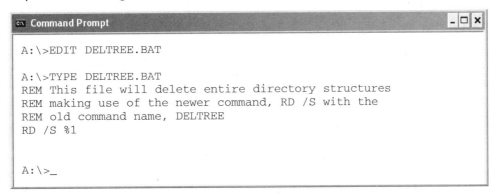

```
A:\>EDIT DELTREE.BAT

A:\>TYPE DELTREE.BAT
REM This file will delete entire directory structures
REM making use of the newer command, RD /S with the
REM old command name, DELTREE
RD /S %1


A:\>_
```

WHAT'S HAPPENING?   You have written a file that re-creates the DELTREE command that "went away" with Windows 2000.

5 Key in the following: A:\>**MD TRYIT** Enter

6 Key in the following: A:\>**MD TRYIT\AGAIN** Enter

7 Key in the following: A:\>**COPY ASTRO*.* TRYIT\AGAIN** Enter

```
A:\>MD TRYIT

A:\>MD TRYIT\AGAIN

A:\>COPY ASTRO\*.* TRYIT\AGAIN
ASTRO\ASTRO.NEW
ASTRO\GALAXY.NEW
ASTRO\ASTRO.TXT
ASTRO\GALAXY.TXT
ASTRO\PLANETS.TXT
```

```
ASTRO\TITAN.TXT
ASTRO\AST.TST
ASTRO\AST.99
ASTRO\AST.BUD
ASTRO\ASTROLGY.FIL
ASTRO\ZODIAC.FIL
       11 file(s) copied.

A:\>_
```

WHAT'S HAPPENING?   You have created a directory TRYIT that contains another directory AGAIN, and have copied some files into the AGAIN directory, in order to test your DELTREE.BAT file.

8   Key in the following: A:\>**DELTREE TRYIT** Enter

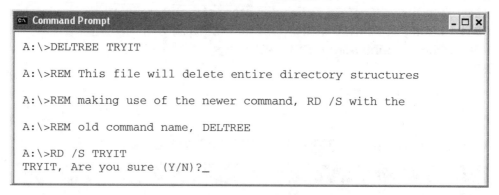

WHAT'S HAPPENING?   The command on the fifth line, RD /S TRYIT, is being executed as if you had keyed it in at the command line. If on the last line you added redirection (RD /S %2 < Y.FIL), then you would not have to enter the Y. The batch file would not need user input. In this case, however, it does.

9   Key in the following: **Y** Enter

10   Key in the following: A:\>**DIR TRYIT** Enter

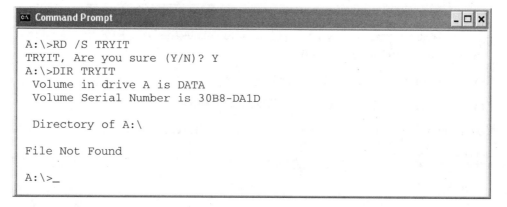

WHAT'S HAPPENING?   The DELTREE batch file works just like the old DELTREE command used to work.

The next batch file you will write will solve a problem. For backup purposes, you often have the same files on more than one subdirectory or floppy disk. You may want to compare which files are in which directory or on which disk. This normally would involve using the DIR command to view each directory or disk, or redirecting the output of the DIR command to the printer and comparing them. Why not let the computer do the work? You can do so with the FC command, which compares two files or sets of files and displays the differences between them. When creating a batch file, you should always test it on unimportant data. To be sure the batch file works correctly, we will set up a duplicate directory, compare it to the original, change the duplicate directories contents, and then compare it to the original again.

11 Key in the following: A:\>**MD ASTRO2** Enter

12 Key in the following: A:\>**COPY ASTRO*.* ASTRO2** Enter

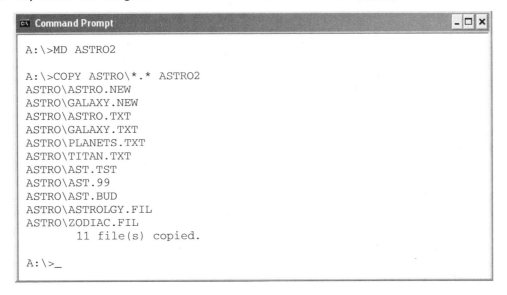

```
Command Prompt                                           _ □ ×

A:\>MD ASTRO2

A:\>COPY ASTRO\*.* ASTRO2
ASTRO\ASTRO.NEW
ASTRO\GALAXY.NEW
ASTRO\ASTRO.TXT
ASTRO\GALAXY.TXT
ASTRO\PLANETS.TXT
ASTRO\TITAN.TXT
ASTRO\AST.TST
ASTRO\AST.99
ASTRO\AST.BUD
ASTRO\ASTROLGY.FIL
ASTRO\ZODIAC.FIL
        11 file(s) copied.

A:\>_
```

WHATS HAPPENING?   You have set up a scenario that enables you to check the viability of the batch file you are going to write.

13 Key in the following: A:\>
EDIT DCOMP.BAT Enter
REM This batch file will compare the file names Enter
REM in two directories. Enter
DIR /A-D /B /ON %1 > SOURCE.TMP Enter
DIR /A-D /B /ON %2 > OTHER.TMP Enter
FC SOURCE.TMP OTHER.TMP ¦ MORE Enter
PAUSE You are about to delete SOURCE.TMP and OTHER.TMP Enter
DEL SOURCE.TMP Enter
DEL OTHER.TMP

14 Press Alt + **F**. Press **X**.

15 Press **Y**.

WHATS HAPPENING?   This batch file uses the FC command to compare two files, each of which contains the file names in a different directory. You want to know if the same files are in each directory, and to do this, the files need to be displayed in the same order. Rather than writing the command line as **DIR ¦ SORT > SOURCE.TMP**, the command line was written as **DIR /A-D /B /ON %1 > SOURCE.TMP**. Why? You will examine each part of the line:

DIR /A-D	This is the command used to display files that do not have the directory attribute, so any subdirectory names will not be displayed.
/B	The /B parameter will eliminate all information in the directory display, such as
	Volume in drive A is DATA
	Volume Serial Number is 3330-1807
	Directory of A:
	as well as the file size, date, time, and long file name information.
/ON	This parameter will order the display by name, sorting the display alphabetically.
> SOURCE.TMP	This redirection character will send the output of the command line to the specified file, first **SOURCE.TMP**, and then **OTHER.TMP**. The files can now be compared to each other.

In addition, you took care to clean up by deleting both **SOURCE.TMP** and **OTHER.TMP** when the program finished executing. You are now going to test this batch file.

16 Key in the following: A:\>**DCOMP ASTRO ASTRO2** [Enter]

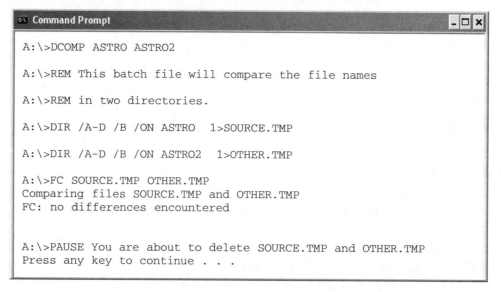

```
A:\>DCOMP ASTRO ASTRO2

A:\>REM This batch file will compare the file names

A:\>REM in two directories.

A:\>DIR /A-D /B /ON ASTRO  1>SOURCE.TMP

A:\>DIR /A-D /B /ON ASTRO2  1>OTHER.TMP

A:\>FC SOURCE.TMP OTHER.TMP
Comparing files SOURCE.TMP and OTHER.TMP
FC: no differences encountered


A:\>PAUSE You are about to delete SOURCE.TMP and OTHER.TMP
Press any key to continue . . .
```

WHAT'S
HAPPENING?   The same files are in each subdirectory.

17 Press [Enter]

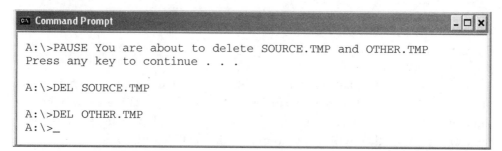

```
A:\>PAUSE You are about to delete SOURCE.TMP and OTHER.TMP
Press any key to continue . . .

A:\>DEL SOURCE.TMP

A:\>DEL OTHER.TMP
A:\>_
```

WHAT'S HAPPENING?   You have deleted the **SOURCE.TMP** and **OTHER.TMP** files. What if there were differences?

18 Key in the following: `A:\>`**DEL ASTRO2\ZODIAC.FIL** [Enter]

19 Key in the following: `A:\>`**DCOMP ASTRO ASTRO2** [Enter]

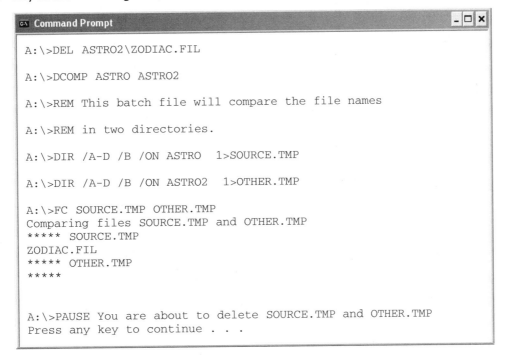

```
A:\>DEL ASTRO2\ZODIAC.FIL

A:\>DCOMP ASTRO ASTRO2

A:\>REM This batch file will compare the file names

A:\>REM in two directories.

A:\>DIR /A-D /B /ON ASTRO   1>SOURCE.TMP

A:\>DIR /A-D /B /ON ASTRO2   1>OTHER.TMP

A:\>FC SOURCE.TMP OTHER.TMP
Comparing files SOURCE.TMP and OTHER.TMP
***** SOURCE.TMP
ZODIAC.FIL
***** OTHER.TMP
*****


A:\>PAUSE You are about to delete SOURCE.TMP and OTHER.TMP
Press any key to continue . . .
```

WHAT'S HAPPENING?   There are differences. The **ASTRO** directory has one more file (**ZODIAC.FIL**) than the **ASTRO2** subdirectory.

20 Press [Enter]

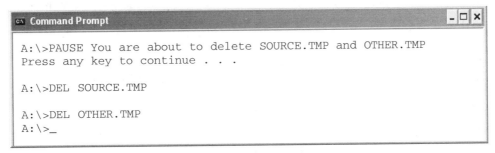

```
A:\>PAUSE You are about to delete SOURCE.TMP and OTHER.TMP
Press any key to continue . . .

A:\>DEL SOURCE.TMP

A:\>DEL OTHER.TMP
A:\>_
```

WHAT'S HAPPENING?   You have deleted the temporary files. You now know you have a tested, working batch file that provides an easy way to compare the files in directories or on disks. You could add an @ECHO OFF statement at the beginning of the batch file so you would not see the REM statements and would see only the results of the command. You will use the DELTREE.BAT file to remove the ASTRO2 directory.

21 Key in the following: `A:\>`**DELTREE ASTRO2** [Enter]

22 Key in the following: **Y** [Enter]

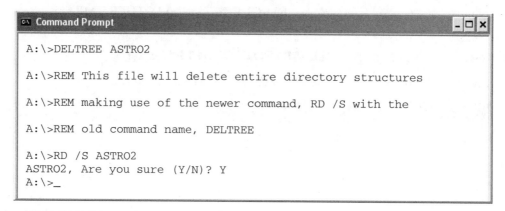

```
Command Prompt                                          - □ ×

A:\>DELTREE ASTRO2

A:\>REM This file will delete entire directory structures

A:\>REM making use of the newer command, RD /S with the

A:\>REM old command name, DELTREE

A:\>RD /S ASTRO2
ASTRO2, Are you sure (Y/N)? Y
A:\>_
```

WHAT'S
HAPPENING?   You have deleted the directory you created for testing purposes.

Chapter Summary

1. Batch processing means running a series of instructions without interruption.
2. Interactive processing allows the user to interface directly with the computer and update records immediately.
3. Batch files allow a user to put together a string of commands and execute them with one command.
4. Batch files have the .BAT or .CMD file extension.
5. Windows looks first internally for a command, then for a .COM file extension, then for a .EXE file extension, and finally for a .BAT or .CMD file extension.
6. Edit is a full-screen text editor used to write batch files.
7. A word processor, if it has a means to save files in ASCII, can be used to write batch files. ASCII files are also referred to as unformatted text files.
8. Batch files must be in ASCII.
9. A quick way to write an ASCII file is to use COPY CON. You copy from the console to a file.
10. Batch files are executed from the system prompt by keying in the batch file name.
11. Batch files are used for many purposes, such as to save keystrokes.
12. To "document" means to explain the purpose a file serves.
13. REM allows the user to document a batch file.
14. When the operating system sees REM, it displays on the screen whatever text follows REM. REM is not a command that executes.
15. ECHO OFF turns off the display of commands. Only the messages from the commands are displayed on the screen.
16. PAUSE allows the user to take some action before the batch file continues to execute.
17. PAUSE does not force the user to do anything. The batch file execution is suspended until the user presses a key.
18. To stop a batch file from executing, press the **Ctrl** key and the letter **C** (**Ctrl** + **C**).
19. Replaceable parameters allow the user to write batch files that can be used with many different parameters. The replaceable parameters act as place holders for values that the user will substitute when executing the batch file.

20. Replaceable parameters are sometimes called dummy, positional, or substitute parameters.

21. The percent sign (%) followed immediately by a numerical value, 0 to 9, indicates a replaceable parameter in a batch file.

Key Terms

batch file	environmental variable	replaceable parameter
batch processing	interactive processing	substitute parameter
documented	place holder	variable
dummy parameter	positional parameter	

Discussion Questions

1. Explain the purpose and function of batch files.
2. Compare and contrast batch processing with interactive processing.
3. You have a batch file called CHECK.BAT. You key in CHECK at the prompt. Where does it look for the file? What does the operating system then do?
4. What is an ASCII file? Why is it important in batch processing?
5. Under what circumstances can a word processor be used to write batch files?
6. Compare and contrast using Edit and COPY CON to write batch files.
7. Explain the purpose and function of the /O and /A parameters when used with the DIR command.
8. Explain the purpose and function of the REM command. What happens when the operating system sees REM in a batch file?
9. In a data-processing environment, what does it mean to document a batch file? Why would it be important to document a batch file?
10. Explain the purpose and function of the ECHO command.
11. Explain the purpose and function of the PAUSE command.
12. Why does the PAUSE command require user intervention?
13. How can you stop a batch file from executing once it has begun?
14. What are parameters?
15. What is a replaceable parameter? Describe how it might be used.
16. What indicates to the operating system that there is a replaceable parameter in a file?
17. What advantages are there to using replaceable parameters in a batch file?
18. Replaceable parameters are sometimes called positional parameters. Explain.
19. There appear to be two prompts when you do not use the ECHO OFF. Explain.

True/False Questions

For each question, circle the letter T if the statement is true and the letter F if the statement is false.

T   F   1. Any command that can be keyed in at the system prompt can be included in a batch file.

T   F   2. Each command in a batch file is on a separate line.

T   F   3. Batch files should be written to complete a process that will need to be done one time only.

T   F   4. The PAUSE command, when used in a batch file, requires user intervention.

T   F   5. In the batch file line COPY MYFILE YOURFILE, COPY would be %1.

Completion Questions

Write the correct answer in each blank space.

6. A word-processing program can be used to write batch files if it has a(n) _____ output mode.

7. The maximum number of replaceable parameters in a batch file is _____.

8. In a data-processing environment, to explain the purpose of a batch file is to _____ it.

9. When you press the Ctrl and C keys simultaneously during the execution of a batch file, you will see _____ on the screen.

10. If you wanted only the output of the command displayed on the screen and not the command itself, you would begin the batch file with the line _____.

Multiple Choice Questions

For each question, write the letter for the correct answer in the blank space.

_____   11. When searching a disk for an external command, the operating system will
              a. choose the command with the extension **.COM** before one with the extension **.BAT**.
              b. choose the command with the extension .BAT before one with the extension .COM.
              c. know automatically which file extension you are seeking.
              d. choose the extension **.BAT** before **.EXE**.

_____   12. To execute a batch file called **THIS.BAT** at the prompt, key in:
              a. THIS %1
              b. %1
              c. THIS
              d. RUN BATCH THIS

_____   13. In a batch file, to display the output of the command but not the command itself, use:
              a. ECHO ON
              b. ECHO OFF
              c. DISPLAY ON
              d. none of the above

_____   14. Which of the following statements is true?
              a. Batch files cannot use variable parameters.
              b. Ctrl + Z interrupts the execution of a batch file.
              c. The PAUSE command will wait until the user takes some action.
              d. either a or b

_____ 15. Quitting a batch file by using **Ctrl** + **C**

    a. erases all the lines of the batch file that come after you quit.

    b. can be done only at a PAUSE during the batch file run.

    c. erases the batch files from the disk.

    d. can be done at any time while the batch file is running.

Writing Commands

Write five lines that would perform the following items in a batch file. Each question represents one line in the file.

16. Document the batch file, explaining that it is a demonstration file.

17. List the files in the **A:\TEMP** directory.

18. Display the contents of a file in the **A:\TEMP** directory that is specified when the batch file is called.

19. Rename the above file to **NAME.NEW**.

20. Display the contents of the **NAME.NEW** file.

Homework Assignments

Problem Set I

Note 1: Place the HOMEWORK disk in Drive A. Be sure to work on the HOMEWORK disk, not the DATA disk. On each batch file you write, be sure and include _your name_, the _name of the batch file_, and the _date_ as part of the documentation.

Note 2: The homework problems will assume Drive C is the hard disk and the HOMEWORK disk is in Drive A. If you are using another drive, such as floppy drive B or hard drive D, be sure and substitute that drive letter when reading the questions and answers.

Note 3: Test all of your batch files before submitting them to be sure they work correctly.

Note 4: To save a file with Edit under a new name, press **Alt** + **F** and choose **Save As**.

Note 5: It will be assumed that the root of the HOMEWORK disk is the default drive and directory, unless otherwise specified.

Note 6: There can be more than one way to write a batch file. If your batch file works correctly, it is most likely written correctly.

Problem A

To Create DD.BAT

A-a   Create a batch file called **DD.BAT**. This batch file should display the files on the root of the HOMEWORK disk in date order with the most current date displayed first, and should pause so that the user may view the display one screenful at a time.

A-b   Document **DD.BAT**. Remember to include *your name*, the *name of the batch file*, and the *date* as part of the documentation.

To Create DDA.BAT

A-c   Edit the batch file called **DD.BAT** and save it under the new name of **DDA.BAT**.

A-d   Edit **DDA.BAT** so that it will look on any drive for files, using a replaceable parameter. It will still be displaying files in date order, with the most current date displayed first.

A-e   Update the documentation.

To Create SD.BAT

A-f   Create a batch file called **SD.BAT** that will display subdirectories only, in order by name, on the root of the A drive.

A-g   Document the file. Remember to include your name, the name of the batch file, and the date as part of the documentation.

To Create SDD.BAT

A-h   Edit **SD.BAT** created above and save the edited file as **SDD.BAT**. The **SDD.BAT** file will display subdirectories on a specified drive\directory in order by name.

A-i   Use replaceable parameters.

A-j   Document the file.

To Print Your Homework

1   Be sure the printer is on and ready to accept print jobs from your computer.

2   Key in the following: A:\>**NAME** Enter

3   Here is an example to key in, but your instructor will have other information that applies to your class. Key in the following:
Bette A. Peat Enter   (*Your* name goes here.)
CIS 55 Enter   (*Your* class goes here.)
T-Th 8-9:30 Enter   (*Your* day and time go here.)
Chapter 10 Homework Enter
Problem A Enter

4   Press F6 Enter

5   If the information is correct, press **Y** and you are back to A:\>.

6 Key in the following:

GO NAME.FIL DD.BAT DDA.BAT SD.BAT SDD.BAT Enter

(These files will not be deleted from your disk after printing.)

7 Press **N** until you see the Notepad window.

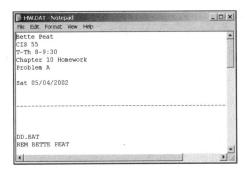

8 In Notepad, click **File**. Click **Print**. Click the **Print** button. Close Notepad.

Problem B

To Create EXTRA.BAT

B-a Copy all the files with the **.TXT** extension from the **WUGXP** subdirectory to the root directory of the HOMEWORK disk. (Overwrite existing files.)

B-b Create a batch file named **EXTRA.BAT** that will do the following:
- Clear the screen.
- Display the root directory of the HOMEWORK disk for any file that has **.TXT** as a file extension.
- Make a copy of the file called **BORN.TXT** and call the copy **BIRTH.STR**.
- Display the contents of the file called **BIRTH.STR**.
- Give the user time to read the file.
- Erase the file called **BIRTH.STR**.

B-c Document **EXTRA.BAT**, including your name, the name of the file, and the date.

To Create EXTRA2.BAT

B-d Edit **EXTRA.BAT**. **EXTRA2.BAT** will do all that **EXTRA.BAT** does but will
- use replaceable parameters so that the user may choose what files to display. (Use only one parameter to represent the entire file specification, such as *.fil or my.fil.)
- allow any existing file to be copied to a new file that the user names.
- display the contents of the newly created file.
- provide a way for the user to change her or his mind and not delete any files.

B-e Save the edited file as **EXTRA2.BAT**.

To Print Your Homework

1 Be sure the printer is on and ready to accept print jobs from your computer.

2 Use Edit to edit **NAME.FIL**. Change the last line from **Problem A** to **Problem B**.

3 Key in the following: **GO NAME.FIL EXTRA.BAT EXTRA2.BAT** Enter

4 Press **N** until you see the Notepad screen.

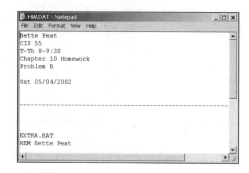

5 In Notepad, click **File**. Click **Print**. Click the **Print** button. Close Notepad.

Problem C

To Create CHECKIT.BAT

C-a Write and document a batch file using replaceable parameters called **CHECKIT.BAT** that will:
- check the status of a specified disk.
- see if any files are noncontiguous on that disk.
- do a wide display of the root directory of that disk.
- pause as necessary so users can view all of each display.

To Create LIST.BAT

C-b Write and document a batch file called **LIST.BAT** that will use replaceable parameters to display the contents of three files. (*Hint*: Think about how many replaceable parameters you will want to use.) Use **JUP.99**, **BORN.TXT**, and **COMEDY.TV** to test your file.

To Print Your Homework

1 Be sure the printer is on and ready to accept print jobs from your computer.

2 Use Edit to edit **NAME.FIL**. Change the last line from **Problem B** to **Problem C**.

3 Key in the following: **GO NAME.FIL CHECKIT.BAT LIST.BAT** Enter

4 Press **N** until the Notepad screen appears.

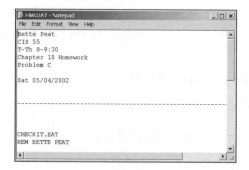

5   In Notepad, click **File**. Click **Print**. Click the **Print** button. Close Notepad.

Problem D: Challenge Assignments

The following three batch file assignments use commands in combination that may not have been specifically discussed or shown by example in the chapter. Research and experimentation may be required in order to write these batch files.

To Create NODEL.BAT

D-a   Using **NOCOPY.BAT**, created in this chapter, as a model, write and document a batch file called **NODEL.BAT** that will
- allow you to delete all the files *except* the file(s) you hide in a specified subdirectory.
- view the files you are about to delete.
- clear the screen when necessary to make it easy for the user to read what is happening in the file.
- give the user an opportunity to cancel prior to deleting the files.
- delete the files.
- unhide the files.
- view which files remain.

D-b   Document the batch file completely, explaining precisely what the file will do, and giving an example of how to run the file.

Hint 1:   Create a practice subdirectory, such as \ **TEMP**, on the HOMEWORK disk. Use the **NODEL** batch file with the files that you copy into this temporary subdirectory, such as the ***.RED** files and the ***.FIL** files. If you make a mistake, you will not delete all the files on your HOMEWORK disk.

Hint 2:   If you do not want to be asked for confirmation from the DEL command, you can use the command DEL *.* < Y.FIL. You will need to copy **Y.FIL** from \ **WUGXP** to the root directory of the HOMEWORK disk.

To Create NEWSUB.BAT

D-c   Write and document a batch file called **NEWSUB.BAT**, using replaceable parameters, that will accomplish what is specified in the following documentation:

```
REM This file will allow the user to create a subdirectory
REM on a drive and with a name specified by the user
REM and then copy files specified by the user from a location
REM specified by the user to the new subdirectory.
REM This batch file is flexible, so any of the elements can be
REM changed by the user when they execute this file.(The 4 elements
REM are entered separately on the command line by the user, and are
REM DRIVE NAME (such as A:), the NEW SUBDIRECTORY NAME,
REM the LOCATION OF FILES TO BE COPIED (such as C:\WUGXP), and
REM the names of the FILES TO BE COPIED.)
REM The newly created subdirectory with its files will then be
REM displayed on the screen. Be sure the user has the opportunity to
REM view all of the display. The command line would read something
REM like    NEWSUB  A:  TEMP  C:\WUGXP  *.99
```

D-d   Include the above lines in the documentation of the file.

D-e   You may want to delete the **TEMP** directory created with the **NODEL.BAT** assignment, and use it again to write and debug **NEWSUB.BAT**.

To Print Your Homework

1   Be sure the printer is on and ready to accept print jobs from your computer.

2   Use Edit to change the last two lines in **NAME.FIL** to read:
Chapter 10 Challenge Homework
Problem D

3   Key in the following: **GO NAME.FIL NODEL.BAT NEWSUB.BAT** Enter

4   Press **N** until you see the Notepad screen.

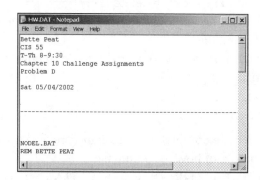

```
HW.DAT - Notepad
File  Edit  Format  View  Help
Bette Peat
CIS 55
T-Th 8-9:30
Chapter 10 Challenge Assignments
Problem D

Sat 05/04/2002

------------------------------------------------


NODEL.BAT
REM BETTE PEAT
```

5   In Notepad, click **File**. Click **Print**. Click the **Print** button. Close Notepad.

CAUTION: If you created a TEMP directory on the HOMEWORK disk, delete that directory before going on to Chapter 11.

Problem Set II—Brief Essay

1. Assume the following scenario:
    On your computer, you have many text files in the C:\MYSTUFF\DOSTEXT subdirectory. You refer to these files frequently at the command line, and you do not want to have to key in the path name each time you want to access one of the files. Instead, you would like to use the unused drive letter F to access this drive. Explain, in detail, how you would go about making the F drive specification available to you each and every time you opened a command line session.

2. Discuss replaceable parameters, including how they work and why they are useful. Include the number of parameters available and the numbering sequence used to represent the command in your discussion.

CHAPTER 11

ADVANCED
BATCH FILES

Learning Objectives

After completing this chapter you will be able to:

1. List commands used in batch files.
2. List and explain batch file rules.
3. Explore the function of the REM, PAUSE, and ECHO commands.
4. Explain the use of batch files with shortcuts.
5. Explain the purpose and function of the GOTO command.
6. Explain the purpose and function of the SHIFT command.
7. Explain the purpose and function of the IF command.
8. Explain the purpose and function of the IF EXIST/IF NOT EXIST command.
9. Explain the purpose and function of the IF ERRORLEVEL command.
10. Explain the purpose and function of writing programs.
11. Explain the purpose and function of the environment and environmental variables.
12. Explain the use of the SET command.
13. Explain the purpose and function of the FOR...IN...DO command.
14. Explain the purpose and function of the CALL command.

Student Outcomes

1. Use the ECHO command to place a blank line in a batch file.
2. Use the GOTO command in conjunction with a label to create a loop.
3. Use a batch file with a shortcut.
4. Use the SHIFT command to move parameters.
5. Use the IF command with strings for conditional processing.
6. Test for null values in a batch file.
7. Use the IF EXIST/IF NOT EXIST command to test for the existence of a file or a subdirectory.
8. Use the SET command.
9. Use the environment and environmental variables in batch files.
10. Use the IF ERRORLEVEL command with XCOPY to write a batch file for testing exit codes.
11. Use the FOR...IN...DO command for repetitive processing.
12. Use the CALL command in a batch file.

Chapter Overview

You learned in Chapter 10 how to write simple batch files and use replaceable parameters. Some commands allow you write even more powerful batch files that act like sophisticated programs.

This chapter focuses on the remaining batch file commands, which will allow you to write sophisticated batch files. You will further refine your techniques in working with the environment.

11.1 Batch File Commands

A quick summary of batch file rules tells us that any batch file must have the file extension of .BAT or .CMD, it must always be an ASCII file, and it must include legitimate commands. In addition, you can use replaceable or positional parameters to create generic batch files. Batch file commands are not case sensitive. You may use any command in a batch file that you can use on the command line, as well as some specific batch file commands. See Table 11.1 for batch file commands.

Command	Purpose
CALL	Calls one batch program from another without causing the first batch program to stop. Beginning with Windows 2000 Professional, CALL accepts labels as the target of the call.
ECHO	Displays or hides the text in batch programs while the program is running. Also used to determine whether commands will be "echoed" to the screen while the program file is running.
ENDLOCAL	Ends localization of environment changes in a batch file, restoring environment variables to their values before the matching SETLOCAL command. There is an implicit ENDLOCAL at the end of the batch file.
FOR	Runs a specified command for each file in a set of files. This command can also be used at the command line.
GOTO	Directs the operating system to a new line that you specify with a label.
IF	Performs conditional processing in a batch program, based on whether or not a specified condition is true or false.
PAUSE	Suspends processing of a batch file and displays a message prompting the user to press a key to continue.
REM	Used to document your batch files. The operating system ignores any line that begins with REM, allowing you to place lines of information in your batch program or to prevent a line from running.
SETLOCAL	Begins localization of environmental variables in a batch file. Localization lasts until a matching ENDLOCAL command is encountered or the end of the batch file is reached.
SHIFT	Changes the position of the replaceable parameter in a batch program.

Table 11.1—Batch File Commands

You have already used ECHO, PAUSE, and REM. You will now learn the remaining batch file commands, which allow you to create complex batch files. Using these commands is similar to using a programming language. Batch files have a limited vocabulary (the commands listed above), a syntax (punctuation and grammar rules), and a programming logic. Batch files are also limited in the kinds of programming they can do. They do not have the power or the flexibility of a "real" programming language such as Visual Basic or C++. Batch files, however, accomplish many things in the Windows environment.

11.2 A Review of the REM, PAUSE, and ECHO Commands

The REM command in a batch file indicates to the operating system that whatever text follows is to be displayed, but only if ECHO has *not* been turned off. If a command follows REM, it will be displayed but not executed. Remarks can be a string of up to 123 characters, and typically they document batch files. Placing REM in front of a command will allow you to execute a batch file or the CONFIG.SYS file without executing the command that follows it. This allows you to disable a line or lines without having to actually delete them.

The PAUSE command stops a batch file from continuing to execute until you press any key. It tells you to press any key to continue, but does not do any *conditional processing*.

Remember, to interrupt a batch file, you can always press Ctrl + C or Ctrl + Break. Pressing this key combination will interrupt the execution of the batch file. There is one warning—if the batch file has called an external command and the operating system is in the middle of executing a command such as FORMAT or DISKCOPY, it will finish executing the command before exiting the batch file. Ctrl + C stops the execution of the batch file itself—it will not stop the execution of a .EXE or .COM program.

The ECHO command can be used either on a command line or in a batch file. It is a special command that turns on or turns off the echoing of commands to the screen. If you key in the command ECHO by itself on the command line or include it in a batch file, it will return the status of ECHO: either ECHO on or ECHO off. When ECHO is on, all the commands in a batch file are displayed on the screen. When ECHO is off, you see the output of the command, but not the command itself. Normally ECHO is on, which is particularly useful when you want to track the operation of a batch file. However, when a batch file runs successfully, the display of commands can clutter the screen.

In a batch file, if you do not wish to see each command on the screen, you can issue the command ECHO OFF. The batch file commands are not displayed, but any messages that a command such as COPY issues will be displayed, for example, "1 file(s) copied." Depending on your preferences, you can key in ECHO ON or ECHO OFF within the batch file to display or not display the commands. In addition, if you precede ECHO OFF with @, the command following the symbol, ECHO OFF, will not appear on the screen.

11.3 Advanced Features of ECHO and REM

There are some interesting features and variations you can implement with both REM and ECHO. One problem with REM is that the operating system recognizes it as a command and must take time to process it. A shortcut is to use a double colon (::) instead of REM in front of a remark, or documentation line. This will save valuable processing time because the operating system treats all lines beginning with a colon as a label and ignores them unless they are "called" elsewhere in the batch file. This will be further explained later.

When you turn ECHO off, you still get the display of messages such as "1 file(s) copied." Sometimes you do not wish to see messages. You can use redirection with standard output to redirect the output of a command to a device called NUL. As the name implies, NUL means send it to "nothing." When you send the output to NUL, it goes nowhere, and it is not displayed on the screen.

Although redirecting the output of a command to the NUL device will suppress messages such as "1 file(s) copied," it will not suppress a message that is generated by the operating system like "File not found."

You often want to place a blank line in a batch file for aesthetic purposes or to highlight particular commands. There is, of course, no such thing as a blank line. In the word-processing world, when you want a blank line, you press the $\boxed{\text{Enter}}$ key, which places a carriage return in the document and prints as a blank line. This does not work in batch files. In a batch file, the operating system simply ignores it when you press $\boxed{\text{Enter}}$. Pressing $\boxed{\text{Enter}}$ does not leave a blank line. If you use REM, you will see nothing if ECHO is off. If you place the word ECHO in the batch file, it will report whether ECHO is on or off. An easy method to get a blank line is to key in ECHO followed by a period. There can be no space between ECHO and the period.

11.4 **Activity: Using ECHO and NUL**

Note: The DATA disk is in Drive A. Open a Command Prompt window. A:\> is displayed.

1   Use an editor to create and save the following batch file called **ONE.BAT**, pressing the $\boxed{\text{Enter}}$ key only where indicated.

:: This is a test of a batch file using $\boxed{\text{Enter}}$
:: different features. $\boxed{\text{Enter}}$
COPY CAROLYN.FIL BOOK.FIL $\boxed{\text{Enter}}$
$\boxed{\text{Enter}}$
TYPE BOOK.FIL $\boxed{\text{Enter}}$
ECHO $\boxed{\text{Enter}}$
DEL BOOK.FIL $\boxed{\text{Enter}}$
COPY NO.FIL BOOK.FIL $\boxed{\text{Enter}}$

2   Close the editor and then key in the following: A:\>**TYPE ONE.BAT** $\boxed{\text{Enter}}$

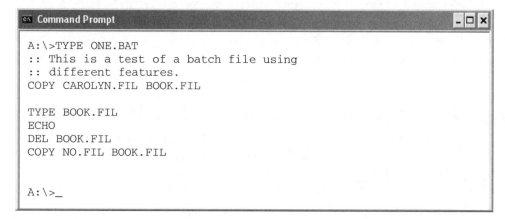

```
A:\>TYPE ONE.BAT
:: This is a test of a batch file using
:: different features.
COPY CAROLYN.FIL BOOK.FIL

TYPE BOOK.FIL
ECHO
DEL BOOK.FIL
COPY NO.FIL BOOK.FIL


A:\>_
```

3   Key in the following: `A:\>`**ONE** Enter

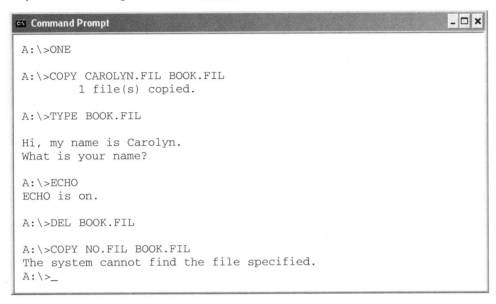

```
A:\>ONE

A:\>COPY CAROLYN.FIL BOOK.FIL
        1 file(s) copied.

A:\>TYPE BOOK.FIL

Hi, my name is Carolyn.
What is your name?

A:\>ECHO
ECHO is on.

A:\>DEL BOOK.FIL

A:\>COPY NO.FIL BOOK.FIL
The system cannot find the file specified.
A:\>_
```

WHAT'S
HAPPENING?   You see messages as well as the output.

4   Edit and save **ONE.BAT** so it looks as follows:

@ECHO OFF
:: This is a test of a batch file using
:: different features.
COPY CAROLYN.FIL BOOK.FIL > NUL
ECHO.
TYPE BOOK.FIL
ECHO.
DEL BOOK.FIL
COPY NO.FIL BOOK.FIL > NUL

5   Key in the following: `A:\>`**ONE** Enter

```
Hi, my name is Carolyn.
What is your name?

A:\>_
```

WHAT'S
HAPPENING?   You now do not see your messages or remarks. You also get some
blank lines. The COPY command could not find **NO.FIL** and the error message was
redirected to the NUL device and was not displayed to the user on the screen.

11.5   The GOTO Command

By using the GOTO command, a batch file can be constructed to behave like a
program written in a programming language such as BASIC or C++. The GOTO
command will branch to a specific part within a batch file. By using the GOTO
statement, you can create a loop. A *loop* is an operation that will repeat steps until

you stop the loop either by using an IF statement or by breaking into the batch file with Ctrl + C.

The GOTO command works in conjunction with a label. This label is not to be confused with a volume label on a disk. A label is any name you choose to flag a particular line, or location in a batch file. A label is preceded by a colon (:) and is ignored by the operating system until called with the GOTO command. A double colon (::), used earlier for REM statements, ensures that the operating system will always disregard the line, even in conjunction with the GOTO statement since a colon may not be used as a label name. A label can be no longer than eight characters. The label itself is not a command, it just identifies a location in a batch file. When a batch file goes to a label, it carries out whatever command follows on the line after the label. GOTO has one parameter—GOTO *label*. Although it is not necessary that labels be exactly the same (i.e., the same case) it is still wise to make them the same case.

11.6   Activity: Using the GOTO Command

Note: The DATA disk should be in Drive A with A:\> displayed.

1   Use any text editor to create and save a batch file called **REPEAT.BAT**. Key in the following using exactly the same case:
REM This file displays many times the contents Enter
REM of a file. Enter
:REPEAT Enter
TYPE %1 Enter
PAUSE Enter
GOTO REPEAT

WHATS
HAPPENING?   You have written a small batch file. The first two lines are remarks that will not execute. You are not including ECHO OFF, because you want to see what is happening in your batch file. Omitting ECHO OFF is a way to "debug" a batch file program. *Debug* means to see and repair any errors. The third line (:REPEAT) is a label, which must be preceded by a colon. The fourth line is a simple TYPE command with a replaceable parameter. The PAUSE command is placed on the fifth line so you may see what is happening. The sixth and last line is the loop. The GOTO tells the batch file to return to the label (:REPEAT). It will then return to line 4 and execute the TYPE command. It will then read lines 5 and 6 and continually repeat the process.

2   You must be at the system prompt, not in the editor. Key in the following:
A:\>**REPEAT ASTRO.TXT** Enter

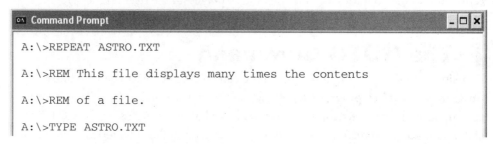

```
A:\>REPEAT ASTRO.TXT

A:\>REM This file displays many times the contents

A:\>REM of a file.

A:\>TYPE ASTRO.TXT
```

```
The study of Astronomy came from Astrology.
Most scientists no longer believe in
Astrology.  The science of Astronomy is
changing every day.

A:\>PAUSE
Press any key to continue . . .
```

WHAT'S HAPPENING?   The first two lines displayed are remarks. The label was ignored, but the TYPE command was executed. The next line has paused the batch file. You need to press **Enter** to continue.

3   Press **Enter**

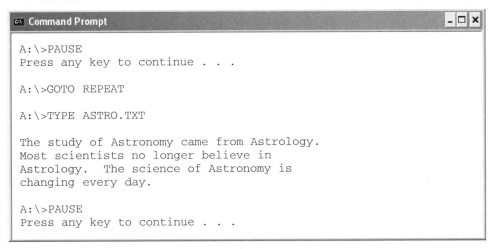

```
A:\>PAUSE
Press any key to continue . . .

A:\>GOTO REPEAT

A:\>TYPE ASTRO.TXT

The study of Astronomy came from Astrology.
Most scientists no longer believe in
Astrology.  The science of Astronomy is
changing every day.

A:\>PAUSE
Press any key to continue . . .
```

WHAT'S HAPPENING?   The next line in the batch file was GOTO REPEAT. The batch file was sent back to the label :REPEAT. The batch file read the next line after the label, which was the TYPE command, then the next line, which was PAUSE. When you press a key, you will again be returned to the label. Now you see a loop in action.

4   Press **Enter** a few times to see the loop in action. Then press **Ctrl** + **C** to break out of the batch file. It will ask you if you want to terminate the batch job. Key in **Y**, then **Enter** for yes. You will be returned to the A:\> prompt.

WHAT'S HAPPENING?   A loop can be very useful. For instance, if you wanted to delete all the files from many floppy disks, you could write a batch file that would look like this:

@ECHO OFF
:TOP
CLS
ECHO Place the disk with the files you no longer want in
ECHO Drive A.
PAUSE
DEL /Q A:*.*
ECHO Press Ctrl + C to stop executing this batch file.
ECHO Otherwise, press any key to continue deleting files.
PAUSE > NUL
GOTO TOP

The /Q parameter makes it so the DEL command does not require a Y or N. You did not want to see the output of the PAUSE command, so you redirected it to the NUL device. Remember, a file like the above which deals with deletion of multiple files can be both convenient and dangerous.

11.7   The SHIFT Command

When you have written a batch file with positional parameters, you key in the batch file name followed by a series of values. When the batch file is executed, the operating system looks to the command line for the values it needs to plug into the batch file. It does this based on the position of particular parameters in the command line. In earlier versions of Windows, the TYPE command was limited to one parameter. Thus, if you wanted to use replaceable parameters, you could create a batch file called LIST.BAT whose contents would be:

TYPE %1

TYPE %2

TYPE %3

Then with this batch file, called LIST.BAT, you would key in the following command line:

LIST APPIL.TXT MAY.TXT JUNE.TXT

With this generic batch file, you could key in only three file names. If you wanted more file names, you would have to re-execute the batch file. You are limited to 10 parameters on a command line—%0 through %9. Since %0 actually represents the batch file name itself, you can have only nine parameters. The SHIFT command allows you to shift the parameters to the left, one by one, making the number of parameters on a line limitless. As the SHIFT command shifts the contents of the parameters to the left, parameter 2 becomes parameter 1, parameter 3 becomes parameter 2, and so on. This allows the batch file to process all the parameters on the command line.

11.8   Activity: Using the SHIFT Command

Note: The DATA disk should be in Drive A with A:\> displayed.

1   Key in the following: A:\>**ECHO a b c d** [Enter]

```
A:\>ECHO a b c d
a b c d
A:\>_
```

WHAT'S HAPPENING?   ECHO on a command line just "echoed" what you keyed in. Thus, the parameters a, b, c, and d on the command line were repeated on the screen. If you wanted to display more than five parameters and place the echoing parameters in a batch file, you would need to use the SHIFT command.

2   Use any text editor to create and save the file **ALPHA.BAT** as follows:

@ECHO OFF
ECHO %0 %1 %2 %3
SHIFT
ECHO %0 %1 %2 %3
SHIFT
ECHO %0 %1 %2 %3
SHIFT
ECHO %0 %1 %2 %3

WHAT'S ▨▨▨
▨▨▨HAPPENING?   You have created a batch file with replaceable parameters. The purpose of the batch file is to demonstrate the SHIFT command. Remember that ECHO just echoes what you keyed in. In your command line, however, even though you have only four parameters (0 through 3), you want to key in more than four values.

3   Remember, you must be at the system prompt, not in the editor. Key in the following: A:\>**ALPHA a b c d e f** Enter

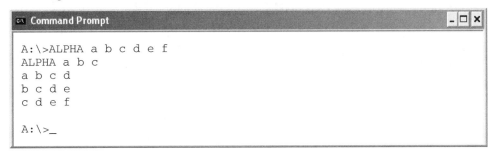

```
A:\>ALPHA a b c d e f
ALPHA a b c
a b c d
b c d e
c d e f

A:\>_
```

WHAT'S ▨▨▨
▨▨▨HAPPENING?   Notice the output. In each case, when the batch file read SHIFT, it moved each parameter over by one position.

Batch File	Supplied Value from Command Line	Screen Display
@ECHO OFF		
ECHO %0 %1 %2 %3	ALPHA is %0	ALPHA a b c
	a is %1	
	b is %2	
	c is %3	
SHIFT	ALPHA is dropped as %0	
	a becomes %0	
	b becomes %1	
	c becomes %2	
	d becomes %3	
ECHO %0 %1 %2 %3	a is %0	a b c d
	b is %1	
	c is %2	
	d is %3	
SHIFT	a is dropped as %0	
	b becomes %0	

	c becomes %1	
	d becomes %2	
	e becomes %3	
ECHO %0 %1 %2 %3	b is %0	b c d e
	c is %1	
	d is %2	
	e is %3	
SHIFT	b is dropped as %0	
	c becomes %0	
	d becomes %1	
	e becomes %2	
	f becomes %3	
ECHO %0 %1 %2 %3	c is %0	c d e f
	d is %1	
	e is %2	
	f is %3	

You should see that you are indeed shifting parameters, but how is this useful? You will write some batch files that use SHIFT so you can see how this technique can be used.

As you know, the operating system stamps each file with the current date and time when it is created or modified. Most often, this means that each file has a unique time and date based on the last time you modified or created the file. Sometimes, you want to place a specific time and date stamp on a file or group of files. For example, if you sell software and you have customers to whom you send files, you might like to ascertain which version of the file they have. By having a particular date and/or time on the file, you can easily keep a date log that is not dependent on the file modification date.

Commands such as XCOPY can back up files after or before a certain date. To ensure that you are backing up all the files you want, you can set the date and update the date stamp on your files. Then you can backup from that date. You need a way to update the dates. You can do this by using the following command:

COPY *filename* **/b +**

Remember, the + sign tells the operating system to concatenate files. The first thing that happens when copying files is a file name is created with the current time and date in the destination directory. At first, the new file is empty. Since there is no specific destination file name, COPY will default to the source file name. It then proceeds to concatenate (add) the existing file to the "new" file name and the new date and time. In essence, it is copying a file onto itself. Since it is a new entry in the directory table, it has the current date and time.

The /B switch tells the operating system to copy the file in binary mode. When you concatenate files with no switches, the files are copied in text mode. The COPY command knows the contents of the file have ended when it sees a special mark called an *EOF (end-of-file) mark*. Typically, the EOF mark is Ctrl + Z. The instant COPY sees this special signal, it thinks there is no more information to copy and will place its own EOF mark at the end of the file—another Ctrl + Z. Unfortunately, this "extra" EOF mark is sometimes interpreted by a program or a data file as something other than the end of the file. Thus, you could be in the situation of not copying the entire file. The alternative is to copy the file in binary mode. When you choose this option—the /B switch—COPY will not read the file but will copy everything in the file, ensuring that the entire file contents are copied without adding an extra **Ctrl** + **Z**. An extra **Ctrl** + **Z** can create problems when you are trying to use the copied file.

Now that you know how and why to update file dates and times, it is easy to place these commands in a batch file. Since you may have more than one file you wish to "stamp," you want to allow for many file names by using the SHIFT command.

4   Use any text editor to create and save a new file. Name the file **UPDATE.BAT** and then key in the following:
:DOIT Enter
COPY %1 /B + > NUL Enter
SHIFT Enter
PAUSE Enter
GOTO DOIT

5   Key in the following: A:\>**DIR JUP.PAR** Enter

6   Key in the following: A:\>**DIR VEN.BUD** Enter

```
Command Prompt                                            _ □ ×

A:\>DIR JUP.PAR
 Volume in drive A is DATA
 Volume Serial Number is 30B8-DA1D

 Directory of A:\

05/07/2002  07:41 AM                 190 JUP.PAR
                1 File(s)            190 bytes
                0 Dir(s)         918,016 bytes free

A:\>DIR VEN.BUD
 Volume in drive A is DATA
 Volume Serial Number is 30B8-DA1D

 Directory of A:\

10/31/2001  07:08 PM                 478 VEN.BUD
                1 File(s)            478 bytes
                0 Dir(s)         918,016 bytes free

A:\>_
```

WHAT'S
HAPPENING?   You want the files **JUP.PAR** and **VEN.BUD** to have today's date and time on them. Remember, the number of bytes free on your DATA disk will not necessarily match the number shown in the directory displays in the book.

7   Key in the following: A:\>**UPDATE JUP.PAR VEN.BUD** Enter

```
Command Prompt                                            _ □ ×

A:\>UPDATE JUP.PAR VEN.BUD

A:\>COPY JUP.PAR /B +   1>NUL
```

```
A:\>SHIFT

A:\>PAUSE
Press any key to continue . . .
```

WHAT'S HAPPENING?   The batch file copied **JUP.PAR**, went to SHIFT, and is now going to copy the next parameter it shifted, **VEN.BUD**.

8   Press **Enter**

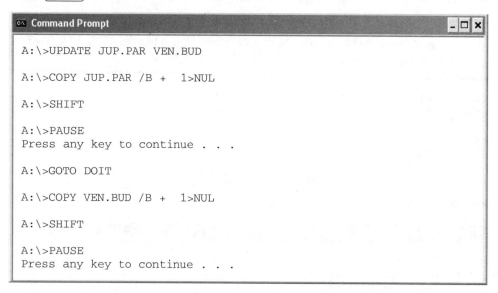

```
A:\>UPDATE JUP.PAR VEN.BUD

A:\>COPY JUP.PAR /B +   1>NUL

A:\>SHIFT

A:\>PAUSE
Press any key to continue . . .

A:\>GOTO DOIT

A:\>COPY VEN.BUD /B +   1>NUL

A:\>SHIFT

A:\>PAUSE
Press any key to continue . . .
```

WHAT'S HAPPENING?   It copied **VEN.BUD**.

9   Press **Enter**

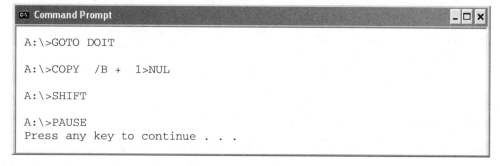

```
A:\>GOTO DOIT

A:\>COPY   /B +   1>NUL

A:\>SHIFT

A:\>PAUSE
Press any key to continue . . .
```

WHAT'S HAPPENING?   This batch file seemed to work effectively when you first initiated it. It copied **JUP.PAR**. It then shifted over to **VEN.BUD** and copied that. However, you created an endless loop. When the batch file finished copying **VEN.BUD**, it again shifted parameters, but there was nothing to shift to. The batch file is continually going to the label and then trying to execute the command. There is something missing here: a condition that you need to insert. First, though, you must break into the batch file.

10   Press **Ctrl** + **C** and answer **Y** to the prompt.

11   Key in the following: A:\>**DIR JUP.PAR** **Enter**

12   Key in the following: A:\>**DIR VEN.BUD** **Enter**

```
┌────────────────────────────────────────────────────────────────┐
│ ▣ Command Prompt                                      - □ x │
├────────────────────────────────────────────────────────────────┤
│ Terminate batch job (Y/N)? Y                                     │
│                                                                  │
│ A:\>DIR JUP.PAR                                                  │
│  Volume in drive A is DATA                                       │
│  Volume Serial Number is 30B8-DA1D                               │
│                                                                  │
│  Directory of A:\                                                │
│                                                                  │
│ 05/05/2002  12:31 PM              190 JUP.PAR                    │
│               1 File(s)           190 bytes                      │
│               0 Dir(s)        918,016 bytes free                 │
│                                                                  │
│ A:\>DIR VEN.BUD                                                  │
│  Volume in drive A is DATA                                       │
│  Volume Serial Number is 30B8-DA1D                               │
│                                                                  │
│  Directory of A:\                                                │
│                                                                  │
│ 05/05/2002  12:32 PM              478 VEN.BUD                    │
│               1 File(s)           478 bytes                      │
│               0 Dir(s)        918,016 bytes free                 │
│                                                                  │
│ A:\>_                                                            │
│                                                                  │
└────────────────────────────────────────────────────────────────┘
```

WHAT'S HAPPENING?   The file worked—the date and time should be the current date and time. You can create a batch file and use SHIFT to identify the size and number of files in a directory so you can determine whether the files will fit on a floppy disk.

13 Use any text editor to create and save a file named **SIZE.BAT** that contains the following:

:TOP
DIR %1 ¦ FIND "Directory" >> TEMP.FIL
DIR %1 ¦ FIND "bytes" ¦ FIND /V "free" >> TEMP.FIL
SHIFT
GOTO TOP
TYPE TEMP.FIL
PAUSE
DEL TEMP.FIL

WHAT'S HAPPENING?   Since you do not care about the names of the files, only the size and the directory they are in, you filtered the output from the DIR command to include only the items that you wanted. In a normal directory display such as the one shown below, you want to capture the highlighted lines:

```
┌────────────────────────────────────────────────────────────────┐
│  Volume in drive C has no label.                                 │
│  Volume Serial Number is 07D1-080F                               │
│                                                                  │
│  Directory of C:\WUGXP                                           │
│                                                                  │
│ 10/30/2001  01:46p              148 AST.99                       │
│ 10/31/2001  07:08p              478 VEN.99                       │
│ 10/30/2001  03:42p              190 JUP.99                       │
│ 10/31/2001  01:08p              406 MER.99                       │
│               4 File(s)        1,222 bytes                       │
│               0 Dir(s)  68,145,774,592 bytes free                │
│                                                                  │
└────────────────────────────────────────────────────────────────┘
```

In order to do so, you had to filter the output. The line in the batch file, **DIR %1 ¦ FIND "Directory" >> TEMP.FIL**, found the first highlighted item. It is the only line with "Directory" in it. The line in the batch file, **DIR %1 ¦ FIND "bytes" ¦ FIND /V "free" >> TEMP.FIL**, was looking for a line with the word "bytes" in it. There are two lines with "bytes." You only want the first line, 4 File(s) 1,222 bytes, so you piped the output eliminating the other line (/V) which removed any line with the word "free" in it (0 Dir(s) 68,145,774,592 bytes free). You then used >> so that you would see both the name of the directory and the bytes in the directory. Had you not used >>, you would have *overwritten* **TEMP.FIL**. At the end of your work, delete **TEMP.FIL** so it will not take space on your disk.

14 Key in the following: A:\>**SIZE CLASS TRIP** [Enter]

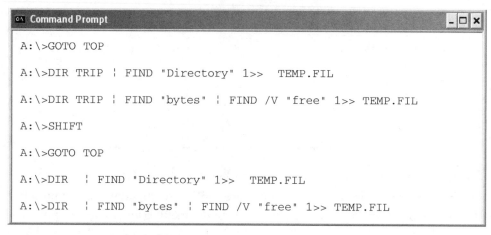

```
A:\>GOTO TOP

A:\>DIR TRIP ¦ FIND "Directory" 1>>  TEMP.FIL

A:\>DIR TRIP ¦ FIND "bytes" ¦ FIND /V "free" 1>> TEMP.FIL

A:\>SHIFT

A:\>GOTO TOP

A:\>DIR   ¦ FIND "Directory" 1>>  TEMP.FIL

A:\>DIR   ¦ FIND "bytes" ¦ FIND /V "free" 1>> TEMP.FIL
```

WHAT'S ▓▓▓▓▓▓
▓▓▓HAPPENING?   Your batch file is running endlessly. You again created an endless loop.

15 Press [Ctrl] + [Break] and answer **Y** to the prompt.

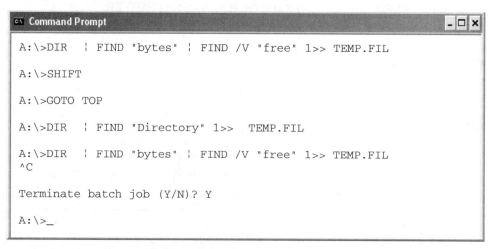

```
A:\>DIR   ¦ FIND "bytes" ¦ FIND /V "free" 1>> TEMP.FIL

A:\>SHIFT

A:\>GOTO TOP

A:\>DIR   ¦ FIND "Directory" 1>>  TEMP.FIL

A:\>DIR   ¦ FIND "bytes" ¦ FIND /V "free" 1>> TEMP.FIL
^C

Terminate batch job (Y/N)? Y

A:\>_
```

WHAT'S ▓▓▓▓▓▓
▓▓▓HAPPENING?   Your display may look different depending on where you broke into the batch file.

16 Key in the following: A:\>**TYPE TEMP.FIL ¦ MORE** [Enter]

```
 Command Prompt                                              _ □ ×

 A:\>TYPE TEMP.FIL | MORE
  Directory of A:\CLASS
             14 File(s)            4,209 bytes
  Directory of A:\TRIP
             19 File(s)            4,860 bytes
  Directory of A:\
             71 File(s)           26,504 bytes
  Directory of A:\
             71 File(s)           26,570 bytes
  Directory of A:\
             71 File(s)           26,636 bytes
  Directory of A:\
             71 File(s)           26,702 bytes
  Directory of A:\
             71 File(s)           26,768 bytes
  Directory of A:\
             71 File(s)           26,834 bytes
  Directory of A:\
             71 File(s)           26,900 bytes
  Directory of A:\
             71 File(s)           26,966 bytes
  Directory of A:\
             71 File(s)           27,032 bytes
 — More  —
```

17 Press [Ctrl] + **C** to stop the processing, if necessary.

WHAT'S
HAPPENING?   Your file may be shorter or longer, depending on the length of time
before you "broke out" with [Ctrl] + [Break]. On some systems, [Ctrl] + C will stop
this file from executing, and on other systems, [Ctrl] + [Break] is necessary. In any
case, you got more information than you wanted. You now know the size of the
CLASS and **TRIP** directories, but the other information is useless. What you are
missing is conditional processing. (The size of your directories may be different,
depending on the work you have done on your DATA disk.)

11.9   The IF Command

The IF command allows for conditional processing. Conditional processing is a
powerful tool in programming. Conditional processing allows a comparison between two items to determine whether the items are identical or whether one is
greater than another. A comparison test will yield one of only two values—true or
false. If the items are identical, the condition is true. If the items are not identical, the
condition is false. Once you establish a true or false value, you can then direct the
program to do something based on that value. Conditional processing is often
expressed as IF the condition is true, THEN do something; IF the condition is false,
THEN do nothing.

In batch files, the IF command will test for some logical condition and then, if the
condition is true, the batch file will execute the command. If the test is false, the
command will not be executed and the batch file will fall through to the next
command line in the batch file. The IF command in batch file processing can check
for three conditions:

1. Whether two sets of characters are or are not identical. The characters are called a string, as in a string of data (sometimes referred to as a character string).
2. Whether or not a file exists.
3. The value of the variable in ERRORLEVEL. ERRORLEVEL is a number that a program can set depending on the outcome of a process, such as checking a true/false condition. ERRORLEVEL can check that number.

Here is the syntax for IF/IF NOT ERRORLEVEL (for complete syntax, see Appendix H):

```
Performs conditional processing in batch programs.

IF [NOT] ERRORLEVEL number command
IF [NOT] string1==string2 command
IF [NOT] EXIST filename command

  NOT                Specifies that Windows XP should carry out
                     the command only if the condition is false.

  ERRORLEVEL number  Specifies a true condition if the last program
                     run returned an exit code equal to or greater
                     than the number specified.

  string1==string2   Specifies a true condition if the specified text
                     strings match.

  EXIST filename     Specifies a true condition if the specified
                     filename exists.
```

11.10 The IF Command Using Strings

You can use the IF command with character strings to test whether or not one string is exactly the same as another. You can tell the IF statement to GOTO a label or to perform an operation when the strings match and the condition is true. Conversely, you can tell the IF statement to GOTO a label or perform an operation when the strings do *not* match and the condition is false. What is to be compared is separated by two equal signs (==).

11.11 Activity: Using the IF Command with Strings

Note: The DATA disk should be in Drive A. The default drive and directory should be A:\>.

1   Use any text editor to create and save a file called **GREET.BAT**. (*Note:* There are no spaces between the two equal signs.) Key in the following:

IF %1==Carolyn GOTO Carolyn Enter
IF %1==Bette GOTO Bette Enter
ECHO Isn't anyone there? Enter
GOTO FINISH Enter
:Carolyn Enter
ECHO Greetings, Ms. Carolyn. Enter
GOTO FINISH Enter

:Bette Enter
ECHO Greetings, Ms. Bette. Enter
:FINISH

WHAT'S HAPPENING? You have created a batch file to test the IF statement using character strings. You did not place ECHO OFF at the beginning of the file so you can see what happens when it executes.

2 Key in the following: A:\>**GREET Carolyn** Enter

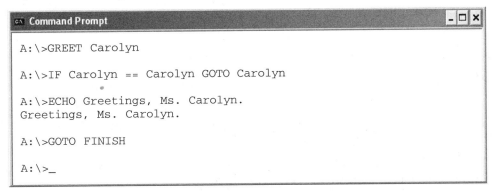

```
Command Prompt                                    _ □ x
A:\>GREET Carolyn

A:\>IF Carolyn == Carolyn GOTO Carolyn

A:\>ECHO Greetings, Ms. Carolyn.
Greetings, Ms. Carolyn.

A:\>GOTO FINISH

A:\>_
```

WHAT'S HAPPENING? You keyed in **GREET Carolyn**. The first line in the batch file was executed. When Carolyn took the place of %1, the line read **IF Carolyn==Carolyn**, which is a true statement because the strings of data matched exactly. Since it is true, it performed the GOTO Carolyn command. The line after the label **:Carolyn** was then displayed: **Greetings, Ms. Carolyn.** The line following said **GOTO FINISH**, which it did. After the label **:FINISH**, there were no more lines, and you were returned to the system prompt.

3 Key in the following: A:\>**GREET Bette** Enter

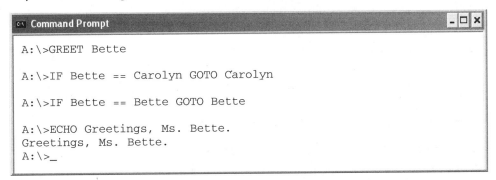

```
Command Prompt                                    _ □ x
A:\>GREET Bette

A:\>IF Bette == Carolyn GOTO Carolyn

A:\>IF Bette == Bette GOTO Bette

A:\>ECHO Greetings, Ms. Bette.
Greetings, Ms. Bette.
A:\>_
```

WHAT'S HAPPENING? When you keyed in **GREET Bette**, it read the first line as **IF Bette==Carolyn GOTO Carolyn**. Bette does not equal Carolyn, so it is a false statement. Therefore, the batch file did not go to the label **:Carolyn** but fell through to the next line. The line then read as **IF Bette==Bette**, which is a true statement because the strings of data match exactly. Since it is true, it performed the GOTO Bette command. The line after the label **:Bette** was then displayed: **Greetings, Ms. Bette.** The line following said **:FINISH**, which it did. After the label **:FINISH**, there were no more lines, and you were returned to the system prompt.

4 Key in the following: A:\>**GREET Juan** Enter

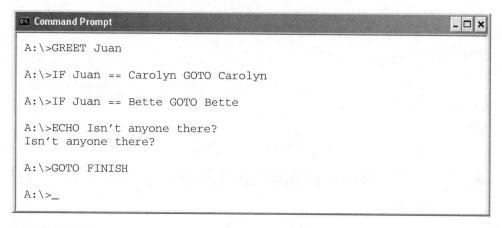

```
A:\>GREET Juan

A:\>IF Juan == Carolyn GOTO Carolyn

A:\>IF Juan == Bette GOTO Bette

A:\>ECHO Isn't anyone there?
Isn't anyone there?

A:\>GOTO FINISH

A:\>_
```

WHAT'S HAPPENING?   You keyed in **GREET Juan**. It read the first line as **IF Juan==Carolyn GOTO Carolyn**. Juan does not equal Carolyn, so it is a false statement. The batch file did not go to the label **:Carolyn** but fell through to the next line. The line then read as **IF Juan==Bette**. This is another false statement, so the batch file did not go to the label **:Bette** but fell through to the next line. The line following said **ECHO Isn't anyone there?** Thus, **Isn't anyone there?** was displayed (echoed) to the screen. It then fell through to the next line, which was **GOTO FINISH**. After the label **:FINISH**, there were no more lines, and you were returned to the system prompt.

5   Key in the following: A:\>**GREET BETTE** Enter

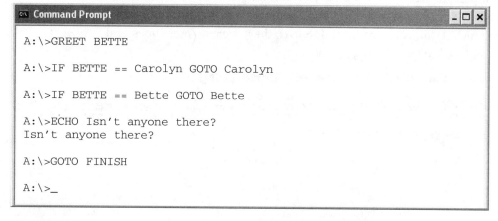

```
A:\>GREET BETTE

A:\>IF BETTE == Carolyn GOTO Carolyn

A:\>IF BETTE == Bette GOTO Bette

A:\>ECHO Isn't anyone there?
Isn't anyone there?

A:\>GOTO FINISH

A:\>_
```

WHAT'S HAPPENING?   You keyed in **GREET BETTE**. It read the first line as **IF BETTE==Carolyn GOTO Carolyn**. BETTE does not equal Carolyn, so it is a false statement. The batch file did not go to the label **:Carolyn** but fell through to the next line. The line then read **IF BETTE==Bette**, which is another false statement. Even though the word is the same, the case is different. Both sides of == must match *exactly*. Because it was not an exact match, the batch file did not go to the label **:Bette**, but fell through to the next line. The line following said **ECHO Isn't anyone there?** Thus, **Isn't anyone there?** was displayed (echoed) to the screen. It then fell through to the next line, which was **GOTO FINISH**. It did. After the label **:FINISH**, there were no more lines, and you were returned to the system prompt. If you wish to ignore case, you can add a parameter, the /I, which when included, tells the batch file to ignore case. The command would be written as

> **IF /I %1= =Carolyn GOTO Carolyn**
> **IF /I %1= =Bette GOTO Bette**

and so on. The /I must immediately follow the IF statement.

11.12 Testing for Null Values

In the above example, you tested for an exact match of character strings. What if you have nothing to test for? For example, in the batch files you wrote, UPDATE.BAT and SIZE.BAT, you used SHIFT. SHIFT kept shifting parameters until all of them were used. When there were no more parameters, you were in an endless loop. You can test to see if a string matches, but what if nothing is there? This is called testing for a *null value*. You are literally testing for nothing. You must have "something" to test for "nothing." Thus, you place a value in the test that will give you nothing.

There are a variety of methods for testing for null values. One method is to use quotation marks so that your statement becomes IF "%1"=="" GOTO LABEL. The second set of quotation marks is keyed in with no spaces. This statement says, "If nothing is there, GOTO somewhere else." You may also make the line read IF %1void==void GOTO LABEL. If you keyed in GREET Carolyn, your line would then look like Carolynvoid==void. This is not true, so it would proceed to the next line. If there was no value, your line would look like void==void. Now this is true, and the GOTO label would execute. You may use any word; "void" was used in this example. Another method is to use \ so that the statement would become IF \%1\==\\ GOTO LABEL. If you keyed in GREET Carolyn, your line would then look like \Carolyn\==\\. This is not true, so it would proceed to the next line. If there were no value, your line would look like \\==\\. Now this *is* true and the GOTO label would execute.

11.13 Activity: Using Null Values

Note: The DATA disk should be in Drive A. The default drive and directory should be A:\>.

1   Edit and save the file called **UPDATE.BAT** to look as follows:

```
:DOIT
IF "%1"=="" GOTO END
COPY %1 /B + > NUL
SHIFT
PAUSE
GOTO DOIT
:END
```

2   Key in the following: A:\>**DIR CAROLYN.FIL** Enter

```
A:\>DIR CAROLYN.FIL
 Volume in drive A is DATA
 Volume Serial Number is 30B8-DA1D
```

```
   Directory of A:\

07/31/1999  12:53 PM                        47 CAROLYN.FIL
                   1 File(s)                47 bytes
                   0 Dir(s)           915,968 bytes free

A:\>_
```

WHAT'S HAPPENING?   The file called **CAROLYN.FIL** has a date of 7-31-99. You are going to update only the date on this file. SHIFT will still work and will shift "nothing" to %1, but now you are testing for a null value. Once the file is updated, you will go to :END.

3   Key in the following: A:\>**UPDATE CAROLYN.FIL** Enter

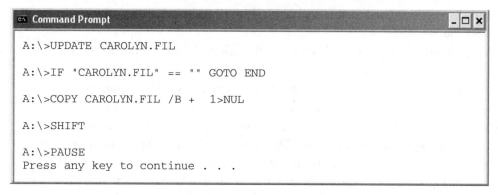

```
A:\>UPDATE  CAROLYN.FIL

A:\>IF "CAROLYN.FIL" == "" GOTO END

A:\>COPY CAROLYN.FIL /B +  1>NUL

A:\>SHIFT

A:\>PAUSE
Press any key to continue . . .
```

WHAT'S HAPPENING?   The batch file updated the file **CAROLYN.FIL**. Prior to your testing for a null value, the file looped endlessly. Now you will see if your test for "nothing" works. Remember, there is a SHIFT that will shift over nothing.

4   Press Enter

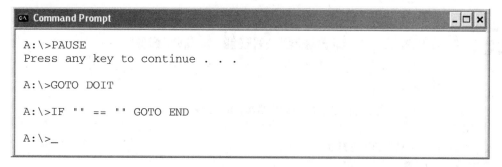

```
A:\>PAUSE
Press any key to continue . . .

A:\>GOTO DOIT

A:\>IF "" == "" GOTO END

A:\>_
```

WHAT'S HAPPENING?   Since nothing, or a null value, was there, it was a true condition, and GOTO told it to go to the label called :END. Thus, it skipped the lines and went directly to the end of the batch file.

5   Key in the following: A:\>**DIR CAROLYN.FIL** Enter

```
A:\>DIR CAROLYN.FIL
 Volume in drive A is DATA
 Volume Serial Number is 30B8-DA1D

 Directory of A:\
```

```
05/06/2002  11:34 AM                47 CAROLYN.FIL
              1 File(s)             47 bytes
              0 Dir(s)         915,968 bytes free

A:\>_
```

WHAT'S HAPPENING?   The date did change to the current date (your date will be different), and you were not in an endless loop. You are now going to try another technique to test for a null value.

6   Edit and save the file called **SIZE.BAT** to look as follows:

:TOP
IF %1nothing==nothing GOTO END
DIR %1 ¦ FIND "Directory" >> TEMP.FIL
DIR %1 ¦ FIND "bytes" ¦ FIND /V "free" >> TEMP.FIL
SHIFT
GOTO TOP
TYPE TEMP.FIL
PAUSE
DEL TEMP.FIL
:END

7   Key in the following: A:\>**DEL TEMP.FIL** Enter

WHAT'S HAPPENING?   You wanted to eliminate **TEMP.FIL**, because the last time you ran this batch file, you were stuck in a loop and **TEMP.FIL** did not get deleted. You never reached that line in the batch file.

8   Key in the following: A:\>**SIZE CLASS TRIP** Enter

```
Command Prompt                                        _ □ ×

A:\>SIZE CLASS TRIP

A:\>IF CLASSnothing == nothing GOTO END

A:\>DIR CLASS   ¦ FIND "Directory"  1>>TEMP.FIL

A:\>DIR CLASS   ¦ FIND "bytes"   ¦ FIND /V "free"  1>>TEMP.FIL

A:\>SHIFT

A:\>GOTO TOP

A:\>IF TRIPnothing == nothing GOTO END

A:\>DIR TRIP    ¦ FIND "Directory"  1>>TEMP.FIL

A:\>DIR TRIP    ¦ FIND "bytes"   ¦ FIND /V "free"  1>>TEMP.FIL

A:\>SHIFT

A:\>GOTO TOP

A:\>IF nothing == nothing GOTO END

A:\>_
```

WHAT'S ▒▒▒▒
▒▒▒▒HAPPENING?   You did not have the problem of an endless loop, but, when you tested for a null value and there was a null value, you told the batch file to GOTO END. It did so, but, by going to the label :END, it never processed the other three lines in the batch file—the lines beginning with TYPE, PAUSE, and DEL. This is why writing batch files (and programs) is a complicated task. You have to think through what you are trying to do and what consequences your instructions will have.

9   Key in the following: A:\>**TYPE TEMP.FIL** [Enter]

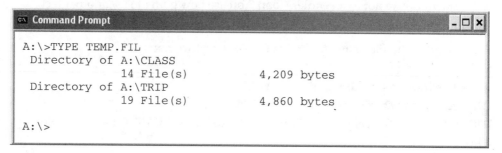

```
A:\>TYPE TEMP.FIL
  Directory of A:\CLASS
            14 File(s)        4,209 bytes
  Directory of A:\TRIP
            19 File(s)        4,860 bytes

  A:\>
```

WHAT'S ▒▒▒▒
▒▒▒▒HAPPENING?   The batch file **SIZE.BAT** worked, to some degree. You got the information in the file **TEMP.FIL**, but the file was never displayed or deleted. Thus, you must find another solution to the problem.

11.14 The IF EXIST/IF NOT EXIST Command

The IF EXIST command uses a file specification for the test. If the file exists, then the condition is true. Processing then passes to the specified GOTO location or to the command that follows the IF statement. If the file does not exist, the condition is false and the operating system ignores the command in the IF clause. The batch process then reads the next line in the file. When you use IF NOT EXIST and the file does not exist, then the condition is true. Processing then passes to the specified GOTO location or to the command that follows the IF NOT statement. If the file does exist, the condition is false and the batch process will fall through to the next line in the batch file. An important part of the IF EXIST / IF NOT EXIST command is that it works only with file names and *not with directory names*.

11.15 Activity: Using IF EXIST to Test for a File

Note: The DATA disk should be in Drive A. The displayed prompt is A:\>.

1   Use any text editor to create and save a file called **RENDIR.BAT**. Key in the following:
IF \%1\==\\ GOTO end [Enter]
IF NOT \%2\==\\ GOTO next [Enter]
ECHO You must include a destination name [Enter]
ECHO for the new directory name. [Enter]
GOTO end [Enter]
:next [Enter]
IF EXIST %1 GOTO message [Enter]
REN %1 %2 [Enter]

GOTO end Enter
:message Enter
ECHO This is a file, not a directory. Enter
:end

WHAT'S ▨▨▨▨▨
▨▨▨ HAPPENING?   This batch file will ensure that you are renaming a directory and
not a file. The following table analyzes the batch file one line at a time. The line
numbers are for purposes of reference only.

1.   **IF \%1\==\\ GOTO end**
2.   **IF NOT \%2\==\\ GOTO next**
3.   **ECHO You must include a destination name**
4.   **ECHO for the new directory name.**
5.   **GOTO end**
6.   **:next**
7.   **IF EXIST %1 GOTO message**
8.   **REN %1 %2**
9.   **GOTO end**
10.   **:message**
11.   **ECHO This is a file, not a directory.**
12.   **:end**

Batch File by Line Number	Test TRUE	Processing	Test FALSE
1. IF \%1\==\\ GOTO end	User keys in nothing for %1. Since test is true, action is to go to line 12.	Testing for null value.	User keys in value for %1. Since test is false, action is to go to line 2.
2. IF NOT \%2\==\\ GOTO next	User keys in nothing for %2. Since test is true, action is to go to line 3.	Testing for null value.	User keys in value for %2. Since test is false, action is to go to line 6.
3. ECHO You must include a destination name		Message for user that he or she did not include a value.	
4. ECHO for the new directory name.		Continuation of the message.	
5. GOTO end		Falls through to the GOTO end statement. Action is to go to line 12.	
6. :next		Label referred to in line 2.	

7. IF EXIST %1 GOTO message	User keys in file name for %1. Since test is true, action is to go to line 10.	Testing for value for %1. Is it a file or a directory?	User keys in directory for %1. Since test is false, action is to go to line 8.
8. REN %1 %2		Since %1 test is false (not a file), re-naming directory can proceed.	
9. GOTO end		After directory is renamed, falls through to GOTO end.	
10. :message		Label referred to in line 2.	
11. ECHO This is a file, not a directory.		Message that user used a file name, not a directory name.	
12. :end			

2   Key in the following: A:\>**RENDIR JUP.PAR LAST** Enter

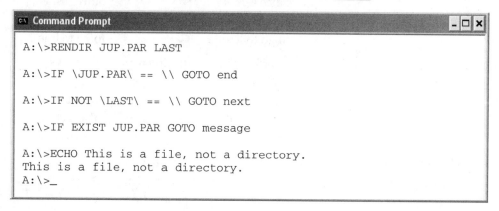

```
A:\>RENDIR JUP.PAR LAST

A:\>IF \JUP.PAR\ == \\ GOTO end

A:\>IF NOT \LAST\ == \\ GOTO next

A:\>IF EXIST JUP.PAR GOTO message

A:\>ECHO This is a file, not a directory.
This is a file, not a directory.
A:\>_
```

WHAT'S ▒▒▒▒▒▒
▒▒▒HAPPENING?   Since **JUP.PAR** is a file, the line **IF EXIST JUP.PAR** is true. Since it is true, the batch file executed GOTO and went to the label **:message**. What if it is a directory and not a file?

3   Key in the following: A:\>**RENDIR TEST OLDER** Enter

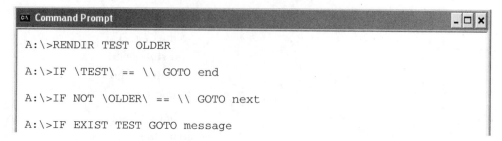

```
A:\>RENDIR TEST OLDER

A:\>IF \TEST\ == \\ GOTO end

A:\>IF NOT \OLDER\ == \\ GOTO next

A:\>IF EXIST TEST GOTO message
```

```
A:\>ECHO This is a file, not a directory.
This is a file, not a directory.
A:\>_
```

WHAT'S HAPPENING?   The if statement identified TEST as a file and therefore went to the message. The directory was not renamed. You cannot use IF EXIST to check for the existence of a directory, as it only works with files. There is a way around this—you can "fool" the IF EXIST command. To check for the existence or nonexistence of a directory, you must use NUL. The null (NUL) device does exist in every directory. NUL is a device that discards anything sent to it. By using %1\NUL, you force IF EXIST/IF NOT EXIST to check for a directory name and not a file name. IF looks for a NUL file (or the nonexistence of a nothing file) in the directory represented by %1. If it cannot get through %1 to look for NUL, then %1 does not exist.

4   Edit the **RENDIR.BAT** file so that you change the line
IF EXIST %1 GOTO message
to read
IF NOT EXIST %1\NUL GOTO message.

5   Key in the following: A:\>**RENDIR TEST OLDER** Enter

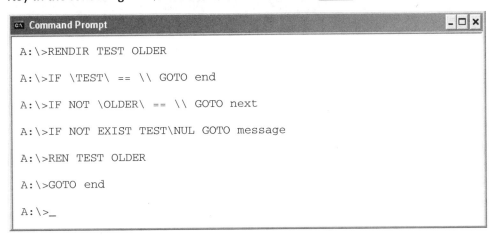

```
A:\>RENDIR TEST OLDER

A:\>IF \TEST\ == \\ GOTO end

A:\>IF NOT \OLDER\ == \\ GOTO next

A:\>IF NOT EXIST TEST\NUL GOTO message

A:\>REN TEST OLDER

A:\>GOTO end

A:\>_
```

WHAT'S HAPPENING?   The question asked with the IF NOT EXIST statement was testing whether TEST was a directory. If this statement were false (a file name), then the batch file would execute the command following IF (the GOTO message). Since TEST does exist (TEST\NUL) the statement is true, the command following IF is ignored, and the batch file falls through to the next line and renames the directory from TEST to OLDER. Using the logic you just learned, you can correct (debug) **SIZE.BAT** so that it processes all the lines in the batch file. There is one more piece of information you need.

6   Edit and save the file called **SIZE.BAT** to look as follows:
IF EXIST TEMP.FIL DEL TEMP.FIL
:TOP
IF %1nothing==nothing GOTO END
IF NOT EXIST %1\NUL GOTO NEXT
DIR %1 ¦ FIND "Directory" >> TEMP.FIL

```
DIR %1 ¦ FIND "bytes" ¦ FIND /V "free" >> TEMP.FIL
:NEXT
SHIFT
GOTO TOP
:END
TYPE TEMP.FIL
PAUSE
DEL TEMP.FIL
```

WHAT'S HAPPENING?   The first line, IF EXIST TEMP.FIL DEL TEMP.FIL, looks for the file called **TEMP.FIL** and delete it if it exists. Then when you create **TEMP.FIL**, it will be a new file every time. The next addition, IF NOT EXIST %1\NUL GOTO NEXT, will see if a directory exists. That is the purpose of %1\NUL. If it is a file, the batch file will go to the :NEXT label, SHIFT, and go back to the :TOP label. The :TOP label is not at the top of the batch file because you want to delete **TEMP.FIL** only the first time you execute the batch file. Notice that you had to move the :END label. In its previous batch file location, you would not have been able to read **TEMP.FIL**.

7   Key in the following: A:\>**SIZE CLASS JUP.PAR TRIP** [Enter]

```
Command Prompt                                          [-][□][×]

A:\>SIZE CLASS JUP.PAR TRIP

A:\>SIZE CLASS JUP.PAR TRIP

A:\>IF EXIST TEMP.FIL DEL TEMP.FIL

A:\>IF CLASSnothing == nothing GOTO END

A:\>IF NOT EXIST CLASS\NUL GOTO NEXT

A:\>DIR CLASS ¦ FIND "Directory" 1>>TEMP.FIL

A:\>DIR CLASS ¦ FIND "bytes" ¦ FIND /V "free" 1>> TEMP.FIL

A:\>SHIFT

A:\>GOTO TOP

A:\>IF JUP.PARnothing == nothing GOTO END

A:\>IF NOT EXIST JUP.PAR\NUL GOTO NEXT

A:\>SHIFT

A:\>GOTO TOP

A:\>IF TRIPnothing == nothing GOTO END

A:\>IF NOT EXIST TRIP\NUL GOTO NEXT

A:\>DIR TRIP   ¦ FIND "Directory"  1>>TEMP.FIL

A:\>DIR TRIP   ¦ FIND "bytes"   ¦ FIND /V "free"  1>>TEMP.FIL

A:\>SHIFT

A:\>GOTO TOP
```

```
A:\>IF nothing == nothing GOTO END

A:\>TYPE  TEMP.FIL
 Directory of A:\CLASS
              14 File(s)              4,209 bytes
 Directory of A:\TRIP
              19 File(s)              4,860 bytes

A:\>PAUSE
Press any key to continue . . .
```

WHAT'S HAPPENING?   Your batch file worked correctly. It used **JUP.PAR**, knew it was a file, and did not include it in the output. The more complicated you want a batch file to be, the more you will have to analyze the logic of what you want to do and how to accomplish it.

8   Press Enter

```
A:\>PAUSE
Press any key to continue . . .

A:\>DEL TEMP.FIL
A:\>_
```

WHAT'S HAPPENING?   The batch file deleted the TEMP.FIL when it completed executing, and you have returned to the system level.

11.16 The IF ERRORLEVEL Command Testing

A program can set an *exit code* when it finishes executing. A batch file can test this exit code with the IF ERRORLEVEL statement. Actually, the name ERRORLEVEL is a misnomer because the number returned does not necessarily mean there was an error. For instance, the test IF ERRORLEVEL 3 will be true if the exit code is greater than or equal to 3. Thus, an exit code is not tested for a match with ERRORLEVEL, but to determine if it is greater than or equal to it. The test IF ERRORLEVEL 0 will *always* be true since every possible exit code is greater than or equal to 0. The trickiest thing about testing ERRORLEVELs in batch files is that the exit codes must be listed in *descending* order when you use IF ERRORLEVEL and in *ascending* order when you use IF NOT ERRORLEVEL. For instance, COPY will set one of the following exit codes:

```
0 Files were copied without error.
1 No files were found to copy.
```

You can write a batch file testing for exit codes.

11.17 Activity: Using IF ERRORLEVEL with COPY

Note: The DATA disk should be in Drive A. The displayed prompt is A:\>.

1   Use any text editor to create and save a file called **ERROR.BAT**. Key in the following:

COPY %1 %2 [Enter]
IF ERRORLEVEL 1 GOTO NOTOK [Enter]
IF ERRORLEVEL 0 GOTO OK [Enter]
:NOTOK [Enter]
ECHO There are no %1 files. Try again. [Enter]
GOTO END [Enter]
:OK [Enter]
ECHO You copied the %1 files successfully. [Enter]
:END

2   Key in the following: A:\>**ERROR *.TXT OLDER** [Enter]

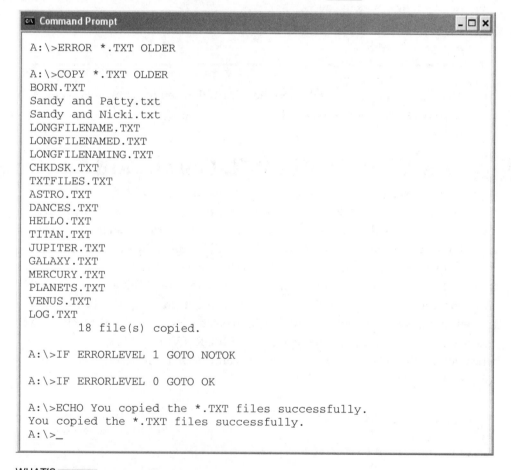

```
A:\>ERROR *.TXT OLDER

A:\>COPY *.TXT OLDER
BORN.TXT
Sandy and Patty.txt
Sandy and Nicki.txt
LONGFILENAME.TXT
LONGFILENAMED.TXT
LONGFILENAMING.TXT
CHKDSK.TXT
TXTFILES.TXT
ASTRO.TXT
DANCES.TXT
HELLO.TXT
TITAN.TXT
JUPITER.TXT
GALAXY.TXT
MERCURY.TXT
PLANETS.TXT
VENUS.TXT
LOG.TXT
        18 file(s) copied.

A:\>IF ERRORLEVEL 1 GOTO NOTOK

A:\>IF ERRORLEVEL 0 GOTO OK

A:\>ECHO You copied the *.TXT files successfully.
You copied the *.TXT files successfully.
A:\>_
```

WHAT'S HAPPENING?   You successfully copied the **.TXT** files to the **OLDER** subdirectory. The exit code that was generated by COPY gave you the message that the copy was successful.

3   Key in the following: A:\>**ERROR *.NON OLDER** [Enter]

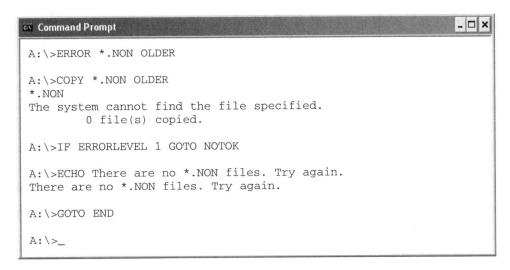

```
Command Prompt                                                    _ □ x

A:\>ERROR *.NON OLDER

A:\>COPY *.NON OLDER
*.NON
The system cannot find the file specified.
        0 file(s) copied.

A:\>IF ERRORLEVEL 1 GOTO NOTOK

A:\>ECHO There are no *.NON files. Try again.
There are no *.NON files. Try again.

A:\>GOTO END

A:\>_
```

**WHAT'S
HAPPENING?**   Again, the exit code was correctly read. As you can see, you can
use the exit codes successfully in a batch file. Since programs like COPY give you a
message anyway when it could not find the file or files, you may ask yourself, why
go to the trouble of writing a batch file? The reason is that you can write a small
program to test for other kinds of information.

11.18 Writing Programs to Test for Key Codes

Rather than being limited to the exit codes that are set by operating system programs, you can write a small program that will create an exit code based on some
activity. For instance, a program can be written that will identify which key was
pressed and report which key it was. You can do this because every time you press a
key, it is identified by a one- or two-digit *scan code*. Actually, two things are reported when you press any key on the keyboard. First, that you pressed a key.
Second, that you released the key. The keyboard controller tells the CPU that some
keyboard activity is occurring. The stream of bytes is converted into the scan code,
which identifies the specific key (see Appendix G for a list of scan codes for all the
keys).

   You are going to write a program that will report the scan code for any key that is
pressed on the keyboard. Once you know the reported code, you can test for a
specific key using ERRORLEVEL in the batch file. The batch file can then act based
on the reported code. In order to do this, you must write a program. Remember, to
be executed, a program must be in "bits and bytes"—the 0s and 1s the computer
understands.

   There are several ways to write a program. One is to know a programming
language and be able to turn the programming language program (source code) into
executable code (object code). This is called compiling a program—turning a
language into code. That task is beyond the scope of this text. Fortunately, there is
an easier way that you can create a small program—using an operating system
utility program called DEBUG.

   DEBUG can directly modify bytes in a file. DEBUG allows you to test and debug
executable files—those with a .COM or .EXE file extension. Remember, you cannot

use TYPE to look at a file with the extension of .EXE or .COM because those file extensions indicate programs that are not ASCII-readable files. DEBUG is a small program that has its own commands and syntax. If you know the commands of the DEBUG program and the rules of programming, you could write a .COM program directly with DEBUG. Unless you are a programming expert, you will probably not want to do this.

The easiest way to use DEBUG is to create a script or a *script file*. A script is a set of instructions that you can write in any ASCII editor. Once you have written the script, you can "feed" it to the DEBUG program via redirection (DEBUG < SCRIPT.FIL). DEBUG will then convert the script file to an executable program with a .COM file extension. Once you have a .COM file, you can execute it as you do any program. This process is the simplest way to create a file that will report the scan code for any key that is pressed. The program you create will be called REPLY.COM.

Since using DEBUG directly can be tricky, the example below shows a .COM program written with DEBUG that will return the scan code of a pressed key. If you want to try to use DEBUG directly, what appears on the screen in this example will be in *this typeface* and what you key in will be in **this typeface**. The hyphen (-) and the colon (:) are prompts presented to you by the DEBUG program. Instructions such as 100 assemble the program at memory address 100 (hexadecimal). 12B3 will vary from machine to machine. In the example shown here, 12B3:0100 represents segment/offset memory address. You must press <enter>after each line and also when <enter>is specified. The following is a summary of commands available within the DEBUG program:

```
assemble      A [address]
compare       C range address
dump          D [range]
enter         E address [list]
fill          F range list
go            G [=address] [addresses]
hex           H value1 value2
input         I port
load          L [address] [drive] [firstsector] [number]
move          M range address
name          N [pathname] [arglist]
output        O port byte
proceed       P [=address] [number]
quit          Q
register      R [register]
search        S range list
trace         T [=address] [value]
unassemble    U [range]
write         W [address] [drive] [firstsector] [number]

allocate expanded memory       XA [#pages]
deallocate expanded memory     XD [handle]
map expanded memory pages      XM [Lpage] [Ppage] [handle]
display expanded memory status XS
```

The following is shown as an example of how to use DEBUG, but you do not have to do this. If you do, note the differences between the letter l and the number 1. Be sure and check with your lab administrator before attempting to key in this example. Be very sure you are at the A:\> prompt.

```
A:\>DEBUG
-a 100 Enter
 158E:0100 mov ah,8 Enter
 158E:0102 int 21 Enter
158E:0104 cmp al,0 Enter
158E:0106 jnz 10a Enter
158E:0108 int 21 Enter
158E:010A mov ah,4c Enter
158E:010C int 21 Enter
158E:010E Enter
-r cx Enter
CX 0000
:e Enter
-n reply.com Enter
 -w Enter
Writing 0000E bytes
-q Enter
```

An easier way to create REPLY.COM is to create a script file. Again, a script file is merely a text file that contains a series of commands that can be redirected into DEBUG to create a .COM file. The script file is not the program. You use any text editor; name the file, in this case REPLY.SCR; and key in the following commands. Then, to make REPLY.SCR an executable program, you redirect it into DEBUG to create REPLY.COM. The next activity will show you how to create REPLY.SCR and REPLY.COM. (*Note:* You may want to check with your instructor to see if he or she has created REPLY.COM for you.)

11.19 Activity: Writing a Script File

Note: The DATA disk should be in Drive A. The displayed prompt is A:\>.

1   Use any text editor to create and save a file called **REPLY.SCR**. Key in the following:
    e 100 b4 08 cd 21 3c 00 75 02 cd 21 b4 4c cd 21 Enter
    rcx Enter
    e Enter
    n reply.com Enter
    w Enter
    q

WHATS
HAPPENING?   Now that you have written **REPLY.SCR**, you must now "assemble" it or convert it into the bytes that make it a program. You do this by redirecting the script file into DEBUG.

2   Key in the following: A:\>**DEBUG < REPLY.SCR** Enter

```
Command Prompt                                           _ □ ×

A:\>DEBUG < REPLY.SCR
-e 100 b4 08 cd 21 3c 00 75 02 cd 21 b4 4c cd 21
-rcx
CX 0000
```

```
:e
-n reply.com
-w
Writing 0000E bytes
-q

A:\>_
```

WHAT'S ▒▒▒▒▒▒
▒▒▒▒ HAPPENING?   You have compiled **REPLY.SCR** into a program called
REPLY.COM.

3   Key in the following: A:\>**DIR REPLY.COM** [Enter]

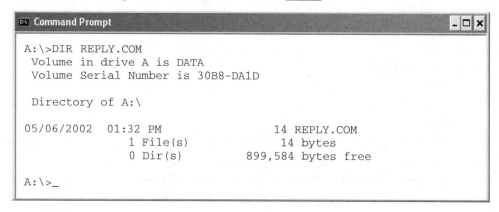

```
A:\>DIR REPLY.COM
 Volume in drive A is DATA
 Volume Serial Number is 30B8-DA1D

 Directory of A:\

05/06/2002  01:32 PM                 14 REPLY.COM
               1 File(s)             14 bytes
               0 Dir(s)         899,584 bytes free

A:\>_
```

WHAT'S ▒▒▒▒▒▒
▒▒▒▒ HAPPENING?   Now that you have written a program, you want to use it in a
batch file.

4   Use any text editor to create and save a file called **KEYING.BAT** that contains
the following:
ECHO PRESS F1 TO CLEAR THE SCREEN.
ECHO PRESS F2 TO DISPLAY THE DIRECTORY.
ECHO PRESS ANY OTHER KEY TO EXIT.
REPLY
IF ERRORLEVEL 61 GOTO END
IF ERRORLEVEL 60 GOTO F2
IF ERRORLEVEL 59 GOTO F1
GOTO END
:F1
CLS
GOTO END
:F2
DIR
:END

WHAT'S ▒▒▒▒▒▒
▒▒▒▒ HAPPENING?   This is a simple batch file that checks the scan codes you generate
by pressing a key. Checking IF ERRORLEVEL codes in descending order is *critical*
because the command is tested to determine if the error code is equal to or greater
than the value specified. In this program, if you press a key that returns a value of
61 or above, you exit the program. If you press [F2], it returns a code of 60. If you
press [F1], it returns a code of 59. If none of those conditions exist, then you exit the
batch file.

5   Key in the following: A:\>**KEYING** [Enter]

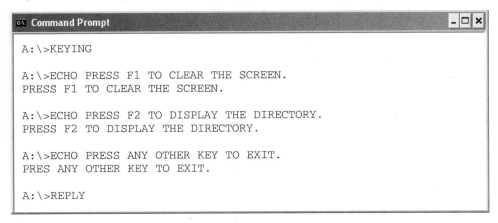

```
Command Prompt                                                _ □ x

A:\>KEYING

A:\>ECHO PRESS F1 TO CLEAR THE SCREEN.
PRESS F1 TO CLEAR THE SCREEN.

A:\>ECHO PRESS F2 TO DISPLAY THE DIRECTORY.
PRESS F2 TO DISPLAY THE DIRECTORY.

A:\>ECHO PRESS ANY OTHER KEY TO EXIT.
PRES ANY OTHER KEY TO EXIT.

A:\>REPLY
```

WHAT'S
HAPPENING?   You have executed the **KEYING** batch file. The program called
REPLY.COM is waiting for you to press a key.

6   Press [F1]

```
Command Prompt                                                _ □ x

A:\>GOTO END
A:\>_
```

WHAT'S
HAPPENING?   Pressing [F1] cleared the screen.

7   Key in the following: A:\>**KEYING** [Enter]

8   Press [F2]

```
Command Prompt                                                _ □ x

04/29/2002    01:32 PM                    9 D.BAT
04/29/2002    01:34 PM                   10 S.BAT
07/06/2002    10:33 AM      <DIR>           BATCH
07/06/2002    10:33 AM      <DIR>           UTILS
07/07/2002    04:44 PM                  190 JUP.PAR
10/31/2001    07:08 PM                  478 JUP.ABC
10/30/2001    12:46 PM                  148 JUP.FIL
07/06/2002    11:37 AM                   13 JUP.XYZ
05/03/2002    02:46 PM                  161 KILLIT.BAT
10/31/2001    07:08 PM                  478 VEN.ABC
10/31/2001    07:08 PM                  478 VEN.PAR
07/07/2002    04:44 PM                  478 VEN.BUD
05/03/2002    03:07 PM                  207 NOCOPY.BAT
07/06/2002    11:59 AM                   30 N.BAT
07/06/2002    12:00 PM                   64 log.bat
07/06/2002    12:00 PM                  111 MULTI.BAT
07/06/2002    12:01 PM                   36 BOG.BAT
07/06/2002    12:02 PM                  113 LOG.TXT
07/06/2002    12:02 PM                  130 TESTING.BAT
07/06/2002    12:03 PM                   35 TEST.BAT
07/06/2002    12:03 PM                  157 TEST2.BAT
07/06/2002    12:59 PM                  149 DELTREE.BAT
05/03/2002    03:48 PM                  253 DCOMP.BAT
05/05/2002    11:24 AM                  182 ONE.BAT
05/05/2002    11:30 AM                  102 REPEAT.BAT
05/05/2002    12:22 PM                  104 ALPHA.BAT
05/05/2002    12:43 PM                  191 GREET.BAT
```

```
               77 File(s)        27,184 bytes
               10 Dir(s)        898,560 bytes free
A:\>_
```

WHAT'S
HAPPENING?   (The above graphic represents only a portion of what scrolled by on your screen.) Pressing [F2] gave you a directory of your disk. As you can see, **REPLY.COM** checked the scan code returned by the key you pressed and followed the instruction in the batch file based on the key you pressed. Remember, the number of files, directories, and bytes free on your DATA disk will not necessarily match the number shown in the directory displays in the book.

11.20 The Environment

The environment is an area that the operating system sets aside in memory. You have used environmental variable PATH in a previous chapter. In Chapter 10, variables that represent the drive and directory used by the operating system were discussed. The environment is like a scratch pad where notes are kept about important items that the operating system needs to know. The environment is like a bunch of post-it notes. Application programs can read any items in the environment and can post their own messages there. A *variable* is a value that can change, depending on conditions or on information passed to the program. Data consists of constants or fixed values that never change and variable values that do change. The *environment* is, in essence, an area in memory where data can be stored. When evaluating an expression in some environment, the evaluation of a variable consists of looking up its name in the environment and substituting its value. In programming, an *expression* is any legal combination of symbols that represents a value. These variables are used by the operating system to discover things about the environment it is operating in. Environment variables can be changed or created by the user or a program.

Programs can get the value of a variable and use it to modify their operation, much like you can use a value in a command line argument. The operating system has the ability to store data in memory. The stored data takes the form of two strings—one is the name of the variable, and the other is the value of the variable. An *environmental variable* is a name assigned to a string (value) of data. You can set your own environmental variables. However, there are some common environmental variables that are set when you start Windows. There are environmental variables that are commonly used which usually have short, easy-to-remember names. These environmental variables store information such as your user name (USERNAME); the location where, by default, your files are saved (USERPROFILE); the search path the operating system uses to look for commands (PATH); what is displayed in your prompt (PROMPT); as well as the name of your Windows directory—where the operating system files are kept (SystemRoot). It also includes the location of the file CMD.EXE. You can also leave messages there via batch files or from the command line. You do this with the SET command. Environmental variables set by the operating system will remain in effect throughout the entire work session at the computer. Those set in the Command Prompt window or in batch files executed in the Command Prompt window will remain in effect *only* during that command prompt session. While values are in effect, you can use the syntax

%VARIABLENAME%, which will use the value of the environment variable. To view the value of an environmental variable, you can use the syntax of ECHO %ENVIRONMENTALVARIABLENAME%. The internal command SET allows you to display what is currently in the environment, set environmental variables, or delete environmental variables. If you use the SET command, followed by a letter, the SET command will list any environmental variables that begin with that letter. The basic syntax is:

```
SET [variable=[string]]

    variable            Specifies the environment-variable name.
    string              Specifies a series of characters to assign to the
                        variable.

Type SET without parameters to display the current environment
variables.
```

11.21 Activity: Using SET and the Environmental Variables

1 Key in the following: A:\>**SET** Enter

Note: If the your environment display is too long to fit on one screen, use the MORE filter.

```
Command Prompt                                                    _ □ ×

ALLUSERSPROFILE=C:\Documents and Settings\All Users.WINNT
APPDATA=C:\Documents and Settings\bpeat\Application Data
CLIENTNAME=Console
CommonProgramFiles=C:\Program Files\Common Files
COMPUTERNAME=ADMIN504
ComSpec=C:\WINDOWS\system32\cmd.exe
HOMEDRIVE=G:
HOMEPATH=\
HOMESHARE=\\Busdiv\User\bpeat
LOGONSERVER=\\BUSDIV
NUMBER_OF_PROCESSORS=1
OS=Windows_NT
Path=C:\WINDOWS\system32;C:\WINDOWS;C:\WINDOWS\system32\WBEM
PATHEXT=.COM;.EXE;.BAT;.CMD;.VBS;.VBE;.JS;.JSE;.WSF;.WSH
PROCESSOR_ARCHITECTURE=x86
PROCESSOR_IDENTIFIER=x86 Family 5 Model 8 Stepping 12,
AuthenticAMD
PROCESSOR_LEVEL=5
PROCESSOR_REVISION=080c
ProgramFiles=C:\Program Files
PROMPT=$P$G
SESSIONNAME=Console
SystemDrive=C:
SystemRoot=C:\WINDOWS
TEMP=C:\DOCUME~1\bpeat\LOCALS~1\Temp
TMP=C:\DOCUME~1\bpeat\LOCALS~1\Temp
USERDNSDOMAIN=BUSINESS.SOLANO.CC.CA.US
USERDOMAIN=BUSDIV1
USERNAME=bpeat
USERPROFILE=C:\Documents and Settings\bpeat
```

WHAT'S
HAPPENING?   Your values will differ from those shown. As you can see, Windows stores much information about your system (your environment) in the operating system environment. For instance, the environmental variable called ComSpec has a value, in this example, of C:\WINDOWS\system32\cmd.exe. This tells the operating system that the location of CMD.EXE is C:\WINDOWS\SYSTEM32. When you execute a program, Windows no longer needs the command processor in memory. However, when you exit the program and need to key in another command, Windows must reload the command processor from disk. In order to do so, it must know where it is located. It looks up the value of ComSpec to find that location. The PATH value tells Windows what directories and in what order it is to search for executable files. The value for SystemRoot, in this example, is C:\WINDOWS. That tells Windows the name of the directory that holds the Windows operating system files.

2   If you used the MORE filter, press the spacebar until you are returned to the prompt or press Q.

3   Key in the following: A:\>**SET U** [Enter]

4   Key in the following: A:\>**SET S** [Enter]

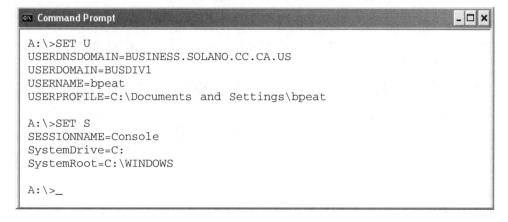

```
A:\>SET U
USERDNSDOMAIN=BUSINESS.SOLANO.CC.CA.US
USERDOMAIN=BUSDIV1
USERNAME=bpeat
USERPROFILE=C:\Documents and Settings\bpeat

A:\>SET S
SESSIONNAME=Console
SystemDrive=C:
SystemRoot=C:\WINDOWS

A:\>_
```

WHAT'S
HAPPENING?   By using the SET command with a letter of the alphabet, all environmental variables that began with that letter were displayed. If you wanted to see the value of an environmental variable, you may do so with the ECHO command, provided that you enclose the environmental variable name you are seeking with percent signs.

5   Key in the following: A:\>**ECHO %PATH%** [Enter]

6   Key in the following: A:\>**ECHO %systemroot%** [Enter]

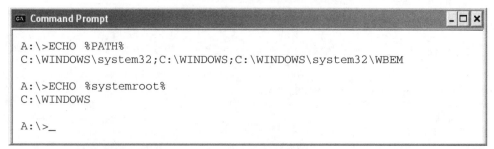

```
A:\>ECHO %PATH%
C:\WINDOWS\system32;C:\WINDOWS;C:\WINDOWS\system32\WBEM

A:\>ECHO %systemroot%
C:\WINDOWS

A:\>_
```

WHAT'S ▨▨▨▨
▨▨▨ HAPPENING?   By surrounding the environmental name with percent signs, you see the value for the variable you requested. As you can see, the case you use does not matter. You may also use the environmental variable with commands.

7   Key in the following: A:\>**C:** [Enter]

8   Key in the following: C:\>**CD %systemroot%** [Enter]

```
A:\>C:

C:\>CD %SYSTEMROOT%

C:\WINDOWS>_
```

WHAT'S ▨▨▨▨
▨▨▨ HAPPENING?   Instead of keying in CD \WINDOWS, you used the environmental variable %SYSTEMROOT%, which changed your location to the value held by the environmental variable %SYSTEMROOT%, in this case, C:\WINDOWS.

9   Key in the following: C:\WINDOWS>**CD %userprofile%** [Enter]

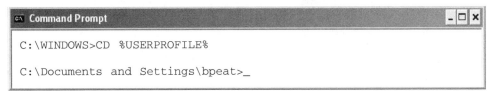

```
C:\WINDOWS>CD %USERPROFILE%

C:\Documents and Settings\bpeat>_
```

WHAT'S ▨▨▨▨
▨▨▨ HAPPENING?   Again, you used an environmental variable to change directories. The displayed prompt represents your personal user directory. Using the environmental variables can be a useful shortcut.

10   Key in the following: C:\Documents and Settings\bpeat>**DIR /AH** [Enter]

```
C:\Documents and Settings\bpeat>DIR /AH
 Volume in drive C is ADMIN504
 Volume Serial Number is 0E38-11FF

 Directory of C:\Documents and Settings\bpeat

12/14/2001  10:08 AM    <DIR>          Local Settings
05/24/2001  11:28 AM    <DIR>          Templates
05/24/2001  11:28 AM    <DIR>          PrintHood
05/24/2001  11:28 AM    <DIR>          NetHood
05/24/2001  11:28 AM    <DIR>          Application Data
05/06/2002  01:40 PM             1,024 ntuser.dat.LOG
05/06/2002  08:10 AM               280 ntuser.ini
12/14/2001  10:08 AM    <DIR>          SendTo
04/29/2002  02:26 PM    <DIR>          Recent
               2 File(s)         1,304 bytes
               7 Dir(s)   6,018,441,216 bytes free

C:\Documents and Settings\bpeat>_
```

WHAT'S ▨▨▨▨
▨▨▨ HAPPENING?   Local Settings is a hidden directory that contains settings that are specific for this user.

11 Key in the following at your personal user prompt:

DIR "Local Settings"\TEMP\~ *.tmp [Enter]

```
┌─────────────────────────────────────────────────────────────────────┐
│ ▣ Command Prompt                                              ─ □ ✕   │
├─────────────────────────────────────────────────────────────────────┤
│                                                                       │
│   12/11/2001    12:04  PM                    512  ~DF451B.tmp         │
│   12/11/2001    09:17  AM                270,336  ~WRS0001.tmp        │
│   12/12/2001    03:07  PM                    512  ~DFFBAA.tmp         │
│   12/12/2001    03:12  PM                    512  ~DF4401.tmp         │
│   12/11/2001    10:29  AM                    512  ~DF9DDB.tmp         │
│   12/12/2001    03:12  PM                278,528  ~WRS0002.tmp        │
│   12/12/2001    03:22  PM                    512  ~DF6860.tmp         │
│   12/12/2001    03:25  PM                    512  ~DF7279.tmp         │
│   12/12/2001    03:25  PM                    512  ~DF8097.tmp         │
│   02/25/2002    12:21  PM                154,148  ~WRS0000.tmp        │
│   03/04/2002    10:44  AM              1,330,970  ~WRS0003.tmp        │
│   03/04/2002    10:44  AM                 32,768  ~WRF3237.tmp        │
│   03/29/2002    10:04  AM                  1,536  ~WRS0004.tmp        │
│   04/17/2002    11:07  AM                 16,384  ~DFB2C1.tmp         │
│   04/19/2002    02:12  PM                 16,384  ~DFD062.tmp         │
│   04/19/2002    02:16  PM                 16,384  ~DF5B19.tmp         │
│   04/17/2002    11:51  AM                 16,384  ~DF1DAB.tmp         │
│   04/19/2002    01:54  PM                 16,384  ~DFF171.tmp         │
│   04/19/2002    01:56  PM                 16,384  ~DFD9CC.tmp         │
│   04/19/2002    02:00  PM                 16,384  ~DF74FF.tmp         │
│   04/19/2002    02:03  PM                 16,384  ~DF6DB2.tmp         │
│   04/19/2002    02:03  PM                 16,384  ~DFA744.tmp         │
│   04/19/2002    02:16  PM                 16,384  ~DF6F57.tmp         │
│   05/06/2002    11:28  AM                    512  ~DFA778.tmp         │
│   05/06/2002    11:35  AM                    512  ~DFF371.tmp         │
│   05/06/2002    11:28  AM                    512  ~DFC219.tmp         │
│   05/06/2002    11:28  AM                 72,704  ~WRS3168.tmp        │
│   05/06/2002    01:40  PM                    512  ~DFB6BB.tmp         │
│               36 File(s)       32,852,800 bytes                       │
│                0 Dir(s)     6,018,441,216 bytes free                  │
│                                                                       │
│   C:\Documents and Settings\bpeat>_                                   │
│                                                                       │
└─────────────────────────────────────────────────────────────────────┘
```

WHAT'S ▓▓▓▓▓
▓▓▓▓HAPPENING?   You may have fewer files then those that are listed here (or no files). The TEMP directory is where Windows keeps temporary files that it is supposed to delete when you finish using a program. Often these files are not deleted. Rather than having to key in a long path name with the DEL command (DEL C:\Documents and Settings\bpeat\"LOCAL SETTINGS"\TEMP\~*.TMP), you can use the environmental variable name.

12 Key in the following:

C:\Documents and Settings\bpeat>**DEL %TEMP%\~ *.tmp** [Enter]

13 Key in the following:

C:\Documents and Settings\bpeat>**DIR %TEMP%\~ *.tmp** [Enter]

```
┌─────────────────────────────────────────────────────────────────────┐
│ ▣ Command Prompt                                              ─ □ ✕   │
├─────────────────────────────────────────────────────────────────────┤
│                                                                       │
│  C:\Documents and Settings\bpeat>DEL  %TEMP%\~*.TMP                   │
│  C:\DOCUME~1\bpeat\LOCALS~1\Temp\~DFA778.tmp                          │
│  Access is denied.                                                    │
│  C:\DOCUME~1\bpeat\LOCALS~1\Temp\~DFF371.tmp                          │
│  Access is denied.                                                    │
│  C:\DOCUME~1\bpeat\LOCALS~1\Temp\~DFC219.tmp                          │
│  Access is denied.                                                    │
│  C:\DOCUME~1\bpeat\LOCALS~1\Temp\~WRS3168.tmp                         │
└─────────────────────────────────────────────────────────────────────┘
```

```
The process cannot access the file because it is being used by another process.
C:\DOCUME~1\bpeat\LOCALS~1\Temp\~DFB6BB.tmp
Access is denied.

C:\Documents and Settings\bpeat>DIR %TEMP%\~*.TMP
 Volume in drive C is ADMIN504
 Volume Serial Number is 0E38-11FF

 Directory of C:\DOCUME~1\bpeat\LOCALS~1\Temp

05/06/2002  11:28 AM                   512 ~DFA778.tmp
05/06/2002  11:35 AM                   512 ~DFF371.tmp
05/06/2002  11:28 AM                   512 ~DFC219.tmp
05/06/2002  11:28 AM               134,144 ~WRS3168.tmp
05/06/2002  01:40 PM                   512 ~DFB6BB.tmp
               5 File(s)          136,192 bytes
               0 Dir(s)     6,051,315,712 bytes free

C:\Documents and Settings\bpeat>_
```

WHAT'S ▨▨▨▨
▨▨▨▨ HAPPENING?   You may or may not get the message "Access Denied" or "The process cannot access the file because it is being used by another process." depending on what is currently in use on your system. You have quickly deleted the ~.TMP files that are not currently in use by the operating system, using an environmental variable.

14 Key in the following: `C:\Documents and Settings\bpeat>`**CD ** `Enter`

15 Key in the following: `C:\>`**A:** `Enter`

WHAT'S ▨▨▨▨
▨▨▨▨ HAPPENING?   You have returned to the root of C, then returned to Drive A.

11.22 Using Set and the Environment in Batch Files

You have been using the built-in environmental variables that Windows sets and uses. You can also set your own environmental variables, giving them both a name and a value in a batch file as well as at the command line. Once you set the variable, you may use it in a batch file. However, any variables that are set are only good for that session of the Command Line window. Once you exit the command prompt, those values are no longer available the next time you open the command prompt.

11.23 Activity: Using SET and the Environment in Batch Files

Note: The DATA disk should be in Drive A. The displayed prompt is A:\>.

1 Close the Command Prompt window, and reopen it to begin a new DOS session. Return to the A:\> prompt.

2 Write and save the following batch file called **TESTIT.BAT**:
@ECHO OFF
ECHO %PATH%
ECHO.

3   Key in the following: A:\>**TESTIT** [Enter]

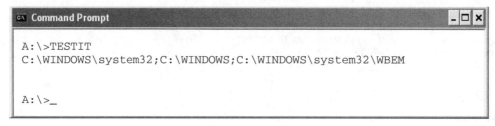

```
A:\>TESTIT
C:\WINDOWS\system32;C:\WINDOWS;C:\WINDOWS\system32\WBEM


A:\>_
```

WHAT'S ▧▧▧▧
▧▧▧ HAPPENING?   The screen display created by this batch file showed the path used in a Command Line window on your system. Notice that it did not return the word PATH but the value stored in the environmental variable "PATH." You can set an environmental value and then use it in a batch file.

4   Key in the following: A:\>**SET TODAY=C:\WUGXP*.FP** [Enter]

5   Key in the following: A:\>**SET** [Enter]

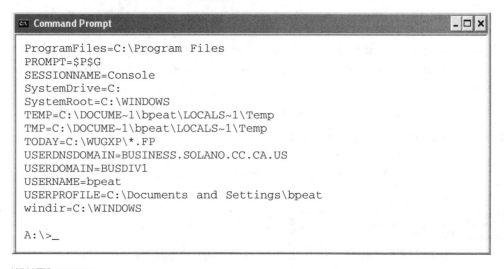

```
ProgramFiles=C:\Program Files
PROMPT=$P$G
SESSIONNAME=Console
SystemDrive=C:
SystemRoot=C:\WINDOWS
TEMP=C:\DOCUME~1\bpeat\LOCALS~1\Temp
TMP=C:\DOCUME~1\bpeat\LOCALS~1\Temp
TODAY=C:\WUGXP\*.FP
USERDNSDOMAIN=BUSINESS.SOLANO.CC.CA.US
USERDOMAIN=BUSDIV1
USERNAME=bpeat
USERPROFILE=C:\Documents and Settings\bpeat
windir=C:\WINDOWS

A:\>_
```

WHAT'S ▧▧▧▧
▧▧▧ HAPPENING?   You now have a value for TODAY, which you set in the environment as **C:\WUGXP*.FP**. Now, as long as you do not close the Command Prompt window, you can use it in a batch file. When you close the Command Prompt window, the environmental variables you set there will disappear.

6   Write and save the following batch file called **SETTING.BAT**:
DIR %today%
ECHO %TODAY%

7   Key in the following: A:\>**SETTING** [Enter]

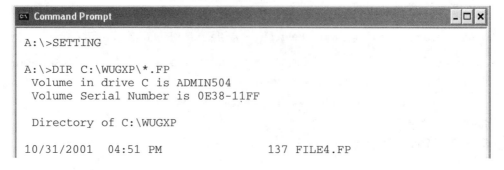

```
A:\>SETTING

A:\>DIR C:\WUGXP\*.FP
 Volume in drive C is ADMIN504
 Volume Serial Number is 0E38-11FF

 Directory of C:\WUGXP

10/31/2001  04:51 PM               137 FILE4.FP
```

```
10/31/2001  04:51 PM                137 FILE2.FP
10/31/2001  04:51 PM                137 FILE3.FP
              3 File(s)            411 bytes
              0 Dir(s)   6,051,553,280 bytes free


A:\>ECHO C:\WUGXP\*.FP
C:\WUGXP\*.FP


A:\>_
```

**WHAT'S
HAPPENING?**   Your batch file needed a value for %today%. The percent signs
indicate that the value was in the environment. It substituted **C:\WUGXP*.FP** for
%today% and for %TODAY%. Case does not matter with environmental variables.
You can use another value.

8   Key in the following: A:\>**SET today=C:\WUGXP*.TMP** [Enter]

9   Key in the following: A:\>**SETTING** [Enter]

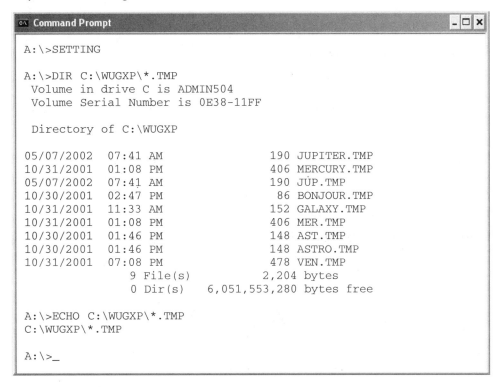

```
A:\>SETTING

A:\>DIR C:\WUGXP\*.TMP
 Volume in drive C is ADMIN504
 Volume Serial Number is 0E38-11FF

 Directory of C:\WUGXP

05/07/2002  07:41 AM                190 JUPITER.TMP
10/31/2001  01:08 PM                406 MERCURY.TMP
05/07/2002  07:41 AM                190 JUP.TMP
10/30/2001  02:47 PM                 86 BONJOUR.TMP
10/31/2001  11:33 AM                152 GALAXY.TMP
10/31/2001  01:08 PM                406 MER.TMP
10/30/2001  01:46 PM                148 AST.TMP
10/30/2001  01:46 PM                148 ASTRO.TMP
10/31/2001  07:08 PM                478 VEN.TMP
              9 File(s)          2,204 bytes
              0 Dir(s)   6,051,553,280 bytes free

A:\>ECHO C:\WUGXP\*.TMP
C:\WUGXP\*.TMP


A:\>_
```

**WHAT'S
HAPPENING?**   Since you changed the value of %TODAY% from
C:\WUGXP*.FP to **C:\WUGXP*.TMP**, the batch file knew to get only the value
in the environment called %TODAY%. To eliminate the value, you must set it to
nothing.

10   Key in the following: A:\>**SET TODAY=** [Enter]

11   Key in the following: A:\>**SET T** [Enter]

```
A:\>SET TODAY=

A:\>SET T
TEMP=C:\DOCUME~1\bpeat\LOCALS~1\Temp
```

```
TMP=C:\DOCUME~1\bpeat\LOCALS~1\Temp

A:\>_
```

You no longer have an environmental value called TODAY. That environmental variable would have been eliminated automatically if you had closed and reopened the Command Prompt window.

12 Key in the following: A:\>**SET TODAY=MONDAY** [Enter]

13 Key in the following: A:\>**ECHO %TODAY%** [Enter]

14 Key in the following: A:\>**SET T** [Enter]

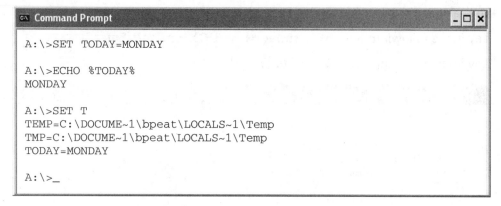

```
A:\>SET  TODAY=MONDAY

A:\>ECHO  %TODAY%
MONDAY

A:\>SET  T
TEMP=C:\DOCUME~1\bpeat\LOCALS~1\Temp
TMP=C:\DOCUME~1\bpeat\LOCALS~1\Temp
TODAY=MONDAY

A:\>_
```

You have set a new environmental variable with the value of MONDAY. You have used the variable syntax %VARIABLENAME% to display the value of the variable. You have also used the SET T command to see any current environment variables that begin with T.

15 Close the Command Prompt window.

16 Reopen the Command Prompt window, and return to the A prompt.

17 Key in the following: A:\>**SET T** [Enter]

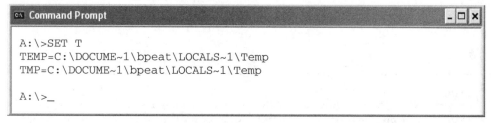

```
A:\>SET  T
TEMP=C:\DOCUME~1\bpeat\LOCALS~1\Temp
TMP=C:\DOCUME~1\bpeat\LOCALS~1\Temp

A:\>_
```

The TODAY variable is no longer there. You can create a useful batch file that you can use during a DOS session. You do not often want to add a directory to your PATH statement, but perhaps you will be doing a lot of work at the Command Prompt using files that are in the root of the A drive. To do this by hand would involve keying in the entire path you currently have and adding your new directory to the end. There is an easier way to do it using the environment. *Note:*   The default prompt is A:\>.

18 Write and save the following batch file called **ADD.BAT**:

IF "%1"=="" GOTO END
PATH > OLDPATH.BAT
:TOP
PATH %PATH%;%1
SHIFT
IF NOT \%1\==\\ GOTO TOP
:END

19 Key in the following: A:\>**PATH > ORIGPATH.BAT** Enter

20 Key in the following: A:\>**ADD A:** Enter

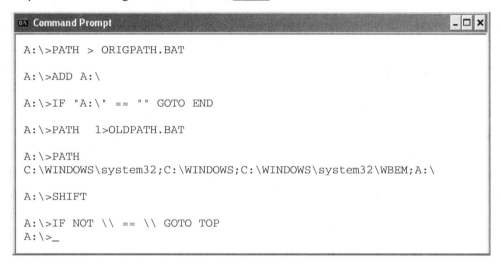

```
 c:\ Command Prompt                                              _ □ ×

A:\>PATH > ORIGPATH.BAT

A:\>ADD A:\

A:\>IF "A:\" == "" GOTO END

A:\>PATH   1>OLDPATH.BAT

A:\>PATH
C:\WINDOWS\system32;C:\WINDOWS;C:\WINDOWS\system32\WBEM;A:\

A:\>SHIFT

A:\>IF NOT \\ == \\ GOTO TOP
A:\>_
```

WHAT'S ▬▬▬▬
▬▬ **HAPPENING?**   To preserve your default path, you saved it to a file called
ORIGPATH.BAT. You then used your new batch file, **ADD.BAT**, and added the **A:**
root directory to the path. You can add more than one directory.

21 Key in the following: A:\>**ORIGPATH** Enter

22 Key in the following: A:\>**ADD A:\;A:\OLDER;A:\CLASS** Enter

```
c:\ Command Prompt                                              _ □ ×

A:\>ORIGPATH

A:\>PATH=C:\WINDOWS\system32;C:\WINDOWS;C:\WINDOWS\system32\WBEM

A:\>ADD A:\;A:\OLDER;A:\CLASS

A:\>IF "A:\" == "" GOTO END

A:\>PATH   1>OLDPATH.BAT

A:\>PATH  C:\WINDOWS\system32;C:\WINDOWS;C:\WINDOWS\system32\WBEM;A:\

A:\>SHIFT

A:\>IF NOT \A:\OLDER\ == \\ GOTO TOP

A:\>PATH  C:\WINDOWS\system32;C:\WINDOWS;C:\WINDOWS\system32\WBEM;A:\;A:\OLDER

A:\>SHIFT
```

```
A:\>IF NOT \A:\CLASS\ == \\ GOTO TOP

A:\>PATH
C:\WINDOWS\system32;C:\WINDOWS;C:\WINDOWS\system32\WBEM;A:\;A:\OLDER;A:\CLASS

A:\>SHIFT

A:\>IF NOT \\ == \\ GOTO TOP
A:\>_
```

WHAT'S
HAPPENING?   You have quickly added new directories to your path.

23 Key in the following: A:\>**PATH** [Enter]

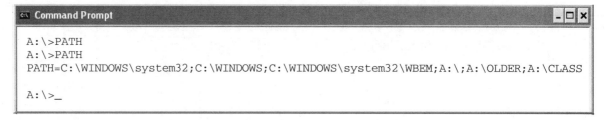

```
A:\>PATH
A:\>PATH
PATH=C:\WINDOWS\system32;C:\WINDOWS;C:\WINDOWS\system32\WBEM;A:\;A:\OLDER;A:\CLASS

A:\>_
```

WHAT'S
HAPPENING?   You keyed in **PATH** to confirm that you added subdirectories. To
return to your original path, you created **ORIGPATH.BAT**.

24 Key in the following: A:\>**ORIGPATH** [Enter]

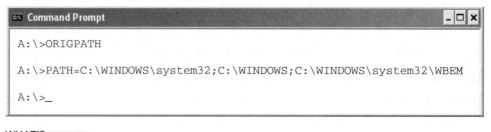

```
A:\>ORIGPATH

A:\>PATH=C:\WINDOWS\system32;C:\WINDOWS;C:\WINDOWS\system32\WBEM

A:\>_
```

WHAT'S
HAPPENING?   You have returned to the original path.

11.24 The DIRCMD Environmental Variable

As has been discussed, the environment is an area that is set aside in memory. In
addition to being able to place and use variables in the environment, you can preset
DIR command parameters and switches by including the SET command with the
DIRCMD environmental variable. Keying in SET by itself will tell you what is in the
environment. You can use the DIRCMD variable and ERRORLEVEL to write a batch
file that will allow you to change the way DIR displays information for the current
command prompt work session.

11.25 Activity: Using DIRCMD

Note: The DATA disk should be in Drive A. The displayed prompt is A:\>.

1 Create the following batch file called **MY.BAT**:
@ECHO OFF
CLS

ECHO.
ECHO.
ECHO How do you want your directory displayed?
ECHO.
ECHO   1.   Files only arranged by file name.   A to Z
ECHO   2.   Files only arranged by file name.   Z to A
ECHO   3.   Files only arranged by file extension. A to Z
ECHO   4.   Files only arranged by file extension. Z to A
ECHO   5.   Directory displays in default mode.
ECHO.
ECHO PLEASE SELECT A NUMBER.
ECHO.
REPLY
ECHO.
IF ERRORLEVEL 49 IF NOT ERRORLEVEL 50 SET DIRCMD=/ON /A-D
IF ERRORLEVEL 50 IF NOT ERRORLEVEL 51 SET DIRCMD=/O-N /A-D
IF ERRORLEVEL 51 IF NOT ERRORLEVEL 52 SET DIRCMD=/OE /A-D
IF ERRORLEVEL 52 IF NOT ERRORLEVEL 53 SET DIRCMD=/O-E /A-D
IF ERRORLEVEL 53 IF NOT ERRORLEVEL 54 SET DIRCMD=

WHAT'S ▓▓▓▓▓
▓▓▓HAPPENING?   You have created a batch file to set the DIRCMD environmental
variable.

2   Key in the following: A:\>**MY** ⌷Enter⌷

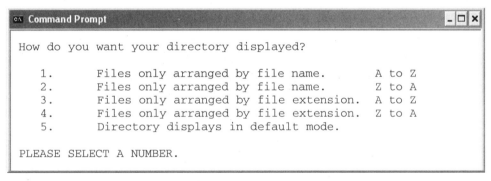

WHAT'S ▓▓▓▓▓
▓▓▓HAPPENING?   The batch file is asking you to select how you want your batch
files displayed. You want your files displayed in file extension order in descending
order (Z–A).

3   Key in the following: **4**

4   Key in the following: A:\>**SET D** ⌷Enter⌷

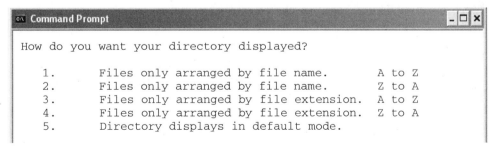

```
PLEASE SELECT A NUMBER.


A:\>SET D
DIRCMD=/O-E /A-D

A:\>_
```

WHAT'S ▒▒▒▒▒
▒▒▒ **HAPPENING?**   The 4 that you keyed in disappeared, but you can see that you did
indeed set an environmental variable. Now, during this Command Line session,
whenever you key in **DIR**, it will automatically arrange the files by extension in
reverse order. You can see that you have established the environmental variable for
DIRCMD to equal the switches /O-E and /A-D.

5   Key in the following: A:\>**DIR CLASS** [Enter]

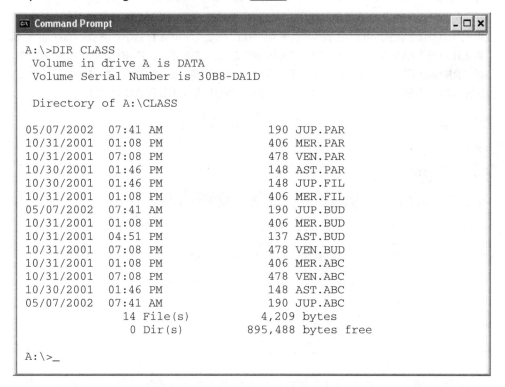

```
A:\>DIR CLASS
 Volume in drive A is DATA
 Volume Serial Number is 30B8-DA1D

 Directory of A:\CLASS

05/07/2002  07:41 AM                190 JUP.PAR
10/31/2001  01:08 PM                406 MER.PAR
10/31/2001  07:08 PM                478 VEN.PAR
10/30/2001  01:46 PM                148 AST.PAR
10/30/2001  01:46 PM                148 JUP.FIL
10/31/2001  01:08 PM                406 MER.FIL
05/07/2002  07:41 AM                190 JUP.BUD
10/31/2001  01:08 PM                406 MER.BUD
10/31/2001  04:51 PM                137 AST.BUD
10/31/2001  07:08 PM                478 VEN.BUD
10/31/2001  01:08 PM                406 MER.ABC
10/31/2001  07:08 PM                478 VEN.ABC
10/30/2001  01:46 PM                148 AST.ABC
05/07/2002  07:41 AM                190 JUP.ABC
              14 File(s)          4,209 bytes
               0 Dir(s)       895,488 bytes free

A:\>_
```

WHAT'S ▒▒▒▒▒
▒▒▒ **HAPPENING?**   The files are arranged by file extension in reverse alphabetical
order. Until you change the values, or close this Command Prompt session, every
time you issue the DIR command it will display file names in reverse alphabetical
order by file extension.

6   Key in the following: A:\>**MY** [Enter]

7   Press **5**

8   Key in the following: A:\>**SET D** [Enter]

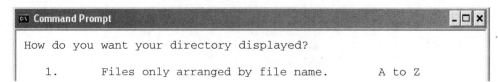

```
How do you want your directory displayed?

   1.     Files only arranged by file name.      A to Z
```

```
   2.        Files only arranged by file name.      Z to A
   3.        Files only arranged by file extension.  A to Z
   4.        Files only arranged by file extension.  Z to A
   5.        Directory displays in default mode.

PLEASE SELECT A NUMBER.



A:\>SET D
Environment variable D not defined

A:\>_
```

WHAT'S ▨▨▨▨
▨▨ **HAPPENING?**   You returned the default DIRCMD environmental variable to its
default value. DIRCMD is no longer defined.

11.26 The FOR...IN...DO Command

The FOR...IN...DO command can be issued at the command line or placed in a batch
file. This command allows repetitive processing. FOR allows you to use a single
command to issue several commands at once. The command can DO something
FOR every value IN a specified set. The basic syntax at the command line is:

```
FOR %variable IN (set) DO command [command-parameters]

   %variable            Specifies a replaceable parameter.
   (set)                Specifies a set of one or more files. Wildcards
                        may be used.
   command              Specifies the command to carry out for each
                        file.
   command-parameters   Specifies parameters or switches for the
                        specified command.
```

```
To use the FOR command in a batch program, specify %%variable
instead of %variable.
```

The FOR command was greatly expanded with the release of Windows 2000 Professional. For full details, see Appendix H or key in FOR /? at the prompt.

The batch file variable is an arbitrary single letter. The double percent sign with a
letter (%%a) distinguishes the batch file variable from the replaceable parameter
(%1). The difference between a variable and a parameter is not complicated. The
FOR statement tells the operating system to get a value from the set you have
chosen. After it executes the command that appears after DO, the FOR command
looks for the next value in the set. If it finds another value, %%a will represent
something new, and the command will be executed with the new value. If there are
no more values in the set, the FOR command stops processing.

If you consider the GOTO label as a *vertical* loop, you can consider the
FOR...IN...DO as a *horizontal* loop. You do not need to use the letter a. You may use
any letter—a, c, x, etc. The parameter value, on the other hand, is set before the
batch file begins processing. Remember, the operating system gets the value from
the position in the command line. The set is always enclosed in parentheses. The
values in the set, either data or file names, will be used to DO some command. The

items in the set must be separated by spaces or commas. You may also use wildcards in a set.

11.27 Activity: Using the FOR...IN...DO Command

Note 1:   The DATA disk should be in Drive A. The displayed prompt is A:\>.

Note 2:   Look at the command line you are going to use in step 1. In English, the command says: Using the variable %a to hold each value in the set (what is in parentheses), do the command (TYPE) to each value in the set (%a).

1   Key in the following: A:\>**FOR %a IN (*.ABC) DO TYPE %a** Enter

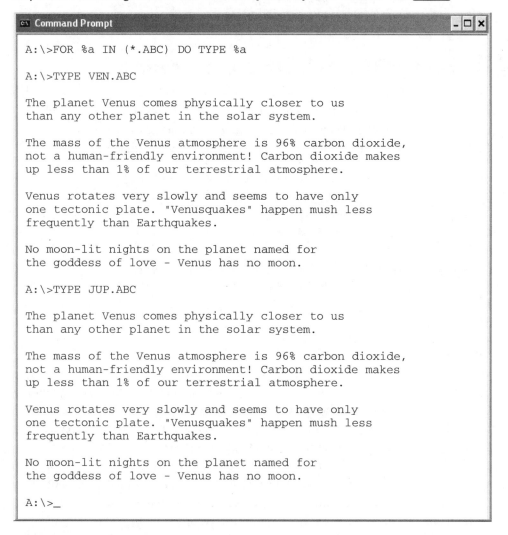

```
A:\>FOR %a IN (*.ABC) DO TYPE %a

A:\>TYPE VEN.ABC

The planet Venus comes physically closer to us
than any other planet in the solar system.

The mass of the Venus atmosphere is 96% carbon dioxide,
not a human-friendly environment! Carbon dioxide makes
up less than 1% of our terrestrial atmosphere.

Venus rotates very slowly and seems to have only
one tectonic plate. "Venusquakes" happen mush less
frequently than Earthquakes.

No moon-lit nights on the planet named for
the goddess of love - Venus has no moon.

A:\>TYPE JUP.ABC

The planet Venus comes physically closer to us
than any other planet in the solar system.

The mass of the Venus atmosphere is 96% carbon dioxide,
not a human-friendly environment! Carbon dioxide makes
up less than 1% of our terrestrial atmosphere.

Venus rotates very slowly and seems to have only
one tectonic plate. "Venusquakes" happen mush less
frequently than Earthquakes.

No moon-lit nights on the planet named for
the goddess of love - Venus has no moon.

A:\>_
```

WHAT'S
HAPPENING?   FOR...IN...DO processed every item in the set as indicated below. Besides using wildcards, you can also be specific.

2   Key in the following:
A:\>**FOR %x IN (VEN.ABC NOFILE.EXT D.BAT) DO TYPE %x** Enter

3   Key in the following:
A:\>**FOR %y IN (VEN.ABC,NOFILE.EXT,D.BAT) DO TYPE %y** Enter

```
┌────────────────────────────────────────────────────────────────────┐
│ ▣ Command Prompt                                        - □ ✕ │
├────────────────────────────────────────────────────────────────────┤
│ A:\>FOR %x IN (VEN.ABC NOFILE.EXT D.BAT) DO TYPE %x                  │
│                                                                      │
│ A:\>TYPE VEN.ABC                                                     │
│                                                                      │
│ The planet Venus comes physically closer to us                      │
│ than any other planet in the solar system.                          │
│                                                                      │
│ The mass of the Venus atmosphere is 96% carbon dioxide,             │
│ not a human-friendly environment! Carbon dioxide makes              │
│ up less than 1% of our terrestrial atmosphere.                      │
│                                                                      │
│ Venus rotates very slowly and seems to have only                    │
│ one tectonic plate. "Venusquakes" happen mush less                  │
│ frequently than Earthquakes.                                        │
│                                                                      │
│ No moon-lit nights on the planet named for                          │
│ the goddess of love - Venus has no moon.                            │
│                                                                      │
│ A:\>TYPE NOFILE.EXT                                                  │
│ The system cannot find the file specified.                          │
│                                                                      │
│ A:\>TYPE D.BAT                                                       │
│ DIR /AD                                                              │
│                                                                      │
│                                                                      │
│ A:\>FOR %y IN (VEN.ABC,NOFILE.EXT,D.BAT) DO TYPE %y                  │
│                                                                      │
│ A:\>TYPE VEN.ABC                                                     │
│                                                                      │
│ The planet Venus comes physically closer to us                      │
│ than any other planet in the solar system.                          │
│                                                                      │
│ The mass of the Venus atmosphere is 96% carbon dioxide,             │
│ not a human-friendly environment! Carbon dioxide makes              │
│ up less than 1% of our terrestrial atmosphere.                      │
│                                                                      │
│ Venus rotates very slowly and seems to have only                    │
│ one tectonic plate. "Venusquakes" happen mush less                  │
│ frequently than Earthquakes.                                        │
│                                                                      │
│ No moon-lit nights on the planet named for                          │
│ the goddess of love - Venus has no moon.                            │
│                                                                      │
│ A:\>TYPE NOFILE.EXT                                                  │
│ The system cannot find the file specified.                          │
│                                                                      │
│ A:\>TYPE D.BAT                                                       │
│ DIR /AD                                                              │
│                                                                      │
│ A:\>_                                                                │
│                                                                      │
└────────────────────────────────────────────────────────────────────┘
```

WHAT'S ▨▨▨
▨▨▨HAPPENING?   There are some important things to notice about these command lines. First, both a space and a comma between items in a set work the same way. Second, the variable letter you choose is not important. In the first case, x was chosen—in the second, y. This command line is case sensitive. If you had keyed in **FOR %b IN (VEN.ABC NOFILE.EXT D.BAT) DO TYPE %B**, the difference between b and B would have made the command line invalid. Even when there was an invalid file (**NOFILE.EXT**), the command line continued processing the other file names in the command. You did not need to worry about testing for null values.

This command works the same when placed in a batch file, only you must use %%. However, it appears that this works no differently than had you keyed in TYPE VEN.ABC NOFILE.EXT.

4   Key in the following: `A:\>`**TYPE VEN.ABC NOFILE.EXT** Enter

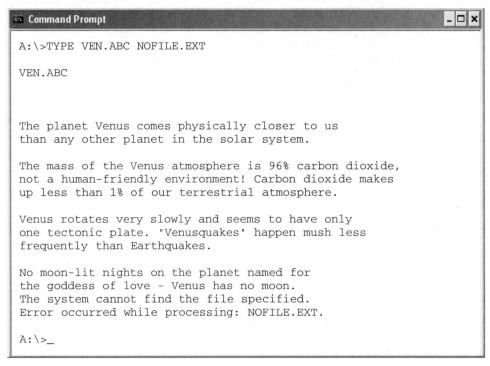

```
A:\>TYPE VEN.ABC NOFILE.EXT

VEN.ABC


The planet Venus comes physically closer to us
than any other planet in the solar system.

The mass of the Venus atmosphere is 96% carbon dioxide,
not a human-friendly environment! Carbon dioxide makes
up less than 1% of our terrestrial atmosphere.

Venus rotates very slowly and seems to have only
one tectonic plate. "Venusquakes" happen mush less
frequently than Earthquakes.

No moon-lit nights on the planet named for
the goddess of love - Venus has no moon.
The system cannot find the file specified.
Error occurred while processing: NOFILE.EXT

A:\>_
```

WHAT'S
HAPPENING?   You see an error message since NOFILE.EXT does not exist. You can use a test to test for an existence of a file in conjunction with the FOR...IN...DO so that the TYPE command will only display the files it finds and will not display any error messages.

5   Key in the following: `A:\>`
FOR %a IN (VEN.ABC,NOFILE) DO IF EXIST %a TYPE %a Enter

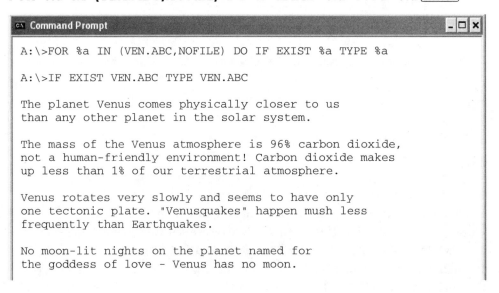

```
A:\>FOR %a IN (VEN.ABC,NOFILE) DO IF EXIST %a TYPE %a

A:\>IF EXIST VEN.ABC TYPE VEN.ABC

The planet Venus comes physically closer to us
than any other planet in the solar system.

The mass of the Venus atmosphere is 96% carbon dioxide,
not a human-friendly environment! Carbon dioxide makes
up less than 1% of our terrestrial atmosphere.

Venus rotates very slowly and seems to have only
one tectonic plate. "Venusquakes" happen mush less
frequently than Earthquakes.

No moon-lit nights on the planet named for
the goddess of love - Venus has no moon.
```

```
A:\>IF EXIST NOFILE TYPE NOFILE

A:\>_
```

WHAT'S HAPPENING?   Now that you checked to see if there is a file, you no longer see the error message. You can also test for character strings supplied in the set.

6   Create and save the following batch file called **DO.BAT** and key in the following:
FOR %%v IN (Patty Nicki Sandy Brian) DO ECHO %%v

7   Key in the following: A:\>**DO** Enter

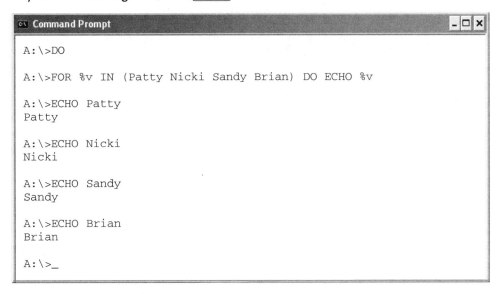

```
Command Prompt                                           _ □ ×

A:\>DO

A:\>FOR %v IN (Patty Nicki Sandy Brian) DO ECHO %v

A:\>ECHO Patty
Patty

A:\>ECHO Nicki
Nicki

A:\>ECHO Sandy
Sandy

A:\>ECHO Brian
Brian

A:\>_
```

WHAT'S HAPPENING?   As you can see, the ECHO command was carried out for each item in the set. It substituted each value (**Patty**, **Nicki**, **Sandy**, and **Brian**) for the replaceable parameter in the ECHO command. In this example, spaces were used to separate the values, but you could have also used commas. The advantage to using this command is that you do not have to write it with a command on each line, as in:

ECHO Patty
ECHO Nicki
ECHO Sandy
ECHO Brian

Another advantage of the FOR...IN...DO method is that you can set values in the environment and then use them in a batch file.

8   Write and save a batch file called **PASS.BAT** and key in the following:
FOR %%a IN (%USERS%) DO IF "%1"=="%%a" GOTO OKAY Enter
:NO Enter
ECHO You, %1, are NOT allowed in the system. Enter
GOTO END Enter
:OKAY Enter
ECHO Welcome, %1, to my world of computers. Enter
:END

WHAT'S
HAPPENING?   You have combined several features in this FOR..IN..DO statement. You have used an environmental variable in the set (**%USERS%**). The percent signs surrounding the value tell the FOR command to use the environmental variable called USERS. You have also used an IF statement. If what the user keys in is in the environment, then it is a true statement and the batch file will go to the :OKAY label. If what the user keys in is false and not equal to the environmental variable, then the batch file falls through to the next line. First, you need to set the environmental variable. (Use upper and lower case exactly as shown.)

9   Key in the following: A:\>**SET USERS=Carolyn,Bette** [Enter]

10   Key in the following: A:\>**PASS Bette** [Enter]

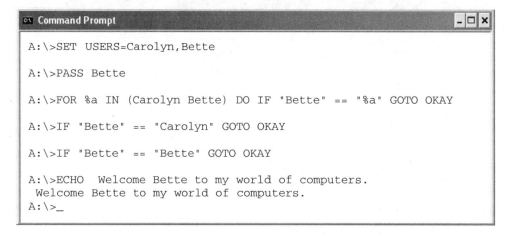

```
A:\>SET USERS=Carolyn,Bette

A:\>PASS Bette

A:\>FOR %a IN (Carolyn Bette) DO IF "Bette" == "%a" GOTO OKAY

A:\>IF "Bette" == "Carolyn" GOTO OKAY

A:\>IF "Bette" == "Bette" GOTO OKAY

A:\>ECHO  Welcome Bette to my world of computers.
 Welcome Bette to my world of computers.
A:\>_
```

WHAT'S
HAPPENING?   You set the environmental values for USERS. You then executed the **PASS.BAT** batch file. It worked as directed because the statement was true. What if it were false?

11   Key in the following: A:\>**PASS Denzel** [Enter]

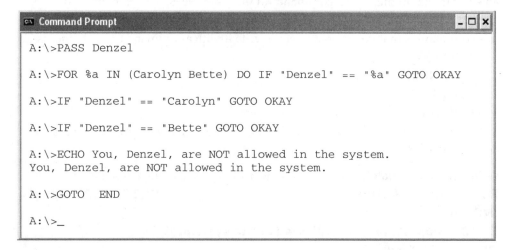

```
A:\>PASS Denzel

A:\>FOR %a IN (Carolyn Bette) DO IF "Denzel" == "%a" GOTO OKAY

A:\>IF "Denzel" == "Carolyn" GOTO OKAY

A:\>IF "Denzel" == "Bette" GOTO OKAY

A:\>ECHO You, Denzel, are NOT allowed in the system.
You, Denzel, are NOT allowed in the system.

A:\>GOTO  END

A:\>_
```

WHAT'S
HAPPENING?   The statement was false and the batch file behaved accordingly. FOR..IN..DO can also be used with replaceable parameters, file names, and wildcards. You are going to take another look at **UPDATE.BAT**.

12   Use any text editor and edit and save the **UPDATE.BAT** file so it looks as follows. Be sure you include two percent signs preceding "v."

```
:DOIT
IF "%1"=="" GOTO END
FOR %%v IN (%1) DO COPY %%v /b + > NUL
SHIFT
PAUSE
GOTO DOIT
:END
```

WHAT'S HAPPENING?   You now can process any number of parameters that appear in the command line. There can be a problem with this batch file. As written, this batch file will copy the newly updated files to the current default directory. Thus, it is a good idea, in general, to place all your batch files in a subdirectory called **BATCH** and set your path to include the **BATCH** directory. If you do not have the BATCH directory on your root of your DATA disk, create it now.

13 Key in the following: A:\>**ADD A:\BATCH** Enter

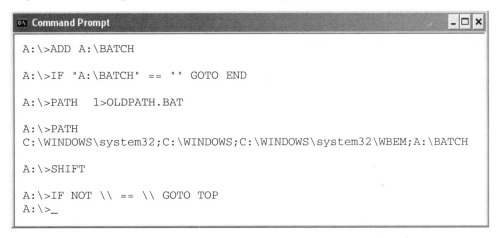

```
A:\>ADD A:\BATCH

A:\>IF "A:\BATCH" == "" GOTO END

A:\>PATH  1>OLDPATH.BAT

A:\>PATH
C:\WINDOWS\system32;C:\WINDOWS;C:\WINDOWS\system32\WBEM;A:\BATCH

A:\>SHIFT

A:\>IF NOT \\ == \\ GOTO TOP
A:\>_
```

WHAT'S HAPPENING?   You have added the **BATCH** subdirectory to your current path. Now you will move all the batch files, as well as the **REPLY** files, into the **BATCH** subdirectory.

14 Key in the following: A:\>**MOVE *.BAT BATCH** Enter

15 Key in the following: A:\>**MOVE REPLY.* BATCH** Enter

16 Key in the following: A:\>**COPY BATCH\ADD.BAT** Enter

```
A:\DCOMP.BAT
A:\ONE.BAT
A:\ALPHA.BAT
A:\ERROR.BAT
A:\SIZE.BAT
A:\GREET.BAT
A:\RENDIR.BAT
A:\KEYING.BAT
A:\TESTIT.BAT
A:\SETTING.BAT
A:\ADD.BAT
A:\ORIGPATH.BAT
A:\OLDPATH.BAT
A:\MY.BAT
```

```
A:\DO.BAT
A:\PASS.BAT
A:\UPDATE.BAT
A:\b.bat
A:\TEST.BAT
A:\EXAMPLE.BAT
A:\D.BAT
A:\S.BAT
A:\BOG.BAT
A:\N.BAT
A:\log.bat

A:\>MOVE REPLY.* BATCH
A:\REPLY.SCR
A:\REPLY.COM

A:\>COPY BATCH\ADD.BAT
        1 file(s) copied.

A:\>_
```

WHAT'S
HAPPENING?   You have moved all your batch files to the **BATCH** subdirectory and you included the **REPLY** files, because batch files use these programs. This grouping allowed you to clean up the root directory of the DATA disk. To ensure that you can use your batch files, you first added the **BATCH** subdirectory to the PATH statement. Then you copied the ADD.BAT file to the root.

CAUTION: If you close the Command Prompt window, you will have to issue the following command to include the A:\BATCH directory in your path: A:\ADD A:\BATCH

17 Key in the following: A:\>**DIR *.SWT** [Enter]

18 Key in the following: A:\>**DIR *.CAP** [Enter]

```
█▀ Command Prompt                                      _ □ x

A:\>DIR *.SWT
 Volume in drive A is DATA
 Volume Serial Number is 30B8-DA1D

 Directory of A:\

10/31/2001  04:50 PM              138 FILE2.SWT
10/31/2001  04:50 PM              138 FILE3.SWT
              2 File(s)           276 bytes
              0 Dir(s)        893,440 bytes free

A:\>DIR *.CAP
 Volume in drive A is DATA
 Volume Serial Number is 30B8-DA1D

 Directory of A:\

07/31/2000  04:32 PM              260 STATE.CAP
04/23/2002  01:01 PM              260 SORTED.CAP
04/23/2002  01:04 PM              260 BYCITY.CAP
              3 File(s)           780 bytes
              0 Dir(s)        893,440 bytes free

A:\>_
```

You can see the dates on these files. Now you are going to update them to the current date.

19 Key in the following: A:\>**UPDATE *.SWT *.CAP** [Enter]

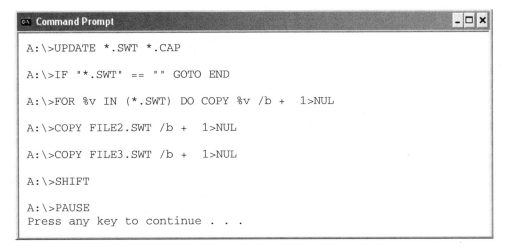

```
A:\>UPDATE *.SWT *.CAP

A:\>IF "*.SWT" == "" GOTO END

A:\>FOR %v IN (*.SWT) DO COPY %v /b +   1>NUL

A:\>COPY FILE2.SWT /b +   1>NUL

A:\>COPY FILE3.SWT /b +   1>NUL

A:\>SHIFT

A:\>PAUSE
Press any key to continue . . .
```

You can see how FOR processed each item in the set, which it got from the command line (%1 was ***.SWT**). Each file that had a **.SWT** file extension was updated. Now the batch file is going to SHIFT and process the new item in the set (***.CAP**).

20 Keep pressing [Enter] until you are back at the command prompt.

21 Key in the following: A:\>**DIR *.SWT *.CAP** [Enter]

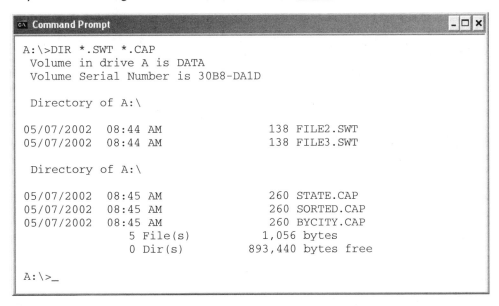

```
A:\>DIR *.SWT *.CAP
 Volume in drive A is DATA
 Volume Serial Number is 30B8-DA1D

 Directory of A:\

05/07/2002  08:44 AM                138 FILE2.SWT
05/07/2002  08:44 AM                138 FILE3.SWT

 Directory of A:\

05/07/2002  08:45 AM                260 STATE.CAP
05/07/2002  08:45 AM                260 SORTED.CAP
05/07/2002  08:45 AM                260 BYCITY.CAP
               5 File(s)        1,056 bytes
               0 Dir(s)       893,440 bytes free

A:\>_
```

Your dates will be different, but you have successfully changed the dates of the files using the FOR.. IN..DO command.

11.28 More Features of the FOR...IN...DO Command

Some of the features in of the FOR...IN...DO command are that you may list environmental variables so that they are divided and appear on separate lines, you may use the special tilde operator (~) to perform such tasks as stripping a file name of quotation marks and to expand a variable, and you may also use the /R parameter. The /R parameter is a recursive parameter. *Recursive* means that the command will search and perform actions on all subdirectories beneath it. You may also select specific text from ASCII files.

11.29 Activity: Using the Additional Features of the FOR...IN...DO Command

1   Key in the following: A:\>**SET PATHEXT** [Enter]

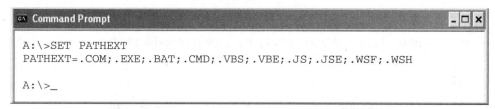

```
A:\>SET PATHEXT
PATHEXT=.COM;.EXE;.BAT;.CMD;.VBS;.VBE;.JS;.JSE;.WSF;.WSH

A:\>_
```

WHAT'S
HAPPENING?   The above list is a list of the file extensions that Windows XP Professional has associated with the application programs on your system. Your list may be different, depending on the software installed on your system. This list is separated by semicolons and appears on one line, sometimes making it difficult to read. You can use FOR...IN...DO to display the list one line at a time.

2   Key in the following:
A:\>**FOR %a IN (%pathext%) DO @ECHO %a** [Enter]

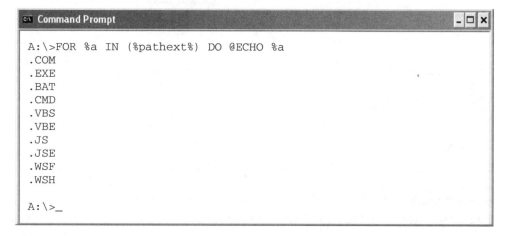

```
A:\>FOR %a IN (%pathext%) DO @ECHO %a
.COM
.EXE
.BAT
.CMD
.VBS
.VBE
.JS
.JSE
.WSF
.WSH

A:\>_
```

WHAT'S
HAPPENING?   Now your extensions are listed one line at a time. Files with spaces in their names provide certain challenges at the command line as well as in batch files.

3   Key in the following: A:\>**FOR %a IN ("Sandy and Patty.txt", MERCURY.TXT) DO @ECHO %a** [Enter]

4   Key in the following: A:\>**FOR %a IN ("Sandy and Patty.txt", MERCURY.TXT) DO @ECHO %~a** [Enter]

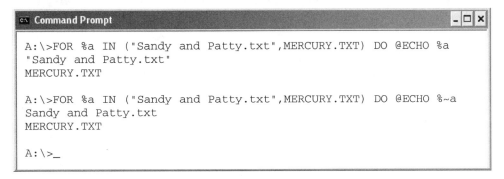

```
A:\>FOR %a IN ("Sandy and Patty.txt",MERCURY.TXT) DO @ECHO %a
"Sandy and Patty.txt"
MERCURY.TXT

A:\>FOR %a IN ("Sandy and Patty.txt",MERCURY.TXT) DO @ECHO %~a
Sandy and Patty.txt
MERCURY.TXT

A:\>_
```

WHAT'S HAPPENING?   In the second command, you added a tilde prior to the variable, a. This stripped the file name of its quotation marks. When you want to add a prefix or suffix to a long file name, you need to use quotation marks. However, if, in the set, you use quotation marks, when you try to rename a file, you will end up with extra quotation marks.

5   Key in the following: A:\>**FOR %a IN ("Sandy and Patty.txt", MERCURY.TXT) DO @REN %a "CZG %a"** [Enter]

6   Key in the following: A:\>**FOR %a IN ("Sandy and Patty.txt", MERCURY.TXT) DO @ECHO %~a** [Enter]

7   Key in the following: A:\>**DIR CZG*.*** [Enter]

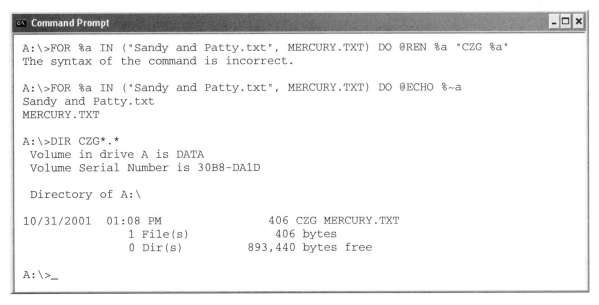

```
A:\>FOR %a IN ("Sandy and Patty.txt", MERCURY.TXT) DO @REN %a "CZG %a"
The syntax of the command is incorrect.

A:\>FOR %a IN ("Sandy and Patty.txt", MERCURY.TXT) DO @ECHO %~a
Sandy and Patty.txt
MERCURY.TXT

A:\>DIR CZG*.*
 Volume in drive A is DATA
 Volume Serial Number is 30B8-DA1D

 Directory of A:\

10/31/2001  01:08 PM                 406 CZG MERCURY.TXT
               1 File(s)            406 bytes
               0 Dir(s)       893,440 bytes free

A:\>_
```

WHAT'S HAPPENING?   The file name with quotation marks did not get renamed because the syntax was incorrect. You had too many quotation marks.

8   Key in the following: A:\>**DEL CZG*.*** [Enter]

9   Key in the following (do not press [Enter] until you see [Enter]):
A:\>**FOR %a IN ("Sandy and Patty.txt", JUPITER.TXT) DO REN %a "Brian %~a"** [Enter]

```
A:\>DEL CZG*.*

A:\>FOR %a IN  ("Sandy and Patty.txt", JUPITER.TXT) DO REN %a "Brian %~a"

A:\>REN "Sandy and Patty.txt" "Brian Sandy and Patty.txt"

A:\>REN JUPITER.TXT "Brian JUPITER.TXT"

A:\>_
```

WHAT'S HAPPENING?   Because you stripped out the quotation marks, you could successfully rename your files. In step 10, overwrite the files, if necessary.

10 Key in the following: A:\>**COPY C:\WUGXP*.TXT TRIP** [Enter]

11 Key in the following:
A:\>**FOR /R %a IN (*SANDY*.*) DO @ECHO %a** [Enter]

12 Key in the following:
A:\>**FOR /R %a IN (*SANDY*.*) DO @ECHO %~nxa** [Enter]

```
A:\>COPY C:\WUGXP\*.TXT TRIP
C:\WUGXP\ASTRO.TXT
C:\WUGXP\BORN.TXT
C:\WUGXP\DANCES.TXT
C:\WUGXP\HELLO.TXT
C:\WUGXP\Sandy and Patty.txt
C:\WUGXP\TITAN.TXT
C:\WUGXP\Sandy and Nicki.txt
C:\WUGXP\LONGFILENAME.TXT
C:\WUGXP\JUPITER.TXT
C:\WUGXP\LONGFILENAMED.TXT
C:\WUGXP\GALAXY.TXT
C:\WUGXP\LONGFILENAMING.TXT
C:\WUGXP\MERCURY.TXT
C:\WUGXP\PLANETS.TXT
C:\WUGXP\VENUS.TXT
        15 file(s) copied.

A:\>FOR /R %a IN (*SANDY*.*) DO @ECHO %a
A:\Brian Sandy and Patty.txt
A:\Sandy and Nicki.txt
A:\TRIP\Sandy and Patty.txt
A:\TRIP\Sandy and Nicki.txt
A:\OLDER\Sandy and Patty.txt
A:\OLDER\Sandy and Nicki.txt

A:\>FOR /R %a IN (*SANDY*.*) DO @ECHO %~nxa
Brian Sandy and Patty.txt
Sandy and Nicki.txt
Sandy and Patty.txt
Sandy and Nicki.txt
Sandy and Patty.txt
```

```
Sandy and Nicki.txt

A:\>_
```

WHAT'S ▓▓▓▓▓
▓▓▓▓ HAPPENING?   You copied files to the **TRIP** directory. You then looked for those files that contained "SANDY" in the filename. The /R parameter searched all the directories on your disk. However, it showed you the entire path name. If you want to use commands such as REN, you need *only* the file name. The options preceded by the tilde allowed you to do so. The *n* forces the variable to expand to only the file name whereas the *x* forces the expansion only of the file extension. You can use these features to write a batch file that will allow you to precede any file name with any prefix you wish.

13 In your batch file directory, create the following batch file called **PREFIX.BAT**. Remember that in a batch file, variable names need to be preceded by two percent signs. Use your name instead of "YourNameHere."

@ECHO OFF
REM YourNameHere
REM Purpose of batch file is to add a new prefix to any file name.
IF "%1"=="" GOTO MESSAGE
IF "%2"=="" GOTO MESSAGE2
FOR /R %%a IN (%2) DO REN "%%~a" "%1 %%~nxa"
GOTO END
:MESSAGE
ECHO You must include a prefix you wish to use.
ECHO Syntax is PREFIX prefix filename
GOTO END
:MESSAGE2
ECHO You must include a file name you wish to rename.
ECHO Syntax is PREFIX prefix filename
:END

14 Be sure that the **BATCH** directory is in your path. You can use **ADD.BAT** to include it.

15 Be sure you are in the root of A:\. Key in the following:
    A:\>**DIR Sandy*.* /S** Enter

```
A:\>DIR Sandy*.* /S
 Volume in drive A is DATA
 Volume Serial Number is 30B8-DA1D

 Directory of A:\

11/16/2000  12:00 PM                 53 Sandy and Nicki.txt
               1 File(s)             53 bytes

 Directory of A:\TRIP

11/16/2000  12:00 PM                 59 Sandy and Patty.txt
11/16/2000  12:00 PM                 53 Sandy and Nicki.txt
               2 File(s)            112 bytes
```

```
Directory of A:\OLDER

11/16/2000  12:00 PM                59 Sandy and Patty.txt
11/16/2000  12:00 PM                53 Sandy and Nicki.txt
               2 File(s)           112 bytes

     Total Files Listed:
               5 File(s)           277 bytes
               0 Dir(s)        883,200 bytes free

A:\>_
```

WHAT'S HAPPENING?   You have five files that have SANDY as the first characters in their names, one in the root of A and the others in a subdirectory called **TRIP** and the others in the OLDER directory. You are going to modify those files so that their names will be preceded by RBP.

16 Key in the following: A:\>**PREFIX RBP SANDY*** [Enter]

17 Key in the following: A:\>**DIR SANDY* /S** [Enter]

18 Key in the following: A:\>**DIR RBP* /S** [Enter]

```
┌─────────────────────────────────────────────────────────────────────┐
│ ▀ Command Prompt                                            _ □ x    │
├─────────────────────────────────────────────────────────────────────┤
│                                                                       │
│ A:\>PREFIX   RBP   SANDY*                                             │
│                                                                       │
│ A:\>DIR SANDY* /S                                                     │
│  Volume in drive A is DATA                                            │
│  Volume Serial Number is 30B8-DA1D                                    │
│ File Not Found                                                        │
│                                                                       │
│ A:\>DIR RBP* /S                                                       │
│  Volume in drive A is DATA                                            │
│  Volume Serial Number is 30B8-DA1D                                    │
│                                                                       │
│  Directory of A:\                                                     │
│                                                                       │
│ 11/16/2000  12:00 PM                53 RBP Sandy and Nicki.txt        │
│                1 File(s)            53 bytes                          │
│                                                                       │
│  Directory of A:\TRIP                                                 │
│                                                                       │
│ 11/16/2000  12:00 PM                59 RBP Sandy and Patty.txt        │
│ 11/16/2000  12:00 PM                53 RBP Sandy and Nicki.txt        │
│                2 File(s)           112 bytes                          │
│                                                                       │
│  Directory of A:\OLDER                                                │
│                                                                       │
│ 11/16/2000  12:00 PM                59 RBP Sandy and Patty.txt        │
│ 11/16/2000  12:00 PM                53 RBP Sandy and Nicki.txt        │
│                2 File(s)           112 bytes                          │
│                                                                       │
│      Total Files Listed:                                             │
│                5 File(s)           277 bytes                          │
│                0 Dir(s)        883,200 bytes free                     │
│                                                                       │
│ A:\>_                                                                 │
│                                                                       │
└─────────────────────────────────────────────────────────────────────┘
```

WHAT'S ▒▒▒▒▒ HAPPENING? You successfully renamed your files. You may also strip out specific fields in a text file. The FOR command also allows you to use the /F parameter. The /F parameter allows you to extract specific data from a text file. It lets you set the rules by which you will extract the data. The basic syntax is:

```
FOR /F "USERBACKQ=option TOKENS=list" %%variable IN ("set")
DO command
```

Using USERBACKQ, you may specify what delimiter you are going to use. If you do not specify a delimiter, then spaces or tabs are used. The TOKENS is a series of numbers telling the command which token on the text line is to be assigned the next %%variable.

19 Create the following batch file called **PERSON.BAT** in the **BATCH** directory:
@ECHO OFF
FOR /F "tokens=1,2,7" %%a IN (%1) DO ECHO %%b %%a, %%c

20 Key in the following, if necessary: A:\BATCH>**CD** \ Enter

21 Key in the following: A:\>**TYPE PERSONAL.FIL** Enter

```
Command Prompt                                                    _ □ ×

Golden     Jane      345 Lakeview  Orange          CA  Nurse
Chang      Wendy     356 Edgewood  Ann Arbor       MI  Librarian
Brogan     Lloyd     111 Miller    Santa Cruz      CA  Vice-President
Brogan     Sally     111 Miller    Santa Cruz      CA  Account Manager
Babchuk    Nicholas  13 Stratford  Sun City West   AZ  Professor
Babchuk    Bianca    13 Stratford  Sun City West   AZ  Professor
Rodriguez  Bob       20 Elm        Ontario         CA  Systems Analyst
Helm       Milton    333 Meadow    Sherman Oaks    CA  Consultant
Suzuki     Charlene  567 Abbey     Rochester       MI  Day Care Teacher
Markiw     Nicholas  354 Bell      Phoenix         AZ  Engineer
Markiw     Emily     10 Zion       Sun City West   AZ  Retired
Nyles      John      12 Brooks     Sun City West   AZ  Retired
Nyles      Sophie    12 Brooks     Sun City West   CA  Retired
Markiw     Nick      10 Zion       Sun City West   AZ  Retired
Washingon  Tyrone    345 Newport   Orange          CA  Manager
Jones      Steven    32 North      Phoenix         AZ  Buyer
Smith      David     120 Collins   Orange          CA  Chef
Babchuk    Walter    12 View       Thousand Oaks   CA  President
Babchuk    Deana     12 View       Thousand Oaks   CA  Housewife
Jones      Cleo      355 Second    Ann Arbor       MI  Clerk
Gonzales   Antonio   40 Northern   Ontario         CA  Engineer
JONES      JERRY     244 East      Mission Viejo   CA  Systems Analyst
Lo         Ophelia   1213 Wick     Phoenix         AZ  Writer
Jones      Ervin     15 Fourth     Santa Cruz      CA  Banker
Perez      Sergio    134 Seventh   Ann Arbor       MI  Editor
Yuan       Suelin    56 Twin Leaf  Orange          CA  Artist
Markiw     Nicholas  12 Fifth      Glendale        AZ  Engineer
Peat       Brian     123 Second    Vacaville       CA  Athlete
Farneth    Nichole   456 Stage     Davis           CA  Dancer

A:\>_
```

WHAT'S ▒▒▒▒▒ HAPPENING? (Some of the file will scroll off your screen.) Here you have a text file. In the batch file you just wrote, you are going to use the /F option. The tokens that you specified are in the first, second, and seventh positions. In other words, you want the first name, last name, and profession extracted from this file. The last name will be **a**, the first name will be **b**, and the profession will be **c**. These are assigned by the FOR command. You will display them so that you see first name, then last name, then profession.

22 Key in the following: A:\>**PERSON PERSONAL.FIL** [Enter]

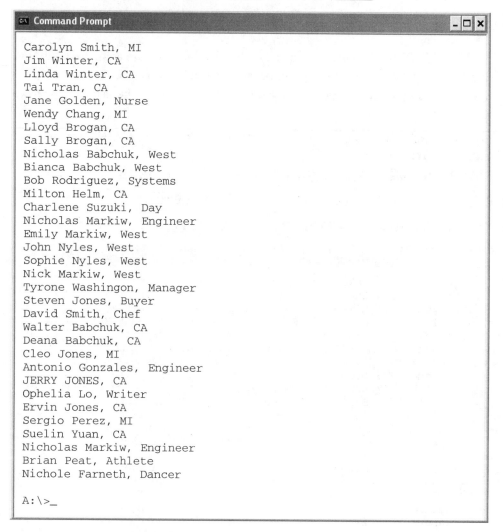

```
Carolyn Smith, MI
Jim Winter, CA
Linda Winter, CA
Tai Tran, CA
Jane Golden, Nurse
Wendy Chang, MI
Lloyd Brogan, CA
Sally Brogan, CA
Nicholas Babchuk, West
Bianca Babchuk, West
Bob Rodriguez, Systems
Milton Helm, CA
Charlene Suzuki, Day
Nicholas Markiw, Engineer
Emily Markiw, West
John Nyles, West
Sophie Nyles, West
Nick Markiw, West
Tyrone Washingon, Manager
Steven Jones, Buyer
David Smith, Chef
Walter Babchuk, CA
Deana Babchuk, CA
Cleo Jones, MI
Antonio Gonzales, Engineer
JERRY JONES, CA
Ophelia Lo, Writer
Ervin Jones, CA
Sergio Perez, MI
Suelin Yuan, CA
Nicholas Markiw, Engineer
Brian Peat, Athlete
Nichole Farneth, Dancer

A:\>_
```

WHAT'S HAPPENING? As you can see, you extracted only two fields from the file. However, they are not all the fields you wanted. You can make your batch file more sophisticated by creating the output in sorted order.

23 Edit the **PERSON.BAT** file in the **BATCH** directory as follows:
@ECHO OFF
SORT < %1 > %2
FOR /F "tokens=1,2,7" %%a IN (%2) DO ECHO %%b %%a, %%c
DEL %2

24 Key in the following: A:\>**PERSON PERSONAL.FIL TEMP.FIL** [Enter]

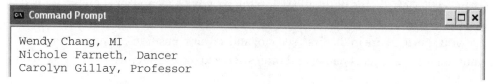

```
Wendy Chang, MI
Nichole Farneth, Dancer
Carolyn Gillay, Professor
```

```
Jane Golden, Nurse
Antonio Gonzales, Engineer
Milton Helm, CA
Cleo Jones, MI
Ervin Jones, CA
JERRY JONES, CA
Steven Jones, Buyer
Ophelia Lo, Writer
Emily Markiw, West
Nicholas Markiw, Engineer
Nicholas Markiw, Engineer
Nick Markiw, West
Kathryn Maurdeff, MI
Sonia Maurdeff, MI
John Nyles, West
Sophie Nyles, West
Frank Panezich, Teacher
Brian Peat, Athlete
Sergio Perez, MI
Bob Rodriguez, Systems
Carolyn Smith, MI
David Smith, Chef
Gregory Smith, MI
Charlene Suzuki, Day
Tai Tran, CA
Steven Tuttle, CA
Tyrone Washingon, Manager
Jim Winter, CA
Linda Winter, CA
Suelin Yuan, CA

A:\>_
```

WHAT'S HAPPENING?   You have a sorted list of people and their professions. However, there is still a problem. Many of the lines have the state listed instead of the profession. The batch file you wrote looks at a space as a delimiter. If you looked at the original data, the seventh position varies, depending on the number of words in the address.

DATA	Yuan	Suelin	56	Twin	Leaf	Orange	CA	Artist	Position
	1	2	3	4		5	6	7	8

The problem here is the data. You can alter the data and choose a delimiter that will set off the fields as actual fields.

25 Open the text editor. Split the screen. With the cursor in the top screen, open **PERSONAL.FIL**. Select the first five lines. Copy them into the bottom screen. Save the new file as **SHORT.FIL**.

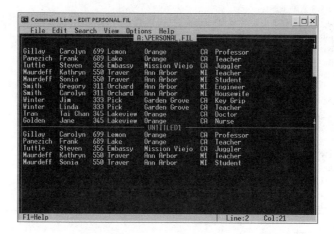

WHAT'S
HAPPENING?   You have a smaller sample of data.

26 Exit Edit and key in the following:

A:\>**PERSON SHORT.FIL TEMP.FIL** Enter

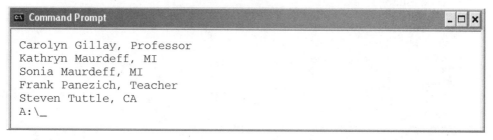

WHAT'S
HAPPENING?   You are still not getting the results that you want. You are going to edit the file, using semicolons to separate the fields.

27 Edit the **SHORT.FIL** file as follows:

Gillay;Carolyn;699 Lemon;Orange;CA;Professor

Panezich;Frank;689 Lake;Orange;CA;Teacher

Tuttle;Steven;356 Embassy;Mission Viejo;CA;Juggler

Maurdeff;Kathryn;550 Traver;Ann Arbor;MI;Teacher

Maurdeff;Sonia;550 Traver;Ann Arbor;MI;Student

Note: A simple way to do this is to place a semicolon at the end of each field, as shown below,

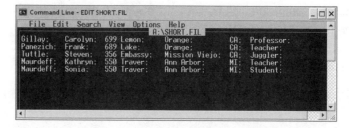

then use Replace on the Search menu to replace a space with nothing,

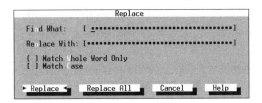

and Replace All and Save your file. Then put a space back between "Ann" and "Arbor" in the two occurrences of "AnnArbor" and between "Mission" and "Viejo" in the one occurrence of "MissionViejo."

WHAT'S
▒▒HAPPENING?   You now have a delimited file. Each field is set off with a semicolon. You could have used any character. If you had used commas, it would be considered a comma-delimited file. But you have to alter your batch file so that it knows that the character you selected is a semicolon. Note that tokens change from 1,2,7 to 1,2,6.

28 Close **SHORT.FIL**, then edit **PERSON.BAT** so it looks as follows:
@ECHO OFF
SORT < %1 > %2
FOR /F "usebackq delims=; tokens=1,2,6" %%a IN (%2) DO ECHO %%b %%a, %%c
DEL %2
Note: When entering the third line (beginning with "FOR"), do not press the [Enter] key until after %%c.

WHAT'S
▒▒HAPPENING?   The statement "usebackq delims" stated that you were going to use the ; as your delimiter. You also had to change the token. The last token is now 6, not 7.

29 Key in the following: A:\>**PERSON SHORT.FIL TEMP.FIL** [Enter]

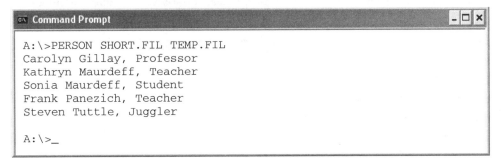

```
A:\>PERSON SHORT.FIL TEMP.FIL
Carolyn Gillay, Professor
Kathryn Maurdeff, Teacher
Sonia Maurdeff, Student
Frank Panezich, Teacher
Steven Tuttle, Juggler

A:\>_
```

WHAT'S
▒▒HAPPENING?   Your data is delimited, and your output is displayed the way you want it.

11.30 The CALL Command

You sometimes need to be able to execute one batch file from within another. If the second batch file is the last line in the original batch file, there is no problem. The second batch file is "invoked" from the first batch file. But invoking a second batch file, executing it, and upon completion of the second file, returning to the first batch file, is not so simple. When the operating system finishes executing a batch file, it returns control to the system level and never returns to the original batch file. There is a solution to this problem, the CALL command. It allows you to call (execute) another batch file and then return control to the next line in the first (calling) batch file.

11.31 Activity: Using CALL

Note: The DATA disk should be in Drive A. The displayed prompt is A:\>. You have executed the command A:\BATCH\>**ADD A:\BATCH** at some point during the current Command Prompt session.

1   Key in the following: A:\>**CD BATCH** ⌈Enter⌋

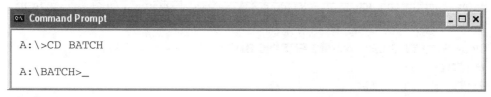

```
A:\>CD BATCH

A:\BATCH>_
```

WHAT'S
HAPPENING?   Your default directory is now the **BATCH** subdirectory. One of the things that you can create is a "noise" to get a user's attention. You can use ⌈Ctrl⌋ + **G** to make a noise. All computers will not make a noise—most do. Although the noise you create sounds like a beep, it is referred to as a bell because in the ASCII character set ⌈Ctrl⌋ + **G** is labeled **BEL**. By using + **G** with ECHO you "ring a bell." Remember that when you see ⌈Ctrl⌋ + **G**, it means press the ⌈Ctrl⌋ key and the letter **G**. When you see ⌈F6⌋, it means press the ⌈F6⌋ function key. Today's computers are very fast— 1.6 GHz is commonplace. The beep sound is very short, and may be difficult to hear. Therefore we will repeat the beep command six times, making it easier for you to hear the generated sound. Even if you cannot hear the sound, you will not get an error message.

2   Key in the following: A:\BATCH>**COPY CON BELL.BAT** ⌈Enter⌋
ECHO ⌈Ctrl⌋ + **G** ⌈Enter⌋
ECHO ⌈Ctrl⌋ + **G** ⌈Enter⌋
ECHO ⌈Ctrl⌋ + **G** ⌈Enter⌋
ECHO ⌈Ctrl⌋ + **G** ⌈Enter⌋
ECHO ⌈Ctrl⌋ + **G** ⌈Enter⌋
ECHO ⌈Ctrl⌋ + **G** ⌈Enter⌋
⌈F6⌋ ⌈Enter⌋

```
A:\>COPY CON BELL.BAT
ECHO ^G
ECHO ^G
ECHO ^G
ECHO ^G
ECHO ^G
ECHO ^G
^Z
```

```
        1 file(s) copied.

A:\BATCH>_
```

Now that you have written **BELL.BAT**, you can execute it.

3   Key in the following: A:\BATCH>**TYPE BELL.BAT** Enter

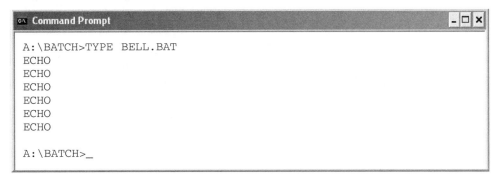

```
A:\BATCH>TYPE  BELL.BAT
ECHO
ECHO
ECHO
ECHO
ECHO
ECHO

A:\BATCH>_
```

Even when you type the file, you hear the bell.

4   Key in the following: A:\BATCH>**BELL** Enter

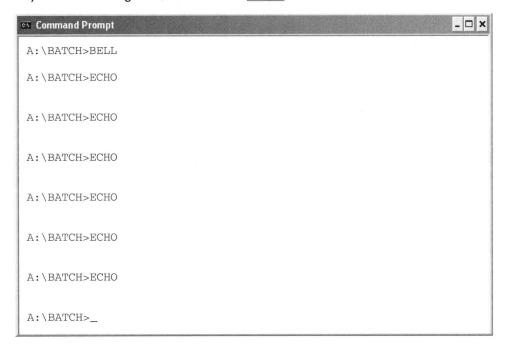

```
A:\BATCH>BELL

A:\BATCH>ECHO

A:\BATCH>ECHO

A:\BATCH>ECHO

A:\BATCH>ECHO

A:\BATCH>ECHO

A:\BATCH>ECHO

A:\BATCH>ECHO

A:\BATCH>_
```

You should have heard the bell beeping or clicking as you ran the
program. Notice, you heard 12 "beeps" instead of only 6. When the command was
read, the "bell" sounded, when the command was executed, the "bell" sounded
again.

5   Use any text editor to create and save a batch file called **BELLING.BAT** in the
BATCH directory. Key in the following:
COPY *.ABC *.XYZ Enter
DEL *.XYZ Enter

BELL [Enter]

(Be sure to hit [Enter] after **BELL**.)

WHAT'S HAPPENING?   This batch file will copy the **.ABC** files to the **BATCH** subdirectory, delete them, and then ring a bell.

6   Key in the following: A:\BATCH>**BELLING** [Enter]

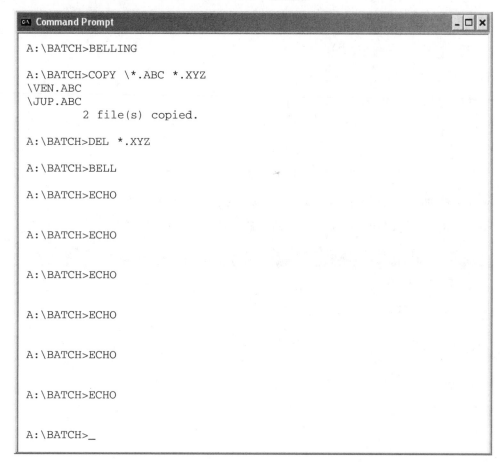

```
Command Prompt                                          _ □ ✕

A:\BATCH>BELLING

A:\BATCH>COPY \*.ABC *.XYZ
\VEN.ABC
\JUP.ABC
        2 file(s) copied.

A:\BATCH>DEL *.XYZ

A:\BATCH>BELL

A:\BATCH>ECHO


A:\BATCH>ECHO


A:\BATCH>ECHO


A:\BATCH>ECHO


A:\BATCH>ECHO


A:\BATCH>ECHO


A:\BATCH>_
```

WHAT'S HAPPENING?   You called one batch file from another. You ran **BELLING**. Its last line was BELL. **BELL** was called and it executed as expected. However, perhaps you would like the bell to sound before the files are deleted.

7   Edit and save **BELLING.BAT** to look as follows:

COPY *.ABC *.XYZ

BELL

REM You are about to delete the *.XYZ files. Are you sure?

PAUSE

DEL *.XYZ

8   Key in the following: A:\BATCH>**BELLING** [Enter]

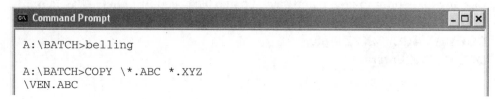

```
Command Prompt                                          _ □ ✕

A:\BATCH>belling

A:\BATCH>COPY \*.ABC *.XYZ
\VEN.ABC
```

```
\JUP.ABC
        2 file(s) copied.

A:\BATCH>BELL

A:\BATCH>ECHO


A:\BATCH>ECHO


A:\BATCH>ECHO


A:\BATCH>ECHO


A:\BATCH>ECHO


A:\BATCH>ECHO


A:\BATCH>_
```

WHAT'S
HAPPENING?   When the **BELLING** batch file reached the line BELL, it called and
executed **BELL**. It turned control over to **BELL.BAT**. Once **BELL.BAT** had control, it
never returned to **BELLING**. Since it never returned to **BELLING.BAT**, your ***.XYZ**
files were not deleted, nor did you see a message.

9   Key in the following: A:\BATCH>**DIR *.XYZ** [Enter]

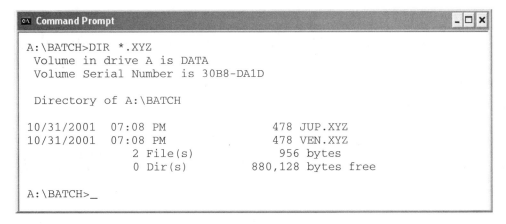

```
A:\BATCH>DIR *.XYZ
 Volume in drive A is DATA
 Volume Serial Number is 30B8-DA1D

 Directory of A:\BATCH

10/31/2001  07:08 PM                 478 JUP.XYZ
10/31/2001  07:08 PM                 478 VEN.XYZ
               2 File(s)             956 bytes
               0 Dir(s)         880,128 bytes free

A:\BATCH>_
```

WHAT'S
HAPPENING?   Indeed, the files are there. This is why you need the CALL com-
mand. CALL will process the batch file **BELL**, but it will then return control to
BELLING so that the other commands in **BELLING** can be executed.

10 Edit and save **BELLING.BAT** to look as follows:
COPY *.ABC *.XYZ
CALL BELL
REM You are about to delete the *.XYZ files. Are you sure?
PAUSE
DEL *.XYZ

11 Key in the following: A:\BATCH>**BELLING** [Enter]

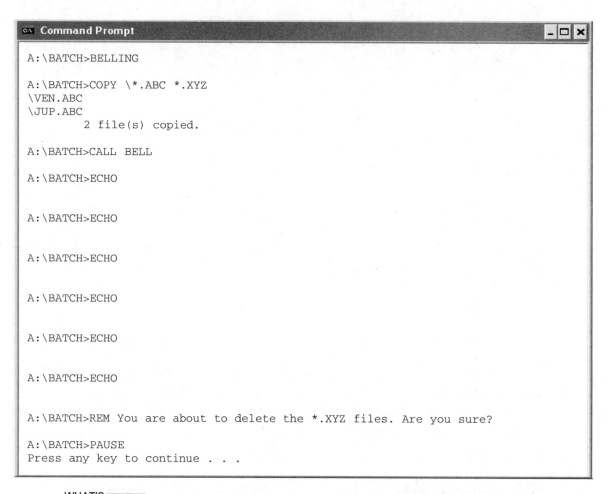

```
A:\BATCH>BELLING

A:\BATCH>COPY \*.ABC *.XYZ
\VEN.ABC
\JUP.ABC
        2 file(s) copied.

A:\BATCH>CALL BELL

A:\BATCH>ECHO


A:\BATCH>ECHO


A:\BATCH>ECHO


A:\BATCH>ECHO


A:\BATCH>ECHO


A:\BATCH>ECHO


A:\BATCH>REM You are about to delete the *.XYZ files. Are you sure?

A:\BATCH>PAUSE
Press any key to continue . . .
```

WHAT'S HAPPENING?   Since you added CALL in front of BELL, the bell sounded. Once **BELL** was finished executing, it passed control back to **BELLING** so that the next commands could be executed.

12 Press **Enter**

13 Key in the following: A:\BATCH>**DIR *.XYZ** **Enter**

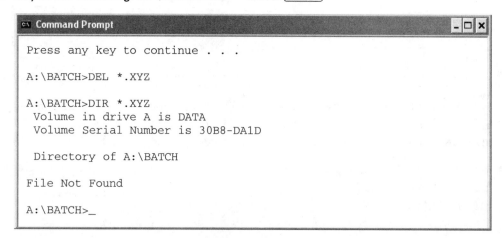

```
Press any key to continue . . .

A:\BATCH>DEL *.XYZ

A:\BATCH>DIR *.XYZ
 Volume in drive A is DATA
 Volume Serial Number is 30B8-DA1D

 Directory of A:\BATCH

File Not Found

A:\BATCH>_
```

WHAT'S HAPPENING?   The CALL command worked as promised. Your **.XYZ** files are gone. A more practical example of using CALL can be seen in the next group of batch files you are going to write. You may find, as you move among directories, that you want to go "home" again. In other words, you want to return to the directory where you were previously. You can create a series of batch files that will remember the directory you were in and return you to it.

Note: In the next file, it is important to press the **F6** key immediately after the command *before* you press **Enter**. Do not press **Enter**, then **F6**. Create the file in the BATCH directory.

14 Use COPY CON to create and save **HOME.DAT** in the BATCH directory. Key in the following:

COPY CON HOME.DAT **Enter**
SET HOME= **F6** **Enter**

15 Use any editor to create and save a batch file called **HOMETO.BAT** in the BATCH directory. Key in the following:

COPY A:\BATCH\HOME.DAT A:\BATCH\HOMESAVE.BAT **Enter**
CD >> A:\BATCH\HOMESAVE.BAT **Enter**
CALL HOMESAVE.BAT **Enter**
DEL A:\BATCH\HOMESAVE.BAT

WHAT'S ▒▒▒▒▒
▒▒▒▒HAPPENING?   The **HOME.DAT** data file you created will create an environmental variable called HOME. The batch file **HOMETO.BAT** that you just created will be used to set the environmental variable to wherever you want HOME to be. The batch file, line by line, breaks down as follows:

Line 1: Copies the contents of the data file to the batch file. **HOME.DAT** now contains SET HOME=. **HOMESAVE.BAT** now contains SET HOME=.

Line 2: Takes whatever directory you are in and appends it to **HOMESAVE.BAT**. If your current directory is **BATCH**, **HOMESAVE.BAT** now has the contents of SET HOME=A:\BATCH.

Line 3: Executes the batch file. **HOMESAVE.BAT** now executes and sets the variable of **HOME** to **A:\BATCH**.

Line 4: Deletes the batch file. Now that you have set the environmental variable, you no longer need the batch file **HOMESAVE.BAT**.

16 Use any editor to create and save a batch file called **HOME.BAT** in the BATCH directory that contains the following:

CD %HOME% **Enter**

WHAT'S ▒▒▒▒▒
▒▒▒▒HAPPENING?   The batch file **HOME.BAT** will change your directory to whatever value is in the environmental variable **HOME** at the time the batch file is executed. In order for this procedure to work correctly, you must include A:\BATCH in your path statement.

17 Key in the following: **PATH** **Enter**

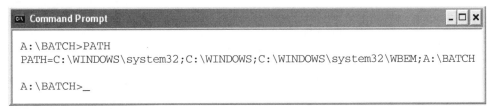

```
A:\BATCH>PATH
PATH=C:\WINDOWS\system32;C:\WINDOWS;C:\WINDOWS\system32\WBEM;A:\BATCH

A:\BATCH>_
```

WHAT'S
HAPPENING?   In this example, A:\BATCH is indeed included in the path. If it is not included in your path, run ADD A:\BATCH before proceeding.

18 Key in the following: A:\BATCH>**SET H** [Enter]

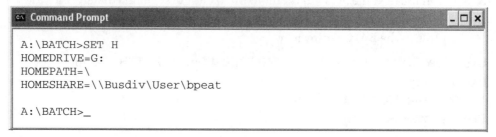

```
A:\BATCH>SET H
HOMEDRIVE=G:
HOMEPATH=\
HOMESHARE=\\Busdiv\User\bpeat

A:\BATCH>_
```

WHAT'S
HAPPENING?   A:\BATCH is included in the path. There is no environmental variable HOME displayed. You are now ready to test "going home."

19 Key in the following: A:\BATCH>**CD ** [Enter]

20 Key in the following: A:\>**CD WORK\ADS** [Enter]

21 Key in the following: A:\WORK\ADS>**HOMETO** [Enter]

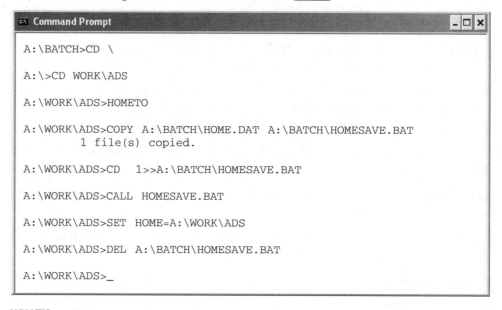

```
A:\BATCH>CD \

A:\>CD WORK\ADS

A:\WORK\ADS>HOMETO

A:\WORK\ADS>COPY A:\BATCH\HOME.DAT A:\BATCH\HOMESAVE.BAT
        1 file(s) copied.

A:\WORK\ADS>CD  1>>A:\BATCH\HOMESAVE.BAT

A:\WORK\ADS>CALL HOMESAVE.BAT

A:\WORK\ADS>SET HOME=A:\WORK\ADS

A:\WORK\ADS>DEL A:\BATCH\HOMESAVE.BAT

A:\WORK\ADS>_
```

WHAT'S
HAPPENING?   You wanted the subdirectory **\WORK\ADS** to be your home directory so you keyed in **HOMETO**.

22 Key in the following: A:\WORK\ADS>**SET H** [Enter]

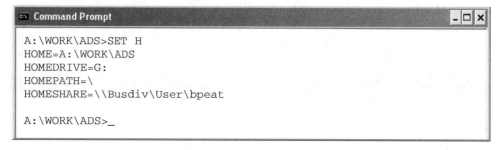

```
A:\WORK\ADS>SET H
HOME=A:\WORK\ADS
HOMEDRIVE=G:
HOMEPATH=\
HOMESHARE=\\Busdiv\User\bpeat

A:\WORK\ADS>_
```

WHAT'S
HAPPENING?   You now have an environmental variable named HOME whose value is **A:\WORK\ADS**. You will go to another directory and then return to **A:\WORK\ADS** by using the HOME command you just wrote.

23 Key in the following: A:\WORK\ADS>**CD \MEDIA\TV** [Enter]

```
A:\WORK\ADS>CD\MEDIA\TV

A:\MEDIA\TV>_
```

WHAT'S
HAPPENING?   Your default directory is now **A:\MEDIA\TV**. You want to return home, which is **A:\WORK\ADS**.

24 Key in the following: A:\MEDIA\TV>**HOME** [Enter]

```
A:\MEDIA\TV>HOME

A:\MEDIA\TV>CD A:\WORK\ADS

A:\WORK\ADS>_
```

WHAT'S
HAPPENING?   You went home—home being the value set in the HOME variable. At any time during the Command Prompt session, you can change the value of home by running HOMETO while in the directory you want home to be, and you can return to it at any time by simply keying in **HOME**.

25 Key in the following: A:\WORK\ADS>**CD ** [Enter]

26 Key in the following: A:\>**ORIGPATH** [Enter]

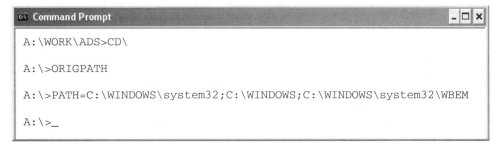

```
A:\WORK\ADS>CD\

A:\>ORIGPATH

A:\>PATH=C:\WINDOWS\system32;C:\WINDOWS;C:\WINDOWS\system32\WBEM

A:\>_
```

WHAT'S
HAPPENING?   You have returned to the root directory of the DATA disk and reset the default path.

Chapter Summary

1. You may substitute a double colon (::) for the REM statement.
2. To place a blank line in a batch file, use the ECHO command followed immediately by a period (ECHO.).
3. The GOTO command used in conjunction with a label creates a loop. The GOTO will process the command following the label.

4. The label in a batch file is not a command, but identifies a location in the batch file.

5. The SHIFT command shifts over command line parameters to the left one position at a time.

6. The SHIFT command is typically used in conjunction with GOTO and a label.

7. The IF command will test for some logical condition. If the condition is true, the command will be processed. If the condition is false, the batch file will fall through to the next line of the batch file.

8. The IF command can test whether or not two character strings are identical.

9. The IF command can test whether or not a file exists.

10. The IF command checks ERRORLEVEL.

11. You may also use IF with NOT. The IF NOT command will test for a NOT condition. If a condition is not true, then the command will process. If the command is true, then the batch file will fall through to the next line in the batch file.

12. You can test for a null value by using quotation marks, a word, or backslashes.

13. To use IF EXIST and to test for the existence of a subdirectory, you may use IF %1\NUL.

14. Many programs set an exit code when finished executing. The IF ERRORLEVEL in a batch file will test if an exit code is equal to or greater than the one in the test.

15. When you use IF ERRORLEVEL in a batch file, the codes must be listed in descending order.

16. When you use IF NOT ERRORLEVEL in a batch file, the codes must be listed in ascending order.

17. You may write programs with DEBUG to set exit codes.

18. You can write programs directly in DEBUG, or you may write a script file that supplies input for DEBUG to create a program.

19. The environment is an area in memory where the operating system leaves messages to itself, including the path and the prompt values.

20. You can create environmental variables that can be used in batch files. When using the variable in a batch file, the syntax is %variable%.

21. The SET command lets you view what is currently in the environment.

22. Environmental variables set in other batch files or at the command line remain in effect only during the current Command Prompt session. When the Command Prompt window is closed, the variable disappears.

23. The DIRCMD command can be used to preset the DIR command parameters and switches.

24. The FOR...IN...DO command allows repetitive processing. The command will execute some command for every value in a specified set.

25. When you use FOR...IN...DO at the command line, the syntax is FOR %variable IN (set) DO command [command-parameter].

26. The /R when used with FOR...IN...DO allows recursive processing. Recursive means that the command will search all the directories.

27. Using the /F parameter with FOR...IN...DO allows you to select specified text using delimiters that you can set.

28. The CALL command allows you to call one batch file from another. When the second batch file is finished executing, it returns control to the first batch file.

Key Terms

debug	environmental	recursive
EOF (end-of-file) mark	variable	scan code
exit code	expression	script file
conditional processing	loop	variable
environment	null value	

Discussion Questions

1. What is the function of the REM, ECHO, and PAUSE commands?
2. What happens in a batch file if ECHO is set to OFF?
3. What happens in a batch file if you precede the ECHO OFF switch with @?
4. What is a NUL device? Why would you use a NUL device?
5. How can you place a blank line in a batch file?
6. How can you create a loop in a batch file? How can you stop a loop from processing in a batch file?
7. What is the purpose and function of the GOTO command?
8. What is a label in a batch file?
9. What is the purpose and function of the SHIFT command?
10. Why is it useful to shift parameters?
11. How can you determine whether or not a file exists?
12. What is the purpose and function of the IF command?
13. Give the syntax of the IF command and explain each part of the syntax.
14. What does it mean to test for a null value?
15. How can you test for a null value? Why would you test for a null value?
16. What is the purpose and function of the IF EXIST / IF NOT EXIST command?
17. Explain the purpose and function of the IF ERRORLEVEL command.
18. What is a script file? How can you create one?
19. What is a scan code?
20. Give the syntax of the SET command and explain each part of the syntax.
21. Explain the purpose and function of the DIRCMD environmental variable.
22. What is the purpose and function of the FOR...IN...DO command?
23. Name two parameters you can use with the FOR...IN...DO command.
24. Describe the purpose of those parameters.
25. Give the basic syntax of the FOR...IN...DO command and explain each part of the syntax.
26. Explain the purpose and function of the CALL command.

True/False Questions

For each question, circle the letter T if the statement is true and the letter F if the statement is false.

T   F   1. The SHIFT command may be used only in batch files.

T   F   2. Environmental variables set at the command line remain in effect until the computer is turned off.

T   F   3. You may alter the way DIR displays by changing the values in DIRCMD.

T   F   4. Keying in SET at the command line shows the correct date and time.

T   F   5. In order to run a batch file from another batch file and then return to the original batch file, you must use the CALL command.

Completion Questions

Write the correct answer in each blank space.

6. In a batch file, to see whether or not the file called MY.FIL is a valid file, you must have the line IF _____ MY.FIL.

7. In a batch file, the line IF "%1"= ="" GOTO END is testing for a(n) _____.

8. You can use the _____ parameter or switch with the FOR command to look at files in different directories.

9. When you key in SET THIS=DIR *.TXT, you are setting a(n) _____.

10. When you use the GOTO command, you must also use a(n) _____.

Multiple Choice Questions

For each question, write the letter for the correct answer in the blank space.

_____ 11. If ECHO. (ECHO followed immediately by a period) is entered into a batch file, it will
   a. display the status of ECHO.
   b. create a blank line.
   c. do nothing.
   d. cause the following command not to execute.

_____ 12. ECHO %PATH% (keyed in at the command line) will
   a. produce an error message.
   b. display the contents of the file named PATH.
   c. display the path for the current session.
   d. display the environmental variables set in the current session.

_____ 13. The following command in a batch file—IF %1none==none GOTO TOP—will
   a. test for a null value.
   b. test for the existence of a file.
   c. test for ERRORLEVEL.
   d. all of the above

_____ 14. A valid batch file label consists of a
   a. percent sign (%) and text chosen by the user.
   b. colon (:) and text chosen by the user.
   c. double colon (::) and text chosen by the user.
   d. any of the above

_____ 15. So that %3 becomes %2, and %2 becomes %1, you must use the _____ command in a batch file.
   a. ROTATE %1
   b. SHIFT %1
   c. SHIFT
   d. none of the above

Homework Assignments

Note 1:   Place the HOMEWORK disk in Drive A. Be sure to work on the HOME-
WORK disk, not the DATA disk.

Note 2:   The homework problems will assume Drive C is the hard disk and the
HOMEWORK disk is in Drive A. If you are using another drive, such as
floppy drive B or hard drive D, be sure and substitute that drive letter
when reading the questions and answers.

Note 3:   Test all of your batch files before submitting them to be sure they work
correctly.

Note 4:   To save a file under a new name with Edit, press `Alt` + F and choose **Save
As**.

Note 5:   There can be more than one way to write a batch file. If your batch file
works correctly, it is most likely written correctly.

Setup

1   Place the HOMEWORK disk in Drive A.

2   Create a **BATCH** subdirectory on the HOMEWORK disk and move any batch files
from the root directory into the **BATCH** subdirectory.

3   Move **GO.BAT** and **NAME.BAT** from the **BATCH** subdirectory back to the root
of the HOMEWORK disk.

4   Create a subdirectory called **CHAP11** off the root directory of the HOMEWORK
disk.

Problem Set I

Problem A

A-a   Make **CHAP11** the default directory.

A-b   Create and save a batch file in the **CHAP11** subdirectory called
DELBAK.BAT that has the following line in it:
FOR %%h IN (*.BAK) DO IF EXIST %%h DEL %%h

____   1. The DELBAK.BAT file will
   a. delete any file in the default drive and directory.
   b. delete any file in the default drive and directory with the .BAK extension.
   c. first check whether or not any files with the .BAK file extension exist in
   the current drive and directory.
   d. both b and c

____   2. If you wanted to use the previous batch file command on the command line,
   what would you have to do?
   a. change %%h to %h
   b. change %%h to %h%
   c. change *.BAK to %h%
   d. none of the above

A-c   Create the following batch file in the **CHAP11** subdirectory and save it as
LIST.BAT:
@ECHO OFF
ECHO.
FOR %%v IN (%PATH%) DO ECHO %%v
ECHO.
ECHO.

_____   3. The **LIST.BAT** file will
   a. display the directory names in the current path.
   b. use an environmental variable.
   c. both a and b
   d. neither a nor b

Problem B

Note: If you are in a lab environment or if your user name has spaces in it,
there may not be a correct answer listed for questions 4 and 5.

B-a   Be sure that **CHAP11** is the default directory on the HOMEWORK disk.

B-b   In the **CHAP11** subdirectory, create and save a batch file called
PASSING.BAT that has the following lines in it:
@ECHO OFF
FOR %%a IN (%USERNAME%) DO IF "%1"=="%%a" GOTO DISPLAY
:NOT
ECHO You used %1. This is not your correct login name.
GOTO END
:DISPLAY
DIR %homepath% /p
:END

B-c   Execute **PASSING.BAT** using your own logon name.

_____   4. When you used PASSING.BAT you
   a. displayed the files in the current default directory.
   b. displayed the files in the root of the HOMEWORK disk.
   c. displayed the files in the root of Drive C.
   d. displayed the message, "You used Bette. This is not your correct login name."

B-d   Execute **PASSING.BAT** using Bette.

_____   5. When you used PASSING.BAT with Bette, you
   a. displayed the files in the current default directory.
   b. displayed the files in the root of the HOMEWORK disk.
   c. displayed the files in the root of Drive C.
   d. displayed the message, "You used Bette. This is not your correct login name."

Problem C

C-a   Be sure that **CHAP11** is the default directory on the HOMEWORK disk.

Note: The following batch file is called **SWAP.BAT**. Its purpose is to allow the user to swap file names between two existing files. If the user keyed in **SWAP MY.OLD MY.NEW**, the file **MY.OLD** would then be named **MY.NEW** and the file **MY.NEW** would then be named **MY.OLD**. However, this batch file has a problem and does not work properly.

C-b   In the **CHAP11** subdirectory, create and save a batch file called **SWAP.BAT** that has the following lines in it:

```
@ECHO  OFF
IF  NOT  EXIST  %1  GOTO  NOFILE1
IF  NOT  EXIST  %2  GOTO  NOFILE2
REN  %1  HOLD
REN  %2  %1
REN  HOLD  %2
GOTO  END
:NOFILE1
ECHO  Cannot find file %1
:NOFILE2
ECHO  Cannot find file %2
:END
```

C-c   If you do not have a subdirectory called **\SPORTS**, create it now. Then copy any file with a **.RED** extension from the **WUGXP** subdirectory to the **\SPORTS** subdirectory on the HOMEWORK disk.

C-d   Key in the following:
A:\CHAP11>**SWAP \SPORTS\LEFT.RED \SPORTS\RIGHT.RED** Enter

____   6. When you used **SWAP.BAT**, you received an error message and **SWAP.BAT** did not work. Why?
   a. You cannot name a file **HOLD**.
   b. The file **\SPORTS\LEFT.RED** does not exist.
   c. The syntax of the REN command is incorrect.
   d. You were immediately sent to the :END label.

____   7. Did any file get renamed in the **\SPORTS** directory?
   a. yes
   b. no

Problem Set II

Note 1:   The HOMEWORK disk is in Drive A and A:\> is displayed as the default drive and the default directory. All work will occur on the HOMEWORK disk.

Note 2:   If **NAME.BAT**, **MARK.FIL**, **GETYN.COM**, and **GO.BAT** are not in the root directory, copy them from the **WUGXP** directory before proceeding.

1   Key in the following: A:\>**NAME** Enter

2   Here is an example to key in, but your instructor will have other information that applies to your class. Key in the following:

Bette A. Peat [Enter]   (*Your* name goes here.)
CIS 55 [Enter]   (*Your* class goes here.)
T-Th 8–9:30 [Enter]   (*Your* day and time go here.)
Chapter 11 Homework [Enter]
Problem A [Enter]

3   Press [F6] [Enter]. If the information is correct, press **Y** and you are back to A:\>.

4   Begin a new Command Prompt session by closing any existing Command Prompt windows and opening a new window.

5   Make A:\> the default directory.

6   Key in the following: A:\>**PATH > MYPATH.BAT** [Enter]

Problem A

A-a   Make **CHAP11** the default directory.

A-b   The following batch file is called **SETPATH.BAT**. Its purpose is to allow the user to add a path to either the front or the back of the existing path. Any number of subdirectory names can be added. When the user keys in **SETPATH /F subdirectory1 subdirectory2** or **SETPATH /f subdirectory1 subdirectory2**, the /F or /f tells the batch file to add the subdirectory name in front of the existing path. If the SETPATH command is keyed in without /F or /f, each subdirectory listed will be added to the end of the path.

A-c   Analyze the following batch file:

```
IF "%1"=="" GOTO DEFAULT
IF "%1"=="/f" GOTO FRONT
IF "%1"=="/F" GOTO FRONT
:ADD
IF "%1"=="" GOTO END
PATH= %PATH%;%1
SHIFT
GOTO ADD
:FRONT
SHIFT
IF "%1"=="" GOTO END
PATH=%1;%PATH%
GOTO FRONT
:DEFAULT
PATH=C:\WINDOWS\SYSTEM32
:END
```

A-d   In the **CHAP11** subdirectory, create and edit a batch file called **SETPATH.BAT** based on the model above.

A-e   Document it with your name and date, and explain the purpose of the batch file.

A-f   Copy the file called **REPLY.COM** that you wrote in Activity 11.XX from the BATCH directory of the DATA disk to the **CHAP11** directory. Then begin the batch file so that you may give the user the opportunity to choose help on how to use this command. The user will press **Y** or **y** if they want help or **N** or **n** if they do not want help. If the user chooses help, provide help on syntax as well as a description on how to use **SETPATH.BAT**. After displaying the description, the user should exit from the batch file. *Note:* The scan code value for Y is 89 and for y is 121. The scan code value for N is 78 and for n is 110.

A-g   Change the :DEFAULT section so that it calls whatever your original path was, rather than **PATH C:\WINDOWS\SYSTEM32** . (*Hint:* Remember, **MYPATH.BAT** is in the root directory of the HOMEWORK disk, created in Problem A.)

A-h   Key in the following: `A:\CHAP11>`**CD** Enter

A-i   Key in the following: `A:\>`**GO NAME.FIL CHAP11\SETPATH.BAT** Enter
Follow the instructions on the screen.

A-j   In Notepad, click **File**. Click **Print**. Click the **Print** button. Click **File**. Click **Exit**.

Problem B

B-a   Make **CHAP11** the default directory.

B-b   Use **SETPATH**, created in Problem A, to add the **A:\CHAP11** and the **A:\BATCH** subdirectories to the path.

B-c   Using as a model **MY.BAT** from Activity 11.XX, create and save a batch file called **DIRS.BAT** in the **CHAP11** subdirectory.

B-d   Document it with your name and date and explain the purpose of the batch file.

B-e   Have the following choices in **DIRS.BAT**:
- Look at directories only, arranged alphabetically by name in the root directory. (Call this Root Directory Only.)
- Look at directories only, arranged alphabetically by name on the entire disk beginning with the root directory. (Call this All Directories.)
- Look at file names only—no dates, no directory information—on the root directory in reverse alphabetic order. (*Hint:* Remember /b.) (Call this **File Names Only**.)
- Look at files only in the root directory arranged by date/time. (Call this **Files by Date/Time**.) *Note:* Do not use date alone in an ECHO line. If you do, you are asking that the DATE command be executed.
- The scan code value for 1 is 49, 2 is 50, 3 is 51, and 4 is 52. If you want to use other key choices, see Appendix C for the scan code values.
- Remove any other choices.
- Be sure no command lines are displayed, only the results of the commands.

B-f   Key in the following: `A:\CHAP11>`**CD** Enter

B-g   Use Edit to modify **NAME.FIL**, changing **Problem A** to **Problem B**.

B-h   Key in the following: A:\>**GO NAME.FIL CHAP11\DIRS.BAT** Enter
Follow the instructions on the screen.

B-i   In Notepad, click **File**. Click **Print**. Click the **Print** button. Click **File**. Click
Exit.

Problem C

C-a   Make **CHAP11** the default directory.

C-b   Check the path to see if **CHAP11** is in the path. If not, use **SETPATH**,
created in Problem A, to add the A:**CHAP11** subdirectory to the path. Add
the **A:\BATCH** subdirectory to the path as well.

Note: The following batch file is called **WORD.BAT**. Its purpose is to allow
the user to key in WORD *filename.ext*. If the file already exists, the user
is immediately taken into Edit with the named file. If, however, the file
is a new file, the user will be told to key in WORD and the new file
name at the command line. This batch file, as written, has a fatal flaw.
Every time the user keys in WORD *newfile.nam* he or she is kicked out of
the batch file.

C-c   Analyze the following batch file:
```
:START
IF EXIST %1 GOTO PROCEED
IF NOT EXIST %1 GOTO NEWFILE
:PROCEED
EDIT %1
GOTO END
:NEWFILE
ECHO  This is a new file, %1. If you
ECHO  wish to create a new file, you must
ECHO  key in WORD and the new file name at the command line.
ECHO  The syntax is:
ECHO  WORD  new.fil
:END
```

C-d   Edit and save a batch file called **WORD.BAT** in the **CHAP11** subdirectory
based on the above model. Document it with your name and date and
explain the purpose of the batch file.

■   If the user keys in WORD with no file name, the batch file should tell the
user what was done wrong and return the user to the system level.

■   If the user keys in WORD filename.ext and it is an existing file, the file
should go directly into Edit using that file name. However, if the file does
not exist, offer the user two choices—either to not create a new file and
exit the batch file or to create a new file and be taken back to the PRO-
CEED label. You will use REPLY and ERRORLEVEL so this choice can be
made. *Note:* The scan code value for Y is 89 and for y is 121. The scan
code value for N is 78 and for n is 110.

C-e   Key in the following: A:\CHAP11>**CD ** Enter

C-f   Use Edit to modify **NAME.FIL**, changing **Problem B** to **Problem C**.

C-g   Key in the following: A:\>**GO NAME.FIL CHAP11\WORD.BAT** [Enter]
Follow the instructions on the screen.

C-h   In Notepad, click **File**. Click **Print**. Click the **Print** button. Click **File**. Click
Exit.

Problem D: Challenge Assignment

The following batch file change is difficult, so do it only if you want a challenge.

D-a   Make **CHAP11** the default directory.

D-b   Check the path to see if **CHAP11** is in the path. If not, use **SETPATH**,
created in Problem A, to add the **CHAP11** subdirectory to the path.

     Note: The following batch file is called **COMPILE.BAT**. Its purpose is to allow
the user to make a list of all the files in all the subdirectories on a
specific removable disk. You will need to ascertain which are your
removable disk drive letters. You obviously will have Drive A but if you
have a Zip drive or CD-ROM drive, you will need to know the drive
letter for each device. Once the user keys in **COMPILE**, the REPLY
command in the batch file asks which drive the user wants to use to
compile a list of files. You will have to use the scan codes in Appendix C
to determine which keys the user may press depending on the drive
letters on your system. The user may also quit once the list of files is
completed. All the information from all the disks that are cataloged is
collected in one file called **TEMP.TXT**.

D-c   Analyze the following batch file:

```
@ECHO OFF
CLS
ECHO.
ECHO Key in a Drive letter to compile a list of files on Drive A.
ECHO Use Q to quit. Use A for Drive A.
ECHO.
REPLY
IF ERRORLEVEL 65 IF NOT ERRORLEVEL 66 GOTO DRIVEA
IF ERRORLEVEL 81 IF NOT ERRORLEVEL 82 GOTO END
IF ERRORLEVEL 97 IF NOT ERRORLEVEL 98 GOTO DRIVEA
IF ERRORLEVEL 113 IF NOT ERRORLEVEL 114 GOTO END
:DRIVEA
SET DRV=A
GOTO LIST
:LIST
CLS
ECHO You are now compiling a list of all the files on Drive %DRV%
ECHO Listing files for Drive %DRV%
ECHO. >> TEMP.TXT
DIR %DRV%:\ /S /A /ON >> TEMP.TXT
ECHO. >> TEMP.TXT
ECHO You have compiled a list of all the files on Drive %DRV%
ECHO to a file called TEMP.TXT on the default drive.
```

PAUSE
:END

D-d   Edit and create a batch file called **COMPILE.BAT** in the **CHAP11** subdirectory based on the above model.

D-e   Document it with your name and date and explain the purpose of the batch file.

D-f   The file TEMP.TXT should first be deleted in the batch file.

D-g   Following REPLY, add more choices for the user. The additional choices will allow the user to choose any removable drive. The user should be able to return to the REPLY line to decide which drive to accumulate more files from. This will give the user the opportunity to either choose a different removable drive, or to choose the same one and place a new disk or CD in it. (*Hint:* Remember, adding choices also means adding more IF ERRORLEVEL.)

D-h   Use the same REPLY in the batch file to allow the user to view the **TEMP.TXT** file on the screen. Remember, the file will be long and you want the user to be able to view the entire file. When finished viewing, the user should be returned to REPLY to either compile more files or to quit. (*Hint:* Remember, every time you add a choice, you must add more IF ERRORLEVEL statements.)

D-i   Key in the following: A:\CHAP11>**CD ** Enter

D-j   Use EDIT to modify **NAME.FIL**, changing Problem C to Problem D.

D-k   Key in the following: A:\>**GO NAME.FIL CHAP11\COMPILE.BAT** Enter
Follow the instructions on the screen.

D-l   In Notepad, click **File**. Click **Print**. Click the **Print** button. Click **File**. Click **Exit**.

Problem E: Challenge Assignment

The following batch file change is difficult, so do it only if you want a challenge.

E-a   Make **CHAP11** the default directory.

E-b   Copy **SWAP.BAT** (created in Problem Set I—Problem C) to a new file called **SWAP2.BAT**.

E-c   Document it with your name and date and explain the purpose of the batch file.

E-d   The batch file should perform as follows:

- When you key in SWAP2 *dirname filename1 filename2*, the file names will be reversed in the specified directory. The batch file will change to the specified directory prior to performing the "swap."

- One of the items you wish to test for is the existence of a directory. (*Hint:* Remember %1\Nul.) If you key in a subdirectory name where a file name is expected, the batch file should take you to a message that tells you that you keyed in a directory name, not a file name.

- If you key in only SWAP2, the batch file will take you to a message that tells the user how to use the command correctly.
- Be sure the batch file returns the user to the **CHAP11** subdirectory.

E-e   Key in the following: `A:\CHAP11>`**CD ** Enter

E-f   Use Edit to modify **NAME.FIL**, changing **Problem C** to **Problem D**.

E-g   Key in the following: `A:\>`**GO NAME.FIL \CHAP11\SWAP2.BAT** Enter
Follow the instructions on the screen.

E-h   In Notepad, click **File**. Click **Print**. Click the **Print** button. Click **File**. Click **Exit**.

Problem F: Challenge Assignment

The following batch file change is very difficult, so do it only if you want a *real* challenge.

F-a   In the **Chap11** directory, copy **SWAP2.BAT** to **SWAP3.BAT**.

F-b   Change **SWAP3.BAT** to allow the user to key in either **SWAP3 dirname file1 file2** or **SWAP3 file1 file2 dirname**.

F-c   Use Edit to modify **NAME.FIL**, changing **Problem D** to **Problem E**.

F-d   Key in the following: `A:\>`**GO NAME.FIL \CHAP11\SWAP3.BAT** Enter
Follow the instructions on the screen.

F-e   In Notepad, click **File**. Click **Print**. Click the **Print** button. Click **File**. Click **Exit**.

Problem Set III—Brief Essay

1. The following is a batch file called **TEST.BAT**:

```
@ECHO OFF
:AGAIN
IF \%1\==\ \ GOTO END
IF %1==LIFE ECHO LIFE
IF %1==MINE ECHO MINE
IF %1==YOURS ECHO YOURS
IF \%1\==\ \ GOTO END
IF NOT EXIST %1 GOTO NEXT
TYPE %1
:NEXT
SHIFT
GOTO AGAIN
:END
```

LIFE, MINE, and YOURS are variables. **MY.FIL** is a file that is on the disk. Analyze this file and describe what will happen and why when you key in each of the following at the command line:

a. **TEST LIFE**
b. **TEST MINE**
c. **TEST YOURS**
d. **TEST MY.FIL**

e. **TEST life**

f. **TEST my.fil**

2. The following is a batch file. The batch file is called **COPI.BAT**. The purpose of this batch file is so that the user may copy many different files to any floppy disk that the user specifies. Thus, if the user keyed in COPY A:*.TXT *.NEW, all the **.TXT** files and all the **.NEW** files would be copied to the disk in Drive A. The contents of **COPI.BAT** are:

IF "%1"=="" GOTO END

FOR %%a IN (a A) DO IF "%%a"=="%1" GOTO drivea

FOR %%b IN (b B) DO IF "%%b"=="%1" GOTO driveb

:drivea

SHIFT

:newa

IF "%1"=="" GOTO END

ECHO copying %1

COPY %1 A:

SHIFT

GOTO newa

:driveb

SHIFT

:newb

IF "%1"=="" GOTO END

ECHO copying %1

COPY %1 B:

SHIFT

GOTO newb

:END

Analyze this file and describe what will happen and why when you key in each of the following at the command line:

a. **COPI**

b. **COPI A C:\WUGXP*.TMP C:\WUGXP*.99**

c. **COPI B C:\WUGXP*.TMP C:\WUGXP*.99**

d. **COPI A:**

e. **COPY B:**

Since most people no longer have a Drive B, how could you modify this batch file so you could use a removable Zip drive with the drive letter of H:?

CHAPTER 12

CONNECTIVITY

Learning Objectives

1. Explain the following terms: client, server, resources, LAN, and WAN.
2. Compare and contrast server-based networks and peer-to-peer networks.
3. List and explain two reasons for setting up a network.
4. Compare and contrast setting up a peer-to-peer network using bus topology and using star topology, and using a hub or router.
5. Explain the purposes of sharing a printer, a folder on a hard drive, and an entire hard drive.
6. Explain the purpose of file and folder permissions on an NTFS drive.
7. Explain the purpose and function of the net commands.
8. Explain the purpose and function of a mapped drive.
9. Explain the purpose and function of the Internet and compare it with the World Wide Web.
10. Explain the role that TCP/IP plays in computer communication.
11. Explain the function and purpose of the Domain Name System.
12. Explain how the TCP/IP utilities can be used to troubleshoot problems.

Student Outcomes

1. Use a network connection.
2. Identify a computer and its workgroup on a network.
3. Share a printer, a folder on a hard drive, and an entire hard drive.
4. Use file and folder permissions, if possible.
5. Use the net commands to gather information about your computer.

6. Map a drive on a network from the command line and the GUI.
7. Use two TCP/IP Utilities.

Chapter Overview

In the computer world, connectivity is a reality. Connectivity can mean connecting to other computers in your home or office, sharing resources such as printers or files on your computer or accessing those resources from another computer, or connecting to resources throughout the world using the Internet. Networks provide these connections. Windows XP Professional is designed for networking; it allows you to network to collect information, exchange files, and share resources.

This chapter introduces the basic concepts and terminology of networking. If you have the appropriate hardware, it will show you how to use your peer-to-peer network and share resources on your network. You will look at a domain-based network to see what information you have access to and how to connect to resources on the domain. You will also look at the command line utilities that allow you to gather information about your network and perform other network-related tasks. Networking also encompasses the Internet. You will be introduced to the basic protocols of the Internet. You will see how the command line provides utilities for you to troubleshoot and diagnosis problems. Again, this will depend on your lab or work environment. If you have the appropriate setup, you will learn how to connect to and navigate the Internet.

12.1 Networks (LANs and WANs)

Today it is more and more common for a small business or even a home to have more than one computer. In this world of so many computers, you will probably want to connect computers together. When you connect computers together, you create what is called a *LAN (local area network)*. In networks, there are servers and clients. A *server* is a computer that provides shared resources to network users. A *client* is a computer that accesses the shared network resources provided by the server. *Resources* refers to the elements that are shared, such as a disk drive, a printer, a file, or a folder. A *server-based network* is one in which security and other network functions are provided by a *dedicated server*. A dedicated server's sole function is to provide network resources.

Server-based networks have become the standard model for networks serving more than 10 users. The key here is 10 or more users. There are many environments that have fewer than 10 users, but would still benefit from a network. Thus, there is an alternative to a server-based network. It is called a *peer-to-peer network*, or a *workgroup*. A peer-to-peer network has neither a dedicated server nor a hierarchy among the computers. All the computers are equal and therefore peers. Each computer can function as either a client or a server.

There are many advantages to setting up a network. If you have only one printer, CD-ROM drive, or Zip drive, every computer in the LAN can use that hardware. You may share an Internet connection among the computers on your network. If you and others are working on the same document, you can access the document without having to copy it to your own computer. If you have several people working on a customer list, for instance, and you can keep that information on one computer, all users can access that information and know that they are working with the most current information. You can set up local email so that you can send messages to any user on the network. If you have notebook computers (portables), you can attach or detach them from the network and update information as you need. If you are away from the office, you can dial in to your network and access the resources you need.

You may also hear the term *WAN (wide area network)*. A WAN consists of computers that use long-range telecommunication links such as modems or satellites to connect over long distances. The *Internet* is a WAN. It is a worldwide network of networks that connects millions of computers.

In order to have any kind of network, including a peer-to-peer network, you must have a *network interface card*, referred to as an *NIC*, installed into a slot in each computer so that a LAN cable connecting all the computers can be installed. One of the most common network cards is an Ethernet card. The card must fit the bus architecture slot you have available. Older desktop computers typically had an ISA (industry standard architecture). Today, most newer desktop computers have a PCI (peripheral component interconnect) slot on a desktop computer and may not have an ISA slot at all, If you have a notebook computer, it most likely has a PCMCIA (Personal Computer Memory Card International Association) slot. You may also get an external adapter that you connect with a USB (Universal Serial Port) cable. The card must support the type of cable you will be using to connect the computers, if you choose a cabled network. If you choose a wireless network, there are no wires dedicated to carrying the network signals. Instead, each computer has a wireless network card, which allow the computers to communicate by radio waves, infrared, power wires in your walls or even by the phone wires in your home. Furthermore, you must consider what design is the most appropriate for your network. A network design is called a *topology*. The two most common topologies for a peer-to-peer network are the *bus topology* and the *star topology*.

The bus topology uses a single coaxial cable and is commonly called Thin Ethernet, 10BASE-2, or Thinnet. If you use this method, you also need *T-connectors* and *terminator plugs*. All the computers connect to a single cable, which is why this topology is called a bus. A T-connector has one end plugged into a network interface card and two open ends (like a T) for connecting the cables that go to other computers. Once the cables are connected to the computers using the T-connectors, each end of the cable uses a terminator plug to complete the networking. Every cable end must be plugged into the network or have a terminator to complete the connection. There can be no end that is unattached. See Figure 12.1.

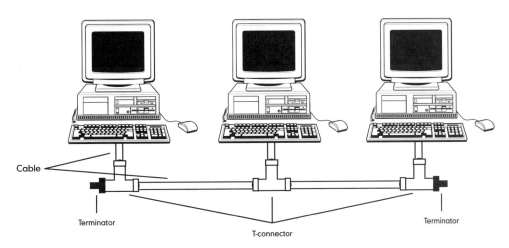

Figure 12.1—A Peer-to-Peer Network with a Bus Topology

The advantages to using a bus topology are that it is easy to install and relatively inexpensive. It is also easy to expand a bus network by adding another length of cable between the terminators. A disadvantage is that if you have three or more components on the bus and one segment of the cable fails, the entire network will fail.

However, bus topology is becoming less and less common. Today, the most popular way to create a peer-to-peer network is to use a hub. This method is considered a star topology. Wireless connections are of the star type. Each connection is like a spoke of a bicycle wheel: one end connects to the hub and the other end connects to a computer or a device such as a printer. There are also two major Ethernet speeds. The original Ethernet has a speed of 10 Mbps (megabits per second). Fast Ethernet, most popular today, has a speed of 100 Mbps. See Figure 12.2.

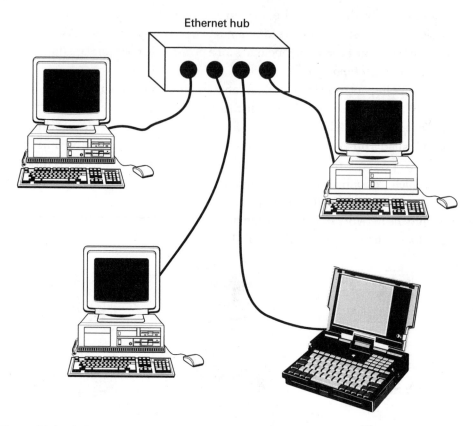

Figure 12.2—A Peer-to-Peer Network with a Star Topology

With a star topology, a single piece of defective cabling affects only the computer it connects, unless it is the hub itself. This kind of problem is known as a ***single point of failure***. Each computer would still work, but there would be no network connection to the computer on the segment of cable that failed. The disadvantages to a star topology include the following: It is more expensive than a bus topology because you must purchase additional hardware, the hub. Expansion of the network may require the purchase of an additional hub if you have used all the connections on the existing hub. Also, the wiring can become unwieldy, especially if you cannot run cable through your walls. However, if you go with a wireless network, then you obviously do not need to run wire. There is a wireless Ethernet standard called 802.11b which is becoming increasingly available and relatively inexpensive. See Figure 12.3.

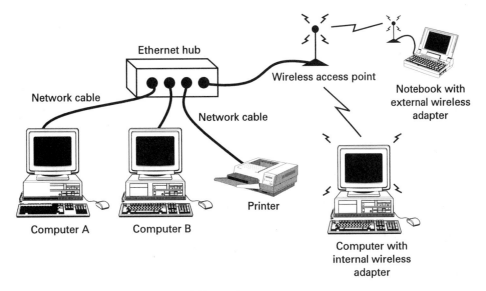

Figure 12.3—A Wireless and Wired Network

With these topologies you can use a networkable printer, or any resource, by connecting it directly to a cable or to a hub. Only the computer that needs to use the printer must be on; no other computers on the network must be turned on. The printer must have a network interface card installed. Most laser printers can have an NIC added, but the common, inexpensive inkjet printers cannot. In that case, the printer must be connected to one of the computers on the network and that computer must be turned on for the printer to be used by any station. Today, most users prefer a hub—basically a box with many connections. You will want at least as many ports as you have computers and devices that you want to connect and you will probably want extra ports in case you add more devices or computers at a later date. Hubs are widely available with 4, 8, 16 or 24 ports. Instead of a hub, you can install a switch which distributes information faster than a hub. And you may even prefer a router, which combines a hub and a small computer that provides Internet sharing. If you use portable hard disks and video cameras, there is another standard to look at—IEEE-1394, also called FireWire.

In a server-based network you must also have software that tells the computers how to communicate with one another. The software is known as a *network operating system (NOS)*. The two most popular network operating systems are Novell NetWare and Microsoft Windows NT. Windows NT, however, is being replaced by Windows 2000 Server or Windows 2000 Advanced Server which is being replaced by Windows .NET Server. An alternative NOS is Linux, a version of an older network operating system, Unix. The server (the computer that serves the other computers on the network) uses this software. In a generic sense, a network operating system is the software you need to make your networked hardware communicate.

You have been introduced to hardware and software. There is a trilogy in networking. The third component is the *network administrator*, sometimes called the system administrator. The administrator is the person who decides how the hardware and software will be used and who will have access to what devices and resources on the network. The administrator also manages the day-to-day operation of the hardware, the network operating system, and the resources of the network.

A server-based network is beyond the scope of this textbook. However, a peer-to-peer network is not. Any computer that is running Windows has the built-in peer-to-peer software to create and administer a small network. A small network still needs the appropriate hardware, software, and administration. In a peer-to-peer network, either each computer can be administered by its user, or there can be a single administrator. The selection of the topology, network interface card, and cable or wireless model is beyond the scope of this textbook. This textbook makes the assumption that these hardware decisions have been made. Many new computer come with a built-in network card. In this chapter you will use a peer-to-peer LAN or a workgroup with the built-in networking software that comes with Windows.

12.2   Looking at Your Network

When Windows XP Professional is installed, it will detect your network card and install the default components. If you add your network later, you may use the New Connection wizard or the Network Setup wizard that allows you to set up your home network. You will have to name your computer. All computers must have a unique name even if they are not on a network. The setup program will provide a cryptic name for your computer. You may override this. Often, a good computer name is the name of the brand of the computer. If you had two computers with the same brand name, you could differentiate between them numerically, such as DellXPS-1 and DellXPS-2. You will also have to enter an administrator password. The administrator password is the most important password in Windows, so be sure to use a secure password as well as write it down and store it in a safe place. This password is what allows you to administer your computer. If you have more than one user on a computer, you will want each user to have a logon name. User names are commonly in the form of first initial and last name, such as Cgillay or Bpeat, or last name and first initial, such as GillayC or PeatB. If you like, you can use your entire name, such as Carolyn Z. Gillay or Bette Peat. Each logon name will have to also have a password. Passwords are case sensitive. Your password should be difficult to guess, but not so difficult that you will forget it. For this reason, you should avoid obvious passwords such as your user name, name, children's names, address, or social security number. Too often a user creates a password and then leaves it on a note taped to the computer—obviously defeating the purpose of any security.

My Network Places is your map to your network. The activities that follow are based on a specific computer configurations. These activities are meant to act as a guide to accomplishing these tasks on your system. You will have to interpret the screen examples to match your specific computer network. The steps given in the activities are related to a specific computer setup. You will not have the same set up. Thus, you will not be able to follow the steps exactly. You may have more or less computers or printers. Your drives may be formatted as FAT32 or as NTFS and so on. This is meant as a guide to how a peer-to-peer network works. You may choose to only read through the steps, particularly when you do not have an equivalent computer setup. You should read through these activities, even if you cannot or choose not to follow them. This way you can see how to manipulate a network. In addition, most schools or work environments do not have the hardware, software, or support staff to allow you to do these tasks in a lab environment. And, in addition, most lab environments are on a server-based network and not a peer-to-peer network. If this is the case, only read the activities, do not do them. In some cases, where appropriate, you will look at your server-based network. Again, what you can or cannot do will depend on your lab or work environment.

12.3 Activity: Looking at Your Network

Note 1:   It is assumed that you have successfully installed the necessary software and hardware.

Note 2:   The activity is based on a specific computer configuration. This configuration is a simple star topology that uses a hub with three computers and two printers. The three printers are part of the BOOKBIZ workgroup. The computer are identified by name. The first is identified as Micron-pc and is running Window XP Professional. The second is identified as Dell-czg and is running Windows 2000 Professional. The third is identified as Dell 8100 (Dell-fp) and is running Windows Me. One printer is a simple inkjet printer (HP Deskjet 895 Cse) that cannot support a network card and is thus physically attached to a Dell 8100(Dell-fp). The other printer (HP Laser Jet 4 Plus) does have a network card and is attached to the hub as well as being physically attached to the Micron-pc computer. Your network will be different and thus your displays will be different.

1   Click **Start**. Right-click **My Network Places**. Click **Properties**. Right-click **Local Area Connection**. Click **Properties**.

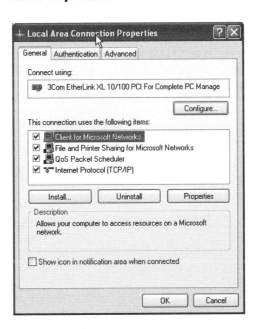

WHAT'S HAPPENING?   The Local Area Connection Properties sheet appears. This computer system is on a peer-to-peer network. When you are on a peer-to-peer network, you have three tabs: General, Authentication, and Advanced. The "Connect using" area shows which type of network card you have. In this example, it is a 3Com Etherlink XL 10/100 PCI. The list box cites what items the network card will use. The first item, Client for Microsoft Networks allows you to access resources on a Microsoft

Network. Its icon is a computer, 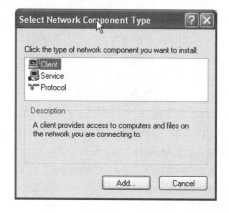, indicating that it is your computer. The next item, File and Printer Sharing for Microsoft Network allows other computers to access resources on your computer. The next item QoS (Quality of Service) Packet Scheduler provides network traffic control. Each of these icons for these items is also a computer but with a hand underneath it, indicating that is it dealing with sharing resources, . And the last item is what protocol is being used. Its icon is representative of a protocol, . You may also choose to display on icon in the notification area on the taskbar when you are connected to the network.

2   Select **Client for Microsoft Networks**. Click **Install**.

WHAT'S
HAPPENING?   There are three types of network component you can install, Client, Service and Protocol. A client allows you access services to other computers on the network. This simply means that when you request access to another computer, you are considered a client that needs service from another computer. A service is work that is provided by a server, When you provide access to your devices or files, you are performing a service to others (clients) on the network. The *protocol* is a set of rules that allows computers to connect with one another and to exchange information. Computers on a network must use the same protocol in order to communicate.

3   Click **Cancel**. Click the **Authentication** tab.

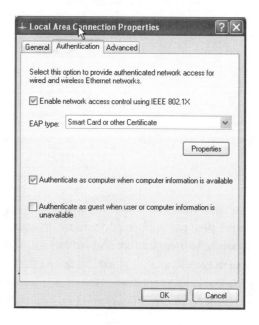

WHAT'S
HAPPENING?   This is the process for verifying that an entity or object is who or what it claims to be. For instance, you would want to verify the identify that a user has access to your computer.

4   Click the **Advanced** tab.

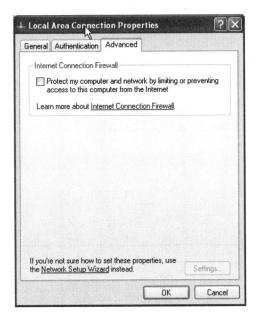

WHAT'S
HAPPENING?   Here you may choose to use the firewall. A *firewall* is a set of programs, located at a network gateway server that protects the resources of a private network from users from other networks. A *gateway* is a network point that acts as an entrance to another network. Here Microsoft provides an Internet Connection Firewall (ICF) which is a specific firewall software that is used to set restrictions on what information is communicated from your home or small office network to and from the Internet to your network. If you are using Internet Connection Sharing (ICS) to provide Internet access to multiple computer, you should enable this feature. If you are a single computer connected to the Internet, this also protects your Internet connection. However, you may have a switch or a router that provides a firewall as well.

5   Click **Cancel**. Close the Network Connections window.

6   Click **Start**. Click **Control Panel**. If you are not in Classic View, click **Switch to Classic View**. Double-click the **System** icon. Click the **Computer Name** tab.

WHAT'S ▓▓▓▓▓
▓▓▓**HAPPENING?**   Here you see the name of your computer and the workgroup you belong to. If you clicked Network ID, Windows would bring up a wizard to help you make a network connection.

7   Click **Change**.

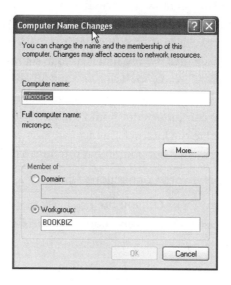

WHAT'S ▓▓▓▓▓
▓▓▓**HAPPENING?**   Here is where you could make changes if you desired. The computer name can be any name you wish, but each computer on the network needs to have a unique name. The name can be longer than 15 characters, but it is best to remain under 15 characters with no spaces. This is because on other network protocols names are limited to 15 characters. Again, for the name of your computer you could use the brand of the computer. But be sure to choose a name that will clearly identify which computer is which on the network. Here, this computer is identified by its brand name—micron-pc.

All computers on your network *must* use the same workgroup name. But a workgroup name cannot be the same name as the computer. The workgroup name must be identical in case and spelling on all computers. Again, you can have up to 15 characters with no spaces. Only computers with the same workgroup name can share resources. In this example, the workgroup name is BOOKBIZ. If you were in a work or school environment that had a domain server, you would click the Domain option button and the domains you could join would be listed.

You would need to take these same steps on every computer on your network. If the other computers were running other versions of Windows such as Windows 98 or Windows 2000 Professional, the steps would be similar but in slightly different locations. However, all of these Windows operating systems will talk to XP and to each other.

8 Click **Cancel**. Click **Cancel**. Close the Control Panel window.

9 Be sure that all your computers are on. Sit at one computer, in this case the Micron-pc. Click **Start**. Click **My Network Places**. Click **View workgroup computers**. Click **View**. Click **Tiles**.

WHAT'S HAPPENING?   You changed the view to Tiles. You see the names for every computer on your network. Be a little patient. It takes some time for the computers to see each other. Each is broadcasting its availability. (*Note:* If you do not see My Network Places or if My Network Places is empty, chances are you have a problem with your network installation, either with the hardware or with the protocols and services. Network troubleshooting is beyond the scope of this textbook. However, a simple mistake that users often make when setting up a network is that they have different workgroup names on each computer. If you are using Windows XP Professional, follow steps 6 and 7 above to make the workgroup the same name. If you are using Windows 2000 Professional or Windows Me, you can also correct this but you need to open the System icon in Control Panel, choosing Networking Identification, and then choosing Properties and ensuring that the workgroup name is the same.)

10 (*Note:* Remember that this activity refers to a specific computer configuration. Your computer network will *not* look exactly like this example.) Double-click the **Dell 8100 (Dell-fp)** computer.

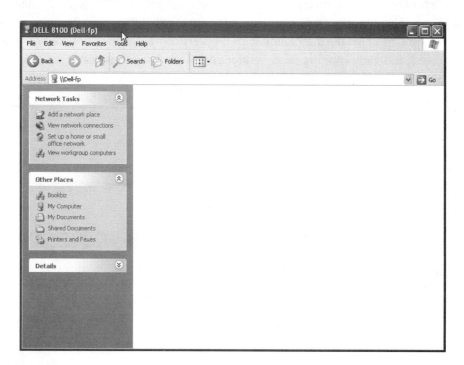

WHAT'S HAPPENING?   Windows XP Professional uses a window like Internet Explorer's. Internet Explorer is a *browser* (a tool to search the Internet). However, the Dell 8100 (Dell-fp) window is empty because you have not shared any of the resources. Also, note the address in the window. The Dell computer is listed as \\Dell-fp. The double backslash is the *UNC* (*universal naming convention*) for locating the path to a network resource. It specifies the share name of a particular computer. The computer name is limited to 15 characters, and the share name is usually limited to 15 characters. The address takes the format of *computer name**share name[**optional path]*. (Brackets are used to indicate items that are optional. They are not actually included in the name.)

11 Close all open windows.

12.4 Sharing Printers on a Network

There are always two parts to sharing resources—the client and the server. The server is the computer that has the resource you wish to share. The client is the computer that wishes to access the resource. The most common items to share are a printer, some other device such as Zip drive, a folder on a hard drive, or an entire hard drive.

When you share a printer, any computer on the network can use that printer. If you do not have a hub, the printer, of course, needs to be connected physically to a computer on the network. That computer then becomes the *print server*. Often, in a large network, there will be one computer dedicated to handling printing, and it will be called the print server. In a small network, the print server is not dedicated only to printing. It can be any computer on the network that has the printer connected to it or a computer that is on the hub. Furthermore, if you have more than one printer, each can be shared. Look at Figure 12.4.

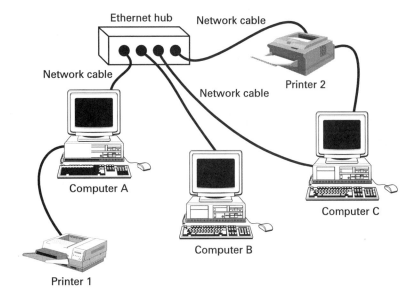

Figure 12.4—Printer Sharing on a Network

Computers A, B, and C and Printer 2 are networked with a simple hub. Computer A has Printer 1 attached to it and Computer C has Printer 2 physically attached to it. If you are sitting at Computer B and want to print, you are the client who wants to use the resource (Printer 1) of Computer A. Computer A, in this case, is the print server because Printer 1 is attached to Computer A. However, Computer A must be on in order for you to use this resource. Printer 1 is not available to you from the hub. Printer 2 is attached to the hub and is a network resource. Any computer on this network can use printer 2 at any time. Only the computer you are sitting at must be on since Printer 2 is always available as a network resource. Printer 2 must have a network card to be attached to the hub and there is special software that will set up this type of network printer connection. If you were sitting at Computer B and Computer A was not turned on, you would not be able to use the printer attached to Computer A. You also have the choice of using a printer *locally*. If you were sitting at Computer A, you could use Printer 1 locally. Locally means without using a network. You could use Printer 1 because it is physically attached to the computer. You would not need to be on the network. In this example, Printer 2 also has a local connection to Computer C. Normally, one connection is all that you would need and you would normally use the network connection. It would be unnecessary to physically attach Printer 2 to Computer C. However, if the network printer software ever failed, by having a local connection, all other computers could still use Printer 2, provided Computer C was turned on and Printer 2 was shared.

12.5 Activity: Sharing Printers on a Network

Note: The following activity is based on a specific computer configuration. Your display will be different or you may not be able to do the steps if you have no network printer. If you cannot do the steps, simply read them so you can learn how to use a network printer.

1   Go to the computer that has the printer physically attached to it (the print server). In this example, it is the Dell 8100 (Dell-fp) computer. In this example, the Dell 8100 (Dell-fp) computer is running Windows Me. You can run different operating system on the different computers on your network.

2   Open My Computer. Open Control Panel. Open the Printers folder. Right-click the printer you wish to share. In this example, it is the HP DeskJet 895Cse.

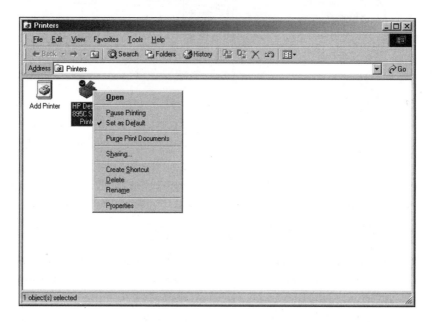

WHAT'S HAPPENING?   In order for others to use this printer, you need to share it. The context menu has a choice Sharing.

3   Click **Sharing**. Click the **Shared As** button.

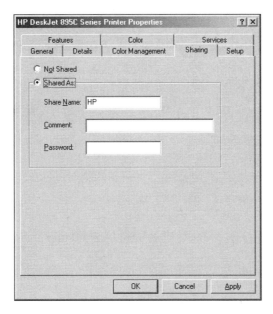

WHAT'S
WHAT'S HAPPENING?   Here you give a name to your shared printer. You again must use the same name across the network and you want the name to be descriptive.

4   In this example, key in **HPCOLOR**.

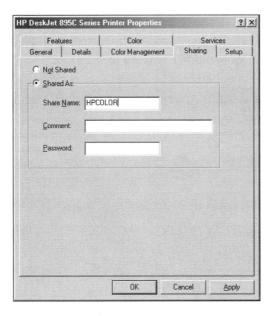

WHAT'S HAPPENING?   You have named your shared printer. If you wanted, you could include a password. However, if you did that, any user who wanted to use this printer would need to know the password.

5   Click **OK**.

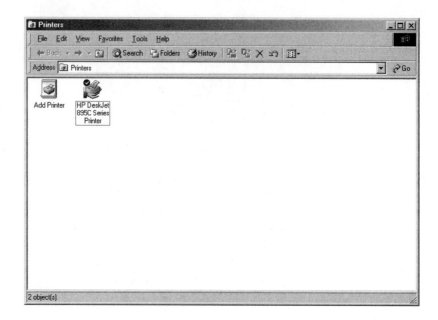

WHAT'S
HAPPENING?   Your printer now has a hand icon under it, indicating that the printer is shared. Now you need to go to each printer client to set up the shared printer. A printer client is any computer on your network that you want to have access to the shared printer. (*Note:* You may need your Windows CD if the printer driver is not installed on the client computer.)

6   Go to a client computer (in this example, the Micron-pc). Open My Computer. Open Control Panel. Double-click **Printers and Faxes**.

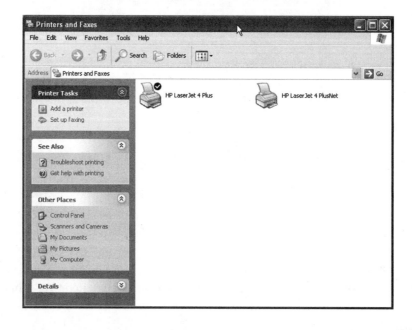

WHAT'S
HAPPENING?   This window has two printer icons. The first printer is called HP Laser Jet 4. This printer is physically attached to the Micron computer. The other printer is called HP Laser Jet 4 PlusNet. This is the same printer as the HP Laser Jet 4. In this example, this is the printer that is "hung" off the network. It has its own

network card and special software that allows it to be attached to the hub and used by the other computers on the network.

7   Right-click the **HP Laser Jet 4 Plus**. Click **Properties**. Click **Ports**.

WHAT'S
HAPPENING?   Your display will not look like this. A port is a connection. The parallel port on your computer is called LPT1. Normally, if you physically connect a printer, it shows up on the port called LPT1. You can see that the HP Laser Jet 4 Plus is assigned to this connection (port) as it has a check mark by it.

8   Click **Cancel**. Right-click the **HP Laser Jet 4 PlusNet** icon. Click **Properties**. Click **Ports**.

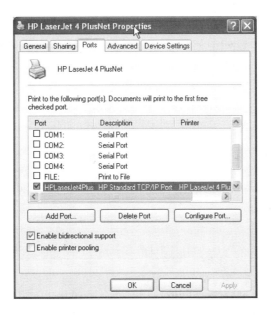

WHAT'S
HAPPENING?   You will not have this display. In this example, the HP LaserJet4 PlusNet has been assigned a new port called HP Standard TCP/IP port with the

printer name HP LaserJet 4 PlusNet. This port was set up by the HP network printer software.

9   If possible, click **Configure Port**.

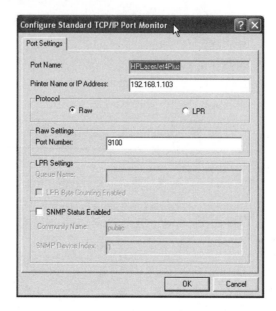

WHAT'S
HAPPENING?   Every device on a network has to be uniquely identified. The IP address 192.168.1.103 is a numeric assignment that is assigned to a port. When you choose to print to this printer, by virtue of the port address, it knows where to send the printer output. You are going to add the printer that is physically attached to the Dell 8100 (Dell-fp).

10 Click **Cancel**. Click **Cancel**. Click **Add a printer**. Click **Next**.

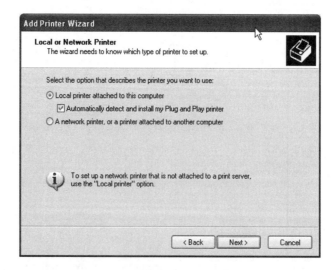

WHAT'S
HAPPENING?   You are asked whether this is a local printer or a network printer or a printer attached to another computer. The information button tells you that if you have a printer that is on hub, you choose Local printer. The reason it is considered a local printer is because of the port assignment. However, in this case, you want to

select A network printer, or a printer attached to another computer. The HP Color printer is attached to another computer.

11 Click **A network printer or a printer attached to another computer**. Click **Next**.

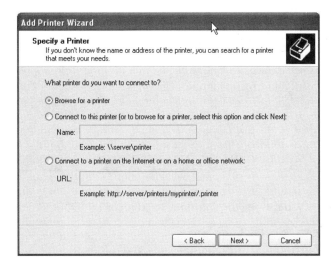

WHAT'S
HAPPENING?   Now you must locate your computer. If you know the name or its URL, you can key it in. Or you can browse for the printer you wish to use. Note the difference in addresses—if you are using a printer off a server, then the correct syntax is \\servername\printername but if you are using the Internet to connect to a printer, then the syntax is http://server/printers/myprinter/.printer.

12 Be sure **Browse for a printer** is selected. Click **Next**.

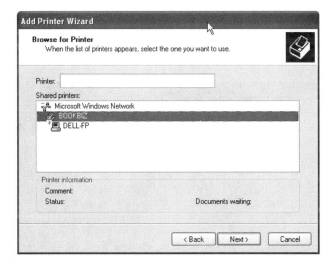

WHAT'S
HAPPENING?   You are looking at your network. You need to find the computer with the printer attached. You wish to select the computer to which the printer is physically attached. In this case it is the DELL-FP.

13 Double-click **DELL-FP**.

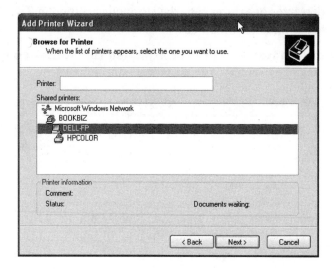

WHAT'S
HAPPENING?   You can see the shared resource, the HPCOLOR printer.

14 Click the printer to select it. Click **Next**.

WHAT'S
HAPPENING?   You may see the following dialog box (Figure 12.5). This dialog box
is telling you that you do not have the printer drivers installed for this printer. If you
see this dialog box, click **OK**. You will then be led through choosing the printer driver.
See Figure 12.5.

Figure 12.5—The Connect to Printer Dialog Box

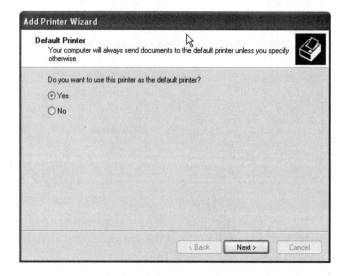

WHAT'S
HAPPENING?   You are asked if you want this to be the default printer.

15 Click **No**. Click **Next**.

WHAT'S
HAPPENING?   You see a summary of your printer choices.

16 Click **Finish**.

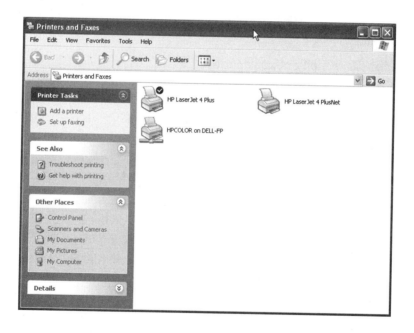

WHAT'S
HAPPENING?   You see your added printer. You know it is a network printer
because the icon has the printer on a cable.

17 Right-click the HPCOLOR on Dell-FP printer. Click **Properties**. Click **Ports**.

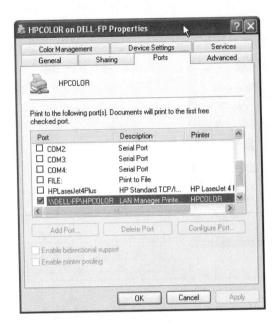

**WHAT'S
HAPPENING?**   You now see your network path. Notice the format—\\DELL-FP\HPCOLOR. The network path always begins with the double backslash (\\). It is in the format of *computer name**share name*.

18 Click **Cancel**. Close the Printers window.

**WHAT'S
HAPPENING?**   You have installed your network printer. You would have to take these steps for each client computer that you wished to access the shared printer.

12.6   Sharing a Hard Drive and a Folder on a Network

When you share a drive, just like a printer, any computer on the network can look into that drive and use the folders and files on that drive. The computer with the drive you wish to share is taking on the role of the *file server*. Again, in a large network, often there will be one computer dedicated to being a file server. In a small network, typically, there is no dedicated file server.

In a peer-to-peer network any computer on the network can share its drive, but first the drive on the server computer has to be shared in the same manner that the printer is shared. You have the choice of sharing an entire drive or selected folders. The process requires two steps. You must go to the server computer, which contains the drive you wish to share, and set up the drive so that you can share it. Then you go to the client computer and access the shared drive via My Network Places. However, when you share a drive, you are now allowing any other users to have full access to your computer.

12.7   Permissions and Rights

If you are in a corporate or lab environment, your local computer is probably part of a domain. A domain is a group of computers that are part of a network and share a common directory database. A domain is administered by a network administrator, as a unit with common rules and procedures. Part of these common rules and procedures for a domain include access control. *Access control*, as it name implies is the process of authorizing users, groups, and computers the ability to access objects (files, folders and devices) on the network. This is a security measure that not only determines who can access an object, but what kinds of access that user is authorized to perform. The management of a network as well as full discussion of permission and rights is beyond the scope of this text but there are elements of these permissions that you can use on a peer-to-peer network.

If your hard drive has been formatted with NTFS (New Technology File System), you can set permissions on files on folders that you will grant to other users. *Permissions* determine which users can access which objects (files and folders and devices) and what kinds of access that user will have to those objects. These permissions include change ownership, full control, modify (read, write and execute), read and execute, or read only. Users can be assigned to groups and you can assign permissions and rights to a group rather than on an individual user by user basis. The permissions that are assigned to an depend on the type of object. In addition, whenever you create an object, such as a file, an owner is always assigned to it. By default, the owner is the creator of the object. No matter what permissions are set on an object, the owner of the object can always change the permissions on that object. In addition, objects inherit permissions. For instance, files within a folder inherit the permissions of the folder.

When you set up permissions, you may specify the level of access for groups and users. This means you could let one user only have read permissions to a file where another user could have read and write permissions. Read permissions mean that a user can only look at a file but not change the contents whereas write permissions allow a user not only look at a file but make changes to that file. You could even deny some users the ability to even look at the file. These permissions can also be assigned to devices so that some users could configure the printer where other users could only print from the printer or you could deny certain users the right to print at all to a specific printer.

If you are using the FAT32 file system, you can provide some security on folders when you share them on a network. You may set some permissions on folders that are shared. However, you cannot assign permissions on a file by file basis as you can with NTFS.

12.8   Activity: Sharing Drives on a Network

Note 1:   The following activity is based on a specific computer configuration. Your display will be different.

Note 2:   This activity also assumes you are using the NTFS file system.

1   Go to the computer with a drive you wish to share. In this example, it is the Micron-pc computer.

2   Click **Start**. Click **My Network Places**. Click **View workgroup computers**. Click **View**. Click **Tiles**. Double-click the **Micron-pc**. Click **View**. Click **Tiles**.

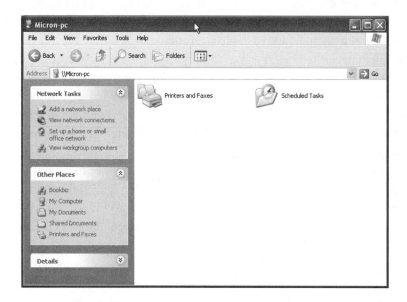

WHAT'S ▓▓▓▓▓
▓▓HAPPENING?   In this example, you are logged onto the Micron-pc computer. You see only the Printers and Faxes folder and the Scheduled Tasks folder. You do not see any drives available through My Network Places even though you are looking at the computer you are logged on to. The reason that you do not see any drives available is because you are looking at your own computer through the network. Nothing has been shared on the network.

3   Click the **Back** button. Double-click the **Dell-czg** computer icon.

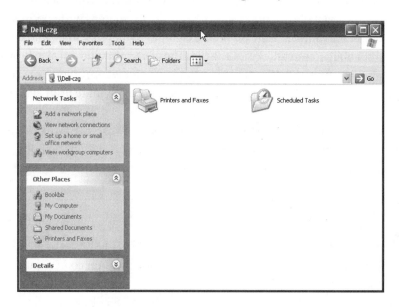

WHAT'S HAPPENING?   If you see a flashlight icon, that icon indicates that Windows is looking for the network connection. Once it finds it, you will see a Printers and Faxes folder and a Scheduled Tasks icons. If you look at the Address, you see that you are looking at the \ \ Dell-czg computer. However, you see no drives. The Dell-czg is a computer running Windows 2000 Professional.

4   Click the **Back** button. Double-click the **Dell 8100 (Dell-fp)** icon. Click **View**. Click **Tiles**.

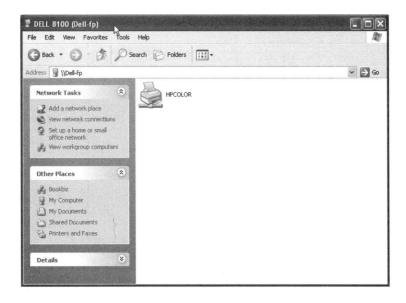

WHAT'S HAPPENING?   You see no folders or drives but you do see the printer you previously shared. No drives were shared on this computer either. This computer is running Windows Me. Each version of Windows will display a slightly different view.

5   Close My Network Places. Open My Computer. Click **View**. Click **Tiles**. Right-click **Drive C**. Click **Sharing and Security**.

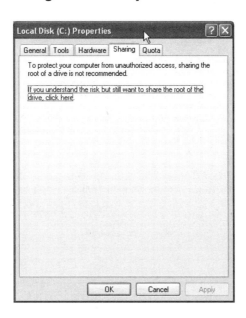

WHAT'S ▓▓▓▓▓
▓▓▓▓HAPPENING?   In this example, Simple file sharing is set. This means that you are sharing everything on your hard drive. As you can see, this is not recommended since you give everyone rights to everything on your hard drive. However, you can be more specific by disabling Simple file sharing.

6   Click **Cancel**. Click **Tools**. Click **Folder Options**. Click the **View** tab. Scroll to the bottom of the window.

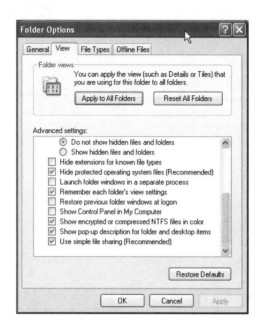

WHAT'S ▓▓▓▓▓
▓▓▓▓HAPPENING?   At the bottom of the window, Use simple file sharing (Recommended) is selected. If you are using the FAT32 file system, you will not see this choice. When Simple file sharing is set, you cannot set more specific permissions on the drive.

7   Clear **Use Simple file sharing (Recommended)**. Click **OK**. Right-click **Drive C**. Click **Sharing and Security**.

WHAT'S
HAPPENING?   In Windows XP Professional, as in versions of Windows, after
Windows 2000 Professional, all drives on your computer, such as Drive C or D, are
automatically shared using the syntax of *drive letter*$, such as D$ or E$. This is known
as an administrative share. This type of share allows administrators to connect the
root directory of a drive over the network. These drives are not shown in either My
Computer or Windows Explorer. These drives are also hidden when users connect to
your computer remotely. But if any user knows your computer name, user name, and
password and if that user is a member of the Administrators, Backup Operators, or
Server Operators group, that user can gain access to your computer over a network or
the Internet, provided that the Administrative share remains a shared folder. It is
shared by default.

8   Click **New Share**.

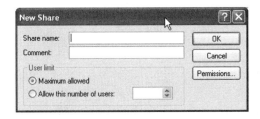

WHAT'S
HAPPENING?   You may name the shared drive anything you like. However, simply
calling it C is not a good idea. All computers have a C drive. You want to name it
uniquely so that it can be identified on the network as the Micron's Drive C. You may
also set how many users may be allowed to share this drive at one time.

9   Click **Permissions**.

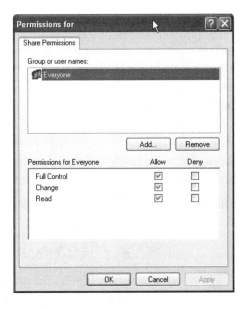

WHAT'S
HAPPENING?   As you can see, Everyone has full permission to do anything to the
shared drive.

10   Click the **Add** button. Click the **Advanced** button. Click **Find Now**.

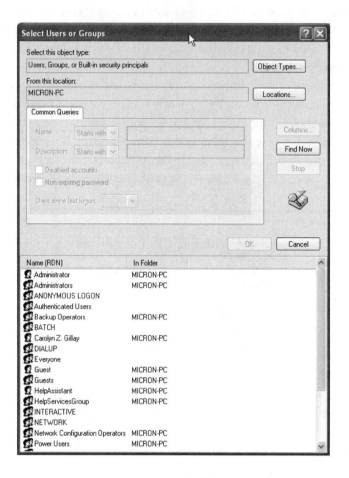

WHAT'S ▨▨▨▨
▨▨▨▨**HAPPENING?**   Windows XP Professional provides groups, whose membership is controlled by the administrator. There is another group called Authenticated Users, whose membership is controlled by the operating system or by the domain, if you are on a domain. Authenticated Users is the same as the Everyone group. By default in Windows XP Professional, any authenticated user is a member of the Users group. Often, an administrator will remove the Everyone group and add specific groups who may access the information so that the environment is more secure. As you can see, as you move into the networking world, administering the system becomes more and more complex. At the moment, you will simply allow Everyone access to this drive.

11 Click **Cancel**. Click **Cancel**. Click **Cancel**. In the Share Name text box, key in **Micron-C**.

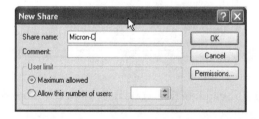

WHAT'S ▨▨▨▨
▨▨▨▨**HAPPENING?**   In this case, you chose to name the drive by the computer brand, and you gave full access to your drive. Note that there is no space between the computer brand and the C. A hyphen was used. A space in a share name can cause

problems in accessing the shared resource. To avoid problems, avoid spaces. The Micron is acting as the server computer. Remember that this is an example. Your drive names and availability will differ from the example.

12 Click **OK**. Click **OK**.

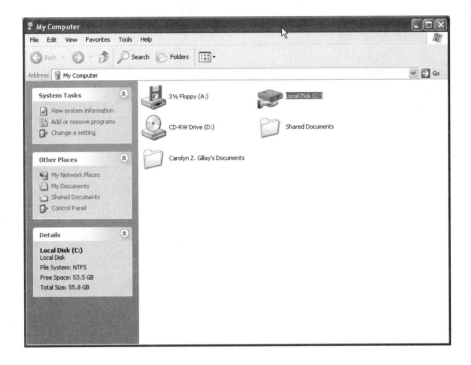

WHAT'S
HAPPENING?   Now on the Micron, you have shared Drive C. You can tell by the hand under the drive icon.

13 Close My Computer. Open My Network Places. Click **View workgroup computers**. Double-click **Micron-pc**.

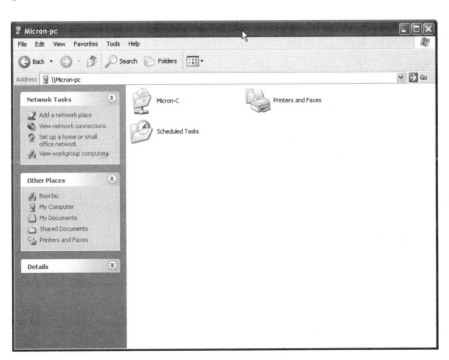

WHATS
HAPPENING?   Now you see your drive represented as a folder icon. You are still the server. To test that you have made the Micron's Drive C available to others on the network, you need to go to a client computer.

14 Close My Network Places. Go to a client computer, in this case, the Dell-czg computer. The Dell-czg is using Windows 2000 Professional as its operating system. Double-click the **My Network Places** icon. Double-click **Computers Near Me**.

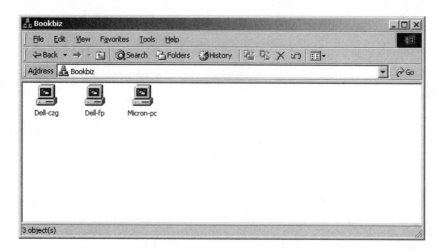

WHATS
HAPPENING?   You are now on the Dell-czg computer, the client, and wish to access the drive on the Micron computer. You should be able to because it is shared.

15 Double-click the **Micron-pc** icon.

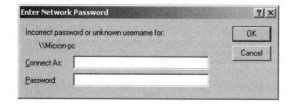

WHATS
HAPPENING?   The server computer, the \\Micron-pc wants to validate who you are. You need to connect as a user. If you have logged onto this computer before, in this work session, you may not see the password dialog box as Windows will remember that you are an authenticated user.

16 If necessary, in the Connect as text box, key in **Everyone**. Click **OK**.

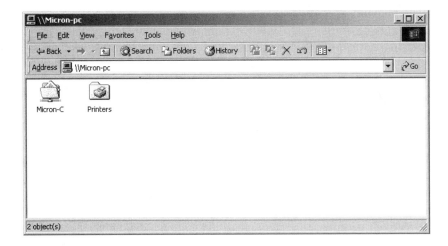

WHAT'S HAPPENING?   Now you have access to Drive C on the Micron computer.

17 Double-click **Micron-C**.

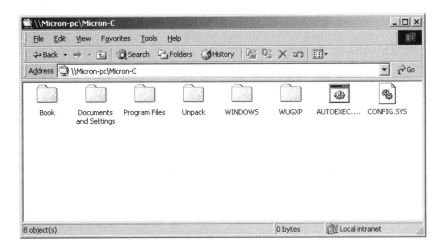

WHAT'S HAPPENING?   You have full access to Drive C on the Micron. Both the title bar and the address (\ \ Micron-pc\ Micron-C) tell you what computer you are accessing. You have been acting as the client computer, because you are logged on to the Dell-czg computer and you are able to access any shared resources (Drive C) of the Micron computer, in this case, the server. However, on a peer-to-peer network, you can switch roles and become the server and share your drives so that other users on the network can access your drives.

18 Click the **Back** button twice. Double-click the **Dell-czg** computer.

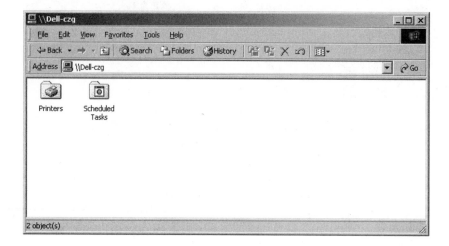

WHAT'S ▨▨▨▨
▨▨ HAPPENING?   Even though you are sitting at the client computer, the Dell-czg, you cannot see any of your drives because you are looking at the Dell-czg computer through My Network Places. Since no drives are shared on the Dell-czg computer, no drives on the Dell-czg computer can be seen through My Network Places.

19 Close My Network Places. Open My Computer on the Dell. Right-click **Drive C**. Click **Sharing**. Click **New Share**. In the Share name text box, key in **Dell-czg-C**. Click **OK**. Click **OK**.

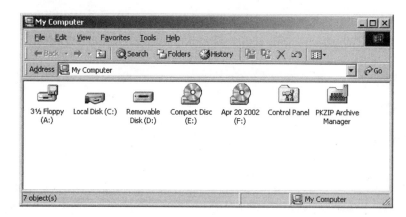

WHAT'S ▨▨▨▨
▨▨ HAPPENING?   You now see that on the Dell, Drive C is shared. Now anyone on another computer connected to the network can access Drive C on the Dell-czg computer. You have just acted as the server.

20 Close My Computer. Open My Network Places. Double-click **Computers Near Me**. Double-click **Dell-czg**.

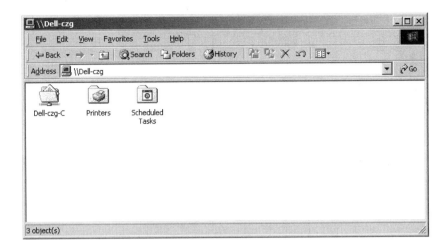

WHAT'S HAPPENING?   As you can see, now the Dell-czg-C drive is available through My Network Places.

21 Close My Network Places. Return to the Micron-pc computer.

22 Open My Computer. Right-click **Drive C**. Click **Sharing and Security**. Click the **Sharing** tab. Click the down arrow in the Share name drop-down list box. Select **Micron-C**. Click **Do not share this folder**.

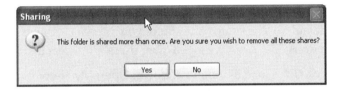

WHAT'S HAPPENING?   Since this folder is shared, you are reminded that you are removing access to the shared drive. It states that this folder is shared more than once – the share you set up and the Administrative share.

23 Click **Yes**. Click **OK**.

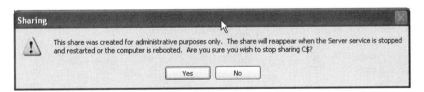

WHAT'S HAPPENING?   The share that is left is the Administrative share. If you ever removed this administrative share (C$), you could recreate it. Although you could recreate it (New Share / C$), it is not necessary, because each time you reboot, the administrative share is always recreated.

24 Click **No**. Open Drive C. Right-click the **WUGXP** folder. Click **Sharing and Security**. Click **Share this folder**.

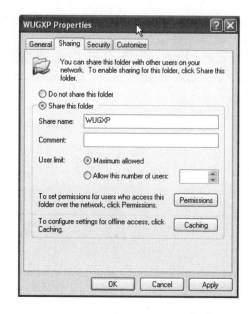

WHAT'S ▓▓▓
▓▓▓HAPPENING?   You do not need to share your entire hard drive. You can elect to
share only a folder and limit other users on the network to accessing only that folder,
not your entire hard drive. In fact, that is often what users do. They opt to share a
folder or folders on their hard drive but do not want to let other users access their
entire hard drive. You are going to share the WUGXP folder. The folder name,
WUGXP, is the default for the share name. Since you did not change permissions, the
default is full for everyone. You have given other users full access to that folder only.

25 Click **Apply**. Click **OK**. Close all open windows. Open My Network Places. Click
View workgroup computers. Open the Micron-pc computer.

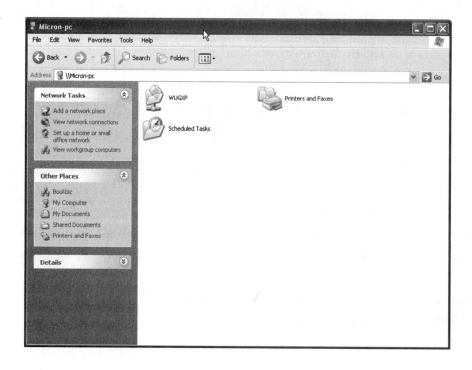

WHATS
HAPPENING? As you can see, the WUGXP folder is now available for other users on the network.

26 Close all open windows. Open My Computer. Open Drive C. Open the WUGXP folder. Right-click **ASTRO.TXT**. Click **Properties**. Click the **Security** tab.

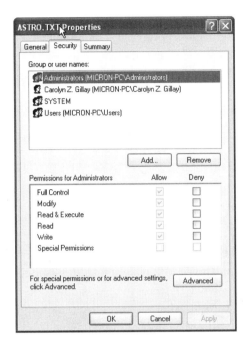

WHATS
HAPPENING? Because in this example the Micron-pc is using the NTFS file system, you can set permissions for each file on your system. In this example, no one is denied access to this file. Everyone may Modify, Read & Execute, Read and Write this file. Deny permissions take precedence over allow entries. If you have users who are members of more than one group, setting a Deny permission for Write will effectively bar them from writing this file to disk. If you deny users all permissions, they will not even be able to look at the file.

27 Click **Cancel**. Click **Tools**. Click **Folder Options**. Click **View**. Set **Use simple file sharing (Recommended)**. Click **OK**.

28 Close all open windows.

WHATS
HAPPENING? You have returned to the desktop.

12.9 Using Net Commands

You may see a list of net commands by keying in **net help** at the command line. See Figure 12.6.

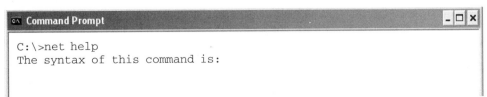

```
C:\>net help
The syntax of this command is:
```

```
NET HELP
command
       -or-
NET command /HELP

   Commands available are:

   NET ACCOUNTS            NET HELP            NET SHARE
   NET COMPUTER            NET HELPMSG         NET START
   NET CONFIG             NET LOCALGROUP       NET STATISTICS
   NET CONFIG SERVER       NET NAME            NET STOP
   NET CONFIG WORKSTATION  NET PAUSE           NET TIME
   NET CONTINUE            NET PRINT           NET USE
   NET FILE               NET SEND             NET USER
   NET GROUP               NET SESSION         NET VIEW

   NET HELP SERVICES lists some of the services you can start.
   NET HELP SYNTAX explains how to read NET HELP syntax lines.
   NET HELP command ¦ MORE displays Help one screen at a time.

C:\>
```

Figure 12.6—List of NET commands

If you want detailed help on a command, at the command prompt, you would use the syntax **net help** *command* where *command* is the specific command of interest. Thus, keying in **net help view** will result in the display shown in Figure 12.7.

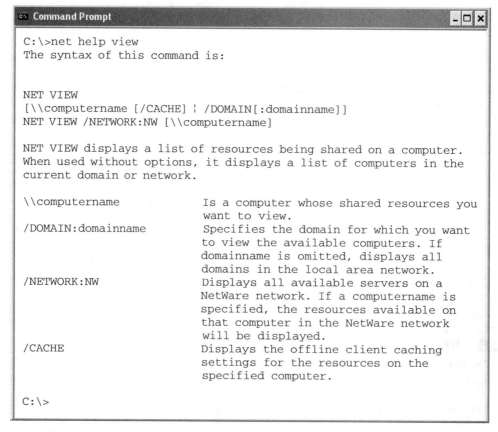

```
C:\>net help view
The syntax of this command is:


NET VIEW
[\\computername [/CACHE] ¦ /DOMAIN[:domainname]]
NET VIEW /NETWORK:NW [\\computername]

NET VIEW displays a list of resources being shared on a computer.
When used without options, it displays a list of computers in the
current domain or network.

\\computername          Is a computer whose shared resources you
                        want to view.
/DOMAIN:domainname      Specifies the domain for which you want
                        to view the available computers. If
                        domainname is omitted, displays all
                        domains in the local area network.
/NETWORK:NW             Displays all available servers on a
                        NetWare network. If a computername is
                        specified, the resources available on
                        that computer in the NetWare network
                        will be displayed.
/CACHE                  Displays the offline client caching
                        settings for the resources on the
                        specified computer.

C:\>
```

Figure 12.7—Using Help with the Net Command

If you want brief help, the usual **net** *command* **/?** will give the syntax of the command of interest. If you are having trouble with your network, and you call technical support, tech support will often ask questions about your network setup which can only be answered by using these commands to locate the necessary information. Most of the net commands can be used on a peer-to-peer or domain based network but some of them are only meaningful on a server or domain based network. The following activity demonstrates the net commands on a server based network. If you are using a peer-to-peer network, you may follow the activities but again, the information's importance will not be as meaningful. Most lab environments will also allow you to execute these commands but you could be limited based on permissions you have and how your network is set up. Obviously your screen displays will vary.

12.10 Activity: Gathering Information with the NET Command on a Domain

Note: The DATA disk is in the A drive.

1 Open a Command Prompt window and make A:\ the default drive/directory.

2 Key in the following: A:\>**NET CONFIG WORKSTATION** [Enter]

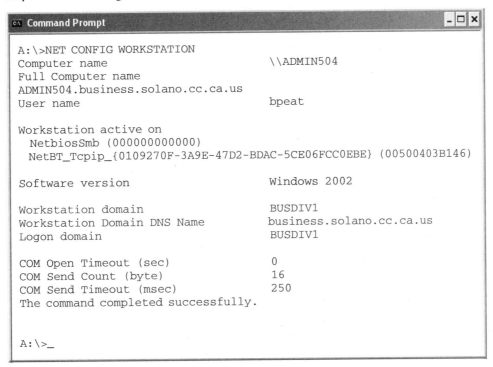

```
A:\>NET CONFIG WORKSTATION
Computer name                        \\ADMIN504
Full Computer name
ADMIN504.business.solano.cc.ca.us
User name                            bpeat

Workstation active on
  NetbiosSmb (000000000000)
  NetBT_Tcpip_{0109270F-3A9E-47D2-BDAC-5CE06FCC0EBE} (00500403B146)

Software version                     Windows 2002

Workstation domain                   BUSDIV1
Workstation Domain DNS Name          business.solano.cc.ca.us
Logon domain                         BUSDIV1

COM Open Timeout (sec)               0
COM Send Count (byte)                16
COM Send Timeout (msec)              250
The command completed successfully.


A:\>_
```

WHAT'S HAPPENING? You have discovered a great deal of the information about your workstation. You see both the short and long names of your workstation, the name of the current user, the software version (operating system) the Domain the workstation belongs to, and the Domain where you are logged in.

3 Key in the following: A:\>**NET CONFIG SERVER** [Enter]

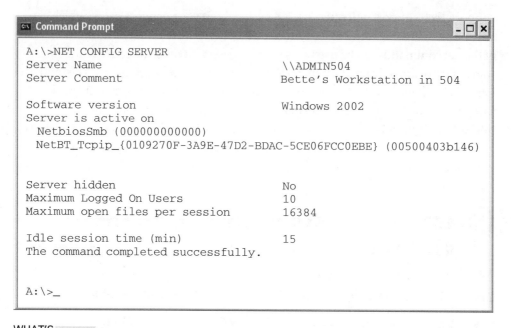

HAPPENING?   In this example, this particular workstation is also a server. Notice the maximum number of logged on users is 10. This workstation has shared resources that are being shared on local workgroup consisting of workstations that are on the same "branch" of the network. The **NET CONFIG SERVER** command issued on an actual Windows 2000 Domain server produces information such as that shown in the Figure 12.8.

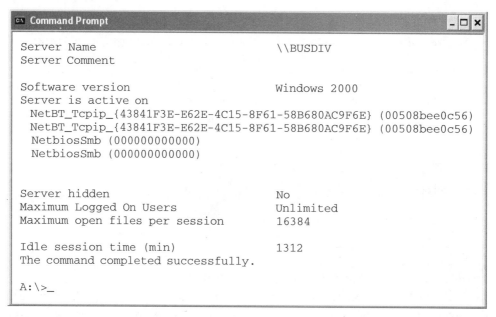

Figure 12.8—Windows 2000 Server

Notice that in this environment, there is no limit to the number of users that can be logged on to the network.

4   Key in the following: A:\>**NET LOCALGROUP** [Enter]

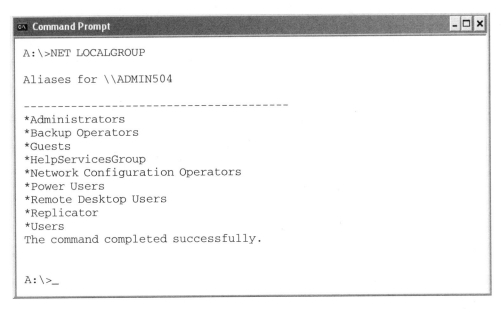

```
A:\>NET LOCALGROUP

Aliases for \\ADMIN504


----------------------------------------
*Administrators
*Backup Operators
*Guests
*HelpServicesGroup
*Network Configuration Operators
*Power Users
*Remote Desktop Users
*Replicator
*Users
The command completed successfully.


A:\>_
```

WHAT'S ▓▓▓▓
▓▓▓HAPPENING?   The **net localgroup** command reports back the "groups" the current user is "a member of." This relates to what permissions or rights the current user has on the network. In this example, all groups are listed because bpeat / ADMIN504 is an administrator for this network.

5 Key in the following: A:\>**NET NAME** Enter

6 Key in the following: A:\>**NET USER** Enter

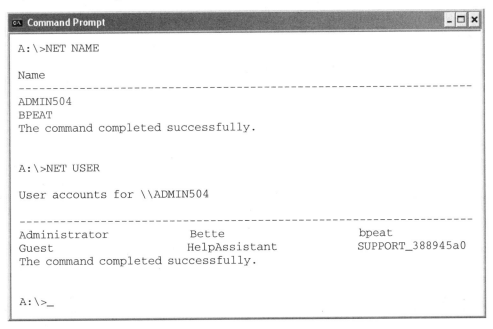

```
A:\>NET NAME

Name
-------------------------------------------------------------------
ADMIN504
BPEAT
The command completed successfully.


A:\>NET USER

User accounts for \\ADMIN504

-------------------------------------------------------------------
Administrator            Bette                    bpeat
Guest                    HelpAssistant            SUPPORT_388945a0
The command completed successfully.


A:\>_
```

WHAT'S ▓▓▓▓
▓▓▓HAPPENING?   You used two more NET commands to determine information about the network. NET NAME returned the name of the Workstation / Server on the Domain, ADMIN504, and the name of the current user, BPEAT. NET NAME can add or delete a messaging name (alias) at a computer. A messaging name is a name to which messages are sent. When used without options, as you did here, the NET NAME command will display all the names that can accept messages at this computer. NET

USER can create and modify user accounts on computers. When you use it without switches, it will list the user accounts for the computer. The user account information is stored in the user accounts database. This command provides useful information only on servers. In this example, since NET USER was used without switches, it returned the user information on the current user. The NET USER command issued on a Windows 2000 Domain server would produce a very different display as shown in Figure 12.9.

```
Command Prompt                                                    _ □ ✕

User accounts for \\BUSDIV


---------------------------------------------------------------
502psrv1               502psrv2               acary
acctg502               acctg503               acctg507
adjunct                Administrator          atulegen
awiller                bmarshal               bpeat
 . . .
dhoggan                dweston                esaw
ewylie                 gkhaja                 glee
gmagnell               gmartin                Guest
 . . .
mengland               mfracisc               mharris
mhiggins               mresende               mtaylor
NewUser                out00                  out01
out02                  out03                  out04
 . . .
out23                  out24                  out25
out26                  out27                  out28
out29                  out30                  pbentley
pceja                  ralexand               rdieter
rkleeb                 smaher                 testuser
tporta                 TsInternetUser         wbadri
wlong                  WS101                  WS102
WS103                  WS104                  WS105
 . . .
WS124                  WS125                  WS126
WS127                  WS128                  WS129
WS130                  WS199                  WS201
WS202                  WS203                  WS204
WS205                  WS206                  WS207
WS208                  WS209                  WS210
WS211                  WS212                  WS213
WS214                  WS215                  WS216
WS217                  WS218                  WS219
WS220                  WS221                  WS222
 . . .
WS327                  WS328                  WS329
WS330                  WS331                  WS332
WS400                  WS401                  WS402
WS403                  WS404                  WS405
 . . .
WS430                  WS505                  WS506
WS603                  WS604                  WS605
WS700                  WS701                  WS702
The command completed successfully.
```

Figure 12.9—Windows 2000 Server Using the NET USER Command (partial display)

Figure 12.9 is an abbreviated display of the user accounts created for the BUSDIV1 Domain, including users and workstations.

7 Key in the following: `A:\>`**NET VIEW** Enter

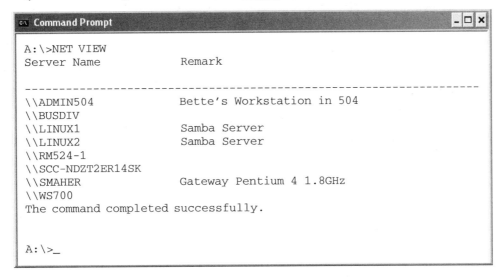

```
A:\>NET VIEW
Server Name            Remark

-----------------------------------------------------------------
\\ADMIN504             Bette's Workstation in 504
\\BUSDIV
\\LINUX1               Samba Server
\\LINUX2               Samba Server
\\RM524-1
\\SCC-NDZT2ER14SK
\\SMAHER               Gateway Pentium 4 1.8GHz
\\WS700
The command completed successfully.


A:\>_
```

WHAT'S HAPPENING?   The NET VIEW command displays a list of resources being shared on a computer. When used without options, it displays a list of computers in the current domain or network. Thus, the NEW VIEW command allows an overview of the servers in the current Domain. In this example, the Domain has a main server, BUSDIV, two LINUX servers, and four Workstations configured as servers.

8 Key in the following: `A:\>`**NET ACCOUNTS** Enter

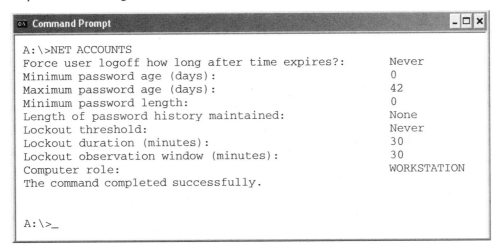

```
A:\>NET ACCOUNTS
Force user logoff how long after time expires?:     Never
Minimum password age (days):                        0
Maximum password age (days):                        42
Minimum password length:                            0
Length of password history maintained:              None
Lockout threshold:                                  Never
Lockout duration (minutes):                         30
Lockout observation window (minutes):               30
Computer role:                                      WORKSTATION
The command completed successfully.


A:\>_
```

WHAT'S HAPPENING?   The NET ACCOUNTS command can update the user accounts database and modifies password and logon requirements for all accounts. When you use it without options, it displays the current settings for password, logon limitations, and domain information. Here it is used without options and the NET ACCOUNTS command returned information on the user. The information presented is for the specific user on a workstation on the Domain, not as a Server on a Domain. Information is related to password and privilege information for that particular user.

9 Key in the following: `A:\>`**NET STATISTICS WORKSTATION** Enter

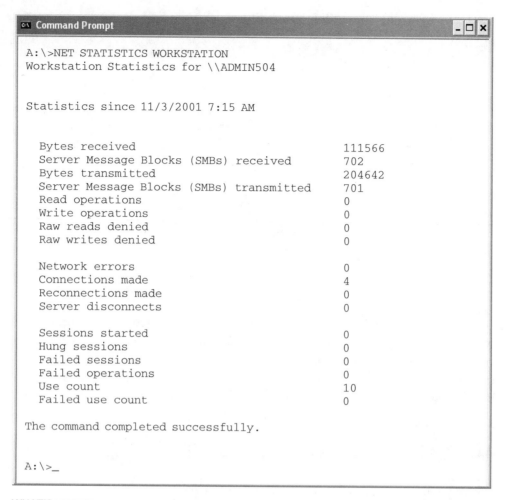

```
CN  Command Prompt                                                          _  □  ×

A:\>NET STATISTICS WORKSTATION
Workstation Statistics for \\ADMIN504


Statistics since 11/3/2001 7:15 AM


  Bytes received                               111566
  Server Message Blocks (SMBs) received        702
  Bytes transmitted                            204642
  Server Message Blocks (SMBs) transmitted     701
  Read operations                              0
  Write operations                             0
  Raw reads denied                             0
  Raw writes denied                            0

  Network errors                               0
  Connections made                             4
  Reconnections made                           0
  Server disconnects                           0

  Sessions started                             0
  Hung sessions                                0
  Failed sessions                              0
  Failed operations                            0
  Use count                                    10
  Failed use count                             0

The command completed successfully.


A:\>_
```

**WHAT'S ▓▓▓▓▓▓
▓▓▓ HAPPENING?**   The NET STATISTICS [WORKSTATION ¦ SERVER] command displays the statistics log for either the local Workstation or the Server service. You must choose either the WORKSTATION or the SERVER to display statistics. Here you used NET STATISTICS WORKSTATION command to display I/O information. If you were having problems sending or receiving data from your workstation, failed read, write, and other session operations would be reported here.

10 Key in the following: A:\>**NET STATISTICS SERVER** Enter

```
CN  Command Prompt                                                          _  □  ×

A:\>NET STATISTICS SERVER
Server Statistics for \\ADMIN504


Statistics since 11/3/2001 7:15 AM


Sessions accepted              1
Sessions timed-out             0
Sessions errored-out           0

Kilobytes sent                 0
Kilobytes received             0

Mean response time (msec)      0
```

```
System errors                          0
Permission violations                  0
Password violations                    0

Files accessed                         0
Communication devices accessed         0
Print jobs spooled                     0

Times buffers exhausted

  Big buffers                          0
  Request buffers                      0

The command completed successfully.


A:\>_
```

WHAT'S █████
█████ **HAPPENING?**   The display is that of a Workstation. Figure 12.10 displays the
results of the NET STATISTICS SERVER command run on a Windows 2000 Domain
Server.

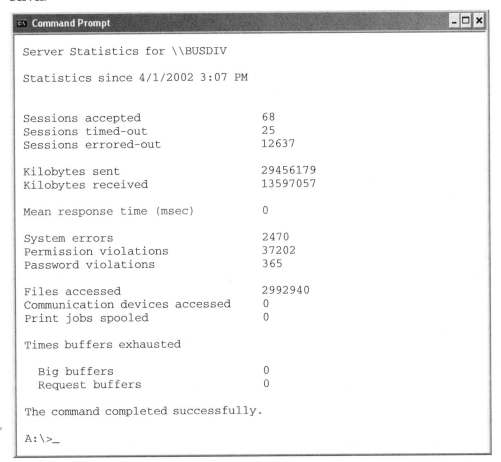

```
Command Prompt                                                    _ □ ×

 Server Statistics for \\BUSDIV

 Statistics since 4/1/2002 3:07 PM


 Sessions accepted                    68
 Sessions timed-out                   25
 Sessions errored-out                 12637

 Kilobytes sent                       29456179
 Kilobytes received                   13597057

 Mean response time (msec)            0

 System errors                        2470
 Permission violations                37202
 Password violations                  365

 Files accessed                       2992940
 Communication devices accessed       0
 Print jobs spooled                   0

 Times buffers exhausted

   Big buffers                        0
   Request buffers                    0

 The command completed successfully.

 A:\>_
```

Figure 12.10—Windows 2000 Domain Server Using the NET STATISTICS SERVER)

As you can see, the statistics on a Domain server involve many errors reported. In
this instance, it represents student workstations that were not logged into and/or out
of correctly.

It is very valuable to have hard copy of this information, especially when trouble-shooting problems on your workstation or on the network. In order to have a hard copy of the information, you can redirect the screen displays into a file and then print the file with Notepad or any text editor.

12.11 Mapping Drives and the NET USE Command

Once a drive or folder is shared, you may map a drive letter to the shared drive or folder. A *mapped drive* is a network drive or folder (one that has been shared) that you assign a local drive letter. When you map a drive or a folder, it appears as a drive on client computers in Windows Explorer, My Computer or in the command prompt window. You no longer need to browse My Network Places to have access to that shared drive or folder. You access directly from My Computer or the command prompt window, using the assigned, or *mapped*, letter. Most often you will map folders rather than entire drives.

The NET USE command is the command line utility that allows you to map drives. NET USE command is one of the more useful net commands. It connects a computer to a shared resource or disconnects a computer from a shared resource. When used without options, it lists the computer's connections. NET USE can thus be used alone to obtain information. The syntax for the NET USE command is

```
NET USE
[devicename ¦ *] [\\computername\sharename[\volume] [password ¦ *]]
        [/USER:[domainname\]username]
        [/USER:[dotted domain name\]username]
        [/USER:[username@dotted domain name]
        [/SMARTCARD]
        [/SAVECRED]
        [[/DELETE] ¦ [/PERSISTENT:{YES ¦ NO}]]

NET USE {devicename ¦ *} [password ¦ *] /HOME

NET USE [/PERSISTENT:{YES ¦ NO}]
[devicename ¦ *] [\\computername\sharename[\volume] [password ¦ *]]
```

It can be used in a multiplicity of ways. For instance, if you wanted to print to a network printer from the command line, using COPY filename LPT1 would not work as you have no printer attached to the port labeled LPT1. Thus, you could key in the following command:

C:\Windows\SYSTEM32\NET.EXE USE LPT1: \\BUSDIV\HP504-1 /YES

which says, in English, go to the Windows\system32 directory, use the NET.EXE command with the USE parameter. Capture everything directed to LPT1 port and send it instead to \\BUSDIV\HP504-1, which is the network name of a printer, and send it there. Thus, you have set up your network printer to act as a "local" printer. As you can see, when you print, you are actually printing to a port which is assigned to a device. In this example, it is important to note the meaning of the last parameter on the /YES. This parameter refers to the "persistent" state of the command. It means that this connection remains in effect until removed with another command. YES or NO are the two possible options for the persistent state. *That state remains in effect until changed.* If the last persistent operator used was /YES, all assignments made will be persistent. To make an assignment temporary, /NO should be used at the end of the NET USE command. Once /NO is used, the persistent state will be off until turned back on by another command.

In addition, you may use the NET USE command to assign or map a drive letter to a network drive or folder, much as SUBST is used to assign a drive letter to a particular subdirectory on your workstation. You can write batch files to simplify certain computer operations you want to perform on a regular basis. For instance, if you have a folder such as C:\WUGXP and you want to back up these files to another folder on another computer on your network, such as called Dell-czg\dell-czg-c\back, you could write a batch file such as this:

```
@echo off
net use  R:  /delete 1>nul 2>nul
net use R: \\Dell-czg\dell-czg-c\back
xcopy C:\WUGXP R: /e /r /c /y
net use R: /delete
exit
```

You could then place this shortcut on your desktop and by double-clicking it, you would perform this task. This is far easier than opening up My Network Places, opening the back folder on the Dell-czg computer, then opening My Computer on the Micron PC, selecting the WUGXP folder and dragging it to the Dell-czg computer. Furthermore, you could add this batch file to your Scheduled Tasks, for total automation.

12.12 Activity: Using the NET USE Command

Note 1: This activity is based on a specific computer network. Your own environment will be significantly different.

Note 2: Be sure and check with your instructor and/or lab technician before attempting to use NET USE in a lab environment.

1   Go to the DELL-CZG computer running Windows 2000 Professional. Open My Computer. Right-click **Drive C**. Click **Sharing**. In the Share name drop down list box, select **Dell-czg-C**. Click **Remove Share**. Click **OK**.

2   Go to the DELL-FP computer running Windows Me. Open My Computer. Right-click **Drive C**. Click **Sharing**. Click **Shared As**. In the Share Name, key in **DELL-FP-C**. Click **OK**.

3   Return to the Micron-PC computer. Open My Network Places. Click **View Workgroup Computers**. Double-click **DELL 8100 (DELL-FP)**.

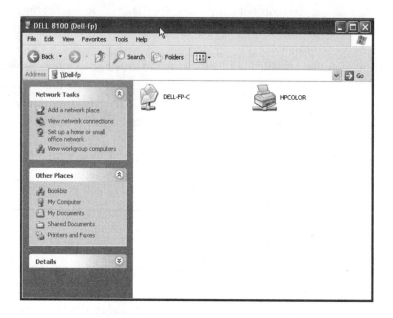

WHAT'S HAPPENING?   You have set up your environment for this activity. No drives or devices are shared on the DELL-CZG (Windows 2000 Professional) computer. The printer and drive C are shared on the DELL-FP (Windows Me) computer.

4   Close the Dell 8100 (Dell-FP) windows. Open a Command Prompt window.

5   Key in the following: C:\>**NET USE** [Enter]

6   Key in the following: C:\>**NET VIEW** [Enter]

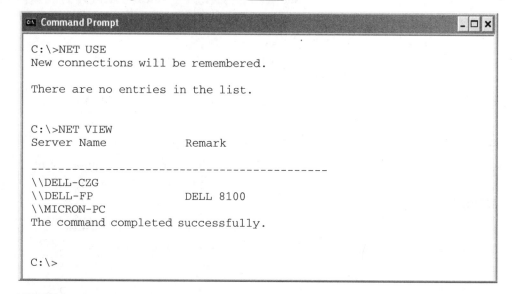

WHAT'S HAPPENING?   Since you have mapped no drives, you see no entries in the list. You must first map a drive in order to see any entries and the drive must be shared. You must select a drive letter that is not an actual physical drive on your system. The NET VIEW command allows you to see.

7   Key in the following: C:\>**NET USE T: \\DELL-FP\DELL-FP-C** [Enter]

8   Key in the following: C:\>**NET USE T:** [Enter]

```
┌─────────────────────────────────────────────────────────────────────────────┐
│ ▨ Command Prompt                                                    _ □ ×      │
├─────────────────────────────────────────────────────────────────────────────┤
│                                                                               │
│  C:\>NET USE T: \\DELL-FP\DELL-FP-C                                            │
│  The command completed successfully.                                          │
│                                                                               │
│                                                                               │
│  C:\>NET USE                                                                   │
│  New connections will be remembered.                                          │
│                                                                               │
│                                                                               │
│  Status       Local     Remote                    Network                     │
│                                                                               │
│  ─────────────────────────────────────────────────────────────────────────  │
│  OK           T:        \\DELL-FP\DELL-FP-C        Microsoft Windows Network   │
│  The command completed successfully.                                          │
│                                                                               │
│                                                                               │
│  C:\>                                                                          │
│                                                                               │
└─────────────────────────────────────────────────────────────────────────────┘
```

WHAT'S HAPPENING?   You see confirmation that the command worked. Then when you used the NET USE command without parameters, the line at the top indicated that *New connections will be remembered.* It is important to note that drive alias assigned with the NET USE command may or may not be "persistent," meaning that the connections created may or may not remain in effect after shutting down the computer. In this example, the persistent state is on. If you were on a domain network or a peer to peer, and had mapped R to a drive, and you keyed in the following series of commands:

> NET USE /PERSISTENT:NO
> NET USE R: /D
> NET USE

Your results would look like Figure 12.11.

```
┌─────────────────────────────────────────────────────────────────────────────┐
│ ▨ Command Prompt                                                    _ □ ×      │
├─────────────────────────────────────────────────────────────────────────────┤
│                                                                               │
│  C:\>NET USE /PERSISTENT:NO                                                    │
│  The command completed successfully.                                          │
│                                                                               │
│                                                                               │
│  C:\>NET USE R: /D                                                             │
│  R: was deleted successfully.                                                  │
│                                                                               │
│                                                                               │
│  C:\>NET USE                                                                   │
│  New connections will not be remembered.                                      │
│                                                                               │
│                                                                               │
│  Status       Local     Remote                    Network                     │
│                                                                               │
│  ─────────────────────────────────────────────────────────────────────────  │
│  OK           F:        \\busdiv\user             Microsoft Windows Network   │
│  OK           G:        \\Busdiv\User\bpeat       Microsoft Windows Network   │
│  OK           H:        \\Busdiv\Workarea         Microsoft Windows Network   │
│  OK           I:        \\Busdiv\Install          Microsoft Windows Network   │
│  OK           M:        \\Busdiv\Datfiles         Microsoft Windows Network   │
│  The command completed successfully.                                          │
│                                                                               │
│                                                                               │
│  C:\>_                                                                         │
│                                                                               │
└─────────────────────────────────────────────────────────────────────────────┘
```

Figure 12.11—Use of Persistent on a Domain Server

In Figure 12.11, notice the line **New connections will not be remembered**. at the top of the display following the NET USE command. The persistent state is now off. It is important to know the persistent state before issuing a NET USE connection so you are aware if the command will be permanent or temporary, or so you can force it to be with the /YES or /NO parameter. Remember, the persistent state will remain in effect. All commands issued will have the same state as the previous command. It is a "from this point forward" parameter.

9   Minimize the Command Prompt window. Open My Computer.

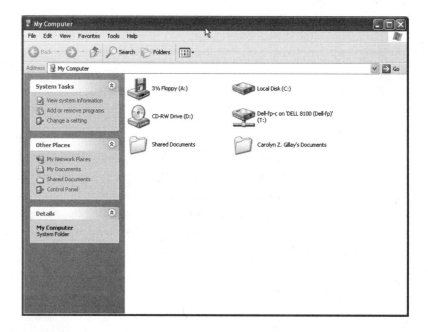

WHAT'S HAPPENING?   You can see the new T drive. The drive icon under for Drive T has a cable. This indicates that this drive is not on the local computer, but is available across the network.

10   Close My Computer and restore the Command Prompt window.

11   Key in the following: C:\>**T:** [Enter]

12   Key in the following: T:\>**DIR** [Enter]

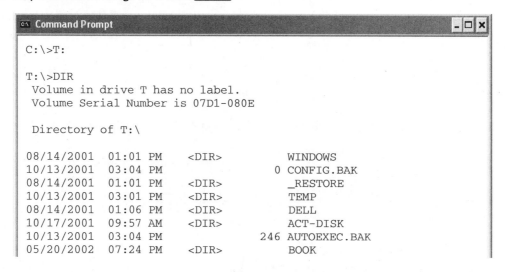

```
04/23/2001   03:38 PM              325,770 8100_A06.EXE
12/01/2000   03:40 PM                2,821 FLASH.BAT
08/14/2001   01:06 PM                   19 OSINFO.ENG
08/16/2000   10:20 AM                  785 VERIFY.BAT
08/14/2001   01:10 PM     <DIR>           BACKUP
12/11/2001   11:08 AM                  616 SCANDISK.LOG
08/14/2001   01:01 PM     <DIR>           Program Files
08/14/2001   01:06 PM     <DIR>           My Documents
08/14/2001   01:28 PM                  967 command.PIF
08/14/2001   01:17 PM                    0 Dumplog.txt
08/14/2001   01:17 PM     <DIR>           DellUtil
10/14/2001   08:25 AM     <DIR>           My Music
04/29/2002   08:42 AM               18,923 vso.log
05/31/2002   09:44 AM                3,523 mcaf.log
              11 File(s)          353,670 bytes
              11 Dir(s)   56,422,825,984 bytes free


T:\>
```

WHAT'S HAPPENING?   As you can see, you can access a mapped drive from the Command Prompt window just as if it was a local drive. Drive C, on the DELL-FP, running Windows Me, was shared. Because it was shared, it could be mapped using NET USE.

13 Key in the following: C:\>**C:** [Enter]

14 Key in the following: C:\>**NET USE T: /DELETE** [Enter]

15 Key in the following: C:\>**DIR T:** [Enter]

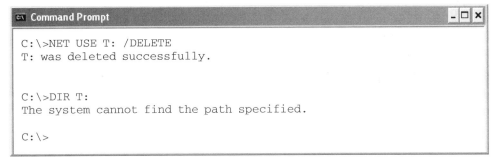

```
C:\>NET USE T: /DELETE
T: was deleted successfully.


C:\>DIR T:
The system cannot find the path specified.

C:\>
```

WHAT'S HAPPENING?   You have successfully disconnected the drive mapping of T: to \\DELL-FP\DELL-FP-C. However, what if a drive is not shared? If for instance, you had one computer downstairs that you were working on and you needed to access a file on a computer upstairs and you had not shared the drive on the upstairs computer, you could still access that computer if you were running Windows 2000 Professional or above, by using the Administrative share to access that upstairs drive. Again, the Administrative share is shared by default. If a user turned off sharing of that Administrative share, you could not access using the *driveletter$*.

16 C:\>**DIR \\DELL-CZG\C$ /P** [Enter]

```
Volume in drive \\DELL-CZG\C$ has no label.
 Volume Serial Number is 07D1-080F

 Directory of \\DELL-CZG\C$
```

```
08/15/2001   12:12 AM   <DIR>           I386
08/15/2001   12:12 AM   <DIR>           BACKUP
08/15/2001   12:12 AM   <DIR>           WINNT
08/15/2001   12:14 AM   <DIR>           DISCOVER
08/15/2001   12:14 AM   <DIR>           DELL
08/15/2001   12:21 AM   <DIR>           DRIVERS
08/15/2001   12:22 AM   <DIR>           Documents and Settings
08/15/2001   12:23 AM   <DIR>           Program Files
09/26/2001   10:36 PM   <DIR>           Unpack
09/27/2001   06:07 AM   <DIR>           QUICKENW
09/27/2001   07:48 AM   <DIR>           Games
09/27/2001   08:02 AM   <DIR>           School
09/27/2001   08:02 AM   <DIR>           Books
09/27/2001   08:02 AM   <DIR>           Personal
09/27/2001   10:05 AM   <DIR>           temp
10/08/2001   07:23 AM   <DIR>           Docs
10/10/2001   09:55 PM   <DIR>           Professional
10/11/2001   10:35 AM   <DIR>           Software
11/01/2001   10:45 AM   <DIR>           Training
11/05/2001   09:42 AM   <DIR>           My Download Files
11/05/2001   09:42 AM   <DIR>           My Music
11/18/2001   11:45 AM   <DIR>           BIOS
11/25/2001   07:26 PM   <DIR>           test
11/25/2001   07:54 PM               239 Owhat.fil
12/06/2001   09:49 AM   <DIR>           WUGXP
12/15/2001   10:50 AM   <DIR>           DELLXPS-OLD
12/16/2001   06:39 PM   <DIR>           FTP-Bookbiz
12/28/2001   09:06 AM   <DIR>           WINDOSBK
12/29/2001   04:16 PM   <DIR>           Pvsw
Press any key to continue . . .
```

WHAT'S HAPPENING?   Even though you did not share Drive C on the DELL-CZG (running Windows 2000 Professional), you were still able to access it using the Administrative share. It is much more convenient to place drive mapping commands batch files and place short-cuts to the batch files on the desktop.

17 Place the DATA disk in the A drive. Change the default to Drive A.

18 Key in the following: `A:\>`**MD CHAP12** Enter

19 Key in the following: `A:\>`**CD CHAP12** Enter

20 Using the Command Line editor, create the following two batch files (MAP-T.BAT and UNMAP-T) in the CHAP12 subdirectory on the DATA disk.

MAP-T.BAT	UNMAP-T.BAT
@ECHO OFF	**@ECHO OFF**
NET USE T: \\DELL-FP\DELL-FP-C	**NET USE T: /DELETE**
PAUSE	**PAUSE**

21 Minimize the Command Prompt window. Open My Computer. Open Drive A. Open CHAP12. Select both **MAP-T.BAT** and **UNMAP-T.BAT**. Right-drag them to the desktop. Click **Create shortcuts here**.

WHAT'S
HAPPENING?   You now have shortcut icons to both MAP and UNMAP-T on the desktop.

22 Double-click the **Shortcut to MAP-T.BAT** icon.

WHAT'S
HAPPENING?   You get the message that the command was successfully completed. The Command Prompt window has not closed, as there is a PAUSE command holding the batch file for user intervention. If not for the PAUSE command, the window would close immediately. If there had been a problem with the mapping, you would have no opportunity to view any error message.

23 Press any key in the Command Prompt window. Open My Computer.

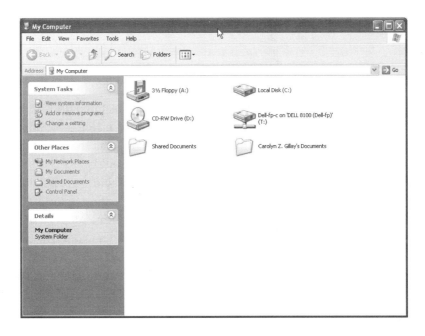

WHAT'S
HAPPENING?   The batch file finishes, and the command prompt window closes. Then, when you opened My Computer window, you see that Drive T is available.

24 Close My Computer. Restore the Command Prompt window and key in the following: C:\>**NET USE** [Enter]

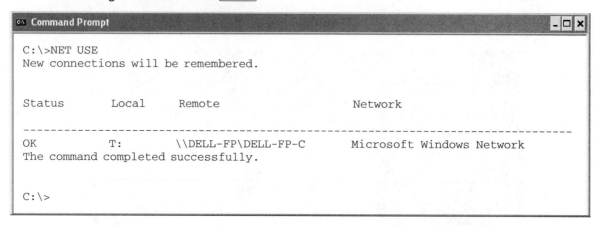

```
Command Prompt                                                    - □ ×

C:\>NET USE
New connections will be remembered.


Status       Local    Remote                 Network

----------------------------------------------------------------------
OK           T:       \\DELL-FP\DELL-FP-C     Microsoft Windows Network
The command completed successfully.


C:\>
```

WHAT'S
HAPPENING?   The NET USE command registers the drive mapping of T.

25 Minimize the Command Prompt window. Double-click the **Shortcut to the UNMAP-T.BAT** icon. Press the space bar when you see the message that the command was successful.

26 Restore the Command Prompt window. Key in the following:
C:\>**NET USE** [Enter]

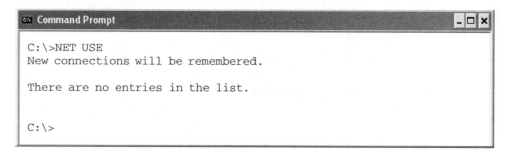

```
Command Prompt                                            - □ ×

C:\>NET USE
New connections will be remembered.

There are no entries in the list.


C:\>
```

WHAT'S
HAPPENING?   The batch file window closed. When you restored the Command Prompt window and used NET USE, you saw that drive T is no longer available. There are endless combinations of useful ways to use drive letter mappings to shared devices. If you have a graphic package with two CDs, you could place one in each computer, map a drive letter to the second computer, and be able to access them quickly without switching disks. You can make backups of critical data "on the fly" by mapping a letter to a subdirectory on the remote computer, and doing a second save to the remote drive. Each situation is different, and only you know the optimum method for your system.

The ability to map drives is especially useful on domain networks. For instance, Figure 12.12 shows the result of a NET USE command on a Domain based network.

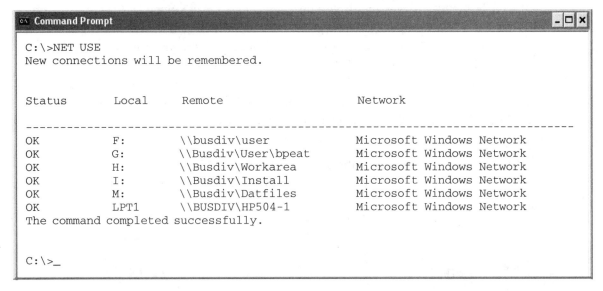

Figure 12.12—Net Use on a Domain

In this example, the connections made to the Network are listed here, including the results of a print command. \\busdiv is the name of the Domain server. Different drive letters are assigned to particular subdirectories on the server. If you then keyed in the command **NET USE LPT1 /D,** you would delete the connection to the printer, LPT1. If you then keyed in the command **NET USE R: \\BUSDIV\USER\BPEAT \GRAPHICS**, you are assigning the drive letter R to the named subdirectory on the server. Then, using **NET USE** would show you the results of these commands which is shown in Figure 12.13.

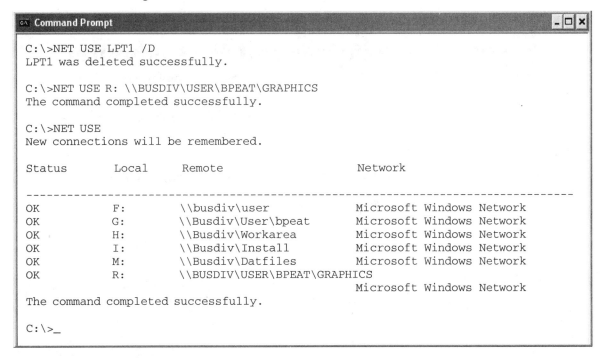

Figure 12.13—Using NET USE on a Domain

Here, in this example, there is a difference in the R: drive name as compared to the other drive names. The R: drive name was assigned by the user, not by the Administrator on the network server. The drive name, however, is valid. Keying in R: will result in and actual change of default drives. This is a valuable tool to use when you, as a user, store your data on a network drive, sometimes many, many directory levels deep, and wish to have a single drive letter to be able access that subdirectory. In this way, when accessing those files you do not have to key in a long drive specification, such as **G:\DATA\2002\CIS55\GRAPHICS***filename*, but can instead use simply **R:***filename*. The NET USE command does not distinguish the type of network. It simply reports the network connections in use.

27   Close all open windows. Delete the shortcuts to the MAP-T.BAT and UNMAP-T.Bat on the desktop.

WHAT'S
HAPPENING?   You have returned to the desktop.

12.13 Mapping Drives Using Windows Explorer and My Computer

You have been using NET USE to map a drive. You may also use the GUI to map drives. Windows XP Professional lets you use My Network Places to map drives using the Internet Explorer–like window. Windows 2000 XP also allows you to map a drive by right-clicking My Computer or My Network from the Start menu and choosing Map Network Drive. If you have icons for My Computer and My Network Places, you may also map a drive from those icons by right-clicking. You may also use the Tools menu in My Computer or Windows Explorer.

12.14 Activity: Mapping Drives with Windows Explorer and My Computer

Note 1:   The following activity is based on a specific computer configuration. Your display will be different.

Note 2:   In this example, you are going to begin with the DELL-czg computer—the computer with a drive you wish to map that is running Windows 2000 Professional.

1   Share the Dell Drive C as Dell-czg-C. Return to the Micron-pc computer.

2   Click **Start**. Right-click **My Network Places**.

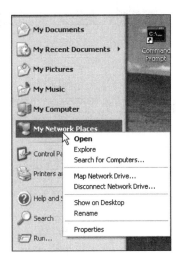

WHAT'S HAPPENING?   You see a shortcut menu listing your choices. The one you are interested in is Map Network Drive.

3   Click Map Network Drive.

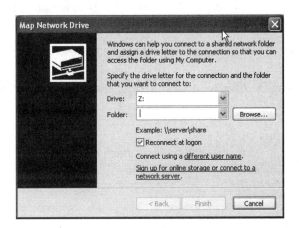

WHAT'S HAPPENING?   The drive listed, in this case, is Z:. The map network drive begins with the last letter of the alphabet as it assumes that is a drive letter not assigned to any real device on this computer. The folder text box is where you key in the UNC path to the drive that you want. The Reconnect at logon box is checked. Thus, every time you connect to the network, Drive Z on your local computer (the Micron-pc, in this example) will actually point to Drive C on the Dell-czg computer.

4   Key in \\Dell-czg\Dell-czg-c. Click Finish.

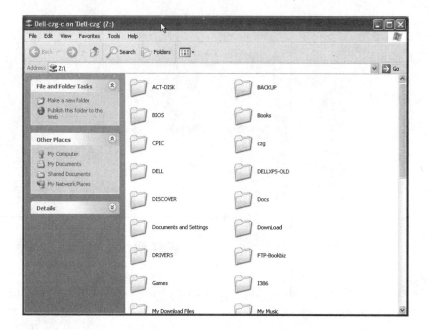

WHATS
HAPPENING?   You see the contents of Drive Z, which is really Drive C on the
Dell-czg computer.

5   Close the window. Open My Computer. Be in Tiles view.

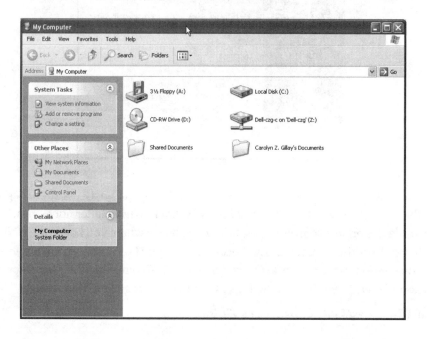

WHATS
HAPPENING?   You can see that Drive Z appears in My Computer as if it were a
drive on your system. You may access it in the usual way, by clicking it. You can tell it
is a network drive by the icon, which looks like a regular drive icon connected to a
cable.

6   Click **Tools** on the menu bar. Click **Disconnect Network Drive**.

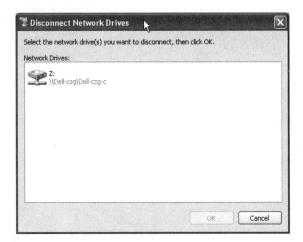

WHAT'S ▒▒▒▒
▒▒▒HAPPENING?   You see a dialog box that tells you which drives are connected. In this case, you have only one. If you had more than one mapped drive, each would be listed and you could select what drives to disconnect.

7   Click **Drive Z (Dell-czg)**. Click **OK**.

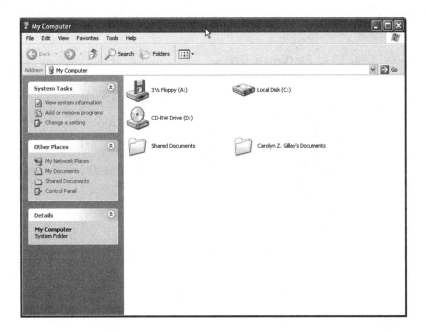

WHAT'S ▒▒▒▒
▒▒▒HAPPENING?   Your mapped drive is no longer available. The drive icon with a cable is gone.

8   Close My Computer. Open My Network Places. Click **View workgroup computers**. Double-click **Dell-czg**. Open Drive C. Scroll so you can see the WUGXP folder. Click **WUGXP**.

WHAT'S
HAPPENING?   Since the entire drive is shared, the WUGXP folder is available. You may map a folder as well.

9   Click **Tools**. Click **Map Network Drive**.

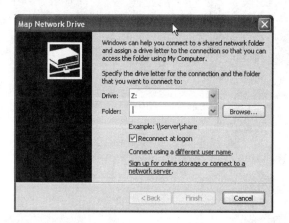

WHAT'S
HAPPENING?   Drive Z is available and needs to be mapped to the folder WUGXP. Again, note that the UNC will be \\Dell-czg\Dell-czg-c\WUGXP.

10   Key in **\\Dell-czg\Dell-czg-c\WUGXP**. Click **Finish**.

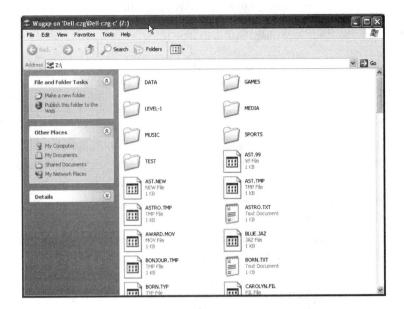

WHAT'S HAPPENING?   Since you shared the drive, you shared all the folders on the drive and could map Drive Z (in this example) to the WUGXP folder on the Dell's Drive C. You may have only one window open—the Drive Z window. What windows remain open are dependent on how many times you did this exercise and whether the Reconnect at logon box was checked.

11 Close the Drive Z window. If necessary, open My Network Places. Click **View workgroup computers**. Double-click **Dell-czg**. Double-click **Dell-czg-C**. Click **Tools**. Click **Disconnect Network Drive**. Click **OK**.

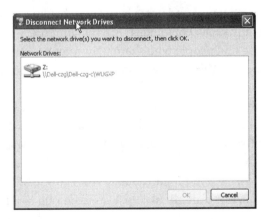

WHAT'S HAPPENING?   Now Drive Z, a network drive, really refers only to the folder WUGXP on the Dell-czg. Notice that the description of the icon tells you this information.

12 Select **WUGXP** in the window (Drive Z). Click **OK**.

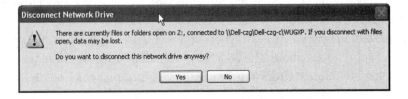

WHAT'S
HAPPENING?   You are warned that you may lose data.

13 Click **Yes**. Close all open windows.

WHAT'S
HAPPENING?   You have returned to the desktop.

12.15 The Internet

The Internet is an enormous, worldwide network of computers. Most simply stated, it is a network of networks. More than 500 million people and organizations are connected to the Internet (**http://www.nua.ie/surveys/how_many_online/world.html**). By accessing this network, you can communicate with all the people who sit at those computers. You can connect to various public and private institutions in order to gather information, do research, explore new ideas, and purchase items. You can access the government, museums, companies, colleges, and universities.

The Internet is part of the *information superhighway*, a term popularized by the media. The Internet is also referred to as *cyberspace*. William Gibson, who coined the term "cyberspace" in his book *Neuromancer*, defined it as "a consensual hallucination experienced daily by billions of legitimate operators, in every nation, by children being taught mathematical concepts. A graphic representation of data abstracted from the banks of every computer in the human system. Unthinkable complexity. Lines of light ranged in the nonspace of the mind, clusters and constellations of data. Like city lights, receding . . ."

When you log on to the Internet, you are in cyberspace. You can use the Internet to communicate by email (electronic mail), chat lines, and forums, which are like bulletin boards where you leave notes or read information about a topic of interest. Email allows you to send letters and notes instantly. Chat lines let you talk to people around the world on any subject of interest, such as computers, sewing, or Ukrainian culture. You are sure to find people who share your interests on the "net." You may connect to the *World Wide Web* (*WWW*) through the Internet. You may even publish your own documents.

For most people, the best-known aspect of the Internet is the Web, an informal expression for the World Wide Web. The Web is a collection of standards and protocols used to access information on the Internet. It is an interconnected collection of millions of *Web sites*. It is a virtual space accessible from the Internet that holds pages of text and graphics in a format recognizable by Web browsers. These pages are linked to one another and to individual files. Using the Web requires a browser to view and navigate through links. The most popular browsers today are Netscape Navigator and Microsoft Internet Explorer.

The World Wide Web is the graphical interface developed at the European Laboratory for Particle Physics in Geneva, Switzerland, by Tim Berners-Lee as a means for physicists to share papers and data easily. Tim Berners-Lee disseminated these tools for free, not taking any personal profit from this world-changing event. He even won a MacArthur "genius" award for the development of the WWW.

The Web and the Internet are not synonymous. The Internet is the actual network used to transport information. The Web is a graphical interface to the Internet. The Web uses three standards: *URLs* (*uniform resource locators*), which tell the location of documents; *HTML* (*Hypertext Markup Language*), which is the programming language used to create Web documents; and the protocols used for information transfer. Most Web traffic uses the protocol *HTTP* (*Hypertext Transfer Protocol*).

URLs are a standard means for identifying locations on the Internet. URLs specify three types of information needed to retrieve a document—the protocol to be used, the server address with which to connect, and the path to the information. The URL syntax is *protocol://server name/path*; examples of URLs are **http://www.netscape.com/netcenter** and **ftp://microsoft.com**. *FTP* stands for *File Transfer Protocol*, and it is used to download or upload files. HTTP is the major protocol used to transfer information within the World Wide Web.

A Web site resides on a server. It is both the virtual and the physical location of a person's or an organization's Web pages. A *Web page* is a single screen of text and graphics that usually has links to other pages. A Web site has an address, its URL. A *home page* is the first page of a Web site. A home page can be thought of as a gateway page that starts you on your search through that Web site.

Web pages usually have hypertext links, referred to as hyperlinks or links. A hypertext link is a pointer to a Web page on the same site or on a different site anywhere in the world. When you click on a link, your browser takes you to the page indicated by the link. If you were at a site about companies that provide electronic commerce solutions for businesses and saw a link called "Reference Desk," you could click it to see what references were available. From the Reference Desk page, you could see a hypertext link to a document called "United States Government Electronic Commerce Policy." Clicking that could take you to the Web site of the Department of Commerce, where you could read the article "Surfing the Net."

A Web site's type is indicated by the "dot" part of its address. Common types include commercial sites, which end in **.com**; educational sites, which end in **.edu**; government sites, which end in **.gov**; military sites, which end in **.mil**; and nonprofit organizations' sites, most of which end in **.org**. Since addresses are being depleted due to the rapid growth of the Internet, new "dots" are being developed, even ones longer than three characters.

Since so much information exists on the Internet, a category of sites called search engines has been developed to help you find what you want. These are essentially indexes to indexes. Popular search engines include Yahoo! (**http://www.yahoo.com**), AltaVista (**http://altavista.com**), Go.com (**http://www.guide.infoseek.com**), Google (**http://www.google.com**), Ask Jeeves (**http://www.askjeeves.com**), Lycos (**http://www.lycos.com**), and WebCrawler (**http://www.webcrawler.com**). Many companies and organizations position themselves as *portals*. A portal is an entry to the Web. Yahoo! and Excite are now expanding beyond being just search engines and are positioning themselves as portals.

There are many ways to access information on the Internet. One common way is to have a modem, communication software, and an online provider. You set up your dial-up network in the Phone and Modem Connections, found in Control Panel. You use your modem to dial out through your telephone line. In order to establish your dial-up account, you have to decide what service you are going to use. You could choose to connect to the Internet by belonging to a service such as MSN (Microsoft Network) or AOL (America Online). Each of these providers would give you detailed instructions on how to set up your dial-up account and would supply you with a local telephone number. If you used a service such as AOL or MSN, you would probably use its preferred browser, although you certainly could use any browser. Both MSN and AOL are now considered portals.

Another popular way to connect to the Internet is to use an ISP. *ISPs (Internet service providers)*, also called *IAPs (Internet access providers)* or service providers, are companies or organizations that provide a gateway or link to the Internet for a fee. EarthLink and XO are examples of this kind of company. You would be given explicit instructions from your provider how to create your dial-up account. You may choose your browser. Most people choose either Netscape Navigator or Microsoft Internet Explorer. The ISP is simply the link to the Internet. On your browser, you can have a home page, the first page that opens when you launch your browser. With some ISPs you can have your own Website, with a home page and one or more Web pages. Many ISPs charge a fee to create a Website, but some provide this service at no additional cost.

There are other ways to connect to the Internet. Some cable companies provide direct cable connections. In this case, you would not use your telephone line. You would always be connected to the Internet and would not have to dial up when you wished to surf the Net. You could use Netscape Navigator or Internet Explorer as your browser, or you could use the cable company's supplied browser. The advantage of a cable connection is speed. Some people joke that when the Internet is accessed over a telephone line, WWW stands for World Wide Wait. A cable connection, on the other hand, is extremely fast.

Another choice is to use an ISDN (Integrated Services Digital Network), which is a high-speed digital phone line that transfers data at a rate five to six times faster than that of a 28.8-kilobits-per-second modem. The phone company must lay the ISDN line to your home or business, and you must have a special modem. A DSL (digital subscriber line) is yet another choice, if available. Here a user can purchase bandwidth that is potentially 10 times faster than a 28.8-kilobits-per-second modem, but still slower than cable. You may be fortunate enough to have your connection through a business or educational institution that has a T1 or T3 leased line, which provides a faster connection than any of the above choices. Another way, not that common yet, is connecting via satellites. This connection provides truly high-speed communications, but it is, at this point, not readily available. A new choice that is gaining in popularity is a wireless connection. Again, you need special types of equipment to connect to a wireless modem.

DSL is becoming more and more popular. The acronym "DSL" stands for Digital Subscriber Line. It is used to refer both categories of DSL—ADSL and SDSL. Both operate over existing copper telephone lies and both need to be relatively close to a central telephone office. Usually you are required to be within 20,000 feet. In many areas there are waiting lists to have DSL installed. When you have DSL installed, the company will usually provide you with a special modem and will run a line directly into your house that looks just like a normal telephone line. They may also provide the network interface card. The installers will "activate" your line with the local company. Some companies will do the software installation as well as the hardware installation. To your computer, the DSL connection is just another link on a LAN. The company will provide you with the IP addresses that you require. DSL uses a static connection. "Static" refers to the fact that the IP address of this computer does not change. This is not the usual home connection, however. Most companies assign a temporary IP address to your computer as you connect.

12.16 An Overview of TCP/IP

When discussing communication, especially the Internet, you will hear the term TCP/IP (Transmission Control Protocol/Internet Protocol). TCP/IP is truly the protocol of the Internet. Data is transferred over the Internet through the protocols called TCP/IP.

Using the Internet is not unlike making a telephone call from Los Angeles to your mother in Phoenix. You know that you do not have a direct phone line connection to your mother's home. You dial and the phone company decides the best way to route your call. If Los Angeles is very busy, the phone company may send your call to Phoenix through Denver because Denver is not as busy and can process the data you are sending faster. It is not important to you how the phone company manages communication as long as you can talk to your mother.

On the Internet, data usually travels through several networks before it gets to its destination. Each network has a *router*, a device that connects networks. Data is sent in *packets*, units of information. A router transfers a packet to another network only when the packet is addressed to a station outside of its own network. The router can make intelligent decisions as to which network provides the best route for the data.

The rules for creating, addressing, and sending packets are specified by the TCP/IP protocols. TCP and IP have different jobs and are actually two different protocols. TCP is what divides the data into packets and then numbers each packet so it can be reassembled correctly at the receiving end. IP is responsible for specifying the addresses of the sending and receiving computers and sending the packets on their way. An *IP address* tells routers where to route the data. Data is divided into packets for two major reasons. The first is to ensure that sending a large file will not take up all of a network's time, and the second is to ensure that the data will be transferred correctly. Each packet is verified as having been received correctly. If a packet is corrupt, only the corrupted packet has to be resent, not the entire file.

A large company, college, or university will maintain a permanent open connection to the Internet (a T1 or T3 line), but this is not the case for a small office or a stand-alone PC. As mentioned previously, a single user often accesses the Internet through a dial-up, cable, or DSL connection instead. This procedure provides a temporary connection known as a *PPP* (*Point-to-Point Protocol*) connection. Another older protocol that accomplishes the same task is *SLIP* (*Serial Line Internet Protocol*). This connection provides full access to the Internet as long as you are online. However, if you are using a cable modem or a DSL connection, you do not need to dial up; you are always connected to your provider (the cable company or phone company). The connection is more like a LAN. You are always connected to the server, which in turn is connected to the gateway to the Internet.

Each computer connected to the Internet must have the TCP/IP protocols installed, as well as a unique IP address. The IP address identifies the computer on the Internet. If you are connected to the Internet through a permanent connection, the IP address remains a static (constant) address. If you have a dial-up account, a cable modem account, or other type of connection, you typically get a dynamic (temporary) IP address. It is a leased address and will change depending on how long the hosting server runs its leases for.

The Internet Corporation for Assigned Names and Numbers (ICANN, **http:// www.icann.org/general/abouticann.htm**) is the non-profit corporation that was formed to assume responsibility for the IP address space allocation, protocol parameter assignment, domain name system management, and root server system management functions previously performed under U.S. Government contract by IANA (Internet Assigned Numbers Authority, **http://www.ican.org**) and other entities. It is a nonprofit organization established for the purpose of administration and registration of IP numbers for the geographical areas previously managed by Network Solutions, Inc. When an organization applies for IP addresses, ICANN assigns a range of addresses appropriate to the number of hosts on the asking organization's network.

An IP address is made up of four numbers separated by periods. An IP address is 32 bits long, making each of the four numbers 8 bits long. These 8-bit numbers are called *octets*. The largest possible octet is 11111111. In decimal notation, that is equal to 255. So the largest possible IP address is 255.255.255.255. This format is called dotted decimal notation, also referred to as "dotted quad."

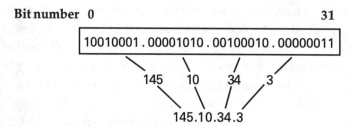

Figure 12.14—A Dotted Quad Address

As originally designed, IP address space was divided into three different address classes: Class A, Class B, and Class C. A Class A network receives a number that is used in the first octet of the address. Class A network numbers range from 0 to 127. If an organization was assigned 95 as its network address, the hosts in the network would have IP addresses like 95.0.0.1, 95.0.0.2, 95.0.0.3, and so forth. There are no Class A network addresses remaining. Class A networks are now referred to as /8 (pronounced "slash eight") or sometimes just 8 since they have an 8-bit network prefix.

A Class B network has its network address assigned as the first two octets. The first octet can range between 128 and 191. The second octet can range between 0 and 255. If an organization was assigned 145.21, the hosts in the network would have IP addresses like 145.21.0.1, 145.21.0.2, 145.21.0.3, and so on. Class B networks are now referred to as /16 since they have a 16-bit network prefix. There are also no Class B network addresses remaining.

Today, Class C network addresses are still available. These are assigned the first three octets as their network address. The first octet can range from 192 to 254. If an organization was assigned 199.91.14, the hosts in the network would have IP addresses like 199.91.14.1, 199.91.14.2, 199.91.14.3, and so on. Class C networks are now referred to as /24 since they have a 24-bit network prefix.

There are two additional classes: Class D, which is used to support multicasting, and Class E, which is reserved for experimental use. With the explosive expansion of the Internet, IP addresses are going to be depleted. The appropriate parties are working on a solution to this problem by developing a new standard, called IP Next Generation (IPv6). In the meantime, the current system remains in place.

Even with the current system, if you had an organization with a large number of computers, you would still run out of IP addresses fairly quickly. A solution is to not assign a permanent (static) IP address to a computer, but rather to assign an IP address to be used for the current work session only when the computer goes online (a dynamic IP address). In this system, when you log off, your IP address is returned to the list of available addresses, and, since not everyone is online at the same time, not as many IP addresses are needed. The server that manages dynamic IP addresses is called a dynamic host configuration protocol (DHCP) server. Some ISPs (Internet service providers) use this method to assign IP addresses to their dial-up clients. Others assign the address to the modem you dial into.

It would be difficult for most people to remember a numeric IP address. People remember names better than numbers. Phone numbers such as 1-800-FLOWERS or 1-800-URENTIT became popular for this very reason. Although you may not name your personal computer, computers in organizations are named so one computer can be distinguished from another. Organizations may choose names such as *pc1*, *pc2*, *mac1*, *mac2* or do it by department such as *sales*. Often, a computer's name will reflect its major role in the company. Thus, a computer devoted to handling electronic mail is often named *mail*, whereas a computer devoted to running the company's World Wide Web service is often called *www*. Both are easy-to-remember host names. These are in-house business names, not IP addresses for the Internet. If the computer is on the Internet, it has an IP address. An IP address can change, but typically it is not an organization's name. To give Internet addresses easy-to-remember names like this, the Internet is divided into domains. A domain is a general category that a computer on the Internet belongs to. A domain name is an easy-to-understand name given to an Internet host, as opposed to the numerical IP address. A user or organization applies for a *domain name* through the Internet Network Information Center (InterNIC) to ensure that each name is unique. InterNIC is now not the only organization responsible for assigning domain names. Some examples of domain names are **saddleback.cc.ca.us**, **solano.cc.ca.us**, **fbeedle.com**, **unl.edu**, **loyola.edu**, **ces.sdsu.edu**, **uci.edu**, **bookbiz.com**, **dell.com**, and **microsoft.com**.

A fully qualified domain name (FQDN) is the host name plus the domain name. As an example, a host name could be **mail** and the domain name could be **fbeedle.com**. The FQDN would be **mail.fbeedle.com**. Another host name could be **www** with a domain name of **microsoft.com**; thus the FQDN would be **www.microsoft.com**. A fully qualified domain name must be resolved into the numeric IP address in order to communicate across the Internet.

The *Domain Name System* (*DNS*) provides this name resolution. It ensures that every site on the Internet has a unique address. Part of its job is to divide the Internet into a series of networks called domains. Each site attached to the Internet belongs to a domain. Large domains are divided into smaller domains, with each domain responsible for maintaining unique addresses in the next lower-level domain or subdomain. DNS maintains a distributed database. When a new domain name is assigned, the domain name and its IP address are placed into a database on a top-level domain name server (domain root server), which is a special computer that keeps information about addresses in its domain. When a remote computer tries to access a domain name and does not know the IP address, it queries its DNS server. If that DNS server does not have the IP address in its database, it contacts a root DNS server for the authoritative server responsible for that domain. Then, the DNS server goes directly to the authoritative server to get the IP address and other needed information, updates its database, and informs the remote computer of the domain name's IP address.

When you use a browser to access a site on the Internet, you key in the URL (uniform resource locator). The browser program contacts the remote server for a copy of the requested page. The server on the remote system returns the page, tells the browser how to display the information, and gives a URL for each item you can click on the page. Figure 12.15 describes the parts of a URL.

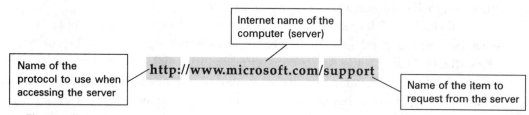

Figure 12.15—The Parts of a URL

The URL in the above figure is for the page that gives you support for Microsoft products.

This somewhat technical discussion is not intended to confuse you, but to give you some idea of Internet jargon. Terms like IP address, URL, and domain name are commonly used in conjunction with the Internet. Having some understanding and familiarity with the terms will help you navigate the Internet.

12.17 TCP/IP Utilities: The Command Line Interface with the Internet

Although the program you will normally use with the Internet is a browser such as Netscape Navigator, Windows also provides a series of commands, also called utility programs, that run at the command line. These are actually TCP/IP commands and are a set of tools that can help you troubleshoot problems as well as offer you connections to computers not connected to the Web, such as Unix system computers. If you are in a lab environment, and are going through a "firewall" (protection software designed to protect the network from unauthorized access) some of the utilities may not function. These utilities are automatically installed when you install the TCP/IP network protocol. Among these tools are:

Command	Purpose
ARP	Displays and modifies the IP to Ethernet translation tables.
FTP	Transfers files to and from a node running FTP services.
IPCONFIG	Displays the IP address and other configuration information.
NETSTAT	Displays protocol statistics and current TCP/IP connections.
PING	Verifies connections to a remote host or hosts.

ROUTE   Manually controls network-routing tables.

TELNET   Starts terminal emulation with a remote system running a Telnet service.

TRACERT   Determines the route taken to a destination.

Table 12.1—Command Line Commands for the Internet

If you want help on any of these commands, at the command line, you key in the command name, a space, and then **/?**, such as **ping /?**. In the next activities, you will look at some of these utilities.

12.18 IPCONFIG

IPCONFIG is a program that displays the current TCP/IP configurations and allows you to request a release or renewal of a DHCP-assigned IP address. This tool presents all the TCP/IP configuration settings in one place. If you have a dial-up service and you dial in, you are assigned an IP address that you might need to know if you are trying to Telnet into a restricted server. Telnet is the utility that emulates a video display terminal. You use it to connect to character-based computers on a TCP/IP network, typically a computer running the Unix operating system. When you Telnet, you log in and use a remote computer interactively. A restricted server denies everyone entry except those who are explicitly permitted into the system. The administrator of the remote system might need to know your IP address in order to allow you into the system.

12.19 Activity: Using IPCONFIG

1   Open a Command Prompt window.

2   Key in the following: C:\WINDOWS>**IPCONFIG** ⌗Enter⌗

```
Command Prompt                                          _ □ x

C:\WINDOWS>IPCONFIG

Windows IP Configuration


Ethernet adapter Internet Connection:

        Connection-specific DNS Suffix  . :
        IP Address. . . . . . . . . . . : 63.109.17.23
        Subnet Mask . . . . . . . . . . : 255.255.255.0
        Default Gateway . . . . . . . . : 63.109.17.254

Ethernet adapter Local Connection:

        Connection-specific DNS Suffix  . :
        IP Address. . . . . . . . . . . : 192.131.0.1
        Subnet Mask . . . . . . . . . . : 255.255.255.0
        Default Gateway . . . . . . . . :

C:\WINDOWS>
```

This computer has two Network Interface cards. You can see all the information for both cards that have TCP/IP bound to them. This computer is on a static DSL connection, so is always on the Web. Consequently, it always has an IP address. If you were not connected and logged on, no IP address would be reported. You can get much more complete information that shown above.

3   Key in the following: C:\WINDOWS>**IPCONFIG /ALL** ⌐Enter⌐

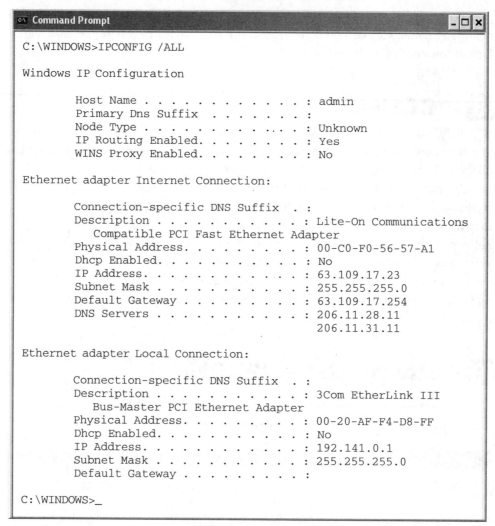

```
C:\WINDOWS>IPCONFIG /ALL

Windows IP Configuration

        Host Name . . . . . . . . . . . . : admin
        Primary Dns Suffix  . . . . . . . :
        Node Type . . . . . . . . . .. . . : Unknown
        IP Routing Enabled. . . . . . . . : Yes
        WINS Proxy Enabled. . . . . . . . : No

Ethernet adapter Internet Connection:

        Connection-specific DNS Suffix  . :
        Description . . . . . . . . . . . : Lite-On Communications
           Compatible PCI Fast Ethernet Adapter
        Physical Address. . . . . . . . . : 00-C0-F0-56-57-A1
        Dhcp Enabled. . . . . . . . . . . : No
        IP Address. . . . . . . . . . . . : 63.109.17.23
        Subnet Mask . . . . . . . . . . . : 255.255.255.0
        Default Gateway . . . . . . . . . : 63.109.17.254
        DNS Servers . . . . . . . . . . . : 206.11.28.11
                                            206.11.31.11

Ethernet adapter Local Connection:

        Connection-specific DNS Suffix  . :
        Description . . . . . . . . . . . : 3Com EtherLink III
           Bus-Master PCI Ethernet Adapter
        Physical Address. . . . . . . . . : 00-20-AF-F4-D8-FF
        Dhcp Enabled. . . . . . . . . . . : No
        IP Address. . . . . . . . . . . . : 192.141.0.1
        Subnet Mask . . . . . . . . . . . : 255.255.255.0
        Default Gateway . . . . . . . . . :

C:\WINDOWS>_
```

By adding the /ALL parameter, you were able to obtain more information about your network and internet connections. (*Note:* The above address have been altered for security purposes, and are not valid.)

12.20 Ping

If you are using your browser and cannot connect to a site, ping is an easy diagnostic tool for checking to see if the computer you are trying to reach is up and running. You can use ping (Packet InterNet Groper) to check out your connection to your service provider or to another computer. Ping sends out a request to see if a computer at the address you specified is there. It affirms whether that computer is up and running. You can ping either the IP address or the host name of the computer you are trying to reach. Ping sends four packets of data to the specified computer. If your ping is successful, you see four replies on the screen display. If any of the packets did not successfully reach their destination or were returned to your computer, you will see a "Request timed out" message. If the IP address is verified but the host name is not, there is some kind of name resolution problem. You can also ping yourself using the special loopback address discussed earlier (127.0.0.1). However, you should be aware that pings are not always reliable. Some servers do not allow themselves to be "pinged," because the server would then be wasting its time responding to pings. Furthermore, some organizations also do not respond to pings for security reasons. Also, many school computer labs do not allow ping requests.

12.21 Activity: Using Ping

Note: This activity assumes you are logged on to the Internet.

1   Open a Command Prompt window.

2   Key in the following: C:\WINDOWS>**PING FBEEDLE.COM** Enter

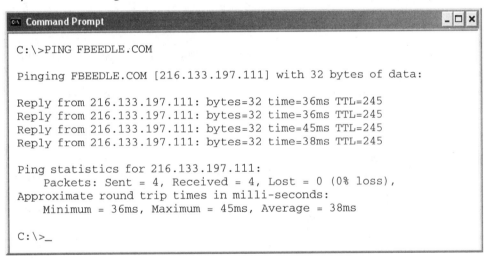

```
C:\>PING FBEEDLE.COM

Pinging FBEEDLE.COM [216.133.197.111] with 32 bytes of data:

Reply from 216.133.197.111: bytes=32 time=36ms TTL=245
Reply from 216.133.197.111: bytes=32 time=36ms TTL=245
Reply from 216.133.197.111: bytes=32 time=45ms TTL=245
Reply from 216.133.197.111: bytes=32 time=38ms TTL=245

Ping statistics for 216.133.197.111:
    Packets: Sent = 4, Received = 4, Lost = 0 (0% loss),
Approximate round trip times in milli-seconds:
    Minimum = 36ms, Maximum = 45ms, Average = 38ms

C:\>_
```

WHAT'S HAPPENING?   You have successfully pinged the publisher of this book. Note the IP address of the requested server is given.

3   Key in the following: C:\WINDOWS>**PING 216.133.197.111** Enter

```
C:\WINDOWS>PING 216.133.197.111

Pinging 216.133.197.111 with 32 bytes of data:

Reply from 216.133.197.111: bytes=32 time=58ms TTL=245
Reply from 216.133.197.111: bytes=32 time=35ms TTL=245
Reply from 216.133.197.111: bytes=32 time=35ms TTL=245
Reply from 216.133.197.111: bytes=32 time=42ms TTL=245

Ping statistics for 216.133.197.111:
    Packets: Sent = 4, Received = 4, Lost = 0 (0% loss),
Approximate round trip times in milli-seconds:
    Minimum = 35ms, Maximum = 58ms, Average = 42ms

C:\WINDOWS>_
```

WHAT'S ▨▨▨▨
▨▨ HAPPENING?   You have pinged both the IP address and the host name. Notice that when you PING-ed the IP address, the HOST name was not returned.

4   Key in the following: C:\WINDOWS>**PING 127.0.0.1** ⏎Enter⏎

```
ⓒ Command Prompt                                               _ □ ✕

C:\WINDOWS>PING 127.0.0.1

C:\WINDOWS>PING 127.0.0.1

Pinging 127.0.0.1 with 32 bytes of data:

Reply from 127.0.0.1: bytes=32 time<1ms TTL=128
Reply from 127.0.0.1: bytes=32 time<1ms TTL=128
Reply from 127.0.0.1: bytes=32 time<1ms TTL=128
Reply from 127.0.0.1: bytes=32 time<1ms TTL=128

Ping statistics for 127.0.0.1:
    Packets: Sent = 4, Received = 4, Lost = 0 (0% loss),
Approximate round trip times in milli-seconds:
    Minimum = 0ms, Maximum = 0ms, Average = 0ms

C:\WINDOWS>_
```

WHAT'S ▨▨▨▨▨
▨▨ HAPPENING?   You have just "pinged" yourself. The IP address of 127.0.0.1 is the loopback address and is the IP address of your computer. If you are having a hardware problem with your NIC, this will usually fail. PING-ing yourself can be a valuable troubleshooting tool.

5   Key in the following: C:\WINDOWS>**PING MICROSOFT.COM** ⏎Enter⏎

```
ⓒ Command Prompt                                               _ □ ✕

C:\WINDOWS>PING MICROSOFT.COM

Pinging MICROSOFT.COM [207.46.197.100] with 32 bytes of data:

Request timed out.
Request timed out.
Request timed out.
Reply from 207.46.129.52: Destination net unreachable.

Ping statistics for 207.46.197.100:
    Packets: Sent = 4, Received = 1, Lost = 3 (75% loss),
Approximate round trip times in milli-seconds:
    Minimum = 0ms, Maximum = 0ms, Average = 0ms

C:\WINDOWS>_
```

WHAT'S ▨▨▨▨
▨▨ HAPPENING?   Microsoft has "blocked" your ping. However, you did attain some information, as the ping did resolve the address. (207.46.197.100)

6   Key in the following: C:\WINDOWS>**PING SUPPORT.MICROSOFT.COM** ⏎Enter⏎

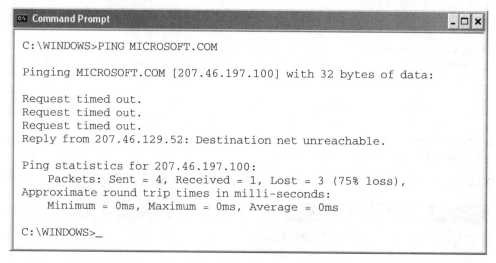

```
ⓒ Command Prompt                                               _ □ ✕

C:\WINDOWS>PING SUPPORT.MICROSOFT.COM

Pinging SUPPORT.MICROSOFT.COM [207.46.196.102] with 32 bytes of data:
```

```
Reply from 207.46.196.102: bytes=32 time=34ms TTL=51
Reply from 207.46.196.102: bytes=32 time=35ms TTL=51
Reply from 207.46.196.102: bytes=32 time=34ms TTL=51
Reply from 207.46.196.102: bytes=32 time=33ms TTL=51

Ping statistics for 207.46.196.102:
    Packets: Sent = 4, Received = 4, Lost = 0 (0% loss),
Approximate round trip times in milli-seconds:
    Minimum = 33ms, Maximum = 35ms, Average = 34ms

C:\WINDOWS>_
```

WHAT'S HAPPENING?   You tried another server, the Microsoft Support Server, and that allowed a response. Large organizations usually have a number of servers.

7   Close the Command Prompt window. If you are going to continue with the activities, remain logged on. Otherwise, log off the system.

12.22 Tracert

Tracert, pronounced "trace route," is a utility that traces the route on which your data is moving. It is a diagnostic utility that determines the route to the destination computer by sending packets containing time values (TTL—Time to Live). Each router along the path is required to decrease the TTL value by 1 before forwarding it. When the value of the TTL is 0, the router is supposed to send back a message to the originating computer. When you use the command, it returns a five-column display. The first column is the hop number, which is the TTL value. Each of the next three columns contains the round-trip times in milliseconds. The last column is the host name and IP address of the responding system. An asterisk (*) means that the attempt timed out. If nothing else, it is fascinating to see the way your data travels. Since tracert uses pings, you may not be able to trace a route if the server you are looking for does not allow pinging.

12.23 Activity: Using Tracert

Note: It is assumed you are logged on.

1   Open a Command Prompt window.

2   Key in the following: C:\WINDOWS>**TRACERT WWW.BOOKBIZ.COM** Enter

```
Command Prompt                                                    _ □ x

C:\WINDOWS>TRACERT WWW.BOOKBIZ.COM

Tracing route to WWW.BOOKBIZ.COM [67.112.148.73]
over a maximum of 30 hops:

  1   30 ms   30 ms   30 ms  adsl-63-199-16-254.dsl.snfc21.pacbell.net [63.109.17.254]
  2   16 ms   17 ms   19 ms  dist4-vlan60.snfc21.pbi.net [216.102.187.133]
  3   19 ms   18 ms   16 ms  bb2-g8-0.snfc21.pbi.net [209.232.130.83]
  4   17 ms   16 ms   16 ms  bb1-p12-0.snfc21.pbi.net [64.161.124.49]
  5   17 ms   19 ms   20 ms  sl-gw11-sj-3-0.sprintlink.net [144.228.44.49]
  6   19 ms   20 ms   19 ms  sl-bb25-sj-6-1.sprintlink.net [144.232.3.133]
  7   17 ms   20 ms   19 ms  sl-bb23-sj-15-0.sprintlink.net [144.232.3.249]
```

```
 8  27 ms   26 ms   26 ms sl-bb23-ana-11-1.sprintlink.net [144.232.18.217]
 9  25 ms   26 ms   26 ms sl-gw22-ana-10-0.sprintlink.net [144.232.1.106]
10  30 ms   30 ms   29 ms sl-swb-34-0.sprintlink.net [144.223.30.202]
11  29 ms   29 ms   29 ms dist3-vlan40.sndg02.pbi.net [206.13.30.10]
12  30 ms   29 ms   30 ms rback12-fe2-0.sndg02.pbi.net [63.200.206.143]
13  41 ms   41 ms   40 ms adsl-67-112-148-73.dsl.sndg02.pacbell.net [67.112.148.73]

Trace complete.

C:\WINDOWS>_
```

WHAT'S HAPPENING?   Your display will be different. In this example, the sending computer is in Fairfield, California. The Web site, **bookbiz.com**, is on a computer in San Diego. It is part of the **bookbiz.net** domain. If you look at the rightmost column, you can see what computers the packets are traveling on. The packets go out first on **pacbell.net**, which is this user's ISP. Notice the DSL notation, reporting the use of ADSL by this computer. It then goes to "pbi" network, to some connections in San Francisco, then to Sprintlink in San Jose and Anaheim, and eventually to San Diego. As you can see, the packets traveled up and down the California coast in milliseconds.

3   Key in the following: C:\WINDOWS>**TRACERT WWW.FBEEDLE.COM** Enter

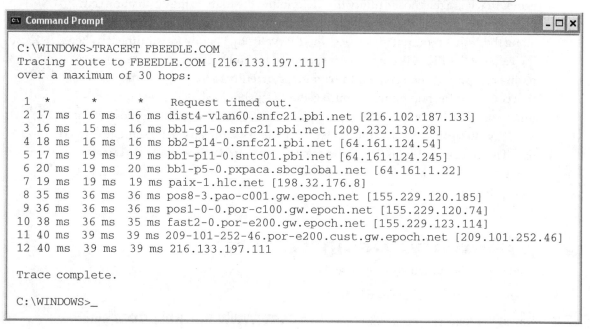

```
C:\WINDOWS>TRACERT FBEEDLE.COM
Tracing route to FBEEDLE.COM [216.133.197.111]
over a maximum of 30 hops:

 1   *        *        *       Request timed out.
 2  17 ms   16 ms   16 ms dist4-vlan60.snfc21.pbi.net [216.102.187.133]
 3  16 ms   15 ms   16 ms bb1-g1-0.snfc21.pbi.net [209.232.130.28]
 4  18 ms   16 ms   16 ms bb2-p14-0.snfc21.pbi.net [64.161.124.54]
 5  17 ms   19 ms   19 ms bb1-p11-0.sntc01.pbi.net [64.161.124.245]
 6  20 ms   19 ms   20 ms bb1-p5-0.pxpaca.sbcglobal.net [64.161.1.22]
 7  19 ms   19 ms   19 ms paix-1.hlc.net [198.32.176.8]
 8  35 ms   36 ms   36 ms pos8-3.pao-c001.gw.epoch.net [155.229.120.185]
 9  36 ms   36 ms   36 ms pos1-0-0.por-c100.gw.epoch.net [155.229.120.74]
10  38 ms   36 ms   35 ms fast2-0.por-e200.gw.epoch.net [155.229.123.114]
11  40 ms   39 ms   39 ms 209-101-252-46.por-e200.cust.gw.epoch.net [209.101.252.46]
12  40 ms   39 ms   39 ms 216.133.197.111

Trace complete.

C:\WINDOWS>_
```

WHAT'S HAPPENING?   In this example, the initial PING was timed out, either blocked or non responsive, but the request was passed on. It is not always easy to know where the route actually goes. You can recognize sfn as San Francisco, and por as Portland, but hlc and pxpaca? Quite often, the location remains a mystery.

4   Close the Command Prompt window.

12.24 FTP

FTP (file transfer protocol) servers store files that Internet users can download (copy) to their own computers. FTP is the communications protocol that these computers use to transfer files. It allows you to transfer text and binary files between a host computer and your computer. FTP requires you to log on to the remote host for user identification. Many FTP servers, however, let you log on as anonymous and use your email address as your password so that you can acquire free software and documents. Most FTP servers contain text files that describe the layout of their entire directory structure to help you find what you need. You can transfer files in either text or binary mode but you must first choose the mode. Text (ASCII) is the default.

One of the major advantages to FTP is that you do not care what operating system is on these remote computers because they all have TCP/IP. The ability to transfer files to and from computers running different operating systems is one of the greatest benefits of FTP. There are still computers out there that only have the character-based interface.

FTP has many commands. To get help from within FTP, you key in **HELP** *command*, where *command* is the name of the command for which you seek help. For a list of the commands, you simply key in **HELP**.

12.25 Activity: Using FTP

Note: It is assumed you are logged on.

1 Open a Command Prompt window. Key in the following:

C:WINDOWS>**ftp ftp.microsoft.com** [Enter]

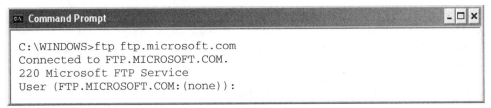

WHATS
HAPPENING?   You have just contacted the FTP server at Microsoft. It is asking for a user name. This server allows anonymous logins.

2 Key in the following: **anonymous** [Enter]

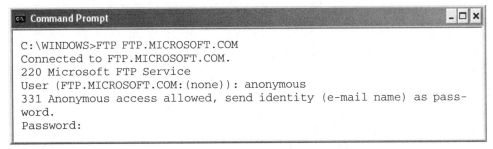

WHATS
HAPPENING?   It asks for your password and tells you that your email name can be used. When you key in your email address, you will not see it on the screen. You may key in anything for the password; you do not really need to key in your email address.

3   Key in the following: **aaaa** Enter (*Note:* The cursor will appear frozen when you key this in, but when you press Enter you will continue on.)

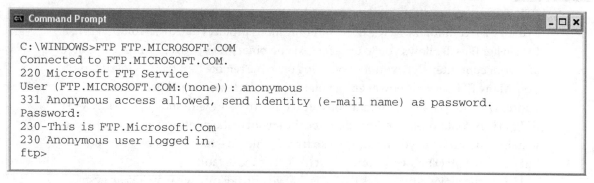

```
C:\WINDOWS>FTP FTP.MICROSOFT.COM
Connected to FTP.MICROSOFT.COM.
220 Microsoft FTP Service
User (FTP.MICROSOFT.COM:(none)): anonymous
331 Anonymous access allowed, send identity (e-mail name) as password.
Password:
230-This is FTP.Microsoft.Com
230 Anonymous user logged in.
ftp>
```

WHAT'S
HAPPENING?   You are logged into the site.

4   Key in the following: ftp>**help** Enter

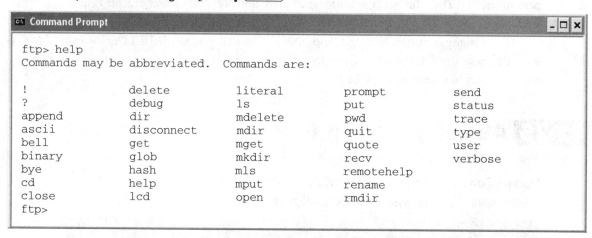

```
ftp> help
Commands may be abbreviated.  Commands are:

!              delete        literal      prompt      send
?              debug         ls           put         status
append         dir           mdelete      pwd         trace
ascii          disconnect    mdir         quit        type
bell           get           mget         quote       user
binary         glob          mkdir        recv        verbose
bye            hash          mls          remotehelp
cd             help          mput         rename
close          lcd           open         rmdir
ftp>
```

WHAT'S
HAPPENING?   These are the FTP commands. For syntax on any command, you would key in **help** plus the command name.

5   Key in the following: ftp>**help bye** Enter

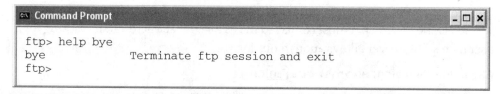

```
ftp> help bye
bye             Terminate ftp session and exit
ftp>
```

WHAT'S
HAPPENING?   The command BYE is how you can terminate the FTP session. You can use commands you are familiar with already, like DIR, to see what is in the directory.

6   Key in the following: ftp>**dir** Enter

```
ftp> dir
200 PORT command successful.
150 Opening ASCII mode data connection for /bin/ls.
dr-xr-xr-x  1 owner     group              0 Feb 13  2001 bussys
dr-xr-xr-x  1 owner     group              0 May 21  2001 deskapps
dr-xr-xr-x  1 owner     group              0 Apr 20  2001 developr
```

```
dr-xr-xr-x   1 owner      group            0 Feb 25    2000 KBHelp
dr-xr-xr-x   1 owner      group            0 Apr 19    2:36 MISC
dr-xr-xr-x   1 owner      group            0 May  2   11:22 MISC1
dr-xr-xr-x   1 owner      group            0 Feb 25    2000 peropsys
dr-xr-xr-x   1 owner      group            0 Jan  2    2001 Products
dr-xr-xr-x   1 owner      group            0 Sep 21    2000 ResKit
dr-xr-xr-x   1 owner      group            0 Feb 25    2000 Services
dr-xr-xr-x   1 owner      group            0 Feb 25    2000 Softlib
226 Transfer complete.
ftp: 745 bytes received in 0.01Seconds 74.50Kbytes/sec.
ftp>
```

WHAT'S HAPPENING?   You see a list of directories. Your listing may be different. You can recognize directories by locating a **dr** on the far left. **Softlib** is a directory that contains Microsoft software files. Files that have the extension **.txt** are ASCII files. Files that have a **.ZIP** extension are compressed. You need a utility like PKZIP to unpack the file. If you key in the command **get** *filename*, it will transfer the file to your default directory. If you key in **get** *filename* **-**, the file name followed by a hyphen acts just like the TYPE command. These commands are Unix commands. As you can see, DOS commands borrow much from Unix commands. If you wanted to transfer a binary file (**.EXE**), you would key in:

> binary
> get file.exe
> ascii

You key in **ascii** to return to text-file mode.

7 Key in the following: ftp>**cd deskapps** Enter

8 Key in the following: ftp>**dir** Enter

```
Command Prompt                                                    [_][□][×]

ftp> cd deskapps
250 CWD command successful.
ftp> dir
200 PORT command successful.
150 Opening ASCII mode data connection for /bin/ls.
dr-xr-xr-x   1 owner      group            0 Feb 25    2000 ACCESS
dr-xr-xr-x   1 owner      group            0 Feb 25    2000 DOSWORD
dr-xr-xr-x   1 owner      group            0 Feb 25    2000 excel
dr-xr-xr-x   1 owner      group            0 Mar 20    2000 games
dr-xr-xr-x   1 owner      group            0 Feb 25    2000 GEN_INFO
dr-xr-xr-x   1 owner      group            0 Feb 25    2000 homeapps
dr-xr-xr-x   1 owner      group            0 Feb 25    2000 ie
dr-xr-xr-x   1 owner      group            0 Feb 25    2000 kids
dr-xr-xr-x   1 owner      group            0 May 21    2001 macofficeten
dr-xr-xr-x   1 owner      group            0 Feb 25    2000 miscapps
dr-xr-xr-x   1 owner      group            0 Feb 25    2000 mmapps
dr-xr-xr-x   1 owner      group            0 Feb 25    2000 MONEY
dr-xr-xr-x   1 owner      group            0 Feb 25    2000 office
dr-xr-xr-x   1 owner      group            0 Feb 25    2000 powerpt
dr-xr-xr-x   1 owner      group            0 Feb 25    2000 project
dr-xr-xr-x   1 owner      group            0 Feb 25    2000 publishr
-r-xr-xr-x   1 owner      group         1791 Aug 30    1994 readme.txt
dr-xr-xr-x   1 owner      group            0 Feb 25    2000 word
dr-xr-xr-x   1 owner      group            0 Feb 25    2000 WORKS
226 Transfer complete.
ftp: 1282 bytes received in 0.01Seconds 128.20Kbytes/sec.
ftp>
```

WHAT'S
HAPPENING?   You changed directories to **deskapps** and are now seeing the contents of that directory.

9   Key in the following: ftp>**get readme.txt** Enter

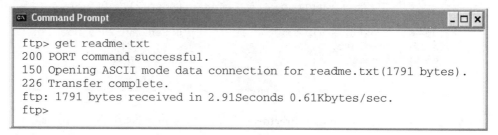

```
ftp> get readme.txt
200 PORT command successful.
150 Opening ASCII mode data connection for readme.txt(1791 bytes).
226 Transfer complete.
ftp: 1791 bytes received in 2.91Seconds 0.61Kbytes/sec.
ftp>
```

WHAT'S
HAPPENING?   You have downloaded the **readme.txt** file to the default directory.

10 Key in the following: ftp>**bye** Enter

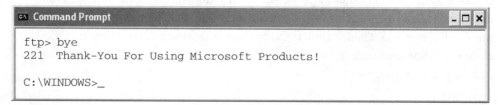

```
ftp> bye
221  Thank-You For Using Microsoft Products!

C:\WINDOWS>_
```

WHAT'S
HAPPENING?   You have logged off from the FTP site at Microsoft as well as quit the FTP program.

11 Key in the following: C:\WINDOWS>**TYPE README.TXT ¦ MORE** Enter

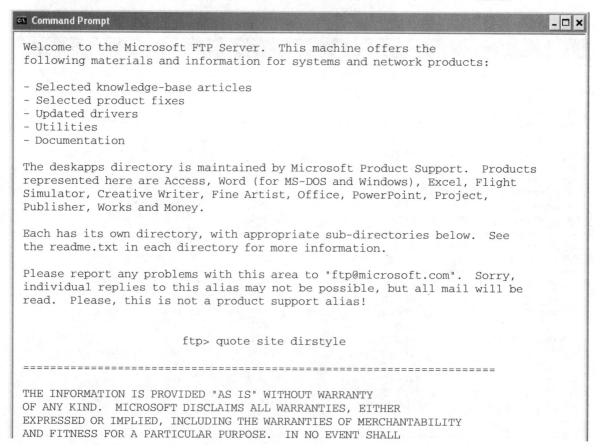

```
Welcome to the Microsoft FTP Server.  This machine offers the
following materials and information for systems and network products:

- Selected knowledge-base articles
- Selected product fixes
- Updated drivers
- Utilities
- Documentation

The deskapps directory is maintained by Microsoft Product Support.  Products
represented here are Access, Word (for MS-DOS and Windows), Excel, Flight
Simulator, Creative Writer, Fine Artist, Office, PowerPoint, Project,
Publisher, Works and Money.

Each has its own directory, with appropriate sub-directories below.  See
the readme.txt in each directory for more information.

Please report any problems with this area to "ftp@microsoft.com".  Sorry,
individual replies to this alias may not be possible, but all mail will be
read.  Please, this is not a product support alias!


                    ftp> quote site dirstyle

=====================================================================

THE INFORMATION IS PROVIDED "AS IS" WITHOUT WARRANTY
OF ANY KIND.  MICROSOFT DISCLAIMS ALL WARRANTIES, EITHER
EXPRESSED OR IMPLIED, INCLUDING THE WARRANTIES OF MERCHANTABILITY
AND FITNESS FOR A PARTICULAR PURPOSE.  IN NO EVENT SHALL
```

```
MICROSOFT CORPORATION OR ITS SUPPLIERS BE LIABLE FOR ANY
DAMAGES WHATSOEVER INCLUDING DIRECT, INDIRECT, INCIDENTAL,
CONSEQUENTIAL, LOSS OF BUSINESS PROFITS OR SPECIAL DAMAGES, EVEN IF
More  --
```

WHAT'S HAPPENING?   You are seeing the file you downloaded from Microsoft's ftp site.

12 Press **Q**.

13 Key in the following: C:\WINDOWS>**DEL README.TXT** Enter

14 Close the Command Prompt window.

12.26 Telnet

Telnet is a connection to a remote computer which makes your computer act like a terminal on the remote machine. This connection type is used for real time exchange of text. Telnet makes your computer into a dumb terminal. It is called a dumb terminal because each time your press a key on your computer, your computer does nothing except transmit your keystroke to some other computer on the Internet. The software performing the commands actually runs at the remote computer and not on your computer. Telnet operates in a client/server environment in which one host (the computer you are using running Client Telnet) negotiates opening a session on another computer (the remote host, running Server Telnet). During the behind-the-scenes negotiation process, the two computers agree on the parameters governing the session. Technically, Telnet is the protocol and is the terminal handler portion of the TCP/IP protocol suite. It tells the remote computer how to transfer commands from the local computer, on which you are working, to another computer in a remote location. Thus, Telnet lets you become a user on a remote computer. Both computers must support the telnet protocol. The incoming user must have permission to use the remote computer by providing a user name and password. Telnet can be used by a system administrator or other professionals to log on to your computer and trouble-shoot problems on your computer. However, Telnet is also most commonly used for connecting to libraries and other informational public databases. You can use a Telnet client to access hundreds of library and government databases. You begin the session in a Command Prompt window.

12.27 Activity: Using Telnet

1 Open a Command Prompt window.

2 Key in the following: C:\>**telnet** Enter

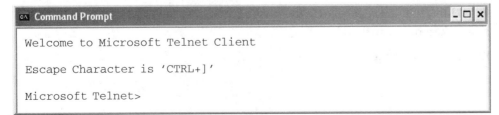

```
Command Prompt                                          _ □ ×

Welcome to Microsoft Telnet Client

Escape Character is 'CTRL+]'

Microsoft Telnet>
```

WHAT'S HAPPENING?   You have started the Telnet program. You need to know the useable commands:

3   Key in the following: **?/help** Enter

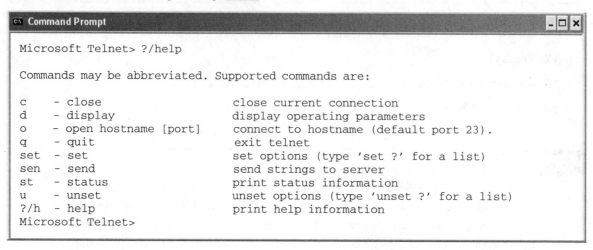

```
Microsoft Telnet> ?/help

Commands may be abbreviated. Supported commands are:

c    - close              close current connection
d    - display            display operating parameters
o    - open hostname [port]  connect to hostname (default port 23).
q    - quit                exit telnet
set  - set                set options (type 'set ?' for a list)
sen  - send               send strings to server
st   - status             print status information
u    - unset              unset options (type 'unset ?' for a list)
?/h  - help               print help information
Microsoft Telnet>
```

WHAT'S HAPPENING?   You see a list of commands you can use in the Telnet environment.

4   Key in the following: **open antpac.lib.uci.edu** Enter

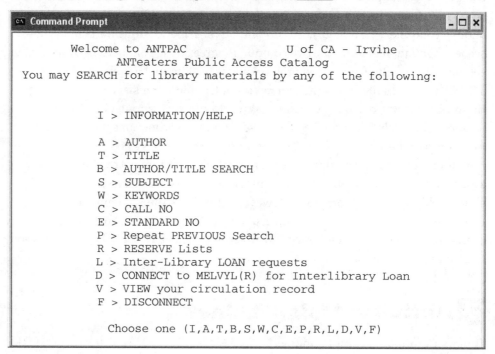

```
          Welcome to ANTPAC              U of CA - Irvine
                 ANTeaters Public Access Catalog
You may SEARCH for library materials by any of the following:


          I > INFORMATION/HELP

          A > AUTHOR
          T > TITLE
          B > AUTHOR/TITLE SEARCH
          S > SUBJECT
          W > KEYWORDS
          C > CALL NO
          E > STANDARD NO
          P > Repeat PREVIOUS Search
          R > RESERVE Lists
          L > Inter-Library LOAN requests
          D > CONNECT to MELVYL(R) for Interlibrary Loan
          V > VIEW your circulation record
          F > DISCONNECT

          Choose one (I,A,T,B,S,W,C,E,P,R,L,D,V,F)
```

WHAT'S HAPPENING?   You have just connected to the University of California at Irvine (UCI) Library Catalog. You are in the public access area and can look up information and make requests to this library.

5   Key in the following: **A.**

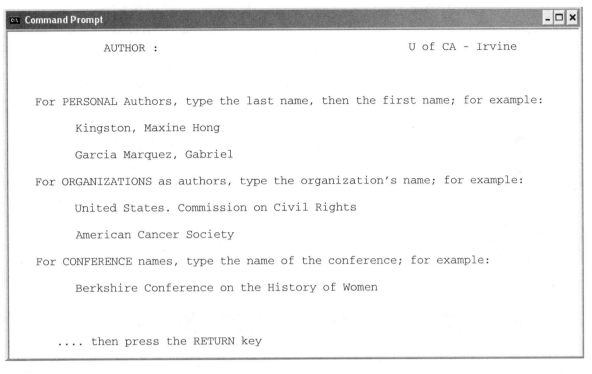

You are on the Author page.

6   At AUTHOR prompt, key in the following: **Babchuk, Nicholas** Enter

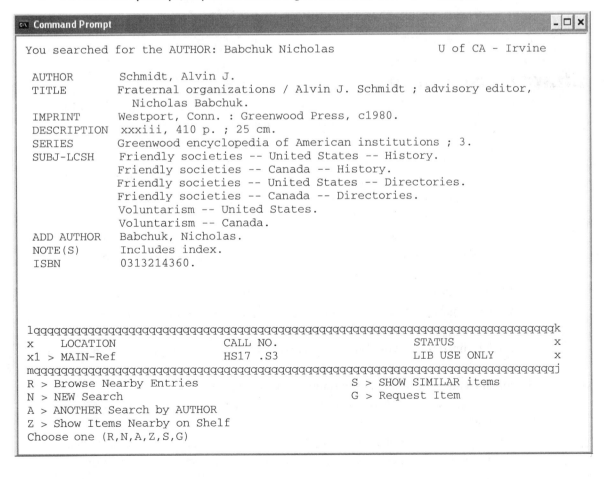

WHAT'S ▓▓▓▓
▓▓▓HAPPENING?   You have found a book, *Fraternal Organizations,* where Dr. Nicholas Babchuk, a renowned sociologist, was the advisory editor. You see the call number, the location, and the status. You could continue to search the UCI catalog for more articles or books. Instead, you will log out. The qqqqqqqqqqqqqqqqqq is the ASCII representation of whatever character they have used in their menu.

7   Press **N**. Press **D**.

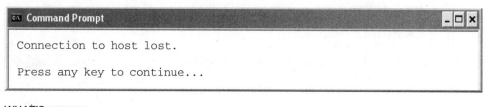

WHAT'S ▓▓▓▓
▓▓▓HAPPENING?   You have logged out of the library.

8   Press Enter

9   Key in the following: **quit** Enter

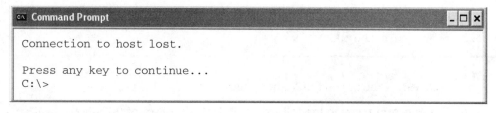

WHAT'S ▓▓▓▓
▓▓▓HAPPENING?   You have had a brief introduction to Telnet.

10 Close all open windows.

Chapter Summary

1. When you connect computers together, it is known as a LAN (local area network).
2. A server is a computer that provides shared resources. A client is a computer that accesses the shared resources provided by the server. Resources are the parts of the computer you share.
3. The standard model for networks with more than 10 users is a server-based network. It is one in which network functions are provided by a computer that is a dedicated server.
4. For networks with fewer than 10 users, the model is a peer-to-peer network, in which all computers are equal. Each computer can function as either a client or server.
5. A WAN (wide area network) consists of computers that use long-range telecommunications links to connect the networked computers over long distances.
6. A network interface card (NIC) is required to set up a network.
7. The NIC must match your bus architecture slot as well as the type of cable or wireless system used to connect your network.
8. You must have the proper networking software for your network to work.
9. A simple network has three parts: the hardware, the software, and the network administrator.
10. All computers on a network must use the same protocol. A protocol is a set of rules that allows computers to connect with one another and exchange information.

11. In a peer-to-peer network, you must name your computer as well as your workgroup. The workgroup name must be identical on all computers in the workgroup.

12. There are two parts to sharing resources: the client and the server. The server has the resource. The client is the computer that wishes to access the resource.

13. When you share devices, any computer on the network can use that device.

14. A *firewall* is a set of programs, located at a network gateway server that protects the resources of a private network from users from other networks.

15. A *gateway* is a network point that acts as an entrance to another network.

16. Common shared devices include printers, drives, and folders.

17. The computer that has the resource must first share it so that others on the network You must name your shared resource. Others on the network will access it by its shared name.

18. My Network Places is a tool to browse the network.

19. A port is a connection. The parallel port on your computer is called LPT1. Normally, if you physically connect a printer, it shows up on the port called LPT1.

20. Access control is the process of authorizing users, groups, and computers the ability to access objects (files, folders and devices) on the network.

21. If you are using the NTFS file system, you can set permissions and rights on individual files and folders. However, you must first clear the Simple file sharing check box to access these features.

22. Permissions determine which users can access which objects (files and folders and devices) and what kinds of access that user will have to those objects.

23. An administrative share allows administrators to connect the root directory of a drive over the network. It uses syntax of *drive letter*$, such as D$ or E$.

24. There is a series of commands that begin with net that deal with network management at the command line.

25. Each of these commands use the syntax of net *command* in which you specify one of the specific net commands substituting the actual command for *command*.

26. The NET VIEW command displays a list of resources being shared on a computer.

27. Once a drive has been shared, you may assign a drive letter to it. This act is called mapping a drive.

28. The NET USE command is the command line utility that allows you to map drives.

29. A drive alias assigned with the NET USE command may or may not be "persistent," meaning that the connections created may or may not remain in effect after shutting down the computer.

30. You may use the Administrative share to access a drive that is not explicitly shared.

31. You may map a drive using Windows Explorer or My Computer.

32. The Internet is a network of networks. You can use the Internet to use email and access chat lines and forums. You may connect to the World Wide Web.

33. The Web is an interconnected collection of Web sites that holds pages of text and graphics in a form recognized by the Web. These pages are linked to one another and to individual files. The Web is a collection of standards and protocols used to access information on the Internet. Using the Web requires a browser.

34. The Web uses three standards: URL (uniform resource locator), HTML (hypertext markup language), and a method of access such as HTTP (hypertext transfer protocol).

35. URLs are a standard format for identifying locations on the Internet.

36. A Web site is both the physical and virtual location of a person's or organization's Web page(s).

37. A Web page is a single screen of text and graphics that usually has hypertext links to other pages.

38. In order to access the Internet, you need a connection, communication software, and an online provider

39. Online providers includes services such as AOL (America Online) or MSN (Microsoft Network). You may also use an IAP (Internet access provider) or an ISP (Internet service provider).

40. You can connect to the Internet using a phone line, a special phone line (ISDN), DSL, through your cable company, wireless or via satellite.

41. TCP/IP is the protocol of the Internet.

42. Protocols are "bound" to specific Network Interface Cards

43. Each network has a router, which is a device that connects networks. A router can make intelligent decisions on which network to use to send data.

44. TCP protocol divides data into packets and numbers each packet.

45. IP protocol specifies the addresses of the sending and receiving computers and sends the packets on their way.

46. Each computer on the Internet uses TCP/IP and must have a unique IP address.

47. An IP address is made up of four numbers separated by periods. This format is called dotted-decimal notation. Each section is called an octet.

48. IP address space is divided into three major address classes: A, B, and C.

49. Each site attached to the Internet belongs to a domain. A user or organization applies for a domain name so that each domain name is unique.

50. Fully qualified domain names are an alphabetic alias to the IP address.

51. The DNS (domain name system) resolves the domain name into the IP address.

52. When you connect to the Internet, you use the URL of the site to which you wish to connect. If you know the IP address, you may use that as well.

53. Included with TCP/IP is a set of command line utilities that can help you trouble-shoot problems as well as offer you connections to computers not connected to the Web, such as Unix system computers. These tools are as follows:

Command	Purpose
arp	Displays and modifies the IP to Ethernet translation tables.
FTP	Transfers files to and from a node running FTP services.
IPCONFIG	Command line utility that displays the IP address and other configuration information
Netstat	Displays protocol statistics and current TCP/IP connections.
ping	Verifies connections to a remote host or hosts.
Route	Manually controls network-routing tables.
Telnet	Starts terminal emulation with a remote system running a Telnet service.
Tracert	Determines the route taken to a destination.

54. If you want help on any of these commands, at the command line you key in the command name, a space, and then /?.

Key Terms

Access control

browser

bus topology

client

coaxial cable

cyberspace

dedicated server

DNS (domain name
    system)

domain name

file server

FTP (file transfer protocol)

home page

HTML (hypertext markup
    language)

HTTP (hypertext transfer
    protocol)

IAP (Internet access
    provider)

information superhighway

Internet

IP address

ISP (Internet service
    provider)

LAN (local
    area network)

locally

mapped drive

network administrator

NOS (network operating
    system)

NIC (network interface
    card)

octet

packet

peer-to-peer network

permissions

portal

PPP (point-to-point
    protocol)

print server

protocol

resources

router

server

server-based network
    services

services

single point of failure

SLIP (serial-line Internet
    protocol)

star topology

T-connectors

terminator plug

Thinnet

topology

twisted-pair cable

UNC (universal naming
    convention)

URL (uniform
    resource locator)

WAN (wide area network)

Web page

Web site

workgroup

WWW (World Wide Web)

Discussion Questions

1. Define the following terms: *client, server, resources,* and *LAN.*
2. Compare and contrast a client computer with a server computer.
3. Compare and contrast a server-based network with a peer-to-peer network.
4. List and explain three reasons why you might set up a network.
5. Compare and contrast a LAN and a WAN.
6. What is the purpose and function of a network interface card?
7. Compare and contrast setting up a peer-to-peer network using bus topology and using star topology.
8. Explain the purpose and function of a hub. Identify one advantage to using a hub.
9. Why is it important that all computers in a peer-to-peer network use the same workgroup name?
10. Explain the difference between using a printer locally and using a print server a network.
11. List and explain the steps you need to take in order to share your drive on a peer-to-peer network.
12. Give the syntax of the network path and explain each part of the syntax.
13. When sharing your drive with another computer, why is it not wise for your share name to be C?
14. What are the net commands? Identify two net commands and how they can be used and what information they will provide.

15. What is an Administrative share? How can it be used?
16. Explain the purpose and function of a mapped drive.
17. Identify two ways you may map a drive.
18. What is the purpose and function of the Internet?
19. How can the Internet be used?
20. Compare and contrast the Internet and the World Wide Web.
21. Explain the purpose of URLs, HTML, and HTTP.
22. List the three types of information a URL needs to retrieve a document.
23. What is a Web site?
24. Compare and contrast a Web site with a Web page.
25. The type of Web site is indicated by its "dot" address. Explain.
26. What is a hypertext link?
27. List and explain three ways a computer user can connect to the Internet.
28. Why is TCP/IP considered the protocol of the Internet?
29. What is a router?
30. Compare and contrast the purposes and functions of TCP and IP.
31. Data is divided into packets when it is transferred over the Internet. Why?
32. What is the purpose of an IP address?
33. Compare and contrast a static versus a dynamic IP address.
34. Why is the format of an IP address called dotted-decimal notation?
35. Describe the format of a Class A, Class B, and Class C IP address.
36. What is a loopback address?
37. Explain the purpose and function of the domain name system.
38. What is the purpose of name resolution?
39. Why can computers have both an IP address and a domain name?
40. Define each part of the following URL—**http://www.amazon.com/books**.
41. Explain the purposes and functions of two utilities that are automatically installed when TCP/IP network protocol is installed.
42. How can you receive help on the TCP/IP utilities?
43. What is the purpose and function of IPCONFIG?
44. What is the purpose and function of ping? tracert?
45. What is the purpose and function of ftp? telnet?

True/False Questions

For each question, circle the letter T if the question is true or the letter F if the question is false.

T	F	1.	LAN is an acronym for Local Area Network
T	F	2.	You may set file permissions on a file located on a drive that is using the FAT32 file system.
T	F	3.	Resources can not be shared on a peer-to-peer network.
T	F	4.	TCP/IP is the commonly used network protocol.
T	F	5.	An IP address is made up of four numbers separated by periods.

Completion Questions

6. The internet is an example of a(n) _____.

7. The address used to connect you to a WEB server is known as its

    _____.

8. To assign a drive letter to a shared resource at the command line, use the
   _____ command.

9. FTP stands for _____.

10. A command line utility used to check your connection to another computer is

    _____.

Multiple Choice Questions

11. What protocol is used to connect to the Internet?
    a. PPP
    b. NetBios
    c. NetBeui
    d. TCP/IP

12. **http://www.solano.cc.ca.us** is an example of
    a. dotted quad notation.
    b. URL.
    c. both a and b
    d. none of the above

13. You can see the path taken by the packets sent on your computer to a
    particular address using
    a. ping
    b. ipconfig
    c. tracert
    d. net use

14. The get command is used with the _____ utility.
    a. telnet
    b. ipconfig
    c. ftp
    d. net use

15. If you give permission to _____, then all users may access to your
    shared folder.
    a. Everyone
    b. World
    c. Power Users
    d. Guest

Homework Assignments

Problem Set I—At the Computer

Note 1:   To do these two activities, you must have access to the Internet as well as a
browser to access the World Wide Web.

Note 2:   Be sure to include your name and class information and the question you
are answering.

1. Visit the site of the magazine Scientific American (**http://www.sciam.com**). You
   will be taken to the home page. Click **Past Issues**. Click **Issues from 1999**. Click

December 1999. Scroll till you see **Technology and Business**. Read the article entitled **Cable-Free** and write a brief report on what it says.

2. Go to **http://antwrp.gsfc.nasa.gov/apod/astropix.html**, which is the Astronomy Picture of the Day site. Use the Search capability of the site to discover the picture of the day for April 21, 2002. Write a paragraph on the picture that was displayed on that date.

3. Visit the site at **http://www.computerhope.com/msdos.htm**. Follow the **MS-DOS History** link. Take a snapshot of the screen with the release dates of MS-DOS versions. Once you have created your snapshot, paste it into WordPad and then write at least a paragraph explaining the snapshot. Print the WordPad document.

    To create a snapshot of the entire screen, press the **Print Screen** key. Then open WordPad. Click **Edit**. Click **Paste**. You will have a snapshot (a picture / graphic) of the entire screen. To create a snapshot of only the active window, press the **Alt** + **Print Screen** keys. Then open WordPad. Cick **Edit**. Click **Paste**. You will then have a snapshot of only the active window.

4. Locate the current weather information for your city. Locate a satellite image of the weather for your area. Describe what steps you took to locate this information. Identify at least two URLs that show weather information.

5. Locate the nearest restaurant to your home that serves Chinese food. Describe what steps you took to locate this information. List the URL for this site.

6. Find out if your city has a Web site. Describe what steps you took to locate this information. Name two items that have links that are on this site. If your city does not have a Web site, locate the website for the city that is closest to you that does have a Web site. Describe what steps you took to locate this information. Name two items that have links that are on this site.

7. Find out if your school has a Web site. Describe what steps you took to locate this information. Name two items that have links that are on this site. If your school does not have a Web site, locate the Web site for another school that does have a Web site. Describe what steps you took to locate this information. Name two items that have links that are on this site. Describe how you might use this site.

Problem Set II—Brief Essay

Be sure to include your name and class information and the question you are answering.

1. A small advertising company has three employees: Mary Brown, Jose Rodriquez, and Jin Li Yu. The office has three computers, a scanner, a laser printer, and a color printer. It has a hub. You have already set up a peer-to-peer network. The laser printer is connected to the hub. Mary's computer is also connected to the laser printer, Jose's computer is connected to the color printer, and Jin Li's computer is attached to the scanner. Mary needs access to the color printer but not the scanner. Jose needs only the color printer. Jin Li needs access to the color printer. Mary and Jose need access to a folder called Clients on Jin Li's computer. Jin Li needs access to a folder on Mary's computer called Parts. Describe what you need to do to accomplish these goals.

2. Briefly describe the importance and use of two command line utilities of your choosing. Describe what they are and how they are used.

CHAPTER 13

FILE AND DISK
MAINTENANCE

Learning Objectives

1. Explain conditions that can cause hardware problems and how to avert these problems.
2. Explain what lost clusters and cross-linked files are.
3. Explain conditions that can cause data errors and how to avert these errors.
4. Explain the purpose and function of Check Disk.
5. Explain the purpose and function of Disk Cleanup.
6. Compare and contrast contiguous and noncontiguous files.
7. Explain how Disk Defragmenter can help optimize a disk's performance.
8. Explain the purpose and function of Task Scheduler.
9. Compare and contrast full, differential, and incremental backups.
10. Explain the importance of and procedures for backing up and restoring files.
11. Explain the purpose and function of the ASR (Automated Recovery System).
12. Explain the purpose and function of initialization files.
13. Explain the purpose and function of the Registry.
14. Explain the purpose and function of System Restore.
15. Explain the purpose and function of a paging file.
16. Explain the purpose and function of plug and play.
17. Explain the purpose and function of Administrative Tools.

Student Outcomes

1. Use Check Disk to repair disk problems.
2. Use Disk Cleanup to remove unneeded files.
3. Use Disk Defragmenter to optimize a disk's performance.
4. Use Task Scheduler to add and remove a scheduled task.
5. Back up and Restore files.
6. Create a restore point with System Restore
7. Use Device Manager to review your driver settings.
8. Use System Information.
9. Use the Computer Management tool.

Chapter Overview

By running programs designed to keep your hard disk in good working order, you can learn much about your system and optimize the performance of your disk. You can repair disk errors, gain more disk space by removing unneeded files, store files more efficiently, run regular maintenance routines, schedule programs to run at specific times and dates, synchronize your files, back up and restore files, and learn other ways to gain more space on your disk.

In this chapter, you will learn to use different file and system programs. You will learn how to use the Check Disk program to check for system errors and bad sectors on your disks. You will learn how Disk Cleanup can delete unnecessary files. You will use Disk Defragmenter to optimize the storage space of a disk. You will see that you can set up a regular maintenance routine as well as use Task Scheduler to run programs. The Backup program will allow you to back up and restore files for data protection and create an ASR (Automated System Recovery) Disk. If you have problems starting your computer, the ASR can assist you in trying to fix the problems.

The Registry keeps track of all of your object linking and embedding (OLE) operations. It stores all the configuration information about the hardware on your specific computer. It also tracks and contains all the preferences for each user of the computer system. Typically, you do not have to deal directly with the Registry. The preferred method for making changes is to use tools such as Control Panel. However, if your Registry becomes corrupt, there are methods to restore it. You can use System Restore. If you add new hardware or software that causes your computer to become inoperable, System Restore allows you to roll back your computer system to a time when your computer was working properly. You will use plug and play as well as Device Manager to determine if all your devices are working properly. Windows XP also offers information about your system in a tool called System Information that tells you about your computer system. In addition, Windows XP Professional provides a set of Administrative Tools to help you manage your system. You will use the Computer Management tool to look at different aspects of your computer system.

13.1   Detecting and Repairing Errors with Check Disk

It is a truism in the computer world that it is not *if* you will have problems with your hard drive but *when*. Hard drives can have physical problems for many reasons. Some of these are:

- Wear and tear on the hard disk. When your computer is on, the hard disk is always spinning. Eventually your hard disk can wear out. This fate of all hard disks is one reason users like computers that support power management. If you use power management features, you can place your computer on standby when it is idle. While on standby, your monitor and hard disks turn off, and your computer uses less power. You can also put your computer in hibernation. The hibernation feature turns off your monitor and hard disk, saves everything in memory on the disk, and turns off your computer. Typically, you use these features to conserve power. You can also use power management features, if your computer supports them, to minimize wear on your system.
- Head crash. The read/write heads of the hard disk float on a cushion of air just above the spinning platters. A severe jolt can cause the heads to crash onto the disk, which can destroy the disk as well as the data on the disk. This event is called a *head crash*. To minimize this problem, place your system unit in a location where it will not get knocked around.

In addition to physical problems, there are also software-related problems. For instance, you can infect your computer with a virus by using an infected floppy disk, unzipping and installing an infected program, using a data file that has a virus embedded in it, or receiving email that has a virus embedded in it. With email, opening a document from an unknown source can infect your computer with a virus.

Viruses are programs that have damaging side effects. Sometimes these side effects are intentionally damaging, sometimes not. Some viruses can destroy a computer's hard disk or the data on the disk. To minimize this problem, you should purchase an antivirus program that will always check your drive for viruses. Popular virus protection programs include Norton AntiVirus and McAfee VirusScan.

The following conditions can cause errors to your data that you may be able to repair. In some cases, these are errors that you have no control over. These include:

- Power surge. Although the current supplied to your computer is usually fairly constant, there can be a sudden and possibly damaging increase in line voltage. This event can occur, for instance, during a severe electrical storm or when the power company has a huge demand such as during a heat wave. To minimize this problem, plug your computer into a surge protector or surge suppressor. A *surge protector (surge suppressor)* is a device that prevents surges from reaching your computer.

- Power outage. If the power suddenly goes out, you will, of course, lose everything in memory, and that could also damage your hard disk. To minimize this damage, use a surge suppressor. There is a more expensive solution—purchase a UPS (Uninterruptible Power Supply). This device provides a backup power supply, usually by battery, so that you can shut down the system properly.

- Improperly closed program or locked system. If you simply turn off your computer without closing application programs or going through the Windows XP Professional shut-down process, information is not properly written to the disk. To minimize this problem, you should always close any open programs and always go through the Windows XP Professional shut-down procedure. However, sometimes your computer will "lock." In other words, your keyboard, mouse, and program become frozen and your only choice is to go through a power cycle (physically turn the computer off, wait at least five seconds, and then turn it back on again).

Windows XP Professional comes with a program called Check Disk, which can check your hard disk for problems and repair those problems. Check Disk checks for logical errors in the file system, such as invalid entries in the tables that keep track of file location and problems that involve the physical disk, lost clusters, or cross-linked files.

Lost clusters are not uncommon. They occur because the file allocation table (FAT) and directory work in conjunction. Every file has an entry in the directory table. This entry points to the starting cluster in the FAT. If the file is longer than one cluster, which it usually is, the FAT has a pointer that leads it to the next cluster, and the next cluster, and so on. These pointers *chain* together all the data in a file. If the chain is broken (a pointer is lost), the disk ends up with lost clusters. Lost clusters are incorrectly marked as used in the FAT and unavailable for new data. A *lost cluster* then is marked by Windows XP Professional as being in use but not representing any part of the chain of a file. In other words, the FAT knows that the clusters are occupied by data, but does not know to which file the clusters belong. Look at Figure 13.1. The FAT looks normal. Clusters 3, 4, and 6 are a chain, but the

FAT does not know to which file this chain belongs. There is no entry in the directory. Hence, these are lost clusters.

Root Directory Table   File Allocation Table

File Name	File Extension	Date	Time	Other Info	Starting Cluster Number

Cluster Number	Status
1	in use
2	in use
3	4
4	6
5	in use
6	end

Clusters 3, 4, and 6 have data, are linked together, but have no file entry in the directory table.

Figure 13.1—Lost Clusters

Since these lost clusters belong to no file, they cannot be retrieved or deleted. The data becomes useless. Windows XP Professional cannot write other data to these lost clusters, so you lose space on the disk. This phenomenon occurs for a variety of reasons. The most common explanation is that a user did not exit a program properly. Often, when a user interrupts this process, the data will not be properly written to the disk. Other times, power failures or power surges cause clusters to be lost.

Check Disk will fix these lost clusters automatically or save them to disk as files. It converts lost file fragments into files so that you may view the contents to determine whether there is any data in them that you want. The files are stored in thea directory and have names such as File0000.chk, File0001.chk, and so on.

A cross link occurs when two or more files claim the same cluster simultaneously or twice in the same file. The files that are affected are called *cross-linked files*. The data in a cross-linked cluster is usually correct for only one of the cross-linked files, but it may not be correct for any of them. Figure 13.2 gives an example of what happens when two files claim the same cluster.

Root Directory Table   File Allocation Table

File Name	File Extension	Date	Time	Other Info	Starting Cluster Number
MY	FIL	4-15-94	11:23		1
HIS	FIL	4-15-94	11:23		3

Cluster Number	Status
1	MY.FIL
2	MY.FIL
3	HIS.FIL
4	MY.FIL HIS.FIL
5	HIS FIL
6	MY.FIL

Figure 13.2—Cross-Linked Files

In the example above, My.fil thinks it owns clusters 1, 2, 4, and 6. His.fil thinks it owns clusters 3, 4, and 5. Both My.fil and His.fil think that cluster 4 is part of their chain. Either one or both of these files are bad.

Figure 13.3 shows an example of a file with two FAT entries that refer to the same cluster. EOF stands for the end-of-file marker.

Cluster number	100	101	102	103	104
Pointer to the next cluster with data	101	102	103	103	EOF

Figure 13.3—Another Cross-Linked File

In the above example, the pointer in cluster 100 says to go to cluster 101 (where there is more data in the chain); the pointer in cluster 101 says to go to cluster 102; the pointer in cluster 102 says to go to cluster 103, but the pointer in cluster 103 says to go again to cluster 103 which is not possible; so again, here is a cross-linked file.

Check Disk can check and repair local hard drives, floppy disks, and removable drives, but cannot find or fix errors on CD-ROMs or network drives. Check Disk can only be used on actual physical drives connected to your computer system. In addition, the system must have exclusive access to the disk to complete its job. If any disk files are in use, you will see an error message asking you if you want to reschedule the task to automatically occur the next time you start your computer. This is true if you are using FAT32 as a file system. It is recommended that Check Disk be run on a regular basis to prevent errors. Remember, before you run Check Disk, you should close any programs that are open, including screen savers, toolbars such as the Microsoft Office toolbar, and virus-checking programs. Since Check Disk is dealing with the disk structure, open programs or open files can cause data loss, corrupt files, and a host of other catastrophic errors.

If the disk or volume (disk partition) is formatted as NTFS (New Technology File System), Windows XP Professional automatically (without running Check Disk) logs all file transactions, replaces bad clusters, and stores copies of key information for all files on the NTFS volume.

13.2 Activity: Using Check Disk

Note: The DATA disk should be in Drive A.

1   Open Windows Explorer. Click **My Computer**. Right-click the Drive A icon. Click **Properties**. Click the **Tools** tab.

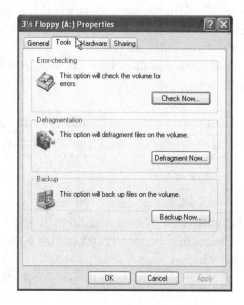

You are interested in error-checking. When you choose error-checking, you execute the Check Disk program.

2   Click **Check Now** in the Tools property sheet.

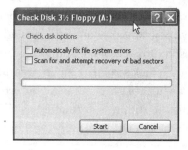

The Automatically fix file system errors option directs Windows to fix file system errors. The Scan for and attempt recovery of bad sectors option attempts to locate bad sectors, record them as bad, recover data from them, and write the recovered data to good sectors on the disk. If this option is selected, it is unnecessary to activate the first option because it is included automatically.

3   Click **Start**.

WHAT'S
HAPPENING?   The status bar indicated the program's progression. When the program has completed its task, a dialog box appears, informing you of the disk's condition. In this case, Check Disk has completed and found no errors.

4   Click **OK**. Click **OK**. Close all open windows.

13.3   Cleaning Up Your Disk

How well your computer system performs depends a great deal on your hard drive. Remember, all your files (programs and data files) primarily are stored on the hard disk. You need to access these files easily and quickly, and you need space for new files, both program and data files. In addition, many programs create temporary files while they are working. You must have sufficient disk space to allow the creation of these files. When you print a document, it is sent to the hard disk, where it is queued in a temporary file until the printer is ready. If you use the Internet, Web browsers cache files on the hard disk to improve your access speed to the sites you frequently visit. A *cache* is a storage area for often-used information. When you delete files from the hard disk, they are sent to the Recycle Bin which, again, is an area on the hard disk.

As you can see, you need hard disk space. You will find that many programs do not delete their temporary files. You will forget to empty the Recycle Bin or delete your cached Internet files. All of these items will not only cause your hard disk to run out of space, but will also slow down your system's performance. Windows XP Professional provides a tool to help you maintain your disk. It is a utility called Disk Cleanup. Disk Cleanup is intended to be run on your hard drives. Disk Cleanup gives you several options to assist you in recovering disk space.

13.4 Activity: Using Disk Cleanup

1   Click **Start**. Point to **All Programs**. Point to **Accessories**. Point to **System Tools**. Click **Disk Cleanup**.

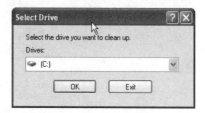

WHAT'S HAPPENING?   A message box appears, asking you which drive you want to clean up. If you have only one drive, go to step 4, as you have no selection to make.

2   Click the down arrow in the drop-down list box.

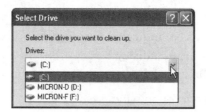

WHAT'S HAPPENING?   Your list will be different depending on how many hard drives you have. If you have only Drive C, you will see no other choices. Notice that no CD, DVD, or floppy drives appear.

3   Click outside the drop-down list to click it. Click **OK**.

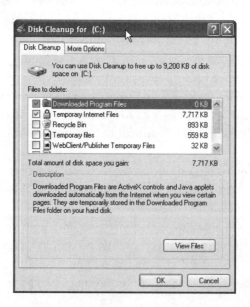

WHAT'S HAPPENING?   A quick message box appears, telling you that your system is being analyzed. Then the Disk Cleanup property sheet appears with the complete analysis. Your computer's analysis will be different. In the example, 9,200 KB can be regained in disk space. You have a choice of seven types of files to remove.

4 If Recycle Bin is not selected, check it now. Then click the **View Files** command button.

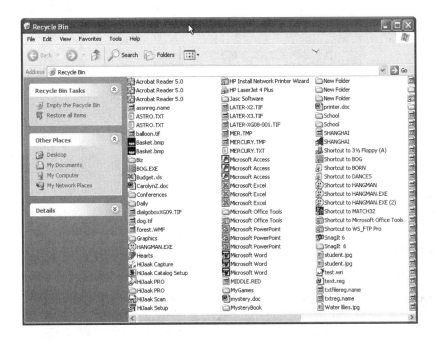

WHAT'S HAPPENING?   Before you delete the files, you can look at them to confirm that you do want to delete them. Your files will vary; you may even have no files to delete. In this example, the Recycle Bin has not been emptied in quite a while.

5 Close the Recycle Bin window. Click the **More Options** tab.

WHAT'S HAPPENING?   Other options are available to free up disk space. The first option is to remove Windows XP Professional components that you seldom or never use.

6   Under Windows components, click **Clean up**.

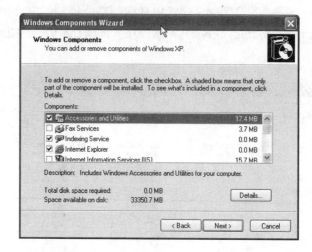

WHAT'S ▒▒▒
▒▒▒HAPPENING?   You are taken to Windows Components Wizard. You may remove
Windows components that you do not use. For instance, if you are using Netscape
Navigator as your browser, you could choose to remove Internet Explorer.

7   Click **Cancel**.

8   In the **Disk Cleanup** window, under Installed programs, click **Clean up**.

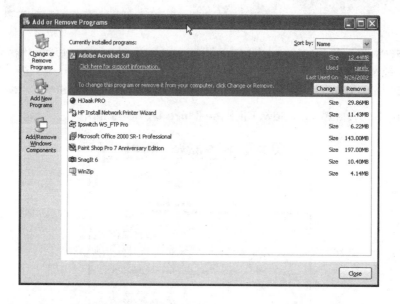

WHAT'S ▒▒▒
▒▒▒HAPPENING?   You are taken to the Add or Remove Programs utility. Here is a list
of programs that are installed on this system. Your list will be different. If you had a
program that you installed but found you did not use or did not like, you can
remove it here.

9   Click **Close**.

10 In the Disk Cleanup window, under System Restore, click **Clean up**.

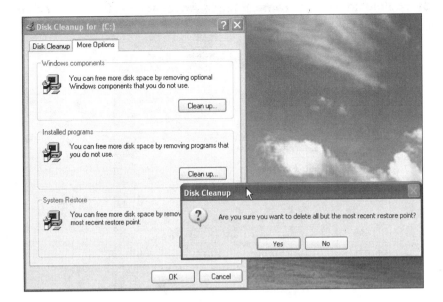

WHATS ▓▓▓▓▓▓
▓▓▓HAPPENING?   System Restore is a utility that you can use to restore your computer to a previous state, if a problem occurs with Windows XP Professional. System Restore works with the Windows XP system files and the registry. Restoring a system does not affect your data files. You will learn to create your own restore points but Windows XP normally creates a restore point daily and at the time of significant events such as when you install a new program or a new device driver. These system restore points can take up much room on your hard disk. Thus, you can opt to keep only the most current Restore Points. In this case, you do not want to run this utilty.

11 Click **No**. Click the **Disk Cleanup** tab.

12 Click **OK**.

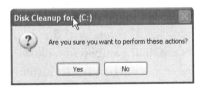

WHATS ▓▓▓▓▓▓
▓▓▓HAPPENING?   You are asked to confirm the Disk Cleanup.

13 Click **Yes**.

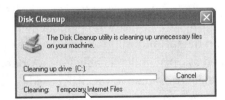

WHATS ▓▓▓▓▓▓
▓▓▓HAPPENING?   You see a progress report on your Disk Cleanup. When it is finished, you are returned the desktop.

14 Click **Start**. Point to **All Programs**. Point to **Accessories**. Point to **System Tools**. Click **Disk Cleanup**. Click **OK**.

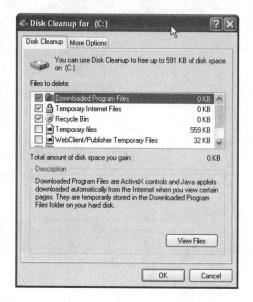

WHAT'S HAPPENING?   Space was gained on the disk in this example. Your results will be different. In this example, there is still space to be regained as every check box was not selected.

15 Click **Cancel**.

WHAT'S HAPPENING?   You have returned to the desktop.

13.5   Contiguous and Noncontiguous

Contiguous means in contact or touching. What does this have to do with files? Windows XP Professional keeps track of data by grouping it into files. In order to store and retrieve files, Windows XP Professional divides a disk into numbered blocks called sectors. Sectors are then grouped into clusters. A cluster is the smallest unit that Windows XP Professional will handle. A cluster is always a set of contiguous sectors. The number of sectors that make up a cluster on a hard disk varies, depending on the size of the hard drive and how it was installed.

Usually, a file will take up more than one cluster on a disk. Thus, Windows XP Professional has to keep track of the location of all the file's parts on the disk. When files are edited and need more space, the file is broken into fragments and stored in open space on the disk. Furthermore, if you are using FAT or FAT32, when a file is deleted, only the entries in the file allocation table (FAT) are deleted and the space the file occupied is marked as open and available for new data.

Windows XP Professional writes data to the disk based on the next empty cluster. It attempts to write the information in adjacent clusters. Windows XP Professional wants all the parts of a file to be next to each other (tries to write to adjacent clusters) because it is easier to retrieve or store information when it is together. When this occurs, the file is considered to be contiguous. When the file is broken up and is no longer stored in adjacent clusters, it is a noncontiguous or *fragmented file*. If a disk is comprised of many noncontiguous files, it can be called a *fragmented disk*. Windows XP Professional will take longer to read a noncontiguous file because the read/write heads must move around the disk to find all the parts of the file.

13.6   Optimizing the Performance of Disks

To fix a fragmented disk, you need a defragmenting utility program, sometimes called a *defragger* or a *disk optimization program*. Sometimes these programs are called disk compression programs, but that is a misnomer. These programs do not compress data. Defragmenting programs literally move data around on a disk to make files contiguous. In System Tools, Windows XP Professional provides a utility called Disk Defragmenter.

The Disk Defragmenter program rearranges files, programs, and empty space on the hard drive. Individual files are stored as a complete unit on the disk. Files are moved around on the disk until all files are stored contiguously on the disk with no space between them.

You should run both Check Disk and Disk Cleanup prior to running Disk Defragmenter. Before you optimize your hard disk, you want to remove all lost or cross-linked clusters and all unnecessary files. Before you run any disk optimizers, it is recommended that you close all open programs, including screen savers and virus-checking programs. In addition, you should be sure to have plenty of time to run Disk Defragmenter. A good time to run the program is overnight when you are away from the computer. If you run it every couple of weeks, depending on your computer use, the program will not take as long to run, because it will have less to do.

You must use the Disk Defragmenter program that comes with Windows XP Professional. Although Disk Defragmenter is safe, it directly manipulates your disk. Therefore, you should back your disk up before beginning Disk Defragmenter. You may use Disk Defragmenter on local drives only, but you cannot run it on floppy disks. You also cannot use it on network drives. In addition, you must have administrator privileges to use this utility program.

13.7   Activity: Using Disk Defragmenter

1   Place the DATA disk in Drive A.

2   Click **Start**. Click **My Computer**. Right-click the Drive A icon. Click **Properties**. Click the **Tools** tab. Click **Defragment Now**.

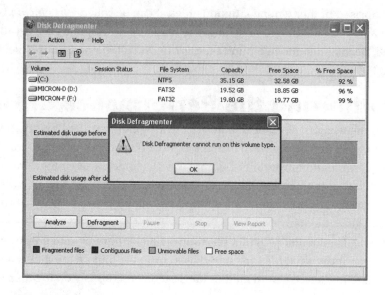

Floppy disks cannot be defragmented. Again, usually you are trying to improve performance on a hard disk. You can start any of these operations from this property sheet, or you can use menus (Start/All Programs/Accessories/ System Tool/Disk Defragmenter).

3   Click **OK**.

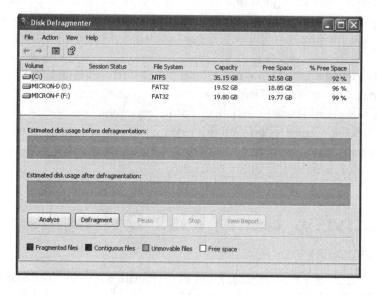

The Disk Defragmenter window opens and displays a list of available hard drives.

4   Click Drive C to select it. Click the **Analyze** command button.

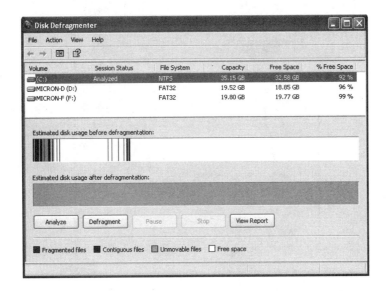

WHAT'S HAPPENING? While your hard disk is being analyzed, vertical lines slowly appear along the Analysis display bar. The line color indicates a file's current status. To interpret the Analysis display bar, refer to the legend along the bottom of the window.

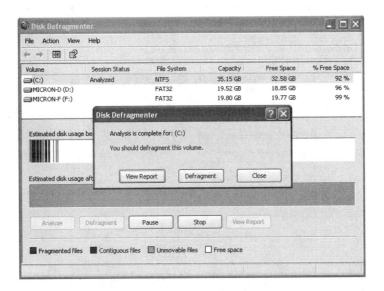

After a few minutes, a dialog box appears indicating whether you should defrag the disk or not. In this example, the analysis determined that defragmenting the disk was necessary.

5 Click the **View Report** command button.

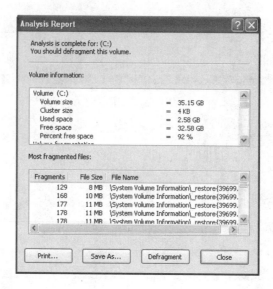

WHAT'S ▒▒▒▒
▒▒▒HAPPENING?   The volume information reports statistics describing the volume size, cluster size, and the used, free, and percentage of free space. The most fragmented files list box describes the most fragmented files, including the file's name, the file's size, and the number of fragments that make up the file. Four command buttons allow you to print the report, save it as a file, go ahead and defrag the disk, or close the Analysis Report dialog box.

6   Scroll to the bottom of the **Volume Information** list box.

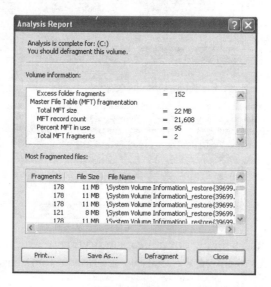

WHAT'S ▒▒▒▒
▒▒▒HAPPENING?   Since this volume (Drive C) uses the NTFS file system, you see the report on the fragmentation of the Master File Table.

7   Click **Close**.

8   If you have another drive, select it and click **Analyze**. When the analysis is complete, click **View Report** and scroll to the bottom of the Volume information list box.

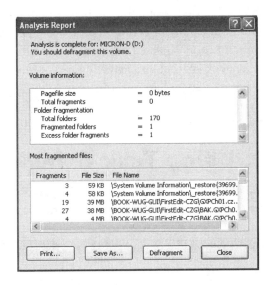

WHAT'S HAPPENING?   Because this volume (Drive D) was formatted as FAT32, there is no information about the MFT (Master File Table). The MFT is only used on NTFS volumes.

9   Click **Close**.

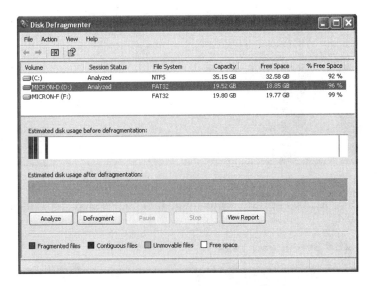

WHAT'S HAPPENING?   In the Disk Defragmenter window, you see that both Drive C and D, in this example, have been analyzed.

10 Close all open windows.

WHAT'S HAPPENING?   You have returned to the desktop.

13.8   Starting Programs Automatically

Windows XP Professional has a wizard for scheduling any program to run at any time. It is called Task Scheduler. For example, you can schedule such programs as Disk Cleanup and Backup to run at a predetermined time when it is most convenient for you. As another example, you might use Task Scheduler to dial into an online service during off hours, look for certain topics, download the results, and then hang up. You would, of course, need a program that could do that task before you could schedule it. Just be sure that you leave the computer on, and that any task you schedule to run when you are not around can operate without user input and can exit cleanly when completed.

13.9   Activity: Using Task Scheduler

1   Click **Start**. Point at **All Programs**. Point at **Accessories**. Point at **System Tools**. Click **Scheduled Tasks**. Click **View**. Click **Tiles**.

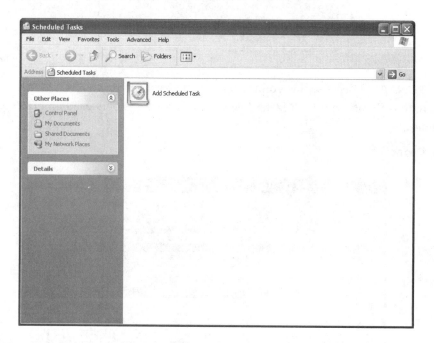

WHAT'S ▒▒▒▒▒▒
▒▒▒▒HAPPENING?   In this example, there are no tasks scheduled. Your display may vary.

2   Double-click **Add Scheduled Task**.

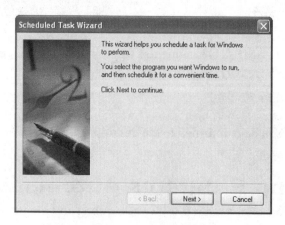

WHAT'S
HAPPENING?   You are presented with Scheduled Task Wizard.

3 Click **Next**.

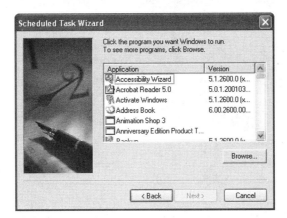

WHAT'S
HAPPENING?   You are presented with a list of programs on your system.

4 Locate **Disk Cleanup**. Click it.

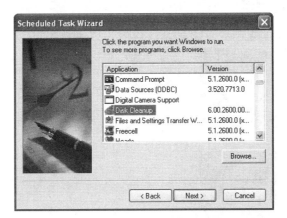

WHAT'S
HAPPENING?   You are interested in scheduling Disk Cleanup.

5 Click **Next**.

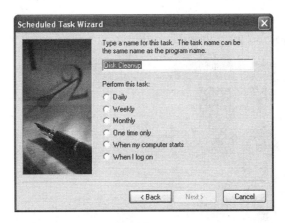

WHAT'S
HAPPENING?   As you can see, you can schedule the program to run at almost
any interval.

6   Click **Weekly**. Click **Next**.

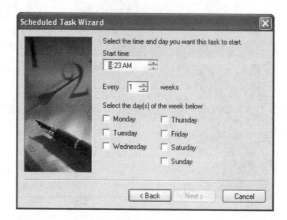

WHAT'S ▨▨▨
▨▨▨HAPPENING?   Your task is scheduled for once a week. The start time is set to whatever the current time is, although you can change that as well. You must pick a day of the week that you want the task to run.

7   Click **Sunday**. Click **Next**.

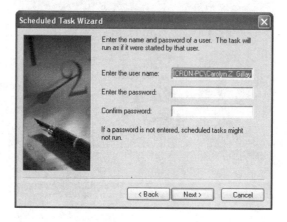

WHAT'S ▨▨▨
▨▨▨HAPPENING?   You must identify the user responsible for starting this task by entering the user's name and logon password. By default, your user name appears in the first text box.

8   Enter your password in the second and third text boxes. Click **Next**.

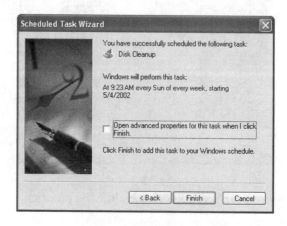

WHAT'S
HAPPENING?   Your task is scheduled. You can open the advanced properties when you are done. In this case you do not need to see them.

9   Click **Finish**. Click **View**. Click **Refresh**.

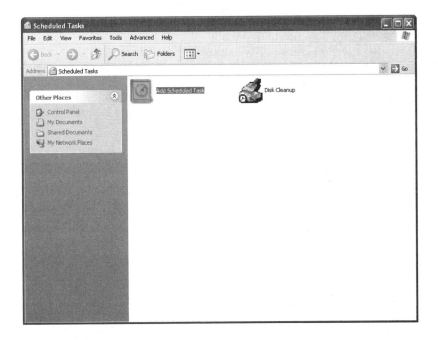

WHAT'S
HAPPENING?   You forced the system to read the disk. That is why you clicked View and then Refresh. Your task has been added to the list of scheduled tasks.

10 Click **Advanced** on the menu bar.

WHAT'S
HAPPENING?   Not only can you pause or stop using Task Scheduler, but you can also look at a log of the tasks that have been done, as well as be notified of any missed tasks. The AT Service account is a program (the "at" program, which can be run at the command line by the administrator.

11 Click somewhere off of the menu to close it. Click **Disk Cleanup** to select it.

12 Press the Delete key.

WHAT'S
HAPPENING?   You are asked to confirm your deletion. Notice that Task Scheduler files have the extension of .job. Windows considers any file with a .job file type to be registered to Task Scheduler.

13 Click **Yes**.

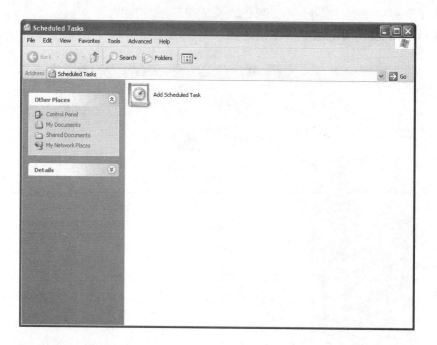

WHAT'S ▨▨▨▨
▨▨▨HAPPENING?   You no longer have any tasks scheduled.

14 Close the **Scheduled Tasks** window. Close all open windows.

WHAT'S ▨▨▨▨
▨▨▨HAPPENING?   You have returned to the desktop.

13.10 Backing Up Your Data

Backing up data is a critical task that users too often neglect. When things go wrong, either through your error or the computer's, rather than having to try to recreate data, you can turn to your backups, but only if you have created them. A *backup* is nothing more than a duplicate of files that are on a disk copied to a medium such as a floppy disk, a CD-R, a CD-RW, a Zip disk, or a tape. You retrieve the files by restoring them, which means copying them back to the original medium. When you copy a file to a floppy disk, you are in effect backing it up. You usually want to back up your entire hard disk, which includes all your files and all your folders. Although you can back up your entire hard disk to floppy disks, it is a very laborious and time-consuming process in this era of 15-gigabyte or larger hard drives. Thus, most users opt to have a tape backup unit or a removable drive with removable media such as a CD-RW, Zip, or Jaz drive. Special tapes must be purchased for use in a tape drive; cartridges for a removable drive. One of the many advantages of using Backup instead of the Copy command is that a backup file can span multiple backup disks. When one disk is full, you are directed to insert another empty disk into the drive.

As you use your computer and programs, you create data. For instance, imagine you are writing a book and you create your first chapter and save it as a file to the hard disk. You back up in January. It is now April, and you have completed 10 chapters. You accidentally delete the folder that contains your chapters. You do not want to rewrite those chapters and, furthermore, you cannot. You turn to your backup, but you have a major problem. The only file you can restore is that first chapter you created in January. The rest of your work is gone. To say the least, backing up your data files regularly is critical. The reason for backing up your entire hard drive may not be as obvious, but it is equally important.

As you work with Windows XP Professional, you create settings, install new programs, and delete old programs. You are also adding and making changes to the system Registry that controls the Windows XP Professional environment. If the Registry becomes corrupt, you will not be able to boot Windows XP Professional. The system itself is ever-changing. If, for instance, you install a new program and it does something to your hard drive, such as cause another program not to work (or worse), you want to return to the working system you had prior to your installation. If the problem is serious, you might have to reformat your hard drive. It can literally take hours, if not days, to reinstall all of your software. If you have backed up your system, you can simply restore what you had before, and a major catastrophe becomes a minor inconvenience. The Backup program supplied with Windows XP Professional supports five methods of backups: Copy Backup, Daily Backup, Differential Backup, Incremental Backup, and Normal Backup.

A *normal backup*, sometimes called a *full backup*, copies all the files from the hard drive to the backup medium, regardless of when or whether anything has changed. Full backup is the "back up everything on my computer" option. In addition, a normal backup will mark each file as having been backed up. Every file has attributes. One of these attributes, also called a flag, is the archive attribute or archive bit. This bit is either off or on. When a file has been backed up using the Normal backup option, the bit is cleared, indicating that the file has been backed up. When you alter the file, the bit is turned back on, indicating that the file has changed since the last backup. When you simply copy a file, the attribute is not altered by the copy routine. Although, the copy operation has "backed" up the file, Windows is not aware of this. The archive bit is only altered by certain programs such as Backup.

An *incremental backup* only copies or backs up the files that have been created or changed since the last normal or incremental backup. Incremental backups mark files as having been backed up by clearing the archive bit.

Backup uses the archive bit to determine whether or not a file needs to be backed up when you are performing incremental backups. If the bit is on, the file needs to be backed up. After the file is backed up, the archive bit may be set to off so that Backup knows that the file has been backed up. When you make create a new file or make any changes to an existing file, the archive bit is automatically turned on, indicating that the file has changed since the last backup.

A differential backup backs up files created or changed since the last normal or incremental backup. However, it does not mark the files as having been backed up. It does not clear the archive bit.

A daily backup backs up all files that have been created or modified the day the daily backup is performed. Again, these files are not marked as having been backed up. The archive bit is not cleared. The daily backup is a quick and dirty way to back up your current work.

A copy backup backs up the files that you select but does not mark each file has having been backed up. The archive bit is not cleared. A copy backup does not affect normal or incremental backups since file attributes are not affected. A copy backup is really no different than simply copying the file to another drive or disk.

You usually backup using a combination of full backups and incremental backups or full backups and differential backups. The choice you make usually has to do with whether you would rather spend less time backing up and more time restoring or more time backing up and less time restoring. You can always do a full backup every time you backup your system but a full backup is slower to perform than an incremental backup because you are backing up your entire system. However, it is faster to restore as you only need the most current full backup storage.

If you use a combination normal (full) backups and incremental backups, when you restore, this method requires that you restore the most recent full backup media, and all incremental media that have changes on them. However, this method requires the least amount of storage space and is the quickest method to use for backing up. Restore will take longer because you will need all the tapes or disks.

Backing up your data using a combination of normal backups and differential backups is more time-consuming, especially if your data changes frequently, but it is easier to restore the data because the backup set is usually stored on only a few disks or tapes.

If you use a combination of normal (full) backups and differential backups, the backup will take more time but it is much easier and faster to restore because your backup data is stored on fewer disks or tapes. This method requires that when you restore your files, you restore the most recent full backup media, and all incremental media that have changes on them. A *differential backup* backs up all selected files that have changed since the last normal or incremental backup. All files that have the archive bit on are backed up. When the backup is complete, the archive bit is left on.

You should have a regular backup schedule. The timing of your backups depends on how much you use your computer and how often you change things. A typical backup schedule might be that once a week you perform a full backup and every day you perform an incremental backup. If you need to restore your data, you need all of the backups, both the full and the incremental. If you are on a network, the network administrator will take care of the full backup; you need to be concerned about your data files only.

When you do backups, it is a good idea to have more than one copy of your backup or backup set. For instance, if you did a full system backup once a week and incremental backups daily, you would want at least two sets of backups. One week, you would back up on one set; the following week you would use the other set. Thus, if Murphy's law was in effect for you—your hard disk and your backup were both corrupted—you would be able to restore files from the other week's backup. The files would not be the most current, but at least you would not have to recreate everything from scratch. Another word of warning: Store at least one copy of your backup away from your computer. If you have your backup tapes at the office and you have a fire or theft, you will lose everything. If you have another set at home, you can recover what was lost at work. The most important thing about backing up is to **DO IT**. Not only do it, but do it on a regularly scheduled basis.

To access Backup, you may right-click a drive, choose Properties, choose the Tools tab, and select the Backup Now command button. You may also access Backup from the Programs submenu. Backup also has other uses. You can use Backup to *archive data*. If your hard disk starts filling up and you want to make more room on it, you can use Backup to copy seldom-used files to a backup medium and then delete them from the hard drive. If you need these files at a later date, you can restore them.

13.11 Activity: Using Backup

Note 1:   Since Backup requires writing information to the hard disk, and since each system is unique, these steps are only one example of how to use Backup. Should you choose to complete this activity on your own computer, be aware that you are going to do only an incremental backup of some files. Under no circumstances should you do this activity if you are on a network, nor will you be able to do it on a network.

Note 2:   Place the DATA disk in Drive A.

1   Click **Start**. Point at **All Programs**. Point at **Accessories**. Point at **System Tools**. Click **Backup**. If you do not see the screen below, click the underlined phrase **Wizard Mode** to switch to the wizard.

WHATS
HAPPENING?   You are welcomed to the Backup or Restore wizard.

2   Be sure **Always start in wizard mode** has a check mark. Click **Next**.

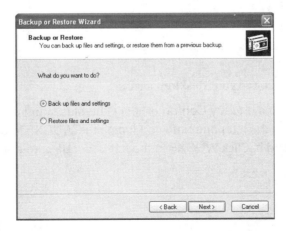

WHAT'S
■■HAPPENING?   You are asked if you want to Backup or Restore.

3   Click **Back up files and settings**. Click **Next**.

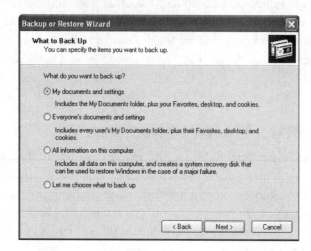

WHAT'S
■■HAPPENING?   Four choices are listed. You may back up your personal documents and settings. You may back up the documents and settings of everyone who is a user on this system. You may choose to back up all information on this computer. This includes the creation of an ASR (Automated System Recovery) disk. When you choose this option, you include the Registry and other key system files. The last choice is what you want to backup. The default setting is to back up My Documents and settings. Since this is just a learning activity, you are going to choose the other option, **Let me choose what to backup.**

4   Click **Let me choose what to backup**. Click **Next**.

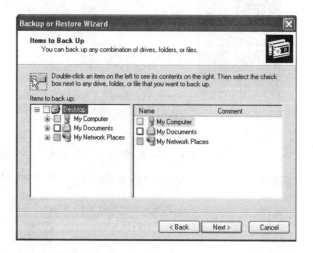

WHAT'S
■■HAPPENING?   You see your desktop objects.

5   Click the plus sign next to My Computer. Click the plus sign next to Drive C: to expand it. Scroll in the left pane until you locate the WUGXP folder. Click on the plus sign to expand it. Click WUGXP in the left pane. Be sure not to place a check mark in the box.

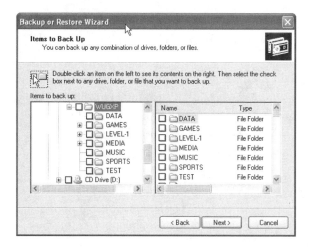

WHATʼS
▓▓▓HAPPENING?   The Backup Wizard window looks somewhat like Windows
Explorer. The left pane shows the structure of your disk, and the right pane shows
the files in the folders. In front of each item is an empty check box. To select an item
for backing up, click in its check box. To expand an entry, double-click it or click the
plus sign next to it. In this example, the left pane shows the structure of the WUGXP
directory. The right pane shows the contents of the WUGXP directory. Placing a
checkmark in the check box next to WUGXP would indicate that that you want to
back up the entire WUGXP folder.

6   Scroll in the right pane until you can see the file that begins with AST. Click the
check boxes in front of **AST.99**, **AST.NEW**, **AST.TMP**, **ASTRO.TMP**, and
ASTRO.TXT.

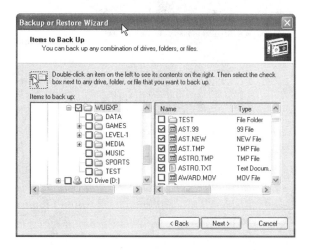

WHATʼS
▓▓▓HAPPENING?   You have selected the files you wish to back up by placing a
checkmark in the box preceding each file.

7   Click **Next**.

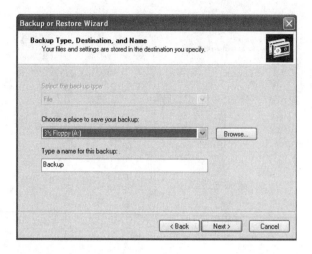

WHAT'S ▨▨▨
▨▨HAPPENING?   The wizard wants to know where to back up to. If you had a tape drive or another backup media type, you could select it here. You could choose to back up to another computer by choosing Browse and selecting My Network Places. You can back up to a CD-R or CD-RW drive but it is a bit more complicated as the files are saved as temporary files so they are saved as "files ready to write to CD"— it is a two step operation. Also, you must have a lot of free disk space. However in this case, since you are backing up to a floppy disk, your only choice is File. Backup creates a file, and you need to tell it what device and what name you are going to use.

8   Select **Backup** and key in the following: **ASTRO**

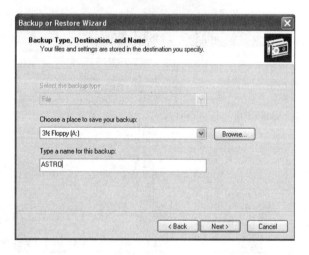

9   Click **Next**.

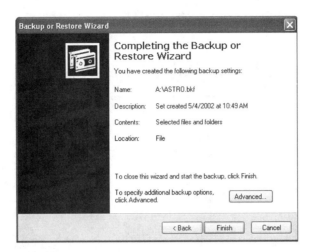

WHATS
HAPPENING?   You have completed your backup of these files. Note that they are
saved as ASTRO.BKF on Drive A.

10 Click **Advanced**.

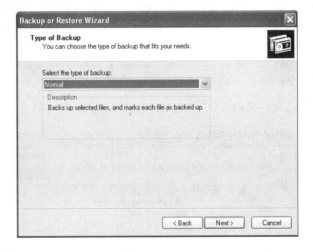

WHATS
HAPPENING?   You may select your type of backup.

11 In the drop-down list box, click the down arrow.

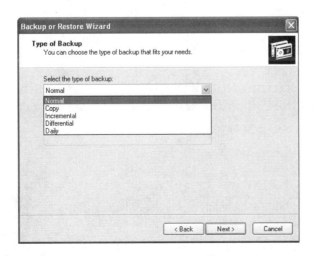

WHAT'S
HAPPENING?   You see your five backup types.

12 Click **Next**.

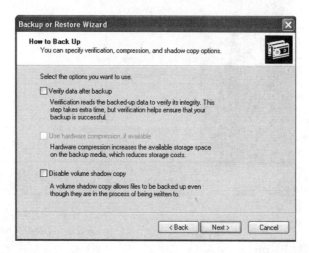

WHAT'S
HAPPENING?   You are asked to make a few more decisions. Windows can verify the data after the backup by reading it and comparing it to the original data, and it can save space on the backup media by compressing the data. In this example, hardware compression is not available, because the drive being backed up is not compressed. You may also disable volume shadow copy. With this option on, you may backup files, even as you are currently using them.

13 Clear all options. Click **Next**.

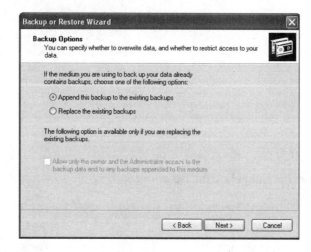

WHAT'S
HAPPENING?   You must decide if you want this backup set to be appended at the end of the data on the backup disk or if it should replace the data on the disk.

14 Click **Next**.

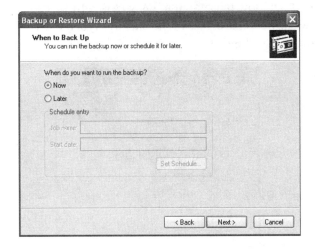

WHAT'S
HAPPENING?   You can do your backup now or schedule it for later.

15   Be sure **Now** is selected. Click **Next**.

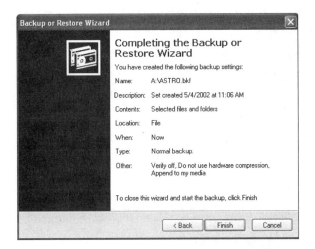

WHAT'S
HAPPENING?   A revised summary appears that includes your new options.

16   Click **Finish**.

WHAT'S
HAPPENING?   A window tells you that Backup is getting ready to do its job.
Another window shows the progress of the backup. When it is complete, you see
the following information box:

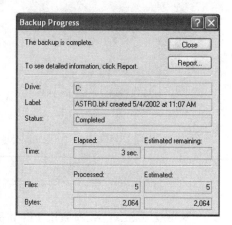

17 Click the **Report** button.

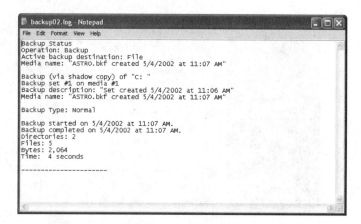

WHAT'S
HAPPENING?   You have opened a document in Notepad that has all the information about your backup.

18 Close Notepad. Click **Close**.

WHAT'S
HAPPENING?   You have returned to the desktop.

19 Open Windows Explorer. Open Drive A.

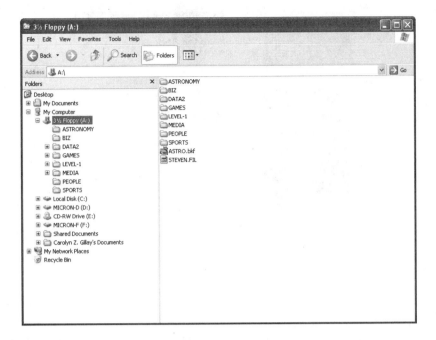

WHAT'S
WHAT'S HAPPENING?   You see your backup file, ASTRO.BKF. However, you cannot use this file or open it except with the Restore portion of the Backup utility.

20 Close the Drive A window.

WHAT'S HAPPENING?   Your backup is complete. You have returned to the desktop.

13.12 Restore

Backup, although called Backup on the menu, is called the Backup or Restore Wizard. You may use the Restore wizard to copy some or all of your files to your original disk, another disk, or another directory. Restore lets you choose which backup set to copy from. Restoring files is as easy as backing them up with the Backup program. You merely choose Restore option and choose the kind of restoration you want. You can use the Restore Wizard, which will lead you through the process of restoring your system.

13.13 Activity: Restoring Files

Note: Since using Restore requires writing information to the hard disk and since each system is unique, these steps are one example of how to restore. Should you choose to complete this activity on your own computer, be aware that you are only going to do an incremental restoration of some files. Under no circumstances should you do this activity if you are on a network, nor will you be able to do it on a network.

1   Click **Start**. Point at **All Programs**. Point at **Accessories**. Point at **System Tools**. Click **Backup**.

WHAT'S HAPPENING?   You saw this screen in the last activity. In this case, you are going to restore the files on the floppy disk to the hard disk.

2   Click Next.

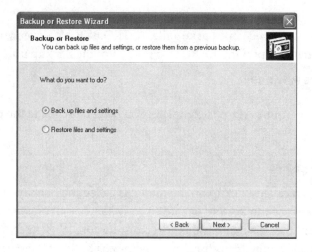

WHAT'S HAPPENING?   Now you choose Restore files and settings.

3   Click Restore files and settings. Click Next.

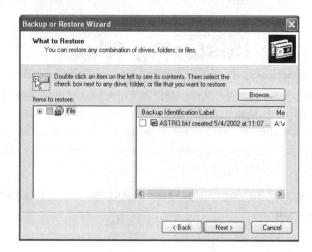

WHAT'S HAPPENING?   The Backup or Restore Wizard is asking you what you want to restore. If the Backup program was previously run on your computer, you may have several items listed.

4   Be sure the DATA is in Drive A. Click the plus sign in the left pane. In the right pane, scroll to the end of the list and click the last entry in the list.

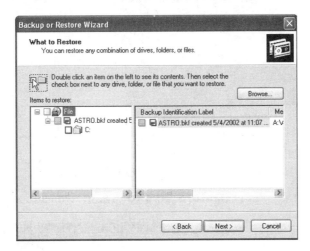

WHAT'S HAPPENING?   The last entry in the list is selected and expanded. Since there is only one item (backup) in the right pane, you can continue.

5   In the left pane, click the check box next to Drive C. Click **Next**.

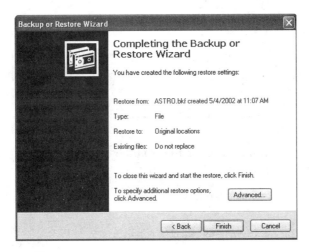

WHAT'S HAPPENING?   The Completion window appears. The choices are preselected in that you are going to use Astro.bkf and restore it to the original location and you are not going to replace any existing files on Drive C.

6   Click the **Advanced** command button.

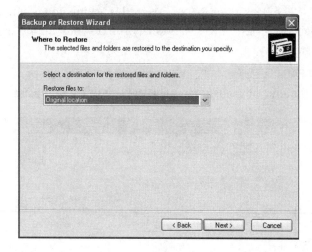

WHAT'S ▒▒▒▒▒
▒▒▒HAPPENING?   Now you can change your options if you wish.

7 Click the down arrow in the **Restore files to** drop-down list box.

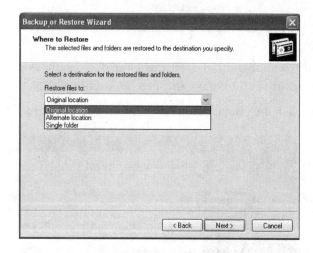

WHAT'S ▒▒▒▒▒
▒▒▒HAPPENING?   You can restore the files to their original location, an alternate location, or a single folder.

8 Click **Original location**. Click **Next**.

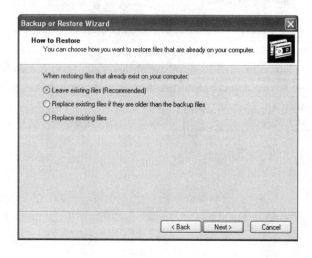

WHAT'S HAPPENING?   Three option buttons allow you to select how to restore files that are already on the disk: Leave existing files (Recommended), Replace existing files if they are older than the backup files, and Replace existing files.

9 Click **Replace existing files**. Click **Next**.

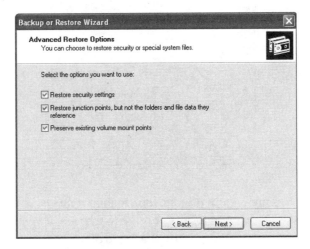

WHAT'S HAPPENING?   Since you want all the files to appear in the same locations with the same security, you will leave the defaults on.

10 Click **Next**.

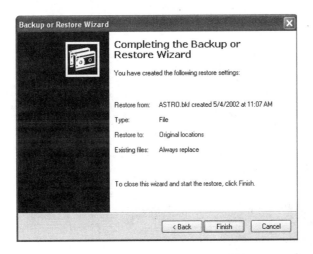

WHAT'S HAPPENING?   The revised settings summary information appears and indicates that existing files are always replaced.

11 Click **Finish**.

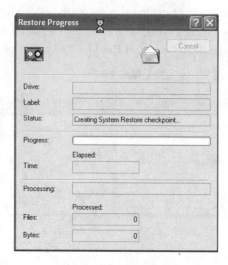

WHAT'S ▨▨▨
▨▨HAPPENING?   Restore is gathering the information it needs. Since there was only one file on the disk in Drive A to restore, it is using that file. If you had multiple backup files, it would ask you to confirm the name of the file to restore. When it is completed restoring files, you see the next window.

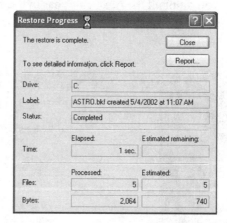

12 Click the **Report** command button.

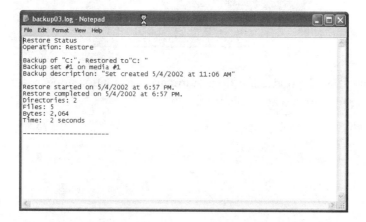

WHAT'S ▨▨▨
▨▨HAPPENING?   The report indicates that the backup set has been restored.

13 Close Notepad. Close the Restore Progress dialog box.

14 Click **Start**. Point to **All Programs**. Point to **Accessories**. Point to **System Tools**. Click **Backup**.

WHAT'S ▓▓▓▓▓▓
▓▓▓▓ HAPPENING?   You do not have to use the wizards to back up and restore files. If you clear the Always start in wizard mode check box, the next time you open Backup and Restore, you will see many more choices. For instance, you can also schedule when Windows will perform the Backup task. To open the Advanced Options, click the underlined phrase.

15 Click **Advanced Mode**.

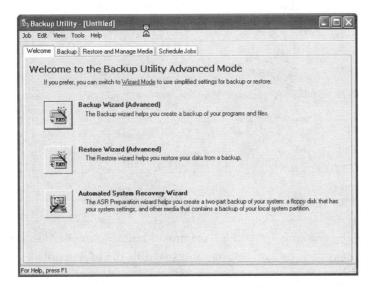

WHAT'S ▓▓▓▓▓▓
▓▓▓▓ HAPPENING?   Here are the advanced options.

16 Click the **Restore and Manage Media** tab.

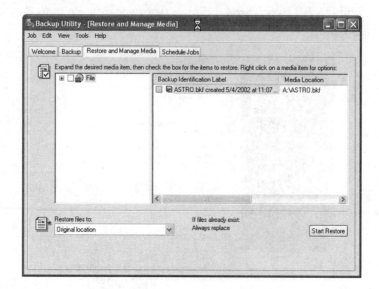

WHATS
HAPPENING?   You can change how you want your restore to function.

17 Click the **Schedule Jobs** tab.

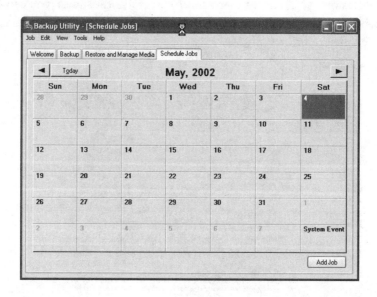

WHATS
HAPPENING?   Clicking the Add Job command button starts Backup Wizard so that you can enter your backup settings and schedule the backup job.

18 Close the Backup window.

WHATS
HAPPENING?   You returned to the desktop.

13.14 Automated System Recovery (ASR)

Windows XP Professional has a built-in repair system for a catastrophic failure of your system. Although the name states it is automated, the process really requires a fair amount of preparation. The purpose of ASR is to restore your system partitions.

It saves the contents of your system drive (where Windows is installed) to some backup media. You do not want to use floppy disks for storing your system information. Although the ASR wizard will prompt you to insert other floppy disks, it would take many floppy disks and many hours to back up the system information to floppy disks. Thus, you should choose a location such as a Zip disk, another drive on a network, or someplace that can handle large files. ASR saves information about your arrangement of disk partitions, system files, and detected hardware. ASR does not save your program files or any of your data files. During the process you also create a floppy disk that is pointing to the location of your backup files. This feature is not available on Windows XP Home Edition. This process is used to solve problems such as when you have a corrupt Registry or when your system will not boot. This repair system relies on the creation of an Automated System Recovery (ASR). It is created in the Advanced Mode of Backup. This disk, and the files that are stored on some media type other than a floppy, along with the CD-ROM used to install Windows XP Professional, repair a corrupted system. The ASR is not a substitute for backing up your data. The ASR is for system problems. It can only restore the system as it was when the ASR was made. It is like a snapshot of your system at a specific point in time. Any time that you make a change to your system, such as installing new programs or hardware, you should update your ASR. The emergency repair process also relies on data saved in the %SystemRoot%\Repair folder. The notation %SystemRoot% indicates a variable name. Windows will substitute the name of your Windows folder, such as \Windows\Repair or \WINNT\Repair.

To repair a damaged version of Windows XP Professional, you would need both the ASR, the availability of those backed up system files, *and* a Windows XP Professional installation CD. You would boot the system from the CD (or from a setup floppy disk). You would then be asked if you wanted to install Windows XP Professional or repair a damaged version. To repair, you would press the F2 key and follow the instructions on the screen. You would be instructed when to insert the ASR disk.

13.15 The Registry

As you are aware, the Windows XP Professional environment is very customizable. You may have different users for one computer, each with his or her own desktop settings, menus, and icons. When you install new hardware, the operating system must know about the new hardware and any drivers for those hardware devices. You can double-click a document icon in Windows to open the correct application program, because, when you install an application program, the program registers its extension with Windows. As you can see, the operating system has much information to keep track of. All this information is the *configuration information.*

In previous versions of Windows, the operating system and most application programs used .INI files to store information about the user environment and necessary drivers. The .INI extension was derived from *initialization files.* Initialization files were broken into two types: system initialization files and private initialization files. Windows itself created the system .INI files such as WIN.INI and SYSTEM.INI, and application programs would also create private .INI files. These configuration files contained the information that Windows needed to run itself, as well as run the programs that were installed on a specific computer. The private .INI files were often added to the Windows directory and kept track of the state of the application, containing such information as the screen position or the last-used files.

The .INI files could specify many items that varied from one computer to the next. Thus, there could not be one set of .INI files that was common to all users. These files contained such items as the name and path of a specific file that is required by Windows, some user-defined variable, or some hardware or software configuration.

Windows itself had two primary initialization files, WIN.INI and SYSTEM.INI. WIN.INI was the primary location for information pertaining to the software configuration and system-wide information added by application software. The SYSTEM.INI file was the primary location for system information that had to do with the computer hardware. One might say that WIN.INI had information for how your system behaved, whereas SYSTEM.INI pointed the Windows operating system to the correct hardware and software components such as device drivers. In order to run Windows, these two files had to be present.

Another file that Windows used was a file called REG.DAT. This file was the *registration database*, but was not an ASCII file and could only be edited by a special application program, REGEDIT. It contained information about how various applications would open, how some of them would print, the information that was needed about file extensions, and how OLE (object linking and embedding) objects were handled.

Instead of using SYSTEM.INI for hardware settings, WIN.INI for user settings, REG.DAT for file associations and object linking and embedding, and all the various private initialization files, Windows XP Professional uses a single location, called the Registry, for hardware, system software, and application configuration information. Windows XP Professional does retain support for both WIN.INI and SYSTEM.INI, although Windows no longer uses these files, so they are available to any legacy application programs that might need to refer to them. Registry information comes from the installation of Windows XP Professional, the booting of Windows XP Professional, applications, and system and user interaction. Every part of Windows XP Professional uses the Registry, without exception. The Registry files are kept in the directory %SystemRoot%\System32\Config. The Registry files that are backed up are kept in %SystemRoot%\Repair\Back.

If you use the ASR disk, there are choices available that do allow you to restore the Registry by using the Recovery Console. The Recovery Console is a text-based command interpreter that allows the system administrator to access the hard disk and files. This process is beyond the scope of this text.

However, you may use some options an alternate method, what is called "Last Known Good Configuration." This option starts Windows XP Professional with the Registry settings that were saved at the last shutdown. This does not solve problems caused by missing or corrupt drivers, but it can be useful in overcoming problems caused by changes you might have made in the current session.

It is always smart to have an ASR so that if something goes wrong, you can always boot and recover. In addition, if you have a problem, you can boot to what is called "safe mode." You access safe mode by pressing and holding the F8 key after your system finished displaying startup messages such as "Keyboard installed" but before the Windows logo appears. When you go to safe mode, you are presented with the Startup menu. See Figure 13.4.

```
Microsoft Advanced Options Menu
Please select an option.
_____

Safe Mode
Safe Mode with Networking
Safe Mode with Command Prompt

  Enable boot logging
  Enable VGA Mode
  Last Known Good Configuration (your most recent settings that worked)
  Directory Services Restore Mode (Windows domain controllers only)
  Debugging Mode

  Start Windows normally
  Reboot
  Return to OS Choices menu

Use the up and down arrows to move the highlight to your choice
```

Figure 13.4—The Startup Menu

This feature allows you to troubleshoot different types of problems. For instance, if you choose an incorrect video driver, you cannot open the property sheet for Display in order to correct your error. You can boot into the Advanced Options menu and choose Enable VGA mode. This would load only the most basic video drivers so that you could then open the property sheet for Display and correct your settings. Safe mode itself loads the minimum amount of drivers and functionality that allows Windows XP Professional to run. If you wanted to return to the last time the system worked, you would use the arrow keys to highlight **Last Known Good Configuration**, and then press **Enter**. However, Windows has included an easier way to solve some of these problems. It is called System Restore.

13.16 System Restore

If you make changes to your hardware, such as adding new hardware, installing a new driver for your hardware, or installing or removing software, you are making changes to your system settings. Any of these changes can cause your computer or your devices to no longer work or to work incorrectly. Sometimes, even removing the hardware, the drivers or uninstalling a program still does not solve your problem. As Microsoft XP Professional states, your computer is now in an "undesirable state." You would like the ability to be able to go back in time to when your system was working properly, when you were in a "desirable state." System Restore allows you to undo the changes you made to your computer. System Restore does all of the following:

Rolls back your computer to a more stable state because System Restore keeps track of changes made at specific times. It also tracks certain events such as when you install a new software program. These times are called *restore points*. You may also create your own personal restore points. Restore points allow you to "roll back" your computer system to a time when you know that everything was working correctly.

System Restore will save your email messages, browsing history and so on. However, be forewarned—System Restore DOES NOT save or restore your documents. System Restore is not a substitute for backing up your data files. System Restore is for your "computer" system, not for your data files. System Restore restores Windows and your programs to a restore point—not your data files.

System Restore saves about one to three weeks of changes depending on how much you use your computer, your hard disk size and how much space has been allocated to store the System Restore information.

You may select which dates you want to restore to by use of a calendar.

System Restore provides several restore points. It creates an initial system checkpoint when you upgrade or install Windows XP Professional. Even if you have not made any changes to your system, regular checkpoints are created daily and at significant events such as when you install a new device driver. If you use Windows Automatic update, restore points are created prior to the update.

All system restores are reversible, so that if the restore point you selected is not successful, you can undo it.

13.17 Activity: Using System Restore

Note: If you are in a lab environment, you will not be able to do this activity.

1   Click **Start**. Point to **All Programs**. Point to **Accessories**. Point to **System Tools**. Click **System Restore**.

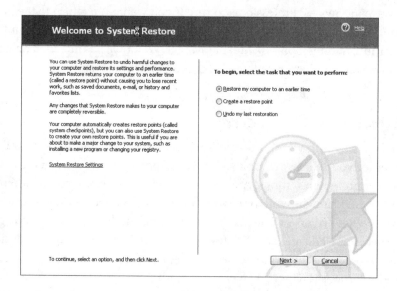

WHAT'S HAPPENING?   The System Restore wizard window opens. You may either create a restore point or restore your computer to an earlier time.

2   Click **Create a restore point**. Click **Next**.

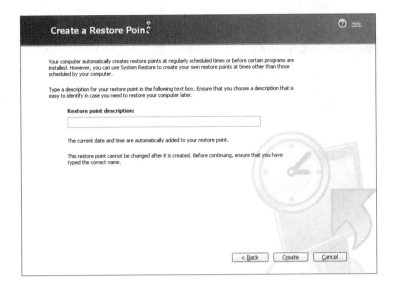

**WHAT'S
▓▓▓HAPPENING?**   Here you name your restore point. The date and time are automatically added. Make your description brief but meaningful. For instance, if you wanted to install a new program, called Wonder Program, you would want to create a restore point prior to your installation and you might call this Pre-Wonder.

3   Key in **Pre-Wonder**. Click **Create**.

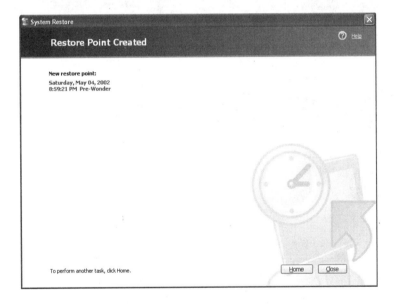

**WHAT'S
▓▓▓HAPPENING?**   The system took a few minutes to create the restore point then presented you with a confirmation window. You may either go back to the opening screen of the System Restore wizard (Home), or close the window.

4   Click **Close**.

**WHAT'S
▓▓▓HAPPENING?**   You are returned to the desktop.

5   Click **Start**. Point to **All Programs**. Point to **Accessories**. Point to **System Tools**. Click **System Restore**.

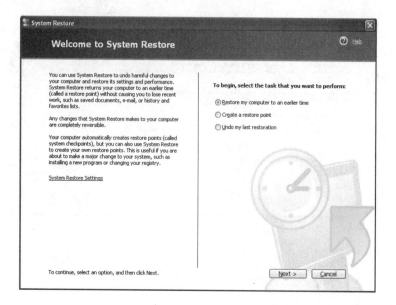

WHAT'S ▓▓▓▓▓
▓▓▓ HAPPENING?   You again opened the System Restore wizard. Now you are going to look at your restore points.

6   Be sure that **Restore my computer to an earlier time** is selected. Click **Next**.

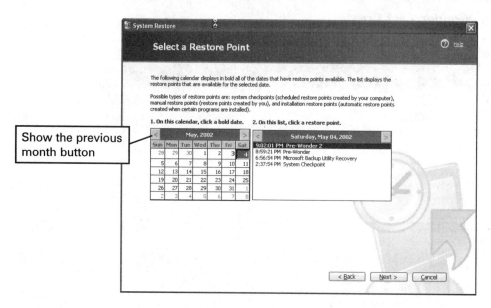

WHAT'S ▓▓▓▓▓
▓▓▓ HAPPENING?   You are presented with a calendar with available restore points. In this example, there are three restore points created by this user (Pre-Wonder, Pre-Wonder 2, and Microsoft Backup Utility Recovery) and a System CheckPoint created by Windows XP Professional. Your display will vary depending on what restore points have been created. Only dates that are bold have a checkpoint.

7   Click the **Show the previous month** button to look at an earlier month.

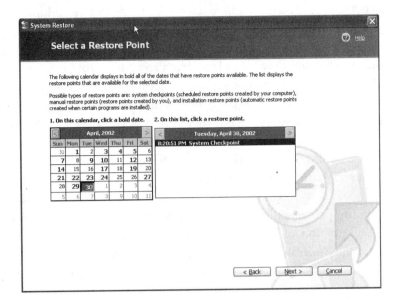

WHAT'S
HAPPENING?   In this example, there is only one restore point, one created by Windows XP Professional. However, any date that is in bold on the calendar holds a restore point. You would select the date you wanted to restore to and then click Next.

8   Click **Cancel**.

WHAT'S
HAPPENING?   You have returned to the desktop. System Restore is another way to protect your system.

13.18 Plug and Play and Device Drivers

Prior to Windows 95, adding new hardware to your system could be a nightmare. If you wanted to add a new piece of hardware such as a sound card, not only would you have to take the cover off the computer and physically add the card, but you would also need to make software changes. Each hardware component needs access to system resources such as IRQ and DMA channels. An IRQ (interrupt request line) signals the CPU to get its attention. DMA (direct memory access) devices use DMA channels to access memory directly, rather than going through the CPU. If different devices contend for the same IRQ or DMA channel, you can have a hardware conflict, which means that the hardware does not work. Furthermore, most hardware devices need software support, contained in driver files that must also be installed. They are called drivers because they "drive" the hardware. A user needs a fair amount of technical expertise to adjust these settings so that the hardware devices work.

Plug and Play is an industry standard developed by Intel and Microsoft, with help from other computer industry leaders, that automates adding new hardware to your computer. Plug and Play in Windows XP Professional is even better than in Windows 95, Windows 98, or Windows 2000 Professional. Windows XP Professional's Plug and Play makes adding new hardware to your system truly user friendly. You install the hardware. Then, when you boot the system, Windows XP

Professional detects that you have added a new hardware device and makes the appropriate adjustments to your system. Hence, the name—you plug it in and it plays. Occasionally, like any new standard, Plug and Play does not work, so sometimes it is called "Plug and Pray." Windows has also added support for new types of devices, including universal serial bus (USB) devices and IEEE 1394 devices. USB devices share a common connector (port) and do not need to be configured manually. IEEE 1394 is a high-speed serial bus that is used by some devices that require fast data transfer, such as scanners or video cameras.

In order for Plug and Play to work, you must have a computer that has a Plug and Play–compatible BIOS (Basic Input Output System). The device you are going to install also needs to be Plug and Play–compatible. Windows XP Professional is Plug and Play–compatible. Full support in Windows XP Professional requires an Advanced Configuration and Power Interface (ACPI)–compliant system board and BIOS, Windows XP Professional as the operating system, the device you want to install, and the drivers for that device. Most computers manufactured after 1998 have an ACPI BIOS. Most computers manufactured between 1995 and 1998 instead use an Advanced Power Management (APM) BIOS or a Plug and Play BIOS. If you have one of these computers, the Plug and Play setting in your BIOS needs to be set to off. See your computer's documentation on how to do this. Hardware that is not Plug and Play–compatible is called *legacy hardware*. If you have an older computer or an older device, you still can get help from Windows XP Professional in resolving hardware conflicts. The Add/Remove Hardware wizard in Control Panel will attempt to assist you in solving hardware conflicts. You may also use Device Manager to add updated drivers or help you identify problems as well as roll back a driver that does not work correctly.

13.19 Activity: Looking at Plug and Play

1   Click **Start**. Right-click **My Computer**. Click **Properties**.

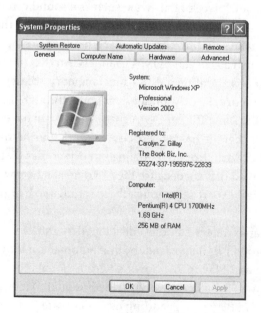

WHATS
HAPPENING?   You are looking at the system properties for your computer.

2   Click the **Hardware** tab. Click the **Device Manager** command button. Expand the Computer entry.

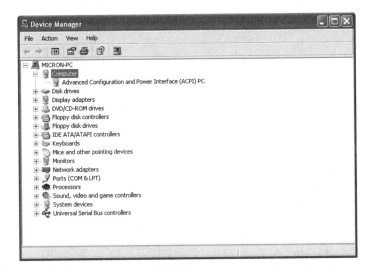

WHATS
HAPPENING?   This compuer has ACPI.

3   Collapse the Computer entry. Scroll to the bottom until you see **System devices**. Double-click **System devices**.

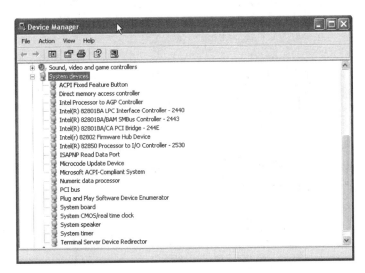

WHATS
HAPPENING?   You see that on this system, one of the entries is Plug and Play Software Device Enumerator. This computer is compatible with Plug and Play. You may see an ISA Plug and Play BIOS or an ISA Plug and Play bus on older systems.

4   Right-click **Plug and Play Software Device Enumerator**. Click **Properties**.

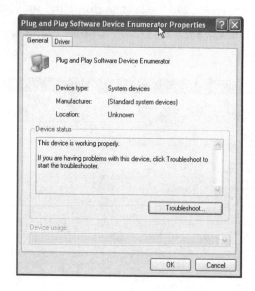

This device is working properly. If it were not working properly,
▓▓▓ HAPPENING? you could click the Troubleshoot command button to open Windows' Help
program's Troubleshooter feature. Not all devices will have a Driver tab, because
devices may or may not have drivers. This is another place you can search to solve
problems.

5   Click the **Driver** tab, if available.

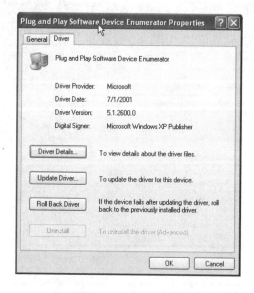

Here is the piece of software that drives this device. Here you may
▓▓▓ HAPPENING? look at the details of the driver (Driver Details), update the driver (Update Driver),
and, if the driver you installed did not work, roll it back to the previous driver
version (Roll Back Driver). You may also, if it is available, uninstall the current
driver (Uninstall). In this example, because this is a Windows system function,
uninstalling is not an option. You can look at each device on your system and review
its properties and attributes as well as update it or roll it back.

6   Click **Driver Details**.

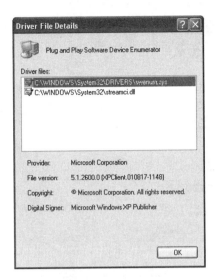

WHAT'S HAPPENING?   This feature tells you what driver file is being used and where it is located.

7   Click **OK**. Click **Cancel**. Click the minus sign (–) next to **System devices**.

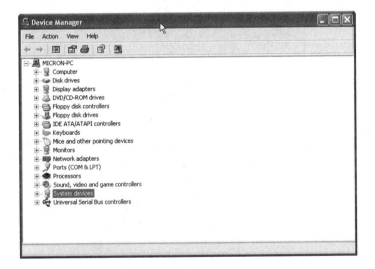

WHAT'S HAPPENING?   You have returned to Device Manager. This window tells you if devices are working properly. If there is a ? next to a device's icon, it means that you have a problem and the device has been disabled. If you have an exclamation point with a circle around it, it means that the device has a problem. The type of problem will be displayed in the Properties dialog box for the device.

8   Click **Sound, video and game adapters** to select it. Click the plus sign (+) next to it to expand it.

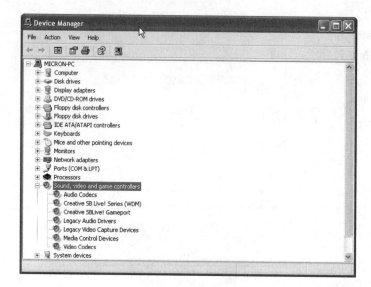

WHAT'S
WHAT'S HAPPENING?   You see what sound card you have. In this case, a Creative Labs Sound Blaster Live is the sound card installed (your sound card may be different).

9   Right-click your sound card to select it. Click **Properties**.

WHAT'S HAPPENING?   You see further details about this sound card. In Device status, you are informed that the device is working properly. If it were not or if you had an updated driver, you could install it.

10 Click the **Driver** tab.

By clicking the Update Driver button, you could install a new driver. If you clicked the Roll Back Driver, you could return to a previous version of the driver. In this example, you could uninstall the driver altogether.

11 Click **Cancel**. Collapse the entry. Close all open windows.

You have returned to the desktop.

13.20 The Paging File

One of the items that has the most impact on the performance of your computer system, other than the processor itself, is the amount of physical memory you have installed. To improve performance, Windows XP Professional uses space on the hard drive as virtual memory. When you run out of physical memory, Windows writes data from physical memory to a hidden file on your disk. When it needs that information again, it reads it back from what used to be called the *swap file* and is now called the *paging file*. The name *swap file* came from the fact that Windows "swaps" information to and from the hard disk when needed. This process is called *demand paging*. This file is dynamic—it can shrink and grow as needed. Perhaps you are writing a book and have an 80-page chapter with color pictures. Such a document can be 20 to 24 MB in size. Even a computer with 128 MB of RAM does not have enough memory available—with the drivers, the running program, and other overhead—to keep a document of that size in memory. So, while you are looking at pages 7 and 8, pages 60 through 80 may be written out to the swap file to free up needed RAM. The swap does slow down performance, but it gives the user more "room" in which to operate.

However, paging does impede performance; any activity is slower when it uses a disk rather than memory. It is possible to set the place and size of the paging file yourself, but it is strongly recommended by Microsoft that you let Windows manage the paging file. There are, however, some instances when it may be advisable to specify where you want the swap file to be. Perhaps you have a second hard drive that is free of executable programs. There would be little I/O (input/output) to this drive. You may want to place your paging file on that drive, freeing up the read/write heads on your main drive. Also, if you elect to modify the placement of your swap file, be sure you place it on your fastest hard drive (the drive with the fastest access time). You may also have a large hard drive that has little information on it. In that case, you may wish to place the swap file on that drive and increase the paging file size.

13.21 Activity: Looking at Setting Up Your Paging File

Note: This activity is specific to the machines used for the demonstration.

1   Click **Start**. Right-click **My Computer**. Click **Properties**. Click the **Advanced** tab.

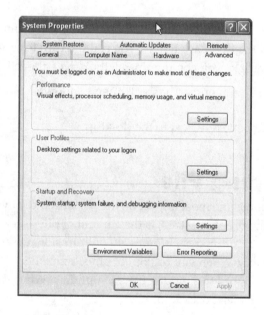

WHAT'S ▓▓▓▓▓
▓▓▓▓ **HAPPENING?**   You are looking at the property sheet that deals with Performance, User Profiles, and Startup and Recover.

2   Click the **Settings** command button in **Performance Options**. Click the **Advanced** tab.

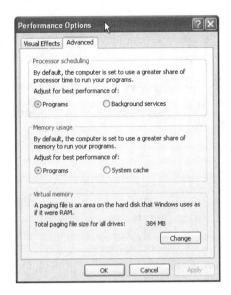

WHAT'S HAPPENING?   The Virtual memory area tells you the current total paging size for all drives. You can change this.

3 Click the **Change** command button.

WHAT'S HAPPENING?   You can set the paging file size.

4 Click the question mark in the title bar, then click the **Initial size (MB)** text box.

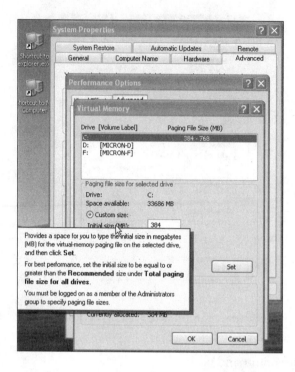

WHAT'S HAPPENING?   As you can see, it is recommended that for best performance you follow Windows's suggestion and set the initial size to be equal or greater than the recommended size. You must also be an administrator to make any changes.

5   Click **Cancel**. Click **Cancel**. Click **Cancel**.

WHAT'S HAPPENING?   You have, in this instance, let Windows manage the paging file.

13.22 Administrative Tools and System Information

System Information is an exceedingly useful tool. It has the ability to collect and display system configuration information for your local computer as well as remote computers. The information includes hardware configuration, computer components, and software, including driver information. You can view this information as well as access different tools by using this program. In addition, if you need technical support, the support technicians require specific information about your computer. You can use System Information to quickly find the information that these technicians need to resolve a system problem. System Information saves data files in files that have an .nfo extension.

Microsoft Management Console (MMC) is a tool used to create, save, and open collections of administrative tools, called consoles. Consoles contain items such as snap-ins, extension snap-ins, monitor controls, tasks, wizards, and documentation required to manage many of the hardware, software, and networking components of your Windows XP Professional system. MMC is a framework that hosts administrative tools. You can add items to an existing MMC console, or you can create new consoles and configure them to administer a specific system component. A full exploration of MMC is beyond the scope of this textbook. But if you look at the Administrative Tools folder found in Control Panel, you will see shortcuts to tools that you frequently use. Many of these tools require that the user have administrator privileges. Figure 13.5 displays the available tools in Control Panel. You may also add Administrative Tools to your Start menu using the Taskbar and Start Menu Properties sheet.

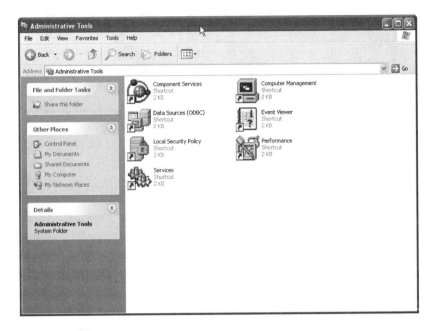

Figure 13.5 • Administrative Tools

- Component Services allows administrators and developers to create, configure, and maintain COM (Component Object Model) applications. This is a programming tool and will rarely be used by the average user.
- Computer Management is for managing disks as well as local or remote computers. It also gives you information about your computer system.
- Data Sources (ODBC) allows you to access data from a variety of database management systems. It is a programming and administrative tool that is rarely used by the average user.
- Event Viewer allows the user to gather information about hardware, software, and system problems, as well as monitor security events.
- Local Security Policy allows a security administrator to configure security levels for local computer policies.
- Performance contains features for logging counter and event data and for generating performance alerts. Counter logs allow you to record data about such items as hardware usage as well as provide alerts. Thus, you can set an alert on a counter defining that a message be sent when a counter's value equals, exceeds, or falls below some specified setting.
- Services allows you to start, stop, pause, or resume services on remote and local computers and configure startup and recovery options. Services include such tasks as running scheduled tasks or starting a network connection.

13.23 Activity: Using System Information and Computer Management

1   Click **Start**. Point to **All Programs**. Point to **Accessories**. Point to **System Tools**. Click **System Information**.

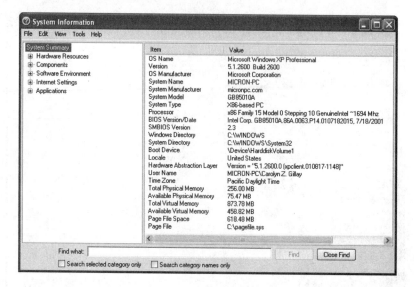

WHAT'S
HAPPENING?   You are looking at the all the information about your computer system, such as your BIOS version and how much memory you have.

2   Expand **Hardware Resources**. Click **IRQs**.

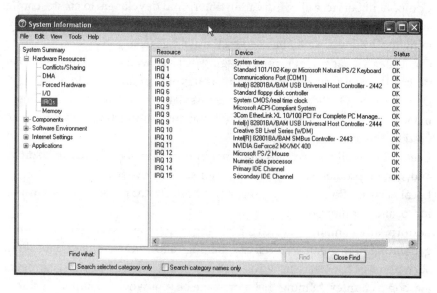

WHAT'S
HAPPENING?   Here you see what devices are claiming which IRQs.

3   Click **Tools**.

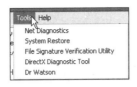

WHAT'S ▨▨▨
▨▨ HAPPENING?   Here are tools you may use. You have used System Restore. The Net Diagnostics will run different tests to check your network connections. The File Signature Verification Utility will help maintain the integrity of your system as critical files have been digitally signed. This utility can see if there have been any changes. DirectX enhances the multimedia capabilities of your computer and provides access to your display and audio cards, which allow programs to provide three-dimensional graphics and various music and audio effects. The DirectX Diagnostic tool will diagnose any problems. Dr Watson detects information about system and program failures and records the information in a log file which can be used by technical support professionals.

4   Collapse hardware resource. Close the System Information window.

5   Click **Start**. Click **Control Panel**. Double-click **Adminstrative Tools**. Double-click **Computer Management**.

6   Expand **Storage**, if it is not expanded. Double-click **Disk Management**.

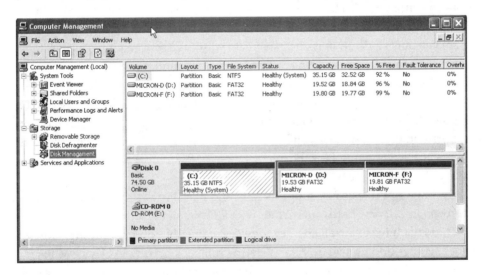

WHAT'S ▨▨▨
▨▨ HAPPENING?   Disk Management is a graphical tool for managing your disks. It provides support for partitions and logical drives. It allows the user to perform online administrative tasks without shutting down the system or interrupting other users. It also provides shortcut menus to show you which tasks you can perform on a selected object. Wizards then guide you through tasks such as creating partitions and volumes and upgrading disks. You must be an administrator to use these tools.

7   Close **Computer Management**. Close Control Panel.

WHAT'S ▨▨▨
▨▨ HAPPENING?   You have returned to the desktop.

Chapter Summary

In this chapter, you learned that errors can happen to disks and also to files. These errors include cross-linked files and lost clusters. Check Disk checks disks for logical errors in the file system and for problems that involve the physical drive. You learned that you can fill up your disk quickly with temporary files that do not get deleted and with cached files. Disk Cleanup helps you keep your disk optimized by removing these unnecessary files.

You also learned that contiguous files are those that have been written to the disk in adjacent clusters. Noncontiguous files have been written in nonadjacent clusters and thereby create a fragmented disk. Fragmentation slows your access to the disk. Disk Defragmenter repairs fragmented files.

Windows XP Professional makes it easy to maintain your disk by letting you run Check Disk, Disk Cleanup, and Disk Defragmenter on a regularly scheduled basis by using Scheduled Task Wizard to schedule the tasks. You are not limited to scheduling only those tasks. Windows XP Professional also provides a tool called Task Scheduler that allows you to schedule any program to run at any time.

Another important aspect of any computer user's routine should be the regular backing up of data. You can easily accomplish this in Windows XP Professional with the Backup program. This program allows you to complete either full or incremental backups. You can back up the whole system or just selected files. You should also create an Automated System Recovery (ASR) disk in case your system fails. In addition, System Restore will restore your system to a working state. Restore points are created automatically, but you can create your own restore points as well.

Virtual memory is space on a hard drive used to simulate an environment in which more memory is available than actually exists on the system board. Additional memory is simulated by means of a virtual paging file on the hard disk. It is advisable to let Windows manage your virtual memory paging file if you have one hard drive in your system. If you have a second, faster hard drive in your system, you may consider taking over the management of the virtual memory paging file and moving it to the faster drive.

Windows XP Professional supports Plug and Play. Plug and Play means that when you install new hardware, Windows XP Professional automatically detects it so you do not have to install any new devices manually. You may review your device settings and update drivers as well as roll back drivers in Device Manager.

System Information allows you to gather information about your system as well as run various diagnostic tools. Microsoft Management Console (MMC) is a tool used to create, save, and open collections of administrative tools, called consoles. The Administrative Tools folder found in Control Panel contains shortcuts to tools that you frequently use. Many of these tools require that the user has administrator privileges. One very useful tool is Computer Management, which lets you explore and manage your computer system.

Key Terms

archive data	chain	defragger
backup	configuration information	demand paging
cache	cross-linked files	differential backup

disk optimization
  program
fragmented disk
fragmented file
full backup
head crash

incremental backup
initialization file
legacy hardware
lost cluster
normal backup
paging file

registration database
restore point
surge protector
surge suppressor
swap file
virus

Discussion Questions

1. What are three occurrences that can cause a loss of data on a hard drive?
2. What is the purpose and function of the Check Disk program that comes with Windows XP Professional?
3. What is a cache?
4. What is the purpose of Disk Cleanup? What benefits do you gain from running this program?
5. Compare and contrast contiguous and noncontiguous files.
6. How does the Disk Defragmenter utility help optimize disk performance?
7. List and explain two factors that should be considered before defragmenting your disk.
8. List and explain two ways that the Task Scheduler wizard could be used.
9. Why is it important to back up data? Programs?
10. Compare and contrast full (normal) and incremental backups.
11. What is the difference between using a differential backup or using the daily option for incremental backups?
12. Why is it wise to have more than one copy of your backup?
13. List and explain two ways that the Backup program can be used.
14. Explain how you can restore files.
15. The Automated System Recovery (ASR) is not a substitute for backing up data. Explain.
16. What is the purpose and function of the Automated System Recovery (ASR)?
17. Compare and contrast system and private initialization files found in previous versions of Windows.
18. What is the purpose and function of the Registry?
19. What is the purpose and function of System Restore?
20. What is a restore point?
21. If you use System Restore, is it still necessary to back up your data files? Why or why not?
22. What is a paging file? Explain some of the advantages and disadvantages of paging.
23. Why would you want to roll back a driver? Where would you accomplish this task?
24. What is system information? Identify two kinds of information you could locate in this tool.
25. What is the Microsoft Management Console (MMC)?

True/False Questions

For each question, circle the letter T if the statement is true or the letter F if the statement is false.

   T   F   1.   Check Disk cannot find or fix errors on CD-ROMs or network drives.

   T   F   2. If you use System Restore, you no longer have to back up your data files.

   T   F   3. You may choose to back up only your documents and settings or everyone's documents and settings when you use Backup.

   T   F   4. A defragmenting program such as Disk Defragmenter compresses data.

   T   F   5. Device manager is a tool that allows you to see if your devices are working properly.

Completion Questions

Write the correct answer in each blank space provided.

6. The tool that allows you to identify your BIOS version is _____.

7. If you are having problems with your system and it is in an unstable state, you may roll it back to a previous working version of your system by using

    _____.

8. The program included with Windows XP Professional that will eliminate cached Internet files and temporary files is _____.

9. The Registry files are kept in the _____ directory.

10. A backup that only backs up files that have changed since the last full backup and turns off the archive bit is called a(n) _____ backup.

Multiple Choice Questions

Circle the letter of the correct answer for each question.

11. The System Information window contains tools that allow you to
    a. change system information.
    b. view system information.
    c. change your monitor settings.
    d. view your monitor settings.

12. Before running the Disk Defragmenter program, be sure you have
    a. plenty of time.
    b. a backup of important files.
    c. a floppy in the drive.
    d. both a and b

13. If you wanted to update a driver for your video card, you would use the _____ tool.
    a. My Computer
    b. Performance
    c. Device Manager
    d. all of the above

14. If you wanted to know about your hard disk file systems, you would open Computer Management. Under Storage, you would select
    a. Removable Storage.
    b. Hardware Resources.
    c. Device Manager.
    d. Disk Management.
15. Which of the following statements is true?
    a. Using Backup will automatically back up the Registry.
    b. The Registry has been replaced by the .ini file.
    c. The Registry is used for configuration information about your computer system.
    d. none of the above

Homework Assignments

Problem Set I—Brief Essay

For all essay questions, use Notepad or WordPad for your answer. Be sure to include your name, your class information, and which problem you are answering. Print your answer.

1. The following files can be deleted in Disk Cleanup. Briefly describe the purpose of deleting each group of files. Determine and explain which options you think are best when using Disk Cleanup.
   - downloaded program files
   - temporary Internet files
   - offline Web pages
   - Recycle Bin
   - temporary files
   - temporary Offline Files
   - Offline Files
   - catalog files for the Content Indexer
2. You are the owner of a small business. You keep your business records on a computer. Develop a plan to schedule Check Disk and Disk Defragmenter on your computer. Describe what tools you will use. Explain the reasons for your choices.
3. Define and explain the use of a paging file. When and why would you want to alter the settings?
4. *Windows XP Professional includes System Restore. This tool is a critical feature for all users.* Describe the purpose and function of System Restore. Then agree or disagree with the statement and provide the rationale for your answer.
5. *It is critical to create an ASR. It is used when* _____. Complete the fill-in portion of the question. Agree or disagree with the first statement. Give your reasons for what you filled in to complete the second statement.

Problem Set II—Scenario

You are the owner of a small business. You have an accounting program installed on the computer. The accounting program is kept in a directory called Quicken. You keep your accounting data files in a directory called Accounting. You are using a word-processing program called Word. The program files are kept in a folder called Winword. You have business letters created in Word that are kept in a folder called Letters. You also use Word to create invoices and you keep those data files in a directory called Invoices.

Develop a backup plan for your computer system. Include which files and directories you will back up and how often.

INSTALLING THE
WUGXP DIRECTORY AND SHAREWARE REGISTRATION

A.1 The WUGXP Directory

The disk supplied with the textbook provides programs and files for you to use as you work through the book. The textbook assumes that the WUGXP directory has been installed on Drive C. If you wish to install the WUGXP directory on a hard drive other than Drive C, you must substitute the correct drive letter in these instructions. If you are working on your own computer, you must be in the Command Prompt window at the command line, not in the Windows XP GUI. You must be at the root of C: and the default drive and directory must be A:\.

If you are in a lab or work environment, the lab instructors should have installed the WUGXP directory on the hard disk. The lab instructors, particularly if the lab is on a network, will have to give you instructions as to the location of the WUGXP directory if it is not on Drive C. If you cannot locate the WUGXP directory, for instructions on what you need to do.

A.2 Activity: Installing the WUGXP Directory

1 Have no disk in any drive. Turn on the monitor and computer. Log in, if necessary.

WHAT'S ▓▓▓▓▓
▓▓▓HAPPENING?   You are at the Windows desktop. You may have more icons displayed on the desktop, depending on how your system was installed.

2   Click **Start**. Point to **All Programs**. Point to **Accessories**. Point to **Command Prompt**.

WHAT'S ▓▓▓▓▓
▓▓▓HAPPENING?   You are going to open the Command Prompt window.

3   Click **Command Prompt**.

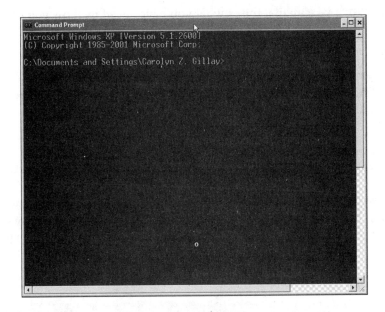

HAPPENING?   You have opened a Command Prompt window. Your directory may differ. In this example, it is C:\Documents and Settings\Carolyn Z. Gillay>.

4 Key in the following:

C:\Documents and Settings\Carolyn Z. Gillay>**CD \ Enter**

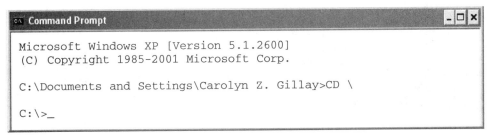

HAPPENING?   You are now at the root of Drive C. If you wanted this folder to be on a drive other than C, you would substitute that drive letter for C.

5 Place the ACTIVITIES disk that came with the textbook in Drive A.

6 Key in the following: C:\>**A:\ Enter**

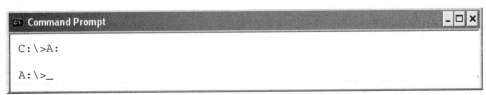

HAPPENING?   You have made the root of A the default drive and directory.

7 Key in the following: A:\>**XCOPY A:*.* /S /E C:\WUGXP**

WHAT'S ▨▨▨
▨▨▨HAPPENING?   Be sure that this is what you have keyed in. Now you can begin
executing the program by pressing [Enter].

8   Press [Enter]

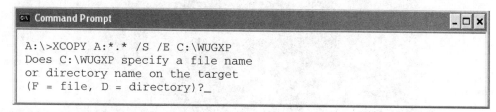

WHAT'S ▨▨▨
▨▨▨HAPPENING?   The XCOPY command is asking you if you want to create a
directory or file called WUGXP. In this case you want to create a directory so you
must specify that by pressing the letter D. Once you press D, the files will be copied
to drive C to the directory called WUGXP.

9   Press **D** [Enter]

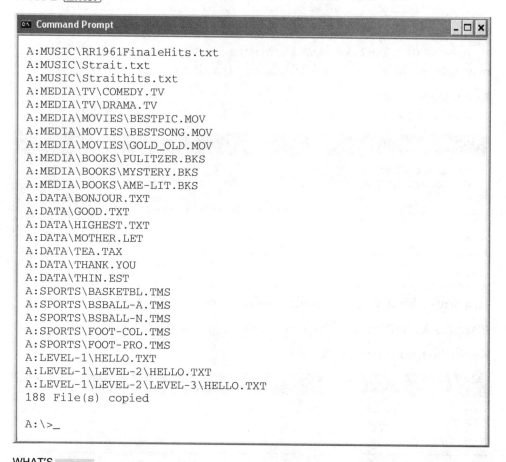

WHAT'S ▨▨▨
▨▨▨HAPPENING?   You now have a directory on Drive C called WUGXP. You need to
have this directory placed on Drive C in order to complete the exercises, activities
and homework.

10   Key in the following: A:\>**C:** [Enter]

11   Key in the following: C:\>**DIR WUG*.*** [Enter]

```
▣ Command Prompt                                              _ □ ✕

C:\>DIR WUG*.*
 Volume in drive C has no label.
 Volume Serial Number is 3CDD-319A

 Directory of C:\

06/11/2002  11:10 AM    <DIR>          WUGXP
               0 File(s)               0 bytes
               1 Dir(s)   57,423,015,936 bytes free

C:\>
```

WHAT'S HAPPENING?   You have successfully installed the WUGXP directory on drive C. Installed means that you created the WUGXP directory on Drive C and copied all the files on the disk in Drive A to the newly created folder called WUGXP.

12 Key in the following: C:\>**EXIT** ⌈Enter⌉

WHAT'S HAPPENING?   You have closed the Command Prompt window and returned to the Windows desktop.

A.3   Removing the WUGXP Directory

If you are working in a lab environment, you should not remove the WUGXP directory. However if you are working on your own computer, when you have completed the textbook, you will probably want to take the WUGXP directory and the files it contains off of your hard drive. You may, of course, use Windows Explorer. You would select WUGXP folder in My Computer or Windows Explorer and then press the ⌈Delete⌉ key. If you want to use the command line, you use the RMDIR /S command.

A.4   Activity: Removing the WUGXP Directory from the Command Line

Note: It is assumed you have booted the system and are at the Windows desktop.

1 Click **Start**. Point to **All Programs**. Point to **Accessories**. Click **Command Prompt**.

2 Key in the following:
C:\Documents and Settings\Carolyn Z. Gillay>**CD ** ⌈Enter⌉

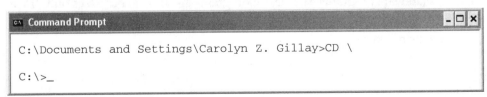

```
▣ Command Prompt                                              _ □ ✕

 C:\Documents and Settings\Carolyn Z. Gillay>CD \

 C:\>_
```

WHAT'S HAPPENING?   You have moved to the root directory of C.

3   Key in the following: C:\>**RMDIR /S \WUGXP**

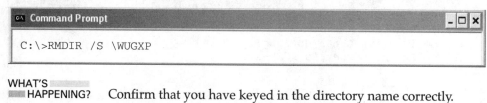

```
C:\>RMDIR /S \WUGXP
```

WHAT'S
HAPPENING?   Confirm that you have keyed in the directory name correctly.

4   Press **Enter**

```
C:\>RMDIR /S \WUGXP
\WUGXP, Are you sure (Y/N)?_
```

WHAT'S
HAPPENING?   You are being asked to confirm if you really want to delete the
directory called WUGXP and all the files and directories that are in it.

5   Press **Y** **Enter**

6   Key in the following: C:\>**DIR WUG*.*** **Enter**

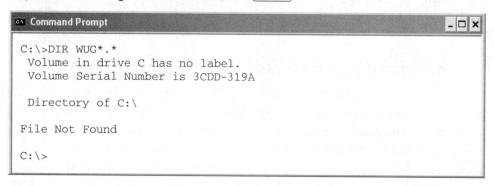

```
C:\>DIR WUG*.*
 Volume in drive C has no label.
 Volume Serial Number is 3CDD-319A

 Directory of C:\

File Not Found

C:\>
```

WHAT'S
HAPPENING?   You have successfully deleted the WUGXP directory.

7   Key in the following: C:\>**EXIT** **Enter**

WHAT'S
HAPPENING?   You have closed the Command Prompt window and returned to
the Windows desktop.

A.5   Shareware Programs Provided with the Textbook

Several programs on the ACTIVITIES disk that are installed to the WUGXP directory are shareware programs. Shareware programs are for trial purposes only. If you
find the programs useful and would like to keep them, you must register them and
pay the registration fee.

ARGH

ARGH.EXE and ARGH.DOC are distributed as shareware. This allows you to try
ARGH before you buy it, but if you continue to use it, you must register. Register by
sending $10.00 to:

David B. Howorth
01960 SW Palatine Hill Road
Portland, Oregon 97219

BOG2

Bog 2 is shareware. To register your copy, please send $10.00 U.S. plus postage and handling to:
Pocket-Sized Software
8547 E. Arapahoe Road
Suite J-147
Greenwood Village, CO 80112 USA
Postage and Handling:
U.S. and Canada: $2.50, overseas: $5.00 (for airmail delivery)

MATCH32 Version 1.1

This game is a shareware. If you like this game and play a lot with it, you should register. Without registration, you could only play a limited part of this game— the first three levels out of the total 17 levels. If you register, you will receive the registration code by mail from the author. After you have received registration code, you could do the following to activate the full version of this game:

- Under the main menu choice Tools, there is a sub-choice Register.
- Click on Register and you will see a dialog box.
- Type in the registration code and press the Enter key or click the OK button.

To register, send $10 of check or money order to:
Yuntong Kuo
P. O. Box 831
Pittsfield, MA 01202

Microlink Shareware

MLSHUT and all the games in the MLINK folder are provided by:
Bob Lancaster
P. O. Box 5612
Hacienda Heights, CA 91745
If you like any of these games, please send $5.00, per game, to Bob Lancaster at the above address.

B.1   An Introduction to Computers

At the most basic level, computers are calculators; but this definition is very narrow. Computers are used to handle accounting chores (spreadsheets), write books (word-processing documents), organize and retrieve information (databases), create and manipulate graphics, and communicate with the world (the Internet). In the visual arts computers have revolutionized the way films are made, games are played, and reality is perceived (virtual reality).

B.2   Categories of Computers

Computers are categorized by a variety of factors such as size, processing speed, information storage capacity, and cost. In the ever-changing technical world, these classifications are not absolute. Technical advancements blur some categories. For instance, many microcomputers today exceed the capabilities of mainframes manufactured five years ago. In addition, the microcomputer now is the dominant computer used by most businesses. These computers are available in sizes ranging from desktop to sub-notebook. Table B.1 shows the major categories of computers.

Computer	Applications
Supercomputer: Very large computer	Sophisticated scientific applications such as nuclear physics, atomic physics, and seismology
Mainframe: Large computer	General purpose business machines. Typical applications include accounting, payroll, banking, and airline reservations
Minicomputer: Small mainframe computer	Specialized applications such as engineering and industrial research
Microcomputer: Small, general-purpose computer	General applications such as word processing, accounting for small businesses, and record keeping. Today, these computers are also known as desktops, PCs, notebooks, subcompacts, and laptops.

Table B.1—Computer Types

B.3   Computer Components

Although types of computers continue to grow, computers operate the same way, regardless of their category. Information is input, processed, and stored and the resulting information is output. Figure B.1 is a graphic representation of this process.

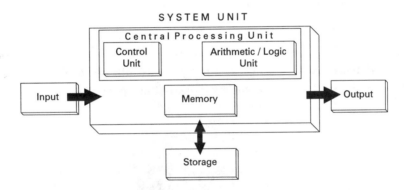

Figure B.1—Components of a Computer System

Figure B.1 shows the process that occurs when using a computer. It represents the physical components of a computer system, referred to as *hardware*. All computer systems, from mainframes to notebooks, have the same basic hardware. Hardware by itself can do nothing—a computer system needs software. *Software* is a set of detailed instructions, called a *program*, that tells the hardware what operations to perform.

Data, in its simplest form, is related or unrelated numbers, words, or facts that, when arranged in a particular way, provide information. Software applications turn raw data into information.

B.4   Microcomputer Hardware Components

This textbook is devoted to single-user computers—microcomputers. Microcomputers, today simply called computers, are also called micros, subcompacts, home computers, laptops, notebooks, personal computers (PCs), or desktop computers. Microcomputers

are comprised of hardware components. Much like a stereo system, the basic components of a complete system, also called a system configuration, include an input
device (typically a keyboard), a pointing device (a mouse or trackball), a system unit
that houses the electronic circuitry for storing and processing data and programs (the
central processing unit/CPU, adapter cards, power supply, and memory/RAM and
ROM), an external storage unit that stores data and programs on disks (disk drives),
and an output device such as a visual display unit (a monitor). Most people also
purchase a printer for producing a printed version of the results. Typically today, a
system also includes speakers for multimedia activities. Figure B.2 represents a
typical microcomputer system.

Figure B.2—A Typical Microcomputer System

If you look at the back of the computer, you can see the input/output devices,
called peripherals. Since they are "peripheral," or outside the case, they must communicate with what is inside the computer through cables attached to a connection that
is called a *port*. Figure B.3 shows some examples of these connections.

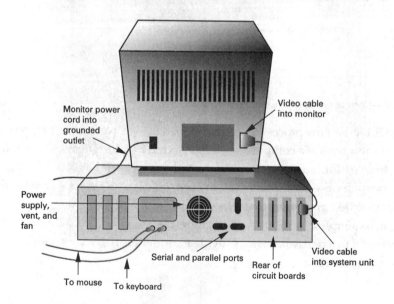

Figure B.3—Cables Attached to a Case

B.5   The System Unit

The system unit, as shown in Figure B.4, is the "black box" that houses the electronic and mechanical parts of the computer. It contains many printed electronic circuit boards, also called interface cards, *cards*, or *adapter cards*. One of these is a special printed circuit board called the *system board* or the *motherboard*. Attached to the system board is a microprocessor chip that is the central processing unit (CPU), random access memory (RAM), and read-only memory (ROM). The system unit is also referred to as the chassis or case. With the outer case removed, the unit looks like the diagram in Figure B.4.

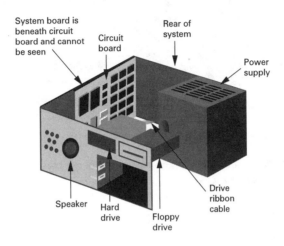

Figure B.4—Inside the System Unit

Inside the typical system unit, you will find the following:

- A system board or motherboard that contains components such as a CPU, RAM, ROM, a chipset, and a system clock.
- Expansion slots that contain adapter cards such as a video card, a sound card, or a network interface card.
- Secondary storage units (disk drives)
- A power supply

A system unit has a power supply (to get power to every single part in the PC), disk drives (including CD-ROM drives, floppy disk drives, removable drives, and hard disk drives), and circuit boards. The motherboard, also called the system board, is the core of the system. Everything in the PC is connected to the motherboard so that it can control every part of in the system. Figure B.5 shows a system board.

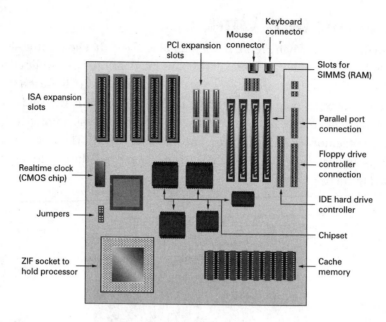

Figure B.5—Components on a System Board

Most modern system boards have several components built in, including various sockets, slots, connectors, chips, and other components. Most system boards have the following components:

■ A processor socket/slot is the place where the CPU is installed.

■ A chipset is a single chip that integrates all the functions of older system chips such as the system timer, the keyboard controller, and so forth.

■ A Super Input/Output chip integrates devices formerly found on separate expansion cards in older systems.

■ All system boards must have a special chip containing software that is called BIOS (basic input/output system) or *ROM-BIOS*. (*ROM* is *read-only memory*.) This chip contains the startup programs and drivers that are used to get your system up and running and acts as the interface to the basic hardware in your system. BIOS is a collection of programs embedded into a chip, called a flash ROM chip. It is nonvolatile, which means that, when you turn off the computer, none of the information stored in ROM is lost. ROM-BIOS has four main functions: POST (power-on self test), which tests a computer's critical hardware components such as the processor, memory, and disk controllers; the bootstrap loader, which finds the operating system and loads or boots your computer; BIOS, which is the collection of actual drivers used to act as a basic interface between the operating system and the hardware (when you run the Windows operating system in safe mode, you are running solely on BIOS drivers); and the CMOS (complementary metal-oxide semiconductor) setup, which contains the system configuration and setup programs. CMOS is usually a menu-driven program that allows you to configure the motherboard and chipset settings along with the date and time and passwords. You usually access the CMOS settings by pressing a special keystroke combination before the operating system loads. The keystroke, such as DEL or F2, depends on the computer. Most ROM is located on the system board, but some ROM is located on adapter boards.

- SIMM/DIMM (single inline memory module/dual inline memory module) slots are for the installation of memory modules. These modules are small boards that plug into special connectors on the motherboard or memory card and replace individual memory chips. If one chip goes bad, the entire module must be replaced.
- System buses are the heart of every motherboard. A *bus* is a path across which data can travel within a computer. A data path is the communication highway between computer elements. The main buses in a system include:
    - The processor bus, the highest-speed bus in the system, is primarily used by the processor to pass information to and from memory.
    - The AGP (accelerated graphics port) bus is a high-speed bus specifically for a video card.
    - The PCI (peripheral component interconnect) bus is a collection of slots that high-speed peripherals such as SCSI (small computer system interface) adapters, network cards, and video cards can be plugged into.
    - The ISA (Industry Standard Architecture) bus is an old bus which appeared in the first computers. Most people use it for plug-in modems, sound cards, and various other low-speed peripherals. ISA slots are gradually being replaced by PCI slots.
    - The voltage regulator is used to drop the power supply signal to the correct voltage for the processor.
    - A battery supplies power for the CMOS chip, which holds the system configuration information.

B.6   Central Processing Unit

A *central processing unit*, most commonly referred to as a *CPU*, is the brain of a computer and is composed of transistors on a silicon chip. It comprehends and carries out instructions sent to it by a program and directs the activity of the computer. The CPU is plugged into the motherboard. The CPU is described in terms of its central processing chip and its model designation. Intel manufactures many of the CPU chips in Windows-based PCs. Intel processors running Windows are commonly called *Wintel* machines. These chips were, for many years, designated by a model number such as 80386 or 80486. Typically the first two numbers were dropped so people referred to a computer as a 386 or 486. With the introduction of the 80586, Intel began referring to its chips as Pentiums such as the Pentium 350. Since that time, Intel has released the Pentium II, the Pentium III, and the Pentium IV. The major competitors to Intel are AMD and Cyrix. A CPU is rated by the following items:

1. Speed. The system clock on the system board times the activities of the chips on the system board. This clock provides a beat that synchronizes all the activities. The faster the beat, the faster the CPU can execute instructions. This is measured in *megahertz (MHz)*, where one MHz is equal to 1,000,000 beats of the clock per second. The original 8088 CPU had a MHz rating of 4.77 MHz. Today, 500 is a common speed, and speeds are available up to 866 MHz or more. In fact, a 1 GHz CPU has been developed, with even faster CPUs coming.
2. Efficiency of the program code built into the CPU chip.

3. Internal data path size (word size) is the largest number of bits the CPU can process in one operation. Word sizes range from 16 bits (2 bytes) to 64 bits (8 bytes).

4. Data path, the largest number of bits that can be transported into the CPU, ranges from 8 bits to 64 bits.

5. Maximum number of memory addresses that the CPU can assign. The minimum is 1 megabyte and the maximum is 4,096 megabytes (4 gigabytes).

6. Internal cache, which is memory included in the CPU. It is also referred to as primary cache or level 1 (L1) cache.

7. Multiprocessor ability. Some chips can accomplish more than one task at a time and thus are multiprocessors.

8. Special functionality. Some chips are designed to provide special services. For example, the Pentium MMX chip is designed to handle multimedia features especially well.

B.7   Input/Output (I/O) Buses

Adapter cards are printed circuit boards, as mentioned previously. They are installed in a system unit either when the unit is purchased or later. Adapter cards allow a user to use a special video display or use a mouse, a modem, or a fax-modem. These items are considered *peripheral devices* and are installed within a system unit in expansion slots. The number of adapter card options you can install depends on how many slots your system unit has. Inexpensive system units usually have only one or two expansion slots, but a costly system unit, especially one designed to be a network server, can have seven, eight, or more.

I/O buses allow your CPU to communicate with your peripheral devices. A peripheral device connected to your computer is controlled by the CPU. Examples of peripherals (also called peripheral device or devices) include such items as a disk drive, a printer, a mouse, or a modem. The original personal computers had nothing built into the computer except a CPU, memory, and a keyboard. Everything else such as floppy disk drivers, hard disk drives, printers, and modems were provided by add-in cards. Nowadays, computer manufacturers have found that it is less expensive to build the most common peripherals into the motherboard. Connectors to which you connect the cables for your devices are called ports. Today, most computers include a parallel port for a printer, two serial ports for devices such as an external modem or a serial mouse, two USB (Universal Serial Bus) ports and controllers for up to two floppy drives and two hard disk drives.

However, not every peripheral has a built-in connection. Data paths often stop at an expansion slot. An *expansion slot* is a slot or plug where you can add an interface card to enhance your computer system. An *interface card* is a printed circuit board that enables a personal computer to use a peripheral device such as a CD-ROM drive, modem, or joystick, for which it does not already have the necessary connections, ports, or circuit boards. Interface cards are also called cards, adapter cards, or adapter boards. The size and shape of the expansion slot is dependent on the kind of bus your computer uses.

Remember, a bus is a set of hardware lines (conductors) used for data transfer among the components of the computer system. A bus is essentially a shared information highway that connects different parts of the system—including the CPU, the disk-drive controller, and memory. Buses are characterized by the number of bits that they can transfer at one time, which is equivalent to the number of wires within a bus. A computer with a 32-bit address bus and a 16-bit data bus can transfer 16 bits of data at a time from any of 2^{32} memory locations. Buses have standards—a technical guideline that is used to establish uniformity in an area of hardware or software development.

Common bus standards include ISA (Industry Standard Architecture), PCI (peripheral component interconnect), local bus, PC Card slots—formerly known as PCMCIA (Personal Computer Memory Card International Association)—primarily used on notebook computers, and VESA (Video Electronics Standards Association) local bus.

The most recent bus standard is the *USB (Universal Serial Bus)*. It is an external bus standard that brings the plug-and-play standard capability of hardware devices outside the computer, eliminating the need to install cards into dedicated computer slots and reconfigure the system. Most computers today include a USB connection. The advantage of USB is that you may daisy chain devices. This connectivity feature means that your first device plugs into the USB connector; then the next device plugs into the first device, and so forth. You only need one USB connection, but most systems come with two. You can use each connection for many devices. In addition, USB devices can be "hot-plugged" or unplugged, which means that you can add or remove a peripheral device without needing to power down the computer. The device, however, must be USB compatible.

FireWire is a recent bus technology. This bus was derived from the FireWire bus originally developed by Apple and Texas Instruments. It is now known as IEEE 1394 rather than FireWire. This bus is extremely fast and suits the demands of today's audio and video multimedia that must move large amounts of data quickly.

B.8 Random Access Memory

RAM (random access memory) is the workspace of the computer. It is often referred to simply as *memory*. The growth in the size of RAM in the last few years has been phenomenal. Whereas 4 MB of memory was more than satisfactory just a few years ago, the demand based on software needs has made 128 MB of RAM commonplace, and 256 or more MB of RAM desirable. Physically, RAM is contained in many electrical circuits. However, a computer's memory is not like a person's memory. RAM is not a permanent record of anything. RAM is the place where the programs and data are placed while the computer is working. Computer memory is temporary (volatile) and useful only while the computer is on. When the computer is turned off, what is in memory is lost.

There are two types of RAM, *dynamic RAM (DRAM)* and *static RAM (SRAM)*. Dynamic RAM chips hold data for a short time whereas static RAM chips can hold data until the computer is turned off. DRAM is much less expensive than SRAM; thus most memory on a motherboard consists of DRAM. Dynamic RAM chips do not hold their data long and must be refreshed about every 3.86 milliseconds. To refresh means that the computer rewrites the data to the chip. The direct memory access (DMA) takes care of refreshing RAM. The DMA controller is on the system board and is part of the chipset. It provides faster memory access because it moves data in and out of RAM without involving the CPU. Today, you also see extended data output (EDO) memory on newer computers. This RAM module works about 20 percent faster then conventional RAM, but the system board must support EDO memory. Since the speed by which you and your computer work is driven by RAM, you can expect improvements in RAM speed to continue.

B.9   Cache Memory

Caching is a method used to improve processing speed. It uses some of the more expensive static RAM chips to speed up data access. Basically, *cache memory* stores frequently used RAM data, thereby speeding up the process of data access. Whenever the CPU needs data from RAM, it visits the cache first to see if the data is available there. If it is, then rapid action occurs. If not, the CPU goes to RAM proper.

The cache will hold data or programming code that is often used or anticipated. This way the CPU has the instructions it needs ready and waiting without having to refresh RAM. Caches can be found in video and printer memory systems as well.

B.10   Controllers

A *controller* is a device on which other devices rely for access to a computer subsystem such as a disk drive. A disk controller, for example, controls access to one or more disk drives. What kind of controller interface you have will determine the number and kinds of devices you can attach to your computer. A common disk-drive controller is the Integrated Device Electronics (IDE), which resides on the drive itself, eliminating the need for a separate adapter card. Another type is the Small Computer System Interface (SCSI), pronounced "skuzzi," which is a very high-speed interface and is used to connect computers to many SCSI peripheral devices such as hard disks and printers. The original SCSI standard is now called SCSI-I, and the new enhanced SCSI standard is called SCSI-II. In addition, new developments include Fast SCSI, Fast/Wide SCSI, and UltraSCSI.

B.11   Connectors

Most computers have a serial port, two USB ports, and a parallel port. See Figure B.6. These connections allow devices to be plugged in. *Serial ports* communicate in series, one data bit after another, and service serial devices such as modems and mouses. *Parallel ports* communicate in parallel, eight data bits at a time, and service parallel devices such as printers. The most common configuration for a personal computer is two serial ports and one parallel port. Serial ports are referred to as COM ports, and on a standard computer they are designated as COM1 and COM2. Parallel ports are called LPT ports. The first LPT port is called LPT1. COM stands for communications and LPT stands for line printer.

A personal computer can have up to five I/O ports, usually three serial and two parallel. Although computers are limited to five ports, there can actually be more than five peripheral devices. USB ports do not figure into the five I/O ports. Today, many devices, such as Zip drives and scanners, that plug into parallel ports have a "through port" so that one LPT port can service two devices. However, today, most Zip drives and scanners are USB. If you have a SCSI interface, you may also connect a series of devices, creating a daisy chain.

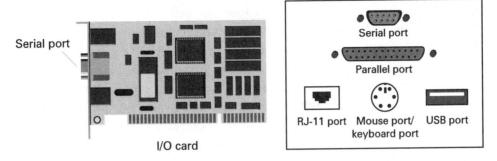

Figure B.6—I/O Ports

Today, many computers come with a built-in modem. If that is the case, you will have a connector called an RJ-11 telephone plug, which is identical to the plug on the back of a telephone. Having an RJ-11 connector frees up a serial port.

B.12 Peripherals: Input Devices

How do software programs and data get into RAM? The answer is input devices. The most common input device is the keyboard, which is attached to a system unit with a cable. By keying in instructions and data, you communicate with the computer. The computer places the information into RAM. Again, most modern computers have a keyboard port to connect the keyboard. See Figure B.6.

You can also input using a pointing device, such as a *mouse*, *trackball*, track pointer, or touchpad to get to the place to enter data. (In this textbook, all such devices will be collectively referred to as a *mouse*.) Data manipulation is as easy as moving the cursor to where you want it on the screen and pressing one of the mouse buttons. Most computers today have a connector for the mouse, most commonly called the PS/2 connector. See Figure B.6.

Other input devices include modems with which data can be downloaded directly into the computer, and scanners for inserting text through optical character recognition (OCR) software and graphics. Disk drives are both input and output devices.

B.13 Peripherals: Output Devices

In addition to getting information into the CPU, you also want to get it out. You may want to see what you keyed in on the monitor, or you might desire a printed or "hard" copy of the data. These processes are known as output. Output devices refer to where information is sent. Thus, you read information in and write information out, commonly known as I/O for input and output.

B.14 Output Devices: Monitors

A *monitor*, also called a terminal display screen, screen, cathode-ray tube (CRT), or video display terminal (VDT), looks like a television. The common monitor size standard used to be 14 inches (measured diagonally). However, today, most users opt for at least a 15-inch monitor. The new standard is becoming the 19-inch monitor, with the 21-inch monitor gaining ground. In addition, the liquid crystal display (LCD) used on notebook computers is now becoming available as a stand-alone monitor to accompany your desktop computer. These monitors take far less space since they are completely flat. Although, these monitors were very expensive when first introduced, the prices have really dropped making this choice an affordable one.

Another important facet to a monitor is the sharpness of its image, referred to as its *resolution*. Resolution is a measure of how many pixels on the screen are addressable by software. It is measured in the number of *pixels* (dots) on the screen. A resolution of 800 by 600 means 800 pixels per line horizontally and 600 pixels vertically. Multiplying 800 by 600 will give you the total number of pixels available (480,000 pixels). The resolution must be supported by the video card controller, and the software you are using must make use of the resolution capabilities of the monitor.

In addition, to determine the sharpness of your image, you must also know the dot pitch of the pixels. *Dot pitch* is the measurement in millimeters between pixels on the screen. The smaller the dot pitch, the sharper the image. Common sizes include .25 to .31. A dot pitch of .28 or .25 will give you the best results.

Another factor in choosing a monitor is the interlace factor. An *interlaced* monitor begins at the top of the screen and redraws (refreshes) every other line of pixels, then returns to the top and refreshes the rest of the lines. A *noninterlaced* monitor refreshes all the lines at one time, eliminating the wandering horizontal line and the flickering screen. Thus, a noninterlaced monitor is the preferred choice. The refresh rate (vertical scan rate) is the time it takes for the electronic beam to fill the screen with lines from top to bottom. Video Electronics Standards Association (VESA) has set a minimum refresh rate standard of 70 Hz (70 complete vertical refreshes per second) as one requirement of Super VGA monitors. Multiscan monitors are also available. These monitors offer a variety of vertical and horizontal refresh rates but cost much more than other monitors.

Information written to the screen by the CPU needs a special kind of circuit board—a video display adapter card, commonly called a video card or a graphics adapter card—which controls the monitor. The video adapter consists of three components:

- A video chip set of some brand (ATI, Matrox, Nvidia, S3, are some of the better known brands). The video chip creates the signals, which the screen must receive to form an image.
- Some kind of RAM (EDO, SGRAM, or VRAM,). Memory is imperative, since the video card must be able to remember a complete screen image at any time. Using AGP, the video card may use the main memory of the motherboard.
- A RAMDAC, a chip converting digital/analog signals. If you have a flat-panel monitor, you do not need a the function of a RAMDAC.

In the early days of computing, the video adapters were only monochrome. The color graphics adapter (CGA) and the enhanced graphics adapter (EGA) came next, but only in 16 colors. Next was the video graphics array (VGA), which generated 256 colors. Next came the Super VGA (SVGA) format, which generated sharper resolution displayed an almost unbelievable 16 million colors. In truth, VGA was the last "real standard" working on any PC. Screen resolution has since improved relative to VGA, and the term SVGA (Super VGA) came into use. Later came XGA and other names, which each described different resolutions. Today, the terms SVGA and XGA are not used much anymore. Instead one looks at resolution, image frequency and color depth. Commonly, a video card has its own "on-board" memory, which is physically on the card. Today, 32 gigabytes of memory on a video card is common, and soon 64 megabytes will be the standard.

The standard CRT monitors will be phased out. They are being replaced by the flat and LCD (Liquid Crystal Display) monitors. The prices are dropping every day—today a 17 inch LCD costs the same as a 21 inch monitor did several years ago. In addition, you get more "viewing" with an LCD. For instance, 17.3" flat panel monitor has a visible area much bigger than that from a traditional 17" CRT monitor—it can be compared to a 19" CRT. The 17.3 inches is the visible diameter. The LCD screen is flat since it has no cathode ray tube (CRT). The screen image is generated on a flat plastic disk where millions of transistors create the pixels. In addition to the size and weight advantage, another big advantage of the LCD monitor is that it does not flicker.

B.15 Output Devices: Printers

A printer is attached to a system unit with a cable, usually to a parallel port. A printer allows a user to have a hard copy (unchangeable because it is on paper) of information.

In the past, *impact printers*, such as dot-matrix printers, were used. An impact printer works like a typewriter. The element strikes some kind of ribbon, which in turn strikes the paper and leaves a mark. A dot-matrix printer forms characters by selecting dots from a grid pattern on a movable print head and permits printing in any style of letters and graphics (pictures). Dot-matrix printers are still used today for multiple-part forms that use carbon paper.

Today, *non-impact printers* are in general use. This category includes thermal printers that burn images into paper using a dot-matrix grid and *inkjet printers* that spray ionized drops of ink to shape characters. Today, inkjet printers that produce very good quality black and white as well as color images have become the most popular personal printer. The *laser printer* is more expensive, but produces fine quality black and white printing. Although laser color is available, it still remains very costly. Laser printers use a laser beam instructed by the computer to form characters with powdered toner fused to the page by heat, like a photocopying machine. Laser printers operate noiselessly at speeds up to 900 characters per second (cps), equivalent to 24 pages per minute.

B.16 Modems

A *modem* (*m*odulator/*dem*odulator) translates the digital signals of the computer into the analog signals that travel over telephone lines. The speed at which the signal travels is called the baud rate—the unit of time for a signal to travel over a telephone line. The rate of transmission has increased to 56,000 baud, and will soon be even faster. The speed at which data packets travel is measured in bits per second (bps) and is usually very near the baud rate. For this transmission to occur, the party on the other end must also have a modem that translates the analog signals back into digital signals. In addition, the computer needs special instructions in the form of a software communication program.

Cable modems are also available in some areas. In this case, the cable company lays high-speed cable lines that require a special modem as well as a network interface card. This greatly increases the transmission speed. Another alternative is an integrated services digital network (ISDN) line—a high-speed telephone data line that also greatly increases speed. A digital subscriber line (DSL) is yet another choice, if available. Here users can purchase bandwidth that is potentially 10 times faster than ISDN lines but still slower than cable. *Bandwidth* can simply be described as a pipe that moves data from point A to point B. It is the data transfer capacity of a digital communications system.

Another choice for organizations such as businesses or educational institutions is a dedicated leased line that provides digital service between two locations at high speeds. A leased line is a permanent 24-hour connection to a specific location that can only be changed by the telephone company. Leased lines are used to connect local area networks to remote locations or to the Internet through a service provider. Leased lines include T-1 and T-3 connections. T-1 is a digital connection running at 1.55 megabits per second (Mbps) and costs several thousand dollars per month. A T-3 connection is equivalent to 30 T-1 lines and connections can run up to 45 Mbps. The cost limits the use to major companies or large universities. There are even satellite modems (wireless) that are incredibly fast and at this time costly but there is no question that wireless is going to be the future.

The growth of online services has made a modem or a digital connection a necessity. CompuServe, America Online, and Internet service providers—all leading to the information superhighway—make all kinds of information available. These services are the libraries of the future.

B.17 Capacity Measurement: Bits and Bytes

A computer is made primarily of switches. All it can do is turn a switch on or off: 0 (zero) represents an off state and 1 (one) represents an on state. A *bit* (short for *binary digit*) is the smallest unit a computer can recognize. Bits are combined in meaningful groups, much as letters of the alphabet are combined to make words. A common grouping is eight bits, called a *byte*. A byte can be thought of as one character.

Computer capacities, such as RAM and ROM, are measured in bytes, originally grouped by thousands of bytes or *kilobytes* (*KB*), but now by millions of bytes or *megabytes* (*MB*, sometimes called *megs*), and *gigabytes* (*GB*, sometimes called *gigs*). A computer is binary, so it works in powers of 2. A kilobyte is 2 to the tenth power

(1,024), and K or KB is the symbol for 1,024 bytes. If your computer has 64KB of memory, its actual memory size is 64 x 1,024, or 65,536 bytes. For simplification, KB is rounded off to 1,000, so that 64KB of memory means 64,000 bytes. Rapid technological growth has made megabytes the measuring factor.

You should know the capacity of your computer's memory because it determines how much data the computer can hold. For instance, if you have 32 MB of RAM on your computer and you buy a program that requires 64 MB of RAM, your computer will not have the memory capacity to use that program. Furthermore, if your computer has a hard disk capacity of 100 MB and the application program you buy requires at least 125 MB of space on the hard disk, you won't be able to install the program. Today, of course, a computer that has a hard disk of only 100 MB is very unlikely, but the principle remains the same—you have a specific amount of space on your hard disk and you can exceed the size of your hard disk if you have many large programs.

Disk capacity is also measured in bytes. A 3½-inch double-density disk holds 720KB. Because high-density and hard disks hold so much more information, they are also measured in megabytes. A 3½-inch high-density disk holds 1.44 MB. Hard disks vary in size, commonly ranging from 10 GB to over 80 GB. Today, most people consider an 20-GB hard disk a minimum requirement; it has a capacity of over twenty billion bytes. Most computer users, when referring to gigabytes, use the term gig. An 38.2 GB hard drive is referred to as an "thirty-eight point two gig" hard drive.

B.18 Disks and Disk Drives

Since RAM is volatile and disappears when the power is turned off, *secondary storage media* or external storage media are necessary to save information permanently.

Disks and disk drives are magnetic media that store data and programs in the form of magnetic impulses. Such media include floppy disks, hard disks, compact discs (CD-ROMs), digital videodiscs (DVDs), removable drives such as Zip and Jaz drives, tapes, and tape cartridges. In the microcomputer world, the most common secondary storage media are floppy disks and hard disks, with removable drives and read/write CD-ROMs rapidly becoming a standard for most users.

Storing information on a disk is equivalent to storing information in a file cabinet. Like file cabinets, disks store information in files. When the computer needs the information, it goes to the disk, opens a file, reads the information from the disk file into RAM, and works on it. When the computer is finished working on that file, it closes the file and returns (writes) it back to the disk. In most cases, this process does not occur automatically. The application program in use will have instructions that enable the user to save or write to the disk.

B.19 Floppy Disks

Floppy disks serve a dual purpose. First, disks provide a permanent way to hold data. When power is turned off, the disk retains what has been recorded on it. Second, floppy disks are transportable. Programs or data developed on one computer can be used by another merely by inserting the disk into the other computer. If it were not for this capability, programs such as the operating system or other application packages could not be used. Each time you wanted to do some work, you would have to write your own instructions.

Floppy disks come in two sizes: 3½ inch and 5¼ inch. The standard size used to be the 5¼ inch, but now the 3½ inch is the standard. The 5¼-inch floppy disk, technically known as a minifloppy diskette, is rarely used today. The 3½-inch diskette is a microfloppy diskette, but both are commonly referred to as floppy disks. Like a phonograph record, the 5¼-inch floppy disk has a hole (called a hub) in the center so that it can fit on the disk drive's spindle.

The disk drive spins the disk to find information on it or to write information to it. Once a disk is locked into a disk drive, it spins at about 300 revolutions per minute. The 3½-inch disk, made of a circular piece of plastic, polyurethane, or Mylar covered with magnetic oxide, is enclosed in a rigid plastic shell. The 3½-inch, 144KB diskette has a plastic shutter–covered hole in the upper-right corner. When the plastic shutter covers the opening, the disk can be written to. When it does not cover the opening, the disk is "write protected" and cannot be written or saved to. It has an opening in the upper-left corner, although this opening does not have a plastic shutter. There is a metal shutter over the area of the disk where the computer writes to the disk. The computer's disk drive opens the shutter only when it needs access. When the disk is not in the drive, the metal shutter is closed. Figure B.7 shows a 3½-inch disk.

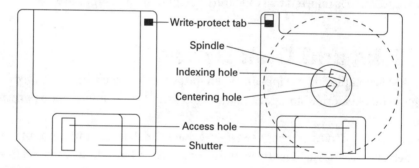

Figure B.7—A Floppy 3½-Inch Disk

B.20 CD-ROM

Today, a common transport device for software is a *compact disc–read-only memory (CD-ROM)*. Borrowed from the music recording business, this disc can hold up to 600 MB of data and retrieves information by laser. Although originally a read-only device, CD-ROM drives are now readily available that both read from and write to a CD (CD-RWs). CD-ROM drives are commonplace, and most software companies are distributing their software via compact disc. The newest technology is *DVD*. It is an enhancement of CD-ROM technology. It provides a new generation of optical-disc storage technology. It encompasses audio, video, and computer data. DVD was designed for multimedia applications with a key goal of being able to store a full-length feature film.

B.21   Removable Disks

Recently, another type of external storage media has been developed—the removable disk. There are now hard disks that you can remove from a computer, making data portable. There are also other types of removable disk media. Two of the most common are Zip drives and Jaz drives. Zip drives come in two forms: permanent drives that are inside the computer, like a floppy drive, and portable drives that attach to the computer via a USB, serial, or SCSI port and can be moved from computer to computer easily. Zip drives use a diskette that is somewhat like a floppy disk in appearance. It can hold 100 MB of information—equivalent to more than 70 3½-inch floppy disks. Jaz drives use a cartridge rather than a disk. Currently, Jaz cartridges hold up to 2 gigabytes of data. The advent of these new disk types makes large amounts of data portable. Zip and Jaz drives read and write data more slowly than a hard disk. Zip drives in particular are becoming the popular alternative to floppy disks for storing and backing up user data.

B.22   Hard Disks

A *hard disk*, also known as a fixed disk or a hard drive, is a non-removable disk that is permanently installed in a system unit (see Figure B.8). A hard disk holds much more information than a removable floppy disk. If a floppy disk can be compared to a file cabinet that holds data and programs, a hard disk can be compared to a room full of file cabinets.

Figure B.8—A Hard Disk

A hard disk is composed of two or more rigid platters, usually made of aluminum and coated with oxide, which allow data to be encoded magnetically. Both the platters and the read/write heads are permanently sealed inside a box; the user cannot touch or see the drive or disks. These platters are affixed to a spindle that rotates at about 3,600 revolutions per minute (rpm), although newer drives rotate at 7200 rpm and even this speed can vary. A hard disk drive is much faster than a standard floppy disk drive. The rapidly spinning disks in the sealed box create air pressure that lifts the recording heads above the surface of the platters. As the platters spin, the read/write heads float on a cushion of air.

Since a hard disk rotates faster than a floppy disk and since the head floats above the surface, the hard disk can store much more data and access it much more quickly than a floppy disk. Today, a common hard disk storage capacity is at least 20 gigabytes.

B.23 Dividing a Disk

A disk's structure is essentially the same whether it is a hard disk or a floppy disk. Data is recorded on the surface of a disk in a series of numbered concentric circles known as *tracks*, similar to the grooves in a phonograph record. Each track on the disk is a separate circle divided into numbered *sectors*. The amount of data that can be stored on a disk depends on the density of the disk—the number of tracks and the size of the sectors. Since a hard disk is comprised of several platters, it has an additional measurement, a *cylinder*. Two or more platters are stacked on top of one another with the tracks aligned. If you connect any one track through all the platters, you have a cylinder (see Figure B.9).

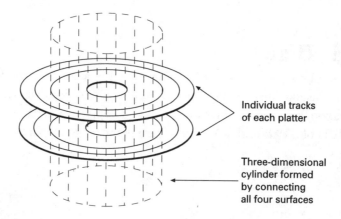

Individual tracks of each platter

Three-dimensional cylinder formed by connecting all four surfaces

Figure B.9—Hard Disk Cylinders

A *cluster* is the basic unit of disk storage. Whenever a computer reads from or writes to a disk, it always reads from and writes to a cluster, regardless of the space the data needs. Clusters are always made from adjacent sectors, from one to eight sectors or more. The location and number of sectors per cluster are determined by the software in a process known as formatting.

A disk is a random access medium, which does not mean that the data and/or programs are randomly arranged on the disk. It means that the head of the disk drive, which reads the disk, does not have to read all the information on the disk to get a specific item. The CPU instructs the head of the disk drive to go directly to the track and sector that holds the specific item of information.

B.24 Disk Drives

A *disk drive* allows information to be written to and read from a disk. All disk drives have read/write heads, which read and write information back and forth between RAM and the disk, much like the ones on tape or video recorders.

A floppy disk drive is the device that holds a floppy disk. The user inserts a floppy disk into a disk drive (see Figure B.10). The hub of the disk fits onto the hub mechanism, which grabs the disk. When the disk drive door is shut, the disk is secured to the hub mechanism. The disk cover remains stationary while the floppy disk rotates. The disk drive head reads and writes information back and forth between RAM and the disk through the exposed head slot. Older disk drives are double-sided and can read from and write to both sides of a disk, but cannot read from or write to a high-density floppy disk. The current generation of high-density disk drives read from and write to both the old style floppy disk and the new style high-density disk.

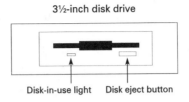

3½-inch disk drive

Disk-in-use light   Disk eject button

Figure B.10—A Floppy Disk Drive

B.25 Device Names

A *device* is a place (a piece of hardware) for a computer to send information (write to) or a place from which to receive information (read from). In order for the system to know which device it is supposed to be communicating with at any given time, each device is given a specific and unique name. Device names, which are also known as reserved names, cannot be used for any other purpose. Disk drives are devices. A disk drive name is a letter followed by a colon.

Drive A: is the first floppy disk drive. Drive C: is the first hard disk drive. All other drives are lettered alphabetically from B: to Z:. You must be able to identify which disk drive you are using. Today, usually users have one floppy disk (Drive A), one hard drive (Drive C), a removable drive (Drive D), and a CD-ROM or a CD-RW drive (Drive E—although often the CD-ROM drive will have an assigned letter near the end of the alphabet such as R: to allow for the addition of more drives, both hard and removable, or for network drives). Today as well it is also common to have a CD-RW drive in addition to the CD-ROM drive. Some common examples are illustrated in Figure B.11.

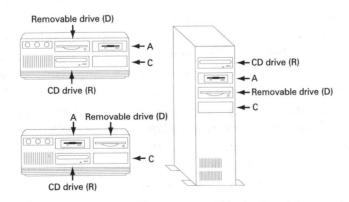

Figure B.11—Disk Drive Configurations

B.26 Software

Up to this point, hardware is what has been discussed. However, software is what makes a computer useful. In fact, without software, hardware has no use. You can think of hardware as a box to run software. Software is the step-by-step instructions that tell the computer what to do. These instructions are called programs. Programs need to be installed or loaded into RAM, so that the CPU can execute them. Programs usually come stored on disks. A program is read into memory from a floppy disk, CD-ROM, or hard disk. Software can also be divided into categories. The most common division is application software and system software.

Application software, as its name suggests, is a set of instructions, a complete program, that directs the computer to solve a particular problem. Application software solves problems and handles information. It is a program designed to assist the user in the performance of a specific task, such as word processing, accounting, money management, or even games. Application software may also be called software packages, off-the-shelf software, canned software, or just software. There are thousands of commercially available application packages. You may have heard of application software by brand names such as WordPerfect (word processing), Excel (spreadsheet), Quicken (money management), or Doom (game). The reason most people purchase a computer is the availability of application software.

System software is also a set of instructions or programs. These programs coordinate the operations of all the various hardware components. System software is usually supplied by the computer manufacturer because it is necessary to run application software. System software is always computer-oriented rather than user-oriented; that is, it takes care of what the computer needs so the computer can run application software.

When you purchase a computer, you usually also purchase the operating system with it, preinstalled on the hard disk. The operating system supervises the processing of application programs and all the input/output of the computer. Running a computer is somewhat analogous to producing a concert. The hardware is the musicians and their instruments. They do not change. The application software is like the score the musicians play, anything from Bach to Ricky Martin. The computer hardware can play any application software from an accounting program to a game. Like the conductor who tells the violins or trumpets when to play and how loudly, the operating system makes the computer work. It is the first and most important program on the computer and *must* be loaded into memory (RAM) before any other program.

Typically, operating systems are comprised of several important programs stored as system files. These include a program that transfers data to and from the disk and into and out of memory and that performs other disk-related tasks. Other important programs handle hardware-specific tasks. These programs check such things as whether a key has been pressed and, if it has, they encode it so that the computer can read it and then decode it so that it may be written to the screen. This program also encodes and decodes bits and bytes into letters and words.

The term *operating system* is generic. Brand names for microcomputer operating systems include System 7, Unix, Linux, MS-DOS, and UCSD-P. The most popular operating system for microcomputers has been Windows 98, which Microsoft Corporation developed and owns. It was the upgrade from Windows 95. Windows 98 is licensed to computer manufacturers, who tailor it to their specific hardware. In addition, users purchased Windows 98 commercially either as an upgrade to Windows 95 or as a complete package (if the user has purchased a computer with no operating system on it).

Microsoft also has a version of Windows called Windows NT Server designed for networked computers, with an iteration called Windows NT Workstation as a desktop interface.

In 2000, Microsoft introduced both Windows 2000 and Windows Millennium Edition (Windows Me). Windows Me was designed for the home computer user and was considered an upgrade to Windows 98. Windows 2000 is a family of operating systems that consists of Windows 2000 Server, Windows 2000 Advanced Server, Windows 2000 Datacenter Server, and Windows 2000 Professional. Windows 2000 Server replaces Windows NT 4.0. Incorporating many new features and functions, Windows 2000 Server is powerful, yet easy to manage, and is designed for the small to medium business organization with many computers that need to share data and resources. Windows 2000 Professional replaces Windows NT 4.0 Workstation, incorporating many new features and functions.

These iterations of Windows have been replaced by Windows XP Home Edition and Windows XP Professional. For the corporate network environment, Microsoft has introduced Windows .NET Server. Windows XP Home edition is typically bundled with computer purchased for home use such as Dell, Compac or Micron PCs. It is intended for the home or a small office where security is not an issue and do not connect to a corporate network. It is compatible with any desktop or notebook computer with a single CPU and a single video display. Windows XP Professional included everything that is in Windows XP Home Edition plus all the networking and security components needed to join a Windows NT/2000/XP domain. Even if you are not a corporate user, you may still prefer to purchase Windows XP Professional for its security and networking capabilities. Also, if you have high-end hardware such as dual processors, you will need Windows XP Professional.

Most people who use a computer are interested in application software. They want programs that are easy to use. If you are going to use a computer and run application packages, you are going to need to know how to use the operating system first. No application program can be used without an operating system.

B.27 Operating System Fundamentals

Windows XP Professional is a program that is always working. No computer hardware can work unless it has an operating system in RAM. When you *boot the system*, you load the operating system software into RAM.

Some of the operating system (OS) software is built into the hardware. When you turn on the computer or "power up," the computer would not know what to do if there were no program directing it. The read-only memory chip called ROM-BIOS (read-only memory–basic input/output system), abbreviated to RIOS, is built into the hardware of the microcomputer system. ROM-BIOS programs provide the interface between the hardware and the operating system.

When you turn on the computer, the power goes first to ROM-BIOS. The first set of instructions is to run a self-test to check the hardware. The program checks RAM and the equipment attached to the computer. Thus, before getting started, the user knows whether or not there is a hardware failure. Once the self-test is completed successfully, the next job or program to execute is loading the operating system.

When the operating system loads, ROM-BIOS checks to see if a disk drive is installed. In today's computers, it is possible to tell the computer where you want it to load the operating system from. It can go first to the A drive to see if there is a disk there. If it finds none, it can then go to the C drive. The OS is looking for a special program called the *boot record*. A computer can also be set up to boot from a CD-ROM or from another peripheral disk drive, such as a Zip or Jaz drive. These drives are attached to the computer by an internal interface card or a parallel port. If ROM-BIOS does not find the boot record in any of the drives it was set to look at or if there is something wrong with the boot record, you will get an error message. If the ROM-BIOS program does find the proper boot record, it reads the record from the disk into RAM and turns control over to this program. The boot record is also a program that executes; its job is to read into RAM the rest of the operating system, in essence, pulling the system up by its bootstraps. Thus, one boots the computer instead of merely turning it on.

The operating system files loaded into RAM manage the resources and primary functions of the computer, freeing application programs from worrying about how the document gets from the keyboard to RAM and from RAM to the screen. This whole process can be considered analogous to driving an automobile. Most of us use our cars to get from point A to point B. We would not like it if every time we wanted to drive we first had to open the hood and attach the proper cables to the battery and to all the other parts that are necessary to start the engine. The operating system is the engine of the computer that lets the user run the application as if driving a car.

B.29 Hardware Requirements for Windows XP Professional Edition

Windows XP Professional is a powerful operating system. Although you can run most of your old programs under Windows XP Professional, you will find yourself buying the new, improved versions of your favorite application programs. These programs will be powerful and large. To run Windows XP Professional, you need at least a Pentium II Processor 233-MHz or faster processor, at least 64 MB of memory, a high-density disk drive, a CD-ROM or DVD drive, and at least a 2-GB hard disk drive with at least 650 MB available. Furthermore, you need a SVGA monitor and SVGA display adapter. You also need a pointing device such as a mouse or trackball. With this hardware, you can run Windows XP Professional and applications written for Windows XP Professional. This configuration is the absolute minimum and is really unrealistic if you want performance from your computer system.

A desirable configuration for Windows XP Professional is listed below:

Processor	Intel Pentium III 600 MHz or better
RAM	256 MB
Hard drive	20 GB with at least 2 GB free
Floppy drive	3½ inch
Removable drive	Zip drive (you may prefer a CD-RW drive instead)

Monitor	SVGA, 19 inch, high resolution, non-interlaced
Graphics	Video card with at least 32 MB of memory
CD	48X CD-ROM or better, DVD if you play many games
CD-RW	24x/10x/40x CD-RW Drive or better
Modem	56K, unless you choose to use a cable or DSL modem
Sound system	Sound card and speakers
Input devices	Keyboard and mouse
Monitor	At least a 15-inch LCD or a 17 Inch CRT

Other features that you might want to use also require other hardware:

- Microphone to record sound files
- TV Tuner card and a TV antenna or cable connection if you want to receive TV stations on your computer
- Digital camera to move graphics to your computer
- Video camera if you want to communicate via conferencing.
- Game controller to play certain video games
- Network Interface Card to set up a home network

In computers, and especially in Windows XP Professional, more is better—a faster processor, more memory, and more disk space. In addition, you must be careful if you are upgrading an existing computer to Windows XP Professional (or Home edition). You must be sure that all of your computer's hardware components are compatible with Windows XP. This is also true with a new computer, although in general, if the new computer comes with Windows XP, its components should be compatible. However, if the hardware is not compatible with Windows XP, your computer (or certain components such as a video card) will simply not work. To find out if your computer and its components are compatible and it can be upgraded, Microsoft maintains a list called the HCL (Hardware Compatibility List). This list will let you know whether Microsoft has tested the hardware (and/or drivers) and stated whether or not the item in question is compatible with Windows XP. You can check **http://www.microsoft.com/hwtest/hcl**, **http://www.microsoft.com/hcl**, or **http://www.microsoft.com/windowsxp** for more information.

B.30 Networks

Today, it is likely that you will be using a network in a work or lab environment. A *network* is two or more connected computers , and it usually has various peripheral devices such as printers. A network allows users to communicate with each other and to share information and devices. Special operating system software and hardware are required for networking. Network software permits information exchange among users; the most common uses are electronic mail (email) and the sharing of files. With email, users can send and receive messages within the network system. Sharing files allows users to share information.

There are two kinds of networks. A *local area network (LAN)* encompasses a small area such as one office. The hardware components such as the server, the terminals, and printers are directly connected by cables. (See Figure B.12.) A *wide area network (WAN)* connects computers over a much larger area such as from building to building, state to state, or even worldwide. Hardware components of the WAN communicate over telephone lines, fiber-optic cables, or satellites. The Internet is an example of a WAN.

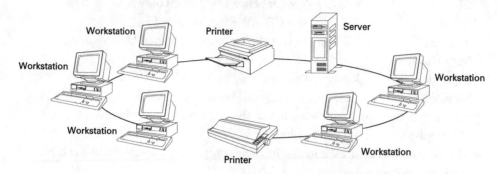

Figure B.12—A Typical Network Configuration

THE RECOVERY
CONSOLE

C.1   The Recovery Console

Windows XP Professional Recovery Console is a command-line repair tool that you can use to start recovery tools, start or stop services, access files on the hard disk, format drives, and repair your system. This tool is not installed by default when you install Windows XP Professional. You may either run it from the Windows XP Professional installation CD or install it as a startup option. To use the Recovery Console you must log in as an Administrator. At one time, you could start the Recovery Console with setup boot floppies. However, now Windows XP Setup boot disks are available only by downloading the appropriate file from the Microsoft web site. You would only need this file to create the setup disks if you have a computer that does not support a bootable CD-ROM or a network-based installation is unavailable. Future Microsoft operating system products will no longer support installation via the setup boot floppy disks.

If you cannot start your computer in Safe Mode or by using Last Known Good Configuration, you can use the Recovery Console by booting from you Windows installation CD. When you boot from the CD, you then choose R for repair. When you do, you will see the following screen. See Figure C.1, Recovery Console.

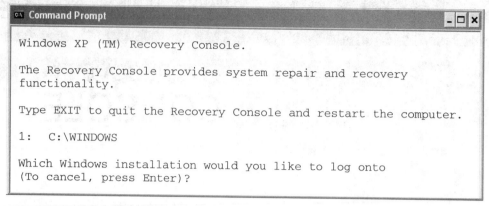

```
Command Prompt                                        _ □ ×

Windows XP (TM) Recovery Console.

The Recovery Console provides system repair and recovery
functionality.

Type EXIT to quit the Recovery Console and restart the computer.

1:   C:\WINDOWS

Which Windows installation would you like to log onto
(To cancel, press Enter)?
```

Figure C.1—Recovery Console

You would then select 1: and press **Enter** to use the Recovery Console. If you had more than one operating system, you would choose the number of operating system you wished to use. Once you start the recovery console, you use a set of commands that are separate from those used in the Command Prompt window. However, you will find that many of the commands are identical in syntax and in usage. When you are Recovery Console mode, you can perform such tasks as starting and stopping services, format drives, read and write data on a local drive which includes drives using the NTFS file system), and perform many other administrative tasks. You should only use Recovery Console if you are an advanced user and you must either be an Administrator or have Administrator privileges.

The other way to start Recovery Console is to install it as a startup option. This is the option that Microsoft recommends which makes it available in case you are unable to restart your system. Once installed, you can then select Recovery Console form the Startup menu.

Once you start the Recovery Console you will have to select which drive you want to log on to if you have a multiple boot system and you will have to log on with the Administrator password. Once you are in the Recover Console, you can get help at the command line by keying in help. Table C.1 Recovery Console commands lists the available commands with a brief description. Remember that the Recovery Console commands are more limited in terms of parameters and options than those in the Command Prompt window. You can get help on individual commands by keying the command name followed by the ? as in DIR /?.

ATTRIB	Changes attributes of a single file or directory. You may not use wildcards.
BATCH	Executes commands placed in a text file.
BOOTCFG	Automatically scans all local disks for Windows installations and configures and repairs entries in the operating system menu (boot.ini).
CD	Changes to a specific directory.
CHDIR	Same as CD.
CHKDSK	Checks a disk and if needed, repairs or recovers it.
CLS	Clears the screen.

COPY	Copies one file at a time. You may not use wildcards.
DEL	Deletes one file at a time. You may not use wildcards.
DELETE	Same as DEL.
DIR	Displays files and directories and includes attributes. You may use wildcards.
DISABLE	Disables a Windows system service or driver.
DISKPART	Manages your hard drives partitions.
ENABLE	Enables a Windows service or driver.
EXIT	Quits Recovery Console and reboots.
EXPAND	Expands compressed files.
FIXBOOT	Rewrites a hard disk boot sector.
FIRXMBR	Repairs the Master Boot Record (MBR) by rewriting it.
FORMAT	Formats a disk.
HELP	Provides help for specific commands. Used alone, lists all commands.
LISTSVC	Lists all available services, drivers, and their start type. Use with Disable and Enable.
LOGON	Restarts Recovery Console.
MAP	Lists all drive letter to the physical device mapping that are currently active.
MD	Creates a directory.
MKDIR	Same as MD.
MORE	Displays the contents of a file. Same as TYPE.
NET	Use NET USE to Map a network share point to a drive letter.
RD	Removes a directory.
REN	Renames a file or directory. You may not use wildcards.
RENAME	Same as REN.
RMDIR	Same as RD.
SET	Displays or modifies Recovery Console environment variables.
SYSTEMROOT	Changes the default directory to the directory that holds the Windows system files. Usually WINNT or WINDOWS.
TYPE	Displays the contents of a file. Same as MORE.

Table 13.4—Recovery Console Commands

C.2 Activity: Installing and Launching the Recovery Console—A Read-Only Activity

Note 1:   It is unlikely in a lab environment that you will be able to do this activity. Remember to install the Recovery Console, you must have the original Windows XP Professional CD as well as have Administrator privileges.

Note 2:   Use the drive letter of your CD-ROM drive. In this example, the CD-ROM drive is Drive D. Your drive letter probably will be different.

Note 3:   If the Windows XP Setup CD window automatically opens, close it.

1   Open a Command Prompt window.

2   Place the Windows XP Professional in the CD-ROM Drive. Open a command prompt window.

3   Key in the following: C:\>**D:** Enter

4   Key in the following: D:>**\i386\winnt32.exe /cmdcons** Enter

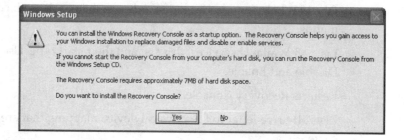

WHAT'S HAPPENING?   You changed drives to your CD-ROM drive. You then keyed in the command name, giving the entire path to the program you wanted to run, / cmdcons, which is Command Console. This program requires about 7 MB of hard disk space. Now you have the opportunity to install the Recovery Console.

5   Click **Yes**.

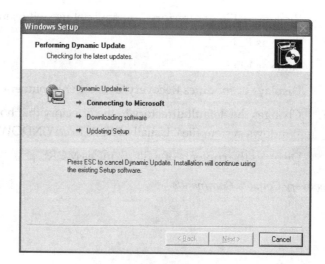

WHAT'S HAPPENING? You see the progress of the program as it is copied to your hard disk. You then see the following message.

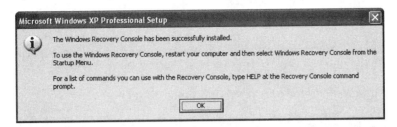

You have now installed the Recovery Console. To use it, you must restart your computer.

6 Click **OK**. Close the Command Prompt window. Remove all disks from all drives. Click **Start**. Click **Turn Off Computer**. Click **Restart**.

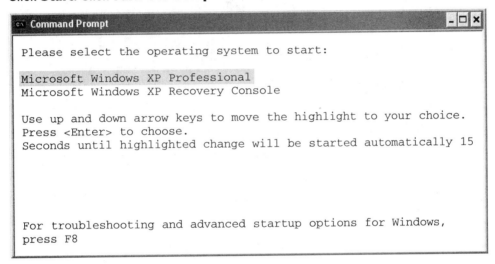

WHAT'S HAPPENING? When you reboot you now have the choices of starting Windows XP Professional normally or choosing the Recovery Console.

7 Select **Microsoft Windows XP Recover Console** and press ⌐Enter¬

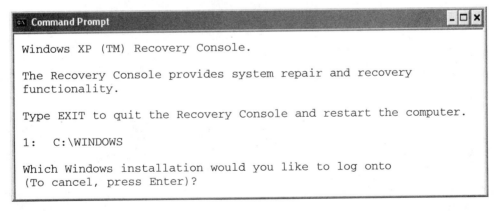

WHAT'S HAPPENING? The Recovery Console wants to know where you want to start it. Normally you select 1.

8 Key in **1** ⌐Enter¬

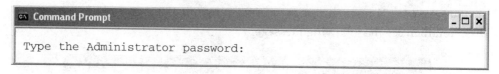

```
Type the Administrator password:
```

WHAT'S HAPPENING?   You must know the administrator password. Here is where you key it in.

9   Key in your administrator password and press **Enter**

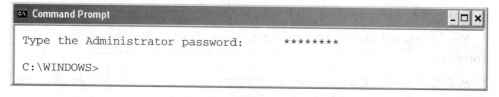

```
Type the Administrator password:      ********

C:\WINDOWS>
```

WHAT'S HAPPENING?   You do not see the password, only the asterisks representing what you keyed in. You are then taken to the Windows system directory. You could have launched the Recovery Console from the boot CD but it is faster to do it the way you just did. In addition, every time you now boot your system, you will always have to choose whether you want to run Windows XP Professional or the Recovery Console. The default choice is Windows XP Professional.

10   Key in the following: C:\WINDOWS>**HELP** **Enter**

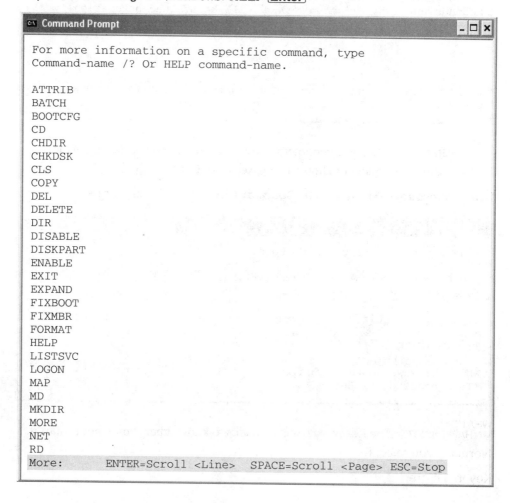

```
For more information on a specific command, type
Command-name /? Or HELP command-name.

ATTRIB
BATCH
BOOTCFG
CD
CHDIR
CHKDSK
CLS
COPY
DEL
DELETE
DIR
DISABLE
DISKPART
ENABLE
EXIT
EXPAND
FIXBOOT
FIXMBR
FORMAT
HELP
LISTSVC
LOGON
MAP
MD
MKDIR
MORE
NET
RD
More:       ENTER=Scroll <Line>   SPACE=Scroll <Page> ESC=Stop
```

WHAT'S HAPPENING?   When you keyed in help, the commands stopped when you filled a screen. To move a line at a time, you press the **Enter** key. To move a page at a time, you press **Space Bar**.

11 Press **Enter**. Press the **Space Bar**.

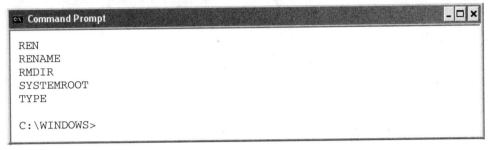

```
REN
RENAME
RMDIR
SYSTEMROOT
TYPE

C:\WINDOWS>
```

WHAT'S HAPPENING?   Although many of the commands look familiar, they are not identical in usage to the commands you have learned.

12 Key in the following: C:\WINNT>**DIR** **/?** **Enter**

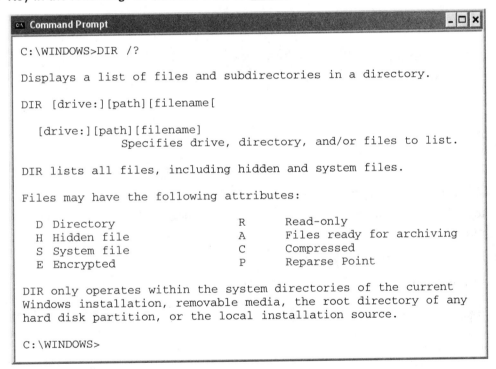

```
C:\WINDOWS>DIR /?

Displays a list of files and subdirectories in a directory.

DIR [drive:][path][filename[

   [drive:][path][filename]
               Specifies drive, directory, and/or files to list.

DIR lists all files, including hidden and system files.

Files may have the following attributes:

   D  Directory              R      Read-only
   H  Hidden file            A      Files ready for archiving
   S  System file            C      Compressed
   E  Encrypted              P      Reparse Point

DIR only operates within the system directories of the current
Windows installation, removable media, the root directory of any
hard disk partition, or the local installation source.

C:\WINDOWS>
```

WHAT'S HAPPENING?   As you can see, you have fewer parameters. You are also restricted to a few directories, most importantly the Windows system directory and any of its subdirectories. Remember, Recovery Console is used primarily for making a failed Window XP Professional installation work again so that is why your access is restricted.

13 Key in the following: C:\WINDOWS>**CD** **\WUGXP** **Enter**

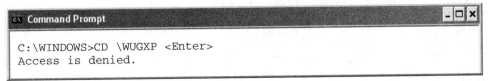

```
C:\WINDOWS>CD \WUGXP <Enter>
Access is denied.
```

WHAT'S
HAPPENING?   This is not a system or Windows directory so you cannot change directories to this location.

14 Key in the following: `C:\WINDOWS>`**DIR SETUPLOG.TXT** `Enter`

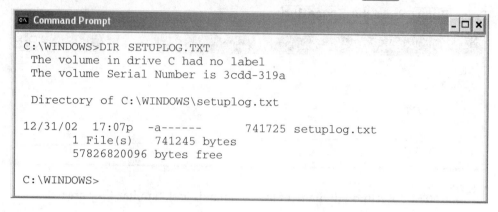

```
C:\WINDOWS>DIR SETUPLOG.TXT
 The volume in drive C had no label
 The volume Serial Number is 3cdd-319a

 Directory of C:\WINDOWS\setuplog.txt

12/31/02  17:07p  -a------          741725 setuplog.txt
        1 File(s)    741245 bytes
        57826820096 bytes free

C:\WINDOWS>
```

WHAT'S
HAPPENING?   The DIR display now displays the file attributes for the selected file.

15 Key in the following: `C:\HELP>`**HELP SYSTEMROOT** `Enter`

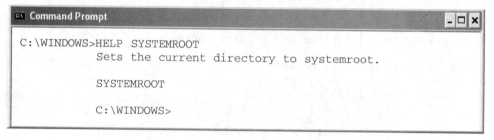

```
C:\WINDOWS>HELP SYSTEMROOT
        Sets the current directory to systemroot.

        SYSTEMROOT

        C:\WINDOWS>
```

WHAT'S
HAPPENING?   The SYSTEMROOT command will change your default directory to wherever the Windows system files are kept. In this case., WINDOWS is the directory where those files are kept.

16 Key in the following: `C:\WINDOWS>`**CD ** `Enter`

17 Key in the following: `C:\>`**SYSTEMROOT** `Enter`

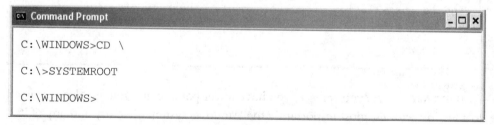

```
C:\WINDOWS>CD \

C:\>SYSTEMROOT

C:\WINDOWS>
```

WHAT'S
HAPPENING?   You first changed the directory to the root of the hard disk. You then keyed in SYSTEMROOT which returned you to the C:\WINDOWS directory where the windows system files are located.

18 Key in the following: `C:\WINDOWS>`**EXIT** `Enter`

WHAT'S ▓▓▓▓▓
▓▓▓**HAPPENING?**   When you keyed in EXIT, your system rebooted. You will have to choose Microsoft Windows XP Professional from the operating system menu to reboot into Windows.

19 Log into Windows XP Professional in the usual way.

C.3   Removing the Recovery Console

If you no longer wish to have the operating system menu appear, you must remove the Recovery Console. The simplest way to do it is to use Help and Support. In Search, key in **Recovery Console**. Choose **Install Recovery Console** as a startup option. Click **Related Topics**. Choose **Delete the Recovery Console**. Then follow the instructions listed.

THE CMOS

A *CMOS (Complementary Metal-Oxide Semiconductor)* is a computer chip built into your computer system. It is specific to your computer system. It is powered by a battery and retains all of your computer settings. The batteries usually last five to seven years.

The CMOS contains the settings that identify the type and specifications of your disk drives—how many and what kind, the assigned drive letters, and any password options. The CMOS also includes the *boot sequence*. The boot sequence is the order in which the BIOS searches drives in order to locate and load the operating system. The normal boot sequence is to search for the operating system on Drive A, then Drive C, and then, on some systems, the CD-ROM. This order can be changed. However, if, for instance, Drive C is set as the only drive to be searched, if your system cannot boot, you cannot use boot floppies to boot the system, as it will never look for Drive A. The CMOS also contains any settings for power management, languages, and so on.

Since the CMOS settings are so critical to the operation of your computer, it is a good idea to know how to access this CMOS as well as how to change the settings. You should also either print the settings, if you can, or write them down. If your battery should ever fail or you have other problems, knowing what the CMOS settings are will allow you to repair your system.

Accessing your CMOS varies from computer to computer, as the CMOS is hardware-dependent, not software-dependent. Usually, when you boot your system, you will see a message displayed telling you what key or combination of keys to press to enter the CMOS utility program, often called Setup. Common keys used are the Delete key, the F2 key or the Esc key. On some computer systems, you see no information displayed on your monitor as you boot (during the POST—Power on Self-Test) until the system says "Starting Windows." Once you see "Starting Windows," you no longer have access to the CMOS utility. If this is the case on your system, and you want to see the POST, often pressing the Esc key when your computer starts to boot will display the POST information and the key or keys necessary to launch the CMOS utility. There are even computer systems that require you to insert a special start-up disk in Drive A to access the CMOS utility. It may be necessary to check the documentation that came with your computer for the key strokes necessary to access the CMOS.

When you launch the CMOS utility, you must be *exceedingly* careful. You do not want to accidently change settings that might stop your computer from working or booting. In most lab environments, the computers will have their CMOS utility programs password-protected so that no one except the network administrator can make changes to the system. Because of this, the next activity is a read-only activity. The activity will describe some functions of two CMOS utilities, but you will not have to do the activity. You are going to look at the opening screen and the screen that allows you to change the boot order. Then you will learn how to exit from the CMOS utility.

Looking at the CMOS (A Read-Only Activity)

1   Turn your computer on.

2   Immediately press the key necessary to access the CMOS.

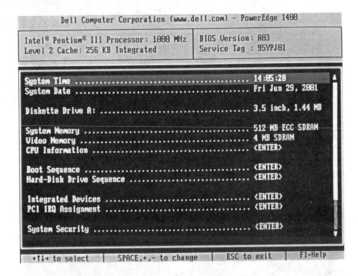

Figure D.1—Pentium BIOS Setup Utility

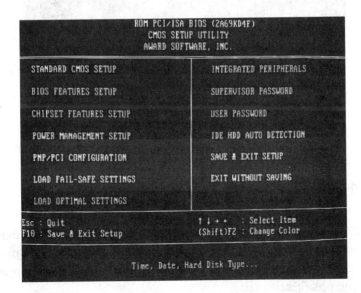

Figure D.2—Award BIOS Setup Utility

WHAT'S
HAPPENING?   Shown above are two common BIOS setup screens. The Pentium
BIOS Setup Utility opening screen display gives you information about the memory,
the language you are using, the system, and other information that is computer-
specific. In the Award BIOS Setup Utility, you must use the up- and down-arrow keys
to select an item. To see memory information and so on, you would select **CHIPSET
FEATURES SETUP**. In both cases, you are interested in the boot order.

3   In a Pentium Processor setup, arrow over to the **Boot** choice on the menu. In an
Award BIOS Setup Utility, down-arrow to **BIOS FEATURE SETUP** and press
Enter

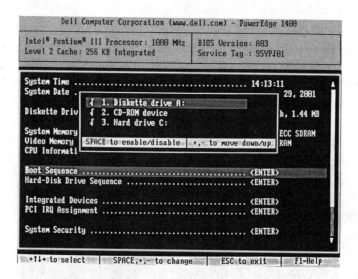

Figure D.3—Pentium BIOS Boot Screen

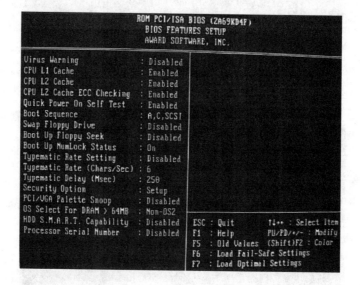

Figure D.4—Award BIOS Boot Screen

WHAT'S
HAPPENING?   The Pentium BIOS screen shows you the boot order on this computer. You use the ↑ and ↓ keys to select an item and then use the PgUp and
PgDn keys to cycle through the available choices. Once you have made your selection, you would press Esc to exit.

In the Award BIOS window, the boot order is listed. In this example, the boot order is first Drive A, then Drive C, then a SCSI drive. In this utility, you would use the down- and up-arrow keys to move to the item of interest, then use the up and down arrow keys within that item to make changes. Once you had selected an item, the arrow keys would cycle through the available choices for that item.

In either example, you could change the boot order so that it might check Drive C first, then Drive A. However, you always want to be able to check Drive A for the operating system so that if you have a problem with Drive C, you can use the different recovery tools available from Drive A.

4   Using either BIOS Setup Utility screen, press [Esc]

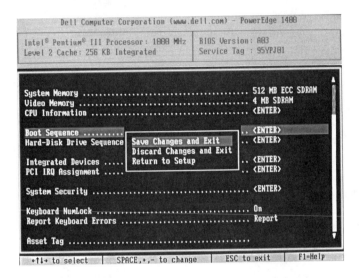

Figure D.5—Pentium BIOS

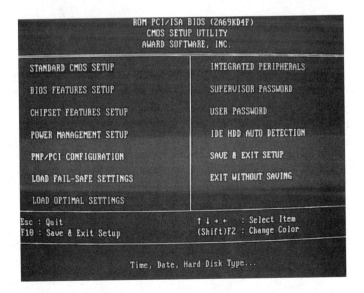

Figure D.6—The Award BIOS Exit Screen

WHAT'S ▓▓▓▓▓▓▓
▓▓▓▓ HAPPENING?   In the Pentium Exit Screen, the default choice is to save the changes. If you want to save the changes, you would press [Enter]. In the Award BIOS, the **Save**

& Exit choice is selected. This will automatically save the changes you made. Note that regardless of the type of BIOS Setup Utility you have, you may restore the default settings. Since you are only looking at the CMOS, you do not want to make any changes.

5   In the Pentium Processor Exit Screen, use the down arrow key to select **Discard Changes and Exit**. Press Enter. In the Award BIOS Exit Screen, down arrow to **Exit without Saving** and press Enter

WHAT'S
HAPPENING?   Your system will reboot.

E.1   An Overview of the Registry

The Registry is the central storage for all configuration data, including the system configuration, the hardware configuration, configuration of most Windows-based applications, and all Windows XP Professional user preferences. Registry information comes from installing Windows XP Professional, booting Windows XP Professional, from applications, system and user interaction such as when you make changes using the Control Panel icons. Every part of Windows XP Professional uses the Registry without exception. Although the Registry is logically one database, it is not one large file. It is, in fact, stored as a number of files. You cannot use or look at these files in their native format but must use the tools that Microsoft supplies.

The Registry files are kept in the directory %SystemRoot%\System32\Config where %systemroot% represents the location of your Windows folder. The registry files that are backed up are kept in %SystemRoot%\Repair\RegBack. The files are:

Autoexec.nt	Used to initialize the MS-DOS environment.
Config.nt	Also used to initialize the MS-DOS environment.
Setup.log	The file that contains a record of all the files that were installed with Windows XP.

The following files are the major registry files and have no file extensions.

Default	The default registry file.
SAM	The Security Accounts Manager registry file.
Security	The security registry file.
Software	The application software registry file.
System	The system registry file.

There are also other files in the %SystemRoot%\System32\Config folder that contain duplicate information or saved files. These will use the .sav file extension. These files contains all the system configuration and settings of data. These are required during system startup to load the device drivers, to determine what hardware you have, and to handle the registration of file types. In addition, user profile information is kept in a file called ntuser.dat which is stored the C:\Documents and Settings folder. There is an ntuser.dat file for each user on your system. In addition, there is a default ntuser.dat, stored in the C:\Documents and Settings\Default User directory.

The simplest, safest, and recommended way to make changes to the Registry is to use Control Panel. When you activate any icon in Control Panel and make changes to an object, you are indeed making changes to the Registry. When you use Add/Remove Hardware or run setup programs for hardware, this information is placed in the Registry. When you use Add/Remove programs or run setup programs for software, again, this information is placed in the Registry. When you use the Open With dialog box, you may change the registered file type. This method is an easy way to update the Registry. You may also open Windows Explorer and use Tools/Folder Options/File Types to alter Registry settings for registered file types.

Most applications programs store their settings in the Registry. You usually can update these settings by changing the options in the application program's property sheet. You may use Device Manager to make changes to system hardware and resource settings. Device Manager displays all the hardware on your computer. It gets this information directly from the Registry. There is also a tool provided by Microsoft called Tweak UI that lets you set some of the most popular entries, such as an entry that controls window animation. You may also go the Microsoft Website to locate and download Tweak UI.

The last choice, and the most dangerous, is to modify the Registry by using the provided tools—RegEdit. Windows 2000 and Windows NT provided two registry editors, RegEdit and RegEdt32. Window XP Professional has combined these two editors and now only provides one Registry editor, RegEdit. When you install Windows, RegEdit is stored in the Windows directory. There is still a RegEdt32, stored in the Windows\System32 directory. However, when you run RegEdt32 at a command prompt, it simply runs a small program whose only function is to execute RegEdit. The Registry can also be modified by a system administrator who can access your computer which makes it possible to diagnose and repair computer problems from a remote site.

There are four primary users and consumers of the data in the Registry. These include the Windows XP Professional operating system itself, the software that is installed on your computer, the hardware that is installed on your computer and you, as the user, can also add or remove data from the Registry. You must be an Administrator or a Power User in order to make changes to the Registry. An ordinary user cannot. In addition, if you are on a network, the system administrator may have made changes that do not allow you to make changes to the Registry. You should also be aware that software applications and hardware that you install are not forced into using the Registry. It is up to the software or hardware developer to decide if and what data will be stored in the Registry. Today, however, most software does use the Registry.

The major uses of the Registry include hardware management, security, software configuration and user preferences. Hardware management includes such information as the device drivers, the I/O ports and the BIOS information used by your computer. The Security area stores information such as the different users, their account information and the groups to which they belong. Examples of what is stored in the software configuration information varies from one application to another. However, typical software configuration information can include the location of the program, the user preferences, what languages are to be used, and licensing information. Windows XP Professional stores user preferences in the Registry, including such information as the printers available, color choices, wallpaper choices, and the mouse double-click speed.

Working with the Registry can be, to say the least, fraught with danger. It is not for the faint of heart. If you in any way damage the Registry files, you will not be able to boot into Windows XP Professional. Your entire computer system will be inoperable. Nonetheless, Windows XP Professional provides tools so that you may change the Registry files. This feature seems to be a contradictory position on the part of Microsoft. What Microsoft knows is what all computer users know. At one point or another, something will happen to your computer, and it will not work. Your only alternative would be to take it to a repair facility (at $100 or more an hour) and hope for the best.

However, there is much you can do yourself to solve your computer problems. You will also find that, as you use your computer, there will be things that you will want to fix. For instance, if you want to delete a program, you will find that it is not as simple as deleting the directory that holds the files. Windows XP Professional application programs leave footprints all over the Registry. To remove a program completely from your disk, you will need to delete the files and may need to modify the Registry to remove all references to the program. There will also be certain types of customizations you will like to do that can only be done by modifying the Registry. For instance, you may wish to add or remove an item from a context or shortcut menu. In order to do so, you will need to modify the Registry.

This appendix differs from most of the other materials in the textbook as it in general, simply an overview. It will provide one activity, with step-by-step instructions, to demonstrate how you could make changes to the Registry. However, if you are in a lab environment or on a network, you will not be able to, nor should you, the activity. No system administrator would ever let changes be made to the system, since one change could bring down the entire lab or the entire network in a company. This section is intended only to be read, as most likely in a lab environment, you probably will not be able to access the Registry. If you are using your own computer, you can do the activity. However, remember, until you know what you are doing, you run a great risk of destroying your computer system and making it totally inoperable. So if you choose to do the activity, proceed at your own risk!

E.2   Backing Up the Registry

Given that the Registry is so critical to the operation of Windows XP Professional, it is imperative that it be backed up. Although most of the time the Registry and, hence, Windows XP Professional, works successfully, the Registry can become corrupted in many ways. How does the Registry become corrupted or "go bad"? The three most common ways the Registry becomes corrupted are as follows:

1. You add new application programs or new drivers to your system.
2. You (or the hardware installation software) make hardware changes from new settings, or your hardware fails.
3. You make changes to the Registry.

Your best protection is to back up the Registry and to take other preventative measures. There are seven major techniques to protecting your system. These include:

1. Use Backup and choose backing up the System State. This is a collection of computer-specific data that can be backed up and restored. System State data includes the Registry, the COM Class registration database and the system boot files.
2. Create System Restore points regularly using the System Restore tool. Be sure to create a system restore point prior to adding new software, new drivers or hardware.
3. Create an Automated System Recovery (ASR) disk.
4. The regedit program provides a tool that allows you to export the Registry (or a part of the Registry.)
5. Use Microsoft Backup or any commercial backup program to perform a full backup of your entire computer system. However, you could have a problem in restoring your system since you might not be able to start Backup to use Restore since you must be able to boot to the desktop to do so.
6. You may use the Recovery Console. Again, remember you want a current version of your ASR disk.
7. You can boot to Safe Mode and choose Last Known Good Configuration. If your problem is a misinstalled application or driver, then this could solve your problem. But if you have a corrupt or missing file, this will not solve the problem. However, you could also use the Roll back Driver or Uninstall Driver if your problem is hardware related.

E.3   Structure of the Registry

The Registry is designed as a hierarchical structure, not unlike Windows Explorer. Keys and subkeys are similar in concept to folders and subfolders in Windows Explorer. The Registry contains three types of objects: *keys*, *values*, and *data*. Each key defines a setting or behavior for Windows or an installed application. Each key can have one or more values. Each value will have a name, a data type and some sort of data.

At the top of the hierarchy are the Registry keys. Registry keys can also have several keys or *subkeys*. The top level keys are also known as *hives* and as a *predefined key*. Keys can contain one or more other keys and values. When this occurs, it is known as nesting. Each key and value must have a unique name within a key or subkey. Keys are case aware but not case sensitive. A key name cannot use backslashes. Backslashes are used as delimiters.

Keys and subkeys contain at least one value with a special name (Default). If the default value has no data, it is read as "value not set." Values have three parts: the data name, the data type, and the data value itself. A value has data like a file has data. There are five major data types as listed in Table E.1, Registry Data Types.

Data Type	Description
REG_BINARY	Binary data. In some cases, you will be able to edit this type of data, such as a value that indicates a true or false condition (0 or False or 1 for True).
REG_DWORD	A 32-bit binary value displayed as an 8-digit hexadecimal value.
REG_SZ	This data type is used to store string information. A string of data is a variable-length set of characters. String data is often enclosed in quotation marks.
REG_EXPAND_SZ	This data type is the same as REG_SZ except that it can contain expressions, macros or environmental variables that would "expand" beyond what is shown if the entry. Thus an entry of %systemroot%\system32 would be interpreted as C:\winnt\system32.
REG_MULTI_SZ	This data type is used to store multiple string values (REG_SZ) for a single entry. Each string value is separated by the Null character. It is usually text but the text has multiple text values.

Table E.1—Registry Data Types

There are also many other data types that can be used such as REG_DWORD_LITTLE_ENDIAN which is the same as REG_DWORD except that the least significant byte of a value is stored first. Unless you are programming Windows, you probably will never make changes to any of these data types.

When you open Registry Editor, you can see the structure of the Registry. My Computer is at the top. Then, in the left pane, you see displayed the hierarchy of the structure with the keys and subkeys. The plus or minus in front of each entry indicates, as in Windows Explorer, whether an item is expanded or collapsed. The right pane shows the current setting of the selected entry or the value. See Figure E.1, Registry Organization.

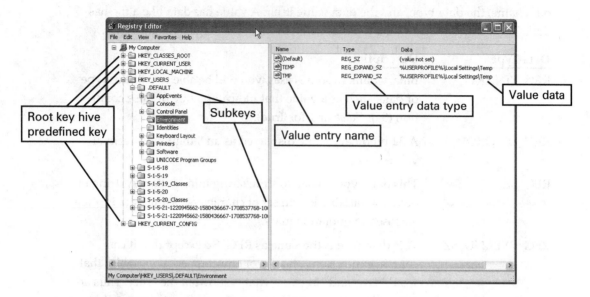

Figure E.1—Registry Organization

There are five root keys. Each root key begins with HKEY. HKEY is an abbreviation for Handle or Hive to a KEY. Although there are five HKEYs that appear, in reality, there are only two keys: HKEY_Local_Machine and HKEY_Users. The other HKEYs are aliases for those two keys. Any change that is made in the aliases is changed in either HKEY_Local_Machine or HKEY_Current_User. Table E.2, Root Keys, lists the pre-determined keys.

Pre-Determined (Root)	Description
HKEY_CLASSES_ROOT	This is an alias for HKEY_Local_Machine. It contains settings for shortcuts, dragging and dropping, and file associations. It is a combined view of HKEY_LOCAL_MACHINE\Software\Classes, which holds settings for all users and HKEY_CURRENT_USER\Software\Classes which holds any settings stored for the current user.
HKEY_CURRENT_USER	This stores user preferences and desktop configuration details for the currently logged on user. The information stored here is reflected in a user's profile. It includes such items as the shortcuts on the user's desktop, contents of the Start menu and the contents of the Favorites menu. It is an alias to either the .DEFAULT user or current user in HKEY_USERS
HKEY_LOCAL_MACHINE	This is a major key that contains configuration data that is specific to your computer, such as what hardware you have installed and what your program settings are. The information in this key applies to every user who uses this computer.

| HKEY_USERS | This is the other major key that contains the configuration information for any user who logs onto the computer. In addition to maintaining information that applies to all users on the machine, it also contains information that is specific to each user. There will be a subkey for each user who has a profile. If a user does not have a profile, .DEFAULT key will be used. The .DEFAULT is the minimum information Windows XP needs to define the workspace when it boots. It is used as a template when a user logs on for the first time. |
| HKEY_CURRENT_CONFIG | This is also an alias for HKEY_Local_Machine, which contains the current configuration for your computer. |

Table E.2—Root Keys

HKEY_CLASSES_ROOT is an alias for HKEY_LOCAL_MACHINE. In this hive, you will see the file associations that associate specific classes with different file extensions. In Figure E.2, shown below, the program WinZip is associated with the ZIP file extension. You can tell your location in the Registry by looking at the status bar.

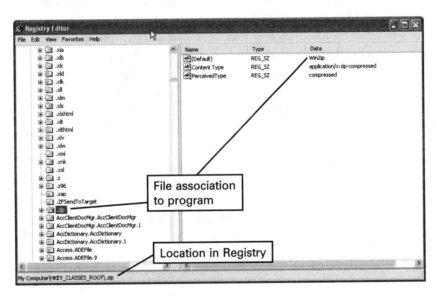

Figure E.2—File Association

This key also includes class definitions that describe all the actions associated with a file's class, such as open or print. In addition, you will find information about the icon that is used, any shell extensions installed, and that class's OLE information. See Figure E.3.

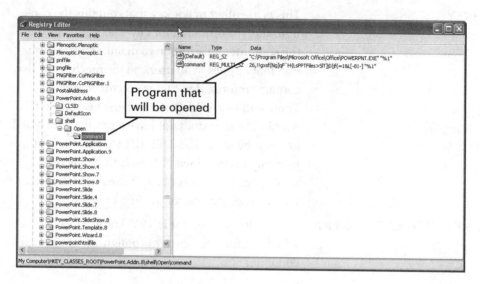

Figure E.3—Shell Extensions and Commands

HKEY_CURRENT_USER is an alias for the current user in HKEY_USERS. If there is only one user on a computer, this will point to the Default subkey. If there is more than one user who maintains a configuration, this key will indicate who is currently logged on.

HKEY_LOCAL_MACHINE relates to the configuration data for this specific machine. This root key information applies to the computer itself, not to each user. This relationship is the reason you would never want to copy the Registry files from one computer to another. In this key you will find individual program settings, such as the path to a program, that would apply to any user who logs on. You would find information about the drive letter assignments for your CD-ROM and removable drives. You would also find information about all the hardware on the computer. Furthermore, you would find data indicating where a program was installed from—the installation path. There are many subkeys which are also aliased by other root keys. Figure E.4 shows system information such as the BIOS date for this computer system.

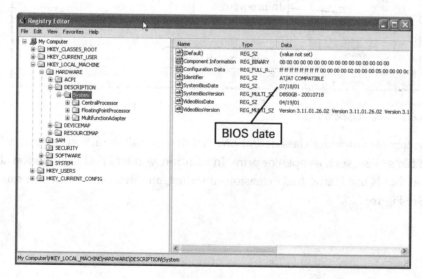

Figure E.4—Local Machine

Some of the major subkeys include the System which stores the data that Windows needs to boot your computer, the Security stores all security specific data for this local machine such as users, groups and so on, and the Software subkey contains all the information about the software installed on the computer, including file associations and program settings. This data is per-computer as opposed to per-user which means you can see all the software installed on this specific machine no matter what user has access to the software.

HKEY_USERS contains the Default subkey which is the minimum amount of information Windows XP Professional needs. It also contains some very long numbers. The first is the Current User SID (Security Identification) for the user who is currently logged on. The last key contains any file extensions association or component embedding that overrides the default settings. See Figure E.5.

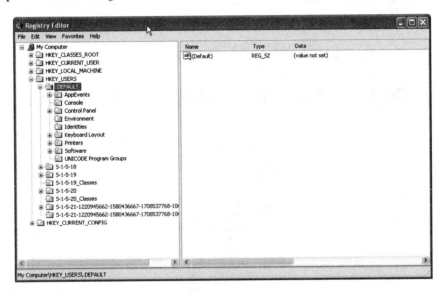

Figure E.5—Default User

Each of the subkeys contains preferences that are specific to that user. Information is written here when you use Control Panel to make changes or when you create settings for specific programs. HKEY_CURRENT_CONFIG is an alias for the currently used hardware configuration found in HKEY_LOCAL_MACHINE.

E.4   REGEDIT

Although Microsoft feels that changes should not be made directly to the Registry, there is a tool to make changes. The tool is REGEDIT.EXE. REGEDIT offers a particular view of the Registry. It is the best general-purpose tool for browsing and modifying the Registry. You may also backup the Registry from here. However, it is a very large file so you need to back it up to either a hard disk, a CD-RW or a Zip disk. When you open the Registry, it shows the primary hives. See Figure E.6.

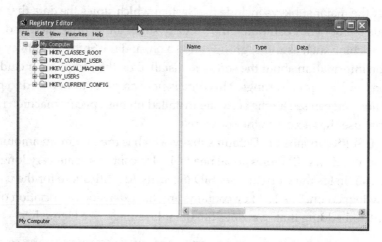

Figure E.6—Primary Keys/Hives

If you have used the Registry, it remembers your last location. See Figure E.7.

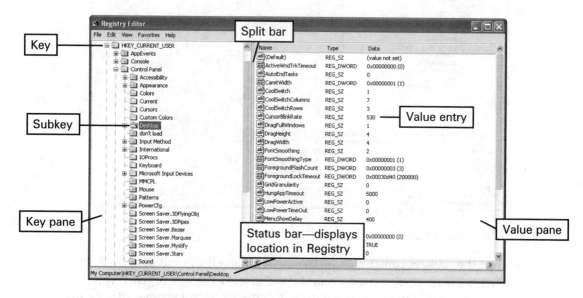

Figure E.7—Registry Location that Remembers Where You Last Were

As you can see, the left pane displays the keys, and the right pane displays the values for a key. The status line shows where you are in the Registry. The split bar allows you to alter the size of the left and right panes. In the value pane one of two icons is displayed. The [ab] icon indicates the text data type, whereas the [binary] icon indicates the binary data type. The display of data in REGEDIT is static rather than dynamic. In other words, the display is showing you the Registry at the specific moment in time that REGEDIT was opened. Any changes made to the Registry after you have opened REGEDIT will not be reflected in the display.

There are only five menu choices—Registry, Edit, View, Favorites and Help.

E.4.1   Registry Menu

You can import and export the entire Registry or a branch of the Registry to a text file by using the Import and Export commands. To export the entire Registry, you would highlight My Computer at the top of the tree, then choose Export Registry File and then in Export Range, choose All. If you wanted to Export a branch, you would select the branch, choose Export and in the Export Range, choose Selected Branch. To import a branch, or the entire Registry, you would choose Import and then select your file.

There are reasons for exporting the Registry. One of these is that, if you export the Registry to a text file, you can safely edit it. However, there is one warning. Windows XP Professional will write the Registry file as a Unicode format (each character is two bytes long). Some text editors do not understand Unicode. To convert the Unicode file to a regular text file, you would key in TYPE regfile.reg > regfile.txt. That way any editor can read it. You can then import the altered file back into the Registry. These files have the .REG extension. This process can be *very* dangerous. If you double-click any file with a .REG extension, the file will *automatically* update the Registry whether you want it to or not. You can also export the Registry before you install a program or make changes, and then export it again after you have made these changes to see the differences. Exporting the Registry is another way to back up the Registry.

You may also Load or Unload Hive. These commands affect only the HKEY_USERS and HKEY_LOCAL MACHINE keys. They are active only when these predefined keys are selected. When you load a hive into the registry, the hive becomes a subset of one of these keys.

If you were on a network, you could connect or disconnect to the network registry. You may also print the Registry.

E.4.2   Edit Menu

This menu allows you create a new key, change, add or delete permission, delete or rename a key as well as coy a key name. In addition, it has the capability to Find entries in the Registry.

E.4.2.1   The Edit/New Submenu

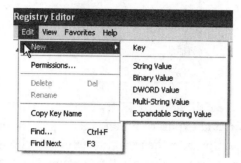

Here you can create a key and determine the data type.

E.4.2.2   The Edit/Permission Dialog Box

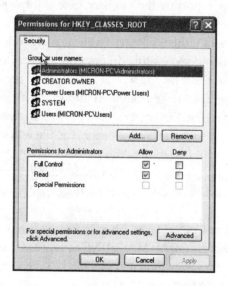

Here you can set up security.

E.4.2.3   The Edit/Find Dialog Box

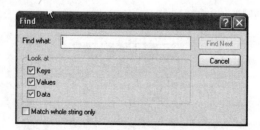

The Find and Find Next option are useful for searching the Registry. You may search for Keys, Values or Data and choose to match the entire string. If you press the **F3**

key, Find will continue searching. If you choose Find Next from the menu, it will also continue searching for what you requested.

E.4.3   View Menu

The View menu allows you to turn the status bar on or off, to adjust the size of the panes with the mouse. If you choose a binary number, you can ask to display that data with Display Binary Data. In addition, you can force a rereading of the Registry (Refresh).

E.4.4   Favorites Menu

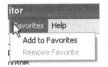

The Favorites menu allows you to quickly return to an item that you often use in the Registry. In this example, there is a favorite—Desktop. You add or remove favorites with the items on the menu.

E.5   Changing the Name and Organization in Windows

An example of how you might use the Registry to make a change that is unavailable in Control Panel or other GUI methods, is a mistake users sometimes make. For instance, if, when you installed Windows XP Professional, you misspelled your name or your company. This means that every time you display the General tab of the System Properties sheet, you see your misspelling. This can be truly annoying. There is no way to make this change through the Windows GUI interface. However, you can make the change in the Registry. In the next activity, you will open the Registry and see where you would make the changes. You will not make the changes. Remember, however, that working with the Registry can be VERY dangerous. If you press a key inadvertently, and save the Registry, you could damage it so severely that you could not even boot your system.

E.6   Activity: Changing the Name and Organization in Windows

1   Click **Start**. Click **Run**. In the run dialog box, key in the following: **REGEDIT**

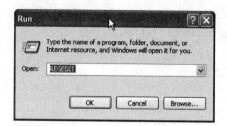

WHAT'S ▓▓▓▓▓
▓▓▓▓HAPPENING?   You can now proceed as you have keyed in the command name.

2   Click **OK**.

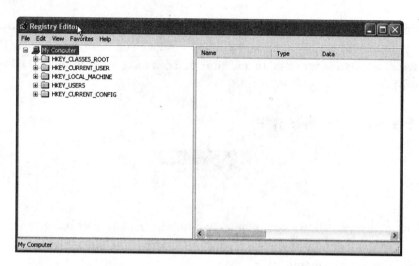

WHAT'S ▓▓▓▓▓
▓▓▓▓HAPPENING?   If your Registry Editor window is not collapsed to its highest level, collapse each branch now.

3   Click the plus sign in front of HKEY_LOCAL_MACHINE to expand it. Then click **HKEY_LOCAL_MACHINE** to select it.

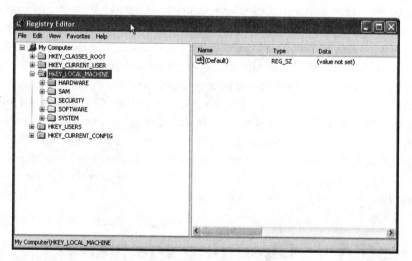

WHAT'S ▓▓▓▓▓
▓▓▓▓HAPPENING?   You need to expand the software key.

4   Click the plus sign in front of Software to expand it.

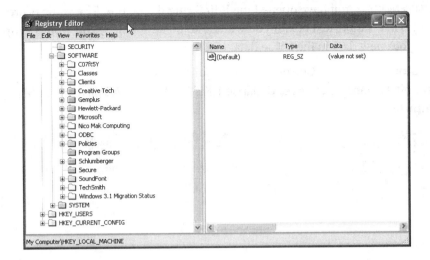

WHAT'S
HAPPENING?   You next need to expand Microsoft and then Windows.

5   Click the plus sign in front of Microsoft to expand it. Scroll until you locate WindowsNT. Click the plus sign in front of WindowsNT to expand it. Click **CurrentVersion** to select it.

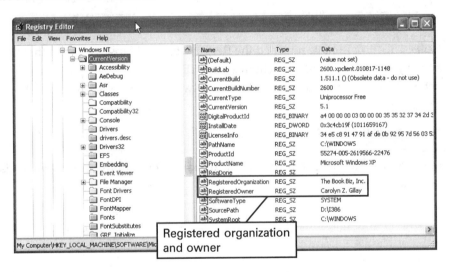

Registered organization and owner

WHAT'S
HAPPENING?   You have found your location in the Registry. The right pane holds the name, the data type and the value. In this example, for organization, the name is RegisteredOrganization, the data type is REG_SZ and the value is The Book Biz, Inc and for owner, the name is RegisteredOwner, the data type is REG_SZ and the value is Carolyn Z. Gillay. Note that the name has no spaces. To make changes, you must change the value.

6   Double-click **RegisteredOwner**.

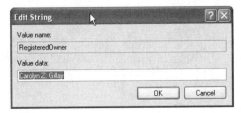

WHAT'S
HAPPENING?   You have opened the Edit String dialog box. The value (Carolyn Z. Gillay) is in a simple text box. If you wanted to make changes, you would simply key in your new data in the Value data: text box.

7   Click **Cancel**. Collapse Current Version. Collapse WindowsNT. Collapse Microsoft. Collapse Software. Collapse HKEY_LOCAL_MACHINE. Click **My Computer**.

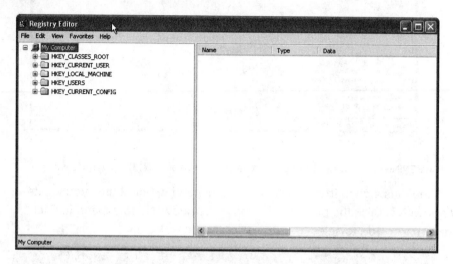

WHAT'S
HAPPENING?   You have returned the Registry to its collapsed form so that the next time you open it, it will open in this view. IF you did not collapse all the branches, the next time you opened RegEdit, it would return you to your last location.

8   Close the Registry Editor.

WHAT'S
HAPPENING?   You have returned to the desktop. You introduction to the Registry is complete.

USING FDISK TO PARTITION THE HARD DISK

Note: Disk partitioning in Windows XP Professional is a part of the Disk Management tool. To partition a new hard drive without using Windows XP Professional Disk Management requires the FDISK program from a previous version of Windows; you should use either Windows 98 or Windows Millennium Edition so that you may have the option of using FAT32.

F.1 Partitioning the Hard Disk

A hard disk is comprised of multiple physical disks called "drive platters." Each platter is divided into concentric rings (tracks), and each track is divided into sectors. On a hard disk, a three-dimensional cylinder is formed by connecting the track-sector "pie wedges" from all the platters.

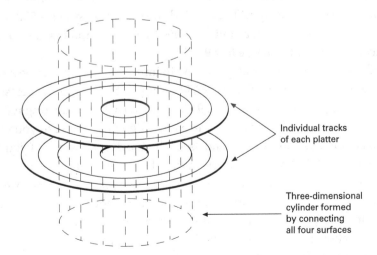

Individual tracks of each platter

Three-dimensional cylinder formed by connecting all four surfaces

Low-level formatting tells the computer where the cylinders and sectors lie on the disk. This process creates the sectors and cylinders by writing the ID numbers of the sectors to the disk surface so that each sector is located and numbered. This identification, or "address," tells the hard-disk controller where the requested information is on the disk.

The numbering of each sector provides two primary benefits (besides the obvious one of giving the controller a place to find the information on the disk). These include the sector *interleave* and the identification of bad sectors on a disk. The sector interleave matches the rotation of the disk to the rate at which the disk controller can physically process data passing underneath the drive head. Thus, sectors will not be consecutively numbered on the disk. This occurs because computers cannot read a sector, write the data to RAM, and get ready to read the next sector by the time the next consecutively numbered sector arrives at the drive head. Rather than waiting for another entire revolution, the sectors are spaced so that when the head is ready to read the next sector, the next consecutively numbered sector is under the drive head. In this way, when the controller is ready to read, it is in the proper place.

Low-level formatting also marks any bad sectors on the disk so that they will not be used to store information. Usually, a disk is low-level formatted only once, at the factory. Rarely, if ever, will an end-user have to deal with low-level formatting.

After low-level formatting, and before the formatting and installation of the operating system, the hard disk must be partitioned. A partition defines what part of the hard disk belongs to which operating system. With some operating systems, you may choose to have more than one operating system on a hard disk. For instance, you could have both DOS and Windows 95 on the same disk in different partitions. They "get along" very well. However, note that only one operating system can be used at one time.

There are three types of partitions: the primary DOS partition, the extended DOS partition, and the non-DOS partition. If you wish to use the Windows operating system on a hard disk, at least one partition is required; this is called the primary DOS partition. The primary DOS partition *must* exist in order to boot from the hard disk. It is the first partition on the disk. Using FAT (FAT16), the primary partition is limited in size to 2 GB. Using FAT32 in Windows operating systems 95B or newer, the primary partition no longer limited. (*Note:* In older computers, the hardware itself may limit the partition size to 7.9 GB.)

With the size of programs today, the FAT16 limitation of 2 GB can be a problem. The only time you would need to use FAT16 is if you have a need to access the drive with an operating system of Windows 95A or older. DOS, and the original Windows 95 can not recognize a disk that is partitioned to FAT32 so you would be unable to boot to DOS on a floppy and "see" the C drive. However, if you use a boot disk created with Windows 95B or newer, this should not be a problem.

After hard disk is partitioned, you can either format it or allow the Windows installation Setup program to format for it you. Please note, however, that formatting the partitions prior to the installation of the Windows operating system speeds up the installation process considerably.

To prepare a disk for Windows XP installation, it is recommended you have a Utility disk that you create with a version of windows from Windows 95B to Windows Millennium. A disk can be created on a computer that is running one of those operating systems by formatting a floppy *with the system on it*, and then copying utility files to the floppy disk. Following is a list of recommended utility programs to include on your Utility disk:

FORMAT.COM
EDIT.COM
DOSKEY.COM
FDISK.EXE
LABEL.EXE
MOVE.EXE
CHKDSK.EXE
XCOPY.EXE
DELTREE.EXE
ATTRIB.EXE

Label the disk with the operating system used and UTILITY DISK and keep it in a safe place. This disk will make it easy to add or replace a hard drive. It will also enable you to boot your system and access your files from FAT16 or FAT32 drives if you are having difficulty and your system won't "boot" from the hard drive.

F.2   How to Use FDISK

Note 1:   These steps are an example *only*. The specifics will vary, depending on the exact version of the OS you are using and the size of your hard drive.

Note 2:   This example assumes that you have a brand new hard disk drive in a computer that contains no other hard drives. You will need to have a boot disk that contains the FDISK.COM file and the FORMAT.EXE file. A utility boot disk created with Windows Millennium is used in this example.

1   Boot with your booting disk. Run FDISK. You will see the following screen:

```
Your computer has a disk larger than 512 MB.
This version of Windows includes improved support for large
disks, resulting in more efficient use of disk space on large
drives, and allowing disks over 2 GB to be formatted as a
single drive.

IMPORTANT: If you enable large disk support and create any new
drives on this disk, you will not be able to access the new
drive(s) using other operating systems, including some versions
of Windows 95 and Windows NT, as well as earlier versions of
Windows and MS-DOS. In addition, disk utilities that were not
designed explicitly for the FAT32 file system will not be able
to work with this disk. If you need to access this disk with
other operating systems or older disk utilities, do not enable
large drive support.

Do you wish to enable large disk support (Y/N)...........? [Y]
```

WHAT'S HAPPENING?   Here you need to decide if you wish to use FAT32. In this example, the answer is **Yes**. After answering **Y** or **N**, you will see the following screen:

```
                    Microsoft Windows Millennium
                     Fixed Disk Setup Program
             (C)Copyright Microsoft Corp. 1983 - 2000

                          FDISK Options

        Current fixed disk drive: 1

        Choose one of the following:

        1. Create DOS partition or Logical DOS Drive
        2. Set active partition
        3. Delete partition or Logical DOS Drive
        4. Display partition information

        Enter choice: [1]
        Press Esc to exit FDISK
```

If you had more than one hard drive in your computer, there would be a fifth option.

```
        5. Change current fixed disk drive
```

2   Select **4** to display the partition information.

WHAT'S
HAPPENING?   You should get a message telling you no partitions are defined.

3   Press **Esc** to return to the main menu.

4   Choose **1** to create a primary partition.

WHAT'S
HAPPENING?   You will be asked if you wish to use the maximum size for a DOS partition and to make the partition active.

5   Press **N** for No.

WHAT'S
HAPPENING?   You will be told the size of the drive, and you can key in what size (either in bytes or by percentage of total drive space) you wish to use for the primary partition.

At this point, you will decide how much space you wish to allocate to each partition. This example will partition the hard drive into two equal halves, and then split the second partition into two equal logical drives.

6   Key in **50%** and press **Enter**

WHAT'S
HAPPENING?   There will now be a choice on the menu to set the active partition.

7   Choose **Set the active partition** and set the number **1** partition as the active (booting) partition.

8   Select **Create DOS partition or Logical DOS Drive** once again.

9   Select **Create Extended DOS partition**.

10   Choose **all the available space**.

WHAT'S
HAPPENING?   Once the partition is created, you will get a message saying "No logical drives defined."

You will now divide the space that you have created as an extended DOS partition into more than one logical (as opposed to physical) drive. You will split this partition into the logical drives D and E, using 50 percent of the available space for each logical drive.

11 Press **Esc** to exit from FDISK and reboot the system. (*Note:* Your booting disk is still in the A drive.)

12 Format the C drive. (To install Windows XP, you do not want to format with the operating system. To make the C drive "bootable" without installing Windows, you would format the drive with the system on it.)

WHAT'S ▒▒▒▒
▒▒HAPPENING?   You *would not* need to place the system on the disk if you were actually preparing the disk for the installation of the OS. The installation process would do this.

13 Format the D drive.

WHAT'S ▒▒▒▒
▒▒HAPPENING?   At this point, if you formatted the disk with the system, you would be able to boot the computer from the Primary DOS partition (Drive C) of the new drive.

ANSI.SYS KEYBOARD
SCANCODE VALUES

Key	Standard	With Shift	With Ctrl	With Alt
A	97	65	1	0;30
B	98	66	2	0;48
C	99	67	3	0;46
D	100	68	4	0;32
E	101	69	5	0:18
F	102	70	6	0;33
G	103	71	7	0;34
H	104	72	8	0;35
I	105	73	9	0;23
J	106	74	10	0;36
K	107	75	11	0;37
L	108	76	12	0;38
M	109	77	13	0;50
N	110	78	14	0;49
O	111	79	15	0;24
P	112	80	16	0;25
Q	113	81	17	0;16
R	114	82	18	0;19
S	115	83	19	0;31
T	116	84	20	0;20
U	117	85	21	0;22

Key	Standard	With Shift	With Ctrl	With Alt
V	118	86	22	0;47
W	119	87	23	0;17
X	120	88	24	0;45
Y	121	89	25	0;21
Z	122	90	26	0;44
1	49	33	N/A	0;120
2	50	64	0	0;121
3	51	35	N/A	0;122
4	52	36	N/A	0;123
5	53	37	N/A	0;124
6	54	94	30	0;125
7	55	38	N/A	0;126
8	56	42	N/A	0;126
9	57	40	N/A	0;127
0	48	41	N/A	0;129
–	45	95	31	0;130
=	61	43	N/A	0;131
[	91	123	27	0;26
]	93	125	29	0;27
Space Bar	92	124	28	0;43
;	59	58	N/A	0;39
'	39	34	N/A	0;40
,	44	60	N/A	0;51
.	46	62	N/A	0;52
/	47	63	N/A	0;53
'	96	126	N/A	0;41
Enter (keypad)	13	N/A	10	0;166
/ (keypad)	47	47	0;142	0;74
* (keypad)	42	0;144	0;78	N/A
- (keypad)	45	45	0;149	0;164
+ (keypad)	43	43	0;150	0;55
5 (keypad)	0;76	53	0;143	N/A
F1	0;59	0;84	0;94	0;104
F2	0;60	0;85	0;95	0;105
F3	0;61	0;86	0;96	0;106
F4	0;62	0;87	0;97	0;107

Key	Standard	With Shift	With Ctrl	With Alt
F5	0;63	0;88	0;98	0;108
F6	0;64	0;89	0;99	0;109
F7	0;65	0;90	0;100	0;110
F8	0;66	0;91	0;101	0;111
F9	0;67	0;92	0;102	0;112
F10	0;68	0;93	0;103	0;113
F11	0;133	0;135	0;137	0;139
F12	0;134	0;136	0;138	0;140
Home	0;71	55	0;119	N/A
↑	0;72	56	0;141	N/A
PgUp	0;73	57	0;132	N/A
←	0;75	52	0;115	N/A
→	0;77	54	0;116	N/A
End	0;79	49	0;117	N/A
↓	0;80	50	0;145	N/A
PgDn	0;81	51	0;118	N/A
Insert	0;82	48	0;146	N/A
Delete	0;83	46	0;147	N/A
Print Screen	N/A	N/A	0;114	N/A
Pause	N/A	N/A	0;0	N/A
Backspace	8	8	127	0
Enter	13	N/A	10	0
Tab	9	0;5	0;148	0;165
Home (directional keypad)	224;71	224;71	224;119	224;151
↑ (directional keypad)	224;72	224;72	224;141	224;152
PgUp (directional keypad)	224;73	224;73	224;132	224;153
← (directional keypad)	224;75	224;75	224;115	224;155
→ (directional keypad)	224;77	224;77	224;116	224;157
End (directional keypad)	224;79	224;79	224;117	224;159
↓ (directional keypad)	224;80	224;80	224;145	224;154
PgDn (directional keypad)	224;81	224;81	224;118	224;161
Insert (directional keypad)	224;82	224;82	224;146	224;162
Delete (directional keypad)	224;83	224;83	224;147	224;163

Following is first a list of command line commands with a brief explanation of their usage, and second a comprehensive listing of commands with syntax.

ASSOC	Displays or modifies file extension associations.
AT	Schedules commands and programs to run on a computer.
ATTRIB	Displays or changes file attributes.
CACLS	Displays or modifies access control lists (ACLs) of files.
CALL	Calls one batch program from another.
CD/CHDIR	Displays the name of or changes the current directory.
CHCP	Displays or sets the active code page number.
CHKDSK	Checks a disk and displays a status report.
CHKNTFS	Displays or modifies the checking of disk at boot time.
CLS	Clears the screen.
CMD	Starts a new instance of the Windows command interpreter.
COLOR	Sets the default console foreground and background colors.
COMP	Compares the contents of two files or sets of files.
COMPACT	Displays or alters the compression of files on NTFS partitions.
CONVERT	Converts FAT volumes to NTFS. You cannot convert the current drive.
COPY	Copies one or more files to another location.
DATE	Displays or sets the date.
DEL/ERASE	Deletes one or more files.
DIR	Displays a list of files and subdirectories in a directory.
DISKCOMP	Compares the contents of two floppy disks.
DISKCOPY	Copies the contents of one floppy disk to another.
DOSKEY	Edits command lines, recalls Windows commands, and creates macros.
ECHO	Displays messages, or turns command echoing on or off.
ENDLOCAL	Ends localization of environment changes in a batch file.
EXIT	Quits the CMD.EXE program (command interpreter).
FC	Compares two files or sets of files, and displays the differences between them.
FIND	Searches for a text string in a file or files.

FINDSTR	Searches for strings in files.
FOR	Runs a specified command for each file in a set of files.
FORMAT	Formats a disk for use with Windows.
FTYPE	Displays or modifies file types used in file extension associations.
GOTO	Directs the Windows command interpreter to a labeled line in a batch program.
HELP	Provides Help information for Windows commands.
IF	Performs conditional processing in batch programs.
LABEL	Creates, changes, or deletes the volume label of a disk.
MD/MKDIR	Creates a directory.
MODE	Configures a system device.
MORE	Displays output one screen at a time.
MOVE	Moves one or more files from one directory to another directory.
PATH	Displays or sets a search path for executable files.
PAUSE	Suspends processing of a batch file and displays a message.
POPD	Restores the previous value of the current directory saved by PUSHD.
PRINT	Prints a text file.
PROMPT	Changes the Windows command prompt.
PUSHD	Saves the current directory then changes it.
RECOVER	Recovers readable information from a bad or defective disk.
REM	Records comments (remarks) in batch files or CONFIG.SYS.
REN/RENAME	Renames a file or files.
REPLACE	Replaces files.
RMDIR/RD	Removes a directory.
SET	Displays, sets, or removes Windows environment variables.
SETLOCAL	Begins localization of environment changes in a batch file.
SHIFT	Shifts the position of replaceable parameters in batch files.
SORT	Sorts input.
START	Starts a separate window to run a specified program or command.
SUBST	Associates a path with a drive letter.
TIME	Displays or sets the system time.
TITLE	Sets the window title for a CMD.EXE session.
TREE	Graphically displays the directory structure of a drive or path.
TYPE	Displays the contents of a text file.
VER	Displays the Windows version.
VERIFY	Tells Windows whether to verify that your files are written correctly to a disk.
VOL	Displays a disk volume label and serial number.
XCOPY	Copies files and directory trees.

ASSOC

Displays or modifies file extension associations

ASSOC [.ext[=[fileType]]]

.ext   Specifies the file extension to associate the file type with
fileType   Specifies the file type to associate with the file extension

Type ASSOC without parameters to display the current file associations. If ASSOC is invoked with just a file extension, it displays the current file association for that file extension. Specify nothing for the file type and the command will delete the association for the file extension.

AT

The AT command schedules commands and programs to run on a computer at a specified time and date. The Schedule service must be running to use the AT command.

AT [\\computername] [[id] [/DELETE] ¦ /DELETE [/YES]]
AT [\\computername] time [/INTERACTIVE] [/EVERY:date[,...] ¦ /NEXT:date[,...]] "command"

\\computername	Specifies a remote computer. Commands are scheduled on the local computer if this parameter is omitted.
Id	Is an identification number assigned to a scheduled command.
/delete	Cancels a scheduled command. If id is omitted, all the scheduled commands on the computer are canceled.
/yes	Used with cancel all jobs command when no further confirmation is desired.
Time	Specifies the time when command is to run.
/interactive	Allows the job to interact with the desktop of the user who is logged on at the time the job runs.
/every:date[,...]	Runs the command on each specified day(s) of the week or month. If date is omitted, the current day of the month is assumed.
/next:date[,...]	Runs the specified command on the next occurrence of the day (for example, next Thursday). If date is omitted, the current day of the month is assumed.
"command"	Is the Windows command or batch program to be run.

ATTRIB

Displays or changes file attributes.

ATTRIB [+R ¦ -R] [+A ¦ -A] [+S ¦ -S] [+H ¦ -H] [drive:][path][filename] [/S [/D]]

+	Sets an attribute.
-	Clears an attribute.
R	Read-only file attribute.
A	Archive file attribute.
S	System file attribute.
H	Hidden file attribute.
[drive:][path][filename]	Specifies a file or files for attrib to process.
/S	Processes matching files in the current folder and all subfolders.
/D	Processes folders as well.

BREAK

Sets or clears extended **Ctrl** + C–checking on DOS system

This is present for compatibility with DOS systems. It has no effect under Windows XP.

If Command Extensions are enabled, and running on the Windows XP platform, then the BREAK command will enter a hard coded breakpoint if being debugged by a debugger.

CACLS

Displays or modifies access control lists (ACLs) of files

CACLS filename   [/T] [/E] [/C] [/G user:perm] [/R user [...]] [/P user:perm [...]] [/D user [...]]

filename	Displays ACLs.
/T	Changes ACLs of specified files in the current directory and all subdirectories.
/E	Edit ACL instead of replacing it.
/C	Continue on access denied errors.
/G user:perm	Grant specified user access rights.

Perm can be:
- R   Read
- W   Write
- C   Change (write)
- F   Full control

| /R user | Revoke specified user's access rights (only valid with /E). |
| /P user:perm | Replace specified user's access rights. |

Perm can be:
- N   None
- R   Read
- W   Write
- C   Change (write)
- F   Full control

| /D user | Deny specified user access. Wildcards can be used to specify more that one file in a command. You can specify more than one user in a command. |

Abbreviations:
CI—Container Inherit.
         The ACE will be inherited by directories.
OI—Object Inherit.
         The ACE will be inherited by files.

IO—Inherit Only.
The ACE does not apply to the current file/directory.

CALL

Calls one batch program from another.

CALL [drive:][path]filename [batch-parameters]

batch-parameters   Specifies any command-line information required by the batch
                        program.

If Command Extensions are enabled CALL changes as follows:

CALL command now accepts labels as the target of the CALL. The syntax is:

CALL :label arguments

A new batch file context is created with the specified arguments and control is passed to the statement
after the label specified. You must "exit" twice by reaching the end of the batch script file twice. The first
time you read the end, control will return to just after the CALL statement. The second time will exit the
batch script. Type GOTO /? for a description of the GOTO :EOF extension that will allow you to
"return" from a batch script.

In addition, expansion of batch script argument references (%0, %1, etc.) have been changed as follows:

%* in a batch script refers to all the arguments (e.g. %1 %2 %3 %4 %5 ...)
Substitution of batch parameters (%n) has been enhanced. You can now use the following optional
syntax:

%~1	expands %1 removing any surrounding quotes (")
%~f1	expands %1 to a fully qualified path name
%~d1	expands %1 to a drive letter only
%~p1	expands %1 to a path only
%~n1	expands %1 to a file name only
%~x1	expands %1 to a file extension only
%~s1	expanded path contains short names only
%~a1	expands %1 to file attributes
%~t1	expands %1 to date/time of file
%~z1	expands %1 to size of file
%~$PATH:1	searches the directories listed in the PATH environment variable and expands %1 to the fully qualified name of the first one found. If the environment variable name is not defined or the file is not found by the search, then this modifier expands to the empty string

The modifiers can be combined to get compound results:

%~dp1	expands %1 to a drive letter and path only
%~nx1	expands %1 to a file name and extension only
%~dp$PATH:1	searches the directories listed in the PATH environment variable for %1 and expands to the drive letter and path of the first one found.
%~ftza1	expands %1 to a DIR like output line

In the above examples %1 and PATH can be replaced by other valid values. The %~ syntax is terminated
by a valid argument number. The %~ modifiers may not be used with %*

CD or CHDIR

Displays the name of or changes the current directory.

CHDIR [/D] [drive:][path]
CHDIR [..]
CD [/D] [drive:][path]
CD [..]

..   Specifies that you want to change to the parent directory.

Type CD drive: to display the current directory in the specified drive.
Type CD without parameters to display the current drive and directory.

Use the /D switch to change current drive in addition to changing current directory for a drive.

If Command Extensions are enabled CHDIR changes as follows:

The current directory string is converted to use the same case as the on disk names. So CD C:\TEMP
would actually set the current directory to C:\Temp if that is the case on disk.

CHDIR command does not treat spaces as delimiters, so it is possible to CD into a subdirectory name that contains a space without surrounding the name with quotes. For example:

cd \winnt\profiles\username\programs\start menu

is the same as:

cd "\winnt\profiles\username\programs\start menu"

which is what you would have to type if extensions were disabled.

CHCP
Displays or sets the active code page number.

CHCP [nnn]

Nnn   Specifies a code page number.

Type CHCP without a parameter to display the active code page number.

CHKDSK
Checks a disk and displays a status report.

CHKDSK [volume[[path]filename]]] [/F] [/V] [/R] [/X] [/I] [/C] [/L[:size]]

Volume	Specifies the drive letter (followed by a colon), mount point, or volume name.
Filename	FAT/FAT32 only: Specifies the files to check for fragmentation.
/F	Fixes errors on the disk.
/V	On FAT/FAT32: Displays the full path and name of every file on the disk. On NTFS: Displays cleanup messages if any.
/R	Locates bad sectors and recovers readable information (implies /F).
/L:size	NTFS only: Changes the log file size to the specified number of kilobytes. If size is not specified, displays current size.
/X	Forces the volume to dismount first if necessary. All opened handles to the volume would then be invalid (implies /F).
/I	NTFS only: Performs a less vigorous check of index entries.
/C	NTFS only: Skips checking of cycles within the folder structure.

The /I or /C switch reduces the amount of time required to run Chkdsk by skipping certain checks of the volume.

CHKNTFS
Displays or modifies the checking of disk at boot time.

CHKNTFS volume [...]
CHKNTFS /D
CHKNTFS /T[:time]
CHKNTFS /X volume [...]
CHKNTFS /C volume [...]

Volume	Specifies the drive letter (followed by a colon), mount point, or volume name.
/D	Restores the machine to the default behavior; all drives are checked at boot time and chkdsk is run on those that are dirty.
/T:time	Changes the AUTOCHK initiation countdown time to the specified amount of time in seconds. If time is not specified, displays the current setting.
/X	Excludes a drive from the default boot-time check. Excluded drives are not accumulated between command invocations.
/C	Schedules a drive to be checked at boot time; chkdsk will run if the drive is dirty.

If no switches are specified, CHKNTFS will display if the specified drive is dirty or scheduled to be checked on next reboot.

CLS
Clears the screen.

CLS

CMD
Starts a new instance of the Windows XP command interpreter.

CMD [/A ¦ /U] [/Q] [/D] [/E:ON ¦ /E:OFF] [/F:ON ¦ /F:OFF] [/V:ON ¦ /V:OFF]
      [[/S] [/C ¦ /K] string]

/C   Carries out the command specified by string and then terminates

/K	Carries out the command specified by string but remains
/S	Modifies the treatment of string after /C or /K (see below)
/Q	Turns echo off
/D	Disable execution of AutoRun commands from registry (see below)
/A	Causes the output of internal commands to a pipe or file to be ANSI
/U	Causes the output of internal commands to a pipe or file to be Unicode
/T:fg	Sets the foreground/background colors (see COLOR /? for more info)
/E:ON	Enable command extensions (see below)
/E:OFF	Disable command extensions (see below)
/F:ON	Enable file and directory name completion characters (see below)
/F:OFF	Disable file and directory name completion characters (see below)
/V:ON	Enable delayed environment variable expansion using ! as the delimiter. For example, /V:ON would allow !var! to expand the variable var at execution time. The var syntax expands variables at input time, which is quite a different thing when inside of a FOR loop.
/V:OFF	Disable delayed environment expansion.

Note that multiple commands separated by the command separator '&&' are accepted for string if surrounded by quotes. Also, for compatibility reasons, /X is the same as /E:ON, /Y is the same as /E:OFF and /R is the same as /C. Any other switches are ignored.

If /C or /K is specified, then the remainder of the command line after the switch is processed as a command line, where the following logic is used to process quote (") characters:

1. If all of the following conditions are met, then quote characters on the command line are preserved:

    no /S switch

    exactly two quote characters

    no special characters between the two quote characters, where special is one of: &<>()@^¦
    there are one or more whitespace characters between the the two quote characters
    the string between the two quote characters is the name of an executable file.
2. Otherwise, old behavior is to see if the first character is a quote character and if so, strip the leading character and remove the last quote character on the command line, preserving any text after the last quote character.

If /D was NOT specified on the command line, then when CMD.EXE starts, it looks for the following REG_SZ/REG_EXPAND_SZ registry variables, and if either or both are present, they are executed first.

    HKEY_LOCAL_MACHINE\Software\Microsoft\Command Processor\AutoRun
and/or

    HKEY_CURRENT_USER\Software\Microsoft\Command Processor\AutoRun

Command Extensions are enabled by default. You may also disable extensions for a particular invocation by using the /E:OFF switch. You can enable or disable extensions for all invocations of CMD.EXE on a machine and/or user logon session by setting either or both of the following REG_DWORD values in the registry using REGEDT32.EXE:

    HKEY_LOCAL_MACHINE\Software\Microsoft\Command Processor\EnableExtensions
and/or

    HKEY_CURRENT_USER\Software\Microsoft\Command Processor\EnableExtensions
to either 0x1 or 0x0. The user specific setting takes precedence over the machine setting. The command line switches take precedence over the registry settings.

The command extensions involve changes and/or additions to the following commands:
DEL or ERASE
COLOR
CD or CHDIR
MD or MKDIR
PROMPT
PUSHD
POPD
SET
SETLOCAL
ENDLOCAL
IF
FOR
CALL
SHIFT
GOTO
START (also includes changes to external command invocation)
ASSOC
FTYPE

To get specific details, type commandname /? to view the specifics.

Delayed environment variable expansion is NOT enabled by default. You can enable or disable delayed environment variable expansion for a particular invocation of CMD.EXE with the /V:ON or /V:OFF switch. You can enable or disable completion for all invocations of CMD.EXE on a machine and/or user logon session by setting either or both of the following REG_DWORD values in the registry using REGEDT32.EXE:

  HKEY_LOCAL_MACHINE\Software\Microsoft\Command Processor\DelayedExpansion

and/or

  HKEY_CURRENT_USER\Software\Microsoft\Command Processor\DelayedExpansion

to either 0x1 or 0x0. The user specific setting takes precedence over the machine setting. The command line switches take precedence over the registry settings.

If delayed environment variable expansion is enabled, then the exclamation character can be used to substitute the value of an environment variable at execution time.

File and Directory name completion is NOT enabled by default. You can enable or disable file name completion for a particular invocation of CMD.EXE with the /F:ON or /F:OFF switch. You can enable or disable completion for all invocations of CMD.EXE on a machine and/or user logon session by setting either or both of the following REG_DWORD values in the registry using REGEDT32.EXE:

  HKEY_LOCAL_MACHINE\Software\Microsoft\Command Processor\CompletionChar
  HKEY_LOCAL_MACHINE\Software\Microsoft\Command Processor\PathCompletionChar

and/or

  HKEY_CURRENT_USER\Software\Microsoft\Command Processor\CompletionChar
  HKEY_CURRENT_USER\Software\Microsoft\Command Processor\PathCompletionChar

with the hex value of a control character to use for a particular function (e.g. 0x4 is Ctrl-D and 0x6 is Ctrl-F). The user specific settings take precedence over the machine settings. The command line switches take precedence over the registry settings.

If completion is enabled with the /F:ON switch, the two control characters used are Ctrl-D for directory name completion and Ctrl-F for file name completion. To disable a particular completion character in the registry, use the value for space (0x20) as it is not a valid control character.

Completion is invoked when you type either of the two control characters. The completion function takes the path string to the left of the cursor appends a wild card character to it if none is already present and builds up a list of paths that match. It then displays the first matching path. If no paths match, it just beeps and leaves the display alone. Thereafter, repeated pressing of the same control character will cycle through the list of matching paths. Pressing the **Shift** key with the control character will move through the list backwards. If you edit the line in any way and press the control character again, the saved list of matching paths is discarded and a new one generated. The same occurs if you switch between file and directory name completion. The only difference between the two control characters is the file completion character matches both file and directory names, while the directory completion character only matches directory names. If file completion is used on any of the built in directory commands (CD, MD or RD) then directory completion is assumed.

The completion code deals correctly with file names that contain spaces or other special characters by placing quotes around the matching path. Also, if you back up, then invoke completion from within a line, the text to the right of the cursor at the point completion was invoked is discarded.

The special characters that require quotes are:
<space>
&()[]{}^=;!'+,'~

COLOR
Sets the default console foreground and background colors.

COLOR [attr]

attr Specifies color attribute of console output

Color attributes are specified by TWO hex digits—the first corresponds to the background; the second the foreground. Each digit can be any of the following values:

0 = Black 8 = Gray
1 = Blue 9 = Light Blue
2 = Green A = Light Green
3 = Aqua B = Light Aqua
4 = Red C = Light Red
5 = Purple D = Light Purple
6 = Yellow E = Light Yellow
7 = White F = Bright White

If no argument is given, this command restores the color to what it was when CMD.EXE started. This value either comes from the current console window, the /T command line switch or from the DefaultColor registry value.

The COLOR command sets ERRORLEVEL to 1 if an attempt is made to execute the COLOR command with a foreground and background color that are the same.

Example: "COLOR fc" produces light red on bright white

COMP
Compares the contents of two files or sets of files.

COMP [data1] [data2] [/D] [/A] [/L] [/N=number] [/C] [/OFF[LINE]]

data1	Specifies location and name(s) of first file(s) to compare.
data2	Specifies location and name(s) of second files to compare.
/D	Displays differences in decimal format.
/A	Displays differences in ASCII characters.
/L	Displays line numbers for differences.
/N=number	Compares only the first specified number of lines in each file.
/C	Disregards case of ASCII letters when comparing files.
/OFF[LINE]	Do not skip files with offline attribute set.

To compare sets of files, use wildcards in data1 and data2 parameters.

COMPACT
Displays or alters the compression of files on NTFS partitions.

COMPACT [/C ¦ /U] [/S[:dir]] [/A] [/I] [/F] [/Q] [filename [...]]

/C	Compresses the specified files. Directories will be marked so that files added afterward will be compressed.
/U	Uncompresses the specified files. Directories will be marked so that files added afterward will not be compressed.
/S	Performs the specified operation on files in the given directory and all subdirectories. Default "dir" is the current directory.
/A	Displays files with the hidden or system attributes. These files are omitted by default.
/I	Continues performing the specified operation even after errors have occurred. By default, COMPACT stops when an error is encountered.
/F	Forces the compress operation on all specified files, even those which are already compressed. Already-compressed files are skipped by default.
/Q	Reports only the most essential information.
Filename	Specifies a pattern, file, or directory.

Used without parameters, COMPACT displays the compression state of the current directory and any files it contains. You may use multiple filenames and wildcards. You must put spaces between multiple parameters.

CONVERT
Converts FAT volumes to NTFS.

CONVERT volume /FS:NTFS [/V] [/CvtArea:filename] [/NoSecurity] [/X]

Volume	Specifies the drive letter (followed by a colon), mount point, or volume name.
/FS:NTFS	Specifies that the volume is to be converted to NTFS.
/V	Specifies that Convert should be run in verbose mode.
/CvtArea:filename	Specifies a contiguous file in the root directory to be the place holder for NTFS system files.
/NoSecurity	Specifies the converted files and directories security settings to be accessible by everyone.
/X	Forces the volume to dismount first if necessary. All opened handles to the volume would then be invalid.

COPY
Copies one or more files to another location.

COPY [/D] [/V] [/N] [/Y ¦ /-Y] [/Z] [/A ¦ /B] source [/A ¦ /B] [+ source [/A ¦ /B] [+ ...]]
       [destination [/A ¦ /B]]

source	Specifies the file or files to be copied.
/A	Indicates an ASCII text file.

/B	Indicates a binary file.
/D	Allow the destination file to be created decrypted
destination	Specifies the directory and/or filename for the new file(s).
/V	Verifies that new files are written correctly.
/N	Uses short filename, if available, when copying a file with a non-8dot3 name.
/Y	Suppresses prompting to confirm you want to overwrite an existing destination file.
/-Y	Causes prompting to confirm you want to overwrite an existing destination file.
/Z	Copies networked files in restartable mode.

The switch /Y may be preset in the COPYCMD environment variable. This may be overridden with /-Y on the command line. Default is to prompt on overwrites unless COPY command is being executed from within a batch script.

To append files, specify a single file for destination, but multiple files for source (using wildcards or file1+file2+file3 format).

DATE
Displays or sets the date.

DATE [/T ¦ date]

Type DATE without parameters to display the current date setting and a prompt for a new one. Press ENTER to keep the same date.

If Command Extensions are enabled the DATE command supports the /T switch which tells the command to just output the current date, without prompting for a new date.

DEFRAG
Usage:
DEFRAG <volume> [-a] [-f] [-v] [-?]

Volume	drive letter or mount point (d: or d:\vol\mountpoint)
-a	Analyze only
-f	Force defragmentation even if free space is low
-v	Verbose output
-?	Display this help text

DEL
Deletes one or more files.

DEL [/P] [/F] [/S] [/Q] [/A[[:]attributes]] names
ERASE [/P] [/F] [/S] [/Q] [/A[[:]attributes]] names

names	Specifies a list of one or more files or directories. Wildcards may be used to delete multiple files. If a directory is specified, all files within the directory will be deleted.
/P	Prompts for confirmation before deleting each file.
/F	Force deleting of read-only files.
/S	Delete specified files from all subdirectories.
/Q	Quiet mode, do not ask if ok to delete on global wildcard
/A	Selects files to delete based on attributes

attributes R Read-only files   S System files
            H Hidden files   A Files ready for archiving
            - Prefix meaning not

If Command Extensions are enabled DEL and ERASE change as follows:

The display semantics of the /S switch are reversed in that it shows you only the files that are deleted, not the ones it could not find.

DIR
Displays a list of files and subdirectories in a directory.

DIR [drive:][path][filename] [/A[[:]attributes]] [/B] [/C] [/D] [/L] [/N] [/O[[:]sortorder]] [/P] [/Q]
    [/S] [/T[[:]timefield]] [/W] [/X] [/4]

[drive:][path][filename]	Specifies drive, directory, and/or files to list.
/A	Displays files with specified attributes.

Attributes   D Directories   R Read-only files
             H Hidden files   A Files ready for archiving
             S System files   - Prefix meaning not

/B   Uses bare format (no heading information or summary).

/C	Display the thousand separator in file sizes. This is the default. Use /-C to disable display of separator.
/D	Same as wide but files are list sorted by column.
/L	Uses lowercase.
/N	New long list format where filenames are on the far right.
/O	List by files in sorted order.
Sortorder	N By name (alphabetic) S By size (smallest first)
	E By extension (alphabetic) D By date/time (oldest first)
	G Group directories first - Prefix to reverse order
/P	Pauses after each screenful of information.
/Q	Display the owner of the file.
/S	Displays files in specified directory and all subdirectories.
/T	Controls which time field displayed or used for sorting
timefield	C Creation
	A Last Access
	W Last Written
/W	Uses wide list format.
/X	This displays the short names generated for non-8dot3 file names. The format is that of /N with the short name inserted before the long name. If no short name is present, blanks are displayed in its place.
/4	Displays four-digit years

Switches may be preset in the DIRCMD environment variable. Override preset switches by prefixing any switch with - (hyphen)—for example, /-W.

DISKCOMP
Compares the contents of two floppy disks.

DISKCOPY
DISKCOMP [drive1: [drive2:]]
Copies the contents of one floppy disk to another.

DISKCOPY [drive1: [drive2:]] [/V]

/V   Verifies that the information is copied correctly.

The two floppy disks must be the same type. You may specify the same drive for drive1 and drive2.

DISKPART
Creates and deletes partitions on a hard drive. The diskpart command is only available when you are using the Recovery Console.

diskpart [/add ¦ /delete] [*device_name* ¦ *drive_name* ¦ *partition_name*] [*size*]

Parameters none

Used without parameters, the diskpart command starts the Windows character-mode version of diskpart.
/add   Creates a new partition.
/delete   Deletes an existing partition.

device_name
The device on which you want to create or delete a partition. The name can be obtained from the output of the map command. An example of a device name is:
        \Device\HardDisk0

drive_name
The partition you want to delete, by drive letter. Used only with /delete. An example of a drive name is:
        D:

partition_name
The partition you want to delete, by partition name. Can be used in place of the *drive_name*. Used only with /delete. An example of a partition name is:
        \Device\HardDisk0\Partition1

size
The size, in megabytes (MB), of the partition you want to create. Used only with /add.

Examples:
The following examples delete a partition:
   diskpart /delete \Device\HardDisk0\Partition3
   diskpart /delete F:

The following example adds a 20 MB partition to your hard drive:
   diskpart /add \Device\HardDisk0 20

DOSKEY
Edits command lines, recalls Windows XP commands, and creates macros.

DOSKEY [/REINSTALL] [/LISTSIZE=size] [/MACROS[:ALL ¦ :exename]] [/HISTORY] [/INSERT ¦ /
OVERSTRIKE] [/EXENAME=exename] [/MACROFILE=filename] [macroname=[text]]

/REINSTALL	Installs a new copy of Doskey.
/LISTSIZE=size	Sets size of command history buffer.
/MACROS	Displays all Doskey macros.
/MACROS:ALL	Displays all Doskey macros for all executables which have Doskey macros.
/MACROS:exename	Displays all Doskey macros for the given executable.
/HISTORY	Displays all commands stored in memory.
/INSERT	Specifies that new text you type is inserted in old text.
/OVERSTRIKE	Specifies that new text overwrites old text.
/EXENAME=exename	Specifies the executable.
/MACROFILE=filename	Specifies a file of macros to install.
Macroname	Specifies a name for a macro you create.
Text	Specifies commands you want to record.

UP and DOWN ARROWS recall commands; [Esc] clears command line; [F7] displays command history;
[Alt] + [F7] clears command history; [F8] searches command history; [F9] selects a command by number;
[Alt] + [F10] clears macro definitions.

The following are some special codes in Doskey macro definitions:
$T	Command separator. Allows multiple commands in a macro.
$1–$9	Batch parameters. Equivalent to %1-%9 in batch programs.
$*	Symbol replaced by everything following macro name on command line.

ECHO
Displays messages, or turns command-echoing on or off.

ECHO [ON ¦ OFF]
ECHO [message]

Type ECHO without parameters to display the current echo setting.

ENDLOCAL
Ends localization of environment changes in a batch file. Environment changes made after ENDLOCAL
has been issued are not local to the batch file; the previous settings are not restored on termination of the
batch file.

ENDLOCAL

If Command Extensions are enabled ENDLOCAL changes as follows:

If the corresponding SETLOCAL enable or disabled command extensions using the new
ENABLEEXTENSIONS or DISABLEEXTENSIONS options, then after the ENDLOCAL, the enabled/
disabled state of command extensions will be restored to what it was prior to the matching SETLOCAL
command execution.

EXIT
Quits the CMD.EXE program (command interpreter) or the current batch script.

EXIT [/B] [exitCode]

/B	Specifies to exit the current batch script instead of CMD.EXE. If executed from outside a batch script, it will quit CMD.EXE
exitCode	Specifies a numeric number. If /B is specified, sets ERRORLEVEL that number. If quitting CMD.EXE, sets the process exit code with that number.

FC
Compares two files or sets of files and displays the differences between them.

FC [/A] [/C] [/L] [/LBn] [/N] [/OFF[LINE]] [/T] [/U] [/W] [/nnnn] [drive1:][path1]filename1
       [drive2:][path2]filename2
FC /B [drive1:][path1]filename1 [drive2:][path2]filename2

/A	Displays only first and last lines for each set of differences.
/B	Performs a binary comparison.
/C	Disregards the case of letters.
/L	Compares files as ASCII text.
/LBn	Sets the maximum consecutive mismatches to the specified number of lines.
/N	Displays the line numbers on an ASCII comparison.
/OFF[LINE]	Do not skip files with offline attribute set.
/T	Does not expand tabs to spaces.
/U	Compare files as UNICODE text files.
/W	Compresses white space (tabs and spaces) for comparison.
/nnnn	Specifies the number of consecutive lines that must match after a mismatch.
[drive1:][path1]filename1	Specifies the first file or set of files to compare.
[drive2:][path2]filename2	Specifies the second file or set of files to compare.

FIND

Searches for a text string in a file or files.

FIND [/V] [/C] [/N] [/I] [/OFF[LINE]] "string" [[drive:][path]filename[...]]

/V	Displays all lines NOT containing the specified string.
/C	Displays only the count of lines containing the string.
/N	Displays line numbers with the displayed lines.
/I	Ignores the case of characters when searching for the string.
/OFF[LINE]	Do not skip files with offline attribute set.
"string"	Specifies the text string to find.
[drive:][path]filename	Specifies a file or files to search.

If a path is not specified, FIND searches the text typed at the prompt or piped from another command.

FINDSTR

Searches for strings in files.

FINDSTR [/B] [/E] [/L] [/R] [/S] [/I] [/X] [/V] [/N] [/M] [/O] [/P] [/F:file] [/C:string] [/G:file]
       [/D:dir list] [/A:color attributes] [/OFF[LINE]] strings [[drive:][path]filename[...]]

/B	Matches pattern if at the beginning of a line.
/E	Matches pattern if at the end of a line.
/L	Uses search strings literally.
/R	Uses search strings as regular expressions.
/S	Searches for matching files in the current directory and all subdirectories.
/I	Specifies that the search is not to be case-sensitive.
/X	Prints lines that match exactly.
/V	Prints only lines that do not contain a match.
/N	Prints the line number before each line that matches.
/M	Prints only the filename if a file contains a match.
/O	Prints character offset before each matching line.
/P	Skip files with non-printable characters.
/OFF[LINE]	Do not skip files with offline attribute set.
/A:attr	Specifies color attribute with two hex digits. See "color /?"
/F:file	Reads file list from the specified file(/ stands for console).
/C:string	Uses specified string as a literal search string.
/G:file	Gets search strings from the specified file(/ stands for console).
/D:dir	Search a semicolon delimited list of directories
strings	Text to be searched for.
[drive:][path]filename	Specifies a file or files to search.

Use spaces to separate multiple search strings unless the argument is prefixed with /C. For example, **FINDSTR "hello there" x.y** searches for "hello" or "there" in file x.y. **FINDSTR /C:"hello there" x.y** searches for "hello there" in file x.y.

Regular expression quick reference:

.	Wildcard: any character
*	Repeat: zero or more occurances of previous character or class
^	Line position: beginning of line
$	Line position: end of line

[class]	Character class: any one character in set
[^class]	Inverse class: any one character not in set
[x-y]	Range: any characters within the specified range
\x	Escape: literal use of metacharacter x
\<xyz	Word position: beginning of word
xyz\>	Word position: end of word

For full information on FINDSTR regular expressions refer to the online Command Reference.

FOR IN DO

Runs a specified command for each file in a set of files.

FOR %variable IN (set) DO command [command-parameters]

%variable	Specifies a single letter replaceable parameter.
(set)	Specifies a set of one or more files. Wildcards may be used.
Command	Specifies the command to carry out for each file.
command-parameters	Specifies parameters or switches for the specified command.

To use the FOR command in a batch program, specify %%variable instead of %variable. Variable names are case sensitive, so %i is different from %I.

If Command Extensions are enabled, the following additional forms of the FOR command are supported:

FOR /D %variable IN (set) DO command [command-parameters]

If set contains wildcards, then specifies to match against directory names instead of file names.

FOR /R [[drive:]path] %variable IN (set) DO command [command-parameters]

Walks the directory tree rooted at [drive:]path, executing the FOR statement in each directory of the tree. If no directory specification is specified after /R then the current directory is assumed. If set is just a single period (.) character then it will just enumerate the directory tree.

FOR /L %variable IN (start,step,end) DO command [command-parameters]

The set is a sequence of numbers from start to end, by step amount. So (1,1,5) would generate the sequence 1 2 3 4 5 and (5,-1,1) would generate the sequence (5 4 3 2 1)

FOR /F ["options"] %variable IN (file-set) DO command [command-parameters]
FOR /F ["options"] %variable IN ("string") DO command [command-parameters]
FOR /F ["options"] %variable IN ('command') DO command [command-parameters]

or, if usebackq option present:

FOR /F ["options"] %variable IN (file-set) DO command [command-parameters]
FOR /F ["options"] %variable IN ('string') DO command [command-parameters]
FOR /F ["options"] %variable IN ('command') DO command [command-parameters]

filenameset is one or more file names. Each file is opened, read and processed before going on to the next file in filenameset. Processing consists of reading in the file, breaking it up into individual lines of text and then parsing each line into zero or more tokens. The body of the for loop is then called with the variable value(s) set to the found token string(s). By default, /F passes the first blank separated token from each line of each file. Blank lines are skipped. You can override the default parsing behavior by specifying the optional "options" parameter. This is a quoted string which contains one or more keywords to specify different parsing options. The keywords are:

eol=c	specifies an end of line comment character (just one)
skip=n	specifies the number of lines to skip at the beginning of the file.
delims=xxx	specifies a delimiter set. This replaces the default delimiter set of space and tab.
tokens=x,y,m-n	specifies which tokens from each line are to be passed to the for body for each iteration. This will cause additional variable names to be allocated. The m-n form is a range, specifying the mth through the nth tokens. If the last character in the tokens= string is an asterisk, then an additional variable is allocated and receives the remaining text on the line after the last token parsed.
Usebackq	specifies that the new semantics are in force, where a back quoted string is executed as a command and a single quoted string is a literal string command and allows the use of double quotes to quote file names in filenameset.

Some examples might help:
FOR /F "eol=; tokens=2,3* delims=, " %i in (myfile.txt) do @echo %i %j %k
would parse each line in myfile.txt, ignoring lines that begin with a semicolon, passing the second and third token from each line to the for body, with tokens delimited by commas and/or spaces. Notice the

for body statements reference %i to get the 2nd token, %j to get the 3rd token, and %k to get all remaining tokens after the 3rd. For file names that contain spaces, you need to quote the filenames with double quotes. In order to use double quotes in this manner, you also need to use the usebackq option, otherwise the double quotes will be interpreted as defining a literal string to parse.

%i is explicitly declared in the for statement and the %j and %k are implicitly declared via the tokens= option. You can specify up to 26 tokens via the tokens= line, provided it does not cause an attempt to declare a variable higher than the letter 'z' or 'Z'.

Remember, FOR variables are single-letter, case sensitive, global, and you can't have more than 52 total active at any one time.

You can also use the FOR /F parsing logic on an immediate string, by making the filenameset between the parenthesis a quoted string, using single quote characters. It will be treated as a single line of input from a file and parsed.

Finally, you can use the FOR /F command to parse the output of a command. You do this by making the filenameset between the parenthesis a back quoted string. It will be treated as a command line, which is passed to a child CMD.EXE and the output is captured into memory and parsed as if it was a file. So the following example:

    FOR /F "usebackq delims==" %i IN ('set') DO @echo %i

would enumerate the environment variable names in the current environment.

In addition, substitution of FOR variable references has been enhanced.

You can now use the following optional syntax:

%~I   expands %I removing any surrounding quotes (")
%~fI   expands %I to a fully qualified path name
%~dI   expands %I to a drive letter only
%~pI   expands %I to a path only
%~nI   expands %I to a file name only
%~xI   expands %I to a file extension only
%~sI   expanded path contains short names only
%~aI   expands %I to file attributes of file
%~tI   expands %I to date/time of file
%~zI   expands %I to size of file
%~$PATH:I   searches the directories listed in the PATH environment variable and expands %I to the fully qualified name of the first one found. If the environment variable name is not defined or the file is not found by the search, then this modifier expands to the empty string.

The modifiers can be combined to get compound results:

%~dpI   expands %I to a drive letter and path only
%~nxI   expands %I to a file name and extension only
%~fsI   expands %I to a full path name with short names only
%~dp$PATH:I   searches the directories listed in the PATH environment variable for %I and expands to the drive letter and path of the first one found.
%~ftzaI   expands %I to a DIR like output line

In the above examples %I and PATH can be replaced by other valid values. The %~ syntax is terminated by a valid FOR variable name. Picking upper case variable names like %I makes it more readable and avoids confusion with the modifiers, which are not case sensitive.

FORMAT

Formats a disk for use with Windows XP.

FORMAT volume [/FS:file-system] [/V:label] [/Q] [/A:size] [/C] [/X]
FORMAT volume [/V:label] [/Q] [/F:size]
FORMAT volume [/V:label] [/Q] [/T:tracks /N:sectors]
FORMAT volume [/V:label] [/Q]
FORMAT volume [/Q]

Volume	Specifies the drive letter (followed by a colon), mount point, or volume name.
/FS:filesystem	Specifies the type of the file system (FAT, FAT32, or NTFS).
/V:label	Specifies the volume label.
/Q	Performs a quick format.
/C	NTFS only: Files created on the new volume will be compressed by default.
/X	Forces the volume to dismount first if necessary. All opened handles to the volume would no longer be valid.

/ A:size   Overrides the default allocation unit size. Default settings are strongly recommended for general use. NTFS supports 512, 1024, 2048, 4096, 8192, 16K, 32K, 64K. FAT supports 512, 1024, 2048, 4096, 8192, 16K, 32K, 64K, (128K, 256K for sector size > 512 bytes). FAT32 supports 512, 1024, 2048, 4096, 8192, 16K, 32K, 64K, (128K, 256K for sector size > 512 bytes).

Note that the FAT and FAT32 files systems impose the following restrictions on the number of clusters on a volume:

        FAT: Number of clusters <= 65526

        FAT32: 65526 < Number of clusters < 4177918

Format will immediately stop processing if it decides that the above requirements cannot be met using the specified cluster size.

NTFS compression is not supported for allocation unit sizes above 4096.

/F:size   Specifies the size of the floppy disk to format (1.44)

/T:tracks   Specifies the number of tracks per disk side.

/N:sectors   Specifies the number of sectors per track.

FTYPE

Displays or modifies file types used in file extension associations

FTYPE [fileType[=[openCommandString]]]

fileType   Specifies the file type to examine or change openCommandString Specifies the open command to use when launching files of this type.

Type FTYPE without parameters to display the current file types that have open command strings defined. FTYPE is invoked with just a file type, it displays the current open command string for that file type. Specify nothing for the open command string and the FTYPE command will delete the open command string for the file type. Within an open command string %0 or %1 are substituted with the file name being launched through the assocation. %* gets all the parameters and %2 gets the 1st parameter, %3 the second, etc. %~n gets all the remaining parameters starting with the nth parameter, where n may be between 2 and 9, inclusive. For example:

        ASSOC .pl=PerlScript

        FTYPE PerlScript=perl.exe %1 %*

would allow you to invoke a Perl script as follows:

        script.pl 1 2 3

If you want to eliminate the need to type the extensions, then do the following:

        set PATHEXT=.pl;%PATHEXT%

and the script could be invoked as follows:

        script 1 2 3

GOTO

Directs cmd.exe to a labeled line in a batch program.

GOTO label

Label   Specifies a text string used in the batch program as a label.

You type a label on a line by itself, beginning with a colon.

If Command Extensions are enabled GOTO changes as follows:

GOTO command now accepts a target label of :EOF which transfers control to the end of the current batch script file. This is an easy way to exit a batch script file without defining a label. Type CALL /? for a description of extensions to the CALL command that make this feature useful.

HELP (command)

Provides help information for Windows XP commands.

HELP [command]

command   Displays help information on that command.

IF

Performs conditional processing in batch programs.

IF [NOT] ERRORLEVEL number command

IF [NOT] string1==string2 command

IF [NOT] EXIST filename command

NOT	Specifies that Windows XP should carry out the command only if the condition is false.
ERRORLEVEL number	Specifies a true condition if the last program run returned an exit code equal to or greater than the number specified.
string1==string2	Specifies a true condition if the specified text strings match.
EXIST filename	Specifies a true condition if the specified filename exists.
Command	Specifies the command to carry out if the condition is met. Command can be followed by ELSE command which will execute the command after the ELSE keyword if the specified condition is FALSE

The ELSE clause must occur on the same line as the command after the IF. For example:

```
IF EXIST filename. (
        del filename.
) ELSE (
        echo filename. missing.
)
```

The following would NOT work because the del command needs to be terminated by a newline:

```
IF EXIST filename. del filename. ELSE echo filename. Missing
```

Nor would the following work, since the ELSE command must be on the same line as the end of the IF command:

```
IF EXIST filename. del filename.
ELSE echo filename. missing
```

The following would work if you want it all on one line:

```
IF EXIST filename. (del filename.) ELSE echo filename. missing
```

If Command Extensions are enabled IF changes as follows:

```
IF [/I] string1 compare-op string2 command
IF CMDEXTVERSION number command
IF DEFINED variable command
```

where compare-op may be one of:

```
EQU - equal
NEQ - not equal
LSS - less than
LEQ - less than or equal
GTR - greater than
GEQ - greater than or equal
```

and the /I switch, if specified, says to do case insensitive string compares. The /I switch can also be used on the string1==string2 form of IF. These comparisons are generic, in that if both string1 and string2 are both comprised of all numeric digits, then the strings are converted to numbers and a numeric comparison is performed.

The CMDEXTVERSION conditional works just like ERRORLEVEL, except it is comparing against an internal version number associated with the Command Extensions. The first version is 1. It will be incremented by one when significant enhancements are added to the Command Extensions. CMDEXTVERSION conditional is never true when Command Extensions are disabled.

The DEFINED conditional works just like EXISTS except it takes an environment variable name and returns true if the environment variable is defined.

%ERRORLEVEL% will expand into a string representation of the current value of ERRORLEVEL, provided that there is not already an environment variable with the name ERRORLEVEL, in which case you will get its value instead. After running a program, the following illustrates ERRORLEVEL use:

```
goto answer%ERRORLEVEL%
:answer0
echo Program had return code 0
:answer1
echo Program had return code 1
```

You can also using the numerical comparisons above:

```
IF %ERRORLEVEL% LEQ 1 goto okay
```

%CMDCMDLINE% will expand into the original command line passed to CMD.EXE prior to any processing by CMD.EXE, provided that there is not already an environment variable with the name CMDCMDLINE, in which case you will get its value instead.

%CMDEXTVERSION% will expand into a string representation of the current value of CMDEXTVERSION, provided that there is not already an environment variable with the name CMDEXTVERSION, in which case you will get its value instead.

LABEL
Creates, changes, or deletes the volume label of a disk.

LABEL [drive:][label]
LABEL [/MP] [volume] [label]

drive:	Specifies the drive letter of a drive.
Label	Specifies the label of the volume.
/MP	Specifies that the volume should be treated as a mount point or volume name.
Volume	Specifies the drive letter (followed by a colon), mount point, or volume name. If volume name is specified, the /MP flag is unnecessary.

MD/MKDIR
Creates a directory.

MKDIR [drive:]path
MD [drive:]path

If Command Extensions are enabled MKDIR changes as follows:

MKDIR creates any intermediate directories in the path, if needed.

For example, assume \a does not exist then:
        mkdir \a\b\c\d
is the same as:
        mkdir \a
        chdir \a
        mkdir b
        chdir b
        mkdir c
        chdir c
        mkdir d
which is what you would have to type if extensions were disabled.

MODE
Configures system devices.

Serial port:	MODE COMm[:] [BAUD=b] [PARITY=p] [DATA=d] [STOP=s] [to=on ¦ off] [xon=on ¦ off] [odsr=on ¦ off] [octs=on ¦ off] [dtr=on ¦ off ¦ hs] [rts=on ¦ off ¦ hs ¦ tg] [idsr=on ¦ off]
Device Status:	MODE [device] [/STATUS]
Redirect printing:	MODE LPTn[:]=COMm[:]
Select code page:	MODE CON[:] CP SELECT=yyy
Code page status:	MODE CON[:] CP [/STATUS]
Display mode:	MODE CON[:] [COLS=c] [LINES=n]
Typematic rate:	MODE CON[:] [RATE=r DELAY=d]

MORE
Displays output one screen at a time.

MORE [/E [/C] [/P] [/S] [/Tn] [+n]] < [drive:][path]filename
command-name ¦ MORE [/E [/C] [/P] [/S] [/Tn] [+n]]
MORE /E [/C] [/P] [/S] [/Tn] [+n] [files]

[drive:][path]filename	Specifies a file to display one screen at a time.
command-name	Specifies a command whose output will be displayed.
/E	Enable extended features
/C	Clear screen before displaying page
/P	Expand FormFeed characters
/S	Squeeze multiple blank lines into a single line
/Tn	Expand tabs to n spaces (default 8)

Switches can be present in the MORE environment variable.

+n	Start displaying the first file at line n
files	List of files to be displayed. Files in the list are separated by blanks.

If extended features are enabled, the following commands are accepted at the
 -- More -- prompt:

P n	Display next n lines
S n	Skip next n lines

F	Display next file
Q	Quit
=	Show line number
?	Show help line
\<space\>	Display next page
\<ret\>	Display next line

MOVE
Moves files and renames files and directories.

To move one or more files:
MOVE [/Y ¦ /-Y] [drive:][path]filename1[,...] destination

To rename a directory:
MOVE [/Y ¦ /-Y] [drive:][path]dirname1 dirname2

[drive:][path]filename1	Specifies the location and name of the file or files you want to move.
Destination	Specifies the new location of the file. Destination can consist of a drive letter and colon, a directory name, or a combination. If you are moving only one file, you can also include a filename if you want to rename the file when you move it.
[drive:][path]dirname1	Specifies the directory you want to rename.
dirname2	Specifies the new name of the directory.
/Y	Suppresses prompting to confirm you want to overwrite an existing destination file.
/-Y	Causes prompting to confirm you want to overwrite an existing destination file.

The switch /Y may be present in the COPYCMD environment variable. This may be overridden with /-Y on the command line. Default is to prompt on overwrites unless MOVE command is being executed from within a batch script.

PATH
Displays or sets a search path for executable files.

PATH [[drive:]path[;...][;%PATH%]
PATH ;

Type PATH ; to clear all search-path settings and direct cmd.exe to search only in the current directory.

Type PATH without parameters to display the current path. Including %PATH% in the new path setting causes the old path to be appended to the new setting.

PAUSE
Suspends processing of a batch program and displays the message:
    Press any key to continue . . .

POPD
Changes to the directory stored by the PUSHD command.

Popd

If Command Extensions are enabled the POPD command will delete any temporary drive letter created by PUSHD when you POPD that drive off the pushed directory stack.

PRINT
Prints a text file.

PRINT [/D:device] [[drive:][path]filename[...]]

/D:device	Specifies a print device.

PROMPT
Changes the cmd.exe command prompt.

PROMPT [text]

Text	Specifies a new command prompt.

Prompt can be made up of normal characters and the following special codes:

$A	& (Ampersand)
$B	¦ (pipe)
$C	((Left parenthesis)
$D	Current date
$E	Escape code (ASCII code 27)
$F	) (Right parenthesis)
$G	> (greater-than sign)
$H	Backspace (erases previous character)
$L	< (less-than sign)
$N	Current drive
$P	Current drive and path
$Q	= (equal sign)
$S	(space)
$T	Current time
$V	Windows XP version number
$_	Carriage return and linefeed
$$	$ (dollar sign)

If Command Extensions are enabled the PROMPT command supports the following additional formatting characters:

$+   zero or more plus sign (+) characters depending upon the depth of the PUSHD directory stack, one character for each level pushed.

$M   Displays the remote name associated with the current drive letter or the empty string if current drive is not a network drive.

PUSHD

Stores the current directory for use by the POPD command, then changes to the specified directory.

PUSHD [path ¦ ..]

Path   Specifies the directory to make the current directory.

If Command Extensions are enabled the PUSHD command accepts network paths in addition to the normal drive letter and path. If a network path is specified, PUSHD will create a temporary drive letter that points to that specified network resource and then change the current drive and directory, using the newly defined drive letter. Temporary drive letters are allocated from Z: on down, using the first unused drive letter found.

RD/RMDIR

Removes (deletes) a directory.

RMDIR [/S] [/Q] [drive:]path
RD [/S] [/Q] [drive:]path

/S   Removes all directories and files in the specified directory in addition to the directory itself. Used to remove a directory tree.

/Q   Quiet mode, do not ask if ok to remove a directory tree with /S

RECOVER

Recovers readable information from a bad or defective disk.

RECOVER [drive:][path]filename

Consult the online Command Reference in Windows XP Help before using the RECOVER command.

REM

Records comments (remarks) in a batch file or CONFIG.SYS.

REM [comment]

REN/RENAME

Renames a file or files.

RENAME [drive:][path]filename1 filename2.
REN [drive:][path]filename1 filename2.

Note that you cannot specify a new drive or path for your destination file.

REPLACE
Replaces files.

REPLACE [drive1:][path1]filename [drive2:][path2] [/A] [/P] [/R] [/W]
REPLACE [drive1:][path1]filename [drive2:][path2] [/P] [/R] [/S] [/W] [/U]

[drive1:][path1]filename	Specifies the source file or files.
[drive2:][path2]	Specifies the directory where files are to be replaced.
/A	Adds new files to destination directory. Cannot use with /S or /U switches.
/P	Prompts for confirmation before replacing a file or adding a source file.
/R	Replaces read-only files as well as unprotected files.
/S	Replaces files in all subdirectories of the destination directory. Cannot use with the /A switch.
/W	Waits for you to insert a disk before beginning.
/U	Replaces (updates) only files that are older than source files. Cannot use with the /A switch.

SET
Displays, sets, or removes cmd.exe environment variables.

SET [variable=[string]]

Variable	Specifies the environment-variable name.
String	Specifies a series of characters to assign to the variable.

Type SET without parameters to display the current environment variables.

If Command Extensions are enabled SET changes as follows:

SET command invoked with just a variable name, no equal sign or value will display the value of all variables whose prefix matches the name given to the SET command. For example:
        SET P
would display all variables that begin with the letter 'P'

SET command will set the ERRORLEVEL to 1 if the variable name is not found in the current environment.

SET command will not allow an equal sign to be part of the name of a variable.

Two new switches have been added to the SET command:
        SET /A expression
        SET /P variable=[promptString]

The /A switch specifies that the string to the right of the equal sign is a numerical expression that is evaluated. The expression evaluator is pretty simple and supports the following operations, in decreasing order of precedence:

()	grouping
! ~ -	unary operators
* / %	arithmetic operators
+ -	arithmetic operators
<< >>	logical shift
&	bitwise and
^	bitwise exclusive or
¦	bitwise or
= *= /= %= += -=	assignment
&= ^= ¦= <<= >>=	expression separator

If you use any of the logical or modulus operators, you will need to enclose the expression string in quotes. Any non-numeric strings in the expression are treated as environment variable names whose values are converted to numbers before using them. If an environment variable name is specified but is not defined in the current environment, then a value of zero is used. This allows you to do arithmetic with environment variable values without having to type all those % signs to get their values. If SET /A is executed from the command line outside of a command script, then it displays the final value of the expression. The assignment operator requires an environment variable name to the left of the assignment operator. Numeric values are decimal numbers, unless prefixed by 0x for hexadecimal numbers, and 0 for octal numbers. So 0x12 is the same as 18 is the same as 022. Please note that the octal notation can be confusing: 08 and 09 are not valid numbers because 8 and 9 are not valid octal digits.

The /P switch allows you to set the value of a variable to a line of input entered by the user. Displays the specified promptString before reading the line of input. The promptString can be empty.

Environment variable substitution has been enhanced as follows:

    %PATH:str1=str2%

would expand the PATH environment variable, substituting each occurrence of "str1" in the expanded result with "str2." "str2" can be the empty string to effectively delete all occurrences of "str1" from the expanded output. "str1" can begin with an asterisk, in which case it will match everything from the beginning of the expanded output to the first occurrence of the remaining portion of "str1."

May also specify substrings for an expansion.

    %PATH:~10,5%

would expand the PATH environment variable, and then use only the five characters that begin at the eleventh (offset 10) character of the expanded result. If the length is not specified, then it defaults to the remainder of the variable value. If either number (offset or length) is negative, then the number used is the length of the environment variable value added to the offset or length specified.

    %PATH:~-10%

would extract the last 10 characters of the PATH variable.

    %PATH:~0,-2%

would extract all but the last two characters of the PATH variable.

Finally, support for delayed environment variable expansion has been added. This support is always disabled by default, but may be enabled/disabled via the /V command line switch to CMD.EXE. See CMD /?

Delayed environment variable expansion is useful for getting around the limitations of the current expansion which happens when a line of text is read, not when it is executed. The following example demonstrates the problem with immediate variable expansion:

```
set VAR=before
if "%VAR%" == "before" (
        set VAR=after
    if "%VAR%" == "after" @echo If you see this, it worked
)
```

would never display the message, since the %VAR% in BOTH IF statements is substituted when the first IF statement is read, since it logically includes the body of the IF, which is a compound statement. So the IF inside the compound statement is really comparing "before" with "after" which will never be equal. Similarly, the following example will not work as expected:

```
set LIST=
for %i in (*) do set LIST=%LIST% %i
echo %LIST%
```

in that it will NOT build up a list of files in the current directory, but instead will just set the LIST variable to the last file found. Again, this is because the %LIST% is expanded just once when the FOR statement is read, and at that time the LIST variable is empty. So the actual FOR loop we are executing is:

```
for %i in (*) do set LIST= %i
```

which just keeps setting LIST to the last file found.

Delayed environment variable expansion allows you to use a different character (the exclamation mark) to expand environment variables at execution time. If delayed variable expansion is enabled, the above examples could be written as follows to work as intended:

```
set VAR=before
if "%VAR%" == "before" (
        set VAR=after
        if "!VAR!" == "after" @echo If you see this, it worked
)

set LIST=
for %i in (*) do set LIST=!LIST! %i
echo %LIST%
```

If Command Extensions are enabled, then there are several dynamic environment variables that can be expanded but which don't show up in the list of variables displayed by SET. These variable values are computed dynamically each time the value of the variable is expanded. If the user explicitly defines a variable with one of these names, then that definition will override the dynamic one described below:

%CD%	Expands to the current directory string.
%DATE%	Expands to current date using same format as DATE command.
%TIME%	Expands to current time using same format as TIME command.
%RANDOM%	Expands to a random decimal number between 0 and 32767.
%ERRORLEVEL%	Expands to the current ERRORLEVEL value
%CMDEXTVERSION%	Expands to the current Command Processor Extensions version number.
%CMDCMDLINE%	Expands to the original command line that invoked the Command Processor.

SETLOCAL

Begins localization of environment changes in a batch file. Environment changes made after SETLOCAL has been issued are local to the batch file. ENDLOCAL must be issued to restore the previous settings. When the end of a batch script is reached, an implied ENDLOCAL is executed for any outstanding SETLOCAL commands issued by that batch script.

SETLOCAL

If Command Extensions are enabled SETLOCAL changes as follows:

SETLOCAL batch command now accepts optional arguments:

ENABLEEXTENSIONS / DISABLEEXTENSIONS

Enable or disable command processor extensions. See CMD /? for details.

ENABLEDELAYEDEXPANSION / DISABLEDELAYEDEXPANSION

Enable or disable delayed environment variable expansion. See SET /? for details.

These modifications last until the matching ENDLOCAL command, regardless of their setting prior to the SETLOCAL command.

The SETLOCAL command will set the ERRORLEVEL value if given an argument. It will be zero if one of the two valid arguments is given and one otherwise. You can use this in batch scripts to determine if the extensions are available, using the following technique:

VERIFY OTHER 2>nul

SETLOCAL ENABLEEXTENSIONS

IF ERRORLEVEL 1 echo Unable to enable extensions

This works because on old versions of CMD.EXE, SETLOCAL does NOT set the ERRORLEVEL value. The VERIFY command with a bad argument initializes the ERRORLEVEL value to a non-zero value.

SHIFT

Changes the position of replaceable parameters in a batch file.

SHIFT [/n]

If Command Extensions are enabled the SHIFT command supports the /n switch which tells the command to start shifting at the nth argument, where n may be between zero and eight. For example:

SHIFT /2

would shift %3 to %2, %4 to %3, etc. and leave %0 and %1 unaffected.

SORT

SORT [/R] [/+n] [/M kilobytes] [/L locale] [/REC recordbytes] [[drive1:][path1]filename1]
        [/T [drive2:][path2]] [/O [drive3:][path3]filename3]

/+n	Specifies the character number, n, to begin each comparison. /+3 indicates that each comparison should begin at the 3rd character in each line. Lines with fewer than n characters collate before other lines. By default comparisons start at the first character in each line.
/L[OCALE] locale	Overrides the system default locale with the specified one. The ""C"" locale yields the fastest collating sequence and is currently the only alternative. The sort is always case insensitive.
/M[EMORY] kilobytes	Specifies amount of main memory to use for the sort, in kilobytes. The memory size is always constrained to be a minimum of 160 kilobytes. If the memory size is specified the exact amount will be used for the sort, regardless of how much main memory is available. The best performance is usually achieved by not specifying a memory size. By default the sort will be done with one pass (no temporary file) if it fits in the default maximum memory size, otherwise the sort will be done in two passes (with the partially sorted data being stored in a temporary file) such that the amounts of memory used for both the sort and merge passes are equal. The default maximum memory size is 90% of available main memory if both the input and output are files, and 45% of main memory otherwise.
/REC[ORD_MAXIMUM] characters	Specifies the maximum number of characters in a record (default 4096, maximum 65535).

/R[EVERSE] [drive1:][path1]filename1	Reverses the sort order; that is, sorts Z to A, then 9 to 0. Specifies the file to be sorted. If not specified, the standard input is sorted. Specifying the input file is faster than redirecting the same file as standard input.
/T[EMPORARY] [drive2:][path2]	Specifies the path of the directory to hold the sort's working storage, in case the data does not fit in main memory. The default is to use the system temporary directory.
/O[UTPUT] [drive3:][path3]filename3	Specifies the file where the sorted input is to be stored. If not specified, the data is written to the standard output. Specifying the output file is faster than redirecting standard output to the same file.

START

Starts a separate window to run a specified program or command.

START ["title"] [/Dpath] [/I] [/MIN] [/MAX] [/SEPARATE ¦ /SHARED]
    [/LOW ¦ /NORMAL ¦ /HIGH ¦ /REALTIME ¦ /ABOVENORMAL ¦ /BELOWNORMAL]
    [/WAIT] [/B] [command/program] [parameters]

"title"	Title to display in window title bar.
Path	Starting directory.
B	Start application without creating a new window. The application has ^C handling ignored. Unless the application enables ^C processing, ^Break is the only way to interrupt the application. The new environment will be the original environment passed to the cmd.exe and not the current environment.
MIN	Start window minimized
MAX	Start window maximized
SEPARATE	Start 16-bit Windows program in separate memory space
SHARED	Start 16-bit Windows program in shared memory space
LOW	Start application in the IDLE priority class
NORMAL	Start application in the NORMAL priority class
HIGH	Start application in the HIGH priority class
REALTIME	Start application in the REALTIME priority class
ABOVENORMAL	Start application in the ABOVENORMAL priority class
BELOWNORMAL	Start application in the BELOWNORMAL priority class
WAIT	Start application and wait for it to terminate command/program. If it is an internal cmd command or a batch file then the command processor is run with the /K switch to cmd.exe. This means that the window will remain after the command has been run.
	If it is not an internal cmd command or batch file then it is a program and will run as either a windowed application or a console application.
parameters	These are the parameters passed to the command/program

If Command Extensions are enabled, external command invocation through the command line or the START command changes as follows:

non-executable files may be invoked through their file association just by typing the name of the file as a command (e.g. WORD.DOC would launch the application associated with the .DOC file extension). See the ASSOC and FTYPE commands for how to create these associations from within a command script.

When executing an application that is a 32-bit GUI application, CMD.EXE does not wait for the application to terminate before returning to the command prompt. This new behavior does NOT occur if executing within a command script.

When executing a command line whose first token is the string "CMD" without an extension or path qualifier, then "CMD" is replaced with the value of the COMSPEC variable. This prevents picking up CMD.EXE from the current directory.

When executing a command line whose first token does NOT contain an extension, then CMD.EXE uses the value of the PATHEXT environment variable to determine which extensions to look for and in what order. The default value for the PATHEXT variable is:

.COM;.EXE;.BAT;.CMD

Notice the syntax is the same as the PATH variable, with semicolons separating the different elements.

When searching for an executable, if there is no match on any extension, then looks to see if the name matches a directory name. If it does, the START command launches the Explorer on that path. If done from the command line, it is the equivalent to doing a CD /D to that path.

SUBST
Associates a path with a drive letter.

SUBST [drive1: [drive2:]path]
SUBST drive1: /D

drive1:	Specifies a virtual drive to which you want to assign a path.
[drive2:]path	Specifies a physical drive and path you want to assign to a virtual drive.
/D	Deletes a substituted (virtual) drive.

Type SUBST with no parameters to display a list of current virtual drives.

TIME
Displays or sets the system time.

TIME [/T ¦ time]

Type TIME with no parameters to display the current time setting and a prompt for a new one. Press **Enter** to keep the same time.

If Command Extensions are enabled the TIME command supports the /T switch which tells the command to just output the current time, without prompting for a new time.

TITLE
Sets the window title for the command prompt window.

TITLE [string]

string   Specifies the title for the command prompt window.

TREE
Graphically displays the folder structure of a drive or path.

TREE [drive:][path] [/F] [/A]

/F	Display the names of the files in each folder.
/A	Use ASCII instead of extended characters.

TYPE
Displays the contents of a text file or files.

TYPE [drive:][path]filename

VER
Displays the Windows XP version.

VER

VERIFY
Tells cmd.exe whether to verify that your files are written correctly to a disk.

VERIFY [ON ¦ OFF]

Type VERIFY without a parameter to display the current VERIFY setting.

VOL
Displays the disk volume label and serial number, if they exist.

VOL [drive:]

XCOPY
Copies files and directory trees.

XCOPY source [destination] [/A ¦ /M] [/D[:date]] [/P] [/S [/E]] [/V] [/W] [/C] [/I] [/Q] [/F] [/L]
        [/G] [/H] [/R] [/T] [/U] [/K] [/N] [/O] [/X] [/Y] [/-Y] [/Z]
        [/EXCLUDE:file1[+file2][+file3]...]

source	Specifies the file(s) to copy.
Destination	Specifies the location and/or name of new files.
/A	Copies only files with the archive attribute set, doesn't change the attribute.

/M	Copies only files with the archive attribute set, turns off the archive attribute.
/D:m-d-y	Copies files changed on or after the specified date. If no date is given, copies only those files whose source time is newer than the destination time.
/EXCLUDE:file1[+file2][+file3]...	Specifies a list of files containing strings. Each string should be in a separate line in the files. When any of the strings match any part of the absolute path of the file to be copied, that file will be excluded from being copied. For example, specifying a string like \obj\ or .obj will exclude all files underneath the directory obj or all files with the.obj extension respectively.
/P	Prompts you before creating each destination file.
/S	Copies directories and subdirectories except empty ones.
/E	Copies directories and subdirectories, including empty ones. Same as /S /E. May be used to modify /T.
/V	Verifies each new file.
/W	Prompts you to press a key before copying.
/C	Continues copying even if errors occur.
/I	If destination does not exist and copying more than one file, assumes that destination must be a directory.
/Q	Does not display file names while copying.
/F	Displays full source and destination file names while copying.
/L	Displays files that would be copied.
/G	Allows the copying of encrypted files to destination that does not support encryption.
/H	Copies hidden and system files also.
/R	Overwrites read-only files.
/T	Creates directory structure, but does not copy files. Does not include empty directories or subdirectories. /T /E includes empty directories and subdirectories.
/U	Copies only files that already exist in destination.
/K	Copies attributes. Normal Xcopy will reset read-only attributes.
/N	Copies using the generated short names.
/O	Copies file ownership and ACL information.
/X	Copies file audit settings (implies /O).
/Y	Suppresses prompting to confirm you want to overwrite an existing destination file.
/-Y	Causes prompting to confirm you want to overwrite an existing destination file.
/Z	Copies networked files in restartable mode.

The switch /Y may be preset in the COPYCMD environment variable. This may be overridden with /-Y on the command line.

absolute path The direct route from the root directory through the hierarchical structure of a directory tree to the subdirectory of interest.

active desktop object A piece of Web content placed on the desktop that needs to be updated on a regular basis, such as stock market prices or a weather map.

active window The window that is currently in use when multiple windows are open.

ActiveX A set of technologies that enables software components to interact with one another in a networked environment, regardless of the language in which the components were created. ActiveX is used primarily to develop interactive content for the World Wide Web, although it can be used in other kinds of programs.

adapter card A printed circuit board that is installed in a computer to allow the installation and control of some type of device, such as a monitor.

add-on An accessory or utility program designed to work with, extend, and increase the capabilities of an original product.

allocation unit See *cluster*.

alphanumeric keys The keys on a keyboard that are letters (A–Z), numbers (0–9), and other characters such as punctuation marks.

ANSI An acronym for American National Standards Institute. A coding scheme used for transmitting data between a computer and peripherals. Each character has a numerical equivalent in ANSI.

app See *application package*.

application package A computer program that is user-oriented and is usually for a specific job, such as word processing. Application packages are also called *packages, off-the-shelf software, canned software,* or *apps*.

application program See *application package*.

application software See *application package*.

application window The window of the application that is currently open and on the desktop. An application window may also contain a document window.

archival backup   A backup procedure in which all the files on a hard disk are backed up by being copied to floppy disks or some other backup medium.

archival data   Information that is stored in archive files.

archive attribute   See *archive bit*.

archive bit   A file attribute that gives the backup history of a file (whether or not a file has been backed up). Archiving to save a file usually refers to long-term storage.

archiving a file   Removing a file from a hard disk and storing it on another medium for historical purposes.

arithmetic/logic unit   The circuitry that a computer uses for mathematical and logical functions and is an integral part of a microprocessor chip.

ASCII   An acronym for American Standard Code for Information Interchange. A coding scheme used for transmitting data between a computer and peripherals. Each character has a numerical equivalent in ASCII.

ASCII editor   A program that is similar to a word-processing program but is unable to perform any special editing. No embedded codes are inserted into documents. ASCII editors can only edit ASCII text files, also called text files or unformatted text files. ASCII editors are also called *text editors*.

asynchronous   Not synchronized; not happening at regular time intervals.

asynchronous communication   A form of data transmission that uses only two wires for communication between computers (generally for communicating via modems). Data is transmitted by the sending of one character at a time with variable time intervals between characters and a start bit and a stop bit to mark the beginning and end of the data.

attachment   An external document included as part of an email message.

AutoPlay   The feature that causes an audio CD placed in a CD-ROM drive to play automatically. To bypass this, hold the `Shift` key down when inserting the disc.

AutoRun   The feature that causes a program CD placed in a CD-ROM drive to execute automatically. To bypass this, hold the `Shift` key down when inserting the disc.

background color   The color that is in the background in Paint. It is not the current drawing color.

background printing   Printing a document in the background while another program is being worked on in the foreground.

background program   In Windows XP, which has multitasking capabilities, background program refers to a program that is being executed in the background at the same time that the user is working with another program in the foreground. For example, printing one document (background program) while at the same time editing another document (foreground program).

backup   The process in which the user makes a copy of an original file or files for safe-keeping.

bandwidth   The data transfer capacity of a digital communications system.

batch file   A text file of DOS commands. When its name is keyed in at the DOS system level, the commands in the batch file are executed sequentially.

batch processing   A manner of running programs without interruption. Programs to be executed are collected and placed into prioritized batches, and then the programs are processed one after another without user interaction or intervention.

baud rate   Measure of how fast a modem can transmit data. Named after the French telegrapher and engineer J.M.E. Baudot.

beta test   A formal process of pretesting hardware and software that is still under development with selected "typical" users to see whether any operational or utilization errors (bugs) still exist in the program before the product is released to the general public.

binary value   A binary value is a variable-length set of hexadecimal digits.

BIOS   An acronym for basic input/output system. A program that controls input/output devices.

BIOS bootstrap   A process that occurs before booting. The program that controls this process is in the BIOS chip and the CMOS setup of the computer. A POST (power-on self test) is performed, wherein the computer checks its physical health. Plug-and-play devices are identified and configured, and a bootable partition is executed.

bit   The smallest unit of information, expressed in binary numbers 0 and 1, that a computer can measure. Eight bits make a byte.

bitmap font   A font that a printer creates dot by dot. When displayed on the monitor, bitmap fonts are created pixel by pixel.

bootable disk   A disk containing the operating system files.

booting the system   The process of powering on a computer. When first turned on (a cold boot) or reset (a warm boot), a computer executes the software that loads and starts the computer's operating system. The computer can be said to pull itself up by its own bootstrap.

boot record   If a disk is a system disk, the boot record contains the bootstrap routine used for loading. Otherwise, the disk will present a message that the disk is a nonsystem disk. Every disk has a boot record. The boot record also contains such information as the type of media, the number of tracks and sectors, and so forth.

boot sector   The first sector on every logical drive.

boot sector virus   A virus that replaces a disk's original boot sector with its own and then loads itself into memory. Once in memory, it infects other disks.

bootstrap   The process a computer uses to get itself ready for loading the operating system into memory. It pulls itself up by its bootstraps.

browser   An application software package that allows you to easily explore the Internet and the World Wide Web.

buffer   A temporary holding area for data in memory.

bug   An error in software that causes the program to malfunction or to produce incorrect results.

built-in font   A resident font that comes with a printer.

bulletin board service (BBS)   A service that users link to using their modems. Some BBSs allow users to read and post messages, download program fixes or other programs, and much more.

bundled   Describes programs included with a larger program to make the larger program more attractive or functional. It is also used to describe a purchase of hardware that includes all devices as well as installed software.

bus   A set of hardware lines (wires) that are used for data transfer among the elements of a computer system.

bus topology   A topology (network design) for a local area network in which all computers or peripherals (nodes) are connected to a main communications line (bus). On a bus network, each node monitors activity on the line.

byte   A unit of measurement that represents one character (a letter, number, or punctuation mark). A byte is comprised of eight bits. Computer storage and memory are measured in bytes.

cache   A place in memory where data can be stored for quick access.

cache memory   A place in memory where data can be stored for quick access.

caching   A process where Windows sets up a reserved area in RAM where it can quickly read and write frequently used data without having to read from or write to the disk.

card   A short name for an adapter card.

cascaded   Windows layered on top of one another.

cascading menu   A menu that opens another menu. A secondary menu will open as a result of a command issued on the first or primary menu. A right-pointing arrow next to the primary menu indicates that a cascade menu is available. Also called a hierarchical menu.

case sensitive   Describes a program that distinguishes between upper- and lowercase characters.

CD-ROM   An acronym for compact disc–read-only memory. It usually refers to a disc that plays in a CD-ROM device.

central processing unit (CPU)   The central processing unit (CPU) is the brain of the computer. It carries out the instructions or commands given to it by a program.

chain   When referring to the file allocation table, a pointer that links clusters together.

channel   A Web site that has been expressly designed for push technology so that content can be delivered to your computer system.

character set   A grouping of alphabetic, numeric, and other characters that have some relationship in common. A font file has character definitions.

character string   A set of letters, symbols, and control characters that are treated as a unit.

checkbox   A box that is clicked to either set or unset a feature.

child directory   An analogous title given to offshoots (subdirectories) of any root or subdirectory.

child menu   A menu in a hierarchical menu structure that is under the parent menu above it. Each subsequent child menu becomes a parent to the next menu in the hierarchy.

child window   A window that belongs to a parent window. A child window can have only one parent but one or more child windows of its own..

clicking   Pressing and releasing the left mouse button once.

client   In networking, a client is a computer that accesses the shared network resources provided by the server.

client application   An application program that is receiving an object from the server application.

clip art   A collection of proprietary or public-domain photographs, maps, drawings, and other graphics that can be "clipped" from the collection and incorporated into other documents.

Clipboard   A special memory area used by Windows that stores a copy of the last information that was copied or cut. A paste operation passes data from the Clipboard to the current program. The Clipboard allows information to be transferred from one program to another, provided the second program can read data generated by the first.

Close button   A button that shuts down a window and closes an application package or dialog box.

cluster   The smallest unit of disk space that DOS or Windows 95/98 can write to or read from. It is comprised of one or more sectors. A cluster can also be called an *allocation unit*.

cluster overhang   Since clusters are made up of one or more 512-byte sectors and Windows reads to or writes from only one cluster at a time, a file will occupy more space than it needs for its data, causing cluster overhang.

CMD.EXE   That part of the operating system that the user actually communicates and interacts with. It processes and interprets what has been keyed in. It is also known as the command processor or the command interpreter.

CMOS   An acronym for complementary metal-oxide semiconductor. CMOS, maintained by a battery pack, is memory that is used to store parameter values, such as the size and type of the hard disk and the number and type of floppy drives, the keyboard, and display type, that are used to boot PCs.

coaxial cable   A type of cable used in connecting network components.

Color box   In Paint, the box that displays the foreground and background colors you may use in your drawing.

combo box   A combination text box and list box.

command   An instruction that is a program that the user keys in at the command line prompt. This instruction executes the selected program.

command button   A button that, when selected by the user, performs the desired action.

command interpreter   See *command processor*.

command processor   That portion of an operating system that interprets what the user keys in.

command syntax   The vocabulary, order, and punctuation necessary to execute a command properly.

communication protocol   A set of communication rules that enable computers to exchange information.

compact disc–read-only memory   See *CD-ROM*.

compound document   A document that contains information, data, or other objects created from more than one application program.

compressed file   A file written (utilizing a file compression utility) to a special disk format that minimizes the storage space needed.

computer virus   A computer program designed as a prank or sabotage that can replicate itself by attaching to other programs and spreading unwanted and often damaging operations. A virus can be spread to other computers by floppy disk and/or through electronic bulletin boards.

conditional processing   A comparison of two items that yields a true or false value. Once the value is determined, a program can be directed to take some action based on the results of the test.

configuration information   Information about your system such as the hardware applications and user preferences.

context menu   A menu that opens with a right-click of the mouse. It is also referred to as a pop-up menu or a shortcut menu.

contiguous   Describes elements that are next to each other. Contiguous files are those files that are written to adjacent clusters on a disk.

control   Provides a way the user can interact (provide input) with available choices. Usually a control is a way to initiate an action, display information, or set the values that you are interested in. Example of controls include command buttons, options buttons, drop-down list boxes, and text boxes.

Control key   The key labeled `Ctrl` on the keyboard that, when held down with another key, causes the other key to have another meaning.

controller   A board that goes into the computer and is needed to operate a peripheral device.

control menu   Has an icon, located in the upper-left corner of a window, that can be opened to provide commands to manipulate the window. These commands are usually keyboard oriented rather than mouse oriented. The icon is referred to as the control-menu icon.

control-menu icon   In Windows, the icon that can be clicked to provide a drop-down menu with additional commands. It is also called the control-menu box.

conventional memory   The first 640KB of memory, where programs and data are located while the user is working.

cookie   On the World Wide Web, a block of data that a Web server stores on your computer system. When you return to the same Web site, your browser sends a copy of the cookie back to the server. Cookies are used to identify users, instruct the server to send a customized version of the requested Web page, or submit account information for the user.

CPU   See *central processing unit (CPU)*.

cross-linked files   Two files that claim the same sectors in the file allocation table (FAT).

current directory   The default directory.

cursor   The location where the user can key in information.

cyberspace   A term used when referring to the Internet; a virtual place where computers can connect and individuals or organizations can communicate.

cylinder   The vertical measurement of two or more disk platters that have the track aligned. It is used when referring to hard disks.

data   Information, in the widest possible sense. Usually it refers to the numbers and text used by a computer to do the work requested by the user.

database   A collection of related information (data) stored on a computer, organized, and structured so that the information can be easily manipulated.

database management program   An application program that allows for manipulation of information in a database.

data bits   A group of bits used to represent a single character for transmission over a modem. A start bit and stop bit must be used in transmitting a group of data.

data file   A file that is usually composed of related data created by the user with an application program. They are organized in a specific manner and usually can be used only by this program.

debugging   Finding and correcting problems in a program. Debug is also a program usable at the command line interface.

dedicated server   A computer in a server-based network that is devoted to providing network resources.

default   What the computer system or computer program "falls back to" if no other specific instructions are given.

default drive   The disk drive that the OS looks on to locate commands or files if no other instructions are given.

default folder   The folder data will be read to or written from unless you change it.

default subdirectory   The subdirectory that the computer "falls back to" when no other specific instructions are given.

defragger   A means to optimize performance on a disk. Running the Disk Defragmenter program rearranges the storage of files on a disk so that they are contiguous.

delimiter   A special character that is used to separate information so that an operating system such as Windows XP can recognize where one part of a parameter ends and the next one begins.

designated drive   See *default drive*.

desktop   The on-screen work area that emulates the top of a desk.

destination file   The desired file that data is to be sent to.

device   A piece of computer equipment, such as a disk drive or a printer, that performs a specific job.

device driver   Software necessary for the use of a hardware device. The program controls the specific peripheral device.

device icon   A small graphic that represents a device such as a printer or a disk drive.

device name   A reserved name that the operating system assigns to a device, such as PRN for printer.

dialog box   In a graphical user interface, a box that either conveys information to or requests information from the user.

differential backup   A differential backup backs up all the selected files that have changed since the last time an All selected files backup was used.

directional keys   Keys used to move the cursor in various directions.

directory   The location or container where documents, program files, devices, and other folders are stored on your disk. The terms *folders* and *directories* are synonymous.

directory tree   The structure of the current disk drive.

disk   A magnetically coated disk that allows permanent storage of computer data.

disk buffer   Acts as the go-between for a disk and RAM.

disk cache   An area in memory where Windows XP looks for information prior to reading from or writing to the disk for the purpose of optimizing performance.

disk compression program   A means to increase disk space by fooling the operating system into thinking that there is more space on the disk.

disk drive   A device that rotates a disk so that the computer can read information from and write information to the disk.

disk file   A file that is stored on a disk.

disk optimization program   A means to optimize performance on a disk. Usually the user runs the Disk Defragmenter program that rearranges the storage of files on a disk so that they are contiguous. It is also called a *disk defragger*.

docucentric   Describes a paradigm or model that designs a computer system or program around the fact that what is most important to the user is the data (the document), not the program that created it.

document   A self-contained piece of work created with an application program and, if saved on a disk, given a unique file name by which it can be retrieved.

documentation   Written instructions that inform the user how to use hardware and/or software.

document file   A data file whose information was created in an application file and saved to a disk.

documenting   Writing the purpose of and instructions for a computer program.

document window   A window that belongs to a program window and is always contained within a program window.

domain name   An alphabetic alias to the IP address. Some examples of domain names are saddleback.cc.ca.us and daedal.net.

Domain Name System (DNS)   The system by which domain names are translated into their IP numeric addresses.

DOS   An acronym for disk operating system, the character-based operating system commonly used on microcomputers. It is also a shorthand way of referring to the command line interface.

dot   A subdirectory marker; a shorthand name; the . for the specific subdirectory name.

dot-matrix printer   A printer that produces text characters and graphics by creating them with a series of closely spaced dots. It uses a print head, platen, and ribbon to form the characters.

dot pitch   In printers, the distance between dots in a dot matrix. In video displays, a measure of image clarity. In a video display, the dot pitch is the vertical distance, expressed in millimeters, between like-colored pixels. A smaller dot pitch generally means a sharper image.

double-clicking   Pressing and releasing the left mouse button twice in rapid succession.

downloading   Receiving a file from a remote computer while connected by a modem, another outside connection, or a network.

downward compatible   Describes software/hardware that can be used on older computer systems.

dragging   Placing the pointer over an object, holding down the left mouse button, and moving the object to another location.

dragging and dropping   Moving or manipulating an object or document across the desktop and dropping it in another location.

drawing area   In Paint, the area where you create your drawing.

drive letter   A letter of the alphabet that identifies a specific disk drive.

driver   A piece of software that tells a piece of hardware how to work.

drop-down list box   A box that contains a default selection. However, if the user clicks on the down arrow, a list box drops down and displays further choices.

drop-down menu   A menu that presents choices that drop down from the menu bar when requested and remain open on the screen until the user chooses a menu item or closes the menu.

DVD   An enhancement to CD-ROM technology. It provides the next generation of optical disc storage technology. It encompasses audio, video, and computer data. DVD is not an acronym but a trademark.

dynamic data exchange (DDE)   A set of standards that supports data exchange among application programs.

dynamic link library (DLL)   A feature that allows executable routines to be stored separately as files with DLL extensions and to be loaded only when needed by a program. A

DLL file does not consume any memory until it is used. Since a DLL file is separate, a programmer can make corrections or improvements to only that module without affecting other programs or other DLLs. Also, the same dynamic link library can be used with other programs.

dynamic RAM (DRAM)   Memory chips that hold data for a short time. DRAM is less expensive than SRAM and thus, most memory is DRAM. See also *static RAM*.

ellipsis   Three dots that can appear after a menu item or on a command button. If you choose the item, a dialog box will open.

email   Short for electronic mail. Email is a note or message that is sent between different computers that use telecommunications services or are on a network.

Emergency Repair Disk   A bootable disk that has critical system files on it.

end-of-file (EOF) marker   A symbol that alerts the operating system when a file has no more data.

enhancement   Increases the capabilities of a computer by adding or updating hardware or software.

event   An action performed by you or by your program that your computer can notify you of. Usually the notification is a sound, such as a beep if you press an incorrect key.

executable   Refers to programs that place instructions in memory. The instructions are followed by the computer.

executing a program   A process where instructions are placed in memory and then followed by the computer.

expansion slot   An empty slot or space inside a system unit that can be used for adding new boards or devices to expand the computer's capabilities.

exporting   Using an existing file or data in the file and sending it to another file.

extension   See *file extension*.

external command   A program that resides on a disk and must be read into RAM before it can be used.

external storage media   Storage devices that are outside the computer system. Floppy, CD-ROM, and removable drives are the most common external storage media.

FAT   See *file allocation table (FAT)*.

FAT file system   The system originally used by MS-DOS to organize and manage files. The FAT (file allocation table) is a data structure is created on a disk when the disk is formatted. When a file is stored on a formatted disk, the operating system places information about the stored file in the FAT so that the operating system (DOS) can retrieve the file later.

file   A program or a collection of related information stored on a disk.

file allocation table (FAT)   A map of the disk that keeps track of all the clusters on a disk. It is used in conjunction with the directory table.

file attributes   Attributes are stored as part of a file's directory entry and describe and give other information about the file.

file extension   The last portion of a file name following the last period. Usually file extensions describe the type of data in the file. See also *file type*.

file format   A special format used to construct a file so an application program can read the data. It consists of special codes that only the creating application program understands.

file infector virus   Adds programming instructions to files that run programs. The virus then becomes active when you run the program.

file name   A label used to identify a file. When most users refer to the file name, they are referring to the file specification.

file server   On a network, a file storage device that stores files. On a large network, a file server is a sophisticated device that no only stores files but also manages them and maintains order as network users request files and make changes to the files.

file specification   The complete name of a file, including the file name and the file extension (file type).

file type   The last portion of a file name following the last period in a file name. Usually file types describe the type of data in the file. See also *file extension*.

firewall   A security system intended to protect an organization's network against external threats, such as hackers. A firewall prevents computers in the organization's network from communicating directly with computers external to the network and vice versa.

fixed disk   See *hard disk*.

fixed parameter   A parameter whose values are specific and limited.

flag   A marker of some type used to process information. File attributes are commonly called flags because they indicate a particular condition of a file.

floating   Describes a toolbar or taskbar that can be positioned anywhere on the screen and does not have to be anchored to a window.

floppy disk   A magnetically coated disk that allows permanent storage of data.

floppy disk drive   See *disk drive*.

folder   The location or container where documents, program files, devices, and other folders are stored on your disk. The terms *folders* and *directories* are synonymous.

folder icon   The graphic representation of a folder that will open when you double-click it.

Folders pane   The left pane of the Explorer window.

font   A typeface (set of characters) that consists of several parts, such as the type size and weight (i.e., bold or italic).

footer   One or more identifying lines printed at the bottom of a page.

foreground   Describes the application or window that the user is currently working on.

foreground application   An application or window that the user is currently working on. It is also referred to as the foreground window or active window.

foreground window   An application or window in which the user is currently working. It is also referred to as the foreground window or active window.

formatting   Preparing a disk for use. It can also refer to the way data looks in a document.

form feed   An operation that advances the hard copy on the printer to the next page.

fragmented   See *fragmented disk*.

fragmented disk   A disk that has many noncontiguous files on it.

fragmented file   A file that is written to a disk in noncontiguous clusters. See also *noncontiguous*.

freeware   A computer program given away free of charge and often made available on the Internet or through newsgroups.

FTP (File Transfer Protocol)   A protocol that allows files to be transferred to and from a node running FTP services.

full backup   A backup procedure that backs up every file on a disk, regardless of whether a file has changed or not.

full system backup   A backup procedure that backs up every file on a disk, including special system files, regardless of whether a file has changed or not.

function keys   Programmable keys on a keyboard. [F1] and [F2] are examples of function keys. Function keys are program dependent.

gig   A colloquial term for gigabyte.

gigabyte (GB)   A unit of measurement equal to approximately one billion bytes.

glide pad   An input device that is a small, smooth object on which you move your finger to control the action of the pointer.

global file specifications   The symbols * and ?, also called wildcards, that are used to represent a single character (?) or a group of characters (*) in a file name.

graphic file   Pictures and drawings that can be produced on the screen or printer and are saved in a file.

grid of cells   Two sets of lines or linear elements at right angles to each other. A spreadsheet is a grid of rows and columns; a graphics screen is a grid of horizontal and vertical lines of pixels. In optical character recognition, a grid is used for measuring or specifying characters.

GUI (graphical user interface)   A display format that allows the user to interact with the computer by using pictorial representations and menu choices to manage the computer resources and work with application programs.

hard copy   A printed paper copy of information that is created when using the computer. It can also be referred to as a printout.

hard disk   A disk that is permanently installed in a computer system and has a larger capacity to store files than a floppy disk. Hard disks are measured in megabytes or gigabytes.

hard disk drive   See *hard disk*.

hard return   Generated when [Enter] is pressed. The system will not move a hard return, but will move a soft return.

hardware   Physical computer components.

hardware interrupt   A request for service or a signal from peripherals to the CPU for attention so the device may be serviced.

head crash   A hard disk failure in which a read/write head, normally supported on a cushion of air, comes into contact with the platter, damaging the magnetic coating in which data is recorded.

header   In word processing or printing, text that is to appear at the top of pages.

head slot   Exposes the disk surface to the read/write heads via an opening in the jacket of a floppy disk.

hexadecimal   A numbering system that uses a base of 16 consisting of the digits 0–9 and the letters A–F.

hidden file   A file that is not displayed in Explorer or My Computer or when the DIR command is used in the DOS window.

hierarchical menu   A menu that opens another menu. A secondary menu will open as a result of a command issued on the first or primary menu. A right-pointing arrow next to the primary menu indicates that a cascade menu is available. It is also called a cascading menu.

hierarchical structure   The logical grouping of files and programs based on pathways between root directories and their subsequent directories. It is also called a tree-structured directory.

hierarchy   A group of things that are ordered by rank. In a disk's structure, it is a dependent relationship where one folder is dependent on the folder above it. Every disk begins with the root directory (folder), with subsequent folders branching from the root.

high-capacity disk   See *high-density disk.*

high-density disk   A floppy disk that can store up to 1.2 MB on a 5¼-inch disk or 1.44 MB on a 3½-inch disk.

high-level formatting   Also known as logical formatting. The process that Windows uses to structure a disk so that files can be stored or retrieved.

highlighting   The process of selecting an object, text, or an icon. Objects must be selected before they can be acted upon. Highlighting is indicated by reverse video.

home page   On a server, the first screen that appears when you select a Web site.

housekeeping task   Any number of routines to keep the environment where programs run in good working order.

hovering   A mouse technique that highlights objects with an underline as you drag your mouse, which indicates that you have selected an object.

HTML (Hypertext Markup Language)   The programming language with which Web documents are created.

HTTP (Hypertext Transfer Protocol)   A common protocol used to access sites on the Internet.

hypertext   A means to easily jump from one logically related topic to the next.

IAP   Internet access provider.

icon   A symbol that represents a more simple access to a program file, a data file, or a task.

impact printer   A type of printer that transfers images onto paper through a mechanism that strikes a ribbon and transfers the images to paper. It is similar to a typewriter.

importing   Bringing information from one program into another. You can import an entire file or part of a file.

incremental backup   A backup process that only backs up files that have changed since the last full or incremental backup.

information superhighway   Refers to the Internet. A worldwide network of networks that provides the ability to gather information, do research, explore ideas, purchase items, send email, and chat with people around the world. See also *cyberspace.*

initialization files   Files that initialize a program or process. In earlier versions of Windows, the operating system and most application programs stored information about the users, environmental parameters, and necessary drivers in .INI files. The .INI extension is derived from initialization files.

initializing   Getting a medium (a disk or a file) ready for use.

initializing a disk   Getting a disk ready for use. It is another term for formatting a disk.

inkjet printer   A nonimpact printer that prints by spraying a matrix of dots onto the paper.

input   Refers to data or information entered into the computer.

input device   A means to get information into RAM by communicating with the computer. Typical input devices include the keyboard and the mouse.

input/output   The process of data and program instructions going into and out of the CPU (central processing unit). It is also referred to as I/O.

insert   A mode that allows the user to enter data in which new text is inserted at the cursor, pushing all text that follows to the right.

install   Copying files (programs) from a CD or floppy disk onto the hard disk.

integrated circuit   An electronic device that combines thousands of transistors on a small wafer of silicon (chip). Such devices are the building blocks of computers.

integrated pointing device   An input device that is an eraser-like object on the keyboard that you can manipulate to control the cursor.

interactive   Describes the ability to update data within the computer system instantaneously.

interactive processing   Sometimes called online or real-time mode, interactive means interacting directly with the computer.

interface   Hardware and/or software needed to connect computer components. Also used as a synonym for interacting with a computer.

interface card   The circuit board that is needed to connect computer components.

interlaced   A technique used in some monitors in which the electron beam refreshes (updates) all odd-numbered scan lines in one vertical sweep of the screen and all even-numbered scan lines in the next sweep. The picture on these monitors tends to flicker. See also *noninterlaced*.

Internet   A network of networks that connects computer users around the world.

intranet   A network designed for information processing within a company or organization.

I/O   See *input/output*.

IP address   A unique numeric address that identifies a computer on the Internet.

ISP (Internet service provider)   A company or organization that provides a gateway or connection to the Internet, usually for a fee. It is also called an access provider or a service provider.

keyboard   A major device used for entering data into a computer consisting of a typewriter-like collection of labeled keys.

kilobyte (KB)   A unit of measurement equal to 1,024 bytes.

LAN   See *local area network (LAN)*.

landscape   A printing orientation that prints horizontally (sideways) on the paper.

laser printer   A high-resolution nonimpact printer that provides letter-quality output of text and graphics. Laser printers are based on a technology in which characters are formed by a laser and made visible by the same technology used by photocopy machines.

legacy hardware   Hardware that is not plug-and-play compatible.

legacy software   Older versions of software that were designed to run on earlier versions of operating system, such as DOS.

light pen   A pointing device (connected to the computer by a cable and resembling a pen) that is used to provide input to the computer by writing, sketching, or selecting commands on a special monitor designed to respond to the light pen.

line feed   An operation that advances the hard copy to the next line of text whether or not the line is full.

list box   A box that presents the user with a list of options. It is used in menus and dialog boxes.

loading   Placing information (data or programs) from storage into memory.

local area network (LAN)   A network of computer equipment located in one room or building and connected by a communication link that enables any device to interact with any other in the network, making it possible for users to exchange information, share peripherals, and draw on common resources.

local bus   See *bus*.

locally   In a networked environment, this means that you are not using the network, but only your own local computer.

local printer   A printer physically attached to your computer.

logical device   A device named by the logic of a software system regardless of its physical relationship to the system.

logical disk drive   A drive named by the logic of the software (operating) system. It is an "imaginary drive" that acts exactly like a real disk drive.

logical formatting   See *high-level formatting*.

logical view   A view of items that are represented by icons rather then by their physical presence.

logo   A distinctive signature or trademark that usually functions as a graphical representation of a company.

long file name (LFN)   The term used to indicate that file names are no longer limited to the 8.3 character file names. In Windows 95 and in Windows 98, file names cannot exceed 255 characters.

loop back   The address 127.0.0.1, which is used to send data to your own computer without using the network card. The data "loops back."

lost cluster   Clusters that have no directory entry in the directory table and do not belong to any file. They are debris that results from incomplete data, and they should be cleaned up periodically with Check Disk.

low-level formatting   Also known as physical formatting. The process of numbering the tracks and sectors of a disk sequentially so that each can be identified. On a hard disk, this process is done by the manufacturer of the hard disk.

macro   A short key code command which stands for a sequence of saved instructions that when retrieved will execute the commands to accomplish a given task.

mandatory parameter   A parameter that must be used with a command.

mapped drive   A network drive or folder (one that has been shared) that you may assign a local drive letter.

master boot record (MBR)   Used before booting. It determines the location of the bootable partition of the hard disk and gives control over to it.

Maximize button   A button that makes the current window fill the entire screen.

meg   A colloquial term for *megabyte*.

megabyte (MB)   A unit of measurement that is roughly equal to one million bytes.

megahertz (MHz)   A unit of measurement used to compare clock speeds of computers.

memory   The temporary workspace of the computer where data and programs are kept while they are worked on. It is also referred to as *RAM (random access memory)*. Information in RAM is lost when the computer is turned off, which is why memory is considered volatile.

menu A list of choices (selections) displayed on the screen from which the user chooses a course of action.

menu bar A rectangular bar, usually in a program, in which the names of the available, additional menus are shown. The user chooses one of these menus and a list of choices for that menu is shown.

message box A type of dialog box that informs you of a condition.

microcomputer A personal computer that is usually used by one person. It is also referred to as a desktop computer or a stand-alone computer.

microfloppy disk A 3½-inch floppy disk encased in a hard plastic shell.

MIDI (Musical Instrument Digital Interface) A way to get input from your musical instruments into a computer and then modify and store the sounds you recorded.

minicomputer A mid-level computer larger than a microcomputer but smaller than a mainframe computer. It is usually used to meet the needs of a small company or department.

minifloppy disk A 5¼-inch floppy disk.

Minimize button A button that reduces the current window to a button on the taskbar.

modem Short for modulator/demodulator. A device that provides communication capability between computers using phone lines. Modems are typically used to access online services, such as AOL (America Online) or an ISP.

monitor A device similar to a television screen that displays the input and output of the computer. It is also called a *screen, display screen, cathode-ray terminal,* or *VDT (video display terminal).*

monospaced typeface A typeface that gives all characters in the set the same width.

motherboard The main computer board that holds the memory and CPU, as well as slots for adapter cards. The power supply plugs directly into the motherboard. It is also called a *system board.*

mouse A small, hand-held device that is equipped with one or more control buttons and is housed in a palm-sized case. It is used to control cursor movement.

mouse pointer An onscreen pointer that is controlled by the movement of the mouse.

mouse trail A "ghost" of the mouse pointer that follows the movement of the mouse around the screen. It is used to improve the visibility of the cursor.

MS-DOS An abbreviation for *Microsoft disk operating system,* a character-based operating system for computers that use the 8086 or above microprocessor.

multitasking Describes the ability to work on more than one task or application program at a time.

naming convention A logical naming scheme for files and folders for facilitating the saving and retrieving of files and folders.

Net A colloquial name for the *Internet.*

netiquette A combination of the words *network* and *etiquette.* It is a set of principles of courtesy that should be observed when sending electronic messages such as email and newsgroup postings.

network A group of computers connected by a communication facility called a server, which permits the sharing and transmission of data. In addition, it allows the sharing of resources, such as a hard drive or a printer.

network administrator The person who decides how the hardware and software will be used on a network.

network interface card (NIC)   An expansion card used to connect a computer to a local area network.

network operating system (NOS)   An operating system installed on a server in a local area network that coordinates the activities of providing services to the computers and other devices attached to the network.

NIC   See *network interface card.*

nonbootable disk   A disk that does not contain the operating system files. The computer cannot boot from it.

noncontiguous   Describes files that are written to a disk in nonadjacent clusters or clusters that are not next to one another.

nonimpact printer   A type of printer that transfers images onto paper by means of ink-jet sprayers, melting ink, or lasers.

noninterlaced   A display method on monitors in which the electron beam scans each line of the screen once during each refresh cycle. Monitors that are noninterlaced generally have clearer images and do not flicker. See also *interlaced.*

NOS   See *network operating system.*

null value   A test for nothing (no data).

numeric keypad   A separate set of keys next to the main keyboard that contains the digits 0 through 9. It also includes an alternate set of commands that can be toggled such as PgUp and the arrow keys. These functions are program dependent.

object   Most items in Windows are considered objects. Objects can be opened, have properties, and be manipulated. Objects can also have settings and parameters.

octet   Refers to one of the four sections of the dotted-decimal notation address.

offline   Describes a printer that may be attached to the computer but is not activated and ready to print. It also refers to not being connected to a network or the Internet.

online   Describes a printer that is not only attached to the computer but also activated and ready for operation. When referring to communication, it refers to being attached to another computer, a network, or the Internet.

online help   On-screen assistance consisting of advice or instructions on utilizing the program's features. It can be accessed without interrupting the work in progress.

open scroll area   An area on a scroll bar to the right or left of the scroll box that will move you in large increments through a document.

operating system (OS)   A master control program or set of programs that manages the operation of all the parts of a computer. An operating system, known as *system software,* is loaded into memory when the computer is booted. It must be loaded prior to any application software.

optional parameter   A parameter that may be used with a command but is not mandatory.

option button   Part of a list of choices presented to the user. Only one option can be selected at a time. Option buttons provide mutually exclusive choices.

overtype   See *typeover.*

overwrite mode   The mode in which newly typed characters replace existing characters to the right of the cursor.

overwriting   Replacing data by writing over old data with new data. Usually when you copy a file from one location to another, the file that is copied overwrites the file that was there.

packet   A unit of information transferred between computers via a network or a modem.

pane   A division in a window.

parallel   In data transmission, it refers to sending one byte (eight bits) at a time.

parallel port   An input/output connector for parallel interface devices.

parameter   A qualifier or modifier that can be added to a command and will specify the action to be taken.

parent directory   The subdirectory above the current subdirectory. The parent directory is always one step closer to the root than the child.

parent menu   A menu in a hierarchical menu structure that is at the top of the menu system. A parent menu may have a child menu; a child menu may become a parent and have child windows of its own.

parent window   A window that is the owner of any objects in it. If there is a folder in the window, it is a child to that parent. A child window can have only one parent, but it can have one or more child windows of its own.

parity   Parity bit is a simple method used to check for transmission errors. An extra bit is added to be sure that there is always either an even or an odd number of bits.

partitioning   Physically dividing a section of the hard disk from other sections of the disk and then having the operating system treat that section as if it were a separate unit.

password   A unique set of text or numbers that identifies the user. Passwords are used when logging onto networks and when Windows 98 has user profiles set up.

path   Tells Windows where to look for programs and files on a disk that has more than one directory.

path name   Information that tells the operating system where to look for program files on a disk that has more than one folder (directory).

peer-to-peer network   A network that has no dedicated servers or a hierarchy among the computers. All the computers are equal, and therefore peers. Each computer can function as either client or server.

pel   See *pixel*.

peripheral device   Any device, such as a keyboard, monitor, or printer, that is connected to and controlled by the CPU.

physical formatting   See *low-level formatting*.

physical memory   The actual memory chips in a computer.

physical view   A view of folders that shows the hierarchy of a file system, indicating drives and where they are located.

pixel   The smallest element on the display screen grid that can be stored or displayed. Pixels are used to create or print letters, numbers, or graphics. The more pixels, the higher the resolution.

Plug and Play   A feature of Windows that automatically detects and configures a new hardware device when it is added to a computer system.

point   Fonts are measured in points. The more points, the larger the font. A point is $1/_{72}$ of an inch.

pointer   An arrow or other indicator on the screen which represents the current cursor (mouse) location.

pointing   Placing the mouse pointer over an object.

Point-to-Point Protocol (PPP)   A temporary dial-up connection that uses this protocol provides full access to the Internet as long as you are online.

pop-up menu   A menu that opens with a right-click of the mouse. It is also referred to as a *shortcut* or *context menu*.

port   A location or place on a CPU to connect other devices to a computer. It allows the computer to send information to and from the device.

portal   An entry point to the World Wide Web (WWW). It is sometimes called a gateway. Search engines such as Yahoo! and service providers such as MSN are positioning themselves as portals.

portrait   The most common printing mode for letters and other documents. This mode prints with the narrower side of the page across the top.

power cycle   Physically turning the computer off, waiting at least five seconds, and turning the computer back on.

PPP   See *Point-to-Point Protocol*.

primary mouse button   The mouse button used for most operatins, usually configured as the left mouse button.

printer   A computer peripheral that produces a hard copy of text or graphics on paper.

printer driver   Software used to send correct codes to the printer. It is also called *driver software* since it drives the printer.

printer font   A font that a printer is capable of printing.

print job   A print job usually consists of a single document, which can be one page or hundreds of pages long.

print queue   A list of files that have been sent to the printer by various applications. The print manager sends the files to the printer as the printer becomes available.

print server   On a network, a computer that is dedicated only to printing.

print spooler   A program that compensates for differences in rates of the flow of data by temporarily storing data in memory and then doling it out to the printer at the proper speed.

process   An executable program or part of a program that is a coherent set of steps. The process consists of the program itself, the memory address space it uses, the system resources it uses, and at least one thread.

program   A set of step-by-step instructions that tells the computer what to do.

program approach   A paradigm of treating programs as central. In order to use data, you must first open your program and then open your file. See also *docucentric*.

program file   A file containing an executable computer program. See also *application software* and *application program*.

progress bar control   See *progress bar indicator*.

progress bar indicator   A control that is a visual representation of the progress of a task.

prompt   A symbol on the screen that tells the user that the computer is ready for the next command. In the DOS window, the prompt usually consists of the letter of the current drive followed by a greater-than sign (e.g., A>, B>, or C>).

property sheet   A special kind of dialog box that allows the user to view or change the properties (characteristics) of an object.

proportional typeface   A typeface that varies the space given to each character. For instance, the *M* will take more space than the *I*.

protected mode   An operating mode in which different parts of memory are allocated to different programs so that when programs are running simultaneously they cannot invade each other's memory space and can access only their own memory space.

protocol   A set of rules or standards designed to enable computers to connect with one another and to exchange information.

push technology   A method of distributing information over the Web by automatically sending updates from Web sites.

queue   A line up of items waiting for processing.

random access memory (RAM)   See *memory*.

read-cache   Intercepts, makes a copy of, and places into memory the file that has been read. When a program makes a request, Windows checks to see if the data is already in the read-cache. Read-cache is used to optimize performance.

read-only attribute   Prevents a file from being changed or deleted.

read-only memory (ROM)   Memory that contains programs written on ROM chips, retained when the computer is turned off. ROM often controls the startup routines of the computer.

real mode   A single-task working environment. DOS runs in real mode.

real time   The actual amount of time the computer uses to complete an operation.

rebooting   Reloading the operating system from a disk.

redirection   A process in which a character-based operating system or the command line in Windows takes standard input or output from devices and sends it to a nonstandard input or output device. The redirection symbol is >.

Registry   A mechanism in Windows that stores user information, application program information, and information about the specific computer. The Registry centralizes and tracks all this information. It is critical to the running of Windows.

relative path   The path from where you are to where you want to go in relation to the directory tree hierarchical structure.

required parameter   See *mandatory parameter*.

resident font   A font stored in a printer.

resolution   The sharpness and clarity of detail attained by a printer or a monitor in producing an image.

resources   In a network environment, resources are what are provided by the server. Resources are the parts of the computer you share, such as a device or file.

Restore button   A button on a window's title bar that returns the window to its previous size.

restoring   Copying some or all of your files to your original disk, another disk, or another directory from your backup media.

Rich Text Format (RTF)   A file format that allows different applications to use formatted text documents.

right-clicking   Pressing the secondary mouse button, usually the right mouse button.

right-dragging   Dragging while holding the secondary mouse button, usually the right mouse button.

ROM   See *read-only memory (ROM)*.

ROM-BIOS (read-only memory–basic input/output system)   A chip built into the hardware of a system. Its functions include running self-diagnostics, loading the boot record, and handling low-level system tasks.

root directory   The directory that Windows creates on each disk when the disk is formatted. The backslash symbol (\) is used to represent the root directory.

router A device that connects networks. A router can make intelligent decisions about which network to use to send data.

RTF See *Rich Text Format (RTF)*.

sample box In a dialog box, an area where a preview of your selections can be seen.

sans serif font A typeface with no serifs.

scale Various sizes a font can be made to print in.

scanner A device that enables a computer to read a handwritten or printed page.

screen capture A picture of a screen. To capture the screen to the Clipboard, you press the `Print Screen` key. To capture the active window, you press `Alt` + `Print Screen`. See also *screen dump*.

screen dump A transfer of the data on the monitor to a printer or another hard-copy device. See also *screen capture*.

screen font A font that is used to display text and graphics on the monitor.

screen saver An image that prevents screen burn-in and provides a modicum of security if passwords are used.

scroll bar A feature used to move through a window when the entire contents will not fit.

scroll box The box in a scroll bar that shows you your relative position in a window or document. It can be dragged with the mouse to move rapidly through the window or document.

scrolling Vertical movement through text.

search criteria The instructions or limitations for a search for files or folders.

search path The set path for searching for program files.

secondary storage media Data storage media other than RAM. Typically disks, tapes, or removable drives such as Zip drives.

sector Data is stored on a disk in concentric circles (tracks) that are divided into sectors. A sector is a portion of a track. A sector is 512 bytes long, based on industry standards.

Serial Line Internet Protocol (SLIP) An older protocol that provides a temporary dial-up connection for full access to the Internet as long as you are online.

serial port A communications port to which a device, such as a modem or a serial printer, can be attached. Data is transmitted and received one bit at a time.

serif font A font with thin lines (serifs) at the ends of each letter.

server On a network, a computer that provides shared resources to network users. It is also used to refer to an application that provides data or an object in object linking and embedding.

server application An application program that provides data (an object) in object linking and embedding. It is also known as the source application.

server-based network A network model in which security and other network functions are provided by a dedicated server.

services A way to allow you to share files and devices on a network. There are other services such as being able to remotely administer a network.

shareware Software that is free on a trial basis with the option to either purchase it or remove it from your hard disk.

shortcut An icon that is created to represent commonly used objects. The icon is placed on the desktop or another location for easy access. A shortcut provides a pointer to the actual object, and it can usually be recognized by a right-bent arrow on top of the object's normal icon or by the word *shortcut*.

shortcut menu   A menu that opens with a right-click of the mouse. It is also referred to as a *pop-up* or *context menu*.

single point of failure   Desribes how, if the hub in a star topology fails, the entire network goes down.

sizing buttons   Allow the user to minimize or maximize a window.

slider   A control that allows you to adjust or set values when there is a range of values. You move the slider with the mouse.

SLIP   See *Serial Line Internet Protocol (SLIP)*.

soft return   A code that is automatically inserted when the end of a line is reached in a document. Unlike a hard return, if text is inserted or removed, software will automatically adjust the text to fit within the margins.

software   Programs that tell the computer what to do.

software package   See *application package*.

spin box   A control that allows you to either key in a number or click on the up or down arrow to increase or decrease a quantity. Usually a control that has numeric quantities to choose will be a spin box.

spinner   A synonym for a *spin box*. See also *spin box*.

splash screen   The first screen that appears when you boot the system or load a program. It is often a decorative screen to look at while the program or system is loading.

split bar   In Explorer, a bar that divides the window to enable the user to see the structure of a disk on the left and the contents on the right.

spool file   Stores a data document in a queue while it waits to be printed. The Windows print manager intercepts a print job on its way to the printer and sends it to disk or memory instead, where the print job is held until the printer is ready for it. The term *spool* comes from "simultaneous peripheral operations online."

spreadsheet program   A program for budget management and financial projections.

standard   A set of detailed technical guidelines used to establish conformity in software or hardware development.

standard error   A process in which a character-based operating system or the command line in Windows writes error messages to the screen.

standard input   A process in which a character-based operating system or the command line in Windows expects to receive information, usually from the keyboard.

standard output   A process in which a character-based operating system or the command line in Windows expects to send information, usually to the screen.

star topology   A local area network (LAN) design in which each device (node) is connected to a central point.

Start button   The first button on the taskbar. Clicking the Start button opens the Start menu, which opens further menus for the user to access programs and data.

static RAM (SRAM)   Memory chips that can hold data until the computer is turned off. See also *dynamic RAM*.

status area   An area located at the right side of the taskbar that is used by Windows and other programs to place information or notification of events. If you were printing, for example, an icon of a printer would appear in the status area.

status bar A bar that supplies information about the current window.

string A string of data is a variable-length set of characters. String values are always enclosed in quotation marks.

stroke weight The thickness of a font.

subdirectory The location or container where documents, program files, devices, and other folders are stored on a disk. The terms *subfolders, folders, directories,* and *subdirectories* are used interchangeably.

subfolder A folder beneath a folder. The terms *subfolders, folders, directories,* and *subdirectories* are used interchangeably.

subscription Sets up a Web browser to check a Web page for new content. The program can then either notify the user about the new content or automatically download it to the user's computer.

supporting Describes a program's ability to read from and write to a specific file format.

surfing the Net Exploring the Internet by moving from topic to topic.

surge protector A device that prevents surges from reaching a computer or other kinds of electronic equipment. It is also called a *surge suppressor.*

surge suppressor See *surge protector.*

switch A modifier that controls the execution of a command. Typically the forward slash (/) is used to indicate a switch. See also *parameter.*

synchronizing files Updating files and folders that are duplicated. It is used with My Briefcase.

syntax The proper order or sequence of a computer's language and commands.

syntax diagram A graphic representation of a command and its syntax.

sysing a disk Placing the operating system files on a disk without removing the data that is there. The command is SYS.

system board Also known as a *motherboard,* it is the main circuit board controlling the major components of a computer system.

system configuration The components that make up a specific computer system.

system date The current date kept by the computer system.

system disk See *bootable disk.*

system prompt A symbol on the screen that tells the user that the computer is ready for the next command. It is used in the command line interface and usually consists of the current drive letter followed by the greater-than sign, as in C:\>.

system resources An area in memory that Windows uses for critical operating system tasks, such as drawing windows on the screen, using fonts, or running applications.

system software A set of programs that coordinates the operations of the hardware components.

system time The current time kept by the computer.

taskbar The bar on the screen that lets you move between any open programs, files, folders, or windows by displaying a button for each open item. The taskbar includes the Start button as well as the status area where Windows and other programs can place notification of events.

taskbar button The button on the taskbar that indicates an open program, file, or window. Clicking the specific button on the taskbar will activate that choice.

T-connector A device used in a network which has one end plugged into the network card and two open ends (like a T) for connecting the cables that go to the computers.

terminator plug A device used with T-connectors so that there is no unplugged end in a network.

text box A place where the user can key in information.

text editor A program that is similar to a word-processing program but is unable to perform any special editing. No embedded codes are inserted into documents. ASCII editors can only edit ASCII text files, also called *text files* or *unformatted text files*. Text editors are also called *ASCII editors.*

text file A file that contains text. It consists of data that can be read, such as letters and numbers, with an ASCII editor such as Notepad or in the DOS window.

Thinnet A single coaxial cable.

tiled A display mode that divides the screen equally among the open windows.

title bar A bar located at the top of a window that contains the name of the program.

toggle switch A switch that turns a function on or off like a light switch.

token A binary shorthand for repetitive words or phrases. When a file is decompressed, the tokens are read and the original characters are restored.

toolbar A toolbar appears in a window or on the desktop and provides shortcuts for entering menu commands. Rather than access the menu, you click a button on the toolbar.

ToolTip A brief description of a button. The user activates a ToolTip by pausing the mouse pointer over a button on a toolbar or the taskbar.

topology A design or configuration formed by the connections between devices on a local area network (LAN).

track A concentric circle on a disk where data is stored. Each track is further divided into sectors. All tracks and sectors are numbered so that the operating system can quickly locate information.

trackball A device used to move the cursor on the monitor. It usually consists of a stationary box that holds a ball that the user rotates to move the cursor.

tracking speed The rate at which the mouse pointer moves across the screen.

transparent to the user Describes a program or process that works so smoothly and easily that it is invisible to the user.

tree structure The organizational properties of a tree that relate to the structure of a disk from the root directory down.

troubleshooter A step-by-step guide to assist you in analyzing and solving a problem.

TrueType font A font that is provided with Windows and is capable of printing on any printer. The font usually looks on the screen like it will when it is printed. See *WYSIWYG.*

tweaking a system Making final changes and fine-tuning a system to improve performance.

twisted-pair cable A type of cable also known as 10BASET, 10BT, Ethernet, TPE, or RJ-45.

typeface The design of a group of letters, numbers, and punctuation, such as Arial or Times New Roman.

typeover The process of deleting existing characters as you key in new ones.

typing replaces selection The process of deleting existing characters by selecting them and keying in data. What you key in replaces your selection.

UNC See *universal naming convention (UNC).*

unformatted text file See *text file*.

Unicode A 16-bit character set intended to accommodate all the commonly used characters in all languages.

uniform resource locator (URL) A standard format for identifying locations on the Internet. URLs specify three types of information needed to retrieve a document: the protocol to be used, the server address with which to connect, and the path to the information. The URL syntax is *protocol/servername/path*; an example of a URL address is **http://www.netscape.com**.

uninterruptible power supply (UPS) A device that ensures electrical flow to the computer is not interrupted because of a blackout and that protects the computer against potentially damaging events, such as power surges and brownouts. All UPS units are equipped with a battery and a loss-of-power sensor; if the sensor detects a loss of power, it switches over to the battery so that the user has time to save his or her work and shut off the computer.

universal naming convention (UNC) A convention used to locate the path to a network resource. It specifies the share name on a particular computer. The computer name is limited to 15 characters, and the share name is usually limited to 15 characters. It takes the format of *computername**sharename*[*optional path*].

universal serial bus (USB) The latest bus standard. It is an external bus standard for the computer that brings plug-and-play capability. It eliminates the need to install cards into dedicated computer slots and to reconfigure the system.

upgrading Purchasing the latest version of software and replacing your existing version with it.

uploading Sending a file to another computer while connected by a modem, another outside connection, or a network.

UPS See *uninterruptible power supply*.

URL See *uniform resource locator*.

user profiles In Windows, enabling profiles allows more than one user to use the same computer and retain his or her own personal settings on the desktop.

utility A program for carrying out specific, vital functions that assist in the operation of a computer or software.

utility program See *utility*.

variable parameter Value/information provided by the user.

vector font A font in which the characters are drawn using arrangements of line segments rather than arrangements of bits.

version A numbering scheme that indicates the progressive enhancements and improvement of software.

VFAT (virtual file allocation table) file system An extension of the file allocation table, with which it is compatible. It provides the ability to handle long file names. See also *file allocation table (FAT)*.

video card A circuit board that controls the capabilities of the video display.

virtual Describes a device, service, or sensory input that is perceived but is not real.

virtual machine (VM) An environment in memory that, from the application's point of view, looks like a separate computer, complete with all the resources available on the physical computer.

virus A program that has damaging side effects. Sometimes the side effects are intentionally damaging, other times not.

volume label   An electronic label for a disk that the user can assign when it is formatted.

volume serial number   A number randomly assigned to a disk when it is formatted.

wallpaper   A graphic image file that serves as a background on the desktop, behind all open windows.

WAN   See *wide area network (WAN)*.

Web   A colloquial expression for the World Wide Web (WWW).

Web browser   A software program for navigating the Internet. Two popular programs are Netscape Navigator and Microsoft Internet Explorer.

Web page   On the Internet, a single screen of text and graphics that usually has hypertext links to other pages.

Web site   Both the physical and virtual location of a person's or an organization's Web page.

What's This?   A feature that allows the user to right-click an item to obtain a brief description of it.

wide area network (WAN)   A network that consists of computers using long-range telecommunication links.

wildcards   The symbols * and ?, also called global file specifications, that are used to represent a character (?) or a group of characters (*) in a file name.

window   A defined work area (rectangular frame) on the screen that is moveable and sizeable; information with which the user can interact is displayed in it.

Wintel   A computer that uses the Microsoft Windows operating system and an Intel central processing unit (CPU).

wizard   A program that uses step-by-step instructions to lead the user through the execution and completion of a Windows task.

word-processing program   Software that allows the user to write, edit, and print any type of text.

word wrap   A feature in software that automatically moves text to the next line when the current line is full.

workgroup   Another name for a peer-to-peer network.

World Wide Web (WWW)   A virtual space accessible from the Internet that holds pages of text and graphics in a recognizable format. These pages are linked to one another and to individual files. The Web is a collection of standards and protocols used to access information on the Internet.

wrapping   Continuing a movement, with the cursor or a search operation, to the beginning or to a new starting point rather than stopping when the end of a series is reached. In a window, a title or an icon label would have additional lines created for the text to be displayed, if necessary.

write-protected disk   A floppy disk that can be only read from, not written to.

WWW   See *World Wide Web (WWW)*.

WYSIWYG   An acronym for *what you see is what you get*. It is displayed on the screen in the manner in which it will be printed.

zip   A type of file. Its contents have been compressed by a special utility program, usually PKZIP or WinZip, so that it occupies less space on a disk or other storage device.